PENGUIN BOOKS

THE THIRD REICH AT WAR

'A vivid narrative . . . The definitive history for our generation'
James Grant, *Herald*

'Masterly . . . an humane account in which scholarly analysis
never obscures the massive suffering which has to be at the heart
of any such study. Evans's trilogy is a monumental achievement
and is to be thoroughly recommended both as a starting point
for those relatively unfamiliar with the period and as a
provocative challenge to those who feel there is nothing left to
say about the much-studied catastrophe of the Third Reich'
Neil Gregor, *History Today*

'The triumphant conclusion to an enthralling trilogy'
Michael Kerrigan, *Scotsman*, Books of the Year

'Readable and compelling, *The Third Reich at War*
is a monumental accomplishment'
The Times Higher Education Supplement

'He seems to stand inside the Third Reich as it self-destructs. He
sees its deeds in all their ghastly perversion. He always strives
magisterially to make us understand – and to sense the demons
within ourselves' Peter Preston, *Observer*

'With this third volume, Richard Evans has accomplished a
masterpiece of historical scholarship'
Antony Beevor, *The Times*

D1339880

Richard J. Evans is one of the world's leading historians of modern Germany. He was born in London in 1947. From 1989 to 1998 he was Professor of History at Birkbeck College, University of London. From 1998 to 2008 he was Professor of Modern History at Cambridge University. He is now Regius Professor of Modern History. In 1994 he was awarded the Hamburg Medal for Art and Science for cultural services to the city, and in 2000 he was the principal expert witness in the David Irving libel trial. His books include *The Feminist Movement in Germany, 1894–1933*, *Death in Hamburg* (winner of the Wolfson Literary Award for History), *In Hitler's Shadow*, *Rituals of Retribution* (winner of the Fraenkel Prize in Contemporary History), *In Defence of History* (which has so far been translated into eight languages), *Telling Lies About Hitler* and *The Coming of the Third Reich* (shortlisted for the *Los Angeles Times* Book Prize), *The Third Reich in Power*, *The Third Reich at War* and *Cosmopolitan Islanders: British Historians and the European Continent*.

RICHARD J. EVANS

The Third Reich at War

*How the Nazis Led Germany
from Conquest to Disaster*

PENGUIN BOOKS

PENGUIN BOOKS

Published by the Penguin Group
Penguin Books Ltd, 80 Strand, London WC2R ORL, England
Penguin Group (USA) Inc., 375 Hudson Street, New York, New York 10014, USA
Penguin Group (Canada), 90 Eglinton Avenue East, Suite 700, Toronto, Ontario, Canada M4P 2Y3
(a division of Pearson Penguin Canada Inc.)
Penguin Ireland, 25 St Stephen's Green, Dublin 2, Ireland
(a division of Penguin Books Ltd)
Penguin Group (Australia), 250 Camberwell Road, Camberwell, Victoria 3124, Australia
(a division of Pearson Australia Group Pty Ltd)
Penguin Books India Pvt Ltd, 11 Community Centre, Panchsheel Park, New Delhi – 110 017, India
Penguin Group (NZ), 67 Apollo Drive, Rosedale, North Shore 0632, New Zealand
(a division of Pearson New Zealand Ltd)
Penguin Books (South Africa) (Pty) Ltd, 24 Sturdee Avenue, Rosebank, Johannesburg 2196, South Africa

Penguin Books Ltd, Registered Offices: 80 Strand, London WC2R ORL, England

www.penguin.com

First published by Allen Lane 2008
Published in Penguin Books 2009
1

Copyright © Richard J. Evans, 2008

The moral right of the author has been asserted

Maps drawn by Andras Bereznay

Typeset by Rowland Phototypesetting Ltd, Bury St Edmunds, Suffolk
Printed in Great Britain by Clays Ltd, St Ives plc

A CIP catalogue record for this book is available from the British Library

978-0-141-01548-4

www.greenpenguin.co.uk

For Matthew and Nicholas

Contents

List of Illustrations

Note: The views or opinions expressed in this book and the context in which the images are used do not necessarily reflect the views or policy of, nor imply approval or endorsement by, the United States Holocaust Memorial Museum.

List of Maps

Preface

This book tells the story of the Third Reich, the regime created in Germany by Hitler and his National Socialists, from the outbreak of the Second World War on 1 September 1939 to its end in Europe on 8 May 1945. It can be read on its own, as a history of Germany during the war. But it is also the final volume in a series of three, starting with *The Coming of the Third Reich*, which deals with the origins of Nazism, the development of its ideas and its rise to power in 1933. The second volume in the series, *The Third Reich in Power*, covers the peacetime years from 1933 to 1939, when Hitler and the Nazis built up Germany's military strength and prepared it for war. The general approach of all three volumes is set out in the Preface to *The Coming of the Third Reich* and does not need to be repeated in detail here. Taken together, they aim to provide a comprehensive account of Germany under the Nazis.

Dealing with the history of the Third Reich during the war poses two special problems. The first is a relatively minor one. After 1939, Hitler and the Nazis became increasingly reluctant to refer to their regime as 'The Third Reich', preferring instead to call it 'The Great German Reich' (*Grossdeutsches Reich*) to draw attention to the massive expansion of its boundaries that took place in 1939–40. For the sake of unity and consistency, however, I have chosen, like other historians, to continue calling it 'The Third Reich'; after all, the Nazis chose to abandon this term silently rather than repudiate it openly. The second problem is more serious. The central focus of this book is on Germany and the Germans; it is not a history of the Second World War, not even of the Second World War in Europe. Nevertheless, of course, it is necessary to narrate the progress of the war, and to deal with the Germans' administration of the parts of Europe they conquered. Within the scope even of so large a book as this, it is not possible to pay equal attention to every phase and every aspect of the war. I have chosen, therefore, to focus on the major turning-points – the conquest of Poland and France and the Battle of Britain in the first year of the war, the Battle of Moscow in the winter of 1941–2, the Battle of Stalingrad in the winter of 1942–3, and the beginning of the sustained strategic bombing of German cities in 1943. In doing so, I have tried to convey something of the flavour of what it was like for Germans to take part in these vast conflicts, using the diaries and letters of both soldiers and civilians. The reasons for choosing these particular turning-points will, I hope, become apparent to readers in the course of the book.

At the heart of German history in the war years lies the mass murder of millions of Jews in what the Nazis called 'the final solution of the Jewish question in Europe'. This book provides a full narrative of the development and implementation of this policy of genocide, while also setting it in the broader context of Nazi racial policies towards the Slavs, and towards minorities such as Gypsies, homosexuals, petty criminals and 'asocials'. I have tried to combine the testimony of some of those it affected – both those who survived, and those who did not – with that of some of the men who implemented it, including the commandants of major death camps. The deportation and murder of Jews from Western European countries is covered in the chapter dealing with the Nazi empire, while the reactions of ordinary Germans at home, and the extent to which they knew about the genocide, are covered in a later chapter on the Home Front. The fact that the mass murder of the Jews is discussed in almost every part of the book, from the narrative of the foundation of the ghettos in Poland in the opening chapter right up to the coverage of the 'death marches' of 1945 in the final chapter, reflects its centrality to so many aspects of the history of the Third Reich at war. Wherever one looks, even for example in the history of music and literature, dealt with in Chapter 6, it is an inescapable part of the story. Nevertheless, it is important to reiterate that this book is a history of Nazi Germany in all its aspects; it is not in the first place a history of the extermination of the Jews, any more than it is a history of the Second World War, though both play an essential role in it.

The book opens where *The Third Reich in Power* left off, with the invasion of Poland on 1 September 1939. Chapter 1 discusses the Germans' occupation of Poland and in particular their ill-treatment, exploitation and murder of many thousands of Poles and Polish Jews from this point to the eve of the invasion of the Soviet Union in June 1941. For the Nazis, and indeed for many Germans, Poles and 'Eastern Jews' were less than human, and this attitude applied, though with significant differences, to the mentally ill and handicapped in Germany itself, whose mass murder in the course of the 'euthanasia' action steered from Hitler's Chancellery in Berlin forms the subject of the last part of the chapter. The second chapter is largely devoted to the progress of the war, from the conquest of Western Europe in 1940 through to the Russian campaign of 1941. That campaign forms the essential backdrop to the events narrated in Chapter 3, which deals with the launching and implementation of what the Nazis called 'the final solution of the Jewish question in Europe'. Chapter 4 turns to the war economy, and looks at how the Third Reich ruled the countries it occupied in Europe, drafting in millions of forced labourers to man its arms factories and pushing ahead with the arrest, deportation and murder of the Jews who lived within the boundaries of the Nazi empire. That empire began to fall apart with the momentous German defeat at the Battle of Stalingrad early in 1943, which is narrated in the concluding part of the chapter. It was followed the same year by reversals in many spheres of the war, from the devastation of Germany's towns and cities by the Allied strategic bombing offensive to the defeat of Rommel's armies in North Africa and the collapse of the Third Reich's main European ally, the Fascist state of Mussolini's Italy. These events form the principal focus of Chapter 5, which goes on to examine the way they affected the armed forces, and the impact they had on the conduct of the war at home. Chapter 6 is largely devoted to the 'Home Front', and looks at how religious, social, cultural and scientific life interacted with the war. It concludes with an account of the emergence of resistance to Nazism, particularly within the Third Reich itself. Chapter 7 begins with an account of the 'wonder-weapons' which Hitler promised would reverse Germany's military collapse, before going on to tell the story of how the Reich was finally defeated, and to examine briefly what happened afterwards. Each chapter interweaves thematic aspects with an ongoing narrative of military events, so that Chapter 1 deals with military action in 1939, Chapter 2 covers 1940 and 1941, Chapter 3 discusses further military events in 1941, Chapter 4 takes the story on through 1942, Chapter 5 narrates the war on land, in the air and at sea in 1943, Chapter 6 moves the narrative on through 1944, and the final chapter gives an account of the closing months of the war, from January to May 1945.

This book is written to be read from start to finish, as a single, if complex, narrative, interspersed with description and analysis; I hope that the ways in which the different parts of the story interact with one another will become apparent to readers as the narrative proceeds. The chapter headings are intended more to provoke reflection on the contents than to provide precise descriptions of what each chapter contains; in some cases they are intentionally ambiguous or ironical. Anyone who wishes to use the book simply as a work of reference is recommended to turn to the index, where the location of the book's principal themes, characters and events is laid out in detail. The bibliography lists works cited in the notes; it is not intended to be a comprehensive guide to the vast literature on the topics dealt with in the book.

Much of this book deals with countries in Central and Eastern Europe where towns and cities have a variety of names and spellings in different languages. The Polish city of Lvov, for example, is spelt L'vov in Russian and L'viv in Ukrainian, while the Germans called it something different altogether, namely Lemberg; there are similar variations in the spelling of Kaunas in Lithuanian and Kovno in Polish, Theresienstadt in German and Terezín in Czech, or Reval in German and Tallinn in Estonian. The Nazi authorities also renamed Lódź as Litzmannstadt in an attempt to obliterate all aspects of its Polish identity altogether and used German names for a variety of other sites, such as Kulmhof for Chelmno, or Auschwitz for Oswiecim. In this situation it is impossible to be consistent, and I have chosen to use the name current at the time about which I am writing, or on occasion simply the name with which English and American readers will be most familiar, while alerting them to the existence of alternatives. I have also simplified the use of accents and diacriticals in place-names and proper names – dropping the Polish character Ł, for instance – to remove what to my mind are distractions for the English-language reader.

In the preparation of this book I have enjoyed the huge advantage of access to the superb collections of Cambridge University Library, as well as to those of the Wiener Library and the German Historical Institute in London. The University of Melbourne kindly appointed me to a Miegunyah Distinguished Visiting Fellowship in 2007, and I was able to use the excellent research collection on modern German history purchased for the University Library from the bequest of the late, and much-missed, John Foster. The Staatsarchiv der Freien- und Hansestadt Hamburg and the Forschungsstelle für Zeitgeschichte in Hamburg kindly permitted consultation of the unpublished diaries of Luise Solmitz. The encouragement of many readers, especially in the United States, has been crucial in spurring me on to complete the book, though it has taken longer to do so than I originally intended. The advice and support of many friends and colleagues has been crucial. My agent Andrew Wylie and my editor at Penguin, Simon Winder, and their teams have been enormously helpful. Chris Clark, Christian Goeschel, Victoria Harris, Sir Ian Kershaw, Richard Overy, Kristin Semmens, Astrid Swenson, Hester Vaizey and Nikolaus Wachsmann read early drafts and made many useful suggestions. Victoria Harris, Stefan Ihrig, Alois Maderspacher, David Motadel, Tom Neuhaus and Hester Vaizey checked through the notes and saved me from many errors. András Bereznáy provided maps that are a model of clarity and accuracy; working on them with him was extremely instructive. The expertise of David Watson in copy-editing was invaluable, and it was a pleasure to work with Cecilia Mackay on the illustrations. Christine L. Corton applied her practised eye to the proofs, and provided essential support in too many ways to mention. Our sons, Matthew and Nicholas, to whom this final volume, like the previous two, is dedicated, have cheered me up on innumerable occasions during the writing of a book the subject matter of which was sometimes shocking and depressing almost beyond belief. I am profoundly grateful to them all.

Richard J. Evans
Cambridge, May 2008

I

'BEASTS IN HUMAN FORM'

LIGHTNING VICTORY

I

On 1 September 1939 the first of a grand total of sixty divisions of German troops crossed the Third Reich's border with Poland. Numbering nearly one and a half million men, they paused only to allow newsreel cameramen from Joseph Goebbels's Propaganda Ministry to film the ceremonial raising of the customs barriers by grinning soldiers of the vanguard. The advance was spearheaded by tanks from the German army's five armoured divisions, with around 300 tanks apiece, accompanied by four fully motorized infantry divisions. Behind them marched the bulk of the infantry, their artillery and equipment pulled mainly by horses – roughly 5,000 of them for each division, making at least 300,000 animals altogether. As impressive as this was, the decisive technology deployed by the Germans was not on the ground, but in the air. The ban imposed by the Treaty of Versailles on German military planes meant that aircraft construction had been forced to start almost from scratch when Hitler repudiated the relevant clauses of the Treaty only four years before the outbreak of the war. The German planes were not only modern in construction, but had been tried and tested in the Spanish Civil War by the German Condor Legion, many of the veterans of which piloted the 897 bombers, 426 fighters and various reconnaissance and transport planes that now took to the skies over Poland.[1]

These massive forces confronted the Poles with overwhelming odds. Hoping that the invasion would be stopped by Anglo-French intervention, and anxious not to offend world opinion by seeming to provoke the Germans, the Polish government delayed mobilizing its armed forces until the last minute. Thus they were poorly prepared to resist the sudden, massive invasion of German troops. The Poles could muster

1.3 million men, but they possessed few tanks and little modern equipment. German armoured and motorized divisions outnumbered their Polish counterparts by a factor of 15 to 1 in the conflict. The Polish air force was able to deploy only 154 bombers and 159 fighters against the invading Germans. Most of the aircraft, particularly the fighters, were obsolete, while the Polish cavalry brigades had scarcely begun to abandon their horses in favour of machines. Stories of Polish cavalry squadrons quixotically charging German tank units were most probably apocryphal, but the disparity in resources and equipment was undeniable all the same. The Germans surrounded Poland on three sides, following their dismemberment of Czecho-Slovakia earlier in the year. In the south, the German client state of Slovakia provided the most important jumping-off point for the invasion, and indeed the Slovak government actually sent some units to fight their way into Poland alongside the German troops, lured by the promise of a small amount of extra territory once Poland had been defeated. Other German divisions entered Poland across its northern border, from East Prussia, while still more marched in from the west, cutting through the Polish Corridor created by the Peace Settlement to give Poland access to the Baltic. Polish forces were stretched too thinly to defend all these frontiers effectively. While Stuka dive-bombers attacked the Polish armies strung out along the border from above, German tanks and artillery drove through their defences, cut them off from each other and broke their communications. Within a few days the Polish air force had been driven from the skies, and German bombers were destroying Polish arms factories, strafing the retreating troops and terrorizing the people of Warsaw, Lódź and other cities.[2]

On 16 September 1939 alone, 820 German aircraft dropped a total of 328,000 kilos of bombs on the defenceless Poles, who possessed a total of only 100 anti-aircraft guns for the whole of the country. So demoralizing were the air attacks that in some areas Polish troops threw down their arms, and German commanders on the ground asked for the bombing to stop. A typical action was witnessed by the American correspondent William L. Shirer, who managed to get permission to accompany German forces attacking the Polish Baltic port of Gdynia:

The Germans were using everything in the way of weapons, big guns, small guns, tanks, and airplanes. The Poles had nothing but machine-guns, rifles, and two anti-aircraft pieces which they were trying desperately to use as artillery against

German machine-gun posts and German tanks. The Poles ... had turned two large buildings, one an officers' school, the other the Gdynia radio station, into fortresses and were firing machine-guns from several of the windows. After a half-hour a German shell struck the roof of the school and set it on fire. Then German infantry, supported – or through the glasses it looked as though they were *led* – by tanks, charged up the hill and surrounded the building ... A German seaplane hovered over the ridge, spotting for the artillery. Later, a bombing plane joined it, and they dived low, machine-gunning the Polish lines. Finally a squadron of Nazi bombers arrived. It was a hopeless position for the Poles.[3]

Similar actions were repeated all over the country as the German forces advanced. Within a week the Polish forces were in complete disarray, and their structure of command was shattered. On 17 September the Polish government fled to Romania, where its hapless ministers were promptly interned by the authorities. The country was now entirely leaderless. A government-in-exile, formed on 30 September 1939 on the initiative of Polish diplomats in Paris and London, was unable to do anything. A single, furious Polish counter-attack, at the Battle of Kutno on 9 September, only succeeded in delaying the encirclement of Warsaw by a few days at most.[4]

In Warsaw itself, conditions deteriorated rapidly. Chaim Kaplan, a Jewish schoolteacher, noted on 28 September 1939:

There is no end to corpses of horses. They lie fallen in the middle of the street and there is no one to remove them and clear the road. They have been rotting for three days and nauseating all the passers-by. However, because of the starvation rampant in the city, there are many who eat the horses' meat. They cut off chunks and eat them to quiet their hunger.[5]

One of the most vivid depictions of the chaotic scenes that followed the German invasion was penned by a Polish doctor, Zygmunt Klukowski. Born in 1885, he was by the outbreak of the war superintendent of the Zamość county hospital in the town of Szczebrzeszyn. Klukowski kept a diary, which he hid away in odd corners of his hospital, as an act of defiance and remembrance. At the end of the second week in September, he noted the streams of refugees fleeing from the encroaching German troops in the middle of the night, a scene that would be repeated many times, in many parts of Europe, in the years to come:

The entire highway was crowded with military convoys, all types of motorized vehicles, horse-drawn wagons, and thousands of people on foot. Everyone was moving in one direction only – east. When daylight came a mass of people on foot and on bicycles added to the confusion. It was completely weird. This whole mass of people, seized with panic, were going ahead, without knowing where or why, and without any knowledge of where the exodus would end. Large numbers of passenger cars, several official limousines, all filthy and covered with mud, were trying to pass the truck and wagon convoys. Most of the vehicles had Warsaw registration. It was a sad thing to see so many high-ranking officers such as colonels and generals fleeing together with their families. Many people were hanging on to the roofs and fenders of the cars and trucks. Many of the vehicles had broken windshields and windows, damaged hoods or doors. Much slower moving were all kinds of buses, new city buses from Warsaw, Cracow, and Lódź and all full of passengers. After that came horse-drawn wagons of every description loaded with women and children, all very tired, hungry, and dirty. Riding bicycles were mostly young men; only occasionally could a young woman be seen. Walking on foot were many kinds of people. Some had left their houses on foot; others were forced to leave their vehicles abandoned.[6]

He reckoned that up to 30,000 people were fleeing the German advance in this way.[7]

Worse was to come. On 17 September 1939 Klukowski heard a German loudspeaker in the market square of Zamość announcing that the Red Army, with German agreement, had crossed Poland's eastern border.[8] Not long before the invasion, Hitler had secured the non-intervention of the Russian dictator, Josef Stalin, by signing secret clauses of a German–Soviet Pact on 24 August 1939 that arranged the partition of Poland between the two states along an agreed demarcation line.[9] In the first two weeks after the German invasion, Stalin had held back while he extricated his forces from a successful conflict with Japan in Manchuria, concluded only in late August. But when it became clear that Polish resistance had been broken, the Soviet leadership authorized the Red Army to move into the country from the east. Stalin was keen to grasp the opportunity to regain territory that had belonged to Russia before the revolution of 1917. It had been the object of a bitter war between Russia and the newly created Polish state in the immediate aftermath of the First World War. Now he could win it back. Faced with a war on two fronts, the Polish armed forces, which had made no plans for such an eventuality, fought a bitter but entirely futile rearguard action to try to delay the inevitable. It was not long in coming. Squashed between two vastly superior armies, the Poles did not stand a chance. On 28 September 1939 a new treaty laid down the final border. By this time, the German assault on Warsaw was over. 1,200 aircraft had dropped huge quanitites of incendiary and other bombs on the Polish capital, raising a huge pall of smoke that made accuracy impossible; many civilians were killed as a result. In view of their hopeless situation, the Polish commanders in the city had negotiated a cease-fire on 27 September 1939. 120,000 Polish troops of the city's garrison surrendered, after being assured that they could go home after a brief and formal captivity as prisoners of war. The last Polish military units surrendered on 6 October 1939.[10]

This was the first example of the still far from perfected 'lightning war', Hitler's *Blitzkrieg*, a war of rapid movement, led by tanks and motorized divisions in conjunction with bombers terrorizing enemy troops and immobilizing enemy air forces, overwhelming a more conventionally minded opponent by the sheer speed and force of a knockout punch through enemy lines. The achievement of the lightning war could be read from the comparative statistics of losses on the two sides. Altogether the Poles lost some 70,000 troops killed in action against the German invaders and another 50,000 against the Russians, with at least 133,000 wounded in the conflict with the Germans and an unknown number of casualties in the action against the Red Army. The Germans took nearly 700,000 Polish prisoners and the Russians another 300,000. 150,000 Polish troops and airmen escaped abroad, especially to Britain, where many of them joined the armed forces. The German forces suffered 11,000 killed and 30,000 wounded, with another 3,400 missing in action; the Russians lost a mere 700 men, with a further 1,900 wounded. The figures graphically illustrated the unequal nature of the conflict; at the same time, however, German losses were far from negligible, in terms not just of personnel but also, more strikingly, of equipment. No fewer than 300 armoured vehicles, 370 guns and 5,000 other vehicles had been destroyed, along with a considerable number of aircraft, and these losses were only partially offset by the capture or surrender of (usually very inferior) Polish equivalents. These were modest but still ominous portents for the future.[11]

For the moment such concerns did not trouble Hitler. He had followed the campaign from his mobile headquarters in an armoured train stationed first in Pomerania, later in Upper Silesia, making occasional forays by car to view the action from a safe distance. On 19 September he entered Danzig, the formerly German city placed under League of Nations suzerainty by the Peace Settlement, to be greeted by ecstatic crowds of ethnic Germans rejoicing in what they saw as their liberation from foreign control. After two brief flights to inspect the scenes of destruction wrought by his armies and airplanes on Warsaw, he went back to Berlin.[12] There were no parades or celebratory speeches in the capital, but the victory met with general satisfaction. 'I have still to find a German, even among those who don't like the regime,' wrote Shirer in his diary, 'who sees anything wrong in the German destruction of Poland.'[13] Social Democratic agents reported that the great mass of people supported the war not least because they thought that the failure of the western powers to assist the Poles meant that Britain and France would soon be suing for peace, an impression strengthened by a much-trumpeted 'peace offer' from Hitler to the French and British in early October. Though this was quickly rejected, the continued inaction of the British and the French kept hopes alive that they could be persuaded to pull out of the war.[14] Rumours of a peace deal with the western powers were rife at this time, and even led to spontaneous celebratory demonstrations on the streets of Berlin.[15]

Meanwhile, Goebbels's propaganda machine had gone into overdrive to persuade Germans that the invasion had been inevitable in the light of a Polish threat of genocide against the ethnic Germans in their midst. The nationalistic military regime in Poland had indeed discriminated heavily against the German ethnic minority in the interwar years. At the onset of the German invasion in September 1939, gripped by fears of sabotage behind the lines, it had arrested between ten and fifteen thousand ethnic Germans and marched them towards the eastern part of the country, beating laggards and shooting many of those who gave up through exhaustion. There were also widespread attacks on members of the ethnic German minority, most of whom had made no attempt to disguise their desire to return to the German Reich ever since their forcible incorporation into Poland at the end of the First World War.[16] Altogether, around 2,000 ethnic Germans were killed in mass shootings or died from exhaustion on the marches. Some 300 were killed in Bromberg (Bydgoszcz), where local ethnic Germans had staged an armed uprising against the town's garrison in the belief that the war was virtually over, and had been killed by the enraged Poles. These events were cynically exploited by Goebbels's Propaganda Ministry to win maximum support in Germany for the invasion. Many Germans were convinced. Melita Maschmann, a young activist in the League of German Girls, the female wing of the Hitler Youth, was persuaded that war was morally justified not only in the light of the injustices of Versailles, which had ceded German-speaking areas to the new Polish state, but also by press and newsreel reports of Polish violence against the German-speaking minority. 60,000 ethnic Germans, she believed, had been brutally murdered by the Poles in 'Bloody Sunday' in Bromberg. How could Germany be to blame for acting to stop such hatred, such atrocities, she asked herself.[17] Goebbels had initially estimated the total number of ethnic Germans killed at 5,800. It was not until February 1940 that, probably on Hitler's personal instructions, the estimate was arbitrarily increased to 58,000, later remembered in rough approximation by Melita Maschmann.[18] The figure not only convinced most Germans that the invasion had been justified, but also fuelled the hatred and resentment felt by the ethnic German minority in Poland against their former masters.[19] Under Hitler's orders, its bitterness was quickly brought into the service of a campaign of ethnic cleansing and mass murder that far outdid anything that had happened after the German occupation of Austria and Czechoslovakia in 1938.[20]

II

The invasion of Poland was indeed the third successful annexation of foreign territory by the Third Reich. In 1938, Germany had annexed the independent republic of Austria. Later in the year, it had marched unopposed into the German-speaking border regions of Czechoslovakia. Both these moves had been sanctioned by international agreement and, on the whole, welcomed by the inhabitants of the areas concerned. They could be portrayed as justifiable revisions of the Treaty of Versailles, which had proclaimed national self-determination as a general principle but denied it to German-speakers in parts of East-Central Europe such as these. In March 1939, however, Hitler had clearly violated the international agreements of the previous year by marching into the rump state of Czecho-Slovakia, dismembering it and creating out of the Czech part the Reich Protectorate of Bohemia and Moravia. For the first time the Third Reich had taken over a substantial area of East-Central Europe that was not inhabited mainly by German speakers. This was in fact the first step towards the fulfilment of a long-nurtured Nazi programme of establishing a new 'living-space' (*Lebensraum*) for the Germans in East-Central and Eastern Europe, where the Slav inhabitants would be reduced to the status of slave labourers and providers of food for their German masters. The Czechs were treated as second-class citizens in the new Protectorate, and those who were drafted into German fields and factories to provide much-needed labour were placed under an especially harsh legal and police regime, more draconian even than that which the Germans themselves were experiencing under Hitler.[21]

At the same time, the Czechs, along with the newly (nominally) independent Slovaks, had been allowed their own civil administration, courts and other institutions. Some Germans at least possessed a degree of respect for Czech culture, and the Czech economy was undeniably advanced. German views of Poland and the Poles were far more negative. Independent Poland had been partitioned between Austria, Prussia and Russia in the eighteenth century and had only come into existence again as a sovereign state at the end of the First World War. Throughout that period, German nationalists mostly believed that the Poles were temperamentally unable to govern themselves. 'Polish muddle' (*Polenwirtschaft*) was a common expression for chaos and inefficiency, and school textbooks commonly portrayed Poland as economically backward and mired in Catholic superstition. The invasion of Poland had little to do with the situation of the German-speaking minority there, which made up only 3 per cent of the population, in contrast to the Czechoslovak Republic, where ethnic Germans had constituted nearly a quarter of the inhabitants. Helped by a long tradition of writing and teaching on the topic, Germans were convinced that they had taken up the burden of a 'civilizing mission' in Poland over the centuries, and it was now time for them to do so again.[22]

Hitler had little to say about Poland and the Poles before the war, and his personal attitude towards them seemed in some ways unclear, in contrast to his long-held dislike of the Czechs, nurtured already in pre-1914 Vienna. What concentrated his mind and turned it sharply against the Poles was the refusal of the military government in Warsaw to make any concessions to his territorial demands, in contrast to the Czechs, who had obligingly caved in under international pressure in 1938, demonstrating their willingness to co-operate with the Third Reich in the dismemberment and eventual suppression of their state. Matters were made worse by the refusal of Britain and France to push Poland into conceding demands such as the return of Danzig to Germany. In 1934, when Hitler had concluded a ten-year non-aggression pact with the Poles, it had seemed possible that Poland might become a satellite state in a future European order dominated by Germany. But by 1939 it had become a serious obstacle to the eastward expansion of the Third Reich. It therefore had to be wiped from the map, and ruthlessly exploited to finance preparations for the coming war in the west.[23]

The decision as to what should be done had still not been taken when, on 22 August 1939, as final preparations were being made for the invasion, Hitler told his leading generals how he envisaged the coming war with Poland:

Our strength lies in our speed and our brutality. Genghis Khan hunted millions of women and children to their deaths, consciously and with a joyous heart. History sees in him only the great founder of a state . . . I have issued a command – and I will have everyone who utters even a single word of criticism shot – that the aim of the war lies not in reaching particular lines but in the physical annihilation of the enemy. Thus, so far only in the east, I have put my Death's Head formations at the ready with the command to send man, woman and child of Polish descent and language to their deaths, pitilessly and remorselessly . . . Poland will be depopulated and settled with Germans.[24]

The Poles were, he told Goebbels, 'more animals than men, totally dull and formless . . . The dirt of the Poles is unimaginable'.[25] Poland had to be subjugated with complete ruthlessness. 'The Poles', he told the Nazi Party ideologue Alfred Rosenberg on 27 September 1939, consisted of 'a thin Germanic layer: underneath frightful material . . . The towns thick with dirt . . . If Poland had gone on ruling the old German parts for a few more decades everything would have become lice-ridden and decayed. What was needed now was a determined and masterful hand to rule.'[26] Hitler's self-confidence grew rapidly as days, then weeks, passed in September 1939 without any sign of an effective intervention by the British and the French to help the Poles. The success of the German armies only increased his feeling of invulnerability. In the creation of

1. Poland and East-Central Europe under the German–Soviet Pact, 1939–41

the Reich Protectorate of Bohemia and Moravia, strategic and economic considerations had played the major role. With the takeover of Poland, however, for the first time, Hitler and the Nazis were ready to unleash the full force of their racial ideology. Occupied Poland was to become the proving-ground for the creation of the new racial order in East-Central Europe, a model for what Hitler intended subsequently to happen in the rest of the region – in Belarus, Russia, the Baltic states and the Ukraine. This was to show what the Nazi concept of a new 'living-space' for the Germans in the east would really mean in practice.[27]

By early October 1939 Hitler had abandoned his initial idea of allowing the Poles to govern themselves in a rump state. Large chunks of Polish territory were annexed by the Reich to form the new Reich Districts of Danzig-West Prussia, under Albert Forster, Nazi Party Regional Leader of Danzig, and Posen (soon renamed the Wartheland), under Arthur Greiser, formerly President of the Danzig Senate. Other pieces of Poland were added on to the existing Reich Districts of East Prussia and Silesia. These measures extended the borders of the Third Reich some 150 to 200 kilometres eastward. Altogether, 90,000 square kilometres of territory were incorporated into the Reich, along with around 10 million people, 80 per cent of them Poles. The rest of Poland, known as the 'General Government', was put under the autocratic rule of Hans Frank, the Nazi Party's legal expert, who had made his name in defending Nazis in criminal cases during the 1920s and since then risen to become Reich Commissioner for Justice and head of the Nazi Lawyers' League. Despite his unconditional loyalty to Hitler, Frank had clashed repeatedly with Heinrich Himmler and the SS, who cared a good deal less for legal formalities than he did, and removing him to Poland was a convenient way of sidelining him. Moreover, his legal experience seemed to fit him well for the task of building up a new administrative structure from scratch. More than 11 million people lived in the General Government, which included the Lublin district and parts of the provinces of Warsaw and Cracow. It was not a 'protectorate' like Bohemia and Moravia, but a colony, outside the Reich and beyond its law, its Polish inhabitants effectively stateless and without rights. In the position of almost unlimited power that he was to enjoy as General Governor, Frank's penchant for brutal and violent rhetoric quickly translated into the reality of brutal and violent action. With Forster, Greiser and Frank occupying the leading administrative positions, the whole area of occupied Poland was now in the hands of hardened 'Old Fighters' of the Nazi movement, portending the unrestrained implementation of extreme Nazi ideology that was to be the guiding principle of the occupation.[28]

Hitler announced his intentions on 17 October 1939 to a small group of senior officials. The General Government, Hitler told them, was to be autonomous from the Reich. It was to be the site of a 'hard ethnic struggle that will not permit any legal restrictions. The methods will not be compatible with our normal principles.' There was to be no attempt at efficient or orderly government. ' "Polish muddle" must be allowed to flourish.' Transport and communications had to be maintained because Poland would be 'an advanced jumping-off point' for the invasion of the Soviet Union at some time in the future. But otherwise, 'any tendencies towards stabilizing the situation in Poland are to be suppressed'. It was not the task of the administration 'to put the country on a sound basis economically and financially'. There must be no opportunity for the Poles to reassert themselves. 'The Polish intelligentsia must be prevented from forming itself into a ruling class. The standard of living in the country is to remain low; it is of use to us only as a reservoir of labour.'[29]

These drastic policies were implemented by a mixture of local paramilitary groups and SS task forces. At the very beginning of the war, Hitler ordered the establishment of an Ethnic German Self-Protection militia in Poland, which soon afterwards came under the aegis of the SS. The militia was organized, and then led in West Prussia, by Ludolf von Alvensleben, adjutant to Heinrich Himmler. He told his men on 16 October 1939: 'You are now the master race here . . . Don't be soft, be merciless, and clear out everything that is not German and could hinder us in the work of construction.'[30] The militia began organized mass shootings of Polish civilians, without any authorization from the military or civil authorities, in widespread acts of revenge for supposed Polish atrocities against the ethnic Germans. Already on 7 October 1939 Alvensleben reported that 4,247 Poles had been subjected to the 'sharpest measures'. In the month from 12 October to 11 November 1939 alone, some 2,000 men, women and children were shot by the militia in Klammer (Kulm district). No fewer than 10,000 Poles and Jews were brought by militiamen to Mniszek, in the parish of Dragass, from the surrounding areas, lined up on the edge of gravel pits, and shot. Militias, assisted by German soldiers, had shot another 8,000, in a wood near Karlshof, in the Zempelburg district, by 15 November 1939. By the time these activities had been brought to an end, early in 1940, many thousands more Poles had fallen victim to the militiamen's rage. In the West Prussian town of Konitz, for example, the local Protestant militia, fired up by hatred and contempt for Poles, Catholics, Jews and anyone who did not fit in with the Nazis' racial ideals, began on 26 September by shooting forty Poles and Jews, without even the pretence of a trial. Their tally of Jewish and Polish victims had reached 900 by the following January. Of the 65,000 Poles and Jews murdered in the last quarter of 1939, around half were killed by the militias, sometimes in bestial circumstances; these were the first mass shootings of civilians in the war.[31]

III

In the course of 1939 Himmler, Heydrich and other leading figures in the SS had been engaged in a lengthy debate about the best way of organizing the various bodies that had come under their control since the beginning of the Third Reich, including the Security Service, the Gestapo, the criminal police and a large number of specialized offices. Their discussions were lent urgency by the prospect of the forthcoming invasion of Poland, in which it was clear that the lines of responsibility and demarcation between the police and the Security Service would need to be redrawn if they were to assert themselves effectively against the mighty power of the German army. On 27 September 1939 Himmler and Heydrich created the Reich Security Head Office (*Reichssicherheitshauptamt*) to pull all the various parts of the police and SS together under a single, centralized directorate. As elaborated over the following months, the Office came to consist of seven departments. Two of these (I and II) ran the administration in all its various activities, from employment conditions to personnel files. The initial director, Werner Best, was eventually pushed aside by his rival Heydrich in June 1940 and his responsibilities divided between less ambitious figures. Heydrich's Security Service itself occupied Departments III and VI, covering respectively domestic and foreign affairs. Department IV consisted of the Gestapo, with sections devoted to dealing with political opponents (IVA), the Churches and the Jews (IVB), 'protective custody' (IVC), occupied territories (IVD) and counter-espionage (IVE). The criminal police was put into Department V, and Department VII was created to investigate oppositional ideologies. The whole vast structure was in a state of constant flux, riven by internal rivalries, and undermined by periodic changes of personnel. However, a number of key individuals ensured a degree of coherence and continuity – notably Reinhard Heydrich, its overall head, Heinrich Müller, the Gestapo chief, Otto Ohlendorf, who ran Department III, Franz Six (Department VII) and Arthur Nebe (Department V). It was to all intents and purposes an independent body, deriving its legitimacy from Hitler's personal pre-rogative power, staffed not with traditional, legally trained civil ser-vants but with ideologically committed Nazis. A key part of its rationale was to politicize the police, many of whose senior officers, including Müller, were career policemen rather than Nazi fanatics. Cut loose from traditional administrative structures, the Reich Security Head Office intervened in every area where Heydrich felt an active, radical presence was needed, first of all in the racial reordering of occupied Poland.[32]

This now proceeded apace. Already on 8 September 1939 Heydrich was reported as saying that 'we want to protect the little people, but the aristocrats, the Poles and Jews must be killed', and expressing his impatience, as was Hitler himself, with the low rate of executions ordered by the formal military courts – a mere 200 a day at this time.[33] Franz Halder, chief of the Army General Staff, believed that 'it's the aim of the Leader and of Göring to annihilate and exterminate the Polish people'.[34] On 19 September 1939 Halder recorded Heydrich as saying there would be a 'clear-out: Jews, intelligentsia, priesthood, aristocracy'. 60,000 names of Polish professionals and intellectuals had been gathered before the war; they were all to be killed. A meeting between Brauchitsch and Hitler on 18 October confirmed that the policy was to 'prevent the Polish intelligentsia from building itself up to become a new leadership stratum. The low standard of living will be maintained. Cheap slaves. All the rabble must be cleared out of German territory. Creation of a complete disorganization.'[35] Heydrich told his subordinate commanders that Hitler had ordered the deportation of Poland's Jews into the General Government, along with professional and educated Poles, apart from the political leaders, who were to be put into concentration camps.[36]

Building on the experience of the occupation of Austria and Czecho-slovakia, and acting on Hitler's explicit orders, Heydrich organized five

Task Forces (*Einsatzgruppen*), later increased to seven, to follow the army into Poland to carry out the Third Reich's ideological policies.[37] Their leaders were appointed by a special administrative unit created by Heydrich and put under the command of Werner Best.[38] The men he appointed to lead the Task Forces and their various sub-units (*Einsatz-kommandos*) were senior Security Service and Security Police officers, mostly well-educated, middle-class men in their mid-to-late thirties who had turned to the far right in the Weimar Republic. Many of the older, more senior commanders had served in the violent paramilitary units of the Free Corps in the early 1920s; their younger subordinates had often been initiated into the politics of the ultra-nationalist, antisemitic far right during their university days in the early 1930s. A good number, though not all, had imbibed violent anti-Polish feelings as members of paramilitary units in the conflicts of 1919–21 in Upper Silesia, as natives of areas forcibly ceded to Poland in the Peace Settlement, or as police officers along the German–Polish border. Best expected his officers not only to be senior, experienced and efficient administrators but also to have military experience of one kind or another.[39]

Typical of these men in most though not all respects was Bruno Streckenbach, an SS brigade leader born in Hamburg in 1902, son of a customs officer. Too young to fight in the First World War, Streckenbach joined a Free Corps unit in 1919 and was involved in fighting against left-wing revolutionaries in Hamburg before taking part in the Kapp putsch of March 1920. After working in various administrative jobs in the 1920s, Streckenbach joined the Nazi Party in 1930 and then in 1931 the SS; in November 1933 he became an officer in the SS Security Service, rising steadily through its ranks and becoming chief of the State Police in Hamburg in 1936, gaining a reputation for ruthlessness in the process. This recommended him to Best, who appointed him head of Task Force I in Poland in 1939. Streckenbach was unusual chiefly in his relative lack of educational attainments; a number of his subordinate officers had doctorates. Like them, however, he had a history of violent commitment to the extreme right.[40]

Streckenbach and the Task Forces, numbering in total about 2,700 men, were charged with establishing the political and economic security of the German occupation in the wake of the invasion. This included not only the killing of 'the leading stratum of the population in Poland' but also the 'combating of all elements in enemy territory to the rear of the fighting troops who are hostile to the Reich and the Germans'.[41] In practice this allowed the Task Forces considerable room for manoeuvre. The Task Forces were placed under the formal command of the army, which was ordered to assist them as far as the tactical situation allowed. This made sense insofar as the Task Forces were meant to deal with espionage, resistance, partisan groups and the like, but in practice they went very much their own way as the SS unfolded its massive campaign of arrests, deportations and murders.[42] The Task Forces were armed with lists of Poles who had fought in one way or another against German rule in Silesia during the troubles that had accompanied the League of Nations plebiscites at the end of the First World War. Polish politicians, leading Catholics and proponents of Polish national identity were singled out for arrest. On 9 September 1939 the Nazi jurist Roland Freisler, State Secretary in the Reich Ministry of Justice, arrived in Bromberg to set up a series of show trials before a special court, which had condemned 100 men to death by the end of the year.[43]

The hospital director Dr Zygmunt Klukowski began recording in his diary mass executions of Poles in his district by the Germans, carried out on the slightest of pretexts – seventeen people in early January 1940, for example.[44] The danger to him as an intellectual, professional man was particularly acute. Klukowski lived in constant fear of arrest, and indeed in June 1940 he was taken by German police from his hospital to an internment camp, where the Poles were put through punishing physical exercises, beaten 'with sticks, whips, or fists', and kept in filthy and insanitary conditions. Under interrogation he told the Germans that there was typhus in his hospital and he had to get back to stop it spreading into the town and possibly infecting them ('In my head I was saying "glory be to the louse",' he later wrote in his diary). He was immediately released to go back to what he portrayed as his thoroughly infested hospital. He had been very lucky, he reflected; he had escaped being beaten or having to run round the prison training field, and he had got out quickly. The experience, he wrote, 'surpassed all the rumors. I was unable before to comprehend the methodical disregard of personal dignity, how human beings could be treated much worse than any animals, while the physical abuses that were performed with sadistic pleasure clearly showed on the faces of the German Gestapo. But,' he went on, '. . . the behavior of the prisoners was magnificent. No one begged for mercy; no one showed even a trace of cowardice . . . All the insults, mistreatment, and abuses were received calmly with the knowledge that they bring shame and disgrace to the German people.'[45]

Reprisals for even the most trivial offences were savage. In one incident in the village of Wawer, a Warsaw physician reported,

A drunken Polish peasant picked a quarrel with a German soldier and in the resulting brawl wounded him with a knife. The Germans seized this opportunity to carry out a real orgy of indiscriminate murder in alleged reprisal for the outrage. Altogether 122 people were killed. As, however, the inhabitants of this village, for some reason or other, apparently fell short of the pre-determined quota of victims, the Germans stopped a train to Warsaw at the local railway station (normally it did not call there at all), dragged out several passengers, absolutely innocent of any knowledge of what had happened, and executed them on the spot without any formalities. Three of them were left hanging with their heads down for four days at the local railway station. A huge board placed over the hideous scene told the story of the victims and threatened that a similar fate was in store for every locality where a German was killed or wounded.[46]

When a thirty-year-old stormtrooper leader and local official arrived drunk at the prison in Hohensalza, hauled the Polish prisoners out of their cells and had fifty-five of them shot on the spot, killing some of them personally, the only effect that the protests of other local officials had was to persuade Regional Leader Greiser to extract from him a promise not to touch any alcohol for the next ten years.[47] In another incident, in Obluze, near Gdynia, the smashing-in of a window in the local police station resulted in the arrest of fifty Polish schoolboys. When they refused to name the culprit, their parents were ordered to beat them in front of the local church. The parents refused, so the SS men beat the boys with their rifle-butts then shot ten of them, leaving their bodies lying in front of the church for a whole day.[48]

Such incidents occurred on a daily basis through the winter of 1939–40 and involved a mixture of regular German troops, ethnic German militias and units from the Task Forces and the Order Police. While the army had not been ordered to kill the Polish intelligentsia, the view most soldiers and junior officers had of Poles as dangerous and treacherous subhumans was enough for them to target a large number of Polish intellectuals and professionals as part of what they thought of as preventive or reprisal measures.[49] Given the fierce if ineffective resistance they encountered from the Poles, German army commanders were extremely worried at the prospect of a guerrilla war against their troops, and took the most draconian retaliatory measures where they suspected it was emerging.[50] 'If there is shooting from a village behind the front,' ordered Colonel-General von Bock on 10 September 1939, 'and if it proves impossible to identify the house from which the shots came, then the whole village is to be burned to the ground.'[51] By the time the military administration of occupied Poland ended on 26 October, 531 towns and villages had been burned to the ground, and 16,376 Poles had been executed.[52] Lower-ranking German soldiers were fuelled by fear, contempt and rage as they encountered Polish resistance. In many units, officers gave pep-talks before the invasion, underlining the barbarism, bestiality and subhumanity of the Poles. Corporal Franz Ortner, a rifle-man, railed in a report against what he called the 'brutalized' Poles, who had, he thought, bayoneted the German wounded on the battlefield. A private, writing a letter home, described Polish actions against ethnic Germans as 'brutish'. Poles were 'insidious', 'treacherous', 'base'; they were mentally subnormal, cowardly, fanatical; they lived in 'stinking holes' instead of houses; and they were under the 'baleful influence of Jewry'. Soldiers waxed indignant about the conditions in which Poles lived: 'Everywhere foul straw, damp, pots and flannels', wrote one of a Polish home he entered, confirming everything he had heard about the backwardness of the Poles.[53]

Typical examples of the ordinary soldier's behaviour can be found in the diary of Gerhard M., a stormtrooper, born in Flensburg in 1914 and called up to the army shortly before the war. On 7 September 1939 his unit encountered resistance from 'cowardly snipers' in a Polish village. Gerhard M. had been a fireman before the war. But now he and the men of his unit burned the village to the ground.

Burning houses, weeping women, screaming children. A picture of misery. But the Polish people didn't want it any better. In one of the primitive peasant houses we even surprised a woman servicing a Polish machine-gun. The house was turned over and set alight. After a short while the woman was surrounded by the flames and tried to get out. But we stopped her, as hard as it was. Soldiers can't be treated any differently just because they're in skirts. Her screaming rang in my ears long after. The whole village burned. We had to walk exactly in the middle of the street, because the heat from the burning houses on both sides was too great.[54]

Such scenes repeated themselves as the German armies advanced. A few days later, on 10 September 1939, Gerhard M.'s unit was fired on from another Polish village and set the houses alight.

Soon burning houses were lining our route, and out of the flames there sounded the screams of the people who had hidden in them and were unable any more to rescue themselves. The animals were bellowing in fear of death, a dog howled until it was burned up, but worst of all was the screaming of the people. It was dreadful. It's still ringing in my ears even today. But they shot at us and so they deserved death.[55]

SS Task Forces, police units, ethnic German paramilitaries and regular German soldiers were thus killing civilians all over German-occupied Poland from September 1939 onwards. As well as observing actions of this kind, Dr Klukowski began to notice more and more young Polish men leaving for work in Germany in the early months of 1940. At the beginning of the year, indeed, the Reich Food Ministry, together with the Labour Ministry and the Office of the Four-Year Plan, had demanded a million Polish workers for the Reich economy. 75 per cent of them were to work in agriculture, where there was a serious labour shortage. These, as Göring decreed on 25 January 1940, were to come from the General Government. If they did not volunteer, they would have to be conscripted. Given the miserable conditions that existed in occupied Poland, the prospect of living in Germany was not unattractive, and over 80,000 Polish workers, a third of them women, were transported voluntarily to Germany on 154 special trains in February, mainly from the General Government. Once in Germany, however, they were sub-jected to harshly discriminatory laws and repressive measures.[56] News of their treatment in Germany quickly led to a sharp decline in the number of volunteers, so that from April 1940 Frank introduced com-pulsion in an attempt to fulfil his quota. Increasingly, young Poles fled into the forests to avoid labour conscription in Germany; the beginnings of the Polish underground resistance movement date from this time.[57] In January the resistance tried to assassinate the General Government's police chief, and over the following weeks there were uprisings and murders of ethnic Germans in a number of villages. On 30 May 1940, Frank initiated a 'pacification action' in which 4,000 resistance fighters and intellectuals, half of whom were already in custody, were killed, along with some 3,000 Poles sentenced for criminal offences.[58] This had little effect. In February 1940 there were still only 295,000 Poles, mostly prisoners of war, working as labourers in the Old Reich. This in no way made good the labour shortages that had been occasioned by the mass conscription of German men into the armed forces. By the summer of 1940, there were 700,000 Poles working as voluntary or forced labourers in the Old Reich; another 300,000 went to the Reich the following year. By this time, Frank was issuing local administrations with fixed quotas to fulfil. Often the police surrounded villages and arrested all the young men in them. Those who attempted to flee were shot. In towns, young Poles were simply rounded up by the police and the SS in cinemas or other public places, or on the streets, and shipped off without further ceremony. As a result of these methods, by September 1941 there were over a million Polish workers in the Old Reich. According to one estimate, only 15 per cent of them had gone there of their own accord.[59]

The mass deportation of young Poles as forced workers to the Reich was paralleled by a wholesale campaign of looting unleashed by the German occupation forces. When German soldiers tried to steal from his hospital, Klukowski managed to get rid of them by telling them once again that several of the patients had typhus.[60] Others were not so quick-witted, or so well situated. The requirement for the troops to live off the land was not accompanied by any kind of detailed rules of requisitioning. From impounding chickens it was but a short step to requisitioning cooking equipment and then to stealing money and jewellery.[61] Typical was the experience of Gerhard M., whose unit arrived in a Polish town and stood on the street awaiting orders:

A resourceful chap had discovered a chocolate shop with its windows boarded over. Unfortunately the owner wasn't there. So we cleared out the shop on tick. Our vehicles were piled high with chocolate until there was no more room. Every soldier ran around with his cheeks stuffed full, chewing. We were mightily pleased with the cheapness of the purchase. I discovered a store of really beautiful apples. All up onto our vehicle. A can of lemons and chocolate biscuits on the back of my bike, and then off we went again.[62]

Leading the way in the despoliation of occupied Poland was the General Governor himself. Frank made no effort to conceal his greed. He even referred to himself as a robber baron. He confiscated the country estate of the Potocki family for use as a rural retreat, and drove around his fiefdom in a limousine large enough to attract critical comment even from colleagues such as the Governor of Galicia. Aping Hitler, he built an imitation of the Berghof in the hills near Zakopane. The magnificent banquets he staged caused his waistline to expand so fast that he consulted a dietician because he could barely fit into his dress uniform any more.[63]

Looting and requisitioning were soon placed on a formal, quasi-legal basis in the territories incorporated into the Reich. On 27 September 1939 the German military government in Poland decreed a blanket confiscation of Polish property, confirming the order again on 5 October 1939. On 19 October 1939 Göring announced that the Office of the Four-Year Plan was seizing all Polish and Jewish property in the incorporated territories. This practice was formalized by a decree on 17 September 1940 that set up a central agency, the Head Office of the Trustees for the East (*Haupttreuhandstelle Ost*), to administer the confiscated enterprises. In February 1941 these already included over 205,000 businesses ranging in size from small workshops to major industrial enterprises. By June 1941, 50 per cent of businesses and a third of the larger landed estates in the annexed territories had been taken over by the requisitioned Trustees without compensation. In addition, the army took over a substantial number of farms to secure food supplies for the troops.[64] Confiscations included the removal of scientific equipment from university laboratories for use in Germany. Even the Warsaw Zoo's collection of stuffed animals was taken away.[65] Metal was at a premium. Along the banks of the Vistula, one German paratrooper reported not long after the invasion, there were great crates 'full of bars of copper, lead, zinc in enormous quantities. Everything, absolutely everything was loaded up and brought back to the Reich.'[66] As had been the case in the Reich itself for some time, iron and steel objects, such as park railings and garden gates, even candelabras and saucepans, were collected to be melted down and used in armament and vehicle production in Germany.[67] When the cold winter really began to bite, in January 1940, Dr Klukowski noted, 'the German police took all sheepskin coats from passing villagers and left them only in jackets'.[68] Not long afterwards the occupation forces began raiding villages and confiscating all the banknotes they found there.[69]

IV

Not all German army commanders, particularly in the senior ranks, where the influence of Nazism was less extreme than lower down the army hierarchy, accepted this situation with equanimity. Some of them indeed were soon complaining of unauthorized shootings of Polish civilians on the orders of junior officers, and of looting and extortion by German troops, and alleging that 'some of the prisoners were brutally beaten'. 'Near Pultusk,' reported a General Staff officer, '80 Jews have been mown down in a bestial manner. A court-martial has been established, also against two people who have been looting, murdering and raping in Bromberg.' Such actions began to arouse concern in the army leadership. Already on 10 September 1939 Chief of the Army General Staff Franz Halder was noticing 'dirty deeds behind the front'.[70] In mid-October, complaints from army commanders led to an agreement that the 'self-protection militias' were to be dissolved, though in some areas it took several months for this to be brought about.[71] But this did not end the senior officers' concerns. On 25 October 1939 Walther von Brauchitsch, Commander-in-Chief of the army, rapped his officers sharply over the knuckles about their conduct in Poland:

A disturbing number of cases, for example of illegal expulsion, forbidden confiscation, self-enrichment, misappropriation and theft, maltreatment or threatening subordinates partly in over-excitement, partly in senseless drunkenness, disobedience with the most serious consequences for the troop unit under command, rape of a married woman, etc., yield a picture of soldiers with the habits of freebooting mercenaries (*Landsknechtsmanieren*), which cannot be strongly enough condemned.[72]

A number of other senior officers, including those whose belief in Hitler and National Socialism was beyond question, shared this view.[73]

In many instances, army leaders, concerned that they might be saddled with the responsibility for the mass murders now in progress, were only too pleased to devolve it onto the SS Security Service Task Force leaders by allowing them a free hand.[74] Yet instances began to multiply of senior army officers taking action against SS units which they thought to be breaching the laws and conventions of war and causing disturbances behind the front that were a general threat to order. General von

Küchler, commander of the German Third Army, ordered the arrest and disarming of a police unit belonging to Task Force V after it had shot some Jews and set their houses on fire in Mlawa. He court-martialled members of an SS artillery regiment who had driven fifty Jews into a synagogue near Rozan after they had finished working on strengthening a bridge, and then shot them all 'without reason'. Other officers took similar measures, even in one case arresting a member of Hitler's SS bodyguard. Brauchitsch had met Hitler on 20 September and Heydrich on 21 September to try to sort out the situation. The only result was an amnesty issued by Hitler personally on 4 October for crimes committed 'out of bitterness against the atrocities committed by the Poles'. Yet military discipline was being threatened, and a number of senior officers were deeply concerned. Rumours spread quickly through the officer corps. At his Cologne base in early December 1939, a thoughtful staff officer in his mid-thirties, Captain Hans Meier-Welcker, heard of the atrocities and wondered, 'How will something like this avenge itself?'[75]

The most outspoken criticism of the occupation policy came from Colonel-General Johannes Blaskowitz, who had played a major part in the invasion and was appointed Commander-in-Chief East, in charge of the military administration of the conquered territories, in late October 1939. Military rule was formally brought to an end on 26 October 1939, and authority passed to the civil administration. Thus Blaskowitz had no general powers over the region. Nevertheless he remained responsible for its military defence. A few weeks after his appointment, Blaskowitz sent Hitler a lengthy memorandum detailing the crimes and atrocities committed by SS and police units in the area under his command. He repeated his allegations at greater length in a memorandum prepared for an official visit by the army Commander-in-Chief to his headquarters on 15 February 1940. He condemned the killing of tens of thousands of Jews and Poles as counter-productive. It would, he wrote, damage Germany's reputation abroad. It would only strengthen Polish national feeling and drive more Poles and Jews into the resistance. It was harming the army's reputation in the population. He warned of 'the boundless brutalization and moral depravity that will spread through valuable German human material like an epidemic in the shortest time' if it was allowed to continue. Blaskowitz instanced a number of cases of murder and looting by SS and police units. 'Every soldier,' he wrote, 'feels himself disgusted and repelled by these crimes that are being committed in Poland by members of the Reich and representatives of its state authority.'[76]

The hatred and bitterness these actions were arousing in the population were driving Poles and Jews together in a common cause against the invader and needlessly endangering military security and economic life, he told the Nazi Leader.[77] Hitler dismissed such scruples as 'childish'. One could not fight a war with the methods of the Salvation Army. He had never liked or trusted Blaskowitz anyway, he told his adjutant, Gerhard Engel. He should be dismissed. The head of the army, Walther von Brauchitsch, brushed aside the incidents detailed by his subordinate as 'regrettable errors of judgement' or baseless 'rumours'. In any case, he was fully behind what he called the 'otherwise unusual, tough measures taken against the Polish population in the occupied territory' that were in his view necessary in view of the need for the 'securing of the German living-space' ordered by Hitler. Lacking support from his superior, Blaskowitz was relieved of his command in May 1940. Although he subsequently served in senior posts in other theatres of war, Blaskowitz never gained his Field Marshal's baton, unlike other generals of his standing.[78]

The generals, now more concerned with military events in the west, knuckled under.[79] General Georg von Küchler issued an order on 22 July 1940 banning his officers from indulging in 'any criticism of the struggle being waged with the population in the General Government, for example the treatment of the Polish minorities, the Jews, and Church matters. The achievement of a final solution of this ethnic struggle,' he added, 'which has been raging for centuries along our eastern frontier, requires particularly tough measures.'[80] Many senior army officers subscribed to this view. What they were concerned about in the main was indiscipline. Given the prevailing attitude of the troops and of junior and middle-ranking officers towards the Poles, it was scarcely surprising that the incidents where officers intervened to prevent atrocities were relatively few in number. The German army hierarchy did not, for example, intend to break the Geneva Convention of 1929 in relation to the nearly 700,000 prisoners of war they took in the Polish campaign, but there were numerous cases of military guards shooting Polish prisoners when they failed to keep up with a forced march, killing prisoners who were too weak or ill to stand, and penning prisoners into open-air camps with inadequate food and supplies. On 9 September 1939, when a motorized German infantry regiment took 300 Polish prisoners after a half-hour exchange of fire near Ciepielów, the colonel in charge, angered by the loss of fourteen of his men during the clash, lined all the prisoners up and had them machine-gunned into a ditch by the side of the road. A later Polish investigation identified a further sixty-three incidents of this kind, and many more must have gone unrecorded.[81] In formal military executions alone at least 16,000 Poles were shot; one estimate puts the figure at 27,000.[82]

THE NEW RACIAL ORDER

I

Hitler had announced before the war that he intended to clear the Poles out of Poland and bring in German settlers instead. In effect, Poland was to serve the same function for Germany as Australia had for Britain, or the American West for the USA: it was to be a colony of settlement, in which the supposedly racially inferior indigenous inhabitants would be removed by one means or another to make room for the invading master race. The idea of changing the ethnic map of Europe by forcibly shifting ethnic groups from one area to another was not new either: a precedent had already been established immediately after the First World War with a large-scale exchange of minority populations between Turkey and Greece. In 1938, too, Hitler had toyed with the idea of including in the Munich agreement a clause providing for the 'repatriation' of ethnic Germans from rump Czecho-Slovakia to the Sudetenland. And the following spring, with the annexation of the rump state, he had briefly considered an even more drastic idea of deporting 6 million Czechs to the east. Neither of these notions came to anything. But Poland was a different matter. As the prospect of an invasion loomed, the Race and Settlement Head Office of the Nazi Party, originally set up by Richard Walther Darré to encourage the movement of urban citizens on to new farms within Germany itself, began to turn its attention to Eastern Europe. Under the slogan 'One People, One Reich, One Leader', Nazi ideologues started to think about bringing back ethnic Germans from their far-flung settlements across Eastern Europe into the Reich, now, from the autumn of 1939, extended to include large areas inhabited by Poles.[83]

On 7 October 1939 Hitler appointed Heinrich Himmler Reich Commissioner for the Strengthening of the German Race. The previous day, Hitler had declared, in a lengthy speech delivered to the Reichstag to celebrate the victory over Poland, that the time had come for 'a new ordering of ethnographic relations, which means a resettlement of the nationalities so that, after the conclusion of this development, better lines of demarcation are given than is the case today'.[84] In the decree of 7 October 1939, Hitler ordered the head of the SS

(1) to bring back those German citizens and ethnic Germans abroad who are eligible for permanent return to the Reich; (2) to eliminate the harmful influence of such alien parts of the population as constitute a danger to the Reich and the German community; (3) to create new German colonies by resettlement, and especially by the resettlement of German citizens and ethnic Germans coming back from abroad.[85]

Over the winter months of 1939–40 Himmler set up an elaborate bureaucracy to manage this process, drawing on preparatory work by the Racial-Political Office of the Nazi Party and the Race and Settlement Head Office of the SS. Two enormous forced population transfers began almost immediately: the removal of Poles from the incorporated territories, and the identification and 'repatriation' of ethnic Germans from other parts of Eastern Europe to replace them.[86]

The Germanization of the incorporated territories began when 88,000 Poles and Jews were arrested in Posen in the first half of December 1939, taken by train to the General Government and dumped there on arrival. Fit and able-bodied men were separated out and taken to Germany as forced labourers. None of them received any compensation for the loss of their homes, their property, their businesses or their assets. The conditions of their deportation, in the middle of winter, with inadequate clothing and supplies, in unheated freight trucks, were murderous. When one trainload arrived in Cracow in mid-December 1939, the receiving officials had to take off the bodies of forty children who had frozen to death on the journey.[87] Dr Klukowski treated evacuees from Posen in his hospital at Szczebrzeszyn in the second week of December 1939: 160 of them, 'workers, farmers, teachers, clerks, bankers, and merchants', had been given twenty minutes' notice then were 'loaded into unheated railroad cars ... The German soldiers were extremely brutal. One of the sick that I received at the hospital, a bookkeeper, had been so severely beaten that he will require long hospitalization.'[88] Another group of 1,070 deportees who arrived on 28 May 1940 were, he reported, in a 'terrible condition, resigned to their fate, completely broken, in particular those whose children had been taken to the labor camps'.[89] The deportations continued, with Klukowski and others like him desperately trying to organize food, medical care and accommodation for the victims on their arrival. By the time they had finished, early in 1941, a total of 365,000 people had been deported from Posen. The same actions took place in other parts of the former Polish Republic. Altogether over a million people were involved, a third of them Jewish. They lost all their property, assets and possessions. 'Hundreds of them who were farmers,' Klukowski wrote, 'became beggars in one hour.'[90]

One of those who observed the arrival of the Polish deportees in the General Government was Wilm Hosenfeld, a German army officer whose relatively poor health had prevented him from taking a direct part in the fighting. Born in 1895 in Hesse, Hosenfeld had spent most of his life to this point not as a military man but as a schoolteacher. His involvement in the German youth movement had led him to join the brownshirts in 1933, and he had also become a member of the National Socialist Teachers' League and, in 1935, the Nazi Party itself. But Hosenfeld's strong Catholic faith was beginning even in the mid-1930s to outweigh his commitment to Nazism. His open opposition to Alfred Rosenberg's attacks on Christianity caused him problems within the Party, and after he was called up on 26 August 1939 and sent to Poland a month later to build a prisoner-of-war camp, the deep religious faith of the Polish inmates began to arouse his sympathy. When he encountered a trainload of Polish deportees in mid-December, he found a way to talk to some of them, and was shocked by the story they had to tell. Surreptitiously he gave them food, and handed some of the children a bag of sweets. On 14 December 1939 he noted in his diary the disturbing effect the encounter had on him:

I want to comfort all these unhappy people and ask their forgiveness for the fact that the Germans treat them the way they do, so terribly without mercy, so cruelly without humanity. Why are these people being torn away from their dwellings when it is not known where else they can be accommodated? For a whole day long they are standing in the cold, sitting on their bundles, their meagre belongings, they are given nothing to eat. There's system in it, the intention is to make these people sick, poor, helpless, they are to perish.[91]

Few Germans thought along these lines. Hosenfeld recorded numerous arrests and atrocities against Poles. A fellow officer told him how he had asked a Gestapo official rhetorically: 'Do you think you can win these men over for reconstruction by these methods? When they come back from the concentration camp they will be the Germans' worst enemies!!' 'Yeah,' replied the policeman, 'do you think then that even one of them will be coming back? They'll all be shot trying to escape.'[92]

Overriding objections from Göring, who was worried that the re-settlement programme was disrupting the war economy, Himmler also deported over 260,000 Poles from the Wartheland in the course of 1940, as well as thousands more from other areas, particularly Upper Silesia and Danzig-West Prussia. Brushing aside the Ministry of the Interior's bureaucratic view that all that was necessary was to enrol the remaining Poles in an inferior category of German nationality, the SS leadership in the Wartheland persuaded Regional Leader Greiser to set up a German Ethnic List. Poles deemed suitable for Germanization would be enrolled in it under a variety of headings such as pro-Nazi ethnic Germans, Germans who had come under Polish influence and so on, and given different levels of privileges accordingly; on 4 March 1941 this system was extended to the whole of the occupied territories.[93]

A whole bureaucracy soon sprang up to assess these people for Germanization along ethnic, linguistic, religious and other lines. The SS saw a problem in the fact that, as it judged, Poles who led the resistance were likely to 'have a significant proportion of Nordic blood which, in contrast to the otherwise fatalistic Slavic strains, has enabled them to take the initiative'. The solution that presented itself was to remove the children from such families to help them escape from the bad influence of their Polish nationalist parents. In addition, all Polish orphanages in the incorporated territories were closed in the spring of 1941 and the children taken off to the Old Reich. As Himmler remarked in a memorandum written on 15 May 1940 and approved by Hitler, this would 'remove the danger that this subhuman people of the east might acquire a leader class from such people of good blood, which would be dangerous for us because they would be our equals'.[94] Thousands of Polish children deemed suitable for Germanization were sent to special camps in the Reich. Here they were given German names and identity papers (including forged birth certificates) and were put through a six-month course of learning the German language and imbibing the rudiments of

Nazi ideology. Many of the children were effectively orphans, whose parents had been shot or deported as forced labourers; a number were simply identified on the street by German police or SS patrols, or by women volunteers for the Nazi People's Welfare organization, which dealt with the minority of these children who were between the ages of six and twelve (the majority, under the age of six, fell under the aegis of the SS 'Well of Life' homes). Eventually they were assigned to ideologically approved German foster-families. All of this led to a kind of officially sanctioned black market in babies and small children, in which childless German couples acquired Polish infants and brought them up as Germans. 80 per cent of the deported children never returned to their families in Poland.[95]

Aware that both Hitler and Himmler wanted the incorporated territories Germanized as fast as possible, Regional Leader Forster in Danzig-West Prussia indiscriminately enrolled whole villages and towns on the official German Ethnic List. One resettlement officer remembered after the war that when a local mayor or Nazi Party branch leader rejected an order by Forster to enrol 80 per cent of the people in his district as Germans on the grounds that 80 per cent of them were in fact Polish, Forster himself came to the village to enforce the enrolment personally. On receiving their papers, the vast majority of those enrolled in this way sent the mayor written rejections. They were enrolled anyway. By the end of 1942, as a result of such actions, 600,000 new applications for Germanization had been received in Danzig-West Prussia.[96] Arthur Greiser, Regional Leader of the Wartheland, disapproved of such ploys by his neighbour and rival, telling Himmler: 'My ethnic policy is . . . being imperilled by that being carried out in the Reich District of Danzig-West Prussia . . .'[97] But arbitrary Germanization continued, not only in the incorporated territories, but increasingly in the General Government too. Early in 1943, faced, like many other Poles in his town, with the demand to fill in a form, entitled *Application for the Issuing of an Identity Card for People of German Descent*, Zygmunt Klukowski crossed out the heading with red ink, and signed himself 'Polish National'.[98]

General Governor Frank became increasingly irritated at the way in which his province was being used as a dumping-ground for unwanted Poles. Already at the end of October 1939 it was estimated that the population of the General Government would have increased from 10 million to 13 million by the following February.[99] From May 1940, in agreement with Hitler, Frank abandoned his initial policy of regarding the General Government as the basis for a rump Polish state and began to prepare for its incorporation in the medium-to-long term into the Reich. In accordance with this new purpose, Frank began to think of his province as a German colony run by settlers with cheap and expendable labour supplied by uneducated Poles. 'We're thinking here in the greatest imperial style of all times,' he declared in November 1940.[100] For all his resentment against the independent power of the SS, Frank made sure that Poles were explicitly excluded from the protection of the law. 'The Pole,' he said in December 1940, 'must feel that we are not building him a legal state, but that for him there is only one duty, namely to work and to behave himself.' Special legal provisions were introduced for Poles in the incorporated territories too, gradually though never completely replacing the arbitrary terror of the early months of German occupation. Poles were subjected to a draconian legal order that prescribed harsher punishments (labour camp, corporal punishment, or the death penalty) for offences that would lead only to imprisonment for German citizens. Appeal was ruled out, and offences such as making hostile remarks about Germans were made punishable by death in some cases. Introduced in December 1941, these measures codified what in fact had been widely carried out in practice in more arbitrary ways, and paralleled the harsh legal measures already introduced in the Reich to deal with Polish and other foreign workers. Poles were second-class citizens, whose inferior position was underlined by a host of local police regulations ordering them to stand aside and remove their hats if Germans passed them on the street, or to serve Germans first in shops and markets.[101]

The Germanization programme began with the Wartheland, on the basis that it had been part of Prussia before 1918, although only 7 per cent of the population consisted of ethnic Germans in 1939. Already under Bismarck in the nineteenth century, strenuous efforts had been made to foster German culture in Prussian Poland and to suppress the Poles' own feelings of national identity. But they did not go nearly as far as the policies implemented from 1939 onwards. Polish schools, theatres, museums, libraries, bookshops, newspapers and all other Polish cultural and linguistic institutions were closed down, and the use of the Polish language was forbidden. Poles were banned from possessing gramophones and cameras, and any Pole found attending a German theatre was liable to arrest and imprisonment. The names of administrative districts, towns and villages were Germanized, sometimes by translating directly from the Polish, sometimes by using the names of prominent local Germans, but wherever possible, in the areas formerly ruled by Prussia, by reverting to the old German names used before 1919. Street names and public notices were similarly Germanized. Regional Leader Greiser launched a radical attack on the Catholic Church, the institution that more than any other had sustained Polish national identity over the centuries, confiscating its property and funds and closing down its lay organizations. Numerous clergy, monks, diocesan administrators and officials of the Church were arrested, deported to the General Government, taken off to a concentration camp in the Reich, or simply shot. Altogether, some 1,700 Polish priests ended up in Dachau: half of them did not survive their imprisonment. Greiser was encouraged in these policies not only by Heydrich and Bormann, but also by the head of his administrative staff, August Jäger, who had made a name for himself in 1934 as the official charged with Nazifying the Evangelical Church in Prussia. By the end of 1941, the Polish Catholic Church was effectively outlawed in the Wartheland. It was more or less Germanized in the other occupied territories, despite an encyclical issued by the Pope as early as 27 October 1939 protesting against this persecution.[102]

Polish culture was assaulted in the General Government too. On 27 October 1939 the mayor of Warsaw was arrested (he was later shot), and on 6 November 182 members of the academic staff of the university and other higher education institutions in Cracow were arrested and taken to Sachsenhausen concentration camp.[103] Universities, schools, libraries, publishing houses, archives, museums and other centres of Polish culture were closed down.[104] 'The Poles,' said Frank, 'do not need universities or secondary schools: the Polish lands are to be changed into an intellectual desert.' 'For the Poles,' he declared on 31 October 1939, 'the only educational opportunities that are to be made available are those that demonstrate to them the hopelessness of their ethnic fate.'[105] Frank only allowed Poles cheap, undemanding entertainment such as sex shows, light opera and drink.[106] Music by Polish composers (including Chopin) was banned, and Polish national monuments were blown up or pulled down.[107] The Germans' assault on Polish educational standards began at the same time as their attempt to suppress Polish culture. In Szczebrzeszyn, following a wider pattern, the German military authorities closed the two local high schools on 20 November 1939.

They did not reopen. Soon after, the German administration began to attack standards of education in the local elementary schools. Dr Klukowski noted on 25 January 1940: 'Today the Germans ordered all school principals to take from the students handbooks of the Polish language as well as history and geography texts. In every Szczebrzeszyn school, in every classroom, children returned books . . . I am in shock and deeply depressed.'[108] Worse was to come, for on 17 April 1941, he reported, 'the Germans removed from the attic of the grammar school buildings all books and teaching supplies. They were piled up on the playground and burned.' Polish intellectuals and teachers did their best to organize advanced lessons informally and in secret, but given the mass murder of so many of them by the German occupiers, such efforts met with only limited success, even if their symbolic importance was considerable.[109] Day after day, Zygmunt Klukowski recorded in his diary the murder of Polish writers, scientists, artists, musicians and intellectuals, many of them his friends. 'Many have been killed,' he noted on 25 November 1940, 'many are still dying in German camps.'[110]

II

Not only were supposedly suitable Poles reclassified as German, but large numbers of ethnic Germans quickly began to be moved in to take over the farms and businesses from which the Poles had been so brutally expelled. Already in late September 1939, Hitler specifically requested the 'repatriation' of ethnic Germans in Latvia and Estonia as well as from the Soviet-controlled eastern part of Poland. Over the following months, Himmler took steps to carry out his wishes. Several thousand ethnic Germans were moved into the incorporated areas from the General Government, but most were transported there from areas controlled by the Soviet Union, under a series of international agreements negotiated by Himmler. So many German settlers arrived in the General Government and the incorporated territories in the course of the early 1940s that another 400,000 Poles were thrown out of their homes from March 1941 onwards, without actually being deported, so that the settlers could be provided with accommodation. Over the course of the following months and years, 136,000 ethnic Germans came in from eastern Poland, 150,000 from the Baltic states, 30,000 from the General

Government and 200,000 from Romania. They were persuaded to leave by the promise of better conditions and a more prosperous life, and the threat of oppression under Soviet Communism or Romanian nationalism. By May 1943 some 408,000 had been resettled in the Wartheland and the other incorporated parts of Poland, and another 74,000 in the Old Reich.[111]

In order to qualify for resettlement, all but a lucky 50,000 of the half-million immigrants were put into transit camps, of which there were more than 1,500 at the height of the transfer, and subjected to racial and political screening, a process personally approved by Hitler on 28 May 1940. Conditions in the camps, which were often converted factories, monasteries or public buildings seized from the Poles, were less than ideal, though an effort was made to keep families together, and compensation was paid in bonds or property for the assets they had been forced to leave behind. Assessors from the SS Race and Settlement Head Office based at the police immigration centre in Lódź descended on the camps and began their work. With only four weeks' training in the basics of racial-biological assessment, these officials were equipped with a set of guidelines, including twenty-one physical criteria (fifteen of them physiognomical) that could never be anything other than extremely rough. The immigrants were x-rayed, medically examined, photographed and questioned about their political views, their family, their job and their interests. The resulting classification ranged from 'very suitable' at the top end, where the immigrants were 'purely Nordic, purely phalian or Nordic-phalian', without any noticeable 'defects of intellect, character or of a hereditary nature', to 'ethnically or biologically unsuitable' at the bottom end, where they were considered to be of non-European blood, or to possess a malformed physique, or to be from 'families who are socially weak or incompetent'.[112] This inevitably meant that the programme of resettlement proceeded only very slowly. Altogether, by December 1942, settlers had taken over 20 per cent of the businesses in the annexed territories, Reich Germans 8 per cent, local Germans 51 per cent, and trustees acting on behalf of the military veterans of the future another 21 per cent. Out of 928,000 farms in these districts, 47,000 had been taken over by settlers; 1.9 million out of a total of 9.2 million hectares of land had been seized from Poles and given to Germans. Yet out of the 1.25 million settlers, only 500,000 had actually been resettled by this point; the vast majority were in camps of one kind or another, and thousands of them had been there for well over a year. 3 million people had registered as Germans in the incorporated territories, but there were still 10 million Polish inhabitants of the Greater German Reich. Clearly, the Germanization programme was far from complete as it entered its fourth year.[113]

The programme continued throughout 1943, as more Polish villages were compulsorily evacuated. Himmler started to use the scheme as a way of dealing with supposedly untrustworthy groups in the borderlands of the Old Reich such as Luxembourg. Families where the husband had deserted from the German army were rounded up in Lorraine and shipped off to Poland as settlers. In 1941 54,000 Slovenes were taken from the border regions of Austria to camps in Poland, where 38,000 of them were found racially valuable and treated as settlers.[114] Travelling through the evacuated villages of Wieloncza and Zawada in May 1943, Zygmunt Klukowski noted that 'German settlers are moving in. Everywhere you can see young German boys in Hitler Youth uniforms.'[115] He continued to list villages in his area that were forcibly evacuated, their Polish inhabitants taken off to a nearby camp, well into July 1943. Visiting the camp in August 1943, Klukowski noted the inmates, behind barbed wire, were malnourished and sick, 'barely moving, looking terrible'. In the camp hospital there were forty children under the age of five, suffering from dysentery and measles, lying two to a bed, looking 'like skeletons'. His offer to take some of them to his own hospital was brusquely rejected by the German officials. In his own town of Szczebrzeszyn, too, Poles were increasingly being turfed out of their homes to make way for incoming German settlers.[116]

The Germanization of the Zamość area, pushed through by Himmler in the teeth of opposition from Frank, was in fact intended to be the first part of a comprehensive programme affecting all of the General Government in due course, though it never got that far. Even so, some 110,000 Poles were forcibly expropriated and expelled from the Lublin region in the process, making up 31 per cent of the population, and between November 1942 and March 1943, forty-seven villages in the Zamość area were cleared to make way for incoming Germans. Many of the Polish inhabitants fled to the forests, taking as much as they could with them, to join the underground resistance.[117] By mid-July 1943 Klukowski's home town of Szczebrzeszyn had been officially declared a German settlement and demoted to the status of a village.[118] 'On the city

2. Population Transfers of Ethnic Germans, 1939–43

streets,' noted Klukowski, who refused to accept this insult to his home town, 'you can see many Germans in civilian clothing, mostly women and children, all new settlers.' New facilities were opened for them, including a kindergarten. Soon he was noting that 'stores are run by Germans; we have German barbers, tailors, shoemakers, bakers, butchers, and mechanics. A new restaurant was opened with the name *Neue Heimat (New Home)*.' Those Poles who had not signed themselves on to the register of ethnic Germans were second-class citizens, used for forced labour, and treated as if their lives meant nothing. On 27 August 1943 Klukowski reported the case of an eight-year-old Polish boy who was found 'lying in an orchard with gunshot wounds. He was taken to the hospital where he died. We learned the boy went there for apples. The new owner, a German locksmith, shot him and left him to die, without telling anyone.'[119]

The Germans who moved into the Wartheland had few reservations about the expulsion of the region's Poles to make way for them. 'I really like the town of Posen,' wrote Hermann Voss, an anatomist appointed to a chair in the Medical Faculty of the new Reich University of Posen, a foundation put at the apex of the German educational system in the occupied territories, in April 1941, 'if only there were no Poles at all, it would be really lovely here.' In May 1941 he noted in his diary that the crematorium in his university department had been taken over by the SS. He had no objections, however – rather the contrary: 'There is a crematorium for burning corpses in the cellar of the Institute building here. It's for the exclusive use of the Gestapo. The Poles they shoot are brought here at night and cremated. If one could only turn the whole of Polish society into ashes!'[120] In addition to the immigrants from the east, some 200,000 Germans moved into the incorporated territories from the Old Reich. A number of these were children and adolescents evacuated from Germany's cities to avoid the dangers of aerial bombardment: thousands were put into military-style camps, where they were subjected to harsh discipline, bullying and a rough, decidedly non-academic style of education.[121]

But many adults went voluntarily to the incorporated territories, seeing them as an ideal area for colonial settlement. Often they regarded themselves as pioneers. One such was Melita Maschmann, sent as press officer for the Hitler Youth in the Wartheland in November 1939. Noticing the absence of educated people amongst the Polish population, she concluded that the Poles were a miserable, poverty-stricken, under-developed people who were incapable of forming a viable state of their own. Their high birth-rate made them a serious threat to the German future, as she had learned from her 'racial science' lessons at school. She sympathized with the poverty and wretchedness of many Polish children whom she saw begging on the streets or stealing coal from the depots, but, under the influence of Nazi propaganda, she later wrote:

I told myself that if the Poles were using every means in the fight not to lose that disputed eastern province which the German nation required as '*Lebensraum*', then they remained our enemies, and I regarded it as my duty to suppress my private feelings if they conflicted with political necessity ... A group which believes itself to be called and chosen to lead, as we did, has no inhibitions when it comes to taking territory from 'inferior elements'.

Though she distanced herself from those Germans who had no doubt that Germans were a 'master race' and Poles destined to be slaves, still, she wrote later: 'My colleagues and I felt it was an honour to be allowed to help in "conquering" this area for our own nation and for German culture. We had the arrogant enthusiasm of the "cultural missionary".'

Maschmann and her colleagues were charged with clearing out and cleaning up Polish farms in readiness for their new German inhabitants, and took part in the SS-led expulsions without asking where the expelled Poles were going.[122] She unashamedly joined in the extensive looting of Polish property during this process, as the departing Poles were obliged to leave furniture and equipment behind for the German settlers. Armed with a forged requisition order and a pistol (which she did not know how to use), she even robbed beds, cutlery and other items from Polish farmers in areas where resettlement had not begun, to give them to incoming ethnic Germans. All this she considered completely justified; the whole experience of her work was entirely positive.[123] These feelings were shared by many other German women who came into the incorporated territories as volunteers or were posted there as newly qualified teachers, junior officials in Nazi women's organizations, or aspiring civil servants. All of them, both at the time and in many cases when interviewed about their work decades later, saw their activities in occupied Poland as part of a civilizing mission and recorded their horror at the poverty and dirt they encountered in the Polish population. At the same time they enjoyed the beauty of the countryside and the sense of being on an exciting mission far from home. As middle-class women they evidently gained fulfilment from cleaning up farms left behind by deported Poles, decorating them, and creating a sense of homeliness to welcome the settlers. For virtually all of them, the suffering of Poles and Jews was either invisible or acceptable or even justified.[124]

III

Melita Maschmann's rosy vision of a new German-dominated civilization rising in Eastern Europe was belied by the realities on the ground. Murder, theft, looting and deportation were only part of the picture. Bribery and corruption were also rife under the German administration of the General Government. In Warsaw in 1940 it was said to cost a Jew a bribe of 125 zloty to an official to obtain exemption from compulsory labour. 500 would purchase dispensation from wearing the yellow star, 1,200 would buy a certificate of Aryan descent, 10,000 release from prison, and 150,000 a fully organized emigration to Italy (this last-named arrangement came to an abrupt end when Italy entered the war on Germany's side in June 1940).[125] Such corruption was made possible not least by the institutional chaos into which the General Government rapidly descended after its creation in 1939. General Governor Hans Frank issued grandiloquent proclamations from his lavishly furnished headquarters in the old royal palace at Cracow, but his authority was constantly undermined by his rival, the SS and police chief for the east, Friedrich Wilhelm Krüger. Krüger was actively encouraged not only by Himmler and Heydrich but also by Hitler himself, who here as elsewhere preferred his subordinates to fight each other for supremacy rather than creating a smoothly efficient, top-down hierarchy of command.

Krüger's area of competence included not only policing but also the implementation of Himmler's population transfer programme. His terrorization of the Polish population of the General Government was carried out more or less without reference to Frank, who became concerned by the hatred and unrest it was arousing amongst the Poles. In 1942 the ambitious Krüger even seemed on the point of displacing Frank altogether. When the former civil governor of Radom was arrested on corruption charges after an official car driven by his father was found transporting carpets, silks, spirits and other goods from the General

Government to the Reich, an investigation set in motion by Himmler quickly revealed this to be the tip of an iceberg. Many if not most officials engaged in practices of this kind. The tone was set by the General Governor. Himmler's investigation established that Frank himself had been enriching members of his own family from state funds and looted property. Two large warehouses were discovered, full of goods such as furs, chocolate, coffee and spirits, all intended for use by Frank and his family. In November 1940 alone Frank had sent back to his homes in the Old Reich 72 kilos of beef, 20 geese, 50 hens, 12 kilos of cheese and much more besides. The General Governor was summoned to Berlin for a dressing-down by Hans-Heinrich Lammers, Reich Minister in the Reich Chancellery and thus the effective head of Germany's civil administration. As the police uncovered further cases of corruption, Frank sought to strike back with a series of speeches in German universities condemning the growing power of the police (headed, of course, by his enemy and chief critic Himmler) only to find himself banned from public speaking and stripped of all his Party offices by a furious Hitler. Yet Frank survived, and by May 1943, with the support of Göring's Four-Year Plan office, he had persuaded Hitler, somewhat late in the day, that the ruthless violence of the police in the General Government was causing so much resentment amongst the Poles that they were refusing to work properly, failing to deliver their quotas of food supplies and disrupting the economy through sabotage. On 9 November 1943, Krüger was replaced by a more amenable police chief. The corruption continued.[126]

Further down the social scale, a huge black market had emerged as a result of the increasingly dire circumstances under which Poles lived. According to one estimate, more than 80 per cent of the Polish population's daily needs were supplied by the black economy. Polish employers circumvented German-imposed wage regulations by paying their workers in kind or by tolerating mass absenteeism, estimated at 30 per cent overall by 1943. Workers in any case could not afford to turn up to their jobs more than two or three days a week because the black market made such demands on the rest of their time. A popular Polish joke from this time recounted two friends meeting each other after a long time: 'What are you doing?' – 'I am working in the city hall.' – 'And your wife, how is she?' – 'She is working in a paper store' – 'And your daughter?' – 'She is working in a plant.' – 'How the hell do you live?' – 'Thank God, my son is unemployed!'[127] Black-marketeers were not only in the business to survive. A few could make huge profits in a few weeks. The dangers of being caught were high. But most risked it because they had no alternative. Besides, they were doing little more than following the example of their German masters, for whom bribery, corruption and profiteering were normal aspects of daily life.[128]

The black market was particularly rampant in the area of food supplies. Food shortages began to occur almost immediately after the invasion, exacerbated by the burning of crops by retreating Polish army units. Conditions were particularly severe in the General Government, which contained Poland's poorer farming areas. In 1940 the German occupation forces in Klukowski's district began registering pigs and other livestock on local farms and ordered that they could only be slaughtered for the German army, not for local inhabitants.[129] Queues outside food stores became commonplace.[130] The Germans began to impose quotas on farmers for delivery of food supplies to them, and punished those who failed to fulfil them.[131] Altogether from 1940 to 1944, 60 per cent of Polish meat production was taken off to feed Germans in the Reich, 10 per cent of grain production, and much else besides.[132] So bad was the food supply situation that even Frank became alarmed. He managed to secure deliveries of grain from the Reich in the first few months of 1940, but here too, the bulk of the supplies went to feed the German occupiers, with Poles working on key installations like the railways coming second, Ukrainians and ordinary Poles next, and Jews bottom of the list. The rations allotted to Poles in Warsaw were down to 669 calories a day by 1941, in comparison to 2,613 for the Germans (and a mere 184 for the Jews).[133] Nobody could live on these quantities. Health deteriorated rapidly, diseases associated with malnutrition spread, death rates soared. Most Poles did their best to provide most of their food intake by other means, and this meant once more the black market.[134]

Dr Klukowski noted with despair the rapid disintegration of Polish society under the impact of such horrifying levels of violence, destruction and deprivation. Bands of robbers were roaming the countryside, breaking into people's houses, terrorizing the inhabitants, looting the contents and raping the women. Poles were denouncing each other, mainly for possessing hidden weapons. Many were volunteering for work in Germany, and collaboration was rife. Polish girls were consorting with

German soldiers, and prostitution was spreading; by November 1940 Klukowski was treating thirty-two women for venereal diseases in his hospital, and noted that 'some are young girls also, even as young as sixteen, who were first raped and later started prostitution as the only way to support themselves'. 'Drunkenness is growing,' he reported in January 1941, 'and naturally there are more drunken fights, but it appears that the Germans are rather pleased about it.' Poles were joining in the looting of Jewish shops, and officers of the prewar Polish police were now working for the Germans. 'I never expected the morale of the Polish population to sink so low,' he wrote on 19 February 1940, 'with such a complete lack of national pride.'[135] 'We are lacking a uniform stand against the Germans,' he complained two months later: 'all the rumours, intrigues, and denunciations are growing.'[136]

IV

Poland's troubles were scarcely any less dire in the area occupied from 17 September 1939 by the Red Army, as a consequence of the Nazi–Soviet Pact.[137] The Soviets occupied 201,000 square kilometres of Polish territory, with a population of 13 million. The 200,000 Polish prisoners of war in the hands of the Red Army were partly released to go home, particularly if they lived in the German part of the country, or transferred to labour camps in south-eastern Poland to work on construction projects. The officers among them, however, were deported to camps in the Soviet Union, where they were joined by Polish customs officials, police, prison guards and military police until they numbered 15,000 in all. During April and early May 1940 some 4,443 of these men were taken in batches by the Soviet secret police, the NKVD, on orders from Moscow, to the Katyń Forest near Smolensk, where they were individually shot in the back of the head and buried in mass graves. The rest of the Polish officers were also killed. Only about 450 out of the 15,000, who were Communists, or deemed capable of being converted to Communism, were spared. The others were shot in a variety of locations or killed in the camps, along with some 11,000 alleged counter-revolutionaries. Some estimates put the total killed at around 20,000; the exact number may never be known. Most of these men were reserve officers, professionals, doctors, landowners, civil servants and the like.[138]

Their extermination was part of a much larger campaign by the Soviets to eradicate Polish national culture. It was accompanied by massive intercommunal violence in which many thousands of Poles were slaughtered by paramilitaries from Ukrainian and Belarussian national minorities in the Polish east, encouraged by the Soviet occupiers. Following a rigged plebiscite, the occupied territories were annexed by the Soviet Union and the economic and social system accommodated to the Soviet model, with businesses and estates expropriated and taken over by the state, and Ukrainians and Belarussians brought in to run them. Polish monuments and street signs were destroyed, bookshops and cultural institutions were closed down. Half a million Poles were imprisoned within Soviet-occupied Poland. Many of them were subjected to torture, beatings, killings and executions. A campaign of mass deportations began. Those singled out included members of political parties, Russian and other exiles, police officers and prison guards, officers and volunteers of the Polish army, active lay members of the Catholic Church, aristocrats, landowners, bankers, industrialists, hoteliers and restaurateurs, refugees, 'persons who have travelled abroad' and even 'persons who are esperantists or philatelists'. Almost all Polish professionals in the occupied area were arrested and deported as well. In many cases their families were sent with them. Altogether the deportees numbered an estimated 1.5 million people. In the first half of 1940, they were packed into cattle-trucks, with standing room only, and taken off in vast train convoys to collective farms in Kazakhstan and other distant locations. Tens of thousands of Poles who had served the previous government or shown themselves unwilling to conform to the occupiers' Marxist-Leninist ideology were arrested, tried on trumped-up charges and sent to labour camps in Siberia. Perhaps a third of the deportees died before the survivors were released after the German attack on the Soviet Union in June 1941. By this time, Soviet policy in occupied Poland had become marginally more lenient, as growing concern in Moscow about the danger of Ukrainian support for a possible German invasion led to a limited encouragement of Polish national identity, which was indelibly anti-German in sentiment. Nevertheless, the outcome of the Soviet occupation was scarcely less disastrous for the Poles than that of the German occupation.[139]

For the 1.2 million Jews who lived in the Soviet-controlled part of Poland, and the 350,000 or so Jewish refugees who had fled there from the advancing Germans, the Soviet takeover of the territory initially provided welcome relief. They would be protected, they thought, not only from the exterminatory racism of the Germans but also from the native antisemitism of the Poles. Even conservative and religious Jews welcomed the Soviet takeover. A substantial, though subsequently disputed, number of Jews took on administrative positions in the Soviet Communist ruling apparatus; however many they were, their number was sufficient to convince many Polish and Ukrainian nationalists that the entire Jewish community was working for the hated Soviet Communists. In fact, the arrest and deportation of wealthy Jews and others, particularly intellectuals and professionals, who refused as Polish patriots to sign on for Soviet citizenship, soon dispelled the Jewish population's illusions about the true nature of Soviet rule. As many as one in three of the Polish citizens deported to Siberia and other remote areas of the Soviet Union was Jewish; 100,000 are estimated to have died in the process. Still, the damage was done; those who remained would pay dearly for their initial enthusiasm for the Soviet invasion when the Red Army was eventually driven out by the Germans. In the meantime, conditions deteriorated so rapidly that Jews who had fled from German-occupied Poland began going back there.[140]

There were, however, crucial differences between the two occupations. Unlike the western part of Poland, annexed by the Nazis, the eastern part contained a majority of non-Poles. These were Ukrainians and Belarussians, mainly peasants whom the occupying power urged to rise up against the supposedly fascist Polish landowning class, and Jews. In pursuit of a social revolution, the Soviet administration expropriated Polish property, nationalized banks and divided up the big estates among peasant smallholders. Formal civil rights were extended to everybody, and younger Jews in particular welcomed their liberation from the antisemitic discrimination practised by the regime of the Polish colonels. When these Jews joined the Communist Party in their enthusiasm for the new regime, they threw off their Jewish identity in the process. The Polish elites were seen as the leaders of Polish nationalism by both occupying powers, to be crushed and eliminated by force; but the main concern of the Soviets was to destroy them politically, and so they were deported not from the Soviet Union altogether, but deep into its interior. From Stalin's point of view, what was being carried out in occupied Poland was a social revolution for the benefit of the majority; from

Hitler's point of view, what was being carried out in occupied Poland was an ethnic revolution for the benefit of a small minority, that of the ethnic Germans; capitalism, property and private enterprise were left in place, but the Poles and Jews were to play no part in them.[141]

'A DREADFUL RABBLE'

I

If Poles were second-class citizens in the General Government, then Jews scarcely qualified as human beings at all in the eyes of the German occupiers, soldiers and civilians, Nazis and non-Nazis alike. The Germans brought with them a fear and contempt for the Jews that had been instilled into the great majority of them by incessant Nazi propaganda over the previous six and a half years. During this time, the Jews of Germany itself, less than 1 per cent of the population, had been subjected to growing government discrimination, dispossession and periodic bouts of violence from Nazi activists. Half of them had emigrated. Those who remained had been deprived of their civil rights and their livelihoods, removed from social interaction with other Germans, drafted into forced labour schemes and effectively cut off from the rest of German society. In November 1938 they had been subjected to a nationwide series of pogroms in which virtually all of Germany's synagogues had been destroyed, thousands of Jewish-owned shops smashed, Jewish flats and houses ransacked, and 30,000 Jewish men arrested and put in concentration camps, where over a period of several weeks they were beaten and terrorized until they were eventually released after giving assurances that they would emigrate. Following this, the remaining Jewish population of Germany was robbed of its last assets. The process by which non-Jewish Germans came to regard their Jewish compatriots as a race apart, despite the fact that Germany's Jews shared all the central aspects of German culture, and looked and dressed no differently from other Germans, had been gradual and uneven, but by 1939 it had gone a long way.[142]

When the Germans invaded Poland, however, they encountered a very different situation. Poland in 1939 contained the largest proportion of Jews living in any European state, numbering almost three and a half million, or 10 per cent of the population, measured by religious affiliation. More than three-quarters of them lived in Poland's towns and cities. There were over 350,000 in Warsaw alone, making up nearly 30 per cent of the capital's population. More than 200,000 lived in Lódź, fully a third of its inhabitants. In more than 30 per cent of towns in the General Government Jews actually formed a majority. 85 per cent of them spoke Yiddish as their first language rather than Polish. The overwhelming majority of them practised Judaism. Many dressed differently from Christian Poles and wore beards or sidelocks on religious grounds. They formed a distinctive national minority against which the antisemitic Polish military government had increasingly discriminated in the second half of the 1930s. Most Polish Jews were small traders and shopkeepers, artisans and tradespeople, or wage labourers; fewer than 10 per cent were professional or other successful members of the middle classes; many of them were very poor, and in 1934 more than a quarter of them had been living off benefits. Just over 2 million Jews lived in the areas taken over by Germany in September 1939, of whom up to 350,000 fled immediately to the eastern part of Poland, to Lithuania or to Hungary. To the incoming Germans these were 'Eastern Jews', a wholly alien and despised minority regarded by most of them as non-European, to be treated with even greater contempt and mistrust than the Jews of Germany itself.[143] Indeed, 18,000 Polish Jews had been forcibly expelled from Germany across the Polish border in October 1938, followed by another 2,000 in June the following year.[144]

In Poland the Nazis' policies of racial suppression and extermination were applied in full for the first time, in a gigantic experiment that would later be repeated on an even larger scale in other parts of Eastern Europe. German rule in Poland was ruthlessly and exclusively designed to further what the Nazis perceived as Germany's interests, including Germany's racial interests. The deliberate reduction of Poland to a state of nature, the boundless exploitation of its resources, the radical degradation of everyday life, the arbitrary exercise of unfettered power, the violent expulsion of Poles from their homes – all of this opened the way to the application of unbridled terror against Poland's Jews. Moreover, the chaotic situation of the country, and Hitler's repeated insistence on the primacy of racial policy in Poland, facilitated from the very beginning the autonomous exercise of power there by the most fanatical and determined elements in the Party and the SS.[145] The Special SS Security Service Task Force under Udo von Woyrsch was particularly active in attacks on Jews. In Bedzin on 8 September 1939 it murdered a number of Jewish children and burned down the local synagogue with flame-throwers, setting light to nearby houses in the town's Jewish quarter; the Task Force troops indiscriminately shot Jews they encountered on the streets. By the time they left, some 500 of the town's Jewish inhabitants were dead. Meeting with Heydrich and Streckenbach in Cracow on 11 September 1939, Woyrsch was told that Himmler had ordered the harshest possible measures to be taken against Jews so that they would be forced to flee to the east and out of the area controlled by the Germans. The Special Task Force redoubled its efforts to terrorize the Jewish population into flight, burning a group of Jews alive in the synagogue at Dynów and carrying out mass shootings in a variety of locations across the land.[146]

Ordinary soldiers and junior officers shared many of the antisemitic prejudices against 'Eastern Jews' encouraged by Nazi propaganda since 1933.[147] German attitudes were well exemplified by the Chief of Staff of General Blaskowitz's Eighth Army, Hans Felber, who on 20 September 1939 described the Jews of Lódź as 'a dreadful rabble, filthy and sly'. They had to be deported, he said.[148] He was echoing the impressions gained by Hitler himself in a visit to the Jewish quarter of Kielce on 10 September 1939: his press chief Otto Dietrich, who accompanied him, noted: 'The appearance of these people is unimaginable . . . They live in inconceivable filth, in huts in which not even a tramp would pass the night in Germany.'[149] 'These are no longer people,' remarked Goebbels after visiting Lódź at the beginning of November 1939, 'these are animals. So the task is not humanitarian but surgical. Steps have to be taken here, and really radical ones too. Otherwise Europe will perish from the Jewish disease.'[150] Goebbels sent film crews in to take pictures for the weekly newsreel show in German cinemas, and Jewish congregations and rabbis were forced to stage special religious services for the German film crews, who also went into Jewish slaughterhouses to get pictures of the ritual slaughter of cattle. All of this material was collected under Goebbels's personal direction and with Hitler's personal involvement for a feature-length documentary entitled *The Eternal Jew*, which was eventually screened a year later, in November 1940.[151]

The general atmosphere of racial hatred and contempt encouraged by Hitler's instructions to the generals before the outbreak of the war gave soldiers clear encouragement to take whatever they wanted from Poland's Jews. As the German army entered Warsaw, the troops immediately began looting Jewish shops and robbing Jews at gunpoint in the street.[152] The Jewish schoolmaster Chaim Kaplan recorded in his diary on 6 October 1939 that German troops had broken into his flat and raped his Christian maid (they were not raping Jewish women because of the Nuremberg Laws, he thought – although in practice this did not prove much of a hindrance). Then they beat her to try to get her to reveal where he had hidden his money (he had in fact already removed it). Kaplan recorded how even officers were manhandling Jews in the street and roughly cutting off their beards. They forced Jewish girls to clean public latrines with their blouses, and committed innumerable other acts of sadism against Warsaw's Jewish inhabitants.[153] Zygmunt Klukowski recorded many instances of theft and looting by German soldiers, often aided and abetted by local Poles, particularly where Jewish shops and premises were concerned. Theft was often followed by arson and wanton destruction, in which local people, their prejudices fed by years of antisemitic propaganda and indoctrination from Polish nationalists, including senior figures in the Polish Catholic Church, participated with enthusiasm.[154]

On 22 October 1939 German troops brought up lorries to cart away the contents of Jewish stores in Zamość, the nearest large town to where Klukowski lived. Eight days later, German army officers began taking away cash and jewellery from Jewish houses in the town.[155] Increasingly, looters and robbers used violence against their Jewish victims.[156] When the Germans settled into Zamość in mid-October 1939, noted Zygmunt Klukowski in his diary, they ordered the Jews to 'sweep the streets, clean all the public latrines, and fill all the street trenches . . . They order the Jews to take at least a half hour of exhaustive gymnastics before any work, which can be fatal, particularly for older people.' 'The Germans are treating the Jews very brutally,' he noted on 14 October 1939: 'They cut their beards; sometimes they pull their hair out.'[157] On 14 November 1939 the town's synagogue was burned down, along with neighbouring Jewish houses. All of this was in direct imitation of the pogrom of 9–10 November 1938 in Germany and its aftermath. The Jewish community was ordered to pay a massive fine as 'compensation'.[158] And from 22 December 1939 all Jews aged ten years and over had to wear a yellow star on their sleeve, and shops had to display signs indicating whether they were Jewish or not.[159] Jews were barred from medical treatment except by Jewish physicians. Called to see a sick Jewish man, Dr Klukowski 'went to him wondering whether anyone was spying on me. I feel terrible,' he wrote in his diary on 29 March 1940. 'On my prescription I even omitted the name of the sick man. So now we come to this: the main goal of every physician is to give medical help, but now it becomes a crime, punishable by imprisonment.'[160]

It was striking that these acts were carried out not by the SS but by regular German army officers and men. Groups of grinning German soldiers fired randomly into houses they marched past in the Jewish quarters of the towns they entered, or gathered around Jewish men in the street, forcing them to smear each other with excrement, setting their beards on fire, compelling them to eat pork, or cutting the Jewish star into their foreheads with knives.[161] For many ordinary soldiers this was their first confrontation with Polish Jews, many of whom in their whole appearance seemed to bear out all the clichés of the propaganda to which Germans had been subjected for the previous six years. These, as one corporal wrote in August 1940, were 'genuine Jews with beards, and filthy, to be precise, even worse than the *Stormer* always describes them as being'.[162] Here, as another corporal wrote in December 1939, were 'Jews – seldom have I seen such unkempt figures wandering around, wrapped in tatters, filthy, greasy. These people seemed to us like a plague. Their nasty way of looking at you, their treacherous questions and deceitful fussing about have often prompted us to reach for our pistols, to recall these over-curious and prying subjects to reality.'[163]

As soon as the war broke out, one Jewish scholar in particular determined to record as much of this behaviour for posterity as he was able to. Born in 1900, Emanuel Ringelblum had trained as a historian, gaining his Ph.D. in 1927. An active left-wing Zionist, he determined to record everything that was happening to the Jews of Warsaw under German rule and kept an extensive diary of daily events. Ringelblum's exact and voluminous notes recorded robberies, beatings, shootings and humiliations of Jews by German troops and SS men on a daily basis. The rape of Polish and Jewish women by German soldiers was common in the early months of the occupation. 'At 2 Tlomackie Place,' he recorded early in 1940, 'three *lords and masters* ravished some women;

screams resounded through the house. The Gestapo are concerned over the racial degradation – Aryans consorting with non-Aryans – but are afraid to report it.'[164] Bribery and corruption quickly spread. 'Only poor people go to the camps,' he noted.[165] Sometimes, Ringelblum reported, Polish Christians came to the defence of Jews attacked by young Polish hooligans; but they were powerless to do anything against the Germans.[166] As the situation of the Jews deteriorated, Ringelblum began to record the bitter humour with which they tried to lighten their burden. A Jewish woman, so one joke related, woke her husband up when he started alternately laughing and yelling in his sleep. 'I was dreaming someone had scribbled on a wall,' the husband said: ' "Beat the Jews! Down with ritual slaughter!" ' 'So what were you so happy about?' asked his wife. 'Don't you understand?' he replied: 'That means the good old days have come back! The Poles are running things again!'[167] Familiar acts of persecution by Poles they could deal with, but not the inhumanity of the Germans: 'A police chief came to the apartment of a Jewish family and wanted to take some things away. The woman cried that she was a widow with a child. The chief said he'd take nothing if she could guess which one of his eyes was the artificial one. She correctly guessed the left eye. She was asked how she knew. "Because that one," she answered, "has a human look." '[168]

In many parts of Poland apart from Warsaw, army units seized Jews as hostages, and in many places there were shootings of Jews as individuals or in groups. The 50,000 Polish prisoners of war whom the army classified as Jewish were drafted like other prisoners on to labour schemes but starved and maltreated to such an extent that 25,000 of them were dead by the spring of 1940.[169] Chaim Kaplan noted on 10 October 1939 that Jewish men were being arrested and taken away to labour schemes.[170] Frank had indeed already ordered the introduction of compulsory labour for the Jews within the General Government and begun to set up labour camps, where Jewish men arrested on the streets or in police raids on their apartments were kept in miserable conditions. A medical report on a group of labour camps at Belzec noted in September 1940 that the accommodation was dark, damp and infested with vermin. 30 per cent of the workers had no shoes, trousers or shirts, and they slept on the floor, 75 to a room measuring 5 metres by 6, so overcrowded that they had to lie on top of one another. There was no soap and no sanitation in the huts: the men had to relieve themselves on the floor during the night, since they were barred from going out. Rations were entirely inadequate for the heavy physical labour the men were required to carry out, mostly on road works and the reinforcement of river banks.[171]

The deteriorating situation was calmly recorded by the Jewish schoolboy Dawid Sierakowiak in his diary. 'The first signs of German occupation,' he noted on 9 September 1939. 'They are seizing Jews to dig.' Although school was starting, his parents stopped him attending because they feared he would be arrested by the Germans. Two days later he was reporting 'beatings and robbings' and noting that the store where his father worked had been looted. 'The local Germans do whatever they wish.' 'All basic human freedoms are being destroyed,' he noted, as the Germans closed the synagogues and forced stores to be open on a Jewish religious holiday. As his mother was obliged to queue for two hours at the bakery at five o'clock every morning to get bread, Sierakowiak reported that the Germans were taking Jews out of food queues. His father lost his job. Then the Germans closed Sierakowiak's school and he had to walk five kilometres a day to another one because his family no longer had the money to pay his tram fare. By 16 November 1939 Sierakowiak was being forced, along with other Jews, to wear a yellow armband when he went out; in early December this was changed to a yellow, 10-centimetre Star of David that had to be worn on the right chest and the back of the right shoulder. 'New work in the evening,' he recorded, 'ripping off the armbands and sewing on the new decorations.' As the first snows of winter began to fall, his school was closed down, and the textbooks were given to the pupils: 'I got a German history of the Jews, a few copies of German poets, and Latin texts, together with two English books.' Dawid Sierakowiak began to witness Germans beating Jews on the streets. The situation was deteriorating on an almost daily basis.[172]

By the autumn of the following year, shocking scenes of violence against the Jews were taking place on the streets of many towns in Poland, including Szczebrzeszyn. On 9 September 1940 Klukowski noted:

This afternoon I was standing by the window in my room when I witnessed an ugly event. Across from the hospital are a few burned-out Jewish homes. An old Jew and a few Jewish women were standing next to one when a group of three

German soldiers came by. Suddenly one of the soldiers grabbed the old man and threw him into the cellar. The women began lamenting. In a few minutes more Jews arrived, but the soldiers calmly walked away. I was puzzled by this incident, but a few minutes later the man was brought to me for treatment. I was told that he forgot to take his hat off when the Germans passed by. German regulations require that Jews must stand to attention and the men have to take their hats off whenever German soldiers pass.[173]

What Klukowski was witnessing was not just the arbitrary exercise of power by an invading force over a despised minority; it was the end-product of a prolonged process of policy-making in Berlin, aided by new institutional structures at the centre of the Third Reich that would play an increasingly important role in the coming years.[174]

II

The Nazi plan for Poland initially envisaged three belts of settlement – German, Polish and Jewish – in three blocks, roughly western, central and eastern. Its implementation was by no means the exclusive prerogative of the SS: already on 13 September 1939, the Quartermaster-General of the Army Supreme Command ordered Army Group South to deport all Jews in the eastern part of Upper Silesia into the area that was shortly to be occupied by the Red Army. But it soon took on a more centrally directed form. The next day, Heydrich noted that Himmler was about to submit to Hitler an overall policy for dealing with the 'Jewish problem in Poland ... that only the Leader can decide'. By 21 September 1939 Hitler had approved a deportation plan that was to be put into effect over the next twelve months. Jews, especially those engaged in farming, were to be rounded up immediately. All Jews – over half a million of them – were to be deported from the incorporated territories along with the remaining 30,000 Gypsies and Jews from Prague and Vienna and other parts of the Reich and Protectorate. This, said Heydrich, was a step in the direction of the 'final aim', which was to be kept totally secret, namely the removal of the Jews from Germany and the occupied eastern areas to a specially created reservation.

In charge of the operation was the head of the SS Central Office for Jewish Emigration (*Zentralstelle für jüdische Auswanderung*) in Prague,

Adolf Eichmann, who set to work energetically, securing the agreement of the relevant regional officials to the deportation plan, and setting up a transit centre at Nisko on the river San. A trainload of more than 900 Jewish men left Ostrava, in the Protectorate of Bohemia and Moravia, on 18 October 1939, followed by another transport of 912 Jewish men from Vienna two days later. At Nisko, however, there were no facilities for them. While a few were detailed to start building barracks, the rest were simply taken a few kilometres away by an SS detachment and then driven off by the guards, who fired their guns and shouted at them, 'Go over there to your Red brothers!' The agreement reached by Himmler with the Soviet Union on 28 September 1939 for the transfer of ethnic Germans to the incorporated territories then put a stop to the whole action, not least because the transport facilities and personnel were needed to deal with German immigrants from the east. In any case, as Hitler pointed out, the creation of a large Jewish reservation in the Nisko area would undermine the future function of the area as a military bridgehead for an invasion of the Soviet Union. Eichmann's grandiose scheme had come to nothing. The stranded Jews stayed where they were, supported by the Jewish community in Lublin, and living in makeshift shelters, until April 1940, when the SS told them to disband and find their own way home: only 300 eventually managed to do so.[175]

The scheme was not regarded as a failure, however. It showed that it was possible to deport large numbers of Jews from their homes in the Reich and the Protectorate to the east, not least by disguising the murderous undertones of the action through the use of euphemisms such as 'resettlement' to self-governing 'colonies' or 'reservations'. Eichmann was promoted to head Department IVD4 of the Reich Security Head Office, in overall charge of 'evacuation' and 'resettlement'.[176] His failure to provide adequate facilities for the proposed reservation at Nisko was no product of organizational incompetence: it was intentional. Essentially, the Jews of Germany and German-occupied Central Europe were simply to be dumped there and left to fend for themselves. As Hans Frank remarked: 'A pleasure finally to be able to tackle the Jewish race physically. The more that die, the better; to strike at the Jews is the victory of our Reich. The Jews have to feel that we've arrived.' A report on a visit of leading officials of the General Government to the village of Cycόw on 20 November 1939 commented: 'This territory, with its strongly marshy nature, could serve as a reserve for the Jews according to District Governor Schmidt. This measure would lead to a major decimation of the Jews.' After all, as a member of the German Foreign Affairs Institute reported from Poland in December 1939, 'the annihilation of these subhumans would be in the interests of the whole world'. It was best, he thought, that this should be achieved by 'natural' means such as starvation and disease.[177]

During the next few months, various alternative plans for the resettlement of the Jews of Central Europe were canvassed in the Reich Security Head Office, the German Foreign Office and other centres of power: all of them involved, implicitly or explicitly, the murder of large numbers of Jews by one means or another. In February and March 1940, virtually the entire Jewish community of Stettin, numbering over a thousand, was deported on Heydrich's orders under such appalling conditions that almost a third of them died of hunger, cold and exhaustion en route. In the course of 1939, 1940 and the first four months of 1941, a series of uncoordinated actions led to the deportation of more than 63,000 Jews into the General Government, including more than 3,000 from Alsace, over 6,000 from Baden and the Saar, and even 280 from Luxembourg. None of these deportations had led to any systematic policy implementation on a larger scale; most of them were the result of the initiatives of impatient local Nazis, most notably the Regional Leader of the Wartheland, Arthur Greiser, whose ambition it was to rid his territory of Jews as fast as possible. The Nisko plan had been aborted, and the size and speed of population transfers in Poland scaled down under the impact of wartime pressures and circumstances. Yet despite all this, the idea of forcing the Jews of Central Europe into a reservation somewhere in the east of the country remained under discussion. As a first step, Hitler envisaged the concentration of all the remaining Jews in the Reich, including the newly incorporated territories, into ghettos located in the main Polish cities, which, he agreed with Himmler and Heydrich, would make their eventual expulsion easier.[178] The American correspondent William L. Shirer concluded in November 1939 that 'Nazi policy is simply to exterminate the Polish Jews', for what else could be the consequence of their ghettoization? If the Jews were unable to make a living, how could they survive?[179]

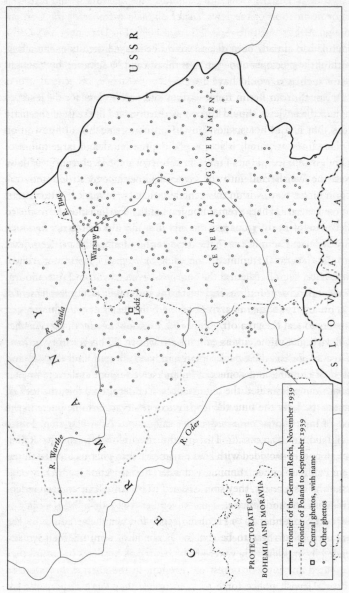

3. Jewish Ghettos in German-occupied Poland, 1939–44

III

Ghettos had already been discussed in Germany in the immediate aftermath of the pogroms of 9–10 November 1938.[180] Because few thought
that the ghettos would have a long-term existence, no central orders
were issued from Berlin for how they were to be managed. Heydrich
proposed that Jews should be confined to certain districts of the main
cities, but he did not suggest how. Conscious that his administration
was far from prepared to accept and administer such a large influx of
penniless refugees, Hans Frank tried to block the deportation of Jews
from the Wartheland into the General Government, so Greiser took
action on his own, within this general policy framework.[181] He ordered
the concentration of the remaining Jews in the Wartheland into a 'closed
ghetto' in the northern part of the city of Łódź, a poor district in which
a considerable number of Jews were already living. On 10 December
1939, the regional administration drew up plans for the boundaries of
the ghetto, the resettlement of non-Jews living there, the provision of
food and other supplies and utilities, and other arrangements. On
8 February 1940 guards arrived at the boundaries and began erecting
barriers to seal the area off. As Dawid Sierakowiak noted, mass arrests
of Jews began in the city as early as December. 'Everyone everywhere,'
he recorded, 'has their backpacks ready packed with underclothes and
essential clothing and domestic equipment. Everyone is extremely nervous.' Many Jews fled the city, taking what they could with them on
handcarts.[182] By the time the ghetto was finally sealed off, on 30 April
and 1 May 1940, it contained some 162,000 of the city's original Jewish
population of 220,000.[183] These people had to live in a district that
was so poorly provided with basic amenities that over 30,000 dwellings
were without either running water or a connection to the sewage
system.[184] As a result, they soon seemed to confirm Nazi associations of
Jews with dirt and disease.

On 21 September 1939 Heydrich had laid down the general principle
that each ghetto was to be run by a council of senior Jewish figures,
headed by an Elder. They were to be treated as hostages to ensure they
prevented any kind of unrest or rebellion in the ghetto; they were to
create a Jewish police force to keep order; they were responsible for
community life; they had to draw up lists of the inhabitants; they had

to arrange the distribution of supplies; and above all they had to carry out the orders of the German administration.[185] As Elder of the Łódź ghetto the Germans chose Chaim Rumkowski, a man who after a series of business failures had ended up as chief administrator of the Jewish orphanages in the city. Now in his seventies, Rumkowski certainly looked the part: white-haired, fit, energetic, with a face and expression that contemporaries often described as noble, majestic or even regal; he quickly took command, becoming in effect the ghetto's dictator. He printed a special currency for exclusive use in the ghetto, he created a system of canteens, nursery schools and social services, and he bargained with the German administration to allow productive work in the ghetto. This involved the import of raw materials for processing, the providing of unskilled Jewish labour for construction work outside and the earning of income that would purchase essential supplies of food and other goods and so allow the ghetto's population to survive. By October 1940 he had largely succeeded, in collaboration with the pragmatic German mayor of Łódź and his ghetto manager, a businessman from Bremen, who wanted to reduce the burden on the public purse of sustaining the Jews, 70 per cent of whom had no other means of feeding themselves. Overcoming opposition within the German administration that saw the ghetto mainly as a means of reducing the Jewish population by a process of attrition, they succeeded in introducing industries and workshops into the ghetto and making it into an element of the German war economy.[186] But power also went to Rumkowski's head. He went round the ghetto surrounded by a retinue of bodyguards, on one occasion throwing sweets to the watching crowds. Making himself indispensable to the Germans as long as the ghetto lasted, he attracted widespread criticism, even hatred, from the Jewish community; yet on the other hand, he could with some plausibility present himself as essential to its survival.[187]

In the General Government, Hans Frank, for all the brutality of his rhetoric, was soon forced to confront the problem of establishing some sort of order, as thousands of destitute Polish and Jewish expellees arrived with no preparations having been made to receive them. While he applied strong and to a large extent successful pressure in Berlin to have the influx stopped, he also began to create ghettos in which the Jewish population would be concentrated prior to their further expulsion to a reservation in some undefined area further east. The first ghetto in the General Government was created at Radomsko in December 1939, followed by many others. Some were small, some lasted only a few months; but the largest quickly took on a more permanent air as, like the ghetto in Łódź, they became important centres of economic exploitation. This was particularly the case after January 1940, when Frank announced that the General Government was no longer to be seen merely as an object of plunder, but had instead to make its contribution to the economy of the Reich.[188] On 19 May 1940 Frank ordered the Jews of Warsaw to be concentrated into an exclusively Jewish area of the city, initially justifying the move with the cynical claim that Jews spread diseases like typhus and had to be quarantined for public health reasons; he also blamed them, in characteristic Nazi fashion, for causing price inflation through their black-marketeering.[189] During the summer, construction work on the ghetto walls was suspended as Frank began to hope that the Jews would be taken to Madagascar instead. But in October it began again.[190] By the time it was sealed off on 16 November 1940, the majority of Jews in the city had been herded, along with many others from outside, into the ghetto area.

The operation was accompanied by scenes of terrifying brutality, as Emanuel Ringelblum reported:

At the corner of Chlodna and Zelazne Streets, those who are slow to take their hats off to Germans are forced to do callisthenics using paving stones or tiles as weights. Elderly Jews, too, are ordered to do push-ups. They [i.e., the Germans] tear paper up small, scatter the pieces in the mud, and order people to pick them up, beating them as they stoop over. In the Polish quarter Jews are ordered to lie on the ground and they walk over them. On Leszno Street a soldier came through in a wagon and stopped to beat a Jewish pedestrian. Ordered him to lie down in the mud and kiss the pavement. – A wave of evil rolled over the whole city, as if in response to a nod from above.[191]

The ghetto area had been created, as a German administrator reported, 'by the utilization of existing walls and by walling up streets, windows, doors and gaps between buildings. The walls,' he added, 'are three metres high and are raised a further metre by barbed wire placed on top. They are also guarded by motorized and mounted police patrols.' There were fifteen checkpoints where Polish and German police regulated traffic in and out of the ghetto, which was divided into a larger and a smaller section separated by an 'Aryan' street crossed by a wooden bridge.[192]

Inside the walls, the ghetto was run, on lines already established in Lódź, by a Jewish Council headed by an Elder, the engineer Adam Czerniaków, a leading member of the local Jewish community now in his mid-sixties. Working long hours, Czerniaków did his best to obtain small concessions by exploiting divisions within the German occupation authorities, and constantly brought the poor conditions in the ghetto to their attention. He was highly critical of the imperious attitude and corrupt practices of the Lódź ghetto Elder Rumkowski ('a conceited and witless man. A dangerous man too since he keeps telling the authorities that all is well in his preserve').[193] Czerniaków's attitude led to his arrest by the SS on 4 November 1940 and again in April 1941. He was tortured and humiliated, but refused to modify his stubborn attempts to defend the interests of the ghetto's inhabitants. Only occasionally was he able to record any success in winning concessions from the Germans. Many of the promises they made to him at the end of lengthy negotiation sessions remained unfulfilled. 'All this toil, as I see it,' he wrote on 1 November 1941, 'bears no fruit. My head spins and my thinking is getting muddled. Not one single positive achievement.'[194]

The creation of the Warsaw ghetto involved the concentration of nearly a third of the city's population into 2.4 per cent of its territory. After a further 66,000 Jews from the surrounding district were brought in during the first three months of 1941, some 445,000 people were crammed into an area of about 400 hectares in extent, with an average density, according to an official German estimate, of over 15 people per apartment or between 6 and 7 to a room, double the density of the population living in the rest of the city. Some rooms no more than 24 square metres in area had to provide living accommodation for as many as 25 or 30 people.[195] Fuel was so scarce that few apartments were heated, even in the coldest winter. The death rate among Warsaw's Jewish population rose from 1 per thousand in 1939 to 10.7 in 1941; in Lódź it was even higher, at 43.3 in 1940 and 75.9 the following year. Children were particularly vulnerable; one in four children in the Warsaw ghetto shelters died in June 1941 alone, and so bad was the situation of children overall that a number of families tried to give their offspring away to non-Jewish families in the surrounding city.[196] Orphaned children began to roam the streets of the ghetto in growing numbers. 'A terrifying, simply monstrous impression is made,' Emanuel Ringelblum confessed, by '. . . the wailing of children who . . . beg for alms, or whine that they have nowhere to sleep. At the corner of Leszno and Markelicka streets,' he reported, 'children weep bitterly at night. Although I hear this weeping every night, I cannot fall asleep until late. The couple of pence I give them nightly cannot ease my conscience.'[197]

Death rates reached a new high in the spring of 1941 as typhus spread amongst the overcrowded, lice-ridden population of the Warsaw ghetto. 'One walks past corpses with indifference,' confessed Emanuel Ringelblum in May 1941. 'The corpses are mere skeletons, with a thin covering of skin over their bones.'[198] Passing through the ghetto, Stanislav Royzicki saw its inhabitants as 'nightmare figures, ghosts of former human beings' and noted 'the prominent bones around their eye sockets, the yellow facial colour, the slack pendulous skin, the alarming emaciation and sickliness. And, in addition, this miserable, frightened, restless, apathetic and resigned expression.' Patients were lying two or three to a bed in the hospitals.[199] In the autumn of 1941 the hospitals were treating around 900 typhus cases a day, with 6,000 more ill in their homes. Tuberculosis spread as well, and contamination of the water supply led to many cases of typhoid. Malnutrition weakened people's resistance to disease, and medical services were unable to cope. Death became an inescapable feature of the ghetto experience in Warsaw; during its whole period of existence, some 140,000 people died inside the ghetto.[200] Travelling through the Jewish ghetto in a tram in early September 1941, Zygmunt Klukowski noted the terrible living conditions and high mortality rate of the Jews. 'It is almost impossible to figure out how something like this can happen,' he wrote.[201] While all this was going on, as Ringelblum recorded, a German film crew visited the ghetto, staging scenes for cinema audiences back home in which kindly German soldiers stepped in to protect Jews from the cruelty of the Polish police.[202]

Hunger led to a deterioration in social relations, and people fought over scraps, forged ration cards, or snatched food from passers-by, eating it as they ran away. Families began to quarrel over rations, and new arrivals sold everything they had to pay for black market food. Small children slipped out of the ghetto where it was only fenced off with barbed wire, risking being shot by the guards as they went off into the surrounding city to scavenge for food. Labourers on work details outside the ghetto often managed to smuggle food back in, while organized gangs of smugglers waged a kind of guerrilla warfare with the German guards.[203] Some 28,000 Jews of all ages managed to find hiding-places outside the Warsaw ghetto, mostly with the aid of non-Jewish Poles, using social contacts, friendships and acquaintanceships that had existed before the Germans came. Parents frequently tried to send their children across the ghetto boundary to safety. Sometimes concealed in attics or cellars, sometimes passed off as 'Aryan', the children lived a precarious life; many were arrested and if, as was often the case, their parents were no longer alive, they were put into prison-like orphanages. Some Poles helped conceal Jews for financial gain, some out of nothing more complicated than human sympathy; others still betrayed them to the German police if they discovered that they were Jewish. A few even employed Jews on work that they succeeded in getting classified as essential, then took more on than they really needed, defending them against all attempts by the Germans to take them away. Most of the 11,000 Jews who survived the war in the Polish capital owed their lives to Polish helpers. The Poles who aided Jews in this, and many other ways, were a small minority, however, far outweighed by the antisemites who willingly participated in, and profited from, the creation of the ghetto and the removal of the Jewish population from the city at large. Neither the Polish nationalist underground 'Home Army' nor the Polish government in exile in London nor, finally, the Polish Catholic Church took a clear stance against the Germans' murderous policies towards Polish Jews; if anything, the opposite was the case, with all three institutions regarding Poland's Jewish population as supporters of 'Bolshevism'. As a semi-official report of the Polish Church to the exiled government declared in the summer of 1941, the Germans 'have shown that liberation of Polish society from the Jewish plague is possible'.[204]

Polish police too played their part in keeping the ghetto sealed off from the rest of the city as far as possible. Walking past the ghetto in September 1941, Wilm Hosenfeld noted:

There are water culverts at the ghetto wall, and Jewish children who live outside the ghetto smuggle potatoes in through them. I saw a Polish policeman beating a boy who was trying to do this. As I caught sight of the emaciated legs under the child's coat, and his face filled with fear, I was seized by an enormous pity. I'd very much have liked to have given the boy my fruit.[205]

But the penalties for such a gesture, even for a German officer, were too severe for him to risk it. Even silent sympathy like Hosenfeld's was extremely rare. German officials, troops, police and SS men frequently came into the ghetto, beating and clubbing the Jews they encountered at will. Looking out of his window one day in February 1941, Chaim Kaplan saw crowds running in wild panic through the street below, before 'a Nazi murderer with a face as red as fire, whose every movement expressed burning wrath, came striding with a singularly heavy step in search of a victim. In his hand was a whip.' When he came across a beggar he started beating him mercilessly, then, when the beggar fell to the ground, the German stamped on him, and kicked and punched him 'for twenty minutes', until long after the man was dead. 'It was hard to comprehend the secret of this sadistic phenomenon,' wrote Kaplan in his diary:

After all, the victim was a stranger, not an old enemy; he did not speak rudely to him, let alone touch him. Then why this cruel wrath? How is it possible to attack a stranger to me, a man of flesh and blood like myself, to wound him and trample upon him, and cover his body with sores, bruises, and welts, without any reason? How is it possible? Yet I swear I saw all this with my own eyes.[206]

For many among the occupying German forces, the ghetto offered the opportunity to vent almost unimaginable violence upon the helpless Jews without the slightest threat of retribution.

Some Germans, indeed, regularly drove through the ghetto singling out victims. Others merely came to watch, to take photographs, or on occasion to take posed pictures for propaganda purposes. It was even claimed by the Polish government-in-exile that the Nazi leisure organization 'Strength Through Joy' organized tourist visits to the ghetto, where the conditions the Germans themselves had created confirmed visitors in their sense of superiority over the ragged, starving and disease-ridden Jews they encountered.[207] Passing a Jewish ghetto in Kutno, Melita Maschmann was shocked to see the lethargic poverty of the people penned in behind the high wire fence. Some children were begging, their hands stretched out through the wire.

The wretchedness of the children brought a lump to my throat. But I clenched my teeth. Gradually I learned to switch off my "private feelings" quickly and utterly in such situations. This is terrible, I said to myself, but the driving out of the Jews is one of the unfortunate things we must bargain for if the "Warthegau" is to become a German country.

She saw some German railway officials going to the fence and gawping at the Jews as if they were animals in a zoo.[208] What they saw, though it was the result of German oppression, confirmed their prejudices against 'Eastern Jews'. As one army NCO wrote on 30 June 1941:

We drove through the quarter of the Jews and the epidemics. I cannot describe the condition of this area and its inhabitants . . . Many hundreds of people were queuing at groceries, tobacconists and liquor stores . . . As we drove by, we saw a man fall over for no obvious cause; it must have been hunger that made him fall, for a number of these riff-raff starve to death every day. A few are still well dressed in prewar clothes, but the most are shrouded in sacks and rags, a terrible picture of hunger and poverty. Children and women run after us and scream 'bread, bread!'[209]

Rare indeed was a German officer like Wilm Hosenfeld, who found 'terrible conditions' in the ghetto when he visited it on business early in 1941, 'all an indictment against us'.[210]

Despite these miserable and often terrifying conditions, the ghetto inhabitants managed to keep some kind of cultural, religious and social life going, even when the pressures imposed by working to survive made observation of the Sabbath difficult, and the desperate state of hygiene and sanitation prevented most Jews from keeping to traditional norms of personal cleanliness. In Warsaw actors and musicians staged theatrical productions and concerts, while in Lódź, true to form, Rumkowski organized all cultural activity himself. Adam Czerniaków recorded in his diary regular visits to chamber music recitals, and as late as 6 June 1942 he was considering having an opera staged – *Carmen*, or perhaps *The Tales of Hoffman*. One of the most important projects in the Warsaw ghetto was devised by the young historian Emanuel Ringelblum, who gathered together people of many different political persuasions to collect an archive of diaries, letters, memoirs, interviews and documents, and to keep a record of the ghetto's history for posterity. He even managed to write a serious study of Polish-Jewish relations during the war while simultaneously trying to survive in the increasingly intolerable conditions of life in the ghetto.[211]

IV

In Germany itself, conditions for the remaining Jewish population continued to deteriorate steadily in the first two years of the war. Numbering
207,000 in September 1939, according to the official racial classification
of the Nazis, it was mostly middle-aged or elderly. Germany's Jews had
been despoiled of almost all their assets. They were effectively ostracized
from German society and dependent on their own organizations for the
maintenance of any kind of collective life. Many of those younger Jewish
men who stayed in Germany had already been drafted into forced-labour
schemes well before the outbreak of war. Compulsory labour, often in
hard and dirty physical jobs such as digging ditches or shovelling snow,
continued through 1940. In the spring of that year, however, the shelving
of plans to create a Jewish reservation in the Lublin area, coupled with
serious labour shortages in the arms industry, led to a change of policy.
Jewish men of military age were banned from emigrating, in case they
took up arms against Germany, and all Jews between the ages of fifteen
and fifty-five for men and fifteen and fifty for women were ordered to
register for labour. By October 1940 there were 40,000 Jews working
on forced labour schemes, increasing numbers of them in war-related
industries. Indeed, Goebbels noted in his diary on 22 March 1941 that
30,000 Jews in Berlin were working in arms factories ('who would ever
have thought that possible?'). Jewish labourers could be got very cheaply,
and they did not require the provision of special accommodation or the
hiring of translators, as did Polish or Czech workers.[212]

Emigration, which had seen more than half Germany's Jewish inhabitants leave since the beginning of 1933, thus became a lesser priority
under the impact of the demand for Jewish labour. Only perhaps 15,000
or so more Jews managed to find refuge in a neutral country in the
course of 1940. Around 1,000 got to Brazil with the help of visas
arranged by the Vatican in 1939, funded by American donors. Somewhat
surprisingly, perhaps, a Japanese consul stationed variously in Lithuania,
Prague and Königsberg in 1939–41, Chiune Sugihara, whose main function was supposed to be observing military matters, began on his own
initiative to issue transit visas to Japan to any Jews who approached
him, even though they had no permission to enter the country; out
of perhaps 10,000 Jews who obtained these documents, possibly half

managed to find their way illegally eventually to Canada, the USA or other destinations.[213] Illegal emigration to Palestine continued, encouraged by the Gestapo, but the British mandate authorities in the country began to put obstacles in its path, fearing that it would alienate the Palestinians: in November 1940 they turned away a shipload of Jewish refugees who had come via the Danube and the Black Sea; the refugees were transferred to another ship to take them back to Romania, and only after the ship had exploded and sunk, killing 251 passengers, did the British authorities allow the rest to disembark and settle. The international treaty port of Shanghai, by contrast, imposed few restrictions on immigration, and remained open until December 1941, when the war in the Pacific broke out; by the summer of 1941, over 25,000 Jewish refugees from a variety of European countries including Germany had managed to flee there, travelling through Hungary or Scandinavia via the Trans-Siberian Railway and thence by sea.[214]

Those who remained in Germany were now overwhelmingly concentrated in Berlin. Despite their extremely difficult situation they were able to continue some sort of social and cultural life not least because of the existence of the Jewish Culture League, which published books and periodicals, staged concerts and plays, arranged lectures and put on film shows. Everything of course had to be approved by its Nazi head, Hans Hinkel, who banned 'German' cultural heritage from being disseminated by the League. Under the restrictive conditions of wartime, it was also more difficult to keep going than before, especially outside Berlin.[215] The overall interests of the Jewish community in the Reich were represented by the Reich Association of Jews in Germany, which was given the task by the regime, on Hitler's explicit orders, of dispensing charity, organizing education and apprenticeships, arranging emigration and finding jobs for members of the Jewish community where possible. In January 1939 the Culture League had been effectively integrated into the Association by order of the Nazis, not least in order to make its financial resources available to the latter to assist Jewish emigration. A new executive committee was installed, consisting of representatives of the Association and the Jewish religious congregations of Berlin and Vienna. Nevertheless, despite its depleted funds, the quality of the League's offerings continued to be high, with performances of classic French plays by Molière and others, symphonies by Mahler and Tchaikovsky, and chamber music groups playing in provincial cities for Jewish audiences.

Religious life, for those who belonged to the Jewish faith, continued too, though after the destruction of Germany's synagogues in the pogrom of 9–10 November 1938, it was obviously on a restricted scale.[216]

No ghettos as such were set up inside the Reich, but in the course of 1940 and 1941, Jews began to be evicted from their dwellings and moved into 'Jews' houses', where they were forced to live under increasingly overcrowded conditions, an echo of what was simultaneously happening on a much larger scale and in a far more brutal manner to Jews in occupied Poland. Basing their actions on a law of 30 April 1939 that allowed landlords to evict Jewish tenants if alternative accommodation was available, municipalities began to concentrate the Jewish population, using further powers created in the same law to compel Jewish homeowners to take in Jewish tenants. In many cases the alternative accommodation was found in disused barracks and similar buildings: in Müngersdorf, near Cologne, 2,000 Jews were put into a dipalidated fort, twenty to a room. Some thirty-eight such 'residence camps' were created after the outbreak of war. War also brought the confiscation of all radio sets from German Jews, followed in 1940 by telephones. New taxes were imposed on their now-meagre incomes. Ration cards for shoes, clothing and fabrics were withdrawn from the Jews. A host of new police regulations and decrees made their lives more difficult and increased their chances of falling foul of the law. Immediately after the outbreak of hostilities, German Jews were subjected to a curfew, and severe restrictions were imposed on the hours during which they could go shopping. They were only allowed to buy supplies in designated, Aryan-owned shops at particular times (there were no more Jewish-owned shops). They were allotted lower rations for food and clothing than non-Jews were and banned from buying chocolates. Himmler announced in October 1939 that any Jew who contravened any regulation, failed to obey any instruction, or showed any kind of resistance to the state and its dictates was to be arrested and put into a concentration camp. The powers of the police and other authorities to harass and persecute Jews grew correspondingly: in the Rhenish town of Krefeld, for instance, cases involving Jews, which had made up 20 per cent of all cases handled by the Gestapo before the war, rose to 35 per cent after the war had started. And in the spring of 1941, Himmler announced that any Jew imprisoned in a concentration camp would remain there for the duration of the war.[217]

Already in October 1940 Hitler personally ordered the deportation of two particular groups of German Jews who lived in the south-western states of Baden, the Saarland and the Palatinate. The Reich Security Head Office was put in charge of the operation. The Jews were rounded up on the basis of detailed lists compiled by the police and put on to buses. They were allowed one 50-kilo suitcase each, bedding and food supplies. They could take a maximum of 100 Reichsmarks each; their dwellings, furniture and valuables had to be left behind and were taken over by the Reich. The same fate had already befallen the Jewish population of Alsace-Lorraine on 16 July 1940, when it was occupied by the Germans after the defeat of France. The Saar, the Palatinate and Alsace-Lorraine were to be put together to form a single new Nazi Party District, which was to be entirely 'Jew-free'. All these people were driven across the French border and dumped into camps in the unoccupied zone; later, more were taken to the General Government. The French authorities promised that the rest would shortly be deported to the French colony of Madagascar. For the time being, these were the only Jews deported from German territory, along with the Jewish inhabitants of Schneidemühl and Stettin, who had been forcibly taken to Lublin the previous February, and the Jews taken from Vienna and the Reich Protectorate to Nisko.[218]

Alongside the remaining Jewish population in the rest of Germany, there was also a significant group of people defined as 'mixed-race', that is, half-Jewish or quarter-Jewish. They were subjected to some of the discriminatory measures introduced by the Nazis over the previous six years, but not all of them. They could not work in state-funded jobs, including schoolteaching and local administration, but they could, until 1941 at least, serve in the army; if they were half-Jewish they were not allowed to marry a non-Jew, and if they practised the Jewish religion they were classified as fully Jewish. On the other hand, a Jew who was married to a non-Jew could escape most of the regime's antisemitic policies provided the couple had children who were not brought up in the Jewish faith; and even if they had no children, they were to some extent exempt, so long as they did not practise the Jewish faith themselves.[219] One such couple were Victor Klemperer, a retired Jewish professor of French literature, and his non-Jewish wife, Eva, a former pianist, whose lives in this period can be reconstructed in great detail thanks to the survival of Klemperer's voluminous diaries. Klemperer had lost his job ostensibly not because he was Jewish but because his post had been declared redundant, so he had a small pension to live off. By 1939, he was no longer allowed to use the libraries in Dresden, where he lived, he was barred from most public facilities in the city, and he had to carry a Jewish identity card with the name 'Israel' added to his own. Writing his memoirs and his diaries and tending his house and garden in the Dresden suburb of Dölzschen were virtually the only remaining activities open to him. He also devoted himself to compiling a list of the linguistic expressions of Nazism, which he called *LTI – Lingua Tertii Imperii*, the language of the Third Reich. His manuscripts and diaries he deposited regularly with a non-Jewish friend, Annemarie Köhler, a doctor who ran a clinic in Pirna, outside Dresden.[220]

The war at first had little impact on Klemperer. His house was raided by the Gestapo, looking for radios and for forbidden literature, but the officers were polite enough, and the main problem he faced was the exorbitant burden of special taxes which the government levied on him as a Jew. On 9 December 1939, however, he was informed that he and his wife would have to rent out their house to a local greengrocer, who would open a shop in it, and move to two rooms in a special house in the city reserved for Jews, which they would share with other families. Under the terms of the rental agreement, which took effect on 26 May 1940, the Klemperers were not allowed to go near their old house, and the greengrocer had first right of refusal on its sale, which was fixed at 16,600 Reichsmarks, a sum Klemperer considered ridiculously low. It was not to be long before the new occupier began to search for a pretext to put the sale into effect. Meanwhile, in the Jews' House, at 15B Caspar David Friedrich Strasse, a detached villa 'stuffed full of people, who all share the same fate', Klemperer was irritated 'by the constant fussing interference of strangers' and the absence of his books, most of which he had been obliged to put into storage. Nerves and tempers became frayed, and he became embroiled in a 'terrible argument' with another inhabitant of the house, who accused him of using too much water.[221]

The Klemperers went out for long walks as much as they could, though shopping was a continual humiliation ('it is always horrible for me to show the J card'). Deliveries from non-Jewish firms were stopped, however, so he now had to go to shops to buy everything, including milk. The Klemperers' life continued in this way for the best part of a year, until, in June 1941, disaster struck. Pedantic, with an attention to detail that was one of the qualities that make his diaries so valuable, Klemperer had survived to this point not least because of his extreme punctiliousness in observing all the rules and regulations to which Jews in the Third Reich were subjected. 'Throughout 17 months of war,' he noted, 'we had always blacked out with the greatest care.' But one evening in February he had come back from a walk after dark and realized he had forgotten to put up the blackout shutters; neighbours had complained to the police about the light coming from his room, the police had reported the incident, and Klemperer was sentenced to eight days in prison. He had never heard of anyone being imprisoned for a first-time offence against the blackout regulations. 'I undoubtedly owed it solely to the J on my identity card.' On 23 June 1940, after his plea for leniency had been rejected, he reported to the police station to begin his sentence. Down in the subterranean world of the cells, the books he had brought with him to while away the time were confiscated, along with his reading glasses, and the warders, shouting at him roughly to hurry up, ushered him into Cell 89, furnished with a fold-up bed and table, some cutlery and crockery, a washbasin, towel and soap, and a WC (flushed twice a day from the outside). The time weighed endlessly upon him, 'the awful emptiness and immobility of the 192 hours'. Conscious of the fact that he was there not least because he was a Jew, he began to wonder if he would ever get out alive.[222]

V

Jews and Poles were not the only objects of the radicalization of Nazi racial policy and practice in the first two years of the war. Germany's 26,000 or so Gypsies were also included in the plans developed by the Nazis for the racial reordering of Central and East-Central Europe in the course of the invasion of Poland. By September 1939, Himmler, persuaded by the criminologist Robert Ritter that mixed-race Gypsies in particular were a threat to society, had instructed every regional criminal police office to set up a special desk dealing with the 'Gypsy problem'. He issued an order banning Gypsies from marrying 'Aryans', and placed some 2,000 Gypsies in special camps [223] On the outbreak of war, Heydrich banned Gypsies from plying their itinerant trades near Germany's western borders. Even before this, some local authorities in these areas had taken the initiative and expelled Gypsies from their districts, expressing a traditional wartime fear of Gypsies as spies; Gypsies who had been conscripted into the army were also now cashiered because of the same fears.[224] In November 1939 Gypsy women were legally prevented from fortune-telling, on the grounds that they were spreading false predictions about the end of the war (the date of which was obviously a matter of intense interest to many of Germans who consulted them). A number were incarcerated in the women's concentration camp at Ravensbrück in consequence. Already in December 1938 Himmler had spoken of 'the final solution of the Gypsy question', and in pursuit of this aim Heydrich informed his senior underlings on 21 September 1939 that as well as the Jews, the Gypsies would also be deported from Germany to the east of Poland. Germany's Gypsies were ordered to remain where they were on pain of being taken off to a concentration camp while a census was taken; subsequently some limited mobility was permitted, essential if Gypsies were to continue to make a living, but it was not much of a concession.[225]

Meanwhile, in January 1940, Himmler began detailed planning for the expulsion of the Gypsies, who were rounded up and placed in collection camps. In May 1940 some 2,500 of them were put on trains and taken to the General Government from a total of seven embarkation centres in the Rhineland, Hamburg, Bremen and Hanover. They were allowed to take a limited amount of luggage, and they were supplied with food and medical care, but the property and possessions they left behind were eventually seized and confiscated. On arrival in the General Government, they were dispersed to towns, villages and work camps; one train even stopped in the middle of the countryside, where the guards threw the Gypsies out and left them to fend for themselves. Many Gypsies died of malnutrition or disease, particularly in the harsh conditions of the camps, and some perished in a massacre near Radom. However, in most cases they were able to move about freely, and a large number found work of one kind or another. Many used the opportunity to return to Germany, where they were generally arrested but not sent back to Poland. Like the planned deportations of the Jews, however, the expulsion of the Gypsies was soon halted; Frank had objected to yet further mass deportations into the General Government, and the supposed military necessity for removing them from the western borders of the Reich disappeared after the conquest of France. For the time being, the Gypsies who remained in Germany were left where they were. Increasing numbers of the fit and able were drafted into forced-labour schemes.[226]

Like the Jews, Germany's Gypsies had experienced a drastic deterioration in their situation since the beginning of the war. It had been made plain to them that their long-term future did not lie in Germany, and that when their deportation en masse finally happened it would be achieved through violence, brutality and murder. Conflicting interests in Poland, coupled with the rapidly changing war situation, had put a temporary halt to the expulsions and given them a respite. Yet Hitler's declared intention of ridding the Reich of all its Jews and Gypsies was in no sense abandoned. Its full realization could only be a matter of time.

'LIFE UNWORTHY OF LIFE'

I

On 22 September 1939, in occupied Poland an SS unit from a paramilitary SS and police group, some 500 to 600 strong, founded in Danzig by Kurt Eimann, a local SS leader, loaded a group of mental patients from the asylum at Conradstein (Kocborowo) into a lorry and drove them to a nearby wood, a killing field where many thousands of Poles had already been shot by the Germans. The SS made them line up, still dressed in their asylum clothing, some of them even wearing strait-jackets, on the edge of a ditch, where Gestapo officers from the Old Reich shot them, one by one, in the back of the neck. The mental patients fell into the ditch as they were executed, and the paramilitaries covered their bodies with a thin layer of soil. Over the next few weeks, more lorry-loads from the asylum arrived, to suffer the same fate, until around 2,000 mental patients had been killed. Relatives were told that the victims had been transferred to other asylums, but the reverse was the case, as mentally and physically handicapped children from institutions in Silberhammer (Srebrzysk), Mewe (Gniew) and Riesenburg (Probuty) were taken to Conradstein for execution. The same thing was happening elsewhere too. In Schwetz (Swiece) and Konitz (Chojnice), German police units and ethnic German 'Self-Protection' squads carried out the killings, while in November 1939 patients from Stralsund, Treptow an der Rege, Lauenburg and Ückermünde were taken to Neustadt in West Prussia (Wejherowo) and shot.[227]

In the Wartheland, Regional Leader Greiser emptied three major psychiatric hospitals of their inmates and had all the Poles and Jews among them killed. Most of them were shot by members of the SS Task Force VI. A special fate, however, was reserved for the patients of the hospital at Treskau (Owińska). They were taken to Posen and crammed into a sealed room in the fort that served as the local headquarters of the Gestapo. Here they were poisoned with carbon monoxide gas, released from canisters. This was the first time in history that a gas chamber had been used for mass killing. Further murders took place in the fort; on one occasion in December 1939, Himmler himself came along to observe. Early in 1940 this murder campaign finished with the transportation of more asylum inmates to Kosten (Kościan) in the Wartheland, where they were loaded into gas chambers mounted on the back of lorries, taken out into the countryside and asphyxiated. All in all, by the time the initial action was over, in January 1940, some 7,700 inmates of psychiatric hospitals and institutions for the mentally and physically handicapped had been killed, along with a number of prostitutes from Gdingen (Gdynia) and Bromberg (Bydgoszcz), and Gypsies from Preussisch-Stargard (Starograd).[228] Such events could hardly be kept secret. Dr Klukowski heard of the killings in February 1940. 'It is hard to believe anything as terrible as this,' he wrote.[229]

The murders continued during the following months. In May and June 1940, 1,558 Germans and 300 or so Poles were taken from an East Prussian mental institution at Soldau and killed by mobile gas wagons in an action organized by a special unit under the command of Herbert Lange, which went on to murder many hundreds more patients in the incorporated territories in the same way. Lange's men received a special bonus of ten Reichsmarks for every patient they killed. The killings even extended to mental patients in the Lódź ghetto, where a German medical commission took away forty to be shot in a nearby wood in March 1940 and another batch on 29 July 1941. So terrible were the conditions in the ghetto by this time that Jewish families still begged the hospital to admit their mentally ill relatives even though they were fully aware of the risks this involved. Altogether well over 12,000 patients were killed in these various actions by Eimann, Lange and their men.[230] Although these murders took place in the context of a war in which many thousands more Poles and Jews were being shot by German army units, SS Security Task Forces and local ethnic German militias, they none the less stand out in some ways as qualitatively different. In Posen the need to free up space to quarter Military SS units may have played a role, and in some cases the accommodation released by the murders was made available to Baltic German settlers. But for the most part, such practical considerations were only of secondary importance or indeed merely served as a way of justifying these actions in seemingly rational terms. The space made available by the killings stood in no relation at all to the numbers of settlers arriving from the east. The real reasons for the killings were not practical or instrumental, but ideological.[231] There was no convincing justification for the murders in security terms either. Unlike Polish intellectuals, the victims could not be regarded as posing a threat to the German occupation or the long-term Germanization of the region. Significantly, those few inmates of asylums deemed capable of work were spared and taken off to Germany. The rest were 'social ballast', 'life unworthy of life', to be killed as quickly as possible.[232]

II

As Himmler's visit to the Posen fort killings suggests, the Nazi leaders in Berlin were well aware of what was going on, and indeed provided the ideological impulse for it to begin. From the mid-twenties at the latest, influenced by the writings of radical eugenicists, Hitler had considered that it was necessary for Germany's racial health and military effectiveness to eliminate 'degenerates' from the chain of heredity. 'If Germany got a million children every year,' he had declared at the 1929 Nuremberg Party Rally, 'and removed 70,000 to 80,000 of the weakest, then the end result would perhaps actually be an increase in its strength.'[233] On 14 July 1933 the regime had introduced compulsory sterilization for Germans considered to be suffering from hereditary weaknesses, including 'moral feeble-mindedness', a vague criterion that could encompass many different kinds of social deviance. Some 360,000 people had been sterilized by the time the war broke out.[234] In 1935, in addition, abortion on eugenic grounds had been legalized.[235] Already, however, well before this time, Hitler had begun to plan for even more radical action. According to Hans-Heinrich Lammers, head of the Reich Chancellery, Hitler had considered putting a provision for the killing of mental patients into the Law of 14 July 1933, but shelved it because it would be too controversial. In 1935, however, as his doctor Karl Brandt recalled, Hitler had told the Reich Doctors' Leader Gerhard Wagner that he would implement such a measure in wartime, 'when the whole world is gazing at acts of war and the value of human life in any case weighs less in the balance'. From 1936, SS doctors began to be appointed in growing numbers as directors of psychiatric institutions, while pressure was put on Church-run institutions to transfer their patients to secular ones. At the end of 1936 or the beginning of 1937, a secret Reich Committee for Hereditary Health Matters was established within the Chancellery of the Leader, initially with a view to drawing up legislation for a Reich Hereditary Health Court. By this time, too, the SS journal *The Black Corps* was openly urging the killing of 'life unworthy of life', while there is evidence that a number of Regional Leaders began to prepare for the murder of institutionalized patients in their areas. All of this suggests that serious preparations for the killing of the handicapped began around this time. It only needed the imminent prospect of war to put them into effect.[236]

Such a prospect finally became real in the summer of 1939. Already in May, as preparations for the war with Poland were under way, Hitler had set up administrative arrangements for the killing of mentally ill children under the aegis of the Reich Committee for Hereditary Health Matters, now renamed more precisely the Reich Committee for the Scientific Registering of Serious Hereditary and Congenital Illnesses. A precedent, or excuse, was found in a petition to Hitler from the father of a baby boy who was born in February 1939 lacking a leg and part of an arm and suffering from convulsions. The father wanted the infant killed, but the Leipzig hospital doctor whom he had first approached had refused to do this because it would have opened him to prosecution for murder. Presented by the Chancellery of the Leader, his personal secretariat, with a dossier on the matter, Hitler ordered Brandt to visit Leipzig and kill the child himself after confirming the diagnosis and consulting with his medical colleagues there. Soon after, Brandt reported back to Hitler that he had got the local doctors to kill the infant on 25 July 1939. Hitler now formally asked Brandt, together with the head of the Leader's' Chancellery, to undertake active preparation of a major programme for killing mentally or physically handicapped children. Hitler's personal physician, Theo Morell, who was closely involved in the planning process, suggested that the parents of the murdered children would prefer it if their death was reported as resulting from natural causes. As a final phase of the planning process, the head of the Leader's Chancellery, Philipp Bouhler, a thirty-nine-year-old long-time Nazi who had built up the office over the years and gradually extended its influence into many of the areas of government touched on by the thousands of petitions addressed to Hitler that it was its job to deal with, invited fifteen to twenty doctors, many of them heads of psychiatric institutions, to a meeting to discuss the planned programme of killing. Although it was to begin with children, Hitler, Bormann, Lammers and Leonardo Conti, the head of the Party's Health Office and 'Reich Health Leader' since the death of the Reich Doctors' Leader Gerhard Wagner on 25 March 1939, decided that Conti should be commissioned with its extension to cover adults as well. Now that the decision had been made to kill the mentally ill and handicapped, a decree dated 31 August 1939 officially brought the programme of sterilizing them to an end in all but a few exceptional cases.[237]

The Leader's Chancellery was from Hitler's point of view the ideal location for the planning and implementation of the killing programme. His own personal office, it was neither subordinate to the Party, like the Party Chancellery, nor part of the civil service, like the Reich Chancellery, so it would be far easier to keep the deliberations over 'euthanasia' secret than it would have been had they taken place in the more formal bureaucratic setting of either of these other two institutions. Morell submitted to Hitler a memorandum on the possibility of formally legalizing the killing of the handicapped, and Hitler gave his personal approval to the idea. Under instructions from Bouhler's office, the Ministry of Justice's official Commission on the Reform of the Criminal Law prepared draft legislation removing penal sanctions from the killing of people suffering from incurable mental illness and confined to institutions. Lengthy discussions within the legal, medical and eugenic bureaucracies continued for many months as the draft was amended and refined. But for Hitler these seemingly endless deliberations were too slow and too pedantic. Like all the rest of the Commission's drafts, the proposed legislation was eventually shelved.[238] Impatient with these delays, Hitler acceded to pressure from Bouhler to transfer responsibility for the killings back from Conti to the Leader's Chancellery, and signed an order in October 1939 charging Bouhler and Brandt 'to extend the powers of doctors to be specified by name, so that sick people who by human estimation are incurable can, on the most critical assessment of the state of their illness, be granted a merciful death'. Although not a formal decree, this order effectively possessed the force of law in a polity where leading constitutional experts had long since been arguing that even Hitler's verbal utterances were legally binding. As a precaution, none the less, the order was shown to Reich Justice Minister Gürtner, to forestall any possible prosecutions; but apart from being made known to a few selected individuals involved in the programme, it was otherwise kept secret. To make clear that it was being introduced as a consequence of the heightened need to purify the German race imposed by the war, Hitler antedated it to 1 September 1939, the day the war broke out.[239]

By the time Hitler signed the order, the murder of adult patients was already under way in Poland; but it would not have begun there had the Regional Leaders in Pomerania, Danzig-West Prussia and East Prussia not been aware of the decisions already taken in Berlin. In Germany itself, the programme was initially directed at children. The secret Reich Committee for the Scientific Registering of Serious Hereditary and Congenital Illnesses, located in Bouhler's Chancellery, ordered the compulsory registration of all 'malformed' newborn children on 18 August 1939.[240] These included infants suffering from Down's syndrome, microcephaly, the absence of a limb or deformities of the head or spine, cerebral palsy and similar conditions, and vaguely defined conditions such as 'idiocy'. Doctors and midwives were paid two Reichsmarks for each case they reported to their superiors, who sent lists of the infants in question to a postal box number in Berlin, next to Bouhler's office. Three doctors in the Leader's Chancellery processed the reports. They then marked the registration forms with a + if the child was to be killed, and sent them on to the nearest public health office, which would then order the child's admission to a paediatric clinic. To begin with, four such clinics were used, but many more were established later on, bringing the eventual total up to thirty.[241]

This whole process of registration, transport and killing was initially directed not at infants and children who were already in hospitals or care institutions, but at those who lived at home, with their parents. The parents were informed that the children would be well looked after, or even that removal to a specialist clinic held out the promise of a cure, or at least an improvement in their condition. Given the hereditarian bias of the diagnoses, a large proportion of the families were poor and ill-educated, and a good proportion of them were already stigmatized as 'asocial' or 'hereditarily inferior'. Those who raised objections to the removal of their offspring from the family home were sometimes threatened with withdrawal of benefits if they did not comply. In any case, from March 1941 onwards, child allowances were no longer paid for handicapped children, and after September 1941 the children could be compulsorily removed from parents who refused to release them. In some institutions parents were banned from visiting their children with the excuse that this would make it more difficult for them to get used to their new surroundings; others found it difficult to visit in any case, since many of the centres were located in remote areas and far from easy to get to by public transport. Once admitted by the social and medical services, the children were put in special wards, away from the other patients. Most of the killing centres carried out their task by starving the children to death or administering overdoses of the sedative Luminal in their food. After a few days the children would develop breathing problems and eventually succumb to bronchitis or pneumonia. Sometimes the doctors left these diseases untreated, sometimes they finished the children off with lethal injections of morphine.[242]

A teacher taken on a tour of the killing ward at the Eglfing-Haar asylum in the autumn of 1939 later testified that the director, Hermann Pfannmüller, a long-time Nazi and an advocate of involuntary euthanasia for many years, told him openly that he preferred to let the children die naturally rather than killing them by injections, because this might arouse hostile comment abroad if news of it ever got out:

As he spoke these words, [Pfannmüller] and a nurse from the ward pulled a child from its crib. Displaying the child like a dead rabbit, he pontificated with the air of a connoisseur and a cynical smirk something like this: 'With this one, for example, it will still take two to three days.' I can still clearly visualize the spectacle of this fat and smirking man with the whimpering skeleton in his fleshy hand, surrounded by other starving children. Furthermore, the murderer then pointed out that they did not suddenly withdraw food, but instead slowly reduced rations.[243]

The programme continued for much of the rest of the war along similar lines, killing an estimated 5,000 children in total. Gradually, the upper age limit for removal and murder was raised, first to eight, then to twelve, and finally to sixteen. In practice some were even older. Many of these children and adolescents suffered from little more than developmental difficulties of one kind or another.[244]

A large number of health officials and doctors were involved in the scheme, whose nature and purpose thus became widely known in the medical profession. Few of them objected. Even those who did, and refused to take part, did not put forward any criticisms on grounds of principle. For many years, and not merely since 1933, the medical profession, particularly in the field of psychiatry, had been convinced that it was legitimate to identify a minority of the handicapped as living a 'life unworthy of life', and that it was necessary to remove them from the chain of heredity if all the many measures taken to improve the health of the German race under the Third Reich were not to be frustrated. Virtually the entire medical profession had been actively involved in the sterilization programme, and from here it was but a short step in the minds of many to involuntary euthanasia. Their views were well represented by an article that appeared in the leading German physicians' journal in 1942 on 'The New German Physician', arguing that it was the task of the medical profession, particularly in wartime, when so many of Germany's best and bravest were dying on the battlefield, 'to come to terms with counter-selection in their own people'. 'Infant mortality,' it went on, 'is a process of selection, and in the majority of cases it affects the constitutionally inferior.' It was the doctors' task to restore this balance of nature to its original form. Without the killing of the incurable, the healing of the majority of the sick and the improvement of the nation's health would be impossible. Many of those doctors involved spoke with pride of their work even after the war, maintaining that they had been contributing to human progress.[245]

III

Hitler's retrospective 'euthanasia' order of October 1939, putting a pseudo-legal gloss on a decision already taken at the end of July, applied not only to children but also to adults in hospitals and similar institutions. Planning for this extension of the killing programme also began before the war. The programme, codenamed 'Action T-4' after the address of the Leader's Chancellery, Tiergartenstrasse 4, from where it was run, was put into the hands of a senior official in the Chancellery, Viktor Brack. Born in 1904, and so in his mid-thirties, Brack, the son of a doctor, was a trained agronomist who had run the estate attached to his father's sanatorium. He joined the Nazi Party and the SS in 1929, and benefited from the fact that his father knew Heinrich Himmler and had delivered one of his children. In the early 1930s he frequently acted as Himmler's driver, before being appointed adjutant and then chief of staff to Bouhler and moving with him to Berlin. Brack was another enthusiast for involuntary euthanasia, declaring after the war that it was based on humane considerations. Such considerations were not powerful enough at the time to overcome his awareness that what he was doing might be regarded as tantamount to murder, so he used the pseudonym 'Jennerwein' when he dealt with the killing programme, just as his deputy, Werner Blankenburg, who succeeded him in 1942 when Brack went off to fight at the front, also disguised his identity (with the pseudonym 'Brenner').[246]

Brack soon created a whole bureaucracy to administer Action T-4, including front organizations with harmless-sounding names to run the registration, transport, personnel and financial sides of the operation. He put Dr Werner Heyde in charge of the medical side of the programme.[247] Born in 1902, Heyde had fought in a Free Corps unit in Estonia before taking up his medical studies, graduating in 1926. He clearly enjoyed strong connections with the far right, and in 1933 it was Heyde whom Himmler had asked to carry out a psychological assessment of the later commandant of Dachau concentration camp, Theodor Eicke, after the latter's violent quarrel with the Regional Leader of the Palatinate, Josef Bürckel, who had committed him to an asylum. Heyde's positive assessment had gratified Himmler, whose backing he now enjoyed. Following this encounter, Heyde had joined the Nazi Party in May 1933. He became an SS officer in 1936. During the 1930s Heyde had acted as an expert medical referee in sterilization cases and he also carried out assessments of concentration camp inmates. Appointed to the staff of Würzburg University in 1932, he became an adviser to the Gestapo in psychiatric matters, lectured on hereditary diseases (or those that were supposedly hereditary) and headed the local branch of the Racial-Political Office of the Nazi Party. In 1939 he became a full professor at the university. Here was an example, then, of a medical man who had built his career in the most ideological areas of Nazi medicine rather than in a more conventional manner. He seemed ideally suited to administer the killing programme.[248]

Already at the key meeting with Bouhler in late July 1933, Heyde, Brandt, Conti and others involved in the planning of the adult involuntary euthanasia scheme had begun to discuss the best method of carrying it out. In view of the fact that Hitler wanted around 70,000 patients to be killed, the methods used to murder the children seemed both too slow and too much likely to arouse public suspicion. Brandt consulted Hitler on the matter, and later claimed that when the Nazi Leader had asked him what was the most humane way of killing the patients, he had suggested gassing with carbon monoxide, a method already put to him by a number of physicians and made familiar through reports of suicides and domestic accidents in the press. Such cases had been investigated in depth by the police, and so Bouhler's office commissioned Albert Widmann, born in 1912, and an SS officer who was the top professional chemist in the Criminal-Technical (or, as we would say, Forensic Science) Institute of the Reich Criminal Police Office, to work out how best to kill large numbers of what he was told were 'beasts in human form'. He worked out that an airtight chamber was required, and had one built in the old city prison at Brandenburg, empty since the construction of a new penitentiary at Brandenburg-Görden in 1932. SS construction workers built a cell 3 metres by 5, and 3 metres high, lined with tiles and made to look like a shower-room so as to dull the apprehensions of those brought into it. A gas pipe was fitted along the wall with holes to let the carbon monoxide into the chamber. And as a last touch, an airtight door was installed, with a small glass window for viewing what was happening inside.[249]

By the time it was finished, probably in December 1939, the gassings in Posen had already taken place, and had been personally observed by Himmler: undoubtedly the method had been suggested by Widmann or one of his associates to local SS officers in Posen, at least one of whom had a chemistry degree and was in touch with leading chemists in the Old Reich.[250] Himmler's subordinate Christian Wirth, a senior official in the Stuttgart police, was one of those who attended the first demonstration of gassing in Brandenburg, along with Bouhler, Brandt, Conti, Brack and a number of other officials and physicians from T4 headquarters in Berlin. They took their turn to watch through the window as eight patients were killed in the gas chamber by carbon monoxide administered by Widmann, who told them how to measure the correct dose. All approved. Several other patients, given supposedly lethal injections by Brandt and Conti, had failed to die immediately – they were later gassed too – and so it was concluded that Widmann's procedure was quicker and more effective. Soon the gas chamber in Brandenburg, which now went into regular service and continued to be used for killing patients until September 1940, was joined by other gas chambers built at the asylum in Grafeneck (Württemberg), which operated from January to December 1940, Hartheim, near Linz, which opened in May 1940, and Hadamar, in Hesse, which began operating in December 1940, replacing Grafeneck. These were former hospitals taken over by T-4 for exclusive use as killing centres; other gas chambers also came into use at hospitals that continued their previous functions, at Sonnenstein, in Saxony, which opened in June 1940, and Bernburg, on the river Saale, which opened in September the same year, replacing the original facility at Brandenburg.[251]

Each centre was responsible for killing patients from a specific region. Local mental hospitals and institutions for the handicapped were required to send in their details to the T-4 office, together with registration forms for long-term patients, schizophrenics, epileptics, untreatable syphilitics, the senile and the criminally insane, and those suffering from encephalitis, Huntington's disease and 'every type of feeblemindedness' (a very broad and vague category indeed). At least to begin with, many physicians in these institutions were unaware of the purpose of this exercise, but before long it must have become clear enough. The forms were evaluated by politically reliable junior medical experts approved by their local Nazi Party offices – very few who were recommended to the T-4 office refused to play their allotted role – and then vetted by a team of senior officials. The key criterion was not medical but economic – was the patient capable of productive work or not? This question was to play a crucial role in future killing operations of other kinds, and it was also central to the evaluations carried out by T-4 physicians when they visited institutions that had failed to submit registration forms. Behind this economic evaluation, however, the ideological element in the programme was obvious: these were, in the view of the T-4 office, individuals who had to be eliminated from the German race for the sake of its long-term rejuvenation; and for this reason the killings also encompassed, for example, epileptics, deaf-mutes and the blind. Only decorated war veterans were exempted. In practice, however, all these criteria were to a high degree arbitrary, since the forms contained little real detail, and were processed at great speed and in huge numbers. Hermann Pfannmüller, for instance, evaluated over 2,000 patients between 12 November and 1 December 1940, or an average of 121 a day, while at the same time carrying out his duties as director of the state hospital at Eglfing-Haar. Another expert, Josef Schreck, completed 15,000 forms from April 1940 to the end of the year, sometimes processing up to 400 a week, also in addition to his other hospital duties. Neither man can have spent more than a few seconds to take the decision on life or death in each case.[252]

The forms, each marked by three junior experts with a red plus sign for death, a blue minus sign for life, or (occasionally) a question mark for further consideration, were sent to one of three senior physicians for confirmation or amendment. Their decision was final. When the completed forms were returned to the T-4 office, the names of the patients selected for killing were sent to the T-4 transport office, which notified the institutions where they were held and sent an official to make the necessary arrangements. Often the lists were so arbitrarily drawn up that they included patients valued by institution directors as good workers, so not infrequently other patients were substituted for them on the spot in order to fill the required quota. Patients who were not German citizens or not of 'Germanic or related blood' also had to be reported. This meant in the first place Jewish patients, who were the subject of a special order issued on 15 April 1940: some thousand Jewish patients were taken away and gassed or, later on, taken to occupied Poland and killed there, over the following two and a half years, on the grounds that Aryan staff had been complaining about them and could not be expected to treat them. Directors of psychiatric hospitals, like Hermann Pfannmüller on 20 September 1940, proudly reported at the appropriate moment that their institution was now 'Jew-free' after the last Jewish inmate had been killed or taken away.[253]

For all categories of patients selected for killing, the procedure was more or less the same. On the appointed day, large grey coaches, of the kind used by the postal service to provide public transport in rural areas, arrived to take the patients away. Although the T-4 doctors and functionaries repeatedly asserted that these patients were insane and incapable of either making decisions for themselves or of knowing what was going on, this was in no sense the case for the great majority of those selected for killing, even if they were supposedly 'feeble-minded'. Some patients initially welcomed the diversion provided by the coaches' arrival, believing the assurances of the staff that they were going on an outing. But many realized only too well that they were being taken to their death. Doctors and nurses were not always careful to deceive them, and rumours soon began to course through Germany's asylums and care institutions. 'I am again living in a state of fear,' wrote a woman from an institution in Stettin to her family, 'because the cars were here again . . . The cars were here again yesterday and eight days ago as well, they took many people away once more, where one would not have thought. We were all so upset that we all cried.' As a nurse said 'See you again!' to a patient in Reichenau as she got on the bus, the patient turned and replied that 'we wouldn't be seeing each other again, she knew what lay before her with the Hitler Law'. 'Here come the murderers!' one patient in Emmendingen shouted as the bus arrived. Staff often injected anxious patients with heavy sedatives so that they were loaded on to the coaches in a semi-comatose state. But some patients began to refuse injections, fearing they contained poison. Others offered physical resistance when they were being loaded on to the coaches, and the brutal violence meted out to them when they did so only increased the anxieties of the others. Many wept uncontrollably as they were hauled on board.[254]

Once they arrived at their destination, the patients were met by staff, led to a reception room and told to undress. They were given an identity check and a perfunctory physical examination aimed mainly at gaining hints for a plausible cause of death to enter in the records; those with valuable gold fillings in their teeth were marked with a cross on the back or shoulder. An identifying number was stamped or stuck on to their body, they were photographed (to demonstrate their supposed physical and mental inferiority) and then, still naked, they were taken into a gas chamber disguised to look like a shower room. Patients still anxious about their situation were injected with tranquillizers. When they were inside the chamber, the doors were locked and staff released the gas. The patients' death was anything but peaceful or humane. Looking through the peephole, one observer at Hadamar later reported that he had seen

some 40 to 50 men, who were pressed tightly together in the next room, and now slowly died. Some lay on the ground, others had sunk into themselves, many had their mouths open as if they could not get any more air. The way they died was so full of suffering that one cannot speak of a humane killing, the more so since many of those killed may well have had moments of clarity about what was happening. I watched the procedure for about 2–3 minutes then left, because I could not bear to look any longer and I felt sick.[255]

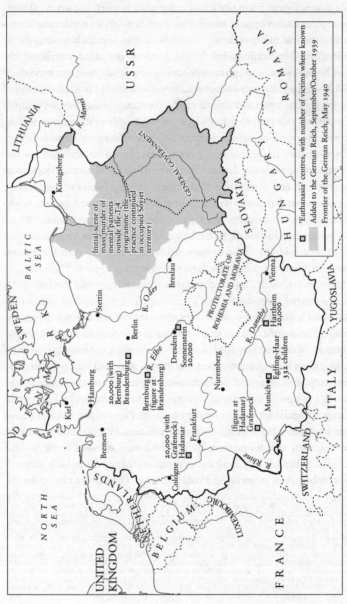

4. Killing Centres of 'Action T-4', 1939–45

The patients were normally killed in groups of fifteen to twenty, though on some occasions many more were crowded into the cramped chambers. After five minutes or so they lost consciousness; after twenty they were dead. The staff waited for an hour or two, then ventilated the chamber with fans. A physician entered to verify death, after which orderlies generally known as 'stokers' (*Brenner*) came in, disentangled the bodies and dragged them out to the 'death room'. Here selected corpses were dissected, either by junior physicians who needed training in pathology, or by others who had orders to remove various organs and send them to research institutes for study. The stokers took the corpses marked with a cross and broke off the gold teeth, which were parcelled up and sent to the T-4 office in Berlin. Then the bodies were put on to metal pallets and taken to the crematorium room, where the stokers often worked through the night to reduce them to ashes.[256]

The families and relatives of the victims were only informed of their transfer to a killing centre after it had taken place.[257] A further letter was sent by the receiving institution registering their safe arrival but warning relatives not to visit them until they had safely settled in. Of course, by the time the relatives received the letter, the patient was in fact already dead. Some time later, the families were notified that the patient had died of a heart attack, pneumonia, tuberculosis, or a similar ailment, from a list provided by the T-4 office and augmented by notes made during their examination on arrival. Aware that they were in some sense acting illegally, the physicians used false names when signing the death certificate, as well as, of course, appending a false date, to make it appear that death had occurred days or weeks after arrival, instead of merely an hour or so. Delaying the announcement of death also had the side-effect of enriching the institution, which continued to receive the benefits, pensions and family subventions paid to the victims between the time of their actual death and the time officially recorded on the certificate. Families were offered an urn containing, they were told, the ashes of their unfortunate relative; in fact, the stokers had simply shovelled them in from the ashes that had accumulated in the crematorium after a whole group of victims had been burned. As for the victims' clothes, they were, the relatives were informed, sent to the National Socialist People's Welfare organization, although in reality, if they were of any quality, they usually found their way into the wardrobes of the killing staff. The elaborate apparatus of deception included maps on which the staff stuck a coloured pin into the home town of each person killed, so that if too many pins appeared in any one place, the place of death could be ascribed to another institution; the killing centres, indeed, even exchanged lists of names of the dead to try to reduce suspicion. Maximum efforts were made to keep the entire process secret, with staff banned from fraternizing with the local population and sworn not to reveal what was going on to anybody apart from authorized officials. 'Anyone who does not keep quiet,' Christian Wirth told a group of new stokers at Hartheim, 'will go to a concentration camp or be shot.'[258]

Within the killing centres, the atmosphere frequently belied the impression of cold calculation conveyed by the numerous forms and documents that it generated. Those who actually carried out the murders were frequently drunk on the special liquor rations they received. They were reported to indulge in numerous casual sexual affairs with one another to take their minds of the all-pervasive stench of death. At Hartheim the staff held a party to celebrate their ten-thousandth cremation, assembling in the crematorium around the naked body of a recently gassed victim, which was laid out on a stretcher and covered with flowers. One staff member dressed as a clergyman and performed a short ceremony, then beer was distributed to all present. Eventually no fewer than 20,000 were gassed at Hartheim, the same at Sonnenstein, 20,000 at Brandenburg and Bernburg, and another 20,000 at Grafeneck and Hadamar, making a total of 80,000 altogether.[259]

IV

Despite the secrecy that surrounded it, the involuntary euthanasia programme could not long remain unnoticed in the world beyond the T-4 bureaucracy and its killing centres. People living near Hadamar noticed clouds of smoke rising from the institution's chimneys not long after the arrival of each transport, while members of staff who went on shopping expeditions or drank in the local inns on the rare occasions on which they were allowed out inevitably talked about their work. Others noticed when the buses arrived in their locality to take mental patients away; on one occasion, early in 1941, coaches loaded up patients from an institution in Absberg not inside the gates but on the town square, in full view of the local people, who began to protest, weeping and shouting abuse, as the patients began to resist and were manhandled on board by burly orderlies.[260] More widespread still were suspicions among relatives of those taken to the killing centres. Some actually welcomed the prospect of their children or dependants being killed; the less perceptive allowed their fears to be dulled by the deceptively reassuring messages that came out of the institutions themselves. But most parents and relatives had their own networks, and knew others in a similar situation to their own, having encountered them at hospital visits or, earlier on, at the doctor's surgery. They knew instinctively what was happening when they learned that their dependants had been transferred to somewhere like Hartheim or Hadamar. Sometimes they tried to take them home before they could be put on a transport list. One mother wrote to the director of her son's institution on hearing that he had been transferred: 'If my son is already dead then I request his ashes, because in Munich all kinds of rumours are going around and for once I want clarity.' Another woman wrote in the margin of the official notification of her aunt's transfer to Grafeneck: 'In a few days we will now receive the news of poor Ida's death . . . I dread the next letter . . . We won't even be able to go to Ida's grave and one doesn't even know whether the ashes that are sent will be Ida's.' With increasing frequency, fear became anger when the official death notice arrived. Why, the sister of one murdered man wrote to the director of the institution from which he had been transported, had he been taken at all if he had been so sick that he had died so soon afterwards? His illness could not 'just have occurred yesterday'. 'In the end,' she told him furiously, 'we are dealing with a poor, sick, human being *in need of help*, and *not with a piece of livestock!!*'[261]

Some judicial officials began to notice the unusual frequency of deaths among the inmates of institutions and some prosecutors even considered asking the Gestapo to investigate the killings. However, none went so far as Lothar Kreyssig, a judge in Brandenburg who specialized in matters of wardship and adoption. A war veteran and a member of the Confessing Church, Kreyssig became suspicious when psychiatric patients who were wards of court and therefore fell within his area of responsibility began to be transferred from their institutions and were shortly afterwards reported to have died suddenly. Kreyssig wrote to Justice Minister Gürtner to protest against what he described as an illegal and immoral programme of mass murder. The Justice Minister's response to this and other, similar, queries from local law officers was to try once more to draft a law giving effective immunity to the murderers, only to have it vetoed by Hitler on the grounds that the publicity would give dangerous ammunition to Allied propaganda. Late in April 1941 the Justice Ministry organized a briefing of senior judges and prosecutors by Brack and Heyde, to try to set their minds at rest. In the meantime, Kreyssig was summoned to an interview with the Ministry's top official, State Secretary Roland Freisler, who informed him that the killings were being carried out on Hitler's orders. Refusing to accept this explanation, Kreyssig wrote to the directors of psychiatric hospitals in his district informing them that transfers to killing centres were illegal, and threatening legal action should they transport any of their patients who came within his jurisdiction. It was his legal duty, he proclaimed, to protect the interests and indeed the lives of his charges. A further interview with Gürtner failed to persuade him that he was wrong to do this, and he was compulsorily retired in December 1941.[262]

Kreyssig was a lone figure in the persistence of his attempts to stop the campaign. Concerned lawyers and prosecutors had their doubts quelled by the Ministry of Justice, and no legal action ensued. More widespread, perhaps, were the concerns of religious leaders. Despite the transfer of many patients to state institutions since 1936, a very large number of the mentally and physically handicapped were still cared for in hospitals and homes run by the Churches and their lay social welfare organizations, the Inner Mission in the case of the Evangelical Church, and the Caritas Association in the case of the Catholic. Some directors of psychiatric institutions run by the Inner Mission tried to delay the registration and transfer of their patients, and one in particular, Pastor Paul Gerhard Braune, director of a group of such hospitals in Württemberg, also enlisted the aid of Pastor Friedrich von Bodelschwingh, a celebrated figure in the world of Protestant welfare organizations. Bodelschwingh ran the famous Bethel Hospital in Bielefeld and refused point-blank to allow his patients to be taken off for killing. The Regional Leader of the Party in his area refused to have him arrested, since his reputation was not only national but even worldwide; Bodelschwingh was legendary for his selfless application of Christian principles of charity. In the middle of the stand-off, shortly after midnight on 19 September 1940, an aircraft appeared over the hospital and proceeded to bomb it, killing eleven handicapped children and a nurse. Goebbels was quick to direct the press to go into overdrive against the barbarity of the British – 'Infanticide at Bethel – Revolting Crime', screamed the headline in the *German General Paper*. How, asked the state-controlled media, could the British single out such a well-known centre of Christian charity? Bodelschwingh himself was only too aware of the irony. 'Should I,' he asked the local state administrator, 'condemn the deed of the English and shortly afterwards take part in an "infanticide" on a far greater scale at Bethel?'[263]

Two days after the attack, a German official who was one of the American correspondent William L. Shirer's informants came to his hotel room and, after disconnecting the telephone, told him that the Gestapo were killing off the inmates of mental institutions. He hinted strongly that the Bethel Hospital had been bombed by a German plane because Bodelschwingh had refused to co-operate. By late November Shirer's investigations had yielded results. 'It's an evil tale,' he noted in his diary. The German government, he wrote, was 'systematically putting to death the mentally deficient population of the Reich'. One informant had given the number as 100,000, which Shirer considered an exaggeration. The American reporter had found out that the killings were taking place on Hitler's written order and were being directed through the Leader's Chancellery. His informants had also noted a bunching of death notices of patients at Grafeneck, Hartheim and Sonnenstein, put in by relatives, sometimes in coded language that made it clear they knew what was going on: 'We have received the unbelievable news . . . After weeks of uncertainty . . . After the cremation had taken place we received the sad news . . .' German newspaper readers, he thought, would know how to read between the lines of such notices, which is why they had now been banned. The programme, Shirer concluded, was 'a result of the extreme Nazis deciding to carry out their eugenic and sociological ideas'.[264]

Bodelschwingh and Braune went to see Brack to protest against the killings, and then, joined by the famous surgeon Ferdinand Sauerbruch, they lobbied Reich Justice Minster Gürtner. Neither meeting had any effect, so Braune compiled a detailed dossier on the murders and sent it to Hitler, apparently in the belief that he knew nothing about it. At the end of his long and detailed exposition, Braune asked for the programme to be brought to a halt. 'If human life counts for so little, will that not endanger the morality of the entire people?' he asked rhetorically. He was told that Hitler was unable to stop the programme. On 12 August

1940, Braune was arrested and imprisoned by the Gestapo; but he was released on 31 October 1940, after a short time, on the condition that he would stop his campaign.[265] Theophil Wurm, Protestant Bishop of Württemberg, wrote to Interior Minister Frick on 19 July 1940, asking for the murders to be brought to a halt:

If so serious a matter as the care of hundreds of thousands of suffering racial comrades in need of care is dealt with merely from the point of view of transient utility and decided upon in the sense of the brutal extermination of these racial comrades, then a line has been drawn under an ominous development and Christianity finally abandoned as a power in life that determines the individual and community life of the German people . . . There is no stopping any more on this slippery slope.[266]

Receiving no reply, he wrote again on 5 September 1940, asking: 'Does the Leader know about this matter? Has he approved it?'[267]

The trouble with such actions is that they did not amount to anything more than the intervention of a few courageous individuals in the end, and so were without effective consequences. Nor did they lead to any wider opposition to the Third Reich in general. Members of the military-conservative opposition were aware of the killings, and strongly disapproved, but they were already critical of the regime for other reasons.[268] Men like Bodelschwingh were not opposed to every aspect of the Third Reich. The Confessing Church was in a parlous state by this time, after years of persecution by the regime. The majority of Protestant pastors and welfare officers either belonged to the pro-Nazi German Christians or kept their heads down in the internal struggles that had convulsed the Evangelical Church since 1933. Fully half of the murdered patients came from institutions run by the Protestant or Catholic Church, and were taken away for killing often with the approval of the people who ran them.[269] The national leadership of the Inner Mission was prepared to go along with the killings so long as they were limited to 'sick people who are no longer capable of mental arousal or human society', a compromise which was acceptable even to Bodelschwingh so long as it was explicitly embodied in a formal public law, though he took the opportunity to build in elaborate safeguards to the selections in his own institution intended to have the effect of causing endless delays to the whole procedure. Doubt, bewilderment and despair racked the consciences of pastors as they debated whether it was right or not to raise their voices in protest against the state, whose fundamental legitimacy none of them questioned. Would it not damage the Church unless it could speak with one voice? If they protested, would this not simply lead to the Inner Mission's institutions being taken over by the state? Many feared that a public protest would give the regime an ideal excuse to intensify its persecution of the Church still further. At one of many meetings and conferences on the matter, Pastor Ernst Wilm, a member of the Confessing Church who had worked in Bodelschwingh's Bethel Hospital, noted: 'We are obliged to intercede and share responsibility for our sick people ... so that it cannot be said: I was in the murderer's hands and you just shrugged your shoulders.' To the few root-and-branch opponents of the killings such as himself, that was how it seemed at the end of 1940 and for most of the following year too.[270]

V

The Catholic Church had also been under fire from the regime for some years already. Many of its lay organizations had been closed down, and numbers of its clergy arrested and imprisoned. Its agreement with the regime, sealed in a Concordat with Pope Pius XI in 1933, supposedly protecting the Church's position in Germany in return for a guarantee of clerical abstinence from political activity, was in tatters. By 1939 the leading German prelates had decided to keep their heads down for fear of something even worse happening to them.[271] Nevertheless, the Catholic Church, under the leadership of the Papacy, was a far more united body than its Protestant equivalent could ever be, while there were some matters of dogma on which it was not prepared to compromise. The Papacy had already complained about the regime's policy of sterilizing the supposedly racially unfit, and it was not likely to let the escalation of this policy into one of outright murder go unmentioned. German bishops had also condemned the sterilization programme and had issued guidelines governing the extent to which Catholic doctors, nurses and officials could participate in it, though these were in practice not implemented. By now there was a new Pope in Rome, Pius XII, elected on 2 March 1939. He was none other than Cardinal Pacelli, who had been the Vatican's representative in Germany for much of the 1920s, read and spoke fluent German, and had played the major part in drafting

Papal protests against violations of the Concordat before the war. In October 1939 his first Encyclical, *Summi Pontificatus*, declared that the state should not try to replace God as the arbiter of human existence. But it was not until the summer of 1940 that Catholic protests against the killing of the handicapped began, sparked initially by the controversial events at the Bethel Hospital.[272]

The Bethel Hospital was located in the diocese of Bishop Clemens August von Galen, whose early accommodation with the regime in 1933–4 had given way by the time of the war to a more critical stance, particularly in view of ideological attacks on Christianity by leading Nazis such as Alfred Rosenberg and Baldur von Schirach.[273] Already supplied with copious information by Bodelschwingh, Galen wrote to Cardinal Adolf Bertram on 28 July 1940 with details of the murder campaign and urging the Church to take a moral position on the issue. Other bishops were also concerned. Conrad Gröber, Archbishop of Freiburg, wrote to Hans-Heinrich Lammers, head of the Reich Chancellery, on 1 August 1940 relaying the concerns of lay Catholics whose relatives had been killed, warning that the murders would damage Germany's reputation abroad, and offering to pay all the costs 'that arise for the state through the care of mentally ill people intended for death'.[274] Many of the institutions from which inmates were being taken away to be killed were run by the German Caritas Association, the principal Catholic welfare organization, and their directors had urgently been asking the Catholic hierarchy for advice. On 11 August 1940 the Fulda Bishops' Conference protested against the killings in another letter to Lammers, and followed this up by commissioning Bishop Heinrich Wienken, from the Caritas Association, to make representations in person. At the Ministry of the Interior, T-4 officials attempted to justify the killings, but Wienken, citing the Fifth Commandment ('Thou shalt not kill'), warned that the Church would go public if the murder programme was not stopped.[275]

At the next meeting, however, Wienken retreated, and merely asked for the assessment of patients to be made more thorough before they were selected for death. He had become afraid that his stand would undermine efforts to get Catholic priests released from Dachau. He was called to order by Cardinal Michael Faulhaber, who told him firmly that the matters that had preoccupied him were mere 'incidentals' to the central fact that people were being murdered. 'If things carry on at the present pace,' the Cardinal warned, 'the work of execution will be completed in half a year.'[276] As for the suggestion, apparently put by Wienken, that the writings of Sir Thomas More justified the killing of the unfit, Faulhaber wrote mockingly that it was 'really difficult not to write a satire. So Englishmen and the Middle Ages have suddenly become role models. One could just as well refer to the witch-burnings and pogroms against the Jews in Strassburg.'[277] Negotiations finally broke down because the Interior Ministry refused to put anything in writing. On 2 December 1940 the Vatican issued a decree declaring roundly: 'The direct killing of an innocent person because of mental or physical defects is not allowed.' It was 'against natural and positive Divine law'.[278] Despite this, the Church hierarchy in Germany decided that further action would be inadvisable. 'Any incautious or precipitous action,' warned Cardinal Bertram's chief adviser on 2 August 1940, 'could in practice have the most deleterious and far-reaching consequences in pastoral and ecclesiastical matters.'[279] The evidence was not sufficient for a protest, Bertram told Galen on 5 August 1940. It was not until 9 March 1941 that Galen printed the decree in his official newsletter. What finally prompted Galen to speak out was the Gestapo's arrest of priests and its seizure of Jesuit property in his home city of Münster to provide accommodation for people made homeless by a bombing raid. This convinced him that the caution advised by Bertram nearly a year before had become pointless. In sermons delivered on 6, 13 and 20 July 1941, he attacked the occupation of Church properties in Münster and the surrounding area and the expulsion of monks, nuns and lay brothers and sisters by the Gestapo. In addition, he also criticized the 'euthanasia' action. The police attempted to intimidate Galen into silence by raiding the nunnery where his sister Helene von Galen was based, arresting her and confining her to a cellar. Undaunted, however, she escaped by climbing out of a window.[280]

Galen was now thoroughly roused. In a fourth sermon, on 3 August 1941, he went much further than he had done before. He was prompted to do so by a secret visit to him by Father Heinrich Lackmann, chaplain at the Marienthal Institution, who told him that patients were about to be taken away for killing, and asked him to do something about it. Galen regarded this as a potential crime, and proceeded on the basis that it was his legal duty to expose it, as indeed it was. In this sermon, he first referred once more to the arrest of priests and the confiscation of Church property, then turned to a lengthy denunciation of the entire euthanasia programme. He provided circumstantial details that he had only hinted at in his sermon of 6 July 1941, including individual cases, and added that the Reich Doctors' Leader Dr Conti 'made no bones about the fact that a large number of mentally ill people in Germany have actually been deliberately killed already and more are to be killed in future'. Such murders were illegal, he declared. On hearing of the transport of patients from the Marienthal Institution near Münster at the end of the previous month, he said, he had formally accused those responsible of murder in a letter to the public prosecutor. People, he told his congregation, were not like old horses or cows, to be slaughtered when they were of no more use. If this principle were applied to human beings, 'then *fundamentally* the way is open to the murder of all unproductive people, of the incurably ill, of people invalided out of work or out of the war, then the way is open to the murder of all of us, when we become old and weak and thus unproductive'. In such circumstances, he asked rhetorically, 'Who can trust his doctor any more?' The facts he had recounted were firmly established. Catholics, he declared, had to avoid those who blasphemed, attacked their religion, or brought about the death of innocent men and women. Otherwise they would become involved in their guilt.[281]

The sensation created by the sermons, not least the last of them, was enormous. Galen had them printed as a pastoral message and read out in parish churches. The British got hold of a copy, broadcast excerpts over the BBC German service, and dropped copies as leaflets over Germany as well as translating them into several other languages and distributing them in France, Holland, Poland and other parts of Europe. Copies found their way into many households. A few people protested as a result, or talked about the killings with their work colleagues; a number were arrested and put into concentration camps, including some of the priests who had duplicated and distributed the sermons. Galen's actions emboldened other bishops, such as Antonius Hilfrich, Bishop of Limburg, who wrote a letter of protest to Justice Minister Gürtner (himself a Catholic) on 13 August 1941 denouncing the murders as 'an injustice that cries out to Heaven'.[282] The Bishop of Mainz, Albert Stohr, sermonized against the taking of life.[283] This was the strongest, most explicit and most widespread protest movement against any Nazi policy since the beginning of the Third Reich. Galen himself remained calm, resigned to martyrdom. But nothing happened. So huge was the publicity he had generated that the Nazi leaders, enraged though they were, feared to take any action against him. Regional Leader Meyer wrote to Bormann demanding that the bishop be hanged, a view in which Bormann himself readily concurred. But both Hitler and Goebbels, when told of these events by Bormann, concluded that to make Galen a martyr would only lead to further unrest, which simply could not be contemplated in the middle of a war. He would be taken care of when the war was over, said Hitler. Ordinary Party members in Münster were uncomprehending: why, they asked, was the bishop not imprisoned, since he was clearly a traitor?[284]

The government's response was oblique: in August 1941 it released a film entitled *I Accuse!*, in which a beautiful young woman stricken with multiple sclerosis expresses the wish to end her suffering, and is helped to die by her husband and another friend, after lengthy discussions of the rights and wrongs of such an action. The discussions also extended to the principle of involuntary euthanasia, justified in one passage by an elaborate lecture from a university professor. 18 million people saw the film, and many, reported the SS Security Service, regarded it as an answer to Galen's sermons. Indeed key scenes had in fact been personally inserted by Viktor Brack from the T-4 office. Older people and especially physicians and the highly educated rejected its message, but younger doctors were more in favour, provided euthanasia was carried out on medical grounds after proper examination, a principle with which many ordinary people agreed. Lawyers were heard to opine that the kind of assisted suicide portrayed in the film needed more careful legal under-pinning, while most people only approved of euthanasia if it was volun-tary. If the person to be killed was 'feeble-minded', a category not dealt with in the film at all, then most people thought this should only happen with the consent of the relatives. The SS Security Service reported that Catholic priests had been visiting parishioners to try to persuade them not to see the film. Ordinary people had no doubt as to the film's purpose. 'The film is really interesting,' said one; 'but things are going on in it just like they are in the lunatic asylums, where they are now bumping all the crazy people off.' The subliminal message, that the T-4 murder programme was justified, clearly did not get through.[285]

What did happen, however, was that the programme was halted. A direct order from Hitler to Brandt on 24 August 1941, passed on to

Bouhler and Brack, suspended the gassing of adults until further notice, though Hitler also made sure that the killing of children, which was on a much smaller and therefore much less noticeable scale, continued.[286] Galen's sermon, and the widespread public reaction it had aroused, made it difficult to continue without creating even further unrest, as the Nazi leaders reluctantly conceded. Nurses and orderlies, especially in Catholic institutions for the sick and the disabled, were beginning seriously to obstruct the process of registration. The killing programme was now public knowledge, and relatives, friends and neighbours of the victims were making their disquiet publicly felt. Moreover, they associated it clearly with the Nazi leadership and its ideology; indeed, despite the naive belief of men like Bishop Wurm that Hitler did not know about it, the danger of Hitler himself taking some of the blame was very real. By mid-1941 even Himmler and Heydrich were criticizing 'mistakes in the implementation' of the action. And the quota set by Hitler, of 70,000 deaths, had already been met.[287]

Yet these considerations do not in the end diminish the significance of Galen's actions.[288] It is impossible to say with any certainty what would have happened had he not ignored the advice of his superiors in the Catholic Church and raised his voice against the killing of the mentally sick and handicapped. But given the propensity of Nazism to radicalize its policies when it met with little or no resistance to them, it is at least possible, even indeed probable, that it would have continued well beyond the original quota after August 1941; finding people to operate the gas chambers at Hadamar and elsewhere would not have been difficult even had some of the existing teams departed for Poland, as indeed they did. In the end it became clear that the Nazis had by no means abandoned their intention of ridding society of those they considered a burden to it. But from August 1941 onwards, if it was to be done at all, it had to be done slowly and secretly. The mentally handicapped, long-term psychiatric patients and others classified by the regime as leading a 'life unworthy of life' were simply too closely bound into the central networks of German society to be isolated and disposed of, the more so since the definitions of abnormality applied by the T-4 experts were so arbitrary and included so many people who were intelligent and active enough to know what was happening to them and tell others all about it.

The same, however, could not be said of other persecuted groups in

German society such as the Gypsies or the Jews. Galen said nothing about them, nor did the other representatives of the Churches, with rare exceptions. The lesson that Hitler learned from the whole episode was not that it was inadvisable to order the wholesale murder of large groups of people, but that, just in case a future action of this kind against another minority ran into similar trouble, it was inadvisable to put such an order down in writing. And the euphemistic propaganda with which Action T-4 had been surrounded, the deceptions, the reassurances to the victims and their relatives, from the description of murder as 'special treatment' to the disguising of the gas chambers as showers, would be strengthened still further when it came to other, larger acts of mass murder. The involuntary euthanasia campaign had been an open secret, in which the employment of euphemisms and circumlocutions had presented people with a choice: to ignore what was really going on by accepting them at face value, or to penetrate to their actual meaning, hardly a difficult or problematical enterprise, and then to be confronted with the difficult choice of whether or not to do anything about it. By the time the main killing programme had ended, in August 1941, a large part of the medical and caring professions had been brought in to operate the machinery of murder. From an initially small group of committed physicians, the circle of those involved had grown inexorably wider, until general practitioners, psychiatrists, social workers, asylum staff, orderlies, nurses and managers, drivers and many others had become involved, through a mixture of bureaucratic routine, peer pressure, propaganda and inducements and rewards of one kind or another. The machinery of mass murder developed in the course of Action T-4, from the selection of victims to the economic exploitation of their remains, had operated with grim efficiency. Having proved itself in this context, it was now ready to be applied in others, on a far larger scale.[289]

VI

The mass murders on which the Third Reich embarked in the autumn of 1939, both in Germany and in the occupied areas of Poland, were far from being a consequence of the outbreak of a war in which the Nazi leadership considered that Germany's very existence was at stake. Still less were they the product of the 'barbarization of warfare', brought on by a life-and-death struggle against a ruthless enemy in harsh conditions. The invasion of Poland took place under favourable conditions, in good weather, against an enemy that was swept aside with contemptuous ease. The invading troops did not need to be convinced by political indoctrination that the enemy posed a huge threat to Germany's future; clearly the Poles did not. Primary group loyalties in the lower ranks of the army remained intact; they did not have to be replaced by a harsh and perverted system of discipline that replaced military values with racial ideology.[290] Almost everything that was to happen in the invasion of the Soviet Union from June 1941 onwards was already happening on a smaller scale in the invasion of Poland nearly two years before.[291] From the very beginning, SS Security Service Task Forces entered the country, rounding up the politically undesirable and shooting them or sending them off to concentration camps, massacring Jews, arresting local men and sending them off to Germany as forced labourers, and engaging in a systematic policy of ethnic cleansing and brutally executed population transfers.

These actions were not confined to the SS. From the very beginning, too, Nazi Party officials, stormtroopers, civilian officials and especially junior army officers and ordinary soldiers joined in, to be followed in due course by German settlers moved into Poland from outside. Arrests, beatings and murders of Poles and especially Jews became commonplace, but what was even more striking was the extent of the hatred and contempt shown towards them by ordinary German troops, who lost no time in ritually humiliating Jews on the street, laughing and jeering as they tore off their beards and made them perform degrading acts in public. Just as striking was the assumption of the invading and incoming Germans that the possessions of the Poles and Jews were freely available as booty. The theft and looting of Jewish property in particular by German troops was almost universal. Sometimes they were aided and abetted by local Poles. More often than not, non-Jewish Poles themselves were robbed as well. All of these actions reflected official policy, of course, directed from the top by Hitler himself, who had declared that Poland was to be totally destroyed, its academically educated and professional classes annihilated, and its population reduced to the status of uneducated helots whose lives were worth next to nothing. The expropriation of Polish and Jewish property was explicitly ordered from Berlin, as were the Germanization of the incorporated territories, the transfers of population, and the ghettoization of the Jews. Nevertheless, the zeal with which the invading Germans, taking their cue from these centrally directed policies, acted on their own initiative, often going far beyond them in the sadistic brutality of their implementation, still requires some explanation.

Popular hatred and contempt for Poles, as for Ukrainians, Belarussians and Russians, and even more for 'Eastern Jews', were deeply rooted in Germany. Even before the First World War, the doctrines of human equality and emancipation inculcated into large parts of the working class by the Social Democratic labour movement had not stretched as far as including minorities such as these. The great mass of ordinary working people regarded Poles and Russians as backward, primitive and uneducated; indeed, the frequent occurrence of antisemitic pogroms in Tsarist Russia was often cited by workers as evidence in support of this view. Fear of invasion from the barbaric east played a major role in persuading the Social Democrats to vote for war credits in 1914. The advent of Communist dictatorship in the Soviet Union had only strengthened and deepened these beliefs. To most Germans, including, ironically, many educated and acculturated German Jews, the 'Eastern Jews' of Poland appeared even more backward and primitive. In the early 1920s they caused resentment out of all proportion to their numbers when a few of them found refuge from the violence of the Russian civil war. Nazi propaganda, ceaselessly reinforcing such stereotypes, deepened prejudice against the Slavs and the Eastern Jews during the 1930s until they appeared to many Germans, particularly in the younger generation, as less than human.[292]

Toughness, hardness, brutality, the use of force, the virtues of violence had been inculcated into a whole generation of young Germans from 1933 onwards, and, even if Nazi education and propaganda in these areas had met with varied success, it had clearly not been wholly without effect. Nazism taught that might was right, winners took all, and the racially inferior were free game. Not surprisingly, it was the younger generation of German soldiers whose behaviour was the most brutal and violent towards the Jews. As Wilm Hosenfeld reported in a letter from Poland to his son in November 1939, 'Jews say: "Old soldier good, young soldier awful." '[293] What the invading and occupying Germans did in Poland from September 1939 was not so much the product of war as of longer-term processes of indoctrination, building on a deep-rooted feeling that Slavs and Eastern Jews were subhumans and that political enemies had no rights of any kind. Typical in this respect was General Gotthard Heinrici, no Nazi fanatic but a dyed-in-the-wool professional soldier, whose letters revealed deep-seated prejudices in their casual association of Slavs, Jews, dirt and vermin. 'Bedbugs and lice are running around here everywhere,' he wrote to his wife from Poland on 22 April 1941, 'also terrible Jews with the Star of David on their arm.'[294] Revealingly, he also saw a historical parallel in the treatment of Jews and Poles by the German occupiers. 'Poles & Jews are serving as slaves,' he reported a few days later. 'Nobody here takes any account of them. Here it's just as it was in Ancient times, when the Romans had conquered another people.'[295] He described the General Government as 'really the rubbish-heap of Europe', full of houses that were 'half-fallen in, dilapidated, filthy, tattered curtains behind the windows, stiff with dirt'.[296] He had evidently never been into the poorer districts of his own country. For Heinrici, as for many others, dirt was Slavic and Polish. 'Just when you're going through the streets,' he reported from Poland in April 1941, 'you already have the feeling you've taken lice and fleas with you. In the Jewish alleyways there's such a stink that you have to clean and blow out your nose when you've been through, just to get rid of the filth you've breathed in.'[297]

Thus when the German forces took what they conceived of as retaliatory actions against the Polish resistance to the invasion, taking hostages, shooting civilians, burning people alive, razing farms to the ground, and much more, they were not acting out of military necessity, but in the service of an ideology of racial hatred and contempt that was to be largely absent in their invasion of other countries further to the west.[298] Violence against racial and political enemies, real or imagined, had become commonplace in the Third Reich well before the outbreak of the war. The violence meted out to Poles and especially Jews from the beginning of September 1939 continued and intensified this line of action established by the Third Reich, as did the looting and expropriation to which they were subjected. The ultimate rationale for such policies in the minds of Hitler and the leading Nazis was to make Germany fit for war by removing the supposed threat of a Jewish presence and thus forestalling the possibility of a 'stab-in-the-back' from subversive elements on the Home Front such as they believed had lost Germany the First World War.[299]

Similar considerations were evident, among others, in the Nazi treatment of occupied Poland, which was designed from the start to be the springboard for the long-envisioned invasion of Soviet Russia. And they were obvious, too, in the mass murder of the mentally ill and handicapped begun in the summer of 1939. This too was no mere product of war, still less was it the outcome of a chance petition to Hitler by the parents of a handicapped baby, as has sometimes been suggested. On the contrary, it too was long planned, foreshadowed by the mass sterilization of nearly 400,000 'unfit' Germans before the war broke out, adumbrated by Hitler ten years before, and in preparation since the mid-1930s. The violence meted out by German forces in Poland was also pre-programmed. It followed logically on from the peacetime policies of the Nazis, extending them and intensifying them in new and terrifying ways.[300] In less than two years they were to be carried even further and implemented on an even larger scale. In the meantime, however great their obsession with ethnic cleansing and the quest for 'living-space' in the east, Hitler and the Nazis were still confronted with the fact that what had begun in September 1939 was not merely the long-dreamed-of eastward extension of Germany's political and ethnic borders, but also, somewhat less encouragingly for them, a world war in which Germany was opposed by the combined might of Britain and France, the two European countries with the largest overseas empires, victors against Germany of the war of 1914–18. To the last, Hitler had hoped that such a conflict could be avoided, and that he would be left to destroy Poland in peace. Now, however, he was confronted with the problem of what to do with Germany's enemies in the west.

2

FORTUNES OF WAR

'THE WORK OF PROVIDENCE'

I

On 8 November 1939, at around eight in the evening, Hitler arrived in the Bürgerbräukeller, the Munich beer-hall where he had launched his unsuccessful putsch in 1923. Here he was scheduled to give his annual speech to the Regional Leaders and 'Old Fighters' of the Nazi movement. At the 1939 meeting he spoke for just under an hour. Then, to everyone's surprise, he left abruptly for the railway station to travel to Berlin, where he needed to be in the Reich Chancellery for discussions on the planned invasion of France, postponed only two days previously because of bad weather. The 'Old Fighters' were disappointed that he did not follow his usual practice of staying behind for half an hour to chat. Most of them slowly went off, leaving a hundred or so staff to clear up. At twenty past nine, less than half an hour after Hitler had departed the building, a huge explosion ripped through the hall. The gallery and roof fell in, and the blast blew out the windows and doors. Three people were killed outright, five died of their injuries later, and sixty-two were wounded. Many of those who struggled out of the wreckage, coughing and spluttering, bruised, bleeding and covered in dust, assumed that they had been victims of a British air raid. Only gradually did they realize that the explosion had been caused by a bomb concealed in one of the hall's central pillars.

The news was brought to Hitler when his train stopped at Nuremberg. Initially he thought it was a joke. But when he saw that nobody around him was laughing, he realized that he had only narrowly escaped death. Once again, he declared, Providence had preserved him for the tasks ahead. But many questions remained. Who, the Nazi leaders asked, had been responsible for this dastardly attempt on Hitler's life? A little over two months into the war, the answer seemed obvious. The British Secret Service had to be behind it. Hitler personally ordered the kidnapping of two British agents whom Heydrich's SS Security Service intelligence chief, Walter Schellenberg, had been keeping under surveillance on the Dutch border, at Venlo. Surely they would reveal the origins of the plot. Schellenberg made contact with the agents, and persuaded them to meet with SS men they thought were representatives of the German military resistance. The SS men shot a Dutch officer who tried to intervene, and whisked the British agents across the German border before anyone could stop them. But although the British officers were persuaded in Berlin to provide the names of numerous British agents on the Continent, they were unable to shed any light on the assassination attempt.[1]

Goebbels's propaganda machine quickly began pumping out denunciations of the British Secret Service. The truth only began to emerge when, in a remote part of south Germany, the border police arrested a thirty-eight-year-old cabinet-maker called Georg Elser, who was trying to cross the Swiss frontier without proper papers. On searching his clothes and effects, they found a postcard of the beer-cellar where the explosion occurred, a fuse and sketches of a bomb. Elser was quickly handed over to the local Gestapo. When news of the explosion reached the Gestapo office, the policemen put two and two together and sent Elser to Munich for interrogation. At first, nobody could believe that the cabinet-maker had worked on his own. Suspects of all kinds were arrested, the process fuelled by a wave of denunciations of characters seen acting suspiciously near the scene of the assassination attempt. Heinrich Himmler arrived at the interrogation centre, kicked Elser repeatedly with his jackboots and had him beaten. But Elser continued to insist that he had acted entirely on his own initiative. The Gestapo even made him build an exact replica of the bomb, which, to their astonishment, he did successfully. In the end, they were forced to admit privately that he had acted alone.[2]

Georg Elser was an ordinary man from a humble background whose brutal and violent father had aroused in him a powerful dislike of tyranny. At one time a member of the Communist Party's Red Front-Fighters' League, he had difficulty in getting work under the Third Reich and blamed Hitler for his misfortunes. In Munich he had reconnoitred the beer cellar where Hitler was to give his annual speech, then set about preparing his assassination attempt. Over many months he pilfered explosives, a detonator and other equipment from his employers, even finding employment in a quarry so that he could have access to the right kind of material. He surreptitiously took measurements in the beer-cellar, though an attempt to get a job there came to nothing. Every evening he would eat his evening meal there at around nine, then hide in a store-room until the cellar closed for the night. During the small hours Elser worked meticulously at the load-bearing pillar he had selected as the best site for the explosion, fitting a secret door into the wooden cladding, hollowing out the bricks, putting in the explosives and the detonator, and fixing the specially made timer. After two months, on 2 November 1939, he inserted the bomb; three nights later he installed the timer, set for 9.20 in the evening of the 8th, when, he thought, Hitler would be in the middle of his speech. Only the fact that Hitler had curtailed his address in order to go off to Berlin prevented the bomb from killing him outright.[3]

The effect on public opinion, the SS Security Service reported syco-phantically, was to provoke a popular reaction against the British. 'Love of the Leader has grown even more, and attitudes to the war have become even more positive in many parts of the population as a result of the assassination attempt.'[4] So widespread was this effect that the American reporter William L. Shirer thought the Nazis themselves had staged the attack in order to win sympathy. Why otherwise, he mused, had the 'bigwigs . . . fairly scampered out of the building' instead of staying to chat?[5] But this theory, though also believed by some later historians, was as little based in fact as was the Nazis' own counter-theory of British inspiration for the attempt.[6] Elser himself was sent to Sachsenhausen concentration camp. A formal trial would have brought into the public domain the fact that he had acted alone, and Hitler and the leading Nazis preferred to maintain the fiction that he had been part of a plot hatched by the British Secret Service. Elser refused steadfastly to tell anything but the truth. Just in case he changed his mind, he was kept in the camp as a special prisoner, and given two rooms for his sole use. He was even allowed to use one of them as a workshop so that he could continue practising his craft as a cabinet-maker. He received a regular supply of cigarettes and whiled away the time by playing the zither. He was not allowed to speak to other prisoners or receive visitors. But his death would not have served any purpose without the kind of confession the Nazis wanted, and this was never forthcoming.[7]

II

The assassination attempt came at a moment when Hitler was turning his attention to the conflict with Britain and France, after the stunning success of his conquest of Poland. Both countries had declared war on Germany immediately after the invasion. But from the very beginning, they realized that there was little they could do to help the Poles. They were already well armed in the mid-1930s, but had only begun to increase the pace of arms manufacture in 1936 and needed more time. In the beginning, they thought, the war would be a defensive one on their part; only later, when they were a match for the Germans in men and equipment, could they go onto the attack. This was the period of the 'phoney war', the *drôle de guerre*, the *Sitzkrieg*, while every combatant nation waited nervously for the start of major action. On 9 October 1939, Hitler told the German armed forces that he would launch an attack in the west if the British refused to compromise. The leadership of the German army warned, however, that the Polish campaign had used up too many resources and it needed time to recover. Moreover, the French and the British would surely be far more formidable opponents than the Poles.[8] Hitler was dismayed by such caution, and on 23 November 1939 he reminded a meeting of 200 senior officers that the generals had been nervous about the remilitarization of the Rhineland, the annexation of Austria, the invasion of Czechoslovakia and other bold policies that had turned out to be triumphs in the end. The ultimate goal of the war, he told them, not for the first time, was the creation of 'living-space' in the east. If this was not conquered, then the German people would die out. 'We can oppose Russia only when we are free in the west,' he warned. Russia would be militarily weak for the next two years at least, so now was the time to secure Germany's rear and avoid the two-front war that had been so crippling in 1914–18. England could only be defeated after the conquest of France, Belgium and Holland and the occupation of the Channel coast. This would have to take place as soon as possible, therefore. Germany was stronger than ever before. More than a hundred divisions were ready to go into the attack. The supply situation was good. Britain and France had not completed their rearmament. Above all, said Hitler, Germany had one factor that made it unbeatable – himself. 'I am convinced of the powers of my intellect and of decision . . . The fate of the Reich depends on me alone . . . I shall shrink from nothing and shall destroy everyone who is opposed to me.' Destiny was with him, he proclaimed, buoyed up by his escape from the beer-cellar bomb a fortnight before. 'Even in the present development I see Providence.'[9]

The leading generals were appalled by this fresh outburst of what they considered Hitler's irresponsible aggressiveness. Time was needed, they pleaded, to train more recruits, and to repair and replenish the equipment damaged or lost in the Polish campaign. The Chief of the Army General Staff, Franz von Halder, was so alarmed that he took up again the conspiratorial plans he had been hatching with fellow officers, discontented spirits in army counter-intelligence and conservative civil servants and politicians, during a similar confrontation over the proposed invasion of Czechoslovakia in the summer of 1938. For a time he even went around with a loaded revolver concealed on his person, in the hope of shooting Hitler when the occasion presented itself. Only Halder's ingrained sense of obedience to his oath of loyalty to the Nazi Leader, and the knowledge that he would have little support from the public or indeed his junior officers, prevented him from using it. During November 1939 the conspirators began again to prepare to arrest Hitler and his principal aides, with the idea of putting Göring in power, since he was known to have serious doubts about a war with Britain and France. On 23 November 1939, however, Hitler addressed his senior generals. 'The Leader,' noted one of them, 'takes a stand in the strongest manner against defeatism of any kind.' His speech betrayed 'a certain mood of ill-humour towards the leaders of the army'. '"Victory," he said, "cannot be won by waiting!"'[10] Halder panicked, believing Hitler had got wind of the plot, and pulled out of it altogether. It fell apart. Ultimately, the lack of communication and co-ordination between the plotters, and the absence of any concrete plans for the period after Hitler's arrest, had doomed the conspiracy to failure from the outset.[11]

In the end, in any case, the confrontation proved unnecessary, for Hitler was forced to postpone the offensive time and again through the winter of 1939–40 because of poor weather conditions. Constant heavy rain turned the ground to mud across large tracts of Western Europe, making it impossible for German tanks and heavy armour to move with the rapidity that had played such a key part in the Polish campaign. The months of delay proved beneficial to German war preparations as Hitler brought about major changes in the armaments programme. In the later 1930s he had been demanding the building of an air force on an enormous scale. But Germany lacked sufficient supplies of aircraft fuel. And by the summer of 1939 shortages of steel and other raw materials, as well as of qualified construction engineers, were leading to a drastic scaling-back of the construction programme. Aircraft production also had to compete for priority with tanks and battleships. In August 1939 Hitler was persuaded by intensive lobbying on behalf of the Air Ministry to put the production of Junkers 88 bombers back on the top of the agenda. A cutback in the naval building programme also allowed Hitler to demand a massive increase in the manufacture of ammunition, especially artillery shells. From this point on, airplanes and ammunition always took up two-thirds or more of arms production resources. But these changes were slow to work their way through the planning and production systems, as fresh blueprints had to be drawn, machines retooled, equipment built, existing factories redeployed and new ones opened. Labour shortages were compounded by the call-up of workers to the armed forces, while under-investment in the German railway system meant that there was not enough rolling-stock to carry armaments, components and raw materials around the country, and coal supplies for industry began to be seriously held up. All these factors took time to overcome.[12]

It was not until February 1940 that ammunition output began to increase significantly. By July 1940 German production of armaments had doubled.[13] By this time, however, Hitler had already lost patience with the armaments procurement system run by the armed forces under the leadership of Major-General Georg Thomas. On 17 March 1940 he set up a new Reich Ministry for Munitions. The man he put in charge of it was Fritz Todt, his favourite engineer, who had masterminded one of Hitler's pet projects in the 1930s, the construction of the new motorway system.[14] So dismayed was the head of the army's procurement office, General Karl Becker, at this development, and the accompanying whispering campaign against the alleged inefficiency of his organization, orchestrated in part by representatives of arms companies like Krupps, who saw an opportunity in the new arrangement, that he shot himself. Todt immediately set up a system of committees for different aspects of arms production, with industrialists playing the leading role. The surge in arms production that took place over the following months was largely the achievement of the previous procurement regime in unblocking supply bottlenecks of vital raw materials such as copper and steel. But the credit went entirely to Todt.[15]

III

The Nazi–Soviet Pact and further negotiations surrounding the invasion of Poland had resulted in a German assignment to the Russian sphere of influence not only of Eastern Poland and the Baltic states but also of Finland. In October 1939, Stalin demanded that the Finns cede to Russia the area immediately north of Leningrad, and the western part of the Rybachi peninsula, in return for a large area of eastern Karelia. But negotiations broke down on 9 November 1939. On 30 November the Red Army invaded, installed a puppet Communist government in a Finnish border town, and got it to sign an agreement ceding the territory that Stalin had been demanding. At this point, however, things began to go seriously wrong for the Soviet leader. Many of the senior Soviet generals had been eliminated in the purges of the 1930s, and the Soviet troops were unprepared and poorly led. Winter had already set in, and white-clad Finnish troops, moving swiftly about on skis, outmanoeuvred raw Soviet conscripts who had not been trained for fighting in deep snow. Indeed, some Soviet officers regarded such camouflage as a badge of cowardice and refused to employ it even when it was available. Trained only to attack, whole Red Army units went to their deaths as they ran straight at machine-gun nests built into the defensive bunkers of the Mannerheim Line, a lengthy series of concrete trenches named after the Finnish Commander-in-Chief.[16]

'They are swatting us like flies,' a Soviet infantryman on the Finnish front complained in December 1939. By the time the conflict was over, more than 126,000 Soviet troops had been killed and another 300,000 evacuated from the front because of injury, disease or frostbite. Finnish losses were also severe, indeed proportionately even more so, at 50,000 killed and 43,000 wounded. Nevertheless, there was no doubt that the Finns had given the Soviets a bloody nose. Their troops showed not only courage and determination, fuelled by strong nationalist commitment, but also ingenuity. Borrowing from the example of Franco's forces in the Spanish Civil War, the Finns took empty bottles of spirits, filled

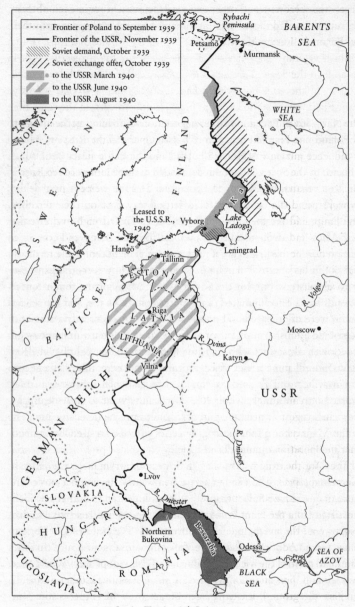

- - - - - Frontier of Poland to September 1939
────── Frontier of the USSR, November 1939
Soviet demand, October 1939
Soviet exchange offer, October 1939
to the USSR March 1940
to the USSR June 1940
to the USSR August 1940

Rybachi Peninsula

BARENTS SEA

Petsamo

Murmansk

NORWAY

WHITE SEA

S W E D E N

F I N L A N D

K a r e l i a

Leased to the U.S.S.R., 1940

Vyborg

Lake Ladoga

Hangö

Leningrad

Tallinn

E S T O N I A

BALTIC SEA

Riga

L A T V I A

R. Volga

LITHUANIA

R. Dvina

Moscow

Vilna

Katyn

G E R M A N   R E I C H

U S S R

R. Dniepr

Lvov

SLOVAKIA

R. Dniester

H U N G A R Y

Northern Bukovina

Bessarabia

Odessa

SEA OF AZOV

YUGOSLAVIA

R O M A N I A

BLACK SEA

5. Soviet Territorial Gains, 1939–40

them with kerosene and other chemicals, stuck a wick in each of them, then lit them and threw them at incoming Soviet tanks, covering them with flames. 'I never knew a tank could burn for quite that long,' said a Finnish veteran. They devised a new name for the projectile, too: in honour of the Soviet Foreign Minister they called them 'Molotov cocktails'.[17] In the end, however, numbers told. After a second offensive thrust had failed, Stalin called in huge reinforcements, at the same time dropping his puppet Finnish government and offering negotiations to the legitimate Finnish regime in Helsinki. On the night of 12–13 March 1940, recognizing the inevitable, the Finns agreed a peace deal which allotted to the Soviet Union a substantially larger amount of territory in the south than it had originally demanded. Despite their eventual defeat, however, and the opening of a Soviet military base on their territory, the Finns had retained their independence. Their tough and effective resistance had exposed the weakness of the Red Army and convinced Hitler that he had nothing to fear from it. For Stalin, Finland would now serve as a subservient buffer-state to insulate Russia against any conflict between Germany and the Allies that might be fought out in Scandinavia. The many setbacks and disasters of the war persuaded Stalin to recall purged and disgraced former officers to active service in senior positions. They also prodded his generals into embarking on sweeping military reforms that they hoped would ensure that the Red Army would put on a better performance the next time it went into action.[18]

In the meantime, however, the conflict in Finland, and the Anglo-French failure to intervene, turned Hitler's attention to Norway. The country's coastal ports could be sites for vital bases for German submarine operations against Britain. They could also provide an essential channel for the export of much-needed iron ore from neutral Sweden to Germany, especially during winter, when Narvik remained ice-free. The lack of any immediate prospect of invading France and the evident possibility of a pre-emptive invasion by the British made a strike against Norway all the more urgent in Hitler's eyes. The head of the German navy, Grand Admiral Raeder, mindful of the consequences of Germany's failure to control the north-west European coast in the First World War, was already pressing such a course upon Hitler in October 1939. To prepare the ground, Raeder made contact with the leader of the Norwegian Fascist Party, Vidkun Quisling. Born in 1887, Quisling, son of a pastor, had passed out from the military academy with the highest marks ever achieved, and joined the army General Staff at the age of twenty-four. In 1931–3 he served as Minister of Defence in a government led by the Agrarian Party, a nationalist group formed not long before to represent small farming communities in this country of 3 million people. Rapid industrialization had led to the rise of a radical, pro-Communist labour movement in the cities, which created great alarm among the peasantry. By this time, Quisling was openly proclaiming the superiority of the Nordic race and warning against the threat of Communism. He presented himself as an advocate of peasant interests. In March 1933, when the government fell, he founded his own National Unity movement, adorning it with ideas such as the leadership principle, borrowed from the newly installed Nazi regime in Germany.[19]

Quisling's movement failed to make any headway in the 1930s. It was undermined by the turn of the Norwegian Social Democrats to a centrist position, based on reconciling the interests of workers and peasants. This brought the Social Democrats a parliamentary majority from 1936 onwards. Quisling took up contacts with the Nazis, visiting Hitler early in 1940 to try to persuade him to back a fascist coup led by himself. The Germans were sceptical, in view of the evidently complete lack of support for Quisling among the Norwegian population. However, Quisling did convince Hitler that an Allied invasion of Norway was likely, and two days after their meeting, Hitler ordered planning for a pre-emptive German strike to begin. Quisling travelled to Copenhagen on 4 April 1940 and met a German staff officer to whom he provided details of Norway's defensive preparations and indicated the best places to invade. Disastrous though it was Quisling's treachery was to prove useful to Allied propaganda in one respect: perhaps because his name was easy to pronounce, it quickly became a handy term for traitors of every kind, replacing the more cumbersome 'fifth columnist', first used in the Spanish Civil War, which British propagandists thought most people had probably already forgotten.[20]

On 1 March 1940, Hitler issued a formal order for the invasion (dubbed 'Weser Exercise'), which for obvious geographical reasons was to encompass not only Norway but also Denmark as well. Brushing aside the objection that the Norwegians and Danes were neutral and likely to remain so, he noted that only a relatively small force would be necessary in view of the weakness of the enemy defences. On 9 April

1940, German forces crossed the land border into Denmark from the south at 5.25 in the morning, while an airborne landing at Ålborg secured the principal base of the Danish air force, and a seaborne invasion took place at five different points, including Copenhagen, the defenders of which were taken completely by surprise. The only problem occurred when the battleship *Schleswig-Holstein* ran aground. At 7.20 a.m., recognizing the inevitable, the Danish government ordered resistance to cease. The invasion had been successfully completed in less than two hours.[21] In Norway, however, the invading forces encountered more serious resistance. German transport ships on their way to Trondheim and Narvik managed to evade the waiting British, but bad weather scattered the accompanying fleet of fourteen destroyers, two battleships (the *Scharnhorst* and *Gneisenau*) and a heavy cruiser, the *Admiral Hipper*. The British battle cruiser *Renown* encountered the two German battleships and damaged them severely enough to cause them to withdraw, but crucially, the British ships were too far away from the Norwegian coast to stop the main German force from entering the Norwegian fjords. Some damage was caused by coastal batteries, and a newly launched heavy cruiser, the *Blücher*, was sunk, but this was not enough to stop German troops taking over all the major Norwegian towns, including the capital. Even so, it was not all plain sailing, and two attacks by the British fleet sank ten German destroyers anchored in and around Narvik on 10 and 13 April 1940. The Germans also lost fifteen transport vessels, forcing them to use a fleet of 270 merchant ships to carry the back-up force of 108,000 troops and their supplies across from Denmark while a further 30,000 were airlifted in. Dependence on airlifting and lack of troop ships meant that the initial invasion was unable to use the overwhelming force it really needed. Coupled with the difficulties of Norway's mostly mountainous terrain, this gave the Norwegians the chance to put up a fight against the invading German forces.[22]

The difficulties of the invasion were compounded by the decision to proclaim Quisling head of a new pro-German government as soon as Oslo was occupied on 9 April. Several of the erstwhile supporters he named as his ministers refused publicly to join him, and the legitimate government roundly condemned his action. The King called for resistance to continue, and left Oslo with the cabinet. He was supported by the army and the great mass of the Norwegian people, outraged by the installation of an obvious German puppet who lacked any kind of significant electoral support. Quisling's proclamation of a 'national revolution' on May Day 1940, when he branded the King and the government as traitors who had sold out to the Jews who ran Britain, and dedicated Norway's future to what he called the 'Germanic Community of Fate', met with nothing but derision.[23] Norwegian troops played a significant part in the fighting around Narvik and the other western ports in the wake of the German invasion. Things were clearly not going as planned for the Germans. But they were even more disastrous for the British. On 14 and 17 April, British forces landed at two points midway along the coast, supported by troops from the French Foreign Legion and a number of Polish units. But there was confusion about where they should go. Many of the soldiers were poorly equipped for winter fighting, and had no snowshoes: others were so overburdened by their winter equipment that they could hardly move. Crucially, they had no effective air support. German airplanes bombarded them mercilessly. After many delays, the Allies occupied Narvik on 29 May 1940, but German reinforcements now finally began to arrive, and a surprise attack that sank the British aircraft-carrier *Glorious* on 4 June along with all the aircraft on board underlined the difficulties of the British position. The Allied forces to the south of Narvik had already withdrawn, and after destroying the harbour, the force occupying Narvik itself sailed for home as well, on 8 June 1940. The day before, the King of Norway and his government had gone into exile on the cruiser *Devonshire*, leaving orders for a ceasefire behind, but making it clear that a state of war would continue between their country and the Third Reich until further notice.[24]

Despite the difficulties they had encountered, the Germans had triumphed through an unprecedented, co-ordinated attack by air, sea and land. They now held a large part of the north-western coast of the Continent, where they established a series of major naval bases, especially for the submarines that were so vital to the disruption of British supplies from America. Not only were Swedish ore deliveries to Germany now assured, but Sweden itself, still nominally neutral, had effectively been reduced to the position of a German client state. Even during the Norwegian campaign the Swedish authorities had allowed German supplies to be transported across Swedish territory; subsequently they permitted the transit of hundreds of thousands of German troops as well. Swedish shipyards built warships for the German navy, and the Swedish economy became the source of supply for practically anything the Germans chose to demand so long as they had it. By contrast, the entire Allied operation had been, as William L. Shirer noted in his diary, a 'debacle'. British plans to lay mines outside the key Norwegian harbours had been repeatedly postponed until it was too late. Co-ordination between the British army and the Royal Navy had been poor. Military planning had been confused and inconsistent. The British forces had been forced to undertake a humiliating withdrawal shortly after landing. In Narvik they had dithered fatally before advancing, thus surrendering the element of surprise and allowing the Germans to bring in reinforcements. None of this seemed to bode well for the future of the British war effort.[25] Indeed, as early as 21 March 1940, the army officer Hans Meier-Welcker noted in his diary a general optimism amongst ordinary Germans that the war would be over by the summer.[26]

Recriminations in London were swift. Defending his conduct of the war in the House of Commons, the Prime Minister, Neville Chamberlain, sounded lame and unconvincing. The leader of the Labour Party opposition, Clement Attlee, came straight to the point. 'It is not Norway alone,' he said. 'Norway comes as the culmination of many other discontents. People are saying that those mainly responsible for the conduct of affairs are men who have had an almost uninterrupted career of failure. Norway followed Czechoslovakia and Poland. Everywhere the story is "too late".' Attlee's typically blunt assessment of the situation was shared by many. The opposition Labour Party decided to force a vote on the issue. 486 members out of 615 voted: some 80 Conservatives were thought to have abstained by staying away from the debate, while 40 of them who were present voted with the Opposition. A government majority of 213 was slashed to 80. The next day, bowing to the inevitable, Chamberlain decided to resign, a broken man. Within a year he was dead.[27] The politician regarded by most as his obvious successor, Foreign Secretary Edward, Lord Halifax, a member of the Upper House, declined to serve because he considered, rightly, that it would be impossible to lead the country from the House of Lords. The choice therefore fell on Winston Churchill. As First Lord of the Admiralty Churchill had been formally responsible for the Norwegian debacle, but, despite having had to defend the government's record during the crucial debate, he had largely escaped criticism because of a widespread feeling that his boldness had been hamstrung by the caution of others. Aged sixty-five at the time of his appointment, Churchill had seen action in the Sudanese War at the end of the nineteenth century and 1914–18. He had held many government offices over the years, but, by the time the Second World War broke out, he had been sitting on the back benches for the best part of a decade, isolated from the government by his reputation as a maverick, and above all by his strident criticisms of the Third Reich and his relentless advocacy of rearmament. He immediately broadened the government into one of national unity. His message to the House of Commons in his first speech after his appointment was uncompromising. Britain, he declared, would fight to the end.[28]

IV

The German assault on Denmark and Norway heralded the launching of a far larger operation against France and the Benelux countries. Discussed over many months, the armed forces' initial, rather conventional, plan for a three-pronged attack on France, Belgium and Holland was reduced to a two-pronged attack, then had to be amended again when the plan fell into enemy hands after the capture of a staff officer who had made a forced landing in Belgium and failed to destroy the documents before he was arrested. Going back to the drawing-board, Hitler began to argue for a single, concentrated, surprise thrust through the Ardennes, a wooded, hilly area generally considered unsuitable for tanks and as a consequence only lightly defended by the French. This would have the advantage of avoiding having to attack strong French defensive emplacements in the heavily fortified Maginot Line, which stretched for many miles along the Franco-German border. The initial doubts of the army high command were overcome when the detailed advocacy of the new, improvised plan by General Erich von Manstein was confirmed by war games and simulations carried out by the General Staff. An officer whose ambition was so irritating to General Halder that he had him transferred to field duties in Stettin, Manstein, born in 1887, was a close aide of General Gerd von Rundstedt, who had led the planning for the invasion of Poland. One of the secondary aims of his new plan was to give Rundstedt's Army Group South the lion's share of the invasion of France. Meeting with Hitler on 17 February 1940,

Manstein demonstrated that it was possible with careful planning to move a major motorized force through the Ardennes. Once through, the main body of the German forces should head for the Channel, cutting the Allied forces off from the south. Meanwhile another invasion force further north would enter Belgium and Holland, deceiving the Allied armies into thinking that this was where the main thrust was coming. The British expeditionary force and the French army would thus effectively be surrounded from the north and south and pinned up against the sea.[29]

By early May the rains had ceased, the Norwegian campaign was clearly drawing to a victorious close, and the moment had come. German troops invaded Holland on 10 May 1940, some being dropped by parachute, the majority simply crossing the land border from Germany itself. The Dutch army retreated, pulling away from the Anglo-French forces in the south. With only eight divisions, it was no match for the massively larger German invading army. A German bombing raid on Rotterdam on 14 May 1940, destroying the centre of the city and killing many hundreds of its civilian inhabitants, persuaded the Dutch that, to avoid further carnage, it was advisable to surrender. They did so the next day. Queen Wilhelmina and the government escaped to London to continue the struggle from across the Channel. At the same time, German paratroopers and glider-borne special forces seized key bridges and defensive emplacements and secured the main routes into Belgium, where the defending troops, failing to co-ordinate their actions with the British and French advancing to assist them, were quickly driven back. The onslaught was sudden and terrifying. William L. Shirer was amazed at the speed of the German advance. Driving into the country with a group of reporters, Shirer saw 'railroad tracks all around torn and twisted; cars and locomotives derailed' around the heavily bombed railway station in the town of Tongres. 'The town itself was absolutely deserted. Two or three hungry dogs nosed sadly about the ruins, apparently searching for water, food, and their masters.'[30]

Further on, they passed lines of refugees trudging along the roads, 'old women,' as Shirer noted, 'lugging a baby or two in their old arms, the mothers lugging the family belongings. The lucky ones had theirs balanced on bicycles. The really lucky few on carts. Their faces – dazed, horrified, the lines frozen in sorrow and suffering, but dignified.' Reaching Louvain, he found that the university library, burned in a deliberate act of reprisal by German soldiers in the First World War for the resistance they had encountered, later reconstructed and restocked with the help of American funds, had been destroyed again. 'The great library building,' Shirer noted on 20 May 1940, 'is completely gutted. The ruins still smoulder.' Goebbels's propaganda machine rushed to claim it had been destroyed by the British, but the local German commander, shrugging his shoulders, told Shirer 'there was a battle in this town . . . Heavy fighting in the streets. Artillery and bombs.' All the books had been burned, he said.[31] The German advance continued amidst heavy fighting. With twenty-two divisions at its command, the Belgian army could put up a tougher resistance than the Dutch. But it too was overwhelmed. On 28 May 1940 the Belgian king, Leopold III, to the dismay of the British and the French, surrendered. Rejecting his government's advice to follow it into exile in London, Leopold stayed on. He was kept in confinement by the Germans for the rest of the war.[32]

The Belgian king's decision to surrender was heavily influenced by events that had been occurring further south. On 10 May 1940, at the same time as German armies invaded Belgium and Holland, a large German force began advancing secretly through the Ardennes. The French felt confident of their ability to withstand a German invasion. Rearmament had been proceeding apace, and by early 1940 the French had around 3,000 modern and effective tanks with which to confront a German armoured force of about 2,500 tanks of generally inferior quality, and around 11,000 artillery pieces to the Germans' 7,400. Altogether, 93 French and 10 British divisions faced a total of 93 German divisions. The French had 647 fighters, 242 bombers and 489 reconnaissance planes at their disposal in France in the spring of 1940, and the British 261 fighters, 135 bombers and 60 reconnaissance planes, making a total of nearly 2,000 combat aircraft altogether; the German air force had around 3,578 combat planes operational at this time, but when the Belgian and Dutch air forces were thrown into the balance this was not enough in itself to overwhelm its opponents. However, despite the recent delivery of 500 modern American aircraft, many of the French planes were obsolete, and neither the British nor the French had learned how to use their planes as tactical support for ground forces in the way that the Germans had in Poland. The result was that in Holland, Belgium and France, German dive-bombers were able to destroy enemy anti-aircraft defences, batter enemy communications and establish air superiority before Allied air forces could react. Moreover, the Allies kept many of their planes in reserve, while the German air force threw almost its entire operational strength into the fray. This was a bold gamble, in which the Germans lost no fewer than 347 planes, including most of the paratroop carriers and gliders used in Holland and Belgium; but it was a gamble that paid off spectacularly.[33]

French intelligence altogether failed to predict how the German invasion would take place. Some preparations were noticed, but nobody put all the information together into a coherent picture, and the generals still assumed that the now obsolete captured plans were the operative ones. Drawing on their experience of the First World War, the French military failed to grasp just how fast and how far the German armoured divisions could move. Since the stalemate of trench warfare in 1914–18, the arrival of air power and tanks had shifted the advantage in warfare from defence to attack, a development which few on the Allied side had followed to its logical conclusion. Locating themselves many miles behind the front line so as to get a better overview, the French generals suffered from poor communications and were slow to react to the fast-moving pace of events. 57 divisions were soon concentrated in the north to fight back the German invasion expected to come via Holland and Belgium. But the German forces here numbered only 29 divisions, and while the French deployed another 36 divisions along the Maginot Line, the Germans only confronted them here with 19 divisions. The strongest German force, 45 divisions, including many of their best-trained and best-equipped forces, was focused on the push through the Ardennes. Not surprisingly, initially at least the French defence in the north held firm, pushing back the Germans in the first tank battle in history, at Hannur. The real issue, however, was being decided further south, where General Ewald von Kleist was leading 134,000 soldiers, 1,222 tanks, 545 half-track armoured vehicles, and nearly 40,000 lorries and cars through the narrow wooded valleys of the Ardennes in what has been called 'the greatest traffic jam known to that date in Europe'.[34]

The enterprise was extremely risky. It left virtually no German armour in reserve. Failure would have opened up Germany to devastating counter-attacks. As Fedor von Bock, the able if conservative general commanding Army Group B to the north, had noted on first learning of the planned invasion through the Ardennes, it was clear that 'it must run into the ground unless the French take leave of their senses'.[35]

But the Germans' luck held. Slowly and painfully, four slow-moving columns, each nearly 400 kilometres long, crawled along narrow roads towards the river Meuse (Maas). They frequently ground to a halt. Traffic managers flew up and down the columns in light aircraft to identify spots where gridlock threatened. The tanks were dependent on fuel stations set up by the advance units at previously designated spots en route. All the crews and drivers had to keep going for three days and nights without a break; crack combat units were dosed up with amphetamines (dubbed 'panzer chocolate' by the troops) to keep them awake. Vulnerable and exposed, the columns were sitting ducks for Allied air attacks. Yet they got away with it because the Allies failed to recognize them for the main German force. Reaching the river Meuse on 13 May 1940, the German forces came under fire from the first real French attempt to stop them. Kleist called up no fewer than 1,000 planes to bombard the French positions, which they did in waves of attacks lasting some eight hours, forcing the French to take cover or withdraw and severely denting their morale. Hundreds of rubber dinghies were now thrown into the river by the Germans, and German troops landed on the other side in three places, destroying French defensive positions and creating a foothold on the left bank large enough for engineers to build a bridge over which the German tanks could start to cross.[36]

This was the crucial breakthrough. True, at this point the German forces were still vulnerable to counter-attack, but the French were again too slow to react, and they were once more surprised when, instead of turning east to assault the Maginot Line from behind, as they expected, Kleist's men turned west, in Manstein's famous 'sickle-cut', designed to pin the Allied forces in Belgium up against the invading German army in the north and jointly drive them into the sea. By the time they got to the Meuse, the French tanks were heavily outnumbered by their German counterparts. Many of them ran out of petrol. Most were destroyed. Allied aircraft were far away, in central and northern Belgium, and when they finally arrived, they found the ground targets difficult to pinpoint. They were also heavily damaged by German anti-aircraft fire: the British lost 30 bombers out of a force of 71. Meanwhile German tanks powered their way rapidly westward across the open plain. In many cases, the German commanders, carried away by the momentum of the attack, advanced farther and faster than their more cautious superiors had intended. French troops marching to the front were amazed to find the

Germans so far west. The French army leadership was in despair. At staff headquarters, generals burst into tears when they learned of the speed and success of the German advance. On the morning of 15 May 1940 the French Prime Minister, Paul Reynaud, telephoned Churchill. 'We have been defeated,' he said. The French had deprived themselves of reserves to throw into the battle by over-committing themselves in Belgium. On 16 May 1940 Churchill arrived in Paris for a hurried conference with the French leaders. 'Utter dejection was written on every face,' he later reported. The French Commander-in-Chief, General Maurice Gamelin, reported despairingly that he could not stage a counter-attack: 'inferiority of numbers, inferiority of equipment, inferiority of method,' he said, accompanying his words, as Churchill later noted, with 'a hopeless shrug of the shoulders'.[37]

On 19 May 1940 Reynaud dismissed Gamelin, whose reputation for caution had proved so fatally well merited, and replaced him with General Maxime Weygand, a much-admired veteran of the First World War who had retired in 1935. It was too late. The next day, the first German tanks reached the Channel. The Allied armies in Belgium were now surrounded by German divisions on three sides, with the sea on the fourth. Weygand decided that the German panzer advance could be broken by a simultaneous attack from north and south, but it soon became clear that the situation had become so chaotic that a co-ordinated offensive was impossible. Meeting with the Belgian king, Weygand concluded correctly that Leopold had already given up the struggle. Communications between the British and French effectively broke down. All attempts to locate the British Commander-in-Chief, Lord Gort, failed.[38] The French general in overall command of the northern forces was killed in a car crash, and no satisfactory replacement could be found. The planned counter-attack foundered amidst a welter of mutual recriminations. The British began to feel that the French were incompetent, the French that the British were unreliable. Things only got worse with the Belgian capitulation on 28 May. On hearing the news, Reynaud was said to be 'white with rage', while Britain's prime minister in the First World War, David Lloyd George, wrote that it would be hard 'to find a blacker and more squalid sample of perfidy and poltroonery than that perpetrated by the King of the Belgians'. As the three-pronged German panzer attack swept up north and west to meet the other German forces advancing through Belgium from the

Frontier of the German Reich, April 1940
Overrun by Germany, April/May 1940
Overrun by Germany, May/June 1940
Main lines of German advance

6. The German Conquest of Western Europe, 1940

east, the British and French began to fall back on the port of Dunkirk.[39]

On the day of Gamelin's dismissal, the British government, anticipating these events, began to assemble a fleet, consisting of almost any boats and ships that could be found along the English coast and could get to the area in time, to carry out the evacuation. Strafed and pounded by German dive-bombers, 860 vessels, some 700 of them British, made their way to the Dunkirk beaches and took off nearly 340,000 soldiers to England. Nearly 200,000 of them were British, the rest mostly French. Far fewer would have escaped had Hitler not personally ordered the German advance to halt, reassured by Göring's boast that his planes would finish off the Allied troops, and advised by Rundstedt to give his tired troops a respite before they turned southwards towards Paris. Neither Brauchitsch, the army chief, nor Fedor von Bock, the commander of Army Group B, on the northern front, could understand it. Bock told Brauchitsch that the attack had to be urgently resumed, 'otherwise it could happen to us that the English can transport whatever they want, under our very noses, from Dunkirk'. But Hitler backed Rundstedt, seeing in this a chance of asserting his authority over the top commanders. By the time Brauchitsch had persuaded Hitler to resume the attack, the evacuation was under way, and the fierce resistance of the defending troops was too much for the weary Germans. 'At Dunkirk,' noted Bock with evident irritation on 30 May 1940,

the English are continuing to leave, even from the open coast! When we finally get there, they will be gone! The Supreme Leadership's halting of the tank units has proved to be a serious mistake! We continue attacking. The fighting is hard, the English are as tough as leather, and my divisions are clapped out.[40]

As the battle finally drew to a close, Bock paid a visit to the scene. He was surprised by the quantity of concrete bunkers and barbed-wire defences that guarded Dunkirk, and dismayed by the quality of the enemy's equipment:

The English line of retreat presents an indescribable appearance. Quantities of vehicles, artillery pieces, armoured cars and military equipment beyond estimation are piled up and driven into each other in the smallest possible space. The English have tried to burn everything, but in their haste have only succeeded here and there. Here lies the *matériel* of a whole army, so incredibly well equipped that we poor devils can only look on it with envy and amazement.[41]

Two days later, Dunkirk finally surrendered. 40,000, mostly French, troops, who formed the rearguard, were left behind to be taken prisoner. Weygand blamed the British for leaving his men behind, though the evacuation had in fact continued for two days after the last British soldiers had left the beach. In any event, the choice of the French to form the rearguard was a natural one given their relatively late arrival on the scene. Nevertheless, Weygand raged bitterly at Churchill's refusal to send any more aircraft or troops to the defence of France. The British in their turn, determined now not to compromise the defence of the British Isles by sacrificing any more of their armed forces or planes, were contemptuous of the French generals and political leaders, whom they regarded as over-emotional, weak and defeatist. British generals did not burst into tears, however dire the situation they were in. Relations were approaching rock-bottom. They were not to recover for some time.[42]

After regrouping, repairing and recovering, the Germans began advancing south with 50 infantry divisions and 10 admittedly somewhat depleted panzer divisions. Forty French infantry divisions and the remnants of three armoured divisions stood in their way. On 6 June 1940 German forces crossed the Somme. Three days later they were in Rouen. The French government had been evacuated to a series of châteaux dotted around the countryside south of Paris, where communications were difficult, working telephones rare, and travel made almost impossible by the endless columns of refugees now clogging the highways. On 12 June 1940, at their first meeting since leaving Paris, the shocked ministers were told by Weygand that further resistance was useless and it was time to request an armistice. In Weygand's view, the British would not be able to hold out against a German invasion of the United Kingdom, so evacuating the French government to London was pointless. Moreover, like an increasing number of other generals, Weygand was beginning to think that it was the civilian politicians who were to blame for the debacle. So it was the army's duty to make an honourable peace with the enemy. Only in this way would it be possible to prevent anarchy and revolution breaking out in France as it had after the previous defeat by the Germans, in 1870, and spearhead the moral regeneration of the country. The hero of the Battle of Verdun in the First World War, the aged Marshal Philippe Pétain, had been brought in as a military figurehead by Reynaud, and he now backed this idea. 'I will not abandon the soil of France,' he declared, 'and will accept the suffering which will be imposed on the fatherland and its children. The French renaissance will be the fruit of this suffering ... The armistice is in my eyes the necessary condition of the durability of eternal France.'[43]

On 16 June 1940, after the government had reconvened in Bordeaux, Reynaud, isolated in his opposition to an armistice, resigned as Prime Minister. He was replaced by Pétain himself. On 17 June 1940 the new French leader announced on public radio that it was time to stop the fighting and sue for peace. Some 120,000 French soldiers had been killed or been reported missing in the conflict (along with 10,500 Dutch and Belgian, and 5,000 British), showing that many did fight and belying claims that French national pride had been destroyed by the politics of the 1930s. But after Pétain's announcement, many gave up. Half of the 1.5 million French troops taken prisoner by the Germans surrendered after this point. Soldiers who wanted to fight on were often physically attacked by civilians. Conservatives like Pétain who abhorred the democratic institutions of the Third Republic did not see in the end why they should fight to the death to defend them. Many of them admired Hitler and wanted to take the opportunity of defeat to re-create France in Germany's image. They were soon to be given the opportunity to do so.[44]

V

Meanwhile France was descending into almost total chaos. A vast exodus of refugees swept southwards across the country. An émigré Russian writer, Irène Némirovsky, who had fled the Bolshevik Revolution to go to France in 1917 at the age of fourteen with her Jewish businessman father, vividly described 'the chaotic multitude trudging through the dust', the luckiest pushing 'wheelbarrows, a pram, a cart fashioned of four planks of wood set on top of crudely fashioned wheels, bowing down under the weight of bags, tattered clothes, sleeping children'.[45] Cars tried to move along the clogged roads, 'full to bursting with baggage and furniture, prams and birdcages, packing cases and baskets of clothes, each with a mattress tied firmly to the roof', looking like 'mountains of fragile scaffolding'. 'An endless, slow-moving river flowed from Paris: cars, trucks, carts, bicycles, along with the horse-drawn traps of farmers who had abandoned their land'.[46] The speed and scale of the German invasion meant there were no official plans for evacuation. Memories of German atrocities in 1914 and rumours of the terrifying effect of bombing created mass hysteria. Whole towns were deserted: the population of Lille is thought to have fallen from 200,000 to 20,000 in a few days, that of Chartres from 23,000 to 800. Looters broke into shops and other premises and took what they wanted. In the south, places of safety were swollen to bursting with refugees. Bordeaux, usually home to 300,000 inhabitants, doubled in population within a few weeks, while 150,000 people crammed into Pau, which normally housed only 30,000. Altogether it is thought that between 6 and 8 million people fled their homes during the invasion. Social structures buckled and collapsed under the sheer weight of numbers. Only gradually did people begin to return to their homes. The demoralization had a devastating effect on the French political system, which, as we have seen, fell apart under the strain.[47]

When the Germans entered Paris on 14 June 1940, therefore, they found large parts of it deserted. Instead of the usual cacophony of car horns, all that could be heard was the lowing of a herd of cattle, abandoned in the city centre by refugees passing through from the countryside further north. Everywhere they went in France, German troops looted the deserted towns and villages. 'Everything's on offer here, just like in a big department store, but for nothing,' reported Hans Meier-Welcker from Elbeuf on 12 June 1940:

The soldiers are searching through everything and taking anything that pleases them, if they are able to move it. They are pulling whole sacks of coffee off lorries. Shirts, stockings, blankets, boots and innumerable other things are lying around to choose from. Things that you would otherwise have to save up carefully for can be picked up here on the streets and the ground. The troops are also getting hold of transport for themselves right away. Everywhere you can hear the humming of engines newly turned on by drivers who still have to become familiar with them.[48]

The French humiliation seemed complete. Yet there was worse to come. On Hitler's personal orders, the private railway carriage of the French commander in the First World War, Marshal Foch, in which the Armistice of 11 November 1918 had been signed, was tracked down to a museum, and, after the museum walls had been broken down by a German demolition team, it was moved out and towed back to the spot it had occupied in the forest of Compiègne on the signing of the Armistice. As the Germans arrived, William L. Shirer noted Hitler's face 'brimming with revenge', mingled with the triumph observable in his 'springy step'. Taking the very same seat occupied by Foch in 1918, Hitler posed for photographs, then departed, contemptuously leaving the rest of the delegation, including Hess, Göring, Ribbentrop and the military leaders, to read out the terms and receive the signatures of the dejected French.[49] In accordance with this agreement, all fighting ceased on the morning of 24 June 1940. France was divided into two, an occupied zone in the north and west, with a nominally autonomous state in the south and east, run from the spa town of Vichy by the existing government under Marshal Pétain, whose laws and decrees were given validity throughout the whole of the country.[50]

German forces had performed the greatest military encirclement in history. No subsequent victories were to be as great, or as cheap in terms of German lives, of which fewer than 50,000 were lost (killed or missing). More prisoners, almost a million and a half, were taken than in any other single military action of the war. The success persuaded Hitler and the leading generals that similar tactics would bring dividends in future actions, notably, the following year, in the invasion of the Soviet Union.[51] Germany's hereditary enemy had been humiliated. Versailles had been avenged. Hitler was beside himself with elation. Before dawn on the morning of 28 June 1940, he flew secretly to Paris with his architect Albert Speer and the sculptor Arno Breker on a brief, entirely personal sight-seeing trip. They visited the Opéra, specially illuminated for his benefit, the Eiffel Tower, which formed the backdrop for an informal photo of the three men taken at first light, the Invalides and the artistic quarter of Montmartre. 'It was the dream of my life to see Paris,' Hitler told Speer. 'I cannot say how happy I am to have that dream fulfilled today.' Pleased with the visit, he revealed to the architect that he had often thought of having the city razed to the ground. After the two men's grandiose building plans for the German capital had turned it from Berlin into the new world city of Germania, however, he said later, 'Paris will only be a shadow. So why should we destroy it?'[52]

Hitler never returned to the French capital. The victory parade was to take place at home. On 6 July 1940 vast, cheering crowds lined Berlin's streets, upon which people had strewn thousands of bouquets of flowers along the route to be taken by the Leader from the station to

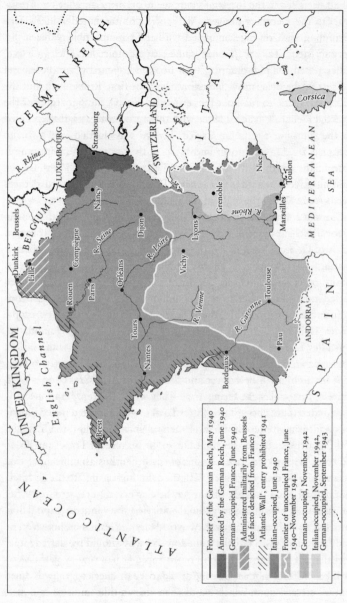

7. The Partition of France, 1940

Frontier of the German Reich, May 1940
Annexed by the German Reich, June 1940
German-occupied France, June 1940
Administered militarily from Brussels
(de facto detached from France)
'Atlantic Wall', entry prohibited 1941
Italian-occupied, June 1940
Frontier of unoccupied France, June
1940–November 1942
German-occupied, November 1942
Italian-occupied, November 1942,
German-occupied, September 1943

the Chancellery. Upon arriving there, he was repeatedly called out onto the balcony to receive the plaudits of the thousands gathered below. There had, as William L. Shirer noted, been little excitement when the news of the invasion of France had been announced. No crowds had gathered before the Chancellery, as usually happened when big events occurred. 'Most Germans I've seen,' he noted on 11 May 1940, 'are sunk deep in depression at the news.'[53] As in previous foreign crises, there had been widespread anxiety about the outcome, underpinned by a general fear at the possibility of Allied bombing raids on German cities. But as on previous occasions too, relief at the ease with which Hitler had achieved his objective flowed together with feelings of national pride into a wave of euphoria. This time it was far greater than ever before. Not untypical was the reaction of the middle-class history student Lore Walb, born in 1919 in the Rhineland and now at Munich University. 'Isn't that tremendously great?' she asked rhetorically as she recorded the victories in her diary on 21 May 1940. She put it all down, as many did, to Hitler: 'It's really only now that we can truly estimate our Leader's greatness. He has proved his genius as a statesman but his genius is no less as a military commander . . . With this Leader, the war cannot end for us in anything except victory! Everyone's firmly convinced of it.'[54]

'Admiration for the achievements of the German troops is boundless,' reported the SS Security Service on 23 May 1940, 'and is now felt even by people who retained a certain distance and scepticism at the beginning of the campaign.'[55] The capitulation of Belgium, the reports continued, 'prompted the greatest enthusiasm everywhere', and the entry of German troops into Paris 'caused enthusiasm amongst the population in all parts of the Reich to a degree that has not so far been seen. There were loud demonstrations of joy and emotional scenes of enthusiasm in many town squares and on many streets.'[56] 'The recent enthusiasm,' it was reported on 20 June 1940, 'gives the impression every time that no greater enthusiasm is possible, and yet with every fresh event, the population gives its joy an even more intense expression.' Pétain's announcement that the French were throwing in the towel was greeted by spontaneous demonstrations on the squares of numerous German towns. Veterans of the First World War were amazed at the speed of the victory. Even those opposed to the regime confessed to a feeling of pride, and reported that the general atmosphere of jubilation made it impossible to continue their underground resistance activities, such as they were.[57] The Catholic officer Wilm Hosenfeld, who had been so critical of German policy in Poland that he had written to his wife that 'I have sometimes been ashamed to be a German soldier',[58] was swept away by the news: 'Boy oh boy,' he wrote to his son on 11 June 1940, 'who wouldn't have been happy to have taken part in it!'[59] In Hamburg, the conservative schoolteacher Luise Solmitz shared in the general euphoria: 'A grand, grand day for the German people,' she wrote in her diary on 17 June 1940 on hearing the announcement that Pétain was suing for peace. 'We were all exhilarated by happiness and enthusiasm.' The victory was 'an unbelievably great national change of fortune, the fulfilment of long-held nationalist dreams'. In comparison with this, the daily cares of wartime, which had dominated her diary up to this point, faded into the background. Only when she remembered the persecution to which she and her Jewish husband Friedrich were subject, despite living in what was classified as a 'privileged mixed marriage', did she pause for thought: 'The successes are so tremendous that the shadow cast by this light is becoming ever darker and more threatening.'[60]

VI

The conquest of France marked the highest point of Hitler's popularity in Germany between 1933 and 1945. People confidently expected that Britain would now sue for peace, and that the war would be over by the end of the summer. Yet the problem of what to do next was not a simple one. Moreover, Hitler's attitude to the British was fundamentally ambivalent. On the one hand, he admired the British Empire, which in the 1930s and 1940s was the world's largest, still covering an enormous area of the globe; and he regarded the English as 'Anglo-Saxon' cousins of the Germans, who in the end would be impelled by the logic of racial destiny to make common cause with them. On the other hand, he realized that there were powerful forces in British politics that regarded Germany under his leadership as a profound threat to the Empire that had to be stopped at all costs. The previous September, these forces had prodded the British Prime Minister Neville Chamberlain into declaring war on Germany immediately after the invasion of Poland. Hitler was aware of the fact that a number of leading figures in the Conservative

Party, notably the Foreign Secretary, Lord Halifax, still hankered after a peaceful solution to the conflict and hoped that he could somehow persuade them to start negotiating a peace settlement. For most of the first months of the war Hitler's policy towards Britain vacillated between aggression and conciliation. Even after Churchill's appointment as Prime Minister made a separate peace much less likely, Hitler continued to hope for one, while preparing invasion plans in case he was unsuccessful.[61]

Foreign Minister Ribbentrop was all in favour of an invasion. After Britain had been invaded and conquered, he envisaged the restoration of the former King Edward VIII, who had been forced to abdicate in 1936 in favour of his younger brother, after declaring his intention of marrying an American divorcée and, gone into exile with the title Duke of Windsor. The Duke had visited Germany not long after renouncing the throne, and was said to have greeted officials with a modified version of the Nazi salute. On more than one occasion he had made it clear that he appreciated what he thought the Nazis were trying to do in Germany. By 1940 he was telling anyone who would listen that Britain had virtually lost the war and it was time to make peace with the Nazis. In the early summer of 1940, the Duke and his wife were residing in Portugal, and Ribbentrop commissioned Walter Schellenberg, the SS intelligence officer who had already made his mark in the Venlo affair, to kidnap them and bring them to Germany via Spain. Pursuing his own agenda, Ribbentrop also thought that kidnapping the Duke of Windsor would make a separate peace with Britain more difficult. The Nazi plot depended on persuading the couple that they were in danger of being kidnapped and perhaps assassinated by British secret agents to stop them falling into German hands. Spanish fascists were recruited behind the back of the neutralist Franco government, which would have been appalled by the damage done to relations with Britain, to spirit the Windsors away once they crossed the border. Inevitably, however, the plot became entangled in the webs of internal Nazi power politics, and neither Schellenberg nor anyone else tried too hard to make it succeed, in case it delivered a major triumph to the hated Ribbentrop. The Duke and Duchess finally sank the plot by acceding to Churchill's suggestion that the Duke should go to the Bahamas as Governor-General of the islands. This put himself and his wife thousands of miles away from intrigues of this kind. Schellenberg's superior, Reinhard Heydrich, congratulated the young intelligence officer on handling his commission from Ribbentrop with just the right mixture of apparent enthusiasm and practical incompetence.[62]

In the meantime, Hitler had been consulting with his army and navy chiefs about the practicalities of an invasion. The German fleet had sustained heavy losses in the Norwegian campaign. Three cruisers and ten destroyers had been sunk, and two heavy cruisers and one battleship had been severely damaged and so were out of action. In the summer of 1940 Admiral Raeder had only one heavy and two light cruisers and four destroyers at his command. This was a woefully inadequate force with which to attempt to win command of an English Channel protected by five Royal Navy battleships, eleven cruisers and thirty destroyers, backed by another major naval force that could sail from Gibraltar at a moment's notice.[63] Moreover, the Germans had failed to add the French fleet to their own naval strength after the capitulation of France. On 3 July 1940, in a bold move that further outraged French opinion, British ships attacked the French naval base at Mers-el-Kébir, near Oran, in French-controlled Algeria, damaging a number of warships and killing 1,250 French sailors, in order to stop the French navy falling into German hands. Raeder was thus left with far too few warships at his disposal. So it would be necessary as a minimum to gain complete air superiority over the English Channel by destroying the Royal Air Force. Only in this way could the potential obstacle posed by British naval dominance be more or less neutralized.[64]

After much deliberation, Hitler signed a directive on 16 July for an invasion, but only 'in case of necessity', and three days later, at an elaborately stage-managed occasion in the Reichstag, he renewed his earlier offer of peace to the British. So vague were the terms in which it was cast, however, that it was rejected by Churchill's government within the hour. Listening to the news of the British rejection of the offer on the radio with a group of military and civilian officials, William L. Shirer was struck by the consternation the announcement produced. The officials, he noted, 'could not believe their ears. One of them shouted at me: "Can you make it out? Can you understand those British fools? To turn down peace now?"' 'The Germans I talk to,' Shirer commented the following day, 'simply cannot understand it. They want peace. They don't want another winter like the last one. They have nothing against Britain . . . They think they can lick Britain too, if it comes to a showdown. But they would prefer peace.'[65] Amongst some Germans, the British refusal to sue for peace unleashed bitter feelings of hatred and revenge, born of disappointment that the war was evidently not coming to an end after all. 'I have never had terrible feelings of hatred,' wrote the student Lore Walb in her diary on 17 June 1940, '– but one thing I do want: this time, the Leader must not be so humane, and he should teach the English a real lesson – for they alone are responsible for all the misfortune and misery into which so many peoples have been plunged.'[66]

Hitler still hoped that Churchill would be overthrown by the advocates of a separate peace in his own government. In reality, however, there was no chance of this happening. Not only Churchill but also his cabinet knew that a peace with a Germany now dominant in Western Europe would open up the way to increasing German interference in Britain's domestic affairs, growing demands for a tougher policy towards the Jews, German backing for the potential British equivalent of Quisling, the fascist politician Sir Oswald Mosley and, in the long run, the undermining and destruction of British independence, especially if in the meantime Germany had managed to conquer the Soviet Union. Time and again Hitler's peace offers had proved to bring not 'peace for our time' but only further demands, as the experience of Czechoslovakia had shown, and by July 1940 few British politicians had any illusions about this fact.[67]

With a reluctance that was obvious to his entourage, therefore, Hitler began preparations for the invasion of Britain. Planning had begun the previous winter for 'Operation Sealion'. A fleet of 2,000 flat-bottomed river barges was assembled in the Channel and North Sea ports (most of them entirely unsuitable for a sea-crossing except in conditions of flat calm), landing manoeuvres were held, and signs erected along the Channel coast showing soldiers the way to the embarkation points.[68] Walter Schellenberg prepared a handbook for German troops and officials as a guide to the British institutions they would encounter.[69] Senior figures in the armed forces were sceptical. The navy, Raeder warned, would not be ready until mid-September at the earliest, but the best course of all would be to wait until the following May. The Chief of the General Staff, Franz Halder, debated interminably with the naval planners on the best place for a landing. While the army wanted to land on a broad front so as to maximize the military advantage, the navy wanted to land on a narrow front so as to minimize the danger of attack by the Royal Navy. But in any case, in order to clear the way for the invasion, Britain's aerial defences had to be destroyed. On 1 August, therefore, Hitler signed the order for the launching of air strikes against Britain. Events in Norway and France had given Hitler the confidence that a mixed airborne and seaborne invasion was in principle feasible provided his planes possessed unchallenged domination of the skies. The British naval control of the Channel and the North Sea might pose an obstacle of a kind not encountered in a land invasion, but without aircraft to protect them, the ships of the Royal Navy would surely be easy prey for German dive-bombers.[70]

German planes had already carried out small-scale bombing raids on British targets from 5–6 June 1940 onwards; the raids became heavier from 10 July, and then intense after 18 August 1940. Although there were scattered raids on a large number of towns and cities, the main thrust of the attack from mid-August onwards was against the airfields of the Royal Air Force's Fighter Command. Contrary to the British myth of 'the few', the two forces were evenly matched: in mid-August 1940 there were 1,379 British fighter-pilots in a state of operational readiness, as against some 870 German pilots, although of course the British pilots were stationed all over the country, while the Germans were concentrated along the Channel coast. German bombers depended on fighter-planes for protection, and were ill equipped to outmanoeuvre and shoot down the British fighter-planes sent to intercept them. The British deployed two of the fastest and most advanced fighter-planes in the world, the Hurricane and the Spitfire, which had been and were being mass-produced at breakneck speed to strengthen Britain's defences. They were 'scrambled' into the air well before the attacking German force arrived, thanks to the invention and deployment of radar, first developed in 1935, to British interception of German radio messages, and to thousands of observers stationed along the Channel coast. Thus the German planes never arrived in time to catch the British fighters on the ground.[71]

As the skies above south-eastern England began to be crisscrossed by the brilliant white vapour trails of aerial dogfights, it gradually became clear that the Germans were not going to achieve their aim. Although the principal German fighter plane, the Messerschmitt Me109, was arguably better than its British equivalents at heights of over 20,000 feet, it lost its advantage because it had to protect the bombers by remaining at lower altitudes, where the Spitfire and Hurricane were more manoeuvrable and could turn and bank more quickly. The Messerschmitt Me110, a heavy fighter designed to escort the bomber squads, was even less capable of evading the attacks of the fast-moving British fighters. The German air force in general was also built to give ground forces close support, and found it difficult to adapt to protecting squadrons of bombers in the air. Air bases from which to launch the attack had to be hurriedly improvised in the recently conquered areas of northern France, supplies were difficult to organize, and repairs often took too long to carry out. There was no difference in skill or standards between the fighter-pilots of the two forces, but both were in relatively short supply. However, while many British pilots whose planes were shot down managed to parachute safely on to British soil and rejoin the fray later on, the same, obviously, was not true of their German counterparts. The outcome of the battle can be read off the casualty figures: almost 900 German planes, including at least 443 fighters, shot down between 8 and 31 August 1940, as against 444 British planes in the slightly longer period from 6 August to 2 September. The British had no difficulty in making good their losses, with 738 Hurricanes and Spitfires operational on 6 September 1940 as against 672 on 23 August. By early September, the British had more than twice as many pilots ready to fly as the Germans did.[72] Crucially, too, German aircraft production by this time was lagging substantially behind that of the British. Immediately after the German annexation of Austria, in April 1938, the British government had pushed through a massive acceleration that was designed to build 12,000 new combat aircraft over the following two years. By the second half of 1940, the British were producing twice as many fighter-planes as the Germans.[73]

Yet the German air force commanders, in particular the two most immediately involved, Field Marshal Albert Kesselring and the former head of the Condor Legion in Spain, Field Marshal Hugo Sperrle, had received very different intelligence about the outcome of the battle. According to the information they were given, 50 per cent of all British fighters had been lost as against only 12 per cent of their German counterparts, or 791 planes as against 169. Many German pilots believed they had won. Already on 17 August 1940, William L. Shirer, encountering a Messerschmitt fighter-pilot in a Belgian café – not, he thought, an inherently boastful character – was impressed when the young man said quietly: ' "It's a matter of another couple of weeks, you know, until we finish with the RAF. In a fortnight the British won't have any more planes." '[74] Ulrich Steinhilfer, a young Me109 pilot, wrote to his mother with unbridled enthusiasm about his missions. On 19 August 1940, attacking an airfield at Manston, he told her, 'I aimed at a fuel tanker which was filling a Spitfire, then at two other Spitfires, one after the other. The tanker exploded and everything began to burn around it. My other two Spitfires began to burn on their own. Only now do I realise what power is given to a pilot with these four guns.'[75] On the last day of August his optimism was undiminished. 'One of the missions today,' he wrote to his mother, 'was a ground-attack on Detling with two sessions of dog-fighting as well. Our squadron bagged three without loss and the Group score was ten. This is the way it should go on with our fighting experience and skill growing. Tally-Ho!'[76]

Such optimism was accepted at face value in Berlin. The moment had come in early September, therefore, it was thought, to launch the next phase of the attack, namely the destruction of British industry, transport and morale by the mass bombing of major British cities. Bombing raids of this kind had already begun, though not in any co-ordinated way, and an attack on the East End of London on 24 August 1940 had prompted the Royal Air Force to launch a counter-raid on Berlin the following night. Although it was not very effective in terms of destructive power, it caused dismay in the German capital, and outraged Hitler, who declared at a public meeting held in the Berlin Sports Palace on 4 September 1940 that if the Royal Air Force dropped a few thousand kilograms of bombs on German cities, 'then we will drop . . . one million kilograms in a single night. And should they declare they will greatly increase their attacks on our cities, then we will erase their cities!'[77] Yet neither the British nor the German raids at this stage of the war, however, were what Hitler on 1 August called 'terror attacks'. He referred to this tactic only in order to insist that it should not be employed except on his explicit orders, which he did not in fact issue until 4 April 1942, after the first major British air raid on a non-military target, the north German city of Lübeck.[78]

Whatever the propagandists said, aircrews on both sides were under orders only to release the bombs when they could see a suitable target of economic or military significance – such as, for example, the London docks. In practice, of course, such instructions were less than wholly realistic, given the impossibility of accuracy with the bombing equipment of the time. Moreover, the bombing of London had begun almost a fortnight before Hitler's speech of 4 September. What was different now was the frequency and intensity of the raids. On 7 September, 350 bombers attacked the London docks in a daylight raid, causing massive damage. Both the bombers and the accompanying fighter squadrons had to fly at high altitude to avoid anti-aircraft fire, so the British withdrew their fighter squadrons westward from the coastal airfields so as to gain time to scramble, and maintained a permanent roster of airborne patrols in anticipation of German raids. As they climbed, the British pilots gave false estimations of their altitude over the radio, so as to fool the German fighter-pilots into staying relatively low. All of this reduced British losses, while the Germans were soon forced to carry out raids mainly at night in an attempt to minimize theirs. Between 7 September and 5 October 1940, the German air force carried out 35 large-scale raids, 18 of them on London. In the week from 7 to 15 September 1940 alone, 298 German aircraft were shot down as against 120 British. On 15 September, more than 200 bombers attacked London, accompanied by a substantial fighter escort. 158 bombers made it to their target, some being shot down before reaching the city, others being forced to turn back for one reason or another. 300 Hurricanes and Spitfires engaged them over the capital, shooting down 34 bombers and 26 fighters and damaging many more.[79]

The Junkers 88, mainstay of the German bomber force, was slow-moving, it was too small to carry a really effective payload, and it lacked the manoeuvrability and the defensive capacity to ward off the British fighters. Other bombers such as the Heinkel 111 and the Dornier 17 were not only relatively small in size but were also antiquated in many respects; indeed they were being replaced by the Junkers 88 over time despite its defects. The German bomber force was simply inadequate to achieve its task. A quarter of the original 200 bombers did not return from the 15 September raid alone. Losses on such a scale were unsustainable.[80] Fighter planes and, still more, pilots were in increasingly short supply. Escorting a 'large raid' over London on 17 September, Ulrich Steinhilfer, in a new, upgraded Me109, 'met amazingly strong fighter opposition'.[81] On 29 September 1940, 'when we got to London and the dog-fighting started I suddenly found that there were only the five aircraft from our squadron with me and about thirty to fifty Spitfires against us'. He only escaped because the British fighters flew off to attack a more important target. By October, he was telling his father that in his Group 'there are only twelve left from the old crew'; they could not take inexperienced newcomers into battle for fear of losing them and there was a new type of Spitfire so fast that 'our Me can hardly keep up with it . . . there is no more talk of absolute superiority'.[82] 'The leadership of our air force,' Chief of the Army General Staff Franz Halder noted after a situation report on 7 October 1940, 'has under-estimated the British fighters by about 100% . . . We need 4 times as much to beat the English down.'[83] By the time Steinhilfer himself was shot down, baling out on 27 October 1940, to spend the rest of the war in captivity, the fighter battle had effectively been lost.

On 14 September 1940, the eve of the original deadline for the launching of 'Operation Sealion', the invasion of Britain, Hitler convened a meeting of the leaders of the armed forces to concede that 'on the whole, despite all our successes, the preconditions needed for Sealion are not yet there . . . A successful landing means victory; but this requires total command of the air', and this had not been obtained. 'Operation Sealion' was postponed indefinitely.[84] Hitler was persuaded by Raeder to continue with night raids, especially over London, to destroy the city's military and economic infrastructure. Increasingly also the raids were justified in terms of their impact on civilian morale. The decision was welcomed by many in Germany. 'The war of annihilation against England has now really begun,' wrote Lore Walb with satisfaction in her diary on 10 September 1940: 'Pray God that they are soon brought to their knees!'[85] This 'war of annihilation' was known in London as 'the Blitz'. In all, some 40,000 British civilians were killed during the Battle of Britain and the Blitz. But morale did not break down. A new German ploy of sending fighters and fighter-bombers flying at high altitudes – 253 such raids were carried out in October 1940 alone – was designed to wear down both civilian morale and British fighter strength. In October 1940, some 146 Spitfires and Hurricanes were lost. But the Royal Air Force had adapted its tactics by mounting high-flying patrols, and in the same month the Germans lost another 365 aircraft, mostly bombers. In November one raid on the midland city of Coventry by a fleet of almost 450 bombers destroyed the entire city centre, including the medieval cathedral, killing 380 civilians and injuring 865; British intelligence had failed to anticipate the raid, and the city had been left effectively without protection.[86]

But this was a rare lapse. Mostly, the German bombers met heavy and well-prepared resistance. Deciding that such attacks achieved little, Raeder persuaded Hitler to switch the bombing campaign to Britain's seaports from 19 February 1941, but while many raids were mounted, Britain's night-time defences quickly became effective here too, as radar and radar-controlled guns came into operation. By May 1941 the raids were being scaled down. British civilian morale, though shaky during the initial phase of the bombing campaign, had not collapsed. Churchill had not come under any significant domestic pressure to sue for peace. British aircraft production had not been seriously affected. 600 German bombers had been shot down. Ordinary Germans began to get depressed about the outcome of the conflict. 'For the first time since the war began,' wrote Lore Walb in her diary on 3 October 1940, 'my constant optimism has begun to waver. We are making no progress against England.'[87] And in December 1940 Hans Meier-Welcker was forced to conclude privately, as many others had already done, that there was no sign of 'a collapse of morale among the English people'.[88] For the first time, Hitler had lost a major battle. The consequences were to be far-reaching.[89]

'PATHOLOGICAL AMBITION'

I

As it became clear that the German air force was not going to win command over the skies between Britain and the Continent, Hitler cast around for alternative methods of bringing the stubborn British to their knees. His attention turned to the Mediterranean. Perhaps it would be possible to enlist Italy, Vichy France and Spain in the destruction of British sea-power and British naval bases there. But a series of meetings held in late October produced nothing of any concrete value. The canny Spanish leader, General Franco, while thanking Hitler for his support during the Spanish Civil War, made no promises at all, but simply said he would come into the war on Germany's side when it suited him. In his view the war was still undecided, and he poured open scorn upon the German belief that Britain would soon be defeated. Even if there was a successful invasion, he said, the Churchill government would retreat to Canada and continue the fight from there with the aid of the Royal Navy. Moreover, it was quite possible that the USA would back Churchill; already, indeed, on 3 September 1940 US President Franklin D. Roosevelt had signed an agreement leasing fifty destroyers to the British navy. Given his unwillingness to force Vichy France to surrender any of its colonial territories in North Africa to the Spanish, Hitler had little or nothing of value to offer Franco in return for his entry into the war, and the Spanish dictator knew it. 'These people are intolerable,' Franco declared to his Foreign Minister after the meeting. 'They want us to come into the war in exchange for nothing.'[90] The meeting broke up without any concrete result. A furious Ribbentrop railed against Franco as an 'ungrateful coward' whose refusal to help was poor thanks for the aid Germany had given him in the Spanish Civil War, while

Hitler told Mussolini a few days later that he would rather 'have three or four teeth taken out' than go through another nine such hours of negotiations with the Spanish dictator.[91]

Hitler fared little better with Marshal Pétain and his Prime Minister, Pierre Laval, who wanted a firm promise of new colonial territory for the Vichy regime in return for lending French support to the attack on Britain. The meeting ended without either side having promised anything. Worse still was the situation in Italy. The Fascist dictator Benito Mussolini had come more closely into the German orbit in the late 1930s, but had stayed out of the war when it began in September 1939. His ambition to create a new Roman Empire in the Mediterranean had gained strength, however, from his defeat and annexation of Ethiopia in 1936 and his successful participation on Franco's side in the Civil War in Spain from 1936 to 1939. By this time, Mussolini had begun to emulate Hitler, introducing German-style racial legislation in the late autumn of 1938.[92] Having started his career as Hitler's teacher, Mussolini was beginning to become his pupil. Every German foreign policy success threatened to put Italian Fascism further in the shade. Soon after the German occupation of rump Czecho-Slovakia in March 1939, therefore, Mussolini invaded Albania, already run by Italy from behind the scenes but never formally annexed. Another piece had been slotted into the jigsaw of the new Roman Empire. Just over a year later, on 10 June 1940, as it became clear that Hitler was achieving complete dominance over Western Europe, Italy finally joined the war in the hope of gaining British and French colonies in North Africa, along the southern shoreline of the Mediterranean. Since Vichy France was, in effect, an ally of the Third Reich, this would not be easy to achieve. The Italian dictator was unceremoniously excluded from the negotiations in the railway carriage at Compiègne, and Hitler rejected his claim on the French fleet even before it was destroyed by the British raid on Mers-el-Kébir.[93] Irritated and disappointed, Mussolini looked around for another opportunity to build his new Roman Empire. He found it in the Balkans. On 28 October 1940, without informing Hitler in advance, Mussolini sent an Italian army across the Albanian border into Greece. The German Leader was furious. The terrain was difficult, the weather was atrocious and would inevitably get worse as winter approached, and the whole venture seemed an unnecessary distraction.[94]

Hitler was right to be concerned. The Italian troops were poorly trained, under-strength and ill prepared. They lacked the winter clothing necessary to brave the rigours of the mountain snows. They were without the naval support that would have made possible amphibious landings of the kind that had proved so effective in Norway and Denmark. They had no maps to help them traverse the largely pathless terrain across the Albanian-Greek border. Italian armour was utterly inadequate to overwhelm the Greek defences. There was no unified line of command. The Italian Foreign Ministry had been unable to prevent information about the invasion leaking out in advance. The Greeks thus had time to take defensive measures. Within a few days the Italians were being repulsed all along the line. On 14 November 1940 the Greeks began a counter-offensive, supported by five squadrons of British planes that bombed key Italian ports and lines of communication. Mussolini's army had been pushed back deep into Albanian territory within a few weeks. The Italians lost nearly 39,000 men out of just over half a million; more than 50,000 were wounded and over 12,000 suffered from frostbite, while a further 52,000 had to be invalided out of the action for a variety of other reasons.[95] The invasion was a fiasco. Despite propaganda attempts to paper over the disaster with rhetoric, Mussolini's humiliation could hardly have been more obvious.

From every point of view it would have made more sense to attack Malta, and possibly Gibraltar and Alexandria as well, rather than Greece, in order to deprive the British of their crucial naval bases in the Mediterranean. But Mussolini was oblivious to this strategic imperative. On 11 November 1940 half the Italian battle fleet was effectively rendered inoperative by a British carrier-based air attack at Taranto. A few months later, on 28 March 1941, alerted by the deciphering of an Italian navy message at the decoding centre in Bletchley Park, the British navy off Cape Matapan in the Mediterranean sank three Italian cruisers and two destroyers on their way to intercept British supply convoys to the Greeks. The British forces lost no more than one aircraft.[96] For the rest of the war, the remainder of the modern and well-equipped Italian fleet stayed close to port for fear of further damage. Well before this time, too, an attempt to invade British-held Egypt from the Italian colony of Libya had been repulsed by a small but well-trained Anglo-Indian force of 35,000 men, who took 130,000 prisoners in December 1940, along with 380 tanks.[97] Perhaps the greatest humiliation came in April 1941, when the Italian occupying force in the Ethiopian capital of Addis

Abeba surrendered to a mixed Allied force that successfully wrested the colony back from its Fascist masters in a campaign far shorter than the original Italian war of conquest in 1935–6. British intelligence had succeeded in deciphering so many of the Italians' battle plans and gained such detailed information about their movements and troop dispositions that the British commanders were aware of everything the Italians were going to do well in advance. A force of 92,000 Italian and 250,000 Abyssinian soldiers was comprehensively defeated by 40,000 British-led African troops. The Ethiopian Emperor Haile Selassie was triumphantly reinstalled on his throne, while Allied forces had overrun Eritrea and Italian Somaliland by May 1941, leaving the whole north-east of Africa in Allied hands.[98]

So comprehensive was the Italian debacle that Hitler had little choice but to intervene. On 19 January 1941 Mussolini arrived at the Berghof for two days of talks. The Italian failures had completely transformed the relationship between the two dictators. Whilst Hitler had previously shown some deference to his former mentor, now, though he did his best to be tactful, there was no doubt that he and his entourage were beginning to hold the Italian dictator in some contempt. On 6 February 1941 Hitler briefed General Erwin Rommel on the task of rescuing the situation in North Africa. Born in 1891, and of middle-class origin, Rommel was not a typical German general. Highly decorated in the First World War, he had attracted attention by a book on infantry tactics published in 1937. He had distinguished himself by his boldness in leading a tank division in the invasion of France. Appointed to head the newly formed Africa Corps, he arrived in Tripoli on 12 February 1941 with a brief to prevent any further Italian collapse in Libya. Nominally under Italian command, in fact Rommel showed little regard for the Italian generals. His troops were well trained and adapted quickly to the peculiar conditions of warfare in the flat, featureless, sandy terrain. Rommel was able to use German decrypts of ciphers from the US military attaché in Cairo to anticipate British moves, while the signals he himself sent to his superiors often said something different to what he actually decided to do. Building on their previous experience of combined air and armoured warfare, Rommel's troops moved swiftly into action, pushing back a British force weakened by the redeployment of many of its best soldiers to defend Greece against the expected German invasion.[99]

By 1 April 1941 Rommel had met with such success that he ignored orders from Berlin and drove on hundreds of miles until he was close to the Egyptian border. Halder considered he had gone 'stark mad', and thought he had spread his forces too wide and opened himself to a counter-attack. He was sharply critical of Rommel's 'pathological ambition'.[100] The British sent a new commander, strengthened their forces, and counter-attacked. Rommel had indeed grossly overstretched his supply lines, and had to withdraw. But he eventually managed to obtain more tanks and fuel and finally took the key Libyan seaport of Tobruk in June 1942. The victory prompted Hitler to promote him to the rank of Field Marshal, the youngest in the German army. In this war of rapid movement across vast distances of largely empty desert, Rommel now forced the British back deep into Egypt. He was within striking distance of the Suez Canal, threatening a major British supply route and opening up the enticing prospect of gaining access to the vast oilfields of the Middle East.[101]

Rommel was widely regarded as a hero not only in Germany but even in Britain. Yet his victories opened up new opportunities for the Nazis and their allies to implement their doctrines of racial superiority on defenceless minorities. The triumphs of the Africa Corps brought terrible suffering to the Jews who lived in often very old-established communities in the major North African cities. 50,000 Jews lived in Tunisia, and as soon as the Germans occupied the country, their homes were raided, their property confiscated, their valuables stolen, and their young men – more than 4,000 of them – sent off to labour camps near the front line. The rape of Tunisian Jewish women by German soldiers was far from uncommon. Walter Rauff, the Gestapo chief in Tunis, transferred from the killing fields of Eastern Europe, quickly instituted a reign of terror against the Jews of Tunis. Many were brutally maltreated; a few were hidden by sympathetic Arabs. The situation of the Jews in the neighbouring Vichy French colonies of Morocco and Algeria was little better. Almost immediately after the regime was established in 1940, some 1,500 Jews serving in the French Foreign Legion were cashiered and imprisoned in a rapidly growing network of labour camps whose number soon exceeded 100. Joined there by internees from a variety of nations, including Poland, Greece and Czechoslovakia, they were forced to work on projects such as the new Trans-Sahara Railway in conditions of considerable brutality. Vichy's harsh discriminatory laws against Jews in France were applied in French North Africa too. Altogether perhaps 5,000 North African Jews died under Axis occupation, roughly 1 per cent of the total. Their numbers would have been far greater had it been possible to transport them across the Mediterranean to the extermination centres of German-occupied Poland.[102]

While these dramatic events were in progress, the Germans tried to gain access to vital oil supplies in the Middle East by fomenting unrest against British rule in Iraq. But the British managed to quell the unrest without too much trouble in the summer of 1941, and built on this success by taking over Syria, a French colony, from the Vichy regime. Thus frustrated, Hitler was reduced to making promises that he had at the moment no chance of fulfilling. The Islamic cleric Haj Amin al-Husseini, Grand Mufti of Jerusalem, fled to Berlin on the defeat of the uprising in Iraq, and Hitler greeted him on 28 November 1941 with an empty promise to destroy Jewish settlements in Palestine.[103] Indeed, in an attempt to avoid offending the Arabs, the Propaganda Ministry for a time recommended replacing the term 'antisemitic' with the more specific 'anti-Jewish' in the media – the Arabs, after all, were Semites too.[104] Yet Rommel's victories ensured that the dream of gaining access to the massive oilfields of the Middle East was still not dead.

II

The search for oil was not confined to North Africa and the Middle East. On 27 May 1940, in the wake of its stunning successes in the west, the Third Reich secured a monopoly over Romanian oil supplies. By July Romanian oil deliveries to Britain, which had previously made up nearly 40 per cent of the output of the Ploesti oilfield, had been completely cut off.[105] But the dictatorship of King Carol of Romania, which had negotiated these deals, ran into trouble when he was forced by Hitler to cede northern Transylvania to Germany's ally Hungary and surrender further territory in the south to Bulgaria (promised because German troops had to pass through Bulgaria to reach Greece). Carol had also been obliged to cede Bessarabia and northern Bukovina to the Soviet Union as part of the deal struck by the Nazi–Soviet Pact the previous year. On 6 September 1940 Carol was forced to abdicate in the face of popular outrage at these concessions, driven out by the army under its leader General Ion Antonescu in alliance with the fascist Iron

Guard. Antonescu became Prime Minister in a new coalition government heavily backed by the military. Early in 1941, however, the Iron Guard staged a violent uprising against the new government, directing its fury especially against the country's 375,000 Jews, whom it blamed, absurdly, for the cession of the lost territories. Under its leader, Horia Sima, the Iron Guard rampaged through Bucharest, hunting down Jews, taking them out into the woods and shooting them. Sima's men also took 200 Jewish men into a slaughterhouse, stripped them naked, made them go through the whole process of the slaughter-line normally used for animals, and hung their corpses up by their throats from meat-hooks, labelling the bodies 'fit for human consumption'. There was some evidence that the SS had backed the revolt in the hope of gaining tighter control over the turbulent Balkan state. But after two days the rebellion was quickly crushed by Antonescu, who now became the country's military dictator. Horia Sima was forced to flee and took refuge in Germany. A rigged plebiscite confirmed the new order. Antonescu, a professional soldier from a military family, now in his fifties, had already established good relations with Hitler, who was deeply impressed with him on a personal level; among other things, the Romanian leader persuaded the Nazis to stop supporting the Iron Guard, thus leaving them at the government's mercy. Hitler in return held out the prospect of assisting the Romanians to recover the substantial territory they had lost to the Soviet Union and maybe more besides. A close alliance emerged between the two countries. German troops entered Romania but the country remained more than merely nominally independent. By 1941 nearly 50 per cent of Romania's crude oil output was produced by German-owned companies and exports of petroleum products nearly tripled in comparison to the previous year. It was not least in order to secure these supplies that Hitler decided it was necessary to extricate the Italians from their problems in neighbouring Greece.[106]

In the composite multinational Kingdom of Yugoslavia, however, the situation had become more difficult for Hitler. On 25 March 1941, the Yugoslav government had yielded to German pressure (which had included the summoning of the Prince Regent Paul to the Berghof for a characteristic piece of bullying by Hitler) and allied itself formally with Germany, thus putting in place another piece of the diplomatic back-ground for the forthcoming invasion of Greece. The reluctant Yugoslav government managed to obtain assurances that no German troops would pass through their country on their way to Greece, and that it would not be asked to provide any military support. As a reward for its goodwill it obtained a commitment that it would be given the Greek port of Salonika once the German conquest of the country was complete. But a German alliance was anathema to the Serb element in the Yugoslav officer corps, who saw in it evidence of excessive Croatian influence in the cabinet and had in any case been deeply committed to the Allied cause and hostile to Germany and Austria since the First World War. In the early hours of 27 March 1941, Serb officers staged a coup d'état, overthrew the Prince Regent and proclaimed Peter II, aged only seventeen, as king. The event was greeted by ecstatic Serbian demonstrations in the streets of Belgrade. An all-party government was formed, for the moment papering over the serious divisions between Serbs and Croats in the face of the likely reaction from Berlin.[107] That reaction was not slow in coming. Hitler was furious. He summoned the leaders of the German army and air force and declared that, in view of this betrayal, Yugoslavia would be smashed. The country must be attacked 'in a lightning operation' and 'with merciless harshness'. Italy, Hungary and Bulgaria would all make territorial gains from the defeated country. The Croats would be given their independence. The plans for the invasion of Greece would have to be revised in the shortest possible time so as to include a parallel invasion of Yugoslavia. Here was another state, like Poland, that had dared to defy him, another state, therefore, that had to be utterly destroyed.[108]

After making the necessary arrangements with Germany's allies Hungary and Italy, the German Twelfth Army entered southern Yugoslavia and northern Greece on 6 April 1941. On 8–10 April 1941 German, Hungarian and Italian forces invaded northern Yugoslavia. With superior numbers and more modern armour and equipment, and backed by 800 aircraft, the German forces overwhelmed their opponents. The Yugoslav army, although over a million strong, was badly equipped, poorly led and riven by ethnic divisions. It crumbled rapidly. As waves of German bombers devastated the Yugoslav capital, Belgrade, German panzer divisions and infantry moved forward rapidly. They took the city on 12 April 1941, leading the Yugoslav government to capitulate five days later. 344,000 Yugoslav troops were captured. German losses amounted to 151 dead. Meanwhile, the Greeks, backed by a British expeditionary force, had put up stiffer resistance, but here too, the tried

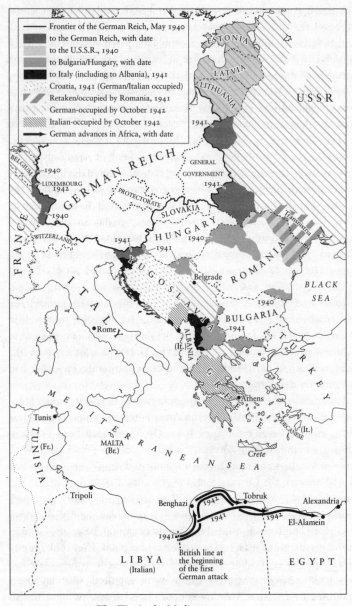

8. The War in the Mediterranean, 1940–42

and tested combination of air command and modern armour over-whelmed the opposition. Split from the Greek army, the retreating British forces decided to evacuate, and a hurriedly assembled naval force, harried by German airplanes, managed to take off about 50,000 troops from the beaches by the end of April, though a number of ships were lost in the process. In despair at the course events were taking, the Greek Prime Minister shot himself on 18 April 1941. German troops entered Athens on 27 April 1941.[109]

The King and the government had already left for Crete, to where the remaining Greek, British and other Allied forces had retreated. But on 20 May 1941 German airborne forces landed on the island and quickly seized the main airfields, where further German troops now landed. The British commander on the island had not appreciated the importance of air defences. Without fighter planes he was unable to intercept the incoming airborne troops. By 26 May he had decided the situation was hopeless. A chaotic evacuation began. With complete command of the skies, German aircraft sank three British cruisers and six destroyers. They forced the Allies to abandon the evacuation on 30 May 1941, leaving some 5,000 men behind. Despite advance warning of these operations from German military signal traffic decoded at Bletchley Park, the British commander simply did not have enough strength on the ground or in the air. He was forbidden to redeploy his troops to the anticipated points of attack in case this should cause the German commanders to suspect their signals were being intercepted. More than 11,000 British troops were captured and nearly 3,000 soldiers and sailors killed. The whole operation was a disaster for the British. Churchill and his advisers were forced to concede that it had been a mistake to send troops to Greece in the first place.[110]

Yet the German victories, spectacular as they were, came at a heavy price. The Greeks and their allies had fought determinedly, and the invading Germans had not escaped without casualties. In Crete, 3,352 out of a total of 17,500 invading German troops had been killed, persuading the German armed forces not to mount a similar airborne operation against Malta or Cyprus.[111] 'Our proud paratroop unit,' wrote one soldier after the victory, 'never recovered from the enormous losses sustained on Crete.'[112] More seriously, the occupation of the conquered territories soon proved to be far from a simple matter. While Bulgaria moved into eastern Macedonia and western Thrace, expelling over

100,000 Greeks from the area and bringing in Bulgarian settlers in a brutal act of 'ethnic cleansing', a puppet government was installed in Greece to maintain the fiction of independence. However, the real power lay with the German army, which occupied key strategic points on the mainland and some of the islands, especially Crete, and the Italians, who were given control over most of the rest of the country. As German troops entered Athens, tired, hungry and without supplies, they began to demand free meals in restaurants, to loot the houses in which they were billeted, and to stop passers-by in the streets and relieve them of their watches and jewellery. One inhabitant of the city, the musicologist Minos Dounias, asked:

Where is the traditional German sense of honour? I lived in Germany thirteen years and no one cheated me. Now suddenly . . . they have become thieves. They empty houses of whatever meets their eye. In Pistolakis's house they took the pillow-slips and grabbed the Cretan heirlooms from the valuable collection they have. From the poor houses in the area they seized sheets and blankets. From other neighbourhoods they grab oil paintings and even the metal knobs from the doors.[113]

While the ordinary troops were stealing what they could, supply officers were seizing large quantities of foodstuffs, cotton, leather and much else besides. All available stocks of olive oil and rice were requisitioned. 26,000 oranges, 4,500 lemons and 100,000 cigarettes were shipped off the island of Chios in the first three weeks of the occupation. Companies such as Krupps and I. G. Farben sent in agents to effect the compulsory purchase of mining and industrial facilities at low prices.[114]

As a result of this massive assault on the country's economy, unemployment in Greece rocketed and food prices, already high because of the damage caused by military action, went through the roof. Looting and requisitioning led to peasant farmers hoarding their produce and attacking agents sent from the towns to collect the harvest. Local military commanders tried to keep produce within their region, disrupting or even cutting off supplies to the major cities. Rationing was introduced, and while the Italians began to send in extra supplies to Greece to alleviate the situation, the authorities in Berlin refused to follow suit, arguing that this would jeopardize the food situation in Germany. Soon hunger and malnutrition were stalking the streets of Athens. Fuel supplies were unavailable, or too expensive, to heat people's houses in

the cold winter of 1941–2. People begged in the streets for food, ransacked rubbish bins for scraps, and in their desperation started to eat
grass. German army officers amused themselves by tossing scraps
from balconies to gangs of children and watching them fight for the
pieces. People, especially children, succumbed to disease, and began
dying in the streets. Overall death rates rose five- or even sevenfold in
the winter of 1941–2; the Red Cross estimated that a quarter of a
million Greeks died as a result of hunger and associated diseases between
1941 and 1943.[115]

In the mountainous areas of northern Greece armed bands attacked
German supply routes and there were some German casualties; the
regional German army commander burned four villages and shot 488
Greek civilians in reprisal. In Crete, stranded British soldiers took part
in resistance activities, and in 1944 a German general was captured by
agents sent from Cairo, including the later writer Patrick Leigh Fermor.
Whether or not the savage reprisals of the German army had any effect
is uncertain. The general state of hunger and exhaustion of the Greek
people meant that there were few attempts at armed resistance in the
first year or so of the occupation, and no co-ordinated leadership.[116]

III

The situation in occupied Yugoslavia was dramatically different. An
artificial creation that had bound together in a single state a variety of
ethnic and religious groups since the end of the First World War, Yugoslavia was torn by bitter inter-communal feuds and rivalries that broke
out in full force as soon as the Germans invaded. The German Reich
annexed the northern part of Slovenia, south of the Austrian border,
while Italy incorporated the Adriatic coast down to (and including some
of) the Dalmatian islands and took over the administration of the bulk of
Montenegro. Albania, an Italian possession since April 1939, occupied a
large chunk of the south-east, including much of Kosovo and western
Macedonia, as well as ingesting part of Montenegro, while the voracious
Hungarians gobbled up the Backa and other areas they had ruled until
1918, and the Bulgarians, as well as seizing most of Macedonia from
the Greeks, marched into the Yugoslav part of Macedonia. The rest of
the country was split into two. Hitler was determined to reward his allies

and to punish the Serbs. On 10 April 1941, the day that German forces entered Belgrade, the Croatian fascist leader Ante Pavelić, with German encouragement, declared an independent Croatia, encompassing all areas inhabited by Croats, including Bosnia and Hercegovina. The newly independent state of Croatia was far larger than rump Serbia. Pavelić immediately allied himself with Germany and declared war on the Allies. Like his equivalent, Quisling, in Norway, Pavelić was an extremist who had little popular support. A nationalist lawyer, he had formed his organization when King Alexander had imposed a Serb-dominated dictatorship in 1929 following demonstrations in which Serb police had killed a number of Croatian nationalists. Known as the 'Ustashe' (insurgents), Pavelić's movement had scored its most spectacular coup in 1934 when its agents had collaborated with Macedonian terrorists in the assassination of the Yugoslav king, along with the French Foreign Minister, during a state visit to France in 1934. The subsequent repression of his organization had meant that Pavelić had been obliged to run it from exile in Italy, where he had converted it into a fully fledged fascist movement, complete with a racial doctrine that saw the Croatians as 'western' rather than Slav. He gave it the mission of saving the Catholic, Christian West against the threat posed by Orthodox Slavs, atheistical Bolsheviks and Jews. By the beginning of the 1940s, however, he is estimated to have won the support of no more than 40,000 out of 6 million Croats in Yugoslavia.[117]

Hitler initially wanted to appoint the leader of the moderate Croatian Peasant Party, Vladko Maček, as head of the new state, but when he refused, the choice fell on Pavelić, who returned from exile and proclaimed a one-party state of Croatians.[118] Pavelić set about recruiting young men from the urban sub-proletariat for the Ustashe, and almost immediately set in motion a massive wave of ethnic cleansing, using terror and genocide to drive out the new state's 2 million Serbs, 30,000 Gypsies and 45,000 Jews or turn them at least into nominal Croats by converting them to Catholicism. Ultra-nationalist students and many Croatian-nationalist Catholic clergy, especially Franciscan monks, joined in the action with gusto. Already on 17 April 1941 a decree proclaimed that anyone guilty of offending against the honour of the Croat nation, either in the past, present or future, had committed high treason and thus could be killed. Another decree defined the Croats as Aryan and banned intermarriage with non-Aryans. Sexual relations between male Jews and female Croats were outlawed, though not the other way round. All non-Croats were excluded from citizenship. While the new treason law was at least paid lip-service in the towns, the Ustashe did not bother even with the appearance of legality in the countryside. After shooting dead some 300 Serbs, including women and children, in the town of Glina in July 1941, the Ustashe offered an amnesty to the inhabitants of the surrounding villages if they converted to Catholicism. 250 people turned up at the Orthodox Church in Glina for the ceremony. Once inside, they were greeted not by a Catholic priest but by Ustashe militia, who forced them to lie down and then beat their heads in with spiked clubs. All over the new Croatia, similarly terrible scenes of mass murder were enacted during the summer and autumn of 1941. On several occasions, Serb villagers were herded into the local church, the windows boarded over, and the building burned to the ground along with everybody in it. Croatian Ustashe units gouged out the eyes of Serbian men and cut off the women's breasts with penknives.[119]

The first concentration camp in Croatia opened at the end of April 1941, and on 26 June a law was enacted providing for a network of camps across the country. The purpose of the camps was not to hold opponents of the regime, but to exterminate ethnic and religious minorities. In the Jasenovac camp system alone, more than 20,000 Jews are thought to have perished. Death was due above all to disease and malnutrition, but Ustashe militia, egged on by some Franciscan friars, frequently beat inmates to death with hammers in night-long sessions of mass murder. At the Loborgrad camp, 1,500 Jewish women were subjected to repeated rape by the commander and his staff. When typhus broke out in the camp at Stara Gradiska, the chief administrator sent sufferers to the disease-free camp at Djakovo so the inmates there could be infected too. On 24 July 1941, the curate of Udbina wrote: 'Up to now, my brothers, we have been working for our religion with the cross and the breviary, but the time has come when we shall work with a revolver and a rifle.'[120] The head of the Catholic Church in Croatia, Archbishop Alojzije Stepinac, a bitter opponent of Orthodox 'schismatics', declared that the hand of God was at work in the removal of the Serbian Orthodox yoke. Pavelić was even granted a private audience with the Pope on 18 May 1941. Eventually, however, Stepinac was moved to protest against forced conversions that were all too obviously achieved through terror, though his condemnation of the killings did not come until 1942, when Father Filipović, who had led murder squads at Jasenovac, was expelled from the Franciscan order. By 1943 Stepinac was condemning the registration and deportation to extermination camps of the remaining Croatian Jews. But this was all rather late in the day. By this time, probably about 30,000 Jews had been killed, along with most of the country's Gypsies (many of whom died working in inhuman conditions on the Sava dike construction project), while the best estimates put the number of Serb victims at around 300,000. Such was the horror generated above all in Italy by these massacres, as reports of the atrocities were publicized by the thousands of Serbian and Jewish refugees who crossed the border into Dalmatia, that the Italian army began to move on to Croatian territory, declaring that it would protect any minorities it found there. But it was too late for most. In the longer term, the Croatian genocide created memories of deep and lasting bitterness among the Serbs. It still had not been forgotten by the time Serbia and Croatia eventually regained their independence after the collapse of the postwar Yugoslav state, in the 1990s.[121]

IV

The half-hearted nature of Hitler's preparations for the seaborne invasion of Britain reflected not least the fact that already before the end of July 1940 his mind was turning to a plan far closer to his heart: the conquest of Russia. This had been at the very centre of Hitler's thinking since the early 1920s. Already in his autobiographical political tract *My Struggle* he had declared in uncompromising terms the necessity of acquiring 'living-space' for the Germans in Eastern Europe. He had repeated this in numerous addresses to his military staff, most notably on 3 February 1933, when he had explicitly promised the army chiefs that he would launch a war to Germanize Eastern Europe some time in the future.[122] Meeting the chiefs of the armed forces towards the end of July 1940, Hitler said that it was time to begin planning for this event. Eighty to 100 divisions would be needed to crush the Red Army. It would be child's play in comparison to the invasion of France.[123] In fact, the army had already carried out feasibility studies and concluded that an invasion was not practicable before the following spring. Further studies were prepared with a view to launching an attack in May 1941.

The prospect of a war on two fronts did not alarm Hitler. France had been eliminated, Britain seemed close to collapse. As for the Red Army, it had been decimated by Stalin's purges, and it had proved hopelessly incompetent in the war with Finland. Slavs in any case were subhumans incapable of putting up serious resistance to a superior race. Bolshevism only made them weaker. Hitler regarded it as a tool of the world Jewish conspiracy, which had succeeded in enslaving the Slavs and bending them to its will. There were, of course, many reasons why this view was little more than a fantasy, not the least of them being the fact that Stalin was himself antisemitic and had dismissed his Foreign Minister, Litvinov, in 1939, among other things because he was a Jew. Still, thought Hitler, if the racially superior Western European nations had been crushed so easily, then what chance did the Slavs stand? 'The Russians are inferior,' Hitler told Brauchitsch and Halder on 5 December 1940. 'The army is leaderless.' The German armed forces would require no more than four or five months to crush the Soviet Union.[124]

Aside from the ideological primacy of 'living-space' there were also pragmatic reasons for attacking the Soviet Union. Throughout 1940 and the first half of 1941, the Third Reich depended heavily on supplies from Eastern Europe. The non-aggression pact signed between Ribbentrop and the Soviet Foreign Minister, Molotov, on 24 August 1939 was still in force at this time, of course.[125] Indeed, on 12 November 1940 Molotov himself arrived in Berlin at Hitler's invitation to discuss future co-operation. On 10 January 1941 the Soviet Union signed a new trade agreement which doubled the quantity of grain exports from the Ukraine to the Third Reich, thus ironically convincing Hitler, if he needed convincing, that the Soviet Union possessed almost limitless supplies of foodstuffs, which would be essential for the further conduct of the war and the general future of the Third Reich. Stalin's concessions to German trade demands thus did little or nothing to affect the timing of the German invasion.[126]

Whatever the Soviets might offer, Hitler had no intention of abandoning his plans. On 18 December 1940 he ordered the armed forces to be ready to crush the Soviet Union in a rapid campaign to begin the following spring. His comparative haste was not least a consequence of his failure to defeat Britain. By 1942, he thought, the USA might well have entered the war on the Allied side. Defeating the Soviets would put Germany in a strong position to deal with the Americans. It would encourage Japan to come into the war against America by eliminating a major threat to Japan's west. And it would isolate the British still further and perhaps finally force them to the negotiating table. This was indeed the primary initial reason for launching the invasion in 1941. 'But if Russia is smashed,' Hitler told his generals on 31 July 1940, 'it is the end of any hopes that might move England still to hope for a change in the situation.'[127] 'The gentlemen in England aren't stupid, you know,' he told Field Marshal Fedor von Bock in early January 1941. 'They'll realize there's no purpose for them carrying on the war when Russia has been beaten and eliminated from it.'[128] Moreover, he added some weeks later, it was necessary to launch the invasion before Britain was defeated; if it came afterwards, the German people would not support it. The code name for the invasion, supplied by Hitler himself, was 'Operation Barbarossa', named after Frederick Barbarossa, Holy Roman Emperor and German crusader in the twelfth century.[129]

As plans became more detailed, the number of divisions to be used in the invasion fluctuated but was eventually set at around 200. The Red Army forces arrayed against the invaders were of a roughly comparable size, but in the minds of Hitler and his military leaders they were far inferior in quality. To be sure, in terms of equipment, the Red Army in the combat zone far outgunned its opponents, with nearly three times as many artillery pieces and the same advantage in tanks. Even in the air, Soviet forces had a strong numerical superiority, with twice as many combat aircraft as the Germans and their allies. But many of these machines were obsolescent, new tank models and new artillery pieces were not yet being produced in any numbers, and Stalin's purges of the 1930s had seriously affected aircraft and munitions production managers and designers, military commanders and senior air force officers.[130] Moreover, German preparations were thorough. Elated by the success of the armoured divisions in the invasion of France, Hitler ordered arms production to focus on tanks. The number of panzer divisions in the German army doubled between the summer of 1940 and the summer of 1941, backed by a corresponding increase in the number of half-track vehicles with which to move the divisions of highly mobile infantry swiftly in behind the tanks to press home the advantage. German arms production in the year before the invasion of the Soviet Union really did concentrate on providing the means to fight a classic war of lightning movement, as it had not done before the invasion of

France. To back this up, production was switched from ammunition, of which there were now plentiful supplies, to machine-guns and field artillery. Despite continued bureaucratic infighting between different procurement and economic management agencies under the control of Fritz Todt, Georg Thomas and Hermann Göring, the arms industry of the Third Reich did therefore operate with some effectiveness in the run-up to Operation Barbarossa.[131]

Over the first half of 1941, railway and other communications in German-occupied Poland were improved, and supplies stockpiled in the border area. Strategic plans finally envisaged cutting off and destroying Soviet forces on the border and advancing rapidly to a line from Arch-angel to Astrakhan. In the north, Finland, bitterly resentful at the loss of territory to the Soviet Union at the end of the 'Winter War' in 1940, agreed to mobilize its sixteen-division army, newly organized and provided with the latest German equipment, though its objectives went no further than the recovery of the lost territory.[132] In the south, Romania supplied eighteen divisions to the invading forces.[133] Romanian troops were joined by a small force of Hungarians, but the two forces had to be kept apart because of the poor relations between the two countries. Most of the Hungarian forces' equipment was obsolete, the rifles used by the infantry frequently jammed, they had only 190 tanks, which were also out of date, and six of the ten 'Alpine' battalions that joined in the invasion of Russia were mounted on bicycles. Far more important was the fact that Hungary was rapidly becoming an important source of petroleum oil for the Germans, until by the middle of the war it was the second-most important supplier after Romania.[134] The participation of the Hungarians was not least the consequence of the anxiety of the Hungarian ruler Admiral Miklós Horthy that the Romanians would steal a march on him and get back some of the territory they had lost to Hungary in 1940. In similar fashion, the participation of the German client state of Slovakia, which sent two divisions intended mainly to provide security behind the front, was intended to gain German goodwill in the face of further Hungarian demands on its territory. By contrast, Mussolini's contribution of 60,000 Italian troops did not take part in the invasion itself, and was made in the vague hope that the Germans would look favourably on Italian aspirations in the postwar peace settlement. 45,000 anti-Communist Spanish volunteers went to join the fray on the Leningrad front, inspired by ideological commitment and sanctioned by Franco as a gesture of gratitude to Hitler for his help in the fighting that had brought him to power. The volunteers cannot have been amused when they were greeted on their arrival by a German air force band mistakenly playing the national anthem of the Republicans, their defeated opponents in the Civil War.[135]

Germany's Balkan ally Bulgaria took a more cautious line than the Hungarians and Romanians. King Boris III, who ran the country's military and foreign policy and much else besides, was realistic enough to recognize that his army of peasant conscripts was not suited for modern warfare and had no interest in fighting far from home. Boris had to perform a delicate balancing act. He once remarked: 'My army is pro-German, my wife is Italian, my people are pro-Russian. I'm the only pro-Bulgarian in this country.'[136] He had eagerly joined in the dismemberment of Greece and Yugoslavia, and begun the Bulgarization of the education system and other aspects of public life in the areas occupied by his forces. But the Bulgarian annexation of Thrace sparked serious resistance, leading to a major uprising at the end of September 1941. Boris claimed with some justification that the army was needed there to put it down, which it did in the following months, killing between 45,000 and 60,000 Greeks and ordering the expulsion or resettlement of many more. Just as important from the king's point of view, however, was the threat of internal revolt by fascist republicans. Partly to ward this off, but also yielding to German pressure, he had introduced antisemitic legislation in October 1940, banning sexual relations between Jews and non-Jews and ousting Jews from a variety of professions and industries. But the Bulgarian legislature had been careful to define Jews in religious terms, and many Jews were able to escape the effects of the legislation by converting, often merely on paper, to Christianity. In addition, the legislation was not very rigorously enforced. Jews were required by law to wear the 'Jewish star' on their clothes, for example, but the government factory commissioned to make them produced so few that the small number of Jews who had started wearing them soon took them off because nobody else was wearing them. The King was also obliged to dissolve the country's Masonic lodges, a favourite target of Nazi and fascist conspiracy theorists, much to the irritation of his ministers, many of whom were Freemasons themselves. But, mindful of the looming power of the Russian colossus on his doorstep, he adamantly refused to provide any troops for the Soviet front, and indeed, although Bulgaria declared war on the Western Allies, it never declared war on the Soviet Union.[137] Half-exasperated, half-admiring, Hitler called him 'a very intelligent, even cunning man', while Goebbels, more bluntly, called him 'a sly, crafty fellow'.[138]

For all its multinational trimmings, therefore, 'Operation Barbarossa' was thus in essence to be a German operation. As the winter snows of East-Central Europe melted and the ground thawed, the German armed forces began moving vast masses of men and equipment up to the Soviet border. Throughout May and early June 1941, Zygmunt Klukowski recorded endless columns of German troops and vehicles passing through his region of Poland, noting the passage of between 500 and 600 vehicles on 14 June alone, for example.[139] Stalin hurriedly launched a futile policy of trying to appease the Germans by stepping up Soviet deliveries of Asian rubber and other supplies under the trade agreement signed in January 1941. As a dogmatic Marxist-Leninist, Stalin was convinced that Hitler's regime was the tool of German monopoly capitalism, so that if he made available everything German business wanted, there would be no immediate reason to invade. Already, under trade provisions agreed under the Nazi–Soviet Pact early the previous year, the Soviet Union was supplying nearly three-quarters of Germany's requirement of phosphates, over two-thirds of its imported asbestos, only a little less of its chrome ore, over half its manganese, over a third of its imported nickel, and, even more crucially, more than a third of its imported oil.[140] Stalin personally vetoed proposals to disrupt the German military build-up by attacking across the Polish demarcation line. Reports from Soviet agents and even from members of the German embassy in Moscow that an invasion was imminent only convinced him that the Germans were playing hard-ball in their drive to extract economic concessions from him.[141]

At the same time, Stalin realized that, as he told graduating military cadets in Moscow on 5 May 1941, 'War with Germany is inevitable.' Molotov might be able to postpone it for two or three months, but in the meantime it was vital to 're-teach our army and our commanders. Educate them in the spirit of attack.'[142] Delivered to young officers as a rhetorical message for the future, this was not a statement of intent. Stalin did not believe that the Red Army would be ready to deal with the Germans until 1942 or perhaps even 1943. Not only had the General Staff not drawn up any plans for an attack on the German forces, it had no plans for a defence against them either.[143] Although the Germans mounted a large and sophisticated deception plan to conceal the true nature of their intentions, Soviet intelligence began to send in accurate reports that the invasion was planned for around 22 June 1941. But Stalin would not listen. Earlier reports that the invasion plans were to become operational on 15 May 1941, though correct at the time, proved wrong when the Germans delayed Barbarossa in order to mount the invasion of Greece and Yugoslavia. Hitler later blamed Mussolini for the consequences, but in fact the weather in East-Central Europe in these weeks would have made an invasion of the Soviet Union inadvisable even had the German Leader not been obliged to step in to rescue his Italian ally from the imbroglio in Southern Europe. The Soviet agents who had made the prediction lost all credibility as a result.[144] The capitalist forces in Britain, including the exiled Polish government, seemed to Stalin's narrow and suspicious mind to be feeding false information to him about German intentions in order to lure him into a battle. Surely in any case the German Leader would not invade while the conflict with Britain was still unresolved. When an ex-Communist soldier deserted the German forces on 21 June 1941 and swam across a river to tell the Russians on the other side that his unit had been given orders to invade the following morning, Stalin had him shot for spreading 'disinformation'.[145]

OPERATION BARBAROSSA

I

As preparations for the invasion were intensifying in Berlin, Hitler's official deputy, Rudolf Hess, became increasingly worried at the prospect of a war on two fronts, a war for which ominous historical precedents, above all in 1914–18, were ever present in the minds of the leading Nazis. Slavishly devoted to Hitler, Hess was convinced, not without reason, that the Nazi Leader's main objective in the west since the conquest of France had been to bring Britain to the negotiating table. Over the past few years, Hess, never the sharpest of the Nazi minds, had lost influence steadily; his access to Hitler had been seriously reduced since the outbreak of the war in September 1939, and the considerable powers of his office had been increasingly wielded by his ambitious deputy, Martin Bormann. Hess had not been involved in the planning for Operation Barbarossa and indeed he had never played any role in foreign policy at all. Yet he considered himself well qualified to do so. Hess's teacher, the geopolitical theorist Karl Haushofer, had instilled in him a belief that it was Britain's destiny to join in the world struggle against Bolshevism on Germany's side. In the resentful and befuddled mind of the Deputy Leader there took shape a daring plan. He himself would fly to Britain to negotiate peace. Delivering an agreement would restore him to Hitler's favour and secure Germany's rear for the forth-coming attack on the Soviet Union. Despite Hitler's explicit orders to the contrary, Hess continued to hone his flying skills in secret. He had a Messerschmitt Me110 specially prepared for his use, and he obtained maps and weather charts for Germany, the North Sea and northern Britain. At six in the evening on 10 May 1941, he put on a fur-lined flying-suit, took off from the airfield of the Messerschmitt works in

Augsburg and headed north-west, in the direction of the British Isles.[146]

Five hours later, Hess parachuted out of the plane near Glasgow, leaving it to continue, pilotless, until eventually it burst into flames and crashed. He landed, somewhat awkwardly, in a field. Approached by a local farmhand, he said his name was Alfred Horn, and he had a message for the Duke of Hamilton, whose home was in the vicinity. The aristocrat had been a member of the Anglo-German Society before the war, and Haushofer's son Albrecht had told Hess that he would be an important addressee for peace overtures. The advice showed both Haushofer's ignorance and Hess's gullibility. In fact, Hamilton was not a particularly significant political figure in British politics. By this time a wing-commander in the Royal Air Force, he was extremely unlikely to act as a willing conduit for German peace overtures. Summoned in response to Hess's request, Hamilton arrived at the Home Guard hut where Hess had been taken and was quickly convinced that he was face-to-face with the Deputy Leader of the Nazi Party. After the stress of his daring flight, Hess's mental confusion was such that he made no real attempt to discuss a separate peace with the Duke, and indeed he could think of nothing more than to repeat Hitler's vague 'peace offer' made the previous July. The diplomat Ivone Kirkpatrick, who had served in the Berlin Embassy from 1933 to 1938 and spoke good German, was sent to Scotland to interrogate Hess, and managed to extract a bit more information. Hess, he said in his report, 'had come here without the knowledge of Hitler in order to convince responsible persons that since England could not win the war, the wisest course was to make peace now.' Hess knew Hitler better than most, and he could assure Kirkpatrick that the German Leader had no designs on the British Empire. This was feeble stuff. 'Hess,' concluded Kirkpatrick, 'does not seem . . . to be in the near counsels of the German government as regards operations.'[147] For the rest of the war, Hess was kept imprisoned in various places, including the Tower of London. His self-imposed 'mission' had been completely pointless. It reflected nothing but his own mental confusion and lack of realism.[148]

Hitler himself knew nothing about Hess's flight until one of the Deputy Leader's adjutants, Karl-Heinz Pintsch, arrived at the Berghof towards midday on 11 May 1941 to deliver a letter in which Hess told the Nazi Leader of his intentions and informed him that he would be in England by the time he read it. If he disapproved of the venture, Hess wrote, then Hitler could simply write him off as a madman. No news had yet leaked out from the British. Appalled, Hitler immediately summoned Bormann and told Göring over the telephone to come straight away from his castle near Nuremberg. 'Something dreadful has happened,' he said.[149] Desperately worried in case the British should break the news first, thus suggesting to Mussolini and Germany's other allies that he was trying to make a separate peace with Britain behind their backs, Hitler sanctioned a radio announcement that was broadcast at eight in the evening on 11 May 1941, taking up Hess's own suggestion and ascribing the flight to the Deputy Leader's mental derangement and hallucination. The broadcast told the German people that Hess had flown off towards the British Isles but had probably crashed en route. On 13 May 1941, the BBC reported Hess's arrival in Scotland and his subsequent capture. In the meantime, on the advice of Otto Dietrich, Hitler's press chief, a second announcement had been put out over German radio underlining Hess's delusional state and mental confusion. Goebbels, arriving at the Berghof later in the day, thought this only compounded the disaster. 'At the moment,' he wrote in his diary, 'the whole thing is still really confused.' 'The Leader is completely crushed,' he added. 'What a spectacle for the world: a mentally deranged second man after the Leader.'[150]

As soon as he received the news of Hess's defection, Hitler abolished the post of Deputy Leader and renamed Hess's office the Party Chancellery, to be led as before by Bormann, but now under the formal supervision of Hess's former éminence grise. This move considerably enhanced Bormann's power. There remained the problem of what spin to put on the event. Hitler had already summoned all the Reich Leaders and Regional Party Leaders to the Berghof. On 13 May 1941 he repeated to them that Hess was mentally ill. In an emotional appeal to their loyalty, he declared that Hess had betrayed and deceived him. At the end of the speech, as Hans Frank, who was present, told his staff in the General Government a few days later: 'The Leader was more completely shattered than I have ever experienced him to have been.'[151] As Goebbels had thought, the idea that his deputy had been mentally deranged for many years did not cast a particularly favourable light upon either him or his regime. Many Party members refused to believe the news at first. 'Depression and uncertainty' were the prevailing feelings noted by Nazi surveillance operatives.[152] 'Nobody believes he was ill,' reported a local official in the rural Bavarian district of Ebermannstadt.[153] No one to whom Field Marshal Fedor von Bock spoke about the 'mysterious story' believed the official account either.[154] 'Why doesn't the Leader say any-thing about the Hess affair?', asked Victor Klemperer's friend Annemarie Köhler. 'He really ought to say something. What excuse will he use – Hess has been sick for years? But then he shouldn't be Hitler's deputy.'[155] Lore Walb, now studying history at Heidelberg University, agreed. 'If he had really been ill for a long time before (mentally ill, from time to time?), then why did he keep his leading position?' she asked.[156] Most people seem to have felt sympathy for Hitler at his deputy's betrayal.[157] They relieved their anxiety, bewilderment and disorientation by telling jokes. 'So you're the madman?' one joke had Churchill saying to Hess as he arrives in the Prime Minister's office for an interview. 'No,' Hess replies, 'only his deputy.' 'British Press Notice: "Today we learned that Hess is indeed insane – he wants to go back to Germany."' 'That our government is mad is something we've known for a long time,' Berliners were reported as saying, 'but that they admit it – that's something new!'[158]

II

The week or so he was forced to spend dealing with the Hess affair was an unwelcome distraction for Hitler. By the middle of May 1941, however, the Nazi Leader was turning his mind back to his plans for the creation of 'living-space' in Eastern Europe. His vision for the future of this vast area, stretching through Poland, the Ukraine and Belarus across wide tracts of European Russia and down into the Caucasus, was articulated most unrestrainedly in the monologues to which he subjected his lunch- and dinner-companions. From early July 1941 onwards, they were noted down on Bormann's orders, and with Hitler's agreement, by a Party official, Heinrich Heim, sitting unobtrusively in a corner of the room (for some periods he was replaced by another junior official, Henry Picker). The notes were later dictated to a stenographer, then handed to Bormann, who corrected them and filed them away for posterity. When Hitler was dead, they would be published, and his successors in the thousand-year Reich would be able to consult them for guidance on what their great Leader had thought on a whole range of political and ideological issues.[159] Despite their tedious repetitiousness, they are indeed valuable as a guide to Hitler's thinking on broad, general issues of policy and ideology. His views at this level changed little over the years, so what he was saying in the summer of 1941 give a good idea of what he must already have been thinking in the spring.

In July 1941, Hitler amused himself by painting castles in the air for his guests on the subject of the future of Eastern Europe. Once conquest was complete, he said, the Germans would annex vast masses of territory for their own racial survival and expansion. 'The law of selection justifies this incessant struggle, by allowing the survival of the fittest.'[160] 'It's inconceivable that a higher people should painfully exist on a soil too narrow for it, whilst amorphous masses, which contribute nothing to civilisation, occupy infinite tracts of a soil that is one of the richest in the world.'[161] The Crimea and the southern Ukraine would become 'an exclusively German colony', he said. The existing inhabitants would be 'pushed out'.[162] As for the rest of the east, a handful of Englishmen had controlled millions of Indians, he said, and so it would be with the Germans in Russia:

The German colonist ought to live on handsome, spacious farms. The German services will be lodged in marvellous buildings, the governors in palaces ... Around the city, to a depth of thirty to forty kilometres, we shall have a belt of handsome villages connected by the best roads. What exists beyond that will be another world, in which we mean to let the Russians live as they like. It is merely necessary that we should rule them. In the event of a revolution, we shall only have to drop a few bombs on their cities, and the affair will be liquidated.[163]

A dense network of roads would be constructed, he went on, 'studded along their whole length with German towns', and around these towns 'our colonists will settle'. Colonists of German blood would come from all over Western Europe and even America. There would be twenty million of them by the 1960s, while Russian towns would be allowed to 'fall to pieces'.[164]

'In a hundred years,' Hitler declared, 'our language will be the language of Europe.' It was not least for this reason that he had replaced Gothic lettering with Roman lettering in all official correspondence and publications in the autumn of 1940.[165] Some months later, he returned to his vision for the new German east. New railways would have to be built to ensure 'rapid communication' between major centres all the way to Constantinople:

I envisage through-trains covering the distances at an average speed of two hundred kilometres an hour, and our present rolling-stock is obviously unsuitable for the purpose. Larger carriages will be required – probably double-deckers, which will give the passengers on the upper deck an opportunity of admiring the landscape. This will presumably entail the construction of a very much broader-gauge permanent way than that at present in use, and the number of lines must be doubled in order to be able to cope with any intensification of traffic ... This alone will enable us to realise our plans for the exploitation of the Eastern territories.[166]

The new railway system would be augmented by an equally ambitious network of six-lane motorways. 'Of what importance will the thousand-kilometre stretch to the Crimea be,' he asked, 'when we can cover it at eighty kilometres an hour along the motorway and do the whole distance easily in two days!' He envisaged a time when it would be possible to go 'from Klagenfurt to Trondheim and from Hamburg to the Crimea along a Reich Motorway'.[167]

As this scenario developed, Russian society would be left far behind. 'In comparison with Russia,' he declared, 'even Poland looked like a civilised country.'[168] The Germans would show 'no remorse' towards the indigenous inhabitants. 'We're not going to play at children's nurses; we're absolutely without obligations as far as these people are concerned.' They would not be provided with medical or educational facilities; not only would they be denied inoculation and other preventive measures, but they should be persuaded that vaccinations were positively dangerous to their health.[169] Eventually Russian society, these views implied, would wither away and disappear, along with other Slavic societies in Belarus, the Ukraine and Poland. In a hundred years' time, the Slavic population of Eastern Europe would have been replaced by 'millions of German peasants' living on the land.[170] What this would mean in more concrete terms was already clear by the beginning of 1941. The aim of the war against the Soviet Union, SS chief Heinrich Himmler told SS leaders at the Wewelsburg Castle in January 1941, was to reduce the Slavic population by 30 million, a figure that was later repeated by other Nazi leaders, including Hermann Göring, who told the Italian Foreign Minister Ciano on 15 November 1941: 'This year, 20–30 million people in Russia will starve.'[171] The 30 million, not just Russians but also other inhabitants of the Soviet Union in areas controlled by the Germans, were to die of hunger, then, and not over the long term, but almost immediately. Soviet cities, many of them created by Stalin's brutal forced industrialization in the 1930, were to be starved out of existence, while practically the entire food production of the conquered areas was to be used to feed the invading German armies and maintain nutritional standards at home, so that the malnourishment and starvation that (Hitler believed) had played such a baleful part in the collapse of the German home front in the First World War would not be repeated in the Second. This 'hunger plan' was developed above all by Herbert Backe, the State Secretary in the Agriculture Ministry, a hardline Nazi who had worked with Reich Agriculture Minister Richard Walther Darré, the leading Nazi ideologue of the peasantry, for many years and was on good personal terms with Heydrich. But it was also agreed by General Georg Thomas, the leading arms procurement figure in the central administration of the armed forces. Meeting with General Thomas on 2 May 1941, the State Secretaries of the relevant ministries agreed that the armed forces would have to live off the resources of the conquered lands in the east, and concluded that 'without doubt, umpteen million people will starve if what is necessary for us is taken out of the country'.[172]

These ideas found concrete expression in the so-called 'General Plan for the East', which Himmler commissioned from the office of the Reich Commissioner for the Strengthening of the German Race on 21 June 1941. The first version of the plan was handed to Himmler on 15 July 1941 by Professor Konrad Meyer, the academic expert in the office who specialized in settlement policy. After a good deal of discussion and further refinement, it was finalized in May 1942, approved by Hitler, and formally adopted by the Reich Security Head Office in July 1942. The General Plan for the East, now the official policy of the Third Reich, proposed to remove between 80 and 85 per cent of the Polish population, 64 per cent of the Ukrainian and 75 per cent of the Belarussian, expelling them further east or allowing them to perish from disease and malnutrition. Not counting the Jewish population of these areas, the Plan thus envisaged the forcible uprooting of at least 31 million people from their homes, in what would no doubt be a murderously violent process of dispossession; some estimates, taking into account projected population increases, put the number at no fewer than 45 million. Not only the Polish territories incorporated into Germany, but also the General

Government, Latvia and Estonia and indeed the greater part of East-Central Europe would become completely German within twenty years. The space vacated by the Slavs would be occupied by 10 million Germans. The borders of Germany would in effect be extended a thousand kilometres to the east.[173]

Himmler and the SS presented this as the resumption and completion of what they saw as the civilizing mission of the Crusading Teutonic Knights of the Middle Ages. But it was to be a mission updated and modernized to suit the conditions of the twentieth century. The new German settlers, Meyer proclaimed, would not be hidebound tradition-alists but progressive farmers, equipped with the latest machinery, dedicated to creating an agricultural wonderland that would keep the new, vastly extended Germany well fed and supplied. They would own farms much like those of the Reich Entailed Farmers back home.[174] A third of them would be retired SS officers, providing an ideological and military underpinning to the whole enterprise. And they would be joined by labourers from the overcrowded peasant regions of the German south-west, since native labour would no longer be available. The Plan took into account Hitler's vision of large, modern towns and industrial centres linked by advanced means of communication, too: it aimed at a farming population little more than a third of the total in the new regions of German settlement. Meyer put the total investment required to realize the Plan at no less than 40 billion Reichsmarks, a sum Himmler revised upwards to 67 billion, equivalent to two-thirds of Germany's Gross Domestic Product in 1941, or half a million Reichsmarks for every square kilometre of the newly settled regions. This gigantic sum would be raised from a variety of sources: the state budget, SS funds, local authorities, the railways and the private sector. The ambition of the Plan was simply staggering. It proposed destruction on a scale never before contemplated in human history.[175]

The invasion of the Soviet Union would transfer to a vastly bigger area the brutal and murderous policies that had already been implemented in Poland since the beginning of the war: ethnic deportation and resettle-ment, population transfer, Germanization, cultural genocide and the reduction of the Slavic population by expropriation, starvation and disease. But it was to be even more radical than the occupation of Poland. Hitler, the Nazis and most of the leading generals saw Poles as little more than Slavic subhumans, but they saw the Soviet Union as a threat, since its Slav inhabitants were led by what they regarded as ruthless and cunning leaders of the 'Jewish-Bolshevik' world conspiracy to undermine the German race and German civilization. While he had nothing but contempt for the Poles and their leaders, Hitler repeatedly expressed his personal admiration for Stalin, 'one of the most extraordinary figures in world history', as he called him in July 1941.[176] 'Stalin, too,' Hitler told his dinner companions a year later, 'must command our unconditional respect. In his own way he is a hell of a fellow! He knows his models, Genghiz Khan and the others, very well . . .'[177] 'Stalin,' said Hitler on another occasion, 'is half beast, half giant . . . If we had given him another ten years, Europe would have been swept away, as it was at the time of the Huns.'[178] Thus, Hitler told army chiefs on 17 March 1941, 'The intelligentsia deployed by Stalin must be annihilated.'[179] Just as the Polish intelligentsia had been killed, now the same fate was to befall its Soviet counterpart. On 30 March 1941 Hitler elaborated on this view in a speech the essential points of which were noted down by General Halder. The coming war would be no ordinary war: 'Struggle of two world-views against one another. Annihilatory judgement against Bolshevism, it's the same as asocial criminality. Communism tremendous danger for the future. We must abandon the standpoint of soldierly comradeship. The Communist is first and last no comrade. This is a war of annihilation.'[180] Political commissars in the Red Army in particular were to be treated not as soldiers but as criminals and dealt with accordingly. Hitler demanded the 'annihilation of the Bolshevik commissars and the Communist intelligentsia . . . The conflict,' he warned, 'will be very different from the conflict in the west.'[181]

III

On 19 May 1941, guidelines issued to the troops for the invasion demanded 'ruthless and energetic action against Bolshevik agitators, irregulars, saboteurs, Jews and total elimination of all active and passive resistance'.[182] The inclusion of 'Jews' as a separate category in this list was of enormous significance. Here was the German army being given licence, in effect, to kill Jews wherever it encountered them, on the assumption that all of them were part of the Bolshevik resistance. The conquest of Poland had already demonstrated the murderous and often sadistic violence regular German troops would visit on 'Eastern Jews'. The invasion of the Soviet Union was to reproduce this violence on a vastly larger scale. The inclusion of the deliberate murder of prisoners in the invasion plan was underlined on 6 June 1941, when Field Marshal Wilhelm Keitel, head of the Combined Armed Forces Supreme Command, issued an order that all political commissars in the Red Army, whom he characterized as the 'originators of barbaric, Asiatic methods of fighting', were to be shot immediately on capture.[183]

By the time of the invasion, the kind of doubts that had assailed senior officers like Johannes Blaskowitz in Poland had long since been quelled. None of the generals raised any open objections to Hitler's orders. The traditional anti-Communism and antisemitism of the officer corps had been augmented by years of incessant Nazi propaganda and indoctrination. The experience of Poland had hardened them to the idea that Slavs and Jews were to be repressed in the most brutal manner possible. Only a very few, such as Field Marshal Fedor von Bock or Lieutenant-Colonel Henning von Tresckow, quietly instructed their officers to ignore the order to kill commissars and civilians as incompatible with international law or dangerous to discipline, or both. The vast majority of the generals transmitted the orders further down the line.[184] Already on 27 March 1941, before Hitler's speech, Field Marshal von Brauchitsch, Commander-in-Chief of the Army, had issued an instruction that the troops 'must be clear about the fact that the conflict is being fought between one race and another, and proceed with the necessary rigour'.[185] The soldiers were instructed accordingly, in a propaganda effort of considerable dimensions that included the inevitable reference to 'the struggle against World Jewry, which [is striving] to arouse all the peoples of the world against Germany'.[186] The normal rules were set aside. Officers were not just officers but also leaders in a racial struggle against 'Jewish Bolshevism'. As General Erich Hoepner wrote in the marching orders for his troops on 2 May 1941:

The war against Russia is a fundamental part of the German people's struggle for existence. It is the old struggle of the Germans against the Slavs, the defence of European culture against the Muscovite, Asiatic deluge, the defence against Jewish Bolshevism. This struggle must aim to smash the Russia of today into rubble, and as a consequence it must be carried out with unprecedented harshness.[187]

Similar orders were issued by a variety of other generals as well, includ-ing Walter von Reichenau, Erich von Manstein and Karl-Heinrich von Stülpnagel (later a member of the military resistance).[188]

Discussions between the Army Quartermaster-General Horst Wagner and SS Security Service chief Reinhard Heydrich resulted in a military order issued on 28 April 1941 giving the SS the power to act on its own initiative in carrying out the Commissar Order and similar 'security' tasks behind the lines. Four SS Security Service Task Forces, A, B, C and D, numbering 600 to 1,000 men apiece, were set up to follow the army into Russia in four zones running from north to south. Behind them came smaller groups of SS and police. Finally, in areas well behind the front line placed under civilian control, battalions of SS soldiers were to provide for 'security'. The police units consisted of 23 battalions with 420 officers and 11,640 men, selected from volunteer applicants and subjected to ideological training by the SS. Most of them were in their thirties, older than the average soldier. A substantial number of the officers had been Free Corps soldiers in the violent years of the early Weimar Republic. Many of them were long-term policemen, drawn from the decidedly right-wing 'Order Police', formed in the Weimar Republic to deal with civil unrest, mostly from paramilitaries on the left. Some of the men were Nazi brownshirts or ethnic-German 'self-protection' militiamen from Poland. A small number of the battalions were drawn from police reservists. All were volunteers, carefully screened by the SS and subjected to a process of indoctrination that included a heavy dose of antisemitism. They were specially selected for service in the Soviet Union. Most of them were recruited from the lower middle class; it was assumed that the Order Police members had small businesses which their wives could carry on in their absence. From the middle of May 1941 they were put into training at the Border Police School in Pretzsch, near Leipzig, where they were subjected to ideological training that would amply reinforce their existing prejudices against Slavs and Jews. These were, therefore, despite claims to the contrary by later historians, neither 'ordinary men' nor 'ordinary Germans'.[189]

On 2 July 1941 the Task Forces and police battalions were told to execute all Communist functionaries, people's commissars, 'Jews in party or state positions' and 'other radical elements (saboteurs, propa-gandists, snipers, assassins, agitators, etc.)'.[190] The order to shoot only one particular category of Jews seemed at first sight to signal a more restricted approach than the one the army had been ordered to take. It directed the Task Forces' attention in the first place to those identified by Hitler as the Communist intelligentsia and the Jewish elite, two categories which he and Heydrich and most other leading Nazis as well as many army generals considered to be more or less identical. And it targeted only men, much as was initially the case in Serbia. However, women and children were not explicitly ruled out. Moreover, the identification of Jews with Communists was encouraged not only by years of antisemitic propaganda but also by the fact that Jews were indeed the largest single national group in key parts of the Soviet elite, including the secret police, a fact that had never been hidden from general view. All of them without exception, at least until the Nazi invasion and its accompanying antisemitic atrocities, had long since repudiated their Jewish ethnic and religious background. They identified completely with the supranational, secular ideology of Bolshevism. Beyond this, the inclusion of ill-defined categories such as 'propagandists' and 'agitators' was an open invitation to kill all male Jews, since Nazi ideology considered in principle that *all* Jewish men fell into these groups. Finally, the treatment of the Jewish population of Poland not only by the SS but also by the army strongly suggested that the Task Forces and police battalions would from the beginning not be too choosy about which Jews they shot, or how many.[191]

IV

By the early hours of 22 June 1941, the months of planning were finally over. At 3.15 in the morning, just before dawn on the shortest night of the year, a huge artillery barrage opened up along a front stretching more than a thousand miles southwards from the Baltic. More than 3 million German soldiers, with another half a million troops from Romania and other allied countries, crossed the Soviet border at numerous points from the Finnish border in the north all the way down to the Black Sea hinterland in the south. They were equipped with 3,600 tanks, 600,000 motor vehicles and 700,000 field guns and other artillery. Some 2,700 aircraft, more than half the entire strength of the German air force, had been assembled behind the lines. As the first motorized ground assaults began, 500 bombers, 270 dive-bombers and 480 fighter planes flew overhead and onwards, to wreak destruction on Soviet military airfields. This was the largest invading force assembled in the whole of human history to this point. The military aim was to trap and destroy the Soviet armies in a massive series of encircling movements, pinning them back against the line of the rivers Dnieper and Dvina, some 500 kilometres from the invasion point.[192] On the first day alone, German air strikes against 66 Soviet airfields destroyed more than 1,200 Soviet aircraft, almost all of them before they had had a chance to take off. Within the first week the German air force had damaged over 4,000 Soviet planes beyond repair. Bombing raids were also carried out on a range of major cities from Bialystok to Tallinn, Kiev to Riga. With the command of the skies assured, the three main army groups pushed forward with their tanks, supported by dive-bombers and followed up by fast-moving infantry, smashing through the Red Army defences, and inflicting huge losses on the ill-prepared Soviet troops. In the first week of the invasion, Army Group Centre broke decisively through Soviet defences, encircling the Red Army troops in a series of battles. It had already taken 600,000 prisoners by the end of the second week in July. By this time, more than 3,000 Soviet artillery pieces and 6,000 tanks had been captured or destroyed, or simply abandoned by the troops. 89 out of 164 divisions in the Red Army had been put out of action. German forces took Smolensk and pushed on towards Moscow. Army Group North seized Latvia, Lithuania and much of Estonia and advanced on Leningrad (St Petersburg). Army Group South was driving towards Kiev, overrunning the agricultural and industrial regions of the Ukraine. Finnish troops, aided by German units, cut off the port of Murmansk and made towards Leningrad from the north, while German and Romanian troops entered Bessarabia in the far south.[193]

Surprise and speed were crucial in throwing the Soviet forces into disarray. The German troops were marching up to 50 kilometres a day, sometimes more. The invasion, wrote General Gotthard Heinrici to his wife on 11 July 1941, 'for us means running, running until our tongues hang out, always running, running, running'.[194] The soldier Albert Neuhaus was astonished by the 'columns of vehicles that roll through here day after day, hour after hour. I can tell you,' he wrote to his wife on 25 June 1941, 'such a thing happens only once in the whole world. One grasps one's head again and again and asks oneself where all these endless millions of vehicles come from.'[195] In the dry summer heat, the

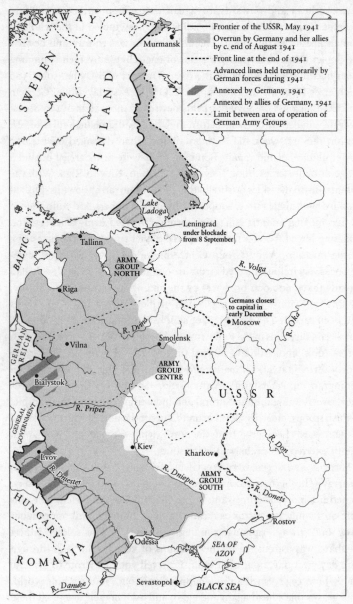

9. Operation Barbarossa and the Eastern Front, 1941

huge German armoured columns threw up vast clouds of choking dust. 'Even after a short while,' wrote one soldier already on the first day of the invasion, 'the dust is lying finger-thick on my face and uniform.'[196] General Heinrici found himself driving along roads 'on which you wade ankle-deep in dust. Every step, every moving vehicle, raises up impenetrable clouds of it. The march routes are characterized by yellow-brown clouds that hang before the sky like long veils.'[197] As the headlong advance continued, the Red Army collapsed in chaos all along the front. Its communications were severed, transport broke down, ammunition and equipment, fuel, spare parts and much more besides quickly ran out. Unprepared for the invasion, officers could not even guess where the Germans would strike next, and there was often no artillery available to blunt the impact of the incoming German tanks. Many of the Red Army's own tanks, from the BT to the T-26 and 28, were obsolescent: more of the total of 23,000 tanks deployed by the Red Army in 1941 were lost through breakdowns than to enemy action. Radio communications had not been updated since the Finnish war and were coded in such a basic manner that it was all too easy for Germans listening in to decrypt them. Worst of all, perhaps, medical facilities were wholly inadequate to deal with the vast numbers of dead and treat the scores of thousands of injured. In the absence of proper military planning, officers could think of little else to do than attack the Germans head-on, with predictably disastrous results. An orderly retreat was made almost impossible by the Germans' prior destruction of roads, railways and bridges behind the lines. Desertion rates rocketed in the Red Army as demoralized soldiers fled in confusion and despair. In a mere three days in late June 1941, the Soviet secret police caught nearly 700 deserters fleeing from the battle on the south-western front. 'The retreat has caused blind panic,' as the head of the Belarus Communist Party wrote to Stalin on 3 September 1941, and 'the soldiers are tired to death, even sleeping under artillery fire . . . At the first bombardment, the formations collapse, many just run away to the woods, the whole area of woodland in the front-line region is full of refugees like this. Many throw away their weapons and go home.'[198]

Some idea of the depth of the disaster can be gauged from the diary of Nikolai Moskvin, a Soviet political commissar, which records a rapid transition from optimism ('we'll win for sure,' he wrote on 24 June 1941) to despair a few weeks later ('what am I to say to the boys?' he asked himself gloomily on 23 July 1941: 'We keep retreating').[199] On 15 July 1941 he had already shot the first deserters from his unit, but they kept on fleeing, and at the end of the month, after being wounded, he admitted: 'I am on the verge of a complete moral collapse.'[200] His unit got lost because it did not have any maps, and most of the men were killed in a German attack while Moskvin, unable to move, was hiding in the woods with two companions, waiting to be rescued. Some peasants found him, nursed him back to health, and conscripted him into helping with the harvest. As he got to know them, he discovered they had no loyalty to the Stalinist system. Their main purpose was to stay alive. After battles, they rushed on to the field to loot the corpses. What in any case would loyalty to Stalin have brought them? In August 1941, Moskvin encountered some Red Army soldiers who had escaped from a German prisoner-of-war camp. 'They say there's no shelter, no water, that people are dying from hunger and disease, that many are without proper clothes or shoes.' Few, he wrote, had given a thought to what imprisonment by the Germans would mean. The reality was worse than anyone could imagine.[201]

In the light of the orders it had received, the German army had no interest in keeping hundreds of thousands of Soviet prisoners of war alive. Hitler and the army leadership had already ordered the Soviet political commissars who accompanied the Red Army to be shot on sight, and the commanders on the ground carried out these orders, often handing them over to the SS for 'special treatment'. Tens of thousands were taken to concentration camps in Germany and killed there by firing squads.[202] During the first weeks, many ordinary troops were also shot immediately on capture as well. 'We are only taking very few prisoners now,' wrote Albert Neuhaus to his wife on 27 June 1941, 'and you can imagine what that means.'[203] There was, as many soldiers reported in their letters, 'no pardon' for Red Army troops who gave themselves up in the first weeks of the campaign.[204] The fate of those who were spared was not much better. In October 1941 Zygmunt Klukowski witnessed a column of 15,000 Soviet prisoners of war passing through his district. He was shocked by what he saw:

They all looked like skeletons, just shadows of human beings, barely moving. I have never in my life seen anything like this. Men were falling to the street; the stronger ones were carrying others, holding them up by their arms. They looked like starved animals, not like people. They were fighting for scraps of apples in the gutter, not paying any attention to the Germans, who would beat them with rubber truncheons. Some crossed themselves and knelt, begging for food. Soldiers from the convoy beat them without mercy. They beat not only prisoners but also people who stood by and tried to pass them some food. After the macabre unit passed by, several horse-drawn wagons carried prisoners who were unable to walk. This unbelievable treatment of human beings is only possible under German ethics.[205]

The following day, as another column of prisoners shuffled through, local people placed bread, apples and other items of food on the pavements for them. 'Even though the soldiers from the convoy started shooting at them while they fought for food,' Klukowski noted, 'the prisoners did not pay any attention to the Germans.' After forcing the local people to remove the food, the Germans subsequently agreed it could be loaded on a cart and distributed to the prisoners. Klukowski thought the prisoners looked 'more like the skeletons of animals than humans'.[206]

Many Soviet prisoners of war died from hunger and exhaustion on their way to the camps. Field Marshal Walter von Reichenau ordered his guards 'to shoot all prisoners who collapse'. Some were transported by rail, but only open freight cars were available for the purpose. The results, particularly as winter set in, were catastrophic. Closed wagons were only deployed on 22 November 1941 after 1,000 out of 5,000 prisoners on a train transport from Army Group Centre froze to death on the journey. Even so, the next month an official German report noted that 'between 25 and 70 per cent of prisoners' died en route to the camps, not least because no one troubled to give them any food. The camps that were erected behind the lines hardly deserved the name. Many were just open fields crudely fenced in by barbed wire. Almost no preparations had been made for dealing with such huge numbers of prisoners, and nothing was done to supply the prisoners with food or medication. One prisoner who escaped and made his way back to the Soviet lines told his police interrogators that he had been penned in a camp in Poland consisting of twelve blocks each housing between 1,500 and 2,000 prisoners. The German guards used the inmates as target practice and set their dogs on them, placing bets on which dog would inflict the worst injuries. The prisoners were starving. When one of them died, the others fell upon the corpse and devoured it. On one occasion, twelve men were shot for cannibalism. All of them were lice-ridden, and typhus spread rapidly. Their light summer uniforms were totally inadequate to protect them from the bitter winter cold. By February 1942 only 3,000 out of the original 80,000 were left alive.[207]

The same experience was repeated in other camps behind the line. Visiting Minsk on 10 July 1941, Xaver Dorsch, a civil servant in the Todt Organization, found that the army had set up a camp for 100,000 prisoners of war and 40,000 civilians, almost the entire male population of the city, 'in an area roughly the size of the Wilhelmplatz' in Berlin:

The prisoners are packed so tightly together in this area that they can hardly move and have to relieve themselves where they stand. They are guarded by a company-strong unit of active soldiers. The small size of the guard unit means that it can only control the camp by using the most brutal level of force. The problem of feeding the prisoners of war is virtually insoluble. Some of them have been without food for six to eight days. Their hunger has led to a deadly apathy in which they only have one obsession left: to get something to eat . . . The only language possible for the weak guard unit, which has to carry out its duties day and night without relief, is that of the gun, and they make ruthless use of it.[208]

Over 300,000 Red Army prisoners had died by the end of 1941. Wilm Hosenfeld was shocked by the way in which the Russian prisoners were left to starve, a policy he found 'so repulsive, inhumane and so naively stupid that one can only be deeply ashamed that such a thing can be done by us'.[209] The inhabitants of the surrounding areas offered to help feed the prisoners, but the German army banned them from doing so.[210] Franz Halder, Chief of the Army General Staff, noted on 14 November 1941 that 'numerous prisoners are dying of starvation every day. Dreadful impressions, but it does not seem possible to do anything to help them at the moment.'[211]

It was practical rather than moral considerations that led to an eventual change of policy. By the end of October 1941, the German authorities had begun to realize that Soviet prisoners could be used as forced labour, and measures were taken to provide proper, though still barely adequate, food, clothing and shelter for them.[212] Many (though not all) were put into disused factories and prisons. A large number were still living in dugouts in January 1942, however. Conditions deteriorated again in 1943, though they never reached the absolute low point of the first months of the war; by this time, there were enough German prisoners in Soviet hands for the German armed forces leadership to be worried about reprisals. Over the whole course of the war, German forces took some 5.7 million Soviet prisoners. Official German records showed that 3,300,000 of them had perished by the time the war was over, or some 58 per cent of the total. The actual number was probably a good deal higher. By comparison 356,687 out of about 2 million German prisoners taken by the Red Army, mostly in the later stages of the war, did not survive, a death rate of almost 18 per cent. This was far in excess of the mortality rates of British, French and other servicemen in German captivity, which were below 2 per cent until the last chaotic months of the war, not to mention those of German servicemen taken prisoner by the Western Allies. But the high mortality rates of German prisoners in Soviet camps reflected the terrible conditions of life in the Soviet Union, and in the Gulag camp system in general, following the massive destruction wrought by the war, and the bad harvests of the immediate postwar period, rather than any particular spirit of revenge towards the Germans on the part of their captors. Indeed, there is no evidence that German prisoners were treated any differently from other prisoners in Soviet camps, except in the intensity with which they were subjected as 'fascists' to programmes of political re-education.[213]

By contrast, Red Army prisoners in German hands perished as a direct consequence of Nazi racial doctrines, shared by the overwhelming majority of the German officer corps, which wrote off 'Slavs' as expendable subhumans, not worth keeping alive while there were hungry German mouths to feed.[214] This was, in a sense, the first stage of the implementation of the 'General Plan for the East'. Only a few German officers protested against the maltreatment of Soviet prisoners of war. One such was Field Marshal Fedor von Bock, leading Army Group Centre. Bock noted on 20 October 1941: 'Terrible is the impression of tens of thousands of Russian prisoners of war who, scarcely guarded, are on the march towards Smolensk. These unfortunate people are tottering along weary unto death and half-starving, and many of them have collapsed along the way, exhausted or dead. I talk to the armies about this,' he added, 'but assistance is scarcely possible.' And even Bock, the epitome of the traditionally 'correct' Prussian officer, was more concerned in the end with preventing such prisoners from escaping and joining the partisan groups formed by the thousands of Red Army soldiers who had been trapped behind the lines by the rapid advance of the German forces. 'They must be supervised and guarded more rigorously,' he concluded after seeing the bedraggled Russian prisoners, 'otherwise we will be nurturing the partisan movement more and more.'[215] Disquiet amongst senior officers like Bock was quelled by Hitler's insistence that the Soviet prisoners of war were not to be treated as ordinary soldiers but as racial and ideological enemies; the junior officers who had them in their charge on a daily basis had few qualms about seeing them die.[216] Those prisoners who were eventually liberated and returned to the Soviet Union – well over one and a half million – had to face extensive discrimination following an order issued by Stalin in August 1941 equating surrender with treason. Many of them were despatched to the labour camps of the Gulag after being screened by Soviet military counter-intelligence. Despite attempts after Stalin's death by top military leader Marshal Georgi Zhukov to end discrimination against former prisoners of war, they were not formally rehabilitated until 1994.[217]

V

At 3.30 a.m. on 22 June 1941 the Chief of the Red Army General Staff, Georgi Zhukov, telephoned Stalin's dacha to rouse the Soviet leader from his sleep. The Germans, he told him, had begun shelling Red Army positions along the frontier. Stalin refused to believe that a full-scale invasion was under way. Surely, he told a small gathering of civilian and military leaders in Moscow later in the morning, Hitler did not know about it. There must be a conspiracy among the leaders of the German armed forces. It was only when the German Ambassador, Count Friedrich Werner von der Schulenburg, met Foreign Minister Molotov in the Kremlin to hand over the German declaration of war that Stalin recognized he had been duped by Hitler. Initially shocked, embarrassed and disoriented, Stalin soon pulled himself together. On 23 June 1941 he worked at his desk in the Kremlin from 3.20 in the morning to 6.25 in the evening, gathering information and making the necessary arrangements for the creation of a Supreme Command to take charge of operations. As the days went by, he became increasingly dispirited by the scale and speed of the German advance. At the end of June, he left for his dacha, saying, in his inimitably coarse way, 'Everything's lost. I give up. Lenin founded our state and we've fucked it up.' He made no address to the Soviet people, he did not talk to his subordinates, he did not even answer the phone. German planes, indeed, dropped leaflets over the Red Army lines claiming that he was dead. When a delegation from the Politburo arrived at the dacha, they found Stalin slumped in an armchair. 'Why have you come?' he asked. With a thrill of terror, two members of the delegation, Mikoyan and Beria, realized he thought they had come to arrest him.[218]

Convinced that the Soviet system was in such bad shape that it needed only one decisive push for it to fall to pieces, Hitler and the leading generals had staked everything on the swift defeat of the Red Army. Like their predecessors in 1914, they expected the campaign to be over well before Christmas. They did not hold major formations in reserve or make any provisions for the replacement of men and equipment lost on the front. Many of the pilots who fought in the campaign expected to be transferred back to the west to fight the British by the beginning of September. The stunning military victories of the first weeks convinced them that they were right. The Soviet armies had surely been completely destroyed. Hitler shared in the general euphoria. On 23 June 1941 he travelled from Berlin to his new field headquarters behind the front, at Rastenburg, in East Prussia. A large compound located deep in the woods, with its own railway spur, along which, from time to time, Göring would trundle in on his luxurious personal train, the headquarters had been under construction since the previous autumn. The compound contained a number of bunkers and huts, hidden from their surroundings and camouflaged from the air. There were barracks for the guards, dining facilities and conference rooms. An airstrip allowed light aircraft to ferry people to and from the headquarters when haste was needed. Two other fenced-off complexes not far away were used by the armed forces chiefs and planning staffs. Hitler called the headquarters the 'Wolf's Lair', a reference to his nickname in the 1920s. It was here that he received briefings from the leaders of the armed forces, and engaged in the lengthy lunch- and dinner-time monologues that Bormann had ordered to be noted down for the benefit of posterity. Hitler did not intend to stay there for more than a few weeks. 'The war in the east was in the main already won,' he told Goebbels on 8 July 1941.[219] He was doing no more than echoing the opinion of the military.

On 3 July 1941, Chief of the Army General Staff Franz Halder, noting that the Red Army appeared to have no more reserves to throw into battle, had already given vent to his euphoria. 'So it's really not saying too much,' he noted in his diary, 'if I claim that the campaign against Russia has been won in 14 days.'[220]

On 16 July 1941, therefore, Hitler held a meeting to make arrangements for the governance of the conquered territories. In nominal overall charge was the Nazi Party's chief ideologue, Alfred Rosenberg, named Reich Minister for the Occupied Eastern Territories. His Baltic German origins made him seem the appropriate man for the job. Rosenberg's office had been planning to co-opt some of the Soviet Union's subject nationalities in the area, and in particular the Ukrainians, as a counter-weight to the Russians. But these plans were futile. Hitler explicitly removed not only the army but also Himmler's SS and Göring's Four-Year Plan organization from Rosenberg's area of competence. And not only Himmler and Göring but also Hitler himself envisaged the ruthless subjugation, deportation or murder of millions of inhabitants in the occupied areas rather than their co-optation into a Nazi New Order. In pursuit of this goal Hitler appointed Erich Koch, the Regional Leader of East Prussia, to lead the Reich Commissariat of the Ukraine, with a brief to be as hard and brutal as possible. He fulfilled it with gusto. His counterparts in the Reich Commissariat of the Eastern Land, which included the former Baltic states, and the General Commissariat of Belarus, Hinrich Lohse and Wilhelm Kube, proved respectively weak and corrupt, and were in the end as widely disregarded as Rosenberg himself. Even more than in Poland, therefore, the SS was allowed to do more or less what it wanted in the newly occupied territories.[221]

Hitler was aware of the possibility that his plans for the racial subjugation and extermination of the indigenous populations of the occupied areas were so radical that they might alienate world opinion. Propaganda, therefore, he said on 16 July 1941, had to emphasize that the German forces had occupied the area in order to restore order and security and liberate it from Soviet control.[222] The invasion was sold to the German people not only as the decisive phase in the war against 'Jewish Bolshevism', but also as a preventive measure designed to forestall a Soviet assault on Germany. Indeed, on 17 September 1941 Hitler told his dinner companions that he had been obliged 'to foresee that Stalin might pass over to the attack in the course of 1941', while

Goebbels already recorded him on 9 July fulminating 'about the Bolshevik leadership clique which had intended to invade Germany'. How
far these statements reflected the two men's real beliefs is a moot point:
both of them knew their words would be recorded for posterity – Hitler's
by Bormann's stenographers, and Goebbels's by his secretaries, for by
this time he had gone over to dictating his diaries rather than writing
them himself, and had signed a contract for their publication after his
death.[223] But this was certainly the line that was fed to the mass of
ordinary Germans.

The announcement of the invasion took most German people almost
completely by surprise. On many previous occasions, the imminence of
war had been obvious in a massive escalation of hostile propaganda
pumped out against the prospective enemy by Goebbels's media
machine. But because Hitler had wanted to deceive Stalin into thinking
there would be no attack, such propaganda had been entirely absent on
this occasion, and indeed in mid-June there were even rumours that
Stalin was about to pay a formal visit to the German Reich. Most
people's attention was still focused on the conflict with Britain and the
hope of reaching a settlement. Not surprisingly, therefore, people's initial
responses to the announcement of the launching of Barbarossa were
mixed. The student Lore Walb captured the public reaction perfectly in
her diary. People felt, she wrote, 'great apprehension and depression at
the same time, but also, somehow, they breathed a sigh of relief'. At
least, she felt, the air had been cleared by the ending of the tactically
necessary but politically false alliance between Germany and Soviet
Bolshevism.[224] The local authorities in the rural Bavarian district of
Ebermannstadt reported that the people were making 'anxious faces'
and were concerned 'that the war was once more dragging itself on long
into the future'.[225] Luise Solmitz too thought that the invasion of the
Soviet Union heralded war without end.[226] 'The first thought we all have
is about the length of the war,' wrote the journalist Jochen Klepper, who
had been enlisted as a reserve officer with German units in Bulgaria and
Romania, 'but then the conviction that a reckoning with Russia was
necessary sooner or later.'[227]

Some were worried that Hitler was biting off more than he could
chew. Melita Maschmann was walking past a beer-garden by Lake
Constance on 22 June 1941, on a visit to her parents, when she heard
Hitler on the radio announcing the invasion of the Soviet Union. She

later remembered that her initial reaction had been one of fear and apprehension. A war on two fronts had never been a good idea, and not even Napoleon had been able to defeat the Russians.

The people round me had troubled faces. We avoided one another's eyes and looked out across the lake. Its farther shore was shrouded in mist under a grey sky. There was something cheerless in the mood of that cloudy summer's morning. Before the broadcast was over it had started to rain. I had a sleepless night behind me and I was cold. I walked along the shore in a fit of depression. The water lapped, grey and indifferent, against the quayside. There was one thing the invasion of Russia would certainly mean. The war would be prolonged for many years, and there would perhaps be immeasurably greater sacrifices.[228]

The stunning victories of the German armies, trumpeted over the media from 29 June 1941 onwards, raised some people's spirits and convinced many of them that the war might not last so long after all; yet enthusiasm continued to be outweighed by apprehension amongst the great major-ity.[229] An official in Ebermannstadt summarized reactions with remark-able honesty some weeks later, on 29 August 1941. The number of people who 'are passionately following the progress of events, from fanatical enthusiasm', he wrote, 'is infinitesimally small. The great mass of people waits for the end of the war with the same longing as the sick person looks for his recovery.'[230]

IN THE TRACKS OF NAPOLEON

I

Within a few days of retreating to his dacha in despair, Stalin recovered his nerve, if indeed he had really lost it. Some thought he had retreated into temporary isolation like Ivan the Terrible centuries before, to demonstrate his indispensability. A State Defence Committee was set up, with Stalin himself in the chair. His retreat had given him the chance to rethink his role. On 3 July 1941, the same day that Franz Halder confided to his diary his belief that victory had already been achieved by the German forces, Stalin spoke to the Soviet people over the radio, for the first time not as Communist dictator but as patriotic leader. 'Brothers and sisters,' he said, 'friends!' This was an entirely new note. He went so far as to admit that the Red Army had been unprepared for the attack. The Germans, he said, were 'wicked and perfidious . . . heavily armed with tanks and artillery'. But they would not prevail. The Soviet people had to organize civil defence and mobilize every ounce of energy to defeat the enemy. It was necessary to form partisan groups behind the lines to cause as much damage and disruption as possible. Silence, lies and evasion, people felt, had at last been replaced with some kind of truth.[231] Communist Party propaganda began to emphasize the defence not of the revolution but of the motherland. The party newspaper, *Pravda* ('Truth'), dropped the slogan 'Workers of the World, Unite!' from its masthead and replaced it with 'Death to the German Invaders!' Nikolai Moskvin noted on 30 September 1941 that 'the mood of the local population has changed sharply'. From constantly threatening to betray him to the Germans, they came round to the patriotic cause after learning that the occupation authorities were keeping the collective farms going because it made it easier to collect the grain for transporting back to Germany.[232]

The speech's patriotic appeal was all the more powerful because people were already beginning to learn the bitter realities of German occupation. Stories of the horrors of the prisoner-of-war camps mingled with eyewitness reports of the mass shooting of civilians and the burning of villages by German troops to produce in the still-retreating ranks of the Red Army a determination to fight the enemy that had been almost entirely absent in the first chaotic days of the war. When the city of Kursk fell, the Germans arrested all the healthy male inhabitants, penned them into open barbed-wire enclosures without food or water, and then put them to work, guarded by Germans wielding rubber truncheons. 'The streets are empty,' noted a Soviet intelligence report. 'The shops have been looted. There is no mains water and no electricity. Kursk has collapsed.'[233] Minsk, reported Fedor von Bock, was little more than a 'heap of rubble, in which the population is wandering about without any food.'[234] Other cities and towns were reduced to a similar state. They were deliberately starved of supplies by their German conquerors, who requisitioned the bulk of foodstuffs for themselves, in a situation already rendered critical by the removal of large quantities of supplies by the retreating Red Army. Hitler declared that it was his firm intention 'to raze Moscow and Leningrad to the ground, so as to prevent people staying there and obliging us to feed them through the winter. These cities are to be annihilated by the air force.'[235] Many people fled the advancing German troops – the population of Kiev, for instance, fell by half, from 600,000 to 300,000 – but even for those who were left, staying alive quickly became a priority in every occupied area. The German military issued a stream of orders imposing curfews, drafting young men into forced labour, requisitioning winter clothing, and executing hundreds of citizens in reprisal for every supposed act of arson or sabotage.[236] Looting by German troops was as widespread as it had been in Poland. 'Everywhere,' wrote General Gotthard Heinrici caustically on 23 June 1941, 'our people are looking for harnesses and take the horses away from the farmers. Great wailing and lamentation in the villages. Thus is the population "liberated".'[237] Their requisitioning of food, he added on 4 July 1941, was thorough and comprehensive. 'But the land will likely soon be sucked dry.'[238] The troops' behaviour quickly alienated even people who had initially welcomed them as liberators from Stalin's tyranny. 'If our people were only a bit more decent and sensible!' lamented Hans Meier-Welcker. 'They are taking everything that suits them from the farmers.' Meier-Welcker saw soldiers stealing chickens, tearing beehives apart to get at the honeycomb, and throwing themselves upon a gaggle of geese in a farmyard. He tried to discipline the looters, but it was a lost cause.[239]

One army officer reported on 31 August 1941 from another part of the front:

The population not only in Orscha, but also in Mogilev and other localities, has repeatedly made complaints concerning the taking of their belongings by individual German soldiers, who themselves could have no possible use for such items. I was told, amongst others, by a woman in Orscha, who was in tears of despair, that a German soldier had taken the coat of her three-year-old child whom she was carrying in her arms. She said that her entire dwelling had been burnt; and she would never have thought that German soldiers could be so pitiless as to take the clothes of small children.[240]

Orders from Army Headquarters threatening punishment for such acts remained a dead letter. In Witebsk troops removed all but eight of the town collective's 200 cattle, paying for only twelve of them. Huge quantities of supplies were stolen, including a million sheets of plyboard from a local timber yard, and 15 tons of salt from a storehouse. When the weather turned cold, troops began stealing wooden furniture from people's houses to use as fuel. In the south, Hungarian troops were said to be 'taking everything that was not nailed down'. The local people referred to them as 'Austrian Huns'. Scores of thousands of troops were forcibly billeted on townspeople, eating them out of house and home. In desperation, many women turned to prostitution. In some areas the incidence of venereal disease among German troops soon reached a rate of 10 per cent. The establishment of 200 official army brothels for the troops in the east did little to alleviate this situation. Rapes were far from uncommon, though rape was not used as a deliberate policy by the army; yet of the 1.5 million members of the armed forces condemned by court-martial for offences of all kinds, only 5,349 were put on trial for sexual offences, mostly as a result of complaints by the female victims. The courts dealt with this kind of offence leniently, and arrests for looting and theft even fell after 22 June 1941. Clearly the army was turning a blind eye to misbehaviour by the troops in the east, so long as it did not affect morale.[241] Theft and rape went alongside wilful acts of destruction. German army units amused themselves in the various palaces that dotted the countryside around St Petersburg by machine-gunning mirrors and ripping silks and brocades from the walls. They took away the bronze statues that adorned the famous fountains of the Peterhof Palace to be melted down, and destroyed the machinery operating the fountains. The houses in which famous Russian cultural figures had lived were deliberately targeted: manuscripts at Tolstoy's Yasnaya Polyana were burned in the stoves, while the composer Tchai-kovsky's house was trashed and army motorcycles driven over the musical manuscripts that littered the floor.[242]

From the outset, the military adopted a reprisal policy that was brutal in the extreme. As in Serbia, German army units raided Ukrainian, Belarussian and Russian villages, burning the houses and shooting the inhabitants, in retribution for even the smallest supposed act of sabotage. They had little compunction in destroying what seemed to them to be scarcely habitable dwellings anyway. 'If one had not seen with one's own eyes these primitive circumstances among the Russians,' wrote the soldier Hans-Albert Giese to his mother on 12 July 1941, 'one could not believe that such a thing still existed . . . Our own cowstalls at home are sometimes like gold in comparison to the best room in the homes in which the Russians choose to live. They are perhaps a worse rabble than the Gypsies.' A few days later he referred to Russian villagers as 'bush negroes'.[243] Senior army officers were equally contemptuous of the civilian population of Russia, which Manstein, entirely typically, described as a land far from Western civilization. Rundstedt was con-stantly complaining of the dirt in the quarters he took up in the southern sector of the front. The inhabitants of the Soviet Union seemed bestial, Asiatic, dull and fatalistic, or cunning and without honour, to officers and men of all ranks alike.[244] On entering the Soviet Union, Gotthard Heinrici felt he had entered another universe: 'I believe that one could only do it justice if we did not, as we have here, enter it gradually, on foot, but instead travelled to it as in a sea-voyage to a strange part of the globe and then, as one left our own shores, cut off all internal ties with the things we are used to at home.'[245] This was a kind of negative tourism: 'There will be hardly anyone in this miserable land,' wrote one soldier from the conquered area, 'who does not think gladly and often of his Germany and his loved ones at home. Things here are really even worse than in Poland. Nothing but dirt and tremendous poverty rule the roost here, and one simply cannot understand how people can live under such circumstances.'[246] It did not matter, therefore, how harshly these miserable, half-human people were treated. Hundreds of civilians were taken as hostages; they were customarily shot when the next act of partisan resistance occurred. 'We are now experiencing war in its entire tragedy,' reported Alois Scheuer, a corporal, born in 1909, who belonged to the older generation among the troops, 'it is humankind's greatest misfortune, it makes people rough and brutal.' Only the thought of his wife and children, and his Catholic faith, prevented him from 'becoming almost without feeling in spirit and soul'.[247] German military violence against civilians soon dissipated the support the invaders had initially won from the local population. Partisan resistance prompted further reprisals, leading more to join the partisans, and so the escalating cycle of violence continued. 'The war is being cruelly fought on both sides,' confessed Albert Neuhaus in August 1941.[248]

A few months later, he reported a commonplace incident of a kind that must have happened many times before. 'In a neighbouring village that we passed through this afternoon, our soldiers had hanged a woman from a tree because she had been stirring up people against the German troops. So we are making short shrift of these people.'[249] A keen photographer, Neuhaus thought nothing of taking a snap of an alleged partisan hanging from a tree and sending it back home to his wife.[250] Everywhere German troops burned villages to the ground and shot civilians by the thousand.[251] The speed of the German advance meant that many Red Army units found themselves cut off; they then continued fighting behind the front, joining with local people to create partisan bands to harry the enemy in the rear. This enraged the German troops, who, just as they had in Poland in 1939, considered this somehow unfair. 'Lost soldiers,' reported General Gotthard Heinrici on 23 June 1941, just one day into the invasion, 'are sitting everywhere in the great forests, in innumerable farmsteads, and often enough shooting from behind. The Russians in general are fighting the war in an insidious manner. Our people have cleared them out several times, without pardon.'[252] 'Our people,' he wrote on 6 July 1941, 'beat and shot dead everything that was running around in a brown uniform.'[253] On 7 November 1941, Heinrici was forced to tell his interpreter, Lieutenant Beutelsbacher, who had been carrying out executions of real or imagined Soviet guerrilla fighters, 'he is not to hang partisans up 100 m in front of my window. Not a pretty sight in the morning.'[254]

Faced with such horrors, Soviet soldiers and civilians began to listen to Stalin's new, patriotic message and fight back. Encouraged by Stalin, more and more young men took to the woods to form partisan bands, raiding German installations and intensifying the vicious circle of violence and repression. By the end of the year, the overwhelming mass of civilians in the occupied areas had come round to supporting the Soviet regime, encouraged by Stalin's emphasis on patriotic defence against a ruthless foreign invader.[255] Escalating partisan resistance went along with a dramatic recovery of the fighting effectiveness of the Red Army. The cumbersome structure of the Red Army was simplified, creating flexible units that would be able to respond more rapidly to German tactical advances. Soviet commanders were ordered to concentrate their artillery in anti-tank defences where it seemed likely the German panzers would attack. Soviet rethinking continued into 1942 and 1943, but already before the end of 1941 the groundwork had been laid for a more effective response to the continuing German invasion. The State Defence Committee reorganized the mobilization system to make better use of the 14 million reservists created by a universal conscription law in 1938. More than 5 million reservists were quickly mobilized within a few weeks of the German invasion, and more followed. So hasty was this mobilization that most of the new divisions and brigades had nothing more than rifles to fight with. Part of the reason for this was that war production facilities were undergoing a relocation of huge proportions, as factories in the industrial regions of the Ukraine were dismantled and transported to safety east of the Ural mountains. A special relocation council was set up on 24 June and the operation was under way by early July. German reconnaissance aircraft reported what to them were inexplicable massings of railway wagons in the region – no fewer than 8,000 freight cars were employed on the removal of metallurgical facilities from one town in the Donbas to the recently created industrial centre of Magnitogorsk in the Urals, for example. Altogether, 1,360 arms and munitions factories were transferred eastwards between July and November 1941, using one and a half million railway wagons. The man in charge of the complex task of removal, Andrej Kosygin, won a justified reputation as a tirelessly efficient administrator that was to bring him to high office in the Soviet Union after the war. What could not be taken, such as coalmines, power stations, railway locomotive repair shops, and even a hydro-electric dam on the Dnieper river, was sabotaged or destroyed. This scorched-earth policy deprived the invading Germans of resources on which they had been counting. But together with the evacuation, it also meant that the Red Army had to fight the war in the winter of 1941–2 largely with existing equipment, until the new or relocated production centres came on stream.[256]

Stalin also ordered a series of massive ethnic cleansing operations to remove what he and the Soviet leadership thought of as potential by subversive elements from the theatre of war. More than 390,000 ethnic Germans in the Ukraine were forcibly deported eastwards from September 1941. Altogether there were nearly one and a half million ethnic Germans in the Soviet Union. 15,000 Soviet secret policemen descended upon the Volga to begin the expulsion of the ethnic Germans living there, removing 50,000 of them already by the middle of August 1941. Similar actions took place in the lower Volga, where a large community of German descent was living. In mid-September 1941, expulsions began from the major cities. By the end of 1942, more than 1,200,000 ethnic Germans had been deported to Siberia and other remote areas. Perhaps as many as 175,000 died as a result of police brutality, starvation and disease. Many of them spoke no German, and were German only by virtue of remote ancestry. It made no difference. Other ethnic groups were targeted too – Poles, as we have seen, were deported in large numbers from 1939, and, later in the war, up to half a million Chechens and other minorities in the Caucasus were removed for having allegedly collaborated with the Germans as well. In addition, as the German forces advanced, the Soviet secret police systematically murdered all the political prisoners in the jails that stood in their path. One hit squad arrived at a prison at Luck that had been damaged in a bombing raid, lined up the political prisoners, and machine-gunned up to 4,000 of them. In the western Ukraine and western Belarus alone, some 100,000 prisoners were shot, bayoneted, or killed by hand-grenades being thrown into their cells.[257] Whatever their impact on the war effort, such actions stored up a bitter legacy of hatred which was to lead within a very short time to horrific acts of revenge.

II

The Soviet will to resist, expressed in these various ways, operating from top to bottom of the hierarchy, quickly became apparent to the German military leaders, who soon realized that the war was not going to end in a matter of weeks after all. Army Group Centre had managed to encircle huge numbers of Soviet troops, but in the north and south the Red Army had only been driven back, and the German advance was slowing down. Far from melting away, the Red Army was beginning to find ways to bring fresh reserves to the front, and it was starting to mount successful counter-attacks on a local basis. Well before the end of July, Field Marshal Fedor von Bock was forced to deal with repeated counter-attacks by the Soviet forces. The Russians were becoming 'impudent', he noted. 'Victory has not yet been won!' 'The Russians are unbelievably tough!!'[258] 'Day by day,' one ordinary soldier wrote in a propaganda tract, the troops had to endure 'the piercing screams of the Bolshevik hordes, who seem to rise from the earth in dense masses'.[259] Particularly around Smolensk, on the way from Minsk to Moscow, to the east of the river Dnieper, the Soviet commanders Zhukov and Timoshenko had begun a series of heavy counter-attacks on 10 July 1941 in an attempt to disrupt the advance of General Heinz Guderian's panzer group towards the city. Poorly equipped, badly co-ordinated and inadequately supplied, the Soviet resistance failed, but it slowed down the German advance and inflicted heavy losses of men and equipment on Guderian's forces, whose supply lines were now seriously over-extended. Ordinary soldiers shared the view that the Russians were unexpectedly tough.[260] The German armies were subjected to constant harassment and repeated attacks. 'The Russians are very strong & fight with desperation,' wrote General Gotthard Heinrici to his wife on 20 July 1941. 'They appear suddenly all over the place, shooting, fall upon columns, individual cars, messengers etc. . . . Our losses are considerable.'[261]

Indeed, the Germans had lost over 63,000 men by the end of the month.[262] On 22 July 1941 Heinrici confided to his wife: 'One does not have the feeling that in general the Russian will to resist has been broken, or that the people want to drive out their Bolshevik leaders. For the moment one has the impression that the war will go on, even if Moscow is taken, somewhere in the depths of this endless land.'[263] Over the next few weeks, he returned again and again in his letters to express his amazement at the Russians' 'astonishing strength to resist' and their astounding 'toughness'. 'Their units are all half-destroyed, but they just fill them with new people and they attack again. How the Russians manage it is beyond me.'[264] German military intelligence had failed to register the presence of the huge Soviet reserve units to the east of the Dnieper, from which fresh troops were constantly being moved to the front.[265] Little more than a month after the invasion had begun, leading German generals were beginning to recognize that the Soviet Union was the Third Reich's 'first serious opponent' with 'inexhaustible human resources'.[266] By 2 August General Halder was already beginning to think of how to supply German troops with winter clothing.[267] Nine days later he was seriously concerned:

In the situation as a whole it is becoming ever clearer that we have underestimated the Russian colossus, which has consciously prepared for the war with the absolute lack of restraint that is peculiar to totalitarian states. This conclusion applies to its economic as well as its organizational forces, to its transport system and above all to its purely military capacity to operate. At the outset of the war we reckoned with about 200 enemy div[isions]. Now we are already counting 360. These div[isions] are certainly not armed and equipped in our sense of the words, and tactically they are often poorly led. But they are there. And when a dozen of them have been destroyed, then the Russians put up another dozen.[268]

And even Halder's gloomy statistic was in fact a substantial under-estimation of the strength of his opponent. Moreover, the German troops were suffering heavy losses – 10 per cent of the invasion force was dead, wounded or missing by the end of July 1941. 'In view of the weakness of our forces and the endless spaces,' he concluded gloomily on 15 August 1941, 'we can never achieve success.'[269]

While the Red Army drew on vast reserves to replace the millions of soldiers lost or captured in the first months of the campaign, the German armed forces had already used up most of the manpower avail-able and had very few fresh troops to throw into the fray. In late July, Guderian pushed on with his armoured forces and took control of the area of land between the two rivers Dvina and Dnieper, but the overstretched German forces left gaps in their defences, and the Red Army, fired with new enthusiasm for the battle, launched a series of counter-attacks that began to give Field Marshal Fedor von Bock, commanding Army Group Centre, serious cause for concern. As the relentless assaults continued, he was forced to concede 'that our troops are tired, and as a consequence of the heavy losses among the officers do not exhibit the necessary steadiness either'. 'I have almost no reserves left to pit against the enemy's massing of strength and his relentless attacks,' he confessed on 31 July 1941. By the end of the first week in August he was seriously worried about 'the slowly declining fighting value of our troops under the impact of constant attacks'. How, he wondered, would his forces ever be able to continue their advance under such conditions?[270]

Quite apart from this, moving around the countryside was far more difficult than it had been in France, Holland or Belgium. Metalled roads were few and far between, totalling only 40,000 miles in all the vast expanse of the Soviet Union. One soldier noted that even the made-up roads were so full of potholes that his unit preferred to march along the ditch that ran along next to it.[271] The railways ran on a broad gauge to which it was difficult to transfer Western European rolling stock after the Red Army had removed virtually all the Soviet locomotives, goods wagons and passenger coaches, and destroyed or sabotaged tracks, bridges and viaducts. And even without these problems, the country was too sparsely supplied with railway lines to transport with any rapidity the huge quantities of men and supplies the Germans brought into the fray. German jeep and truck production was still relatively low despite the motorization drive of the 1930s, and motor vehicles in any case were restricted in their use by the shortage of fuel. In these circumstances, the German and allied armies relied heavily on horses – at least 625,000 of them on the Eastern Front – for basic transport, hauling artillery pieces, carrying ammunition and pulling supply carts. Horses were often better able to negotiate the muddy and treacherous tracks that passed for roads in Eastern Europe. 'Thank God for our horses!' exclaimed Meier-Welcker some months later:

At times they are the last and only thing we can rely on. Thanks to them we made it through the winter, even if they died in their thousands from exhaustion, lack of fodder and their tremendous exertions. Horses are especially important in the wet summer of this year and the often thickly wooded, boggy and impass-able terrain of our present sector. The motorized troop units in our area shrank to miserable objects last winter and spring.[272]

But horses were also slow-moving, unable to go at much more than walking pace for most of the time. The vast bulk of the infantry, as always, trudged along on foot.

As the invasion proceeded, the wear and tear of flying almost continual missions began to tell on the German aircraft. By the end of July 1941 there were only just over 1,000 planes in operation. Command of the air counted for little if there were too few bombers to inflict significant damage on Soviet war production. The expanse of Russia was too vast for the German air force to establish permanent air superiority, however great its effectiveness in a tactical role. Stuka dive-bombers terrified enemy infantry by the screaming noise of their engines as they plunged out of the sky, but they were extremely vulnerable to attack from fighter planes, while the bombers most commonly deployed, the Dornier 17 and the Junkers 88, lacked the range to be effective against Soviet installations. Troop losses by this time, including missing, wounded and killed, were over 213,000. The rest, as Bock had observed, were beginning to suffer from exhaustion after more than a month of non-stop combat. Spare parts for tanks and armoured personnel carriers were in short supply. On 30 July 1941 the Army Supreme Command ordered the advance to pause and regroup. Little more than a month after it had begun, the invasion had started to lose its momentum.[273]

Dividing the invading forces into Army Groups North, Centre and South, intended to advance tangentially to one another, was a measure partly necessitated by the presence in the area of invasion of the vast and impenetrable Pripet marshes. But it meant that the German armed forces were unable to concentrate on a single, unstoppable, knockout blow. By August 1941, it was already clear that the advance could not resume on all three fronts simultaneously. A choice had to be made between putting the weight of the next phase of the assault in the north, towards Leningrad, the centre, towards Moscow, or the south, towards Kiev. The leading German generals, following the classic Prussian military doctrine of going for the enemy's centre of gravity, wanted to continue on to Moscow. But Hitler, whose contempt for the Russian troops was boundless, did not think this would be necessary; for him, securing the economic resources of the western parts of the Soviet Union was the primary aim; the Soviet state would crash into ruin in any case. After the victories in France and the west, neither Halder nor the other generals who thought like him felt able to gainsay the Leader. On

21 August 1941, after a good deal of debate, Hitler rejected the army's request to continue pushing on towards Moscow, and ordered the generals to divert forces from Army Group Centre to strengthen the attack in the south, take Kiev, secure the agricultural resources of the Ukraine, and then head on for the Crimea, to deprive the Russians of a possible base for air attacks on the Romanian oilfields. Further troops and resources were detached from the centre to bolster the drive towards Leningrad. But Germany's Finnish allies lacked the resources, the manpower and indeed the political will to push the Soviet forces back very far beyond the old Russo-Finnish border, and the German advance was slowed down by fierce Soviet resistance. A frustrated Hilter announced on 22 September 1941 that he had 'decided to erase the city of Petersburg from the face of the earth. I have no interest in the further existence of this large city after the defeat of Soviet Russia'.[274] The threat proved to be empty bluster.

Field Marshal Fedor von Bock telephoned Halder and told him that the decision to focus on the southern sector was misconceived,

above all because it puts in question the attack on the east. The War Directives are always saying that the point is not to capture Moscow! I don't want to capture Moscow! I want to destroy the enemy army, and the mass of this army is standing in front of me!! The turn away towards the south is a sideshow, however large it might be, through which a question-mark is placed over the execution of the main operation, namely the destruction of the Russian armed forces before the winter – it does not help at all!![275]

A disappointed Bock could only give vent to his frustration in the pages of his diary: 'If the eastern campaign after all its successes now fades away into a dreary defence,' he wrote, 'that's not my fault.'[276] Halder was just as irritated, criticizing in his diary the 'zigzag in the Leader's individual orders' that the switch of target involved.[277] Yet at first, Hitler's decision to weaken his forces in the centre did not seem to pose a problem. German armoured divisions from Army Groups Centre and South under the command of Heinz Guderian, who had caused Bock considerable irritation with his insistent and intemperate demands, broke through the Soviet lines, repelled a massive counter-offensive launched in late August and early September, and captured a further 665,000 prisoners, along with 884 tanks and over 3,000 artillery pieces. Kiev, Kharkov and most of central and eastern Ukraine were occupied in late September and October, and on 21 November 1941 German forces took Rostov-on-Don, opening up the prospect of cutting off oil supplies to the Red Army from the Caucasus and harnessing the industrial resources of the Donets Basin. These were among the greatest German military victories of the war.[278]

Even before the assault on Kiev, German losses in terms of killed, missing, wounded or invalided out had mounted to nearly 400,000, and half the German tanks were out of commission or under repair. Bock hailed the operation as 'a brilliant success' but added that 'the main strength of the Russians is standing unbroken in front of me, and – as before – the question remains open as to whether we will succeed in smashing it and exploiting the victory before winter comes in such a way that Russia cannot recover in this war'.[279] Hitler thought this was still possible. The German forces, he told Goebbels on 23 September 1941, had achieved the breakthrough they had been looking for. German troops would soon encircle Moscow. Stalin, Hitler thought, was bound to sue for peace, and this would inevitably bring Britain to the negotiating-table too. The way was open to a final victory. Yet Hitler did not now expect this to occur immediately. He was already resigned to accepting that the war would go on until the following spring. But the huge victories of the preceding months left him optimistic that the war would be over by the middle of 1942 at the latest.[280] Substantial numbers of troops were transferred back to Army Group Centre, now reinforced with fresh supplies, and strengthened by more forces from the north for a resumption of the march on Moscow. Bock had got his wish.[281] 2 million German soldiers and 2,000 tanks, backed by massive air-power, advanced on the Soviet capital in October 1941 in a fresh campaign named 'Operation Typhoon', once again encircling the Red Army forces and taking 673,000 prisoners and enormous quantities of equipment. Addressing the traditional annual assembly of Party Regional Leaders and 'Old Fighters' in Munich on 8 November 1941, the anniversary of the failed 1923 beer-hall putsch, Hitler declared: 'Never before has a giant empire been smashed and struck down in a shorter time than Soviet Russia.'[282]

But this was another illusion. For the weeks of delay proved fatal. In retrospect, many considered that had they pressed on towards Moscow in August and September, the German forces might well have taken the Soviet capital, despite growing problems of keeping their supply lines open at such a distance from their bases further to the west. And, as Bock wished, they might have inflicted enormous, perhaps fatally demoralizing losses on the main forces of the Red Army in doing so. But in the end, this was hindsight with a grossly distorted vision. Generals like Bock, Halder and the others who championed, both then and later on, the idea of a knockout blow against the Soviet forces massed before Moscow were reflecting above all the dogma of the Prussian military tradition in which they had been brought up and spent most of their lives: the tradition that prescribed attack as the king of military operations, and the total destruction of the enemy armies as the only proper end of any military campaign. Bock knew better than almost anybody that his troops were tired, his units depleted, his supplies intermittent, his equipment unfitted for a winter campaign. But like many senior commanders in the German army, he was haunted by the memory of the Battle of the Marne, the failure of the western offensive in 1914. Like Hitler, he was determined that it would not be repeated. And like Hitler, too, he fatally underestimated the strength of the enemy, an enemy the depth of whose reserves of manpower and *matériel* he was aware of, but lightly brushed aside, just as, in the end, he discounted the new fighting spirit of the Red Army that had inflicted so many casualties on his forces.[283]

III

By October, as Bock had feared, the Soviet leadership had rethought and reorganized its whole way of conducting the war. After issuing draconian orders for the punishment of shirkers and deserters and having Dmitri Pavlov, the commander of the Red Army on the Western Front at the time of the invasion, tried by a summary court-martial and shot, Stalin began to realize, as he told his officers in October 1941, that 'persuasion, not violence' should be used to motivate the troops. He began to allow his commanders greater freedom of action in conducting their campaigns. Meanwhile, after reading a biography of the Tsarist general Kutuzov, who had abandoned Moscow in the face of Napoleon's invasion, the Soviet leader decided that to leave the capital would cause panic. It was one thing to burn a small early nineteenth-century town to the ground, another thing altogether to surrender the vast conurbation that had become the modern Soviet capital. 'No evacuation,' Stalin said. 'We'll stay here until victory.'[284] Under Stalin's leadership, the new State Defence Committee began to get a grip on the situation. On 10 October 1941 Stalin appointed General Georgi Zhukov to command the armies defending the capital. Zhukov's forces, numbering about a million men, were forced on to the defensive as Bock pushed rapidly forward towards Moscow. Panic broke out among the population in some quarters of Moscow, though the city was spared the horrors of aerial bombardment, as German planes concentrated their efforts on attacking Soviet troops on the ground.[285]

At this point, the autumn rains arrived with a vengeance, turning the unmade Russian roads into impassable sludge. On 15 October 1941, Guderian told Bock that he had to order a pause in the advance. The Field Marshal blamed it not only on stiff enemy resistance but also on the 'indescribable state of the roads, which makes almost any movement of the motorized vehicles impossible'.[286] Because of the 'temporary impassability of the roads and tracks for vehicles', noted Meier-Welcker, 'we have not received any deliveries of fuel, munitions or foodstuffs', and the troops were living off whatever they could find, mainly potatoes, baking their own bread and slaughtering local livestock themselves.[287] Driving along a road in the area on 16 October 1941, General Heinrici found 'a continual line of sinking, bogged-down, broken-down motor vehicles, which were hopelessly stuck fast. Almost as many dead horses lay beside them in the mire. Today,' he was forced to admit, 'we've simply come to a halt because of the difficulties of the roads.'[288] By late October the German armies had been stuck in the mud for three weeks.

Zhukov seized the opportunity to restore order, declaring martial law on 19 October 1941 and putting nine reserve armies into place behind the river Volga. Although they consisted mostly of raw recruits and previous military rejects, they numbered 900,000 men in all and would, Stalin and Zhukov hoped, provide a serious obstacle to any German attempt to encircle the city. Moreover, a report from Richard Sorge, Stalin's spy in Tokyo, not long before his arrest on 18 October 1941, convinced the Soviet leader that the Japanese were not going to attack Russia (indeed, they had other targets in mind). Backed by further intelligence reports, this led to a decisive move: on 12 October Stalin ordered 400,000 experienced troops, 1,000 tanks and 1,000 planes westward across Siberia into position behind Moscow, replacing them with enough newly recruited soldiers to deter the Japanese should they change their minds.[289] The new reinforcements brought up by Stalin were not only unanticipated by the Germans, they also proved decisive. Field Marshal Bock feared the worst: 'The splitting of the Army Group,' he wrote on 25 October 1941, 'in combination with the terrible weather has led to our getting stuck. Through this, the Russians are winning the time to fill up their shattered divisions and to strengthen their defences, the more so as they command the mass of roads and railway lines around Moscow. That's very bad!'[290]

By 15 November 1941, as winter began to set in, the ground was hard enough for Bock to resume his advance. The tanks and armoured vehicles rolled forward once more, reaching positions within 30 kilometres of the suburbs and cutting off the Moscow–Volga canal. But soon it began to snow, and on the night of 4 December the temperature plummeted to minus 34 degrees Celsius, freezing German equipment and penetrating the troops' inadequate winter clothing. The next night the thermometer fell still further, reaching minus 40 in some places. In the midst of the Russian winter, the German troops, equipped for a campaign that had been confidently expected to last only until the autumn, were poorly clad and ill prepared. 'All armies,' noted Bock already on 14 November 1941, 'are complaining about considerable difficulties in bringing fresh supplies of every kind – foodstuffs, ammunition, fuel and winter clothing.'[291] Soon Reich Propaganda Minister Goebbels began a campaign to collect winter clothes for the troops. Hitler issued a personal appeal on 20 December 1941, and the same evening Goebbels broadcast a helpful list of the items needed. Woollen and fur clothing was confiscated from German Jews in late December 1941 and sent to the freezing troops on the Eastern Front. But it was all too late; and in any case, transport difficulties meant that much of the clothing would not reach the front. Meier-Welcker was reduced to hoping in late January that the 'wool collection' would at least reach the front by the following winter. Cases of frostbite were occurring with increasing frequency among the German troops. 'Their feet are so swollen,' he noted, 'that their boots have to be cut open. That reveals that their feet or at least their toes are blue or already black, and are starting to be affected by frostbite.'[292]

The senior generals had been aware of the problem, but with blind optimism they had thought it would be solved by the occupation of major Russian cities like Moscow and Leningrad, where they could take up warm winter quarters. Winter had come, and they were still encamped on the open steppe. The wind, wrote General Heinrici, 'stabs you in the face with needles, and blasts through your protective headgear and your gloves. Your eyes are streaming so much that you can hardly see a thing.'[293] In one infantry division, 13 per cent of the unit's average strength were invalided out with frostbite between 20 December 1941 and 19 February 1942.[294] After weeks without washing or changing their clothes, the men were dirty and verminous. 'Everybody is swarming with lice, and is constantly itching and scratching,' wrote Heinrici. 'Many have suppurating wounds from the eternal scratching and scraping. Many have got bladder and bowel infections through lying on the cold ground.' His troops were 'extremely exhausted'.[295] Such conditions were well suited to the Soviet armies, who had learned the lesson of the bitter Winter War against Finland and were now properly equipped for fighting in these terrible conditions, deploying ski battalions to move swiftly over the snow-covered ground, and light cavalry to advance quickly over waterlogged terrain impassable to tanks. The German army's defensive tactics were based on the assumption that counter-attacks could be met with sufficient forces to provide defence in depth, that the Red Army would mainly use infantry, and that it would be possible for senior officers to choose their ground and make tactical withdrawals where necessary. All these assumptions proved to be wrong from the outset and contributed to the disaster that was about to overtake the German forces. On 5 December 1941 Zhukov ordered a counter-offensive, aiming initially at the German pincers north and south of Moscow, to eliminate the danger of it being surrounded. Soviet troops, he ordered, were not to waste time and lives in frontal attacks on fortified positions but were simply to pass them by, leaving covering forces, and make for the German lines of withdrawal. On 7 December 1941 Bock noted that he was now facing twenty-four more Red Army divisions than there had been in his theatre of war in mid-November. The odds were stacking up fast against him. Without supplies, weakened in numbers, lacking in reserve forces, weary and exhausted, the troops could not be deployed rapidly to meet the onslaught of an enemy 'who is mounting a counter-attack with the reckless commitment of his inexhaustible human masses'.[296]

Unable to decide whether to continue the advance or break it off,

Bock could think of nothing better than sending Halder a continual stream of demands for reinforcements. The next day Hitler recognized the seriousness of the situation by ordering a halt to the advance. Meanwhile, Bock's dithering began to spread uncertainty among the troops. If they could not advance any further, what were they to do next?[297] Morale began to plummet. Already on 30 November 1941 the corporal Alois Scheuer wrote to his wife from his position 60 kilometres from Moscow:

I am sitting with my comrades in a dugout, in the half-dark. You have no idea how lousy and crazy we all look, and how this life has become a torment for me. It can't be described in words any more. I've only got one thought left: when will I get out of this hell? . . . It has been and is simply too much for me, what I've got to take part in here. It is slowly destroying us.[298]

By Christmas Day 1941, Scheuer estimated that 90 per cent of his original company were gone – dead, wounded, missing, ill or suffering from frostbite. His own toes were beginning to turn black. Scheuer survived the experience, lasting until February 1943, when he was killed, still fighting on the Eastern Front.[299] Amidst wild blizzards that brought down the German field telephone lines and blocked the roads, confusion began to set in amongst Bock's troops. Only a single railway line was available to serve a retreat, and the roads became blocked with immobilized tanks and vehicles, many of which had to be abandoned as the German forces, shocked and surprised by the counter-attack, began to fall back in the face of Zhukov's onslaught. Smaller counter-attacks in the far north and south, at Tikhvin and Rostov, prevented the Germans from moving reinforcements to the battle-front.[300]

German tanks and armoured vehicles were in many cases out of fuel. Ammunition and rations were in short supply. Combat aircraft could not fly in the driving snow. On 16 December 1941, after pushing back the German salients to the north and south of the city, Zhukov ordered a full advance to the west. Within ten days the situation for the Germans had become desperate. 'We have a difficult day behind us,' wrote Meier-Welcker on 26 December 1941:

Hampered by the snow and especially the snowdrifts, often shovelling ourselves out metre by metre, and travelling with vehicles and equipment that is by no means adequate for the Russian winter, behind us the enemy pressing on, concern to bring the troops to safety in time, to carry the wounded along, not to let too many weapons or too much equipment fall into enemy hands, all this was sorely trying for the troops and the leadership.[301]

Worst of all were the 'snowstorms, which very quickly rendered impassable roads we had just dug free'.[302] The Russian advance was unstoppable. 'Equipped with fabulous winter equipment, they are everywhere pushing through the wide gaps that have opened up in our front,' observed Heinrici on 22 December. 'Although we saw the disaster of encirclement coming, again and again the command came from above to halt.' But there was no alternative to moving if they were not to be completely cut off. The result was a chaotic instead of an orderly retreat. 'The retreat in snow and ice,' wrote Heinrici, 'is absolutely Napoleonic in its manner. The losses are similar.'[303]

IV

Faced with the failure of their grand offensive, Bock and the senior commanders had little idea of what to do next. One minute they ordered a retreat, the next they thought it was better to make a stand. Guderian confessed he did not know how to extricate the army from the situation it was now in. While he dithered, failing altogether to prepare proper defensive positions for overwintering, Bock remained almost absurdly optimistic about the possibility of a further advance. However, he now thought the issue of whether or not to retreat was more political than military. The generals' desperation began to take its toll. The crisis of the German army before Moscow prompted the first major upheaval in the senior ranks of the German armed forces during the war. The first to go was Field Marshal Gerd von Rundstedt, the commander of Army Group South. He had been ordered by Hitler, via the Commander-in-Chief, Field Marshal Walther von Brauchitsch, to stop the beleaguered armoured divisions of General Ewald von Kleist from withdrawing from the outskirts of Rostov further than the German Leader had been prepared to allow. But, fearing they would be encircled, he refused. An angry Hitler fired Rundstedt on 1 December 1941, replacing him with Field Marshal Walter von Reichenau. Only when he visited the area on 2–3 December 1941 did Hitler concede that Rundstedt had been right.

But he did not reinstate Rundstedt. Reichenau's command was only a brief one, since he died of a heart attack on 17 January 1942. His death was a sign of the severe mental and physical strain under which the senior commanding officers, mostly men in their late fifties and early sixties, were now labouring. In early December Rundstedt, already ailing, also suffered a heart attack, though it did not prove fatal. The next to suffer a collapse in his health was Bock himself. Already on 13 December 1941 he told Brauchitsch that he was 'physically very low'. 'The "Russian sickness" and a definite over-exertion has brought me so low,' he wrote a few days later, 'that I must fear that I will fail in my command.' On 16 December 1941 he asked Hitler for permission to go on sick leave. There was no question, however, of any difference of opinion between the two men. Before he left the front on 19 December 1941, handing over the command of Army Group Centre to Field Marshal Günther von Kluge, Bock issued orders to his troops to hold the line. His meeting with Hitler on 22 December 1941 was 'very friendly', he noted in his diary. That this was a real rather than a diplomatic illness was made crystal-clear by Bock's request to Hitler to be reinstalled in a front-line command when he had recovered, as indeed he soon was.[304]

On 16 December 1941, in the most important of these changes of top-ranking military personnel, Hitler accepted the resignation of Field Marshal Walther von Brauchitsch, Commander-in-Chief of the army. Brauchitsch, buffeted by the competing demands of his Leader and his generals, had been unable to cope with the stress of defeat. He too suffered a heart attack in mid-November. After some discussion, Hitler decided that he would replace him not with another general, but with himself.[305] Hitler's announcement that he had replaced Brauchitsch and taken over the direction of military operations himself was greeted with relief by many of the beleaguered German troops. 'Now the Leader has taken our fate into his own hands,' reported Albert Neuhaus to his wife on 21 December 1941, 'after v. Brauchitsch has resigned because of illness. And the Leader will know how to deploy his soldiers where it's right to do so.'[306] The generals too breathed a sigh of relief. Responsibility for getting the army out of the mess before Moscow had at last been taken from their shoulders. Guderian hoped now for 'quick and energetic' action from Hitler's 'accustomed energy', while another tank commander, General Hans-Georg Reinhardt, welcomed the fact that there was 'finally a Leader's Order' that would bring 'clarity' about what to do next. Only a few remained sceptical, amongst them General Heinrici, who wrote to his wife on 20 December 1941 that Hitler had now taken over command but 'he too will probably not be in a position to turn the situation around'.[307]

But nearly all the generals considered that Hitler had already proved his genius as a military commander in 1940, and trusted him to cut the Gordian knot. Stepping in eagerly to fill the decision-making vacuum, Hitler ordered reinforcements to be brought up from the west and told his troops on the Eastern Front to hold their positions until they arrived. 'The fanatical will to defend the ground on which the troops are standing,' he told the officers of Army Group Centre four days later, 'must be injected into the troops with every possible means, even the toughest.' 'Talk of Napoleon's retreat is threatening to become reality,' he warned on 20 October 1941. Napoleon's retreat was the beginning of the end for the French Emperor. The same thing was not going to happen to him.[308] His order to stand firm not only created clarity about what the army was doing but also had some effect in improving morale. On the other hand, the rigidity with which he now implemented it began to have an effect on the smaller-scale tactical withdrawals that the desperate situation frequently necessitated at various parts of the front. Gotthard Heinrici in particular became increasingly frustrated at the repeated orders to stand firm, when all this brought was a repeated danger of being surrounded. 'The disaster continues,' he wrote to his wife on Christmas Eve 1941:

And at the top, in Berlin, at the very top, nobody wants to admit it. Whom the gods wish to destroy they first make blind. Every day we experience this anew. But for reasons of prestige nobody dares to take a determined step backwards. They don't want to admit that their army is already completely surrounded before Moscow. They refuse to recognize that the Russians can do such a thing. And in complete blindness they are keeling over into the abyss. And they will end in 4 weeks by losing their army before Moscow and later on by losing the whole war.[309]

Heinrici railed against his superiors, who refused to order a retreat 'for fear of offending the top leadership'.[310]

This was the beginning of a long-lived legend, repeated by many of Hitler's surviving generals after the war, according to which if only they had been left by Hitler to get on with it, they could have achieved victory. Professional generalship was what won wars; the interference of an amateur like Hitler, however gifted he might be, could only bring ruin in the end. The truth, however, was very different. The generals' blind insistence on attack through the autumn and early winter of 1941, their failure to prepare defensive positions for overwintering, their naive optimism in the face of what they knew to be a determined and well-equipped enemy, their studious refusal to draw the consequences from the increasing tiredness of their troops, the growing difficulties of supply and the failure of much of their equipment in the bitter cold of the Russian winter brought them to a situation by December where they were paralysed by despair and indecision. Hitler's stabilization of the situation only increased his contempt for them. 'Once more a dramatic scene with the Leader,' recorded Halder in his diary on 3 January 1942, 'in which he casts doubt on the generals' ability to screw up their courage to take tough decisions.'[311] Hitler was now determined not to allow the generals any more freedom of action. Field Marshal Wilhelm Ritter von Leeb, in command of Army Group North, found himself under fire from Hitler when he visited him on 12 January 1942 to ask permission to withdraw from some positions he thought were indefensible, in order to avoid further losses. Hitler, backed by Halder, thought this would weaken the Army Group's northern flank and make the coming summer campaign more difficult. When he failed to get his way, he tendered his resignation, which was accepted on 16 January 1942. His replacement, General Georg von Küchler, was told firmly by Halder that he would be expected to obey the orders emanating from Hitler's headquarters.[312]

Disobedience to Hitler's orders now carried with it severe consequences. General Heinz Guderian met Hitler on 20 December 1941 to plead for permission to retreat. Hitler told him he would have to get the troops to dig in and fight. But, Guderian objected, the ground was frozen solid five feet down. Then the troops would have to sacrifice themselves, Hitler countered. He was backed by Kluge and Halder, both of whom disliked the arrogant, wilful tank commander, as Bock had also done, and saw in the contretemps an opportunity to get rid of him. Disobeying Kluge's express command, Guderian carried out a major withdrawal operation, telling his commander: 'I will lead my army in these unusual circumstances in such a manner that I can answer for it to my conscience.' Kluge thought he should answer to his superior officers, and told Hitler that either Guderian would have to go, or he would. On 26 December 1941 Guderian was dismissed. The lack of solidarity shown by the leading generals with one another fatally undermined any attempt they might have made to take a stand against Hitler's rigid insistence on resistance at any price.[313] The tank commander General Erich Hoepner noted perceptively: ' "Fanatical will" alone won't do it. The will is there. The strength is lacking.'[314] Faced with the encirclement of the Twentieth Army Corps, Hoepner requested permission to withdraw and to retreat to a more defensible line. The new commander of Army Group Centre, Field Marshal Günther von Kluge, told him he was referring the matter to Hitler and ordered him to prepare for an immediate retreat. Thinking this meant Hitler would give his approval and not wanting to court disaster by delaying any further, Hoepner began the retreat anyway, moving his troops out on the afternoon of 8 January 1942. Appalled, and terrified at what Hitler might think, Kluge reported his action immediately to the Leader, who dismissed Hoepner from the army without a pension the same evening.[315]

With these changes, and others lower down the chain of command, Hitler had succeeded in establishing a complete dominance over the top army commanders. From now on they would do his will. Their much-vaunted professionalism had failed before Moscow. Military operations would now be directed by Hitler himself. With this victory over the generals, he could now afford to relax his rigid insistence on holding the line. By the middle of January 1942 Field Marshal Kluge had won Hitler's approval for a series of adjustments of the front including a number of local retreats to its 'winter position'. Fighting continued as the Red Army mounted continual assaults on the narrow German communication line with the rear. General Heinrici gained a considerable reputation as a defensive tactician as he held it until the Russian attacks ran out of steam; it was to return to haunt him at the end of the war, when Hitler would put him in charge of the defence of Berlin.[316] Nevertheless, the scale of the disaster before Moscow was clear to all. Zhukov had pushed the Germans back to the point from which they had launched Operation Typhoon two months before. For the German army, this was, as General Franz Halder put it, 'the greatest crisis in two world wars'.[317] The losses inflicted on the German armed forces were enormous. In 1939, only 19,000 had been killed; and in all the campaigns of 1940, German losses had totalled no more than 83,000

– serious enough, indeed, but not irreplaceable. In 1941, however, 357,000 German troops were reported killed or missing in action, over 300,000 of them on the Eastern Front. These were huge losses that could not easily be replaced. Only Stalin's decision to attack all along the front instead of pushing home the advantage by concentrating his forces in an all-out assault against the retreating German Army Group Centre prevented the disaster from being even worse.[318]

For all their advances since 22 June 1941, the Germans had everywhere failed to achieve their objectives. The overweening optimism of the first weeks of Operation Barbarossa had given way to an increasing sense of crisis, reflected in Hitler's repeated dismissals of his leading generals. German military forces had for the first time been shown to be vulnerable. After Moscow, Hitler was still optimistic about the chances of victory. But he now knew it would take longer than he had originally envisaged.[319] The invasion of the Soviet Union had changed the face of the war irrevocably. A series of easy victories in the west had been followed by an increasingly grim struggle in the east. What happened on the Soviet Front dwarfed anything seen in France, Denmark, Norway or the Low Countries. From 22 June 1941 onwards, at least two-thirds of the German armed forces were always engaged on the Eastern Front. More people fought and died on and behind the Eastern Front than in all the other theatres of war in 1939–45 put together, including the Far East. The sheer scale of the struggle was extraordinary. So too was its bitterness and its ideological fanaticism, on both sides. It was in the end on the Eastern Front, more than any other, that the fortunes of war were decided.[320]

3

'THE FINAL SOLUTION'

'NO PITY, NOTHING'

I

As he entered Kovno (Kaunas) in Lithuania on 27 June 1941, Lieutenant-Colonel Lothar von Bischoffshausen, a regular army officer, noticed a laughing and cheering crowd of men, women and children gathered in the forecourt of a petrol station by the side of the road. Curious, he stopped to see what was going on. Bischoffshausen, a much-decorated career soldier and former Free Corps fighter, born in 1897, was no humanitarian liberal, but as he approached the crowd, even he was shocked by what he saw:

On the concrete forecourt of the petrol station a blond man of medium height, aged about twenty-five, stood leaning on a wooden club, resting. The club was as thick as his arm and came up to his chest. At his feet lay about fifteen to twenty dead or dying people. Water flowed continuously from a hose washing blood away into the drainage gully. Just a few steps behind this man some twenty men, guarded by armed civilians, stood waiting for their cruel execution in silent submission. In response to a cursory wave the next man stepped forward silently and was then beaten to death with the wooden club in the most bestial manner, each blow accompanied by enthusiastic shouts from the audience.[1]

Some of the women, he noted, were lifting up their children so that they could see better. Later on, Bischoffshausen was told by army staff officers that the murders were a spontaneous action by local people 'in retaliation against the collaborators and traitors of the recently ended Russian occupation'. In fact, as other eyewitnesses reported, the victims were all Jews. A German photographer managed to take pictures of the event. Waving his army pass, he warded off an SS man's attempt to confiscate the film, thus preserving a record of these events for posterity.

Bischoffshausen reported the massacre to his superiors. Although he discovered that members of the SS Security Service had been in the area since 24 June 1941, and it was not hard to guess that they had been instrumental in inciting the massacre, the general commanding the German army in the area said this was an internal matter for the Lithuanians and refused to intervene.[2]

What he had witnessed was no chance, localized or spontaneous act of violence. As soon as the German forces had entered the Soviet Union and the various territories it controlled, followed by the four SS Security Service Task Forces and subordinate Task Units including a number of police battalions, they had begun to carry out the orders Heydrich had given them to kill civilian resisters, Communist Party officials and Jews, along with all Jewish prisoners of war, in order, as they thought, to eliminate any possibility of resistance or subversion from 'Jewish Bolsheviks'. Initially, the killings were, if possible, to be done by local people, who the Nazis expected to rise up against their Communist and Jewish oppressors, as they saw them.[3] In a report written in mid-October 1941, the head of Task Force A, Walther Stahlecker, noted Heydrich's instruction to set in motion what he called 'self-cleansing efforts' by the local population, or in other words anti-Jewish pogroms that were to appear as spontaneous actions by patriotic Lithuanians. It was important 'to create as firmly grounded and provable for posterity the fact that the liberated population took the toughest measures against the Bolshevik and Jewish enemy on its own initiative, without any direction from the German end being recognizable'. 'It was initially surprisingly difficult to set a fairly large-scale pogrom in motion there,' he reported, but in the end a local anti-Bolshevik partisan leader managed 'without any German orders or incitement being discernible' to kill more than 1,500 Jews on the night of 25/26 June and a further 2,300 the following night, also burning down sixty Jewish houses and a number of synagogues. 'The armed forces units,' he added, 'were briefed and showed full understanding for the action.'[4]

Pogroms of this kind took place in many areas in the first few days of German occupation. Antisemitism in the Baltic states had been fuelled by the experience of Soviet occupation since the spring of 1940, under which native elites and nationalists had been persecuted, arrested, deported or killed. Stalin had encouraged the Russian and Jewish minorities to help build the new Soviet states of Latvia, Lithuania and Estonia, and two-thirds of the Central Committee of the Latvian Communist Party were either Russian or Jewish in origin, though like all Communists, of course, they rejected their previous ethnic and religious identities in favour of secular Bolshevik internationalism. For their part, the Nazis regarded the Baltic peoples not as subhuman Slavs but as potentially assimilable to the German master race. Yet only a tiny minority of extreme nationalists in these countries vented the hatred of Communism they had accumulated over the period of Soviet occupation on the local Jewish population.[5] Task Force A, for example, had to get auxiliary police rather than local civilians to kill 400 Jews in Riga. It is more than likely that in practice the same procedure had to be followed in other areas such as Mitau, where the local Jewish population of 1,550 was, it was reported, 'disposed of by the population without any exceptions'. Finally, in Estonia, the Jewish population was so tiny – a mere 4,500 people – that such actions were not possible at all, and most of the Jews managed to flee to safety.[6] By the time German troops reached Estonia, SS Security Task Forces and other units in Latvia and Lithuania had in any case gone over to killing Jewish men themselves. In the Lithuanian border town of Garsden (Gargzdai), where the German troops had encountered fierce resistance from the Red Army, security was left to a unit of German border police from Memel, who arrested between 600 and 700 Jews. Acting under the orders of the Gestapo chief in Tilsit, Hans-Joachim Böhme, they marched 200 Jewish men and one Jewish woman (the wife of a Soviet political commissar) to a nearby field, where they forced them to dig their own graves and then, on the afternoon of 24 June 1941, shot them all. One of the victims was a boy of twelve. Now known as the Tilsit Task Unit, Böhme's group then moved eastwards, killing over 3,000 civilians by 18 July 1941.[7]

On 30 June 1941 the group was visited by Himmler and Heydrich, who gave its actions their approval. Böhme and his men were clearly carrying out their wishes. German forces treated all Jewish men as Communists, partisans, saboteurs, looters, dangerous members of the intelligentsia, or merely 'suspicious elements', and acted accordingly. Antisemitism also led regular German troops to shoot captured Jewish soldiers rather than send them into captivity behind the front. 'Up here in what was Lithuania,' wrote the ordinary soldier Albert Neuhaus from Münster, born in 1909 and therefore a little older than the average soldier, on 25 June 1941, 'things are pretty much Jewified, and in this case no quarter is given.'[8] The mixture of ideologically preconceived antisemitism and military or security rationalization, as well as the involvement of a variety of different agencies in the massacres, was evident in a letter written to his parents by a regular German soldier on 6 July 1941 from Tarnopol in eastern Galicia. After describing the discovery of the mutilated bodies of German soldiers taken prisoner by Red Army troops, the soldier went on:

We and the SS were merciful yesterday, for every Jew we caught was shot right away. It's different today, for we again found the mutilated bodies of 60 comrades. Now the Jews had to carry the corpses out of the cellar, stretch them out neatly, and then they were shown the atrocities. Then after inspecting the victims they were beaten to death with truncheons and spades. Up to now we have sent about 1,000 Jews into the hereafter, but that's too few for what they've done.[9]

The Jews of course had no demonstrable connection with the atrocities at all. Nevertheless, altogether some 5,000 of the town's Jewish population were massacred, including a small number of women and children.[10]

In late June and through the first weeks of July, the Task Forces set about killing ever-increasing numbers of Jewish men in the occupied territories in the east, encouraged by frequent visits of Himmler and Heydrich to their areas of operation. The SS leaders began to provide the Task Forces with quotas to fill. In Vilna (Vilnius), at least 5,000 and probably as many as 10,000 Jews were killed by the end of July. Most of them were taken out to pits previously dug by the Red Army for a tank base, made to bind their shirts over their heads so they could not see, then machine-gunned in groups of twelve. Three SS Security Service units in Riga, assisted by local auxiliary police, had killed another 2,000 Jews in a wood outside the town by the middle of July, while thousands more Jews were shot in a similar way in other centres of population. As the grisly business proceeded, the gestures towards legal formalities that had often accompanied the early mass shootings, including the conventional rituals of the firing-squad, were quickly abandoned.[11] Already on 27 June 1941, men from a variety of units under the overall command of the army's 221st Security Division had driven more than 500 Jews into a synagogue in Bialystok and burned them alive, while army units blew up the surrounding buildings to stop the fire spreading. Other Jewish men were arrested in the streets. Their beards were set on fire and they were forced to dance before being shot. At least 2,000 Jews were killed in all. Shortly afterwards, a German police battalion entered what was left of the Jewish quarter and took out twenty truckloads of loot. Himmler and Heydrich arrived in Bialystok early in July 1941 and are said to have complained that despite these killings not enough was being done to combat the Jewish menace. Almost immediately, over 1,000 Jewish men of military age were arrested, taken out of the city and also shot.[12]

The Task Force reported that it aimed to 'liquidate' the entire 'Jewish-Bolshevist leadership cadre' in the area, but in practice it rounded up and killed virtually the whole adult male Jewish population without distinction of occupation or educational attainment.[13] The German invasion of 1941 had initially come as a surprise to the Jews as well as to Stalin, and most Jews had not fled, unless they had some connection with the Communist Party. Many of them had relatively positive memories of the German occupation in the First World War, and they had been alienated by the Soviet suppression of Jewish institutions, the Communist expropriation of their businesses, and the anti-religious campaigns that had forced them to abandon their traditional dress and stop celebrating the Sabbath.[14] One German soldier reported that his unit had been welcomed in eastern Poland not only by villagers offering them milk, butter and eggs but also by Jews, who, he remarked, 'haven't yet realized that their hour has come'.[15] But this situation soon changed. News of the massacres spread quickly, and the Jewish population began to flee en masse as the German forces approached. The speed of the German army's advance was such that they were often overtaken, and so were then unable to escape the SS Task Forces following hard behind.[16] Nevertheless, a report filed by Task Unit 6 of Task Force C on 12 September 1941 noted that 90 or even 100 per cent of the Jewish population in many Ukrainian towns had already fled. 'The expulsion of hundreds of thousands of Jews,' it added, ' – from what we hear, in the most cases across the Urals – has cost nothing and constitutes a considerable contribution to the solution of the Jewish question in Europe.'[17]

II

Felix Landau, a thirty-year-old Austrian cabinet-maker, was in the area of Lemberg (Lvov) in early July. Landau had joined the SS in April 1934 and taken part in the murder of the Austrian Chancellor Dollfuss in 1934.[18] He was a committed Nazi and antisemite, therefore. He had volunteered for service in Task Force C, and it was with one of the Task Force's units that he arrived in Lemberg in the wake of the advancing German armies on 2 July 1941. Landau kept a diary in which he recorded his unit's progress. German troops entering Lemberg, he reported, had discovered the mutilated bodies of Ukrainian nationalists killed by the Soviet secret police after an attempted uprising, along, it was alleged, with a number of captured German airmen treated in the same way.[19] Indeed, in Lemberg as in other towns, the Soviet secret police had tried to evacuate 'counter-revolutionary elements' from the prisons in advance of the German invasion, and massacred all those whom they were unable to march off. The murdered men included a number of German prisoners of war. Many of the victims had been beaten to death and were exhumed with broken bones, though common reports that they had had their eyes put out or their genitals mutilated more likely reflected the depredations of rats and other scavenging beasts. There is also some evidence that Ukrainian nationalists in Lemberg nailed bodies to the prison wall, crucified them or amputated breasts and genitals to give the impression that the Soviet atrocities were even worse than they actually were.[20] The discovery of the mutilated corpses led to an orgy of violence by the military, the Ukrainians and the Task Force unit alike.[21] 'Shortly after our arrival,' Landau recorded, 'the first Jews were shot by us.' He did not particularly like doing this, he said – 'I have little inclination to shoot defenceless people – even if they are only Jews. I would far rather good honest open combat' – but on 3 July 1941 his unit shot another 500 Jews, and on 5 July 1941 another 300 Poles and Jews.[22]

Soon after arriving in the town, Landau's unit was informed that local Ukrainians and German soldiers had taken 800 Jews to the former citadel of the Soviet secret police and started attacking them, holding them responsible for the prison massacres. As he made his way towards the citadel, Landau saw hundreds of Jews walking along the street with blood pouring down their faces, holes in their heads, their hands broken and their eyes hanging out of their sockets. They were covered in blood. Some of them were carrying others who had collapsed. We went to the citadel; there we saw things that few people have ever seen. At the entrance of the citadel there were soldiers standing guard. They were holding clubs as thick as a man's wrist and were lashing out and hitting anyone who crossed their path. The Jews were pouring out of the entrance. There were rows of Jews lying one on top of the other like pigs, whimpering horribly. The Jews kept streaming out of the citadel completely covered in blood. We stopped and tried to see who was in charge of the unit. Someone had let the Jews go. They were just being hit out of rage and hatred.[23]

Landau found such violence 'perfectly understandable' in view of what had gone before. The hatred of some Ukrainians for the Jews was fuelled by religious prejudice and nationalist resentments derived from the fact that many Jews had worked for Polish landlords. It found expression in support for antisemitic and extreme nationalist militias that marched into eastern Galicia alongside the advancing German troops. Above all, however, the Jews were blamed by both Ukrainian militiamen and German troops for the massacres of prisoners carried out by the retreating Soviet secret police. Ukrainians took what they believed to be their revenge by beating the Jews to death, in one place, Brzezany, using clubs studded with nails. In Boryslaw, the commanding German general, seeing the corpses of young men killed in the prison by the Soviet secret police laid out on the town square, gave an enraged crowd twenty-four hours to do what they wanted with the local Jews. The Jews were rounded up, made to wash the corpses, forced to dance, then beaten to death with lead pipes, axes, hammers and anything else that came to hand.[24] Altogether, 7,000 Jews were murdered in Lemberg alone in these early weeks of the invasion. The participation of Ukrainian nationalists was widely noted, and Ukrainians indeed murdered a further 2,000 Jews in the city at the end of the month. Even so, these operations were generally unsystematic.[25] Only a relatively small minority of Ukrainians were out-and-out nationalists keen to take revenge against the Soviet Communists for years of oppression and the mass starvation of the early 1930s. Task Force C was obliged to conclude that 'The attempts which were undertaken cautiously to incite pogroms against Jews have not met with the success we hoped for . . . A decided antisemitism on a racial or spiritual basis is, however, alien to the population.'[26]

After leaving Lemberg, Landau's unit went on to Cracow, where the shootings resumed.[27] As he took twenty-three Jews, some of them refugees from Vienna, including two women, out to a wood to be shot, he asked himself as the Jews began to dig their own graves: 'What on earth is running through their minds during those moments? I think that each of them harbours a small hope that somehow he won't be shot. The death candidates are organized into three shifts as there are not many shovels. Strange, I am completely unmoved. No pity, nothing,' he wrote.[28] After digging the graves, the victims were made to turn round. 'Six of us had to shoot them. The job was assigned thus: three at the heart, three at the head. I took the heart. The shots were fired and the brains whizzed through the air. Two in the head is too much. They almost tear it off.'[29] Following these killing actions, Landau was placed in charge of recruiting Jews for forced labour. He had twenty shot for refusing to appear on 22 July 1941, after which, he reported in his diary, everything ran smoothly.[30] Aside from such cool descriptions of mass murder, much of Landau's journal was devoted to worrying about his girl-friend, a twenty-year-old typist he had met in Radom. By the end of the year he was living with her in a large villa, where he commissioned the Jewish artist and writer Bruno Schulz, whose work impressed him, to paint a mural. This temporarily preserved the artist's life, though Schulz was shot dead shortly afterwards by one of Landau's rival officers in the local SS.[31] If Landau showed any remorse, he did not record it.

These mass murders and pogroms often took place in public, and were not only observed and reported by participants and onlookers, but also photographed. Soldiers and SS men kept snapshots of executions and shootings in their wallets and sent them home to their families and friends, or took them back to Germany when they went on leave. Many such photos were found on German troops killed or captured by the Red Army. The soldiers thought that these reports and photos would show how German justice was meted out to a barbaric and subhuman enemy. The Jewish population seemed to confirm everything they had read in Julius Streicher's antisemitic tabloid paper *The Stormer*: everywhere the soldiers went in Eastern Europe they found 'filthy holes' swarming with 'vermin', 'dirt and dilapidation', inhabited by 'unending quantities of Jews, these repulsive *Stormer* types'.[32] In the southern sector of the front, Field Marshal Gerd von Rundstedt found himself confronted with quarters that he roundly condemned as a 'filthy Jewish hole'.[33] 'Everything is in a condition of horrifying dilapidation,' wrote General Gotthard Heinrici to his wife on 11 July 1941. 'We are learning to treasure the blessings of Bolshevik culture. The furnishings are only of the most primitive kind. We are living mostly in empty rooms. The Star of David is painted all over the walls and blankets.'[34] Heinrici's casual equation of dirt, Bolshevism and 'the Star of David' was typical. It informed the actions of many officers and men of all ranks in the course of the eastern campaign.

III

On 16 July 1941, speaking to Göring, Lammers, Rosenberg and Keitel, Hitler declared that it was necessary 'to shoot dead anyone who even looks askance' in order to pacify the occupied areas:[35] 'All necessary measures – shooting, deportation etc. – we will do anyway ... The Russians have now given out the order for a partisan war behind our front. This partisan war again has its advantage: it gives us the possibility of exterminating anything opposing us.' Foremost amongst those opponents of course, in Hitler's mind, were the Jews, and not just in Russia but also in the rest of Europe, indeed the rest of the world. The following day he issued two new decrees on the administration of the newly conquered territories in the east, giving Himmler complete control over 'security measures' including, it went without saying, the removal of the threat of 'Jewish-Bolshevik subversion'. Himmler understood this to mean clearing all the Jews from these areas by a mixture of shooting and ghettoization. From his point of view, this would pave the way for the further implementation of his ambitious plans for the racial reordering of Eastern Europe, as well, of course, as vastly increasing his own power in relation to that of the nominally responsible administrative head of the region, Alfred Rosenberg. He ordered two SS cavalry brigades to the region, numbering nearly 13,000 men, on 19 and 22 July 1941 respectively.[36]

On 28 July 1941 Himmler issued guidelines to the First SS Cavalry Brigade to assist them in their task of dealing with the inhabitants of the vast Pripet marshes:

If the population, looked at in national terms, is hostile, racially and humanly inferior, or even, as will often be the case in marshy areas, composed of criminals who have settled there, then everyone who is suspected of supporting the partisans is to be shot; women and children are to be taken away, livestock and foodstuffs are to be confiscated and brought to safety. The villages are to be burned to the ground.[37]

It was understood from the outset that the partisans were inspired by 'Jewish Bolshevists' and that therefore a major task of the cavalry brigades was the killing of the Jews in the area. On 30 July 1941 the First SS Cavalry Brigade noted at the end of a report: 'In addition, up to the end of the period covered by this report, 800 Jewish men and women from the ages of 16 to 60 were shot for encouraging Bolshevism and Bolshevik irregulars.'[38] The extension of the killing from Jewish men to Jewish women and children as well ratcheted up the murder rate to new heights. The scale of the massacres carried out by the newly assigned SS cavalry brigades in particular was unprecedented. Under the command of the Higher SS and Police Leader for Central Russia, Erich von dem Bach-Zelewski, one brigade shot more than 25,000 Jews in under a month, following an order issued at the beginning of August by Himmler, who was visiting the area, that 'all Jewish men must be shot. Drive Jewish women into the marshes.' Women were no longer to be spared, in other words, they were to be drowned in the Pripet marshes. Yet, as the SS cavalry reported on 12 August 1941: 'Driving women and children into marshes did not have the success it was meant to, since the marshes were not deep enough for them to sink in. In most cases one encountered firm ground (probably sand) below a depth of 1 metre, so that sinking-in was not possible.'[39]

If it was not possible to drive Jewish women into the Pripet marshes, then, SS officers concluded, they too had to be shot. Already in the first half of August, Arthur Nebe, the commander of Task Force B, which operated in Bach-Zelewski's area, ordered his troops to start shooting women and children as well as men. Further south, Himmler's other SS brigade, under the command of Friedrich Jeckeln, began the systematic shooting of the entire Jewish population, killing 23,600 men, women and children in Kamenetsk-Podolsk in three days at the end of August 1941. On 29 and 30 September 1941, Jeckeln's men, assisted by Ukrainian police units, took a large number of Jews out of Kiev, where they had been told to assemble for resettlement, to the ravine of Babi Yar, where they were made to undress. As Kurt Werner, a member of the unit ordered to carry out the killings, later testified:

The Jews had to lie face down on the earth by the ravine walls. There were three groups of marksmen down at the bottom of the ravine, each made up of about twelve men. Groups of Jews were sent down to each of these execution squads simultaneously. Each successive group of Jews had to lie down on top of the bodies of those that had already been shot. The marksmen stood behind the Jews and killed them with a shot in the neck. I still recall today the complete terror of the Jews when they first caught sight of the bodies as they reached the top edge of the ravine. Many Jews cried out in terror. It's almost impossible to imagine what nerves of steel it took to carry out that dirty work down there. It was horrible . . . I had to spend the whole morning down in the ravine. For some of the time I had to shoot continuously.[40]

In two days, as Task Force C reported on 2 October 1941, the unit killed a total of 33,771 Jews in the ravine.[41]

By the end of October, Jeckeln's troops had shot more than 100,000 Jewish men, women and children. Elsewhere behind the Eastern Front, the Task Forces and associated units also began to kill women and children as well as men, starting at various times from late July to early September.[42] In all these cases, the few men who refused to take part in the murders were allowed time out without any disciplinary consequences for themselves. This included even quite senior officers, for example the head of Task Unit 5 of Task Force C, Erwin Schulz. On being told at the beginning of August 1941 that Himmler had ordered all Jews not engaged in forced labour to be shot, Schulz requested an interview with the head of personnel at the Reich Security Head Office, who, after hearing Schulz's objections to participating in the action, persuaded Heydrich to relieve the reluctant officer of his duties and return him to his old post at the Berlin Police Academy without any disadvantage to his career. The great majority of officers and men took part willingly, however, and raised no objections. Deep-seated antisemitism mingled with the desire not to appear weak and a variety of other motives, not the least of which was greed, for, as in Babi Yar, the victims' possessions in all these massacres were looted, their houses ransacked, and their property confiscated. Plunder, as a police official involved in the murders later admitted, was to be had for all.[43]

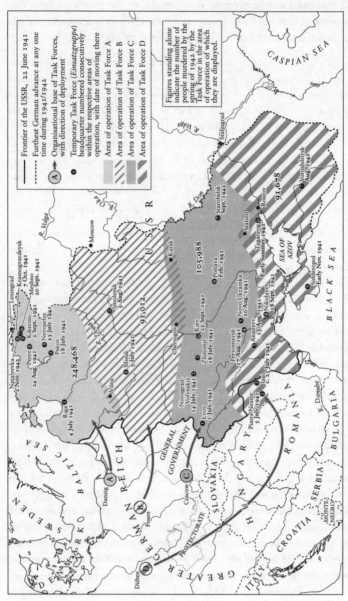

10. Killing Operations of the SS Task Forces, 1941–3

In the town of Stanislawów in Galicia, Hans Krüger, the head of the Security Police, was informed by the local German authorities that the ghetto they were about to set up was not going to be able to house anything like the entirety of the town's Jewish population, which numbered around 30,000, possibly more. So he rounded up the town's Jews on 12 October 1941 and lined them up in a long queue that reached to the edge of prepared open ditches in the town cemetery. Here they were shot by German police, ethnic Germans and nationalist Ukrainians, for whom Krüger provided a table laden with food and alcoholic spirits in the intervals between the shootings. As Krüger oversaw the massacre, striding round with a bottle of vodka in one hand and a hot-dog in the other, the Jews began to panic. Whole families jumped into the ditches, where they were shot or buried by bodies falling on top of them; others were shot as they attempted to climb the graveyard walls. By sunset, between 10,000 and 12,000 Jews, men, women and children, had been killed. Krüger then announced to the remainder that Hitler had postponed their execution. More were trampled in the rush to the cemetery gates, where they were again rounded up and taken to the ghetto.[44]

In some cases, as in the town of Zloczów, local German army commanders protested and managed to get the murders stopped, at least temporarily.[45] By contrast, in the village of Byelaya Tserkow, south of Kiev, the Austrian field commander, Colonel Riedl, had the entire Jewish population registered and ordered a unit of Task Force C to shoot them all. Together with Ukrainian militiamen and a platoon of soldiers from the Armed SS, the Task Force troops took several hundred Jewish men and women out to a nearby firing range and shot them in the head. A number of the victims' children were taken in lorries to the firing range shortly afterwards, on 19 August 1941, and shot as well, but ninety of the youngest, from small babies up to six-year-olds, were kept behind, unsupervised, in a building on the outskirts of the village, without food or water. German soldiers heard them crying and whimpering through the night, and alerted their unit's Catholic military chaplain, who found the children desperate for water, lying around in filthy conditions, covered in flies, with excrement all over the floor. A few armed Ukrainian guards stood about outside, but German soldiers were free to come and go as they pleased. The chaplain enlisted the aid of a regimental staff officer, Lieutenant-Colonel Helmuth Groscurth, who, after inspecting the building, posted soldiers round it to prevent the children being taken away. Outraged at his authority being overridden, Riedl protested to the regional commanding officer, Field Marshal von Reichenau, that Groscurth and the chaplain were departing from proper National Socialist ideology. 'He explained,' Groscurth reported, 'that he held the extermination of the Jewish women and children to be urgently required.' Reichenau backed Riedl and ordered the children's murder to go ahead. On 22 August 1941 the children and infants were taken out to a nearby wood and shot on the edge of a large ditch dug in preparation by Riedl's troops. The SS officer in charge, August Häfner, later reported that, after objecting that his own men, many of whom had children themselves, could not reasonably be asked to carry out the shootings, he obtained permission to get Ukrainian militiamen to do the deed instead. The children's 'wailing', he recalled, 'was indescribable. I shall never forget the scene throughout my life. I find it very hard to bear. I particularly remember a small fair-haired girl who took me by the hand. She too was shot later ... Many children were hit four or five times before they died.'[46]

Groscurth's horror at these events reflected the moral doubts that had led him to take up contacts with the conservative-military resistance. He protested that such atrocities in effect were no better than those committed by Soviet Communists. Reports of the events in the village were bound to reach home, he thought, damaging the standing of the German army and causing problems for morale. A devout Protestant and conservative nationalist, his courageous stand in August 1941 earned the wrath of his superiors, and he was duly reprimanded by Reichenau. To some extent he may well have phrased his objections in such a way as to make them count with his superiors. Yet his report to Reichenau on 21 August 1941 concluded that the outrage lay not in the shooting of the children but in the fact that they were left in appalling conditions while the responsible SS officers dithered. Once the decision had been made to kill the adults, he saw no option but to kill the children as well. 'Both infants and children,' he declared, 'should have been eliminated immediately in order to have avoided this inhuman agony.'[47]

IV

On 12 June 1941, during a visit to Munich, the Romanian army chief and dictator Ion Antonescu received 'guidelines' from Hitler as to how to deal with the Jews in the areas under Soviet control into which the Romanian army was scheduled to march ten days later as part of the plan for Operation Barbarossa. Under his orders, Romanian police commanders began the ghettoization of Jews living in towns and the 'extermination on site' of Jews found in the countryside. 100,000 Jews fled from these areas into the Soviet Union, but not before the Romanians had begun killing them in large numbers.[48] Already before the invasion, Antonescu had ordered the registration of all Romanian Jews and their banning from a wide variety of professions. Jewish property was expropriated and Jews were subjected to forced labour orders. From 8 August 1941 all Jews had to wear the yellow star. These and other orders reflected not only Hitler's urgings but also Antonescu's own deep-seated and violent personal antisemitism. Senior members of the Romanian regime justified the treatment of the Jews in terms of an Orthodox Christian crusade against unbelievers, fortified by the Orthodox Patriarch Nicodim's declaration that it was necessary to destroy the Jews, servants of Bolshevism and killers of Christ. Antonescu, too, often expressed his antisemitism in language tinged with religious phraseology ('Satan is the Jew,' he wrote in one virulently antisemitic diatribe). But he also repeatedly spoke of what he saw as the need for the racial 'purification' of Romania, and the discriminatory laws he introduced were racial, not religious, in character.[49] He was obsessed with the image of the Jews as the prime movers of that most anti-religious of political movements, Bolshevism. He blamed Romanian military losses, food and supply shortages, and any other problems he faced, on the Jews. He was encouraged in these beliefs by the German leadership.

On 26 June 1941 a pogrom was begun in the north-eastern Romanian town of Iaşi, organized by Romanian and German intelligence officers and involving the local police force. At least 4,000 local Jews were killed before the rest were packed into two goods trains in sealed wagons and then taken on a journey with no fixed destination; by the time the trains finally came to a halt, 2,713 of the Jews on them had died of thirst or suffocated to death. Even German observers were shocked by the violence. 'Everything is going according to plan, including the slaughter of the Jews,' wrote one from Iaşi on 17 July 1941, but he added: 'The atrocities that are taking place here and can be observed going on are unspeakable – and we, I and others, tolerate and must tolerate them.'[50] After the massacres in Iaşi, which killed possibly as many as 10,000, Antonescu ordered the expulsion of all Jews from Bessarabia and Bukovina, along with other supposedly treacherous elements. Machine-guns were to be used, he said: the law did not exist here. Thousands of Jews were shot, and the survivors were incarcerated in squalid, poorly provisioned camps and ghettos, principally in the Bessarabian capital of Kishinev, before being expelled to Transnistria, in the southern Ukraine, which was occupied by the Romanian army. Forced marches, hunger and disease took a terrible toll; in December 1941 and January 1942 the Romanian authorities ordered the shooting of thousands of the Jewish expellees out of hand.[51] At one camp in Transnistria, the commandant fed the inmates on a type of pea usually given to cattle. After Jewish doctors reported that the peas caused paralysis of the lower limbs, followed in most cases by death, the commandant ordered the feeding of the inmates with the peas to continue. They had nothing else to eat. At least 400 Jews were reported to have suffered paralysis before the food supply was eventually changed.[52]

There were more massacres when Romanian troops occupied Odessa. On 22 October 1941, a time-bomb previously laid by the Russian secret service blew up the Romanian army headquarters, killing sixty-one mostly Romanian officers and staff, including the city's military commander. Antonescu ordered savage reprisals. 200 'Communists' were to be hanged for every officer killed in the explosion. Romanian troops took this as a licence to launch a pogrom. Over the next two days, 417 Jews and alleged Communists were hanged or shot, and some 30,000 Jews were rounded up and force-marched out of the city to the town of Dalnic. But then, on the intervention of the mayor of Odessa, they were marched back to the city harbour. Here 19,000 of them were herded into four large sheds, where they were all machine-gunned. After this, the sheds were set on fire to ensure there were no survivors.[53] Thousands of the remaining Jewish inhabitants of Odessa were now taken out of the city preparatory to deportation into German-held Ukraine. 52,000 Jews from Odessa and southern Bessarabia were crammed into forty or so cowsheds at Bodganovka, or held in open pens. At nearby Domanovka and Akmecetka there were 22,000 more, many of them herded with deliberate sadism into pigsties on a large, abandoned Soviet state farm. Their money and jewellery were seized and taken off to the Romanian state bank. Typhus broke out in the insanitary conditions and the Jews began dying in large numbers.[54]

The Romanians expected to be able to transport these Jews into German-held Ukraine, but when it became clear that this was not going to happen, the guards at Bogdanovka, aided by local Ukrainian police, crammed around 5,000 elderly and sick Jews into stables, scattered hay on the roofs, doused it with petrol and burned them alive inside. Those Jews who could walk, around 43,000 of them, were taken to a nearby ravine and shot one by one in the back of the neck. 18,000 more were shot by Ukrainian policemen on Romanian orders at Domanovka. The pigsties at Akmecetka were used to house the sick and emaciated, and up to 14,000 were deliberately starved to death on the orders of the Romanian regional commander, Lieutenant-Colonel Isopescu. Thousands more Romanian Jews were deported to improvised, chaotically run and poorly supplied ghettos and camps in Transnistria, where death rates reached between a third and a half in the winter of 1941–2. In the Warsaw ghetto, by contrast, which for all its overcrowding and deprivation at least had a functioning social and administrative infrastructure, death rates were running at about 15 per cent at this time.[55]

Faced with desperate pleas from the surviving leaders of the Jewish community in Romania at these massacres, Antonescu took refuge in familiar claims that the Jews had previously tortured and murdered Romanian soldiers, so they deserved their fate. 'Every day,' he wrote to a Jewish community leader on 19 October in an open letter published in the Romanian press, 'the horribly mutilated bodies of our martyrs are brought out of the cellars of Chisinau . . . Did you ask how many of our people fell, murdered in a cowardly manner by your co-religionists? – and how many were buried alive . . . These are acts of hatred,' he went on, 'bordering on madness, which your Jews have displayed towards our tolerant and hospitable people . . .'[56] Within a year of beginning their campaign, the Romanian forces, sometimes in conjunction with German SS and police units, more often acting on their own, had killed between 280,000 and 380,000 Jews, the largest number murdered by any independent European country during the Second World War apart from Germany.[57]

SS Task Force D, dissatisfied with the chaotic nature of many of these killings, attempted to channel what it called 'the sadistic executions improperly carried out by the Romanians' into a 'more planned procedure'.[58] Ohlendorf complained to Berlin that the Romanian forces had 'driven thousands of children and frail old people, none of whom is capable of working, from Bessarabia and Bukovina into the German sphere of interest'. His men drove many back into Romanian territory, killing a substantial number of them in the process. By the end of August, as one of his subordinates later reported, Ohlendorf was carrying round with him 'a paper with a broad red border marked "Secret Reich Business". . . from which he informed us that all Jews without distinction were from now on to be liquidated'.[59] In mid-September, following this order, a sub-unit of the Task Force murdered all the Jews in the town of Dubossary, forcing mothers and their children with blows from their rifle-butts to stand on the edge of specially dug pits, where they were made to kneel down before being shot in the back of the neck. Around 1,500 people were murdered in this way in a single mass execution, one of many similar actions committed by the Task Force and its various subdivisions around this time. Once more, Himmler was present in the area when these massacres took place.[60] For Ohlendorf and Himmler, the Romanian forces' murder operations were neither thorough nor systematic enough and attended by an excess of inefficiency, corruption and randomly sadistic brutality. As Task Force D moved southwards, eventually reaching the Crimea, it searched every town and village, killed every Jewish man, woman and child it found, and reported back proudly in due course that it had rendered the area completely 'Jew-free'.[61]

V

The explicit inclusion of the mass murder of Bolshevik commissars, Jews, partisans and others in the orders developed in Berlin in the spring of 1941 for the invasion of the Soviet Union helped put genocide on the agenda in other parts of the Balkans too. In Yugoslavia the atmosphere was poisoned still further by the violence taking place in the area controlled by the fascist Ustashe regime in Croatia. As the Ustashe began massacring Serbs in huge numbers in the spring of 1941, thousands of refugees fled across the border to German-occupied Serbia, where they joined the nascent resistance movement, composed mainly of former soldiers and policemen who had taken to the hills in April 1941. Generally known as Chetniks, after anti-Turkish armed bands in the Balkan Wars earlier in the century, these groups gradually fell under the leadership of Colonel Dragoljub Mihailović, a Serbian nationalist in touch with the government-in-exile of the young King Peter. In late June 1941 the disparate actions of the Chetniks coalesced into a general uprising, the first in any German-occupied country in Europe. The rebels were joined by Communist partisans under Josip Broz Tito, who had been organizing their forces for some months. While the Chetniks were fuelled as much as by Serb hatred of the Croats than by the desire to resist the Germans, Tito's Communists aimed to unite all ethnic and religious groups in the struggle against the occupying forces. The situation was inflamed not only by the continuing genocidal violence in neighbouring Croatia, but also by the draconian policies adopted from the outset by the German army. General Halder, the Chief of the Army General Staff, had issued orders that were not dissimilar to those previously carried out in Poland, but more comprehensive and more severe still. The armed forces were to co-operate with the incoming German police and the Security Service of the SS in arresting known or suspected terrorists, saboteurs and German émigrés, to which Halder personally added two further categories: Communists and Jews.[62]

Within a few weeks of the invasion, the military occupation authorities had forced the registration of Serbian Jews, and in some places enforced the compulsory wearing of the Jewish star. The German army ordered the exclusion of Jews from a variety of occupations, expropriated much of their property without compensation, and extended these measures to Serbia's Gypsies. Army officers moved into well-furnished villas after the Jewish owners had been evicted, imprisoned or shot, while the rank-and-file soldiers began buying up confiscated Jewish goods at knock-down prices.[63] As soon as the Chetnik uprising started, the military commander in Belgrade ordered the Jewish community to provide forty hostages a week, to be shot if the resistance persisted. As a result, the 111 people who had been executed by the Germans by 22 July 1941 in 'reprisals' included many Jews. From 27 July 1941 Serbs were also held 'co-responsible' if they provided a supportive environment for the rebels. As far as the German troops were concerned, all the rebels were Communists or Jews. In mid-August the Jews of the

Banat area were deported to Belgrade, where all male Jews and Gypsies were interned at the beginning of September. By this time, according to an official German report, despite the fact that 'approximately 1,000 Communists and Jews had been shot or publicly hanged and the houses of the guilty burned down, it was not possible to restrain the continued growth of the armed revolt'.[64]

The 25,000 German soldiers left behind in Yugoslavia while the bulk of the armed forces moved on to Greece were without battle experience, and their average age was thirty. The officers were all from the reserve. The small number of German auxiliary and police regiments stationed in Serbia had also never been involved in the combating of guerrilla insurgency. They had little idea of how to deal with a well-supported and effective resistance movement. What they did do, however, was not dissimilar to what the German army was doing elsewhere in Eastern Europe. 'It is understandable,' explained a senior German army commander in Serbia, General Bader, on 23 August 1941,

that the troops who are often shot at from the rear by Communist bands are crying out for vengeance. Often in such a case any people found in the fields are arrested and shot. In most cases, however, they do not apprehend the guilty parties, who have long since disappeared; they catch innocent people and thus cause a population that up to this point has been loyal to go over to the bandits out of fear or embitterment.[65]

His warning fell on deaf ears. German soldiers continued to carry out brutal acts of revenge for attacks they were unable to counter. 'Today was a record!!' wrote one lieutenant on 29 July 1941. 'This morning we shot 122 Communists and Jews in Belgrade.'[66] The appointment of a puppet Serb government under Milan Nedić, a pro-German and anti-Communist Serb politician, did little to help the situation. The overall commander in the region, Field Marshal Wilhelm List, a Bavarian Catholic and a professional soldier of long standing, became increasingly frustrated. The Serbs, in his view, were naturally violent and hot-blooded and could only be tamed by force. In August 1941 Hitler personally underlined the need for 'the harshest intervention' in the military suppression of the revolt.[67] Goebbels was less convinced. On 24 September 1941, he noted with some concern that the 'bloody reign of terror' of the Croats against the Serbs was driving them 'to desperation . . . so that the movements of revolt are reaching out ever further'.[68]

And indeed the Chetniks became ever bolder, capturing 175 Germans in two separate incidents in early September 1941. List elbowed aside the serving military commander in Serbia, an air force general, and imported an Austrian, General Franz Böhme, as Commander-in-Chief. Böhme was trusted by Hitler, who indeed had put him forward as Commander-in-Chief of the Austrian army at one point during his negotiations with the Austrian dictator Schuschnigg shortly before the German invasion of Austria in 1938. Böhme shared the anti-Serb and antisemitic prejudices and resentments of the Austrian officer corps in full measure. 'Your mission,' he told his troops on 25 September 1941,

is to be carried out in a country in which in 1914 rivers of German blood flowed because of the treachery of the Serbs, men and women. You are the avengers of the dead. An intimidating example has to be created for the whole of Serbia, one that hits the whole population in the severest manner. Anyone who shows mercy is betraying the lives of his comrades. He will be called to responsibility without respect of his person and put before a court-martial.[69]

Böhme systematized the existing practice of violent retaliation. He ordered punitive expeditions to towns and villages, the opening of concentration camps for alleged 'Communists' and Jews at Šabac and Belgrade, and the shooting of all suspected Bolsheviks – over 1,000 of whom had already been killed by 4 October 1941. On 16 September 1941 Field Marshal Wilhelm Keitel, the head of the Combined Armed Forces Supreme Command, had ordered fifty to 100 Communists to be shot in retaliation for every single German soldier killed in German-occupied areas all across Europe. Böhme issued an even more far-reaching command on 10 October 1941: 'Communists or male inhabitants who are suspected of being Communists, all Jewish men, and a specified number of nationalistic and democratically inclined inhabitants' were to be seized as hostages and killed in the ratio of 100 to every German soldier killed by the partisans and fifty to every one wounded.[70]

Böhme was exceeding Keitel's orders, which did not mention Jews. There was a general assumption that because of their treatment in Germany and Poland the Jews would automatically be enemies of the German occupation of Serbia. A similar reasoning was applied to the Gypsies, though those who had a regular job and whose family had ceased to be nomadic since 1850 at the latest were explicitly exempted.

Without presenting any concrete evidence at all, the military administration claimed 'that the Jewish element participates to a considerable extent in the leadership of the bands and that it is Gypsies who are responsible for particular atrocities, and for espionage activities'.[71] On Böhme's orders, 2,200 prisoners from the Šabac and Belgrade concentration camps were shot, 2,000 of them Jews, 200 Gypsies. There were plenty of witnesses. Milorad Jelesić, a Serb interned in another, nearby camp, was taken out to a field near Šabac and with others was ordered to dig an open ditch while a detachment of German soldiers ate their lunch. Then, he later testified,

A group of fifty people who I could see were Jews were led from behind a field of corn ... An officer gave the command and then the Germans would aim at the back of the head – two soldiers for each Jew. We then had to run to the open grave and throw the dead into it. Then the Germans ordered us to go through all their pockets and take out any items of value ... If we couldn't get the rings off, the Germans gave us a little knife and we had to cut off their fingers and give them the rings like that.[72]

Another group of fifty Jews was then led out, and the operation repeated over the next two days, with Gypsies making up an increasing proportion of the victims. Some of the Jews were Austrian refugees, who with grim historical irony thus found themselves being killed by mainly Austrian troops in reprisal for acts of resistance carried out by Serbian partisans on the German army.[73]

Böhme's measures, directed against people who had nothing to do with the partisan uprising, had crossed the line that separated military reprisals, however excessive, from gratuitous mass murder. Further shootings followed. In many cases they were filmed for propaganda purposes. In the two weeks after the order of 10 October was issued, army units in Serbia shot more than 9,000 Jews, Gypsies and other civilians. Some soldiers even took part in the killings as if they were some kind of sport. When one Viennese soldier returned to his regiment in Belgrade from leave, he was greeted by his regimental comrades with the flippant inquiry: 'Are you going along with us to shoot Jews?'[74] If the troops ran out of supposed Communists, democrats, nationalists, Jews and Gypsies to kill in any particular place to which they had been ordered, they simply rounded up the rest of the male inhabitants and shot them too. In this way, for example, units of the 717th Infantry

Division shot 300 men in the town of Kraljevo who seemed to belong
to the categories outlined in Böhme's order, before going on to round
up indiscriminately a further 1,400 Serbs and shooting them too in order
to reach their quota of 100 'hostages' for every dead German.[75] Like
Böhme, almost all the senior army officers and SS commanders in occupied Yugoslavia were Austrians; so too were many army units, including
the 717st Infantry Division. The extreme violence they meted out to
the local population, Serbs, Gypsies and Jews, reflected not least their
deep-rooted hostility towards the Serbs, and the particularly virulent
nature of antisemitism in the country from which, like Hitler himself,
they came.[76]

Across the whole of Eastern Europe by the end of 1941, the overall
numbers of murders, above all of Jews, carried out by the army, the SS
Security Service Task Forces and their associates had reached hundreds
of thousands. Task Force A reported that by the middle of October it
had killed more than 118,000 Jews, a figure that had increased to nearly
230,000 by the end of January 1942. Task Force B had reported exactly
45,467 Jews shot by the end of October, rising to just over 91,000 by
the end of the following February. Task Force C had shot around 75,000
by 20 October 1941, and Task Force D reported nearly 55,000 by
12 December 1941 and a total of almost 92,000 by 8 April 1942. How
accurate these figures were cannot be precisely ascertained; they may in
some cases have been exaggerated, or double-counted. On the other
hand they did not include all the Jews killed by local militias or units of
the German army, whose commanders had issued orders to kill 'Jewish
Communists' and other 'Jewish elements'. The fact that senior army
officers repeatedly felt it necessary to ban their troops from taking part
in pogroms, looting and mass shootings of Jewish civilians indicates
how commonplace such actions were. In some instances, indeed, as in
that of the 707th Army Division in Belarus, the extermination of Jews
was actually organized by the military in the name of combating partisan
activity.[77] In all, it is probable that around half a million Jews were shot
by the Task Forces and associated military and paramilitary groups by
the end of 1941.[78]

Unevenly, but unmistakeably, an important step had been taken:
the extension of the killings to women and children, and the effective
abandonment of the pretext or in many cases indeed the belief that Jews
were being killed because they had organized resistance to the invading

German forces. The timing, manner and extent of the murders were more often than not a matter for local SS commanders on the ground. Himmler's role in ordering this extension and then, sometimes jointly with Heydrich, in driving it on through inspection visits to the areas where the killings were taking place, and in strengthening the SS forces in the area to enable more killing to be done, was nevertheless central.[79] It was Himmler who, in repeated verbal orders issued to his subordinates, accomplished the transition to the indiscriminate killing of Jews of both sexes and all ages in July and August 1941. He clearly believed, now and later, that he was carrying out Hitler's own wish of 16 July to shoot 'anyone who even looks askance'. Here too, as in other instances, the Nazi chain of command worked indirectly. There was no one specific, precise order; Hitler set the overall parameters of action, Himmler interpreted them, and the SS officers on the ground, with his encouragement, used their initiative in deciding when and how to put them into effect, as the uneven timing of the transition from shooting Jewish men to shooting Jewish women and children clearly showed. Nevertheless, it is clear that the mass murder of Eastern European Jews that began at this time was above all a reflection of Hitler's own personal desires and beliefs, repeatedly articulated both in public and in private during these months.[80]

Thus, for example, on 25 October 1941 Hitler was having dinner with Himmler and Heydrich, and so his thoughts naturally turned to the massacres they had set in motion in Russia, and in particular Himmler's order of early August to 'Drive Jewish women into the marshes':

In the Reichstag, I prophesied to Jewry, the Jew will disappear from Europe if war is not avoided. This race of criminals has the two million dead of the [First World] war on its conscience, and now hundreds of thousands again. Nobody can tell me: But we can't send them into the morass! For who bothers about our people? It's good if the terror that we are exterminating Jewry goes before us.[81]

On 1 August 1941, Heinrich Müller, head of the Gestapo, ordered the Reich Security Head Office to forward the reports it was receiving from the Task Forces to Hitler. Altogether, forty to fifty copies of each report were usually circulated to Party and government offices.[82] The 'Event Report number 128', issued on 3 November 1941 and containing the first six full reports of the Task Forces from July to October, was for example distributed in fifty-five copies not only to the Party Chancellery but to government departments as well, including the Foreign Office, where it was countersigned by no fewer than twenty-two officials.[83] Thus not only Hitler but also many people in the senior ranks of the Party and state administration were fully informed of the massacres being carried out by the SS Task Forces in the east.

LAUNCHING GENOCIDE

I

Given Hitler's reference on 25 October 1941 to his own prophecy of the annihilation of the Jews in the event of a world war, it is not surprising that he was thinking on a global scale at this time. In the background of Hitler's mind throughout Operation Barbarossa and what followed was the thought that the rapid defeat of the Soviet Union would also bring about the capitulation of the British. The attempt to bomb the British into submission in 1940 had clearly failed. But there were other ways of bringing them to the negotiating table. Chief among these was the disruption of their supplies, which by necessity had to come by sea, partly from Britain's far-flung Empire, but principally from the United States. The US President, Franklin Delano Roosevelt, had up to now won considerable domestic support by keeping America out of the war. But for some time he had privately thought that the USA would have to act to stop further German aggression.[84] Roosevelt therefore began a large-scale programme of arms manufacture, with Congress voting through huge sums of money for the construction of aircraft, ships, tanks and military equipment. Already on 16 May 1940, Roosevelt had brought to Congress a proposal to build no fewer than 50,000 military airplanes a year, starting immediately. This was many times the output that any of the European combatants could achieve. Secret technical discussions with the British ensured these aircraft would be of direct benefit to the British war effort. Not long afterwards, Congress also passed the Two Oceans Navy Expansion Act, inaugurating the construction of enormous Atlantic and Pacific fleets grouped around aircraft carriers that would enable the US Navy to strike at America's enemies around the world. Conscription was next, starting with the drafting and training of an army of 1.4 million men. In November 1940, Roosevelt was re-elected. Buoyed by bipartisan support in Congress, he transferred increasing quantities of military and naval supplies, as well as foodstuffs and much else, to Britain under 'lend-lease' arrangements. In 1940 alone, the British were able to purchase more than 2,000 combat aircraft from the USA; in 1941 the number rose to more than 5,000. These were significant quantities. In the middle of August 1941 Roosevelt and Churchill met to sign the 'Atlantic Charter', which included the provision that US submarines would accompany convoys to Britain for at least half of their Atlantic passage.[85]

From June 1941 the USA also began shipping supplies and equipment to the Soviet Union in ever-increasing quantities; if the USSR was defeated, then Roosevelt feared, with some justification, that Germany would return to the attack on Britain and then move on to challenge America.[86] The pace and scale of American rearmament in 1940–41, and the German invasion of the Soviet Union, which tied up Soviet forces in the west, helped persuade the aggressively expansionist Japanese government that its drive to create a new Japanese empire in South-east Asia and the Pacific required the elimination of American naval forces in the region sooner rather than later. On 7 December 1941, six Japanese aircraft carriers sent their planes to bomb the American naval base at Pearl Harbor, in Hawaii, where they sank, grounded or disabled eighteen ships, before moving on to the invasion of Thailand, Malaya and the Philippines. The attack united the American people behind intervention in the war. And it also prompted Hitler to throw off the restraint he had hitherto shown towards the USA. He now authorized the sinking of American ships in the Atlantic, to disrupt and if possible cut off US supplies to Britain and the Soviet Union. Then, gambling on America's preoccupation with the Pacific, he issued a formal declaration of war on 11 December 1941. Italy, Romania, Hungary and Bulgaria declared war on the USA as well. Hitler believed that the Japanese attack would weaken the Americans by dividing their military efforts. This would offer the best chance of defeating the USA in the Atlantic and cutting off supplies to Britain and the Soviet Union. Moreover, it would consume important British resources in the Far East as the Japanese moved on British colonies from Malaya to Burma and maybe eventually India as well. Above all, Hitler's move was governed by the realization that it was vital to strike sooner rather than later, before the vast military build-up in the USA reached its full, overwhelming extent.[87]

These events had a direct bearing on Nazi policy towards the Jews. The rapidly increasing American aid to Britain and the Soviet Union deepened Hitler's conviction that the USA was effectively participating in the war in a secret, Jewish-dominated alliance with Churchill and Stalin. On 22 June 1941, the day of the launching of Operation Barbarossa, Hitler announced that the hour had come, 'in which it will be necessary to enter the lists against this conspiracy of the Jewish-Anglo-Saxon instigators of the war and the equally Jewish rulers of the Bolshevik Moscow Central'.[88] Propaganda aimed at persuading the German people that the Roosevelt administration was part of an international Jewish conspiracy against Germany had already got under way in the spring of 1941. On 30 May and 6 June 1941 the Propaganda Ministry told the papers to emphasize that 'England [is] ultimately ruled by Jewry; same is true of the USA' and urged 'clarity about the aim of Jews in the USA at any price to destroy and exterminate Germany'.[89] Now the propaganda barrage was dramatically intensified.

Operation Barbarossa had been intended from the outset as a surprise attack, so it had not been preceded by the kind of propaganda build-up that had presaged the move against Poland in 1939. In the weeks following the invasion of the Soviet Union on 22 June 1941, the Nazi leadership thus thought it necessary to launch a propaganda offensive designed to win the retrospective approval of the German people. Almost immediately, Hitler focused his attention on the Jews. The coincidence of Operation Barbarossa with the escalation of American aid to Britain and Russia formed the central focus of the media blitz that followed. It was personally directed by Hitler himself and reflected his deepest convictions.[90] On 8 July 1941, Hitler told Goebbels to intensify media attacks on Communism. 'Our propaganda line,' wrote Goebbels the next day, 'is thus clear: we must continue to unmask the collaboration between Bolshevism and Plutocracy and now more and more expose the Jewish character of this Front as well.'[91] Instructions were duly issued to the press, and a massive campaign got underway, reinforced by further encouragement given by Hitler to his Propaganda Minister on 14 July 1941.[92]

This campaign was spearheaded by the Nazi Party's daily newspaper, the *Racial Observer*, edited since 1938 by Wilhelm Weiss. With a circulation of nearly 1.75 million, it had semi-official status. Its stories owed much to the press directives issued by Otto Dietrich, the Reich press chief, from Hitler's headquarters following his daily meeting with the Leader. Throughout the whole of 1940 it had carried not one single front-page headline of an antisemitic nature. In February and March 1941 there were three, but then there were no more for three months until a concentrated outburst began in July. On 10 and 12 July the paper carried front-page headlines on 'Jewish Bolshevism', on 13 and 15 July it turned its attention to Britain ('Jewry Floods England with Soviet Lies'), and on 23 and 24 July it carried stories about Roosevelt as the tool of Jews and Freemasons who were out to destroy Germany. There were further front-page stories on 10 and 19 August ('Roosevelt's Goal is World Domination by Jews') and there were more lurid headlines attacking Roosevelt on 27 and 29 October and 7 November, with a general lead on 'The Jewish Enemy' on 12 November. After this, the campaign died down, with only four antisemitic headlines in 1942.[93] In similar fashion, the 'Word of the Week' wall-posters, issued since 1937 in editions of 125,000, pasted up on walls and kiosks all over Germany, or mounted in specially designed glass display boxes, and changing their topic every week, had only mentioned antisemitic subjects in three out of 52 editions in 1940, but between 1941 and their cessation in 1943 attacks on the Jews were carried in about a quarter of them. In contrast to the *Racial Observer*, the wall-posters continued the campaign into 1942, with twelve out of twenty-seven issued up to July devoted to antisemitic themes.[94] Thus there was an undoubted peak in antisemitic propaganda of all kinds in the second half of 1941, reflecting Hitler's order to Goebbels on 8 July to focus his propaganda machine's attention on the Jews. The propaganda had an almost immediate effect. Already on 23 June 1941, for example, a German army NCO stationed in Lyon reported: 'Now the Jews have declared war on us all along the line, from one extreme to the other, from the London and New York plutocrats all the way to the Bolsheviks. Everything that is in thrall to the Jews is lined up in a front against us.'[95]

Much play was made in this campaign with a pamphlet by the American Theodore N. Kaufman, issued earlier in the year under the title *Germany Must Perish*, which demanded the sterilization of all German men and the parcelling-out of all Germany's territory amongst its European neighbours. Kaufman was an eccentric (to put it no more strongly than that), who had already earned the ridicule of the press in the USA by urging the sterilization of all American men to stop their children becoming murderers and criminals. Nevertheless, Goebbels seized upon his new pamphlet, portrayed Kaufman as an official adviser to the White House and trumpeted it as a Jewish product that revealed the true intentions of the Roosevelt government towards Germany: 'Enormous Jewish Extermination Programme,' announced the *Racial Observer* on 24 July 1941. 'Roosevelt Demands Sterilization of German People: German People to be Exterminated within Two Generations.'[96] 'Germany Must be Annihilated!' declared the 'Word of the Week' poster for 10 October 1941. 'Always the Same Aim.'[97] Goebbels declared he would have Kaufman's book translated into German and distributed in millions of copies, 'above all on the front'. A booklet containing translated extracts was duly published in September 1941, in which the editor declared it was proof that 'World Jewry in New York, Moscow and London agrees on demanding the complete extermination of the German people'.[98] The Propaganda Minister coupled this with repeated press reporting of alleged atrocities against German soldiers by troops of the Red Army. The message was clear: the Jews were conspiring across the world to exterminate the Germans; self-defence demanded that they be killed wherever they were found.[99] In response to the threat, as Goebbels declared on 20 July 1941 in an article for *The Reich*, a weekly journal he had founded in May 1940 and which had reached a circulation of 800,000 by this time, Germany and indeed Europe would deliver a blow to the Jews 'without pity and without mercy' that would bring about 'their ruin and downfall'.[100]

That blow fell in stages in the late summer and early autumn of 1941. From late June onwards the Task Forces and their auxiliaries were, as we have seen, killing increasing numbers of Jewish men, then, from mid-August, Jewish women and children as well, in the east. But it was already clear by this time that the Nazi leaders were thinking not just on a regional but on a European scale. On 31 July 1941 Heydrich took to Göring, who was formally in charge of Jewish policy, a brief document to sign. It gave Heydrich the power 'to make all necessary preparations in organizational, practical and material respects for a total solution of the Jewish question in the German sphere of influence in Europe'. The key point about this order, which also empowered Heydrich to consult all other central Party and government offices if their areas of competence were affected, was that it extended Heydrich's brief to the entire

Continent. It was not a command to initiate, still less to implement, a 'total solution of the Jewish question', it was a command to make preparations for such an action. But, on the other hand, it was a good deal more than the commission that some historians have seen in it merely to undertake 'feasibility studies' that might or might not be used some time in the future – the subsequent reports and references to the outcome of such studies that one might expect in the documentary record are simply not there.[101]

The matter hung fire for a few weeks while Hitler and the generals argued about whether to move on Moscow or divert the German armies further north and south; and then for much of early August Hitler was seriously ill with dysentery.[102] By mid-August, however, he was well enough to launch a fresh diatribe against the Jews, recorded by Goebbels in his diary entry of 19 August 1941:

The Leader is convinced that the prophecy he made then in the Reichstag, that if Jewry succeeded again in provoking a world war, it would end with the annihilation of the Jews, is confirming itself. It is becoming true in these weeks and months with a certainty that seems almost uncanny. The Jews are having to pay the price in the east; it has to a degree already been paid in Germany, and they will have to pay it still more in future. Their last refuge remains North America, and there in the long or short run they will one day have to pay it too.[103]

It was remarkable how Goebbels here let slip the global scope of Nazism's ultimate geopolitical ambitions. More immediately these remarks coincided, not by chance, with a marked escalation in the killings carried out by the Task Forces in occupied Eastern Europe. Moreover, from February to April 1941, Hitler had sanctioned the deportation of some 7,000 Jews from Vienna to the Lublin district at the request of the Nazi Regional Leader of the former Austrian capital, Baldur von Schirach, who had come to prominence in the 1930s as the head of the Hitler Youth. Schirach's main aim was to obtain their houses and apartments for distribution to the non-Jewish homeless. At the same time, his action stood in a continuity of ideologically driven antisemitic measures that went back to the first days of the German occupation of Vienna in March 1938.[104] For some months this remained a relatively isolated action. In order to avoid any possible disturbance at home while the war was still in progress, Hitler for the time being vetoed Heydrich's proposal to begin evacuating German Jews from Berlin as well.[105]

But in mid-August Hitler once more took up the idea that he had rejected earlier in the summer of 1941, of starting to deport Germany's remaining Jews to the east. By mid-September his wishes had become widely known in the Nazi hierarchy. On 18 September 1941, Himmler told Arthur Greiser, the Regional Leader of the Wartheland: 'The Leader wants the old Reich and the Protectorate [of Bohemia and Moravia] to be emptied and liberated of Jews from west to east as soon as possible.'[106] Hitler may have thought of the deportations, which were to be carried out openly, as a warning to 'international Jewry', especially in the USA, not to escalate the war any further, or worse things would happen to the Jews of Germany. He had come under pressure to take retaliatory measures against 'Jewish-Bolshevik' Russia following Stalin's forcible deportation of the Volga Germans.[107] Regional Leaders, notably Karl Kaufmann in Hamburg, were pressing for Jews to be evicted to make room for bombed-out German families. Joseph Goebbels, in his capacity as Regional Leader of Berlin, was determined 'that we must evacuate the Jews from Berlin as quickly as possible'. This would be possible 'as soon as we have cleared up the military questions in the east'.[108] The fact that vast tracts of territory had already been conquered east of the General Government had already opened up the possibility of deporting Jews there from Central Europe. They would, Goebbels said after a meeting with Heydrich, be put into the labour camps already set up by the Communists. 'What is more obvious than that they should now be peopled by the Jews?'[109] Overriding all other possible motives in Hitler's mind was that of security: in his memory of 1918, the Jews had stabbed Germany in the back, and ever since he had come to power he had been attempting by increasingly radical means to prevent this recurring by driving them out of the country. On the one hand, the threat had seemingly increased following the invasion of the Soviet Union and the growing involvement of America in the war. On the other, the opportunity for mass deportation now presented itself with the new territorial annexations in the east. The moment seemed to have come for action on a European scale.[110]

II

During this period, conditions of life deteriorated rapidly for those Jews who remained in Germany. One of them was Victor Klemperer, whose position was still to some extent protected by his marriage to a non-Jew, his wife Eva, and his record as a war veteran. Imprisoned in a police cell in Dresden on 23 June 1941 for violating blackout regulations, Klemperer found the time in jail weighed heavily on his mind. But he was not badly treated, and, despite his obsessive worry that he had been forgotten, he was released on 1 July 1941. He settled back into life in the overcrowded Jews' House he was forced to share with his wife and other, similar, couples in Dresden.[111] Soon his diary was filled with the growing difficulties he and his non-Jewish wife experienced in what he called 'the hunt for food'. In April 1942 he recorded despairingly that 'we are now facing complete starvation. Today even turnips were only "for registered customers". Our potatoes are finished, our bread coupons will last for perhaps two weeks, not four.'[112] They began to beg and barter.[113] By the middle of 1942 Klemperer was feeling constantly hungry and had been reduced to stealing food from another inhabitant of the house ('with a good conscience', he confessed, 'because she needs little, allows much to go to waste, is given many things by her aged mother – but I feel so demeaned').[114]

From 18 September 1941, following a decree issued by the Reich Ministry of Transport, German Jews were no longer allowed to use dining cars on trains, to go on excursion coaches, or to travel by public transport in the rush hour.[115] As his wife sewed the Jewish star on to the left breast of his coat on 19 September 1941, Klemperer had 'a raving fit of despair'. Like many other Jews, he felt ashamed to go out (ashamed 'of what?', he asked himself rhetorically). His wife began to take over the shopping.[116] Klemperer's typewriter was confiscated and from 28 October 1941 onwards he had to write his diary and the remainder of his autobiography by hand.[117] More petty privations followed. Jews were denied coupons for shaving-soap ('do they want to reintroduce the medieval Jew's beard by force?' Klemperer asked ironically).[118] A list he compiled of all the restrictions to which they were subjected ran by this time to over thirty items, including bans on using buses, going to museums, buying flowers, owning fur coats and woollen blankets, entering railway stations, eating in restaurants, and sitting in deck chairs.[119] A law issued on 4 December 1941 laid down the death penalty for virtually any offence committed by a Jew.[120] On 13 March 1942 the Reich Security Head Office ordered a white paper star to be pasted on the entrance to every dwelling inhabited by Jews.[121] A further blow came in May 1942 when the authorities announced that Jews would no longer be allowed to keep pets, or to give them away; with a heavy heart, Klemperer and his wife took their cat Muschel to a friendly vet and had it put to sleep illegally, to spare it the suffering they thought it would be subjected to if they handed it over in the general round-up.[122] All of these measures, as their timing makes clear, were intended to prepare for the mass deportation of Germany's Jews to the east.[123]

To underline the firmness of the deportation decision, Himmler ordered on 23 October 1941 that Jews were no longer to be allowed to emigrate from the German Reich or any country occupied by it.[124] The end of the Jewish community in Germany was also signalled by the Gestapo's dissolution of the Jewish Culture League on 11 September 1941; its assets, musical instruments, possessions and property were distributed to a variety of institutions including the SS and the army.[125] All remaining Jewish schools in the Reich had already been closed down.[126] The round-ups and deportations got under way on 15 October 1941; according to decrees issued on 29 May and 25 November 1941 and personally approved by Hitler, the deported were deprived of their German nationality and their property was confiscated by the state. By 5 November 1941, twenty-four long trainloads of Jews – some 10,000 from the Old Reich, 5,000 from Vienna and 5,000 from the Protectorate – had been transported to Łódź, along with 5,000 Gypsies from the rural Austrian territory of the Burgenland. By 6 February 1942, a further thirty-four trainloads had taken 33,000 Jews to Riga, Kovno and Minsk.[127] This still left a substantial number who were performing forced-labour tasks thought important to the war economy. Goebbels was disappointed and pressed for the deportations to be speeded up. On 22 November 1941 he was able to note in his diary that Hitler had agreed to further deportations on a city-by-city basis.[128]

To prepare the deportations, the Gestapo would obtain lists of local Jews from the Reich Association of the Jews in Germany, pick out the names of those to be deported, give each of them a sequenced number, and inform them of the date on which they were to depart and the arrangements to be taken for the journey. Each deportee was allowed to take 50 kilos of luggage, and provisions for three to five days. They were taken by the local police to a collection centre, from where, after waiting often for many hours, they were transported to an ordinary passenger train for the journey. These measures were intended to prevent the Jews becoming alarmed about their fate. Yet the trains began their journey at night, in shunting yards instead of passenger stations, and not infrequently the deportees were roughly pushed on to the train by the police, with curses and blows. A police guard accompanied each transport on the journey. When the deportees reached their destination, their situation deteriorated radically. The first trainload to leave Munich, for instance, set out on 20 November 1941, and after being diverted from its original destination of Riga, where the ghetto was full, it arrived in Kovno three days later. Informed that the ghetto there was full too, the police took the deportees to the nearby Fort IX, where they were made to wait in the dry moat surrounding the building for two days until they were all shot.[129]

In January 1942 the order came for the Jews of Dresden to be deported to the east. Victor Klemperer's relief was palpable, therefore, when he learned that holders of the Iron Cross, First Class, who lived in 'mixed marriages', such as himself, were exempt.[130] For those who remained, life became still harder. On 14 February 1942 Klemperer, aged sixty and in less than perfect health, was ordered to report for work clearing snow off the streets. Arriving at the venue, he discovered that he was the youngest of the twelve Jewish men on the site. Fortunately, he reported, the overseers from the municipal cleansing department were decent and polite, allowed the men to stand around chatting, and told Klemperer: 'You must not over-exert yourself, the state does not require it.'[131] They were paid the meagre sum of just over 70 Reichsmarks a week after tax.[132] When this service was no longer required, Klemperer was sent to work in a packing factory.[133] The Gestapo became ever more brutal and abusive, and Jews came to dread house-searches by the authorities. When Klemperer's own Jews' House was searched, he was fortuitously out visiting a friend. He returned to find the house had been turned over. All the food and wine had been stolen, along with some money and some medication. The contents of cupboards, drawers and shelves had been emptied on to the floor and stamped on. Anything they wanted to steal, including bed-linen, the Gestapo men had stowed into four suitcases and a large trunk, which they ordered the inhabitants to take to the police station the following day. Eva Klemperer had been insulted ('You Jew's whore, why did you marry the Jew?') and repeatedly spat at in the face. 'What an unthinkable disgrace for Germany,' was Victor Klemperer's reaction.[134] '*These* are no longer house searches,' his wife commented, 'they're *pogroms*.'[135] Desperately worried that the Gestapo would find his diaries ('one is murdered for lesser misdemeanours'), Klemperer started to get his wife to take them at more frequent intervals to his non-Jewish friend, the doctor Annemarie Köhler, for safe keeping. 'But I shall go on writing,' he declared in May 1942. 'This is *my* heroism. I intend to bear witness, precise witness!'[136]

In Hamburg, thankful that his privileged status as the war-decorated husband of a non-Jew and bringing up a daughter as a Christian meant that her Jewish husband Friedrich did not have to wear the yellow star, Luise Solmitz recorded bitterly on 13 September 1941: 'Our luck is now negative – everything that doesn't affect us.' The Solmitzes secured a ruling from the Gestapo that people in privileged mixed marriages such as theirs were not obliged to accommodate Jews in their houses. Cuts in pensions, benefits and rations they shared with other Germans. Otherwise they lived much as they had done before, though necessarily more privately, since Friedrich was effectively barred from taking part in the social life of the non-Jewish circles in which they had previously moved. Luise Solmitz and her husband steadily lost weight as food supplies became shorter in the course of 1941. By 21 December 1942 she weighed 96 pounds. Yet her principal worry about changes in rationing arrangements was not so much that their diet would become even more restricted, but that she would be banned from collecting the family's ration cards, and Friedrich would have to go to the ration office himself as a Jew, with his 'evil, impossible epithet' imposed by the government ('Israel') and queue 'amidst all the people who one has never had anything to do with', or in other words Hamburg's remaining population of Jews. Her concern for the safety of her half-Jewish daughter Gisela grew as rumours circulated that people classified as mixed-race were to be deported. 'We are already the playthings of dark and malicious powers,' she recorded gloomily in her diary on 24 November 1942.[137]

III

It is clear that by October 1941 the deportation idea encompassed in principle the whole of Europe, and was intended to begin almost immediately.[138] On 4 October 1941 Heydrich referred to 'the plan of a total evacuation of the Jews from the territories occupied by us'.[139] In early November 1941, he defended his approval of antisemitic attacks on Parisian synagogues that had taken place four days earlier in view of the fact that 'Jewry has been identified at the highest level with the greatest clarity as the fire-raiser responsible for what has happened in Europe, and must finally disappear from Europe.'[140] Hitler himself sharply increased his rhetorical attacks on the Jews once more, not just in the Soviet Union and the USA but also in Europe as a whole. On 28 November 1941, meeting the Grand Mufti of Jerusalem, Haj Amin al-Husseini, Hitler declared: 'Germany is determined to press one European nation after the other to solve the Jewish problem.' In Palestine too, he assured the Mufti, the Jews would be dealt with once Germany gained control of the area.[141]

By this time, the surviving Jews in the regions conquered by the German forces in Eastern Europe were being rounded up and confined in ghettos in the principal towns. At Vilna (Vilnius), beginning on 6 September 1941, 29,000 Jews were crammed into an area formerly housing only 4,000 people. Visiting the Vilna ghetto at the beginning of November 1941, Goebbels noted that 'the Jews are squatting amongst one another, horrible forms, not to be seen, let alone to be touched ... The Jews are the lice of civilized humanity. They have to be exterminated somehow ... Wherever you spare them, you later become their victim.'[142] Another ghetto was set up at Kovno on 10 July 1941, where a Jewish population of 18,000 was subjected to frequent, violent raids by German and Lithuanian forces searching for valuables.[143] Smaller ghettos were established around the same time in other towns in the Baltic states in the wake of major massacres of the local Jewish population. Since these massacres had mainly, at least in the initial phase, been directed against men, these ghettos often had a preponderance of women and children: in Riga, for example, where the ghetto was set up towards the end of October 1941, there were nearly 19,000 women compared to just over 11,000 men when the ghetto was closed just over a month later. 24,000 were taken out and shot on 30 November and 8 December 1941, the remainder, mostly men, being sent off to Germany as industrial labourers. A similar mass killing happened on a larger scale in Kovno on 28 October 1941, when Helmut Rauca, head of the Jewish Department of the Gestapo in the town, ordered its 27,000 Jewish inhabitants to assemble at six in the morning on the main square. All day long, Rauca and his men separated those who could work from those who could not. By dusk, 10,000 Jews had been sorted into the latter category. The rest were sent home. The next morning, the 10,000 were marched out of the city on foot to Fort IX and shot in batches.[144]

Almost all of the ghettos created in occupied Eastern Europe following the invasion of the Soviet Union were improvised and relatively short-lived, designed as little more than holding areas for Jews destined for death in the very near future. In Yalta, a ghetto was created on 5 December 1941 by partitioning off an area on the edge of the city: on 17 December 1941, less than two weeks later, it was shut down and its inhabitants killed. A similar pattern could be observed in other centres too.[145] Clearly, the Jews of Eastern Europe were not expected to live much longer. The ghettos were to be cleared in order to make way for the Jews whose expulsion Hitler was now repeatedly urging from the 'Old Reich' and the Protectorate of Bohemia and Moravia, and following this from the rest of German-occupied Europe. Some historians have tried to identify a precise date on which Hitler ordered the expulsion and extermination of Europe's Jews. Yet the evidence for this is unpersuasive. Much has been made of the fact that, long after the war, Adolf Eichmann recalled that Heydrich had summoned him in late September or early October to tell him that 'The Leader has ordered the physical extermination of the Jews.' Himmler was also to refer to such a command on more than one occasion in the future. But it is extremely doubtful whether it was given to Himmler or Heydrich or indeed anyone else in so many words. Hitler's statements, recorded in a number of sources, most notably the public record of his speeches and the private notes of his conversations in Goebbels's diary and the *Table Talk*, represent both the style and the substance of what he had to say on this issue. It is a mistake to look for, or imagine, an order, whether written or spoken, of the kind issued by Hitler in the case of the compulsory euthanasia programme, where it was required to give legitimacy to the actions of professional doctors rather than committed SS men, who scarcely needed it anyway.[146] As the Nazi Party's Supreme Court had noted early in 1939, under the Weimar Republic, Party leaders had become accustomed to evading legal responsibility by ensuring 'that actions . . . are not ordered with absolute clarity or in every detail'. Correspondingly, Party members had become accustomed 'to read more out of such a command than it says in words, just as it has become a widespread custom on the part of the people issuing the command . . . not to say everything' and 'only to hint' at the purpose of an order.[147]

Thus Hitler is extremely unlikely to have gone any further than issuing the kind of statements which he repeatedly made from the middle of 1941 onwards in respect of the Jews, backed up by virulently antisemitic propaganda from Goebbels and his co-ordinated mass media. Such statements were often widely broadcast and publicized, and those made in public at least would have been familiar to virtually every member of the Party, the SS and similar organizations. When added to the explicit orders given in advance of Barbarossa to kill Soviet commissars and Jews, and the murderous policies already implemented in Poland since September 1939, they created a genocidal mentality in which Himmler in Berlin and his senior officers on the ground in the east competed to see how thoroughly and how radically they could put Hitler's repeated promise, or threat, to annihilate the Jews of Europe into effect. Often they were faced with severe food shortages, and, as in Poland, they established a hierarchy of food rationing in which the Jews were inevitably bottom of the heap. From here to active extermination was but a short step for many zealous local and regional commanders, who – as in Belarus – also ordered the killing of other people seen as unable to work and therefore 'useless eaters', as the phrase had it. Among these were the mentally ill and the handicapped. They were murdered not for racial reasons, though the German 'euthanasia' campaign had provided an important precedent, but for economic ones. The SS did not object to 'degenerative' influences on Slavic heredity; they simply considered the mentally ill and handicapped in these areas surplus to requirements.[148]

The concrete results of such a mentality were evident by the middle of October 1941 at the latest. By this time, Jews from the Greater German Reich and the Protectorate were being deported to the east, and Jews from the rest of German-occupied Europe were to follow. No Jews were allowed to emigrate. There are numerous statements from this time at various levels of the Nazi hierarchy testifying that there was common agreement that all Europe's Jews were to be deported to the east. Task Forces were indiscriminately shooting huge numbers of Jews all across occupied Eastern Europe. In a lecture delivered to senior military, police, Party, Labour Front, academic, cultural and other figures at the German Academy on 1 December 1941, Goebbels reported that Hitler's prophecy of 30 January 1939 was now being fulfilled.

Sympathy or even regret is wholly out of place. World Jewry in unleashing this war made a completely false assessment of the forces at its disposal. It is now suffering a gradual process of annihilation that it intended for us and that it would without question have carried out if it had the power to do so. It is now perishing as a result of Jewry's own law: 'An eye for an eye and a tooth for a tooth'.[149]

Although the mass murder, as Goebbels hinted, was, for obvious reasons of practicality, to be carried out in stages, there was now no doubt that, as Alfred Rosenberg put it, speaking at a press conference on 18 November 1941, that the aim was the 'biological extermination of the whole of Jewry in Europe'.[150]

By this time, it was clear that military authorities, police units, SS and civil administrators were co-operating without difficulty in the implementation of the extermination programme. According to a report compiled by the Arms Inspectorate of the Armed Forces, Ukrainian militia, 'in many places, regrettably, with the voluntary participation of members of the German armed forces', had been shooting Jewish men, women and children in a 'horrible' manner. Up to 200,000 had been killed already in the Reich Commissariat of the Ukraine, and in the end the total would reach nearly half a million.[151] But already it was becoming clear that mass shooting could not achieve the scale of extermination that Himmler was demanding. Moreover, complaints were coming in from Task Force leaders that continual mass shootings of defenceless women and children were placing an intolerable strain on their men. As Rudolf Höss, a senior SS officer, later recalled, 'I always shuddered at the prospect of carrying out exterminations by shooting, when I thought of the vast numbers concerned, and of the women and children.' Many members of the Task Forces, 'unable to endure wading through blood any longer, had committed suicide. Some had even gone mad. Most . . . had to rely on alcohol when carrying out their horrible work.'[152] The numbers of Jews to be shot were so great that one Task Force report concluded on 3 November 1941: 'Despite the fact that up to now a total of some 75,000 Jews have been liquidated in this way, it has nevertheless become apparent that this method will not provide a solution to the Jewish problem.'[153]

IV

A solution to the problem, however, presented itself immediately. After the enforced termination of the T-4 'euthanasia' action on 24 August 1941, following its denunciation by Bishop Clemens von Galen, its lethal gas technicians became available for redeployment in the east.[154] Specialists from the T-4 unit visited Lublin in September; so too did Viktor Brack and Philipp Bouhler, its two leading administrators. Dr August Becker, who described himself as 'a specialist in the gassing processes involved in exterminating the mentally sick', later remembered:

I was transferred to the Reich Security Head Office in Berlin as a result of a private conversation between Reich Leader SS Himmler and Senior Service Leader Brack. Himmler wanted to deploy people who had become available as a result of the suspension of the euthanasia programme and who, like me, were specialists in extermination by gassing, for the large-scale gassing operations in the east which were just beginning.[155]

In addition, Albert Widmann, who had devised the standard gas chamber used in the 'euthanasia' programme, visited Minsk and Mogilev, where Task Force B had requested technical assistance in killing the patients of the local mental hospitals. Such murders were a standard part of Task Force activities in the east, as they had been in Poland in 1939–40, and several thousand mental patients fell victim to them. After a number of patients had been killed by carbon monoxide gases from car exhaust fumes being pumped into a sealed room, Arthur Nebe, the head of the Task Force, conceived the idea of killing people by putting them in an airtight van and piping the exhaust fumes into it. Heydrich gave his approval.[156]

On 13 October 1941, Himmler met regional police chiefs Globocnik and Krüger in the early evening and agreed that a camp should be built at Belzec, to serve as a base for the gas vans. It was, in other words, to be a camp created for the sole purpose of killing people.[157] Construction began on 1 November 1941, and specialists from the T-4 operation were sent there the following month.[158] The inhabitants of the Polish ghettos were now being systematically killed to make space for the Jews who were to be taken there from other parts of Europe. A similar centre was set up at Chelmno in the Wartheland, from where Jewish prisoners, transported from the Lódź ghetto, would be taken out in the vans to be gassed. The three gas vans based at Chelmno could kill fifty people each at a time, driving them out from the camp to woods about 16 kilometres distant, asphyxiating the people inside along the way. There they halted to unload their grisly cargo into ditches dug by other Jewish inmates of the camp. Occasionally a mother inside the van managed to wrap up her baby tightly enough to keep it from breathing in the deadly fumes. Jakow Grojanowski, one of the gravediggers employed by the SS, reported how German guards picked up any babies who had survived the journey and smashed their heads against nearby trees. Up to 1,000 were killed every day; 4,400 Gypsies from the Lódź ghetto were also murdered. Altogether, 145,000 Jews were put to death in the first period of Chelmo's existence; more followed, and another 7,000 were murdered when the camp briefly reopened in the spring of 1944; the total killed in the camp exceeded 360,000.[159]

These gas wagons were among thirty built by a small vehicle manufacturer in Berlin. The first four were delivered to the Task Forces in November–December 1941; all four Task Forces were using them by the end of the year.[160] The van operators later described how up to sixty Jews, often in a poor physical state, hungry, thirsty and weak, were herded into the back of each van, fully clothed. 'It did not seem as if the Jews knew that they were about to be gassed,' one later said. 'The exhaust gases were fed into the inside of the van,' remembered Anton Lauer, a member of Police Reserve Battalion number 9. 'I can still today hear the Jews knocking and shouting, "Dear Germans, let us out."' 'When the doors were opened,' another operator recalled, 'a cloud of smoke wafted out. After the smoke had cleared we could start our foul work. It was frightful. You could see that they had fought terribly for their lives. Some of them were holding their noses. The dead had to be dragged apart.'[161]

One gas van was also sent to Serbia, where General Franz Böhme, busily exterminating Jews in reprisal for what he supposed was their part in the Chetnik uprising in progress since the previous July, reported in December 1941 that 160 German soldiers killed and 278 wounded had been avenged by the killing of between 20,000 and 30,000 Serbian civilians, including all adult male Jews and Gypsies. Up to this point the murders had encompassed only men; Böhme envisaged that the remaining 10,000 Jewish women, children and old people, as well as any surviving Jewish men, would be rounded up and put into a ghetto. Over 7,000 Jewish women and children, 500 Jewish men and 292 Gypsy women and children were herded by the SS into a camp at Sajmiste, across the river from Belgrade, where they were kept in insanitary conditions in unheated barracks while the SS arranged for a mobile gassing unit to be sent from Berlin. While the Gypsies were released, the Jews were told that they were being transferred to another camp where better conditions prevailed. No sooner had the first batch of sixty-four climbed into the lorry than the doors were sealed and the exhaust pipe swung round to pump its deadly fumes into the interior. As the lorry drove through the centre of Belgrade, past the unsuspecting crowds of pedestrians and through the daily traffic, to the firing-range at Avela on the other side of the capital, the Jews inside were all being gassed to death. A police unit at Avela removed them and threw them into an already excavated mass grave. By the beginning of May 1942 all the camp's 7,500 Jewish inmates had been killed in this way, along with the inmates and staff of the Jewish hospital in Belgrade and Jewish prisoners from another, nearby camp. Serbia, the leading SS officer in the country, Harald Turner, declared with pride in August 1942, was the only country in which the Jewish question had so far been completely 'solved'.[162]

THE WANNSEE CONFERENCE

I

On 29 November 1941 Reinhard Heydrich ordered Adolf Eichmann to draft an invitation to a variety of senior civil servants from ministries with responsibilities of one kind or another for the Jewish question, together with representatives of key SS and Nazi Party departments involved in the area. 'On 31 July 1941,' the invitation began, 'the Reich Marshal of the Greater German Reich commissioned me, with the assistance of the other central authorities, to make all necessary organizational and technical preparations for a comprehensive solution of the Jewish question and to present him with a comprehensive proposal at an early opportunity.'[163] In order to finalize the details of such a proposal, all the interested agencies needed to meet. Heydrich was particularly concerned to include representatives of institutions and departments with which the SS had experienced some problems. The Foreign Office was asked to send a senior official, belying later claims that the conference was intended only to deal with German Jews; indeed, although Heydrich did not go into any details about what exactly the conference would be discussing, the Foreign Office assumed that it would focus on arranging the round-up and deportation of Jews in every country in Europe under German occupation.[164]

The meeting was scheduled for 9 December 1941 and was to take place in a lakeside villa in the tranquil Berlin suburb of Wannsee. But the day before, on hearing of the Japanese attack on Pearl Harbor, Heydrich's staff telephoned all the invitees and postponed the conference, since it was likely that he and other participants would be called to the session of the Reichstag that this new development in international politics clearly warranted.[165] This did not mean, however, that policy towards the Jews was to take a back seat. Speaking to a meeting of senior Party officials the day after he had declared war on the USA, Hitler, as recorded in Goebbels's diary, repeated his sentiments of the previous August in more precise form:

As far as the Jewish question is concerned, the Leader is determined to clear the decks. He prophesied to the Jews that if they brought about another world war, they would thereby experience their own annihilation. That was not just waffle. The world war is here, the annihilation of Jewry must be the necessary consequence. This question is to be contemplated without any sentimentality. We are not here to pity the Jews but to pity our own German people. Now that the German people have lost another 160,000 dead on the Eastern Front, the originators of this bloody conflict will have to pay for it with their lives.[166]

On 14 December 1941 Rosenberg agreed with Hitler for reasons of international policy not to mention 'the extermination of Jewry' in a public speech he was about to deliver, even though, as Hitler remarked, 'they saddled us with the war and brought destruction; it's no wonder that they are the first to bear the consequences'.[167]

By this time, it had become clear to Hitler and everyone else in the Nazi hierarchy that the war was not going to come to an end as soon as they had expected. They now accepted that it would last through the winter, though they still thought that the Soviet Union would collapse some time in the summer of 1942. The deportation of European Jews to the east would now therefore take place before the end of the war. Hitler's radical rhetoric in November and December 1941 was designed to push on the detailed planning and implementation of this policy as quickly as possible.[168] Since the Jews were already being exterminated in the occupied territories of eastern Europe, including those like the Wartheland that had been incorporated into the Reich, it was clear that the earlier plans to deport them to the Reich Commissariat of the Ukraine, or to some undefined area further east, had now been abandoned. As Hans Frank told his staff in the General Government of Poland on 16 December 1941, after returning from the 12 December conference of Nazi leaders with Hitler in Berlin:

With the Jews – I want to say that to you with complete frankness – an end has to be made in one way or another . . . We were told in Berlin, why are you raising all these objections; we can't do anything with them in the [Reich Commissariat of the] Eastern Land or in the Reich Commissariat [of the Ukraine], liquidate them yourself!! Gentlemen, I have to forearm you against any thought of pity. We must annihilate the Jews wherever we come upon them and wherever it is at all possible, in order to sustain the total structure of the Reich here.[169]

How was this to be done, however? The number of Jews in the General Government that Frank had been told to kill was impossibly large, some three and a half million in all according to Frank (something of an exaggeration; his staff later put the number at two and a half million): 'We can't shoot these 3.5 million Jews,' complained Frank to his staff on 16 December 1941, 'we can't poison them, but we will be able to take measures that somehow lead to their successful annihilation, namely in connection with large-scale measures that are to be discussed from the Reich.'[170] What these measures were would soon become clear.

The mass murder of Eastern European Jews that began in the summer of 1941 owed something to the ideological zeal of men such as Arthur Greiser, Regional Leader of the Wartheland, and police chiefs and Task Force Leaders who on their own initiative carried out large-scale mass-acres of Jews in a number of centres. At the same time, however, they were framed by an overall policy the parameters of which were set by Hitler and implemented in practical terms by Himmler. When, for example, the police chief in Riga, Friedrich Jeckeln, had a trainload of Jewish deportees from Berlin shot on their arrival, Himmler, whose order not to kill them, sent on 30 November 1941, reached Jeckeln too late, was furious. Shooting Berlin Jews would alarm those who were still in the capital. The intention was to keep them in the Riga ghetto for the time being. Himmler disciplined Jeckeln and told him not to act on his own initiative again.[171] For the most part, however, local and regional initiatives fell well within the overall purposes of the regime. The general transfer of gassing technology to the east, along with the experts who knew how to set it up and operate it, and the participation of institutions like Frank's General Government administration, the army, the Leader's Chancellery (which supplied the gas technologists) and the Reich Security Head Office, led by Himmler, spoke of a broadly co-ordinated policy under central direction. So too did the timing of the regional killing oper-ations, which coincided with the beginnings of the organized deportations of Jews from the Reich and the commissioning of special camps near the major ghettos in the east with the sole purpose of killing their inhabitants.

No operation of this size and scale could have taken place in the Third Reich without the knowledge of Hitler, whose position as Leader made him the person to whom all these institutions were ultimately responsible. It was Hitler's murderous, but deliberately generalized, antisemitic rhetoric, repeated on many occasions in the second half of 1941, that gave Himmler and his subordinates the essential impulse to carry out the killings.[172] On occasion, Hitler confirmed his approval of the murders directly. Meeting with Himmler on 18 December, for example, he told the SS leader, according to the latter's notes, 'Jewish question/to be exterminated as partisans'.[173] The extermination of Soviet Jews was thus to be continued, under the pretext that they were partisans. The fruits of this policy were visible just over a year later in 'Report number 51', dated 29 December 1942, sent by Himmler to Hitler and, as a marginal note by Hitler's adjutant confirms, seen and read by him. Entitled 'the fight against bandits', it noted under the sub-heading of 'those assisting bandits or suspected of banditry' that the number of 'Jews executed' in southern Russia, the Ukraine and the Bialystok district in the months from August to November 1942 was no less than 363,211.[174] The sheer extent of the killings became a factor in itself, suggesting powerfully to leading Nazis that the mass extermination of Jews on a hitherto unimaginable scale was now a real possibility. By this time, the Nazi net had widened to encompass not only Polish and Soviet Jews, but Jews in the whole of occupied Europe as well.[175]

II

On 20 January 1942 the meeting of senior officials called by Heydrich the previous November finally took place. The fifteen men gathered round a table in the Wannsee villa included representatives of Rosenberg's Reich Ministry for the Occupied Eastern Territories, Frank's Office of the General Government of Poland and the SS Security Service in Poland, Latvia and the Reich Commissariat of the Eastern Territory, all of whom would be concerned with the actual operation of the extermination programme; the Reich Ministries of the Interior and Justice, the Party Chancellery and the Reich Chancellery, covering legal and administrative questions; the Foreign Office, dealing with Jews living in nominally independent countries outside Germany, particularly in Western Europe; the Four-Year Plan, to cover economic aspects; and the SS departments of the Reich Security Head Office and the Head Office for Race and Settlement, who would be in charge of the exterminations. There had been some argument between various Nazi satraps, notably Hans Frank and Alfred Rosenberg, as to who should have control over the 'Jewish question' in the occupied territories, and Heydrich wanted to assert the authority of the SS. He began, therefore, by reminding the meeting that Göring had charged him on 31 July 1941 with making the detailed arrangements for the final solution of the European Jewish question, and that overall responsibility lay with his superior, Heinrich Himmler. After outlining the measures taken over the previous several years to get Jews to emigrate from Germany, Heydrich noted that Hitler had, more recently, approved a new policy, of deporting them to the east. This, he emphasized, was only a temporary measure, though it would provide 'practical experience that is of great significance for the coming final solution of the Jewish question'.[176]

Heydrich then went on to enumerate the Jewish population of every country in Europe, including many outside the German sphere of influence. There were, for instance, he noted, 4,000 Jews in Ireland, 3,000 in Portugal, 8,000 in Sweden and 18,000 in Switzerland. All of these were neutral countries, but their inclusion in the list strongly suggested that, at some point in the not-too-distant future, the Third Reich hoped to be in a position to put pressure on them to surrender their Jewish populations for extermination. Altogether, Heydrich reckoned, the Jewish population of Europe totalled around 11 million, though, he noted disapprovingly, these were in many cases only people who practised Judaism, 'since some countries still do not have a definition of the term *Jew* according to racial principles'.[177] 'In the course of the final solution and under appropriate leadership,' he said, 'the Jews should be put to work in the East. In large, single-sex labour columns, Jews fit to work will work their way eastward constructing roads.' But this was in practice to be another form of extermination, for, Heydrich continued: 'Doubtless the large majority will be eliminated by natural causes.' Any who survived the experience would be 'dealt with appropriately because, by natural selection, they would form the germ cell of a new Jewish revival (see the experience of history)'. Those deemed 'fit to work' would in any case only be a small minority. The representative of the General Government pointed out that 'the two and a half million Jews in the region were in any case largely unable to work'. Jews over sixty-five – nearly a third of the remaining Jewish population of Germany and Austria – and Jews with war decorations or severely wounded in the First World War were to be sent to an old-age ghetto. The meeting discussed the problems of persuading occupied or allied countries to give up their Jewish populations. An 'adviser for Jewish questions' would have to be forced on the Hungarian government for this purpose. Pausing to note that the 'Jewish question' had already been 'solved' in Slovakia and Croatia, the meeting then plunged into a pedantic and inconclusive discussion about what to do with people who were 'racially mixed' – a matter that continued to be discussed in follow-up meetings and discussions, notably on 6 March 1942. It then concluded with what the minutes coyly described as 'various possible kinds of solution'. According to later testimony, this included the use of gassing vans.[178]

It has been argued that the main concern of the conference was to organize the provision of labour for the huge road-building schemes envisioned by the General Plan for the East. Thus it was not really about mass murder.[179] But in fact, Task Force C had already some months before recommended the drafting of Jews into labour projects and commented that this would 'result in a gradual liquidation of Jewry'. Jewish slave labourers would be deprived of adequate rations and worked till they dropped. Given the labour shortage under which the German war economy was increasingly suffering, using Jewish workers seemed unavoidable; but this was not in the end an alternative to killing them, merely a different way of doing it. The almost parenthetical reference to the fact that the Jews of the General Government were mostly unable to work, along with the statement that those who survived the labour columns would be killed, meant that the major purpose of the meeting was to discuss the logistics of extermination. The men sitting round the table in the Wannsee villa were well aware of this.[180]

The stress laid in the conference on 'extermination through labour' had significant administrative consequences over the following weeks. In February 1942 the administration of all the concentration camps was restructured, with the economic, construction and internal administrative divisions being merged into the new SS Economy and Administration Head Office under Oswald Pohl. Group D of Pohl's Head Office, under Richard Glücks, was now in charge of the whole system of concentration camps. These changes marked the fact that the camps were now being seen as a significant source of labour to be supplied to Germany's war industries. This had in fact already begun before the war, but it was now to become far more systematic. Nevertheless, the SS did not approach the need to utilize prisoner labour for the war economy in a rational manner. Getting the most out of such men was not, for them, a matter of improving their conditions or paying them wages. Instead, they were to be forced to increase their labour input by violence and terror. The prisoners were regarded by the SS not just as expendable, but in the medium to long term as obstacles to the racial reordering of Eastern Europe. Hence they were subjected to 'extermination through labour'. Those who became unproductive would be killed, and replaced by fresh slave labourers. This was what the SS also envisaged would happen to millions of Slavs once the war was over. The selection of able-bodied Jews for work duties provided a convenient justification for the mass killing of the millions not deemed fit to work.[181]

The talk at the Wannsee Conference, as Eichmann, who took the minutes, later admitted, had been of killing, often expressed 'in very blunt words ... totally out of keeping with legal language'.[182] The minutes had played this down, but at key points they made it clear that all the Jews of Europe would perish in one way or another. Almost all of the men round the table had at some time either given direct orders for Jews to be killed – four of them had ordered or directed the mass killings carried out by the SS Security Service Task Forces, both Eichmann and Martin Luther of the Foreign Office had explicitly called for all the Jews of Serbia to be shot, a number of participants, including the representatives of the Party Chancellery and the Foreign Office, had most probably seen the murder statistics compiled by the Task Forces and sent back to Berlin, and the officials sent to Wannsee from the General Government and the Ministry for the Occupied Eastern Territories had already sanctioned the murder of Jews deemed unfit for work – or created conditions in the ghettos that they knew to be fatal to many of their inhabitants.[183] So they had no problems in planning genocide.

At the end of the meeting, the participants stood around for a while, drinking brandy and congratulating themselves on a successful day's work. Heydrich sat down by the fireplace with Eichmann and with Heinrich Müller, the Gestapo chief, all three of them from the Reich Security Head Office. Heydrich started smoking and drank a cognac, something which, Eichmann later said, he had not seen him do before, or at least not for many years. The Ministry of the Interior and the General Government had both come into line, and Heydrich's overall authority in the 'final solution' had been unambiguously affirmed. Sending out thirty copies of the minutes to a variety of officials, Heydrich noted that 'happily the basic line' had been set down 'as regards the practical execution of the final solution of the Jewish question'.[184] On reading his copy of the minutes, Joseph Goebbels noted: 'The Jewish Question must now be solved on a pan-European scale.' On 31 January 1942, Eichmann sent out new deportation orders. Transport problems delayed matters for some weeks, so he ordered a fresh series of deportations of German Jews in March.[185] They were taken, not to extermination camps, but to ghettos in the east. Here they would be confined for a while, possibly until the end of the war, before being killed. In the meantime, those who were capable of it would be used as labour. To make room for them, the Polish and East European Jews in the ghettos would have to be taken out and exterminated in the nearby camps that were already being prepared for this purpose.[186]

III

The Wannsee Conference and its aftermath took place in an atmosphere of violent antisemitic propaganda, led by Hitler himself. On 30 January 1942, in his traditional speech marking the anniversary of his appointment as Reich Chancellor in 1933, Hitler reminded his audience at the Sports Palace in Berlin that he had prophesied in 1939 that if the Jews started a world war, they would be annihilated: 'We are . . . clear that the war can only end either by the Aryan peoples being exterminated or by Jewry disappearing from Europe . . . This time the true old Jewish law "an eye for an eye, a tooth for a tooth" is being applied for the first time!'[187] Privately, Hitler assured Himmler and Lammers that the Jews would have to leave Europe altogether. 'I don't know,' he told them on 25 January 1942,

I'm colossally humane. In the days of Papal rule in Rome the Jews were badly treated. Every year up to 1830, eight Jews were driven through the city with donkeys. I'm only saying, they have to go. If they perish in the process, I can't do anything about it. I only see total extermination if they don't leave of their own free will. Why should I regard a Jew any differently from a Russian prisoner? Many are dying in the prison camps because we have been driven into this situation by the Jews. But what can I do about it? Why then did the Jews provoke the war?[188]

Here was a moment in which Hitler admitted the killing of large numbers of Soviet prisoners of war, declaring that the same fate was befalling the Jews of Europe, while at the same time verbally washing his hands of responsibility for both acts of mass murder: in his own imagination, it was the Jews who were responsible.

Hitler's justification of the genocide continued through the early months of 1942, couched in terms that wanted for nothing in clarity. His repeated insistence on the need to destroy, remove, annihilate, exterminate the Jews of Europe constituted a series of impulses to his subordinates, headed by Himmler, to press on with the extermination of the Jews even before the war was over.[189] On 14 February 1942 Hitler told Goebbels

that he is determined to clear up the Jews in Europe without compunction. It is impermissible to have any kind of sentimental emotions here. The Jews have deserved the catastrophe they are experiencing today. As our enemies are annihilated so they will experience their own annihilation too. We must accelerate this process with cold ruthlessness, and in so doing we are rendering an incalculable service to a human race that has been tormented by Jewry for millennia.[190]

Goebbels himself was well aware of the process by which the killing programme was being implemented. On 27 March 1942 he confided to his diary the details he had learned – or at least some of them; even Goebbels was too cautious to put everything down on paper. The passage is a crucial one, for Hitler's views as much as for those of his Propaganda Minister, and deserves to be quoted at length:

The Jews are now being pushed out of the General Government, beginning in Lublin, to the east. A pretty barbaric procedure is being applied here, and it is not to be described in any more detail, and not much is left of the Jews themselves. In general one may conclude that 60% of them must be liquidated, while only 40% can be put to work. The former Regional Leader of Vienna [Globocnik], who is carrying out this action, is doing it pretty prudently and with a procedure that doesn't work too conspicuously. The Jews are being punished barbarically, to be sure, but they have fully deserved it. The prophecy that the Leader issued to them on the way, for the eventuality that they started a new world war, is beginning to realize itself in the most terrible manner. One must not allow any sentimentalities to rule in these matters. If we did not defend ourselves against them, the Jews would annihilate us. It is a struggle for life and death between the Aryan race and the Jewish bacillus. No other government and no other regime could muster the strength for a general solution of the question. Here too the Leader is the persistent pioneer and spokesman of a radical solution, which is demanded by the way things are and thus appears to be unavoidable.[191]

The ghettos in the General Government, he went on, would be filled by Jews from the Reich as they became free (in other words, when their inhabitants had been killed), and then the process would repeat itself.[192] His insistence that the Jews were hell-bent on the extermination of the German race provided an implicit justification for killing them en masse.

This series of antisemitic tirades culminated in a speech delivered by Hitler to the last-ever meeting of the Reichstag, on the afternoon of 26 April 1942. The Jews, he said, had destroyed the cultural traditions of human society. 'What then remains is the animal part of the human being and a Jewish stratum that, having been brought to leadership, in the end parasitically destroys its own source of nourishment.' Only now was the new Europe declaring war on this process of the decomposition of its peoples by the Jews.[193] On the same day, Goebbels noted in his diary: 'Once more I talk through the Jewish question with the Leader, at length. His position with regard to this problem is unrelenting. He wishes to expel the Jews from Europe absolutely.'[194] Hitler's speeches in these months were accompanied by a swelling chorus of antisemitic addresses by other Nazi leaders and anti-Jewish diatribes in the press. In a speech delivered in the Sports Palace in Berlin on 2 February 1942, German Labour Front Leader Robert Ley declared that 'Jewry will and must be exterminated. That is our holy mission. That is what this war is about.'[195] Crucial here were the Nazi leaders' ideologically driven anxieties about the security threat that Jews were believed to pose. These were dramatically illustrated by a bomb attack, organized by a group of Communist resisters under the leadership of Herbert Baum, on an anti-Soviet exhibition in Berlin on 18 May 1942. Little damage was done and nobody was hurt. But the action made a considerable impression on the Nazi leadership. The Gestapo succeeded in tracking down and arresting the perpetrators, among whom, Goebbels wrote on 24 May

1942, there were five Jews and three half-Jews as well as four non-Jews. 'One sees from this composition how correct our Jewish policy is,' he noted. Goebbels thought this showed that all remaining Jews had to be removed from Berlin as a security measure. 'Of course, liquidation would be the best thing.'[196] Baum committed suicide after being tortured, the other members of the group were executed, and 250 Jewish men incarcerated in Sachsenhausen were shot as a 'reprisal', to be replaced by another 250 Jewish men from Berlin taken there as hostages. On 23 May 1942 Hitler told Nazi leaders assembled in the Reich Chancellery that the bomb attack demonstrated 'that the Jews are determined to bring this war to a victorious conclusion for themselves under all circumstances, since they know that defeat also means personal liquidation for them.'[197] In conversation with the Propaganda Minister on 29 May 1942, Hitler agreed to override objections to the deportation of Jewish forced labourers from Berlin. They could be replaced by foreign workers. 'I see a great danger,' said Goebbels, 'in the fact that 40,000 Jews who have nothing more to lose are at large in the capital of the Reich.' The experience of the First World War, Hitler added, showed that Germans would only take part in subversive movements when persuaded to do so by Jews. 'In any case,' wrote Goebbels, 'it is the Leader's aim to make the whole of Western Europe Jew-free.'[198]

These radical diatribes against the Jews were translated into action by Heinrich Himmler, who met Hitler on a number of occasions in these months for confidential discussions. In the late winter and early spring of 1942, following the Wannsee Conference, Himmler repeatedly pushed on the killing programme. He visited Cracow and Lublin on 13–14 March, when the programme of mass killings by poison gas began. A month later, on 17 April 1942, a day after talking with Hitler, he was in Warsaw, where he ordered the murder of the Western European Jews who had arrived in the Lódź ghetto. After further consultation with Hitler on 14 July 1942, Himmler travelled eastwards again to accelerate the killing programme. At Lublin, he sent an order to Krüger, the Chief of Police in the General Government, to organize the killing of the remaining Jews in the General Government by the end of the year. Himmler even issued a written order for the extermination of the last Ukrainian Jews, which began in May 1942. As in the previous autumn and winter, Himmler, busily travelling around the occupied areas of Poland, pushed on the killings time and again. The Wannsee Conference had made the process easier to co-ordinate and implement, but it had neither inaugurated it nor made it into an automatic sequence of events.[199] Himmler's restless activity ensured that it was put into effect. As he noted on 26 July 1942, in response to an attempt by Rosenberg to interfere, as he saw it, in policy towards the Jews: 'The occupied eastern territories will be Jew-free. The Leader has laid the implementation of this very difficult order on my shoulders. Therefore I forbid anyone else to have a say in it.'[200]

At the same time, in the Reich Security Head Office, Adolf Eichmann was following up the Wannsee Conference by issuing a stream of orders intended to set the trains rolling to the ghettos of Eastern Europe once more. On 6 March 1942 he told Gestapo chiefs that 55,000 more Jews would have to be deported from the 'Old Reich', the Protectorate and the 'Eastern March' (i.e., the former Austria). Some sixty trains, each loaded with up to 1,000 deportees, made their way to the ghettos during the following weeks. The removal of most of the employees of the remaining Jewish institutions began, with the first trainload going on 20 October 1942, to be followed by Jewish inmates of concentration camps in the Reich. Following the decision to begin deporting Jewish munitions workers in Germany and replace them with Poles, the police began rounding up the remaining 'full Jews' and their families in Germany on 27 February 1943. The first trainload left on 1 March 1943 and by the end of the first week of the action nearly 11,000 Jews had been transported, including 7,000 from Berlin, where most remaining German Jews now lived. Between 1,500 and 2,000 Berlin Jews who had been arrested had been able to show the police that they were exempted from deportation, mostly because they were married to non-Jewish partners. While the authorities worked out the details of where they were to be sent to work – not in munitions factories any more, for security reasons, but in the few remaining Jewish institutions in the capital, such as hospitals – the internees' wives, relatives and friends gathered on the pavement across from the building at Rosenstrasse 2–4 where they had been detained, waiting for the decision, calling out to them, and occasionally trying to get food parcels into the building. By 8 March 1943 most of the internees had been reassigned to new jobs; the rest followed. The small crowd dispersed. Subsequent legend elevated this incident into a rare public protest that had secured the internees' release; but there had never been any intention of sending these particular Jews east for extermination, and the crowd had not engaged in any kind of explicit protest.[201] By this time, the last remnants of Jewish community organizations in Germany had finally been destroyed; the only Jews left were those in a privileged position (mostly through marriage to non-Jews) or those who had gone underground.

For some, suicide seemed the only dignified way out. The devout Protestant writer Jochen Klepper, whose wife and stepdaughters were Jewish, had rejected the idea of resistance, as so many did, for patriotic reasons. 'We cannot wish Germany's downfall out of bitterness against the Third Reich,' he wrote in his diary on the outbreak of war.[202] As one fresh antisemitic measure after another impinged on his immediate family, Klepper managed to secure permission for one of his stepdaughters to emigrate, but the other daughter, Renate, stayed on. In 1937 he had sent Reich Interior Minister Wilhelm Frick copies of his successful historical novel The Father: The Novel of the Soldier King, and in October 1941 used Frick's appreciation of his work to secure an official letter certifying that Renate would be exempted from deportation. On 5 December 1942, Renate obtained an immigration permit from the Swedish Embassy in Berlin, but when Klepper visited Frick to try to obtain permission for his wife to leave with her, the Interior Minister told him: 'I can't protect your wife. I can't protect any Jews. Such things can't by their very nature be carried out in secret. They'll come to the Leader's ears and then there'll be a murderous row.'[203] It was likely, said Frick, that the two women would be deported to the east. 'God knows,' wrote Klepper despairingly, 'that I can't bear to let Hanni and the child go on this cruellest and most dreadful of all deportations.'[204] There remained one last chance. Since Frick had in any case lost the power to grant emigration permits, Klepper pulled some more strings and obtained a personal interview with Adolf Eichmann, who told him that while his daughter probably would be able to leave, his wife would not. Klepper, his wife and his daughter did not want to be separated from each other. 'We will now die – oh, that too is in God's hands,' wrote Klepper on 10 December. 'We will go to our deaths together tonight. Above us stands in our last hours the image of Christ in blessing, and he will fight for us. In the sight of it, our life will end.'[205] A few hours later, they were dead.

Many Jews killed themselves rather than be deported at this time; others did so more out of despair at their increasingly unbearable situation. Among them was Joachim Gottschalk, a well-known movie actor who had been banned by Goebbels from appearing in films because he refused to divorce his Jewish wife. On 6 November 1941 he killed himself with his wife and daughter when the two women received a deportation order. Another was the widow of the painter Max Lieber-mann, who killed herself in 1943 when she received a deportation order. She was buried in the Jewish cemetery at Weissensee, where 811 suicides had been interred the previous year, compared with 254 in 1941. Up to 4,000 German Jews killed themselves in 1941–3, with the number rising to 850 in the fourth quarter of 1941 alone. By now, Jewish suicides made up almost half of all suicides in Berlin, despite the tiny numbers of the surviving Jewish community. Most of them were elderly, and saw taking poison, the commonest method, as a way of asserting their right to end their own life when and how they wanted to, rather than being murdered by the Nazis. Some men put on their First World War service medals before committing suicide. Such acts continued almost until the end of the war. On 30 October 1944, for example, a Jewish woman in Berlin whose non-Jewish husband had been killed on the Eastern Front refused to accept her situation, and failed to collect her 'Jewish star' from the Gestapo office in her home town, preferring to take her own life instead.[206]

Long before this time, the extermination programme had been extended to other parts of Europe. The deportations began on 25 March 1942. Over the following weeks, some 90,000 Jews, first young men intended for labour, then older men, women and children, were sent from the puppet-state of Slovakia to ghettos in the Lublin district, and to camps in the east. Visiting Bratislava, the Slovak capital, on 10 April 1942, Heydrich told Minister-President Tuka that his was merely 'one part of the programme' for the deportation of half a million Jews from European countries including Holland, Belgium and France.[207] On 27 March 1942, 1,112 Jews were deported east from Paris, to be held as hostages as a deterrent to the French resistance (with which, in reality, very few of them had any connection at all). Five more trainloads, the departure of which had already been proposed by Heydrich in the spring, followed in June and July 1942. In July it was decided to request the Croatian government to deliver the country's Jews to Germany for extermination; 5,000 were duly deported the following month. Pressure was put on other allies of Germany, including Hungary and Finland, to do the same. The 'final solution of the Jewish question in Europe' was now under way.[208]

IV

Some months earlier, towards the end of September 1941, Hitler had retired the Reich Protector of Bohemia and Moravia, the old-conservative former Foreign Minister Konstantin von Neurath, ostensibly on health grounds. The German occupiers had begun to encounter mounting resistance from the Czechs, and Communist sabotage and other acts of subversion were multiplying in the wake of the German invasion of the Soviet Union. The situation, Hitler thought, required a firmer and more thorough approach than Neurath was able to offer. The new Reich Protector was Reinhard Heydrich, who thus now added the running of Bohemia and Moravia to his many other duties. Heydrich lost no time in announcing that the Czechs would be divided into three basic categories. The racially and ideologically unsound would be deported to the east. Those judged racially unsatisfactory but ideologically acceptable would be sterilized. Racially impeccable but ideologically dubious Czechs would be Germanized. If they refused, they would be shot. Before he could launch this bizarre programme, however, Heydrich had to deal with the swelling tide of resistance. He began to have Czechs arrested and executed for their part in the movement – 404 in his first two months of office alone. Over the same period he sent 1,300 more to concentration camps in the Reich, where most of them perished. In October 1941 he staged a show trial of the figurehead Czech Prime Minister Alois Eliáš, who was sentenced to death in a blaze of publicity for supposedly making contact with the Czech government in exile and encouraging the local resistance. Eliáš was eventually executed in June 1942. These measures effectively destroyed the Czech resistance movement, earning Heydrich the nickname of 'the Butcher of Prague'. Commissioned among other things to improve the productivity of Czech workers and farmers in the interests of supplying German agriculture and industry, however, he also raised food rations for over 2 million employees, and made 200,000 much-needed pairs of new shoes available to munitions workers. He reorganized and improved the Czech social security system, and engaged in a series of public gestures to woo the

Czech masses away from the nationalist intelligentsia, including a scheme to send workers to luxury hotels in Czech spa towns. All of this, he considered, would prevent the re-emergence of any kind of serious resistance movement, now that the existing resistance had effectively been destroyed.[209]

Alarmed at the apparent success of Heydrich's policies, the Czech government-in-exile in London urged that he should be killed. This would have the additional benefit of calling down harsh repression that would in turn get the resistance movement going again. Without an active resistance movement working for it in the Protectorate, the exiled Czech government might find itself in a weak negotiating position when the war finally ended. The British government went along with this plan. Two Czech exiles, Jozef Gabčík and Jan Kubiš, were selected to do the job by the exiled Czech government in December 1941. They were given training in sabotage and espionage techniques by the British, and flown to the Protectorate in a plane supplied by the British Special Operations Executive in May 1942, parachuting down into a field on the outskirts of Prague. On the morning of 27 May 1942, Heydrich left his home, twelve miles outside Prague, to drive to his office at the Hradčany Castle in the city centre. Despite being the leading security official in the Reich, he took no pains at all over his own personal safety. He travelled alone, without an escort; the only person with him in the car was his chauffeur. At this particular time, enjoying the pleasant spring weather, Heydrich had asked to be driven to work in an open-top car. The assassins had established that Heydrich travelled the same route every day, at the same time. Although he was a little later than usual on this particular morning, they were still lying in wait as the car slowed down to take a sharp bend in the road in a suburb of the Czech capital. Gabčík's sten-gun jammed as he tried to fire it, but Kubiš managed to throw a grenade which hit the rear wheel and went off, bringing the car to a standstill. Heydrich leaped out, drew his revolver and started shooting at Kubiš, who ran behind a passing tram, leaped on to a bicycle and pedalled away from the scene. Thwarted, Heydrich turned on Gabčík, who returned fire with a revolver, missing him but shooting the chauffeur in both legs. Then Heydrich put his hand to his hip and staggered to a halt. Gabčík left the scene and made good his escape by getting onto a crowded tram. The look-out, who had flashed a mirror to warn the assassins that the car was coming, calmly walked away from the scene of carnage.[210]

Heydrich had been badly injured. The grenade had blown bits of leatherwork and horsehair and shards of steel springs from the car's upholstery into his ribs, stomach and spleen. The foreign objects were removed in an operation, but the cut was too wide, the wound became infected, and on 4 June 1942 he died.[211] He was, the SS newspaper the *Black Corps* declared in an obituary, 'a man without defects'.[212] Hitler called him 'indispensable'.[213] He certainly appeared to many as the incarnation of all the SS virtues. Even his own men sometimes called him, with a touch of irony, 'the blond beast'. Yet his character remained elusive, hard to pin down. Most historians have characterized him as a technician of power, a 'craftsman of pragmatism', or the 'incarnation of the technology of government by brute force'. Certainly, there can be no doubt about his consuming ambition to make a career for himself under the Third Reich. Ideology, it has been argued, was something that he was too intelligent to take seriously. Yet anyone who reads his written memoranda and statements must surely be impressed by their mindless and total assimilation of Nazi ideology, their permeation by the thought-patterns of Nazism, their lack of recognition of any possible alternative to the Nazi world-view.[214] His extraordinary scheme for classifying and dealing with the Czech population was a case in point.

What was absent from Heydrich's rhetoric was the coarseness and crudity that so often characterized the language used by 'Old Fighters' like Hans Frank, Hermann Göring or Heinrich Himmler. Nazi ideology appeared to be for Heydrich something utterly impersonal, an unquestioned set of ideas and attitudes that it was his ambition to put into effect with cold, passionless efficiency. Most of his subordinates and colleagues were afraid of him, even Himmler, who was only too aware of his intellectual inferiority to his subordinate. 'You and your logic,' he shouted at him on one occasion: 'we never hear about anything but your logic. Everything I propose you batter down with your logic. I'm fed up with you and your cold, rational criticism.'[215] Yet, on the other hand, Heydrich was also, as many remarked, a passionate man, a keen sports-man, a musician who was often clearly deeply moved when he played the violin. His divided personality did not escape the attention of con-temporaries, many of whom (quite wrongly) explained it in terms of a divided, part-Jewish ancestry – 'an unhappy man, completely divided against himself, as often happened with those of mixed race', as Himmler was reported to have observed.[216] Carl J. Burckhardt, the League of

Nations Commissioner in Danzig during the 1930s, said to himself on meeting Heydrich, 'Two people are looking at me simultaneously.'[217] One of Heydrich's colleagues told Burckhardt a story of how Heydrich, coming home drunk, looked through an open door into the bathroom, where the lights were on, and saw his own image in the full-length mirror on the opposite wall. Drawing his revolver, he fired twice at the reflection, shouting, 'At last I've got you, scum!'[218]

Hitler accorded Heydrich a suitably solemn and pompous memorial ceremony. Privately, he was furious at the security lapse that had given the assassins their chance. Heydrich's habit of indulging in 'such heroic gestures as driving in an open, unarmoured vehicle' were, he said, 'stupid and idiotic'.[219] Heydrich was replaced in the Protectorate by Karl Hermann Frank, who had been his deputy as well as Neurath's. The champion of a less subtle, more crudely repressive approach than Heydrich, Frank was eventually named German State Minister for Bohemia and Moravia in August 1943. It was Frank who presided over the fearful revenge Hitler now visited upon the Czechs. The assassins themselves, hiding in the St Cyril and Methodius Orthodox Church in Prague, were betrayed to the Gestapo by a local agent of the British Special Operations Executive for a large reward. Together with five other agents who had also been parachuted into the Protectorate by the British, they fought a bitter gun-battle that raged for several hours. Eventually, realizing their situation was hopeless, they turned their guns on themselves. Hitler initially wanted to shoot 10,000 Czechs out of hand in reprisal for the murder, and to eliminate the entire Czech intelligentsia just as he had done the Polish. He told the puppet Czech President Hácha that if another similar incident occurred, 'we should have to consider deporting the whole Czech population'.[220] Flying swiftly to Berlin, Hermann Frank persuaded the Leader that these measures would cause immense damage to Czech arms production. Among the papers found on another Czech agent of the Special Operations Executive was one mentioning the Czech village of Lidice. Frank suggested that making an example of the village would be a sufficient reprisal. Hitler agreed. On 10 June 1942, the entire population of Lidice, charged with providing shelter to the assassins, was rounded up, the men shot, the women sent to the Ravensbrück concentration camp, and the children taken away for racial cataloguing. Eighty-one of them were deemed racially inferior, taken off and killed; the other seventeen were given new identities and placed with German families for adoption. The village was burned to the ground. A further twenty-four men and women were shot in the hamlet of Lezacky, and their children sent to Ravensbrück. Another 1,357 people were summarily tried and executed for their supposed involvement in the resistance. 250 Czechs, including entire families, were killed in the Mauthausen concentration camp. And 1,000 Jews were rounded up in Prague and taken off to be killed. Altogether, some 5,000 Czechs perished in this orgy of revenge. Only the desperate need of the Nazi regime for the products of the sizeable and advanced Bohemian arms industry prevented the terror from going further. For the time being, at least, it had achieved its object.[221]

The assassination of Heydrich reinforced the fear in the Nazi leadership that the Jews (who in fact had had nothing to do with it) posed a growing security threat on the Home Front. Some historians have also argued that growing food shortages in the Reich were what prompted an acceleration of the killing programme at this time. The daily rations allocated to the German population at home had been cut in April 1942. These cuts were not only unpopular, but also obliged the government to reduce the rations allotted to foreign labourers in Germany still further, to avoid hostile comment by native Germans. This damaged their productivity. Such was the severity of the cuts that Hitler took the unusual step of forcing the retirement of his Agriculture Minister, Richard Walther Darré, who had proved more of an ideologue than an administrator, and promoting the Ministry's top civil servant, Herbert Backe, to the post of Acting Minister. After meeting with Hitler and Himmler in May 1942, Backe secured their agreement to stop provisioning German armed forces from Germany. Henceforth they would have to live off the land. In the east, where most of them were stationed, this meant cutting still further the rations of the local population, and this was ordered by Backe on 23 June 1942. As for the region's remaining Jews, whose food supplies had already been cut to starvation rates by many local administrators, their rations would be stopped altogether. The General Government, said Backe, would be 'sanitized' of Jews 'within the coming year'.[222] But this, of course, was not a statement of intent, more a report of what was in any case expected, given the scale of the killing programmes already in operation. Nor is there any evidence to suggest a direct causal link between the food situation and any decisive acceleration of the extermination programme.

Security considerations remained uppermost in the minds of the Nazi leadership.

On 19 July 1942 Himmler ordered Friedrich Wilhelm Krüger, the Chief of Police in the General Government, to ensure 'that the resettlement of the entire Jewish population of the General Government is carried out and completed by 31 December 1942'. The ethnic reordering of Europe demanded a 'total cleaning-out'.[223] Hitler too was now determined, as he said in September 1942, that Jewish workers should as far as possible be removed from munitions factories in the Reich and that all remaining Jews in Berlin should be deported.[224] He returned to his 'prophecy' of 30 January 1939 in a speech at the Berlin Sports Palace on 30 September 1942. He had predicted, he told his audience, 'that if Jewry provokes an international world war for the extermination of the Aryan peoples, then it will not be the Aryan peoples who are exterminated, but Jewry.' But now, 'an antisemitic wave' was going round Europe 'from people to people', and every state that entered the war would become an antisemitic state.[225] In a private discussion with Bormann on 10 October 1942, Göring, it was reported, 'believes the steps undertaken by the Reich Leader of the SS, Himmler, to be absolutely correct', despite the fact that there had (probably for economic reasons) to be at least some exceptions.[226] A few days previously, in a speech delivered at the Berlin Sports Palace, Göring had told his audience that Churchill and Roosevelt were 'drunken and mentally ill people who dangle from the Jews' wires'. The war was a 'great race war ... about whether the German and Aryan will survive or if the Jew will rule the world'.[227] He too, therefore, presented the extermination as a necessary act of self-defence on the part of the German people. Hitler's annual speech to the Nazi 'Old Fighters' at Munich on 8 November 1942, broadcast over German radio, repeated yet again his 1939 prophecy, this time saying bluntly that the war would end in their 'extermination'. He added that the Jews who (he thought) had laughed at him then 'are laughing no longer'.[228]

Immediately after this speech, Hitler's press chief Dietrich stepped up antisemitic propaganda once more. Over the coming months, Goebbels also returned repeatedly to this theme. A significant part of his speech in the Sports Palace in Berlin on 18 February 1943, which was broadcast on all German radio stations, was devoted to it:

Behind the onrushing – [excited shouts of interjection] – behind the onrushing Soviet divisions *we can already see the Jewish liquidation squads*, which loom behind *terror*, the spectre of millions going hungry and total anarchy in Europe. Here international Jewry is once more proving itself to be the *devilish* element of decomposition . . . *We have never been afraid of Jewry and we are less afraid today than ever!* [shouts of 'Hail!', loud applause] . . . The aim of Bolshevism is the world revolution of the Jews . . . Germany at least does not intend to quail before this Jewish threat; rather, to meet it with the *timely*, if necessary *total* and *most radical exter* . . . [correcting himself] *exclusion* of Jewry! [loud applause, wild shouting, laughter].[229]

Goebbels's deliberate slip enlisted the complicity of his audience across the nation, not only in the mass murder of the Jews, but also in their understanding that euphemistic language had to be employed when referring to it. Hitler spoke, less explicitly, along the same lines on 24 February and 21 March 1943. He instructed Goebbels to intensify antisemitic propaganda in foreign broadcasts, especially to England.[230] In a lengthy monologue addressed to the Propaganda Minister on 12 May 1943, after Goebbels had drawn his attention to the Tsarist forgery *The Protocols of the Elders of Zion* (a work that Hitler insisted was undoubtedly genuine), the Nazi Leader insisted that the Jews were everywhere working on the basis of their racial instinct to undermine civilization. 'Modern peoples have no choice remaining but to exterminate the Jews.' Only by fighting the Jewish race 'with all the means at our disposal' was victory possible. 'The peoples who have rumbled the Jews first and fought them first will rule the world in their place.'[231] The apocalyptic tone of this speech was remarkable. Hitler was now justifying the extermination of the Jews as a necessary precondition of world domination by Germans.

On 3 May 1943, Goebbels issued a confidential circular to the German press demanding that more attention be devoted to attacks on the Jews. 'The possibilities for exposing the true character of the Jews are endless,' he opined. 'The Jews must now be used in the German press as a political target: the Jews are to blame; the Jews wanted the war; the Jews are making the war worse; and, again and again, the Jews are to blame.'[232] After only four front-page headlines of an antisemitic nature in the *Racial Observer* in the whole of 1942, there were seventeen in the first five months of 1943 alone. Altogether in 1943, indeed, the paper carried thirty-four front-page headlines referring to the Jews.[233] The propaganda offensive repeated ad nauseam the now-familiar diatribes against Churchill, Roosevelt and Stalin as puppets of a Jewish world conspiracy aimed at the annihilation of the German race – a kind of projection, it has been argued, of Nazism's own drive to annihilate the Jews.[234] As the military situation worsened and Allied bombing raids on German cities began to have a serious impact, propaganda warnings that a victory for the Allies would mean a genocidal extermination of the German people became steadily more shrill. Great play was made with the discovery of the graves of Polish officers massacred by the Soviet secret police at Katyń earlier in the war – a massacre inevitably attributed not to the Russians but to the Jews. Anti-Jewish propaganda, which had gone through its first period of concentrated intensity in the second half of 1941 as a way of launching what the Nazis called the 'final solution of the Jewish question in Europe', was now becoming a means of rallying the German people to continue fighting.[235]

Thus the pace, justification and mode of implementation of the genocide changed repeatedly from its inception in the summer of 1941. Examining the origins of 'the final solution' in terms of a process rather than a single decision uncovers a variety of impulses given by the Nazi leadership in general, and Hitler and Himmler in particular, to the fight against the supposed global enemy of the Germans. Overriding all of them, however, was the memory of 1918, the belief that the Jews, wherever and whoever they might be, threatened to undermine the German war effort, by engaging in subversion, partisan activities, Communist resistance movements and much else besides. What drove the exterminatory impulses of the Nazis, at every level of the hierarchy, was not the kind of contempt that stamped millions of Slavs as dispensable subhumans, but an ideologically pervasive mixture of fear and hatred, which blamed the Jews for all of Germany's ills, and sought their destruction as a matter of life and death, in the interests of Germany's survival.

'LIKE SHEEP TO THE SLAUGHTER'

I

Already some time before the Wannsee Conference, Himmler had appointed Odilo Globocnik, the SS and Police Leader in Lublin, to organize the systematic killing of all the Jews in the General Government. The ghettos would have to be emptied to make room for Jewish deportees from the west. Globocnik was to set up a series of camps to achieve this aim in the 'Reinhard Action'.[236] Globocnik was an Austrian Nazi. His deep antisemitism had brought him a conviction for murdering a Jew in 1933. He had been appointed Regional Leader of Vienna after the annexation, but in January 1939 he had been reduced to the ranks for speculating in foreign currency. Himmler, however, did not lose sight of him, and appointed him to his post in Lublin the following November. In 1940, Globocnik built up a small economic empire on the basis of Jewish slave labourers, and in July 1941 he commissioned the building of a huge labour camp at Majdanek. For the Reinhard Action, Globocnik recruited a large number of people from the former T-4 Action, including Christian Wirth. They continued to be paid by the headquarters of the euthanasia programme at the Chancellery of the Leader in Berlin, though they took orders from Globocnik. Nearly all of the twenty or thirty SS men employed in each of the camps Globocnik now began to establish to carry out his mission fell into this category. This set the camps apart from the normal run of SS establishments. All of the SS men were officers or NCOs. Basic manpower was provided by Ukrainian auxiliaries, many of whom had been drafted in from prisoner-of-war camps and given a brief training before being sent on to work for Globocnik.[237]

The three 'Reinhard Action' camps set up to carry out the extermination programme were all based at remote sites to the west of the river Bug, but with good railway connections to other parts of Poland and within relatively easy reach of the major ghettos. Construction of the first of these death camps, at Belzec, began on the site of an existing labour camp on 1 November 1941. It was carried out under the supervision of a former euthanasia operative, who stayed on to assist Christian Wirth on the latter's appointment as camp commandant in December 1941. He had a railway spur built, running into the camp from the nearby station. There were houses for the SS, barracks for a small number of longer-term prisoners such as cobblers, tailors or carpenters, who would work for the SS, and quarters for the Ukrainian auxiliaries. The gas chambers were constructed of wood but were made airtight and supplied with pipes through which petroleum exhaust from cars would be pumped, killing anyone inside. Wirth chose this procedure because pure carbon monoxide canisters such as had been used in the euthanasia action were difficult to obtain in quantity, and might arouse the suspicion of incoming victims if they saw them. By February 1942 the facilities were ready. They were tried out on small groups of Jews; then the Jewish workers who had helped build them were also gassed. On 17 March 1942 the first deportees were delivered to the camp and gassed immediately on arrival. Within four weeks, 75,000 Jews had been put to death, including 30,000 of the 37,000 inhabitants of the Lublin ghetto, and more from other regions of the General Government including Zamość and Piaski.[238]

The murderous brutality of the round-ups and transports to Belzec was noted by Dr Zygmunt Klukowski, whose diary provides a graphic though not completely accurate account of their impact on local Jewish populations in Poland. On 8 April 1942 he learned

that every day two trains, consisting of twenty cars each, come to Belzec, one from Lublin, the other from Lvov. After being unloaded on separate tracks, all Jews are forced behind the barbed-wire enclosure. Some are killed with electricity, some with poison gases, and the bodies are burned. On the way to Belzec the Jews experience many terrible things. They are aware of what will happen to them. Some try to fight back. At the railroad station in Szczebrzeszyn a young woman gave away a gold ring in exchange for a glass of water for her dying child. In Lublin people witnessed small children being thrown through the windows of speeding trains. Many people are shot before reaching Belzec.[239]

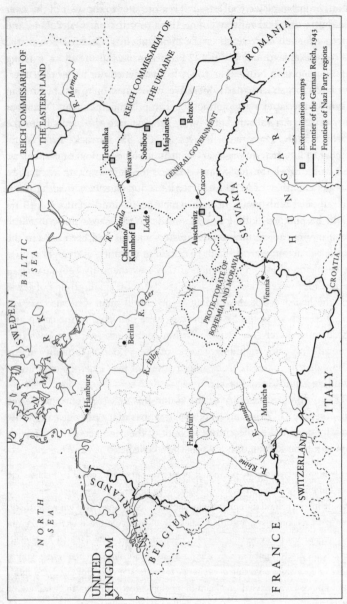

11. Extermination Camps, 1941–5

Shortly afterwards, 2,500 Jews were taken from Zamość; several hundred were shot on the streets. The Jewish inhabitants of Szczebrzeszyn were in a state of complete panic, sending their children to live with Poles in Warsaw, and bribing Poles to keep them in hiding. Crowds were gathering in order to loot their homes when they were deported.[240] On 8 May 1942, reported Klukowski, a German police unit arrived in Szczebrzeszyn and started shooting Jews 'like ducks, killing them not only on the streets but also in their own houses – men, women, and children, indiscriminately'. Klukowski began to organize help for the wounded, but then he was told he was not allowed to give help to Jews, so, reluctantly, he posted people outside the hospital to turn them away. 'I was lucky that I did so,' he noted later: soon afterwards the police arrived at the hospital, carrying machine-guns, and went through the wards looking for Jews: had there been any, Klukowski and probably some of his staff would almost certainly have been shot. The whole massacre left him deeply upset, as he recorded in his diary:

I am saddened that I had to refuse to give any help at all. I did this only because of strict orders by the Germans. This was against my own feeling and against a physician's duties. With my eyes I can still see the wagons filled with the dead, one Jewish woman walking along with her dead child in her arms, and many wounded lying on the sidewalks across from my hospital, where I was forbidden to give them any help.[241]

He was appalled by the behaviour of some Poles, who looted the houses of the victims, and even laughed as they saw them being shot. Later, too, the German police ordered the local Jewish council to pay for the ammunition used in the massacre.[242]

Wirth tried to design the camp at Belzec in such a way as to allay the suspicions of the Jews arriving there. They were told it was a transit centre and that they would be disinfected before receiving clean clothes and getting their valuables returned to them. The gas chambers themselves were designed to look like showers. All this followed the original pattern devised for the euthanasia gassings, though on a much larger scale. But the ruses were little more than gestures. The very brutality with which they were rounded up must have left the Jews with few illusions as to the fate in store for them. Another Austrian SS officer, Franz Stangl, described what he saw at Belzec in the spring of 1942:

I went there by car. As one arrived, one first reached Belzec railway station, on the left side of the road. The camp was on the same side, but up a hill. The commandant's office was 200 metres away, on the other side of the road. It was a one-storey building. The smell . . . Oh God, the smell. It was everywhere. Wirth wasn't in his office. I remember, they took me to him . . . He was standing on a hill, next to the pits . . . the pits . . . full, they were full. I can't tell you; not hundreds, thousands, thousands of corpses . . . One of the pits had overflowed. They had put too many corpses in it and putrefaction had progressed too fast, so that the liquid underneath had pushed the bodies on top up and over and the corpses had rolled down the hill. I saw some of them . . . oh God, it was awful.[243]

Stangl himself was subsequently to play a central role in the Reinhard Action. Born in 1908, the son of a brutal ex-soldier, he had grown up in small-town poverty, and trained as a weaver. In 1931 he had joined the police, undergoing a tough training before being involved in pursuing and arresting members of the illegal socialist opposition during the Schuschnigg dictatorship. At some point he had become an active, secret member of the Nazi Party, and after the absorption of Austria into the Reich in 1938 he was promoted, before being transferred to work in the central administration of the 'euthanasia' murder programme in Berlin in 1940. Here he had got to know Christian Wirth, who summoned him to Belzec to get him acquainted with the Reinhard Action on the ground.[244] Stangl thought the programme was operating with lamentable inefficiency. The gas chambers at Belzec were crude constructions. They were constantly breaking down, leaving deportees waiting for days without food or water; many died. Eventually this was too much even for Wirth. In June 1942, he temporarily halted the transports and dismantled the wooden gas chambers, replacing them with a concrete construction containing six gas chambers with a total capacity at any one time of 2,000 people. They came into operation in mid-July; transports continued arriving until mid-December. By the end of 1942 some 414,000 Jews from occupied Poland had been killed in the camp, and more from other parts of Central Europe who had been taken to the ghettos in the Lublin district; the total may have been as high as 600,000.[245]

The second of the Reinhard Action camps was constructed near the village of Sobibor, where up to this point there was nothing but a small labour camp for Jewish women. Construction began in March 1942, but fell behind schedule, so Wirth appointed Franz Stangl camp commandant with the initial brief of finishing the building on time. By the middle of May 1942 the gas chambers were ready. They were housed in a brick building and could each hold 100 people, who were killed by engine exhaust fumes piped in from outside. The camp was built in imitation of Belzec, with administration and reception areas near the railway spur and the extermination area some distance away, out of sight and reached through a narrow passage 150 metres long known as the 'tube'. Behind the gas chamber building were burial pits. A narrow-gauge tramway went from the railway to the pits with the bodies of people who had died on the journey. The usual gestures were made to reassure the arriving victims, but, as in Belzec, they were often ineffective, since the SS and particularly the Ukrainian guards shouted at the victims and beat them as they ran through the 'tube'. Some SS men trained a dog to bite the naked Jews, increasing their panic. Stangl ran the camp efficiently according to his lights, and it was not overwhelmed by vast numbers of transports as Belzec had been. Nevertheless, within the first three months of the camp's operation, nearly 100,000 Jews from Lublin, Austria, the Protectorate of Bohemia and Moravia, and the Old Reich had been killed there.[246]

Work on the main railway line brought the transports to a temporary halt in the summer of 1942. At the same time, the hot weather caused the tightly packed layers of bodies buried in the pits behind the extermination area to swell up and rise above the ground, as had been the case in Belzec, causing a terrible stench and attracting large numbers of rats and other scavenging animals. The SS men also began to notice a rancid taste in the water. The camp water supply was taken from wells and they were clearly becoming contaminated. So the camp administration constructed a large pit which they filled with wood and ignited; a mechanical excavator was brought in to dig up the corpses, which were placed on grilles above the pit and cremated by a Jewish Special Detachment whose members were afterwards put to death themselves. Meanwhile, the transports resumed in October 1942 and continued until the beginning of May 1943. One transport of 5,000 arrived from Majdanek, with prisoners in striped uniforms already weakened by hunger and maltreatment. On this occasion, the gas chambers had broken down, so the prisoners were kept in the open through the night. 200 of them died from exhaustion or from beatings and shootings administered by the SS during the hours of darkness. The remainder were herded into the gas chambers the next day. Another transport arrived in June 1943 with the prisoners already naked because the SS in Lvov thought this would make it more difficult for them to escape: the journey had been a long one, and twenty-five out of the fifty freight cars contained nothing but corpses. They had died of hunger and thirst, and as an eyewitness later recalled, some of them had been dead for as long as a fortnight by the time they arrived.[247]

Jews still had some personal effects with them. These, along with their clothing and the contents of their suitcases, were taken from them. Valuables were impounded by the camp authorities. Many of them found their way into the pockets of individual SS men and their auxiliaries. The most valuable jewellery was sent together with the gold extracted from the tooth fillings of the dead to a central sorting office in Berlin, where the precious metals were melted down into bars for the Reichsbank and the jewellery exchanged in occupied or neutral countries for industrial diamonds needed for German arms factories.[248] From August 1942 the collection and delivery of these objects was organized by Pohl's Economy and Administration Head Office. The confiscation of the furniture and other effects the Jews had left behind, including clothing, crockery, carpets and much else besides, was carried out by Rosenberg's office and the confiscated items auctioned off in Germany.[249] A report to Pohl's office estimated the total value of Jewish possessions confiscated in the Reinhard Action up to 15 December 1943 at not far short of 180 million Reichsmarks.[250]

By this time, almost 250,000 victims had been killed at Sobibor. When Himmler visited the camp early in 1943, the operation was already winding down. Although no new regular transports were scheduled to arrive, the camp administration arranged a special transport from a labour camp in the district in order for him to observe a gassing in action. Pleased with what he saw, he gave promotions to twenty-eight SS and police officers including Wirth, Stangl and other senior functionaries. He also ordered preparations to be made for the closure of the camps and the removal of all traces of their activity once the final batches of victims had been killed. Sobibor was to be transformed into a storage depot for ammunition captured from the Red Army. Jewish labourers were put to work constructing the new facilities. In the meantime the cremation of the victims' corpses continued apace. It became clear to the Jewish construction workers, many of them battle-hardened Soviet prisoners of war who arrived on 23 September 1943 and formed a cohesive, well-disciplined group, that they were doomed. They began to organize an escape. On 14 October 1943 they managed to entice most of the camp's SS personnel and a number of the Ukrainian auxiliaries into the camp workshops on a variety of pretexts and kill them with daggers and axes without attracting the attention of the guards on the watch-towers. The resisters cut the camp's telephone wires and electicity supply. As they made a break for the main gate, the Ukrainian guards opened fire with automatic weapons, killing many; others broke out through the perimeter fence. Some were killed in the minefield outside the fence but more than 300 out of a total of 600 inmates succeeded in breaking out of the camp (all those who did not succeed were shot the following day). 100 of the escapees were caught and killed almost immediately as the SS and police mobilized a large search operation including spotter planes. But the rest eluded capture, and a number of them eventually found their way to partisan units. Shortly afterwards, a fresh detachment of Jewish prisoners arrived to dismantle the camp. The buildings were razed, trees planted, a farm constructed, and when the work was completed, the Jews were forced to lie down on the roasting grilles and were shot one by one. After December 1943 there was no one left at the camp, and all obvious traces of it had disappeared.[251]

II

The third of the Reinhard Action camps was located at Treblinka, north-east of Warsaw, in a remote wooded area at the end of a single-track branch line running to an old quarry from the railway station at Malkinia, a station on the main railway line from Warsaw to Bialystok. In the spring of 1941 the German occupiers opened a labour camp near the quarry, to excavate materials for use in fortifications on the Soviet–German border in Poland. A year later, the SS selected it as the site of a new death camp. Construction began at the beginning of June 1942, overseen by Richard Thomalla, the SS officer who had built Sobibor. By the time it was begun, the death camps at Belzec and Sobibor were already in operation, so Thomalla tried to improve on them. Jewish workers were brought in to build the new camp; many of them were randomly shot by the SS as they worked, or made to stand in the line of trees as they were felled to clear the ground, so progress was often interrupted. They built a railway spur and station, from which arriving Jews were taken to an undressing room near the 'ghetto' where the longer-term prisoners lived. Once they got there, the naked Jews were quickly herded through a narrow fenced-in alleyway (called by the SS the 'Road to Heaven') to a large, carefully concealed brick building in the upper camp. This housed three gas chambers, into which the victims were driven with shouts and curses, to be killed by fumes pumped in from diesel engines through a system of pipes. Behind the building was a set of ditches, each 50 metres long, 25 metres wide and 10 metres deep, dug out by a mechanical excavator. Special Detachments of prisoners pushed the bodies in small wagons from the processing area along a narrow-gauge railway and dumped them in the ditches, which were earthed over when they were full.[252]

As in Sobibor, arriving Jews were told they had come to a transit camp and that they would receive clean clothes and their safeguarded valuables after going through a disinfection shower. Initially, around 5,000 Jews or more arrived each day, but in mid-August 1942 the tempo of killing increased, and by the end of August 1942, 312,000 Jews, not only from Warsaw but also from Radom and Lublin, had been gassed at Treblinka. Less than two months had passed since the first gassings in the camp on 23 July 1942. The first commandant of the camp, Irmfried Eberl, an Austrian doctor who had worked on the 'euthanasia' action, had declared his ambition of exceeding the number of killings in any other camp. The transport trains were unventilated and, without water or sanitation, thousands died en route in the hot weather. The pressure of numbers was such that all pretence was abandoned. Oskar Berger, who arrived on a transport on 22 August 1942, noted 'hundreds of bodies lying all around' on the platform, 'piles of bundles, clothes, suitcases, everything mixed together. SS soldiers, Germans and Ukrainians were standing on the roofs of barracks and firing indiscriminately into the crowd. Men, women and children fell bleeding. The air was filled with screaming and weeping.' The survivors were driven up to the gas chambers by SS men who beat them with whips and iron bars. In case their screams were heard by those waiting below, the SS set up a small orchestra playing Central European hit songs, to drown out the noise. So many victims arrived that the gas chambers were unable to cope, and, as in the case of the transport that arrived on 22 August 1942, the SS guards shot large numbers of the Jews in the reception area instead. Even this did not work, and newly arrived trains were left standing for hours, even days, in the summer heat. Many of those inside died of thirst, heatstroke or asphyxiation. The gas chambers frequently broke down, sometimes when the victims were already inside, where they would be forced to wait for hours until repairs were completed. The ditches were rapidly filled, and new ones could not be excavated quickly enough, so that soon there were unburied bodies everywhere.[253]

Eberl and his staff confiscated large quantities of the Jews' possessions for themselves, and gold and money were said to be lying around on the sorting yard in great heaps along with huge piles of clothes and suitcases, which were accumulating far too rapidly to be processed. Ukrainian guards, lacking proper accommodation, had set up tents around the camp, where they partied with local prostitutes. Eberl was reported to have made a Jewish girl undress and dance naked in front of him; she was later shot. Reports of the chaos reached Globocnik and Wirth, who paid a surprise inspection visit and dismissed Eberl on the spot. Wirth had been appointed as general inspector of the three death camps in August 1942, with the brief of streamlining the killing operations. He transferred the command to Franz Stangl, the commandant of Sobibor, at the beginning of September. On his arrival, Stangl established what he thought of as an orderly regime. Neatly dressed, in a smart white jacket, dark trousers and jackboots, he habitually carried a riding-crop, though he did not use it, or take part in any violence personally. He built a fake railway station, complete with timetables, ticket booths and a station clock, though the hands were painted on and never moved. He established gardens, built new barracks and set up new kitchens, all to deceive the arriving victims into thinking they were at a transit camp. Standing, as he regularly did, on a vantage point between the lower and upper camps, he would watch the naked prisoners being driven brutally up the 'Road to Heaven', thinking of them, as he confessed later, as 'cargo' rather than as human beings. Every so often, Stangl would go home on leave to visit his wife and family. He never told her what his job was, and she thought he was engaged only on construction work.[254]

At the camp, scenes of sadism and violence continued. Jewish work details were constantly beaten, and when their term of duty came to an end, they were shot in front of their replacements. Ukrainian auxiliaries would commonly seize and rape young Jewish women, and one, Ivan Demjanjuk, who supervised Jews going into the gas chambers and worked the diesel motor outside, was reported to have sliced off the ears and noses of elderly Jews as they went in.[255] In September 1942, one prisoner, Meir Berliner, who was in fact an Argentinian citizen, knifed an SS officer to death at a roll-call. Wirth was called in; he had 160 men executed randomly as a reprisal, and stopped all the work prisoners' food and water for three days. The incident did not interrupt the flow of victims to the gas chambers. The number of transports fluctuated during the early months of 1943, but by the end of July 1943, the small number of work details kept alive in the camp were becoming conscious that the amount of work to do was declining. Already in the spring of 1942, Himmler had decided that the bodies buried at the extermination camps should be dug up and burned so as to destroy the evidence of the murders. Globocnik resisted the implementation of this policy, except where it was obviously necessary for other reasons, as at Sobibor. Instead of digging up the bodies, he is said to have remarked, they should 'bury bronze tablets stating that it was we who had the courage to carry out this gigantic task'.[256]

In December 1942, however, the cremations began at Chelmno and Belzec, to be followed in April 1943 by Treblinka. Himmler took the decision to close the camps down, since the vast majority of the Jewish inhabitants of the Polish ghettos had now been killed. By late July 1943, after four months, the task of digging up and incinerating some 700,000 corpses that had been crudely buried in mass pits was almost complete. Fewer and fewer transports were arriving at Treblinka. The workers themselves realized that they were next in line for the gas chambers. Clandestine resistance groups were set up in both parts of the camp, and though the plan formed to co-ordinate their actions did not work out in the end, they managed on 2 August 1943 to set part of the camp on fire, acquire weapons and enable almost half of the 850 camp inmates to break through the perimeter fencing and escape. Looking out of his window, Stangl suddenly saw Jews beyond the inner perimeter fence, shooting. The phone wires had not been cut, so Stangl called in reinforcements from outside. The Jewish fighters had not managed to secure many weapons or collect much ammunition, and 350 to 400 were killed by the better-armed SS guards as they returned fire. Only half a dozen guards were shot. Of the men who escaped, half were recaptured shortly afterwards, and perhaps 100 disappeared into the nearby woods; how many of them survived is not known. Almost the only building left intact after the fire was the solid brick house containing the gas chambers.[257]

Stangl initially intended to rebuild the camp, but three weeks later, he was summoned by Globocnik, who told him that the camp was to be closed down immediately and he was to be transferred to Trieste to organize the suppression of partisans. Back at the camp, Stangl packed his bags, then called together all the remaining Jewish labourers 'because', he said later without the slightest trace of irony, 'I wanted to say goodbye to them. I shook hands with some of them.'[258] After he left, they were killed. Meanwhile, the uprisings at Sobibor and Treblinka had strengthened Himmler's belief that Jews anywhere were a security risk. The numbers of inmates in the two camps were small, but there were some 45,000 Jews, including women and children, in three labour camps in the Lublin area run by Reinhard Action staff, especially at Travniki and Poniatowa, and a large number of Jews at the Majdanek concentration camp as well. Himmler decided they should all be killed immediately. In a carefully planned, military-style operation codenamed 'Operation Harvest Festival', thousands of police, SS and Military SS men surrounded the camps, where the men had already been made to dig trenches on the pretext that they were building defensive fortifications. When the German forces arrived, they made all the inmates undress and go to the trenches, where they were all shot. A clandestine Jewish resistance group at Poniatowa seized a barrack building and opened fire on the SS, but the Germans set the barracks on fire and burned all the Jews inside alive. At Majdanek, all the Jewish inmates were selected and, together with many more Jews brought in from the smaller labour camps in the Lublin district, were made to undress, driven to previously prepared trenches and shot. As the trenches filled up, the newly arriving naked victims were made to lie on top of the dead bodies before they were shot themselves. Beginning around six in the morning, the killings continued until five in the afternoon. Some 18,000 Jews were murdered in the camp on this single day. At Travniki and Majdanek, camp loudspeakers broadcast dance music at full volume throughout the action, to drown out the sound of the shooting and the cries of the victims. All in all, 'Operation Harvest Festival' killed a total of 42,000.[259]

Little or no trace of the Reinhard Action camps remains today. Following the uprising, the remaining buildings at Treblinka were demolished, the land was grassed over and planted with flowers and trees, and the bricks from the gas chambers were used to build a small farm, designed to be lived in by a Ukrainian who promised to tell visitors that he had been there for decades.[260] But local Polish people knew what had been there, and in the summer of 1944 rumours spread that Jews had been buried there without having had their gold teeth removed, and that their clothing, full of jewellery and valuables, had been buried with them. For many months, large numbers of peasants and farm workers scoured the area, looking for buried treasure. When a member of the Polish state war crimes commission visited the site of Treblinka on 7 November 1945 she found 'masses of all kinds of pilferers and robbers with spades and shovels in their hands ... digging and searching and raking and straining the sand. They removed decaying limbs from the dust [and] bones and garbage that were thrown there.' The macabre treasure-hunt ended only when the Polish government set up official memorials on the camp sites and posted guards around them.[261]

According to a report sent to Eichmann on 11 January 1943 and intercepted by British monitoring services, the number of Jews killed in the Reinhard Action camps by the end of the previous year totalled nearly one and a quarter million.[262] A more complete list of all Jews 'evacuated' or 'sluiced through the camps' in the east was provided on Himmler's orders by his 'Inspector for Statistics', Richard Korherr, on 23 March 1943; it put their number at 1,873,539, though this included killings outside the Reinhard camps as well. A shorter version of the report, updated to 31 March 1943 and prepared in the large type used for documents intended to be read by the short-sighted Hitler, was presented to the German Leader on the eve of his fifty-fourth birthday, on 19 April 1943.[263] Modern estimates put the total number killed at Belzec, Sobibor and Treblinka at around 1,700,000.[264]

III

The conquest of Poland and the victory over France, with the re-annexation of Alsace and Lorraine, had led to the creation of new concentration camps in the incorporated territories at Stutthof, near Danzig in September 1939 (locally run until January 1942), Natzweiler in Alsace in June 1940, and Gross-Rosen in Silesia in August 1940 (initially as a sub-camp of Sachsenhausen). Another camp was set up in April 1940 in an old collection centre for migrant labourers near the town of Oswiecim, known in German as Auschwitz, now part of the German Reich. It was built to house Polish political prisoners. On 4 May 1940 the former Free Corps fighter and camp officer in Dachau and Sachsenhausen, Rudolf Höss, was appointed as commandant. In his memoirs Höss complained about the poor quality of the staff he was given, and the lack of supplies and building materials. Not without a touch of pride, he recorded that when he was unable to obtain enough barbed wire to seal the camp off, he pilfered it from other sites; he got steel from old field fortifications; and he had to 'organize' the trucks and lorries he needed. He had to drive 90 kilometres to acquire cooking-pots for the kitchen. In the meantime prisoners had started to turn up; on 14 June 1940 the first batch arrived to be sorted, to serve a period of quarantine, and then to be sent on to other camps. Most of them were drafted into construction work while they were in Auschwitz. But Auschwitz soon became a permanent centre for the Polish political prisoners, of whom there were to be up to 10,000 in the camp. Over the entrance, Höss placed a wrought-iron archway with the words *Arbeit macht frei*, 'work liberates', a slogan he had learned in Dachau.[265]

In November 1940, Himmler told the commandant that 'Auschwitz was to become *the* agricultural research station for the eastern territories ... Huge laboratories and plant nurseries were to be set out. All kinds of stock-breeding were to be pursued there.'[266] The camp grew still further after Barbarossa. On 26 September 1941 Himmler ordered the building of a vast new camp at Birkenau (Brzezinka), 2 kilometres from the main Auschwitz camp, to house Soviet prisoners of war and use them for labour projects: up to 200,000 were to be imprisoned there according to his plans, though these were never fully realized. 10,000 Soviet prisoners of war arrived in October 1941. Höss put them in a separate compound in the main camp, and tried to use them to build the new camp at nearby Birkenau, but he found them too weak and malnourished to be of any use. 'They died like flies,' he later noted, especially in the winter. There were many cases of cannibalism. 'I myself,' he recalled, 'came across a Russian lying beween piles of bricks, whose body had been ripped open and the liver removed. They would beat each other to death for food ... They were no longer human beings. They had become animals, who sought only food.' It evidently did not occur to Höss to give it to them. Of the 10,000, only a few hundred were left alive by the following spring.[267]

The new camp at Auschwitz-Birkenau was one of a pair, paralleled by the construction of another labour centre for Soviet prisoners in the eastern part of the city of Lublin. This was unofficially known as the Majdanek camp. But the project did not go well, and the camp only ever reached a fifth of its projected extent (even more grandiose plans for it to hold a quarter of a million inmates were quickly abandoned). Instead of the planned 50,000 Soviet prisoners, only 2,000 arrived to construct the camp. As it developed, Majdanek took on a variety of functions, holding not only prisoners of war but also members of the Polish resistance, hostages, deportees, and later on sick prisoners transported from other camps to be killed there. It contained a wide variety of workshops and small factories but the camp management never managed to integrate them into German war production, and the employment of Jews was treated mainly as a means of killing them by forcing them to work long hours at exhausting tasks. When Himmler decided to quicken the pace of the extermination of the Jews in July 1942, some seven gas chambers were constructed at Majdanek, of which at least three were in use by September 1942. Some 50,000 Jews were put to death in these gas chambers by exhaust fumes over the following months. In addition, following the revolt at Sobibor, 18,000 Jews were shot in the camp as part of the 'Harvest Festival' operation. Altogether 180,000 people were eventually to be killed at Majdanek; up to 120,000 of these were Jews, not only from the Lublin district but also from further afield, including Western Europe. That Majdanek did not become larger was in part at least the consequence of its continual maladministration. The camp administration soon became widely known for its corruption and brutality. Two of its commandants, Karl Otto Koch and Hermann Florstedt, not only stole on a massive scale but also completely neglected their administrative duties, preferring to enforce their commands by naked terror. They eventually went too far even for the Reich Security Head Office, and were arrested and executed. Their successor, Max Koegel, had convictions for peculation and deception dating from the 1920s and was not much better. Many of the guards were Croatians and Romanians, who were difficult to control. Their cruelty towards the Jewish inmates was notorious. As an unstable, badly run and inefficient camp, Majdanek never achieved its originally intended potential as a multifunctional centre of labour and extermination. That achievement, if achievement it was, belonged to Auschwitz.[268]

Auschwitz was destined, indeed, to become the largest mass killing centre in the history of the world, larger even than the killing centres at Belzec, Sobibor and Treblinka. Summoning Höss to see him, according to the latter's subsequent recollection, some time in the summer of 1941, but most probably several months later, at the very end of the year or the beginning of 1942, Himmler informed the camp commandant that, since the existing extermination facilities in the east were not extensive enough to carry out the final solution of the Jewish question, he was designating Auschwitz as an additional centre, most notably because of its combination of good communications and relative remoteness from major centres of population. Shortly after this, Eichmann arrived at the camp and discussed the plans in more detail. Whereas the Reinhard Action camps had been set up to kill the Jews of Poland, the eventual function of Auschwitz was to kill the Jews brought from the rest of occupied Europe, including not only neighbouring parts of the former Poland but also, once these Jews had been killed, from Germany, the Reich Protectorate of Bohemia and Moravia, and western countries like France, Belgium and Holland. From the outset, the methods used in Auschwitz differed from those employed in the other camps. Initially, this was a matter of a chance discovery; but soon it became systematic.[269]

In July 1941 a team of prisoners and their SS guards was disinfecting some clothes and bedding with the chemical pesticide known as Zyklon-B, the main constituent of which was hydrongen cyanide, when they noticed that a cat that strayed into the room was rapidly killed by the gas. One of the guards speculated that the chemical might be useful for killing people too. The idea, which had been briefly considered by the T-4 team in 1939 but rejected as impractical, was taken up by the camp management. Early in September 1941 it was tried out on some 600 Soviet prisoners of war who had been classified by a Gestapo commission the previous month as 'fanatical Communists', along with 250 sick inmates of the camp. They were taken into a cellar in Block 11, in the main camp, and gassed. The experiment was then repeated later the same month with 900 healthy Red Army prisoners in the camp morgue.[270] Höss later remembered observing the gassing. The men were herded into the room, the doors were sealed, then powdered Zyklon-B was shaken down through holes in the roof. The warmth generated by the bodies packed into the chamber below quickly turned it into a deadly gas. 'For a little while,' he recalled, 'a humming sound could be heard. When the powder was thrown in, there were cries of "Gas!", then a great bellowing, and the trapped prisoners hurled themselves against both the doors. But the doors held.' All the prisoners died.[271] On Eichmann's next visit to the camp, it was agreed to use the gas in a systematic way. But the camp morgue was so close to the main administration building that when the Soviet prisoners were killed, their screams in the gas chamber could be heard by the personnel. So Höss decided that the killings would have to be carried out away from the main camp, at Auschwitz-Birkenau. Soon there were two provisional gas chambers ready for operation there, in buildings known as Bunker I and Bunker II, or the 'red house' and the 'white house'. They killed their first victims on 20 March 1942.[272]

On arriving at the camp, the surviving deportees were roughly bundled out of the trains by SS guards and auxiliaries with dogs and whips, yelling at them: 'Out! Out! Fast! Fast!' They were made to line up – in the early months by an open field 2.5 kilometres from the camp, at the end of a goods siding, and in the later stages of the camp's existence, on the infamous 'ramp' leading from the railway siding to the camp – and undergo a 'selection'. 'The process of selection,' Höss later remembered without a trace of self-consciousness, '. . . was in itself rich in incident.'[273] Selections were carried out by SS doctors, who asked the arrivals a few questions and gave them a cursory medical examination. Those under the age of sixteen, mothers with children, the sick, the old and the weak were moved to the left, loaded on to lorries and taken straight to the gas chambers, after being told they were to be 'disinfected' there. Families, recalled Höss, tried to stick together, and rushed back from one line to rejoin one another. 'It was often necessary to use force to restore order.' Able-bodied men and women were taken to the camp, tattooed with a serial number on the left arm, and registered. In many transports they were in a minority. In the main camp and the labour camps, periodic 'selections' were carried out, to eliminate those deemed no longer fit to work. Unlike many of the new arrivals, these victims knew what lay in store for many of them; terrible scenes often followed, as they wept, begged for mercy, or tried to resist attempts to push them into the gas chamber.[274]

Those selected for killing were marched over to the gas chamber from the selection area. The two bunkers had a capacity of 800 and 1,200 people respectively. Over the course of 1942–3, the gassing facilities at Auschwitz-Birkenau were extended and refined. A purpose-designed gas chamber already ordered for the main camp in October 1941 was delivered to Birkenau instead, and three more crematoria were also built. All four were redesignated Crematoria I, II, III and IV when the two gas chambers in the main camp were closed down in July 1943 (one was destroyed, the other mothballed). More were planned but never built. All the new crematoria were located some distance from the prisoners' barracks. They were disguised by trees and shrubs. Two of them were known by the SS as the 'forest crematoria'. The new gas chambers were completed between March and June 1943. Small transports of fewer than 200 people were taken into a washroom in Crematorium II or III after 'selection' and shot in the back of the neck. Larger groups were gassed. In each facility, the gas chamber was mostly below surface level, disguised in the usual fashion as a shower and sealed by an airtight door with a peephole. The Jews selected for killing were taken to a disrobing room, told they would go into a disinfecting shower, and made to undress. 'It was most important that the whole business of arriving and undressing should take place in an atmosphere of the greatest possible calm,' Höss wrote later. Members of the Special Detachments of Jewish prisoners detailed to deal with the bodies after the gassing chatted to the victims and did their best to reassure them. Those who were reluctant to undress were 'helped', and the refractory were 'calmed down', or, if they began to shout and scream, taken out and shot in the back of the neck. Many were not deceived. Mothers sometimes tried to hide their babies in the piles of clothes. Children often cried, but most 'entered the gas chambers, playing or joking with one another and carrying their toys', Höss noted. Occasionally Jews would address him as he stood supervising the procedure. 'One woman approached me as she walked past,' he recalled later, 'and, pointing to her four children who were manfully helping the smallest ones over the rough ground, whispered: "How can you bring yourself to kill such beautiful, darling children? Have you no heart at all?"'[275]

Once the victims had been herded into the gas chamber, SS men standing on the reinforced concrete roof lowered canisters of Zyklon-B pellets through four openings into wire-mesh columns, which allowed the pellets to release the cyanide gas as soon as the body-heat of the victims had warmed up the air. After twenty minutes or so, the canisters were pulled up again, to remove the possibility of any more gas escaping, while the chamber was ventilated and a Special Detachment of Jewish prisoners dragged the corpses out into another room, pulled out gold teeth and fillings, cut the women's hair off, removed gold rings, spectacles, prosthetic limbs and other encumbrances, and put the bodies into elevators that took them up to the crematorium room on the ground floor, where they were put into the incinerating ovens and reduced to ashes. Any remaining bones were ground up and the ashes used as fertilizer or thrown away in nearby woods and streams. These facilities, designed and supplied by the firm Topf and Sons of Erfurt, were patented for future use by their inventor, the engineer Kurt Prüfer, who came to Auschwitz on numerous occasions to supervise their construction, testing and initial operation. He introduced numerous small technical innovations, including, for example, the installation of heating in Crematorium II to speed up the dissolution of the Zyklon B on cold winter days. His plans have survived and have provided historians with important documentary evidence for the Crematorium's modus operandi.[276] Yet Prüfer's designs did not withstand the test of constant use. Very soon, the numbers of corpses proved too great for the crematorium ovens to deal with. The brickwork began to crack, and the ovens were damaged by overheating. Before the construction of the new facilities, most corpses had been buried in the ground, but from September 1942 onwards the SS, under the command of Paul Blobel, who was in charge of similar operations at other camps, began to have them dug up by the Special Detachments of prisoners and burned on metal grilles laid over ditches, in the manner followed in the Reinhard Action camps shortly afterwards. By the end of the year, he had disposed of 100,000 bodies in this way, in an attempt to conceal the traces of the murder from posterity. This method also had to be used whenever the crematorium ovens proved unable to cope with the numbers of corpses arriving.[277]

In Auschwitz, as in the Reinhardt Action camps, the Special Detachments were killed at regular intervals and replaced by other young, able-bodied prisoners. Some of these, including former members of the French resistance and the Polish Communist underground, formed a clandestine prisoners' organization that managed to make contact with a larger secret resistance movement among the regular prisoners some time during the late summer of 1943. A rebellion aimed at opening the way for a mass breakout was frustrated by the drafting-in of SS reinforcements. However, in 1944, after the SS camp guards had killed 200 members of the Special Detachments following an unsuccessful escape attempt, a further 300 who were selected for gassing on 7 October 1944 attacked the SS men as they approached Crematorium IV, using whatever they could lay their hands on, including stones and iron bars. They set the building alight and destroyed it. The smoke alerted other members of the camp resistance, and some managed to break through the barbed wire surrounding Crematorium II, though none succeeded in reaching freedom; they were all killed, including a group who had sought shelter in a barn and were burned alive by the SS. Meanwhile, the SS had set up machine-gun positions in the camp and started firing indiscriminately; altogether some 425 Special Detachment prisoners were murdered over the next three days.[278]

IV

The first transports to arrive at Auschwitz, in March 1942, were from Slovakia and from France. Initially they were registered and admitted, in the belief that they might be used for labour purposes; but before long, in May 1942, systematic extermination began, killing not only the French and Slovakian Jews but also other Jews from Poland, Belgium and the Netherlands. It was a transport from Holland that Himmler watched being selected and murdered during his visit on 17 and 18 July 1942. 'He had no criticisms to make,' recorded Höss; indeed, the visit ended with the Reich Leader of the SS awarding the camp commandant a promotion. At an evening reception, Höss noted that Himmler 'was in the best of spirits, took a leading part in the conversation and was extremely amiable, especially towards the ladies'. The next day Himmler went to the women's camp, 'attended the whipping of a female criminal' and 'talked with some female Jehovah's Witnesses and discussed with them their fanatical beliefs'. In his final address before departing, Himmler ordered an intensification of the killing and urged Höss to complete the construction of the new camp at Birkenau as quickly as possible.[279] From July onwards, German Jews began to arrive, first from Vienna and then, in November and December, from Berlin. Trains began to deliver Jews from Romania, Croatia, Finland, Norway, then

Bulgaria, Italy and Hungary, Serbia, Denmark, Greece and southern France.[280]

Most of the Jews were transported directly to Auschwitz from their country of origin, but some came from a special camp set up in the northern Czech town of Terezin, known to the Germans as Theresienstadt, where the central prison of the Gestapo in the Protectorate had been established. Work began on this new camp in November 1941, and the first 10,000 Jews arrived at the beginning of January 1942. Its initial purpose was to act as a collection centre for Czech Jews, and it was organized on the lines of a ghetto, with a Jewish Council led by an Elder, the Zionist Jakob Edelstein, who was well known to Adolf Eichmann as a leading figure among Czech Jews. Under Edelstein's leadership, the camp developed a wide range of cultural and sporting activities, established a welfare system, and received sufficient money from the German authorities to function as a kind of model ghetto, to be filmed for international newsreels and displayed to visiting delegations of organizations like the Red Cross. One movie completed towards the end of November 1944 showed parks, swimming pools, sporting activities, schools, concerts and happy faces everywhere. Entitled *The Leader Gives the Jews a Camp*, it was never actually shown. Its director was the German-Jewish actor Kurt Gerron, who had achieved fame towards the end of the Weimar Republic by singing the part of Mack the Knife in the first recording of Bertolt Brecht and Kurt Weill's *Threepenny Opera* and starring with Emil Jannings opposite Marlene Dietrich in the film *The Blue Angel*. In 1933 he had fled first to Paris and then to Holland, where he continued making films; but following the Nazi invasion he was interned along with other Jews and sent to Theresienstadt. Gerron organized a cabaret show in the camp, entitled *The Carousel*, an enterprise so successful that he seemed a natural choice to direct the film, which he did under duress. After it was completed, Gerron was taken to Auschwitz on the last transport to leave the camp, on 18 October 1944, and gassed.[281]

The portrayal of the ghetto-camp's active cultural life, unlike other aspects of the movie, did not lie. On the same transport as Gerron in October 1944 was the Czech-Jewish composer Viktor Ullmann, a follower of Arnold Schoenberg, who had been taken to Theresienstadt two years previously. Among other things Ullmann composed an opera, *The Emperor of Atlantis*, that was performed successfully in the camp, along with chamber music and piano works. Later on, Ullmann was reduced to writing his compositions on the back of lists of inmates slated for deportation to Auschwitz. Friends somehow managed to preserve many of them until the war was over. Jewish artists in the camp gave drawing and painting lessons to the children among the inmates; many of their drawings too have survived. Despite such cultural activities, conditions in the camp were generally poor and deteriorated as time went on. From July 1942, trainloads of elderly Jews from the Reich began to arrive in the camp. Many were weak, exhausted or sick, and they died in their hundreds. In September 1942 alone, 3,900 people died out of a total of 58,000. The inmates of Theresienstadt also included Jewish veterans from the First World War with their families, and Jewish spouses from 'mixed marriages' that had been dissolved. On 8 September 1943, no fewer than 18,000 inmates were taken to Auschwitz. They were allowed to keep their clothes and effects. They were housed there in a specially designed 'family camp' with a school and a kindergarten, living in relatively superior accommodation which they were allowed to decorate. The purpose of the 'family camp' was to impress visitors and provide material for international propaganda. After six months it was closed down; in two separate actions in March and July 1944, the inmates were almost all taken to the gas chamber, except for 3,000 who were transferred to another camp.[282] Then in October 1944 twelve transports alone left Theresienstadt for Auschwitz, leaving a population of just over 11,000 where there had been nearly 30,000 in mid-September. Within a few weeks, however, the numbers had risen to 30,000 again with a fresh influx of deportees from Slovakia, the Czech lands and the Reich, many of them 'mixed-race'. In February 1945 the camp authorities built a huge hall that could be hermetically sealed, and an enormous covered pit. The remaining inmates could all be exterminated on the spot if it was felt desirable or necessary. In the event this did not happen. Nevertheless, out of just over 140,000 people who had been transported to Theresienstadt in the course of its existence, fewer than 17,000 were left alive by the end of the war.[283]

If Theresienstadt was a model ghetto, then Auschwitz in many ways was a model German town in the newly conquered east. By March 1941 there were 700 SS guards working in the camp, a number that had grown to more than 2,000 by June 1942; in all, over the period of the camp's existence, some 7,000 SS men worked there at one time or another. The SS and their families, if they had them, lived in the town, along with secretaries and administrators; there were concert parties, theatrical performances by visiting companies like the Dresden State Theatre, a pub (with an upstairs flat for Himmler, which in fact he never used) and a medical centre. The SS men were supplied with plenty to eat, and were allowed regular periods of leave. If they were unmarried, they could receive visits from their girl-friends, or, if they were married and their families lived elsewhere in the Reich, from their wives, usually during the warmer weather in summer. New houses were built for the camp staff, and nearby there was the gigantic I. G. Farben chemical plant at Monowitz, which made Auschwitz into a major economic centre and employed German managers, scientists, administrators and secretaries. The creation in a single complex of a residential area, a factory, a labour camp and an extermination centre looked forward to the kind of urban community that might have been founded in other parts of the German east, at least until the General Plan for the East was carried out completely. The only cause for complaint on the part of the town's inhabitants was the unpleasant smell that wafted across to the town and the SS living quarters from the camp crematoria.[284]

Over the whole period of the camp's existence, at least 1.1 million and possibly as many as 1.5 million people were killed at Auschwitz; 90 per cent of them, probably about 960,000, were Jews, amounting to between a fifth and a quarter of all Jews killed in the war. They included 300,000 Jews from Poland, 69,000 from France, 60,000 from Holland, 55,000 from Greece, 46,000 from Czechoslovakia (the Protectorate of Bohemia and Moravia), 27,000 from Slovakia, 25,000 from Belgium, 23,000 from Germany (the 'Old Reich'), 10,000 from Croatia, 6,000 from Italy, the same number from Belarus, 1,600 from Austria and 700 from Norway. At a late stage in the war, as we shall see, some 394,000 Hungarian Jews were taken to the gas chambers and put to death. More than 70,000 non-Jewish Poles were killed, 21,000 Gypsies, 15,000 Soviet prisoners of war, and up to 15,000 people of a whole variety of nationalities, mainly East Europeans. The minority who were 'selected' for work on arrival were registered, and a number tattooed on their forearm. There were about 400,000 of these, and about half of them were Jewish. At least half of the registered prisoners died from malnutrition, disease, exhaustion or hypothermia.[285]

Rudolf Höss later confessed he had found his duties as commandant of the biggest murder factory in the history of the world difficult to carry out with equanimity.

I had to see everything. I had to watch hour after hour, by day and by night, the removal and burning of the bodies, the extraction of the teeth, the cutting of the hair, the whole grisly, interminable business ... I had to look through the peephole of the gas-chambers and watch the process of death itself, because the doctors wanted me to see it. I had to do all this because I was the one to whom everyone looked, because I had to show them all that I did not merely issue the orders and make the regulations but was also prepared myself to be present at whatever task I had assigned to my subordinates.[286]

His subordinates often asked him 'is it necessary that we do all this? Is it necessary that hundreds of thousands of women and children be destroyed?' Höss felt that he 'had to tell them that this extermination of Jewry had to be, so that Germany and our posterity might be freed for ever from their relentless adversaries'.[287] Antisemitic to the end, Höss reflected after the war that antisemitism had 'only come into the limelight when the Jews have pushed themselves forward too much in their quest for power, and when their evil machinations have become too obvious for the general public to stomach'.[288] Bound by these beliefs to his job, Höss felt he had to suppress any doubts in carrying out what he believed to be Hitler's orders. He owed it to his subordinates not to show any sign of weakness. 'Hardness' was after all a core value of the SS. 'I had to appear cold and indifferent to events that must have wrung the heart of anyone possessed of human feelings,' he later recalled. 'I had to watch coldly, while the mothers with laughing or crying children went into the gas-chambers.'[289] Particularly after an evening's drinking with Adolf Eichmann, who 'showed that he was completely obsessed with the idea of destroying every single Jew that he could lay his hands on', Höss felt he had to suppress his human feelings: 'after these conversations with Eichmann I almost came to regard such emotions as a betrayal of the Leader'.[290]

Höss could not help thinking of his own wife and children as he watched Jewish families go into the gas chamber. At home, he was haunted by memories of such scenes. But he also felt beleaguered in Auschwitz. The constant demands for expansion, the incompetence and deceitfulness of his subordinates and the ever-increasing number of prisoners to manage drove him into himself and he turned to drink. His wife, who lived in a house just outside the camp perimeter with him and their four children (a fifth was born in 1943), tried to organize parties and excursions to improve his quality of life, but Höss quickly became known for his bad temper, despite the fact that he was able to requisition whatever he wanted (illegally) from the camp stores. 'My wife's garden,' he wrote later, 'was a paradise of flowers . . . The children were perpetually begging me for cigarettes for the prisoners. They were particularly fond of the ones who worked in the garden.' Höss's children kept many animals in the garden, including tortoises and lizards; on Sundays he walked the family across the fields to visit their horses and foals, or, in summer, went swimming in the river that formed the eastern boundary of the camp complex.[291]

V

Many of the Jews who arrived in Auschwitz-Birkenau, especially in the later phases of the camp's existence, were taken there directly from their home countries. But many others went through the transitional stage of confinement in a ghetto, as did all the Jews who were killed in the Reinhard Action camps. There they might survive for months or even years. The largest of the ghettos, as we have seen, were founded shortly after the conquest of Poland in 1939. Some of them lasted well into the second half of the war. In practice, of course, the conditions in the ghettos were so terrible that they already meant a slow death for many of their inhabitants. Starved of supplies, even for those in them who worked for the German war economy, they were desperately over-crowded, deprived of proper sanitation and rife with disease. Throughout the winter of 1941–2, Adam Czerniaków, the Jewish Elder of the Warsaw ghetto, continued to do his best to combat the rapid deterioration of the situation under the impact of hunger and disease. 'In the public assistance shelters,' he noted on 19 November 1941, 'mothers are hiding dead children under the beds for 8 days in order to receive a larger food ration.' Meeting a group of children on 14 June 1942, Czerniaków noted despairingly that they were 'living skeletons . . . I am ashamed to admit it,' he wrote, 'but I wept as I have not wept for a long time.' As large contingents of Jews deported from Germany began to arrive and stay in the ghetto for a few days before being transported to

Treblinka, and rumours of the death camps began to spread, Czerniaków did his best to try to halt the mounting panic. He even organized play activities for the ghetto children, comparing himself to the captain of the *Titanic* ('a ship is sinking and the captain, to raise the spirits of the passengers, orders the orchestra to play a jazz piece. I had made up my mind to emulate the captain').[292]

Assured repeatedly by the German authorities that the 'terrifying rumours' of imminent deportations were untrue, he toured the ghetto, trying to 'calm the population' ('what it costs me they do not see'). But on 21 July 1942 the German Security Police began arresting members of the Jewish Council and other officials in his presence in order to hold them hostage for the collaboration of the rest. The next morning, the deportation specialist of the regional SS, Hermann Höfle, called Czerniaków and the remaining leading Jewish officials in the ghetto to a meeting. While his young Jewish interpreter, Marcel Reich-Ranicki, typed the minutes, the sound of Johann Strauss's *Blue Danube* waltz, played by the SS on a portable gramophone in the street outside, drifted in through the open window. Czerniaków was officially told that all the Jews would be deported, in consignments of 6,000 a day, starting immediately. Anyone who tried to stop the action would be shot. Throughout his time as Elder, Czerniaków had kept a cyanide tablet ready to use if he received any orders he could not reconcile with his conscience. One of the SS officers in charge of the deportations had told him that children were included, and Czerniaków could not agree to hand them over to be killed. 'I am powerless,' he wrote in a final letter, 'my heart trembles in sorrow and compassion. I can no longer bear all this. My act will show everyone the right thing to do.' Refusing to sign the deportation order, he swallowed the tablet and died instantly. Doubts about him in the ghetto community were immediately quelled. 'His end justifies his beginning,' wrote Chaim Kaplan. 'Czerniaków earned eternity in one moment.'[293]

The Catholic German army officer Wilm Hosenfeld, stationed in Warsaw and charged with organizing sporting activities for the troops, became aware of the deportations to Treblinka almost as soon as they began. 'That a whole people, men, women, children, are simply being slaughtered, in the twentieth century, by us, us of all people, who are fighting a crusade against Bolshevism: this is such a dreadful blood-guilt that one wants to sink into the ground with the shame of it.'[294] 30,000

Jews were transported for mass extermination in the last week of July 1942 alone, he reported. Even in the days of the guillotine and the French Revolutionary Terror, he noted caustically, 'such virtuosity in mass murder was never achieved'.[295] The Jews, he told his son in August 1942, 'are to be exterminated, and it's already being done. What immeasurable quantities of human suffering are coming to light on the one hand, of human malice and bestiality on the other. How many innocent people have to die, who is demanding justice and legality? Does this all have to happen?'[296] 'Death paces the streets of the ghetto,' Chaim Kaplan reported in his diary in June 1942. 'Every day Polish Jewry is being brought to slaughter. It is estimated, and there is some basis for the figures, that three-quarters of a million Polish Jews have already passed from this earth.' Kaplan recorded terrible scenes as people were rounded up and taken off to Treblinka every day in the repeated deportations of the summer of 1942. On 5 August 1942 it was the turn of the children living in orphanages and other children's homes. These actions were neither orderly nor peaceful. German troops, SS men and auxiliaries used unbridled force in rounding up the Jews and forcing them on to the trains. Over 10,000 Jews were shot in the ghetto during the round-ups; some of them must have tried to resist. In early August 1942, visiting Warsaw, Zygmunt Klukowski was kept awake by the sound of machine-gun fire coming from the ghetto. 'I was told that about 5,000 people a day were being killed.'[297] By the time the round-ups came to an end on 12 September 1942, more than 253,000 inhabitants of the ghetto had been taken to Treblinka and gassed. Already in August 1942, fearing the worst for himself, Kaplan gave his diary to a friend. His friend smuggled it out of the ghetto and passed it on to a member of the Polish underground, who took it with him when he emigrated to New York in 1962, after which it was finally published. Kaplan's own fears had been more than justified: he was rounded up not long after he passed the diary on, and perished with his wife in the gas chambers of Treblinka in December 1942 or January 1943.[298]

By November 1942, only 36,000 Jews were left in the Warsaw ghetto, all engaged on labour schemes of one kind or another.[299] Few now doubted what would happen to those who were taken off in an 'action'. They knew they were going to their death even if they were hazy about the way it was done. The mass deportations gave rise to anguished self-examination amongst politically active Jews. 'Why did we allow ourselves to be led like sheep to the slaughter,' was the agonized question that Emanuel Ringelblum asked himself.[300] Ringelblum thought that the Jews had been terrorized by the extreme violence of the Germans into passivity. People knew that if they tried to revolt, many others who had not been involved would also be the target of German reprisals. Religious Jews, who probably formed the majority of the ghettos' inhabitants, were perhaps inclined to regard suffering and death as merely transient, and to accept what was happening as the outcome of the Divine Will, however difficult that may have been. The role of the Jewish police in carrying out selections and deportations also made resistance more difficult. Often people trusted the ghetto leadership, which almost always tried to reassure them about the future rather than create problems by spreading alarm. Arms were hard to come by, the Polish resistance was often (though not always) reluctant to supply them, and weapons frequently had to be purchased on the black market at very high prices. There was always hope, and the need for it frequently meant that ghetto inhabitants preferred to disbelieve the stories of extermination camps that were told to them. Often, particularly in the early stages of the murder programme, the German authorities convinced those selected for deportation that they were merely being moved to another ghetto or another camp. The vast majority of Jews were too weakened by prolonged hunger, privation and disease, and too preoccupied with the daily struggle to stay alive, to offer any resistance. Nevertheless, young and politically active Jews in a number of ghettos formed clandestine resistance movements to prepare for armed revolt or to organize an escape to the forests to join the partisans, the favoured tactic of the Communists (but which also undercut the possibility of resistance within the ghetto itself). A group of this kind was particularly active in Vilna, but it was generally unable to act because of internal political divisions between Communists, socialists and Zionists, the disapproval of the Jewish Councils that ran the ghettos, and the violent intervention of the German authorities at the slightest hint of resistance.[301]

In Warsaw, however, the resistance did come to fruition. In the course of 1942, Jewish underground organizations began to form, and Polish Communists supplied them with arms. On 18 January 1943 insurgents attacked the German guards accompanying a deportation column, and the deportees escaped. Himmler now regarded the ghetto as a security risk and ordered its final 'liquidation' on 16 February 1943. But the raid had made the resistance movement widely known and admired amongst the remaining Jewish population in Warsaw, which now began collecting and hoarding food supplies and preparing for an uprising despite the hostility of the ghetto's Jewish Council to any armed action. Alarmed at the prospect of an armed confrontation and concerned at the left-wing politics of some of the underground leaders in the ghetto, the Polish nationalist resistance rejected their call for help and offered instead to smuggle the Jewish fighters out to safety; the offer was refused. Fundamental to the resistance was the certainty that the entire population of the ghetto was about to be killed; there was no hope left, and the resisters, overwhelmingly young men, became convinced that it would be better to go down fighting and die with dignity than submit meekly to extermination. As the SS marched in to begin the final round-up on 19 April 1943, they were fired on at several points, and had to work their way forward in a series of bitter street-fights.[302]

Jürgen Stroop, the SS officer in charge of putting down the revolt, described how his men fought day and night against the desperate resistance. On 23 April 1943, Himmler ordered him to proceed with 'the greatest harshness, ruthlessness and toughness'. 'I now therefore decided,' Stroop wrote,

to undertake the total annihilation of the Jewish residential quarter by burning down all the housing blocks, including those belonging to the armaments factories ... The Jews then almost always came out of their hiding-places and bunkers. Not infrequently the Jews stayed in the burning houses until, because of the heat and because they were afraid of being burned to death, they decided to jump out of the upper storeys, first flinging mattresses and other upholstered objects out of the burning houses onto the street. With broken bones they still tried to crawl across the street to housing blocks that were not yet alight or only partly in flames.[303]

Some fighters fled into the sewers underneath the ghetto, so Stroop had scores of manhole covers opened and put smoke-sticks down them, driving the fighters underground towards an area of the city where they could be cornered and shot. A few managed to flee across the boundary on to the Polish side of the city. The great majority were killed. By 16 May 1943, Stroop announced the end of the action by blowing up the main synagogue. The fight had been an unequal one. A mere fifteen German and auxiliary troops had been killed. This was almost certainly an underestimate, but with equal certainty the actual number, whatever it was, was out of all proportion to the number of Jews killed. 7,000 Jews, reported Stroop, had been 'annihilated' in the street-fighting, and up to 6,000 had been 'annihilated' as buildings were burned down or blown up. The rest of the ghetto's inhabitants had been taken to Treblinka.[304] 'The last remnants of the Jewish inhabitants of the ghetto have been eradicated,' reported Wilm Hosenfeld on 16 June 1943. 'An SS Storm Leader told me how they had mown down the Jews who rushed out of the burning houses. The whole ghetto is a fiery ruin. This is the way we intend to win the war. These beasts.'[305]

On 11 June 1943 Himmler ordered the ruins of the Warsaw ghetto to be razed to the ground. Cellars and sewers were to be filled in or walled up. After the work was completed, soil was to be poured over the site and a park constructed. Although the park was never even begun, the ruined buildings were destroyed over the next few months. Himmler and the SS pursued the survivors of the uprising relentlessly. Stroop offered a reward of a third of the ready cash found in the possession of any Jew in the Polish part of the city to the arresting policeman, and threatened execution to any Pole found sheltering a Jew. Warsaw's Polish population, Stroop reported, had 'in general welcomed the measures carried out against the Jews'. A substantial number of Jews survived for a time in hiding, protected by Poles. Among them was Marcel Reich-Ranicki, who had stolen a good deal of money from the safe of his employers, the Jewish Council, and handed most it over to the resistance. With the remainder, he and his wife bribed their way out of the ghetto in February 1943, and found a hiding place with a Polish typesetter and his wife on the outskirts of the city. Every time he ventured out, Reich-Ranicki felt himself in acute danger from young Poles who sought to earn money, or sometimes even just the jewellery or the winter clothing worn by their victims, by identifying Jews on the street and handing them over to the police.[306]

Emanuel Ringelblum, the historian whose assiduous collection of diaries, letters and documents has provided us with much of what we know about the Warsaw ghetto, also went into hiding. Ringelblum was arrested during the uprising and taken to Travniki Camp, from where a Polish railway worker and a Jewish contact sprang him in July 1943. Dressed as a railwayman, and equipped with false papers by the Polish underground, he made his way with his wife and twelve-year-old son back to Warsaw, where they were hidden along with thirty other Jews in a bunker under the greenhouses of a Polish market garden. From here he re-established contact with the Jewish resistance, and resumed his work of gathering information and writing reports on the evolving situation for posterity. On 7 March 1944, however, the bunker was betrayed, and the Gestapo arrested the inhabitants. Ringelblum was tortured for three days, then taken to the site of the ghetto, where he was forced to watch his wife and son being killed before being executed himself. The Germans had learned of the archive he had assembled, but they were unable in the end to lay their hands on it; Ringelblum had buried it under the ghetto during the uprising, but refused to reveal its whereabouts. Part of it was eventually located and dug up in September 1946; the rest was discovered in December 1950, with Ringelblum's *Notes* sealed inside a milk-churn.[307]

Well before Ringelblum's death, the original leaders of most of the Jewish ghetto communities had long since been removed from office and replaced by men more easily intimidated into doing the Germans' bidding.[308] Virtually the only choice open to such men was to try to preserve a minority of the ghetto inhabitants from the exterminatory zeal of the Nazis by arguing for their economic indispensability. Even this, however, would not count in the end, since Hitler and Himmler increasingly considered the security risk posed by the Jews to outweigh any value they might have for the war economy.[309] The insoluble dilemmas faced by ghetto leaders by this time were graphically illustrated by Chaim Rumkowski, the controversial, self-willed Elder of the Lódz ghetto. Rumkowski had initially preserved the ghetto by persuading the Germans to regard it as a centre of production. But this did not prevent the Germans from systematically depriving it of food supplies. The young student Dawid Sierakowiak's diary recorded 'hunger everywhere' in the Lódz ghetto already in April 1941. Life for him, as for others, was reduced to a never-ending quest for something to eat – mostly carrots and other root vegetables. Sierakowiak relieved the boredom by learning Esperanto with a group of Communist friends, before he was able to enrol in the ghetto school and start lessons again. With other inmates, Sierakowiak kept in touch with world events through listening in secret to BBC radio broadcasts and reading German newspapers smuggled in from outside. The news he heard only dampened his spirits further: one German victory followed another seemingly without end.

On 16 May 1941 he reported that a medical check-up had left him seriously concerned about his health: the doctor 'was terrified at how thin I am ... Lung disease is the latest hit in ghetto fashion; it sweeps people away as much as dysentery and typhus. As for the food, it's worse and worse everywhere; it's been a week since there were any potatoes.' Somehow he managed to survive the year, occupying his mind by translating Ovid into Polish, and earning some money by giving private tutorials. Frequently ill, he stuck doggedly to his studies, completing them successfully in September 1941 and finding a job in a saddlery.[310]

Meanwhile, as more and more ghetto inmates were taken away by the Jewish ghetto police, never to return, Jews from other parts of Europe started to be shipped in. Rumkowski tried to persuade the German authorities that there was no room for them, but without effect. To the 143,000 Jews living in the Lódź ghetto in the autumn of 1941 were now added, in October, 2,000 more from small towns near by, then 20,000 from the Reich and the Protectorate of Bohemia and Moravia, along with 5,000 Gypsies. Sierakowiak thought the new arrivals looked spectacularly well dressed. Yet the newcomers were soon reduced to selling their bespoke-tailored suits for small quantities of flour and bread. Meanwhile, on 6 December 1941, the gas vans at the newly constructed camp in Chelmno had begun operation. Rumkowski was ordered to register 20,000 ghetto residents supposedly for labour service outside the ghetto walls. He managed to persuade the Germans to halve this number and with a special committee selected prostitutes, criminals, people on welfare, the unemployed and Gypsies. In an attempt to reassure people, Rumkowski declared in a public address on 3 January 1942 that honest people had nothing to fear. On 12 January 1942 the first deportations took place. By 29 January 1942, more than 10,000 Jews had been taken from the ghetto straight to Chelmno and put to death in gas vans. By 2 April 1942 another 34,000 had been taken away and murdered; by May, the total had reached 55,000, including now over 10,000 Jews deported to Lódź from the west.[311]

All the while, new transports of Jews were arriving, particularly from the Wartheland. The ghetto population thus remained at well over 100,000.[312] By the middle of 1942, reported Sierakowiak, people were dying in large numbers of 'ghetto disease': 'A person becomes thin (an "hourglass") and pale in the face, then comes the swelling, a few days in bed or in the hospital, and that's it. The person was living, the person is dead; we live and die like cattle.' In September 1942 2,000 patients were seized from the ghetto hospitals with the co-operation of Rumkowski's ghetto administration and taken off to be gassed; then all children under the age of ten, everybody over the age of sixty-five and all the unemployed, making another 16,000 in all. Sierakowiak's mother was among them. Many were shot, suggesting growing resistance to deportations. Rumkowski justified his co-operation in the action in a speech to ghetto inhabitants on 4 September 1942: 'I must amputate limbs in order to save the body!' he said, weeping as he spoke. It was not clear whether he really believed this or not. Fearful and depressed, the majority of the remaining inhabitants were too concerned with the daily struggle for survival to react with anything but dull resignation. By November 1942 Sierakowiak's father was ill, 'completely covered with lice and scabs'; in March he died. In April 1943 things began to look up for Dawid Sierakowiak: he found a job in a bakery, a much-sought-after position since it enabled him to eat his fill of bread on the job. But it was too late. He was already sick with fever, malnutrition and tuberculosis, lice-ridden and suffering from scabies, so weak that he was sometimes unable to get out of bed in the morning. 'There is really no way out of this for us,' he wrote on 15 April 1943. It was his last diary entry. On 8 August 1943 he died, just two weeks after his nineteenth birthday.[313]

By this time, the days of the Lódź ghetto were already numbered. Following the Warsaw ghetto uprising, Himmler had ordered the 'liquidation' of all remaining ghettos in the east on 21 June 1943. All remaining Jews in the Reich were to be deported.[314] 26,000 inhabitants of the Minsk ghetto were killed in the following months, and a further 9,000, all engaged on labour schemes, were dead by the end of the year.[315] In Bialystok the final 'liquidation' began on 15 August 1943, taking the resistance movement that had formed there by surprise. Deep divisions between the Communists and Zionists in the resistance further hampered concerted action, and the resisters had little support from the general ghetto population. Nevertheless, the fighting lasted five days. Globocnik, who took personal charge of the operation, sent in tanks and, copying Stroop, burned all the buildings in the ghetto to the ground.[316] In other ghettos, the process of dissolution had already begun before Himmler issued his order.[317] In Lvov, 40,000 Jews were taken from a labour camp in mid-August 1942 and gassed in Belzec; the remaining Jews were put into a newly created ghetto in the city while twelve members of the Jewish Council were publicly hanged from lamp-posts in the street, or from the roof of the Council's office building. Over the next few months, further actions took thousands more inhabitants of the ghetto off to the gas chambers of Belzec, until early in 1943 the ghetto was closed down and the remaining Jews transferred back to the labour camp. Only 3,400 out of a total population of 160,000 survived the war.[318] Round-ups began in Vilna in April 1943, prompting, as elsewhere, the flight of many young members of the resistance, especially those with Communist beliefs, for whom the principal objective was to aid the Red Army by tying down German forces, into the nearby woods. Most of the ghetto's remaining 20,000 inhabitants were taken off to be killed, many of them in Sobibor.

The last major ghetto to be closed was the Lódź ghetto, which was wound down in the summer of 1944. Over 73,000 people were still living there. Deportations to Chelmno began in mid-July, even at this point still carried out with the participation of the Jewish ghetto police, and then from 3 August some 5,000 Jews were ordered to assemble at the railway station every day, with the promise that they would be relocated to better conditions. The trains all went directly to extermination camps. The last one, leaving the now virtually empty ghetto on 28 August 1944, carried on it the Ghetto Elder Chaim Rumkowski and his family. On arrival at Auschwitz-Birkenau, they were all sent to the gas chamber. Of nearly 70,000 Jews still living in the ghetto at the end of July 1944, only 877 were still there the following January, charged with the task of clearing up.[319] All in all, over 90 per cent of Poland's 3.3 million Jews had been killed by this time.[320]

VI

The extermination of the Jews has sometimes been seen as a kind of industrialized, assembly-line kind of mass murder, and this picture has at least some element of truth to it. No other genocide in history has been carried out by mechanical means – gassing – in specially constructed facilities like those in operation at Auschwitz or Treblinka. At the same time, however, these facilities did not operate efficiently or effectively, and if the impression given by calling them industrialized is that they were automated or impersonal, then it is a false one. Men such as Höss and Stangl and their subordinates tried to insulate themselves from the human dimension of what they were doing by referring to their victims as 'cargo' or 'items'. Talking to Gerhard Stabenow, the head of the SS Security Service in Warsaw, in September 1942, Wilm Hosenfeld noted how the language Stabenow used distanced himself from the fact that what he was involved in was the mass murder of human beings: 'He speaks of the Jews as of ants or other vermin, of their "resettlement", that means their mass murder, as he would of the extermination of bedbugs in the disinfestation of a house.'[321] But at the same time such men were not immune from the human emotions they tried so hard to repress, and they remembered incidents in which individual women and children had appealed to their conscience, even if such appeals were in vain. The psychological strain that continual killing of unarmed civilians, including women and children, imposed on such men was considerable, just as it had been in the case of the SS Task Forces, whose troops had been shooting Jews in their hundreds of thousands before the first gas vans were deployed in an attempt not only to speed up the killing but also to make it somehow more impersonal.

What kept such men going was a belief that they were doing Hitler's bidding, and killing the present and future enemies of the German race. They were not faceless bureaucrats or technologists of death; nor was the killing at any level simply the product of impersonal pressures to obey superior orders or the cold pursuit of material or military advantage for the Third Reich. The careers of SS men like Eichmann, Stangl and Höss revealed them to be hardened antisemites; the racial hatred of their subordinates, stoked and fuelled by years of propaganda, training and indoctrination, was scarcely less extreme. Translating visceral hatred of Jews in the abstract to violent acts of mass murder in reality proved not to be difficult for them, nor for a number of the SS Security Service bureaucrats who took over the leadership of the Task Forces in the east. Particularly in the lower ranks of the SS, but also in the regular army, Jews, when encountered individually or in small groups, frequently aroused a degree of personal, sadistic brutality, a desire to humiliate as well as destroy, that was seldom present when they dealt with ordinary Poles, Russians or other Slavs. Slav prisoners were not made to perform gymnastics or dance before they were shot, as Jews were; nor were they made to clean out latrines with their clothes or bare hands, as Jews were. Slavs were mere tools; it was the Jews who were supposedly behind the Stalin regime, who ordered the Soviet secret police to commit bestial massacres of German prisoners, who inspired the partisans to launch cruel and cowardly attacks on German troops from the rear. Rank-and-file German troops, both regular soldiers and SS men, were heavily influenced by propaganda and indoctrination and, if they were young, years of education in the school system of the Third Reich, to believe that Jews in general, and Eastern Jews in particular, were dirty, dangerous dishonest and diseased, the enemies of all civilization.[322]

The atrocities of the Soviet secret police confirmed German soldiers in their belief that Jews, whom they held to blame, were bestial killers who deserved no mercy. 'Jewry is good for only one thing,' wrote one sergeant,

annihilation ... And I have confirmed to myself that the entire leadership of all [Soviet] institutions consisted of Jews. So their guilt is huge, the suffering they have caused unimaginable, their murderous deeds devilish. This can only be expiated by their annihilation. Up to now I have rejected this way of doing things as immoral. But after seeing the Soviet Paradise for myself I don't know any other solution. In these Eastern Jews there live the dregs of every kind of criminality, and I am conscious of the uniqueness of our mission.[323]

Abusing and humiliating Jews could also serve as a compensation for the lowly status and daily privations of the ordinary soldier. 'The best thing here,' wrote one from an occupied eastern town in May 1942, 'is that all the Jews doff their hats to us. If a Jew spots us 100m away, he already doffs his hat. If he doesn't, then we teach him to. Here you feel yourself to be a soldier, for here we rule the roost.'[324] Higher up the chain of command, the army often rationalized the killing of Jews as a step necessary for the maintenance of its own essential food supplies,[325] but this claim should not be taken simply at face value. The need to feed the army and the German civilian population at home did at particular junctures create a perceived need to operate what in medical terms might be called a *triage*, distinguishing those thought to need food most urgently and in greatest quantities from those with a lower priority. But what put Jews at the bottom of this hierarchy was not any rationalistic calculation based on an estimate of their contribution to the economy. It derived above all from an obsessively pursued ideology that regarded the Jews not simply as the most dispensable of the inhabitants of occupied Eastern Europe, but as a positive threat to Germany in every respect, conspiring with Jews everywhere else in the world, and especially in Britain and the USA, to wage war on the Third Reich. Had the Jews merely been surplus consumers of scarce resources, Himmler would hardly have undertaken a personal journey to Finland to try to persuade the government there to hand over the very small number of Jews under its control for deportation and extermination.[326]

As this suggests, the extermination programme was directed and pushed on repeatedly from the centre, above all by Hitler's continual rhetorical attacks on the Jews in the second half of 1941, repeated on other occasions as the Jews loomed in his mind as a threat once more. There was no single decision, implemented in a rationalistic, bureaucratic way; rather, the extermination programme emerged in a process lasting several months, in which Nazi propaganda created a genocidal mentality that spurred Himmler and other leading Nazis to push forward with the killing of Jews on an ever-wider scale. Altogether during the war, some 3 million Jews were murdered in the extermination camps. 700,000 were killed in mobile gas vans and 1.3 million were shot by SS Task Forces, police units and allied forces or auxiliary militias. Anything up to a million Jews died of hunger, disease or SS brutality and shootings in the concentration camps and especially the ghettos that the Third Reich established in the occupied territories. A precise total is impossible to arrive at, but it is certain that at least 5.5 million Jews were deliberatedly killed in one way or another by the Nazis and their allies. Since the opening of the archives in the former Soviet bloc in the 1990s it has become clear that the probable total is around 6 million, the figure given by Adolf Eichmann at his trial in Jerusalem in 1961. 'With this terrible murder of the Jews,' wrote Wilm Hosenfeld on 16 June 1943, 'we have lost the war. We have brought upon ourselves an indelible disgrace, a curse that can never be lifted. We deserve no mercy, we are all guilty.'[327]

1. The German Army enters Lódź in September 1939 to an ecstatic welcome from ethnic Germans, while the city's Polish inhabitants look silently on.

2. Redrawing the racial map of Europe: ethnic Germans from Lithuania cross the border with Germany at Eydtkau in East Prussia in February 1941, entering the Reich under a banner bidding them 'Welcome to Greater Germany'.

3. Polish Jews are assembled for road-sweeping duties by German troops, September 1939.

4. German air force troops round up a group of terrified Jews in the diarist Zygmunt Klukowski's home town of Szczebrzeszyn.

5. This still from *I Accuse* (1941), directed by Wolfgang Liebeneiner, shows the concert pianist Hanna Heyt, who is suffering from multiple sclerosis, asking her friend Dr Lang for advice; his opposition to assisted suicide is used as a foil for the film's justification of the killing of the incurably ill.

6. An assassination attempt that failed: the destruction caused in a Munich beer-cellar on the evening of 8 November 1939 by a bomb planted by the lone left-winger Georg Elser. Hitler left the hall shortly before the bomb went off.

7. Rudolf Hess visits the Krupp armaments factory on 1 May 1940, flanked by Robert Ley (*left*) and Alfred Krupp (*right*).

8. 'The biggest traffic jam in history': German armour squeezes through the narrow gorges of the Ardennes on its way to France on 11 May 1940.

9. Hitler, with Albert Speer (*left*) and Arno Breker (*right*), at the Trocadéro in Paris during a brief private visit to the conquered city on 28 June 1940.

10. Spying out the land: Field-Marshal Fedor von Bock (*left*) gauges the situation in the Crimea in May 1942, accompanied by General Fritz Lindemann.

11. Operation Barbarossa: infantrymen of the SS 'Death's Head' tank division drive along a dusty road near Smolensk, September 1941.

12. German soldiers burn a Ukrainian farm in September 1941 while the farmer's wife protests in vain.

13. Atrocity tourism: German troops take snaps as an alleged partisan is hanged in a Belarussian town in January 1942.

14. Three and a third million Red Army prisoners of war died in German captivity, many of them while being transported from the front in open goods wagons like this one, photographed at Witebsk railway station on 21 September 1941: when winter set in, these wagons became death-traps.

15. Bogged down before Moscow: German soldiers try to free a car from the mud in November 1941.

16. The propaganda war against the 'global enemy': a Ministry of Propaganda poster shows Churchill and Stalin joining hands across the Continent in a 'Jewish Conspiracy Against Europe' in the summer of 1941.

17. Gestapo chief Heinrich Müller (*right*), Security Service boss Reinhard Heydrich (*middle*) and Heinrich Himmler (*left*), overall head of the SS, meet in November 1939 to discuss Georg Elser's attempt on Hitler's life.

4

THE NEW ORDER

THE SINEWS OF WAR

I

In the small hours of February 1942, Hitler's favourite architect and close friend Albert Speer was going over his plans for the rebuilding of Berlin with Hitler in his field headquarters at Rastenburg in East Prussia. The conversation, he recalled later, visibly cheered up the tired Leader, who had spent the previous hours in a dispiriting conference with the Minister of Armaments, Fritz Todt. The Armaments Minister had already concluded during the Battle of Moscow in November–December 1941 that the war could not be won. Not only were British and American industrial resources stronger than Germany's, but Soviet industry was producing better equipment on a larger scale, better adapted to fighting in the depths of winter. German supplies were running short. Industrialists were advising Todt that they would not be able to match the military production of Germany's enemies. But Hitler would not listen. The Japanese attack on Pearl Harbor seemed to him to defer American involvement in the European theatre and give Germany a new chance of victory. On 3 December 1941 he had issued an order for 'simplification and increased efficiency in armaments production' intended to bring about 'mass production on modern principles'. At Hitler's behest, Todt had reorganized the system of arms production administration into five Principal Committees, respectively for ammunition, weapons, tanks, engineering and equipment, and set up a new advisory committee with industrialists and air force representatives. His visit to Hitler on 7–8 February 1942 is likely to have involved discussions of these new structures and of the benefits they could bring. Despite all these changes, Todt most probably cautioned Hitler during his visit to Rastenburg on 7–8 February 1942 that the situation remained serious if not critical; hence the Leader's air of despondency when he emerged from their meeting.[1]

Chatting briefly with Speer over a glass of wine, Todt offered him a seat on the plane that was to take him back to Berlin at 8 a.m. on 8 February. The architect was only in Rastenburg by chance, having been prevented by heavy snow from returning to Berlin from Dnepropetrovsk by rail. He had accepted instead a lift by air to Hitler's field headquarters, which at least got him closer to his destination. So he was looking for transport, and Todt's offer was therefore a tempting one. But by the time Hitler and Speer went to bed it was 3 a.m., and Speer sent word that he wanted to sleep in and would not be travelling with the Armaments Minister. Speer was still asleep when the phone beside his bed rang shortly after eight in the morning. Todt's plane, a converted twin-engined Heinkel 111, had taken off normally but then crashed into the ground, where it had burst into flames. It had been completely destroyed. Everyone on board was killed.[2] A later commission of inquiry suggested that the pilot had pulled a self-destruct mechanism in error; but in fact this particular plane did not carry such a mechanism, nor was there any reliable evidence of a mid-air explosion. Nicolaus von Below, Hitler's air force adjutant, later remembered that Hitler had banned the use of such small twin-engined planes by his senior staff and had been sufficiently concerned about the Heinkel's airworthiness that he had ordered the pilot to take it up for a trial spin before Todt embarked. Below thought that the poor weather conditions in which the plane had taken off meant that the inexperienced pilot had been unable to see properly and had flown it into the ground. The mystery was never satisfactorily solved. Had Speer planted a bomb on board? It seems unlikely, for while the account of the crash he gave in his memoirs was full of inaccuracies, there is no reason to doubt his story that he was in Rastenburg entirely by chance, and so would not have had the time to plan Todt's death. Nor, despite a certain strain in the relationship between the two men, was there any obvious reason why he should want him dead. Had Hitler, then, decided to kill his Armaments Minister because he could not stand the constant pessimism of his reports? Had he, perhaps, privately told Speer not to travel on the plane? This speculation too is implausible; this was not the way Hitler dealt with uncomfortable or inconvenient subordinates, and had he wanted to get rid of Todt, he would have been far more likely simply to have dismissed him, or, in an extreme case, had him arrested and shot.[3]

Todt was an engineer and a committed Nazi who had come to prominence as the builder of Germany's famous motorways in the 1930s. Hitler respected and admired him and had put him in charge not only of weapons and munitions production but also of energy and waterways and some aspect of the organization of forced labour during the war. Todt had headed the construction industry under the aegis of Göring's Second Four-Year Plan administration. He had run his own outfit, the Todt Organization, building roads across all the occupied territories, continuing with the creation of the West Wall defences and constructing U-boat bases on the Atlantic coast. Within the Party, Todt was in charge of the Head Office for Technology, controlling voluntary associations of many kinds in the field. In the spring of 1940, Hitler had created a new Ministry of Armaments and appointed Todt to run it. This accumulation of offices had given Todt considerable power over the economic management of the war, though he had had to contend with a range of rivals, especially Hermann Göring.[4] He would be a difficult man to replace.

Over breakfast at the Leader's headquarters on 8 February 1942, the talk was all of who should be his successor. Speer realized that he would be asked to take over at least some of Todt's functions, since as General Building Inspector for Berlin he already had some responsibilities in this area, including the repair of bomb damage and the provision of air-raid shelters. Todt had assigned him the task of improving the transport system in the Ukraine, which is indeed why he had been in Dnepropetrovsk. Hitler had told him more than once that he wanted to entrust him with some of Todt's existing tasks. But Speer was unprepared when, as he later remembered, he was 'summoned to Hitler as the first caller of the day at the usual late hour, around one o'clock in the afternoon' and told that he was being appointed to succeed Todt in all his capacities, not just that of construction overlord. Although 'thunderstruck', Speer had the presence of mind to ask Hitler to issue a formal command, which he would be able to use to impose his authority on his new sphere of operations. There was, however, one last obstacle to overcome. Just as he was leaving, Göring 'bustled in'. He had boarded his special train at his hunting lodge 60 miles away as soon as he had learned of Todt's death. 'Best if I take over Dr Todt's assignments within the framework of the Four-Year Plan,' he said. But it was too late. Hitler repeated his formal appointment of Speer to all of Todt's jobs. And Göring's authority over the economy was further downgraded when Speer persuaded Hitler to sign a decree on 21 March 1942 ordering that all other aspects of the economy had to be subordinated to arms production, run by himself.[5]

In his memoirs, written many years after these events, Speer, not without a dash of sincerity, professed to have been amazed by the 'recklessness and frivolity' of his appointment. After all, he had no military experience and no background in industry. It was, he wrote,

in keeping with Hitler's dilettantism that he preferred to choose nonspecialists as his associates. After all, he had already appointed a wine salesman as his Foreign Minister, his party philosopher as his Minister for Eastern Affairs, and an erstwhile fighter pilot as overseer of the entire economy. Now he was picking an architect of all people to be his Minister of Armaments. Undoubtedly Hitler preferred to fill positions of leadership with laymen. All his life he respected but distrusted professionals such as, for example, Schacht.[6]

But the choice was not as irrational as Speer claimed later on. As an architect, he was not so much a lone artist sitting at his drawing-board making sketches of buildings, as a manager of a large and complex office engaged in major, indeed gargantuan, projects of construction and design.[7] As General Building Inspector for Berlin, he was already familiar with the havoc bombing could wreak and, as the man responsible for restoring the roads and railways in the Ukraine, he knew all about the problems posed by poor communications and the need to organize an adequate supply of labour. He had worked closely with Todt in a number of areas. His duties had already acquainted him with the power-plays of men like Göring, and his initial reaction to his appointment showed quite clearly that he was fully able to cope with them. Above all, however, he was Hitler's own man. He was Hitler's personal friend, perhaps his only one. Together they continued even after his appointment to pore over models of the new Berlin, and dream of the transformation of German cities they would achieve together after the war was over. Long before his appointment, Speer had on his own admission fallen totally under his Leader's spell. He would do unquestioningly anything he wanted.[8]

In contrast to Speer's unquenchable optimism, others besides Fritz Todt had begun by this time to have serious doubts about the German capacity to continue the war to victory. A few months before his appointment, Speer had visited the General Manager of the Junkers factory at Dessau, Heinrich Koppenberg, to discuss the buildings needed to house the gigantic new aircraft factory he was planning in the east. Speer later recalled that Koppenberg had led him 'into a locked room and showed me a graph comparing American bomber production for the next several years with ours. I asked him,' Speer went on, 'what our leaders had to say about these depressing figures. "That's just it, they won't believe it," he said. Whereupon he broke into uncontrollable tears.'[9] General Georg Thomas, chief of procurement at the Combined Armed Forces Supreme Command, had become increasingly pessimistic from the summer of 1941 onwards. By January 1942 he was more worried about whom to blame for the disastrous supply situation facing the army in the east than how to rescue the situation, 'since', as he said, 'some day somebody will be held responsible'.[10] General Friedrich Fromm, who commanded the reserve army at home and had responsibility for the army's armaments supplies, told Chief of the Army General Staff Franz Halder on 24 November 1941 that the arms economy was on a 'descending curve. He thinks,' Halder noted in his diary, 'of the necessities of making peace!'[11] Manpower reserves were being exhausted, and oil supplies were running short, and Fromm advised Hitler to send all available new troops to Army Group South, so that it could make a dash for the oilfields of the Caucasus. The despair of some ran even deeper. On 17 November 1941 the head of the procurement organization for the air force, Ernst Udet, a former flying ace, shot himself after failing repeatedly to convince Hitler and Göring that aircraft production in Britain and America was growing so fast that the German planes would face overwhelming, impossible odds within a few months.[12] In January 1942 Walter Borbet, the head of the Bochum Association, a major arms manufacturing concern where he had pioneered new methods of production, also shot himself, convinced both that the war could not be won and that Germany's leadership would never be persuaded to make peace.[13]

These men had good cause for concern. Despite all the Germans' efforts, the British were continuing to out-produce them in tanks and other weapons. The armed forces procurement officials insisted on technological sophistication at the expense of mass production, and there was constant bickering between the army, the navy and the air force, each with its very plausible rival claims for priority in the allocation of resources. Focusing on complex weaponry brought higher profits to business than cheap mass production. All this slowed down production and reduced the quantities of armaments and equipment available to the armed forces. At the same time, Hitler continued to demand ever-greater efforts from industry as the military situation failed to deliver the anticipated breakthrough. In July 1941 he ordered the construction of a new high seas battle fleet, at the same time as a fourfold increase in the air force and the expansion of the number of motorized divisions in the army to thirty-six. He was all too aware of the rapidly increasing quantities of American arms and equipment that were managing to reach Britain. Already by the time America formally became a combatant nation, in December 1941, it was churning out quantities of armaments that Germany had so far shown no signs that it would be able to match. Army officers early in 1942 began to notice an improvement in Soviet military equipment and weaponry as well. To demand that German arms production match all this seemed completely unrealistic.[14]

Unlike Todt and the other economic managers who thought that the war was already lost in economic and therefore also in military terms, Speer believed, with Hitler, that it could still be won. He had a blind faith in Hitler's powers. At every stage, Hitler's will had triumphed over adversity, and it would do so again. Speer was not a technocrat; he was a true believer.[15] Speer was not so blind, of course, that he failed to realize that this was a major reason for his appointment. Hitler, indeed, confided in him more than once that the death of Todt at a moment when Speer was visiting his headquarters was providential. As Speer wrote later,

In contrast to the troublesome Dr. Todt, Hitler must have found me a rather willing tool at first. To that extent, this shift in personnel obeyed the principle of negative selection which governed the composition of Hitler's entourage. Since he regularly responded to opposition by choosing someone more amenable, over the years he assembled around himself a group of associates who more and more surrendered to his arguments and translated them into action more and more unscrupulously.[16]

This principle had already been at work in the changes Hitler had made in the senior ranks of the army after the Moscow debacle. Now it was at work in the management of the war economy too. But Speer was no amateur in one respect at least. In the following weeks, he warded off one attempt after another by Göring to restrict his powers. He repeatedly called on Hitler to back him and even to transfer the armaments functions of the Four-Year-Plan to the Armaments Ministry. In all this, he showed that his instinct for power was as strong as that of anyone in the Nazi hierarchy.[17]

II

Speer had several major advantages in his mission to galvanize German war production into greater efficiency. He had the support of Hitler, which he used whenever he ran into serious opposition, and he had good relations with key figures in the Nazi hierarchy. As General Buildings Inspector, for instance, Speer had worked closely with Himmler and the SS, and depended for his grandiose schemes on the supply of stone quarried by the inmates of the concentration camps at Flossenbürg and Mauthausen.[18] He also had good contacts in the armaments management hierarchy (especially the State Secretary in the Air Ministry, Field Marshal Erhard Milch, nominally Göring's man but in practice much more willing to work with Speer). Speer also came into office when the drive to rationalize had already begun, spurred on by Hitler's insistent criticisms of inefficiency and facilitated by the changes in economic management inaugurated by Todt in December 1941. He worked hard to eliminate overlaps in arms production between the three armed services. He subordinated the leading industrial producers directly to himself and gave them a degree of delegated responsibility in improving their production methods. He fought against excessive bureaucracy and introduced streamlined methods of mass production. The result, he claimed later, was a significant increase in production in every area within six months. 'Total productivity in armaments increased by 59.6 per cent . . . After two and a half years, in spite of the beginning of heavy bombing, we had raised our entire armaments production from an average index figure of 98 for the year 1941 – admittedly a low point – to a summit of 322 in July 1944.'[19]

In taking over the management of armaments production, Speer trumpeted the virtues of rationalization. He brought in a number of industrialists to man the new committee structure set up by Todt. A typical example of Speer's use of industrialists to increase efficiency could be found in the production of submarines, where he appointed a car manufacturer to reorganize the assembly process in 1943. The new submarine supremo broke down the production of each vessel into eight sections, got a different firm to make each section with standard parts to a timetable co-ordinated with the others, assembled the final product at a central plant, and thereby reduced the time it took to make each U-boat from forty-two weeks to sixteen. Speer also implemented a new system of fixed-price contracts introduced by Todt in January 1941, which forced prices down and offered exemption from corporation tax for those who reduced costs and therefore prices by a significant amount. Speer demanded that companies exploit their workers more effectively, with double shifts being introduced, and tried to reduce costs by using existing plant more intensively instead of constructing new factories. No fewer than 1.8 million men were employed in setting up new plant, but much of the extra capacity could not be used because of shortages of energy and lack of machine tools; Speer terminated contracts for new industrial facilities costing 3,000 million Reichsmarks. And he introduced a drastic concentration and simplification of the production of arms and arms-related products across the economy. The number of mostly small firms engaged in producing prismatic glass for use in viewfinders, telescopes, binoculars, periscopes and the like was reduced from twenty-three to seven, and the variety of different types of glass from a staggering 300 to a mere fourteen. Speer found that no fewer than 334 factories were making firefighting equipment for the air force; by early 1944 he had reduced this to sixty-four, which was reckoned to have saved 360,000 man-hours per month. The number of companies producing machine-tools was cut from 900 in early 1942 to 369 by October the following year. Speer even extended the rationalization principle to consumer goods industries. When he found that five out of the 117 carpet manufacturers in Germany were producing 90 per cent of the carpets made, he had the other 112 closed down, and their factories and labour put to use in the war economy. In the competition for resources, the different armed forces and their associated manufacturers had exaggerated their needs, so that, for example, aircraft factories had demanded four times the amount of aluminium per aircraft than was actually needed. The metal was being stockpiled or put to non-essential uses such as making ladders or greenhouses. Speer made the companies surrender their stockpiles, and tied the allocation of raw materials to production targets.[20]

Arms production required massive quantities of steel, which Hitler ordered to be directed above all towards the army, rather than the navy or the air force. Introducing greater efficiency into the organization of steel production was not least the achievement of the Reich Economics Ministry and its leading official Hans Kehrl. He set up a new system of ordering and production at a meeting on 15 May 1942 of the new central planning body he had established with Milch to co-ordinate arms production. At the same time, Speer appointed savings engineers to advise firms on how to use steel and other raw materials more efficiently. Better machines and more automation reduced wastage. By May 1943 Speer could claim that less than half the iron and steel was used to produce an average ton of armaments than had been used in 1941. By the end of the war, each ton of steel was being used to produce four times the quantity of munitions than had been the case in 1941. However, steel production needed large quantities of coking coal, and this proved impossible to obtain, given the difficulties facing the railway system and the low productivity of forced labour in the mines. Moreover, the mines were still short of more than 100,000 workers, while the railways needed another 9,000 men to load and operate the trains transporting the coal. Told of these problems on 11 August 1942, Hitler declared bluntly: 'If, due to the shortage of coking coal, the output of the steel industry cannot be raised as planned, then the war is lost.'[21]

More coal was obtained by cutting allocations to domestic consumers by 10 per cent. Steel output was boosted to 2.7 million tons a month in early 1943 in the Greater German Reich. With the increase in steel allocations to ammunition factories, and the introduction of fresh incentives to industrialists, Speer was able to boast that arms production as a whole doubled in his first year of office. At the same time, Erhard Milch and the Air Ministry were able to double the monthly output of aircraft, not least by concentrating production in a small number of mammoth factories. Bringing the main producers into line by forcing them to make changes in their senior management, Milch pushed through a rationalization programme in which the development of new, more advanced fighters and bombers was sacrificed to the mass-production of huge numbers of existing models, thus achieving significant economies of scale. An advanced fighter plane, the Messerschmitt Me210, was already being manufactured, but the Air Ministry had pushed on too fast, leaving crucial problems of design and development unsolved. The aircraft was unstable, and yet hundreds were being produced. Milch cancelled the project and focused resources on producing planes such as the twin-engined Heinkel 111. This medium bomber had first flown in 1934 and had proved ineffective in the Blitz, so it was redeployed as a night interceptor over Germany, where it met with some success. Similarly, Milch directed resources towards bringing more Me109 fighter planes off the production lines. The number of factories making the fighter was reduced from seven to three, and production boosted from 180 a month to 1,000. These changes meant that twice as many aircraft were being produced per month in the summer of 1943 than had been the case a year and a half before.[22]

The air force had repeatedly demanded modifications and improvements to existing aircraft, thus slowing down production; by the end of 1942, indeed, the number of design changes recommended for the Junkers Ju88 bomber had reached 18,000, while the specifications for changes to the Heinkel He177 heavy bomber stored in Heinkel's design offices filled no fewer than fifty-six stout files. Working together with Milch, Speer did his best to ward off new demands for design changes, but it was not until early 1944 that he managed to reduce the number of models of combat aircraft in production from forty-two to thirty, then to nine, and eventually to five. The number of different types of tanks and armoured vehicles was slashed in January 1944, with the reluctant and much-delayed agreement of the army, from eighteen to seven, and a single type of anti-tank weapon replaced the existing twelve. Speer found a total of 151 different types of lorry being manufactured for military use; in 1942 he cut this down to twenty-three. This simplification process extended to coal-mining and machine-tools too, where a total of 440 different types of mechanical and hydraulic presses was reduced to thirty-six. Components were a particular problem, complicating and slowing down the production process; the Ju88 for example used more than 4,000 different types of bolt and screw. Its eventual replacement, the Ju288, used only 200. Here, and where possible in other areas too, automatic riveting machines replaced manual labour, and the simplification process also meant that workers required shorter and more elementary training than they had previously needed. All of this boosted productivity, which in the arms industries was more than 50 per cent higher in 1944 than it had been two years previously.[23]

Speer also rationalized the production of tanks. Early in the war the

German army had relied on two medium tanks, the Mark III and the Mark IV, and a Czech-designed tank, the T-38, all of which proved their worth in the invasion of Poland and Western Europe in 1939–40. But in 1941 they encountered the superior Soviet T-34, which was fast, manoeuvrable and at the same time better armoured and equipped with more effective guns. This led to a major rethink, resulting in the production of two new tanks, the 56-ton Tiger and 45-ton Panther. These were formidable weapons, much more than a match for the T-34, and far more heavily gunned than their American counterparts. Speer managed to have them rolling off the production lines in considerable quantities by 1943. But almost as soon as they began to be built in any numbers, Allied bombing began to destroy the factories where they were made, so they could never be turned out in sufficient numbers. By contrast Soviet industry was turning out four tanks to every one manufactured by the Germans by the beginning of 1943. The relocation of Soviet industry to the Urals had finally paid off.[24] The German economy might have been able in some areas at least to produce better weapons than the economies of its enemies, but it was quite unable to match them for quantity. The move to standardized mass production came later in Germany than elsewhere; in the end, indeed, it came too late.[25]

The difference in other areas of armaments production was similarly striking, if not quite so dramatic. Even the United States was only producing half as many infantry weapons as the Soviet Union in 1942, and hardly any more combat aircraft and tanks. The American rationalization method was the same as the German, concentrating production in a limited variety of gigantic plants turning out a small number of standardized armaments. Yet German rationalization in some areas was achieved at the cost of quality. The Me109 fighter plane, for example, was too slow to cope with its more manoeuvrable Soviet counterparts. The Junkers bombers were also too slow, and too small to carry a really devastating payload. The new Tiger and Panther tanks were superior products, but, as so often, they were rushed into battle before all the design problems had been ironed out. They had a worrying tendency to break down. And all too often they ran out of fuel and could not be resupplied.[26] At the same time, the Soviet people paid dearly for their Herculean production efforts: hundreds of thousands of workers, in a manner that had already become familiar in Stalin's drive to industrialize during the 1930s, were drafted in from the farms, agricultural production suffered, and there was widespread malnutrition and even starvation. The fever-pitch of Soviet economic mobilization evident in 1942 could not be kept up for very long. But American lend-lease arrangements provided the Soviet armies with large quantities of food, raw materials and communications equipment, especially radios and field telephones, and were making a huge difference to British equipment and supplies as well. Soon the Americans would enter the war in Europe and North Africa directly. Speer's efforts at rationalization, Todt's efficiency drive, Milch's organizational reforms, Kehrl's administrative changes, all were insufficient in the end.[27]

By the middle of the war, the American economy was producing quantities of weapons, aircraft, warships, ammunition and military equipment that the Third Reich could not hope to match. In 1942, US factories produced nearly 48,000 aircraft; the following year saw nearly 86,000 roll off the production lines and in 1944 more than 114,000. Of course, a large proportion of these went to fight the Japanese in the Pacific. But this still left huge numbers to be deployed in the European theatre of war. Moreover, both the Soviet Union and the United Kingdom were out-producing Germany as well. Thus in 1940 the Soviet Union produced more than 21,000 aircraft, in 1943 nearly 37,000. The British Empire produced, in 1940, 15,000 aircraft, in 1941, just over 20,000, in 1942, more than 23,000, in 1943, around 35,000, and in 1944, roughly 47,000: the overwhelming majority of these were produced in the UK itself. This compared to 10,000 new aircraft built in Germany in 1940, 11,000 in 1941, and getting on for 15,000 in 1942. The rationalization measures taken by Speer and Milch and the increasing concentration of resources on aircraft production only had an effect from 1943, when more than 26,000 rolled off the production lines, and 1944, where the figure reached nearly 40,000. This was still fewer than Britain and the Dominions produced, and less than a fifth of the combined production of the three main Allied powers.[28]

It was the same in other areas. According to the German Combined Armed Forces Supreme Command, for instance, Germany managed to manufacture between 5,000 and 6,000 tanks a year from 1942 to 1944, thus failing significantly to increase output. This compared to Britain and the Dominions, where some 6,000 to 8,000 tanks were produced a year. The Soviet Union, however, produced around 19,000 tanks a year during this period, and US tank production rose from

THE NEW ORDER 333

17,000 in 1942 to more than 29,000 in 1944. In 1943 the combined Allied production of machine-guns came to 1,110,000, compared to 165,527 in Germany. Not all of the Allied military hardware was deployed against the Germans, of course: in particular, the British and Americans were waging hard-fought wars in Asia and the Pacific. Nevertheless, large quantities of American arms and equipment did find their way to Britain and the Soviet Union, to bolster what was already a massive Soviet superiority in tanks and aircraft. The writing was already on the wall in 1942, as Todt had realized.[29] By 1944, it was clear for all to read.

III

The strain on the German economy could be gauged from the fact that, by 1944, 75 per cent of GDP was being devoted to the war, in comparison to 60 per cent in the Soviet Union and 55 per cent in Britain.[30] Yet Germany could also benefit from the annexation or occupation of a large part of Europe in the first half of the war. As we have already seen, the takeover of Poland offered opportunities for enrichment that few were able to withstand. More importantly perhaps, the conquest of affluent countries in Western Europe, with their advanced industrial and prosperous agricultural sectors, held out the promise of making a major difference from 1940 onwards. Altogether, it has been estimated, the German sphere of influence in Europe in 1940 had a population of 290 million, with a prewar GDP greater than that of the USA. Among the conquered countries, France, Belgium and the Netherlands also had extensive overseas empires that added further potential to the Third Reich's economic power. The German authorities began to set about exploiting the resources of the conquered countries with an abandon that did not augur well for the future well-being of the subject economies. In the initial euphoria of victory, looting and plunder were the order of the day. After the defeat of France, the German armies sequestered for their own use over 300,000 French rifles, more than 5,000 pieces of French artillery, nearly 4 million French shells and 2,170 French tanks, many of which were still being used by the German army in the later phases of the war. All of this constituted no more than a third of the total booty seized from the French by the Germans. Another third was supplied by the seizure of thousands of railway engines and vast quantities of rolling stock. The German railway system had been starved of investment in the years before the war, leading to severe delays in moving bulk supplies such as coal around the country. Now, however, it was able to replenish its depleted stocks with 4,260 locomotives and 140,000 freight cars and wagons from the French, Dutch and Belgian railways. Finally, the German armed forces confiscated massive quantities of raw materials for the arms industry back home, including 81,000 tons of copper, a year's supply of tin and nickel and considerable quantities of petrol and oil. Altogether, the French estimated that 7.7 billion Reichsmarks' worth of goods was taken from them during the occupation.[31]

It was not only the German government and German armed forces that took advantage of the conquest of other countries: ordinary German soldiers, as we have already seen, did so as well. The scale of their depredations in Poland, the Soviet Union and Western and Southern Europe was considerable. The letters written by German soldiers are full of reports and promises of goods, looted or purchased with their German Reichsmarks, being sent to their families in Germany. Heinrich Böll, later to become famous as a Nobel prize-winning novelist, sent packets of butter, writing-paper, eggs, ladies' shoes, onions and much more besides. 'I've got half a suckling pig for you,' he announced triumphantly to his family just before coming home on leave in 1940. Mothers and wives sent money in the post to their sons in France and Belgium, Latvia and Greece, intended for them to buy supplies to take or send home. Soldiers seldom returned to Germany without carrying bags and suitcases of presents, purchased or purloined. After the regime lifted restrictions on how much could be taken or sent home in this way, the number of packages sent from France to Germany by military post soon ran at more than three million a month. Soldiers' pay was increased towards the end of 1940 explicitly in order to help them pay for foreign goods for their families. Still more important were the massive quantities of goods, equipment and above all foodstuffs officially requisitioned and sequestered by the German army and civilian authorities in occupied Eastern Europe.[32]

The Third Reich also began to exploit the economies in subtler, less obvious ways. The exchange rate with the French and Belgian franc, the Dutch guilder and other currencies in occupied Western Europe was set at a level extremely favourable to the German Reichsmark. It has been estimated, for example, that the purchasing power of the Reichsmark in France was more than 60 per cent above what it would have been had the exchange rate been allowed to find its own level on the markets instead of being artificially fixed by decree.[33] Germany imported huge quantities of goods legitimately from the conquered countries as well as simply looting them, but it did not pay for them by increasing its own exports commensurately. Instead, French, Dutch and Belgian firms exporting goods to Germany were paid by their own central banks in francs or guilders, and the sums paid marked up as debts to the Reichsbank in Berlin. The debts, of course, were never paid, so that by the end of 1944, the Reichsbank owed 8.5 billion Reichsmarks to the French, nearly 6 billion to the Dutch, and 5 billion to the Belgians and Luxembourgers.[34] Altogether French payments to Germany amounted to nearly half of all French public expenditure in 1940, 1941 and 1942, and as much as 60 per cent in 1943.[35] Germany, it has been estimated, was using 40 per cent of French resources by this time.[36] Altogether, well over 30 per cent of the wartime net production of the occupied countries in the west was extracted by the Germans.[37] The effects of these exactions on the domestic economies of the occupied countries were significant. German control over central banks in the occupied countries led to the end of restrictions on the issuing of banknotes, so that 'occupation costs' were paid not least by simply printing money, leading to serious inflation, made worse by the shortages of goods to purchase because they were being taken to Germany.[38]

German companies were able to use the overvalued Reichsmark to gain control of rival firms in France, Belgium and other parts of Western Europe. They could be helped by German government regulation of trade and raw materials distribution, which generally worked to their advantage. Yet the enormous deficit Germany ran up through the non-repayment of debts to the central banks of the occupied countries obviously made it more difficult to export the capital needed to buy up companies in the conquered countries. I. G. Farben, the German Dye Trust, did manage to seize control of much of the French chemical industry, and German firms, above all the state-sponsored Hermann Göring Reich Works, snapped up much of the mining and iron and steel industries in Alsace-Lorraine. German state sponsorship of the Hermann Göring Reich Works gave it an obvious advantage over private enterprise in the acquisition of foreign firms. Many of the enterprises taken over were state-controlled or foreign-owned; the Aryanization of Jewish firms also played a role here, though in overall terms they did not amount to very much. Many of the biggest private enterprises, however, escaped takeovers, including major Dutch multinationals like Philips, Shell and Unilever, or the huge steel combine that went under the name of Arbed. Of course, the German occupiers supervised the activities of these firms in many ways, but in most cases they were unable to exert direct control or reap direct financial benefits.[39]

This was not least because in the occupied countries in Western Europe, national governments remained in existence, however limited their powers might be, and property laws and rights continued to apply as before. From the point of view of Berlin, therefore, economic co-operation, however unequal the terms on which it was based, was what was required, not total subjugation or expropriation along the lines followed in Poland. The occupation authorities, civil and military, set the overall conditions, and opened up opportunities for German firms, for instance through Aryanization (though not in France, where Jewish property was controlled by the French authorities). All that German companies looking to expand their influence and reap the profits of the occupation could do, therefore, was to ingratiate themselves with the occupying authorities in the attempt to steal a march on their rivals.[40] The policy of co-operation dictated from Berlin limited the freedom of action of such companies. It was born not simply of expediency – the desire to win the co-operation of France and other Western European countries in the continuing struggle against Britain – but also of a grander vision: the concept of a 'New Order' in Europe, a large-scale, pan-European economy that would mobilize the Continent as a single block to pit against the giant economies of the USA and the British Empire. On 24 May 1940 representatives of the Foreign Office, the Four-Year Plan, the Reichsbank, the Economics Ministry and other interested parties held a meeting to discuss how this New Order was going to be established. It was clear that it had to be presented not as a vehicle of German expansionism but as a proposal for European co-operation. Germany's policy of trying to wage war with its own resources was clearly not working. The resources of other countries had to be harnessed as well. As Hitler himself told Todt on 20 June 1940: 'The course of the war shows that we have gone too far in our efforts to achieve autarky.'[41] The New Order was intended to reconstitute autarky, self-sufficiency, on a Europe-wide basis.[42]

What was required, therefore, as Hermann Göring, head of the Four-Year Plan, put it on 17 August 1940, was 'a mutual integration and linkage of interests between the German economy and those of Holland, Belgium, Norway and Denmark', as well as intensified economic co-operation with France. Companies such as I. G. Farben leaped in with their own suggestions as to how their own particular industrial needs could be met, as a memo from the company put it on 3 August 1940, by the creation of 'a large economic sphere organized in terms of self-sufficiency and planned in relation to all the other economic spheres of the world'.[43] Here too, as a representative of the Reich Economics Ministry explained on 3 October 1940, circumspection was necessary;

One can take the view that we can simply dictate what is to happen in the economic field in Europe, i.e. that we simply regard matters from a one-sided standpoint of German interests. This is the criterion which is sometimes adopted by private business circles when they are dealing with the questions of the future structure of the European economy from the point of view of their own particular sphere of operations. However, such a view would be wrong because in the final analysis we are not alone in Europe and we cannot run an economy with subjugated nations. It is quite obvious that we must avoid falling into either of two extremes: on the one hand, that we should swallow up everything and take everything away from the others, and, on the other, that we say: we are not like that, we don't want anything.[44]

Steering such a middle course was roughly the line taken by the visionary economic imperialists who had developed thinking about a German sphere of economic interest – sometimes known as *Mitteleuropa*, 'Central Europe' – before the First World War. It would, economic planners thought, involve the creation of Europe-wide cartels, investments and acquisitions. It might require government intervention to abolish customs barriers and regulate currencies. But from the point of view of German industry, the New Order had to be created above all by private enterprise. European economic integration under the banner of the New Order was to be based not on state regulations and government controls, but on the restructuring of the European market economy.[45]

Pursuing such a goal meant avoiding as far as possible giving the impression that the conquest of Western European countries amounted

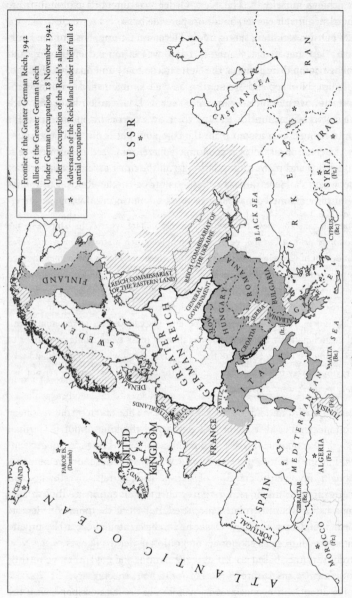

Frontier of the Greater German Reich, 1942

Allies of the Greater German Reich

Under German occupation, 18 November 1942

Under the occupation of the Reich's allies

Adversaries of the Reich/land under their full or
partial occupation

12. The New Order in Europe, 1942

to nothing more than their economic subjugation and exploitation. At the same time, however, German economic planners were clear that the New Order would be set up above all to serve German economic interests. This involved a sleight of hand that could sometimes be quite sophisticated. Mindful, for example, of the bad name that had clung to the concept of reparations since 1919, the Third Reich did not demand financial compensation from the defeated countries; how could it anyway, since the reparations Germany had had to pay from 1919 to 1932 had been to compensate for the damage done to France and Belgium by the German invasion of these two countries in 1914, and nobody had invaded Germany in 1940. So instead the victorious Germans imposed what were called 'occupation costs' on the defeated nations. These were ostensibly meant to pay for the upkeep of German troops, military and naval bases, airfields and defensive emplacements in the conquered territories. In fact, the sums extracted under this heading exceeded the costs of occupation many times over, amounting in the case of France to some 20 million Reichsmarks a day, enough, according to one French calculation, to support an army of 18 million men. By the end of 1943, nearly 25 billion Reichsmarks had found their way into the German coffers under this heading. So enormous were these sums that the Germans encouraged the French to contribute to their payment by transferring shares, and, before long, majority control over vital French-owned enterprises in the Romanian oil industry and Yugoslavia's huge copper mines had passed to Party-dominated enterprises in Germany such as the ubiquitous Hermann Göring Reich Works and the newly established 'multinational', Continental Oil.[46]

IV

What this all reflected was the fact that from the point at which serious preparations began to be made for the invasion of the Soviet Union, ideas of economic co-operation began to take second place to the imperatives of economic exploitation. Some, like Speer, took these ideas relatively seriously.[47] But as far as Hitler was concerned, they were little more than a smokescreen. On 16 July 1941, for example, he devoted some attention to a declaration in a Vichy French newspaper that the war against the Soviet Union was a European war and therefore should benefit all European states. 'What we told the world about the motives for our measures,' he said, 'ought . . . to be conditioned by tactical reasons.'[48] Saying that the invasion was a European enterprise was such a tactic. The reality was that it would be in Germany's interests. This had long been clear to the Nazi leaders. As Goebbels declared on 5 April 1940: 'We are carrying out the same revolution in Europe as we carried out on a smaller scale in Germany. If anyone asks,' he went on, 'how do you conceive the new Europe, we have to reply that we don't know. Of course we have some ideas about it, but if we were to put them into words, it would immediately create more enemies for us.'[49] On 26 October 1940 he made it brutally obvious what these ideas boiled down to: 'When this war is over, we want to be masters of Europe.'[50]

By 1941, therefore, the conquered countries of Western Europe were being exploited by the Germans for all they were worth. Most of them had advanced industrial sectors that were intended to contribute to the German war effort. Yet it soon became clear that the French contribution was falling far short of what German economic and military leaders hoped for. Attempts to get French factories to produce 3,000 aircraft for the German war effort repeatedly stalled before an agreement was signed on 12 February 1941. Even after this, production was slowed down by shortages of aluminium and difficulties in obtaining coal to provide power. Only 78 planes were delivered by factories in France and the Netherlands by the end of the year, while at the same time the British had purchased over 5,000 from the USA. The following year, things improved somewhat, with 753 planes delivered to the German air force; but this was only a tenth of the quantity the British got from the Americans. Low morale, poor health and nutrition among workers, and probably considerable ideological reluctance as well, ensured that labour productivity in French aircraft factories was only a quarter of what it was in Germany. Altogether the occupied western territories managed to produce only just over 2,600 airplanes for German military use during the whole of the war.[51]

Even with the addition of the substantial natural resources of the conquered areas of Western Europe, the economy of the Third Reich remained woefully short of fuel during the war. Particularly serious was the lack of petroleum oil. Attempts to find a substitute were unsuccessful. Synthetic fuel production only rose to 6.5 million tons in 1943, from 4 million in four years before. The Western European economies occupied in 1940 were massive consumers of imported oil, producing not a drop themselves, and so they merely added to Germany's fuel problems as they were abruptly cut off from their former sources of supply. Romania supplied 1.5 million tons of oil a year, and Hungary almost as much, but this was by no means enough. French and other fuel reserves were seized by the occupying forces, reducing the supply of petroleum in France to only 8 per cent of pre-war levels. Germany's Italian ally consumed further quantities of German and Romanian oil, since it too was cut off from other sources. German oil reserves never exceeded 2 million tons during the entire war. By contrast, the British Empire and the USA provided Britain with over 10 million tons of oil imports in 1942, and twice as much in 1944. The Germans failed to seize other sources of oil in the Caucasus and the Middle East.[52]

Coal, which still provided the basic fuel for electricity generation, industrial power and domestic use, was present in Western and Central Europe in huge quantities, but production in occupied countries plummeted as workers slowed down. Some even went on strike in protest against impossibly low food rations and deteriorating conditions. In 1943–4, about 30 per cent of the coal used in Germany came from occupied areas, particularly Upper Silesia, but far more could have been obtained, particularly from the rich coal seams of northern France and Belgium. The British blockade cut off imports of grain, fertilizer and animal fodder from overseas, while German confiscations of these materials from French, Dutch and Belgian farms, together with the drafting of farmworkers into forced labour schemes in Germany, had a disastrous effect on agriculture. Farmers had to slaughter pigs, chickens and other animals in vast quantities because there was nothing to feed them with. The grain harvest in France fell by more than half in the two years from 1938 to 1940. The German occupiers introduced food rationing. By 1941, official rations in Norway were down to 1,600 calories a day, in France and Belgium a mere 1,300. This was not enough for anybody to live off, and, as in occupied Eastern Europe, a black market rapidly emerged, as people began to break the law in order to stay alive.[53] All this meant that the addition of the economies of Western Europe did far less than had been hoped to strengthen the German war effort. Not only did productivity in the coalmines decline, but the confiscation of French, Belgian and Dutch rolling stock and railway engines also severely disrupted the movement of coal supplies across the country, hampering industrial production. As coal supplies fell, steelworks, starved of the coke essential for smelting, began to get into trouble as well. Not only was the German economy unable to take much advantage of the acquisition of coalmines in France and Belgium, but conditions in the German mines began to deteriorate too. Matters were not helped by the drafting of many key workers into the armed forces, and attempts to induce men to go down the mines by raising wages were undermined by already long hours, including Sunday working, dangerous conditions and above all the poor food rations on which miners had to subsist.[54] All in all, therefore, the German war economy gained far less from the conquest of other European countries than might have been expected.

All of this reflected, in the end, the primacy of ruthless exploitation dictated by the state. Some economists, such as Otto Bräutigam, a senior official in Rosenberg's Ministry for the Eastern Territories, considered that Germany could have extracted far more from the economies of the countries it had conquered, above all in Eastern Europe, if its leadership had followed the ideas of a collaborative economic New Order in Europe rather than policies of racial subjugation, oppression and mass murder.[55] Some businessmen and capitalists may have thought along similar lines, but on the whole they took the regime's policies towards its subject peoples as a given, and tried to gain what they could out of them. This was clearly, as the exiled political scientist Franz Neumann put it during the war, a *command economy*, a capitalist market economy increasingly subjected to direction and control from above.[56] Was it any more than that? Was the Nazi economy moving away from free enterprise capitalism altogether? There is no doubt that, in the course of the war, the regime intervened ever more intrusively in the economy, to an extent that amounted to far more than merely steering it in certain directions, or forcing it to work within the political context of a global war. Price and exchange controls, the regulation of labour and raw materials distribution, the capping of dividends, forced rationalization, the setting and resetting of production targets and much more besides constituted a drastic deformation of the market. The state's vast and precipitous increase in armaments expenditure distorted the market by pulling resources away from consumer goods production and towards arms-related and heavy industries. Industry thus came increasingly to serve the purposes and interests of an ideologically driven political regime.[57]

Moreover, as time went on, state and Party interests owned a growing proportion of the economy. Practically the whole newspaper and magazine industry had already fallen into Nazi ownership before the war, for instance, and other media, including film studios and book publishers, were similarly largely owned by branches of the Nazi Party organization. In some regions like Thuringia, regional Party bosses had been able to lay their hands on key industries. After 1939, state or Party agencies were able to take over companies with foreign owners whose countries were at war with Germany, and the Aryanization of Jewish firms in occupied countries provided still further opportunities. The state-run Hermann Göring Works spread its tentacles ever further in this way. The SS Economy and Administration Head Office under Oswald Pohl mushroomed into a complex network of businesses covering an astonishing variety of fields. The holding company set up by Pohl in 1940, the so-called German Economic Enterprise (*Deutscher Wirtschaftsbetrieb*), owned or leased and effectively controlled housing corporations, furniture, ceramics and cement manufacturers, a quarry and stone business, munitions works, woodworks, textile factories, book publishers and much more besides. Often these reflected Himmler's own particular, sometimes rather eccentric personal interests. Thus, for example, Himmler was concerned to reduce alcohol consumption in Germany and particularly in the SS, so he arranged for the Apollinaris mineral water company at Bad Neuenahr, which was British-owned before the war, to be leased from its German trustees to the SS holding company, rewarding it with a large contract to supply mineral water to the SS. The existing manager could not be ousted, but he was forced to work with a deputy appointed by the SS, giving it a large measure of control. Other companies fell under direct ownership. The SS economic empire expanded very quickly as a result of such developments.[58] At the same time, however, it had no clear overall conception of what it wanted its role to be. It simply grew by accretion, in a haphazard way, as the example of the Apollinaris mineral water company suggests. Nor was the eventual domination of the German economy a significant aim of the SS; this always took second place to security and racial policy.[59] In the last two years of the war, indeed, these latter aims pushed the economic ambitions of the SS into the background.[60]

Striking though these developments were, however, they did not do much to alter the fact that Germany was still a capitalist economy,

dominated by private enterprise. Regulation was widespread and intrusive, but it was carried out by many different, often competing
institutions and organizations.[61] Industrial managers and company
executives managed to preserve at least some freedom of action, but
they were acutely aware that their autonomy was being increasingly
restricted during the war along with the operation of a free market
economy, and they were deeply worried that the regime would go over
to a fully 'socialist', state-run economy; Joseph Goebbels, widely
regarded as a 'socialist', was a particular bogey-man in this respect, but
the growing economic empires of the SS and the Hermann Göring
Works, among others, were a cause of anxiety as well. Such concerns
drove many businessmen and industrialists to co-operate with the regime
as much as they could, in order to ward off, as they thought, even more
drastic encroachments on their decision-making powers.[62]

Thus managers, executives and company chairmen were more than
willing to take advantage of the many inducements the state had to
offer, most notably of course the provision of lucrative arms contracts.
German businesses benefited from the activities of the SS as well. The
Dresdner Bank, for example, issued credits to the SS, and senior executives were rewarded by being made officers in the organization. Its
services to the SS included providing loans for construction works in
Sachsenhausen and finance for the building of Crematorium II in Auschwitz.[63] Huta, the small firm that built the gas vans used to kill Jews at
Chelmno and elsewhere, the engineering company of Topf and Sons, who
provided the ovens for the crematoriums at Auschwitz, and many other
firms were only too happy to profit from the business of death. Some, such
as the company that supplied Zyklon-B to Auschwitz, may possibly have
been unaware of the use to which their products were being put, but in
most cases it was only too obvious. Those who processed the gold from
the dental fillings extracted from the corpses of Jews killed at Auschwitz
and other death camps can have had few doubts as to the provenance.
After collection at the camps, the fillings were sent to a refinery operated
by the Frankfurt-based Degussa firm, Germany's leading company for
the processing of precious metals. The gold was melted down and made
into bars, along with other gold materials, jewellery and the like, taken
from Jews and others in the conquered areas of Europe. Altogether, it
has been estimated, Degussa earned about 2 million Reichsmarks from
the plundering of the Jews between 1939 and 1945; 95 per cent of the

firm's gold intake between 1940 and 1944 came from loot.[64] Degussa earned such profits by selling the gold on via the Reichsbank to finance houses such as the Deutsche Bank.[65] The origin of much of this gold was clear enough to those who processed it on the factory floor. The fillings arrived at the Degussa factory for processing, as one worker recalled long after the war, in a condition that made it all too clear where they had come from: 'The crowns and the bridges, there were those where the teeth were still attached ... That was the most depressing, the fact that everything was still there. It was probably just like it had been when broken out of a mouth. The teeth were still there and sometimes still bloody and with pieces of gum on them.'[66]

'NO BETTER OFF THAN PIGS'

I

Speer's achievement in galvanizing the war economy into increased production, futile though it was to prove in the end, rested not least on the effective use of the labour force. The proportion of the industrial workforce engaged in arms manufacture had grown by 159 per cent from 1939 to 1941 and by the time Speer took up office, there was little room left for any further growth in this area. Speer encouraged the more efficient use of labour, not only through increasing the amount of shift-work but also through his general rationalization of production, halving the number of man-hours needed to make a Panzer III tank, for example. The number of combat aircraft made in German factories quadrupled between 1941 and 1944, and even if the choice of terminal dates for the statistics maximized the increase, the growth in production was still real enough. Yet this was achieved with an aircraft factory workforce that in 1944 was not much larger than it had been three years previously, at 390,000 instead of 360,000.[67]

At the same time, fresh labour was poured into the armaments industries, increasing the size of the workforce dramatically in a few key areas. In 1942 the number of workers engaged in producing tanks grew by nearly 60 per cent. A 90 per cent increase in the number of employees in railway locomotive factories in the same year helped boost production from under 2,000 in 1941 to more than 5,000 two years later. The crucial growth came in ammunition production, where 450,000 workers were employed by the autumn of 1943, compared to 160,000 in tank factories and 210,000 in the manufacture of weapons. Here too there were major increases, although they had been inaugurated not by Speer, but by a programme announced on 10 January 1942 under Todt.[68] The task of recruiting these new workers was allotted to the man whom Hitler appointed as General Plenipotentiary for Labour Mobilization on the creation of this new post on 21 March 1942: Fritz Sauckel. Sauckel was a very different character from a smooth, cultivated bourgeois professional like Speer. Born on 27 October 1894, the son of a post office worker, Sauckel grew up in poor circumstances in Franconia, left school at the age of fifteen, became a cabin boy on a freighter and spent the First World War in a prison camp when his ship was sunk by a French warship as soon as hostilities broke out. Back in Germany in 1919, he worked as a lathe operator in a ball-bearing factory before studying engineering. Here, therefore, was a real plebeian, in both his origins and his lifestyle. Unlike some of the other leading Nazis, Sauckel appears to have had a happy marriage, during which he fathered no fewer than ten children. In 1923 he heard Hitler speak and was converted by his message of the need for national unity. Sauckel remained loyal to Hitler after the failed beer-hall putsch of the same year, and Hitler rewarded him by appointing him Regional Leader of Thuringia in 1927. Elected to the Thuringian legislative assembly in 1929, Sauckel became Minister-President of Thuringia when the Nazis came out of the 1932 state elections as the strongest party.[69]

In the 1930s, he not only led the Aryanization of one of the biggest arms manufacturers in Thuringia but also ensured that it was taken over by his own holding company, the Wilhelm Gustloff Foundation. Despite his origins, therefore, Sauckel was no stranger to the world of business and industry. His experience was to stand him in good stead in 1942. Sauchel's plebeian populism found dramatic expression on the outbreak of war, when, after Hitler had turned down his request to be allowed to serve in the armed forces, he smuggled himself on to a U-boat as a stowaway, only being discovered after the submarine had put to sea. Given his prominence, the head of the U-boat fleet, Admiral Karl Dönitz, recalled the vessel to port, but the episode did Sauckel's reputation no harm. A close ally of Martin Bormann, he seemed both to Bormann and, indeed, to Hitler to possess the qualities of energy and ruthlessness needed to solve the labour problem in 1942. His record as a hardline Nazi would reassure the Party that he was not going to be soft on 'subhuman' Slavs even if their labour was vital to the German war effort. The new post was directly subordinate to Hitler, which gave Sauckel, like Speer, enormous clout. He used it, at least to begin with, to work closely with Speer in organizing the recruitment above all of foreign workers, though the tensions between the two men were palpable, later turning into a real power-struggle. Other institutions that had previously played a role in labour mobilization, including the Reich Labour Ministry, the Four-Year Plan and the German Labour Front, were effectively sidelined. On the other hand, the element of coercion needed to put the mobilization into effect necessarily involved the Reich Security Head Office, whose head, Heinrich Himmler, thus became a third major player in this field alongside Sauckel and Speer.[70]

There were already large numbers of foreign workers in Germany – over a million of them Polish – when Sauckel took up his newly created post. As Himmler and Göring considered Poles inferior racially and in every other way as well, they were thought only capable of working in simple, unskilled jobs in agriculture, where indeed they were badly needed because of the drafting of German labourers into the army and the longer-term migration of rural workers into the towns.[71] Of the 1.2 million prisoners of war and foreign civilians working in Germany in May 1940, 60 per cent were employed in agriculture. The 700,000 Poles amongst them worked almost exclusively as farm labourers, though a few were employed in road construction. Attempts to draft them into the mines had met with little success; the Polish workers were inexperienced, many were in poor health, malnourished or unfit for the heavy physical labour required of coalminers, and their productivity was low.[72] While Polish labourers had overwhelmingly been drafted into agriculture, however, the need by mid-1940 was for more workers in the arms industry – the deficit according to some armaments inspectors was as high as a million. The large numbers of French and British prisoners of war taken during the western campaign of May–June 1940 seemed eminently suitable. By early July 1940, some 200,000 of these had already been sent to work in Germany; the number increased to 600,000 by August 1940 and 1,200,000 by October 1940.[73]

Yet attempts to identify skilled workers for deployment into the arms industry were less than wholly successful. By December 1940 over half of the prisoners were employed, like the Poles, in agriculture. The deficit had to be made up by civilian volunteers. They were recruited from the occupied western countries and from countries allied to Germany, and they were supposed in theory at least to have the same wages and conditions as German workers. By October 1941, there were 300,000 civilian workers in Germany from the western countries, 270,000 from Italy, 80,000 from Slovakia and 35,000 from Hungary. The Italians quickly made themselves unpopular with complaints about German food and with rowdy behaviour in the evenings, while the privileges they were accorded aroused resentment amongst native Germans. Nor did the foreign workers live up to their employers' expectations. Most of them, as the Security Service of the SS complained, put little effort into their work. The reason was obvious: their wages were kept lower than those of their German counterparts, and were not tied to performance.[74]

The invasion of the Soviet Union, however, introduced a whole new dimension to the deployment of foreign labour. Hitler, Göring and the economic managers of the Reich began, as we have seen, by regarding the people of the territories conquered in Operation Barbarossa as dispensable. Victory would be swift, so their labour would not be needed. By October 1941, however, it was clear that victory would not come that year, and industrialists in Germany were beginning to put pressure on the regime to supply Red Army prisoners of war, for example in the mines, where manpower shortages had caused a fall in production. On 31 October 1941, Hitler ordered that Russian prisoners of war should be drafted into work for the war economy. Using them as unskilled labourers would enable skilled German workers to be redeployed where they were most needed.[75] So many Soviet prisoners of war had died by this time, however, and the condition of the rest was so poor, that only 5 per cent of the 3,350,000 Red Army troops captured by the end of March 1942 were actually used as workers.[76] Thus the recruitment of civilians became even more urgent.

Using a mixture of advertising and inducements on the one hand, and coercion and terror on the other, the German civil and military authorities in the occupied eastern territories launched a massive campaign to recruit civilian workers even before Sauckel came into office. Armed recruitment commissions roamed the countryside arresting and imprisoning young, able-bodied men and women, or, if they had gone into hiding, maltreating their parents and families until they surrendered. By the end of November 1942 Sauckel himself claimed to have recruited over a million and a half extra foreign workers since his appointment, bringing the total up to nearly 5.75 million. Many of these, notably from the west, were on six-month contracts, and a proportion had been released as unfit, so that the actual number of foreign workers (including prisoners of war) employed in Germany in November 1942 was in fact no more than 4,665,000. This was a substantial achievement by Sauckel's own lights.[77] But it was still not enough. By 1942 the war in the east had turned into precisely the kind of war of attrition that Hitler had tried to avoid. From June 1941 to May 1944 the German armed forces were losing on average 60,000 men killed on the Eastern Front each month. In addition, hundreds of thousands more were put out of action by capture, wounds or disease.[78] Replacing them was far from easy. Nearly a million more recruits were gained in 1942 by lowering the age of conscription; 200,000 more men were drafted in from jobs in the arms industry previously ruled exempt; raising the age of conscription to include the middle-aged had also been necessary to bring many of them in. But these measures in turn exacerbated the existing shortages of labour in the arms industry and in agriculture.[79]

The more German soldiers died on the Eastern Front, the more the army drafted in fresh groups of previously protected German workers from the arms industries, and the more those industries needed to replace the departing employees with new cohorts of foreign workers. Unwilling to offend popular opinion in Germany by improving wages and conditions for foreign workers, the regime went over increasingly to compulsion even in the west. On 6 June 1942 Hitler agreed with Pierre Laval, the Vichy French Prime Minister, that he would release 50,000 French prisoners of war in return for the despatching of 150,000 civilian workers to Germany, in a scheme that was subsequently considerably expanded still further. Early in 1942 Sauckel demanded that a third of all French metalworkers, amounting to some 150,000 skilled labourers, be relocated to Germany, along with another quarter of a million workers of all kinds. By December 1943 there were over 666,000 French workers employed in Germany, along with 223,000 Belgians and 274,000 Dutch. The more determinedly Sauckel's roving commissions seized workers from French factories, the more difficult it became to keep those factories producing munitions and equipment for the German war effort. Increasing compulsion led to growing resistance, just as had previously happened in Poland.[80]

The scope Sauckel felt he had for forced recruitment in the east was considerably greater than in the west. As the military situation on the Eastern Front became more difficult, the army, the occupation authorities and the SS all began to abandon any remaining scruples in the recruitment of local inhabitants for labour. Speaking in Posen in October 1943, Heinrich Himmler declared: 'Whether 10,000 Russian women collapse with exhaustion in the construction of an anti-tank ditch for Germany only interests me insofar as the ditch gets dug for Germany.'[81] The SS burned down whole villages if the young men evaded labour conscription, picked up potential workers off the streets, and took hostages until sufficient candidates for conscription came forward – all measures that further fuelled recruitment for the partisans. Meanwhile, the military authorities in the east devised a plan ('Operation Hay') to seize up to 50,000 children between the ages of ten and fourteen for employment in construction work for the German air force, or for deportation to Germany to work in arms factories. By such methods, the number of foreign workers from the occupied areas of the Soviet Union employed in Germany was boosted to more than 2.8 million by the autumn of 1944, including over 600,000 prisoners of war. By this time, there were nearly 8 million foreign workers in the Reich as a whole. 46 per cent of workers in agriculture were foreign citizens, 33 per cent of workers in mining, 30 per cent in the metal industries, 32 per cent in construction, 28 per cent in the chemical industry, and 26 per cent in transport. More than a quarter of the workforce in Germany consisted of citizens of other countries in the final year of the war.[82]

II

This massive influx of foreign labour changed the face of Germany's towns and cities from the spring of 1942 onwards. Camps and hostels were set up all over Germany to house these workers. In Munich alone, for example, there were 120 prisoner-of-war camps and 286 camps and hostels for civilian foreign workers. In this way, 80,000 beds were made available for foreign workers. Some firms employed very large numbers: towards the end of 1944 the motor vehicle manufacturer BMW was housing 16,600 foreign workers in eleven special centres.[83] The Daimler-Benz factory at Untertürkheim, near Stuttgart, which made aircraft engines and other war products, had a workforce of up to 15,000 during the war. Excluding the company's research and development section, the proportion of foreign workers increased from roughly nil in 1939 to more than half by 1943. They were housed in seventy different facilities, including improvised barracks set up in an old music hall and a former school.[84] In the Krupp steelworks in Essen, which had lost more than half its male German workers to the armed forces by September 1942, while at the same time having to cope with a doubling of turnover since 1937 in response to huge increases in military orders, nearly 40 per cent of the workforce consisted of foreigners by the beginning of 1943. They were there because the firm had put in repeated requests to the relevant government authorities (latterly Sauckel's office), and because the company itself had gone on a recruiting drive for skilled workers in Western Europe. Top Krupp officials pulled strings in the German occupation administration in France to secure an allocation of nearly 8,000 workers, many of them highly skilled, in the autumn of 1942. Sauckel's office even began to suspect that the company preferred skilled foreign workers to less well-trained and experienced German ones. In the Krupp company town of Essen, the foreign workers lived in private lodgings, or – if they were prisoners of war, or drafted from the east – in specially constructed and heavily guarded camps. The camps for Soviet workers were particularly badly built, with inadequate sanitation and a lack of bed-linen and other equipment. A large number of the civilians were under the age of eighteen. The diet they were allocated was markedly worse than that provided for other nationalities. One foreman at the Krupp vehicle manufacturing plant, who was also a sergeant in the SS and thus not likely to be sympathetic to Soviet workers, complained that he was supposed to get a decent day's work out of men whose daily ration was 'nothing but water with a couple of turnips floating in it, just like dish-water'. Another Krupp manager pointed out: 'These people are starving and in no position to do the heavy labour in boiler construction for which they were assigned to us.'[85]

Corruption was rife in the foreign workers' camps, with commandants and officers siphoning off supplies and selling them on the black market, or hiring out skilled workers to local tradesmen in return for schnapps or food for themselves. There was a lively trade in leave permits, often forged by educated inmates working in the camp administration. At one camp, a German-Polish interpreter established a widespread prostitution ring, using young female inmates and bribing the German guards to turn a blind eye with food stolen from the camp kitchens. Sexual liaisons were common between German camp officials and female inmates; they were often coerced, and rape was not uncommon. For the sexual needs of the foreign workers, sixty brothels had been specially established by the end of 1943, with 600 prostitutes, all (at least according to the Security Service of the SS) volunteers from Paris, Poland or the Czech Protectorate and all earning a tidy sum of money by providing sexual services for the workers. Whether their work was quite as lucrative as the SS supposed was questionable. At one camp brothel in Oldenburg, for example, some six to eight women clocked up 14,161 visits by clients in the course of 1943, earning 200 Reichsmarks a week, with 110 deducted for living costs.[86] If these measures were intended to prevent liaisons between foreign workers and German citizens, they failed. Social contact between Germans and western foreign labourers was not banned if the latter were not prisoners of war, and there were inevitably many sexual encounters, so many, indeed, that the Security Service of the SS estimated that at least 20,000 illegitimate children were born to German women as a result, so that the 'danger of foreign contamination of the blood of the German people was constantly increasing'.[87]

The situation of Polish workers in the Reich was particularly bad. In the countryside, as the secret observers of the exiled German Social Democrats reported in February 1940, villagers were giving assistance to Polish labourers in all sorts of ways. Especially in eastern areas, Germans had been used to Poles as seasonal migrant labourers for many decades. The regime was appalled by such fraternization, and responded with propaganda detailing the atrocities supposedly committed by Poles and presenting evidence of their alleged racial inferiority and the threat that this allegedly posed.[88] Building on the experience of dealing with Czech workers drafted into the Reich after March 1939,[89] the Nazi regime, following discussions between Hitler, Himmler and Göring, issued a series of decrees on 8 March 1940 to ensure that the racial inferiority of the Poles was clearly recognized in Germany. Polish workers in Germany were issued with leaflets warning them that they risked being sent to a concentration camp if they slacked at work or attempted industrial action. They were paid lower wages than their German counterparts doing the same work, they were subject to special taxes, and they got no bonuses and no sick pay. Polish workers had to wear a badge designating them as such – a forerunner of the 'Jewish star' introduced the following year. They had to be housed in separate barracks and to be kept clear of German cultural institutions and places of amusement such as bars, inns and restaurants. They were not to use the same churches as German Catholics. Sexual liaisons with German women were to be prevented by recruiting equal numbers of both sexes from Poland, or alternatively where this was not possible by establishing brothels for the men. Polish workers were not allowed to use public transport. They were subject to a curfew. Sexual intercourse with a German was punishable by death for the Polish man involved, on the personal orders of Hitler himself. Any German women who had entered into a relationship with a Polish worker were to be publicly named and shamed, among other things by having their heads shaved. If they were not condemned to a prison sentence by a court, they were to be sent to a concentration camp anyway. The sexual double standard in operation under the Nazi regime ensured that similar punishments were not decreed for German men who had sexual relations with Polish women. During the first phase of the war, these decrees were widely distributed to local authorities and acted upon in a number of places, sometimes as a result of denunciations from members of the public, although ritual acts of humiliation such as the shaving of German women's heads also caused widespread popular disquiet.[90] A typical incident occurred on 24 August 1940 in Gotha, when a seventeen-year-old Polish worker was publicly hanged without trial in front of fifty Poles (who were forced to attend) and 150 Germans (who attended voluntarily). His offence was to have been caught having sexual intercourse with a German prostitute. Such incidents became more common from the autumn of 1940 onwards.[91] In every way possible, the Poles were to be kept apart from German society. Small wonder, therefore, that many absconded, and that resistance to recruitment in Poland itself spread rapidly.[92]

Soviet prisoners of war working in Germany were treated even more harshly than their Polish counterparts.[93] At a meeting held on 7 November 1941, Göring laid down the basic guidelines:

The place of German skilled workers is in the armaments industry. Shovelling dirt and quarrying stones are not their jobs – that is what the Russian is there for . . . No contact with German population, in particular no 'solidarity'. German worker always basically the boss of the Russians . . . *Food provision* a matter for the Four-Year Plan. Russians to arrange own food (cats, horses, etc.). Clothing, housing, maintenance a bit better than what they had back home, where some still live in caves ... Supervision: members of the Armed Forces during work, as well as German workers, acting as auxiliary police ... Range of punishment: from cutting food rations to execution by firing squad; generally nothing in between.[94]

Part of the intention of these regulations was to co-opt the German working class into the ideology of the regime, from which many of its members still remained distant, by enrolling them as members of the master race in their dealings with the Russians. The broader compromise they represented, between the exterminatory racist impulses of the SS on the one hand, and the need for labour on the other, was expressed here as elsewhere by conscripting the supposedly subhuman as workers, but continuing to treat them as subhuman by denying them decent living conditions and imposing on them a draconian regime of supervision and punishment. On 20 February 1942, after weeks of negotiation, Heydrich signed a draft decree ordering that Soviet prisoners of war and forced labourers, who – it was claimed – had been brought up under Bolshevism and were therefore inveterate enemies of National Socialism, would be segregated from Germans as far as possible, made to wear a special badge, and punished by hanging if they engaged in sexual intercourse with German women.[95]

Whether they had come voluntarily or not, Soviet forced labourers were all treated the same: herded into barracks, subjected to the humiliating rituals of delousing, and fed on bread and watery soup. 'We're no better off here than pigs,' complained two young Russian women who had come voluntarily and were therefore allowed to write to their relatives at home early in 1942. '. . . It's like being in jail, and the gate is shut . . . We're not allowed to go out anywhere . . . We get up at 5 a.m. and go to work at seven. We finish at 5 p.m.'[96] Tuberculosis and similar diseases were rife.[97] Employers soon began to complain that the eastern workers were so malnourished that more than 10 per cent were absent every day due to sickness and the rest were barely fit to work. Some women collapsed from hunger as they worked. Reports of their treatment reached their friends and relatives at home and led to a rapid decline in the number of volunteers. Rosenberg's Eastern Ministry demanded an improvement in their treatment; and when on 13 March 1942 Speer reported on the situation to Hitler, the Leader ordered that the civilian Russian workers should not be kept confined and that they should be given better wages, performance bonuses and improved rations. On the other hand, any insubordination was punishable by death. On 9 April 1942 these orders found expression in a new set of regulations which Sauckel immediately put into effect, dressing them up in brutal rhetoric designed to reassure Nazi ideologues that racially inferior Russians were not being treated in a humanitarian spirit. If they disobeyed orders, he said, they should be handed over to the Gestapo and 'hanged, shot!' If they were now being given decent rations, it was because 'even a machine can only perform if I give it the fuel, lubricating oil and care it needs'. Otherwise the Russians would become a burden on the German people or even a threat to their health.[98]

Such rhetoric was able to overcome the hostility of the SS to the recruitment of Soviet civilians. However, it was regarded as vital for political purposes that their wages and conditions were not substantially improved at a time when rations for Germans were being reduced. This would have caused hostile reactions among the German population. Their standard of living in the east had in any case been lower, it was argued. On the other hand, it was just as important not to make their wages so low that employers would dismiss German workers in order to take them on. To prevent this, employers were made to pay a special surtax on eastern workers. And to improve work-rates, the workers were paid piece-rates and productivity bonuses, especially when it was realized that Stalin's forced industrialization programme of the 1930s had equipped many of them with skills badly needed in German industry. Despite limited improvements of this kind, increasing numbers of them were now drafted. Sauckel nevertheless found it necessary to remind local Nazi officials in September 1942 that 'flogged, half-starved and dead Russians do not mine coal for us, they are totally useless for making iron and steel'.[99] By the end of 1942, therefore, foreign workers were becoming vital for industry as well as agriculture in Germany. At the same time, however, the SS and the law enforcement and Party agencies were becoming increasingly concerned about what they saw as the security threat posed by the presence of enormous numbers of men and women from conquered countries in the cities and towns of Germany and were trying contain it by any means possible. With the agreement of the Reich Security Head Office, Martin Bormann set up a special surveillance operation, with units of reliable Party members, ex-soldiers, SS and SA men, to monitor foreign workers, and report them if they broke regulations by, for example, using public transport, visiting bars, or riding bicycles.[100]

Not only were conditions poor for these workers, security was also in practice very lax, despite draconian punishments for infractions of the rules. In April 1942, as Sauckel's programme of importing foreign labour was getting under way, just over 2,000 Soviet prisoners of war and civilian workers escaped from their camps and hostels; three months later the figure had multiplied more than tenfold. In August 1942 the Gestapo despairingly predicted there would be at least another 30,000 escapes by the end of the year. Even if their claim to be recapturing some three-quarters of the escapees was correct, the situation was clearly spiralling out of control. Taking charge of the situation the following month, Gestapo chief Heinrich Müller had road-blocks and cordons set up all over the country, instituted checkpoints at railway stations and posted men in inner cities to check the papers of suspicious-looking pedestrians. Thus the mass influx of foreign labourers was now having a drastic effect on the lives of ordinary Germans, as police checks and controls became more intrusive than ever before. There were so many foreign workers in Hamburg by the spring of 1943, Luise Solmitz noted in her diary, that there was 'a confused babel of languages wherever you hear people speaking'.[101]

In the meantime, Fr.[iedrich Solmitz] saw a miserable procession of foreign workers in Ostmark Street: blonde girls, young people, amongst them unmistakeable Asiatics, old people, staggering under their burden, without an eastern smile, loaded down with their meagre possessions, close to dying from exhaustion. 'Get down off the pavement, you bandits!'[102]

Such sympathy was not uncommon, even though, as Luise Solmitz's reference to 'Asiatics' suggests, German people frequently felt a sense of racial superiority over Soviet prisoners and forced labourers.[103] When, a few months later, he gave some food to a starving forced labourer, Friedrich Solmitz was denounced anonymously to the police and arrested by the Gestapo; he was lucky to escape with nothing more than a warning.[104]

III

A major reason for the mass recruitment of foreign labour to the German arms industry lay in the fact that, for a variety of reasons, the regime did not bring a sufficient number of German women into the workforce. The possibilities here were indeed rather limited. For many decades, women's participation in the workforce had been much greater in Germany than in the more advanced industrial economy of Britain. By 1939 just over half of all women between the ages of fifteen and sixty in Germany were in work, compared to only a quarter in the UK. Thanks to a considerable effort, the British participation rate increased to 41 per cent by 1944; but it never reached that of Germany. Women's share of the German labour force was also greater than the equivalent in the USA, which stood at 26 per cent. The basic reason was that the small farms so characteristic of many agricultural regions in Germany depended heavily on female labour, the more so as men departed for the front or were sucked into the munitions industry. In 1939, no fewer than 6 million German women worked on farms, compared to a mere 100,000 in Britain. As men were drafted into the army, or into arms production, the proportion of women in the native German agricultural labour force increased from 55 per cent in 1939 to 67 per cent in 1944; such work was a vital part of war production, and the women engaged in it were helped at crucial times such as the harvest months by the drafting-in of additional temporary female labour, involving, for example, nearly 950,000 women in the summer of 1942. Above and beyond this, hundreds of thousands of women worked as unpaid family assistants on farms or in shops. 14 million women were in employment by 1941, constituting 42 per cent of the native workforce (there were already substantial numbers of foreign women workers in Germany before the war, and their numbers increased too). How much higher could the rate go?[105] Economic managers considered that even with the most vigorous efforts to mobilize women for war production, it would not be possible to recruit more than about 1.4 million extra pairs of hands in this way. This was a mere fraction of the numbers actually needed.[106]

When the war began. Germany actually experienced a fall in female employment as half a million women left the labour market between

May 1939 and May 1941. This was largely because of cutbacks in the textile, footwear and consumer goods industries in general, which employed very large numbers of women. Some 250,000 women workers had been transferred from such areas into war industries by June 1940. Between May 1939 and May 1942 the number of women working in producer goods industries rose from 760,000 to just over 1.5 million, while in the consumer goods industries it fell from just over 1.6 million to just under 1.3 million. The German Labour Front therefore lobbied strongly for an improvement in conditions for women workers in order to attract more to the arms industry. In May 1942 it succeeded in getting an increase in government funding for crèches for married women workers, and an improved allowance for women workers for the weeks before and after they gave birth, as well as new restrictions on the working hours of expectant and breast-feeding mothers. But the effect of such inducements was more than countered by the generous allowances provided to the wives and widows of men on active service; in some cases these added up to as much as 85 per cent of the men's wages in their previous civilian occupations. Hitler himself was also personally opposed to the conscription of German women into the war industries because he thought working in munitions factories might damage their childbearing prospects or indeed discourage them from having children altogether. He personally vetoed the idea of conscripting German women between the ages of forty-five and fifty for labour service in November 1943, declaring that this would affect their ability to look after their husbands and families; the previous year, he had also intervened to try to ensure that German women who volunteered for war-related employment were given relatively undemanding office jobs. Mobilizing women with young children was not considered acceptable in any belligerent country, and in any case by 1944 more than 3.5 million such women in Germany were in part-time jobs, which was four times the number in the UK. More fundamentally, perhaps, Hitler was obsessed, as always, with the precedent, as he saw it, of the 'stab-in-the-back' that he considered had caused Germany's defeat in 1918. Women on the home front had been discontented because they had resented being forced into poorly paid, dangerous and exhausting factory work, and some had taken part in the strikes that Hitler thought had undermined morale on the home front. Inadequate welfare support had led women to take part in food riots and spread anti-war sentiment among the population more widely. He was determined that was not going to happen in the Second World War.[107]

On 1 September 1939, to be sure, Hitler called on women to join in Germany's 'fighting community' and make their contribution to the war effort. But what was that contribution?[108] The regime's attempts to boost the role of the mother in the German 'national community' continued unabated during the war: Nazi women's organizations carried on with the travelling exhibitions on motherhood, courses on child-rearing, and celebrations of Mother's Day that they had organized before the war.[109] Alongside the ongoing publication of literature praising the German mother, new collections of essays now appeared, intended for consumption by women, recounting the lives of heroic German women of the past. Their heroism, however, consisted not of warlike deeds which they carried out on their own behalf, but of nobly assisting their menfolk, sending their husbands and sons off to battle, or protecting their children when the enemy loomed. Women's courage in wartime was shown mainly by their refusal to give in to despair when told of the death of a loved one in battle. As housewives, so propaganda in various media insisted, women could contribute to the war effort by behaving responsibly as consumers and keeping the family clothed and fed in difficult economic circumstances. If women were to be persuaded to engage in war work, then it had to be war work in keeping with what Nazi ideology regarded as their feminine essence. If they served as air-raid wardens, then they did so to protect the German family; if they made munitions in a factory, then they were supplying the nation's sons with the arms they needed to survive in battle. Selfless sacrifice was to be their lot. 'Earlier,' one woman who worked in a factory while her son was serving at the front was reported as saying, 'I buttered bread for him, now I paint grenades and think, this is for him.'[110]

There was no German equivalent of the much-vaunted American propaganda icon 'Rosie the Riveter', who cheerfully rolled up her sleeves to help the war effort by doing what had traditionally been regarded as a man's job in a man's industrial world.[111] For all the welfare measures designed to protect working mothers, the fact remained that in Germany, as in other countries, the majority of women in full-time paid work were young and unmarried. Organizations like the League of German Girls and the German Labour Front went to some lengths to recruit women in various kinds of war-related jobs, and the extent to which committed

lay above all in the principles of rationalization introduced by Speer and his allies and pushed through with such determination that 1944 was to prove the high-water mark of the German war economy.

IV

A key part of Speer's management of the arms economy was his collaboration not only with the SS but also with German industry. Here, a nexus of common interests soon emerged. In their search for cheap and pliant labour, industrial firms across Germany looked beyond the available foreign workers and began to recruit concentration camp inmates. By October 1944, for example, the 83,300 foreign workers employed by the giant chemicals combine I. G. Farben – 46 per cent of the total workforce – included not only 9,600 prisoners of war but also 10,900 prisoners supplied by the camp system. Among the key industrial sites set up by the combine during the war was a large buna (synthetic rubber) factory at Monowitz, three miles from the town of Auschwitz. It was far enough to the east to be out of range of bombing raids, but enjoyed good railway connections and was close to good supplies of water, lime and coal. Once its construction had been agreed, on 6 February 1941, Carl Krauch, the I. G. Farben director who was also head of research and development for Hermann Göring's Four-Year Plan organization, got Göring to ask Himmler to supply labour both from resettled ethnic Germans in the area and from inmates of the nearby concentration camp (at this time Polish political and military prisoners) in order to speed up construction. The company agreed to pay the SS 3 to 4 marks for each nine-to-eleven-hour shift completed by each prisoner, while the camp commandant Rudolf Höss agreed to provide, train, feed and guard the inmates and to build a bridge and rail spur from the camp to the site. By the spring of 1942 there were 11,200 men working on the site, 2,000 of them from the camp. Otto Ambros, who led the buna programme within I. G. Farben, declared that the company would 'make this industrial foundation a strong cornerstone for a virile, healthy Germanism in the east'. 'Our new friendship with the SS,' he reported privately to his boss within the company, Fritz terMeer, 'is proving very beneficial.'[119]

By late 1943, however, the building was still far from complete. Up to 29,000 workers were employed at Monowitz, roughly half of them foreigners, about a quarter ethnic Germans and the rest camp inmates. Maltreatment of the prisoners by SS guards, together with the poor rations they received and the lack of basic medical and sanitary facilities at the construction site barracks, where they were sleeping two or three to a bed, meant that increasing numbers of them fell sick or were unable to do the long hours of heavy physical labour required on the site. By this time, too, the great majority of camp inmates were Jewish. Most likely at the invitation of company managers on the spot, an SS officer was summoned from the camp, inspected the 3,500 prisoners engaged on construction work and sent those judged no longer fit to work back to the main Auschwitz camp to be gassed. From now on, these 'selections' were repeated at frequent intervals, so that in 1943–4 a total of 35,000 inmates passed through Monowitz, of whom 23,000 are known to have died from disease or exhaustion or been sent to the gas chambers; the total may have been as high as 30,000. In their living quarters, the company managers were exposed to a continual stench from the crematoria chimneys and even more, at intervals from September 1942 onwards, from the grilles on which large numbers of dead bodies were sometimes burned in the open air. I. G. Farben overseers and managers knew of the mass extermination in progress at Birkenau, and of the fate that awaited those identified by the SS as unfit to work on the Monowitz site: indeed, some of them even used the gas chambers as a threat to prisoners they did not think were working hard enough. Meanwhile, the SS was garnering a tidy income from its collaboration with the giant chemicals firm, altogether collecting something like 20 million Reichsmarks in payments for these labourers from the company.[120]

The use of concentration camp prisoners as workers was the outcome of a significant change in the nature, extent and administration of the camps that took place early in 1942. Almost as soon as the war broke out, Theodor Eicke, who had been running the camps since the early days of the Third Reich, was transferred to military duties; he was killed in action in Russia on 16 February 1943. Under his successor, Richard Glücks, the overall population of the camp system expanded rapidly from a total of 21,000 on the eve of war to 110,000 in September 1942. This total did not of course include the Reinhard Action extermination camps, where prisoners were not registered but went straight to the gas chambers, except for a small number employed for a time in the Special

Detachments. Large numbers of the new inmates were Polish workers, and from 1940 also known or suspected opponents of the German occupation regime in the Protectorate of Bohemia and Moravia, France, Belgium, Norway, Holland and Serbia. Workers, professionals and clergy were a particular target. With the invasion of the Soviet Union came further arrests. A table of the arrests made by the Gestapo in October 1941 across the Reich showed that the month's total stood at 544 arrests for 'Communism and Marxism', 1,518 for 'opposition', 531 for 'prohibited association with Poles or prisoners of war', and no fewer than 7,729 for 'ceasing work'. Smaller numbers were arrested for religious opposition to the regime, or because they were Jews who had been released from a camp after the pogrom of November 1938 on condition that they emigrated and had then failed to do so.[121]

The expansion of the system in the first two and a half years of the war involved the establishment of new camps, including Auschwitz, Gross-Rosen and Stutthof. Despite Himmler's attempt to insist that some of the new foundations were really labour camps, the distinction between a concentration camp, a labour camp and a ghetto became rather blurred as the war progressed. This was not least because the rapidly growing need for labour in the German war economy made the camp population an increasingly obvious source of workers for war-related industries. The most important change in this respect came as part of the general reorganization of the war economy following the defeat of the German army before Moscow and then the appointment of Albert Speer as Armaments Minister. On 16 March 1942, Himmler transferred the Inspectorate of the Concentration Camps to the Economy and Administration Head Office of the SS, run by Oswald Pohl. This became the channel through which firms requested the provision of labour, and the SS put more and more Poles and eastern workers in the camps so that they could meet this demand. On 30 April 1942 Pohl wrote to Himmler summarizing the change of function that was now taking place in the camps:

The mobilization of all camp labour at first for military tasks (to raise armaments production) and later for peace-time building programmes is becoming increasingly important. This realization demands action which will permit a gradual transformation of the concentration camps from their old one-sided political form into an organization suited to economic requirements.[122]

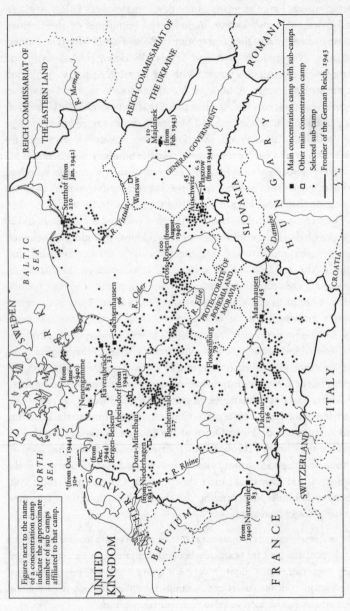

REICH COMMISSARIAT OF
THE EASTERN LAND

REICH COMMISSARIAT OF
THE UKRAINE

ROMANIA

R. Memel

c.10
Majdanek
(from
Feb. 1943)

Stutthof (from
Jan. 1942)
210

GENERAL GOVERNMENT

Warsaw

c. 5
Plaszow
(from 1944)

45
Auschwitz

BALTIC
SEA

SWEDEN

SLOVAKIA

HUNGARY

R. Danube

R. Vistula

Gross-Rosen (from
August,
1940)
100

CROATIA

Sachsenhausen
96

R. Oder

R. Elbe

PROTECTORATE OF
BOHEMIA AND
MORAVIA

Mauthausen
45

Ravensbrück
33

Neuengamme
(from
June
1940)
83

Flossenbürg

ITALY

Arbeitsdorf (from
1942)

Bergen-Belsen
(from
Dec.
1944)

Buchenwald
127

Dachau
136

*(from Oct. 1944)
30*

Dora-Mittelbau

NORTH
SEA

*Niederhagen
(from
1941)

R. Rhine

SWITZERLAND

NETHERLANDS

BELGIUM

Natzweiler
(from
1940) 83

UNITED
KINGDOM

FRANCE

■ Main concentration camp with sub-camps
□ Other main concentration camp
• Selected sub-camp
— Frontier of the German Reich, 1943

Figures next to the name
of a concentration camp
indicate the approximate
number of sub camps
affiliated to that camp.

13. Concentration Camps and Satellites, 1939–45

Himmler was in broad agreement with this radical change, though he continued to insist that the camps should carry out political re-education, 'otherwise the suspicion might gain ground that we arrest people, or if they have been arrested keep them locked up, in order to have workers'.[123]

The labour was provided under broadly the same arrangements as obtained at Monowitz: the SS received payment for it, and in return supervised and guarded the labour detachments, made sure they worked hard and supplied them with clothes, food, accommodation and medical assistance. Himmler ordered that skilled workers in the camp population should be identified, and that others where appropriate should receive training. The bulk of them were used in construction projects, for heavy and relatively unskilled physical labour, but where they did possess expertise, Himmler intended that it should be exploited. Ever since 1933, many camp inmates had been marched out on work duties on a daily basis, but such was the scale of the system's expansion from this point onwards that it soon became necessary to establish sub-camps near workplaces more than a day's march from the main camp. By August 1943 there were 224,000 prisoners in the camps; the largest was the complex of three camps in Auschwitz, with 74,000, then Sachsenhausen, with 26,000, and Buchenwald, with 17,000. By April 1944 the inmates were housed in twenty camps and 165 sub-camps. By August 1944 the number of inmates had climbed to nearly 525,000. Increasingly, too, forced labourers in the occupied territories were transferred to the Reich, so that on January 1945 there were nearly 715,000 inmates, including more than 202,000 women.[124]

By this stage, the proliferation of sub-camps, many of them quite small, had reached such dimensions that there was scarcely a town in the Reich that did not have concentration camp prisoners working in or near it. Neuengamme, for example, had no fewer than eighty-three sub-camps, including one on Alderney, in the Channel Islands. Auschwitz had forty-five. Some of these were very small, for example at Kattowitz, where ten prisoners from Auschwitz were engaged through 1944 on the construction of air-raid shelters and barracks for the Gestapo. Others were attached to major industrial enterprises, such as the anti-aircraft factory run by the Rheinmetall-Borsig company at the Laurahütte, where roughly 900 prisoners were working at the end of 1944 alongside 850 forced labourers and 650 Germans. Many of the prisoners were picked for their skill and qualifications, and these were relatively well treated; others worked in the kitchens, provided clerical services, or did unskilled labour loading and unloading products and equipment. The camp where they lived was run by Walter Quakernack, a guard seconded from the main camp at Auschwitz and known for his brutality; he was executed for his crimes by the British in 1946.[125] But this situation soon changed when the SS lost control over the distribution and employment of camp inmates, which was finally taken over by the Armaments Ministry in October 1944. In the final months of the war, the SS was reduced, in effect, to the role of simply providing 'security' for the prisoners' employers.[126]

A vast range of German arms companies made use of camp labour. Such was the demand from business, indeed, that in contravention of the most basic ideological tenets of the SS and the camp administrations, even Jewish prisoners were commandeered if they had the right skills and qualifications.[127] Businesses were indifferent to the prisoners' welfare, and the SS continued to treat them in the same way as in the camps, so that malnourishment, overwork, physical stress and not least the continual violence of the guards took their toll. At the Volkswagen factory in Wolfsburg, 7,000 camp inmates were employed from April 1944 onwards, mostly on construction work; the miserable conditions under which they lived were of little concern to the company management, and the SS continued to prioritize the suppression of the prisoners' individuality and group cohesion over their maintenance as effective workers.[128] Prisoners were drafted in to the Blohm and Voss shipyards in Hamburg, where the SS set up another sub-camp. Here too the economic interests of the company conflicted with the repressive zeal of the SS.[129] At the Daimler-Benz factory in Genshagen, 180 inmates from Sachsenhausen were put to work from January 1943, to be joined by thousands more from Dachau and other camps in a variety of plants. The deployment of camp labour was the motor driving the creation of sub-camps across the country, reflecting in its turn the increasing dispersal of arms production over many different sites, some underground, others in the countryside, in an effort to evade the attention of Allied bombing raids. Business needed a quick injection of labour to build the new facilities, and the SS was more than willing to supply it.[130]

Deaths in forced labour camps were common, and conditions were terrible. Everywhere, prisoners who were too weak or too ill to work were killed by shooting or, in some cases, gassing. Unlike the other camps, the Auschwitz complex continued to the end to serve the dual function of labour and extermination camp, and mass gassing facilities elsewhere only found relatively restricted use in comparison, as at Sachsenhausen or Mauthausen. However, SS camp doctors in general were given instructions to kill inmates who were too ill or too weak to work, by giving them lethal injections of phenol. The cause of death in such cases was given as typhus or some similar ailment.[131] On 16 December 1942 the deputy commandant of Auschwitz, Hans Aumeier, was recorded as telling the SS officer in charge of deportations from Zamość:

Only able-bodied Poles should be sent in order to avoid as far as possible any useless burden on the camp and the transport system. Mentally deficient persons, idiots, cripples, and the sick must be removed as quickly as possible by liquidation so as to lighten the load on the camp. Appropriate action is, however, complicated by the instruction of the Reich Security Head Office that, unlike Jews, Poles must die a natural death.[132]

Thus, in effect, Aumeier was saying that only when Poles were killed did the records have to be falsified to record death by natural causes. Death rates were indeed high. No fewer than 57,000 out of an average total of 95,000 prisoners died in the second half of 1942 alone, a mortality rate of 60 per cent. In some camps, notably Mauthausen, where 'asocial' and criminally convicted Germans were sent for 'extermination through labour', death rates were even higher. In January 1943 Glücks ordered camp commandants 'to make every effort to reduce the mortality figure', thus 'preserving the prisoners' capacity for work'. Death rates did indeed decline somewhat after this. Nevertheless, a further 60,000 prisoners died in the camps between January and August 1943 from disease, malnutrition and ill-treatment or murder by the SS.[133] A continual tension existed between the SS, which was unable to abandon the ingrained concept of the camps as instruments of punishment and racial and political oppression, and employers, who saw them as sources of cheap labour; it was never satisfactorily resolved.[134]

How far did business profit from the employment of forced and prisoner labour? Certainly it was indeed cheap. A Soviet prisoner of war, for instance, cost less than half to employ than a German worker did. Up to 1943 German business most probably gained financially from using foreign workers. But their productivity was low, particularly if they were prisoners of war. In 1943/4, for example, the productivity of prisoners of war in the coalmines was only half that of Flemish workers.[135] But foreign labour was increasingly used on construction projects that did not yield significant profits before the war came to an end. The giant chemicals plant at Auschwitz-Monowitz, for example, was never completed, and never managed to produce any buna, though a facility to manufacture methanol, used in aircraft fuel and explosives, began operating in October 1943; by late 1944, it was producing 15 per cent of Germany's total output of the chemical. In the longer term, the Monowitz factory did become a major producer of artificial rubber, but only well after the war was over, and then under Soviet occupation.[136] A similar enterprise built using the labour of concentration camp inmates, among others, at Gleiwitz, cost the chemical firm Degussa 21 million Reichsmarks by the end of 1944, while sales from the products it was beginning to turn out netted no more than 7 million, and the facilities constructed by the prisoners were dismantled for their own use by the Soviet forces, after which what was left was nationalized by the Polish government. The eagerness of business to use the concentration camp system as a source of cheap labour, especially in the last two years of the war, reflected longer-term goals than the gaining of instant profits . By 1943, most business leaders realized that the war was going to be lost. They began to look ahead and position their enterprises for the postwar years. The safest way of investing was to acquire real estate and plant, and for this their factories had to expand to gobble up more land and get more armaments orders from the government. This in turn required the recruitment of more workers, and business leaders did not mind too much where they got them from. Once they acquired the workers, businesses often made their own decisions as to how they were to be exploited, regardless of the instructions of central planning bodies. The provision of forced labour, and still more the murderous conditions under which it was used, was the responsibility of the SS and the Nazi state. But a large part of the responsibility for its rapid expansion and exploitation lay with the businesses who demanded it.[137] Altogether in the course of the war, some 8,435,000 foreign workers were drafted into industry; only 7,945,000 of them were still alive in mid-1945. Prisoners of war fared even worse: of the 4,585,000 who found themselves engaged in forced labour during the war, only 3,425,000 were still alive when the war ended.[138] The survivors had to wait nearly half a century until they were able to claim compensation.

Speer never achieved total domination over the economy. Although his influence was enormous, much of it depended on smooth co-operation with other interested parties, involving not only Göring and the Four-Year Plan but also the armed forces and their procurement officers such as Milch and Thomas, Sauckel and his labour mobilization operation, the Reich Ministry of Economics and the SS. In his memoirs, Speer drew a sharp contrast between the years when he was in charge and what he portrayed as the administrative chaos that preceded them; the contrast was overdrawn.[139] On the one hand, Fritz Todt had already achieved a degree of centralization before his death; on the other hand, the administrative 'polycracy' that many historians have identified in the arms economy before Speer continued right up to the end of the war.[140] Speer did his best to master it, but he never quite succeeded. Just as importantly, Speer was able to benefit from Nazi conquests. When taken together with the looting and forced requisitioning of vast amounts of foodstuffs, raw materials, arms and equipment, and industrial produce from occupied countries, with the expropriation of Europe's Jews, with the unequal tax, tariff and exchange relations between the Reich and the nations under its sway, and with the continual purchase by ordinary German soldiers of goods of all kinds at an advantageous rate, the mobilization of foreign labour made an enormous contribution to the German war economy. Probably as much as a quarter of the revenues of the Reich was generated by conquest in one way or another.[141]

Yet even this was insufficient to boost the German war economy enough to enable it to compete with the overwhelming economic strength of the USA, the Soviet Union and the British Empire combined. No amount of rationalization, efficiency drives and labour mobilization would have worked in the long run. The German military successes of the first two years of the war depended to a large extent on the element of surprise, on speed and swiftness and the use of unfamiliar tactics against an unprepared enemy. Once this element was lost, so too were the chances of victory. By the end of 1941 the war had become a war of attrition, just like the First World War. Germany was simply being out-produced by its enemies, and in the end there was nothing Speer could do to rescue the situation, however hard he tried. This had been clear to many economic managers even before Speer took over in 1942.

At no point in the war was the ratio of the GDP of the Allies to that of the Axis countries, including Japan, less than 2:1, and by 1944 it was more than 3:1.[142] By the beginning of 1944, even Speer was starting to realize that the odds were hopeless. All his efforts simply postponed the inevitable. They were directed not at managing the arms supply crisis, but at disguising it. The mass recruitment of foreign labour, the rationalization, the desperate efforts at co-ordinating armaments production, all were fundamentally irrational undertakings that ignored the basic impossibility of Germany's out-producing its enemies.[143] On 18 January 1944, worn out by the strain of trying to achieve the impossible, Albert Speer fell seriously ill and was taken to hospital. It was nearly four months before he recovered sufficiently to be able to return to work. In the intervening period, his rivals, from Himmler to Sauckel, gathered like vultures around what they thought was his political corpse, hoping to pick off parts of his empire for themselves.[144]

UNDER THE NAZI HEEL

I

In some versions, the New Order in Europe was not merely an economic idea but also encompassed political restructuring as well.[145] Faced with the problem of administering the areas of Europe it dominated, the Third Reich came up with a characteristic hodge-podge of different arrangements.[146] While some areas like western Poland and small chunks of eastern France and Belgium were incorporated directly into the Reich, others, intended for later absorption, like Alsace-Lorraine, Luxembourg or Bialystok, were placed under the authority of the nearest German Regional Leader. A third category, with a somewhat indeterminate status, included the Reich Protectorate of Bohemia and Moravia and the Reich Commissariats of the Ukraine and the 'Eastern Land' (the Baltic states and Belarus), was run by a specially created German administration, although in the Protectorate there was also a large Czech element in the bureaucracy. In other countries under German occupation, there was a military administration if they were considered strategically important like Belgium, occupied France or Greece; countries considered 'Germanic', like Norway, Denmark and the Netherlands, were run by a civilian Reich Commissioner, using the native administration as far as possible. Only in Norway was a native fascist leader placed in power, although in another nominally independent state, Vichy France, a regime emerged which bore distinctly fascist traits. A fifth category consisted of client states such as Croatia or Slovakia, where there was a limited German military presence but German agents of one kind or another wielded huge power. Finally there were Germany's allies, notably Hungary, Italy and Romania, where there was German influence but no German domination. The situation was fluid, however, changing partly with the military situation and partly with local conditions, so that countries sometimes moved from one category into another.[147]

Economic exploitation was not the only priority for the occupying authorities. The 'New Order' demanded the racial restructuring of Europe as well as its economic rearrangement for Germany's benefit. A major purpose of the German administration of occupied countries as well as of German representatives in client states and allied nations was to implement there as well as at home 'the final solution of the Jewish question in Europe'. Everywhere that they could, German administrators, civilian, military and SS, moved quickly to secure the passing of anti-Jewish laws, the Aryanization of Jewish property and finally the round-up of the Jewish population and its deportation to the killing centres of the east. Reactions to these policies varied widely from country to country, depending on the zeal of the Germans, the strength of antisemitic feeling in the local authorities, the degree of national pride in the population and the government and a variety of other factors. Almost everywhere, Jewish refugees from other countries were the first victims. They were generally offered little or no protection by the administration of the country in which they had sought safety from persecution in Germany or elsewhere; even native Jewish organizations were reluctant to do anything to help them. When the Germans moved against the native Jewish population of these countries, however, reactions turned out to be more complex, and more divided.

Such moves generally began in 1941–2 and so came before the emergence of any widespread resistance movements in occupied Western Europe. The speed and scale of the German military victories in 1940 had left most Western Europeans in a state of shock and despondency. Millions of refugees had to find their way home; the physical damage caused by military action had to be repaired; normal life had to be restored. Hardly anyone thought in 1940 or 1941 that Britain would survive the onslaught that Hitler would sooner or later undoubtedly unleash. Most people in the occupied countries of Western Europe decided to wait and see what would happen, and in the meantime get on with their lives as best they could. Those who undertook any form of resistance were very few. Before June 1941 the continued existence of the German–Soviet Pact also made it difficult for Communists to take action. Small groups of independent leftists and right-wing nationalists did engage in various kinds of resistance, but these did not include violent action, and overall they had little effect. For the great majority, Germany's victories made it a country to be admired, or at least respected. They had demonstrated the effectiveness of dictatorship and the weakness of democracy. The prewar political order was discredited. Working with the occupying authorities seemed unavoidable.[148] And for some, at least, defeat provided the spur to national regeneration.

This was most obvious in France, where the armistice had been followed by a division of the country into an occupied zone in the north and along the western coast, and an autonomous area in the south and east, run by the government of Marshal Pétain from the spa town of Vichy. Technically this was the last government of the defeated and discredited Third Republic, but the parliament quickly voted Pétain full powers to draft a new constitution. The aged Marshal abolished the Third Republic but he did not create any formal replacement. Everything centred on himself. 'Ministers are only responsible to me,' he said on 10 November 1940. 'History will judge me alone.'[149] He developed a leadership cult. His portrait was everywhere, and he required all public servants to take a personal oath of loyalty to him. In Vichy France, mayors and other officials were appointed rather than elected, and it was Pétain who controlled the appointments process. Public opinion regarded him as the saviour of France. His regime took on a fascist tinge, proclaiming a 'national revolution' that would regenerate French society and culture. A new youth movement was to mobilize and discipline young people in the service of their country. Vichy proclaimed the virtues of the traditional family, with women in their proper place as wives and mothers. Catholic values were intended to replace the Godlessness of the Third Republic, and the clergy, high and low, duly lent their support to the regime. But Vichy never had the time or the coherence to develop into fully fledged fascism. Moreover, many of its policies soon began to alienate popular opinion. Vichy's moral repressiveness was not popular among young people, and labour requisitioning by the Germans began to turn people against the idea of collaboration. The Deputy Premier, Pierre Laval, who liked to think of himself as a realist and therefore regarded the 'national revolution' with a healthy degree of scepticism, did not get on with Pétain and was dismissed in December 1940, but on 18 April 1942 Pétain recalled him to office as Prime Minister, and he remained there, increasingly taking over the reins of government from the aged Marshal, until the end of the war.[150]

The triumph of Marshal Pétain and the far-right nationalists in France brought to power in the unoccupied zone a regime that was shot through to its core with antisemitism. This tradition derived partly from the military opposition to the campaign to exonerate the Jewish officer Alfred Dreyfus, who had been accused of spying for the Germans in the 1890s, partly from the antisemitic fallout of a series of notorious financial scandals in the 1930s, partly from the broader influence of the rise of European antisemitism under the impact of Hitler.[151] The polarization of French politics during the Communist-supported Popular Front in 1936–7 under the Premiership of Léon Blum, who happened to be Jewish, added further fuel to the flames of antisemitic feeling on the right. And the immigration into France of some 55,000 Jewish refugees from Central Europe, bringing the total Jewish population of the country to 330,000 by 1940, ironically stoked fears among the military of a 'fifth column' of agents working secretly for the German cause, along the lines they still believed had been followed by Dreyfus.[152] More than half the Jews living in France were not French citizens, and a high proportion of those who were had acquired their citizenship after the First World War. These now became the first target of state discrimination. Already on 18 November 1939, well before the defeat, a new law provided for the internment of anyone who was considered to be a danger to the French Fatherland, and some 20,000 foreigners resident in France, including many Jewish immigrants from Germany, Austria and Czechoslovakia, were put into prison camps; many were released after a short time, but as soon as the German invasion began, all German citizens, most of them Jewish, were arrested once more and taken again to the camps. Jews from Alsace-Lorraine, France and the Benelux countries were among the millions who took to the road in terror, fleeing to the south. At the same time, antisemitic campaigners like Charles Maurras and Jacques Doriot plumbed new depths in their rhetorical attacks on the Jews, whom they now blamed for the French defeat, a view shared by many senior figures on the political right as well as large parts of the French population in general and, not least, by the Catholic Church hierarchy in France.[153] In the following wartime years, other antisemitic writers, such as Louis-Ferdinand Céline, Pierre Drieu La Rochelle or Lucien Rebatet in his bestseller *Les Décombres*, were to echo such views and, in Rebatet's case at least, to describe French Jews as weeds that had to be destroyed root and branch.[154]

After the French defeat and the creation of the Vichy regime in the unoccupied zone, Pétain's government first repealed legislation banning incitement to racial or religious hatred, then on 3 October 1940 passed its first formal measure against the Jews, whom it defined as people with three or four Jewish grandparents, or two if they were married to a Jew. Jews were banned in particular from owning or managing media concerns. Jewish professors were with a few exceptions dismissed from their posts. These measures had validity for the whole of France, including the occupied zone; in addition, when the German authorities in the occupied zone took steps against the Jews, the Vichy regime frequently followed suit under the pretext of preserving the administrative unity of France. On 4 October 1940 another law created special internment camps for all foreign Jews in the Vichy zone. 40,000 Jews were interned in them by the end of 1940.[155] Native French Jews and their leading representatives assured the Vichy regime that the fate of the foreign Jews was not their concern.[156] For the moment, they remained relatively unaffected. But this would not last. As early as August 1940 the German Embassy in Paris had begun urging the military authorities to remove all Jews from the occupied area.[157] Action soon followed.

In the occupied zone of France, the German Ambassador, Otto Abetz, urged immediate measures against the Jews. With Hitler's explicit approval, Jewish immigration to the occupied zone was banned, and preparations were made for the expulsion of all Jews who were still there. On 27 September 1940, with the agreement of the army Commander-in-Chief von Brauchitsch, Jews who had fled to the unoccupied zone were banned from returning, and all Jewish persons and property were to be registered in preparation for expulsion and expropriation. From 21 October 1940 all Jewish shops had to be marked as such. By this time the registration of around 150,000 Jews in the occupied zone was essentially complete.[158] The Aryanization of Jewish businesses was now driven rapidly forwards, while the economic foundation of the Jews' existence was increasingly undermined by a series of ordinances that banned them from a whole variety of occupations. Jews were forbidden to enter bars where members of the German armed forces were customers. And the SS began to take an increasingly active role, led by Theodor Dannecker, the officer responsible for the 'Jewish question' in the Security Service of the SS in France. Dannecker ordered the arrest and internment in camps of 3,733 Jewish immigrants on 14 May

1941. The Vichy regime also began carrying out Aryanization measures along the same lines, confiscating Jewish assets and businesses. By early 1942 some 140,000 Jews had been officially registered, enabling the authorities to pick them up whenever they wanted to.[159] Preparations to deport them began in October and November 1941, following a series of meetings between Himmler and senior figures in the French occupation administration, including Abetz, in September 1941.[160]

Many of these refugees had been opponents of the Nazi regime, and a good number were hunted down ruthlessly by the Gestapo. A special fate was reserved for one Jewish refugee in particular. In June 1940, a Gestapo unit arrived in Paris to secure the young Pole Herschel Grynszpan, whose assassination of a German diplomat there had been the pretext for the launching of the pogrom of 9–10 November 1938. Grynszpan had in fact been moved by the French prison authorities to Toulouse. En route he had actually escaped, perhaps with the connivance of his captors, or perhaps he had simply got lost, but, amazingly, he turned up at a police station not long afterwards to present himself to the authorities. The Gestapo were quickly on the scene. After interrogating him in their notorious cellars in the Prinz Albrecht Street in Berlin, no doubt about his supposed but in fact purely imaginary Jewish backers, they took him to Sachsenhausen concentration camp, where he was admitted on 18 January 1941 and seems to have received relatively privileged treatment. In March 1941 he was transferred to Flossenbürg, and in October to the Moabit prison in Berlin to await trial by the People's Court under Otto-Georg Thierack. Meanwhile a legal team had been sent to Paris to try to find evidence for the claim, put forward in 1938 as justification for the pogrom, that he had been acting as part of a Jewish conspiracy. It failed to find any. Worse still, it now became clear that the man he had shot, vom Rath, was homosexual, and rumours were circulating that the two had been involved in a sexual relationship. There was no truth in the allegations, but the danger of embarrassment was still considerable, so Goebbels decided to abandon the idea of a trial. Grynszpan was transferred to the penitentiary at Magdeburg in September 1942, where he seems to have died early in 1945, whether or not from natural causes is uncertain.[161]

Tensions meanwhile were mounting in Paris and other parts of the occupied zone of France. The senior army commander in the occupied zone, Otto von Stülpnagel, was replaced on 16 February 1942 by his cousin Karl-Heinrich von Stülpnagel, a hardline antisemite transferred from the Eastern Front. The new commander ordered that future reprisals were to take the form of mass arrests of Jews and their deportation to the east. Following an attack on German soldiers, 743 Jews, mostly French, were arrested by the German police and interned in a German-run camp at Compiègne; with another 369 Jewish prisoners they were eventually deported to Auschwitz in March 1942.[162] On 1 June 1942, in addition, a new Chief of the SS and Police took over in Paris – another transfer from the east, Carl Oberg. Finally, in the Vichy zone, the return of Pierre Laval to head the government in April 1942 signalled an increased willingness to co-operate with the Germans, in the belief that this would lay the foundations for a Franco-German partnership in building a new Europe after the war. With the growing radicalization of German policy towards the Jews, Laval correspondingly appointed a radical antisemite, Louis Darquier (who called himself, somewhat pretentiously, 'Darquier de Pellepoix'), to run Jewish affairs in the unoccupied zone, with the assistance of an effective and unscrupulous new chief of police, René Bousquet. It was Bousquet who asked Heydrich during the latter's visit to France on 7 May 1942 for permission to transport another 5,000 Jews from the transit camp at Drancy to the east. By the end of June, 4,000 had already gone to Auschwitz.[163]

On 11 June 1942 a meeting was called by Eichmann in the Reich Security Head Office, with the heads of the Jewish Affairs departments of the SS Security Service in Paris, Brussels and The Hague. It was informed that Himmler demanded the transport of Jewish men and women from Western Europe for labour duties, together with a substantial number of those judged unfit for work. For military reasons it was not possible to deport more Jews from Germany during the summer. 100,000 were to be taken from both French zones (later reduced to 40,000 for reasons of practicality), 15,000 were to come from the Netherlands (a number subsequently increased to 40,000 to make up some of the shortfall from France), and 10,000 from Belgium.[164] By this time, the wearing of the Jewish star had become compulsory in the occupied zone, calling forth many individual demonstrations of sympathy from French Communists, students and Catholic intellectuals.[165] On 15 July 1942 the arrest of stateless Jews began. French police used previously compiled files to identify and begin the round-up of 27,000 Jewish refugees in the Paris region. The scale of the action was so large that it could scarcely remain a secret even in the planning stage, and many Jews went underground. Just over 13,000 had been arrested by 17 July 1942. After sending all the unmarried people or childless couples to the collection camp at Drancy, the police penned up the remaining 8,160 men, women and children in the bicycle-racing stadium known as the Vél d'Hiv. For three to six days they stayed there, without water, toilets or bedding, in temperatures of 37 degrees Celsius or above, subsisting only on one or two bowls of soup a day. Together with another 7,100 Jews from the Vichy zone, they were eventually sent via further collection centres to Auschwitz – a total of 42,500 altogether by the end of the year. Among them was a transport sent on 24 August 1942 consisting mainly of sick children and adolescents between the ages of two and seventeen who had been kept in hospital while their parents had been sent to Auschwitz; all 553 were gassed immediately on their arrival at the camp.[166]

The leading representatives of the French Jewish community did little to protest against these deportations of foreign Jews, still less to try to prevent them. Only when the majority had already been deported, and the Germans began to turn their attention to native French Jews, did their attitude begin to change.[167] A similar evolution took place in the approach of the Catholic Church in France. Meeting on 21 July 1942, the French Cardinals and Archbishops resolved to do nothing to prevent foreign Jews being deported to what they now knew to be their death. Those who protested were, they noted, enemies of Christianity, especially Communists. It would be wrong to make common cause with them. The letter they sent to Marshal Pétain on 22 July 1942 merely criticized the maltreatment of the internees, especially at the Vél d'Hiv. Some prelates were less mealy-mouthed. On 30 August 1942 the Archbishop of Toulouse, Jules-Gérard Saliège, issued a pastoral letter declaring roundly that both French and foreign Jews were human beings and should not be loaded on to trains like cattle. Others encouraged rescue attempts behind the scenes, particularly where Jewish children were the targets. But the Catholic Church in France as an institution had traditionally been deeply conservative, even monarchist in sentiment; and it stood broadly behind the ideas that underpinned the Vichy regime. Only when the regime came under pressure to reclassify as foreigners all Jews who had been naturalized as French citizens since 1927 did the Cardinals and Archbishops declare their opposition. It was clear, too, that this policy would encounter substantial popular criticism, and Pétain and Laval rejected the proposal in August 1943. Their reluctance was no doubt strengthened by their realization that Germany was on the way to losing the war by this time.[168]

On 11 November 1942, symbolically marking the anniversary of the armistice that had ended the First World War, German troops crossed the border from the occupied zone into the area controlled by Vichy and proceeded to take it over. The Vichy regime had failed to prevent the Allied invasion of the territories it controlled in North Africa, notably Algeria, and its ineffective fighting forces, which Hitler now ordered to be disbanded, clearly offered no prospect of a defence against Allied attacks on the southern French coast across the Mediterranean.[169] This presaged a further dramatic worsening of the situation for France's remaining Jewish population. On 10 December 1942 Himmler noted that at a meeting with Hitler the two men had agreed 'Jews in France/ 600–700 000/do away with.' [170] This was double the number of Jews actually in France. Nevertheless, on the same day, Himmler told his subordinates: 'The Leader has given the order for the Jews and other enemies of the Reich in France to be arrested and taken away.'[171] Deportations resumed in February 1943. But the German authorities' efforts to arrest and deport French Jews ran into increasing difficulties. Popular willingness to protect or hide them was growing, and some 30,000 also found their way to relative safety in the Italian-occupied portion of south-eastern France. In the summer of 1943, determined that the French Jews should be exterminated, Eichmann sent Alois Brunner directly from carrying out similar work in Salonika with a staff of twenty-five SS officers to replace the French officials in charge of the transit camp at Drancy. Over the next few months, the Gestapo arrested most of the leaders of the French Jewish community and deported them to Auschwitz or Theresienstadt; the last trainload left for Auschwitz on 22 August 1944.[172] Altogether, some 80,000 out of 350,000 French Jews, or just under a quarter, were killed; this was a far greater proportion than in other largely self-governing countries in Western Europe such as Denmark or Italy.[173]

The German takeover of the previously unoccupied area of France presaged the decline of the Vichy regime. Pétain now became little more than a figurehead for Laval, whose radical right-wing views had free rein. He shocked many French people by openly proclaiming his desire for Germany to win the war. But increasingly he had to rely on repression to impose his views. In January 1943 he set up a new police force, the French Militia (*Milice française*) under Joseph Darnand, whose own Fascist paramilitary Legionaries formed its active and radical core. With nearly 30,000 members, all bound to a code of honour that obliged them to fight against democracy, Communism, individualism and the 'Jewish leprosy', the Militia bore more than a passing resemblance to Michael Codreanu's Legion of the Archangel Michael in Romania. Darnand joined the SS and as a reward Himmler's organization began to supply him with money and arms. Laval was being outflanked on the right, and in December 1943 the French Militia was authorized by the Germans to operate across the whole of France. These developments deepened the unpopularity of the occupation and the Vichy regime. Growing economic problems, a rapidly falling standard of living and ever more intrusive labour drafts all undermined its credibility still further. Waiting across the Channel in London was the Free French movement under Colonel Charles de Gaulle. By 1943 the Vichy regime had lost most of its power, and the idea of national regeneration on which it had based its appeal to the French people had been rendered meaningless by the German takeover of the unoccupied zone.[174]

II

In Belgium, the chaos that accompanied the German invasion was such that the majority of people were simply concerned to re-establish some kind of normality. Two million Belgians, a fifth of the entire population, had fled south to France when the German forces marched in, and despite the relative brevity of the conflict, the damage done to property by military action was considerable. Seen from Belgium, the situation looked very different from how it appeared across the Channel. King Leopold III, whose precipitate surrender had caused such anger in London, was seen by Belgians as a unifying figure, and his presence, albeit in confinement, in Brussels during the war provided a focal point for national unity. The government that had fled to London was blamed for the defeat, along with the parliament. The prewar order was unpopular even with the small groups on the far left and right who tried, without much success, to resist the German occupation. Given the importance of the Belgian coast as a jumping-off point for a possible invasion of Britain, either in 1940 or at some time in the future, Hitler decided to leave the military in charge, as they were also in the French departments of the Nord and the Pas-de-Calais. This led to a different and to some extent milder form of occupation than it might have been had a civilian Nazi commissioner been in charge. From the German point of view, the role of Belgian heavy industry was also important to the war economy, so it was vital not to alienate the working population. The overall result was that the existing Belgian establishment, the civil service, lawyers, industrialists, the Church and those political leaders who had not gone into exile, worked with the German military administration to try to preserve peace and calm and maintain the existing social order. The vast majority of ordinary Belgians saw little alternative but to go along with this, making what accommodations with the occupying powers they thought necessary.[175]

The German occupiers also tended to view the Flemish inhabitants of Belgium as Nordic in their racial constitution, and held the same view of the vast majority of the inhabitants of the Netherlands. In the long term, indeed, Holland was slated for incorporation into the Reich. In consequence, the German administration was relatively conciliatory, and took care not to alienate the population. In any case, as in Belgium, the prewar order was popularly blamed for the defeat, and the vast majority of Dutch people saw little alternative to coming to terms with the occupation, at least in the short-to-medium term. The best thing to do seemed to be to reach a modus vivendi with the Germans and wait and see what would happen in the long run. Queen Wilhelmina and the government had fled into exile in London, so a civil administration was imported under the Austrian politician Arthur Seyss-Inquart, who proceeded to appoint fellow Austrians to all the top civilian posts except one. For good measure, the head of the SS and the German police in Holland, Hanns Rauter, was also Austrian. The military administration, run by an air force general, was relatively weak. Thus Nazi Party appointees and the SS had far more room to impose extreme policies than did their counterparts in Belgium. In the absence of a Dutch government, Seyss-Inquart issued a stream of edicts and injunctions, and established comprehensive control over the administration. The consequences of this were soon to become apparent.[176]

There were 140,000 Jews living in the Netherlands when the German armed forces invaded in 1940, of whom 20,000 were foreign refugees. The native Dutch Jews belonged to one of the oldest established Jewish communities in Europe, and antisemitism was relatively limited in scope and intensity before the German occupation. But the strong position of the Nazi and in particular the SS leadership in the absence of a Dutch government, and the antisemitic convictions of the almost wholly Austrian occupation administration, lent a radical edge to the persecution of Dutch Jews. In addition, ironically, since Hitler and the leading Nazis regarded the Dutch as quintessentially Aryan, the need to remove the Jews from Dutch society seemed particularly urgent. The German administration began almost immediately to institute anti-Jewish measures, limiting and then in November 1940 ending Jewish participation in state employment. Jewish shops had to be registered and so too, on 10 January 1941, were all Jewish individuals (defined roughly as in the Nuremberg Laws). With the inevitable emergence of a native Dutch Nazi Party, tensions began to mount, and when the Jewish owners of an ice-cream parlour in Amsterdam attacked a pair of German policemen under the mistaken impression that they were Dutch Nazis, German forces surrounded the Jewish quarter of the city and arrested 389 young men, who were deported to Buchenwald and then to Mauthausen. Only one of them survived. Numerous protests were directed by Dutch academics and from the Protestant Churches (except the Lutherans) at the antisemitic policies of the occupiers. The Dutch Communist Party declared a general strike that brought Amsterdam to a virtual standstill on 25 February 1941. The German occupying authorities responded with massive and violent repression, in which a number of protesters were killed and the strike brought to a swift end. Another 200 young Jews, this time refugees from Germany, were tracked down, arrested and sent to their deaths in Mauthausen after a small group of resisters launched bold but futile attack on a German air force communications centre on 3 June 1941.[177]

The situation of Dutch Jews became truly catastrophic following the Eichmann conference of 11 June 1942. Already on 7 January 1942, acting on German orders, the Jewish Council of Amsterdam, responsible for the Jews in the whole country since the previous October, began ordering unemployed Jews into special labour camps at Amersfoort and elsewhere. Run mainly by Dutch Nazis, the camps quickly became notorious centres of torture and abuse. Another camp, at Westerbork, where German-Jewish refugees were detained, became the main transit centre for non-Dutch deportees to the East, while Dutch Jews were collected in Amsterdam before being loaded on to trains bound for Auschwitz, Sobibor, Bergen-Belsen and Theresienstadt. After fresh anti-semitic legislation had been introduced, including a Dutch version of the German Nuremberg Laws and, in early May 1942, the compulsory wearing of the Jewish star, it became easier to identify Jews in Holland. The main burden of the business of rounding up, interning and deporting the Jews fell on the Dutch police, who participated willingly and, in the case of a 2,000-man force of voluntary police auxiliaries recruited in May 1942, with considerable brutality. In the usual way, the German Security Police in Amsterdam – about 200 men in all – forced the Jewish Council to co-operate in the deportation process, not least by allowing it to establish categories of Jews who would be exempt. Corruption and favouritism rapidly spread as desperate Dutch Jews used every means in their power to obtain the coveted stamp on their identity cards granting them immunity. Such immunity was not available to non-Dutch Jews, mostly refugees from Germany, many of whom therefore went into hiding – amongst them the German-Jewish Frank family, whose adolescent daughter Anne kept a diary that became widely known when it was published after the war.[178]

Two members of the Jewish Council managed to destroy the files of up to a thousand mostly working-class Jewish children assembled in a central crèche and smuggled the children into hiding. But help from the mass of the Dutch population was not forthcoming. The civil service and the police were used to working with the German occupiers, and took a strictly legalistic view of the orders they were asked to implement. The leaders of the Protestant and Catholic Churches sent a collective protest to Seyss-Inquart on 11 July 1942, objecting not only to the murder of Jewish converts to Christianity but also to the murder of unbaptized Jews, the overwhelming majority. When the Catholic Bishop of Utrecht, Jan de Jong, refused to give in to intimidation from the German authorities, the Gestapo arrested as many Jewish Catholics as they could find, and sent ninety-two of them to Auschwitz. Despite this clash, however, neither the Churches nor the Dutch government in exile did anything to rouse the population against the deportations. Reports about the death camps sent to Holland both by Dutch SS volunteers and by two Dutch political prisoners who had been released from

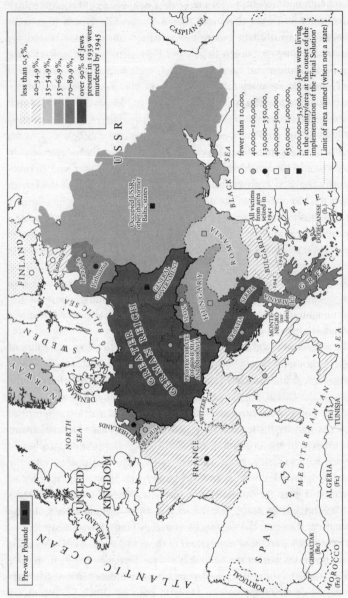

14. The Extermination of the European Jews

Auschwitz had no effect. Between July 1942 and February 1943 fifty-three trains left Westerbork, carrying a total of nearly 47,000 Jews to Auschwitz: 266 of them survived the war.[179] In the following months, a further 35,000 were taken to Sobibor, of whom a mere nineteen survived. A trainload of 1,000 Jews left the transit camp at Westerbork every Tuesday for week after week through all this period, and beyond, until over 100,000 had been deported to their deaths by the end of the war.[180] The Nazi administration in Holland went further in its anti-semitism than any other in Western Europe, reflecting not least the strong presence of Austrians among its top leadership. Seyss-Inquart even pursued the sterilization of the Jewish partners in the 600 so-called mixed marriages registered in the Netherlands, a policy discussed but never put into action in Germany itself.[181]

The contrast with neighbouring Belgium was striking. Between 65,000 and 75,000 Jews lived in Belgium at the beginning of the war, all but 6 per cent of them immigrants and refugees. The German military government issued a decree on 28 October 1940 compelling them to register with the authorities, and soon native Jews were being dismissed from the civil service, the legal system and the media, while the registration and Aryanization of all Jewish assets got under way. The Flemish nationalist movement set light to synagogues in Antwerp in April 1941 following a showing of an antisemitic film.[182] However, the German military government reported that there was little understanding of the Jewish question amongst ordinary Belgians, and feared hostile reactions should native Belgian Jews be rounded up. Most Belgians, it seemed, regarded them as Belgians. Himmler was willing for the moment to agree to a postponement of their deportation, and when the first train left for Auschwitz on 4 August 1942, it contained only foreign Jews. By November 1942 some 15,000 had been deported. By this time, however, a newly founded Jewish underground organization had made contact with the Belgian resistance, whose Communist wing already contained many foreign Jews, and a widespread action began to bring the country's remaining Jews into hiding; many local Catholic institutions also played an important part in concealing Jewish children. In Holland, on the other hand, the Jewish community leadership was less active in assisting Jews to go underground. Quite possibly, too, the fact that the Belgian monarchy, government and civil service and police administration had remained in the country provided a buffer against the genocidal zeal of the Nazi occupiers, as did the effective control of Belgium by the German military, in contrast to the dominance in Holland of the Nazi Commissioner Seyss-Inquart and the SS. Certainly the Belgian police were less willing to assist in the round-up of Jews than were their colleagues in the Netherlands. As a consequence of all this, only 25,000 Jews were deported from Belgium to the gas chambers of Auschwitz; another 25,000 found their way into hiding. All in all, 40 per cent of Belgian Jews were murdered by the Nazis, an appalling enough figure; in the Netherlands, however, the proportion reached 73 per cent, or 102,000 out of a total of 140,000.[183]

III

In pursuit of Hitler's declared purpose of ridding Europe of the Jews, the pedantically thorough Heinrich Himmler also turned his attention to Scandinavia, where the number of Jews was so small as to have virtually no political or economic importance, and native antisemitism was far less widespread than in other Western European countries. He even visited Helsinki in July 1942 to try to persuade the government, which was allied to the Third Reich, to hand over the 200 or so foreign Jews who lived in Finland. As the Finnish police began compiling a list, news of the forthcoming arrests spread, and voices were raised in protest both within the government and beyond. Eventually the number was whittled down to eight (four Germans and an Estonian with their families), who were deported to Auschwitz on 6 November 1942. All save one were killed. The 2,000 or so native Finnish Jews were not affected, and after the Finnish government assured Himmler that there was no 'Jewish question' in the country, he abandoned any attempt to secure their delivery to the SS.[184]

In Norway, under direct German occupation, Himmler's task was simpler. The King and the government elected before the war had gone into exile in Britain, from where they broadcast regularly to the population. Resistance to the German invasion had been strong, and the installation of a puppet government under the fascist Vidkun Quisling had failed to produce the mass popular support for collaboration with the German occupiers that its leader had promised. Growing shortages of food and raw materials, like everywhere else in Western Europe, had done little to win over the population. The majority of Norwegians remained opposed to the German occupation, but unable for the moment to do much about it. Behind the scenes, the country was effectively ruled by Reich Commissioner Josef Terboven, the Nazi Party Regional Leader in Essen. There were about 2,000 Jews in Norway, and in July 1941 the Quisling government dismissed them from state employment and the professions. In October 1941, their property was Aryanized. Shortly afterwards, in January 1942, the Quisling government ordered the registration of the Jews according to the definition of the Nuremberg Laws. In April 1942, however, recognizing Quisling's failure to win public support, the Germans dismissed his government, and Terboven began to rule directly. In October 1942 the German authorities ordered the deportation of the Jews from Norway. On 26 October 1942 the Norwegian police began arresting Jewish men, following this on 25 November with women and children. 532 Jews were shipped to Stettin on 26 November, followed by others; in all, 770 Norwegian Jews were deported, of whom 700 were gassed in Auschwitz. 930, however, managed to flee to Sweden, and the rest survived in hiding or escaped in some other way.[185] Once the deportations of Jews from Norway began, the Swedish government decided to grant asylum to any Jews arriving in the country from other parts of Europe.[186] Neutral Sweden now took on a significant role for those trying to stop the genocide. The Swedish government was certainly well enough informed about it. On 9 August 1942 its consul in Stettin, Karl Ingve Vendel, who worked for the Swedish secret service and had good contacts with members of the German military resistance to the Nazis, filed a lengthy report that made it clear that Jews were being gassed in large numbers in the General Government. The authorities continued to grant asylum to Jews who crossed the Swedish border but refused to launch any initiative to stop the murders.[187]

Hitler considered the Danes, like the Swedes and Norwegians, to be Aryans; unlike the Norwegians, they had offered no noteworthy resistance to the German invasion in 1940. It was also important to keep the situation in Denmark calm so that vital goods could pass to and fro between Germany and Norway and Sweden without hindrance. Denmark's strategic significance, commanding a significant stretch of the coast opposite England, was vital. For all these reasons, the Danish government and administration were left largely intact until September

1942, when King Christian X caused Hitler considerable irritation by replying to his message of congratulation on his birthday with a terseness that could not be considered anything but impolite. Already irritated by the degree of autonomy shown by the Danish government, an angry Hitler immediately replaced the German military commander in the country, instructing his successor to take a tougher line. More significantly, he appointed the senior SS officer Werner Best as Reich Plenipotentiary on 26 October 1942. By this time, however, Hitler had calmed down, and Best was fully aware of the need not to offend the Danes, their government or their monarch by being too harsh. Somewhat unexpectedly, therefore, he operated to begin with a policy of flexibility and restraint. For several months he even urged caution in the policy adopted towards the Danish Jews, of whom there were about 8,000, and little was done to them apart from minor measures of discrimination, to which the leaders of the Jewish community did not object.[188]

But as Germany's military fortunes began to decline, acts of resistance in Denmark began to multiply. Sabotage, strikes and various kinds of unrest had become widespread by the summer of 1943. Hitler ordered the declaration of martial law, and this was followed shortly afterwards by the withdrawal of co-operation by the Danish government. There was clearly no possibility of an alternative, more willing administration being formed to take its place, although this was the course favoured by the German Foreign Minister Ribbentrop. Best now moved to assume total power himself, using the Danish civil service to implement his own personal rule. For this he needed a massive increase in police powers, and the means to this seemed obvious to him: the implementation of the long-delayed deportation of the Danish Jews. On 17 September 1943 Hitler gave his approval, confirming the deportation order on 22 September 1943. In his mind, the Jews were in any case responsible for the growth of Danish resistance, and their removal would be crucial in putting an end to it. Swiftness and surprise were vital. But news of the impending arrests began to leak out. The Swedish government, which had been told the date by its ambassador in Copenhagen, issued a public offer to grant asylum to all Danish Jews, who now began to go into hiding. In a country where collaborationism was weak and there was little native antisemitism, a police action now seemed to Best to be counter-productive. A police sweep would probably take weeks and would arouse widespread public anger. Best tried to get Berlin to call off the action, but without results. So he himself now ensured that the planned date of the action, 2 October 1943, leaked out as widely as possible. On 1 October 1943, after a good deal of secret preparation, Danes everywhere and in every situation of life worked together to ship around 7,000 Jews across the straits to Sweden and safety. Only 485 were arrested in the following day's 'action'. Best intervened with Eichmann to ensure that almost all those arrested were taken not to Auschwitz but to Theresienstadt, where the great majority of them survived the war.[189]

Best presented this action as a triumph for German policy. 'Denmark,' he wrote to the German Foreign Office, 'has been freed of Jews, since there are no more Jews active and living here legally who fall under the relevant decrees.'[190] His action was motivated not by any moral considerations, but by power-political calculation, within the overall context of a virulent and murderous antisemitism propagated and implemented by the organization to which he himself belonged, the SS. It was already clear that martial law would soon come to an end, and, when it did, Best instituted a regime of what might be called behind-the-scenes terror, in which he proclaimed in public the continuation of a flexible approach, but – acting on Hitler's orders to take reprisals – used clandestine armed bands, including on occasion SS men dressed as civilians, to kill those he believed were responsible for the growing campaign of sabotage against German military and economic installations. His policy met with little success; on 19 April 1944, indeed, his own chauffeur was assassinated. As the situation threatened to deteriorate into a state of unbridled civil war, and Copenhagen looked like becoming a European version of 1920s Chicago, Best backpedalled once more. Ignoring orders from Hitler and Himmler for show trials and on-the-spot killings of suspects, he carried out individual executions but, even after a mass strike in Copenhagen, refused to implement a policy of mass counter-terror. From the Danish perspective, however, there was little difference between the two policies. As Ulrich von Hassell noted on 10 July 1944, after meeting with a friend stationed in Denmark, Best was 'a very sensible man': 'The murder of German soldiers or of Danes friendly to the Germans is not met by punishment or the shooting of a hostage. Instead a simple policy of revenge murder is carried out, that is some innocent Danes are killed. Hitler wanted a ratio of 5 to 1; Best reduced it to 2 to 1. The hatred created everywhere is boundless.'[191] The effect was thus the same. Normal life continued in Denmark after a fashion, with the civil administration continuing to function, but the hold of the German occupiers on the country became steadily more shaky. And although Best had gone back on his instrumentalization of 'Jewish policy' for the scrapping of existing forms of collaboration and the introduction of a regime of naked terror, it was to be introduced in other countries to deadly effect.[192]

At the same time, the obsessive pursuit of the Jewish population all over occupied Europe continued, irrespective of the economic utility or otherwise of their extermination. A clear case in point was Greece, where there was a substantial Jewish community – 55,000 in the German occupation zone, 13,000 in the area controlled by the Italians, whose reluctance to co-operate in antisemitic measures frustrated the ambitions of the Reich Security Head Office until 1943. In 1942, however, the German army began to draft Jewish men into forced labour projects, and in February 1943 the wearing of the Jewish star was made compulsory. The large Jewish population of the northern city of Salonika was herded into a tumbledown district of the city as a preparation for deportation. Meanwhile, senior officials in Eichmann's department had arrived in Salonika to prepare the action, including Alois Brunner. On 15 March 1943 the first train left with 2,800 Jews on board; others followed until, within a few weeks, 45,000 out of the city's 50,000 Jewish inhabitants had been taken off to Auschwitz, where the majority were killed immediately on arrival. Taken by surprise, and poorly if at all informed about what was going on in Auschwitz, they offered no resistance; nor was there any Greek organization in existence that might have offered to help them. The leader of the religious community in Salonika, Rabbi Zwi Koretz, merely tried to assuage the fears of his congregation. Objections from the Red Cross's representative in Athens, René Burckhardt, were met by a successful German request to the organization's headquarters to have him transferred back to Switzerland. The Italian consul in Salonika, Guelfo Zamboni, supported by the ambassador in Athens, intervened to try to obtain as many exemptions as he could, but he could only save 320 of Salonika's Jews in all. Meanwhile, the Germans razed the Jewish cemetery and used the gravestones to pave new roads in the area.[193]

Several months went by before the deportations could be extended to the capital, since the Jewish community's list of members had been destroyed. On 23 March 1944, however, 800 Jews who had gathered in the main synagogue after the German authorities had promised to distribute Passover bread were arrested and deported to Auschwitz; and in the course of July 1944, the Germans rounded up the tiny Jewish communities living on the Greek islands, including ninety-six from Kos and 1,750 from Rhodes, who were shipped to the mainland and similarly deported to Auschwitz.[194] As in the case of Finland, the obsessiveness with which the SS, aided by the local German civilian and military authorities, hounded the last Jews to their deaths, irrespective of any military or economic rationality, was a stark testimony to the primacy of antisemitic thinking in the ideology of the Third Reich.

IV

The situation of the Jewish populations of countries allied to Nazi Germany was complex, and altered with the changing fortunes of war. In some of them, native antisemitism was strong, and in the case of Romania, as we have seen, it led to pogroms and killings on an enormous scale. By the middle of 1942, however, the Romanian dictator Ion Antonescu was beginning to have second thoughts about the extermination of the Romanian Jews, who formed a large proportion of the country's professional classes. Interventions from the USA, the Red Cross, the Turkish government, the Romanian Queen Mother, the Orthodox Metropolitan of Transylvania and the Papal Nuncio all began to have an effect on the dictator. There is also some evidence that wealthy Romanian Jews had bribed Antonescu and some of his officials to postpone their deportation. Moreover, behind the scenes, Romanian intellectuals, professors, schoolteachers and others forcefully reminded Antonescu that Romania was the only European country apart from Germany to have carried out a large-scale extermination of the Jews on its own initiative. When the war was over, and the Germans, as now seemed increasingly likely to many leading Romanians, had been defeated, this would endanger Romanian claims over northern Transylvania, since in December 1942 Churchill and Roosevelt declared the punishment of countries that had persecuted the Jews to be an Allied war aim. Initially, Antonescu had acceded to the German request to allow the deportation to occupied Poland not only of Romanian Jews living in Germany or German-occupied Europe, but also of the 300,000 Jews left in Romania itself. But he was irritated by repeated German attempts to get him to surrender what were, after all, despite his record of reducing their civil equality and much more besides, Romanian citizens. Warned by the German Foreign Office that they were a serious threat, he still dithered. After playing for time, Antonescu first halted the deportation of Jews to Transnistria, then late in 1943 began repatriating the surviving deportees back to their Romanian homeland.[195] Hitler did not give up trying to persuade him to resume the genocide, warning him as late as 5 August 1944 that, if Romania was defeated, it could not expect Romanian Jews to defend it or do anything but put a Communist regime in power.[196] But Antonescu was no longer willing to listen to him.

Concerns about sovereignty were also decisive in Bulgaria, where King Boris refused to surrender the country's Jews to the SS after widespread popular protest against the plan. There was still a functioning parliament in the country, imposing limits on the authoritarian monarch's freedom of action, and deputies objected forcefully to the deportation of Bulgarian citizens, despite having bowed to German pressure earlier by introducing antisemitic legislation. 11,000 Jews in the annexed Thracian and Macedonian territories were deprived of their citizenship, rounded up and handed over to the Germans for killing. Yet there was little endemic antisemitism in Bulgaria, where the Jewish minority was small. There was widespread outrage when 6,000 Jews from the prewar Bulgarian kingdom were listed for deportation along with the others by an over-zealous antisemitic official. The Orthodox Church stepped in to protect the Jews, declaring that Bulgaria would remember the war with shame if they were deported. On a visit to Germany on 2 April 1943, King Boris explained to Foreign Minister Ribbentrop that the remaining 25,000 Jews in Bulgaria would be put in concentration camps rather than delivered to the Germans. Ribbentrop insisted that in his view only 'the most radical solution was the right one'. But he was forced to admit that nothing more could be done.[197]

In similar fashion, the Hungarian government, which had nationalized Jewish-owned land and begun discussions with the German government about the deportation of Hungarian Jews, also began finding excuses for failing to co-operate with the increasingly insistent demands of the German Foreign Office. In October 1942 the Hungarian Regent and effective Head of State, Miklós Horthy, and his Prime Minister, Miklós

Kallay, rejected a German request to introduce the wearing of the Jewish star for Hungarian Jews. While Hitler did not want to offend either Romania or Bulgaria, he became increasingly irritated with the failure of Hungary to deliver up its Jewish population of 800,000 for extermination and the confiscation of its assets. In addition, Horthy was now pulling troops out of the German-led army on the Eastern Front, in the belief that Germany was on the way to losing the war. On 16 and 17 April 1943, therefore, Hitler met with Horthy near Salzburg, in the presence of Foreign Minister Ribbentrop, to put some pressure on him on both these issues. Among other things, Horthy made it clear during the first day's discussion that any Hungarian solution of the 'Jewish question' would have to take the specific circumstances of Hungary into account. Dismayed by his reluctance to accede to their request, Hitler and Ribbentrop returned to the topic on the second day. Both sides now dropped the diplomatic circumlocutions. According to the interpreter's minutes, Ribbentrop told Horthy 'that the Jews must either be annihilated or taken to concentration camps. There was no other way.' Hitler weighed in with a lengthier series of arguments:

Where the Jews were left to themselves, as for example in Poland, gruesome poverty and degeneracy had ruled. They were just pure parasites. One had fundamentally cleared up this state of affairs in Poland. If the Jews there didn't want to work, they were shot. If they couldn't work, they had to perish. They had to be treated like tuberculosis bacilli, from which a healthy body could be infected. This was not cruel, if one remembered that even innocent natural creatures like hares and deer had to be killed so that no harm was caused. Why should one any more spare the beasts who wanted to bring us Bolshevism? Nations who did not rid themselves of Jews perished.[198]

But Horthy would not budge. He would soon pay the price for his intransigence.

The small and predominantly agricultural Catholic state of Slovakia, set up as an autonomous state after the Munich agreement in 1938, had been led since March 1939, when it had become nominally independent, by the Catholic priest Jozef Tiso as President and the extreme nationalist law professor Vojtech Tuka as Minister-President. The radical wing of the nationalist movement, which Tuka led, had moved steadily closer to National Socialism, and was able to rely on a paramilitary force known as the Hlinka Guard, named after the priest Andrej Hlinka, who had long encouraged the growth of Slovakian nationalism. At a meeting with Hitler on 28 July 1940, Tiso, Tuka and Interior Minister Mach had been told to put in place legislation to deal with Slovakia's small Jewish minority – 80,000 people, making up 3.3 per cent of the country's total population. They agreed to the appointment of the German SS officer Dieter Wisliceny as their official adviser on Jewish questions, and soon after his arrival in the Slovakian capital Bratislava, the government began a comprehensive programme of expropriating the Jewish population, driving them out of economic life, removing their civil rights and drafting them into forced labour schemes. Slovakian Jews were forced to wear the Jewish star, just as it was being introduced in the Reich. Within just a few months, the country's Jewish population had largely been reduced to a state of destitution. Responding early in 1942 to a request from the German government for 20,000 Slovakian workers for the German arms industry, the government offered 20,000 Jewish workers instead. The matter thus passed into the hands of Eichmann, who decided they could be used to build the extermination camp at Auschwitz-Birkenau. He also offered to take their families, or in other words, to ensure, in a manner that was to become customary, that the men who could work would be drafted into labour schemes on arrival at the camp, and anyone who could not work would be taken straight to the gas chamber. On 26 March 1942, 999 young Slovakian Jewish women were loaded with blows and curses on to cattle-trucks by the Hlinka Guard, assisted by local ethnic German units, and taken to Auschwitz. More men, women and children swiftly followed. Unusually, the Slovakian government paid 500 Reichsmarks to the German authorities for each 'unproductive' Jew to cover the costs of transportation and as compensation for being allowed to keep their property. Eichmann assured the Slovakians that none of the deportees would ever return. And indeed by the end of June 1942 some 52,000 Slovakian Jews, well over half the country's entire Jewish population, had been deported, the vast majority to Auschwitz; even those spared to work on construction projects at Birkenau did not live very long.[199]

By this time, however, the deportations, undertaken, it must be remembered, on the initiative of the Slovakian government itself, not in response to any request issued by the Germans, were running into trouble. Distressing and violent scenes at the railway yards, as Jewish deportees were beaten up by the Hlinka Guard, were causing mounting protests from ordinary Slovakians, voiced in addition by some leading churchmen, such as Bishop Pavol Jantausch, who demanded that the Jews be treated humanely. The formal position of the Slovakian Catholic Church was somewhat more ambivalent, since it coupled a demand for the Jews' civil rights to be respected with an indictment of their alleged responsibility for the death of Jesus on the Cross. The Vatican called in the Slovakian ambassador twice to inquire privately what was going on, an intervention that, for all its moderation, caused Tiso, who after all was still a priest in holy orders, to have second thoughts about the programme. More important by far was the initiative of a group of still-wealthy Slovakian Jewish community leaders, who systematically bribed key Slovakian officials to hand out exemption certificates. By 26 June 1942 the German ambassador in Bratislava was complaining that 35,000 of these had been issued, as a result of which there were virtually no more Jews left to be deported. At the German Foreign Office, Ernst von Weizsäcker responded by telling the ambassador to remind Tiso that 'Slovakia's co-operation in the Jewish question up to now has been greatly appreciated' and that the halting of the deportations would thus cause some surprise. Nevertheless, apart from a brief and temporary resumption in September 1942, the Slovakian deportations were now brought to an end. In April 1943, when Tuka threatened to resume them, he was forced to backtrack by public protests, especially from the Church, which by this time had been convinced of the fate that awaited the deportees. Pressure from the Germans, including a direct confrontation between Hitler and Tiso on 22 April 1943, remained without effect.[200] However, in 1944 the Slovakian resistance movement, which had been growing in strength and determination, made a disastrous attempt to overthrow Tiso, and was brutally suppressed by the Hlinka Guard aided by German troops. At this point, Tiso ordered the deportation of the country's remaining Jews, some of whom were sent to Sachsenhausen and Theresienstadt, but most to Auschwitz.[201]

V

All over occupied Europe, resistance movements were beginning to gain headway by 1943, and in some parts well before that. In France, the labour draft led to the formation of the Maquis, resistance groups so named because they originally emerged in the eponymous brushwood of Corsica. Resisters were sometimes advised, trained and supplied by British agents of the Special Operations Executive. They undermined support for the German occupiers by distributing propaganda leaflets and spreading rumours, encouraging various forms of non-cooperation all the way up to strikes. They attacked individual German soldiers or significant local collaborators, including the police, and increasingly engaged in acts of sabotage and subversion. Early in 1944, Joseph Darnand, head of the Vichy militia, replaced René Bousquet as Chief of police, while Philippe Henriot, for many years a well-known right-wing extremist, took over the management of the regime's propaganda. Henriot began pumping out virulently antisemitic literature, branding the rapidly growing French resistance as a Jewish conspiracy against France. At the same time, Darnand's police tortured and murdered numerous prominent Jews and resistance fighters. The resistance responded in June 1944 by assassinating Henriot.[202] German military authorities in France operated a policy of reprisal, arresting and shooting 'hostages'. In early June 1944 the military ordered an escalation of reprisals, which the Second SS Tank Division took to mean implementing the kind of policy that had long been standard in the east. On 10 June 1944 its troops entered the village of Oradour-sur-Glane, shot all the male inhabitants, and herded the women and children into the church, which they set alight, burning them all alive. Altogether 642 villagers perished in the massacre. Supposedly a reprisal for recently committed, violent attacks on German troops, it took place in a community which in fact was completely unconnected with the resistance. Its only effect was to send a wave of revulsion through France and alienate people still further from the German occupation.[203]

As the resistance spread, it worked in ever closer co-operation with regular Allied forces. At the same time, however, resistance movements almost everywhere were deeply divided amongst themselves. Stalin's injunction to Communists to form partisan groups in July 1941 galvanized them into action, but at the same time rival, nationalist and often right-wing partisan and resistance movements emerged that often owed their allegiance to governments in exile in London. And Nazi antisemitism, sometimes echoed by nationalist resisters, prompted Jews in some places to form their own partisan units as well. The scene was set for a complex struggle in which, for many partisans, the Germans were far from being the only enemy.[204] Perhaps the most serious divisions between resistance movements occurred in South-east Europe. In Greece, the Communist resistance launched successful attacks on German communication lines and had effectively taken over much of the mountainous and inaccessible interior by the middle of 1944. In August 1943, serious fighting broke out between its forces and its smaller right-wing rival, led by the ambitious, aptly named Napoleon Zervas, backed by the British as a counterweight to the Communists. The conflict was eventually to descend into a full-blown civil war. A rather similar situation emerged in the former Yugoslavia, where the Yugoslav Communist partisans under Tito won the backing of the British because they were more active than the Serb nationalist Chetniks. By 1943 Tito's forces numbered some 20,000 men. As in Greece, the Communist partisans managed in the teeth of ferocious reprisals from the German occupying forces to take over immense tracts of the inhospitable and remote interior of the country. Yet even more than in Greece, the two resistance movements spent as much time fighting each other as they did the Germans. Indeed, Tito even negotiated with the Germans, offering his services in crushing the Chetniks if the German occupying forces agreed to suspend their anti-partisan campaigns, which they did for a time until Hitler personally vetoed the deal.[205]

Behind the Eastern Front, German rule began to disintegrate within a year of the invasion of the Soviet Union. Already by the spring of 1942 the security situation in some parts of Poland was out of control. In his diary, the hospital director Zygmunt Klukowski recorded one robbery after another; partisans, he noted, were everywhere, taking food and killing people working for the German administration. 'It is nearly impossible to find out who they are,' he wrote, 'Polish, Russian, even German deserters or plain bandits.' The police had given up trying to intervene.[206] Many partisan groups were well armed and organized and some Polish officers were forming regular units of the Home Army. Villagers thrown out of their homes to make way for ethnic Germans swelled their ranks, thirsting for revenge. Often they went back to their villages to burn down their own homes before the Germans could occupy them.[207] The Home Army liaised with the Polish government in exile in London, whose advice to be patient it seldom heeded. From January 1943 onwards, Klukowski devoted an increasing number of his diary entries to describing its acts of military resistance and sabotage. Already some local railway lines were made impassable by constant explosions and machine-gun attacks. German settler villages were attacked, the livestock was expropriated and anyone who protested was beaten up. Local partisan leaders became folk heroes; Klukowski met one of them and agreed to provide medical supplies for the movement.[208] After this, his contacts with the Home Army became more frequent. Using the code name 'Podwinski', he provided its fighters with money, wrote down reports on events in his area and acted as a postbox for partisan units. He also treated wounded partisans, ignoring the German requirement that he report any cases of gunshot wounds to the police. He remained characteristically cautious: when commanders of partisan units visited him, he made them undress 'so that in the event of German intrusion it would appear to be a normal physical examination'.[209]

Rival partisan groups, notably those organized by the Russians, were now active too. Some of them were several hundred strong.[210] Partisan activity led to radical reprisals from the German occupying forces, who took hostages from the local population and threatened publicly to kill ten or twenty of them for every German shot by the resistance, a threat they carried out repeatedly, adding to the general atmosphere of terror and apprehension in the local population.[211] The German and Polish auxiliary police were increasingly unable to mount effective operations against either the resistance movement or the rising tide of violence, robbery and disorder. The brutality of German rule in Eastern Europe from the very beginning had completely alienated the majority of the population.[212] The argument, supported by Alfred Rosenberg among others, that this was the main reason for the spread of partisan resistance, cut no ice either with Himmler or with the army hierarchy. Partisan activity further fuelled the antisemitism of civilian administrators as well. One official in Belarus wrote in October 1942 that Jews had in his view a 'very high participation in the success of the whole campaign of sabotage and destruction . . . One operation carried out on a single day . . . revealed 80 armed Jews amongst the 223 bandits who were killed. I am happy,' he added, 'to see that the 25,000 Jews who were originally in the territory have shrunk to 500.'[213] Some 345,000 people, making roughly 5 per cent of the population of Belarus, died in the partisan war. It has been estimated that over the whole period of the German occupation, about 283,000 people in Belarus took part in partisan groups of one kind or another.[214] Similar loss of life was caused by German military reprisals in other parts of Eastern Europe.

Jewish partisan groups, consisting of men and women who had taken to the deep forests of eastern Europe in flight from the machine-guns of the SS Task Forces, also began to emerge early in 1942.[215] Many individual Jews escaped to the forest on their own, but failed to link up with the partisans. Often robbers stole their clothes, and many starved. So badly did they fare that, as Zygmunt Klukowski noted, 'it is a common occurrence that Jews come on their own to the gendarme post and ask to be shot.'[216] Villagers, he reported, were often hostile to these partisans. 'There are many people who see the Jews not as human beings but as animals that must be destroyed.'[217] Nevertheless, Jewish involvement in the partisan movement was widespread. The first Jewish resistance group in Eastern Europe was started by the twenty-three-year-old intellectual Abba Kovner in Vilna on 31 December 1941. At a meeting of 150 young people disguised as a New Year's Eve party, Kovner read out a manifesto, in which, basing his reasoning on the mass shootings and killings that had been in progress since the previous summer, he declared: 'Hitler plans to annihilate all the Jews of Europe . . . We don't want to allow ourselves to be led like sheep to the slaughtering-block.'[218] By early 1942, another group had been set up by the four Bielski brothers, villagers in Belarus whose parents had been killed by the Germans in December 1941. Based in a secret camp deep in the endless woods of the region, the brothers set up an elaborate system of procuring weapons and were joined by other Jews; their number reached 1,500 by the end of the war. Many more Jews joined local Communist-led partisan units as individuals.[219]

The New Order in Europe was beginning to crumble. Its early ambition of a broad sphere of economic and political co-operation had vanished in the face of the grim realities of war. German rule everywhere had grown harsher. Executions and mass shootings, the fruits of a belief that terror was the only way to combat resistance, had replaced informal mechanisms of co-operation and collaboration. Regimes friendly to the

Third Reich, from Vichy to Hungary, were distancing themselves or losing their autonomy and falling into the same pattern of repression and resistance that was undermining German control in directly occupied countries. The insatiable demands of the German war economy for labour and materials, and the ruthless exploitation of subject economies, were driving more and more young men and women into resistance movements whose spreading campaigns of non-cooperation, disruption, sabotage and assassination were calling forth ever harsher reprisals, engendering in turn a further alienation of subject peoples and a further escalation of resistance. Yet this cycle of violence was also a reflection of the generally deteriorating position of Germany in the war itself, above all from early 1943 onwards. The early belief across Europe that there was no alternative to German domination was beginning to disappear. At the heart of the new preparedness of Europeans to resist was the perception that Hitler might, after all, lose the war. The turning-point was provided by a single battle that more than any other showed that the German armed forces could be defeated: Stalingrad.

TOTAL WAR

I

The extension of the Nazi programme of extermination in 1942 took place in a military context in which the German armed forces were on the offensive once more. To be sure, the German army's defeat before Moscow meant that Hitler's belief in the fragility of the Stalinist regime in the Soviet Union had been proved decisively wrong. Operation Barbarossa had signally failed to achieve the aims with which it had set out in the confident days of June 1941. After stemming the German tide before Moscow, the Red Army had gone on to the offensive and forced the German army to retreat. As one German officer wrote to his brother: 'The Russians are defending themselves with a courage and tenacity that Dr Goebbels characterizes as "animal"; it costs us blood, as does every repulse of the attackers. Apparently,' he went on with a sarcasm that betrayed the German troops' growing respect for the Red Army as well as a widespread contempt for Goebbels among the officer class, 'true courage and genuine heroism only begin in Western Europe and in the centre of this part of the world.'[220]

The bitter cold of the depths of winter, followed by a spring thaw that turned the ground to slush, made any fresh campaigning difficult on any scale until May 1942. At this point, emboldened by the victory over the Germans before Moscow, Stalin ordered a series of counter-offensives. His confidence was further strengthened by the fact that the industrial facilities relocated to the Urals and Transcaucasus had begun producing significant quantities of military equipment – 4,500 tanks, 3,000 aircraft, 14,000 guns and more than 50,000 mortars by the start of the spring campaign in May 1942. Over the summer and autumn of 1942, the Red Army command experimented with a variety of ways of deploying the new tanks in combination with infantry and artillery, learning from its mistakes each time.[221] But Stalin's first counter-attacks proved to be as disastrous as the military engagements of the previous autumn. Massive assaults on German forces in the Leningrad area failed to relieve the beleaguered city, attacks on the centre were repulsed in fierce fighting, and in the south the Germans held fast in the face of repeated Soviet advances. In the Kharkov area a large-scale Soviet offensive in May 1942 ended with 100,000 Red Army soldiers killed and twice as many taken prisoner. The Soviet commanders had seriously underestimated German strength in the area, and failed to establish air supremacy. Meanwhile, Field Marshal Fedor von Bock, back from his sick leave on 20 January 1942 as commander of Army Group South, had decided that attack was the best form of defence, and fought a prolonged and ultimately successful campaign in the Crimea. But all the time he remained acutely aware of the thinness of the German lines and the continuing tiredness of the troops, noting with concern that they were 'fighting their way forward with great difficulty and considerable losses'.[222] In a major victory, Bock took the city of Voronezh. The situation seemed to be improving. 'I saw there with my own eyes,' wrote Hans-Albert Giese, a soldier from rural north Germany, 'how our tanks shot the Russian colossi to pieces. The German soldier is just better in every department. I also think that it'll be wrapped up here this year.'[223]

But it was not to be. Hitler thought Bock dilatory and over-cautious in the follow-up to the capture of Voronezh, allowing key Soviet divisions to escape encirclement and destruction. Bock's concern was with his exhausted troops. But Hitler could not accept this. He relieved Bock of his command with effect from 15 July 1942, replacing him with Colonel-General Maximilian von Weichs.[224] The embittered Bock spent the rest of the war in effective retirement, obsessively trying to defend his conduct in the advance from Voronezh, and hoping against hope for reinstatement. Meanwhile, on 16 July 1942, in order to take personal command of operations, Hitler moved his field headquarters to a new centre, codenamed 'Werewolf', near Vinnitsa, in the Ukraine. Transported from East Prussia in sixteen planes, Hitler, his secretaries and his staff spent the next three and a half months in a compound of damp huts, plagued by daytime heat and biting mosquitoes. Here too were now located for the time being the operational headquarters of the Supreme Command of the army and of the armed forces.[225] The main thrust of the German summer offensive was aimed at securing the Caucasus, with its rich oilfields. Fuel shortages had played a significant role in the Moscow debacle the previous winter. With typically dramatic overstatement, Hitler warned that if the Caucasian oilfields were not conquered in three months, Germany would lose the war. Having previously divided Army Group South into a northern sector (A) and a southern sector (B), he now ordered Army Group A to finish off enemy forces around Rostov-on-Don and then advance through the Caucasus, conquering the eastern coast of the Black Sea and penetrating to Chechnya and Baku, on the Caspian, both areas rich in oil. Army Group B was to take the city of Stalingrad and push on to the Caspian via Astrakhan on the lower Volga. The splitting of Army Group South and the command to launch both offensives simultaneously while sending several divisions northwards to help in the attack on Leningrad reflected Hitler's continuing underestimation of the Soviet army. Chief of the Army General Staff Franz Halder was in despair, his mood not improved by Hitler's obvious contempt for the leadership of the German army.[226]

Whatever they thought in private, however, the generals saw no alternative but to go along with Hitler's plans. The campaign began with an assault by Army Group A on the Crimea, in which Field Marshal Erich von Manstein defeated twenty-one Red Army divisions, killing or capturing 200,000 out of the 300,000 soldiers facing his forces. The Red Army command had realized too late that the Germans had, temporarily at least, abandoned their ambition to take Moscow and were concentrating their efforts in the south. The main Crimean city, Sevastopol, put up stiff resistance but fell after a siege lasting a month, with 90,000 Red Army troops being taken prisoner. The whole operation, however, had cost the German army nearly 100,000 casualties, and when German, Hungarian, Italian and Romanian forces moved southwards they found the Russians adopting a new tactic. Instead of fighting every inch of the way until they were surrounded and destroyed, the Russian armies, with Stalin's agreement, engaged in a series of tactical retreats that denied the Germans the vast numbers of prisoners they had hoped for. They took between 100,000 and 200,000 in three large-scale battles, many fewer than before. Undaunted, Army Group A occupied the oilfields at Maykop, only to find the refineries had been systematically destroyed by the retreating Russians. To mark the success of their advance, mountaineering troops from Austria climbed Mount Elbrus, at 5,630 metres (or 19,000 feet) the highest point in the Caucasus, and planted the German flag on the peak. Hitler was privately enraged, fuming at what he saw as a diversion from the real objectives of the campaign. 'I often saw Hitler furious,' reported Albert Speer later, 'but seldom did his anger erupt from him as it did when this report came in.' He railed against 'these crazy mountain climbers who belong before a court-martial'. They were pursuing their idiotic hobbies in the midst of a war, he exclaimed indignantly.'[227] His reaction suggested a nervousness about the advance that was to turn out to be fully justified.

In the north, Leningrad (St Petersburg) had been cut off by German forces since 8 September 1941. With over 3 million people living in the city and its suburbs, the situation soon became extremely difficult as supplies dwindled to almost nothing. Soon the city's inhabitants were starving, eating cats, dogs, rats and even each other. A narrow and precarious line of communication was kept open across the ice of Lake Ladoga, but the Russians were not able to bring in more than a fraction of what was needed to feed the city and keep its inhabitants warm. In the first winter of the siege, there were 886 arrests for cannibalism. 440,000 people were evacuated, but, according to German estimates, a million civilians died during the winter of 1941–2 from cold and starvation. The city's situation improved in the course of 1942, with everyone growing and storing vegetables for the coming winter, half a million more people being evacuated, and massive quantities of supplies and munitions being shipped in across Lake Ladoga and stockpiled for when the freeze began. A new pipeline laid down on the bottom of the lake pumped in oil for heating. 160 combat planes of the German air force were lost in a futile attempt to bomb the Soviet communication line, while bombing raids on the city itself caused widespread damage but failed to destroy it or break the morale of the remaining citizens. Luck also came to the Leningraders' aid at last: the winter of 1942–3 was far less severe than its calamitous predecessor. The frost came late, in mid-November. As everything began to freeze once more, the city still stood in defiance of the German siege.[228]

Further south, a Soviet counter-attack on the town of Rzhev in August 1942 was threatening serious damage to Army Group Centre. Halder asked Hitler to allow a retreat to a more easily defensible line. 'You always come here with the same proposal, that of withdrawal,' Hitler shouted at his Chief of the General Army Staff. Halder lacked the same toughness as the troops, Hitler told him. Halder lost his temper. He was tough enough, he said. 'But out there, brave musketeers and lieutenants are falling in thousands and thousands as a useless sacrifice in a hopeless situation simply because their commanders are not allowed to make the only reasonable decision and have their hands tied behind their backs.'[229] In Rzhev, Hans Meier-Welcker noticed an alarming improvement in Soviet tactics. They were now beginning to co-ordinate tanks, infantry and air support in a way they had not succeeded in doing before. The Red Army troops were far better able than the Germans to cope with extreme weather conditions, he thought. 'We are amazed,' he wrote in April 1942, 'by what the Russians are achieving in the mud!'[230] 'Our columns of vehicles,' wrote one officer, 'are stuck hopelessly in the morass of unfathomable roads, and further supplies are already hard to organize.'[231] In such conditions, German armour was often useless. By the summer, the troops were having to contend with temperatures of 40 degrees in the shade and the massive dust-clouds thrown up by the advancing motorized columns. 'The roads,' wrote the same officer to his brother, 'are shrouded in a *single* thick cloud of dust, through which man and beast make their way: it's troublesome for the eyes. The dust often swirls up in thick pillars that then blow along the columns, making it impossible to see anything for minutes at a time.'[232]

Impatient with, or perhaps unaware of, such practical problems, Hitler demanded that his generals press on with the advance. 'Discussions with the Leader today,' recorded Halder despairingly at the end of August 1942, 'were once more characterized by serious accusations levelled against the military leadership at the top of the army. They are accused of intellectual arrogance, incorrigibility and an inability to recognize the essentials.'[233] On 24 September 1942, finally, Hitler dismissed Halder, telling him to his face that he had lost his nerve. Halder's replacement was Major-General Kurt Zeitzler, previously in charge of coastal defences in the west. A convinced National Socialist, Zeitzler began his tenure of office by demanding that all members of the Army General Staff reaffirm their belief in the Leader, a belief Halder had so self-evidently long since lost. By the end of 1942, it was reckoned that one and a half million troops of various nationalities had been killed, wounded, invalided out or taken prisoner on the Eastern Front, nearly half the original invading force. There were 327,000 German dead.[234] These losses were becoming increasingly hard to replace. The eastern campaign had stalled. To try to break the impasse, the German army advanced on Stalingrad, not only a major industrial centre and key distribution point for supplies to and from the Caucasus, but also a city whose name lent it a symbolic significance that during the coming months came to acquire an importance far beyond anything else its situation might warrant.[235]

II

The young fighter pilot Count Heinrich von Einsiedel, a great-grandson of Reich Chancellor Otto von Bismarck in the maternal line, was flying over Stalingrad on a clear, warm day on 24 August 1942, looking for signs of enemy activity. 'A light haze lay over the steppes,' he wrote, 'as I circled high over them in my Me109. My eyes scanned the horizon, which faded into formless mists. The sky, the steppes, the rivers and the lakes, which could only be seen dimly in the distance, lay peacefully, links with eternity.' Einsiedel, who had just turned twenty-one years of age, shared in full the romantic image of the fighter-pilot, knight of the air, which attracted aristocratic young men like him to this branch of the armed forces. The excitement of the fight far outweighed the doubts he had about the justice of the cause. Yet his account conveyed too the sheer strength of numbers of the Russian air force, against which bravery and skill were useless in the end. As the enemy came up towards him, he wrote,

Every German Stuka, every combat aeroplane was surrounded by clusters of Russian fighters ... We throw ourselves into the tumult at random. A two-star Rato crossed my track. The Russian saw me, went into a nose-dive and tried to get away by flying low. Fear seemed to have crippled him. He raced ten feet above ground in a straight course and did not defend himself. My machine vibrated with the recoil of its guns. A streak of flame shot from the petrol tank of the Russian plane. It exploded and rolled over on the ground. A broad, long strip of scorched steppe-land was all that it left behind.[236]

Spotting a group of Soviet fighters above him, he pulled out of his dive and raced up towards them. 'The love of the chase,' he confessed, 'and a sense of indifference had taken hold of my reactions.' Flying in a steeply banked curve, he got behind one and shot it down. It was a foolhardy action. 'As I turned round to look for the Russian fighters,' he wrote in his diary after the incident, 'I saw their blazing guns eighty yards behind me. There was a terrific explosion and I felt a hard blow on my foot. I twisted my Messerschmitt and forced it up into a steep climb. The Russian was shaken off.' But Einsiedel's plane was badly damaged, his guns had been put out of action, and he had to limp back to base.[237] Such incidents occurred on a daily basis over Stalingrad during the late summer and autumn of 1942 and inevitably took their toll. Senior officers disapproved of spectacular individual actions, which, they said, wasted fuel. From now on, Einsiedel's unit was ordered to support the German infantry and to avoid engaging Soviet fighters. It was a losing battle. 'Breakdowns reached enormous proportions . . . A fighter group of forty-two machines seldom had more than ten machines operational.' The odds were impossible. On 30 August a shot penetrated Einsiedel's engine cooler as he was flying low over the Russian lines, and he crash-landed. Miraculously, Einsiedel was unhurt. But Soviet troops quickly arrived on the scene. They stole all his personal belongings before taking him off to be interrogated.[238]

As Einsiedel had noted, the German planes had failed to establish complete air superiority in the area; as fast as they lost planes to the German air aces, the Soviets rushed replacements to the combat zone from other fronts. Yet, on the other hand, the Soviet air force had not achieved domination either. Throughout the spring and summer of 1942, while the German fliers continued to dispute the command of the skies with Soviet fighter-pilots, the German ground forces of Army Group B were advancing steadily on the city of Stalingrad, the gateway to the lower Volga river and the Caspian Sea. The Germans had so far failed to take either Moscow or Leningrad. For Hitler in particular, it was all the more important, therefore, that Stalingrad should be captured and destroyed. On 23 August 1942 wave after wave of German planes carpet-bombed the city, causing massive damage and loss of life. At the same time, German tanks advanced virtually unopposed, reaching the Volga to the north. As the bombing continued, now reinforced by German artillery, Stalin allowed civilians to begin evacuating the city, which was rapidly crumbling into uninhabitable ruins. On 12 September 1942 German troops from General Friedrich Paulus's Sixth Army, backed by General Hermann Hoth's Fourth Panzer Army, entered Stalingrad. It only seemed a matter of weeks before the city fell. But the

German commander was in some ways less than ideally suited for the job of taking the city. Paulus had been deputy chief of the Army General Staff before being given his command early in the year. Born in 1890, he had spent almost his entire career, including the years of the First World War, in staff posts, and had almost no combat experience. In this situation, he depended heavily on Hitler, whose achievements as a commander filled him with awe. On 12 September, as his troops were entering the city, Paulus was conferring with the Leader at Vinnitsa. The capture of Stalingrad, the two men agreed, would give the German forces command of the entire line along the Don and Volga rivers. The Red Army had no more resources; it would collapse, leaving the Germans free to devote their efforts to speeding up the advance into the Caucasus. The city, Paulus assured the Leader, would be in German hands within a few weeks.[239] After that, Hitler had already decided, the entire adult male population of the city would be killed, and the women and children would be deported.[240]

By 30 September 1942 Paulus's men had overrun about two-thirds of the city, prompting Hitler to announce publicly that Stalingrad was about to fall. Hitler's speech did a good deal to strengthen the troops' faith in ultimate victory. 'The Leader's great speech,' reported Albert Neuhaus from the Stalingrad front to his wife on 3 October 1942, 'has only strengthened our belief in it by another 100%'.[241] But speeches would not overcome the Soviet resistance, whatever their effect on morale. Senior generals, including Paulus and his superior Weichs, and Halder's successor Zeitzler, all advised Hitler to order a withdrawal, fearing the losses that would be incurred in a lengthy period of house-to-house fighting. But for Hitler the symbolic importance of Stalingrad now far outweighed any practical considerations. On 6 October 1942 he reaffirmed that the city had to be taken.[242] Similar considerations ruled on the other side. After a year of almost continuous defeat, Stalin had decided to throw as many of his resources as possible into the defence of what was left. The city bore his name, and it would be a major psychological blow if it fell. At the same time, feeling battered by the defeats of the previous months, he decided to give a free hand to the chief of the general staff, General Aleksandr Vasilevskii, and Georgi Zhukov, the general who had stopped the German forces at Moscow a year before, in organizing the overall campaign in the south. Stalin gave the command over Red Army forces in the city itself to General Vasili

Chuikov, an energetic professional soldier in his early forties. Chuikov had had a chequered career, having been sent off to China in disgrace, as Soviet Military Attaché, following the defeat of his Ninth Army by the Finns in the Winter War in 1940. Stalingrad, where he was put in charge of the Sixty-Second Army, was his chance to prove himself. Chuikov understood that he had to 'defend the city or die in the attempt', as he told the regional political boss, Nikita Khrushchev. He stationed armed Soviet political police units at every river crossing to intercept deserters and execute them on the spot. Retreat was unthinkable.[243]

German aircraft and artillery continued to attack the Soviet-occupied part of Stalingrad, but the bombed-out ruins of the city provided the Soviet troops with ideal conditions for defence. Digging in behind heaps of rubble, living in cellars and posting snipers in the upper floors of half-demolished apartment blocks, they were able to ambush the advancing German troops, break up their mass assaults, or channel the enemy advance into avenues where they could be disposed of by concealed anti-tank guns and heavy weaponry. They laid thousands of mines under cover of darkness, bombed German positions at night and set up booby-traps to kill German soldiers as they entered houses. Chuikov formed machine-gun squads and arranged for supplies of hand-grenades to be shipped into the city.[244] Often the fighting was hand-to-hand, using bayonets and daggers. The struggle rapidly became a battle of attrition. Constant, unremitting combat increasingly took its toll and many soldiers fell sick. Their letters home are full of bitter disappointment at being told they were having to spend a second consecutive Christmas in the field. Despite the danger of being discovered by the military censor, many were quite frank. 'I've only got one big wish left,' wrote another on 4 December 1942, 'and that is: that this shit soon comes to an end ... We're all so depressed.'[245] Yet it was in the rear of Paulus's forces, rather than in the city itself, that the Soviet breakthrough would come. Zhukov and Vasilevskii persuaded Stalin to bring in and train large quantities of fresh troops, fully equipped with tanks and artillery, to try to mount a huge encirclement operation. The Soviet Union was already producing over 2,000 tanks a month to Germany's 500. By October the Red Army had created five new tank armies and fifteen tank corps for the operation. Over a million men were assembled ready for a massive assault on Paulus's lines by early November 1942.[246]

Zhukov and Vasilevskii saw their chance when Paulus's superior,

General Maximilian von Weichs, in command of Army Group B, decided to help Paulus concentrate his forces on taking the city itself. Romanian forces would take over about half the German positions to the west of Stalingrad, freeing up German forces for the assault on the city itself. He thought of them as more than a rearguard. But Zhukov knew that the Romanians had a poor military record, as did the Italians who were stationed alongside them in the north-west. He moved two armoured corps and four field armies to confront the Romanians and Italians to the north-west of Hoth's armoured forces, and another two tank corps to face the Romanians in the south-east, on the other side of the German armour. Strict secrecy was maintained, radio traffic reduced to a minimum, troops and armour moved up at night and camouflaged during the day. Paulus failed to strengthen his defences, preferring to keep his tanks close to the city, where they were of little use. On 19 November 1942, their preparations finally complete, and with favourable weather conditions, the new Soviet forces attacked at a weak point in the Romanian lines almost 100 miles west of the city. 3,500 guns and heavy mortars opened fire in the early morning mist, blasting a way through for the tanks and infantry. The Romanian armies were unprepared, lacking in anti-tank weapons, and were overwhelmed. After putting up an initial fight, they began to flee in panic and confusion. Paulus reacted too slowly, and when he eventually sent tanks to try to shore up the Romanian lines, it was too late. They were no match for the massed columns of T-34 tanks now pouring through the gap.[247]

Soon the rapid Soviet advance was pushing back the German lines as well, driving back Paulus's men towards the city. None of the German generals had reckoned with a Soviet attack in such strength, and it was some time before they realized that what was in progress was a classic encirclement manoeuvre. So they failed to move troops up to prevent the Soviet tank thrusts from meeting up with one another. On 23 November 1942 the two tank columns met up at Kalach, completely cutting off Paulus and his forces from the rear and leaving Hoth's armour marooned outside the encircled area. With twenty divisions, six of them motorized, and nearly a quarter of a million men in total, Paulus's first thought was to try to break out to the west. But he had no clear plan, and once more he hesitated. The idea of a breakout would have meant a retreat, abandoning the much-trumpeted attempt to capture Stalingrad, and Hitler was unwilling to sanction a withdrawal because he had already announced in public that Stalingrad would be taken.[248] Speer reported him at the Berghof in November 1942 complaining privately that the generals consistently overestimated the strength of the Russians, who he thought were using up their last reserves and would soon be overcome.[249] Acting on this belief, Hitler organized a relief force under Field Marshal von Manstein and General Hoth. Manstein's belief that he could succeed in breaking the encirclement strengthened Hitler in his refusal to allow Paulus to withdraw. On 28 November 1942 Manstein sent a telegram to the beleaguered forces: 'Hold on – I'm going to hack you out of there – Manstein.' 'That made an impression on us!' exclaimed one German lieutenant in the Stalingrad pocket. 'That's worth more than a trainload of ammunition and a Ju[nkers] full of food supplies!'[250]

III

Manstein's forces, two infantry divisions, together with three panzer divisions, all under Hoth's command, advanced on the Red Army from the south on 12 December 1942. To counter this, Zhukov attacked the Italian Eighth Army in the north-west, overrunning it and driving south to cut off Manstein's forces from the rear. By 19 December 1942 the German relief armour had been stopped in its tracks, 35 miles away from Paulus's rear lines. Nine days later it was virtually surrounded, and Manstein was forced to allow Hoth to retreat. The relief operation had failed. There was nothing left for Paulus but to attempt a breakout, as Manstein told Hitler on 23 December. But this still looked like abandoning the entire attempt to take the city, and so, once again, Hitler refused. But Paulus told him that the Sixth Army had only enough fuel for its armour and transport to go for 12 miles before it ran out. Göring had promised to airlift 300 tons of supplies into the pocket every day to keep Paulus's men going, but in practice he had managed little more than 90, and even Hitler's personal intervention failed to boost it to anything more than 120, and that only for about three weeks. Planes found it difficult to land and take off in the heavy snow, and airfields were under constant attack from the Russians.[251] Supplies were getting low, and the situation of the German troops in the city was becoming increasingly desperate. By now, they were doing little except trying to stay alive. Most of them were living in cellars or underground bunkers

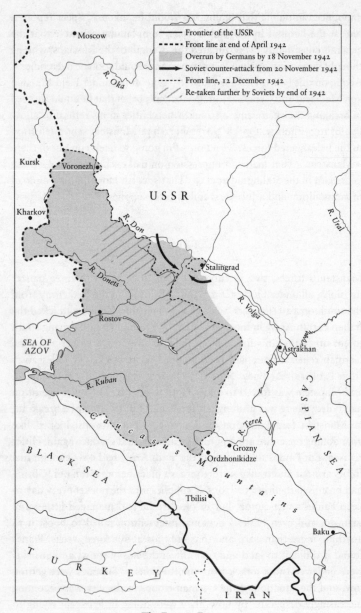

15. The Eastern Front, 1942

or in foxholes in the open, which they tried to line and cover with brick and wood as best they could. Often they furnished and decorated them to try to re-create a homely atmosphere. As one soldier reported to his wife on 20 December 1942:

We're squatting here with 15 men in a bunker, i.e. in a hole in the ground roughly the size of the kitchen in Widdershausen [his home in Germany], everyone with his clobber. You can well picture for yourself the terrible overcrowding. Now the following picture. One man is washing himself (insofar as water is available), a second is delousing himself, a third is eating, a fourth is cooking a fry-up, another is asleep, etc. That's roughly the milieu here.[252]

In underground holes like these, they waited for the regular Soviet attacks, conserving their ammunition and supplies as best they could.[253]

By the time the festive season arrived, Paulus's army was effectively doomed. Christmas provided the occasion for an enormous outpouring of emotion in the troops' letters home, as they contrasted their desperate situation with the peace and calm they had known in their family circle in past years. They lit candles and used broken-off branches to make Christmas trees. Not untypical was the letter of one young officer to his mother on 27 December 1942:

Despite everything, the little tree had so much Christmas magic and homely atmosphere about it that at first I couldn't bear the sight of the lighted candles. I was really affected, to such an extent that I cracked up and had to turn my back for a minute before I could sit down with the others and sing carols in the wonderful sight of the candlelit tree.[254]

The troops took comfort from radio broadcasts from home, especially when they played sentimental songs, which they sometimes learned by heart and sang themselves. 'There's a song we often sing here,' one soldier wrote to his family on 17 December 1942. 'The refrain goes: "It'll all soon be over – it'll end one day – after every December will come a May" etc.'[255] Writing letters home became a way of keeping human emotions going; the thought of getting back to Germany and to their families held despair at bay. Nearly 3 million letters made their way from the encircled army to Germany during the months of the conflict, or were found, unposted, on troops killed in action or taken into captivity.[256]

The troops did not freeze to death as they had the previous winter.

'By the way,' wrote Hans Michel from Stalingrad on 5 November 1942, 'we're well supplied with winter things; I've also got hold of 1 pair of socks, a fine woollen scarf, a second pullover, fur, warm underwear etc. They are all things from the wool collection. You have to laugh when you see one or other of the men wearing a ladies' jumper or something similar.' Those on watch were supplied with felt boots and fur coats in addition. The veterans of the Moscow campaign also noted that the winter was initially much milder in 1942–3 than it had been the previous year.[257] But the warmth created by layers of clothing was an ideal breeding-ground for lice. 'Your red pullover,' wrote one soldier to his wife on 5 November 1942, 'is a proper louse-trap; I've caught quite a few there already (excuse the jump in my thoughts, but one bit me just now).' Another wrote that although he was not the worst affected, 'I've already snapped a few thousand.' Some tried to make light of the problem in letters home ('one can genuinely say "everyone has his own zoo",' quipped one), but in the long run the physical irritation and discomfort they caused added to the growing demoralization of the German troops. 'They can drive you mad,' wrote one infantryman on 28 December 1942. 'You can't sleep properly any more . . . You gradually get filled with disgust for yourself. You don't have any opportunity to wash yourself properly and change your underwear.' 'The damned lice,' complained another on 2 January 1943, 'they totally eat you up. The body is totally consumed.'[258]

Far worse, however, was the growing shortage of food, which weakened the men's resistance to the cold, however warmly dressed they might have been. 'We're mainly feeding ourselves just with horsemeat,' wrote one German soldier on 31 December 1942, 'and I myself have eaten even raw horsemeat because I was so hungry.'[259] 'All the horses have been eaten in a few days,' reported the staff officer Helmuth Groscurth on 14 January 1943, adding bitterly: 'In the tenth year of our glorious epoch we are standing before one of the greatest catastrophes in history.'[260] 'Although I am exhausted,' wrote another soldier on the same day, 'I cannot sleep at night but dream with open eyes again and again of cakes, cakes, cakes. Sometimes I pray and sometimes I curse my fate. In any case, everything has no meaning or point.'[261] 'I only weigh 92 pounds. Nothing more than skin and bones, the living dead,' wrote another on 10 January 1943.[262] By this time, the weather had deteriorated sharply, and the weakened troops were unable to resist the cold. Fighting in such circumstances was virtually impossible, and the troops became steadily more depressed. 'You're nothing more than a wreck any more ... We're all completely desperate.'[263] 'The body is gradually losing its capacity for resistance as well,' was the observation in another letter, written on 15 January 1943, 'because it can't go on for long without fat or proper food. It's now lasted 8 weeks and our situation, our sad predicament, is still unchanged. At no point in my life up to now has fate been so hard on me, nor has hunger ever tormented me so much as now.'[264] One young soldier reported that his company had been given only a single loaf for six men to last three days. 'Dear Mummy ... I can't move my legs any more, and it's the same with others, because of hunger, one of our comrades died, he had nothing left in his body and went on a march, and he collapsed from hunger on the way and died of cold, the cold was the last straw for him.'[265] On 28 January 1943 the order was issued that the sick and wounded should be left to starve to death. The German troops were in effect suffering the same fate that Hitler had planned for the Slavs.[266]

Even faith in Hitler now began to fade. 'None of us is yet abandoning his belief or his hope,' wrote Count Heino Vitztbum, an aristocratic officer, on 20 January 1943, 'that the Leader will find a way to preserve the many thousands in here, but unfortunately we have already been bitterly disappointed many times.'[267] Not only was food running out, so too was ammunition. 'The Russians,' complained one soldier on 17 January 1943, 'have built their weapons properly for winter; you can take a look at whatever you like: artillery, grenade-throwers, Stalin organs and airplanes. They are attacking without a break day and night, and we've got to save every shot because the situation doesn't allow it. How much we wish we could really shoot properly once again.'[268] Men began to wonder if it would be better to be taken prisoner than to continue the hopeless struggle, although, as one remarked on 20 January 1943, it would not be so bad, 'if it was Frenchmen, Americans, Englishmen, but with the Russians you don't really know whether it would be better to shoot yourself.' 'If it all goes wrong, my love,' wrote another to his wife, 'then don't expect me to be taken prisoner.' Like others, he began to use his letters to say his farewells to his loved ones.[269] Enough letters of this kind were opened by the SS Security Services back in Germany to provide a realistic picture of their effect on morale. Already in mid-January, the confidential reports of the SS Security Service on

morale on the home front noted that people did not believe the propaganda emanating from Berlin. Field-post letters from the front were seen
as the only reliable source of information. 'If the situation in the east is
currently regarded by large parts of the population with a disproportion-
ately greater concern than it was a week ago, this is to be explained
by the fact that the field-post letters that are now arriving at home
overwhelmingly sound very serious and to some extent extremely
gloomy.'[270]

By this time, Marshal Konstantin Rokossovskii, an experienced officer
who had been purged and imprisoned by Stalin in the 1930s but
reinstated in 1940 and given command of the Red Army troops to the
west of Stalingrad, had begun advancing across the pocket from west to
east, capturing the last airfield on 16 January 1942. Aerial bombardment, artillery fire and tanks, backed by massed infantry, overwhelmed
the weakened German defences. In the southern sector, the Romanian
troops simply ran away, leaving a huge hole in the defensive line through
which the Red Army poured its T-34 tanks. The weather had turned
cold, and many German soldiers collapsed from exhaustion and froze
to death on the ground as they retreated. Others pulled the wounded
along on sledges, passing along icy roads littered with abandoned or
shattered military equipment. In a few sectors the German forces put up
a fight, but very soon they were all driven back into the ruins of the
city, where 20,000 wounded were crowded into makeshift underground
hospitals and cellars which had to be entered past piles of frozen corpses.
Bandages and medication ran out, and there was no chance of ridding
the patients of the lice that crawled over them. Even those who were
not hospitalized were sick, starving, frostbitten and exhausted.[271]

Eight days before, the Soviet High Command had made Paulus an
offer of honourable surrender. 100,000 German troops had been killed
in the battle by this point. The situation of the rest had clearly been
hopeless since the failure of Manstein's breakthrough attempt. Senior
officers were beginning to surrender to the enemy. But once more, Hitler
ordered Paulus to fight on. The general ordered that in future all Soviet
approaches should be met with gunfire. On 22 January 1943 Paulus
suggested all the same that surrender was the only way of saving the
remainder of the troops. Once more, Hitler rejected his request. Meanwhile, Rokossovskii's advance drove further forward, splitting the
pocket into two and forcing the remaining 100,000 German troops into

two small areas of the city.[272] Goebbels's propaganda machine was now abandoning its earlier talk of victory. Increasingly, newspaper and newsreel stories emphasized the heroism of the encircled soldiers, a lesson for all in the glory of continuing to fight, never giving in even when the situation seemed hopeless. The telegram sent by Paulus the night before the tenth anniversary of Hitler's appointment as Reich Chancellor on 30 January 1933 was grist to the propaganda mill: 'On the anniversary of your seizure of power, the Sixth Army greets its Leader. The swastika flag is still flying over Stalingrad. May our struggle be an example for the present and coming generations that we should never capitulate even when we have lost hope. Then Germany will win. Hail my Leader. Paulus, Colonel-General.'[273] The same day, Hermann Göring gave a speech, broadcast over the radio, in which he compared the Sixth Army to the Spartans who died defending the pass at Thermopylae against the invading Persian hordes. This, he said, 'will remain the greatest heroic struggle in our history'. It did not escape the attention of many of the troops crouching round their radios in bunkers scattered around Stalingrad and its outskirts that the Spartans at Thermopylae were all killed. To underline the message, Hitler promoted Paulus to Field Marshal on 30 January 1943, a measure intended – and understood clearly enough by its recipient – as an invitation to commit suicide.[274]

But Paulus, at the very end, finally turned against his master. On 31 January 1943, instead of committing suicide, he surrendered, along with all the remaining troops in the part of Stalingrad he still occupied. Rokossovskii arrived to take the formal surrender, accompanied by a photographer and an interpreter, secret policemen and army officers and Marshal Voronov from the Soviet Supreme General Staff. Paulus's dark hair and incipient beard had begun to turn white under the strain of the past months, and he had developed a tic in his facial muscles. The Soviet generals asked him to order all his remaining troops to give themselves up, to prevent further bloodshed. In a last remnant of deference towards Hitler, Paulus refused to order the other pocket of resistance to cease fire. The remnants of six divisions were holed up in it; Hitler ordered them to fight to the end. But the Russians bombarded them mercilessly, and they surrendered on 2 February 1943. Altogether some 235,000 German and allied troops from all units, including Manstein's ill-fated relief force, were captured during the battle; over 200,000 had been killed. Dressed in rags, filthy, unshaven, lice-ridden and often barely able to walk, the 91,000 German and allied troops left in Stalingrad were lined up and marched off into captivity. Already weak, starving and ill, demoralized and depressed, they died in their thousands on their way into prison camps. The Russians were unprepared for such large numbers of prisoners, food supplies were inadequate, and over 55,000 prisoners were dead by the middle of April 1943. Among their number was Helmuth Groscurth, whose diaries from 1939–40 gave later historians important insights into the early development of the military-conservative resistance to Hitler; captured in the pocket that surrendered on 2 January 1943, he succumbed to typhus and died on 7 April 1943. Altogether, fewer than 6,000 of the men taken prisoner at Stalingrad eventually found their way back to Germany.[275]

IV

It was impossible to explain away a defeat of these dimensions. The retreat from Moscow the previous year could be presented as a temporary measure, a tactical withdrawal that would be made good later on. But it was scarcely possible to take such a line in the case of Stalingrad. The complete encirclement and destruction of an entire German army could not be glossed over. In private, Hitler railed against the weakness of the Romanian and Italian troops, but most of all he was furious at what he saw as the cowardice of Paulus and his senior officers, who had preferred to lose their honour by surrendering rather than save it by killing themselves. Worse was to come, for, beginning almost immediately after the invasion, the Russians began attempts to 're-educate' German prisoners of war as 'anti-fascists', starting with NCOs and then moving on to the officers. A judicious mixture of the carrot and the stick won over a growing number of prisoners to the cause, the majority of them going along with it because it was the easiest thing to do. A small number of convinced German nationalists among them were persuaded that Hitler was destroying Germany, and that joining his enemies was the quickest way to save their country. A few opportunists, many of them ex-Nazis, were particularly vocal in their support for 'anti-fascism'. By July 1942 the Soviet secret police had met with sufficient success to start building an organization of converted prisoners, turning it the following year into a 'National Committee "Free Germany"'. The young pilot Friedrich von Einsiedel became one of its leading figures, gravitating towards the Communist wing of the organization along with a few others who had entertained serious doubts about the Nazi cause even before they had been taken prisoner. Most spectacularly, however, the National Committee was also joined by Field Marshal Friedrich von Paulus, who was persuaded by the Russians to make a series of propaganda broadcasts to Germany on their behalf. The broadcasts probably had little effect, but the mere fact that Paulus was making them was a deep embarrassment to the Nazi leadership, and provided further proof to Hitler, if he needed any, that the army leadership was not to be trusted.[276]

Goebbels had already begun to prepare the German people for the bad news even before the final surrender at Stalingrad. From all the co-ordinated media there poured out the elements of a new myth: 'They died so that Germany could live,' as the *Racial Observer* put it on 4 February 1943. The self-sacrifice of the troops would be a model for all Germans of the future. Quite what their sacrifice had achieved was, however, difficult to say. The young student Lore Walb, for example, accepted the official propaganda image of the 'heroism' of the troops at Stalingrad, and the need for 'holding out'. But this did not stop her from noting on 3 February 1943: 'Today is the blackest day for Germany in the history of our war.'[277] And many people derided the rhetoric emanating from the Propaganda Ministry.[278] The Security Service of the SS reported a 'general feeling of deep shock' amongst Germans at home. People were talking about the huge losses, and arguing over whether the Soviet threat to the Sixth Army had been recognized soon enough:

Above all, people are saying that the enemy's strength must have been underestimated, otherwise the risk of continuing to occupy Stalingrad even after it was surrounded would not have been undertaken. National comrades cannot understand how it was not possible to relieve Stalingrad, and some of them are not precisely enough informed about the whole development in the southern sector of the Eastern Front to have the correct understanding of the strategic significance of these battles ... There is a general conviction that *Stalingrad* signifies a *turning-point* in the war.[279]

Some people, indeed, the report was forced to admit, saw in Stalingrad 'the beginning of the end', and in Berlin's government offices there was said to be 'to some degree a decided atmosphere of head-hanging despair'.[280]

In Franconia, people were said to be directing 'the most serious criticism against the army leadership' and asking why the Sixth Army had not been withdrawn while there was still a chance. Moreover, 'people are saying on the basis of letters [from the front] that many soldiers have died just of exhaustion, and that others again present such an appearance that you cannot recognize them because they have lost so much weight. Rumours are circulating,' the report concluded, 'which depress the morale of the population very deeply indeed.'[281] Reports from other areas suggested a 'visibly serious, if not yet desperate mood' as a result of the defeat.[282] In the rural district of Ebermannstadt, in Bavaria, where many people had sons, brothers or husbands in the Sixth Army, the criticism was said to be 'to a degree very hard and strong, even if people are careful in their choice of words, so as not to become liable to criminal prosecution'. Thus people were criticizing Hitler without actually naming him, though the import of what they said was clear: he would not rest until everything had been destroyed, he had overestimated Germany's strength, he should have tried to make peace.[283] For the first time, as the disaffected diplomat Ulrich von Hassell noted in his diary on 14 February 1943, 'critical rumours' were being directed at Hitler himself.[284] People were asking why he did not save the lives of the remaining men of the Sixth Army by ordering them to capitulate.[285] Germany's few remaining persecuted and battered Jews drew hope from the defeat. On 5 February 1943 Victor Klemperer learned that 'the debacle in Russia is said to be a real and decisive one'. The public shock was so great, a non-Jewish acquaintance told him, that there was every possibility of an internal uprising against the Nazis.[286]

The crisis in morale brought about by the defeat at Stalingrad did not end soon. 'The popular mood is not good any more,' reported one local official in Bavaria on 19 March 1943. 'The word Stalingrad is still in the foreground.'[287] Other reports observed 'that many are now condemning the war'. Many wanted it brought to an end, and opined that the English and Americans would not let the Russians take Germany over; even if they did, it would only be the Party men who would suffer.[288] By mid-April, the Security Service of the SS was reporting that people were demanding to see more of Hitler. 'A picture of the Leader from which people could assure themselves that he has not – as rumour once had it – gone completely white-haired, would have a more positive effect on the attitude of national comrades than many aggressive slogans.'[289]

Hitler's charisma was beginning to fade. Regional Party officials reported that jokes were beginning to circulate about him. 'What's the difference between the sun and Hitler?' went one, to which the answer was: 'The sun rises in the east, Hitler goes down in the east.'[290]

By July 1943 the Security Service of the SS was noting that '*the most nonsensical and ill-intentioned rumours about leading men in the Party or the state are circulating very quickly and can last weeks and months*'.[291] Thus, for example, Baldur von Schirach was said, quite wrongly, to have fled to Switzerland with his family. Worse still:

Telling jokes that are nasty and detrimental to the state, even jokes about the Leader's person, has become much more common since Stalingrad. When national comrades talk in public houses, on the shop-floor, or in other places where they meet, they tell each other the 'latest' political jokes, and in doing so they often make no distinction between those that are relatively harmless in content and those that are clearly oppositional. Even national comrades who hardly know one another are exchanging political jokes. Clearly they are assuming that anyone *can tell any joke today without having to reckon with being rebuffed, let alone being denounced to the police*.[292]

Similarly, the report continued, people were now openly criticizing the regime, declaring it to be inefficient, poorly organized and corrupt. It was clear, too, 'that *listening to foreign radio stations* has obviously *become a lot more common* in the last months'. The Security Service of the SS found in this fact an explanation for the widespread pessimism people were showing about the eventual outcome of the war. As a clear symbolic sign of the growing distance of people from the regime, '*The use of the German greeting*, as shopkeepers and officials who deal with the public are reporting, has *declined* strikingly in the past months. It must also be confirmed *that many Party members no longer wear their Party badge*.'[293]

V

Propaganda Minister Joseph Goebbels was acutely aware of the need to do something dramatic to raise morale and turn the situation around. He knew, as did everyone else in the Nazi leadership, that the decisive underlying factor in the downward turn in Germany's military and naval fortunes was the failure of the economy to produce enough equipment, enough tanks, enough guns, enough planes, enough submarines, enough ammunition. Even before the full extent of the catastrophe at Stalingrad had become clear, he was beginning to declare 'that only a more radical civil prosecution of the war will put us in a position to win military victories. Every day provides further proof,' he told his ministerial conference on 4 January 1943, 'that we are confronted in the east with a brutal opponent who can only be defeated by the most brutal methods. In order to achieve this, the total commitment of all our resources and reserves is necessary.'[294] Goebbels now repeatedly pressed Hitler to declare 'total war', including the mobilization of women for work, the closing of 'luxury shops' and 'luxury cafés', and much more besides. Dissatisfied with the slow progress being made following Hitler's initial decision to back the idea, he decided to turn up the pressure with a major public demonstration.

On 18 February 1943 Goebbels delivered a major, nationally broadcast speech in the Berlin Sports Palace before a hand-picked audience of 14,000 Nazi fanatics representing, as he said, 'a cross-section of the whole German nation, at the front and at home. Am I right? [loud shouts of "Yes!" Lengthy applause] But Jews are not represented here! [Wild applause, shouts]'[295] After outlining the measures that had been taken against luxuries and amusements, he declared that Germans now wanted 'a Spartan way of life for everybody', the kind of life, indeed, lived by the Leader himself. Everyone had to redouble his efforts to achieve victory. At the climax of his speech, he put a series of ten rhetorical questions to his by now thoroughly roused audience. They included the following exchanges:

Are you and the German people determined, if the Leader orders it, to work ten, twelve and, if necessary, fourteen and sixteen hours a day and to give your utmost for victory? [Loud shouts of 'Yes!' and lengthy applause] . . . I ask you: Do you want total war? [Loud cries of "Yes!' Loud applause] Do you want it, if necessary, more total and more radical than we can even imagine it today? [Loud cries of 'Yes!' Applause]

Linking the idea of total war to loyalty to Hitler, the Propaganda Minister had the crowd shouting enthusiastically for the mobilization of every last resource, including women workers, in the final struggle for victory. He was interrupted more than 200 times with wild shouts and choruses, slogans ('Hail, Victory!', 'Leader command – we follow you!'), and hysterical applause. The whole event was subsequently described as 'a feat of mass hypnosis'. The speech was listened to by millions of people who had been waiting for some kind of lead from the regime. To underline its importance, it was printed in the daily papers the following morning and broadcast again the following Sunday. It was presented as an imposing demonstration of the German people's will to fight to the end.[296]

In all likelihood, Hitler had given his approval to Goebbels's initiative in general terms beforehand. But he had not been consulted about the detailed contents of the speech, so he immediately had a copy sent to him and declared his complete approval.[297] But what did 'total war' actually mean in concrete terms? Within the Nazi leadership, it was seen first and foremost as a bid by Goebbels, aided and abetted by Speer, to seize control of the home front. Hitler's initial response to the crisis had been to create a 'Committee of Three', consisting of Martin Bormann, Hans-Heinrich Lammers and Wilhelm Keitel to initiate 'total war' measures; Goebbels's speech was among other things an attempt to sideline this group, and he followed it up by intriguing with Hermann Göring to claim back the management of the 'total war' from it. But Göring by this time had lost much of his earlier energy, weakened by heavy doses of morphine, to which he had now become addicted. Hitler refused to give either Goebbels and Speer or the Lammers group the authority over the home front that they were competing for. By the autumn of 1943 the Committee of Three had effectively ceased to function. Its initiatives to simplify the civil administration of the Reich by reducing duplication, for example between the Reich and Prussian Finance Ministries (it advocated abolishing the latter), ran into the sands, and it spent much time arguing over trivialities such as whether or not to ban horse-racing.[298] As for the economic realities of 'total war', it was difficult to see what could be done. The problem, as was evident across the whole range of defeats and setbacks in the war during 1943, was not that people were not working hard enough, it was that raw materials were lacking. There was no point in demanding a boost in production if there was not enough coal and steel to build planes and tanks, or enough petrol to fuel them. And the labour shortage, as we have seen, could only be dealt with to a very limited degree by the mobilization of women; in the event, it was tackled by the ruthless expansion of foreign labour. In purely practical terms, 'total war' boiled down to an attempt to suppress domestic consumption in order to divert resources to war production. Here too the possibilities were limited.

A series of decrees issued early in 1943 did, to be sure, crack down on non-war-related production and consumption. On 30 January 1943 the Committee of Three ordered the closure of non-essential businesses. This measure led to the shutting-down of 9,000 mostly small businesses in the Brandenburg region alone, causing widespread resentment in the lower middle class as independent workshop-owners were now forced to become wage-labourers in arms factories. Many were worried that they would not be able to reopen after the war. Within a few months, the implementation of the policy had to be stopped, at the insistence of the Propaganda Ministry, because of widespread resistance and evasion.[299] In Berlin it was reported that the Melody Bar on the Kurfürstendamm had closed down, only to reopen immediately as a restaurant, with the same waiters. The Gong Bar renamed itself the Café Gong and carried on business with coffee and cakes instead of beer and cocktails. The measure also created problems for munitions and other war-related workers who were forced to spend the week away from their families and so depended on restaurants for their evening meal. Many bars and small restaurants were by this time run by people who had reached retiring age and could scarcely be expected to be drafted in to munitions factories. While working-class bars were being closed down, widespread resentment was aroused by the fact that top hotels like the Four Seasons in Hamburg, with its expensive grill-room, and classy restaurants like Schumann's Oyster Cellar in the same city remained in business.[300] The crackdown on conspicuous consumption was in any case only symbolic. It was all very well saying that Germans had to live like Spartans, but in 1943 many thought they were already doing so.

The shift from consumer to war-related production and investment had in fact already begun in the 1930s, but when the war broke out it accelerated even further. By the end of the first year of the war, military expenditure had increased from a fifth of national output to over a third. Hoping to avoid giving the German public the feeling that they were being bled dry to feed the military machine, the Reich Economics Ministry dropped its initial thoughts of imposing a hefty tax hike, and opted for controlling consumer expenditure by rationing instead. By the end of August 1939, per capita consumption had fallen by 11 per cent; it dropped another 7 per cent in the following year.[301] Almost as soon as the war broke out, food and clothing were rationed. Of course, this was nothing new in principle. Already in the 1930s, some foodstuffs and other items in short supply had been rationed.[302] In October 1939 an official food ration of 2,570 calories a day was set for civilians, with 3,600 calories allocated to each member of the armed forces and 4,652 to labourers engaged in particularly heavy physical work. Civilians had to present their ration cards in shops, colour-coded for each different item (red for bread, for example) and their purchases were marked so that they would not get more than the prescribed maximum. These ration cards lasted for a month, so that new ones could be issued with different maxima if necessary.[303]

In concrete terms at the beginning of the war this meant, for example, just short of 10 kilos of bread a month for a normal adult, 2,400 grams of meat, 1,400 grams of fatstuffs including butter, 320 grams of cheese, and so on. As the war went on, these allowances began to be reduced. The bread ration held more or less steady, but meat was down to 1,600 grams a month by the middle of 1941, and rationing began to be introduced around the same time for fruit and soon after for vegetables and potatoes. By the beginning of 1943 allowances stood at 9 kilos a month of bread, 600 grams of cereals, 1,850 grams of meat, and 950 grams of fats. In general, these levels roughly held, with fluctuations both up and down, until the final phase of the war, when the bread allowance fell from 10.5 kilos a month in January 1945 to 3.6 kilos in April, the cereal ration from 600 to 300 grams, meat fell sharply to a mere 550 grams, and fats from 875 grams to 325 grams. Only potatoes, with a regular allowance of around 10 kilos a month through the war, seemed to stay in plentiful supply. But not only were these quantities insufficient for most people's needs, it was also frequently impossible to obtain them because of shortages. Rationing also covered a wider range of articles than in Britain, and tight restrictions on clothing reduced average German consumption to a quarter of peacetime levels by October 1941; many clothes were made of inferior synthetic materials, and people often had to use wooden clogs because of the shortage of leather. 'A man who is tired of life tries in vain to hang himself,' went a joke recorded in April 1942, ' – impossible: the rope is made of synthetic fibre. Then he tries to jump into the river – but he floats, because he's wearing a suit made from wood. Finally he succeeds in taking his own life. He has been existing for two months on no more than he got from his ration card.'[304]

Even relatively small cuts in food rations could lead to discontent. In March 1942, for instance, the Security Service of the SS reported that the announcement of forthcoming ration cuts by the equivalent of around 250 calories a day for normal civilians and 500 a day for heavy labourers had been 'devastating', indeed 'to a greater degree than scarcely any other event in the war'. Workers in particular did not understand the need for the cuts, since they had already considered the existing rations very short. 'The mood in these parts of the population,' the report warned, 'has reached a point lower than any previously observed in the course of the war.' And there was widespread resentment at the ability, as many saw it, of the better off to use their connections to get food above and beyond the rationed amount.[305] If starvation such as had occurred during the First World War was avoided – virtually an obsession on the part of the regime, since Hitler considered this to have been one of the main factors behind the mythical 'stab-in-the-back' in 1918 – this was not least because of massive imports from abroad, principally from 1940 onwards from the occupied territories. These were particularly vital for maintaining the bread ration at an acceptable level, given the fact that this was the main staple of many Germans' diet, and that its cutting in April 1942 had been 'felt to be particularly hard in all sectors of the population'.[306]

Imports of bread grain rose from 1.5 million tons in 1939–40 to 3.6 million in 1942–3 and stayed at roughly the same level the following year. Nevertheless, there was no denying that the great majority of people continued to find food rations barely enough to survive on, and every time the regime made them tighten their belts, there was widespread grumbling and discontent. Food parcels from relatives and friends in the army in France or Western Europe helped, but they were never decisive, and in some situations, particularly at Stalingrad and on the Eastern Front more generally, food parcels tended to go in the other direction. Overall, the contribution of the economies of the occupied countries, east and west, to the German economy through the war was probably not much more than 20 per cent of the whole. It was not enough to make people feel they were living well. 'What's the difference between India and Germany?' went one popular joke reported in the spring of 1943. 'In India, one person [Gandhi] starves for everybody, in Germany everybody starves for one person [Hitler].'[307]

Goebbels's rhetoric of suffering and sacrifice failed to convince because living standards had already been severely depressed long before 1943. Indeed, the rhetoric was not even new. Goebbels had issued an appeal for 'total war' at the beginning of 1942, after the debacle before Moscow.[308] As early as March 1939, Hitler had declared that 'any mobilization must be a total one', including the economy. In the pursuit of rearmament, living standards had already been depressed even before this. There are few more durable historical legends than that of the *Blitzkrieg* as an economic strategy designed to wage war cheaply and quickly, without putting the economy on a war footing.[309] The economy was on a war footing well before the war began.[310] Private consumption declined from 71 per cent of national income in 1928 to 59 per cent in 1938, and real earnings failed to recover to their pre-Depression levels by the time the war broke out. Real wages in Germany had grown by 9 per cent in 1938 compared to their 1913 levels, but the comparable figure in the USA was 53 per cent and in the UK 33. The quality of many goods in Germany, from clothing to foods, declined under the impact of import restrictions during the 1930s. When the war began, the Finance Ministry and the Four-Year Plan agreed that personal consumption had to be limited, mainly through rationing, to no more than the minimum necessary for staying alive. Taxes on beer, tobacco, cinemas, theatres, travel and other aspects of consumption were increased, and all taxpayers had to pay an emergency war surtax. As a result, taxes increased by 20 per cent on average for people, mostly working-class, who were earning between 1,500 and 3,000 Reichsmarks a year between 1939 and 1941, and 55 per cent for those earning between 3,000 and 5,000. Taxation provided half the income needed for military expenditure, the other half being covered by exactions from the occupied territories and by government loans.[311]

Hitler vetoed any further increases in income tax because of the popular hostility he feared they might arouse. Instead, additional funds were raised by raiding people's savings. The government was well aware of the fact that from early 1940 more and more money was flowing into the deposit accounts of Germany's local savings banks and insurance funds. Within a year, investors were putting more than a billion Reichsmarks into savings annually. The government silently creamed this off to pay for arms, while forcing severe cutbacks on the kind of programmes that it would normally have financed, such as housing construction, which fell from just over 320,000 new dwellings in 1937 to a mere 40,000 five years later. As early as 1940, 8 billion Reichsmarks flowed from savings banks into arms construction, a figure that increased to 12.8 billion the following year. This system of war financing was far preferable to public appeals for loans, which had had such a disastrous effect in the First World War, when patriotic investors lost all their savings in the postwar inflation. It did not, as has sometimes been claimed, signify public trust in the government, or certainty of victory. As government restrictions on other forms of investment tightened, people were left with no alternative. Rather than make long-term investments, they preferred as far as possible to put their money where it would be easy to get hold of it when they needed it – after the war was over.[312] Apart from this, there seemed little that they could do with it. As Mathilde Wolff-Mönckeberg, a woman from a prominent Hamburg family, wrote on 25 March 1944, everyone had taken to bartering:

I have exchanged the table for fat and meat and quite a number of other delicacies, which the new owner will bring from her canteen. But what else can one do these days? The stomach demands its due and money does not buy a thing. Everyone has oodles of money . . . You can only persuade workmen into your house if you press cigarettes into their hands or treat them to a glass of brandy. The man from the gas board, whom I tried to inveigle into letting us have a new cooker, had to be softened with a can of beer, two sausage sandwiches and finally a cigar.[313]

Two months earlier, the Security Service of the SS had devoted a special report to the spread of bartering. So many essential goods and services were in short supply that 'the black marketeering of small quantities of goods has become such a way of life for many people that most dismiss any reservations about it with the remark: "Those who do not help themselves will never improve their situation."' Only trading and bartering for profit met with popular disapproval. Despite this, it was but a small step from here to the emergence of a black market on a very substantial scale.[314]

The rapid increase in savings in the early part of the war reflected the fact that consumer spending fell most sharply up to 1942, then remained relatively stable thereafter until the last months of the war. Per capita consumption in Germany (in its prewar boundaries, including Austria, the Sudetenland and Memel) fell by a quarter between 1939 and 1942, then stabilized. If the incorporation of relatively poor areas of Poland into the Reich is taken into account, then real per capita consumption had fallen to 74 per cent of its 1938 level by 1941, then levelled off at 67–8 per cent in the following two years, while per capita retail sales dropped by roughly similar amounts. Real per capita output of all consumer goods fell by 22 per cent from 1938 to 1941. After an initial rise caused by panic buying, sales of textiles and metal and household goods in June 1940 were 20 per cent lower than in the previous year, sales of furniture 40 per cent lower.[315] And these figures disguised the fact that the first claim on consumer goods went to the armed forces. In 1941–2, for instance, per capita meat consumption in the armed forces was more than four times higher than among civilians, bread-grain consumption two and a half times higher. Soldiers could drink real coffee while civilians had to make do with substitutes, and they had plentiful supplies of cigarettes and alcohol. This was a matter of policy. Soldiers' meat ration was three and a half times that of civilians, and they were entitled to twice the daily ration of bread. Most of the non-armaments parts of the economy were working mainly for the armed forces, and by January 1941 90 per cent of furniture manufactured went to the military, while in May 1940 half of all textile sales were made to the armed forces, the SS and other uniformed organizations. 80 per cent of consumer-related chemicals went to the armed forces (including toothpaste and shoe-polish).[316] So much coal was reserved for industrial production that people did not have enough to heat their homes during the winter. 'In Germany,' went one joke told widely in 1941, 'the temperature is still being measured according to the foreign standards of Celsius and Réaumur. Hitler orders that, in future, measurements will be taken on the German Fahrenheit scale. In this way the temperature goes up by 65 degrees and the coal shortage is automatically solved!'[317]

Goebbels's rabble-rousing effort inspired some, both at home and at the front. 'It's 02.00 hours,' wrote the paratrooper Martin Pöppel in his diary from the Eastern Front on 19 February 1943. 'I can't get the Goebbels speech calling for total war out of my mind. The speech was so tremendous and fantastic that I feel I have to write home with my own response. Everyone was carried away by his words, all of us were under his spell. He spoke to us from the heart.'[318] Goebbels won widespread praise for making clear how serious the military situation was. Many had apparently not realized before. They were impressed by the fact that, as they thought, the regime was being honest, yet others were more sceptical. A few considered that Goebbels 'has painted the situation "blacker than it is", in order to lend emphasis to the *totalizing measures*'. His speech contained little that was new in concrete terms, some thought. 'To be sure,' reported the Security Service of the SS, 'people generally recognized the effectiveness of the 10 questions, but national comrades and Party members in every walk of life expressed the thought that the propagandistic purpose of these questions and answers was all too obvious to readers and listeners.'[319] Small farmers could be heard complaining that they 'had been compelled to work at a superhuman level for a long time already', so that they found the demands made in the speech more or less incomprehensible.[320] In Würzburg, indeed, it was reported that some people 'are characterizing the peroration of the speech with its questions as a comedy, since those present at the meeting were not the people [in general] but groups ordered there, who obviously were shouting yes to everything.'[321] Clearly a staged propaganda event, the Sports Palace speech had largely failed to convince because people knew that economic mobilization had already gone about as far as it could. The impulse given by the speech largely dissipated itself in attacks on 'luxury' establishments the impact of which on the war economy as a whole was minimal. Within a few months of Goebbels's speech, however, total war was to be visited on the home front in a sense that neither the Propaganda Minister nor anybody else had anticipated: and its impact, both in economic and in human terms, was to be devastating.

5

'THE BEGINNING OF THE END'

GERMANY IN FLAMES

I

On 9 November 1934 a Dresden schoolboy, writing an essay on aerial warfare, imagined what it would be like if in some future war the enemy decided to bomb the city. The sirens, he wrote, howled, and the people fled into their air-raid shelters. The bombs fell with a deafening noise, blowing in windows and destroying all the houses. 'Vast flames rage over Dresden.' A second wave of enemy planes came over, dropping gas bombs. Almost everyone in the bomb shelters was killed. Ashes and rubble were all that remained. The raid was a total catastrophe. But the boy did not gain high marks for his prescience. 'It can't get any worse!' wrote his teacher on the essay in furious disbelief. 'Stupid!' 'Evil! It's not so simple to lay waste to Dresden! You write almost nothing about defences. The essay is crawling with errors.'[1] Just over a decade later, the schoolboy was to be proved right in the most dramatic manner possible. Yet his teacher was not without a point either. From the very beginning of the Third Reich, in 1933, the regime had begun preparing defences against bombing. Air-raid wardens were appointed, warning sirens installed, and the population in urban centres forced to engage in repeated exercises and practice runs. Anti-aircraft batteries began to be constructed, in the belief that ground-to-air fire ('flak') would be decisive. However the construction of air-raid shelters and bomb-proof bunkers did not go forward with much vigour until the autumn of 1940, and, even then, shortages of labour and raw materials meant that it did not get very far. It was effectively abandoned two years later.[2]

When the war began, frequent alarms, very often false, caused disruption, discomfort and irritation, but, initially at least, damage inflicted by bombing was relatively light. As their military situation in France deteriorated in May 1940 the British decided to attack by selecting targets east of the Rhine: the seaport and industrial and trading centre of Hamburg, Germany's second city, easily reachable across the North Sea, became a favourite target. The first attack on the city, on 17–18 May 1940, was the first on any large German town, and it was followed by 69 further raids and 123 alarms to the end of the year. Hamburg's inhabitants had to spend virtually every other night in bunkers and air-raid shelters during this period. But the damage done was relatively small: 125 deaths and 567 injuries. In 1941 and the first half of the following year, the raids continued, but at greater intervals: altogether, by the middle of July 1942, the city had suffered 137 attacks costing 1,431 lives and 4,657 injured. Just over 24,000 people had been made homeless in a city of 2 million. By this time, after a late start, the Hamburg authorities had reinforced most of the city's cellars. In the areas near the River Elbe where the water-table was too high to allow them to be built it had erected solid bunkers above ground. Similar precautions were taken in other towns and cities across the Reich.[3] But soon British bombers were ranging even further afield. Night-time air raids against Berlin in 1940–41 were neither very large-scale nor very destructive, but they were a nuisance, and they became so frequent that the inhabitants of the capital began to make light of them. People were officially advised to snatch some sleep in the late afternoon before the bombings started. The joke then ran that when someone came into the air-raid shelter and said 'good morning', this meant that they had indeed been sleeping. If someone arrived and said 'good evening', this meant they hadn't. When a few arrived and said 'Hail, Hitler!', this meant they had always been asleep.[4]

Despite all the preparations, the rulers of the Third Reich, like their counterparts in the Soviet Union, did not set much store by large-scale, strategic bombing. Both used bombers tactically, either in support of ground forces or to prepare the way for them. The German raids on London and other cities in 1940 were intended above all to bring Britain to the conference table, and when they did not succeed, they were discontinued. The idea of destroying the enemy heartland by a persistent, long-term and large-scale bombing campaign was not entertained in Berlin. Only on the Eastern Front was anything like a campaign of this sort undertaken, but it had strictly limited military objectives and did not last for very long. In 1943–4 the German air force launched a strategic bombing offensive against Soviet industrial targets and communications. It scored some successes, most notably in the destruction of 43 US-built B-17 bombers and nearly a million tons of aviation fuel delivered to the Soviet Union and parked on an airfield at Poltava in June 1944, thus effectively eliminating the threat of American bombers attacking Germany from the east as well as from the west. But shortages of fuel and the switch of airplane production to fighters for the defence of Germany's cities against bombing raids by the British and Americans prevented the offensive from being taken any further.[5] Likewise, Stalin thought of bombing as useful mainly to help front-line troops on the ground. He did not develop a fleet of large-scale strategic bombers, and the destruction eventually wrought on German cities in the line of the Red Army's advance in the last two years of the war came from British and American bombers, not Russian ones. But Stalin was indeed keen for the Western Allies to relieve the Red Army by developing a major bombing campaign against the German homeland.[6]

Fear of aerial bombardment had been widespread in Europe in the 1930s, especially after the destruction of Guernica by German and Italian bombers in the Spanish Civil War. Bombers could never attain precision in hitting targets, not least because they had to be big if they were to carry an adequate payload, and this made them slow and difficult to manoeuvre, so they had to fly as high as they could in order to avoid being hit by flak. This often took them above the clouds, which made identifying targets even more difficult. Daylight raids were virtually impossible because of the very heavy losses inflicted on the planes by fighters and ground defences. There were a few early in the war, but they were quickly abandoned. Night-bombing was far from easy, especially since all belligerent nations went to some lengths to enforce the 'blackout', masking or turning off public and private lighting in towns and cities so that enemy bombers could not see them. Often, too, bombers had to fly considerable distances to reach their targets, and the difficulty of navigation was another problem the crews had to overcome. The best that pilots could do was to steer their way towards where they thought their target was, and release their bombs in its general direction. While small dive-bombers like the Stuka could lend more precise tactical support to ground forces, they could only carry very limited payloads and so were useless for large-scale, strategic bombing. Thus in practice all major bombing raids were more or less indiscriminate; it simply was not possible to be precise. Almost from the very outset, therefore, strategic bombing served two purposes that it was impracticable in reality to disentangle: to destroy enemy military and industrial resources on the one hand, and to weaken enemy civilian morale on the other. In many raids in 1941 – all of them small by later standards – most of the bombs missed their intended targets. Only very large targets, in practice entire towns and cities, were likely to be hit by planes flying high at night, and this was the strategy that Churchill and the British leadership finally decided on late in 1941. To implement it they appointed Arthur Harris, an energetic and determined officer, to lead Bomber Command. Harris decided to focus on major German cities, where his bombers could be certain without looking too closely to find war-related industries and the houses of the people who manned them. In 1942, when ground fighting on the Continent and in North Africa did not seem to be going well for the British, the destruction wrought by Harris's bombers on German cities gave a boost to British military and civilian morale. At the same time, however surprising it may seem, few British people saw in the bombing of Germany an opportunity for avenging the destruction of Coventry and the 'Blitz' on London.[7]

The British and Americans, unlike the Germans or the Russians, had already decided in the late 1930s that heavy bombers were the strategic weapon of the future. By 1942 British production of heavy bombers, notably the four-engined Avro Lancaster, first flown only a year before, and the Handley Page Halifax, introduced in 1940, was in full swing, augmenting lighter, two-engine models such as the Wellington, a staple of Bomber Command with over 11,000 manufactured altogether. When Harris took up office there were only sixty-nine heavy bombers at his disposal. By the end of the year there were nearly 2,000. They became the mainstay of British raids on Germany. Eventually more than 7,000 Lancasters and 6,000 Halifaxes were produced, replacing the less successful four-engined Stirling. They were joined from late 1942 onwards by American bombers based in UK airfields, in particular by the rugged B-17 Flying Fortress, of which more than 12,000 were produced, and the faster, lighter but more vulnerable Liberator, which was mass-produced on an enormous scale, with over 18,000 eventually coming off the production lines. Harris's first demonstration of his new tactic of mass bombing raids on large urban targets was against Lübeck on the night of 28–9 March 1942. The city had no military or economic significance worth mentioning, but its old brick and wooden buildings made it a good subject for a demonstration of what bombing could achieve. 234 Wellington, Lancaster and Stirling bombers, flying low because Lübeck was virtually undefended and easily accessible from the sea, dropped large explosive bombs to break open buildings in the city, following them with incendiaries to set them on fire. 50 per cent of the town was destroyed; 1,425 buildings were effectively razed to the ground and 10,000 were damaged, nearly 2,000 severely. 320 people were killed and 785 wounded. Harris followed the raid up with further attacks on other small cities along the Baltic coast in April 1942, including the medieval town of Rostock.[8]

These raids provoked Hitler in April 1942 to announce what he called 'terror raids' on British targets, aiming to 'produce the most painful effects on public life . . . within the framework of retribution'.[9] After the best part of a year without any serious attacks on British cities, he ordered the German air force to launch a counter-campaign on similar British cities, known as the 'Baedeker raids' after a well-known series of tourist handbooks. These were carried out with only small numbers of aircraft – only thirty fighter-bombers were available for daytime raids, and 130 bombers for use during the hours of darkness – on small, more or less undefended historic towns. They caused little damage to the British war effort and achieved nothing of military significance.[10] They were an entirely emotional response on Hitler's part. There was no way that he could match the huge forces being assembled by 'Bomber' Harris. Yet despite the devastation caused by the raid on Lübeck, morale in the town did not seem to have been damaged. The day after the raid, many shops reopened with signs such as 'Life goes on here!'[11] Nor did the raids seem to cause outrage against the British. Luise Solmitz recorded the bombing raids impersonally in her diary, as if they were natural disasters or acts of God. 'We are no longer in control of our fate, we are forced to allow ourselves to be driven by it and to take what comes without confidence or hope,' she wrote resignedly on 8 September 1942.[12] The destruction of the old red-brick north German Hanse town of Lübeck saddened her, but at the same time she also recorded the bombing of York and Norwich, 'a terrible pity about all those Germanic cultural possessions . . . Suffering and annihilation everywhere'.[13]

The openness of Lübeck to attack was unusual. British night attacks on the Ruhr in 1940 had prompted the appointment of an air force general, Josef Kammhuber, to organize a national system of air-raid defences. By the end of the year he had set up a line of radar stations stretching from Paris to Denmark, backed by Me110 night-fighters directed by a central control room and supplemented by ground-based searchlights and anti-aircraft guns. Over 1,000 British bombers were lost in 1941 as a result. Matters only began to improve for the British in 1942 with the introduction of the Lancasters and the installation of a new radio navigation device that allowed them to stick together in formation, swamping the German defences. Harris began deploying 'pathfinders' in advance of the bomber fleets, to locate the targets and light them up with incendiaries. From early 1943 they were equipped with airborne radar and radio target-finders that helped them fly in poor visibility, though it was not until the following year that these were perfected. Harris put a bomb-aimer as a member of the crew in each plane so that the navigator could be left to concentrate on finding the way there and back. And from the middle of 1943, after a long delay due in part to the fear that the Germans might get the same idea, bombers were equipped with a device known as 'Window'. This consisted of packets of strips of aluminium foil to drop out of the bomb-bays and confuse enemy radar. To counter these measures, the German air force developed its own aerial radar that enabled night-fighters to fly in groups, locate the enemy bombers and shoot them down. It moved large numbers of fighters to the west, leaving less than a third of the fighter force to confront the Red Army. Anti-aircraft batteries were manufactured on a large scale: by August 1944 there were 39,000 of them, and their nightly use absorbed a force of no fewer than a million gunners. German defences managed to knock out a substantial number of enemy bombers; the death rate amongst the men of Britain's Bomber Command was as high as 50 per cent overall; more than 55,000 men were killed over the course of the war. Yet Hitler's characteristic preference for attack over defence made him consistently favour retaliation by ordering fresh bombing raids over Britain and downgrading the production and deployment of fighter planes in defensive positions. And in any case, fighters found it took so long to climb up to a position where they could attack bombers flying at anything up to 30,000 feet that they were often unable to confront them until after they had dropped their payload.[14]

Initially, however, there was no sustained bombing campaign against Germany. To demonstrate that larger raids could be carried out on bigger targets, Harris staged a thousand-bomber attack on Cologne on 30 May 1942, destroying over 3,300 buildings and leaving 45,000 people without homes. 474 people were killed and 5,000 injured, many of them seriously. The raid proved that large fleets of bombers could reach their targets without mishap and overwhelm local defences.[15] A thousand-bomber raid on Essen in the summer of 1942 was relatively unsuccessful, however, and was not repeated; among other things, it had only been possible to mount it by including aircraft normally used for training – and crewed by men who were doing courses in them. British bombers then concentrated not on urban targets but on U-boat pens on the Atlantic coast of France, which were so heavily protected by reinforced concrete that little damage was done. However, preserving Atlantic convoys seemed the highest priority. Only when Churchill and Roosevelt met at Casablanca in January 1943 was a decision taken to begin the strategic bombing campaign in earnest. The Second Front demanded by Stalin, the two leaders agreed, would have to be postponed until 1944; in its place would come the invasion of Italy and a new campaign of bombing the aim of which, to quote the Combined Chiefs-of-Staff in their order to the British and US air forces on 21 January 1943, was to effect 'the progressive destruction and dislocation of the German military, industrial and economic system, and the undermining of the morale of the German people to a point where their capacity for armed resistance is fatally weakened'.[16] The new Combined Bombing Offensive began with a series of attacks on the Ruhr. On 5 March 1943, 362 bombers attacked Essen, where the Krupp arms factory was located; this was followed up with a whole series of further raids on the town over the following months. In between, there were attacks on Duisburg, Bochum, Krefeld, Düsseldorf, Dortmund, Wuppertal, Mülheim, Gelsen-kirchen and Cologne, all of them major centres of industry and mining. The attack on Dortmund was particularly heavy. 800 bombers dropped twice the tonnage that had fallen on Cologne in the thousand-bomber raid the previous year. 650 people were killed, and the town's library, with over 200,000 volumes and a unique newspaper archive, went up in flames. A further raid on Cologne on 28–9 June 1943 caused nearly 5,000 deaths. Altogether some 15,000 people were killed in the indus-trial cities of western Germany in this series of raids. In addition, on 16 May 1943 the 'dam-buster' squadron, flying low towards major dams on the Eder and Möhne rivers, launched its 'bouncing bombs' which shattered the concrete barriers and released huge quantities of water, severely disrupting water supplies to the Ruhr area and flooding large tracts of countryside as well as cutting off electricity supplies to industrial plants. Just over 1,500 people were killed, the majority of them foreign workers and prisoners of war; panic rumours in the German population put the figure at anything up to 30,000. To complete the devastation, fast-moving Mosquito fighter-bombers, made of wood to give greater speed and range, flew into the Ruhr between the major raids to ensure there was no respite.[17] Reich Propaganda Minister Goebbels was shocked by the devastation. 'We find ourselves in a situation of helpless inferiority,' he confided to his diary after the attack on Dortmund, 'and have to receive the blows of the English and Americans with dogged fury.'[18]

Armaments Minister Albert Speer was seriously alarmed. He visited the Ruhr repeatedly to organize the relocation of the workforce to camps from which they could be sent to other factories if their own was destroyed, and he did what he could to repair the damage and get things started again. He drafted in 7,000 men from the West Wall to rebuild the dams. The German Labour Front, the Todt Organization and the regional Nazi Party created special teams to clear up the mess and get miners and munitions workers back to work, while the National Socialist People's Welfare organization mobilized itself to care for those who had been made homeless.[19] Despite all these efforts, there could be no doubting the scale of the damage the bombers had inflicted on the war economy. Arms production had been growing at an average of 5.5 per cent a month in Germany since June 1942; now the growth stopped altogether. Steel production fell by 200,000 tons in the second quarter of 1943 and ammunition quotas had to be cut. There was a crisis in supplies of components for aircraft, and from July 1943 until March 1944 production of aircraft stagnated.[20] A raid by American bombers on Schweinfurt on 17 August 1943 badly damaged a number of factories producing ball-bearings and led to a fall of 38 per cent in their production. 'We are approaching the point of total collapse ... in our supply industry,' Speer told the Air Force Procurement Office. 'Soon we will have airplanes, tanks, or trucks lacking certain key parts.' If the raids on Germany's industrial centres continued, he warned Hitler, then Germany's arms production would come to a total halt.[21]

II

The attacks on the Ruhr were followed by a massive raid on Hamburg, Germany's largest seaport and a leading shipbuilding and industrial centre. This was the first time that Window was used, and it proved highly effective. On the night of 24–5 July 1943, 791 bombers took off from forty-two airfields in the east of England and made their way north-east towards the mouth of the river Elbe. Forty-five had to turn back because of mechanical problems, dumping their bombs into the sea. The bulk of the fleet veered south-east and flew towards Hamburg from the north, which the city's defenders did not expect, throwing out packets of aluminium foil strips at one-minute intervals and severely disrupting ground radar. There was very little resistance, and only twelve of the aircraft were lost. Pilots reported ground searchlight beams waving about aimlessly, looking for targets. The pathfinders dropped their markers, and the main force began releasing its bombs over the city centre shortly before one in the morning. People rushed to their shelters. Many bombs fell on sparsely populated outlying suburbs and villages, but the city centre and the shipyards in the harbour were hit as well, and fire-engines and clearance teams began their work according to a prearranged plan even before the attack was over. But the assault on Hamburg was a new kind of operation, not a single raid but a series of raids designed to destroy the city in stages. The next day, 109 American Flying Fortresses flew in over the city for another attack. Daylight raids were far more dangerous than night attacks, and no fewer than seventy-eight of the planes were hit by anti-aircraft fire, causing many to drop their bombs short of the target, though some damage was caused in the harbour and outlying suburbs. A smaller raid the following night kept up the pressure, then on the night of 27–8 July 1943, 735 British bombers flew in, this time from the east. The pathfinders dropped their markers in a concentrated area to the south-east of the city centre and the main force offloaded 2,326 tons of bombs before returning home. Seventeen planes and crews were lost, but most escaped because a third of the way through the raid the anti-aircraft gunners on the ground had been instructed to restrict their fire to 18,000 feet to allow night-fighters to attack the enemy aircraft: all the bombers apart from the Stirlings, which had already done their work, could fly above this level, and there were too few German night-fighters to make much of an impact.[22]

The weather was unusually hot and dry that night, and the fire-fighters were mostly over on the western area of the city still dealing with the smouldering remains of the previous raids. In the first twenty-three minutes of the raid, the bombers dropped so many incendiaries, blast-bombs and high explosives on such a small area in the south-east area of the city that the fires merged into one, sucking air out of the surrounding area until the whole square mile became one huge blaze, with temperatures reaching 800 degrees Celsius at the centre. It began to draw in air at hurricane force from all around, extending another two miles to the south-east as the bombers continued to drop their payloads there. The force of the howling, spark-filled wind created by the firestorm uprooted trees and turned people on the streets into living torches. The firestorm sucked the air out of the basement shelters in which thousands of people were cowering, killing them with carbon-monoxide poisoning, or trapping and suffocating them by reducing the buildings above to heaps of rubble that covered the air-vents and exits. 16,000 apartment-block buildings with a frontage of 133 miles were ablaze by three in the morning, until the firestorm finally began to subside. By seven a.m. it was over. Many people survived by sheer good fortune. Fifteen-year-old Traute Koch described how her mother wrapped her in wet sheets, pushed her out of the air-raid shelter, and said 'run!'

I hesitated at the door. In front of me I could see only fire – everything red, like the door to a furnace. An intense heat struck me. A burning beam fell in front of my feet. I shied back but then, when I was ready to jump over it, it was whirled away by a ghostly hand. I ran out onto the street. The sheets around me acted as sails and I had the feeling that I was being carried away by the storm. I reached the front of a five-storey building in front of which we had arranged to meet again. It had been bombed and burnt out in a previous raid and there was not much left in it for the fire to get hold of. Someone came out, grabbed me in their arms, and pulled me into the doorway.[23]

They descended into the cellar, and survived. Others were not so fortunate. Johann Burmeister, a greengrocer, recorded how people leaped into one of Hamburg's many canals to extinguish their burning clothes. Some committed suicide. A nineteen-year-old milliner described how her aunt had dragged her through the spark-filled streets until their progress was stopped because the asphalt had melted. 'There were people on the roadway, some already dead, some still lying alive but stuck in the asphalt . . . Their feet had got stuck and then they had put out their hands to try to get out again. They were on their hands and knees screaming.' Eventually she decided to roll down a bank by some burning trees. 'I took my hand out of my aunt's and went. I think I rolled over some people who were still alive.' At the bottom she found a blanket and pulled it over her. The next morning, she found her aunt's body; she could identify it only by the blue-and-white sapphire ring she always wore. Many corpses were found black and shriveled; some were lying in a mess of coagulated human body fat.[24]

This was far from being the end of Hamburg's misery. As the wind cleared away the smoke from the still-burning ruins, Bomber Command decided to mount a third raid. On the night of 29–30 July, 786 bombers set off for Hamburg. Forty-five had to turn back because of mechanical problems, and a few more were shot down on the way, but the majority reached their target, identifying the city by the glow of its fires, which could be seen even over the horizon. Extra searchlights had been rushed to the city and the area around it, and both anti-aircraft batteries and night-fighters took full advantage of the light they threw on the bombers, thus getting round the need to depend on radar readings still confused by the boxes of Window aluminium foil streamers they were dropping. This time, the bombs were released over a much wider area; strong winds had blown the pathfinders off course. As a result, the north-east of the city was devastated, rather than the area further west that had been intended. Even now, however, Harris was not satisfied; after a delay caused by adverse weather conditions, he launched a fourth and final major attack on the city on 2–3 August 1943. Two groups of bombers took off. The first, with 498 aircraft preceded by 54 pathfinders, was to attack the wealthy residential areas to the west of Hamburg's central lake, the Alster, while the second, consisting of 245 bombers and 27 pathfinders, was to destroy the industrial area of Harburg, to the south. This time the German defences had learned how to deal with Window by allowing the night-fighters to fly freely and operate visually, guided by a continuous commentary from the ground about the bombers' position and by their own airborne radar. Weather conditions worsened and the bombers flew into a huge electrical storm that turned their propellers into giant firewheels, as one pilot reported, and blew them all over the sky. The bomber waves were broken up, many dropped their payloads on small towns and villages, or on the countryside, and turned back before they ever got to Hamburg. Some crashed. Enemy fighters and anti-aircraft fire took their toll. Altogether 35 aircraft failed to return, and little serious damage was done to the city. Nevertheless, in the four great raids taken all together, Allied bombers had flown more than 2,500 missions over the city, dropping over 8,300 tons of incendiaries and high explosives on to their target. 59 had been brought down by night-fighters, 11 by anti-aircraft 'flak', and another 17 by a combination of causes including storm damage in the final raid. The devastation was staggering. The city's shipyards were pulverized, so that between twenty and twenty-five U-boats planned for or already under construction were never built. Industrial output from the city, so it was later calculated, returned to 80 per cent of its previous levels within five months, but the loss of war production caused by the bombing was reckoned to have amounted to the equivalent of nearly two months' output from the city as a whole. The disruption was far-reaching. All the city's railway stations were destroyed, the harbour and the river were blocked by sunken ships, the rivers and canals by fallen debris. The city's supplies of gas, water and electricity were all cut off and could not be restored until the middle of August. Nevertheless, the major cost was human. Partly by accident and partly by design, the bulk of the bombs had fallen on residential areas. In particular, the firestorm had devastated the working-class areas to the south-east of the city centre, inhabited by people who were traditionally opposed to the Nazis, while the wealthy villa quarter to the north-west, where the pro-Nazi elite lived, was largely untouched, though its destruction had been one of the aims of the final, unsuccessful raid. Altogether 56 per cent of Hamburg's dwellings, around 256,000 of them, had been destroyed and 900,000 people were made homeless. Some 40,000 people lost their lives and a further 125,000 required medical treatment, many of them for burns.[25]

14,000 firemen, 12,000 soldiers and 8,000 technical experts laboured night and day to deal with the fires and repair the worst damage, bringing in emergency supplies of food and water. People began to flee the city already after the first raid. There was, as Mathilde Wolff-Mönckeberg noted in an unsent letter written for her children abroad, 'panic and chaos . . . There were no trams, no Underground, no rail-traffic to the suburbs. Most people loaded some belongings on carts, bicycles, prams, or carried things on their backs, and started on foot, just to get away, to escape.'[26] 840,000 of the homeless wandered out of the centre of the city and were guided by the police to still-intact railway stations or river jetties on its outskirts. Nazi Party Regional Leader Karl Kaufmann arranged for them to be evacuated to rural areas to the north and east. 625 trains carried off more than three-quarters of a million people to new, mostly temporary homes. Despite Kaufmann's plea for officials to stay at their posts, many of these fled too. Three weeks after the raids, 900 out of 2,500 officials of the city's food distribution office were still away from their posts, absent or dead. Many local Nazi Party bosses acted on their own initiative, commandeering trains for evacuees from their own city precinct, and not a few seized cars and lorries to get their own families and what they could of their own possessions out of the city. The Party apparatus seemed to be in a state of collapse. In the all-embracing paternal state of the Third Reich, people had come to expect assistance in a crisis as a matter of course, and its widespread failure in the catastrophe aroused much hostile comment. Popular anger was directed not against the British for their 'terror raids', although Goebbels's propaganda did its best to arouse feelings of revenge, but against Göring and the German air force, which had patently failed to defend the homeland, and against the Nazi Party, which had brought this destruction on Germany. 'People who were wearing Party badges,' noted Mathilde Wolff-Mönckeberg, 'had them torn off their coats and there were screams of "Let's get that murderer." The police did nothing.'[27]

The raids so shocked Luise Solmitz that she was unable to find words to describe them. When she and her husband ventured out of doors on to the streets of the city at the beginning of August 1943, they saw 'nothing but rubble, rubble in our path'. In horror and fascination she observed the slowness with which the superheated buildings gradually cooled:

The coal bunker at Rebienhaus on the corner finally, finally burnt out. A fantastic drama. The shops [on top of the bunker] destroyed, glowing red and rosy-red. I went into the cellar staircase, it was an irresponsible thing to do; the enormous house loomed steeply above me, all destroyed, and down below I could see the lonely, blazing hell, filled with flames raging with their own life. Later only the bunker shafts were aglow, the shops were black, dead caves. At the end the flame was burning blue. During the daytime the air was shimmering with heat.[28]

Visiting Hamburg a few days earlier, on 28 July 1943, the soldier and former Nazi stormtrooper Gerhard M., as always travelling with his bicycle, found it deserted. 'Where are all the people now?' he asked himself. In the working-class area of the Hammerbrookstrasse, near the harbour, he encountered

a deathly quiet. Here there are no people looking for their belongings, for here the people too are lying underneath the rubble. Here the street is no longer passable. I have to carry my bike over my shoulder and clamber over the rubble. The houses have been levelled. Everywhere I cast my eye: a field of ruins, still as death. Nobody got out of here. Here incendiaries, air-mines and time-bombs have lodged at the same time. You can still see dead bodies lying on the street. How many must still be lying on what used to be the surface of the street, under the rubble?[29]

When, he asked himself, would it all be rebuilt and people live there again? As a long-time stormtrooper, he knew only one answer: 'When we have won the war. When we can once more go about our work in Germany undisturbed. When a stop has been put to the envy of people abroad.'[30] He took comfort in the fact that Hamburg had recovered from the previous devastation of the Great Fire of 1842, just over a century before. And – forgetting, perhaps, the damage and loss of life caused by the Blitz – he imagined that London, where people were rejoicing 'in ignorance of the strength of Germany' and living a 'carefree' life, would some day soon suffer the same fate: 'one day arrogant London will feel the effects of war, and it will do so far, far more than has now been the case in Hamburg'.[31] Yet such a reaction was unusual. In the air-raid shelters, attempts to fan the flames of hatred against the British frequently met with rebuffs. 'Almost 3 hours in the bunker,' Luise Solmitz reported on a subsequent occasion. 'Bunker warden Söldner: "The Londoners have to sit in their bunkers for 120 hours. I hope they never get out – they deserve not to!" – "They've got to do what their government wants. What else are they to do?" said a woman's voice.'[32] 'Despite everything that we have suffered in the attacks,' she wrote later, 'there's not much hatred in Hamburg for the "enemy".'[33]

What people did feel was despair. 'We have lost courage and are filled only with a dumb kind of passive apathy,' wrote Mathilde Wolff-Mönckeberg. 'Practically everyone knows that all that bluff and rubbish printed in the newspapers and blazoned out on the wireless is hollow nonsense.'[34] The Security Service of the SS reported that 'large parts of the people are *sealing themselves off against propaganda* in its present form'.[35] Many people eventually returned to Hamburg, so that the population of the city recovered from 600,000 to over a million by the end of the year, but large numbers of refugees remained in other parts of the Reich, intensifying what the Security Service of the SS called the 'shock-effect and huge consternation' in the 'population of the whole territory of the Reich'. 'The stories the evacuated national comrades have been spreading about the effects of the damage in Hamburg have strengthened existing fears even more.'[36] The anxiety was intensified to a degree by the common Allied practice of dropping leaflets on German cities, warning people that they would be destroyed: sometimes they contained menacing rhymes, such as 'Hagen [a town in the Ruhr], you're lying in a hole, but we'll still find you all.' In 1943 Allied planes dropped huge quantities of forged food ration cards, which did indeed cause confusion among ordinary citizens and made extra work for the local authorities. The destruction caused in the Hamburg raids of July–August 1943 dealt a severe blow to civilian morale, already weakened as it was by the catastrophic defeat of the German army at Stalingrad. After August 1943, people carried on less out of enthusiasm for the war than out of fear of what might happen if Germany lost, a fear played on increasingly by the propaganda pumped out by Goebbels's co-ordinated media.[37]

At the same time, the Propaganda Ministry's exhortation to ordinary Germans to redouble their efforts in the campaign for 'total war' were undermined by the obvious lack of preparedness of the regime. 'They're lying to us through their teeth,' complained one junior army officer after his family home had been bombed in Hamburg. 'The events in Hamburg demonstrate that "total war" might have been proclaimed but it hasn't been prepared.'[38] On 17 June 1943, following raids on Wuppertal and Düsseldorf, people, as the Security Service of the SS reported, were 'totally exhausted and apathetic'. But some (or so the SS cautiously guessed) blamed the regime. In Bremen two stormtroopers had come upon a woman weeping in front of the cellar of her bomb-damaged house, in which lay the corpses of her son, her daughter-in-law and her two-year-old granddaughter. As they attempted to console her, she shouted: 'The brown cadets are to blame for the war. They would do better to have gone to the front and made sure the English don't come here.'[39] It was noteworthy, the report went on, that people in bombed cities were using the old-fashioned 'Good morning!' instead of 'Hail, Hitler!' when they met. A statistically minded Party member reported that the day after an attack on Barmen, he had greeted fifty-one people with the words 'Hail, Hitler!' and had the same greeting returned by only two. 'Anyone who brings five new members into the Party,' went a joke reported by the SS Security Service in August 1943, 'is permitted to join it himself. Anyone who brings 10 new members into it is even given a certificate saying he never belonged to it.'[40] Another popular joke told in many parts of the Reich went as follows:

A man from Berlin and a man from Essen are discussing the extent of the bomb damage in their respective cities. The man from Berlin explains that the bombardment of Berlin was so terrible that window-panes were still falling out of the houses five hours after the attack. The man from Essen answers, that's nothing, in Essen, even a fortnight after the attack, portraits of the Leader were flying out of the windows.[41]

In Düsseldorf someone had hung a picture of Hitler from a home-made gallows.[42] Disillusion with Hitler was particularly strong in towns such as this, where the Social Democratic and Communist labour movements had been entrenched before 1933. But it had been widespread in virtually all large towns and cities, including Hamburg and Berlin. Discontent came easily to the surface here because belief in the Nazi system had never gone very deep into the masses.

III

The mass evacuation of Hamburg's inhabitants had its parallels in other towns and cities of the Reich. Every major attack led to an exodus. But there was also in each case an evacuation plan. It focused initially on the young, on people in other words who were not directly useful to the war economy. An elaborate programme of 'Children's Evacuation to the Countryside' (Kinderlandverschickung) was developed, with urban children over the age of ten being sent to camps in south Germany, Saxony, East Prussia and to some extent also Poland, Denmark, the Reich Protectorate of Bohemia and Moravia and the Baltic states. By the end of 1940 some 300,000 had already been sent to a total of nearly 2,000 camps, most of them for a few weeks; children under the age of ten were billeted on local families. By 1943 they were staying for longer periods, sometimes months on end, and there were more than a million children in some 5,000 camps at any one time.[43] The scheme was intended not least to allow the Hitler Youth, who ran it in conjunction with the National Socialist People's Welfare organization, to remove children from the influence of their families and especially the Church, and provide them with a rigorously Nazi education. Priests and pastors were banned from the camps, and bishops began complaining about the absence of religious education in them.[44] So successful did the scheme appear in this respect to Baldur von Schirach, the Hitler Youth leader, and his staff that plans were even drawn up to extend it after the war had been won.[45] However, the scheme ran up against considerable hostility from countryfolk, especially those on whom cheeky and unruly children and teenagers from run-down working-class areas of Germany's great cities were billeted, and many refused to accept them even when offered financial inducements to do so. The closure of bomb-damaged urban schools and the evacuation of pupils and teachers to the country-side remained relatively limited in scope. Even at the end of 1943 only 32,000 school pupils had been evacuated in this way from Berlin, out of a total population of 249,000 school pupils; 85,000 remained in the city, while 132,000 had been sent by their parents to stay with relatives in other parts of Germany. Thus, up to this point, self-help remained more important than state or Party direction in the removal of children from bombed-out areas of German towns and cities.[46]

Throughout 1944 and early 1945, as bombing raids intensified and made ever larger numbers of people homeless, the number of evacuees and refugees increased until it reached more than 8 million, including not only children but mothers and babies, and old people.[47] On 18 November 1943 the Security Service of the SS summarized the effects to date. While most of the women and children who had been evacuated were reasonably satisfied with their lot, it noted that a minority were not, particularly those who had been forced to leave their menfolk behind. Similar complaints could be heard from men, especially in the working classes, whose families had been evacuated to the countryside: they felt abandoned and neglected, lonely and deprived. One miner in the Ruhr was reported as saying to his mates after his shift had ended: ' "I am in agony again thinking about the evening ahead. As long as I'm in the factory, I don't think about it, but when I come home I'm overcome with dread. I miss my wife and the laughter of my kids." And,' the report went on, 'the man wept as he was saying this, openly and without shame.'[48] Particular problems were caused by the tensions that arose between working-class families evacuated to Catholic areas and the pious local inhabitants upon whom they were billeted. 'We can thank you Hamburgers for that,' some Bavarians were said to have remarked to people evacuated from the north, after Munich and Nuremberg had been attacked as well. 'That's happened because you don't go to Church!'[49] Added to such tensions came the fact that, as the report noted, 'Most of the evacuated women and children have been accommodated in small villages and rural communities in the most primitive circumstances.' They often had to walk miles to get supplies, 'in wind and weather, ice and snow', leaving their children unsupervised and so causing further anxiety. Local and Party authorities in rural areas were often felt to be unhelpful. Widespread resentment was caused by the obvious fact that middle- and upper-class houses were left with empty rooms while peasants and craftsmen had to make room for evacuees in their cramped cottages. Evacuation caused further worries about the fate of the damaged property people had left behind in the city.[50]

Problems of this kind led many women to take their children back to their home towns, a move which the authorities tried to discourage by ordering that their ration cards would not be accepted there. As a result, 300 women staged an open, public demonstration in the industrial town of Witten, near Dortmund, on 11 October 1943, and the police had to be called in to restore order. On arriving at the scene, however, the police refused to do anything since they were persuaded that the women were right to protest. Similar, if less dramatic scenes, took place elsewhere in the Ruhr. 'The abuse of official and leading persons,' the report noted in a shocked tone, 'was on the agenda.'[51] One woman was reported as saying, in an obvious allusion to the fate of German Jews: 'Why don't you just send us to Russia, turn machine-guns on us, and polish us off?'[52] People wanted their houses to be repaired as quickly as possible, or new ones built.[53] But this was scarcely possible, given the scale of the damage. Some officials, like the Regional Leader of Hamburg, Karl Kaufmann, urged the deportation of Jews to make more dwellings available for people who had lost their homes in the bombing, but the Jewish minority in Germany was so small – it had never been more than 1 per cent of the population even at its height – that, although this opportunity was indeed used, among others by Albert Speer in his search for accommodation for his workers, it was in no way enough even to make a small dent in the problem. Local authorities made plans to build emergency accommodation, including quick-to-build two-storey wooden barracks, but these fell foul of the official prioritization of war-industrial construction. On 9 September 1943 Hitler issued a decree setting up a 'German Housing Aid' under Robert Ley, and the regime provided grants for the erection of prefabricated barracks, some of which were constructed by Jewish concentration camp prisoners. But these made little impact either. By March 1944 an official estimate put the number of homeless at 1.9 million, needing a total of 657,000 new dwellings. By the end of July 1944 only 53,000 had been built. Some employers provided simple new accommodation for their German workers, but even this was very limited in scale. Visiting Bochum in December 1944, Goebbels noted that the city still had 100,000 inhabitants dwelling there, then corrected himself: 'it's too much to say "dwelling"; they're camping out in cellars and holes in the ground'.[54]

Goebbels himself had played an increasingly important role in dealing with air raids since his appointment by Hitler as Chairman of the Inter-Ministerial Bomb Damage Committee in January 1943. This gave him wide-ranging powers to send emergency aid into stricken cities, including for example even the confiscation of army camps to provide temporary accommodation for people who had lost their homes. When an air raid on Kassel on 22 October 1943 created a huge firestorm that rendered 63 per cent of the town's houses and flats uninhabitable, Goebbels sent in a team that reported almost immediately that the local Party boss Karl Weinrich was completely unable to deal with the situation. At Goebbels's request, Weinrich was soon after retired on health grounds. The experience prompted Goebbels to persuade Hitler to set up a Reich Inspectorate for Civil Air War Measures on 10 December 1943, with himself in charge. All of this allowed him to criticize Party officials he did not like, and use his influence to override them or even get them replaced. But of course he never achieved total control over this area; in some ways, indeed, it only brought him up against other powerful figures such as Göring, who controlled civil defence, and Himmler, who was in charge of the police and fire services. Unexploded bombs, of which there were many, were dealt with by the Reich Ministry of Justice, which, following an order issued by Hitler in

October 1940, sent prisoners from state penal institutions to try to defuse them. By July 1942, as the Ministry told Hitler, they had already defused more than 3,000 bombs; this number increased dramatically as the raids intensified in the following months. The death rate among the prisoners engaged in this work was around 50 per cent. For those who survived, the promise of a remission of their sentence that had inveigled many of them into agreeing to serve in bomb disposal never materialized. Many other emergency measures following major air raids lay in the hands of the National Socialist People's Welfare organization, which ferried in field-kitchens to provide people with food, helped sometimes by the army. The war transformed the organization into a rescue operation, dealing with the effects of total war, placing evacuees, caring for the old, finding homes for orphans, setting up a finding service for missing children, and much more besides. Over a million volunteers were working for it and the closely allied German Red Cross by 1944. It had successfully eliminated the competition of Church welfare groups.[55] But it still had a rival in the Nazi women's organization, which also played its part in caring for bombed-out families with children.[56] The Nazi Party Regional Leaders were empowered to raise ration allocations and distribute extra food supplies as well as issuing substitute ration cards to those who had lost theirs in a raid. Supplies were often short, however, and the demand for cooking utensils and other domestic goods ran up against shortages of materials and the higher priority given to war production. The financial compensation paid by the government (according to two decrees issued in November 1940) to bombed-out people to allow them to rent new accommodation and replace essential household items was strictly limited in scope.[57]

Nor did it prove easy to boost the provision of air-raid protection facilities to the desired level. Despite frequent inspections by senior Party officials like Karl Kaufmann, Regional Leader of Hamburg (who severely criticized the lack of bunkers on an inspection tour of Dresden in January 1945), little was done to improve matters as a result. Hitler had originally planned the construction of up to 2,000 bomb-proof bunkers at the end of September 1940, and by the end of August 1943 over 1,700 had been completed. At the height of the construction programme in Berlin, in the middle of 1941, more than 22,000 workers were engaged on building bunkers in the capital city, many of them foreign forced labourers. But of course even 2,000 was a pathetically tiny number for the protection of Germany's large urban population. Concrete was needed for U-boat bases, labour for the arms industry and the West Wall, transport for arms-related materials, money to build planes and tanks. In consequence, those bunkers that were completed, particularly the thick-walled, reinforced-concrete structures built above ground, became desperately overcrowded when there was a raid – 5,000 people crammed into a bunker in Hamburg-Harburg early in 1945 that had been built to accommodate 1,200, for example. In small towns as in large cities, air-raid protection was only available for a fraction of the population – 1,200 people out of a population of 38,400 in Lüdenscheid, for instance, or 4,000 out of a population of 25,100 in Soest. People began to complain as early as 1943 that the regime had done nothing to build them when money, men and materials were ready to hand, early in the war. Rumours soon became rife that Party bosses had constructed their own private bunkers, as the Saxon Regional Leader Martin Mutschmann had done with SS pioneer labour beneath his private villa in Dresden – the only bomb-proof air-raid shelter in the entire city. The most spectacular of these was of course Hitler's own bunker complex beneath the Reich Chancellery in Berlin. An air-raid shelter had existed there since 1936, but early in 1943 a vast extension programme was undertaken. Consisting of two floors located 40 feet below the surface, and protected by a reinforced concrete roof some 12 feet thick, it had its own diesel generator used to provide heating and lighting and pump water in and waste matter out. Its construction by the Essen firm of Hochtief, together with that of the command bunker in Hitler's field headquarters and the underground headquarters complex at Ohrdruf in Thuringia, had consumed more concrete and used up more labour (28,000 men in all) than the entire public programme of civil defence bunker construction for the whole of Germany in the years 1943 and 1944 put together.[58]

People's lives in Germany's towns and cities during the second half of the war were increasingly lived for much, even most, of the time in air-raid shelters, bunkers and cellars, as Goebbels's comments on Bochum suggested. Air-raid warnings sent people scurrying into them with growing frequency, day and night. In Münster, for example, the sirens sounded 209 times in 1943 and 329 in 1944; in the latter year, no fewer than 231 of these alarms were sounded during the day. And in the first three months of 1945 the town's air-raid warnings went off on

293 occasions, more than in the whole of 1943. Other towns and cities had similar experiences. The disruption to people's daily lives, to their sleep, to the economy, was enormous and in the final months of the war in many places it became almost unbearable. People tried to relieve the tension with jokes: ' "Whom do we have to thank for the night-fighters?" "Hermann Göring." "For the whole air force?" "Hermann Göring." "Upon whose orders did Hermann Göring do all this?" "On the orders of the Leader!" "Where would we all be if it were not for Hermann Göring and the Leader?" "In our beds!" '[59] As the enemy armies advanced through occupied Europe in 1944–5, German advance radar stations fell silent, and the interval between air-raid alarms and the start of bombing raids grew ever briefer. People began to panic, rushing into the shelters in wild disorder; increasingly, there were injuries and even deaths in the crush. In January 1944, indeed, thirty people were trampled to death in the scramble to get into a bunker at the Hermannplatz in Berlin; the following November, thirty-five people were killed in similar circumstances in the town of Wanne-Eickel.[60]

Those who stayed in their own homes placed bags of sand and buckets of water in position to try to put out fires caused by bombs. They knew well enough that there was no protection against a direct hit. Cellar walls were broken through to allow escape into a neighbouring house in case a bomb fell on their own. One diarist described a night in his air-raid cellar during a raid in the following terms:

To begin with, a series of incendiary bombs fell in our vicinity. Then there came detonation after detonation, heavy, heavy explosions. Since we don't have a deep cellar, we crouched on the floor, on mats, near the hole that we had broken through [for escape purposes, into the next house, as required in regulations]. Everyone had a wet cloth wound round their head, a gas-mask on their arm, matches in their pocket, and a wet towel that we placed over our face on the command 'attention!' that signalled the audible approach of heavy bombs, pressing it down with our thumbs and little fingers over our mouths and nostrils so that our eyes, also closed, and our mouths were protected against air-pressure and mortar-dust. Although no high-explosive bombs or mines fell on to our street, the walls still shook worryingly. The lights went out, and we lit our lanterns. There was a noise of breaking glass and falling tiles, window-frames etc. We expected to find nothing more than rubble in the house. There was a penetrating smell of fire.[61]

In the public shelters, admittance and behaviour were carefully regulated and controlled by air-raid wardens, but in the last phase of the war, the rules were increasingly disregarded. They were supposed to be for people who had none in their own homes, and Jews and Gypsies were not allowed to enter them. In 1944 Goebbels ordered that priority had to be given to workers in vital war industries. People entering a public shelter had to show an admission card. By the second half of 1943 few paid much attention to such rules. People crowded indiscriminately into the bunkers, where ventilation facilities devised for only a few soon proved inadequate, the fetid air made people sweat, scabies and other dirt-related diseases and infestations spread, and people began to lose all sense of order, as one sanitary officer in Hamm noted in January 1945: 'They are grabbing at other people's possessions, they don't respect women and children, any sense of order or cleanliness disappears. People who were otherwise well groomed don't bother to wash themselves or comb their hair all day . . . In the bunkers they don't go to the toilets any more but just relieve themselves in the dark, in the corners of the room.'[62]

Meanwhile, above ground, the police struggled to restore order in the aftermath of major bombing raids. Dangerous ruins were sealed off, streets cleared, bodies collected, if possible identified, and buried, sometimes just wrapped in paper, in mass graves: although Hitler had forbidden this, it was impractical in most cases to do anything else, since the numbers of corpses far exceeded the capacity of cemeteries to take them, and religious objections to cremation over the years meant that facilities were not available to incinerate them. People left messages for missing relatives chalked up on the walls of their ruined houses, in the hope that they might still be alive. People's possessions lay everywhere in the wreckage: beds, furniture, pots and pans, clothes, jars and cans of food, and everything imaginable besides. Special detachments went around collecting them and took them to depots for storage until their owners, if they were still alive, reclaimed them: in Cologne alone there were 150 such depots, most of which were subsequently themselves destroyed in air raids.[63] In this situation, with desperate and dispossessed people roaming the streets, the temptation to help oneself to some of these goods was often overwhelming. The penalties for those who were caught were severe. A decree issued on 5 September 1939 against 'national pests' (*Volksschädlinge*) prescribed death for theft under cover of the blackout. As a Hamburg newspaper noted on 19 August 1943, not long after the great air raids on the city,

The police and the courts are getting down to the job energetically and in continual session are succeeding ever more in giving their just deserts to all those who have selfishly exploited the distress of our comrades by looting. Anyone who loots and thereby offends in the most serious way against the community will be eradicated![64]

A minor, insignificant case of looting might lead to a period of one or two years' imprisonment in a state penitentiary, but repeated or large-scale thefts carried with them the sentence of death, particularly if the offender belonged to a clear-up detachment.

The Special Court at Bremen sentenced a man to fifteen years' in a penitentiary on 4 March 1943 on fifteen counts of stealing clothing, radio sets, food and other items from bomb-sites after dark and selling them on to a fence. The court noted he had previous convictions and declared him to be a dangerous habitual criminal. The prosecutor considered the sentence too lenient, however, and appealed for it to be increased to death by decapitation. The day before the appeal was due to be heard, the offender committed suicide.[65] In another case, heard on 23 January 1945, a labourer with ten previous convictions was sentenced to death for stealing from the bodies of people killed in an air raid the previous June. His haul consisted of a wristwatch, a pipe, a tin of tobacco, a shaving-brush, a bunch of keys, a pair of nail-scissors, two lighters and a cigarette-holder and case. He was executed on 15 March 1945.[66] Such cases came before the Special Courts with growing regularity. Thirty-two out of fifty-two death sentences passed by the Special Courts in Dortmund, Essen and Bielefeld in 1941 were for crimes against property; in 1943, a quarter of all death sentences passed in Germany as a whole were for property offences, the great majority of them looting from bomb-sites.[67] But this was a losing struggle. The more the fabric of Germany's cities was destroyed, the more the fabric of German society began to fall apart. In 1943 it began the transition from a 'people's community' to a 'society of ruins'. It was to end in 1945 in a state of almost complete dissolution.

IV

The successful bombing operations carried out by the Allies in the spring and summer of 1943 were a serious indictment of Göring's air defences. Not only his standing in the Nazi leadership but also his reputation in the population at large began to decline steeply. Soon jokes of all kinds were circulating about him. Since he had once boasted that he would change his name to Meier if so much as a single enemy bomb fell on the Fatherland, people now began habitually calling him 'Mr Meier'. However, the Reich Marshal, as Speer reported later, merely buried his head in the sand. When General Adolf Galland, in charge of the fighters, reported the alarming development that American fighter planes with added-on fuel tanks had been able to accompany bombers as far as Aachen, Göring dismissed the report. He himself was an old fighter-pilot and knew this was impossible. A few planes must have been blown east by the wind. When Galland persisted, noting that some fighters had been shot down and identified on the ground, Göring lost his temper: 'I herewith give you an official order that they weren't there!' he shouted. Galland, a long cigar clamped between his teeth, gave way with deliberate irony. 'Orders are orders, sir,' he replied with, as Speer noted, 'an unforgettable smile'. The raids were so serious that they left the Chief of Staff of the German Air Force, Hans Jeschonnek, in a state of deep depression. On 18 August 1943 he committed suicide, leaving a note saying that he did not want Göring to attend his funeral. Of course, the Reich Marshal could not avoid doing so, and indeed he laid a wreath on Hitler's behalf. But the suicide, coming after that of Ernst Udet two years before, was another indication that Göring's sublime complacency was driving his subordinates to despair.[68]

Instead of continuing their attacks on the Ruhr in 1943, however, the Allies turned their attention to Berlin. As well as being the Reich's capital city, it was also by some distance the largest industrial centre in Germany. But it was much further away from the English airfields than Hamburg or the Ruhr, and bombers had to travel a long and roundabout way to get there. Thus German defences had time to locate them. Berlin was also beyond the range of the most effective navigational aids because it was hidden by the curvature of the earth. Undaunted, more than 700 bombers flew over the capital on the night of 22–3 November 1943, dropping their payloads through heavy cloud, guided by radar. Although many missed their target, the raid destroyed a large number of familiar landmarks, including most of the major railway stations, and ironically also the former British and French Embassies. Watching a raid from a flak tower, Albert Speer had a grandstand view of 'the illumination of the parachute flares, which the Berliners called "Christmas trees", followed by flashes of explosions which were caught by the clouds of smoke, the innumerable probing searchlights, the excitement when a plane was caught and tried to escape the cone of light, the brief flaming torch when it was hit.' When day dawned, the city was shrouded in a cloud of smoke and dust rising to 20,000 feet.[69]

Over the next few months, Bomber Command attacked the capital a further eighteen times. In all, the raids killed more than 9,000 and made 812,000 people homeless. But the cost to the Allies was high. More than 3,300 British pilots and crew were killed, and nearly 1,000 had to bale out into captivity. In the raid of 24 March 1944, 10 per cent of the bombers were destroyed and many others hit. This was the last of these British raids. Earlier in the month, the Americans had begun to mount daylight attacks, which continued through April and May 1944.[70] By this time, the Americans had learned to reduce their losses by getting fighter planes to accompany the raids in order to deal with German defences in the air. But the fighters' limited range forced them to turn back at the German border. On 14 October 1943 a fleet of nearly 300 B-17s flew into the German Reich via Aachen. As soon as the escorting American fighters had turned back, a swarm of German fighter planes appeared, aiming cannon and rocket fire at the bombers, breaking up their formations then finishing them off singly. 220 American bombers reached Schweinfurt and caused further devastation to the ball-bearing factories, but altogether 60 were shot down and another 138 damaged. Similarly, in a raid on Nuremberg on 30 March 1944, 795 bombers, flying on a clear moonlit night, were identified by their vapour trails before they even got to Germany, and attacked by squadrons of night-fighters as they flew the long route towards their target. 95 were destroyed, or 11 per cent of those who had set out. Harris warned that such losses could not be sustained.[71]

Bombers clearly needed to have fighter escorts to deal with the German night-fighters. American P-38 Lightning and P-47 Thunderbolt fighter planes had already been fitted with extra fuel tanks under the wings, but the real difference was made by the P-51 Mustang, a plane built with an American frame and a British Rolls-Royce Merlin engine. Equipped with extra fuel tanks, it could fly up to 1,800 miles, allowing it to escort bombers all the way to Berlin and get back with fuel to spare. Soon thousands of these aircraft were rolling off the production lines. The first flew into Germany on a raid on Kiel in December 1943, and soon all bombing raids were escorted by squadrons of fighters that were fast and manoeuvrable enough to deal with their German counterparts despite the extra load of fuel they were carrying. Already in November 1943, German fighter-plane losses were beginning to climb as the new tactic began to be employed. In December nearly a quarter of the strength of the German fighter fleet was lost. Production could not keep pace with these losses, which were running at something like 50 per cent a month by the spring of 1944; aircraft factories too were affected by bombing raids, with production falling from 873 in July 1943 to 663 in December 1943. Moving fighter planes to the west to deal with the bombers denuded the Eastern Front, where by April 1944 the German air force had only 500 combat aircraft left, confronting more than 13,000 Soviet planes. The German Air Ministry thought that 5,000 planes a month would have to be produced to stand a chance of winning these confrontations. Instead, Allied bombers destroyed not only airplane factories but also oil refineries and fuel production facilities, leaving the German air force dependent on stockpiled fuel by June 1944. By this time, indeed, the German air force had effectively been defeated and the skies were open to a further escalation of the strategic bombing offensive.[72]

Of course, even with the reduction of German fighter defences to no more than a marginal threat, bomber squadrons still had to contend with anti-aircraft batteries in large numbers, and flying over German towns and cities continued to be a dangerous and often deadly business. But losses were reduced to numbers that Allied air force chiefs found acceptable, and were more than made good by a huge expansion of aircraft production in Britain and America. By March 1945 there were over 7,000 American bombers and fighter planes in operation, while the British were deploying more than 1,500 heavy bombers in virtually continual sorties across the whole of Germany. Of the 1.42 million tons of bombs dropped on Germany during the war, no fewer than 1.18 million tons fell between the end of April 1944 and the beginning of

May 1945, the war's final year. But it was not merely a matter of quantity. The decline of German defences allowed smaller fighter-bombers to come in and attack their targets with more precision than the Lancasters or Flying Fortresses ever could, and in the second half of 1944 they directed their attention at the transport system, attacking railways and communications hubs. By the end of the year, they had halved the number of goods journeys on the German railway system. Arms factories suffered even more severely than before. By the end of January 1945 Speer's Ministry calculated that the economy had produced 25 per cent fewer tanks than planned, 31 per cent fewer aircraft and 42 per cent fewer lorries, all because of the destruction wrought by bombing. Even had those production targets been met, they would in no way have matched the staggering military-industrial output of the United States, let alone the additional production of the war economy in Britain and the Soviet Union. Moreover, the need to combat the bombing absorbed more and more German resources, with a third of all artillery production going on anti-aircraft guns by 1944, and 2 million people engaged on anti-aircraft defence or repairing and clearing up after raids. German air superiority was lost on the Eastern Front, where fighters and bombers were no longer present in numbers sufficient to offer the ground forces the support they needed to defeat the Red Army, support that had played such a key role in the early stages of the war. Allied bombers were able to pulverize the roads, bridges and railways behind the Normandy beaches in 1944, making it impossible for the German army to bring up adequate reinforcements. Had the German air force retained the command of the skies, the invasion could not have taken place.[73]

It has been argued, therefore, that bombing helped save lives by shortening the war, and in particular that it saved Allied lives by weakening German resistance. Nevertheless, it also caused between 400,000 and half a million deaths in Germany's towns and cities, the overwhelming majority of them civilian. Of these people, some 11,000 were killed up to the end of 1942, perhaps 100,000 in 1943, 200,000 in 1944 and between 50,000 and 100,000 in the last months of the war, in 1945. Around 10 per cent were foreign workers and prisoners of war. All these figures are extremely approximate, but about their concentration in the last two years of the war there can be no doubt. On the Allied side, some 80,000 airmen were killed in the bombing raids, along with 60,000 British civilians in German raids, and quite possibly as many again in

German aerial attacks on Warsaw, Rotterdam, Belgrade, Leningrad, Stalingrad and other European cities. About 40 per cent of housing stock in German towns and cities with more than 20,000 inhabitants was destroyed; in some cities, like Hamburg and Cologne, the figure was as much as 70 per cent, and in some smaller towns like Paderborn or Giessen virtually every single dwelling was rendered uninhabitable. The devastation was enormous, and took many years to make good.[74]

The German dead were not mere 'collateral damage', to adopt the phrase made familiar by wars in later years and other places. Undermining civilian morale, even wreaking revenge on Germany and the Germans, unquestionably belonged among the aims of the strategic bombing offensive, although attacks on civilians have customarily been regarded as a war crime. Even if one does not accept that the entire bombing campaign was unnecessary, then it is at least arguable that it was continued longer than was strictly necessary, and conducted, especially in the final year of the war, in a manner that was too indiscriminate to be justifiable.[75] Arguments will no doubt continue to rage over this difficult question. What is undeniable, however, is that the bombing had a huge effect on civilian morale. The hope of some in Britain that it would inspire ordinary Germans to rise up against the Nazis and bring the war to an early end by an act of revolution was unrealistic. Most Germans affected by the bombing were too busy trying to survive amidst the ruins, to reconstruct their shattered homes and disrupted lives, and to find ways of avoiding getting killed to bother about things like revolution. Asked after the war what the hardest thing had been for civilians in Germany to put up with, 91 per cent said the bombing; and more than a third said that it had lowered people's morale, including their own.[76] It did even more than the defeats at Stalingrad and in North Africa to spread popular disillusion about the Nazi Party. One not untypical example in this respect can be seen in the correspondence of the paratrooper Martin Pöppel, by now serving in a unit fighting the invading Allied forces after D-Day. In 1944 he was receiving increasingly despairing letters from his wife at home in Germany. She could no longer understand or support the Nazis. 'What have they made of our beautiful, magnificent Germany?' she asked. 'It's enough to make you weep.' Allied bombs were destroying everything. It was surely time to call a halt to the war. 'Why do people let our soldiers go to their death uselessly, why do they let the rest of Germany be ruined, why all the misery, why?'[77]

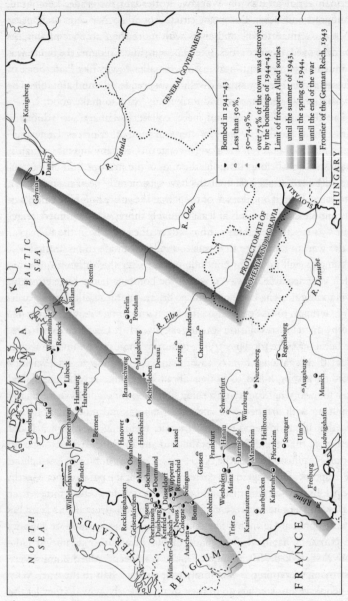

Bombed in 1941–43
- ◐ Less than 50%,
- ◖ 50–74.9%,
- ⬥ over 75% of the town was destroyed by the bombings of 1944–45

Limit of frequent Allied sorties
- until the summer of 1943,
- until the spring of 1944,
- until the end of the war

— Frontier of the German Reich, 1943

16. Allied Bombing Raids on German Cities, 1941–5

Goebbels's Propaganda Ministry poured out bile against the Allied bombing crews and their political masters. The Americans were gangsters, their air crews uncultivated mobsters taken out of the prisons. By contrast, the German media claimed, the British fliers were drawn mainly from the effete ranks of the aristocracy. Both, however, in the view propagated by the Nazi media, were in the service of Jewish conspirators, who were also manipulating Roosevelt and Churchill in their quest for the total destruction of Germany.[78] The propaganda did have an effect.[79] There were widespread reports from 1943 at the latest of people demanding reprisal attacks on London; but this was not so much in anger, rather in the belief that only this could prevent further raids on Germany and even defeat in the war in general.[80] 'Again and again,' reported the Security Service of the SS, 'one could hear: "If we don't do something soon, nothing will help us any more," or "We can't watch much longer as everything we have is smashed to bits." '[81]

In 1944 there was some popular anger against the pilots and crew of Allied bombers, under the psychological pressure of constant alarms, raids, death and destruction, and encouraged by Goebbels's mass media. It began to express itself in violence against Allied airmen who were forced to bale out after their plane had been hit. On 26 August 1944 seven American airmen who had baled out over Rüsselsheim were beaten to death by an angry crowd, while on 24 March 1945 a British airman who landed by parachute in a field near Bochum was attacked by a soldier with his rifle-butt. He fell over and was surrounded by a crowd who kicked him, hurting him badly. Someone tried to shoot the airman but the gun jammed, so he was dragged away until a member of the crowd produced a hammer and beat him to death. Three other British airmen who had also landed in the area were arrested by the Gestapo, tortured and then shot. One local works fireman who protested to his workmates against these murders was denounced, arrested and shot by the Gestapo. Not only did the police fail to intervene to stop such incidents, but anyone who did was likely to be arrested and tried for 'forbidden contact with prisoners of war'. The Party Regional Leader for Southern Westphalia ordered on 25 February 1945 that pilots 'who have been shot down are not to be protected from the people's anger'. Altogether at least 350 Allied airmen were lynched in the last two years of the war and a further sixty or so injured without being killed. In a particularly notorious incident, when fifty-eight British airmen had escaped on 24 March 1944 from a prisoner-of-war camp near Sagan in Lower Saxony, all those who were recaptured were shot by the Gestapo on the explicit orders of Heinrich Himmler. Yet these incidents have to be kept in perspective. The total number of Allied airmen who were lynched or shot by the Gestapo made up no more than 1 per cent of the total captured.[82] The hatred that animated such actions was a product above all of the last phase of the bombing, and was, as the Security Service of the SS noted, not really present before 1944. The Security Service's observers noted calls among the population, especially those who had been bombed out of their homes, for the British to be gassed or 'annihilated', but added that 'hate-filled-sounding words against England are often more an expression of desperation and the belief that the annihilation of England is the only rescue . . . *One cannot speak of hatred for the English people as a whole.*' And they quoted one woman who had lost her home in a raid as saying: 'It hurts me that all my things have gone for good. But that's war. Against the English, no, I don't have anything against them.'[83]

THE LONG RETREAT

I

The sharp decline of morale amongst the German population in 1943 was not just the result of the intensification of Allied bombing raids on German cities, it also reflected a series of dramatic reverses in other areas of the war as well. Amongst these, one of the most disheartening was in North Africa. In the summer of 1942 Field Marshal Erwin Rommel had succeeded in capturing the key North African seaport of Tobruk and driving the British back into Egypt. But difficulties in supplying his troops by either land or sea weakened Rommel's position, and the British stood their ground at El Alamein, where they prepared deep defensive positions and massed their forces ready for a counter-attack. On 23 October 1942, under yet another new general, the meticulous Bernard Montgomery, the British attacked the German forces with over twice the number of infantry and tanks that Rommel could assemble. Over twelve days they inflicted a decisive defeat on them. Rommel lost 30,000 men captured in his headlong retreat across the desert. Little over two weeks later the Allies, their command of the Mediterranean virtually unchallenged, landed 63,000 men, equipped with 430 tanks, in Morocco and Algeria. The German bid to gain control of North Africa and penetrate from there to the oilfields of the Middle East had failed. Rommel returned to Germany on sick leave in March 1943.[84] Defeat in North Africa turned into humiliation in mid-May, when 250,000 Axis troops, half of them German, surrendered to the Allies.[85] Its complete failure to disturb British control over Egypt and the Middle East denied the Third Reich access to key sources of oil. These failures once more signalled not only the fact that the British were determined not to give in, but also the massive strength of the far-flung British

Empire, backed to an increasing degree by the material resources of the United States.[86] Reflecting privately on these failures in 1944, Field Marshal Rommel still believed that, if he had been provided with 'more motorized formations and a secure supply line', he could have seized the Suez Canal, thus disrupting British supplies, and gone on to secure the oilfields of the Middle East, Persia and even Baku on the Caspian Sea. But it was not to be. Bitterly, he concluded that 'the war in North Africa was decided by the weight of Anglo-American material. In fact, since the entry of America into the war, there has been very little prospect of our achieving ultimate victory.'[87] It was a view that many ordinary Germans shared. Rommel was a brilliant general, the student Lore Walb confided to her diary. But, she went on: 'What can he do with limited forces and little ammunition?' After the recapture of Tobruk by the Allies in November 1942, she was beginning to wonder if this was 'the beginning of the end', and a few days later she began to fear that the entire war was being lost: 'Will Heaven then permit us to be annihilated???'[88]

The Third Reich was now beginning to lose its allies. In March 1943, King Boris III of Bulgaria decided that the Germans were not going to win the war. Meeting with Hitler in June, he thought it politic to agree to the German dictator's request for Bulgarian troops to replace German forces in north-east Serbia so that they could be redeployed to the Eastern Front. But he refused to render any further assistance, and behind the scenes he began to put out peace feelers to the Allies, rightly fearing that the Soviets would disregard Bulgaria's official stance of neutrality in the wider conflict. Hitler continued to put pressure on him, meeting with him again in August 1943. But before anything could come of their talks, events took an unexpected turn. Shortly after arriving back in Sofia, Boris fell ill, dying on 28 August 1942, aged only forty-nine. In the feverish climate of the times, rumours immediately spread that he had been poisoned. An autopsy carried out in the early 1990s revealed, however, that he had died of an infarction of the left ventricle of the heart. He was succeeded by Simeon II, who was only a boy, and the regency largely continued Boris's policy of disengaging from the German side, spurred on by increasing numbers of Allied bombing raids on Sofia, starting in November 1943. Popular opposition to the war spread rapidly, and armed partisan bands formed under the leadership of the Soviet-inspired Fatherland Front, causing increasing disruption; British agents arrived to assist them, but the partisan movement failed to make much headway, and some of the British agents were betrayed and shot. Nevertheless, under these pressures, the government began to backtrack, repealing anti-Jewish legislation, and declaring full neutrality the following year.[89]

Far more alarming to many Germans were the dramatic events that unfolded in Italy after their defeat in North Africa. On 10 July 1943 Anglo-American forces, ferried across by sea and backed by airborne assaults on defensive positions behind the beaches, landed in Sicily, which was occupied by a combination of Italian and German troops. Despite extensive preparations, the attack was far from perfectly executed. The landing forces mistook the planes flying overhead for enemy aircraft and started firing on them, weakening the airborne thrust. The British commander Montgomery split his forces in the east into a coastal and an inland column, as a result of which they only made slow progress against heavy German resistance. Syracuse was captured, but because of the delays in the British advance, the Germans managed to evacuate most of their troops across to the mainland. Still, the island eventually fell to the Allied forces. Ominously for the Italian Fascist dictator Mussolini, too, the citizens of Palermo had waved white flags at the invading Americans, and there were growing indications that ordinary Italians no longer wanted to continue fighting. Hitler visited Mussolini in northern Italy on 18 July 1943 to try to bolster his confidence, but his two-hour monologue depressed the Italian dictator and made him feel he lacked the will to carry on. The dictator's prestige and popularity had never recovered from the catastrophic defeats of 1941, most notably in Greece. His relationship with Hitler had changed fundamentally after this: even Mussolini himself referred to Fascist Italy as no more than the 'rear light' of the Axis, and he soon acquired a new nickname: the Regional Leader of Italy. Hitler, always late to bed, had taken to sending him messages in the middle of the night, obliging him to be woken up to receive them; and the Italian dictator began to complain that he was becoming fed up with being summoned to meetings with him like a waiter by a bell.[90]

While Italian troops continued to fight, they were losing their faith in the cause for which they were being asked to lay down their lives. Mussolini himself began to complain privately that the Italians were letting him down. Distrusting the ability of the Italians to carry on fighting, Hitler had already made plans to take over Italy and the territories it occupied in southern France, Yugoslavia, Greece and Albania. He put Rommel in charge of the operation.[91] As Allied planes began to bomb Italian cities, the prospect of an invasion of the Italian mainland by the Allies became imminent. German forces moved into the peninsula, indicating by their mere presence whose cause the Italians were now fighting for. Serious opposition to Mussolini's dictatorship surfaced for the first time in many years and came to a head towards the end of July. In February 1943 Mussolini had carried out a purge of leading figures in his increasingly discontented Fascist Party. It had been growing ever more critical of his political and military leadership. This was virtually his last decisive act. Disoriented and demoralized, he began suffering from stomach pains that sapped his energy. He spent much of his time dallying with his mistress Clara Petacci, translating classic Italian fiction into German, or devoting himself to minor administrative issues. Since he was not only Commander-in-Chief of the armed forces but also held several major ministries, this meant that a vacuum began to appear at the centre of power. The sacked party bosses began to intrigue against him. Those in the Fascist Grand Council who either wanted more radical measures taken to mobilize the population or sought to place the further conduct of the war entirely in the hands of the military decided to strip him of most of his powers at a meeting held on 24–5 July 1943 (the first since 1939). Few details were made known of this dramatic, ten-hour marathon. The leading moderate Fascist, Dino Grandi, who proposed the motion, later confessed that he had been carrying a live grenade throughout, in case of emergencies. But it was not necessary. Mussolini's reaction to the criticisms levelled at him was feeble and confused. He hardly seemed to know what was going on and failed to put a counter-proposal, leading many to think he had no objections to Grandi's motion. In the early hours of the morning, it was voted through by nineteen votes to seven.[92]

The Grand Council's vote played right into the hands of the leading military men, whose dissatisfaction with the war prompted them to get the King to dismiss Mussolini (as he was constitutionally entitled to do, since Mussolini's formal position was still that of Prime Minister), and have him arrested the very next day. There was no resistance, and the now ex-dictator was carried off to prison without any serious protest. Only one Fascist zealot is known to have committed suicide on hearing the news. As Mussolini's successor, the monarch appointed Marshal

Pietro Badoglio to lead a new government. The Fascist Party more or less fell to pieces under the impact of these dramatic events, and was swiftly declared illegal. Badoglio and the King assured the Germans that Italy would stay in the war, and as a token of goodwill, or perhaps a recognition of the inevitable, the new government allowed them to take over key Alpine passes and other significant positions and begin pouring large numbers of troops and equipment into the peninsula. While the Germans withdrew their forces from Corsica and Sardinia, they also used the troops they had extricated from Sicily to start preparations to defend the southern part of the mainland. Amidst a rapidly disintegrating situation, Badoglio began secretly negotiating an armistice with the Allies, which he signed on 3 September 1943. The same day, Allied troops landed in Calabria, in Italy's far south, and then on 9 September 1943 at Salerno, further up the coast. On the previous day, 8 September 1943, the Italian government announced its surrender to the Allies. Badoglio, the King and the government fled south, into Allied protection. Ordinary Germans at home were reported as expressing their disappointment that the Italian leaders had not been captured and hanged. Neither the Italian army nor the Italian government had any instructions for the million or more Italian troops still under arms.[93]

Faced with battle-hardened German troops taking up positions all over the peninsula, Italian soldiers flung down their weapons, threw off their uniforms, or simply surrendered. Only a few units tried to resist, most notably on the Italian-controlled island of Cephalonia, off the Greek coast, where fighting went on for a week and ended with the German occupiers executing more than 6,000 Italian soldiers and sailors, shooting almost all the Italian officers in batches over a four-hour period of cold-blooded carnage. Half a million Italian servicemen were lucky enough to find themselves in areas already under Allied control. They were disarmed and eventually sent home. But 650,000 Italian soldiers were seized by the German military as prisoners of war, and then deported to Germany as forced labourers in December 1943. Their situation was far from enviable. Goebbels declared that the Italians were 'a Gypsy people gone to pot'. Hitler thought they were utterly decadent. Many Germans were bitter at what they regarded as Italy's betrayal of the Axis, which they compared with similar events in the First World War, when Italy had also changed sides. The Security Service of the SS reported that there are *marked* feelings of hatred in all parts of the Reich and all strata of the population *against* one people, namely *the* Italians. Basically people don't hold the enmity of our real opponents against them. It is felt to be a matter of fate. But people can never forgive the Italians for the fact that after they have gone to great lengths to assure us through their chosen representatives of their friendship, they have now betrayed us so 'despicably' a second time. The *hatred* against the Italian people springs from the most profound feelings.[94]

The German authorities treated the Italians particularly harshly, exacting from them a severe revenge for Italy's repudiation of the German alliance. In terms of food rations and general treatment they were placed on the same footing as Soviet workers. At the Krupp factory in Essen, the average weight loss of the Italian prisoner-of-war workers was 9 kilograms in the first three months of 1944; some lost as much as 22 kilos. Death rates were higher than for any other group except Soviet workers.[95] Up to 50,000 Italian prisoners of war died in these conditions. At seventy-seven deaths per thousand, this was five times the death rate of British prisoners of war; it was, indeed, the highest death rate of all western prisoners of war in Germany.[96]

In Italy itself, the Germans' outrage at the defection of the Italians found expression in numerous acts of gratuitous vandalism and vengeance. On 26 September 1943, after encountering some minor resistance as they marched into Naples, German troops poured kerosene over the shelves of the university library and set it alight, destroying 50,000 books and manuscripts, many of them irreplaceable. Two days later, while the library was still burning, German soldiers discovered 80,000 more books and manuscripts from various archives deposited for safe keeping in Nola and set them alight, along with the contents of the Civic Museum, including forty-five paintings. The German military commander of Italy, the air force Field Marshal Albert Kesselring, hurriedly organized the evacuation of art treasures from museums in Florence and other cities likely to become battlegrounds if the Allies succeeded in advancing up the peninsula. Soldiers and SS men took jewellery, furs and silver from palaces and country houses, or occupied them as billets, turfing out the owners. The Marchesa Origo, an Anglo-American woman married to an Italian aristocrat, arriving at her villa after the occupying German troops had retreated, described the scene that greeted her eyes:

The Germans have stolen everything that took their fancy, blankets, clothes, shoes and toys, as well, of course, as anything valuable or eatable, and have deliberately destroyed much of sentimental or personal value . . . In the dining room the table is still laid, and there are traces of a drunken repast: empty wine-bottles and smashed glasses lie beside a number of my summer hats (which presumably have been tried on), together with boot-trees, toys, overturned furniture and W.C. paper . . . The lavatory is filled to the brim with filth, and decaying meat, lying on every table, adds to the foul smell. There are innumerable flies. In our bedroom, too, it is the same.[97]

Her experience, suffering from the indifference of tired and exhausted German troops, many of whom had earlier fought on the Eastern Front, was typical of many Italian property-owners at this time.

In political terms, the Germans did not stand idly by. In September 1943 the deposed dictator Mussolini had been taken on the new government's orders first of all to the island of Ponza, then to another island, and finally to an isolated ski hotel in the Apennine mountains of central Italy. Depressed and ill, he tried on one occasion to kill himself. In the meantime, Hitler had begun organizing a search and rescue operation, determined that his ally should not fall into Anglo-American hands, with all the possibilities for bad publicity and embarrassing revelations that this might entail. He was aware of the fact that, as the SS Security Service was reporting, many Germans thought that, if Mussolini's regime could collapse overnight, then so too could Hitler's. The Italian dictator's mystique somehow had to be restored. And something had to be done to dampen the disastrous effects of his overthrow on popular morale in Germany, where, it was reported at the end of July, people were regarding it as another turning-point in the war, and the majority were now depressed and saw 'no real way out any more'.[98] Mussolini's location was not hard to find – it was revealed by intercepted radio traffic. The hotel was staffed with a large force of armed military police. But they were under instructions to act with extreme caution, and in any case the occupation of Italy by the Germans made them extremely unwilling to offend the peninsula's new rulers. The way seemed open for a rescue operation.[99]

On 12 September 1943, after carrying out air reconnaissance of the area, an SS commando unit consisting of paratroopers led by Otto Skorzeny, an Austrian SS officer, flew silently over the peak on gliders and parachuted down to the hotel, leaving the planes to crash into the nearby mountains. In five minutes they had overrun the complex without firing a shot. Skorzeny found Mussolini and announced he had been sent by Hitler. Clearing a landing-strip on a small, sloping meadow in front of the hotel, the commandos called up a small Stork reconnaissance and liaison aircraft, which was able to land at very low speeds: Mussolini was bundled in and taken first to Rome and thence to Hitler's field headquarters at Rastenburg. Hitler was disappointed when he was confronted by an obviously broken man. But he persuaded the former Italian dictator to set up a puppet regime in northern Italy, based in the town of Salò. Here, prompted by the Nazis, he had five of the leading Fascists who had voted against him on the Grand Council, including his son-in-law and former Foreign Minister Galeazzo Ciano, tried for treason and executed. His regime soon degenerated into a morass of violence, corruption and terror. Meanwhile, Skorzeny's daring exploit cheered people up in Germany, as indeed it had been intended to. It showed, people were reported as saying, that Germany was still capable of getting out of a tricky situation by improvising in grand style.[100]

II

The German takeover and the establishment of the puppet Fascist regime at Salò plunged Italy's 43,000 Jews, of whom 34,000 were located in the German zone, into a crisis far worse than they had so far experienced. They had been subjected to considerable official discrimination by the Fascist regime since the introduction of racial laws in 1938 along the lines of the Nuremberg Laws in Germany. Yet antisemitism had never been very intense or widespread in Italy. In Greece, southern France and Croatia, indeed, the Italian army had gone to some lengths to protect Jews from murder and deportation. Now such protection was no longer possible. To begin with, the Germans concentrated on robbery. Shortly after the German occupation of Rome, the SS Security Service chief in the Italian capital, Herbert Kappler, ordered the Jewish community to deliver 50 kilos of gold within thirty-six hours. If they did this, he assured the community leaders, they would not be deported. And indeed, although Himmler had already telephoned Kappler on 12 September 1943 to tell him to organize the deportation of the Italian Jews, the

Security Service boss himself was of the opinion that the Italian police posed a far greater security threat, and intended if possible to devote his own rather limited manpower to dealing with them first. While the Jewish community leaders gathered the gold, delivering it to Kappler for transportation to the Reich Security Head Office in Berlin on 7 October 1943, Alfred Rosenberg's staff arrived in the city and began loading the contents of the community's library onto two railway wagons for transportation to Germany. This open robbery caused widespread alarm amongst Rome's Jews, who were aghast at the impunity with which it was carried out. It did not seem to bode well for their own safety. Soon, indeed, fifty-four Jews were murdered by SS troops in the far north, in the area of Lake Maggiore, and deportations began from Merano and Trieste. And on 6 October 1943, Theodor Dannecker arrived in Rome with an armed escort, under orders from Berlin to override Kappler and organize the arrest and transport of the Jews to Auschwitz for extermination.[101]

His arrival caused considerable concern among the leading German officials in Rome. The acting representative of the German Foreign Office, Eitel Möllhausen, and the head of the German armed forces in the area, Field Marshal Albert Kesselring, joined forces with Kappler to press the Foreign Office in Berlin to use the Jews on fortification work instead of being 'liquidated', as Möllhausen incautiously put it in a telegram sent to Berlin on 6 October 1943. Moreover, the newly appointed German Ambassador to the Vatican, Ernst von Weizsäcker, warned the Foreign Office that Pope Pius XII, under whose windows, as it were, the deportation was to take place, might issue a public protest; in order to avoid this, he too advised that it might be preferable to employ the Jews on labour projects in Italy instead. Hitler's reaction was not slow in coming. On 9 October 1943 the Foreign Office told Möllhausen in no uncertain terms that Ribbentrop insisted, 'on the basis of a Leader instruction', the Jews of Rome were to be taken away and he was to 'keep out of all questions concerning Jews', which were the business of the SS.[102] This effectively squashed the opposition. With the support of regular German troops, Dannecker's SS men arrested 1,259 Roman Jews on 16 October 1943, including 200 children under the age of ten. The majority of those arrested were women. After releasing twenty-nine of the prisoners because they were not Italian, or they were 'mixed-race' or married to non-Jews, Dannecker shipped them off to

Auschwitz. Fifteen of them survived the war. Many other Jews went into hiding, assisted by non-Jewish Italians who were outraged by the action. Several thousand Jews found refuge in the Vatican and in monasteries and convents in other parts of Rome, but the predicted public protest from the Pope did not materialize; it might have given a lead to Italians and caused the Germans to stop their action for fear of arousing public opposition. But the Pope was nervous that an outright condemnation might endanger the position of the Church or even, indeed, the Vatican itself. An article that subsequently appeared in the official Vatican organ, the *Roman Observer*, praising the Pope for his attempts to mitigate the suffering caused by the war was cast in such vague and general terms that, as Weizsäcker noted, very few people indeed would interpret it as a reference to the Jewish question at all.[103]

In Mussolini's rump Fascist state in north Italy, the government ordered all Jews to be interned in concentration camps, and the police began arresting Jews in Venice in December 1943 and again in August and October 1944, taking them out of an old people's home and a hospital as well as their own houses. After the second and third of these raids, which took place, unlike the first, with German participation, the weakest of the internees were killed and the rest deported to Auschwitz. Altogether another 3,800 Jews were taken to Auschwitz in 1944, while another 4,000 Jews and partisans were rounded up by Odilo Globocnik, who had transferred from the east, on the Adriatic coast and killed at a concentration camp near Trieste, some of them in a mobile gas van.[104] Nevertheless, some 80 per cent of Italy's Jews survived the war, not least thanks to help from ordinary, non-Jewish Italians.[105] The German occupation led to the immediate formation of partisan groups, numbering 10,000 fighters by the end of 1943 and 100,000 by October 1944. Roughly half of them were Communists, and there was little overall unity or co-ordination between the others. Their activities spawned a variety of counter-organizations inspired by the Salò regime; they roamed the countryside, hunting down the regime's opponents and carrying out bloody reprisals. SS units joined in, and in one notorious incident on 24 March 1944 they rounded up 335 people, including seventy-two Jews, in Rome, took them out to the Ardeatine caves, a labyrinth of early Christian catacombs, made them kneel down, and shot them all in the back of the neck as a reprisal for a daring partisan attack the day before. Other massacres followed, all of them with the same pretext, including one in which 771 people were shot at Marzabotto. Altogether, it has been estimated, nearly 45,000 partisans were killed in shoot-outs with Fascist or German police, paramilitary, SS and army units, and nearly 10,000 people were executed in reprisals.[106] Among the partisans caught up in these actions was the young industrial chemist Primo Levi, who had fled to the Alpine foothills to avoid arrest and then joined a group that called itself 'Justice and Liberty'. Captured by Fascist militia, he admitted to being Jewish and was taken to the internment camp for Jews at Fossoli, near Modena, and thence to Auschwitz, where he survived for several months thanks to his knowledge of German and the help of a fellow Italian prisoner. In November 1944 Levi was transferred to Monowitz, where his scientific expertise was put to use on the buna project. After the war, Levi's reminiscences and reflections, gathered in his book *If This Is a Man* and other publications, attracted worldwide attention for the detail and subtlety of their eyewitness account.[107]

Meanwhile, Allied troops continued to fight their way slowly up the peninsula. In their path lay the Pontine marshes, which Mussolini had drained at huge expense during the 1930s, converting them into farmland, settling them with 100,000 First World War veterans and their families, and building five new towns and eighteen villages on the site. The Germans determined to return them to their earlier state, to slow the Allied advance and at the same time wreak further revenge on the treacherous Italians. Not long after the Italian surrender, the area was visited by Erich Martini and Ernst Rodenwaldt, two medical specialists in malaria who worked at the Military Medical Academy in Berlin. Both men were backed by Himmler's Ancestral Heritage research organization in the SS; Martini was on the advisory board of its research institute at Dachau. The two men directed the German army to turn off the pumps that kept the former marshes dry, so that by the end of the winter they were covered in water to a depth of 30 centimetres once more. Then, ignoring the appeals of Italian medical scientists, they put the pumps into reverse, drawing sea-water into the area, and destroyed the tidal gates keeping the sea out at high tide. On their orders German troops dynamited many of the pumps and carted off the rest to Germany, wrecked the equipment used to keep the drainage channels free of vegetation and mined the area around them, ensuring that the damage they caused would be long-lasting.[108]

The purpose of these measures was above all to reintroduce malaria into the marshes, for Martini himself had discovered in 1931 that only one kind of mosquito could survive and breed equally well in salt, fresh or brackish water, namely *anopheles labranchiae*, the vector of malaria. As a result of the flooding, the freshwater species of mosquito in the Pontine marshes were destroyed; virtually all of the mosquitoes now breeding furiously in the 98,000 acres of flooded land were carriers of the disease, in contrast to the situation in 1940, when they were on the way to being eradicated. Just to make sure the disease took hold, Martini and Rodenwaldt's team had all the available stocks of quinine, the drug used to combat it, confiscated and taken to a secret location in Tuscany, far away from the marshes. In order to minimize the number of eyewitnesses, the Germans had evacuated the entire population of the marshlands, allowing them back only when their work had been completed. With their homes flooded or destroyed, many had to sleep in the open, where they quickly fell victim to the vast swarms of *anopheles* mosquitoes now breeding in the clogged drainage canals and bomb-craters of the area. Officially registered cases of malaria spiralled from just over 1,200 in 1943 to nearly 55,000 the following year, and 43,000 in 1945: the true number in the area in 1944 was later reckoned to be nearly double the officially recorded figure. With no quinine available, and medical services in disarray because of the war and the effective collapse of the Italian state, the impoverished inhabitants of the area, now suffering from malnutrition as well because of the destruction of their farmland and food supplies, fell victim to malaria. It had been deliberately reintroduced as an act of biological warfare, directed not only at Allied troops who might pass through the region, but also against the quarter of a million Italians who lived there, people now treated by the Germans no longer as allies but as racial inferiors whose act of treachery in deserting the Axis cause deserved the severest possible punishment.[109]

III

The Allied invasion of Italy was made possible by what had by now become a complete Allied domination of the Mediterranean Sea. In 1942–3 the British and Americans were able to land their armies in North Africa, Sicily and Italy with impunity. The German and Italian navies were unable to attack them. During the 1930s, Hitler had intended to build a large surface fleet, but the fate of the relatively few ships that had been constructed by 1939 was not encouraging. Early in the war, the British Royal Navy outmanoeuvred the German pocket battleship *Count Spee* and forced it to scuttle off the coast of Uruguay. Another Royal Navy unit boarded a German prison ship, the *Altmark*, off Norway on 16 February 1940 and freed 300 captured British sailors. More German ships were destroyed in the invasion of Norway, as we have seen. The German navy never managed to build an aircraft carrier, so aerial attacks on British shipping were limited by the range of land-based bombers. Aircraft based in Norway did attack convoys en route for Russia's ports in the Arctic, but they were in short supply. The damage had to be done by German ships. So the commander of the German navy, Grand Admiral Raeder, sent out capital ships to attack the British. But they met with mixed fortunes. A new battleship, the *Bismarck*, sank the British cruiser *Hood* and badly mauled the battleship *Prince of Wales*, but it was located by a British flying boat and sunk on 27 May 1941. The pocket battleship *Lützow* was torpedoed on 13 June 1941, while the battleships *Scharnhorst* and *Gneisenau* were damaged by British mines while slipping through the English Channel on their way from France to Norway early the following year, and were effectively put out of action. A British commando raid on the port of St Nazaire destroyed the only Atlantic dock capable of repairing the one remaining battleship, *Tirpitz*, which was repeatedly attacked in its Norwegian bolt-hole until it was hit by a British mini-submarine raid in September 1943 and then put permanently out of action by bombing. The lessons were clear. Conventional naval forces would not succeed. Grand Admiral Raeder, who had continued to advocate surface attacks throughout this period, was summarily dismissed on 30 January 1943 and replaced by Admiral Karl Dönitz, commander of the submarine fleet, who only just managed to dissuade Hitler from decommissioning all the German navy's remaining big ships and using their guns for coastal defence.[110]

Hitler had in fact long since focused resources on the construction of U-boats. But, in the early part of the war, hampered by shortages of essential raw materials such as copper and rubber, and by the concentration of resources on planning for the land invasion of France, the ambitious plans of Dönitz to construct 600 U-boats had stood no chance of being realized. In fact, only twenty were built between the outbreak of the war and the summer of 1940. The infiltration of a submarine into the British naval base at Scapa Flow, where it sank the battleship *Royal Oak*, was a spectacular propaganda coup. But far more serious was the fact that the U-boats, few in number though they were, immediately launched submarine attacks on Allied shipping in an attempt to disrupt supplies. They were helped by their success in breaking the codes into which the British encrypted their radio transmissions. By March 1940 they had sunk nearly 680,000 tons of British shipping. This caused serious alarm in London. Yet this was only a fraction of the total. Losses, breakdowns and lengthy periods in port for repairs meant that there were only twenty-five U-boats operating in the Altantic by the summer of 1940. This was nowhere near sufficient to cut off Britain's transatlantic supply lines.[111]

As well as being few in number, German submarines were also not much more technically advanced than they had been in the First World War. They still had to sail mostly on the surface, where they moved slowly and could easily be spotted by enemy planes; diving was only possible for relatively short periods of time. They were also disadvantaged by their lack of air reconnaissance support, so that they had to find the ships themselves. The British set up a convoy system almost immediately, providing destroyer protection for vulnerable merchant ships. Scanning the horizon anxiously for the tell-tale columns of smoke from British ships rising faintly over the horizon, German submariners had to take visual aim before releasing their torpedoes. Diving was a defensive tactic, a last-resort measure undertaken to evade the attentions of the accompanying destroyers and their depth-charges. It was easy to be spotted, and only a few losses among the U-boat fleet would severely damage the attempt to destroy Britain's seaborne supply lines.[112] A really major construction campaign might have given the U-boats the upper hand. They were far cheaper to build than surface warships. Hitler ordered the rate of construction to be stepped up to twenty-five sub-marines a month in July 1940. But the effects were slow in coming through. By the end of the year, an observer like the intellectual soldier Hans Meier-Welcker was forced to admit: 'We cannot break English sea-power.'[113] Other, more senior, figures agreed. A short time after-wards, Hitler changed priorities back to the army, and by March 1941 only seventy-two additional submarines had been delivered. Over the same period, the twenty-odd U-boats cruising the Atlantic at any one time none the less managed to sink more than 2 million tons of British shipping. However, the convoy system was then reinforced, and the British succeeded in deciphering German radio codes, so that losses had fallen to below 100,000 tons a month by the summer of 1941.[114]

In the first months after war was declared on the USA, German submarines lurking off the American coast and around the Caribbean took advantage of the Americans' failure to dim the lights of coastal towns to sink large quantities of supply ships setting out across the Atlantic without armed naval escort. By the end of August 1942, 485 ships had been sunk, totalling more than two and a half million tons. For most of 1942, until it was finally broken in December 1942, a new German cipher prevented the British from decoding naval messages while the Germans for their part were able to decipher British radio traffic. In November 1942 alone 860,000 tons of Allied shipping were sunk, 720,000 of them by submarines. By this time, the number of U-boats at sea had increased from twenty-two in January 1942 to more than 100. Already on 27 June 1942 the Arctic convoy PQ17, carrying military supplies to the Soviet Union, had been largely destroyed by German planes and submarines with the loss of twenty-six out of thirty-nine ships after the naval authorities in London had ordered it to scatter in the erroneous belief that the battleship *Tirpitz* had left port to attack it. Many lessons were learned from this debacle, and after a short break the Arctic convoys resumed in September 1942, this time with a greater degree of success. However, attempts to bomb the shipyards where the U-boats were built and the harbours where they rested proved a costly failure. The 'Battle of the Atlantic', as it was dubbed, reached a climax in the first four months of 1943 in a series of hard-fought engagements between convoy escorts and German submarines, of which there were now more than 120 in the North Atlantic.[115] The outcome seemed in the balance.

But the British were able to decode German naval signals traffic again from December 1942 and route their convoys away from the waiting U-boats.[116] The submarines were forced to search for Allied convoys mainly by sailing in loosely knit groups ('wolf-packs') which converged when one of them spotted the enemy. Shore-to-ship radio traffic with the convoys was also intercepted by the German navy from 1941 until June 1943, when a new code was introduced, thus helping the submarines find the convoys or at least work out where they were heading. But the radio signals used by the wolf-pack U-boats to communicate with one another were intercepted by the convoy escort ships. The submarines could not send and receive radio signals while submerged, and when under water they could only move very slowly, so they spent most of their time on the surface, making them vulnerable to location and attack. Under water, they could be located by echo-sounding and damaged by depth-charges. Submarines generally attacked from the surface and at night, so the convoy escorts developed a searchlight system to locate them. From 1943 small aircraft carriers accompanied the convoys. This made a huge difference, not least to the Arctic convoys. In February 1943 for the first time the Allies, above all the Americans, were building more ship tonnage than the Germans were sinking. By May 1943 U-boat losses were running at one a day and submarine commanders were becoming reluctant to engage the enemy. On 24 May 1943 Admiral Dönitz conceded defeat and ordered the submarine fleet to move out of the North Atlantic. U-boats continued to be constructed in substantial numbers, new, more advanced types were commissioned, and the war at sea continued, but the threat to Allied supplies across the Atlantic and through the Arctic Ocean was never really significant again.[117]

'HELL HAS BROKEN OUT'

I

On the Eastern Front, the defeat of the German Sixth Army at Stalingrad marked the beginning of a long retreat that was only to end with total defeat in Berlin just over two years later. It was the decisive turning-point of the war in the east.[118] Even before Paulus and his bedraggled forces had surrendered, Army Group A (the other half of Army Group South) was also getting into trouble. In the summer of 1942 Army Group A had made rapid advances through the Caucasus as the Red Army retreated while the Soviet generals desperately tried to organize reinforcements of men and supplies. By the early autumn, the German armies were exhausted, reduced in numbers, dependent on long and precarious supply lines, and weakened by being split into a number of different spearheads. By mid-September 1942, despite their rapid advances, they were still hundreds of miles away from their objectives, the oilfields at Grozny and Baku. The commander of Army Group A, Field Marshal Wilhelm List, concluded that he simply did not have the resources to drive the Russians back across the mountain passes before winter set in. Told of the situation, Hitler flew into a towering rage and sacked List, temporarily taking over command of Army Group A himself, though he did not trouble to visit the scene of operations. Hitler still thought that he would be able to conquer the Caspian oilfields. But even he eventually had to admit that this would not happen in 1942. The Red Army finally organized itself enough to make a stand. For many German soldiers, the advance through the fragrant orchards, the vineyards and the maize fields, with snow-capped mountains on the horizon, had seemed almost idyllic. But at the city of Ordzhonikide, they met with insurmountable resistance. 'None of us,' wrote one young artilleryman on 2 November, 'has experienced days such as these. Hell has broken out.'[119] 'What we have experienced in the last two weeks,' he wrote on 14 November 1942, 'was dreadful.'[120] Surrounded by Red Army troops, the German forces fought their way out; but there was nowhere to go but backwards. The offensive was not just stalled, it was over.[121]

Retreat now became the only option, as the Soviet thrust to the west of Stalingrad not only cut off Paulus's Sixth Army but also threatened other German positions. Army Group A would be isolated as well if Soviet forces managed to capture Rostov and seal off the Caucasus on the northern side. As he became increasingly preoccupied with Stalingrad, Hitler appointed Field Marshal Ewald von Kleist to command Army Group A. Kleist immediately saw the danger of being cut off. On 27 December 1942 Manstein persuaded Zeitzler to ask Hitler for permission to withdraw from the Caucasus. Hitler reluctantly gave his assent. Perhaps he realized that with the Sixth Army tied up in Stalingrad and key units sent earlier to the north, it would not be possible to get reinforcements to the Caucasus. Shortly afterwards, he changed his mind; but it was too late: Zeitzler had telephoned through the order and the retreat had begun. Pursued by relatively weak Soviet forces, the German troops marched all the way back to Rostov-on-Don, and then, as the Red Army advanced westwards in the wake of its victory at Stalingrad, the Germans were forced to retreat even further.[122] The retreat depressed many of the troops. 'You could almost break into tears,' wrote Albert Neuhaus to his wife on 16 February 1943, 'when you think what the conquest of these territories has cost in sacrifice and effort. You mustn't think about it . . . There seems to be a real crisis at the moment and you could almost lose your courage if you didn't have a devout heart.'[123] This was one of his last letters home. Albert Neuhaus fell to a Red Army bullet just under a month later, on 11 March 1943.[124]

The Eastern Front had been reconstructed and to some extent stabilized by these withdrawals. Fresh troops were transferred from Western Europe, while Manstein reorganized and re-equipped his forces ready for a counter-attack. On 19 February 1943, Army Group South sent two panzer armies northwards, pulverizing the Soviet advance forces and retaking Kharkov, while another panzer army destroyed the Soviet armour further east. A month later, the spring thaw turned everything to mud and stopped further movement for the time being. But neither Hitler nor the army leadership had any illusions about these limited gains. After Stalingrad, they knew, for all the bold rhetoric in which the Nazi leadership continued to indulge, that Germany had gone over to the defensive on the Eastern Front. The main priority was now to preserve control over the heavy-industrial areas of the Donets Basin, with its rich and essential deposits of coal and ores. Its loss would mean the end of the war, Hitler told the generals.[125] What was needed was a tactical offensive designed to straighten out the German front, sacrificing as little in men and armaments as possible, and weakening the Red Army sufficiently to stop it launching a successful summer offensive. The possibilities were limited. The German generals knew that the Red Army now had nearly twice as many men and three or four times as many artillery pieces and tanks as they did on the Eastern Front. Where in these circumstances would it be safest to launch the offensive? As they had done before Moscow, the generals argued amongst themselves and were unable to take a united decision. The Combined Armed Forces Supreme Command disagreed with the Army Supreme Command on whether it was in any case more important to strengthen defences in Italy and the west. And as before Moscow, Hitler was eventually forced to take the decision himself. The blow, he ordered, would fall at Kursk, where a salient in the front line exposed the Soviet forces to a classic encircling manoeuvre.[126]

While they waited for the ground to harden, the German commanders moved up large quantities of the new Tiger and Panther tanks, together with other heavy armour – especially another new weapon, the Ferdinand self-propelled gun – and combat aircraft, in preparation for an assault on the salient. Manstein wanted to move quickly, before the Red Army could make its preparations, but he was frustrated by the problems the railway system experienced in getting the reinforcements to the front, and the attacks carried out on the transports by partisans. Field Marshal Model, commander of the Ninth Panzer Army to the north of Kursk, warned repeatedly that his forces were too weak to carry out their part of 'Operation Citadel', as it was called. Hitler therefore delayed the attack while his armies gathered their strength. But the vulnerability of the Kursk bulge was obvious to all, so the Red Army brought in massive reinforcements of men and armour. Soviet intelligence managed to discover not only where the German offensive thrusts would be launched, but when they would begin as well. The element of surprise essential to the original concept of the attack had been lost. The consequences were to prove fatal for the German armies.[127]

By the beginning of July, the forces were assembled for what was to be the greatest land battle in history. The statistics were staggering. The Battle of Kursk, including Operation Citadel and two Soviet counter-offensives, involved a total of more than 4 million troops, 69,000 artillery pieces, 13,000 tanks and self-propelled guns, and nearly 12,000 combat aircraft. In the initial assault of Operation Citadel the Red Army outnumbered the German forces by a factor of almost three to one (1,426,352 men against roughly 518,000). 2,365 tanks and self-propelled guns on the German side faced 4,938 Soviet vehicles of the same kind. The Soviet defenders possessed 31,415 artillery pieces of various categories, including rocket-launchers, to put up a wall of fire that the Germans would find it hard to penetrate, while the 7,417 artillery pieces deployed by the German armies had no chance of destroying the Soviet defences. The German forces on the Eastern Front had long since lost the command of the skies, and with only 1,372 combat aircraft to put against their opponents' 3,648, they were unlikely to regain it. In addition to all this, the Red Army held vast quantities of men and equipment in reserve nearby, ready to throw into the fray if and when it became necessary. Realizing this, Model kept significant panzer forces back from the battle in case the Soviets brought on their reserves to threaten his rear. Altogether in the whole area of the battle, the Red Army outnumbered its German opponents by 3:1 in men, 3:1 in tanks and armour, 5:1 in artillery and 4:1 in aircraft. And it was far better prepared and organized than it had been in previous encounters.[128]

II

On the morning of 5 July 1943, the Germans attacked simultaneously from both sides of the salient. The Russians were ready for them. In three months of feverish work, 300,000 civilian conscripts had helped the Soviet troops construct defensive systems 300 kilometres deep, with barbed wire, deep ditches, tank traps, bunkers, machine-gun emplacements, flame-throwers and artillery arranged in eight lines, one behind the other. Nearly a million landmines had been laid, in some sectors more than 3,000 per kilometre. One German panzer commander commented: 'What happened at Kursk was unbelievable. I've never experienced anything like it in war, either before or since. The Soviets had prepared a defensive system whose extension in depth was inconceivable to us. Every time we broke through one position in bitter fighting, we found ourselves confronted with a new one.'[129] Nevertheless, the battle began badly for the Red Army. Misled by false information from a captured German soldier as to the time of the intended assault, the Soviet artillery opened up first, thus betraying to the Germans the fact that they knew the assault was coming. Soviet bombers took to the air in a surprise attack on the German airfields, which were crowded with combat aircraft, but they were spotted by German radar, and the German air force scrambled its fighter planes, which shot down 425 Soviet aircraft for the loss of only thirty-six of its own. As a result, the Germans obtained temporary air supremacy, despite the far greater strength of the Soviet air forces in the area.[130]

Meanwhile, in the north, Field Marshal Walter Model pushed forward with the Ninth Panzer Army. Mindful of the huge Soviet reserves in his rear, and the massive superiority of the forces that faced him, he was uncharacteristically hesitant. He tried to preserve his tanks by using them to follow up the infantry instead of deploying them to punch through the deep Soviet defences. This slowed up the advance, and then Model began to lose his tanks as they were blown up by mines. After five days of ferocious combat, the advance ground to a halt.[131] To the south, Manstein deployed his considerably larger panzer army, with more than 200 Tiger and Panther tanks, in the classic manner, pushing them through the Soviet defences. But they too were slowed down by minefields, which destroyed twenty-five of them on the first day. Mechanical failure crippled another forty-five Panthers, in another illustration of the dangers of deploying a new weapon before it had been fully tried and tested. Nevertheless, the heavy Tigers proved strongly resistant to attempts to destroy them, and even the Panthers soon proved their superiority over the Soviet T-34s, shooting them to pieces at distances well in excess of 2,000 metres. Manstein and Hoth's forces advanced steadily, and the Soviet generals began to panic. They decided to bury a large proportion of their tanks in the ground, up to the turret, for protection. This caused enormous difficulties for the German tanks, which now had to approach extremely close in order to destroy their Soviet opponents; the well-camouflaged Russian tanks frequently let the Tigers and Panthers pass by before destroying them at close quarters from behind. The southern attack began to slow down, its situation worsened by the transfer of a large number of combat aircraft to assist the beleaguered Model in the north. Still, by 11 July 1941, Manstein's forces had broken through the Soviet defences and were within reach of their first major objective, the town of Prochorovka.[132]

Here the Soviet generals launched a counter-attack, with the aim of encircling and destroying the German forces. The leading Soviet tank general Pavel Rotmistrov sent in fresh forces, advancing up to 380 kilometres from the rear in a mere three days with more than 800 tanks. Keeping some in reserve, he sent 400 of these in from the north-east, and another 200 from the east, against the battle-weary German forces, who were taken completely by surprise. With only 186 armoured vehicles, a mere 117 of them tanks, the German forces faced total destruction. But the Soviet tank-drivers, tired after three days' driving and perhaps also fired up, as Red Army troops often were, by liberal doses of vodka, failed to notice a massive, 4.5-metre-deep anti-tank trench dug not long before by Soviet pioneers as part of Zhukov's preparations for the battle. The first lines of T-34s fell straight into the ditch, and when those following on finally saw the danger, they veered aside in panic, crashed into one another and burst into flames as the Germans opened fire. By the middle of the day the Germans were reporting 190 wrecked or deserted Soviet tanks on the battlefield, some of them still burning. The number seemed so unbelievable that a senior general arrived personally to verify it. The loss of so many tanks enraged Stalin, who threatened to have Rotmistrov court-martialled. To save his skin, the general agreed with his commanding officer and with the senior political commissar in the area – Nikita Khrushchev – to claim that the tanks had been lost in a vast battle in which more than 400 German tanks had been destroyed by the heroic Soviet forces. Stalin, whose idea it had originally been to send Rotmistrov's forces into the fray, was obliged to accept their report. It became the source of a long-lived legend that marked Prochorovka as the 'greatest tank battle in history'. In reality it was one of history's greatest military fiascos. The Soviet forces lost a total of 235 tanks, the Germans three. Despite all this, Rotmistrov became a hero, and today a large monument marks the site.[133]

The missing German tanks had disappeared in response to a redeployment order by Hitler. The rapidly deteriorating situation in the Mediterranean, and above all the Allied landings in Sicily on 10 July 1943, convinced the German Leader that it was necessary immediately to

withdraw key forces from the Eastern Front, and above all the tank
divisions that were taking part in Operation Citadel, and transport them
to the Italian peninsula to prepare to defend it against the looming Allied
invasion. Manstein still believed it would be possible to pull a limited
success out of the Kursk offensive, particularly in view of the heavy
Soviet losses. But on 17 July 1943 the tank commanders received the
order to withdraw. Manstein and other generals bitterly reproached
Hitler in later years for allegedly throwing away the prospect of victory.
But the fact was that the fiasco at Prochorovka made little real difference
to the overall balance of strength at Kursk. The losses sustained by the
German forces in the battle as a whole were relatively light: 252 tanks
against nearly 2,000 Soviet tanks, perhaps 500 artillery pieces against
nearly 4,000 of their Soviet counterparts, 159 airplanes as against nearly
2,000 Russian fighters and bombers, 54,000 men compared to nearly
320,000 Russian troops. Far from being the graveyard of the German
army, as it has sometimes been described, the battle had only a relatively
minor impact. It had, to be sure, demonstrated that the Tiger and Panther
tanks were far superior to the T-34. But this made little difference; they
were simply too few in number compared to their Soviet counterparts.
The aims of Operation Citadel had been limited and modest. But it had
failed. Its failure convinced many German soldiers that there would be
no reversal of fortune after Stalingrad. For the first time, a German
summer offensive had been repulsed, not least because a two-front war
was now in progress.[134]

This was far from being the end of the Battle of Kursk. On 12 July
1943, while the German offensive was still in progress, the Red Army
launched its counter-blow. More than a million fresh troops were
thrown into the battle, along with 3,200 tanks and self-propelled guns,
25,500 artillery pieces and grenade-throwers and nearly 4,000 aircraft.
Together with the forces already fighting in defence, this meant that
the numbers involved on the Soviet side were now overwhelming and
unprecedented: more than two and a quarter million men, of whom just
over one and a half million were combat troops; 4,800 tanks and
self-propelled guns; and 35,200 artillery pieces. This was more than
twice the size of the victorious Red Army force at Stalingrad. The
numerical superiority of the Red Army was so great that it could still
afford to open fresh offensives in other sectors of the Eastern Front at
the same time, backed by a massive partisan operation in the German

rear that tied down large numbers of German troops. The Red Army, advancing on a broad front instead of following the classic principle of trying to punch through the German lines and surround the enemy in an encircling manoeuvre, sustained horrific losses. By the time the counter-offensives were over, on 23 August 1943, it had altogether lost approximately 1,677,000 men dead, wounded or missing in action against the Germans' 170,000; more than 6,000 tanks in comparison to the Germans' 760; 5,244 artillery pieces compared with perhaps 700 or so on the German side; and over 4,200 aircraft against the Germans' 524. All in all, in July and August 1943, the Red Army lost nearly 10,000 tanks and self-propelled guns, the Germans just over 1,300.[135] The profligacy of Stalin and his generals with the lives of their men was breathtaking.

Yet the Germans were far less able to sustain their much smaller losses. On 2 September 1943, Otto Wöhler, a German infantry general, confessed:

While we were forced to adopt the most difficult tactics of conserving our ammunition, the enemy could command unlimited munitions for his artillery and grenade-throwers. He thinned out our ranks to such an extent that it was no longer possible to preserve the m[ain] c[ombat] l[ine], but only to construct it from security groups linked by patrols . . . The 39th I[nfantry Division] only had 6 officers and around 300 men in the fight this morning . . . The commanders reported to me that over-tiredness had led to such apathy amongst the troops that draconian measures were not leading to the desired effect at the moment, and neither the example set by the officers nor 'gentle encouragement' had any success.[136]

The German generals were forced to retreat. Hitler was furious, and issued a stream of orders to hold the line. But the situation was impossible, and even Hitler's favourite commander, Walter Model, disregarded his Leader's wishes and carried out a series of tactically skilled withdrawals that managed to reduce German losses. As the Soviet troops advanced on Kharkov, Hitler ordered the town to be held at all costs: Manstein and Werner Kempf, his commander on the spot, told him it was not possible. Hitler reacted by dismissing Kempf, but his replacement said the same thing, and Hitler was forced to agree to the evacuation of the city. As the German troops withdrew from the Kursk battlefield, they left behind a scene of apocalyptic devastation, a 'battlefield', as one German soldier described it, 'upon which every tree and shrub was torn to shreds, the area was covered in wrecked artillery pieces, burned-out tanks and shot-down planes . . . Pictures of the end of the world, the experience of which threatened to drive to despair the men it affected, unless they possessed nerves of steel.'[137]

III

The months between the Battle of Kursk in July–August 1943 and the Normandy landings in June 1944 have sometimes been called the 'forgotten year' of the war.[138] The generals were well aware of their desperate situation, and repeatedly asked Hitler for freedom of action so that they could use the vast open spaces of the steppe to perform large-scale tactical movements, hoping to cut off advancing Soviet armies and destroy them. To Hitler, however, this seemed merely an excuse for a cowardly retreat, and as time went on he became ever more insistent on holding the line. This meant, increasingly, that German withdrawals were not integrated into any overall strategy, and took place suddenly, in reaction to the threat of encirclement by Soviet armies. Too often, German army units abandoned their position in panic flight instead of planned withdrawal.[139] Throughout the whole period, the German forces were in almost permanent retreat, burning and destroying everything as they went. One young infantryman described the scene to his wife at home, as his unit withdrew across the Dnieper:

On the other side of the river everything has been burning fiercely for days already, for you must know that all the towns and villages in the areas that we are now evacuating are being set ablaze, even the smallest house in the village has to go. All the large buildings are being blown up. The Russians are to find nothing but a field of rubble. This deprives them of every possibility of accommodating their troops. So it's a horrifyingly beautiful picture.[140]

Troops were possessed by a kind of lust for destruction, as this letter suggests, often leading to a breakdown in discipline and the mass looting of buildings before they were burned to the ground. Burning buildings signalled only too clearly to the advancing Soviet troops where the Germans were going, and the work of destruction wasted time and resources that might have been better spent on organizing defensive lines. Increasingly, troop units retreated on their own without waiting to be told to, as soon as their situation began to look critical.[141]

Nevertheless, the German armies held together against the reckless assaults of the Soviets, whose repeated frontal attacks caused them to suffer five times the losses of their opponents, sometimes more. Superior intelligence, the preparation of strong points and defence in depth enabled key parts of the front to hold the line again and again before they were overwhelmed by superior numbers and forced to retreat.[142] What kept German soldiers fighting one losing battle after another? Increasingly, they felt they were fighting for Germany rather than for Hitler or for Nazism. Fear and loathing of the 'Bolshevik hordes', of Soviet 'subhumans', made them more than willing to kill and destroy. The very recklessness of their enemy cheapened life more than ever. The nearer the retreat got to the borders of Germany itself, the more desperate became the fight to save it, independently of the soldiers' own allegiance to the principles of Nazism. At the same time, the nationalist beliefs that sustained the troops had become ever more strongly infused over the previous decade with the ideology of Nazism. It filled them with its contempt for Slavs, its assertion of German superiority and, crucially, its willingness to use violence in the pursuit of its aims.[143]

The intermingling of Nazism with a more traditional kind of nationalism was strongest amongst the youngest and most junior troops, and weakest in the older generations, which meant above all the top ranks of the officer corps. The majority of the generals, born in the 1880s, were nationalists of the traditional kind. They had grown up in the reign of the last Kaiser, when they had belonged unthinkingly to the ruling caste of officers, aristocrats, senior civil servants, Protestant churchmen, university professors and conservative businessmen. Many had lived in rural districts or small towns, and mixed only with the families of other officers or members of the local elite. Particularly if they came from East-Elbian Prussia, they were likely to have cast their eyes fearfully towards the looming colossus of 'half-Asiatic' Russia. The long military training through which they had passed had confirmed their conservative, monarchist and nationalist values just as it cut them off even further from the rest of society. Characteristic in this respect was Gotthard Heinrici, a general unusual only in the assiduity with which he kept a journal and the colourful detail in which he described what he saw and experienced. Born in 1886 in Gumbinnen, on the Polish border, he had enrolled as a military cadet in 1905, fought in the First World War and made his way up through the ranks in a typical alternation of staff and operational positions between the wars, becoming a Lieutenant-General in 1938, a full General in June 1940, and a Colonel-General on 1 January 1943. Heinrici had lived his entire life within the confines of the military elite, with no real knowledge of, or contact with, the rest of German society. His whole world had collapsed in November 1918, like that of other members of the Wilhelmine elite. He blamed the defeat on a Jewish-socialist revolutionary conspiracy on the home front and, not surprisingly, supported the Kapp putsch, hoped for the downfall of the Weimar Republic and longed for a war of revenge against Germany's enemies. Suspicious at first of what he regarded as the vulgar radicalism of the Nazis, he was won over by Hitler's support of rearmament and his suppression of Social Democracy and Communism. Heinrici was no Nazi ideologue, but he did come to admire Hitler, and stuck to the regime out of an innate conformism and a sense of patriotic loyalty. He supported Hitler's aim of achieving European dominance for Germany and using it to challenge the British Empire and the United States for global hegemony, though, unlike Hitler, he remained sceptical as to whether this could be achieved. What comes through in his diary is not only his exemplary concern for the well-being of his troops, whose privations he made sure he shared, but also his narrow-mindedness, which would admit of no priority greater than the military. His casually expressed but deep-rooted prejudices against Jews and Slavs were entirely typical of his caste. His loyalty to Hitler and to his own ideas of Germany was to keep him fighting almost to the very end.[144]

Cast in a similar mould was Fedor von Bock, whose career, unlike that of the more pedestrian Heinrici, eventually took him to the rank of Field Marshal. Born in 1880 in Küstrin, another town on the eastern borders of Germany, he came from a military family, had fought on both fronts in the First World War and remained in the army throughout the Weimar years. In 1938 he had commanded the Eighth Army on the march into Austria, then took Army Group North into Poland in 1939. His late marriage, in 1936, to a widow who already had children seems to have been successful, although his active service meant that he saw little of his family. Bock admired Hitler for restoring Germany's national and military pride, but he too was no Nazi ideologue. His war diaries reveal a narrowly professional soldier, oblivious of almost everything apart from military action and military planning. His monarchism was no secret. In the Netherlands in May 1940 he drove to Doorn, where the elderly ex-Kaiser Wilhelm II continued to live in exile; but he found that the troops guarding the residence had been instructed not to allow him in to pay his respects. Bock's military professionalism gave him a basic belief in the laws of war, respect for civilians, concern for the welfare of prisoners-of-war and much else besides. He thought, for example, that occupied areas should be under military government and did not like the intrusion of the SS. He was concerned about Nazi policies towards the Jews in occupied France and Belgium, and his diaries do not reveal any open or even implicit antisemitism. But Bock conceded that Hitler would get his way in the areas the army had conquered, and in any case, all these issues were of very minor importance for him, compared to the dictates of military necessity. His time and energies were taken up almost entirely by commanding armies on active campaign, so he never did anything about these violations of military propriety.[145]

Professionalism and conservative nationalism were joined by material interest in keeping the generals in line. As in other countries, so too in Nazi Germany, a range of new honours and medals was established to reward bravery in combat during the war, and successful field commanders were rapidly promoted, twelve of them to the rank of Field Marshal after the victory in the west in 1940. Hitler never completely trusted the army, and saw such promotions as a means of binding senior officers to his will even if they disapproved of Nazi ideology. Rapid promotion made little difference, however, to the essentially aristocratic make-up of the senior levels of the officer corps.[146] Promotion brought not only a salary increase but also bonuses – 4,000 Reichsmarks a month, tax-free, for a Field Marshal or a Grand Admiral. Hitler did not scruple to use his own considerable personal fortune to steer far larger sums their way. On 24 April 1941 he gave Grand Admiral Raeder a one-off donation of 250,000 Reichsmarks, on his sixty-fifth birthday, to help cover the costs of building a new house. Such gifts were usually made discreetly and behind the scenes, as with another cheque for 250,000 Reichsmarks handed over by Hitler's principal adjutant, Rudolf Schmundt, to Field Marshal Wilhelm Ritter von Leeb to mark the latter's sixty-fifth birthday on 5 September 1941. As Hitler knew, Leeb was far from uncritical in his stance towards the way he was conducting the war. The sum helped reassure the Field Marshal, and even after he was sent into retirement at the beginning of 1942 following the defeat before Moscow, he actively looked for property to buy with his gift, repeatedly seeking the help of a variety of civil authorities in his search, which finally succeeded in 1944.

Earlier on, Leeb had been so disillusioned with Hitler's proposed violation of Belgian neutrality in 1940 that he had put out feelers to the military opposition that was crystallizing once more around Chief of the Army General Staff Franz Halder. But this was the only contact he had, and he did not repeat it. Other senior officers who received the same sum on reaching the age of sixty or sixty-five included Field Marshal Gerd von Rundstedt, Field Marshal Wilhelm Keitel and Field Marshal Hans-Günther von Kluge. Some, like Guderian or Kleist, were given valuable landed estates, or the money with which to buy them. The Deipenhof estate, which Guderian received, was valued at almost one and a quarter million Reichsmarks. Previously a critic of Hitler's conduct of the war, Guderian returned from enforced retirement towards the end of the conflict as one of the most determined supporters of a fight to the finish. No doubt the hope of a gift on this scale from Hitler influenced the conduct of many other senior officers. Yet these were men who often made a point of advertising their adherence to the traditional Prussian military virtues of modesty, probity, frugality and a keen sense of honour. As the disaffected diplomat Ulrich von Hassell remarked, 'for the majority of the generals, a career and the Field Marshal's staff are more important than the great practical principles and moral values that are at stake'.[147]

At the divisional level, the more junior members of the officer corps showed some of the same characteristics, but there were also differences too, largely stemming from the fact that they mostly came from younger age-groups. In the 253rd Infantry Division, for instance, which has been the subject of an exhaustive statistical analysis, only 9 per cent of the officers were born before 1900, and 8 per cent in the years 1900–1909; fully 65 per cent were born in the years 1910–19, the remaining 19 per cent belonging to the post-1919 generation. The Protestant domination of the military elite was reflected in the fact that 57 per cent of the officers in the division described themselves as Protestants and only 26 per cent as Catholics, in sharp contrast to the religious affiliation of the troops they commanded, where Catholics were in a majority; the influence of Nazism came through strongly in the fact that 12 per cent of the officers described themselves as 'Deists', the vague, non-confessional term preferred by the regime. The divisional officers came overwhelmingly from the educated and professional middle or upper-middle class and had already served in the army for some years, in many cases going back to the Weimar Republic. 43 per cent were members of a Nazi organization of one kind or another. They were more likely to be decorated for bravery than the men were, and they had better career prospects, assuming they survived: nearly half of them achieved battalion command during the war, or rose even higher, and even the most junior could expect to be promoted to the rank of Captain or Major. This meant, however, that they were far more likely than their men to be transferred to another division or other duties.[148]

For the great mass of ordinary soldiers the institutional setting in which they lived and fought was surprisingly stable for most of the war years. Roughly half of all German forces at any one time were not engaged in combat duties; either they were in reserve or on security work in occupied areas behind the front or employed in any one of a huge variety of administrative, supply, support or other ancillary tasks. For every tank regiment, for example, there had to be not only men who drove the tanks but also men who repaired them, supplied them with petrol and ammunition, transported them to and from the front, and kept track of where they were. In addition, there were always considerable numbers of troops who were undergoing training, or convalescing after being invalided out with wounds or illnesses of one kind or another. Of the other half, engaged on active combat duty, some 80 per cent served in infantry divisions, which might be regarded therefore as the typical combat unit of the armed forces. From the outbreak of the war to the invasion of the Soviet Union, the army underwent a lengthy initial period of expansion, training and organization, during which military losses, at around 130,000 dead or missing, were relatively low, amounting indeed to only 2.5 per cent of total German military losses during the war. New divisions were continually being formed by mixing experienced troops from existing divisions with fresh recruits, thus ensuring a high degree of continuity. From ninety infantry divisions at the beginning of the war, the army grew to contain some 175 in June 1941. The troops mostly took part in actual combat only intermittently, in short-lived lightning wars such as the invasion of Poland, the western campaigns of 1940 and the Balkan victories of the following year. All this meant that they remained relatively cohesive and a sense of stability underpinned the loyalty of the 'comrades' in each unit to one another.[149]

This picture of relative stability changed dramatically with the heavy losses that began to hit the army following the invasion of the Soviet Union. The military administration tried to mitigate the disruptive effects of these losses in a variety of ways, for example by ensuring that new recruits came from the same part of Germany as the troops in the units they joined, and that men who had recovered from their wounds were sent back to their old regiments, so that the social and cultural composition of each regiment remained relatively homogeneous, thus (it was thought) improving its cohesion and its fighting power. The insistence of the armed forces on thorough training continued to ensure that troops went into battle as effective fighting men. Despite this, mounting losses meant that many regiments were unable to bring themselves back up to full strength, and some indeed ceased to exist as effective fighting units altogether. Morale also began to suffer with the series of major defeats that began with Stalingrad. However, up to the late summer of 1944, it is clear that the German armed forces remained relatively intact in their organization, structure and recruitment patterns. Defeat came not through their disorganization or inefficiency but through the military and economic superiority of the Red Army (or, in North Africa and Italy, and later Normandy, the British and the Americans).[150]

Who were the men who fought in these infantry divisions? The soldiers and NCOs of the 253rd Infantry Division ranged widely in age. 19 per cent were born between 1901 and 1910 and had experienced the Weimar years as adults; 68 per cent were born between 1911 and 1920 and thus, like the remaining 11 per cent who were born between 1921 and 1926, had been wholly or partially socialized and educated under the Third Reich. What is striking despite the steadily declining average age of the soldiers over the course of the war is the dominance of the generation born shortly before or during the First World War. In other words, the character, behaviour and morale of this, as in all probability of other infantry divisions too, were shaped by a dominant cohort of men who were in their mid-to-late twenties.[151] As might be expected from this age structure, the majority of the troops – 68 per cent at the start of the war, 60 per cent towards the end – were unmarried. Many of the older troops already had children, and the divisional command tended to hold them back from the front as a result, sending the younger men without family ties of this kind into the most dangerous situations. Similarly, marriage and fatherhood may well have proved restraining factors in the behaviour of the older soldiers when it came to dealing with the civilian populations, especially women and children, of the conquered territories.[152]

59 per cent of the soldiers in the division who were born after the end of the First World War had belonged to a Nazi organization. 69 per cent of those born from 1916 to 1919 had been members of the Reich Labour Service. 83 per cent of those born in 1913–17 had already been serving in the armed forces before 1939. The proportion of those born in 1910–20 who had gone through one of these institutions by the time the war broke out averaged 75 per cent; indeed, 43 per cent had gone through more than one. These were precisely the age-groups that formed the core of the division for the greater part of the war.[153] As the war went on, moreover, the army itself intensified the political indoctrination to which it subjected its officers and NCOs and through them its ordinary troops. The idea of an unpolitical army, so loudly and insistently proclaimed under the Weimar Republic, had long ceased to exist. By the time the war broke out, the armed forces regarded enlistment and training in their ranks as the final and highest stage in a process of ideological education that had begun long before. The soldier was trained not just to be a fighter but also to be a full member of the racial community of Germans, even, according to some training guidelines, a new kind of man. All officers were required to learn and convince themselves of the correctness of the National Socialist world-view. A flood of books, pamphlets and manuals was published to assist them in mastering this task. In many of these works, officers were informed about the world conspiracy of the Jews against Germany and told that the Jew was the most dangerous and deadly of all the enemies they were going to have to fight. Arrangements were put in place to ensure the continued 'spiritual conduct of war' in the spirit of National Socialism. Intensive ideological training added to the indoctrination the men had already received from school, from the Hitler Youth, and from Goebbels's mass media. It was hardly surprising that many of the men went into battle against the soldiers of the Red Army describing them as 'subhumans who've been whipped into frenzy by the Jews'.[154]

Particularly after the army's sense of invincibility began to wear thin, from December 1941 and then, far more dramatically, after Stalingrad, senior commanders redoubled their efforts to convince the soldiers that they were fighting for a worthy cause. The German officer, Hitler declared in 1943, had to be a political officer. Especially when things were going badly, it was vital that officers draw deep from their well of National Socialist convictions to remind themselves of what it was all about. On 22 December 1943 Hitler ordered the creation of a team to co-ordinate 'National Socialist Leadership in the Armed Forces'. The measure, as he told Goebbels and a few others privately early the following month, was to ensure that all the troops inhabited the same mental world, one where they would possess the 'fanatical will' to fight for the Nazi cause to the end. The provision of Nazi political education officers was centralized and extended. Similar measures were taken in the navy and the air force. In effect, the Nazis were introducing into the German armed forces a kind of parallel to the political commissars who were so important in the Red Army. Their role was inculcated at numerous special political education courses held behind the front, and discussed in conferences organized by the army. Increasingly, as time went on and defeat followed defeat, officers' orders and commands became more National Socialist in content, in an attempt to inspire the men to ever more fanatical resistance to an overwhelmingly powerful enemy.[155] Of course, this still left a considerable number of officers and men indifferent, or even hostile, to Nazi ideology, depending on their age, their circumstances and their pre-existing beliefs. Yet overall, there can be little doubt that political education and indoctrination did have an effect on the troops, and played a role in pushing them to fight to the end.

Some indeed kept fighting out of antisemitic commitment. Propaganda and indoctrination had instilled in them the firm belief that, as a soldier working in the Leader's military messenger service on the Eastern Front wrote on 1 March 1942, 'This is a matter of two great world-views. Either us or the Jews.'[156] This belief kept some going when German victory began to look in doubt. 'It surely cannot be,' wrote one army man stationed in southern France at the end of May 1942, 'that the Jews will win and rule.'[157] Mingled with such incredulity was an ever-stronger dose of fear. If Germany was defeated, wrote another soldier in August 1944, 'the Jews will then fall on us and exterminate everything that is German, there will be a cruel and terrible slaughter.'[158] Yet Nazi ideology played little or no role in the commitment of many others. Why, for example, did a man like Wilm Hosenfeld carry on serving in the army, when he hated Nazism so much? It was not only Eastern Europeans and Jews whom the regime he served were persecuting and murdering, but also, he realized in December 1943, Germans themselves. Coming from rural Hesse, Hosenfeld had perhaps not realized the extent of the Nazis' maltreatment of their internal opponents in the 1930s. A conversation with his new assistant, a former Communist whose health had been broken by repeated torture in the cells of the Gestapo, stripped him of this last illusion. It was clear, wrote Hosenfeld, that the men who led the regime approved of such behaviour:

Now it becomes clear to me why they can only carry on working through force and lies, and why lies have to be the protection for their whole system . . . Ever more violent acts have to follow, war is only the logical continuation of their policy. Now the entire [German] people, who did not exterminate this ulcer at the appropriate moment, must perish. These rogues are sacrificing us all . . . The atrocities here in the east, in Poland, Yugoslavia and Russia, are only continuing in a straight line the process that began with their political opponents in Germany . . . And we idiots believed they could bring us a better future. Every person who approved of this system even to the smallest degree has to be ashamed today of having done so.[159]

For Hosenfeld, the Nazis were a tiny clique of criminals who did not represent the German people as a whole. He carried on performing his duties not for them, but for Germany, to preserve it from Bolshevism. A good many other officers most probably felt similarly. By July 1943, for example, General Heinrici was becoming concerned that Germany was in danger of losing the war. It was, he wrote, as if to bolster up his own commitment to continuing the fight, 'clear that there must be no defeat in this war, since what would come afterwards is not even to be thought of. Germany would go under, and we ourselves with it.'[160]

There is little evidence to suggest that Nazi ideology spread through the army to fill a gap left by the disintegration of military values and the men's basic loyalty to one another as 'comrades'. The relative homogeneity of each division in most respects meant that primary group loyalties remained intact within the division for most of the war. It was not so much the disintegration of such loyalties as their persistence, in a mixture of experienced and increasingly cynical and brutalized veterans with a continual and, from early 1943, increasing stream of ideologically deeply

Nazified younger men that formed the basis for the barbarous conduct of the war by German troops in the east. Even in times of heavy losses, such as the end of 1941 and the beginning of 1942, the social cohesion of the 253rd Infantry Division companies was damaged but not destroyed, and with the return of convalescent soldiers and the arrival of fresh recruits it was soon restored.[161] These were groups of men bound together by ties of mutual loyalty forged in the heat of battle. Even when, as they increasingly did after Stalingrad, they began to doubt whether victory could ever be attained, they continued to fight out of a sense of comradeship and mutual support in adversity.[162] Here they could create emotional bonds in small groups that provided a substitute, at least to some extent, for the families they had left at home, caring for the wounded, decorating their bunkers and living quarters and, like the troops who invested so much emotional capital in the celebration of Christmas at Stalingrad, providing some kind of meaning to life amidst the senselessness of war. Here, in another way perhaps, was the organic national community, the *Volksgemeinschaft*, in miniature; and correspondingly, all the soldiers' aggressive masculinity was directed outwards, towards the enemy, and towards a population that, in the east at least, they regarded as racially inferior, indeed as barely human.[163]

The men also kept fighting out of sheer fear – fear of what would happen to them if they surrendered to the enemy, fear of their superiors should they show signs of flagging. The armed forces had their own courts-martial, which were freely used by officers in all three services to prosecute offences ranging from the theft of food parcels sent in the field post at one extreme to desertion of the colours at the other. Any of these offences could land the offender before a firing-squad. Numerous prosecutions were brought for the vaguely defined offence of 'undermining military strength' (*Wehrkraftzersetzung*), which could include anything from defeatist utterances to self-mutilation in the hope of being invalided out; and, as in civilian life, criticism of the regime and its leaders was also a criminal offence. By contrast, as we have already seen, there were relatively few prosecutions for offences against the civilian population of occupied areas, such as looting, rape or murder, and shooting captured enemy soldiers instead of taking them prisoner was widely tolerated, especially in the initial stages of Operation Barbarossa. Courts-martial were, therefore, overwhelmingly used as a means of enforcing discipline and the will to fight. Over the whole course of the war, it has been estimated that courts-martial tried the staggering total of 3 million cases, of which some 400,000 were brought against civilians and prisoners of war.[164] Of all these cases, no fewer than 30,000 ended in a member of the German armed forces being condemned to death. This compared with a mere forty-eight executed in the German forces during the First World War. Of those 30,000 death sentences, some were commuted, and a few were pronounced *in absentia*. But the great majority – at least 21,000 according to the most thorough estimate – were carried out. In all other combatant countries with the exception of the Soviet Union, death sentences pronounced by courts-martial during the Second World War can be numbered in hundreds at most, rather than thousands.[165]

A prisoner brought before a court-martial was supposed to be tried by three judges. Regulations required the accused to be provided with a defence counsel, but in the heat of the battle such rules were widely disregarded. One participant recalled for example that in a part of the Stalingrad front covered by four army divisions, 364 death sentences were handed out by drumhead courts-martial in the space of just over week, for offences including cowardice, desertion and the theft of food parcels.[166] Acting in his capacity as Commander-in-Chief, Hitler issued a set of guidelines that prescribed the most draconian levels of punishment. 'The death penalty is recommended,' according to one of the guidelines, 'if the offender acted out of fear of personal endangerment or if it is necessary in the particular circumstances of the individual case for the maintenance of manly discipline.'[167] Military judges by and large shared the view of the civilian judicial apparatus under Nazism that, as one of them declared:

Whatever serves the people is just . . . In the narrower sense of military law, it follows that 'whatever serves the armed forces is just'. . . Now it becomes clear why there can be no 'average soldier'. To be a soldier means to raise the National Socialist conception of honour and soldierly behaviour to a professional ethos.[168]

This meant, for example, that 6,000 executions were carried out for 'undermining military strength'. The commonest offence bringing men before the firing-squad was desertion, which led to 15,000 executions. In many cases, the offence in effect amounted to little more than absence without leave (*unerlaubte Entfernung*). Sentences, following orders issued by the Combined Armed Forces Supreme Command in December 1939 and again in July 1941, were carried out as soon as possible after being passed. 'The faster a pest in the armed forces (*Wehrmachtschädling*) receives the punishment he has earned, the easier it will be to prevent other soldiers from committing the same or similar deeds and the easier it will be to maintain manly discipline among the troops.'[169]

IV

Terrorizing the troops through the draconian application of military justice may well have helped keep them fighting long after they knew the war was lost. But what the regime increasingly required was a military force that fought out of fanatical National Socialist commitment. This was in fact available, in the shape of the Military SS (*Waffen-SS*). Its history went back to the early days of the Third Reich, when Hitler had formed an armed personal bodyguard, which later became the so-called 'Adolf Hitler Standard' (*Leibstandarte Adolf Hitler*). Conceived mainly as a ceremonial unit, it was commanded by a rough Bavarian Nazi, Josef ('Sepp') Dietrich, whose previous jobs had included working as a petrol-pump attendant, a waiter, a farm labourer and a foreman in a tobacco factory. Born in 1892, he had served in a tank unit, but otherwise had no serious military experience, as army generals repeatedly but vainly pointed out. Soon, however, Dietrich's boss Heinrich Himmler set up another, larger organization and began recruiting army men to provide the unit with proper military training, which from 1938 was provided to Dietrich's men as well. By the end of 1939, these various military units of the SS had been joined by groups from the Death's Head Units formed by Theodor Eicke to provide guards for the concentration camps. The SS forces grew in number from 18,000 on the eve of war to 140,000 in November 1941, including tank regiments and motorized infantry. They were intended from the outset to be an elite, ideologically committed, highly trained, and – unlike the army – unconditionally loyal to Hitler. Senior officers were notably younger than their army counterparts, mostly being born in the 1890s or early 1900s and so in their forties or early fifties at the time of the war. Military SS regiments were given names such as 'The Reich', 'Germany', 'The Leader' and so on. Again unlike the army, the Military SS was an institution not of the German people but of the Germanic race, and its leading figure, Gottlob Berger, a long-time Nazi and First World War veteran who was one of Himmler's closest intimates, set up recruiting offices in 'Germanic' countries like Holland, Denmark, Norway and Flanders, forming the first non-German division ('Viking') in the spring of 1941. Further recruits from Eastern European countries followed, as numbers began to take priority over supposed racial affinities. By 1942 the Military SS numbered 236,000 men; in 1943 it exceeded half a million; and in 1944 it was approaching a strength of 600,000, of whom some 369,000 were active in the field.[170]

Regular army commanders were disparaging of the Military SS, whose commanders they considered lacking in professionalism and over-inclined to sacrifice the lives of their men. Although the SS divisions were placed under their command, the army generals could do little to rein in their fanatical desire for self-sacrifice. When told by Eicke that his men's lives had counted for nothing in an attack he had just carried out, the army general Erich Hopner, under whose command Eicke had been placed, roundly condemned this attitude: 'That is the outlook of a butcher.'[171] However, the senior generals were not wholly averse to the Military SS spearheading attacks and taking the bulk of the casualties: it preserved the lives of their own men and reduced the strength of a serious rival force. Himmler complained in August 1944 that 'people of ill-will' in the army were conspiring to 'butcher this unwelcome force and get rid of it for some future development'.[172] Army commanders also alleged that members of the Military SS were more likely than their own troops to commit massacres of innocent civilians, especially Jews, and carry out other crimes, above all on the Eastern Front. An official army investigation in August 1943 noted that out of eighteen proven cases of rape reported to it, twelve had been committed by members of the Military SS. How accurate such reports were cannot be ascertained. The Military SS tended to provide something of an excuse for regular army commanders wishing to conceal, or pass over, the crimes committed by their own men. On the other hand, even officers from other branches of the SS were known to complain about its brutality. When the commander of the 'Prince Eugene' division tried to excuse to a minister of the puppet government in Croatia some atrocities committed by his men as 'errors', another SS officer told him: 'Since you arrived there has unfortunately been one "error" after another.'[173] Attempts after 1945 by former Military SS officers to portray their troops as nothing more than ordinary soldiers failed to carry conviction, since there could be no doubt about their elite status or their fanatical ideological commitment. On the other hand, the mass of evidence that has come to light since the early 1990s about the conduct of regular troops on and behind the Eastern Front undermines claims that the Military SS was wholly exceptional in its disregard for the laws and conventions of warfare.

The undoubted fanaticism of the Military SS, as well as the tendency of military commanders to put its units into the front line, led to heavy losses among its troops. A total of 900,000 Military SS men served in the war, of whom more than a third – 34 per cent – were killed.[174] On 15 November 1941 the 'Death's Head' division reported losses of 60 per cent amongst officers and NCOs. Its backbone was gone, a report complained. The general view of the Military SS among the German people was, as the Security Service of the SS reported in March 1942, that it was poorly trained and its men were often 'recklessly sacrificed'. Its men were thrown into battle because it wanted to show itself better than the army.[175] Moreover, parents were beginning to try to stop their sons from enlisting because of the anti-Christian indoctrination to which they would be subjected in the Military SS. 'Influence of parents and Church negative,' reported one recruitment centre in February 1943. 'Parents generally anti-Military SS,' reported another. In Vienna one man told the recruiting officer: 'The priest told us that the SS was atheist and if we joined it we should go to hell.'[176] Volunteers from Flanders, Denmark, Norway and Holland began to apply to be discharged, complaining of the arrogant and overbearing treatment of foreign recruits by German SS officers. Recruiting officers began to go to Labour Service camps and force young men to 'volunteer'. Relatives complained about such actions, while Military SS officers soon declared themselves dissatisfied with the results, as many of the new recruits were 'intellectually sub-standard' and 'inclined to insubordination and malingering'. The Military SS was rapidly deteriorating in quality towards the end of the war. But in this, it was doing no more than following the course taken by the regular armed forces themselves.[177]

A NEW 'TIME OF STRUGGLE'

I

On 7 November 1942 Albert Speer was travelling with Hitler to Munich on the Leader's own train. 'In earlier years,' Speer recalled, 'Hitler had made a habit of showing himself at the window of his special train whenever it stopped. Now these encounters with the outside world seemed undesirable to him; instead, the blinds on the station side of the train would be lowered.' Late that evening, the train was halted in a siding and Hitler and the rest of the Leader's entourage sat down to dinner. Speer reported what happened next:

The table was elegantly set with silver cutlery, cut glass, good china and flower arrangements. As we began our ample meal, none of us at first saw that a freight train was stopped on the adjacent track. From the cattle wagon, bedraggled, starved, and in some cases wounded German soldiers, just returning from the east, stared at the diners. With a start, Hitler noticed the sombre scene two metres from his window. Without as much as a gesture of greeting in their direction, he peremptorily ordered his servant to draw the blinds. This, then, in the second half of the war, was how Hitler handled a meeting with ordinary front-line soldiers such as he himself had once been.[178]

Hitler, indeed, withdrew increasingly from public view from 1942 onwards. Goebbels and Speer both tried to persuade him to visit bombed-out areas of German cities to boost morale, but without success.[179] There were rumours that he had fallen ill or been wounded. Yet when he did speak, it no longer had the effect it had once been able to produce on popular opinion. A speech broadcast on 21 March 1943, for example – his first public address since Stalingrad – was so brief, and delivered at such speed and in such a dull monotone, that people wondered whether he had been racing to get it finished in case it was interrupted by an air raid, or indeed whether it had been spoken by a stand-in.[180]

Even to his intimates, Hitler became less openly friendly. From the autumn of 1943 onwards, Speer thought that lunch with him was 'an ordeal'. His dog, an Alsatian, was, Speer noted, 'the only living creature at headquarters who aroused any flicker of human feeling in Hitler'. His distaste for bad news meant that his subordinates played up positive reports and presented insignificant, temporary successes as if they were major victories. He did not visit the front, and had no contact with the harsh realities of the fighting. He always assumed that the divisions marked on the maps he used to direct strategy were up to full strength. Equipped with the latest technology, with telephone and two-way radio, he was able to communicate with the generals on the ground, but the real communication was all one-way; if any generals objected, or tried to bring him back to reality, he would bawl them out and, in some instances, dismiss them. He bullied and browbeat the General Staff officers at his headquarters, and lost his temper when bad news was presented to him. The generals were cowards, he would rage, 'the training of the General Staff is a school of lying and deception', the information the army was conveying to it was false, 'the situation is deliberately being represented as unfavourable – that's how they want to force me to authorize retreats!'[181]

Underneath it all, Hitler was aware that the military situation was deteriorating, but outwardly he always presented a façade of optimism. His will had triumphed before: it would triumph again. With his concentration of power in military affairs, he now, for the first time in his life, had to work extremely hard, abandoning the casual and chaotic lifestyle of his earlier years as dictator, with its social evenings listening to music, watching old movies or playing with the architectural models created by Speer. Now he spent his time conferring with, or rather arguing with and browbeating, his generals, poring over military maps and thinking out military plans, often down to the last detail. Convinced more than ever of his own infallible genius, he became increasingly consumed by suspicion and distrust of his subordinates, expecially in military matters. No major decisions could be taken without him. Never one to take physical exercise, he relied increasingly on pills and remedies prescribed him by Dr Theo Morell, his personal physician since 1936:

over twenty-eight different pills a day by the later stages of the war, and
so many injections that Göring dubbed Morell 'The Reich Master of
Injections'. Morell controlled Hitler's diet as well as he could in the face
of his patient's vegetarianism and his liking for foods such as pea soup,
which caused him indigestion. Morell was a qualified physician, and no
quack, and all the medicines he prescribed Hitler were clinically
approved. His bedside manner enabled him to deal effectively with his
patient, who relied on him increasingly as the war went on, and indeed
he kept Hitler on his feet for virtually the whole time, apart from one
bout of illness in early August 1941. But he was unable to deal effectively
with Hitler's physical deterioration under the strain to which he was
now subjecting himself. From 1941 onwards electrocardiograms began
to show progressive heart disease, probably caused by sclerosis of the
coronary arteries. Beginning in the spring of 1943 Hitler suffered from
chronic indigestion, with periodic stomach cramps (at least twenty-four
bouts by the end of 1944), which may have been made worse by Morell's
treatment. A tremor began in his left hand, becoming markedly worse
from the end of 1942, and accompanied by a growing stoop and jerking
movements in his left leg. By 1944 he was shuffling rather than walking,
and the symptoms of a mild but generally worsening case of Parkinson's
disease were becoming clear for all medically informed observers to
note. Even Morell, whose preference was for psychosomatic diagnoses,
accepted this early in 1945 and began applying the standard treatment
available at the time. More generally, observers began to note how
rapidly Hitler was ageing, with his hair turning grey and his appearance
no longer that of a vigorous and energetic middle-aged man, but – thanks
not least to his Parkinsonism – of an elderly, increasingly debilitated one.
Hesitation about revealing this to the outside world may have been an
important factor in his growing refusal to appear in public.[182]

Hitler gave nine public addresses in 1940, seven in 1941, five in 1942,
and only two in 1943. On 30 January 1944, the eleventh anniversary of
his appointment as Reich Chancellor, he delivered a radio broadcast,
and on 24 February, the anniversary of the promulgation of the Nazi
Party programme, he spoke in Munich to 'Old Fighters' of the Party,
but he declined Goebbels's offer to broadcast this speech, and it was not
even reported in the newspapers. After this he was heard no more in
public, except briefly, under special circumstances (as we shall see) on
21 July 1944. Otherwise, he made no attempt to communicate directly

with the German people by word of mouth, and even his traditional speech in Munich on 8 November 1944 was read out to the 'Old Fighters' by Heinrich Himmler. Most of his time he spent at his field headquarters, almost entirely preoccupied with the conduct of the war, repairing to his mountain retreat on the Berghof, in the Bavarian Alps, for three months in 1943 and again from late February to mid-July 1944.[183] Letters began arriving in growing numbers at the Propaganda Ministry asking, as Goebbels noted on 25 July 1943, 'why the Leader does not even speak to the German people to explain the current situation. I regard it,' the Propaganda Minister confided to his diary, 'as most necessary that the Leader does that.' Otherwise, thought Goebbels, the people would cease to believe in him.[184] Hitler's admirers amongst ordinary Germans became impatient too. Why didn't Hitler speak on the 'dramatic' military situation in September 1944, asked one supporter in a letter to the Propaganda Ministry.[185] Goebbels became increasingly critical of Hitler's preoccupation with military affairs to the evident neglect of domestic politics. His absence from Berlin was creating a 'leadership crisis', he complained. 'I can't influence him politically. I can't even report to him about the most urgent measures in my area. Everything goes through Bormann.'[186] The shadowy Bormann's power became even greater when, on 12 April 1943, he was given the title of 'Secretary of the Leader'. Goebbels began to feel that Hitler had largely lost his grip on domestic affairs.[187]

Superficially, at least, it seemed as if the gap might be filled by the 'second man in the Reich', Hermann Göring. On 30 August 1939 Göring had succeeded in persuading Hitler to set up a Ministerial Council for the Defence of the Reich, whose role was to co-ordinate the civil administration. Hitler retained the power of veto over its orders, but in effect he had largely handed over control of domestic affairs to Göring, who became the Council's chairman. The Council's obvious importance attracted a number of key figures to its meetings, including Goebbels, Himmler, Ley and Darré, and by February 1940 it was beginning to look like a kind of substitute cabinet. Alarmed, Hitler ordered that it should not meet again, and it never did. Göring did not attempt to revive it: the right he had acquired to append his signature to laws and decrees after Hitler's was enough to satisfy his vanity. Despite his wide-ranging powers as head of the Four-Year Plan, Göring was becoming less energetic and decisive, perhaps under the influence of his morphine addiction.

He spent more and more time in his various hunting lodges and castles, and devoted a good deal of what energy he had left to building an opulent, extravagant mode of life for himself. In March 1943 a visitor who spent a day with Göring at Carinhall reported on the Reich Marshal's now 'grotesque' lifestyle:

He appeared early in a Bavarian leather jacket with full white shirt sleeves. He changed his costume often during the day, and appeared at the dinner table in a blue or violet kimono with fur-trimmed bedroom slippers. Even in the morning he wore at his side a golden dagger which was also changed frequently. In his tiepin he wore a variety of precious stones, and around his fat body a wide girdle, set with many stones – not to mention the splendour and number of his rings.[188]

In these circumstances, there was no chance of Göring taking over the day-to-day management of domestic affairs in the Reich. In addition, the poor performance of the air force, of which he was the head, caused a sharp fall in his reputation from 1942 onwards, not only with the general public, but also with Hitler himself.

The Third Reich was clearly becoming increasingly leaderless on the home front. Yet somehow the machinery of government continued to function. The civil administration, staffed largely by traditional, conscientious and hard-working bureaucrats, carried on business on its own right up to the end of the war, ministers and state secretaries implemented policies the broad lines of which had been laid down by Hitler before the war, and responded to changes initiated by him when they came. They did not dare to formulate policies on major issues without his express approval. As before, Hitler's own interventions in policy were intermittent, arbitrary and often contradictory. Finding it increasingly difficult to gain access to him, ministers, beginning with Goebbels, started sending him regular briefing papers on matters of importance. Hitler sometimes took note of them, more often not; it is very unlikely that he actually read all the 500 or so briefing papers sent to him by the Propaganda Ministry, for example, or every one of the 191 that reached him from the Reich Ministry of Justice during the war. Conscious, perhaps, of the fact that he had less time than before to intervene in the conduct of domestic affairs, he issued orders in May 1942 and again in June 1943 that he was to be known exclusively as the 'Leader' and not 'Leader and Reich Chancellor', even when signing official laws and decrees. Hitler was unable to provide any kind of overall direction of domestic affairs, so that government departments found it increasingly necessary to issue their own regulations on matters of detail, often without consulting other departments about their contents. In 1941, for example, 12 formal laws were passed, after consultation with ministries, 33 decrees were issued by Hitler, 27 decrees were ordered by the Ministerial Council for the Defence of the Reich, and 373 regulations and orders were issued by individual government departments. In the absence either of a formal cabinet or of any consistent direction by Hitler, government was becoming more and more fragmented. 'Everybody does and leaves undone what he pleases,' complained Goebbels in his diary on 2 March 1943, 'because there's no strong authority anywhere.'[189] A co-ordinating 'Committee of Three' (Bormann, Keitel and Lammers) was, as we have seen, established early in 1943, but it ran up against the hostility of powerful figures like Goebbels and Speer, and ceased to meet after August.[190]

As time went on, the Nazi Party began to move into the domestic power vacuum. On 20 August 1943, Hitler dismissed Interior Minister Frick, providing him with a meaningless title (Reich Protector of Bohemia and Moravia, where Karl Hermann Frank, now appointed State Minister for Bohemia and Moravia, continued in practice to be in charge). Goebbels had been arguing for Frick's dismissal for years. He was old and worn out, the Propaganda Minister said, and the decline in popular morale needed a tougher approach to the home front. The man Hitler chose to replace Frick was Heinrich Himmler, whose elevation implied an escalation of police repression to confront the possibility of demoralization turning into open resistance.[191] At the same time, Martin Bormann effectively used his control over access to Hitler to sideline the civil administration and many of its ministers. By the beginning of 1945, Lammers was complaining that he had not seen Hitler since September the previous year and that he was 'continually being pressed from all quarters to obtain the numerous decisions which are urgently awaited from the Leader'.[192] The head of the civil service was thus reduced to asking the head of the Party Chancellery to allow him to see the head of state. The eclipse of the traditional state administration in comparison to the Party could not have been made more obvious. And it was underlined still further by the growing power of Goebbels, whose initiative for 'total war' in 1943 succeeded, among things, in bringing him closer to the centre of economic management than ever before.[193]

As soon as the war began, the Party's Regional Leaders had been appointed to the new posts of regional Reich Defence Commissioners, a position that enabled them to act independently of the existing civil governors and regional military authorities. The subsequent quarrels over competence ended in victory for the Party on 16 November 1942, as the number of Reich Defence Commissioners was increased from thirteen to forty-two and the regions they covered made identical to the Party Regions. Further struggles for power ensued as Bormann's attempts to control them from the Party Chancellery were frustrated by the direct access they enjoyed to Hitler. Increasingly, they tended to use their own people to put their orders into effect, rather than going through regional state administrations as they were supposed to. After March 1943 they ran up against the new Reich Interior Minister Heinrich Himmler, surely a more formidable opponent than his predecessor, Wilhelm Frick, but Himmler too was faced with the loss of effectiveness of the civil administration under the impact of war. A report he commissioned from Ernst Kaltenbrunner, Heydrich's successor as head of the SS Security Service, submitted on 26 August 1944, confirmed that the Regional Leaders were bypassing state administrators with their own staff. Kaltenbrunner noted despairingly:

The public does not appreciate it when, in the present situation, comradely co-operation does not always have priority and instead people take the opportunity of contriving shifts in the domestic balance of power. The constant necessity for the local government organs to defend their position causes a loss of energy, inhibits initiative, and on occasion produces a sense of helplessness.[194]

As the military situation deteriorated, Party officials became ever more concerned to shore up morale and isolate 'grumblers' and complainers. Each Block Warden, according to a set of instructions issued by Robert Ley in his capacity as Reich Organization Leader of the Party on 1 June 1944, had to visit every household at least once a month and reassure himself that the inhabitants had the correct level of political and ideological commitment. The worse things got, the more the Party tried to re-create the atmosphere of the 'time of struggle' before 1933.[195] The growing power and influence of the Nazi Party was welcomed by many in its ranks, who had seen themselves overshadowed to this point by the military. 'On the whole,' wrote Inge Molter, whose father had joined the Nazi Party in Hamburg in 1932, to her husband, Alfred, on 7 August

1944, 'these times remind me at the moment strongly of the time of struggle. Just like in those days, Papa has to give every free minute to the Party.'[196]

II

The higher levels of ideological commitment demanded during the war were enforced by a whole new raft of legal sanctions. As Roland Freisler, State Secretary in the Reich Justice Ministry, declared in September 1939:

Germany is engaged in a fight for honour and justice. More than ever, the model of devotion to duty for every German today is the German soldier. Anyone who, instead of modelling themselves on him, sins against the people has no place in our community . . . Not to apply the most extreme severity to such pests would be a betrayal of the fighting German soldier![197]

Looming behind such considerations was the perennial spectre of 1918. Another statement from the Reich Justice Ministry in January 1940 made the point clear:

During the war, the task of the judicial system is the elimination of the politically malicious and criminal elements who, at a critical moment, might try to stab the fighting front in the back (e.g. the Workers' and Soldiers' Councils of 1918). This is all the more important in that experience shows that the sacrifice of the lives of the best at the front has the effect of strengthening the inferior elements behind the front.[198]

The Social Darwinist thinking in statements such as this was reflected in a further move towards the prosecution and punishment of offenders because of who they were, not because of what they had done. The new laws, often cast in vague terms, replete with references to 'national pests' (*Volksschädlinge*) made this clear. As soon as the war broke out, the death penalty was applied to anyone convicted of 'publicly' trying to 'subvert or cripple the will of the German or of an allied people to military self-assertion'.[199] A Decree Against National Pests issued on 5 September 1939 subjected to capital punishment anyone convicted of crimes against property or persons committed during the blackout, including looting, and anyone damaging the will of the German people to fight. The use of guns in committing violent crimes was made punishable by death from 5 December 1939. The Reich Criminal Code was amended to apply the death penalty to anyone causing a 'disadvantage' to Germany's war effort. These offences included, for example, making 'defeatist' comments. Another decree made the hoarding or concealment of food supplies punishable by death. This was also the sanction applied to anyone found deliberately damaging military equipment or producing faulty munitions. Altogether, by early 1940, more than forty different offences, some of them, like the above, extremely vaguely defined, were punishable by execution. In 1941 the death penalty was extended to cover serious 'habitual criminals'.[200]

Not surprisingly, executions for criminal offences now began to increase. In 1939 329 people were sentenced to death in the Greater German Reich; in 1940 the figure went up to 926, and in 1941 to 1,292, before leaping dramatically to 4,457 in 1942 and 5,336 in 1943. Altogether, the courts of the Third Reich, and especially the regional Special Courts and the national People's Court, handed down 16,560 death sentences, of which 664 were passed in 1933–9 and 15,896 during the war. Roughly 12,000 of them were carried out, the rest being commuted to life imprisonment. The People's Court itself handed down more than 5,000 death sentences during the whole course of its life, over 2,000 in 1944 alone. Since 1936, executions in Germany had been carried out by the guillotine, but by 1942 the official state executioners were also using hanging, on the grounds that it was quicker, simpler and less messy. So many executions were taking place in Germany's state prisons by this time that the Ministry of Justice allowed them at any time of the day instead of, as previously, only at dawn. New executioners were hired, virtually all of them from the long-established milieu of the professional executioner, with its connections to the old trades of butchery and horse-knacking. By 1944 there were ten principal executioners at work, with a total of thirty-eight assistants working for them. One subsequently claimed to have dispatched more than 2,800 offenders during his term of office from 1924 to 1945. The time that was now allowed to elapse between sentencing and execution was often no more than a few hours, certainly not long enough for appeals for clemency to be prepared and considered. Nevertheless, the death rows in German prisons began to suffer from serious overcrowding. Roughly half the executions carried out up to the end of 1942 were of non-

Germans, mainly Polish and Czech forced labourers, who, as we have seen, were subject to particularly draconian legal sanctions. On the night of 7–8 September 1943, the Ministry of Justice ordered the immediate hanging of 194 prisoners in the Plötzensee jail in Berlin to reduce the overcrowding, which had become worse since an air raid had damaged a number of cells in the prison. After seventy-eight had been killed, in batches of eight, it was discovered that the wrong files had been taken out of the prison office, and six of the prisoners executed had not been sentenced to death at all. Characteristically, the Ministry officials focused not on dealing, even if retrospectively, with this injustice but on finding the six other prisoners who should have been executed. By the morning of 8 September the executioner, his request for a twenty-four-hour break in the middle of the process having been brusquely rejected, had completed his work with a further 142 hangings. The bodies were left lying about in the open, in very hot weather, for several days until they were removed.[201]

Such measures, especially when applied to native Germans, reflected not least Hitler's own long-held belief that the German judicial system was too lenient. On 8 February 1942, for example, he complained privately that too many burglars and thieves were sent to prison, where they were 'supported at the expense of the community'. They should be 'sent to a concentration camp for life or suffer the death penalty. In time of war,' he added, 'the latter penalty would be appropriate, if only to set an example.' But the judicial system was still obsessed with 'finding extenuating circumstances – all in accordance with the rites of peacetime. We must have done with such practices.'[202] In March 1942 he was so outraged when he read a newspaper report of a five-year prison sentence handed down by a court in Oldenburg to a man who had beaten and abused his wife until she had died that he phoned up State Secretary Schlegelberger in the Justice Ministry 'in the greatest passion' to complain about it.[203] The matter obviously still rankled when he came to deliver a major speech in the Reichstag on 26 April 1942, broadcast all over Germany. 'From now on,' he declared to vigorous applause, 'I am going to intervene in these cases and relieve of their office judges who are obviously failing to realize the requirements of the day.'[204] The judges were appalled. Not even the Nazis had up to this point suggested breaching the long-established principle of the irremoveability of judges. Such a threat made them all the more amenable to the pressure that was now put on them to impose harsher sentences on offenders. In many cases, it had already come from Hitler. He had ordered the Ministry to be telephoned on some eighteen occasions since the beginning of the war to demand that criminals whom he had read about in the morning papers as having been sentenced to imprisonment should be 'shot while trying to escape'. The conservative Minister of Justice, Franz Gürtner, had tried to impose some sort of regular procedure on these interventions, but in January 1941 he had died, and his office had been handed over to Franz Schlegelberger, the senior civil servant in the Ministry. This made the Ministry extremely vulnerable. On 20 August 1942 Hitler finally replaced him with Otto-Georg Thierack, a hardline Nazi and President of the People's Court; the State Secretary in the Ministry, Roland Freisler, moved over to the People's Court to take his place.[205]

At the lunchtime meeting held to mark this transition, Hitler made clear his belief that justice was essentially a matter of eugenics. In war, he said, 'it's always the best men who then get killed. All this time, the absolute ne'er-do-well is cared for lovingly in body and spirit' in prison. Unless something was done, there would be 'a gradual shift in the balance of the nation' towards inferior and criminal elements. The judge, he concluded, thus had to be 'the bearer of racial self-preservation'.[206] Thierack sprang into action right away. At the beginning of September 1942 he began issuing 'Judges' Letters', outlining to the courts cases in which their alleged leniency had run into criticism from Hitler, the SS or elements in the Party, and instructing them on how to handle similar cases in future.[207] He dispensed advice on general principles too. On 1 June 1943, for instance, he told them that 'the purpose of sentencing lies in the protection of the people's community', and that punishment 'in our time has to carry out the popular-hygienic task of continually cleansing the body of the race by the ruthless elimination of criminals unworthy of life'.[208] In pursuit of this objective, Thierack also moved to regulate the relationship between the judicial system and the SS, which – not only at Hitler's behest – had been taking offenders condemned to terms of imprisonment and shooting them 'while trying to escape', or indeed executing offenders on its own initiative before they even got to court. What the Ministry delicately termed the 'correction of insufficient judicial sentences through special treatment by the police' was to cease; Bormann and Himmler would refer such cases to the Ministry, along with appeals for clemency, so that Hitler's time would no longer be taken up with such trivial matters. Local and regional Party and SS offices were ordered from now on to cease interfering in the judicial process. As a quid pro quo, Thierack agreed at his meeting with Bormann and Himmler on 18 September 1942 that 'asocials' would be handed over from state prisons to the SS 'for extermination through labour'. 'Persons in protective custody will be delivered without exception, Czechs or Germans with sentences of more than eight years on the recommendation of the Reich Minister of Justice.'[209]

Large numbers of non-German offenders were from this point onwards dealt with by the SS, though others continued to pass through the courts. This largely accounts for the fact that the officially registered number of death sentences in the Reich fell from 5,336 in 1943 to 4,264 the following year, though part of the reason for the drop may also lie in the fact that fanatically Nazi judges of the younger generation were being called up to the front, leaving the courts in the hands of older judges who retained at least some vestigial allegiance to the judicial process.[210] The statistical decrease, in other words, marked a continued growth in the number of native Germans sentenced to death. To their number were added the 'asocials' and 'habitual criminals' consigned by Thierack to the SS for 'extermination through labour'. After Hitler had approved of the killings on 22 September 1942, the transfer of prisoners from state jails and penitentiaries began. Most of them were 'security confined', repeat offenders who had been in prison since the early years of the Third Reich. Gypsies and Jews in the prisons were also included in the process. Individual prisoners whose transfer to a concentration camp had to be recommended by the Ministry were examined in their prison by officials, usually in a very brief session lasting no more than a few minutes. Some were kept in prison beyond their release date so that they could be examined in this way. Prison governors tried, and in many cases succeeded, in retaining prisoners whose labour was particularly economically valuable to the prison. Altogether more than 20,000 prisoners were handed over. Most were taken to Mauthausen, where they were savagely beaten, sometimes to death, on their arrival, then, if they survived this ordeal, they were forced to haul stones weighing up to 50 kilograms each up the 186 broad steps of the camp quarry. If they staggered and fell, the prisoners were shot by the SS guards, who would sometimes throw them down into the quarry from 30 or 40 metres up, or force them to empty trucks of stones on to the men working below.

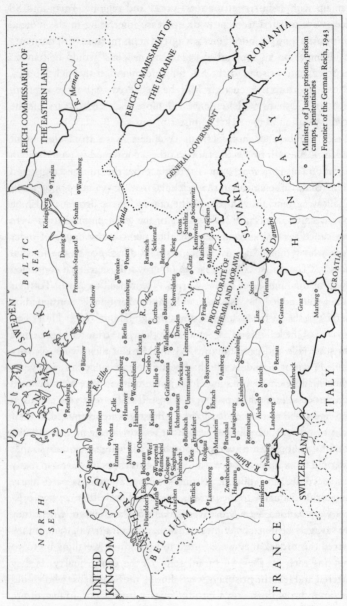

17. German Prisons and Penitentiaries

A number of prisoners put an end to their suffering by jumping off the cliff into the quarry depths. By the end of 1942, the mortality rate of the transferred prisoners stood at 35 per cent, far greater than that of any other group of camp inmates apart from Jews.[211]

III

Those inmates who remained behind in Germany's state prisons experienced steadily deteriorating conditions as the war progressed. The need for labour sharply increased the pressure on the Justice Ministry to effect what Thierack called the 'mobilization' of prisoners. They were increasingly lent out to arms manufacturers, for a suitable fee, in the same way that concentration camp inmates were. Similarly, this often involved their being sent out to sub-camps rather than staying in prison. In the prisons themselves, food supplies started running low, and inmates were sometimes reduced to eating animal fodder and mouldy vegetables. Thus in 1943, for example, prisoners at Plötzensee were reported to be grabbing leaves from the trees in the prison yard as they went round it on their daily exercise, to add nourishment to their soup. Weight loss and vitamin deficiencies weakened the prisoners and made them susceptible to infection.[212] Food supplies were not keeping pace with the increase in the prison population, particularly among women. The number of women convicted of criminal offences rose from 46,500 in 1939 to 117,000 in 1942, and that of juvenile offenders from 17,500 to 52,500. Many of these were sentenced for offences against wartime laws and regulations, particularly economic offences, which increased from under 3,000 in 1940 to more than 26,500 two years later. Convictions for illegal association with prisoners of war, a new offence, reached 10,600 by 1943. But the number of people sentenced for other crimes was on the rise too: theft convictions rose from 48,000 in 1939 to nearly 83,000 in 1943, for example. By contrast, sexual offences declined steeply, with pimping convictions down by over 50 per cent, rape by more than 65 per cent, and sexual offences with minors by more than 60 per cent. Evidently the police were so concerned to enforce wartime restrictions that they were starting to neglect other areas of the criminal law, though the fall in sexual offences would also have reflected the departure of millions of young men to the battle-front.[213]

Inevitably in these circumstances, overcrowding became a serious problem in Germany's state penal institutions during the war. The total prison population grew from just under 110,000 in mid-1939 to 144,000 in mid-1942 and 197,000 in mid-1944. In the Old Reich – the area within the borders of 1937 with some small additions during the war – the number rose from around 100,000 at the beginning of the war to 140,000 in September 1942 and 158,000 two years later. The proportion of female inmates increased from 9 per cent of the prison population in 1939 to 23 per cent four years later, by which time German penal institutions were keeping more than 43,000 women behind bars. These numbers were far higher than the prisons had been designed to hold. Dirt and disease were the result, as prisoners were packed in several to a cell, hygiene facilities were strained beyond their limit, and washing and showering, particularly in the final year of the war, became nigh impossible. Infestations with scabies and lice became common, and several prisons were hit by epidemics of typhus and other infectious diseases. Prison warders became increasingly short-tempered and prone to use violence to maintain order, as the ratio of warders to prisoners deteriorated from 1:6 (in 1939) to 1:14 (in 1944). In some cases, prisoners were chained to the wall or floor when they were being punished. Beatings, relatively uncommon in the 1930s, became commonplace in the last two years of the war. The prison authorities' decision to help the collection of winter clothing to assist the German troops freezing before the gates of Moscow in December 1941 netted more than 55,000 socks and nearly 5,000 jumpers confiscated from inmates, exposing prisoners to cold and leading to a rise in the death rate. Prisons did not possess air-raid shelters, and those in or near the centre of large towns and cities were particularly prone to destruction in bombing raids, leading to more deaths and further overcrowding as the number of cells was further reduced.[214]

Even after 1943, more Germans were held in state prisons than in concentration camps. But conditions in the latter deteriorated too. From the mid-1930s, the camps had begun to function mainly as centres of detention for 'asocials' and other minorities, after most of the political opponents of the regime for whom they had originally been intended had been released on good behaviour. As soon as the war began, however, the camps began to resume their earlier function as centres of detention and deterrence for the wider German civilian population, above all former

Communists and Social Democrats. At the beginning of the war, Hitler gave Himmler new powers of arrest and detention, which he used, with the Leader's agreement, to apprehend people suspected of opposing the regime. On 26 October 1939 the Gestapo ordered that if anyone from an arms factory was taken off to a camp for behaviour hostile to the state or likely to undermine the morale of the workforce, a notice had to be put up in the factory announcing the fact, adding in severe cases that he had been put in a punishment block. Care should be taken, the order added, not to announce the length of the sentence or the date of release. If corporal punishment in the camp was ordered for the worker, this should be publicized too.[215] If this was not enough of a deterrent, the camps began to function as places of execution for people arrested by the police as 'saboteurs' or 'shirkers'. Executions were widely publicized. While he was still at Sachsenhausen, Rudolf Höss later reported, an ex-Communist at the Junkers aircraft factory was arrested after refusing to carry out air-raid protection work; Himmler personally ordered his execution, which was to take place at the nearest concentration camp. The man was taken to Sachsenhausen, where it fell to Höss to carry out the execution. He ordered a post to be erected in a sandpit near the camp workshops and had the man tied to it. 'The man was completely resigned to his fate,' he remembered later, although 'he had not expected to be executed. He was allowed to write to his family, and was given cigarettes, for which he had asked.' A firing-squad shot him through the heart and Höss 'gave him the *coup de grâce*'. 'In the days to come,' he added, 'we were to have plenty of experiences of this kind. Almost every day I had to parade with my execution squad.'[216]

Most Germans sent to the camps became long-term inmates. Thus 'political' prisoners once again became an important part of the camp population. They had to wear a red triangle on their uniforms to distinguish them from the other categories of prisoner, such as the green-triangled 'criminals'. Political prisoners' later accounts of their experiences in the camps portrayed the 'criminals' in particular as brutal and ruthless men who were deliberately put in positions of responsibility by the SS in order to intimidate the rest. The reality was rather different. Both 'criminals' and 'politicals' were used by the SS to work with the camp administration in controlling the other inmates because they were Germans and thus fulfilled the racial criteria demanded by the SS for positions of responsibility. Benedikt Kautsky, son of a leading Social

Democrat of the Imperial era, later recalled from his own time as a prisoner in a variety of concentration camps that a 'bitter struggle' was constantly being waged between the 'reds' and the 'greens', in which each side would denounce members of the other to the SS, engage in 'despicable intrigues' and stage 'palace revolutions' against their opponents. The winners were able to get relatively safe jobs in the camp office, better food, better clothing, more freedom of action, more power and more status. Attaining the position of 'block leader' or 'capo' meant a better chance of surviving. By such means, the political prisoners succeeded in some camps, notably Buchenwald and Neuengamme, in dominating the internal self-administration of the inmates themselves. There is no convincing evidence that the 'criminals' were any more brutal or unscrupulous than other, political capos. The survival of all of them depended on carrying out the orders of the SS.[217]

The vast expansion of the camps as they were converted from centres of punishment to suppliers of forced labour transformed their character. From 21,000 mostly German inmates in mid-1939, the system grew to hold 110,000 by September 1942 and nearly 715,000 in January 1945, including over 202,000 women. At Buchenwald, for instance, nearly 100,000 new prisoners were admitted in 1944 alone. The camp contained prisoners from more than thirty different countries, and foreigners outnumbered Germans many times over.[218] In these circumstances, as camp authorities were unable to keep pace with building programmes to cater for the massive influx of new prisoners, death and disease, aided by the brutality of the camp guards, became more common even than before. Below the camp aristocracy of 'greens' and 'reds', the broad mass of prisoners lived in a state of continual fear and privation. Camp life was, with rare exceptions, a war of all against all for the survival of the fittest, in which the worst jobs were given to those least able to defend themselves. Jews and Slavs received the lowest rations and the least adequate accommodation, and hunger, overwork, beatings and disease turned the weakest into 'Moslems' (*Muselmänner*), the inmates' designation for those who had given up. Such people no longer tried to keep clean or to stop other prisoners stealing their food or survive the blows that were inevitably rained down on them by the guards and the capos, until they died of ill-treatment and exhaustion.[219]

The transformation of the camps into centres of labour supply for industry, and the influx of hundreds of thousands of new prisoners, provided opportunities for self-enrichment that commandants and officers were not slow to exploit. Aware of the corruption problem, Himmler addressed senior SS leaders in Posen on 4 October 1944, reminding them that they had taken from the Jews 'what wealth they had' and handed it over to the Reich.

We have taken none of it for ourselves. Individual men who have lapsed will be punished ... A number of SS men – there are not very many of them – have fallen short, and they will die without mercy. We had the moral right, we had the duty to our people, to destroy this people which wanted to destroy us. But we have not the right to enrich ourselves with so much as a fur, a watch, a mark, a cigarette or anything else. We have exterminated a bacterium because we do not want in the end to be infected by the bacterium and die of it. I will not see so much as a small area of sepsis appear here or gain a hold. Wherever it may take hold, we will cauterize it. [220]

Himmler was referring here, at least implicitly, to a commission of investigation under an SS judge, Konrad Morgen, that had uncovered widespread evidence of corruption in the administration of a number of camps. Only a few of those responsible were, in fact, shot out of hand; most were usually dismissed or transferred to other duties. The most prominent among them was the commandant of Auschwitz, Rudolf Höss, who was transferred to administrative duties in the concentration camp inspectorate on 22 November 1943. Several other camp commandants were disciplined in a similar way, including, as we have seen, at Majdanek and Treblinka. The case of Karl Otto Koch, who was dismissed as commandant of Buchenwald at the end of 1941, was unusual in its severity. Morgen's extensive investigations during the course of 1942 and 1943 revealed that Koch had not only embezzled large sums of SS money but also allowed prisoners to escape, destroyed vital evidence of his corruption and had key witnesses murdered. With Himmler's approval, Morgen arrested Koch on 24 August 1943, brought him before an SS tribunal and had him condemned to death: he was eventually shot in Buchenwald a few days before the camp was liberated by US forces.[221]

IV

As overcrowding got worse in the camps, disease began to spread, and the malnourished and ill-treated inmates increasingly succumbed to infections, including at times murderous epidemics of typhus. Hospital blocks in the camps began to suffer under the strain. Early in 1941, therefore, Himmler approached the T-4 'euthanasia' unit in Berlin with a request for help. Initially, because they were fully occupied in killing the mentally handicapped and mentally ill, the members of the T-4 team were unable to assist. But when the killing programme was halted in August 1941 following the intervention of Bishop von Galen, the unit's two leading administrators, Philipp Bouhler and Viktor Brack, began sending T-4 doctors to assess camp inmates who had become seriously ill. They operated under the bureaucratic designation 'Special Treatment 14f13', devised by the head of the concentration camp inspectorate, where 'Special Treatment' meant killing, '14' referred to reported deaths in the camps and '13' to the cause of death, namely gassing (other file series were labelled '14f6', suicide, '14f7', natural death, and so on).[222] Under the 14f13 programme, commissions of doctors from the euthanasia organization visited the camps from September 1941 onwards. After a merely visual inspection of the prisoners paraded before them by the SS, they filled out forms of the kind usually employed in the T-4 Action for those they singled out for killing. The forms went to Brack's office in Berlin, from where they were sent to a selected killing centre (Bernburg, Hartheim or Sonnenstein), which then requested that the relevant camp should deliver the designated inmates. As a letter from one of the medical referees, Friedrich Mennecke, to his wife on 26 November 1941, written from the concentration camp at Buchenwald, made clear, in many cases the selection process was a 'purely theoretical task' that had little to do with medicine. This applied particularly to 'in total 1,200 Jews', he wrote, 'who don't all have to be "examined", but whose reasons for being arrested (often very extensive) have to be taken from the files and copied on to the forms'. Mennecke diagnosed the non-Jewish inmates he selected for killing with phrases such as 'compulsive, rootless psychopath, anti-German mentality', or 'fanatical German-hater and asocial psychopath'. Under the heading 'symptoms', Mennecke put descriptions like 'dyed-in-the-wool Communist, not worthy to join the armed forces', or 'continual racial defilement'.[223]

Those selected for killing were told they were being moved to better conditions. After the first inspection, the remaining inmates knew better, and told their fellow prisoners to take off their spectacles before they paraded before the doctors, and not to register with minor injuries if they could manage it. The fact that the selected inmates were told to leave their spectacles behind, along with artificial limbs and other accoutrements of the disabled, before they embarked on the transport, was rightly taken as a clear indication of the fate to which they were going. The numbers of those selected were considerable. Already in the first trawl, of the camps in the Old Reich and the former Austria – Buchenwald, Dachau, Flossenbürg, Mauthausen, Neuengamme and Ravensbrück – the doctors selected no fewer than 12,000 victims. This was not altogether to the liking of Himmler, who instructed the camp commandants that only those inmates incapable of work should be killed; in April 1943 this was restricted still further to the mentally ill. Nevertheless, the total number of concentration camp inmates murdered in the gas chambers of the T-4 programme has been put at around 20,000. From April 1944 the concentration camp at Mauthausen, where 10,000 out of some 50,000 inmates were registered sick, began to send inmates directly to the gas chamber at Hartheim without involving the euthanasia organization in Berlin; an unknown number of inmates were killed in this way. The programme was important enough for the planned demolition of the gas chamber to be put off until 12 December 1944.[224]

This was not the only purpose for which Hartheim and the other killing centres of the T-4 programme were used after August 1941. Brack and Bouhler not only sent their experts to the camps, or seconded them to the Reinhard Action in the east, they also used them to carry on the original killing programme in secret. Galen's protest had weakened the political position of their organization, which became the object of bureaucratic in-fighting between the T-4 group, based in the Leader's Chancellery, and the Interior Ministry, ending in an uneasy compromise in which the programme was put under the formal control of Herbert Linden, who filled the new post of Reich Commissioner for Healing and Care Institutions within the Ministry of the Interior. But the T-4 group continued to do its work. Viktor Brack, its leading figure, explained to those involved 'that the "Action" was not ended by the stop that happened in August 1941 but will continue'.[225] Subsidiary organizations such as the transport group that moved the patients to the killing centres also remained in existence. It was clear to all that the mass killings now had to give way to individual murders, so as not to arouse public suspicion. For the closure of the gas chambers had not quelled public unease. On 18 November 1941, for example, in what was undoubtedly the strongest open attack on the programme by any medical man in the course of the Third Reich, Franz Büchner, a professor of medicine at Freiburg University, asked rhetorically in a lecture on the Hippocratic Oath: 'Is the human being of the future only to be assessed for his biological value?' His answer was unambiguously negative. 'Every physician who thinks Hippocratically will resist the idea that the life of the incurably ill should be described in the sense of Binding and Hoche as a life not worth living.' Binding and Hoche, the authors of an influential tract advocating involuntary euthanasia, were thus in his view advocating the violation of basic medical ethics. 'The only master the physician has to serve,' declared Büchner, 'is life.'[226]

But medical staff at the T-4 headquarters in Berlin and in psychiatric and care institutions continued to be committed to the idea of killing 'life unworthy of life'. The murder of children through fatal injections or deliberate starvation continued as before, but these methods were now applied to adult patients as well, and in a far wider range of institutions than the original killing centres. At Kaufbeuren-Irsee, patients who could work on the asylum farm or in some other capacity were fed what was categorized as a 'normal diet', and those who could not were given a 'basic diet', consisting of small amounts of root vegetables boiled in water. After three months of ingesting virtually no fats or proteins, they would be so weak that they could be killed with an injection of a small quantity of sedatives. By late 1942 so many were dying that the director of the asylum banned the ringing of the chapel bell during burials, in case its frequency alarmed local people. Conferences were held between the directors and staff of different institutions to determine the best way of starving inmates to death, and orders were issued, for example by the Bavarian Interior Ministry, providing for the food rations of the 'unproductive' to be cut. At Eglfing-Haar, patients selected for killing were isolated in special pavilions, soon dubbed 'hunger houses'. The director, Hermann Pfannmüller, was quite open about the purpose of these diets, and regularly inspected the asylum kitchens in order to ensure that they were enforced. Aware of what was going on, the cook added fats to the cooking-pot after he left. Nevertheless, from 1943 to 1945 some 429 inmates died in the hunger houses. At Hadamar, patients deemed incapable of working were fed on a diet of nettle soup, just three times a week; relatives who received letters from them asking for food parcels were told that feelings of hunger were a symptom of their illness, and that in any case soldiers and people who were working for the nation had to get priority in the distribution of food supplies. 4,817 patients were transported to Hadamar between August 1942 and March 1945: no fewer than 4,422 of them died.[227]

By this time, starvation and lethal injections were also being used to kill poorly disciplined and refractory patients, as well as any whom the asylum directors felt would be poor workers, irrespective of the form-filling operations run by T-4 headquarters. At Kaufbeuren-Irsee, for example, a fifteen-year-old Gypsy who stole from hospital stores was killed with a lethal injection, which he was told was a typhus inoculation; at Hadamar, in December 1942, an inmate who worked on the estate was found to be telling stories about the asylum in the local town, confined to quarters, and died within three days. Corruption played a part too: patients who owned a good watch or a stout pair of shoes would sometimes be killed by nurses eager to acquire their possessions, while in the Kalmenhof psychiatric reformatory, produce from the institution's 1,000-acre estate frequently went to the director and the staff instead of the inmates, who had to survive on about half their planned allocation of milk, meat and butter.[228] The killing programme even became more intensive in 1944–5, and continued in some institutions all the way up to the end of the war; in Kaufbeuren-Irsee, indeed, one killing was recorded on 29 May 1945, nearly a month after the war had officially ended.[229]

In the intervening period, new categories of victims had been added to the original list. Towards the end of 1942 the central directorate of the euthanasia programme began to organize the killing of foreign forced labourers, particularly Poles, who had become mentally ill or had contracted tuberculosis; over a hundred of them were murdered in Hadamar between the middle of 1944 and the end of the war, and more in Hartheim and other established killing centres as well as new camps and institutions designated for the purpose. The killings extended to babies born to female forced labourers who had resisted the pressure to have an abortion; sixty-eight children under the age of three were killed at the Kelsterbach institution from 1943 to 1945 because they were classified as the racially undesirable offspring of such women.[230] At Hadamar, more than forty healthy children moved there in April 1943 were killed because they had been classified as 'mixed-race of the first degree', that is, one parent was Jewish. Often they had been taken into care because their parents were dead, or the Jewish parent had been killed and the remaining parent had been ruled incapable of caring for them. The chief physician at Hadamar, Adolf Wahlmann, justified these murders by classifying the victims as 'congenitally feeble-minded' or 'difficult to educate', although there was no medical or psychiatric justification for such a designation at all.[231]

The killing of psychiatric patients also extended beyond the Reich. Already in 1939–40 it had encompassed asylums in occupied Poland. From the summer of 1941 it also operated in the parts of the Soviet Union conquered and occupied by the German armies in the course of Operation Barbarossa. As well as killing large numbers of Jews and Communist Party officials, the SS Task Forces that followed the German army sought out psychiatric hospitals and systematically killed the inmates by shooting them, poisoning them, depriving them of food, or putting them outside in the winter cold to die of exposure. From August 1941, on Himmler's instructions, they began to look for other means, in view of the stress that these direct methods placed on the SS men, some of whom were turning to drink or suffering from nervous exhaustion. With the help of equipment provided by Albert Widmann and the Criminal-Technical Institute, the SS first tried locking patients into a building and blowing them up with explosives. This turned out to be too messy for their taste. So they went over to gassing them with carbon monoxide in mobile gas vans as suggested by Widmann. Carried out in this way, the Task Force killings of psychiatric patients in the occupied Soviet Union continued sporadically until late 1942. Although the exact number will never be known, Soviet sources suggest that about 10,000 people were exterminated in this way.[232]

Increased efforts were made after August 1941 to keep such murder programmes from attracting public attention. The transportation of patients was now justified as a means of removing them from the danger posed by air raids, for example. Yet the killings could not be kept entirely secret. On 21 October 1943 Herbert Linden complained to the President of Jena University that his staff were being too open about the continuing 'children's euthanasia' programme:

According to Director Kloos in Stadtroda, the mother of a young idiot boy was told the following in the clinic at Jena: 'Your boy is an idiot, without any prospect of developing, and he must therefore be transferred to the regional hospital in Stadtroda, where three physicians from Berlin examine the children at certain intervals and decide whether they should be killed.'[233]

This laxness had to be stopped, he said. 'As you know,' he added in a second letter, 'the Leader wants all discussion of the question of euthanasia to be avoided.'[234] Voices were also raised in protest from within the Confessing Church, most notably in October 1943, when a synod in Breslau stated publicly: 'The annihilation of human beings simply because they are relatives of a criminal, old, or mentally ill, or belong to a foreign race, is not wielding the sword of state given to the authorities by God.'[235] Protestant welfare institutions like Bodelschwingh's Bethel Hospital sometimes tried to delay the transport of patients to the killing centres, or to send them out of harm's way, but even Bodelschwingh met with only limited success in these efforts.[236] The Catholic Church was initially hesitant, though it soon realized that the killing programme was continuing. A joint pastoral letter on the topic, drafted in November 1941 by a group of bishops, was suppressed by Cardinal Bertram, who was reluctant to exacerbate the situation still further in the wake of Galen's sermon. Instead, early in 1943, the bishops instructed Catholic institutions not to co-operate with the registration of patients for the Reich Ministry of the Interior, which had ordered it at the end of the previous year with the obvious intention of compiling lists of people to be killed.[237] On 29 June 1943 Pope Pius XII issued an Encyclical, *Mystici Corporis*, condemning the way in which, in Germany, 'physically deformed people, mentally disturbed people and hereditarily ill people have at times been robbed of their lives . . . The blood of those who are all the dearer to our Saviour because they deserve the greater pity,' he concluded, 'cries out from the earth up to Heaven.'[238] Following this, on 26 September 1943, an open condemnation of the killing of 'the innocent and defenceless mentally handicapped and mentally ill, the incurably infirm and fatally wounded, innocent hostages and disarmed prisoners of war and criminal offenders, people of a foreign race or descent' by the Catholic bishops of Germany was read out from the pulpit in churches across the land. The breadth of the terms in which it was couched was remarkable. Its overall effects were minimal.[239]

V

Among the many people whom the Nazis regarded as racially inferior, a special position was reserved for the Gypsies. Himmler regarded them as particularly subversive because of their itinerant lifestyle, their alleged criminality and their aversion to regular, conventional employment. Racial mixing with Germans posed a eugenic threat. By September 1939 German Gypsies had been rounded up and registered with a special office in Berlin. Many of them were in special camps. As soon as the war broke out, the SS took the opportunity to put into effect what Himmler had already called the 'final solution of the Gypsy question'.[240] Restrictions were placed on their movements, and many were expelled from border areas in the belief that their wanderings and their supposed lack of patriotism made them suitable for recruitment by foreign intelligence agencies. A plan to resettle them in occupied Poland was shelved while Himmler sorted out the resettlement of ethnic Germans there, but a meeting of SS officials chaired by Heydrich on 30 January 1940 decided that it was time for the plan's implementation. In May 1940 some 2,500 German Gypsies were rounded up and deported to the General Government. In August 1940, however, it was decided to postpone further deportations until the Jews had been dealt with. While the SS dithered, the persecution of those Gypsies who remained in the Reich intensified. Gypsy soldiers were cashiered from the army, Gypsy children were expelled from schools, Gypsy men were drafted into forced labour schemes. Early in 1942 Gypsies in Alsace-Lorraine were arrested, and some of them were taken to concentration camps in Germany as 'asocials'. 2,000 Gypsies in East Prussia were loaded on to cattle cars at the same time, and taken to Bialystok, where they were put in a prison, from which they were later moved to a camp in Brest-Litovsk. Meanwhile, Dr Robert Ritter's research team, based in the Reich Health Office, was painstakingly continuing its registration and racial assessment of every Gypsy and half-Gypsy in Germany. By March 1942 the team had assessed 13,000; a year later the total assessed in Germany and Austria had reached more than 21,000; and by March 1944 the project was finally completed, with a final tally of precisely 23,822. However, by this time, many of those who had been assessed by Ritter and his team were no longer alive.[241]

The killings began in 1942. The previous year, the Reich Criminal Police Office, which had already concentrated Gypsies from the Austrian Burgenland into a number of camps in the province, had persuaded Himmler to allow the deportation of 5,000 of them to a specially cordoned-off section of the Lódź ghetto. Plans to use the adult Gypsies for labour duties came to nothing, however. As typhus began to rage in the ghetto, particularly affecting the overcrowded and insanitary quarter where the Gypsies lived, the German administration decided to take them all to Chelmno, where the great majority – more than half of them children – were killed in mobile gas vans. Around the same time, SS Task Forces in occupied Eastern Europe were shooting large numbers of Gypsies as 'asocials' and 'saboteurs'. In March 1942, for instance, Task Force D reported with evident satisfaction that there were no more Gypsies left in the Crimea. The killings commonly included women and children as well as men. They were normally rounded up together with the local Jewish population, stripped of their clothes, lined up alongside ditches and shot in the back of the neck. The numbers ran into thousands and included sedentary as well as itinerant families, despite the fact that Himmler made a clear distinction between the two. In Serbia, as we have seen, the regional army commander Franz Böhme included Gypsies in his arrests and shootings of 'hostages'. One eyewitness of a mass shooting of Jews and Gypsies by men of the 704th Infantry Division of the regular German army on 30 October 1941 reported: 'The shooting of the Jews is simpler than that of the Gypsies. One has to admit that the Jews go to their death composed – they stand very calmly, whereas the Gypsies cry, scream and move constantly while they already stand at the place of the shooting. Several even jump into the ditch and pretend to be dead.' Harald Turner, the head of the SS in the area, alleged (without any evidence) that Gypsy men were working for the Jews in partisan warfare and were responsible for many atrocities. Several thousand were killed, although when the gassing of the remaining Serbian Jews in the Sajmiste camp began in February 1942, the Gypsy women and children held there were released.[242]

The killing of Gypsies was also carried out by Germany's Balkan

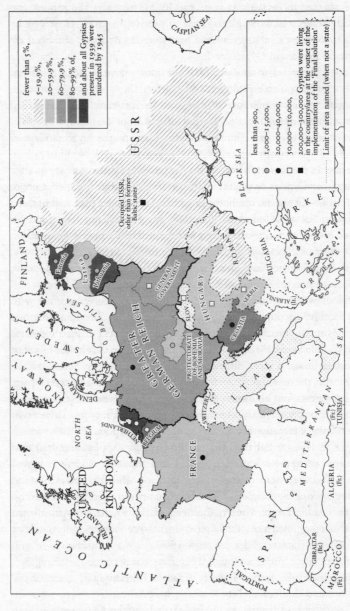

18. The Extermination of the Gypsies

allies. In Croatia, as we have seen, the Ustashe massacred large numbers of Gypsies as well as Serbs and Jews. Similarly, the antisemitic regime of Ion Antonescu in Romania ordered some 25,000 out of a total of 209,000 Romanian Gypsies to be deported to Transnistria, along with 2,000 members of a religious sect, the Inochentists, who refused on grounds of conscience to do military service. Those who were rounded up were mainly itinerant Gypsies, whom Antonescu made largely responsible for crime and public disorder in Romania. In practice, the arrests were often quite arbitrary in character, and the Romanian army protested successfully against the inclusion of some First World War veterans in the deportations. The deportees were described in 1942 as living in conditions of 'indescribable misery', without food, emaciated and covered in lice. Increasing numbers died of hunger, cold and disease. Their bodies were found on local highways; thousands had perished by the spring of 1943, when they were transferred to better housing in a number of villages and given jobs on public works projects. Only half of the deportees survived long enough to return to Romania from Transnistria with the retreating Romanian army in 1944.[243]

Although these killings were on a large scale, they were far less systematic than those carried out by the Germans. On 16 December 1942 Himmler ordered the deportation of more than 13,000 German Gypsies to a special section of the Auschwitz camp.[244] The camp commandant Rudolf Höss recalled that the arrest of Gypsies was chaotic, with many decorated war veterans and even Nazi Party members being rounded up simply because they had some Gypsy ancestry. In their case there was no classification as a half- or quarter-Gypsy; anyone with even a small amount of Gypsy ancestry was regarded as a threat. The 13,000 constituted under half the Gypsy and part-Gypsy population of the Reich; many of the others were exempted because they worked in armaments and munitions factories, so that a considerable proportion of those deported were children. Thousands more were deported to Auschwitz from the Protectorate of Bohemia and Moravia. At Auschwitz-Birkenau they filled a special family camp. It eventually contained nearly 14,000 Gypsies from Germany and Austria, 4,500 from Bohemia and Moravia, and 1,300 from Poland. Hygiene was poor, conditions filthy, malnutrition rife, and inmates, especially children, rapidly succumbed to typhus and tuberculosis. The sick were selected on a number of occasions and sent to the gas chambers. Some 1,700 who came in from

Bialystok on 23 March 1943 were killed shortly after arrival. Early in 1944 the majority of the Gypsy family camp's men and women were taken to other camps in Germany for use as forced labourers. On 16 May 1944 the SS surrounded the family camp with the intention of sending the remaining 6,000 inmates to the gas chambers. Forewarned by the camp's German commandant, the Gypsies armed themselves with knives, spades, crowbars and stones, and refused to leave. Fearful of causing a pitched battle, the SS withdrew. Over the following weeks, more Gypsies were taken in small batches for work in Germany. On 2 August 1944 Rudolf Höss, now reinstated as the main camp commandant, ordered the SS to round up the remaining 3,000 or so Gypsies, who were given food rations and told they too were being deported to another camp. His real intention, however, was to free up the Gypsy camp accommodation for large numbers of new incoming prisoners. The Gypsies were taken to the crematoria and put to death. Another 800, mostly children, were sent from Buchenwald in early October 1944 and killed as well. This brought the total number of Gypsies who died at Auschwitz to more than 20,000, of whom 5,600 had been gassed and the rest had died from disease or maltreatment. In his memoirs, unbelievably, Höss described them as 'my best-loved prisoners', trusting, good-natured and irresponsible, like children.[245]

Gypsies in Nazi Germany were arrested, sent to concentration camps and killed not because, like Jews, they were thought to be so potent a threat to the German war effort that they all had to be exterminated, but because they were considered to be 'asocial', criminal, and useless to the 'national community'. In Nazi Germany, of course, these supposed characteristics were thought to be largely inherited, and thus racial in origin. But this does not make the mass murder of German and European Gypsies a genocide in the same way as the mass murder of German and European Jews was. In most concentration camps, Gypsies were classified as asocial and made to wear the black triangle that denoted them as such. Sometimes, as we shall see in the next chapter, they were specially selected for medical experimentation; in Buchenwald there is no doubt that they were singled out for especially harsh treatment. At least 5,000 and possibly up to 15,000 remained in Germany during the war, and in January 1943 the police ordered that they were to be sterilized if they agreed to the operation. They were offered the inducement of permission to marry non-Gypsy Germans if they consented.

However, those who refused were liable to be put under heavy pressure to give their consent. A number were threatened with being sent to a concentration camp. Others successfully appealed on the grounds that the admixture of Gypsy blood in their veins was insignificant. Altogether, between 2,000 and 2,500 Gypsies were sterilized during the war, most of them classified by Ritter and his team as 'asocial mixed-race Gypsies'. They fell into a similar category to that of so-called mixed-race Jews, a group that caused perpetual uncertainty amongst the Nazis as to what should be done with them. Overall, the Gypsies were not, in other words, the subject of a concerted, obsessive and centrally directed campaign of physical extermination that sought to eliminate them all, without exception. But the fact that the majority of them were also classified as 'asocial' imposed on them a double burden of discrimination and persecution. That is why so many of them were killed, while the vast majority of so-called mixed-race Jews were not. In the long run, of course, race laws and sterilization programmes were intended to eliminate both categories from the chain of heredity in what some have called a 'delayed genocide'.[246]

VI

The various categories of camp inmates also included homosexuals, designated by a pink triangle. Male homosexuality was illegal, under a definition whose scope had already been considerably expanded before the war. The head of the SS, Heinrich Himmler, was almost obsessed with hunting down homosexuals, whom he thought undermined the masculinity of the SS and the armed forces; he was supported in this by Hitler, who in August 1941 declared that 'homosexuality is actually as infectious and as dangerous as the plague' and urged the use of 'barbaric severity . . . wherever symptoms of homosexuality appear among young people'.[247] On 4 September 1941 the death penalty was introduced for sex with a minor.[248] Then, in November 1941, at Himmler's behest, Hitler issued a confidential order prescribing execution for a member of the SS found committing 'unnatural acts with another man'.[249] It had, Himmler decreed the following March, to be explained to all members of the SS and police and they had to sign a form saying they had read and understood it. In practice, this policy was not implemented very thoroughly, and relatively few cases were brought; in the last few months of the war, indeed, Himmler commuted the sentences of some of the SS men condemned for homosexual behaviour on condition that they joined the Military SS and fought at the front.[250]

The armed forces were also concerned to combat homosexuality among the troops, and, after a good deal of internal debate, decided on 19 May 1943 to punish serious cases, however these might be defined, with the death penalty, and others by a dishonourable discharge from the forces, incarceration in a field punishment camp or referral to the police. Within the armed forces there were just over 1,100 convictions for contravention of the law against homosexual acts in 1940, rising to around 1,700 a year for the rest of the war. More generally, convictions of civilian men in Germany for contravening section 175 of the Reich Criminal Code, which outlawed homosexuality, fell from around 8,200 in 1939 to just over 4,000 in 1940, reflecting the enlistment of millions of men in the armed forces. Civilian offenders were initially sent to prison after trial, but Himmler ordered in 1940 that all homosexuals found to have had more than one sexual partner were to be taken straight to a concentration camp at the end of their prison sentence.[251] Ernst Kaltenbrunner of the SS Security Service wanted to go even further. In July 1943 he pressed the Ministry of Justice to issue an emergency edict ordering the compulsory castration of homosexuals, since too few prisoners had come forward to voluntarily request it. The Ministry pointed out that the lack of volunteers had been caused by its own ban on castrations since the beginning of the war, but added that the ban had now been revoked. Kaltenbrunner was satisfied with this explanation, but he also managed to get the army to review nearly 6,000 prosecutions for homosexuality that had been brought against soldiers since September 1939, with a view to cashiering 'incorrigibles' (many of whom would undoubtedly have then been arrested by the Gestapo and put into the camps).[252]

This meant that at least 2,300 homosexuals were put in one or other of the main German concentration camps every year during the war.[253] Here they were housed apart from other prisoners, and forced to work outdoors in all weathers in the hope that this would sort out those who were really 'manly' from those who were not. At Sachsenhausen, Rudolf Höss thought that, by treating them in this way, young men who had become male prostitutes just for the money 'were soon brought to their senses by hard work and the strict discipline of camp life'. Those he thought of as genuine homosexuals, however, 'gradually broke down physically' under the strain.[254] In Dachau, some 31 prisoners were incarcerated because of their homosexuality in 1939, 50 in 1940, 37 in 1941, 113 in 1942, 81 in 1943, 84 in 1944, and 19 in 1945. 109 were still in the camp on the eve of liberation in 1945.[255] Sometimes left-wing men who happened to be homosexual were put in a camp because of their homosexuality when the Gestapo was unable to pin a political offence on them. Thus, for example, the clerk H.D., born in 1915, was arrested in 1938 while trying to communicate with the Soviet Embassy in Prague. His partner was arrested and tortured into admitting that he had a sexual relationship with H.D. The Gestapo could not get a conviction for treason, but managed to secure a condemnation in the courts under the law banning homosexuality, and H.D. was sent to a penitentiary for three and a half years. On his release in November 1941, he was immediately rearrested and taken to Buchenwald, where he was made to wear the pink triangle, put to work in the camp quarry and singled out for particularly brutal maltreatment by a capo who was known for his hatred of homosexuals. Only the capo's own release from the camp saved him. The homosexuals' block in the camp was ruthlessly exploited by the SS guards, who regularly stole the food packets some of its inmates received from friends and relatives. Homosexuals were also regularly singled out during work at the quarry and 'shot while trying to escape'. The growing demand for camp labour from the autumn of 1942 onwards put an end to this practice, though not to the everyday brutality of the guards and capos. H. D. was eventually able to secure lighter duties, and survived. Many others did not.[256] Altogether, between 5,000 and 15,000 homosexuals were put into the concentration camps over the whole period of the Third Reich, of whom up to a half are thought to have perished.[257]

There is little doubt that Nazi policy towards homosexuals was becoming more radical and more exterminatory during the war; and indeed, more generally, the vast expansion of the concentration camp system in this period was not just a symptom of the insatiable demand of the war economy for fresh sources of labour but also reflected the growing radicalism of the Nazi regime as a whole. By February 1944, the Ministry of Justice was preparing to introduce a law that would allow the police to arrest, imprison and indeed eventually eliminate anyone who they considered a 'community alien'. As the legal definition in the draft legislation put it:

A community alien is: (1) anyone who, by his personality and way of life ... shows himself unable to satisfy the minimal demands of the national community by his own efforts; (2) anyone who (a) from work-shyness or frivolity leads a useless, spendthrift, or disorderly life ... or (b) from a tendency or inclination to ... minor criminal offences, or from a tendency to disorderliness while drunk, grossly violates his duty to sustain the national community, or (c) persistently disturbs the general peace through irritability or pleasure in quarrelling; or (3) anyone whose personality and way of life make it clear that their natural tendency is to commit serious crimes.[258]

In a draft preamble, the criminologist Edmund Mezger noted that the Law would be applied to 'failures' and the 'immoral' as well as 'criminals' and the 'work-shy'.[259] The Law was never implemented. It would, Goebbels thought, have made a bad impression abroad, at a time when Germany desperately needed the goodwill of neutral countries. Others within the higher echelons of the regime blocked it because it would have given Himmler's police system virtually unlimited powers over the whole of German society, enforcing Nazi ideology through a reign of unbridled terror.[260] But it was a characteristic product of the era. It breathed the radical spirit of the 'time of struggle' that was re-emerging in the final phases of the war: a spirit that now had the entire apparatus of state and Party at its disposal.

6

GERMAN MORALITIES

FEAR AND GUILT

I

On the night of 10 March 1941 a fifteen-year-old girl was woken up suddenly by a noise in another part of the flat where she lived with her family in a working-class area of Düsseldorf. 'I heard my stepfather fighting with my mother,' she later told the Gestapo. 'He was drunk and I heard him say: "Now it makes no difference. England will definitely win. Germany has no ammunition left." On this my mother retorted: "When you talk like this, you are not a German and I shall report you to the police." ' By this time, the girl had got out of bed and was watching the quarrel through the kitchen door. 'I observed,' she went on, 'that my stepfather took out a knife and pointed it at my mother, saying, "Before you betray me, I will kill you." I came out to help my mother, but when my stepfather saw me, he put the knife away and tried to hit me with a chair ... He was later taken away by the police.'[1] His wife told the Gestapo that he had said, among other things: 'Hitler is responsible for our hunger and the war' and 'Hitler wanted to hang the Jews, but they should hang him first'. The man denied the allegations and said he could not remember uttering any treasonable statements, since he had been insensibly drunk at the time. Like many similar (if less dramatic) incidents, there was more to this than a woman's simple disapproval of her husband's politics. The Gestapo officers assigned to the case realized that, as the stepdaughter said, the man was frequently inebriated and abusive, and concluded that domestic disharmony rather than hard-core political opposition was at the heart of the case. They decided that there was not enough evidence to prosecute, and let the man off after confiscating the knife. In such cases, they usually took the side of the husband: battered wives were not very high on the Gestapo's list of priorities.[2]

In other cases, the Gestapo took women's complaints more seriously. In March 1944, for instance, a Düsseldorf woman who was bombed out of her home went to seek refuge in her sister's house. The sister, Frau Hoffmann, had been married to a policeman since 1933, and was away at the time on a visit to her mother in Bavaria. As she entered the house, the woman was shocked to discover the policeman sharing the marital bedroom with an Estonian woman. She contacted her sister in Bavaria to tell her of the situation. When she got back, Frau Hoffmann tried to get her husband to end his relationship with his mistress. But it was to no avail. The marriage went rapidly downhill, with frequent heated arguments and shouting matches. In desperation, Frau Hoffmann unearthed some letters her husband had sent her when he was away. In them, he had written among other things that Germany would never win the war. She also reported that he had been making defeatist statements at his office. Her husband was duly arrested and interrogated. Under pressure from the Gestapo, he was unable to argue away the contents of his letters, and he confessed that what his wife alleged was true. He was tried for undermining popular morale, sentenced to death early in 1945 and executed shortly afterwards.[3]

Here too, the denunciation sprang from personal circumstances, but the motive did not really matter as far as the Gestapo was concerned. Only about 30 per cent of denunciations to the police in fact came from women. In the vast majority of these cases, the women had suffered abuse or violence from men. Since 1933 the Nazi state had intruded ever deeper into family and private life, and women experiencing difficulties with their relationships were responding by crossing the border between the private and the public in the other direction, thus allowing the regime effectively to co-opt them in its suppression of defeatist or oppositional states of mind. Often, in the aggressively masculine atmosphere of the Third Reich, the women seem to have felt there was no alternative. A woman employee being sexually harassed by her boss, or a wife being beaten and abused by her husband, was unlikely to get a hearing unless she denounced him for a political offence of some kind.[4] The state was particularly keen to keep soldiers' wives in line when their husbands were at the front, and was not going to listen to them if they complained. In propaganda and the mass media, the wives of soldiers, sailors and airmen (*Kriegerfrauen*) were portrayed as pure, asexual, self-sacrificing, hard-working and above all faithful. Thus Block Wardens, local Party officials and employers all kept a vigilant eye on their conduct. As a result, there were numerous denunciations of women who failed to live up to the saintly image to which they were supposed to conform. A typical case was recorded by the Düsseldorf branch of the Gestapo in November 1941, when a Frau Müller was confronted by the foreman in the packing factory where she worked with allegations about her relationship with a Belgian worker. A shouting match ensued, she slapped the foreman in the face, and he denounced her to the police. Interviewed by the Gestapo, she reported that her husband, a soldier, had had relationships with other women, and had even had children by some of them. Nevertheless, the Gestapo warned her officially that she must behave herself and end her relationship with the Belgian, otherwise they would take much harsher action against her.[5]

Despite its pressures on soldiers' wives to lead a chaste life while their menfolk were serving in the armed forces, the Nazi state was far from being the sexually repressive and prudish regime portrayed by exiled adherents of the Frankfurt School of sociology, or the followers of the Marxist Freudian Wilhelm Reich. During the war, people were naturally cautious about having children. With husbands at the Front, there was less opportunity for conception anyway, and many women were reluctant to become what were in effect single mothers. Births fell from more than 1,413,000 in 1939 to only just over a million on average in each of the later war years, while the number of new marriages dropped from almost 775,000 to less than 520,000.[6] As war losses mounted, Hitler became increasingly concerned about Germany's demographic future. On 15 August 1942 he issued an order recalling from the front line the last surviving son in every family where more than one son had been killed, because, he said, in view of the obviously strong hereditary strain of bravery and self-sacrifice in such families, 'nation and state have an interest in your families not dying out'.[7] Heinrich Himmler had already ordered his SS men to have children whether inside wedlock or 'beyond the limits of bourgeois laws and conventions', as he put it.[8] They had, of course, to be racially pure, and indeed restrictions on marriage to this end were actually tightened up in 1941, perhaps in response to the large numbers of foreign workers now in Germany.[9] In January 1944, too, reporting Hitler's own views on the topic, Martin Bormann issued a memorandum warning of the 'catastrophic' position Germany would be in after the war, with the 'loss of blood' to the nation consequent upon the mass death of the bravest young men at the battlefront. He suggested a variety of remedies, including educating women in the benefits of having children and relaxing the laws on illegitimacy in a situation where there would be a large surplus of women over men.[10]

The Nazi regime's espousal of population growth, extending even to encouraging racially suitable women to bear children outside wedlock, led it to issue popular manuals on how to achieve a happy sex life. One such tract was written by Dr Johannes Schultz; his 1940 book *Sex-Love-Marriage* gave detailed instructions to both men and women on, among other things, how best to achieve orgasm during intercourse. At the same time, Schultz's gung-ho attitude to heterosexual sex had a grim obverse side, as he endorsed the extermination of the handicapped in the T-4 Action and staged 'examinations' at the Göring Institute for Psychological Research and Psychotherapy during which men accused of homosexuality were forced to have sex with a female prostitute, and were sent to a concentration camp if they failed to perform satisfactorily. As far as racially approved heterosexual sex was concerned, Nazi encouragement combined with the circumstances of war to produce what many commentators described as a loosening of sexual morals between 1939 and 1945.[11] The Hamburg social worker Käthe Petersen complained in 1943 that women's behaviour had undergone a marked deterioration during the war; loose morals, debauchery, even prostitution had become common:

Many previously respectable wives have been alerted to the existence of other men through going out to work. In many firms – the tram company is a particularly good example – the male workers seem to have acquired the habit of going after the soldiers' wives. In many factories too, soldiers' wives have been led astray by the corrosive influences of some of their ruder female co-workers. Women who previously devoted themselves to their household chores, and were good mothers, have been led by such influences to neglect their housework and children, and to interest themselves only in night-time adventures and the quest for male company.[12]

The Security Service of the SS reported on 13 April 1944 that soldiers at the front were becoming upset at stories of the infidelities of married women at home. There was a marked increase in female immorality, it claimed, and it was particularly worrying that young women saw nothing wrong in indulging in sexual relationships with racially inferior foreign workers or prisoners of war. Denunciations often led to such women being arrested, and, as Himmler had instructed in January 1940, being put into a concentration camp for a minimum period of one year if their behaviour offended 'popular feelings'.[13]

The SS Security Service report of 1944 laid the responsibility for female immorality on female idleness not female employment, especially

the comparatively *high family benefits given to soldiers' wives and widows* ... These women do not have to find a job, since in many cases the level of family benefits even guarantees them a higher standard of living than that which they had before the war. The time and money at their disposal seduce them into spending their afternoons and evenings in coffee houses and bars, they need not give a second thought to treating themselves to expensive wines and spirits, and above and beyond that they are in a position to treat men – mainly soldiers – to them as well.[14]

Other factors included the eroticization of public life through hit songs and popular films and revues, and a feeling among some women that if soldiers were, as was probably the case, having 'a bit on the side', women 'had equal rights and were also entitled to amuse themselves'.[15] Sex was even becoming a commodity, with young women in particular bartering it for scarce foodstuffs and luxuries such as chocolate, silk stockings or cigarettes. Particularly in the final air raids, there was a widespread feeling that life was cheap and could easily be cut short, so women and girls decided to live it to the full while they could.[16]

Whether all this was part of a general increase in women's power and freedom of action, however, as some feminist historians have claimed, may be doubted. Certainly, during the war women had to fend for themselves, run their families without the controlling presence of their husbands and develop new levels of resourcefulness and initiative in managing their daily lives. But they did so in circumstances of increasing difficulty, with shortages of fuel and food creating worry and concern, bombing raids or enforced evacuation turning their lives upside down, and the general struggle to survive leading to weariness and exhaustion. Soldiers' wives who deserted or denounced their husbands were very much a minority. Most kept up regular correspondence with them, asked for their advice in their letters and longed for their return: 'Ah,' as one wrote to her husband on 17 April 1945, 'if only you were here with us, then everything would be much, much better and easier.'[17] Men came home on leave at increasingly infrequent intervals in the latter part of the war. Married women customarily kept photographs of their husband prominently displayed in the home to remind the children of his existence, talked regularly about him, and tried as much as possible to make him a presence in family life. For their part, fathers often dispensed advice and encouragement, or censure and criticism, from the front, controlling their family as far as they were able from afar. They even discussed their school reports. 'Klaus's mark for English has gone down due to laziness,' wrote one father, admittedly a schoolteacher, to his wife from the front. 'He lacks the disciplining influence of a father.'[18] 'I am sending your exercise book back,' wrote another father from the front to his nine-year-old son in 1943. 'Carry on so diligently and you'll make your parents very proud. Your essay on local history is very good.'[19]

II

One reason for the relative lack of success of Himmler's attempt to procure more children for the nation by encouraging illegitimate births lay in the fact that the overwhelming majority of Germans still steered their moral life mainly by the compass of the Christian religion. In 1939 95 per cent of Germans described themselves either as Catholics or as Protestants; 3.5 per cent were 'Deists' (gottgläubig), and 1.5 per cent atheists: most people in these latter categories were convinced Nazis who had left their Church at the behest of the Party, which had been trying since the mid-1930s to reduce the influence of Christianity in society.[20] Especially in rural areas and amongst older generations, the overwhelming predominance of Christianity encouraged conservative attitudes towards sexual morality, reinforced by the preaching of pastors and priests. This was not welcome to the Nazi hierarchy. During the 1930s Hitler had curtailed the autonomy of the Catholic Church, which had most adherents in the south and west of Germany, as far as he was able, and relations between the Third Reich and the Church had seriously deteriorated as a result. In Protestant north and central Germany, the attempt to create a fusion of Nazi ideology and a Church purged of its 'Jewish' elements in the German Christian movement had largely failed, not least because of fierce opposition from fundamentalist pastors in the self-styled Confessing Church. The Church minister Hans Kerrl, an enthusiastic supporter of German Christians, died a disappointed man aged fifty-four on 12 December 1941. The situation within German Protestantism as the war began was something of a stalemate, as neither side really won the battle, and the great mass of ordinary Protestants tried to find some kind of middle way between the two.[21]

Hitler's hostility to Christianity reached new heights, or depths, during the war. It was a frequent theme of his mealtime monologues. After the war was over and victory assured, he said in 1942, the Concordat he had signed with the Catholic Church in 1933 would be formally abrogated and the Church would be dealt with like any other non-Nazi voluntary association. The Third Reich 'would not tolerate the intervention of any foreign influence' such as the Pope, and the Papal Nuncio would eventually have to go back to Rome.[22] Priests, he said, were 'black bugs', 'abortions in cassocks'.[23] Hitler emphasized again and again his belief that Nazism was a secular ideology founded on modern science. Science, he declared, would easily destroy the last remaining vestiges of superstition. 'Put a small telescope in a village, and you destroy a world of superstitions.'[24] 'The best thing,' he declared on 14 October 1941, 'is to let Christianity die a natural death. A slow death has something comforting about it. The dogma of Christianity gets worn away before the advances of science.'[25] He was particularly critical of what he saw as its violation of the law of natural selection and the survival of the fittest. 'Taken to its logical extreme, Christianity would mean the systematic cultivation of human failure.'[26] It was indelibly Jewish in origin and character. 'Christianity is a prototype of Bolshevism: the mobilization by the Jew of the masses of slaves with the object of undermining society.'[27] Christianity was a drug, a kind of sickness: 'Let's be the only people who are immunized against the disease.'[28] 'In the long run,' he concluded, 'National Socialism and religion will no longer be able to exist together.' He would not persecute the Churches: they would simply wither away. 'But in that case we must not replace the Church by something equivalent. That would be terrifying!'[29] The future was Nazi, and the future would be secular.

Nevertheless, when the war broke out, Hitler initially soft-pedalled his anti-Christian policies, concerned that a further worsening of Church–state relations might undermine national solidarity in the prosecution of the war. The regime put pressure on the ecclesiastical leaders of both Churches to come out in public support of the war effort, which they did. A brief suspension of Church meetings by order of the Gestapo in the first weeks of the war was soon lifted. Military chaplains were quickly appointed to troop units and proved popular with the men. But the truce did not last long. As Hitler and the leading Nazis became more confident in the outcome of the war, they began to resume their attacks on the Churches. Protestant church visitation reports in Franconia in the spring of 1941 began recording that 'the struggle against the Church has been noticeably resumed'. Anti-Christian literature was being distributed by the Party once more.[30] Martin Bormann circularized the Party Regional Leaders in June 1941 reminding them that National Socialism was incompatible with Christianity and urging them to do all they could to reduce the influence of the Churches.[31] Many of the Regional Leaders, like Arthur Greiser in the Wartheland for example, were already rabidly anti-Christian, and needed little encouragement to follow Bormann's initiative. Soon churches were being permanently closed if they were too far away from air-raid shelters, church bells were being melted down for gun-metal, Church periodicals were being wound up because of the paper shortage, and Hermann Göring, the one leading Nazi who was in overall charge of a branch of the armed forces, banned chaplains from the air force. Citing the need for an intensified war effort, the state abolished some religious feast-days and moved others from weekdays to Sundays. The last vestiges of religious education were formally wound down in Saxony. Church property all over Germany was seized for conversion into maternity homes, schools for evacuated children, or hospitals for wounded soldiers. In September 1940 a blanket ban was placed on new novices joining any monastic order. Then, beginning in December 1940, monasteries and nunneries were expropriated and the monks and nuns expelled. By May 1941 some 130 had been taken over by the Party or the state.[32]

Expropriations of this kind were, as we have seen, the trigger to Bishop von Galen's denunciation of the 'euthanasia' action in 1941. And indeed, these measures aroused wide disquiet among the faithful. On 31 May 1941, for instance, it was reported in the rural district of Ebermannstadt, in Bavaria, that people were simply ignoring the injunction to work on religious feast-days:

The greatest part of the rural population is still sticking faithfully to its religious community. All attempts to shatter this loyalty have met with ice-cold rejection, and in part arouse discontent and hatred. The (legally abolished) feast-day of the Ascension was just one solid demonstration against the state ban, in the Protestant as well as in the Catholic population. The abolition of Ascension Day as well as the ban on the holding of processions, pilgrimages etc. on workdays is regarded as a mere excuse for the gradual and ongoing general removal of Church festivals altogether, as part of the total extermination of the Christian religious communities.[33]

Some fifty-nine priests were arrested in Bavaria alone for protesting against the abolition of holy days. This opposition was serious enough. But no anti-Christian measure was more widely resented than a decree issued by the Bavarian Education Minister, Adolf Wagner, on 23 April 1941 ordering school prayers to be replaced by Nazi songs, and crucifixes and religious pictures to be removed from school walls. Crowds of outraged mothers gathered outside the schools where the crucifixes had been taken down, demanding their reinstatement. Shaken by this public opposition, Wagner withdrew his decree after only two weeks. He did not publicize this because he did not want to lose face. Local Nazi hotheads persisted with the action, therefore, incurring even more widespread parental protests and demonstrations when the new school year began in the autumn of 1941. Women gathered thousands of signatures for petitions demanding that the crosses be put back. How could they support their husbands in the fight against Godless Bolshevism, they asked rhetorically, if religion was being attacked at home? They were backed by a powerful pastoral letter from Cardinal Faulhaber, read out from church pulpits on 17 August 1941. The opposition was clearly not going to go away. Humiliated, Wagner had to issue a public revocation of the order, release the fifty-nine priests, order all crucifixes to be put back in the schools, and permit a prayer (with an officially approved wording) to be read out in morning assembly. Hitler carpeted Wagner after this fiasco, and told him he would be sent to Dachau if he did anything so stupid again.[34]

The protesters' success was evidence of the depth of their convictions. It was also a product of the piecemeal nature of the measures. Had Wagner implemented them in a concerted overnight action they might have stood a better chance of success. Hitler, Goebbels and even Bormann now realized that the final solution of the Church question would have to wait until the war was over. It was simply too distracting and too damaging to national unity and morale to launch such attacks, especially after the war began going badly. By 1942, Protestant church visitation reports in Franconia were saying that all was quiet once more.[35] Pressure on active Party members to leave the Church was continuing, but few were heeding the call. On the other hand, the deteriorating situation of Germany during the war did not seem to cause many people to rediscover religion. 'The seriousness of the times,' according to the same report, 'has led only a few isolated members of the parish who have stayed remote from the Church to return to church services. In general, one can observe only a general apathy in most of the population . . . Regrettably, there is a considerable inclination amongst young people to regard the Church as a *quantité négligeable.*'[36] This suggested that Hitler had some reason to suppose that Christianity would wither away if the Third Reich lasted long enough into the future. Nazi education and indoctrination were taking the younger generation away from it.

Persecution, as experienced above all in 1941, made the Catholic Church hierarchy extremely wary of engaging in public protests against the regime. Those bishops who were concerned about matters such as the 'Jewish question, treatment of the Russian prisoners of war, atrocities of the SS in Russia etc.', as an unsigned memorandum discovered later in Cardinal Faulhaber's files put it, decided to approach the Nazi leadership with their concerns only in private, confining themselves in public to protesting in general terms about the persecution of the Church and the regime's attacks on the basic rights, the property, the freedom and the lives of German citizens. A public protest to this effect, dated 15 November 1941, was, however, suppressed on the orders of the senior Catholic cleric in Germany, Cardinal Bertram.[37] Bertram was more concerned to keep his head down than most, but throughout the war years, Catholic bishops showed little concern publicly for the mass murder of Jews or Soviet prisoners of war. Even Clemens von Galen remained silent. In his famous sermon of 3 August 1941 condemning the euthanasia campaign he had also referred to the Jews, but only by asking rhetorically whether Jesus had only wept over Jerusalem, or whether he wept over the land of Westphalia as well. It was absurd to think, he implied, that Jesus wept only over the people 'that rejected God's truth, that threw off God's law and so condemned itself to ruin'.[38] Even though he was indeed approached by at least one Jew in the hope that he would do something to help the Jews, he did and said nothing, not even in private.[39]

Conrad, Count Preysing, Bishop of Berlin, was perhaps the most persistent advocate within the Catholic Church of a policy of openly condemning the regime's maltreatment of the Jews. In August 1943 he had a petition to the regime drawn up which he hoped all the Catholic bishops in Germany would sign. Condemning the brutal evacuation of the Jews from Germany, it did not, however, mention their extermination, and only asked for the deportations to be carried out in a manner that respected the human rights of the deportees. But the Catholic bishops rejected the petition, opting instead for a pastoral letter that asked their flock to respect the right to life of people of other races. Preysing approached the Papal Nuncio, only to be told: 'It is all well and good to love thy neighbour, but the greatest neighbourly love consists in avoiding making any difficulties for the Church.'[40] The relative silence of the Catholic Church in Germany reflected not least the growing concern of Pope Pius XII about the threat of Communism, a concern that became greater as the German forces got into difficulties on the Eastern Front and the Red Army began to advance. The Pope had never forgotten his experiences as Papal Nuncio in Munich during the Communist and anarchist revolutions in 1919, events to which he referred when receiving the new German Ambassador to the Vatican, Ernst von Weizsäcker, in July 1943. As the war went on, Pius XII came to regard the German Reich as Europe's only defence against Communism, especially after the overthrow of Mussolini and in view of the growing strength of Communist partisan groups in northern and central Italy, and he privately condemned the Allied demand for unconditional surrender. He directed his efforts at using the internationally neutral status of the Vatican to work for a compromise peace that would leave an anti-Communist Germany intact. In pursuit of this goal, he considered it best not to raise his voice against the extermination of the Jews, for fear of compromising the Vatican's neutrality. Yet this did not prevent him from issuing a series of sharp condemnations of the 'euthanasia' programme in letters sent to his bishops in Germany; nor did it stop him from issuing in May and June 1943 public statements of his sympathy with the sufferings of the Polish people, as he had already done in December 1939.[41]

As he wrote to Preysing in April 1943, the Pope feared that public protests would lead to renewed persecution of the Church in Germany.

He was not willing to intervene to help the Jews. A public stance against the killings would not stop them, he thought, and indeed might simply speed them up. With the Germans in Rome, too, open criticism might bring German troops into the Vatican. The most he could do, he told Preysing, was to pray for the 'non-Aryan or half-Aryan Catholics . . . in the collapse of their external existence and in their spiritual need'. Contrary to what some of his critics have claimed, there is no convincing evidence that Pius XII was an antisemite, or that he had concluded from his experience in Munich in 1919 that Communism was part of a world Jewish conspiracy.[42] But on the other hand, he was fully aware by April 1943 that the Jews, including Catholics of Jewish origin, were not just suffering in spiritual and material terms, but were being murdered in vast numbers by the Germans. Pius XII knew, of course, that many Catholic priests in Italy, including some in the Vatican City, were giving refuge to Jews as the Germans began to threaten their existence from the autumn of 1943 onwards. He did nothing to stop such actions, but he took no part in them himself, nor did he utter a single word that might have encouraged priests to undertake them. Ever the cautious career diplomat, Pius XII did what he thought best in the interests of the Catholic Church both in Italy and elsewhere.[43]

Things were only a little different among German Protestants. On 4 April 1939 the German Christians issued a declaration in Bad Godesberg that affirmed the Church's 'responsibility for keeping our people racially pure' and insisted that there was 'no sharper contradiction' than that between Judaism and Christianity. The following month, the Confessing Church replied with a similar document agreeing that 'the preservation of the purity of our people demands an earnest and responsible racial policy'. Few will have noticed much difference between the two.[44] On occasion the Confessing Church did raise its voice in protest. When the Church Chancellery, formally the leading body of the Evangelical Church, together with three bishops, issued an open letter demanding 'that baptized Non-Aryans stay away from the Church activities of the German congregation', the leadership of the Confessing Church asked pointedly whether in that case Christ and the Apostles would have been ejected from the Church on racial grounds had they lived in the Third Reich. And as persecution turned to mass murder, one leading Protestant tried to stop the persecution of the Jews. Bishop Theophil Wurm wrote to Goebbels in November 1941, warning him that the campaign against the Jews was helping enemy propaganda. Goebbels threw the letter into his wastepaper basket. Another letter, which Wurm attempted to have passed to Hitler by a senior civil servant, made a similar point in respect of what he called 'the growing harshness of the treatment of Non-Aryans'.[45] On 16 July 1943 Wurm tried again. By this time, as he noted, he had lost both his son and his son-in-law on the Eastern Front. Writing personally to Hitler, he declared that the 'measures of annihilation' directed against 'Non-Aryans' stood 'in the sharpest contradiction to God's Commandment and violate the basis of all Western life and thought: people's God-given, fundamental right to life and human dignity in general'. Although it was ostensibly a private letter, Wurm had it copied and distributed within the Church. On 20 December 1943 Wurm repeated its main points in a letter to Hans-Heinrich Lammers, the head of the Reich Chancellery. 'I hereby caution you emphatically,' Lammers replied, 'and request you in future to be most punctilious in remaining within the bounds of your profession.' Politics were not the bishop's business. Nobody apart from Wurm attempted such an intervention, and shortly after his protest, he was banned from writing or speaking in public for the rest of the war, though he contined to preach and take services despite the ban.[46]

III

If the Churches did not openly condemn the Nazi genocide of the Jews, or undertake anything to try to stop it, then what was the attitude of the mass of ordinary Germans in this respect? Finding out about the killings was not difficult. Obviously, news travelled fast to the few Jews who remained in Germany.[47] In January 1942 Victor Klemperer was reporting rumours that 'evacuated Jews were *shot* in Riga, in groups, as they left the train'.[48] On 16 March 1942 his diary mentioned for the first time 'Auschwitz (or something like it), near Königshütte in Upper Silesia, mentioned as the most dreadful concentration camp'.[49] By October 1942 he was referring to it as a 'swift-working slaughter-house'.[50] 'The will to extermination is growing all the time,' he noted at the end of August 1942.[51] The mass murders in Auschwitz and elsewhere had, he noted, 'now been reported too frequently, and by too many consistent Aryan sources, for it to be a legend'.[52] As this suggests, knowledge of the mass killings of Jews, Poles and others in the east was not hard to come by. It could be obtained from a variety of sources. The Security Service of the SS reported in March 1942 that soldiers returning from Poland were talking openly about how the Jews were being killed there in large numbers.[53] The Nazi Party Chancellery complained on 9 October 1942 that 'discussions' about ' "very harsh measures" against the Jews, particularly in the Eastern Territories' were 'being spread by men on leave from the various units deployed in the east, who have themselves had the opportunity to observe such measures'.[54] Civil servants at many levels of the central Reich administration read the Task Force reports or were in contact with administrators in the east.[55] Railway timetable clerks, engine drivers and train drivers and other staff on stations and in goods yards could all identify the trains and knew where they were going. Policemen rounding up the Jews or dealing with their files or their property knew as well. Housing officials who reassigned the Jews' dwellings to Germans, administrators who dealt with the Jews' property – the list was almost endless.

Some Germans reacted with open enthusiasm to discrimination against the Jews. After putting on his yellow star, Victor Klemperer experienced for the first time being shouted at in the streets by young members of the Hitler Youth.[56] In his minutely detailed account of everyday life as a Jew in Nazi Germany during the war, Klemperer recorded a wide variety of reactions by ordinary Germans on the street as they encountered him wearing the star. While one asked him brusquely 'why are you still alive, you rogue?', others, complete strangers, would come up to him and shake him by the hand, whispering 'you know why!', before passing quickly on.[57] Such encounters became more dangerous after late October 1941, when the Reich Security Head Office ordered the arrest of any German who demonstrated any kind of friendliness towards a Jew in public, along with the arrest and incarceration in a concentration camp of the Jew in question.[58] Some persisted, however. Sometimes Klemperer was able to identify friendly workers as 'old SPD men at least, probably old KPD men', but he received abuse from other workers too.[59] On a visit to the Health Insurance Office Klemperer noticed a worker catching sight of his Jewish star and saying, 'They should give them an injection. Then that would be the end of them!'[60] By contrast, in April 1943 a worker removing the effects of an 'evacuee' from the Jews' House in Dresden where Victor Klemperer lived murmured to him, 'These damned swine – the things they're doing – in Poland – they drive me into a rage too.'[61] Jewish rations were worse than inadequate, but, while some shopkeepers stuck stony-faced to the rules, others showed some willingness to bend them.[62]

When they forced Jews to wear the yellow star on their clothing, the better for people to identify them, many non-Jewish Germans did not react in the way that Goebbels wanted them to. Jews reported being greeted on the street with unusual politeness, people coming up to them and apologizing, or offering them a seat on the tram. Foreign diplomats, among them the Swedish Ambassador and the US Consul-General in Berlin, noted similarly sympathetic reactions on the part of the majority population, particularly from older people. The public advertisement of the Jews' persecuted status produced feelings of shame and guilt when it was attached to visible, living human beings.[63] Popular reactions to the introduction of the Jewish star were overwhelmingly negative, and those who took it as the opportunity to abuse and attack Jews were in a small minority.[64] When, not long afterwards, the police began rounding up Jews in German cities and taking them to the local railway station for deportation to the east, negative public reactions outweighed the positive ones again. Older Germans in particular found the deportations shocking. The Security Service of the SS reported in December 1941 that people in Minden were saying that it was 'incomprehensible how human beings could be treated so brutally; whether they were Jews or Aryans, all of them in the end were people created by God.'[65] The religiously inclined were particularly critical of the deportations.[66] In Lemgo a crowd gathered to see the last transport of Jews off at the end of July 1942. Many citizens, particularly in the older generations, were critical, and even Nazi Party members said it was too hard on the Jews, who had been living in the town for many decades, even centuries.[67]

'On the train,' noted Luise Solmitz in Hamburg on 7 November 1941, 'people are craning their necks; apparently a fresh trainload of Non-Aryans to be sent away is being put together at Logenähs.'[68] Not long afterwards, she heard a passer-by comment as an elderly Jewish woman was taken away from a Jewish old people's home, 'driven together in such a little pile of misery': 'Good, that the rabble is being cleaned out!' But another witness to the action took exception to this comment: 'Are you talking to me?' he asked. 'Please shut up.'[69] All through the summer of 1942 Luise Solmitz witnessed the repeated deportations of elderly Jews to Theresienstadt. 'The whole of Hamburg is filled with the deportation even of the oldest people,' she noted. An acquaintance reported that 'whooping children had accompanied the removal', although Solmitz herself had never seen such behaviour. 'Once more, Jews have gone to Warsaw,' she reported on 14 July 1942. 'I found confirmation of this in the rubbish-bins outside their home, which were full to the brim with the miserable remains of their few possessions, with coloured tin cans, old bedside lamps, torn handbags. Children were rummaging about in them, cheering, making an indescribable mess.'[70]

An unexpected new challenge was posed to the Solmitz family when Friedrich and Luise's daughter Gisela fell in love with a Belgian man working in a Hamburg factory and they decided to marry. At the Registry Office, an official told Luise that the Reich Ministry of Justice had turned down the couple's application to marry, adding:

'Do the young man's parents know that your daughter is a half-breed of the first grade? I'm sure they've given their consent, but do they know that?' – 'Belgium doesn't recognize such laws or such views.' – 'What do you mean, "Belgium"? Today we don't even use the term "Germany". We think: "Europe". No Jew is to remain in Europe. This is my personal view – not the official one, but I notice it from signs that the Jews will be dealt with even more severely than before.' He said that to me twice. And there I sat, defenceless. 'Look,' he continued to lecture me, 'at what the Jews have done in Russia, in America. Now we're noticing it for the first time.'

When Luise Solmitz made so bold as to mention her Jewish husband, the official was thoroughly taken aback. 'Your husband is still here?!' he exclaimed in disbelief.[71]

IV

A few people tried to rescue such Jews as they could. The story of the businessman Oskar Schindler is well known: a Czech German and member of the Nazi Party, he obtained an enamel factory in Cracow when its Jewish owner was dispossessed, and employed 1,100 Jewish forced labourers there while also engaging in widespread black market activities, trading in looted art and pursuing other forms of corruption. As time went on, however, Schindler began to be outraged at the treatment meted out to Polish Jews, and managed to use his money and connections to protect those who were working for him. As the Red Army approached, he obtained permission to evacuate his workers to an arms factory in the Sudetenland, although it never produced any arms. The Jews survived the war, but Schindler had lost most of his fortune in protecting them, and he did not prosper in the more orderly business world of the postwar years. He moved to Argentina in 1948, but was forced into bankruptcy a decade later, and returned to Germany, living first in Frankfurt then in Hildesheim, and dying a relatively poor man in 1974, aged sixty-six.[72]

Another rescuer, the Catholic German army officer and former school-teacher Wilm Hosenfeld, also began employing Poles and Jews in his army sports administration in Warsaw, to protect them from arrest. 'How many have I already helped!' he wrote to his wife on 31 March 1943, adding a few months later: 'I don't have such a bad conscience that I must be afraid of any retribution.'[73] On 17 November 1944 Hosenfeld stumbled upon a starving Jewish survivor of the ghetto, living in an abandoned house that Hosenfeld was prospecting for use as the new army command headquarters.[74] The man turned out to be a well-known professional pianist, Wladyslaw Szpilman, whose radio recitals had made him a household name in Poland before the war. Hosenfeld hid him in the attic while the German army command moved in down-stairs, and kept him supplied with food and winter clothing until the Germans left the city. He never told Szpilman his name, nor did he, for obvious reasons of security, make any mention in his diary of what he had done. It was not until the 1950s that the pianist, who by this time had revived his career in Poland, discovered his rescuer's identity.[75]

There were others, less well known, who helped keep a total of several thousand Jews in hiding in Berlin, Warsaw, Amsterdam and many other occupied cities. They included clandestine groups stimulated by socialist or religious or sometimes simply humanitarian beliefs, such as scouting troops, charitable organizations, student clubs and a whole variety of pre-existing networks. A number of Jews, especially in France, were able to hide in the countryside with the help of friendly or compassionate farmers and villagers. One of many groups devoted to rescue was the Organization for Rescuing Children and Protecting the Health of Jewish Populations, founded in Russia in 1912. Its French branch hid several hundred Jewish children, many of them refugees from Germany and Austria, provided them with false identity papers, dispersed them to non-Jewish families who were willing to take the risk, or smuggled them into Spain or Switzerland. All in all, underground groups such as this managed to hide many thousands of Jews or send them into safety outside German-occupied Europe.[76] But these thousands, of course, have to be set against the millions who did not survive.

A small number of individuals also tried to get news of the extermination to the world outside German-dominated Europe. At the end of July 1942 the German industrialist Eduard Schulte, who enjoyed good relations with leading members of the regime, travelled to Zurich, where he told a Jewish business friend that Hitler had planned the complete annihilation of Europe's Jews by the end of the year. Up to 4 million would be transported to the east to be killed, possibly by sulphuric acid, he said. The information reached Gerhart Riegner of the Jewish World Congress, who organized the British and US embassies to transmit it via telegram to his headquarters in New York. Such reports frequently encountered scepticism amongst those to whom they were addressed. The enormity of the crime seemed beyond belief. The US government advised the Congress to keep Riegner's report confidential until it could be independently verified.[77] More reliable and precise information could only come from an eyewitness. One of the most extraordinary of these was Kurt Gerstein, a disinfection expert in the Hygiene Institute of the Military SS. Gerstein was sent by the Reich Security Head Office in the summer of 1942 to deliver 100 kilos of Zyklon-B to Lublin for an undisclosed purpose. On 2 August 1942 he arrived in Belzec and was present as a trainload of Jews from Lvov came in, were forced to undress, and were driven by Ukrainian auxiliaries into the gas chambers, where they were told they would be disinfected. There they had to wait for two and a half hours, weeping and crying, while mechanics outside tried to get the diesel motor going. Once it started working, Gerstein noted punctiliously, it took thirty-two minutes to kill the people inside the chamber. A devout Protestant, Gerstein was shocked by what he witnessed. On the journey back from Warsaw to Berlin, he told it all to Göran von Otter, a Swedish diplomat, who reported the details in a dispatch to the Swedish Foreign Office after discreetly checking Gerstein's credentials. The dispatch languished there until the end of the war, kept secret by officials who feared it would offend the Germans. Back in Berlin, Gerstein pestered the Papal Nuncio, the leaders of the Confessing Church and the Swiss Embassy with his story, all to no effect. Gerstein did not, however, as one might have expected, resign his post or ask for a transfer. He continued to deliver consignments of Zyklon-B to the camp, while redoubling his futile efforts to spread information about what was going on. Finally he wrote three separate reports on what he had seen, augmented by information gained by talking to others involved. He kept them secret, however, and it was only at the end of the war that he made them public by handing them over to the Americans. Arrested as an alleged war criminal, Gerstein hanged himself in his cell on 25 July 1945, most probably out of remorse at his failure, or guilt at not having done more.[78]

It was from Poland that the most determined attempts to inform the world of the extermination programme came. Members of the resistance sent information about the gassings at Treblinka to the exiled Polish government in London almost as soon as they began. On 17 September 1942 the Polish government in exile approved a public protest against the crimes the Germans were committing against the Jews, but it undertook no concrete action, encouraging neither Poles to give shelter to the Jews, nor Jews to seek refuge with Poles. Drawing too much attention to the Jews would in the exiled Polish government's view distract world opinion from the sufferings of the Poles, undermining the government's attempt to fight Stalin's policy of getting the Allies to recognize the Nazi–Soviet border agreed before the partition of Poland in September 1939. Some politicians in the exiled government believed that Jewish influence stood behind not only Stalin but also Churchill and Roosevelt. It might be exerted in favour of the recognition of the Curzon Line.[79] The situation only changed when, in 1942, Jan Karski, a member of the Polish underground, was commissioned by the resistance to go to the west and report on Poland's plight. The murder of the Jews was fairly low on the list of priorities he was given. Hearing of his mission, however, two members of a Jewish underground group persuaded him to visit the Warsaw ghetto and most probably also the camp at Belzec. Karski reported what he had seen when he eventually reached London.[80]

His report had a dramatic effect. On 29 October 1942 the Archbishop of Canterbury chaired a large public protest meeting at the Albert Hall in London, with representatives of the Jewish and Polish communities in attendance. On 27 November 1942 the Polish government-in-exile in London finally gave official recognition to the fact that Jews from Poland and other parts of Europe were being murdered on the territory it claimed for its own. Representatives of the government informed Churchill, and on 14 December 1942 Foreign Secretary Eden delivered an official report on the genocide to the British Cabinet. Three days later, the Allied governments issued a joint declaration promising retribution to those responsible for the mass murder of Europe's Jews.[81] The Allies concluded that the best way to stop the genocide was to concentrate everything on winning the war as quickly as possible. Bombing the railway lines to Auschwitz and other camps would only have achieved a temporary respite for the Jews, and distracted attention and resources from the larger purpose of overthrowing the regime that was killing them.[82] What the Allies did do, however, was to direct a massive propaganda campaign against the Nazi regime. Beginning in December 1942, British and other Allied propaganda media bombarded German citizens with broadcast and written information about the genocide, promising retribution.[83] In Berlin, faced with these accusations, Nazi propagandists did not even trouble any more to issue a denial. In terms of counter-propaganda, Goebbels said,

there is no question of a complete or partial refutation of the Jewish atrocity claims but simply a German action that will concern itself with English and American acts of violence in the whole world . . . It must be so, that every party accuses every party of committing atrocities. This general clamour will in the end lead to this topic being removed from the programme.[84]

The mass murder of the Jews thus became a kind of open secret in Germany from the end of 1942 at the very latest, and Goebbels knew that it would be futile to deny it.

The evidence does not, therefore, support the claim made by many Germans immediately after the war that they had known nothing about the extermination of the Jews. Nor does it, however, support the argument that Germans as a whole were enthusiastic supporters of the regime's murderous antisemitism or the claim that hatred of the Jews was a significant force in holding the 'people's community' together either before or during the war.[85] Strikingly, the voluminous surveillance reports of the SS Security Service had relatively little to say on the subject. There were good reasons for this. As the clandestine reporting service of the Social Democratic Party noted in March 1940:

The comprehensive terror compels 'national comrades' to conceal their real mood, to hold back from expressing their real opinions, and instead to feign optimism and approval. Indeed, it is obviously forcing ever more people to conform to the demands of the regime even in their thinking; they no longer dare to bring themselves to account. The outer shell of loyalty that forms in this way can last a long time yet.[86]

Open discussion of the persecution and murder of the Jews was thus relatively rare, and seldom reported even by the Security Service of the SS.[87] Nevertheless, the available evidence suggests that, on the whole, ordinary Germans did not approve. Goebbels's propaganda campaigns carried out in the second half of 1941 and again in 1943 had failed to convert them. But if people could not be made to approve of the murder of the Jews, then perhaps their evident knowledge of it could be used to persuade them to carry on fighting for fear of what the Jews might do to them in revenge, particularly if, as Nazi propaganda claimed, the Jews were in charge of Germany's enemies: Britain, the United States and the Soviet Union.[88]

The last two years of the war were filled with atrocity propaganda emanating from Goebbels's mass media: the Red Army in particular was portrayed, not entirely inaccurately, as hell-bent on raping and killing Germans as it advanced. Yet the effects of this were not what Goebbels intended. Far from leading to a strengthening of resolve amongst ordinary Germans, this propaganda only served to reveal deep-seated feelings of guilt that they had done nothing to prevent the Jews being killed. Such a feeling was an unexpected by-product of the continuing Christian convictions of the great majority of German citizens. In June 1943, for example, 'clerical groups' in Bavaria were reported to be reacting in this way to Goebbels's propaganda campaign centred on the Soviet massacre of Polish officers at Katyń. The Party Chancellery in Munich reported them as saying:

The SS used similar methods of butchery in its fight against the Jews in the east. The dreadful and inhumane treatment of the Jews by the SS virtually demands the punishment of our people by the Lord God. If these murders are not avenged upon us, then there is no longer any Divine justice! The German people has taken such a blood-guilt upon itself that it cannot count on any pity or forgiveness. Everything is bitterly avenged here on Earth. Because of these barbaric methods there is no more possibility of a humane conduct of the war on the part of our enemies.[89]

When Cologne cathedral was bombed the following month, people said this was in retribution for the burning of synagogues in 1938.[90] On

3 August 1943 an SS Security Service agent reported that people in Bavaria were saying 'that Würzburg was not attacked by enemy airmen because no synagogue was burned down in Würzburg. Others again said that the airmen were now coming to Würzburg as well because the last Jew left Würzburg a short while ago.' On 20 December 1943 the Protestant Bishop of Württemberg, Theophil Wurm, wrote to Hans-Heinrich Lammers, the long-time civil servant heading up Hitler's Reich Chancellery, reporting that in many cases the German people regarded

the sufferings that they have had to endure from enemy air attacks as retribution for what has been done to the Jews. The burning of houses and churches, the crashing and splintering on bombing nights, the flight with a few meagre possessions from houses that have been destroyed, the perplexity in searching for somewhere to take refuge, all this reminds the population in the most painful way of what the Jews had to suffer on earlier occasions.[91]

Just over a year later, on 6 November 1944, the Security Service of the SS reported from Stuttgart that Goebbels's propaganda graphically portraying the lootings, killings and rapes carried out by Red Army troops in Nemmersdorf, in East Prussia,

in many cases achieved the opposite of what was intended. Compatriots say it is shameless to make so much of them in the German press . . . 'What does the leadership intend by the publication of such pictures as those in the National Socialist Courier on Saturday? They should realise that the sight of these victims will remind every thinking person of the atrocities we have committed in enemy territory, even in Germany itself. Have we not murdered thousands of Jews? Don't soldiers again and again report that Jews in Poland have had to dig their own graves? And how did we treat the Jews in the concentration camp in Alsace? Jews are human beings too. By doing all this we have shown the enemy what they can do to us if they win.' (The opinion of numerous people from all classes of the population.)[92]

'The Jews alone will repay us for the crimes we have committed against them,' predicted one anonymous letter to the head of news at the Propaganda Ministry on 4 July 1944.[93] Fear and guilt were driving the great mass of Germans to dread the retribution of the Allies. From 1943 onwards, they were mentally preparing themselves to deflect this retribution as far as they were able, by denying all knowledge of the genocide once the war was lost.

CULTURES OF DESTRUCTION

I

During the Second World War, as before it, Nazi propaganda could seem all-pervasive and inescapable, corralling a supine nation into unthinking adulation of Hitler, unconditional enthusiasm for Nazi ideology, and unquestioning support for the military conquest and racial supremacy that were the primary aims of the German war effort. This at least was the impression that Goebbels liked to give. Yet it was a false one.[94] To begin with, propaganda was far from all-pervasive. Even Goebbels realized that it had to have its limits. Entertainment and relaxation also had a role to play. 'It's important for the war to keep our people in a good mood,' he noted in his diary on 26 February 1942. 'We failed to do that during the [First] World War, and we had to pay for it with a terrible catastrophe. This example must under no circumstances be repeated.'[95] In taking this view, Goebbels was among other things learning from experience, as popular distaste for the over-politicized media and a constant diet of speeches and exhortations had already led to widespread indifference to Nazi propaganda before the war.[96] By 1939, therefore, the Nazi Propaganda Minister knew very well that his initial ambition to achieve a total spiritual and emotional mobilization of the German people could not be fulfilled. The purpose of Nazi propaganda during the war was thus more modest: it was to keep people fighting and make sure they conformed, even if only outwardly, to the demands the regime made on them.[97]

As Propaganda Minister, Goebbels had huge power over the arts, culture and the media, but he did not have it all his own way. He had a major rival in Otto Dietrich, whom Hitler had appointed head of the Reich Press Office of the Nazi Party in 1931. In 1938 Hitler also made him President of the Reich Press Chamber. Unlike Goebbels, Dietrich worked in Hitler's office and was therefore in a position to receive the Leader's direct orders virtually on a daily basis. It was one of Dietrich's tasks to give Hitler a digest of the international news media every morning. From 1938 onwards Dietrich and his staff also gave daily noontime press conferences at which they issued directives to the editors of the German papers. In order to try to circumvent Dietrich's growing influence, Goebbels timed his own daily Minister's Conference for 11 a.m. This only made matters worse. In 1940 Dietrich began to outflank Goebbels by issuing 'Daily Slogans of the Reich Press Chief' from Hitler's headquarters. Relations between the two men deteriorated still further. On one occasion, as they sat round Hitler's lunch table, Dietrich said: 'My Leader, this morning, while I was taking a bath, I thought of a good idea.' Quick as a flash, Goebbels interrupted him: 'Mr Dietrich, you should take more baths.'[98]

A particularly serious clash occurred in October 1941, when Hitler sent Dietrich to Berlin to announce to an international press conference that the Soviet Union had been defeated. Although this reflected a widespread perception in the higher echelons of the Nazi leadership at the time, Goebbels was furious: such over-optimistic declarations were in his view hostages to fortune.[99] He was right, as it turned out. By 23 August 1942 the tension between Goebbels and Dietrich was so acute that Hitler himself felt it necessary to order all press directives, including Goebbels's, to be channelled through Dietrich's office, ruling that Dietrich's noontide press conferences were the only ones that legitimately represented the Leader's opinions. Not long afterwards, Dietrich succeeded in getting one of his men appointed Deputy Reich Press Chief with an office in the Propaganda Ministry. Goebbels complained to Bormann, whose power was now considerable. This dangerous move prompted a threat to resign from Dietrich, turned down brusquely by Hitler. It was only towards the end of the war that Goebbels finally gained the upper hand, winning the power of veto over Dietrich's daily press directives in June 1944 and finally persuading Hitler to sack the press chief on 30 March 1945, much too late to make any difference.[100] By this time, the Propaganda Minister had also successfully sidelined other rivals as well. These ranged from the press division of Ribbentrop's Foreign Office to the 'propaganda companies' formed by the armed forces. The management of propaganda had always been riven by rivalries, but in the last two years of the war, Goebbels finally did achieve almost total control over it.[101]

While these quarrels were going on in the background, the Propaganda Ministry pumped out enormous amounts of material in every medium of communication as part of its effort to boost morale. An official Propaganda Ministry report noted that in the year beginning September 1939 it had produced nine slide shows that had been seen by 4.3 million people in evening entertainments organized by regional Party offices. Themes covered included 'Germany's Racial Policies' and 'World Pirate England'. In the first sixteen months of the war, the Party organized some 200,000 political meetings, mainly for morale-boosting purposes. Picture posters for pasting on walls were printed in huge numbers (a million for 'Down with Germany's Enemies', for example); text-posters appeared in editions of up to half a million. The Ministry issued 32.5 million copies of the Nazi Party 'Word of the Week', and produced no fewer than 65 million leaflets on a wide variety of subjects. Not to be forgotten either, 700,000 photographs of Hitler had been distributed by the end of 1940. Journalists, Otto Dietrich told representatives of the press on 3 September 1939, were no longer just reporters but also 'soldiers of the German people'.[102] By 1944 the Nazi Party controlled almost the entirety of the German press. Here was a medium that was far more propaganda than entertainment. The need to ration paper supplies led the Reich Press Chamber to close down 500 newspapers in May 1941 and a further 950 two years later (including the formerly respectable *Frankfurt Newspaper*). Yet people were avid for news during the war, and the circulation of the major papers increased substantially as their number fell. The total circulation of daily papers rose from 20.5 to 26.5 million between 1939 and 1944. The flagship daily of the Party, the *Racial Observer*, was selling 1,192,500 copies by 1941; and it was joined by significant new weeklies, above all *The Reich*, founded by Goebbels in 1940 and printing 1.5 million copies of each edition three years later. The growing size and importance of the SS were reflected in the fact that its own weekly, *The Black Corps*, founded in 1935, was the second-biggest-selling weekly by this time with a circulation of 750,000 copies. Yet people did not just read the press for information or to hear the latest news of the Party or the SS. They also read it for entertainment and relaxation, and so sales of illustrated magazines and weeklies rose from 11.9 to 20.8 million between 1939 and 1944.[103]

The regime placed considerable emphasis on literature as a spur to patriotic commitment, reviving and marketing appropriate classics like Schiller's *William Tell* with a new enthusiasm. 45,000 front-line libraries supplied reading matter to the troops in their idle moments, if they had any. Germans donated no fewer than 43 million books to stock them. 25,000 public libraries at home catered for the reading needs of civilians. What, then, did people read during the war? William L. Shirer reported in October 1939 that the best-selling novels in Germany at this time were Margaret Mitchell's *Gone with the Wind* and A. J. Cronin's *The Citadel*. The Swedish explorer Sven Hedin's *Fifty Years of Germany* was attracting readers who sought reassurance that Germany was not wholly despised in the non-fascist world.[104] This situation obviously could not last. The war offered the Reich Chamber of Literature considerably increased opportunities to exercise control over writers and publishers. Censorship was tightened up in 1940, and the need to ration paper supplies provided an excuse for requiring publishers to give advance notice of new books and their authors for approval after this time. All books and periodicals from enemy states were banned, except for purely scientific ones, and those by authors who had died before 1904 (provided they were not Jewish). Living German authors still interested in publishing in the Third Reich faced an uncertain future unless they produced books with titles like *We Fly Against England*, the top item in the borrowing statistics of Hamburg libraries in 1940–41. William L. Shirer reported that anti-Soviet books were still selling well in 1939–40, despite the Hitler–Stalin Pact, and detective stories were also very popular. Historical war-books were much sought after, including *The Total War*, a celebrated tract on the First World War by the now safely dead Erich Ludendorff, and propaganda accounts of England and Poland were also selling well. The biggest seller of all was still Hitler's *My Struggle*, which had provided its author with the royalties from no fewer than 6 million copies by 1940.[105]

Escapist literature of various kinds became more important than ever after the war began. Goebbels encouraged the publication of erotic literature and soft pornography, especially for the troops, while humorous fiction and collections of jokes also sold well. The Wild West novels of Karl May – widely known to be Hitler's own favourite author – enjoyed a revival, prompting in some military readers the reflection that they had taught them a lot about how to fight Soviet partisans behind the Eastern Front. In this situation, literary writers increasingly took refuge in 'inner emigration', either lapsing into silence or producing historical romances. Werner Bergengruen, whose work before 1939 had been taken by the reading public as a veiled criticism of the Nazi regime, sold 60,000 copies of his 1940 novel *Heaven as It Is on Earth* before it was banned the following year. Deprived of the opportunity to reach his public in the conventional way, he wrote poems anonymously and had them distributed privately and, in effect, illegally. *The Realm of Demons*, by Frank Thiess, was also banned after its first edition had sold out in 1941. His next novel, *The Neapolitan Legend*, published the following year, met with more toleration because of its less obvious applicability to the present. The problem with these works of 'inner emigration' was that their message for the present could only be discovered by the most assiduous reading between the lines, often indeed reading into them things that the reader wanted to see rather than the author wanted to be understood. After the war was over, Thiess was to claim in an angry exchange with the exiled Thomas Mann that only writers who had stayed in Germany to oppose the regime could lay claim to be the spiritual founders of postwar democracy. But their works, like that of other tolerated writers, had as much effect in distracting readers from the realities of wartime life in the Third Reich as they did in expressing a widely held desire to acquire an inner distance from it.[106]

II

Of all the mass media used by the Propaganda Ministry, it was, perhaps surprisingly, the theatre to which it devoted the most money, steering towards it more than 26 per cent of the subsidies it issued to the arts, in comparison, for example, to under 12 per cent for the cinema. In the early part of the war, there were no fewer than 240 theatres in Germany run by the state or regional, local or municipal authorities, with a total of 222,000 seats, together with another 120 or so privately funded theatres of one kind or another. In 1940 some 40 million tickets were sold; roughly a quarter of the tickets were block bookings for groups of soldiers or munitions workers. Demand was high, buoyed up by the closure of many other sources of amusement and relaxation.[107] Although private and individual tourism continued to a degree during the war, the Labour Front's 'Strength Through Joy' programme was drastically curtailed, its foreign and domestic tourism operations cut back, its ships and transport facilities converted for use by troops and its funding of entertainment directed towards catering for members of the armed forces.[108] Theatre became an important substitute.

The Security Service of the SS noted early in 1942 that 'during the war, very many theatres can report visitors in numbers that have scarcely been experienced before. In the big cities it is hardly possible any more to obtain theatre tickets through regular box-office sales.'[109] Goebbels declared at the beginning of the war that the repertoire must now avoid 'exaggeration and stylelessness that go against the seriousness of the times and the national feeling of the people'.[110] However, he was aware that most theatre-goers, especially new ones, were in search above all of entertainment. Theatre directors were told that pessimistic or depressing plays were not to be put on. There was also a ban on performances of plays by authors belonging to enemy states (though occasional exceptions were made for Shakespeare). Chekhov was allowed before 22 June 1941, but not thereafter. Theatre directors did their best to get round such regulations. They mounted new productions of German classics, including tragedies, and thereby created, so many of them later claimed, a theatrical oasis in the Nazi cultural desert. None of this could disguise the fact that the ban on many foreign authors impoverished the repertoire. Responding to public demand for comedies and light entertainment further depressed the standard of what the German stage offered in these years. And of course, as in other areas of culture in wartime Germany, what was found in the theatre was above all escape from reality.[111] From 1943 onwards escape in this form became progressively more difficult, as one theatre after another was destroyed by bombing, not infrequently leading to the actors and stagehands being drafted into the armed forces or munitions work. In August 1944, when, in his new capacity as Reich Plenipotentiary for the Total War Effort, Goebbels ordered the closure of all theatres, music halls and cabarets, he was doing little more than making a virtue of necessity.[112]

As with the theatre, cinema increased dramatically in popularity in the early part of the war.[113] In 1942 over a billion tickets were sold, more than five times more than in 1933. Every German went to the movies on average some thirteen to fourteen times a year. Young people's attendance was particularly high – in 1943 a sample survey reported that over 70 per cent of ten-to-seventeen-year-olds went to the cinema at least once a month, and 22 per cent at least once a week. Cinema-goers were catered for not only by more than 7,000 picture-houses but also large numbers of mobile cinemas that toured country areas and also found their way to the battle-front to entertain the troops. Every year from 1939 to 1944, German studios produced some sixty to seventy new films, shown in every country in Europe where German troops were stationed.[114] The studios were state-owned, centrally organized from 1942, and equipped to use the most modern techniques. In the cinema, each programme had by order of the Propaganda Ministry to contain an educational 'cultural film', dealing with natural history, showing German 'cultural work' in Poland, or, from 1943, giving instructions on air-raid protection.[115]

Audiences were said to have found these rather boring. What they really wanted to see was the latest newsreel. From 7 September 1940 all existing newsreels were merged into one, entitled from November 1940 onwards the 'German Weekly Review' (Deutsche Wochenschau), which formed a compulsory part of every movie programme. The producers were able to show a forty-minute newsreel within two weeks of the film being taken by cameramen and journalists 'embedded' in regiments serving at the front. This gave newsreels an immediacy and an authenticity that made them very popular. Up to 3,000 copies were made of each issue, and each issue was seen by some 20 million people in Germany alone. The newsreels satisfied public demand for first-hand information about the progress of the war, and many people went to the cinema mainly to see them rather than the feature film. Skilful use of music, a focus on images rather than words and careful editing gave them a powerful and to some degree aesthetic appeal. Of course, soldiers always appeared in a heroic light, fighting off demonic enemies hell-bent on Germany's destruction, the descriptions of the strategic situation were generally vague and always optimistic, and blood and guts, dead bodies and anything likely to produce horror or revulsion were banished from the screen. Hitler's personal request to the Propaganda Ministry on 10 July 1942 for shots of Russian atrocities to be included in the newsreel ('He specifically asks that such atrocities should include genitals being cut off and the placing of hand-grenades in the trousers of prisoners')[116] does not seem to have been followed, perhaps fortunately for cinema audiences. Nevertheless, the viewers were drawn into the action almost as virtual participants, often breaking out into spontaneous applause and shouts of 'Hail!' during the reports of victories in the first two years of the war.[117]

Goebbels buttressed the informative and propaganda impact of the newsreel with a series of major feature films aimed at popularizing key elements of Nazi ideology. In 1941 he commissioned four anti-Bolshevik films, including *GPU*, premièred on 14 August the following year. Its title was already out of date: the Russian political police by this time was known by the initials NKVD. Predictably, the emphasis in the film was on the machinations of the supposed Jewish conspiracy behind the murderous activities of the Soviet police. Goebbels attempted to win over audiences by having a love-story put at the centre of the drama, but the film was not a success: its portrayal of the Russians as sadistic torturers was simply too cliché-ridden and too crude, and after it was released Goebbels put a stop to further anti-Soviet feature films. Just as mixed were the fortunes met by the films he commissioned that were directed against the British, whom he wanted shown as controlled by Jews and ruled by plutocrats. In 1940 *The Rothschilds' Shares in Waterloo* pilloried the imaginary financial manipulations of a Jewish bank during the Battle of Waterloo in 1815 (which it showed, of course, as being won by the Prussians, under General Blücher). The film was a failure with the public, since it was not clear whether it was intended to be anti-British or antisemitic, and it was withdrawn in 1940 and re-edited. Other films, like *My Life for Ireland*, *Carl Peters* and *Uncle Kruger*, all released in 1941, attacked the British colonial record. *Uncle Kruger* was particularly impressive. A film about the Boer War, it was well acted (it starred Emil Jannings) and had high production values. However, a good many of the figures in the film were crude caricatures – Queen Victoria was shown as addicted to medicinal whisky, Cecil Rhodes as decadent, waited on by slaves and obsessed with gold, the monocled Austen Chamberlain as hypocritical and effete, General Kitchener as ruthless and inhumane, and the young Winston Churchill, a concentration camp commandant, as a sadistic murderer who feeds his bulldog on beef steaks and shoots starving inmates if they complain about their lack of food. Uncle Kruger, the Boer leader, was depicted as an honest, simple national hero who leads successful resistance against overwhelming odds – a lesson Goebbels considered made it worth ordering the film to be re-released in 1944.[118] Critics of the original showing were indeed in a minority, and those who felt that some scenes were 'not historically genuine' were outnumbered by those who saw it as 'a kind of historical document'. The more knowledgeable amongst the audience wondered, however, whether it was wise to portray the 'Boer people' in such a heroic light. 'The character of this hybrid people is ambiguous and cannot be presented as an ideal image of the Germanic race if only in view of the colonial tasks that will face Great Germany after the final victory.'[119]

Almost as soon as the war began, Goebbels ordered the preparation of two major antisemitic films: *Jew Süss* and *The Eternal Jew*, both designed to win the support of the German public for the Nazi leadership's stepping up of anti-Jewish measures as soon as the war began, particularly in Poland. *Jew Süss*, directed by Veit Harlan and released on 24 September 1940, was a historical film based on a novel of the same name by the (now exiled) Jewish writer Lion Feuchtwanger. While Feuchtwanger had wanted to highlight the role of the Jew as scapegoat, Harlan turned the character of Süss, an eighteenth-century moneylender hanged for his alleged crimes, into a villain who not only extorted money from honest Germans but also abducted and raped a beautiful young German girl. Harlan contrasted the civilized-looking, socially integrated character of Süss not only with fair-haired Germans but also with all the other Jewish characters in the film, who were depicted as ugly and dirty. Süss's hanging at the end of the film conveyed the clearest possible message as to the fate the Jews merited in the present. The much-praised performances of the principal actors were so powerful that one of them actually got Goebbels to announce in public that he was not Jewish because many cinema-goers were convinced that he was. Himmler was so enthusiastic about the film that he ordered all SS men to watch it, and it was also specially shown to non-Jewish audiences in Eastern Europe in the vicinity of concentration and extermination camps, and in Germany in towns where a new deportation was scheduled.[120]

The Eternal Jew, directed by Fritz Hippler under Goebbels's personal supervision, was a feature-length documentary that also purported to show how Jews really were. Pictures of Jews on the streets of Polish towns were intercut with film sequences of 'rats, which,' the synopsis said, 'are the parasites and bacillus-carriers among animals, just as the Jews occupy the same position among mankind'. Film of kosher butchering, taken in Poland shortly after the invasion of 1939, was edited to suggest the brutality of the Jews, while mock-up sets of Jewish homes showed dirt, neglect and infestation with vermin. Just like rats, Jews had migrated across the world, and everywhere, the film claimed, citing a whole series of invented statistics, the Jews committed crimes, spread revolution and subversion, and undermined cultural values and standards. So radical was the film's antisemitism that the Propaganda Ministry had doubts about showing it to the public, and certainly it was most successful among Party activists; the general public was less impressed. Many were reported to have walked out half-way through the screening, and others were recorded as thinking it 'boring'. Most people preferred the subtler and dramatically more interesting images portrayed in a drama such as *Jew Süss*, which was so powerful in its effect on audiences that people spontaneously sprang to their feet during performances, especially in the rape scene, and shouted curses at the screen. In Berlin, there were shouts from the audience of 'Get the last Jews out of Germany!'[121]

What the success of *Jew Süss* and the comparative failure of *The Eternal Jew* showed was that Germans did not want mere propaganda. With the coming of war, people needed distraction from their daily cares more than ever. William L. Shirer recorded in October 1939 that 'in the movie world the big hit at the moment is Clark Gable in *Adventure in China*, as it's called here. It's packing them in for the fourth week at the Marble House. A German film,' he added, 'is lucky if it holds out a week.'[122] Shirer was exaggerating: not all German films were failures. Goebbels was well aware of the popularity of films like *Request Concert* and *The Great Love*, each of which attracted more than 20 million cinema-goers. Both had an implicit ideological content, depicting couples separated by war and conquering their own personal desires in the service of the wider community, and coming together once more at the end. At the same time as showing episodes of military action, they bracketed out the more violent and destructive aspects of war, presenting to the audience a sanitized version of conflict that it was meant to find reassuring.[123] The huge success of these films persuaded Goebbels to order that four out of five films made should be 'good entertainment films, secure in their quality'. And indeed, no fewer than forty-one out of the seventy-four movies made in Germany in 1943 were comedies.[124] By this time, people were flocking to see lavishly costumed operettas, revues, detective films and melodramas. At the very same time as Goebbels was delivering his 'total war' speech to the Party faithful in the Sports Palace, ordinary Germans were settling down in Berlin's cinemas to watch *Two Happy People*, *Be Fond of Me* and *The Big Number*. The next year, escapism reached new heights with *The White Dream*, a review on ice featuring a song that advised people: 'Buy a colourful balloon / Take it firmly in your hand / See it flying off with you / to a foreign fairyland.'[125]

By 1943, neither the proliferation of entertainment movies nor the hectoring tones of the voice-over in the weekly newsreel could disguise the fact that the war was going badly. As the Security Service of the SS reported on 4 March 1943, it was clear that 'people are no longer going to the cinema just for the sake of the newsreel and don't want any more to take on all the unpleasant secondary burdens that a visit to the movies often brings with it, such as queuing for tickets'.[126] The more the propaganda began to lose touch with reality, the more the newsreels' repetitious insistence on the inevitability of final victory met with scepticism among audiences. In mid-1943 Goebbels tried to offset this disenchantment by commissioning a colour film from Veit Harlan on the siege of the German town of Kolberg, on the Baltic, by Napoleon's armies in 1806. After the shattering military defeats of Jena and Auster-litz, the garrison had decided to surrender the town, but the mayor had rallied the citizens to a last-ditch defence. Many Nazi propaganda themes of the second half of the war came together here: the Party's distrust of the army, the populist appeal to ordinary Germans to rally round the flag, the belief in sacrifice, the stoicism of the people in the face of death and destruction. 'Death is entwined with victory,' as the mayor says at one point. 'The greatest achievements are always borne in pain.' 'From the ashes and rubble,' another character says, anticipating defeat and implicitly exhorting audiences to go down fighting, 'a new people will rise like a phoenix, a new Reich.'

Many of the speeches in the film were written not by Harlan but by Goebbels himself. He allocated it a budget of 8.5 million Reichsmarks, twice the normal production costs for a feature film. In a graphic illustra-tion of the priority he attached to propaganda, Goebbels requisitioned 4,000 sailors and 187,000 soldiers from the army to play the battle scenes, at a time when they were badly needed at the front. The incident it portrayed was sufficiently obscure for most people not to know that Kolberg had in fact been taken by Napoleon: the screenplay had the

French Emperor withdrawing in dismay, confounded by the unyielding resistance of the citizens. But it was all too late. The film was not ready until 30 January 1945, when it was shown in Berlin on the anniversary of Hitler's appointment as Reich Chancellor twelve years previously. By this time many cinemas had been destroyed – 237 of them by August 1943 already. In Hanover, only twelve out of thirty-one cinemas were still working. The breakdown of railway communications meant that the possibility of getting copies of Kolberg out to the rest of the country had more or less disappeared. Hardly anybody saw it. The town of Kolberg itself was taken by the Red Army less than two months after the première. 'I will ensure,' wrote Goebbels in his diary, 'that the evacuation of Kolberg is not mentioned in the Combined Armed Forces Supreme Command's report.'[127]

III

It was Joseph Goebbels's ambition to bring the Nazi message into the home of everyone in Germany, and for this purpose no institution was better suited than the radio.[128] In August 1939 the Reich Propaganda Ministry took over all radio stations in Germany, and from July 1942 the Reich Radio Society (the main broadcaster) was directly run by the Ministry. Broadcasts were used, as in other belligerent countries, to give practical advice to listeners on how to eke out their food rations, how to economize in their lifestyle, and generally how to cope with wartime conditions. Front-line reports conveyed a positive picture of the heroism of the troops, while in the later stages of the war, broadcasts began to urge listeners to carry on fighting regardless of bad news from the front. Radio suffered from the call-up of staff to the armed forces, however, and whole programmes and even frequencies were turned over to propaganda directed in foreign languages to audiences abroad. As before, Goebbels insisted that propaganda was far from being the only or even the principal function of German radio. In 1944, for instance, out of 190 hours of broadcasts a week, 71 were devoted to popular music, 55 to general entertainment, and 24 to classical music, leaving 32 hours a week for political broadcasts, 5 hours for a mixture of words and music, and 3 hours a week for 'culture'. Some listeners took the view that popular music should not be broadcast in such difficult times, and, in the countryside in particular, the 'modern offerings' of crooners and dance-music were widely frowned on. But the broadcasters insisted (with some justification) that such programmes were popular with the troops and with Germans performing Labour Service, so they were retained. The Security Service of the SS reported that programmes with a mixture of humour and popular music were especially successful. The broadcasters took care to cater for regional tastes, and Bavarian listeners were said to welcome the broadcast of local songs such as 'the steam-noodle song of the Tegernsee musicians'.[129]

Some songs, however, transcended regional boundaries and were a hit with troops and civilians alike. Sentimental numbers like Zarah Leander's 'I know one day a miracle will come' comforted people in hard times and implicitly promised a better future. As we have seen, the troops at Stalingrad huddled around their radios to listen to the popular *chanteuse* Lale Andersen singing 'It'll all soon be over / It'll end one day'. Like other, similar numbers, this was directed at strengthening the emotional bonds between couples and families separated by the war. Andersen's 1939 hit song 'Lili Marleen' cast a nostalgic glow over its listeners as it described a soldier saying goodbye to his girl-friend underneath a street-lamp outside his barracks. Would they ever meet again? Would she find someone else? Would he survive the war? And if he did not, who would then be standing with Lili underneath the lamp-post? The song encapsulated the personal anxieties as well as the linger-ing hopes of men far away from their loved ones. Further piquancy was added by the fact that, while the words were those of a man, they were sung by an attractive woman. Yet Goebbels disliked its pessimistic and nostalgic tone. At the end of September 1942 he had Andersen arrested for undermining the troops' morale. Her correspondence with friends in Switzerland, including exiled German Jews, was intercepted, and her refusal to accede to Goebbels's request to pay a visit for publicity purposes to the Warsaw ghetto was held against her. Goebbels had her banned from making any further public appearances. Eventually, from the middle of 1943 onwards, she was allowed to sing again in public, provided she did not put 'Lili Marleen' on the programme. At her first concert after the ban was lifted, the audience yelled for her to sing the song, and when it became clear that she was not going to, they sang it themselves. In August 1944 it was finally banned altogether. Long before this, British and American troops had started listening to the

song as it was broadcast from the powerful German forces' radio trans-
mitter in Belgrade. The Allied military authorities had it translated
into English. 'My Lili of the Lamplight' was sung by Marlene Dietrich,
Vera Lynn and (in French) Edith Piaf, and towards the end of the
war the British forces radio broadcast the German version across the
enemy lines to the German troops to try to depress them, thus perhaps
inadvertently confirming Goebbels's belief that it was damaging to
morale.[130]

By this time, it was becoming increasingly difficult for Germans to
hear not only 'Lili Marleen' but anything at all on the radio. The cheap
'People's Receivers' often broke down, and batteries and spare parts
were hard to get. A thriving black market in them soon developed.
Bombing raids interrupted electricity supplies in the towns, sometimes
for days on end. And as the war began to go badly for Germany, listeners
grew increasingly distrustful of German radio's reports on it.[131] As early
as January 1942 the Security Service of the SS bemoaned the fact that
people were indifferent to political broadcasts. Yet people were also
worried about the lack of detailed reports of the progress of the war on
the Eastern Front and in Africa. They felt they did not know what was
going on. 'An open statement on these questions, which move and
oppress everyone, would get rid of the present feeling of uncertainty.'[132]
In the search for reliable information, German listeners turned to foreign
radio stations, above all the BBC. The popular People's Receivers, sold
cheaply before the war, could only receive short-wave broadcasts, and
this made it difficult to listen to foreign stations. However, they
accounted for under 40 per cent of radios in Germany in 1943. Most
people with a radio could receive the German-language service of the
BBC without too much difficulty, and even the People's Receivers could
sometimes succeed in tuning in. By August 1944 the BBC reckoned that
up to 15 million Germans were listening in to it on a daily basis.[133]

Germans listened to the BBC and other foreign stations at considerable risk to themselves. The moment the war broke out, tuning in to
foreign stations was made a criminal offence punishable by death. It was
all too easy, in apartment blocks poorly insulated for sound, for listeners
to face denunciation to the authorities by fanatical or ill-intentioned
neighbours who overhead the sonorous tones of BBC newsreaders
coming through the walls. Some 4,000 people were arrested and pros-
ecuted for 'radio crime' in the first year of the law's operation, and the

first execution of an offender came in 1941.[134] A typical case was that of a Krefeld worker who was sentenced to a year in prison in December 1943 for listening to the BBC and passing on what he heard to his workmates. Like most people punished for this offence, he had formerly been active in left-wing politics. Ordinary offenders were seldom punished very harshly, and prosecutions and sentences from 1941 onwards were relatively uncommon. In 1943, for instance, only eleven death sentences were passed in the whole of the Greater German Reich for 'radio crime', or 0.2 per cent of the total.[135] Nevertheless, people went to extraordinary lengths to avoid being heard listening to the BBC, locking themselves in the toilet or covering themselves, and the radio, with a blanket, or sending other family members out of the room. Not long after the war began William L. Shirer noted, with a pinch of exaggeration: 'Many long prison sentences being meted out to Germans who listen to foreign radio stations, and yet many continue to listen to them,' including a family with whom he had recently spent an afternoon. 'They were a little apprehensive when they turned on the six p.m. BBC news,' he recorded. The porter was 'the official Nazi spy for the apartment house', and there were others too. 'They played the radio so low that I could hardly catch the news,' Shirer wrote, 'and one of the daughters kept watch by the front door.'[136]

No such precautions were needed in Britain or other countries when it came to listening to the propaganda broadcasts emanating from Germany. Goebbels ensured that increased resources were assigned to English-language broadcasts, and employed British and American pro-Germans, often with fascist beliefs, to make them: the most notorious of these was William Joyce, whose plummy accent earned him the nickname of 'Lord Haw-Haw' from his British listeners. These propaganda broadcasters found an audience not least because their style was more intimate and relaxed than that of the stiffly formal BBC; but overall their effect on morale was minimal, and as time went on, people began to tire of Joyce's continual sarcasm and contempt. The most surprising of these broadcasts, perhaps, were put on by Goebbels in defiance of all the Nazis' cherished beliefs about the racial degeneracy of jazz music, when a German swing band, led by the crooner Karl ('Charlie') Schwedler, went on to the air with popular British and American songs, adapting the words into parodies of the original for propaganda purposes. A favourite theme was the unreliability of the BBC ('talking the wishful talk', as a parody of the 'Lambeth Walk' put it).[137]

Jazz and swing were not just used by the regime for its own purposes, they became expressions of opposition to it as well. In Hamburg, the well-off 'Swing Youth' of the prewar years were not deterred from holding dances and parties by the mere outbreak of a war. Early in 1940 the Gestapo discovered 500 of them swinging away in a dance-hall in an Altona hotel to the sound of English music, even with English lyrics. The next time this happened, the police were prepared. On 2 March 1940 forty Gestapo agents raided another dance, in the Curio-Haus in the city's university quarter, locked the doors and fingerprinted 408 participants, all but seventeen of them under the age of twenty-one. Further public dances had to be cancelled, but the gilded youth of Hamburg continued their partying in private. Until December 1941 they gathered in the Waterloo cinema near the Dammtor railway station to watch American films, with the young Axel Springer, a future newspaper publisher, acting as projectionist. As the police became more intrusive, the Swing Youth retreated to the plush suburban villas of their parents, where they celebrated in the cellars in what the Gestapo described disapprovingly as an 'erotic ambience'. In June 1942 a summer party in one such villa included a cabaret with impersonations of Hitler and Goebbels. The Hitler Youth, who feared the Swing Youth as rivals to their own popularity, such as it was, sent spies to the party, and the cabarettist was arrested.

The arrogance and insouciance of the Swingers, their provocative dress, such as Hannelore Evers's grey suit, man's waistcoat and open jacket with shoulder-pads ('an absolute knock-out,' as one veteran of the Swing Youth recalled later), or Kurt-Rudolf Hoffmann's habit of wearing the American flag on his lapel, combined with their open admiration of British style, were eventually reported to Himmler and Heydrich, who on 26 January 1942 ordered them to be arrested, beaten and put to work. Their parents were to be interrogated and sent to a concentration camp if it was found that they had encouraged the 'Anglophiliac tendencies' of their offspring. Within a few weeks, up to seventy Swingers had been arrested and sent to camps including Ravensbrück and Sachsenhausen. There they were classified as political prisoners, though many denied they had acted out of political conviction. 'We were long on hair and short on brains,' one later confessed, and as for their habit of booing at the newsreel when they went to the cinema, one of them said they did it because 'we were going to tell these dumb bastards that we were different, that's all'. Yet the disregard for the regime's racism that led a number of the Swing boys to carry on sexual relationships with Jewish girls, the hatred of the war some of them showed in their letters (intercepted by the Gestapo) and their open contempt for the Nazi leaders and the Hitler Youth, gave the Gestapo some reason to regard them as political. Many of the younger Swing boys were conscripted into the army after serving their time in a camp for juveniles, but at least three of them, according to their own later accounts, managed to avoid ever shooting at the enemy, and two of them crossed the lines and gave themselves up.[138]

IV

As the popularity of musical films and radio broadcasts suggests, musical life was initially relatively unaffected by the war.[139] Escapist operas were popular on the stage as well as on the cinema screen: the most notable written during these years was Richard Strauss's *Capriccio* (1942). Hitler himself had recently acquired a passion for the music of Anton Bruckner, whose manuscripts he planned to collect in the magnificent library at the vast Austrian monastery of St Florian, where Bruckner had played the organ and where his body was buried. The monastery was located near Hitler's favourite town, Linz. Hitler had the monks summarily expelled ready for the building's conversion to its new function. He paid for the restoration of the organ out of his personal funds and also subsidized the publication of the Haas edition of Bruckner's collected works. He bought a number of additional items for the library, and had a Bruckner study centre set up at the monastery, also supporting it from his own coffers; it was intended in the long run to be the nucleus of a major music conservatory. Hitler prompted the foundation of a Bruckner Symphony Orchestra, which began playing concerts in the autumn of 1943. His design for a bell-tower in Linz that would play a theme from Bruckner's Fourth Symphony, the *Romantic*, was, however, never realized.[140]

Despite all this, there was ultimately, in Hitler's view, still no substitute for Wagner. In 1940, on his way back from his brief visit to Paris, he called in at Bayreuth to attend a performance of *Twilight of the Gods*.

It was to be his last. Immersed in the conduct of the war, and increasingly reluctant to appear in public, he went to no more live musical performances after this. Yet he never lost his belief in the power of music. In the same year he established a 'War Festival' at Bayreuth, to which he invited – or forced the attendance of – specially chosen guests, 142,000 of them in all during the five years of the Festival. 'The war,' he reminisced in January 1942, 'gave me the opportunity to fulfil a desire dear to Wagner's heart: that men chosen amongst the people – workers and soldiers – should be able to attend his Festival free of charge.'[141] By 1943, *Twilight of the Gods* no longer seemed appropriate, in view of the rapidly deteriorating military situation, and, after consulting with Winifred Wagner, Hitler had it replaced by *The Mastersingers of Nuremberg* at the remaining two Festivals. In his own quarters, he had stopped listening to Wagner altogether after Stalingrad, and sought escape in *The Merry Widow*, his favourite operetta, by Franz Lehár, conveniently disregarding the fact that the librettist was Jewish, as indeed was Léhar's own wife.[142]

Bayreuth and its festivals always occupied something of an anomalous place in the Third Reich, not least because they were in practice run by the Wagner family in direct consultation with Hitler, whereas other aspects of German musical life all fell under the aegis of the Reich Chamber of Music and therefore Joseph Goebbels's Propaganda Ministry. In 1940 the Ministry claimed that there were 181 permanent orchestras at work in the Reich, employing a total of 8,918 musicians.[143] They had to adapt themselves to wartime conditions, playing in munitions factories and appearing at charity events for the troops. Political considerations continued to trump the regime's general hostility to musical modernism; the fact that Hungary was an ally of Germany, for instance, allowed the Munich Philharmonic under its conductor Osvald Kabasta to play Béla Bartók's *Music for Strings, Percussion and Celeste* in concert in 1942, although the composer himself had never wanted his music to be performed in Nazi Germany (he had by this time gone into exile in the USA). But political considerations also entailed – or offered an opportunity to orchestras to set out on – tours of occupied countries, spreading German culture and proselytizing for German music. The repertoire was heavily German, with the music of Richard Strauss and Hans Pfitzner taking pride of place amongst living composers. Conductors such as Eugen Jochum, Hans Knappertsbusch and younger men like Herbert von Karajan and Karl Böhm ensured that standards were maintained until the destruction of concert halls and opera houses and the drafting of players and administrators into the armed forces began to take their toll from 1943 onwards. Böhm did his career no harm by giving the Nazi salute from the podium at the start of his concerts, while Karajan, a member of the Nazi Party since 1933, benefited from the fact that he was considered politically more reliable than the senior figure he began to rival for concert-goers' affections during the war, Wilhelm Furtwängler.[144]

Hitler remained, however, a fan of Furtwängler ('the only conductor whose gestures do not appear ridiculous,' he said in 1942, 'is Furt-wängler').[145] Such approval further cemented Furtwängler's commitment to the Third Reich: indeed, on 13 January 1944 Goebbels wrote in his diary: 'To my pleasure I find that with Furtwängler the worse things go for us, the more he supports our regime.'[146] During the war, Furtwängler became a kind of court conductor to the Nazi elite. He took an orchestra to Norway a week before the German invasion in 1940, an event described by the German Embassy in Oslo, which knew that German forces were about to launch an attack on the country, as 'very suited to awaken and animate sympathy for German art and for Germany'. In 1942 he conducted a performance of Beethoven's Ninth Symphony for Hitler's birthday. All of this he did voluntarily. His conservative nationalism kept him in the Reich until January 1945, when he encountered Albert Speer in a concert interval. 'You look so very tired, maestro,' said Speer with a knowing look: perhaps, he suggested, it would be a good idea to stay in Switzerland after a forthcoming concert and not come back. Furtwängler took the hint and did not return.[147]

Many people who went to his concerts, or more generally listened to music on the radio, were, as Furtwängler pointed out after the war, thereby enabled to take refuge for a while in a world of higher spiritual values than those purveyed by the Nazis. Yet music's significance could vary enormously according to who was playing it or listening to it. 'When I hear Beethoven,' wrote one journalist in a radio magazine in 1942, for example, 'I become brave.'[148] A woman who attended the War Festival in Bayreuth in 1943 reported that the performance had given her 'fresh courage and strength for the work to come'.[149] Local towns-people in Bayreuth, by contrast, found the opulence of the Festival abhorrent. Seeing a group of War Festival guests drinking cognac, a group of soldiers agreed: 'There you see it again: we're always the stupid ones.'[150] The spectacle was particularly annoying for people who had been bombed out of their homes. 'These shits,' said one of them, observing the guests at the theatre restaurant, 'gobble and glug themselves up to the brim here, while those of us who've lost everything don't get a single drop of wine to drink.'[151] Even outside Bayreuth, people were reported to be complaining about the resources devoted to the Festival at a time when everybody was being exhorted to live frugally: the hard-pressed rail service was forced to transport 30,000 people to Bayreuth, many of them given leave from their jobs in munitions factories for the best part of a week.[152] For those who attended, however, the Festival seemed a gift from Hitler of almost incredible generosity. Their expressions of gratitude were recorded at suitable length in the Security Service report. Yet for most of them, it was only a brief, if welcome, break. Music in the abstract has very little to do with life; and in listening to it, opera- and concert-goers were taking the very route of escapism that Goebbels had laid down for them. As one of the munitions workers who attended the Bayreuth Festival in 1943 confessed: 'After the curtain went down, we were unable to find the way back to reality for ourselves at all quickly.'[153] Many others must have felt the same.

The Third Reich's record of producing new music of its own was far from convincing. Richard Strauss was undoubtedly the best-known German composer during the Third Reich, but the Nazis took particular exception to the fact that his son had married a woman whom they classified as Jewish. In 1938, when Austria, where he and his family were domiciled, was incorporated into the Reich, stormtroopers specifically targeted his Jewish daughter-in-law Alice in the pogrom of 9–10 November 1938, harassing her mercilessly and raiding her house. Strauss's protests and his good relations with Baldur von Schirach, the Regional Leader of Vienna, a personal friend of the Strauss family through his upbringing as the son of a theatre director in Weimar, bore some fruit, but the composer was unable to prevent Alice's grandmother from being deported to Theresienstadt. Strauss drove up in his limousine to the camp gates, where he grandly announced: 'I am the composer Richard Strauss.' Sceptical guards turned him away. The grandmother died, along with twenty-five other Jewish relatives of Strauss's daughter-in-law. Meanwhile, at Goebbels's prompting, the Gestapo raided Alice's home and took her off to interrogation with her husband, whom they put under pressure to divorce her. He stood firm. Repeated letters from the composer to Himmler and others failed to achieve clarity about the inheritance that he wished to pass on to his half-Jewish grandsons. Strauss was still the most frequently performed living opera composer in Germany in 1942, but he lived under straitened circumstances, he was no longer – unlike some other prominent musicians – privileged by the regime, and he had to contend with the constant threat to the life of his daughter-in-law and his grandsons.[154]

The true nature of the composer's relationship with the regime was brutally revealed at a meeting of leading composers with Goebbels on 28 February 1941, at which Strauss attempted to persuade the Propaganda Minister to rescind a recent decision to reduce copyright payments to serious composers in favour of rewarding the writers of more frequently performed light music like that of Hitler's favourite Franz Lehár, whose work Strauss dismissed out of hand, with something like their full income. Goebbels had an incriminating sentence from Strauss's letter to his librettist Stefan Zweig of 17 June 1933, criticizing the regime, read out loud, then shouted at Strauss: 'Be quiet, and take note that you have no idea of who you are and who I am! Lehár has the masses, you don't! Stop babbling about the significance of serious music! This will not revalue your stock! Tomorrow's culture is different from that of yesterday! You, Herr Strauss, are of yesterday!'[155] In 1943, Strauss got into further trouble because he refused to accommodate evacuees in his home. When he refused again the following year, Goebbels tried to have his operas banned. He was overruled by Hitler. But the composer's eightieth birthday in June was studiously ignored by the regime and the Party. He had become something of an unperson.

The second most popular German composer in the concert-halls, Hans Pfitzner, fared little better. Curmudegonly and self-pitying, he complained in March 1942 that the regime was behaving as if he did not exist, 'and it's not a good sign for this Germany that important positions are filled by men of decidedly inferior character and intelligence and nobody looks to me for them even once.'[156] He found sympathy not in Germany but in occupied Poland, where Regional Leader Greiser awarded him the Wartheland Prize, worth 20,000 Reichsmarks, and General Governor Frank invited Pfitzner to conduct a special concert of his own and other music in Cracow in May 1942. Invited again the following year, he was so pleased that he wrote a special six-minute

'Cracow Greeting' for the occasion. Pfitzner survived the war, dying in an old people's home in Salzburg in 1949, at the age of eighty.[157] More successful by far was Werner Egk, who had won Hitler's approval during the 1930s for work that echoed Nazi ideological themes, even if it was written in a distinctly modern style. His opera *Peer Gynt* was played in numerous German opera houses in 1939–40, in Prague in 1941 and at the Paris Opera in 1943. By this time Egk was heading the composers' division of the Reich Music Chamber and earning 40,000 Reichsmarks a year. A new stage work, *Columbus*, could clearly be understood as drawing a parallel between the European conquest of America and the creation of the German empire in the east. In February 1943 he wrote in the *Racial Observer* that he was confident that Germany would win the war, achieving after it was over a 'marriage between idealistic politics and realistic art'.[158] By contrast the stock of Carl Orff, whose *Carmina Burana* had been a sensational success on its first performance in 1937, went down during the war. His opera *The Wise Woman*, first performed in February 1943, was received with much less enthusiasm. Was it for such culture, asked a critic after the work opened in Graz in March 1944, that German soldiers were sacrificing themselves at the front? At the second performance the local Nazis turned up and greeted the piece with a chorus of whistling. But Orff's later claims that the opera was a bold act of resistance to Nazi tyranny lacked all plausibility: the libretto's denunciation of tyranny and injustice was put in the mouth not of heroic figures but of a chorus of villains and good-for-nothings, and was clearly intended to be understood ironically.[159]

In the end, little music of any value was composed in Germany during the war years. The most powerful compositions came from an entirely different source: the Jewish composers imprisoned in Theresienstadt. Besides Viktor Ullmann and Kurt Gerron, many other inmates wrote and performed music in a variety of genres during the brief years of the camp's existence. Some of the most moving of these compositions were by Ilse Weber, who wrote both music and lyrics and sang them, accompanying herself on a guitar, as she did her night rounds in the children's ward of the camp hospital, carrying out her duties as a nurse. Born in 1903, Weber had worked as a writer and radio producer in Prague before her deportation in 1942. Her husband and younger son were in the camp with her; they had succeeded in getting their older son to safety in Sweden. The popular songs of Zarah Leander and Lale Andersen spoke of the time when friends, relatives, partners and lovers would see one another again: Weber's songs harboured no such illusions:

> Farewell, my friend, we have come to the end
> Of the journey we took together.
> They've found me a place on the Poland express,
> And now I must leave you for ever.
> You were loyal and true, you helped me get through,
> You stood by my side in all weather.
> Just feeling you near would quiet every fear,
> We bore all our burdens together.
> Farewell, it's the end; I'll miss you, my friend,
> And the hours we spent together.
> I gave you my heart; stay strong when we part,
> For this time our farewell's for ever.[160]

The warm simplicity of her settings was never more moving than in her lullaby 'Viegala', which she reportedly sang to children from the camp, including her son Tommy, as she accompanied them voluntarily into the gas chamber at Auschwitz on 6 October 1944: 'Viegala, viegala, vill: now is the world so still! No sound disturbs the lovely peace: my little child, now go to sleep.'[161]

V

Theresienstadt and other camps and ghettos did not, it was thought, present suitable subjects for the German painters and sculptors who were at work during the wartime years. Heroic war was what Goebbels and the Reich Chamber of Culture wanted artists to depict.[162] The fourth Great German Art Exhibition, opened by the Propaganda Minister in 1940, devoted a number of rooms to war art, and battle scenes now took pride of place amongst the 1,397 works by 751 artists displayed in the show. War, as one commentator noted, 'is a great challenger. German visual arts have met the challenge.'[163] Opening the 1942 exhibition, Hitler reminded his listeners that 'German artists too have been called upon to serve the homeland and the front.'[164] Those who visited the exhibitions mounted during the war years, or saw newsreel reports on them in the cinema, could admire pictures such as *The*

Flame-Throwers by Rudolf Liepus, *Sniper Aiming a Rifle* by Gisbert Palmié, or *Lookout on a U-boat* by Rudolf Hausknecht. Forty-five official war artists were appointed by a committee under Luitpold Adam, who had already served as a war artist in 1914–18; by 1944 there were eighty artists on his staff. The artists were attached to units of the armed forces, they were paid a salary, and their paintings and drawings became the property of the government. Special touring exhibitions of their work were sent round Germany to demonstrate the undiminished creativity of German culture in time of war. The artists themselves, indeed, were regarded as soldiers: 'Only a soldier-like character,' as one commentator remarked in 1942, 'filled with intense feelings, is able to transmit the experience of war in artistic form.'[165]

War artists employed a variety of techniques, and some of them painted landscape scenes that were a world away from the realities of war. Franz Junghans's *Sunset on the Duna River* (1942), for example, was almost abstract in its use of colours merging into one another over the flat and featureless landscape. Olaf Jordan's *Two Russian Prisoners of the Germans* portrayed its subjects with some sympathy and compassion, while Wolfgang Willrich's sketch of a Bavarian villager serving on the Eastern Front showed more of the peasant than the soldier in his rough, humorous features. But the great majority of the war artists' paintings depicted optimistic scenes of heroic soldiers gazing defiantly at the enemy, manning their machine-gun posts, or leading the troops onwards with gestures that implicitly included the spectator, and thus the whole German people, in their invitation to join the assault. The paintings of one of the most popular war artists, Elk Eber, whose work was endlessly reproduced in propaganda magazines, 'had', as an obituary in the *Racial Observer* noted in 1941, 'basically only one theme: the soldierly, heroic masculinity of our time'.[166] Eber's *The Dispatch Courier* was a particular favourite, often shown on postcards: it showed a steel-helmeted soldier, his rifle slung horizontally across his back, rushing heroically out of a foxhole, determination mingled with enjoyment of his role stamped on his features. Whatever they depicted, however, the war artists made sure to avoid displaying the horrors of battle. There were no wounded, no dead bodies, no soldiers with missing limbs, there was no blood, no suffering, indeed almost no real violence at all in their works. The contrast to the gut-wrenching pictures painted by anti-war German artists in 1914–18 was noted with approval. The new work was eminently suitable for use in schools, it was agreed. 'Show the pupils the pictures of soldiers painted by Erler or Spiegel,' remarked one commentator, 'compare them with the vulgar and horrid works by Dix or Grosz. Every pupil will recognise immediately what decadent art is . . . The strength of the real artist is in his blood, which leads him to heroism.'[167]

The leading German artist of the war years, however, was not a painter but a sculptor. Arno Breker had already created a number of monumental, aggressive and militaristic figures before the war.[168] His European reputation was considerable. In 1941 Hitler persuaded a group of French artists, including André Derain, Kees van Dongen and Maurice Vlaminck, to visit him in his studio. One of their number, the director of the École des Beaux-Arts, wrote on his return in glowing terms of the way in which 'a great country honours its artists and their work, its intellectual culture and the dignity of human existence'.[169] Breker seemed the ideal subject for a major retrospective, which was held in April 1942 not in Berlin but in occupied Paris. Jean Cocteau wrote a fulsome introduction to the catalogue, praising him as a worthy successor to Michelangelo.[170] Knowing his high standing with Hitler, prominent Nazis vied with each other for his friendship, and he was on good terms not only with Hermann Göring and Joseph Goebbels but also with Heinrich Himmler, who discussed with him commissions to adorn various premises of the SS with his work. In April 1941 Breker was appointed Vice-President of the Reich Chamber for the Visual Arts. He played a key role in Speer's plans for the reconstruction of Berlin, and Speer set him up with what was virtually a factory to produce his sculptures, bas-reliefs and other three-dimensional objects, subsidizing it with vast sums of money. Hitler told his companions at dinner one night that Breker deserved an income of a million Reichsmarks a year, and Martin Bormann gave him a tax-free honorarium of 250,000 Reichsmarks in April 1942. Hitler and Speer paid for the refurbishment of his castle near the river Oder, where Breker advertised his privileged status by displaying his collection of paintings by Léger, Picasso and other artists officially regarded as 'degenerate' on the walls. The German ambassador in Paris put the confiscated house of the Jewish cosmetics manufacturer Helena Rubinstein at his disposal, and Breker spent a good deal of his substantial income on buying up works by Rodin and other artists as well as quantities of fine wines, books and perfume.[171]

Breker was far from being alone in his avid pursuit of paintings, sculptures and other cultural objects in the occupied countries. Indeed, he was heavily outclassed in this respect by Hitler and Göring. Both were wealthy men by the time the war broke out.[172] Hermann Göring owned ten houses, castles and hunting lodges, all provided and maintained at the taxpayer's expense. In all these locations, and particularly in his vast and ever-expanding principal hunting lodge at Carinhall, named after his first wife, Göring wanted to display artworks, tapestries, paintings, sculptures and much else besides, to emphasize his status as the Reich's second man. Göring spent large sums of money on acquiring cultural objects of all kinds, using whatever means he could.[173] By contrast, Hitler himself made a point of avoiding ostentatious displays of personal wealth, preferring instead to accumulate an art collection for public use. Hitler had long planned to turn his home town of Linz, in Austria, into the cultural capital of the new Reich, even drawing sketches for the new public buildings and museums he hoped to construct there. Linz would become the German Florence, with a comprehensive collection above all of Germanic art housed in a range of purpose-built galleries and museums. Berlin, too, had to have art museums suitable for its new status as the coming capital of the world. On 26 June 1939 Hitler engaged the services of an art historian, Hans Posse, a museum director in Dresden, to amass the collection he needed for this purpose. Posse was provided with almost limitless funds, and by the middle of the war he was acquiring art objects from all over German-occupied Europe, amassing an almost incredible total of more than 8,000 by 1945. Armed with full powers from Hitler, he was able to outbid or outmanoeuvre other agents, such as Kajetan Mühlmann, who were working for Göring, or for other major German museums, or indeed for themselves. By December 1944, Posse and the man who succeeded him shortly after Posse's death from cancer in December 1942, Hermann Voss, director of the Wiesbaden Museum, had spent a total of 70 million Reichsmarks on buying for the Linz collection. Not surprisingly, dealers used by Hitler and Posse, such as Karl Haberstock, made considerable profits out of their business.[174]

This spending spree did not take place in normal art market conditions. Many countries for example had rules and regulations controlling the export of art treasures, but during the war Hitler was easily able to ignore them or brush them aside. Moreover, the high prices offered in many cases for the old German Masters he wanted for the Linz Museum were not quite what they seemed, at least not from 1940 onwards, since the Germans fixed exchange rates with the French franc and other currencies in occupied countries at rates that were extraordinarily favourable to the German Reichsmark. But in many cases it was not necessary to spend any money at all. Artworks had already been confiscated from German-Jewish collectors in large quantities, especially after the pogrom of 9–10 November 1938, allegedly for 'safe-keeping'; they were registered and subsequently appropriated by the German state. A precedent had been set in March 1938 with the invasion of Austria. Here as in other occupied countries, Jewish emigrants had to leave their assets behind if they emigrated, to be taken over by the Reich. After the conquest of France in 1940 the property of citizens who had fled the country also fell to the German Reich; the same applied eventually to all Jews deported to Auschwitz and other extermination camps in the east from every occupied country in Europe, offering widespread opportunities for plunder.[175]

Looting extended far beyond the expropriation of the Jews when the Nazis invaded countries inhabited by people they regarded as subhuman, uncultured Slavs. Already during the invasion of Poland, German troops ransacked country houses and palaces for cultural objects of all kinds. Soon, however, the despoliation of Poland's cultural heritage was put on an organized basis. Kajetan Mühlmann, who had previously carried out similar duties in Vienna, was put in charge of the process. By the end of November 1940 the registration was complete, and Posse arrived to select prime specimens for the Leader. He was followed in due course by art museum directors from Germany, anxious for their share in the spoils. Quarrels broke out, as Hermann Göring tried to obtain pictures for himself while Hans Frank objected to the removal of prize loot from his headquarters. Perhaps this was not such a bad idea, however, since Frank had no idea of how to display or preserve Old Masters, and was once reprimanded by Mühlmann for hanging a painting by Leonardo da Vinci above a radiator. Private collections were ransacked as well as state museums, and the vast collection amassed by the Czartoryski family, including a Rembrandt and a Raphael, was systematically despoiled.[176] Meanwhile Hans Frank was busy decorating his headquarters with looted artworks, and shipping trophies back to his home in Bavaria. When American troops arrived there in 1945, they found a

Rembrandt, a Leonardo, a fourteenth-century Madonna from Cracow, and looted vestments and chalices from Polish churches.[177]

This process of looting and expropriation was repeated on an even larger scale when Germany invaded the Soviet Union on 22 June 1941. As in Poland, ethnic cleansing was accompanied by cultural cleansing. Special units were attached to the incoming SS forces, armed with lists of 'Germanic' art for confiscation and shipping back to the Reich. Among the most famous of these items was the celebrated amber room given to Peter the Great by King Friedrich Wilhelm I of Prussia and subsequently augmented by further gifts from his successor. The Soviets had taken away all the furniture and movable items but left the amber panelling in place, and the room, installed in the Catherine Palace in the town of Pushkin, was dismantled and returned to Königsberg in East Prussia, where it was put on display until being packed away for protection against air raids. The Soviets of course had removed many cultural treasures out of reach of the invading armies, there were no great private collections left in the Soviet Union, since all had been confiscated by the Communist state, and the Germans never managed to conquer Moscow or St Petersburg; but much still remained to be looted; 279 paintings were carried off from Kharkov alone, for example, and Himmler requisitioned considerable quantities of artworks to decorate and furnish the SS's headquarters at Wewelsburg. Individuals could often pick up treasures at bargain rates: one SS officer sent Himmler a collection of antique jewellery he had bought from the widow of a Soviet archaeologist, starving in war-torn Kiev, for 8 kilograms of millet.[178]

The greatest art treasures, however, were to be found in the conquered countries of Western Europe. On 5 July 1940 Hitler commissioned a subsection of Alfred Rosenberg's Foreign Policy Office of the Nazi Party, the Task Staff of Reich Leader Rosenberg, to collect artworks from Jewish owners and confiscate anti-German material along with any documents that might be valuable for Reich. Based initially in Paris, and backed by the authority of Hitler himself, Rosenberg's unit quickly took the lead in the rush to acquire cultural objects for the Linz Museum and other collections. On 1 March 1941 it relocated to Berlin, from where it sent out emissaries to supervise the spoliation of museums and libraries in the east in the wake of Operation Barbarossa. By the time Rosenberg's staff arrived in Holland in September 1940, however, Kajetan Mühlmann was already there, as was Hermann Göring's art

18. Inside a women's barracks at Auschwitz: this photograph, taken in January 1945, shortly after liberation, can only give a faint idea of the squalor and overcrowding to which the inmates were subject.

19. Camp commandant Richard Baer, camp doctor Josef Mengele and former camp commandant Rudolf Höss in relaxed mood at the SS retreat known as the 'Sun Huts' outside Auschwitz in 1944.

20. Albert Speer demonstrates the increase in the production of artillery pieces under his management of the war economy in 1943.

21. StuG III assault guns in production, summer 1943.

22. House-to-house fighting in Stalingrad at the end of 1942; but where have the houses gone?

23. The face of defeat: a German soldier is taken prisoner at Stalingrad in January 1943.

24. The long march into captivity: German soldiers pass before the ruined city of Stalingrad, January 1943.

25. Germany in flames: Allied air-raids on Hamburg in July and August 1943 destroyed a large part of the city and killed 40,000 of its inhabitants. When this photo was taken, on 2 December 1943, all that remained of much of the city was dust and rubble.

26. Strategic bombing caused widespread disruption of communications: a photo of Hamburg's main railway station not long after the raids.

27. General Gotthard Heinrici (*right*) and Field-Marshal Günther von Kluge (*left*) plan the next retreat.

28. Red Army soldiers advancing on Warsaw in August 1944 pursue German troops running away from their shattered tank.

29. V-1 pilotless bombs sometimes carried propaganda leaflets such as this: the message on the reverse told Londoners that they were being 'continually blasted day and night by those mysterious flying meteors'. 'What good are all your planes, warships and tanks against that new German weapon?' it asked.

30. The gates of hell: workers going through the entrance to the underground factory where the V-2 rockets were made in the later stages of the war.

31. Hitler with officers of the 9th Army on a brief visit to Wriezen, behind the Oder front, 3 March 1945. With him, standing in the front row, from left: Wilhelm Berlin, Robert Ritter von Greim, Franz Reuss, Job Oderbrecht and Theodor Busse.

32. The German 'Dad's Army': not all members of the 'People's Storm' were as smartly dressed and well equipped as in this photograph taken in Hamburg on 29 October 1944, though many of them were probably as short-sighted.

33. The young were drafted in to the 'People's Storm' as well: Joseph Goebbels meets a teenage soldier at Lauban, Lower Silesia, in March 1945.

34. Hermann Göring breakfasting in his Nuremberg cell on 26 November 1945. He committed suicide rather than face the hangman.

35. Joachim von Ribbentrop contemplates his fate in the same prison. He was sentenced to death and hanged.

36. Berlin's Tauentzienstrasse after the end of the war, with the ruins of the Kaiser Wilhelm church in the background. The absence of able-bodied men meant that the responsibility for clearing the wreckage fell mainly to civilian women. The signs on the left mark the border between the British-occupied sector and the US sector of the city.

curator, Walter Andreas Hofer. Hitler authorized Hans Posse to go to Holland on 13 June 1940, and Hermann Göring travelled to Amsterdam in person. A frenzy of competitive buying ensued, and large quantities of actual or alleged German artworks made their way from Dutch collectors, dealers and museums to repositories in the Reich. Mühlmann's team tracked down collections taken to Holland by German-Jewish owners fleeing persecution in the 1930s, and confiscated them. A 1669 self-portrait by Rembrandt was among a number of works sent back to Germany on the grounds that they had been illegally exported: no compensation was given to Jewish owners of such works. In addition, the artworks of Jews who had fled the country to take refuge in England were confiscated, and crates of artworks about to be shipped abroad were opened and the contents removed and confiscated.[179]

Even richer pickings were to be had in France. On 30 June 1940 Hitler ordered that art objects owned by the French state were to be put under German guard. Ambassador Abetz prepared to seize artworks in large quantities, telling the military that Hitler or Ribbentrop would decide what was to be taken to Germany. The latter category included works looted by Napoleon from the Rhineland, already listed in a 300-page document drawn up by German art historians touring French museums and libraries in the 1930s posing as academic researchers. But the army command had employed its own art historian, the Francophile Count Franz Wolff-Metternich, who persuaded the military authorities to withhold co-operation on the grounds that the 1907 Hague Convention forbade looting. Enlisting the support of army Commander-in-Chief Brauchitsch, he frustrated all Abetz's attempts to sequester artworks in the ownership of the French state. With Jewish dealers and collectors, whose possessions Hitler had also ordered to be confiscated, matters stood very differently. The property of fifteen major Jewish dealers was seized, along with that of Jewish owners such as the Rothschilds, which was stored in the Jeu de Paumes, a small gallery used by the Louvre for temporary exhibitions. Rosenberg's Task Staff arrived to administer the collection, and soon Hermann Göring too descended upon the museum, spending two days there selecting twenty-seven works by Rembrandt, van Dyck and others for his private collection. He prudently agreed, however, that Hitler was to have first choice of items from the Jeu de Paumes. Rosenberg and the German museums could have most of the rest. Everything had to be paid for and the profits made over to a fund for French war orphans. While Hans Posse, inspecting the list of works piled up at the museum, had fifty-three artworks taken off to Germany for eventual inclusion in the Linz Museum, Göring chose over 600 paintings, pieces of furniture and other items, which he had valued at very low prices if they were to go on display at Carinhall, or high prices if he intended to sell them. Göring peremptorily brushed aside Wolff-Metternich's objections, and the army formally absolved itself of any further responsibility for the artworks.[180]

By the end of the war, Hitler's own collection included 75 Lenbachs, 58 Stucks, 58 Kaulbachs, 52 Menzels and 44 Spitzwegs. Besides nineteenth-century German and Austrian painters, he also had 15 Rembrandts, 23 Breughels, 2 Vermeers, 15 Canalettos and paintings by Titian, Leonardo, Botticelli, Holbein, Cranach, Rubens and many others. Their rarity alone had prevented Hitler from purchasing works by Bosch, Grunewald and Dürer. He frequently referred to the works he had obtained, but he hardly ever saw them; they were all put into storage.[181] So obsessed was he with the idea of the Linz Museum that he was to issue instructions for its foundation in his will. 'I never bought the paintings that are in the collections that I built up over the years for my own benefit,' he declared, 'but only for the establishment of a gallery in my home town of Linz.' In the end, however, Hitler's fantasy of a world centre for Germanic art was in reality little more than a wish-fulfilment of his own rehabilitation as an artist, after the failures and humiliations of his years in Vienna before the First World War.[182]

DEADLY SCIENCE

I

In March 1940 William Guertler, Professor of Metallurgy at the Technical University of Berlin and a long-time Nazi, wrote a personal petition to Hitler. There were many such petitions, and they were routinely dealt with by Hitler's staff. There is no evidence that Hitler ever read what Guertler had to say. But it was regarded as sufficiently significant to be forwarded to Hans-Heinrich Lammers, head of the Reich Chancellery, who had it copied and distributed to a number of ministers, including Hermann Göring. What concerned Guertler, seven months into the war, was a decline in educational standards so precipitate that it was leading, in his opinion, to catastrophe. As soon as the war had begun, the Education Ministry had decreed, in the interests of the most efficient use of students' time, that the traditional two-semester university year should be replaced by a three-term year, without any diminution in the length of the term. The university year had thus been increased from seven and a half months to ten and a half. So, Guertler complained,

we teachers received the order to ensure that the students would learn in one year as much as they used to learn in one and a half. We did our utmost. It was completely in vain. The students' capacity for learning had already long been overtaxed. Even before this, we had been unable to maintain the level of training, but now every examination told us of a catastrophic decline in the knowledge they had acquired. Young students had long since been forced to give up those pleasures even of the most industrious years of study that had once been so celebrated – and so well-deserved. They tormented themselves outrageously – it was beyond their strength.[183]

Neither Lammers nor any of the petition's other readers disagreed. Even Reich Education Minister Bernhard Rust accepted the professor's alarming diagnosis.[184]

The decline in educational standards had begun long before the war and affected schools as well as universities. In 1937 the nine years of secondary education had been reduced to eight. The influence of the Hitler Youth had reduced the authority of many teachers, and the emphasis of Nazi education on sport and physical exercise had curtailed the time available for academic study. Even had they managed to acquire a reasonable knowledge in this situation, school students were liable to forget much of it in the two and a half years or so they were obliged to spend doing labour service and serving in the armed forces before they were allowed to matriculate at a university.[185] The war saw a further increase in the ideological content of the curriculum; more than 150 hastily issued pamphlets, for example, replaced previous textbook accounts of English history and institutions with hostile propaganda branding Britain as a Jewish-run country that had committed countless atrocities in its murky past. Textbooks became increasingly difficult to obtain, and school buildings in many towns and cities were either requisitioned for use as military hospitals or, especially from 1942 onwards, destroyed in bombing raids.[186] Teachers went off to the front and were not replaced, so much so that by February 1943 the National Socialist Teachers' League was closed down for lack of activity and funds. Older pupils were forced to spend more and more time helping with air-raid work, collecting clothes, rags, bones, paper and metal for the war economy, or, in the summer, going to the countryside to help with the harvest for as long as four months at a stretch. From February 1943 classes in Berlin schools took place only in the mornings as all the children spent the afternoons either in military drill and education or going off to man anti-aircraft batteries if they were fifteen or older. The last school examinations were held in 1943, and in the last months of the war most schools ceased teaching altogether.[187]

Nazi elite schools were just as badly affected. The Order Castle at Vogelsang, for example, lost almost all its students and teachers to military service as soon as the war began, and its premises were used for billeting troops and then providing indoctrination courses for recuperating war-wounded.[188] The National Political Educational Institutions, or Napolas, another form of elite school, suffered similarly. The fanatically

Nazi students saw the war as an opportunity for showing their commitment, demonstrating their bravery, and winning medals. By March 1944 some 143 Napola students or graduates had been decorated for bravery; 1,226 had been killed. Student numbers thus fell sharply, and by the end of 1944, the Napolas were being used for training officer cadets and members of the Military SS. Nevertheless, some teaching continued, and on one occasion at the Oranienstein school, towards the end of the war, students incongruously found themselves taking yachting lessons as American bombers flew overhead, 'a totally crazy scene in a totally crazy world', as one student later recalled.[189]

In this situation, it was not surprising that educational standards at universities suffered as well. But they had their own problems too. All German universities were closed down on 1 September 1939, and when they reopened ten days later, they registered a dramatic fall in student numbers, from 41,000 to 29,000, reflecting the enlistment of many male students in the armed forces. Numbers slowly began to recover thereafter – to 38,000 in 1942, and 52,000 in 1943; in higher education institutions of all kinds, there was an increase from 52,000 in 1940 to 65,000 in 1944. The students who made up these numbers now included war-wounded soldiers, men certified as unfit for service for one reason or another, soldiers on leave (many of whom had forfeited their places at university on enlisting), foreign students, medical students required by their army units to continue their studies, and, increasingly, women – 14 per cent of the student body in all institutions of higher education in 1939, 30 per cent in 1941, and 48 per cent in 1943. As before the war, medicine was in a position of absolute dominance in Germany's universities. 62 per cent of all students were enrolled in Medical Faculties in 1940; all of them had to serve six months at the front as ordinary soldiers to prepare for service as army medics when they qualified. Thus a perception amongst some (typically anti-intellectual) Nazi activists that those who went to university during the war were 'slackers' trying to avoid military service was incorrect; almost all male students, in fact, were members of the armed forces in one capacity or another.[190]

Educational standards at university did not just fall during the war as a consequence of the decline of educational standards in the schools. Students were obliged to spend increasing amounts of their time on work duties, helping with the harvest or working during the vacations in factories. The Ministry of Education did recognize in 1941 that the three-semester year, in combination with labour service during the vacations, was imposing an impossible strain on students, and restored the traditional two-semester year.[191] But there were widespread complaints from professors that students were either too tired to work or too lazy and apathetic. The Nazi Party's open contempt for learning, hammered into them in their formative years, lowered their respect for their teachers. After the war, there would be a huge demand for lawyers and doctors, they thought, so why bother to work anyway? As the Security Service of the SS reported on 5 October 1942:

It is unanimously reported from every university town in the Reich *that the performance level of the students is continually falling.* Their written work, their participation in classes and seminars, as well as their examination results, have reached a real low point . . . Many students *don't even possess the simplest, most elementary knowledge.* Orthographic, grammatical and stylistic mistakes are encountered ever more frequently in written work.[192]

Knowledge of foreign languages, the report added, was so poor that students were unable to follow lectures that used Latin words to denote different parts of the human body. Professors were asked by students to avoid using foreign words, and began to lower standards, making examinations easier to pass, and reducing the demands on their own time by marking student work less rigorously.[193]

The student body, already disparaged by many active Nazis as politically apathetic before the war, did not find any new commitment to National Socialism when the war began. If it committed itself to the conflict, it was as much on behalf of Germany as it was in the cause of National Socialism. The National Socialist German Students' League went into decline, though it did score one success by persuading the remaining traditional fraternity members in its ranks to abandon the practice of duelling on the grounds that it was no longer necessary to demonstrate one's manly courage by standing unflinchingly still as an opponent gouged a scar in one's cheek with a sabre: one could now prove one's valour by fighting in a real battle.[194] The war, however, increasingly came home to the universities themselves, especially to those located in the larger towns and cities. By July 1944, twenty-five out of sixty-one higher education institutions in the Greater German Reich had been damaged in bombing raids. The disruption to teaching was considerable, as it took time to find new classrooms and lecture theatres, and these too were then often damaged by bombing. Frequent false alarms caused further disruption. By the end of the war, in 1945, bombing had effectively put an end to higher learning almost everywhere in Germany: only Erlangen, Göttingen, Halle, Heidelberg, Marburg and Tübingen were undamaged. Many other universities had been totally destroyed. Long before this, study had been made more difficult by the understandable decision of many university libraries to move their precious collections out to coalmines or similar sites for safe-keeping. Bookshops fell victim to the bombing raids as well, so that journals and textbooks became increasingly difficult to find.[195]

When Goebbels was appointed Reich Plenipotentiary for the Total War Effort in 1944, university education effectively came to an end. 16,000 students were drafted to the front, and 31,000 were conscripted for service in war industries. Goebbels had wanted to close all the universities down, but he had been prevented from doing this by Himmler on the grounds that some, at least, of their activities were of direct benefit to the war effort. Thus the only students allowed to continue their studies were either those about to take their final examinations or those enrolled in courses on subjects like physics, maths, ballistics and electronics. There were still 38,000 German students in university at the end of 1944, though this was many fewer than the number of students who had been there a year before. But they could no longer study to any effect, even had they wanted to. Disillusion with the regime was widespread. The use of the 'Hitler greeting' was said to have virtually ceased many months before this. Yet open opposition to Nazism was still rare. Dull apathy was far more common.[196]

II

In these circumstances, continuing with research and publication was extremely difficult for university teachers. The longer teaching year in 1939 and 1940 indeed made it virtually impossible for many. Only if research could be shown to be of direct benefit to the war effort, or to projects associated with it, would it be given any kind of priority. Publication in the arts and humanities was reduced to little more than propaganda. For most professors, conservative nationalists as they were, the war presented a spiritual call to arms to fight for Germany, however much they may have disliked Nazism and its ideas. A case in point was the Freiburg historian Gerhard Ritter, whose writings, public and private, of the war years were torn between his moral revulsion for Nazism and his patriotic commitment to the German cause. Like many others in his situation, he was enthused by the victories of 1939 and 1940, but increasingly disillusioned by the military setbacks and disasters of the following years. His behaviour was strongly coloured by the death of his own son on the Eastern Front. In his public lectures and publications he did his best to bolster morale both at home and in the forces; he went on tours of France and other occupied countries and lectured to the armed forces as well as continuing to teach in his own university. Increasingly, however, he larded his lectures and articles with appeals for moderation and implicit criticisms of what he saw as Nazi extremism. Introducing a reissue of his biography of Martin Luther in 1943, for instance, he insisted on the importance of retaining a pure conscience and a strong legal order. Ritter was bitterly opposed to the attempts of the German Christians to Nazify German Protestantism, and began to write private memoranda about the need to re-establish a moral order after the war was over. In November 1944 he was finally arrested by the Gestapo, but he was not badly treated in prison; he survived the war and became a prominent member of the West German historical establishment in the 1950s. His complex and often contradictory position during the Third Reich typified that of many other academics in the humanities, and he was not the only one whose views evolved gradually from a positive though always conditional support of the regime towards a deepening opposition based on the Christian, conservative and patriotic values that he thought it was violating.[197]

Other historians and social scientists, however, and especially younger ones, were only too keen to participate in the war in the interests not so much of Germany as of Nazi ideology. Specialists in the history of East-Central Europe like the young Theodor Schieder and his colleague Werner Conze declared large parts of the region to be historically German and urged the clearing-out of the Jewish population in order to make room for German settlers. In a memorandum presented to Himmler, Schieder advocated the deportation of the Jews overseas, and the removal of part of the Polish population further east. Other, more senior historians including Hermann Aubin and Albert Brackmann offered their services in the identification of historically 'German' parts of the region, as a prelude to the expulsion of the rest of the population. Statisticians calculated the proportion of Jews in the region, demographers worked out the details of possible future population growth following Germanization, economists engaged in cost-benefit analyses of deportation and murder, geographers mapped out the territories to be resettled and redeveloped. All of this ultimately fed into the General Plan for the East, with its almost limitless ambition for racial reordering and extermination.[198] These various enthusiastic contributions reflected the eagerness of a variety of scholars and institutions to exert an influence on, or at least play a part in, the reconstruction of Eastern Europe under Nazi rule. Beyond this, they rushed to take part in the grand schemes developed by the Nazi leadership for the reshaping of the whole economic, social and racial structure of Europe. 'Scholarship cannot simply wait until it is called upon,' wrote Aubin to Brackmann on 18 September 1939. 'It must make itself heard.'[199]

Some of these scholars and scientists were still based in universities during the war, but even more than had been the case in the peacetime years, research activity, particularly in the natural and physical sciences, was concentrated in non-university institutes funded by major national bodies, notably the German Research Community and the Kaiser Wilhelm Society. These survived, with their very substantial budgets, in the first part of the war not least because nobody in power paid very much attention to them. German military victories generated a widespread sense of complacency. The victories in the west in 1940 and the rapid advances across the Soviet Union the following year demonstrated not only the superiority of German arms but also the world-beating stature of German science and technology. Only when things began to go badly did Nazi leaders turn to scientists for help. Albert Speer in particular was keen on co-ordinating scientific research and focusing it on war-relevant projects. In the summer of 1943 a Reich Research Council was established to co-ordinate and focus scientific efforts across the wide variety of research institutes and funding bodies that were competing with one another in the effort to deliver new weapons and new technologies. But this still left a number of rival institutions, as the air force and the army insisted on running their own research centres and the decentralization and dissipation of military-related research defied all attempts of the Reich Research Council to develop a coherent research strategy that would avoid the same areas being covered by parallel groups of researchers.[200]

Scientific research during the war ranged across the whole spectrum of Nazi plans and ambitions. Scientists at a specially created institute in Athens carried out research into improving crop yields and food supplies for future use by German settlers in the east, while an SS botanical unit collected plant specimens behind the Eastern Front to see if any of them were of nutritional value.[201] Such work involved a two-way bargain: scientists were not just being co-opted by the regime, but also willingly used the research opportunities it provided to build their own research careers and further their own scientific work. So intensive was the collaboration indeed that some even spoke ironically of 'war in the service of science'.[202] In 1942, the creation of a Reich Institute for Psychological Research and Psychotherapy set the seal on the efforts of Matthias Göring (a cousin of the Reich Marshal, whose name was of considerable help to him in his campaign) to gain recognition for a profession long associated by the Nazis with Jewish doctors such as Sigmund Freud. The Institute investigated war-relevant matters such as the reasons for neuroses and breakdowns among the troops; but it is also, as we have seen, researched homosexuality, which the army and the SS regarded as a genuine threat to the German soldier's fighting prowess.[203]

Racial-biological research was carried out not only by Kaiser-Wilhelm-Institutes but also by Himmler's Ancestral Heritage organization, the research arm of the SS.[204] Himmler's men ranged far and wide both before and during the war in search of proof for his often wild racial and anthropological theories. The organization mounted expeditions to Scandinavia, Greece, Libya and Iraq looking for prehistoric remains, and two scholars worked their way through a variety of sites in the Middle East, sending back reports to German intelligence as they went. Most remarkably of all, Ancestral Heritage staffers Ernst Schäfer and Bruno Beger led an SS expedition to remote Tibet, where they photographed some 2,000 of the inhabitants, measured 376 individuals and took plastic casts of seventeen Tibetan faces. Heinrich Harrer, already well known for his conquest of the Eiger mountain, achieved greater fame on another expedition sent by Himmler to the Himalayas. Arrested by the British on the outbreak of war, he escaped and spent seven years in Tibet, later writing a best-selling account of his experiences.

Encountering problems in identifying who was Jewish and who was not in the ethnically and culturally mixed regions of the Crimea and the Caucasus when they were overrun by German forces, Himmler dispatched Schäfer and Beger to the area to try to sort things out so that the Jews could be separated out and killed. Before long, Beger was engrossed in a large-scale study of supposedly Jewish racial characteristics. Unable to continue his work because of the advance of the Red Army in 1943, he relocated to Auschwitz, where he selected and measured Jewish prisoners and took casts of their faces, in full knowledge of their impending fate. Then he moved on to the concentration camp at Natzweiler. Here he was assisted by the ghoulish anatomist August Hirt, whose features had been severely disfigured by a wound to his upper and lower jaw during the First World War. At Natzweiler the two men started a collection of Jewish skulls, first taking x-rays of selected inmates, then, after having them gassed, macerating their flesh in a chemical solution before adding the skeletal remains to the Ancestral Heritage archive at Mittersill castle. These macabre activities were only brought to an end by the arrival of the advancing Allied armies.[205]

III

Medical science also came into the service of waging war. Military and civil planners urgently needed medical answers to a wide range of questions. Some of these were of direct relevance to the war: how to combat typhus more effectively, how to stop wounds from becoming infected, how to improve the chances of survival for seamen drifting in lifeboats after their vessel had been sunk. Such problems faced all combatant nations during the war. In Germany, medical science felt able to use experimentation on concentration camp inmates in the search for answers to these problems. Nobody forced medical scientists to do this work; on the contrary, they took part in it willingly or even asked to do so. That this was so should not be surprising: for some years, doctors had been among the most committed supporters of the Nazi cause.[206] From their point of view, the inmates of concentration camps were all either racially inferior subhumans or vicious criminals or traitors to the German cause or more than one of these at the same time. Whatever they were, they seemed to Nazi doctors – two-thirds of the medical profession in the Third Reich – to have no right to life or well-being, and were thus obvious subjects for medical experimentation that could, indeed in many cases quite clearly would, cause pain, suffering, illness and death.

The first use of camp inmates for medical experimentation was at Dachau, where the leading figure was an ambitious young SS doctor, Sigmund Rascher. Born in 1909, Rascher had joined the Nazi Party in 1933 and by the outbreak of war was working for Himmler's Ancestral Heritage research organization. Rascher's partner Karoline Diehl, a former singer sixteen years older than himself, was an old personal friend of Himmler's, and the SS leader therefore reacted positively when the doctor presented him with a project for the early diagnosis of cancer. Rascher held out the prospect of creating an infectious form of cancer that could be used as a rat poison. In order to carry out the research, he obtained Himmler's permission to take regular blood tests from long-term inmates at the Dachau concentration camp. In 1941, Rascher, who in the meantime had been appointed as a medical officer in the air force reserve, further persuaded the SS leader to let him carry out experiments on prisoners in Dachau designed to test the human body's reactions to rapid decompression and lack of oxygen at high altitudes, with the aim of working out how to keep a pilot alive when he was forced to parachute out of a pressurized aircraft cabin at heights of 18 or 21 kilometres. Up to 300 experiments were carried out on ten or fifteen criminal prisoners in a mobile decompression chamber in Dachau from February to May 1942. The suffering inflicted on the prisoners was considerable, and at least three are known to have died during the experiments. When the senior colleague seconded by the air force was absent, Rascher carried out further, as he called them, 'terminal experiments', in which the subject's death was planned from the start: these consisted of seeing how long someone could stay alive when the air supply was gradually thinned out. Some of the subjects, described by Rascher as 'race-defiling, professionally criminal Jews', were made unconscious in a simulated parachute jump without oxygen at the equivalent of 14 kilometres above ground, and were then killed by drowning before they recovered. Rascher reported on these experiments directly to Himmler, who visited Dachau in order to observe them. The experiments were also filmed, and the results shown to a gathering of air force medical personnel in the Air Ministry on 11 September 1942. Between seventy and eighty prisoners were killed in the course of this project.[207]

So pleased was Himmler with Rascher's work that he set up an Institute for Applied Research in Defence Science in the summer of 1942, as part of the Ancestral Heritage division of the SS, with the express purpose of carrying out medical research in the concentration camps. Rascher's operation in Dachau became part of this organization. Already in June Himmler, prompted by the air force, had commissioned Rascher to carry out experiments on prisoners to determine how best to promote the survival of pilots who came down in the icy waters of the North Sea. As they floated in large tanks filled with water at various (but always low) temperatures, dressed in air force uniforms and life-jackets, prisoners' bodies were closely monitored while a variety of simulated rescue attempts was undertaken. By October 1942 between fifteen and eighteen out of the fifty or sixty inmates subjected to this treatment had died. The average time before death was seventy minutes. Removal and plunging into a warm bath did not cause a shock to the system, as Rascher had expected, but brought about an immediate improvement. He presented the results to a large conference of ninety-five medical scientists in Nuremberg on 26 and 27 October 1942; none of them raised any objections to the use of camp inmates as subjects, or to the fact that many of them had been killed by the experiments.[208]

This marked perhaps the high point of Rascher's career. Its progress had depended almost exclusively on the favour shown him by Himmler. When the SS chief had initially objected to his marriage to Karoline Diehl on the grounds that she was too old to bear children, the couple had proved him wrong by announcing that she was pregnant. When Rascher informed Himmler that his fiancée had given birth to two sons, the marriage was approved, and Himmler even sent the couple a bouquet of flowers with his fulsome congratulations. However, the SS leader was being deceived, and when Karoline Rascher announced that she had given birth to another infant early in 1944, even Himmler smelt a rat: surely at fifty-two a woman was too old to bear children? An investigation revealed that she had stolen the infant from its mother on Munich's main railway station, and that she had acquired her other children in much the same way. Himmler, furious at being made to look a fool, had her arrested, confined to Ravensbrück and then executed. Rascher himself was dismissed from all his posts and imprisoned in Buchenwald; at the end of the war he was transferred back to Dachau and shot there three days before the camp's liberation.[209]

Rascher's disgrace by no means ended medical experimentation of this kind, however. The German air force and navy were also concerned about the survival of airmen and sailors who had succeeded in getting into a dinghy or life-raft but had no water to drink. Air crew in particular faced this problem since water supplies in any quantity were too heavy to carry on board their planes. A number of experiments with converting seawater for drinking purposes proved fruitless because they involved subjects whose health could not be compromised because they were genuine volunteers, Professor Oskar Schröder, a leading air force doctor, asked Himmler on 7 June 1944 for forty healthy subjects from concentration camps. The young men were selected from 1,000 Gypsies transferred from Auschwitz to Buchenwald and told that if they volunteered for special duties in Dachau they would be well fed and that the experiments would not be hazardous: the doctor in charge of the experiments, Wilhelm Beiglböck, told them he himself had drunk seawater without any ill effects. After being fed air-force rations for a week, the subjects were put on a diet of seawater that had been treated in a variety of different ways, or in some cases not treated at all. Soon they were all suffering from unbearable thirst. If they refused to take any more seawater it was force-fed to them. One man was driven mad with desperation and had to be put in a straitjacket, while another was tied to his bed. Others lay around apathetically, or screamed with pain. When the floor was cleaned, the men threw themselves on to it to lap up the traces of liquid left by the mop. While nobody actually died from these experiments, the pain and suffering they inflicted was as considerable as the results were meagre.[210]

Further experiments were conducted by medical scientists interested in the treatment of wounds received in battle. Following the death of Reinhard Heydrich from septicaemia, Himmler, acting on Hitler's instructions, ordered experiments to be carried out under the supervision of the Reich Physician SS, Ernst-Robert Grawitz, to see whether and under what conditions a variety of sulphonamides might be effective against an infection of this kind. These were antibacterial drugs, the forerunners of antibiotics, and they had already been developed by the Bayer pharmaceutical company with some success; the medical scientist Gerhard Domagk had been awarded the Nobel Prize for Medicine for his role in developing a commercial variety known as Prontasil in 1939, though Hitler had forbidden him to accept the prize. In July 1942 Karl

Gebhardt, Himmler's personal SS physician, began experimenting in the Ravensbrück camp on fifteen male inmates and forty-two young female prisoners from Poland, most of them students. Gebhardt's reputation, severely dented by the failure of his sulphonamides to save Heydrich's life, depended on the success of this work. He went at it with enthusiasm and commitment. First, he simulated war wounds by cutting open the subjects' calves, crushing the muscles, and sewing infectious material into the wounds, along, in some cases, with splinters of glass and wood or pieces of gauze impregnated with a variety of bacterial cultures. Gebhardt treated the patients with sulphonamides then reopened the wounds after four days to gauge their effect. They had had no effect at all. Similar experiments were carried out at the same time in Dachau, where ten people died of the gangrene brought about by the artificially induced infections. Grawitz was not satisfied that the Ravensbrück experiments had been thorough, however, since the wounds had only been light, so Gebhardt took another twenty-four women and injected gangrenous tissue into them; three died, but the rest survived, most probably because of the sulphonamide treatment. Gebhardt conducted further experiments in the camp, even smashing the women's bones with a hammer to simulate war wounds. The sulphonamide treatment was sufficiently effective for Himmler to rehabilitate Gebhardt and allow him to resume his career. At Dachau, SS doctors carried out similar work, injecting forty mostly Polish Catholic priests with pus and treating some but not others, not only recording the effects but also photographing them. Twelve died, and all of them suffered terribly. Many of the sulphonamide experiments left their subjects with serious health problems or physical disabilities for the rest of their lives.[211] In May 1943 the results of the experiments were presented to a medical conference at which no attempt was made to conceal the fact that the subjects had not given their consent to the work carried out on them.[212]

Not only wounds but also diseases were the subject of medical experimentation in the camps. Foremost among these was typhus, which research carried out shortly before the First World War had shown to be transmitted by the human body louse. Apart from killing the louse, there was no means of defence against the disease until Polish researchers developed a vaccine in the early 1930s; but its production was difficult, costly and time-consuming. The German army began making it, but was unable to produce the quantities needed. The danger that German soldiers would become lousy through contact with the military and civilian populations of the east led to an intensification of German research, including at the laboratories of I. G. Farben. A variety of vaccines was produced, but the dosage they required remained uncertain, and their effectiveness in doubt. Human experimentation seemed to German medical scientists the obvious method of answering these questions. After being approved on 29 December 1941 at a meeting of representatives of various interested parties, including the Army Sanitary Inspectorate, the Military SS, the Reich Health Leader and the Robert Koch Institute (the leading centre for bacteriological research), experiments were set in motion at the Buchenwald concentration camp. In the initial experiment, 145 inmates were first given a course of injections of the vaccine, or (if they belonged to a control group) not, and were then, a fortnight or so after the final dose, injected again, this time with the blood of a patient infected with the most virulent form of typhus. The experiment was repeated a further eight times with different vaccines. For 127 out of the 537 camp inmates subjected to these procedures the results were fatal.[213]

The Battle of Stalingrad, where German troops had died of malnutrition in their thousands, had suggested to Hitler that new ways had to be found of feeding the soldiers. Hitler's doctor Karl Brandt, the SS chief Heinrich Himmler and a variety of nutrition experts discussed what might be done. Eventually, a sort of artificial pâté called 'Eastern Nutrition' (Östliche Kostform), made of cellulose remnants, was developed and fed to 450 apparently healthy prisoners at Mauthausen in 1943. The prospect of being able to use it for the entire population of concentration camp inmates was particularly enticing. The prisoners found the paste revolting but had no choice. In a second experiment at Mauthausen, 150 prisoners were made to live on the paste for six months. 116 died, although given the conditions under which they were held, it was not possible to say how far their diet had contributed to their demise.[214] Almost as serious at Stalingrad had been the high rate of infection from epidemic jaundice, or hepatitis, which affected up to 6 million soldiers on the Eastern Front between June 1941 and the end of 1942, according to one army estimate. Kurt Gutzeit, a medical professor at Breslau and adviser to the army who was an expert in the disease, wanted to show that it was infectious, and obtained permission from the SS to carry out experiments on camp inmates. In June 1943, with the backing of Karl Brandt and Heinrich Himmler, Gutzeit's assistant Arnold Dohmen went to Auschwitz, where he selected a group of young Jews on the arrival ramp. On 10 August he took eleven of them, dressed in civilian clothes and travelling by scheduled passenger trains, to Berlin and thence to Sachsenhausen. After taking time off to get married and go on his honeymoon, Dohmen arrived at the camp in October, but he began to have doubts about the ethics of the experiment, and it was not until a year later when, having been subjected to heavy pressure by his superiors, he injected the subjects with hepatitis and performed liver punctures on two of them to see whether they had caught the disease. None is known to have suffered any long-term physical effects, but then infectious hepatitis does not usually cause these. The distress from which they suffered, particularly from being separated from their parents, about whose fate they were kept in the dark, was considerable.[215]

Experiments were also carried out to try to find a way of treating phosphorous burns caused by incendiary bombs. With Himmler's approval, Ernst Grawitz got an SS doctor to smear phosphorous on the arms of five inmates of the Buchenwald camp in November 1943 then set it alight. The pain, according to survivors, was excruciating. The ointment then put on the wounds seems to have had little effect, and some of the subjects died.[216] At Sachsenhausen and Natzweiler, mustard gas, which had caused such suffering in the First World War, and which, it was feared, might be used in Allied bombing raids, was injected into some inmates, while others were made to drink it in liquid form, or forced to inhale it. Some had wounds inflicted on them and infected with the gas. Three inmates had died in the experiments by early 1943, but the scientists, working for the SS Ancestral Heritage organization, reported some success with treatment. In subsequent experiments involving phosgene gas, four Russian prisoners were killed, and there were further prisoner deaths in December 1944 in mustard gas experiments conducted at the Neuengamme camp. Carried out under the auspices of Karl Brandt and the SS, in many cases with the knowledge of Hitler himself, these dangerous, often painful, and sometimes fatal experiments were inflicted on people who had no choice about undergoing them. None of this research ever brought any benefit to the German soldiers, sailors and airmen it was intended to help.[217]

IV

Camp inmates were also used for pure research without any obvious or immediate practical implications. The leading figure here was Dr Josef Mengele, camp doctor in Auschwitz. Mengele was a scientific assistant to the prominent racial hygienist Otmar Baron von Verschuer at the University of Frankfurt am Main. Mengele had published scientific articles arguing for racial differences in the structure of the lower jaw, cleft palate and a deformity of the ear known as *fistulae auris*. He was a member of the Nazi Party and the SS, and joined the Military SS in 1940, where he served as a medical officer on the Eastern Front. Here he won the Iron Cross, First Class, and was wounded in action. In May 1943 he was transferred to the Economy and Administration Head Office of the SS and at the end of the month posted to Auschwitz, where he made an immediate impression on the inmates with his youthful, handsome appearance, his well-tailored uniform and highly polished boots, his politeness and his elegance. All of this set him apart in the most dramatic possible way from the mass of the ill-kempt and under-nourished inmates. He saw in Auschwitz the chance to resume his career as a scientific researcher after his break at the front. One of his research projects focused on noma, a disease in which severe malnutrition caused the lining of the cheek to atrophy and a gangrenous hole to open up, exposing the teeth and the jaw. In the search for supposed hereditary elements in the disease, which he thought might affect Gypsies more than other groups, Mengele treated a large number of children suffering from this disease at Auschwitz, giving them vitamins and sulphonamide and effecting a considerable improvement in their condition.[218]

For Mengele, however, such treatment was a means to a scientific end, not an end in itself. As soon as it had brought about an improvement sufficient to provide convincing evidence of its effectiveness, he stopped it, and the children returned to their former condition and fell victim to the disease again. For him they were experimental subjects, not medical patients. Energetic and workaholic, Mengele developed many further research projects, some of which were supported by the Kaiser Wilhelm Institute for Anthropology in Berlin, where his teacher Verschuer received regular reports on his work in the camp.[219] He considered his most important project to be the one that built on Verschuer's proposal that hereditary influences could best be studied by research on twins. Auschwitz offered Mengele a unique opportunity for collecting subjects for this research. He could often be found inspecting new arrivals on the selection ramp even when he was off duty, looking for fresh sets of twins. Plunging into the mass of arriving Jews, shouting 'twins out!', he would pluck twins of any age out of the mêlée of frightened families and take them off to one of the three offices he used for the project. Here he would have each of them tattooed with a special prisoner number, and put into living quarters separated from the rest of the camp. They were allowed to keep their own clothes and did not have to have their heads shaved. If they were very young, their mother was saved from the gas chamber in order to look after them.

Mengele did not allow the twins to be beaten or maltreated in case this interfered with his experiments. He would have them measured in minute detail before injecting them, sometimes in the spine, with a variety of chemicals to see if they reacted differently, or applying chemicals to the skin to observe their effect. Such experiments caused deafness, collapse or even, if the children were very young, death. On occasion, if twins fell ill and there was a disputed diagnosis, Mengele would give them a fatal injection and carry out an autopsy to determine the nature of their ailment. On the whole, however, he kept the twins alive. The older ones were evacuated from Auschwitz in January 1945 and their fate is uncertain. One estimate puts the proportion of those who died as a result of experimentation at around 15 per cent. Although Mengele intended his research to form the basis for his 'Habilitation', the second doctorate required in Germany to qualify for an academic career, its value was dubious in scientific terms. He was, for example, unable to determine whether the twins he collected were identical or not, and indeed some siblings who were close in age and appearance to one another managed to save themselves from the gas chamber by passing themselves off as twins even though they were not.[220]

Mengele acquired his notoriety among camp survivors not so much from his experiments as from his role in selecting prisoners for extermination. Standing on the ramp, often alone, immaculate in his appearance, and carrying a riding-crop, he would cast his glance briefly at each arrival before pronouncing 'left' or 'right' according to what he perceived to be their physical state and usefulness (or otherwise) for the camp's labour programmes. So frequently was he there that many inmates assumed, quite wrongly, that he was the only camp doctor to carry out this duty. Some thought he looked like a Hollywood movie star. Only if he encountered resistance would he break his elegant pose, beating people with his riding-crop if they refused to be separated from their family, or on one occasion drawing his gun and shooting a mother who physically attacked an SS man trying to separate her from her daughter. Mengele shot the daughter as well and then, as a punishment, sent all the people from the transport to the gas chamber, shouting: 'Away with this shit!' Touring the wards in the camp hospital, with a spotless white coat over his SS uniform, smelling of eau de Cologne and whistling snatches of Wagner, he would indicate with a thumbs-up or a thumbs-down which patients were to be selected for the gas chamber. Often he would select them on merely aesthetic grounds, consigning them to their death if they had an ugly scar or a rash on their body. On one occasion he drew a horizontal line on the wall of the children's block and sent all those whose heads could not reach the line to the gas chamber. Sometimes he would not wait, but would inject people with a deadly solution of phenol himself. What struck inmates was the evident sense of enjoyment with which Mengele approached his work. Here was a man completely at ease with the power he was wielding over life and death.[221]

Mengele did not confine his hereditarian researches to work on twins. He also collected people with physical abnormalities, hunchbacks, transsexuals, and the like, some of whom he had shot so that he could anatomize their bodies on the dissecting table. He was particularly enthusiastic in his search for dwarfs, whom he kept in the twins' quarters for experimentation in his search for hereditary causes of their condition. Mengele also used his position to supply eyes from dead inmates to a research project at his institute in Berlin, where scientists were studying the phenomenon of heterochromia (the two eyes of one person having different colours). If Mengele discovered any inmates with this condition, he ordered them to be killed. On one occasion, when his prisoner assistant put the eyes of all eight members of a Gypsy family together after their death, for shipment to Berlin, the clerk in charge of the shipment discovered that it only contained seven pairs of eyes; the assistant, terrified of what Mengele might do if he found out, scoured the morgue for Gypsy corpses, excised one blue eye from one and one black eye from another, and had them packed up with the rest. Here too, therefore, the scientific work was less than wholly reliable. Characteristically, Mengele took his work a step further, and tried to create perfect Aryan specimens from children he found with blond hair and brown eyes by injecting their eyes with methylene blue. The procedure, of course, failed to bring about any permanent change of eye-colour; but it did cause considerable pain, in some cases damage to the children's eyesight, and in at least one recorded instance, death. In all of these projects, Mengele regarded himself as a normal scientist, even holding a regular research seminar with his assistants, who included medically qualified camp prisoners. Mengele would chair the meeting and ask the prisoner-doctors to discuss particular cases. Freedom of debate was naturally restricted, however, by the fact that, as one of them later remarked, they were reluctant to disagree with Mengele because he could have any of them killed at any moment and on the slightest whim.[222]

Josef Mengele has come to stand in the decades since the Third Reich as a symbol for the perversion of medical science. Yet his experiments were only a few among a much greater number carried out by a variety of doctors on the inmates of the camps. These included research conducted by Dr Kurt Heissmeyer in the concentration camp at Neuengamme, in which twenty Jewish children between the ages of five and twelve, taken from Auschwitz, were infected with virulent tuberculosis and treated in a variety of ways, including the surgical removal of swollen glands. At the end of the war, in order to try to destroy the evidence of these experiments, the surviving children were taken on 20 April 1945 by one of the doctors to a sub-camp at Bullenhuser Damm and injected with morphine, after which an SS man accompanying them hanged the sleeping children from a hook one by one, pulling on their bodies to make sure they would die. Other medical experiments were carried out at the direct behest of Himmler, for policy rather than scientific purposes. At Auschwitz, for example, doctors working for Himmler experimented on female inmates with injections and x-ray treatment in the search for a quick and cheap means of mass sterilization, resulting in many cases in the loss of their hair and teeth, the complete disappearance of sexual feeling, or in the most serious cases the onset of cancer. Men were bombarded with x-rays aimed at their testicles, often leading to impotence or causing serious physical damage that made it difficult for them to urinate. Senior SS officers fantasized about such methods being applied to 10 million racially inferior people, or to Jewish men needed for labour, but they never got beyond the experimental stage.[223] Medical scientists at the Kaiser Wilhelm Institutes also carried out research on the brains of hundreds of patients killed in the 'euthanasia' action, to see whether they exhibited any consistent signs of degeneracy.[224] And in November 1942 complaints by the anatomical institutes of German universities that they did not have enough cadavers for dissection in teaching and research led to a ruling of the Ministry of Justice that they could have the remains of offenders executed in German prisons without having to obtain the permission of their relatives, a ruling that less than a year later was leading to further complaints by the institutes, this time that 'the massive deliveries of corpses of executed offenders during the last months has led to a complete overcrowding of our storage facilities'.[225]

Were any of the medical experiments carried out in the camps of any medical or scientific value? Some, like Mengele's, were clearly scientifically flawed. Others obviously had no defensible medical application. So it was, for example, with the experiments at the SS hospital in Hohlenlynchen, where a way of injecting people with live tuberculosis bacilli was developed that would kill them quickly and allow physicians to record tuberculosis as the cause of death; this was required because the usual method of killing people by injecting them with phenol or gasoline caused the corpse to emanate a suspicious smell. Sigmund Rascher's invention of small cyanide capsules for suicides was to have wide application at the end of the war, but could hardly be called scientifically or medically useful. However, other experiments carried out on concentration camp inmates in Germany were regarded in Germany as normal science, their results presented at conferences and published in reputable medical journals. Standard experimental protocols were employed in evaluating the experiments carried out, for example, by the Bayer Pharmaceutical Company on women inmates of Auschwitz whom it had purchased for this purpose from the SS at a premium of 700 Reichsmarks each. When Karl Gebhardt and Fritz Fischer had women prisoners injected with gas bacilli, staphylococcus or malignant oedema at Ravensbrück and then tested new drugs on them, the results were discussed at a subsequent conference and with leading physicians such as the famous surgeon Ferdinand Sauerbruch. Yet to suggest that such work was in accordance with the normal scientific protocols of the day in no way legitimizes the methods it employed. Medical research in these cases was unethical because it caused pain and often death in people who had no choice but to participate in it: indeed, it would still have been unethical had the subjects participated in it of their own free will, given the fundamental moral commitment of medicine to preserve life and not to end it.[226]

RESISTANCE

I

On 4 October 1943, in Posen, Heinrich Himmler gave a speech to senior SS officers, which he repeated in more or less the same form two days later to Party Regional Leaders and other prominent figures, including Joseph Goebbels and Albert Speer.[227] The speech contained what have since become some of his most notorious utterances. 'The evacuation of the Jews,' he declared, '. . . is a laudable page in our history that will never be written.' The Jews were a threat to the Reich, he declared. Therefore they were being killed, and not just the men:

We were approached with the question, what about the women and children? – I decided to find an absolutely clear solution here too. Thus I did not feel I had the right to exterminate – let's say then, kill them or have them killed – the men while I allowed their avengers, in the form of their children, to grow up and avenge them upon our sons and grandsons. The really difficult decision had to be taken to make this people disappear off the face of the Earth. For the organization that had to carry out the task, it was the most difficult we had so far had.[228]

Several months later, on 5 May 1944 and again on 24 May 1944, he repeated these sentiments in addresses to senior army officers at Sonthofen, describing how difficult he found 'the fulfilment of this soldierly command that was issued to me' to exterminate the Jews. Killing the women and children as well as the men, he implied, was his own interpretation of Hitler's order; the reference to a 'soldierly command' could only be a reference to Hitler himself, since there was nobody else from whom Himmler would accept commands of any kind. Hitler himself was clear enough about his own overall responsibility, however. As he remarked to senior military personnel on 26 May 1944: 'By removing the Jews, I have removed from Germany the possibility of the construction of any kind of revolutionary cell or nucleus . . . Humanitarianism would mean the greatest cruelty towards one's own people, here as in general, everywhere.'[229] It was a life-or-death struggle. If the Jews were not eliminated, they would exterminate the entire German people. Not only the generals and Party satraps, but also Himmler himself seemed to share the view that the extermination of the Jews was a crime, a necessary crime in their view, but a crime none the less: for why, otherwise, would the history books to be written in the future never dare to mention it? Such a crime would invite retribution should Germany lose the war. So these speeches, delivered at a time when Germany's military situation was becoming steadily more desperate, were designed not least to remind the senior Party figures and generals of their complicity in the genocide, in order to ensure that they would carry on fighting to the end, a point fully grasped by Goebbels, who wrote in his diary on 9 October 1944 that Himmler in his speech 'pleaded for the most radical solution and the toughest, namely to exterminate Jewry, bag and baggage. That is certainly the most consistent solution, even if it is also a brutal one. For we have to take on the responsibility of completely solving this question for our time.'[230]

To SS leaders, on 4 May 1944, Himmler had an even more explicit message. He had no doubt that they would continue the struggle to the bitter end. He wanted to remind them, however, that the extermination of the Jews had to be carried out wherever and whenever it was possible, and without any exceptions:

'The Jewish people will be exterminated', says every Party comrade. 'It's clear, it's in our programme. Elimination of the Jews, extermination and we'll do it.' And then they come along, the worthy eighty million Germans, and each one of them produces his decent Jew. It's clear the others are swine, but this one is a fine Jew. Not one of those who talk like that has watched it happening, not one of them has been through it. Most of you will know what it means when a hundred corpses are lying side by side, or five hundred or a thousand are lying there. To have stuck it out and – apart from a few exceptions due to human weakness – to have remained decent, that is what has made us tough.[231]

Even the SS men who carried out the murders, therefore, were told by Himmler that what they were doing went against the wishes of the great majority of Germans.

Most of Europe's Jews had already been murdered by this time; but one very large Jewish community remained more or less untouched, namely the Jews of Hungary, whom Hitler had for some time been pressing the Horthy regime to hand over. With the rapidly worsening military situation, the signs that Horthy was preparing to switch sides began to multiply. Still the major source of petroleum for the Reich, Hungary could not be allowed to slip out of German control. Hitler summoned Horthy to meet him on 18 March 1944 and told him that German forces would occupy his country immediately. The only question was whether it was to be done without bloodshed. Horthy had no option but to accept the ultimatum, and to agree to install the pro-German Ambassador in Berlin, Döme Sztójay, as Prime Minister. Not the least of Hitler's complaints against Horthy was, as he told the Hungarian Regent at their meeting, that 'Hungary did nothing in the matter of the Jewish problem, and was not prepared to settle accounts with the large Jewish population in Hungary.' Now all this was about to change.[232]

German troops marched into Hungary on 19 March 1944. On the very same day, Adolf Eichmann arrived in Budapest, to be followed shortly by a special unit led by Theodor Dannecker, charged with the arrest and deportation of the Hungarian Jews. Two radical antisemites, László Endre and László Bary, were appointed as the top civil servants in the Interior Ministry, to assist in the round-up. In the usual way, a Jewish Council was established, and on 7 April 1944 the compulsory wearing of the Jewish star was introduced. The first arrests of Jews now began in Hungarian Transylvania and Carpatho-Ukraine, where ghettos and camps were quickly erected, all with the full co-operation of the Hungarian police. In the meantime, the Gestapo arrested several thousand Jewish professionals, intellectuals, journalists, left-wing or liberal politicians and other prominent figures, mostly in Budapest, and sent them off to concentration camps in Austria. Their further fate remained for the moment uncertain. The same was not the case with the provincial Jews now being herded into the new temporary camps and ghettos in Hungary. Although the Council and also many individual Jews knew full well from personal contacts, the Hungarian service of the BBC and many other sources what awaited Jewish deportees who got on to the trains destined for Auschwitz, no steps were taken to warn Jews outside Budapest not to embark on them. Printed and widely distributed reports from four escapees from the camp did not change this situation. Most likely the Jewish Council did not want to cause unrest, and hesitated before urging people to break the law. At the same time, however, several Council members used their contacts with the SS to enable them, their families and their friends to flee to Romania or in some cases to other neighbouring countries. Up to 8,000 Jews managed to escape in this way.[233] Meanwhile, in Berlin, the Propaganda Ministry began directing the German press to carry stories about the 'Jewification' of Hungary, which was now finally being rectified by the measures taken after the German invasion.[234]

The first trainloads of Jews left for Auschwitz on 14 May 1944. From now on, between 12,000 and 14,000 were packed into cattle-trucks and sent to the camp every day. Four gas chambers and crematoria were brought into action again and worked round the clock without a break. New Special Detachments were recruited to pull the bodies of the dead out of the gas chambers as fast as they could, to allow the next contingent of victims to be driven in. One prisoner in the buna factory nearby saw flames up to ten metres high roaring out of the crematoria chimneys at night, while the smell of burning flesh reached as far as the factory itself. One crematorium broke down under the strain, and the Special Detachments began burying bodies in pits. Visiting Hitler on 7 June 1944, Prime Minister Sztójay sought to convince the German Leader that the deportations were causing resentment in Hungary because they were widely perceived as resulting from foreign intervention in the country's internal affairs. Hitler responded with a tirade against the Jews. He had warned Horthy, he said, that the Jews had too much influence, but the Regent had done nothing. The Jews were responsible for killing tens of thousands of Germans in Allied bombing raids, he claimed. For this reason 'nobody could demand of him that he should have the least pity for this global plague, and he is now only sticking to the old Jewish saying: "An eye for an eye, a tooth for a tooth" '.[235] By this time, the King of Sweden and US President Franklin D. Roosevelt had both protested to Horthy and asked him to bring the deportations to an end. However, Pius XII's intervention, on 25 June 1944, neither mentioned the Jews by name nor specified the fate to which they were being sent. The leading figures in the Hungarian Catholic hierarchy refused to issue any public condemnation of the deportations; one of them, the Archbishop of Eger, considered that 'what is currently happening to the Jews is nothing other than an appropriate punishment for their misdeeds in the past'.[236] On 7 July 1944, finally overcoming the opposition of the most pro-Nazi members of the Hungarian government, Horthy ordered them to stop. Eichmann managed none the less to send two more trainloads of Hungarian Jews to Auschwitz, on 19 and 24 July. By this time, in little over two months, no fewer than 438,000 Hungarian Jews had been taken to Auschwitz, where some 394,000 of them had been gassed immediately on arrival.[237]

II

These tragic and desperate events took place in a rapidly deteriorating military situation for the Third Reich. On 3 November 1943 Hitler issued a general directive for the conduct of the war over the coming months. The Red Army might be advancing in the east, but German forces were still deep inside Soviet territory, so for the moment there was no direct threat to the survival of the Reich itself. The danger posed by the imminent Allied invasion of Western Europe, on the other hand, was far more acute, given the relatively short distance the Anglo-American armies would have to traverse before they got to the German border once they had succeeded in landing on the Continent. Priority therefore had to be given to building up defences in the west; the east could for the time being look after itself. At the same time, however, Hitler was unwilling to sacrifice territory in the east that provided Germany with major supplies of grain, raw materials and labour. And the Red Army was pressing on relentlessly, driving the German Army Group South under Manstein back west of Kiev and forcing Kleist's Army Group A back from the Dnieper river bend. All along the front, from the Pripet marshes to the Black Sea, Soviet armoured divisions were pushing through the German armies, now depleted by the transfer of more forces and equipment to the west, outflanking their defences and advancing towards the borders of Hungary and Romania. The 120,000 German and Romanian troops cut off in the Crimea were annihilated by a Soviet pincer movement in April and May 1944. As in the past, Hitler blamed his generals for these defeats, sacking Manstein and Kleist on 28 March 1944 and replacing them with two of his favourite senior officers, Ferdinand Schörner and Walter Model.[238]

These defeats showed that the Red Army had now completely seized the initiative. German counter-attacks on any scale were effectively out of the question. All that Schörner, Model and the other field commanders could do was try to guess where the Red Army would strike next. But guessing was not easy. Stalin, Zhukov and the leading Soviet generals decided to deceive their German counterparts into thinking that the push would come in the Ukraine, building on the victories achieved in the spring. Model persuaded Hitler to move substantial reinforcements and equipment to support his own forces (now renamed Army Group North Ukraine), taking reserves away from Army Group Centre in Belarus under Field Marshal Ernst Busch. The central sector of the front was now bulging out to the east after the spring successes of the Red Army to the north and south. Previous attempts by the Soviet forces to reduce the bulge had been unsuccessful. Under conditions of great secrecy, Stalin and his commanders moved massive reinforcements of men, tanks and armaments into this area, concentrating on one big push – codenamed 'Operation Bagration' – rather than dissipating their forces over disparate sectors of the front. Lulled into complacency by repeated and deliberate deceptions carried out on German intelligence by the Russians, Busch went away for a few days, ignoring a massive spread of partisan activity to the rear of his forces. From the night of 19–20 June 1944 onwards pro-Soviet partisans blew up hundreds of railway lines and roads to make it more difficult for the Germans to bring up reinforcements. One and a half million Soviet troops, equipped with enormous quantities of tanks, armour and artillery, began a huge encirclement, of the kind so successfully practised by the Germans earlier in the war, with a series of armoured thrusts. Busch returned to the front, but Hitler refused his appeal to withdraw. In less than two weeks 300,000 German troops were killed or captured as the Red Army swept on. By the middle of July, the Soviet forces had advanced 200 miles in the central sector of the front and had to stop to regroup. On 17 July 1944 some 57,000 German prisoners were paraded through the middle of Moscow in a kind of Roman Triumph. Many of them had simply given themselves up. They were not prepared to undergo another Stalingrad. It was one of the greatest and most spectacular victories of the war.[239]

'Operation Bagration' opened the way for further victories all along the line. In the north, Soviet troops advanced as far as the Baltic, west of Riga; sent to rescue the situation, Schörner managed to fight back

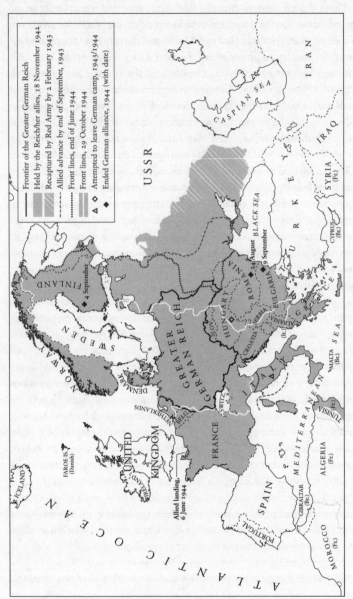

19. The Long Retreat, 1942–4

and recapture enough of the coastline to restore the line of communication, but his forces still had to retreat from Estonia and much of Latvia to avoid getting cut off. On 5–9 October 1944, Soviet troops pushed through again to the sea. The German forces lacked the resources for a counter-attack, but supplies and reinforcements came in by sea. A new note of desperation characterized their fighting as they defended the German territory of East Prussia. Soviet lines of communication were now over-extended. The German forces managed to slow down the Soviet advance until it ground to a halt. However, the Red Army had also launched an attack on Finland in June 1944, completing the relief of Leningrad and convincing the Finns that there was no option but to sue for peace. On 4 September 1944 a new government under Marshal Mannerheim signed an armistice under which the 1940 borders were to be restored and any German troops in the country arrested and interned. Further south, Model's Army Group North Ukraine, weakened by the transfer of troops and equipment to Army Group Centre, was attacked by a series of savage armoured blows that sent it reeling back to the Carpathian mountains. Red Army commanders were helped by a massive superiority in arms and equipment, and by supremacy in the air after Germany's fighter force had been redeployed to deal with Allied bombing raids from the west. Soviet artillery was being produced in huge quantities to pulverize the enemy before the tanks moved in. Particularly feared was the Katyusha rocket launcher, first used at Smolensk in 1941. It had been kept absolutely secret, so that when it came into action for the first time, firing dozens of rockets against the enemy with a huge noise, not only German troops but also Red Army soldiers fled in panic. Initially rather inefficient, with a range of less than 10 miles, by 1944 the device had been improved and was being manufactured en masse. German soldiers called it the 'Stalin Organ' from the appearance of its closely packed launch-tubes. They had no equivalent to use in return.[240]

By the autumn of 1944 Soviet forces were fast approaching the gates of Warsaw. Stalin announced the appointment of a puppet Polish government, a rival to the exiled Polish regime in London. The exiled regime's underground Home Army, a nationalist organization opposed to the communists, was being crushed by the Red Army as it moved into Polish territory. Nevertheless, when Stalin called upon the citizens of Warsaw to rise up against their German oppressors, in the expectation that Soviet forces would shortly be entering the city, the Home Army in the city decided to stage an uprising on 1 August 1944, fearing that, if it did not, Stalin would brand it pro-German, and hoping in any case to gain political influence by taking control of the traditional capital of Poland. The Home Army in Warsaw was poorly equipped, since most of its weapons and ammunition were being used for partisan activities in the countryside, and it was ill prepared. Its commanders had paid little attention to the ghetto uprising the previous year, and learned nothing from its fate. With 'Molotov cocktails', pistols and rifles, the Poles fought a stubborn defence against tanks, artillery, machine-guns and flame-throwers. For two months, the terrible scenes of 1943 were repeated on a larger scale, as German SS and police units commanded by Erich von dem Bach-Zelewski confined the insurgents to isolated areas, then reduced them to pockets of resistance, and finally wiped them out altogether, razing most of the city to the ground in the process. 26,000 German troops were killed, wounded or missing, but the Polish dead, men, women and children, numbered more than 200,000. Bach-Zelewski, employing Ukrainians, Soviet renegades and convicts drafted in from the concentration camps, massacred everyone he could find. An insurgent nurse described a typical scene as German and Ukrainian SS troops entered her hospital,

kicking and beating the wounded who were lying on the floor and calling them sons of bitches and Polish bandits. They kicked the heads of those lying on the ground with their boots, screaming horribly as they did it. Blood and brains were spattered in all directions . . . A contingent of German soldiers with an officer at its head came in. 'What is going on here?' the officer asked. After driving out the murderers, he gave orders to clear up the dead bodies, and calmly requested those who had survived and could walk to get up and go to the courtyard. We were certain they would be shot. After an hour or two another German-Ukrainian horde came in, carrying straw. One of them poured some petrol over it . . . There was a blast, and a terrible cry – the fire was right behind us. The Germans had torched the hospital and were shooting the wounded.[241]

Similar and worse incidents repeated themselves throughout the Polish capital during these weeks. Himmler had ordered the whole city and its population to be destroyed. The centre of Polish culture would exist no longer. If the uprising was seen historically, he told Hitler, 'it is a blessing that the Poles are doing it.' It would enable Germany to bring the 'Polish problem' to a decisive end.[242]

Stalin held back the Red Army while it focused on establishing bridge-heads on the Vistula and Narva rivers. He did nothing to assist the few Anglo-American planes that tried to airlift supplies to the insurgents. Most of the drops fell into German-held territory, and Stalin's refusal to allow the planes to use Soviet airfields, along with the reluctance of the air force commanders, ensured that the airlift had no effect. From Stalin's point of view, the uprising was a success: it inflicted heavy losses on the Germans, and it wiped out the politically inconvenient Polish Home Army as well. Once the last resisters surrendered, on 2 October 1944, he moved his forces in to take over the devastated city.[243] 'You have to seal your eyes and your heart,' wrote the Warsaw-based German army officer Wilm Hosenfeld as the unequal fight continued. 'The population is being pitilessly exterminated.'[244] After the Warsaw uprising was finally defeated, he watched the 'endless columns of the captured rebels. We were totally amazed by the proud bearing they showed when they came out.' The women in particular impressed him, marching past, heads held high, singing patriotic songs.[245] His attempt to get the captured resisters recognized as enemy combatants and so subject, at least in theory, to the laws of war, was predictably rebuffed by his superiors. Hosenfeld was ordered to interrogate the survivors. 'I try to rescue everyone,' he wrote, 'who can be saved.'[246]

Resistance was also mounting in the west, and particularly in France, where the Maquis now numbered scores of thousands of men and women, engaged in sabotaging German military installations in preparation for the invasion of France across the English Channel. Elaborate deception measures mounted by British and American intelligence services persuaded the German commanders that the invasion would come in Norway or near Calais or some other seaport. Over a million British, American, French, Canadian and other Allied troops were assembled in southern England under the general command of US general Dwight D. Eisenhower. On the night of 5–6 June 1944, more than 4,000 landing craft and over 1,000 warships convoyed the troops across the Channel while three airborne divisions began parachuting down behind the German defences. With the German navy effectively out of action, the German air force seriously weakened by losses in the preceding months and German forces dispersed over other areas and lacking the crack divisions concentrated on the Eastern Front, resistance was weaker than expected. Pulverized by naval and aerial bombardment, German defences were overwhelmed by the force of the landings, and except on Omaha Beach the resistance was quickly overcome. By the end of 6 June 1944, 155,000 men and 16,000 vehicles had been safely landed by the Allied operation. Prefabricated 'Mulberry harbours' were towed in and assembled, and more Allied forces landed and joined up from their five beachheads before the German army could rush in sufficient reinforcements to repel them. The capture of Cherbourg by 27 June 1944 provided them with a seaport, and huge quantities of men and equipment began to come over. German reinforcements were rushed to the front and began to put up stiff resistance, but the German commanders, Rundstedt and his subordinate Rommel, had no effective strategic plan for dealing with the invading forces, who now began to fight their way slowly across Normandy. This was now a war on two fronts.[247]

Hitler reacted predictably by blaming this situation on the generals. They were constantly plying him with pessimistic assessments of the situation, he raged, and demanding withdrawals and retreats instead of staying put and fighting to the last. On 1 July 1944, worn out by the constant arguments with the Leader, Chief of the Army General Staff Kurt Zeitzler broke down, and simply abandoned his office. Hitler had him drummed out of the army in January 1945 and denied the right to wear a uniform. General Heinz Guderian was appointed his replacement on 21 July 1944. In the west, Field Marshal von Rundstedt was sacked two days later, along with Hugo Sperrle, the air force commander who had made a name for himself in the bombing of Guernica during the Spanish Civil War, but was now blamed by his Leader for failing to mount an effective airborne defence against the Allied invasion. Field Marshal Günther von Kluge was appointed to replace Rundstedt. On the Eastern Front, Field Marshal Ernst Busch was sacked because of the catastrophic defeat of his Army Group Centre in Operation Bagration, and replaced by Field Marshal Walter Model, one of the few senior officers whom Hitler held in continuing high esteem. As he left the Berghof for the last time on 14 July 1944 to return to his field headquarters at the 'Wolf's Lair' in Rastenburg, Hitler's contempt for so many of his generals was becoming even more open than before.[248]

III

The military catastrophes of the spring and early summer of 1944 led to an upsurge of resistance not only in occupied Europe but also in the German Reich itself. Already, the defeats of the previous year had spread disillusion with the regime. The devastating effects of the bombing weakened the authority of the regime still more. Nevertheless, open acts of resistance or defiance were still rare. Individual acts of defiance were met with arrest, trial and not infrequently execution. Collective resistance was difficult in the extreme. Social Democratic and Communist resistance organizations had been crushed by the Gestapo by the mid-1930s and the leading figures in both parties were either in exile or in prison or concentration camp. Not only the more restrictive police regime of the war years but also the Nazi–Soviet Pact had a dampening effect on the will of former labour movement activists to organize any kind of oppositional activity before June 1941. And the euphoria created by the stunning military victories of 1939 and 1940 was shared by many in the working class, including former Social Democrats. As a precaution, too, the Gestapo arrested and incarcerated a number of former Communist functionaries on the invasion of the Soviet Union in case they should start a campaign of subversion. It was only in 1942, after the defeat of the German army before Moscow, that clandestine Communist resistance groups began to emerge again, in strongholds of the industrial working class like Saxony, Thuringia, Berlin and the Ruhr. Some of them were able to establish contact with the exiled party leadership in Moscow, but it was only intermittent, and in general there was little central co-ordination. The Communists managed to put out some leaflets urging opposition to the Nazis and even advocating acts of sabotage, but in general they achieved relatively little before they too were smashed by the Gestapo. The most spectacular action was undoubtedly that mounted by a group of young Jewish Communists and their sympathizers, led by Herbert Baum, who, as we have seen, managed to blow up part of an anti-Soviet exhibition staged by Goebbels in Berlin, though without causing any serious damage or any casualties. They too were quickly betrayed to the Gestapo; thirty were arrested and tried by the People's Court; fifteen of them were executed.[249]

Since the mid-1930s, the official party line from Moscow had emphasized the need for Communists to collaborate with Social Democrats in a 'popular front'. But this tactic faced severe difficulties on both sides. The Social Democrats justifiably suspected the clandestine Communist groups of being under far more intensive surveillance than they were themselves, and the dangers of collaboration were dramatically illustrated on 22 June 1944 when a meeting in Berlin between the Social Democrats Julius Leber and Adolf Reichwein and a group of Communist functionaries resulted in the arrest of all those involved. As far as the Communists were concerned, it was more than likely that when the war was over the Social Democrats would re-emerge as their major rivals for the allegiance of the industrial working class, so that any co-operation could only be strictly tactical and temporary and should not involve concessions to a likely future political enemy. Within the concentration camps, and above all in Buchenwald, Communists formed their own groups, which could at times achieve a limited degree of prisoner self-management. The appointment of Communists as capos and block leaders was encouraged by the SS camp management, who saw the Communists as reliable and effective in this role. For their part, the Communist prisoners tried to maintain solidarity amongst themselves and protect their comrades, devolving difficult and dangerous work on to other categories of prisoner such as the 'asocials' and criminals. Through maintaining good relations with the SS they also hoped to improve conditions generally in the camp and so benefit all the inmates in the long run. In such a situation there were only limited prospects of meaningful co-operation with Social Democratic or other political prisoners. Solidarity within the Communist group was all-important. This precarious strategy, trying to strike a balance between ideological purity on the one hand, and self-protection through collaboration with the SS on the other, was to lead to widespread and sometimes bitter controversy after the war.[250]

One exceptional group with Communist connections, though subject neither to Communist discipline nor to Stalinist ideology, had managed to survive since early on in the Third Reich. This was known by the Gestapo as the 'Red Orchestra' (*Rote Kapelle*), though it was in fact a series of overlapping and functionally rather different clandestine groups. Beginning late in 1941, German military counter-espionage in Brussels and Paris began to uncover an extensive network of Soviet intelligence agents. It had links to a resistance circle in Berlin, grouped around a civil servant in the Reich Economics Ministry, Arvid Harnack, and an attaché in the Air Ministry, Harro Schulze-Boysen. Harnack was a Marxist economist who believed in a peaceful, socialist Germany, while Schulze-Boysen was a radical nationalist revolutionary who had been arrested and tortured by the Nazis in 1933 but then released on good behaviour. Some of their followers were members of the Communist Party, but the group was essentially independent of any central direction from Moscow. Women played a particularly prominent role in it, notably Harnack's American wife Mildred Harnack-Fish, a literary historian, and Schulze-Boysen's wife Libertas, who gained a critical view of Nazi propaganda through her work in the film section of the Propaganda Ministry. In order to give himself 'cover', Harnack joined the Nazi Party in 1937. The group helped political fugitives to escape from Germany, distributed leaflets not only to Germans but also to foreign forced labourers, and took up contact with both the US and the Soviet embassies, whom they kept informed about the crimes of Nazism. The Soviets were impressed enough to supply them with radio equipment, and they managed to convey some information on the war economy to the Russians, but Stalin refused to believe the group's warning of an imminent invasion in June 1941. Their leaflets became longer and more ambitious, including one written by Schulze-Boysen warning percipiently that Hitler would suffer the same fate in Russia as Napoleon had done. However, their clandestine radio messages to the Russians were intercepted by German military counter-intelligence. This led to Schulze-Boysen's arrest on 30 August 1942 and Harnack's on 7 September 1942. Other arrests followed, eventually numbering more than 130. After a series of rapid trials, more than fifty members of the group were executed, including both the Harnacks and the Schulze-Boysens. On Hitler's personal insistence, the death sentences were carried out by hanging.[251]

The so-called 'Red Orchestra' was not the ring of Soviet spies portrayed in subsequent Nazi propaganda but a home-grown resistance movement whose contacts with Soviet intelligence were made on its own terms. It was far from being the only left-wing group of this kind, though it was larger than most. One of the most remarkable was a tiny, little-known but tightly knit organization called the 'League: Community for Socialist Living'. Formed in the early 1920s by the adult education lecturer Artur Jacobs, it set up a number of centres where it held discussions, offered dance and movement classes, and tried to build a lifestyle that crossed class boundaries and transcended the egotism of the individual. Some of its members were Communists; others were Social Democrats; a good number had no party affiliation at all. In any case its members, as it were, left their party cards at the door when they entered the League's premises. From the very beginning they identified antisemitism as the core of Nazi ideology, and in 1933 the League and its members went underground and began helping Jews to escape arrest and, from 1941, deportation. Here its small size – there were never more than a few hundred members even at the height of its popularity in the 1920s – and the close personal ties that had grown up between its members helped the League stay intact and to carry on its work undetected by the Gestapo. Its members organized false identities for Jews in hiding, ferried them secretly from one location to another, and helped them evade the attentions of the Gestapo. From the point of view of the League's members, this was a way of keeping the spirit of social and racial equality alive in the face of Nazi persecution. In this way, they provided a practical alternative to the usual activities of left-wing resistance groups, which focused on the largely futile attempt to rouse popular opinion against the Nazis.[252]

The milieu from which the League emerged in the 1920s, in which small groups of various political hues tried to build new lifestyles of one kind or another, also gave rise, at a greater distance, to a far better-known resistance movement, the self-styled 'White Rose', some of whose members had been involved in the autonomous youth movement of the Weimar years. Any initial enthusiasm they might have had for the Nazi regime was quickly dispelled by its racism and its antisemitism, its restrictions on personal freedom, and above all the extreme violence it unleashed on the Eastern Front in 1941–2. While they were studying medicine at Munich University, some of the young men who played a key role in forming the group had been sent to work in the army medical service on the Eastern Front. The group gradually expanded to include not only Kurt Huber, a Munich professor who acted as a kind of mentor to many of its members, but also friends, colleagues and students in other university towns from Freiburg to Stuttgart, and especially Hamburg. Leading members included the Scholl siblings, Hans and Sophie, as well as a number of other Munich students, Alexander Schmorell, Christoph Probst and Willi Graf. Some of them tried to take up contact with Falk

Harnack, brother of the key figure in the 'Red Orchestra' network, in Chemnitz in November 1942 and again in early February 1943. As it expanded, the group became bolder, typing, cyclostyling and posting to a wide and more or less random range of recipients a series of six leaflets in quantities ranging from just a hundred up to several thousand. Their aim, like that of traditional left-wing resistance groups, was to rouse popular opinion so that the masses would rise up and bring an end to the war by overthrowing Hitler and his regime. They roundly condemned the mass murder of the Jews and the Polish elites, and pilloried the apathy of the German people in the face of the Nazis' crimes. After Stalingrad they began daubing graffiti on the walls of public buildings in Munich ('Hitler Mass Murderer', 'Freedom' and so on). On 18 February 1943, however, Hans and Sophie Scholl were observed by a university porter scattering copies of their latest leaflet in the courtyard. He reported them to the Gestapo, and they were arrested. During a lengthy interrogation, they admitted that Schmorell, Graf and others had also been involved in writing, printing and distributing the leaflets, and the police quickly arrested the rest of the group. Hitler wanted a quick trial. Probst and the Scholls were brought before the People's Court on 22 February 1943, found guilty of treason and beheaded; Huber, Schmorell and Graf were condemned on 19 April and also executed. Ten others were given prison sentences. The Hamburg group continued to distribute the leaflets but it was also eventually discovered by the Gestapo; the last of its members was arrested in June 1944. Copies of the final leaflet reached the British via Sweden, and the Royal Air Force dropped hundreds of thousands of copies over Germany in the spring of 1943.[253] Thus the message of the 'White Rose' did not go unread.

For the most part, however, moral and political critics of the regime sat tight, hoping for better times, and keeping their beliefs to themselves. It is impossible to say with any certainty how widespread such behaviour was. One example can be found in the diary of Erika S., born in Hamburg in 1926, into a formerly Social Democratic family. Her journal mixed in unselfconscious juxtaposition with her own daily cares her moral outrage at the larger damage she thought the war was causing. 'Ah,' she wrote on 4 June 1942, 'if only this unholy war were soon at an end! Nothing to eat and then these many cruel murders, it's too terrible, especially when you think of all the victims and those left behind. Nobody knows how many young people have already had to sacrifice their lives for Hitler's devilish cause, it's no longer anything but one huge campaign of murder.'[254] Such sentiments were doubtless shared by her father, who was taken into custody by the Gestapo on more than one occasion, the last time on 23 August 1944. Undaunted by this final arrest, Erika sat down and wrote a letter to Himmler, assuring him that her parents had 'brought me and my 14-year-old brother up in a completely National Socialist way'. She reminded the SS chief that she was a member of the League of German Girls and had joined the Nazi Party the previous April. So she could not understand why her father had been taken into custody. After waiting in vain for a reply, she went to the nearest Gestapo office to pursue her quest. The officers were polite, but made no concessions. 'It just can't be borne any longer,' she wrote in her diary, 'how one is treated in Germany. And all the same, one still does everything to avoid attracting attention.'[255]

IV

None of this was ever likely to achieve the overthrow of the Nazi regime. Only one group was in a position to do this, and that was the military resistance that had originally emerged in 1938 among senior army officers concerned about what they saw as Hitler's rashness in risking a general European war by the invasion of Czechoslovakia, when Germany was unprepared for one. The victories of 1939–40 seemed to prove them wrong.[256] Only a few, such as the former Ambassador to Italy, Ulrich von Hassell, remained convinced of what he called the criminal irresponsibility of the regime and were appalled at the destruction it was visiting upon Eastern Europe. Hassell found it intolerable, as he wrote in his diary on 8 October 1940, that 'the Jews are systematically being exterminated, and a devilish campaign is being launched against the Polish intelligentsia with the express purpose of annihilating it'.[257] Other Foreign Ministry officials, including State Secretary Ernst von Weizsäcker, Adam von Trott zu Solz and Hans-Bernd von Haeften, had long shared Hassell's views. Hassell regularly discussed this and other issues with a small number of like-minded civilians who had occupied senior positions in government and administration, notably Carl Goerdeler, the former Price Commissioner and ex-Mayor of Leipzig, and Johannes Popitz, Prussian Minister of Finance. The group included the former

Chief of the Army General Staff Ludwig Beck, who was one of the few senior military figures who were not bowled over by the military triumphs of the first phase of the war; others who had once contemplated arresting Hitler and installing a military regime, like Franz Halder, no longer went beyond grumbling about Hitler's conduct of the war even when the going began to get tough in 1941, as we have seen. Like the vast majority of senior officers, Halder supported the concept of a crusade against the Soviet Union and considered the harshest measures justified. The circle around the head of the Military Intelligence, Admiral Wilhelm von Canaris, and his chief of staff, Hans Oster, had also been concerned for some time about Hitler's reckless military ambition. But they bided their time, considering it was pointless trying to undertake anything while popular support for Hitler was so high. The group also included the young theologian Dietrich Bonhoeffer, who had been an inspirational figure in the Confessing Church but missed its main confrontation with the Nazi regime in the mid-1930s because he had been serving as a pastor in London. Bonhoeffer had been drafted into Military Intelligence in 1940, and soon began working with the oppositional group there.[258]

A small number of mostly aristocratic officers of the younger generation, however, like Fabian von Schlabrendorff and Henning von Tresckow, on the staff of Army Group Centre, were so outraged by the atrocities being committed in the east that they determined to take action. Tresckow in particular, though he had initially supported Hitler, had soon been appalled by the brutality and lawlessness of his regime. A Prussian officer in the classic mould, he considered that enemy soldiers should be treated according to the laws of war, and tried to circumvent the orders he was given to shoot Soviet political commissars on sight. His commanding officer, Field Marshal Günther von Kluge, expressed an interest in joining the military opposition but was too cautious to commit himself. Moral objections to Nazism were also at the root of the growing opposition expressed (in private) by the Kreisau Circle (a name given to it later by the Gestapo). This was a loose network of intellectuals, eventually numbering over a hundred, who met at the estate of Count Helmuth von Moltke at Kreisau, in Lower Silesia, for discussions about the situation. On three occasions in 1942–3 the group held larger conferences that included theologians, lawyers, former Social Democratic politicians, and others from a wide variety of backgrounds.

A number of members of the circle held minor government posts, among them Count Peter Yorck von Wartenburg (a civil servant in the Price Commissioner's office) and Count Fritz-Dietlof von der Schulenburg, who was Deputy Police President of Berlin. Moltke himself worked in the prisoner-of-war department of the Combined Armed Forces Supreme Command. A number of the Kreisau Circle's members had experience of other countries, which strengthened their critical perspective on Nazism. Their views were strongly idealistic. On 9 August 1943 they agreed a set of basic principles to be implemented after the collapse of Nazism. These emphasized Christianity as the basis for a moral regeneration of the German people. Basic freedoms had to be restored. Politically, Germany was to become a federal state with a weak central power. It was to be divided into provinces of between 3 and 5 million inhabitants each, which would be further divided into self-governing communities, organized into districts. The regions would have parliaments elected by the district assemblies, and a national Reichstag would be elected by the provincial parliaments. The minimum voting age was to be twenty-seven. The Kreisau Circle also wanted some kind of international community of states, to reduce the risk of war happening again. All of this expressed a kind of radical-conservative idealism, grounded in the suspicion of modern 'mass society' and aimed at re-creating a sense of rootedness and belonging based on Christian values and local identities. The members of the Kreisau Circle were suspicious of capitalism, and wanted both common ownership of vital industries and 'co-responsibility' in the individual plant. What they thought of as the excesses of urbanism would be overcome by the state guaranteeing to provide every family with a garden.[259]

The Kreisau Circle and its members developed multiple and shifting contacts with members of the military and civilian resistance, and on 8 January 1943 a meeting took place between representatives of the two groups. It did not go well. Moltke considered Goerdeler a reactionary, while more politically experienced men like Hassell thought many of the 'youngsters' unrealistic.[260] Various attempts by Moltke, Trott and others to forge contacts with the Western Allies and persuade them to work together with them to rebuild Germany after victory came to nothing.[261] The Allies had their own plans. Distrust of Western parliamentary models of democracy, which the Kreisau Circle regarded as having failed under Weimar, was almost universal in the various arms of the German resistance, and this alone was hardly likely to recommend their constitutional plans to the British or the Americans. Goerdeler and the military conspirators were even less likely to win Allied approval. Leading figures in the group hammered out and repeatedly revised a set of aims that became steadily more modest as Germany's military situation worsened, but even in May 1944 they included a negotiated peace on the basis of the German frontiers of 1914 plus Austria, the Sudetenland and the South Tyrol, autonomy for Alsace-Lorraine, and the retention of an effective defence force in the east.[262]

The constitutional ideas of the conspirators ranged from an authoritarian, quasi-corporatist state, as suggested by Hassell, to a more parliamentary model advocated by Goerdeler in an attempt among other things to satisfy Social Democrats in the group like Julius Leber. Even here, however, Goerdeler wanted a strong corporative element, with candidates coming from economic interest groups and indirect elections to the Reichstag, which was to be restricted in influence by being granted only advisory powers and subordinated to a second chamber nominated by the head of state. Extra votes were to be given to fathers of families. Like the Kreisau Circle, Goerdeler and the military conspirators were determined to avoid the party-political animosities that had so undermined the Weimar Republic, so open electoral campaigning was not supposed to take place in the state they hoped to found. And like the Kreisau Circle, the military-conservative resistance regarded Christian values as the all-important foundation for the re-emergence of a morally upright Germany, though Leber and the Social Democrats were unhappy about this idea. The Social Democrats' influence, which grew stronger over time, could be found in a degree of overlap with the Kreisau Circle's emphasis on the need to control the capitalist economy. However, the vision of Goerdeler and his group, of a Germany in which class antagonisms would be overcome by the creation of a true national community dominated by the traditional aristocracy (the 'stratum that carries the state', as Schulenburg put it), was never likely to be accepted by the working-class followers of the Social Democrats. The hostility of the military-conservative resistance to a parliamentary constitution and a pluralist, open society demonstrated its backward-looking character and its lack of potential appeal to the masses. Indeed, given the participation of Prussian officers and conservative Prussian politicians in the group, it was hardly surprising that they looked back, as many in the Kreisau

Circle also did, to the Prussian reforms of Baron Karl vom Stein at the beginning of the nineteenth century as a model for the future development of Germany. Here, too, their lack of realism was palpable.[263]

One of the factors motivating the German resistance was undoubtedly outrage and shame at the regime's treatment of the Jews. Already in late August 1941, Helmuth von Moltke was writing to his wife about the mass murder of Jews and Soviet prisoners of war in the east. This was, he said, burdening the German people 'with a blood-guilt that can never be expunged in our lifetime and can never be forgotten'.[264] In similar vein, Ulrich von Hassell confided to his diary on 4 October 1941 that General Georg Thomas, the chief procurement officer of the armed forces, had reported on his return from the Eastern Front on 'the continuance of repulsive cruelties, particularly against the Jews, who were shamelessly shot down in batches'.[265] 'Hundreds of thousands of people have been systematically killed just because of their Jewish descent', noted an outraged memorandum penned by Goerdeler and others on the postwar future of Germany in November 1942. After the fall of Nazism, the authors promised that the Nuremberg Laws and all laws specially affecting the Jews would be abolished. Yet the reason they gave was not that they were unjust, but that they were unnecessary because the very small number of Jewish survivors would no longer constitute a 'danger for the German race'. Nor, significantly, did this prevent the resisters from drawing up plans to classify the surviving Jews on the basis of their race as much as their religion.[266]

Moreover, a number of the military participants in the conspiracy had themselves ordered actions against the Jews, including for example Karl-Heinrich von Stülpnagel, army commander in Paris. As the senior official in Regional Leader Wagner's Silesia, Fritz-Dietlof von der Schulenburg had implemented antisemitic and anti-Polish policies with enthusiasm, including the forced labour conscription or deportation of Poles and Jews. It was above all the German military defeat at Stalingrad, which he took as evidence of Hitler's military incompetence, that drove Schulenburg into the opposition; and indeed for many of the military figures among the resisters, the belief that Hitler was responsible for the worsening situation of Germany in the war was also crucial.[267] Wolf Heinrich, Count Helldorf, Police President of Berlin, also involved in the conspiracy, had actually taken a leading part in persecuting the capital city's Jews in the 1930s.[268] The plot even included among its supporters and informants Arthur Nebe, commander of SS Task Force B in the Soviet Union, responsible for the murder of scores of thousands of Jews; his motives for joining the opposition were particularly obscure. Some of the conspirators, including Johannes Popitz, disapproved of the methods used by the Nazis to deal with 'the Jewish question' because they were too extreme, not because the idea of discriminating against the Jews was wrong in itself. As this suggests, it was not surprising that many of them had initially supported the Nazis for their racial policies as well as for other reasons. Well before 1944, however, such views had been all but obliterated by the view that, as Goerdeler put it, 'the Jewish persecution . . . has taken the most inhuman, merciless and deeply shaming forms, for which no recompense can be adequate'.[269]

There was one crucial difference between the military conspirators and the Kreisau Circle. Moltke and most of his friends were against an assassination attempt on Hitler on religious grounds, preferring to wait for the military collapse of the Third Reich before putting their plans into action. To a degree, this view was shared by other members of the civilian resistance. The military had no such scruples. In particular, Henning von Tresckow was convinced that Hitler had to be killed if the Nazi regime was to be overthrown. He began to organize a series of assassination attempts shortly after Stalingrad. On 13 March 1943 he tried to blow up Hitler's plane on a flight between his field headquarters with explosives supplied by Admiral Canaris and military counter-intelligence and smuggled into the plane's hold. But the attempt failed because the detonator would not work in the extremely low temperature of the hold at high altitude. The bomb, disguised as a package containing two bottles of cognac, was still in the hold when the plane landed. In the nick of time, Tresckow's co-conspirator Fabian von Schlabrendorff managed to fly to the scene, get hold of the package and defuse it. On 21 March 1943 another young conspirator, Colonel Rudolf-Christoph, Baron von Gersdorff, took a bag of explosives along to an exhibition of captured Soviet equipment in Berlin, hoping to kill Hitler during his planned visit. But the Nazi Leader rushed through the building at such a pace that the opportunity did not present itself. As one attempt after another came to nothing, Goerdeler pressed the military to move quickly, otherwise millions more lives would be lost and Germany would be so thoroughly defeated that the new regime he envisaged would be in no position to make terms with the Allies. That he believed this would still be possible despite the decision of the Allied leaders at Casablanca early in 1943 to accept nothing other than unconditional surrender from Germany shows the conspirators' lack of political realism; and even had Churchill and Roosevelt been prepared to negotiate, there was no chance that they would accept the terms that Goerdeler and his co-conspirators were offering.[270]

Moreover, the conspiracy began to get into serious trouble as its members began for one reason or another to come to the attention of the Gestapo. Military Intelligence under Canaris and Oster, which the conspirators viewed as the key logistical centre of their operation, was increasingly threatened by the ambitions of Walter Schellenberg's foreign intelligence department of the SS Security Service. This led to increased surveillance by the Gestapo. In the spring of 1943 Oster and some of his key officers, including Bonhoeffer, were arrested over allegations of currency offences. In January 1944 Hitler's suspicions led to his ordering the takeover of foreign military intelligence, which Oster had been running until his arrest, by the Security Service of the SS. Canaris, an emigmatic figure who some suspected of betraying military secrets to the Allies, was interned. In a further blow, Moltke was arrested in January 1944. Meanwhile, Popitz, in an extraordinary act of political unrealism, approached Himmler with a view to winning him over to the idea of toppling Hitler on his own initiative. The initiative met with a vague expression of interest from the SS chief, but no more. Horrified, Goerdeler and the other civilian conspirators did their best to avoid contact with Popitz after this. Important figures dropped out – Kluge suffered serious injuries in a car accident, the Social Democrat Mierendorff and the retired army chief Hammerstein both died of natural causes. All of this set back the conspiracy by many months and reduced the coherence and potential effectiveness of the plot.[271]

Deeper problems faced the conspirators as they tried to revive their assassination plans. In order for the plot to succeed, they had to persuade key units of the reserve army to move on Berlin and take over the major institutions of government, but, though they made some headway with the delicate negotiations, there were still many uncertainties. While General Friedrich Olbricht, who headed the armed forces reserve section in Berlin, was with them, actively planning the troop movements that would secure power once Hitler was dead, his boss, General Friedrich Fromm, commander of the reserve army, a man with an eye to the main chance, decided to play a waiting game when he was told about the conspiracy, though he did not betray the conspirators for the time being. Together with the former Chief of the Army General Staff Ludwig Beck, and Tresckow, Olbricht drew up plans for 'Operation Valkyrie', a military coup to be launched immediately Hitler was pronounced dead. But who would kill the Leader? This was the final problem to be solved. It required someone who combined access to Hitler's person with commitment to the resistance – a difficult if not impossible combination to find. On more than one occasion, an attempt had to be abandoned because the man who had agreed to carry it out could not get near the target. But in the late summer of 1943, a new figure entered the conspiracy who fulfilled all these qualities. Claus Schenk, Count von Stauffenberg, was a lieutenant-colonel who had been badly injured in North Africa, losing his right hand and the third and fourth fingers of his left. He wore a black patch over one eye. He was due to take up his appointment as chief of staff of the Army General Office on 1 October 1943. An able and extremely energetic officer, Stauffenberg had, like a few others in the military hierarchy, initially supported Nazism, and been enthused by the early victories of German arms in Poland and France. But he had become disillusioned with Hitler's recklessness on the Eastern Front and thought, above all after Stalingrad, that it was taking Germany into the abyss. Stauffenberg also had an unusual kind of moral and patriotic commitment, derived from his youthful membership of the circle around the poet Stefan George. What turned him decisively against Hitler were the atrocities committed by the SS on and behind the Eastern Front against Slavs and Jews, and his feeling that they had to be stopped became ever stronger. With Tresckow, Stauffenberg became the central energizing and organizing figure in the conspiracy. They set up one new assassination attempt after another, only to see them all fail, often by pure chance. In the end, Stauffenberg resolved to kill Hitler himself.[272]

As the Gestapo began to close in on the plotters, finding a way of getting to Hitler became ever more urgent. On 1 July 1944 it presented itself out of the blue when Stauffenberg was promoted to a colonelcy and appointed chief of staff to Fromm, head of the army reserve. This gave him access to Hitler as Fromm's emissary. At the same time, the purpose of the assassination was changing with the fast-moving military situation. After the Normandy landings, Stauffenberg doubted whether killing Hitler would serve any useful political purpose. Surely there was no hope any longer, if there had ever been any, of reaching a negotiated settlement with the Allies and rescuing something of Germany from the ruins. But, as Tresckow told him: 'The assassination must be attempted at any cost. Even should that fail, the attempt to seize power in the capital must be undertaken. We must prove to the world and to future generations that the men of the German resistance movement dared to take the decisive step and to hazard their lives upon it. Compared with this object, nothing else matters.'[273] On 20 July 1944 Stauffenberg visited Hitler's field headquarters at Rastenburg, carrying a briefcase containing two bombs. With only a thumb and two fingers at his disposal, he was slow in priming the time-delayed detonator, and he only had time to prepare one of the bombs before being ushered in to the barracks where Hitler was conducting a review of the military situation with his staff; the other bomb he entrusted to his companion Werner von Haeften, who later threw it out of his car. Putting the case down next to the large wooden map-table over which Hitler was leaning, Stauffenberg left the room, saying he had to make a phone call. He watched from a distance as the bomb exploded, wrecking the barracks. Then he bluffed his way through the SS security cordons, got into a plane and flew back to Berlin.[274]

Assured by Stauffenberg over the phone that Hitler could not have survived the explosion, Olbricht and the leading conspirators at army headquarters in Berlin launched the military takeover. But very quickly things began to go wrong. Had Stauffenberg been able to prime both bombs, or even left the unprimed one in his briefcase along with the other, there is no doubt that Hitler would have been killed. But the force of one explosion was not enough. The blast was not contained by the flimsy wooden walls of the barracks but blew them out together with the windows, while the heavy wooden map-table protected Hitler, who was standing on the other side. Even so, four of those present, standing near where the bomb went off, were either killed instantly or died later of their wounds. Hitler staggered out of the door, putting out the flames that were burning on his trousers. He ran into Keitel, the sycophantic Chief of the Armed Forces General Staff, who burst into tears, crying: 'My Leader, you are alive, you are alive!' Hitler's clothing was torn and he had burns and abrasions on his arms and legs and some splinters of wood in his legs. Like everyone else in the hut apart from Keitel, he had burst ear-drums. But he had no serious injuries. This was to prove decisive. Almost as ominous for the conspirators was the fact that, while they had managed to sever some communications with the Rastenburg field headquarters, they had been unable to cut them all off. Within a short time, members of Hitler's staff were able to telephone Berlin and pass on the news that Hitler was still alive.

In Berlin, the cautious General Fromm, asked by the conspirators to set the military coup in motion, telephoned Rastenburg to see if their claim that Hitler was dead was correct. He was told that it was not. Trying to arrest Olbricht and the other conspirators at army head-quarters, he was himself placed under arrest as they attempted to go on with the coup. Amid mounting confusion, some army units went into action according to the planned 'Operation Valkyrie', but others were stopped in their tracks as Hitler began to have instructions transmitted from Rastenburg countermanding the conspirator's orders. Caught in the cross-fire of claim and counter-claim, Major Otto Ernst Remer, commander of a guards battalion in the capital, and a fanatical Nazi, had obeyed orders to surround the government quarter with his troops, in the belief that Hitler was dead. With machine-gunners taking up positions near the Brandenburg Gate, things looked bad for ministers, such as Goebbels, who were caught in the trap. Fearing the worst, Goebbels pocketed a supply of cyanide pills before moving into action. He persuaded Remer to come and discuss the situation with him, in the presence of Albert Speer, who later remembered the Propaganda Minister's nervousness as the major entered his room. Hitler was not dead, Goebbels assured Remer: and surely the Leader could override the orders of any general. He telephoned Hitler's direct line in Rastenburg. Hitler spoke to Remer in person and ordered him to restore order. Remer withdrew his troops from the government ministries. Those of Olbricht's subordinates who had not been taken into his confidence now joined forces with Remer. Shooting broke out at army headquarters, and Stauffenberg was wounded. Fromm was released, and now arrested Olbricht, Stauffenberg and the other conspirators in turn. Beck produced a revolver and shot himself twice; as he lay injured on the floor, Fromm ordered a sergeant to take him into the next room and finish him off. Then he hurriedly condemned the other conspirators to death. If they were left alive to talk to the Gestapo, his own earlier complicity in the plot would have been revealed. A firing-squad lined up Olbricht,

Stauffenberg, Haeften and their fellow-plotter Colonel Albrecht Mertz von Quirnheim in the courtyard and shot them one by one. As he was about to be killed, Stauffenberg shouted: 'Long live sanctified Germany!'[275]

V

The news of Hitler's survival torpedoed the conspiracy not only in Berlin but also in Prague and Vienna, where some of the conspirators had also tried to stage a coup. In Paris, the military commander of occupied France, General Karl-Heinrich von Stülpnagel, put the coup in motion as soon as Stauffenberg telephoned him to say Hitler was dead. Over a thousand SS officers were arrested, including the top commanders of the SS and its Security Service in Paris, Carl-Albrecht Oberg and Helmut Knochen. But before any more could be done, the vacillating Field Marshal Kluge discovered that Hitler was after all alive, and stopped the measures in their tracks. The SS men were released. For Oberg and Knochen, their detention and their failure to take any steps against the conspiracy were deeply shaming and potentially dangerous. Kluge's representative in Paris, General Günther Blumentritt, took advantage of their evident embarrassment to patch up a deal over several bottles of champagne in the Salon Bleu of the Hôtel Raphaël. He put the main events down to a misunderstanding and prevented the complicity of most of the conspirators in Paris from being discovered. For Stülpnagel, however, there was no reprieve. 'So, Herr General,' Oberg had said to Stülpnagel on entering the hotel, 'you seem to have bet on the wrong horse.' Indeed, Kluge had already reported Stülpnagel's actions to Berlin. Guessing the fate that was in store for him, the general drove out of Paris towards the First World War battlefield of Verdun, where he stopped his car, got out and shot himself in the head. Like Beck, however, he did not succeed in killing himself. Blinded and badly disfigured, he was taken to Berlin under arrest.[276]

News of the bomb and Hitler's survival had already been broadcast over the radio by this time. Shaken but not badly injured, Hitler managed to find time for a prearranged meeting with Mussolini at his field head-quarters, showing him proudly round the scene of the explosion, before broadcasting to the nation just before one in the morning of 21 July

1944. Reassuring Germans that he was alive and unharmed, he declared that 'a tiny clique of ambitious, unscrupulous and at the same time criminally stupid officers hatched a plot to remove me, and together with me, virtually to exterminate the staff of the German Supreme Command.' Providence, he continued predictably, had preserved his life. Privately, he fulminated against the conspirators, raging that he would 'annihilate and exterminate' every one of them. He appointed Himmler to replace Fromm, whose attempt to cover up his own complicity had not fooled anyone. Guderian became Chief of the Army General Staff. All Germans, said Hitler, had to join in hunting down those responsible. By this time, Remer and Ernst Kaltenbrunner, head of the SS Security Service, had arrived at army headquarters in Berlin, and Otto Skorzeny, who had sprung Mussolini from captivity a year before, turned up with an armed squad of SS men. They stopped any other executions from taking place. Meanwhile, Fromm attempted to telephone Hitler from Goebbels's office, but the suspicious Propaganda Minister made the call himself, and received orders to put the general under arrest. Goebbels instructed the media to emphasize again that only a small group of reactionary aristocrats had been involved. Public demonstrations had to be organized to celebrate the failure of the coup.[277]

Meanwhile, Himmler and the Gestapo moved into action to identify and arrest the surviving conspirators. As the investigation gathered pace, it became apparent that Hitler's first estimation that the plot was the work of no more than a handful of reactionary officers was mistaken. Soon Canaris, Oster and the Military Intelligence group were brought in for questioning, along with many army officers involved in the conspiracy. Arrests of civilians followed, including Hjalmar Schacht, the former economic supremo of the Third Reich. Schacht had been in touch with the plotters, but even before he knew this, Hitler ordered him to be taken in because, he still felt, Schacht had sabotaged rearmament in the 1930s. Hess too would be arrested when England was finally beaten, he raged. He would be 'mercilessly hanged' because he had given the others an 'example of treason'. Johannes Popitz and the Social Democratic participants and sympathizers, including Gustav Noske and Wilhelm Leuschner, were also arrested. Carl Goerdeler went into hiding, then made his way eastwards, camping out in forests, until he was finally recognized, denounced and arrested in his turn. Exhausted, demoralized and subjected to sleep deprivation by his captors, and like some of the other resisters in thrall to a moral conviction not only that the truth had to be told but also that it would have a persuasive effect on those who heard it, he gave the Gestapo the names of other members of the conspiracy, making it clear that it was far more than a plot hatched by a handful of military malcontents. He never wavered from his now openly expressed conviction that Hitler was a 'vampire' and that 'the bestial murder of a million Jews' was a crime that besmirched the name of Germany.[278]

Himmler organized a huge sweep of known opponents of the regime, arresting in the end as many as 5,000 people. As late as 23 September 1944, documents came to light implicating the earlier conspirators, including top army officers such as Halder, Brauchitsch and the armed forces' chief procurement officer, General Georg Thomas. Many others had already given themselves up, like Ulrich von Hassell, or courted death by resisting arrest, or committed suicide by shooting themselves. Henning von Tresckow, still on the Eastern Front, drove out towards the enemy lines on the morning of 21 July and blew himself up with a grenade after learning that the plot had failed. Worried that torture might force him to name names, he told Fabian von Schlabrendorff before he set out: 'Hitler is the arch-enemy not only of Germany but of the whole world.'[279] Others took poison, or shot themselves for similar reasons. One army officer who had joined the coup attempt in Berlin put a grenade in his mouth and pulled the pin as he was about to be led away by the Gestapo. A number of the resisters were severely beaten. Metal spikes were driven underneath their fingernails to make them talk. But they did not reveal the names of their co-conspirators. Hitler's growing suspicion of Kluge, who he feared would negotiate a surrender with the invading Allies, led him on 17 August 1944 to appoint the ever-faithful Model Commander-in-Chief in the west in his stead. Knowing the game was up, Kluge drove off eastwards, and near the spot where Stülpnagel had tried to kill himself, he stopped the car and swallowed a phial of poison. The popular Field Marshal Erwin Rommel, who had known of the conspiracy but not approved of it, had nevertheless told Hitler to his face that he should bring the war to an end. Rommel was still convalescing from war wounds when Hitler presented him with the alternatives of suicide disguised as death from his injuries and followed by a state funeral, or arrest, trial and public humiliation. As the SS surrounded the house where he was resting, Rommel realized he would never reach Berlin alive, and took poison. The state funeral duly followed. Twenty-two other military conspirators were dismissed with dishonour from the army by a court-martial hastily convened on Hitler's orders and presided over by Field Marshal von Rundstedt.[280]

On 7 August 1944 the trial of the first eight conspirators, including General Erwin von Witzleben, who had been involved in military conspiracies against Hitler since 1938, and Yorck von Wartenburg, opened before the People's Court in Berlin. Subsequent trials were held over the following weeks, involving many other conspirators, including Schulenburg, Trott, Goerdeler, Leuschner, Hassell and the blinded Stülpnagel. The trial of Leber, Popitz and the former Württemberg state president, Eugen Bolz, and members of the Kreisau Circle, including Moltke, took place as late as January 1945. Many of the conspirators had hoped that a trial would give them the opportunity to expound their views, and indeed Hassell among others had probably given himself up in this expectation. But the President of the People's Court, Roland Freisler, bullied and hectored the accused men, showered them with crude insults, and did not allow them to speak more than a few words at a time. His conduct was so outrageous that even Nazi Minister of Justice Otto-Georg Thierack complained about it. Most of the lawyers appointed to defend them prudently accepted the prosecution's case from the start and made no attempt to plead mitigation. To try to ensure they would appear as pathetic and undignified as possible, the accused had been physically maltreated beforehand, were forbidden to wear neckties, and were banned from using belts or braces to hold up their trousers. Nevertheless, a few managed to get a word in edgeways. When Freisler told one of them he would soon roast in hell, the defendant bowed and responded swiftly: 'I'll look forward to your own imminent arrival, your honour!' Another told Freisler that though his own neck would shortly be on the block, 'in a year it will be yours!' But Hitler had personally ordered that they should be hanged, a dishonouring punishment generally reserved by this time for foreign workers, though also applied to the 'Red Orchestra'. The first group of men were hanged from crude hooks suspended from the ceiling in an outbuilding at the Plötzensee prison in Berlin. Specially thin rope was used so that they would die of slow strangulation. As they died, their trousers were pulled down in a last act of humiliation. Hitler had the executions filmed and watched them in his headquarters at night.[281]

Some of the conspirators escaped death and lived on after the Third Reich was over, to tell their story to posterity. They included Fabian von Schlabrendorff, who was sheltering in the cellar of the People's Court with the judge and legal officials on 3 February 1945 when an Allied bombing raid demolished the courthouse. A beam crashed through the floor into the cellar below. Freisler was killed instantly. His was the only injury, but the trial had to be postponed; by the time it restarted, in mid-March, the court was beginning to temporize in the face of imminent defeat, and acquitted him because he had been illegally tortured, a scruple that had not troubled it at all in the months before. Altogether perhaps 1,000 people were killed or committed suicide in the wake of the failed coup attempt. In addition, Himmler, declaring that anyone involved in such a heinous crime against Germany must have bad blood, drew on what he said was the old Germanic tradition of punishing criminals' families as well as the criminals themselves, and arrested the wives and children, and in some cases brothers and sisters, parents, cousins, uncles and aunts of a number of the conspirators. Stauffenberg's wife was sent to Ravensbrück concentration camp and her children given a new identity and put into an orphanage. Those whose families were treated in similar fashion included Goerdeler, Hammerstein, Oster, Popitz, Tresckow, Trott and others. The property and assets of the conspirators and their families were confiscated by the state.[282]

The plot, the most serious and widespread attempt to overthrow Hitler since he had come to power in 1933, had failed, with the most disastrous possible consequences for almost everybody involved in it, for a variety of reasons, both specific and general. The conspirators had not managed to kill Hitler, nor had they succeeded in preventing news of his survival being broadcast from his field headquarters to the outside world. Their preparations were careless and paid too little attention to detail. Although it was fast fading, Hitler's charismatic authority, backed by Goebbels, Göring, Himmler and Bormann, was still enough to prevent vacillating senior officers like Fromm and Kluge from throwing their weight behind the coup attempt. Goebbels, Hitler, Himmler and the SS acted quickly and decisively, while the conspirators were dilatory. The plotters had not managed to persuade enough key military commanders to back the coup; although the majority of senior officers knew by now that there was little hope of Germany winning the war, most of them were still locked into a rigid military mentality in which orders from above had to be obeyed, the oath they had taken to Hitler was sacrosanct, and killing the head of state was an act of treachery. Typical was the attitude taken by General Gotthard Heinrici, who in his diary insisted on the sacred nature of the personal oath of allegiance he had taken to Hitler, as had all other German soldiers, and strongly disapproved of the July 1944 bomb plot.[283]

Those who backed the coup attempt were always in a small minority. Some top officers were no doubt influenced by the money lavished on them by Hitler. Many officers were deterred by the fear that they would be blamed for Germany's defeat in the kind of 'stab-in-the-back' which many of them thought had been responsible for Germany losing the First World War. More generally, the ideas of the conspirators were backward-looking, and for all their attempts to forge a unified pro-gramme, they were deeply divided on many central issues. As the most clear-headed among them already recognized in June 1944, the assassin-ation attempt was more a moral gesture than a political act. Had they succeeded in their earlier attempts on Hitler's life, in 1943, they might have made more of a difference. But they were dogged by ill-fortune from the start. Had Stauffenberg managed to kill Hitler, the result would most likely have been a civil war between army units backing the plotters, and those which opposed them, supported by the SS. Even then, it seems unlikely that the plotters would have won: the forces at their command were simply not strong or numerous enough. The Allies had no intention of negotiating with them, and indeed, when the news of the attempt reached London and New York, it was quickly dismissed as a meaning-less squabble within the Nazi hierarchy. Some of the conspirators had hoped that a coup would enable them to make a separate peace with the Western Allies, but the British and Americans were aware of this, and were concerned about the damage it would do to their alliance with the Soviet Union if they gave any kind of positive response to the conspiracy. A separate peace would have raised the alarming prospect of a conflict with the Soviet Union, and this was something that Churchill and Roosevelt were not prepared to contemplate.[284]

The plotters' aim was to stage a military coup, and despite Stauffen-berg's attempts to gain wider backing by negotiating with Social Demo-crats like Leber, the military-conservative resistance had very little support in the German population at large.[285] Yet the death of Hitler might well have hastened the disintegration of the regime, loosened the bonds of loyalty that tied so many Germans to it still in mid-1944, and shortened the war by some months, saving millions of lives on all sides by doing so. This alone was more than enough justification for the undertaking. It was not easy for the conspirators to reach the conclusions they reached or take the actions they took. In the end, however, they acted. Count Peter Yorck von Wartenburg implicitly spoke for them all when he wrote in his last letter to his mother, shortly before his execution, that 'it was not ambition or lust for power which determined my actions. My actions were influenced solely by my patriotic feeling, my concern for my Germany as it has grown over the past two thousand years.'[286] His, like theirs, was the Germany of the past, above all the Prussian past, and he had come to recognize that Hitler, in myriad different ways, was destroying it.

7

DOWNFALL

'A LAST SPARK OF HOPE'

I

At the end of July 1943, when the cleaning-up squads were sifting through the ruins of Hamburg after the Allied bombers had departed, they pulled a fifteen-year-old schoolboy out of the rubble, alive and unharmed. Thanking his rescuers, Ulrich S. joined a column of refugees making their way out of the city and after a few days found refuge with an uncle who lived in the nearby countryside. The child of passionately Social Democratic parents, he wanted nothing more to do with the war, and hid himself away in the attic of his uncle's house in the woods to evade the attentions of the Hitler Youth. He followed events by listening on the radio to the BBC and wrote a diary to ward off the inevitable sense of isolation, giving it the title: 'The Enemy Speaks!' His diary entry on the failed assassination attempt of 20 July 1944 was typical of its tone in general: 'Unfortunately, as if by a miracle, the pig-dog was not wounded . . . Hitler might have escaped his just punishment this time, but this mass-murderer will get what he deserves before too long.'[1] After the first trials, he wrote of the condemned conspirators: 'Their enterprise will be carried on to the end. The Nazis want to sacrifice an entire people just to postpone their own downfall a little longer.'[2]

The boy's reactions were extreme, to say the least. It is of course impossible to know how far they were shared in a milder form by other members of former Social Democratic and Communist families. For many men from such backgrounds fighting at the front, however, the attempt seemed like a betrayal; for if they approved of it, what then were they fighting for? 'We know,' wrote one soldier on 7 August 1944, 'that these soundrels are all Freemasons and thus in cahoots with, or, better put, in thrall to, international Jewry. A pity that I couldn't take part in the action against these rogues.'[3] Convinced Nazis were deeply shocked. The long-term Austrian brownshirt Alfred Molter, who served on the ground staff with the German air force, wrote to his wife Inge on 20 July 1944 from Vienna, where he was visiting his mother:

Darling, have you heard the news about the attempt to assassinate the Leader? Darling, I had the feeling I just had to run somewhere and pray. Thank heavens that the Leader has been preserved for us. Inge, if the Leader was killed, then the war would be lost, and Göring would surely be killed as well. And that's what the bandits were looking to achieve. What venal pig must have raised his hand to do this! When I heard about it, I couldn't be alone. So I waltzed off to the SA.[4]

Here, reminiscing with an old brownshirt comrade about the days when they had fought together against the Austrian dictator Schuschnigg, he found reassurance. 'Nothing can shake our belief in the Leader.'[5] Yet many troops mixed feelings of shock and outrage with other sentiments too. The paratrooper Martin Pöppel, by now promoted from the ranks to the officer corps, did not approve of the assassination attempt. Soldiers had a duty to carry on fighting. But, he thought by now, Hitler had let them down badly. He should have left the conduct of the war to the professionals. As the Allied troops advanced, the situation of Pöppel's unit in northern France became steadily more hopeless. But, when he told his men they would have to surrender, many of them felt ashamed at the prospect. 'As paratroopers,' they asked, 'how will we be able to look our wives in the face if we surrender voluntarily?' Eventually Pöppel was able to persuade them that they had no alternative. But their despairing question indicated the power of the sense of military duty and masculine honour that were among the factors that kept many German soldiers fighting on the Western Front to the bitter end.[6]

Reactions on the home front were mixed as well. On 28 July 1944, the Security Service of the SS dutifully claimed general popular relief that Hitler had escaped with his life, and the determination of the German people to carry on fighting. 'We hear again and again the view expressed that, if the attempt had succeeded, the only result would be the creation of another 1918.' People were anxious to know more. How long had the conspiracy been brewing? Who was behind it? Were British secret agents involved? For some, the leading role taken by Prussian aristocrats was a cause for anger. They were reported as saying 'that the aristocracy should be completely exterminated'. The involvement of so many army officers suggested to many an explanation for Germany's continuing defeats – they had been sabotaging the German war effort for months by holding back troops and munitions. Some even alleged that the problems of the war economy were also the result of sabotage.[7] These views were strongly encouraged by Goebbels, who told Nazi Party officials on 8 August 1944 that the bomb plot explained why the German armies had been doing so badly over the past months. It was clear that traitorous generals had not wanted to win. They had been in league with the Allies to bring about Germany's defeat.[8] The public meetings that Goebbels had called for attracted large crowds, anxious to hear more details of the attempt. They were indeed described in one report as an implicit plebiscitary endorsement of Hitler and his regime. Goebbels himself concluded that the failed coup had had a cleansing effect, doing the regime more good than harm.[9]

It was hardly surprising, however, that convinced Nazis and agents of the regime rushed to declare their faith in Hitler, in a situation in which anyone who showed the slightest sympathy with the conspirators was liable to be arrested, tortured, tried and executed. There was no possibility of an open reaction to the attempt. As the gendarmerie in the rural Bavarian district of Bad Aibling and Rosenheim reported on 23 July 1944:

When the evening news was broadcast at 8 o'clock on Thursday the 20.7.1944 and before it the special announcement of the violent attack was made, there were among others some twelve farmers from the present reporting area sitting in a local inn. They listened to the special announcement quietly and with rapt attention. After the announcement, nobody dared say anything, and everyone sat silently at the tables.[10]

In Berchtesgaden, the Security Service of the SS reported that women in particular were desperate for the war to come to an end, and that some thought that Hitler's death might bring this about. 'In an air-raid bunker, after the alarm had sounded, one could hear a female voice in the dark: "Well, if only it had got him." '[11] People could only trust themselves to say such things under cover of anonymity. In general, despite a temporary upsurge of relief, the attempt had no *general* effect on popular morale. 'Nobody believes any more,' the gendarmerie report continued, 'that the war can be won.' And the popular mood was 'the worst imaginable'.[12] Most people had more important things to worry about than the coup attempt. Two days after Stauffenberg exploded his bomb, the SS Security Service reported that the worsening military situation was causing a continuing deterioration in morale. Worse still, 'a kind of creeping mood of panic has gripped numerous national comrades, especially a large number of women. The comments we have collected predominantly reflect dismay, perplexity and despondency.'[13]

Even in western Germany, events on the Eastern Front were said to be putting everything else into the shadow. At best, people were still expressing their confidence in Hitler; at worst, they were saying that the military situation was more desperate than they could imagine – 'and,' one report noted, 'the pessimists are in the majority'.[14] Letters from soldiers on the Eastern Front, and reports from those invalided out, were making clear that the German forces were not engaged in a planned withdrawal but a wholesale retreat. Entire units were running away or giving themselves up to the enemy, and the troops 'already have no more desire to fight'.[15] 'The mood in many troop units is said by men on leave to be even worse than at home because the great majority of the soldiers do not believe in victory any more.'[16] The deterioration in popular morale continued through the remaining months of the war unaffected by the news of the bomb plot. People were beginning to flee from the territories that lay in the path of the advancing Red Army, taking their money and possessions with them. On 10 August 1944 the SS Security Service was reporting 'war-weariness amongst the majority of national comrades', alongside a willingness (the reporter felt perhaps obliged to add) to fight on to victory in what he revealingly called the 'final battle'.[17] Hitler and Goebbels might have blamed the generals for systematically undermining the war effort for years, but if this had been the case, some asked, then either the Nazi leaders had been extremely stupid or careless in allowing this to happen or they had known about it but not chosen to let the German people into their confidence. The consequence, so the Security Service of the SS reported from Stuttgart at the beginning of August 1944, was 'that most national comrades, even those who up to now have believed unwaveringly, have now lost all faith in the Leader'.[18] By November 1944, the same office was reporting that Hitler's reputation had, if possible, declined still further. One citizen said: 'It's always being claimed that the Leader was sent to us by God. I don't doubt it. The Leader was sent to us by God, not to rescue Germany but to destroy it. Providence has decided to annihilate the German people, and Hitler is its executioner.'[19]

Successive reports could only note a further decline in morale as the Red Army moved ever further towards, and then into, Germany itself. A seemingly endless series of defeats against the invading Allied armies in the west only added to the deepening gloom. Diplomatically, too, the Reich was becoming increasingly isolated. Turkey broke off diplomatic relations with Germany on 2 August 1944 and Bulgaria declared war on Germany as Soviet troops entered the country on 8 September 1944. After the remnants of the Romanian army disintegrated in the face of the Soviet advance, leading to the annihilation of eighteen German divisions in Romania by the Red Army, Marshal Antonescu was ousted from power on 23 August 1944 and Romania went over to the Allies, hoping to regain the territory it had lost to Hungary in 1940. All this threatened to cut off German forces in Greece, and on Hitler's authorization they withdrew into Macedonia in October, also evacuating Albania and southern Yugoslavia. The defection of Turkey in particular caused yet further demoralization in Germany itself.[20] The loss of Romania brought the Red Army to the borders of Hungary, where the ruler, Admiral Horthy, organized fierce resistance to the invaders. Horthy realized, however, that the game was up and wrote to Stalin claiming, somewhat implausibly, that he had joined the war on the German side in 1941 as a result of a misunderstanding. On 15 October 1944 he announced that Hungary was no longer allied to the Reich.[21]

Hitler had already planned his counter-move to this long-anticipated defection. On the same day as Hungary left the alliance, Otto Skorzeny, acting on Hitler's orders, broke into the fortress in Budapest where Admiral Horthy and his government were ensconced, and kidnapped the Hungarian leader's son, also called Miklós, rolling him up in a blanket and rushing him out of the building to a waiting lorry. Within a short time, the younger Horthy was incarcerated in the concentration camp at Mauthausen. Hitler now informed Horthy that his son would be shot and the fortress stormed unless he surrendered. The admiral gave in, resigned and was taken off to a relatively comfortable exile in a Bavarian castle. In the meantime, Ferenc Szálasi, the leader of the fascist Arrow Cross, seized power with the backing of the Germans. Szálasi lost no time in passing new laws reconstructing the state along fascist-style, corporate lines. His men began murdering surviving Jews across Budapest, assisted in some cases by Catholic priests, one of whom, Father Kun, got into the habit of shouting 'In the name of Christ, fire!' as the Arrow Cross paramilitaries levelled their guns at their Jewish victims. As 35,000 Jewish men who had been rounded up into labour battalions to construct fortifications around the Hungarian capital started crossing the Danube into the city in a hasty retreat before the oncoming Red Army, Arrow Cross units blocked their way, killed them on the banks or bridges and threw the bodies into the water. So many bodies were found lying around in the streets that even the police complained. On 18 October 1944 Adolf Eichmann arrived in Budapest again and organized the arrest of another 50,000 Jews, who were sent out of the city on foot in the direction of Vienna with the idea of working on fortifications there: they were poorly provisioned and brutally mal-treated, and many thousands died on the futile march – so many, indeed, that Szálasi stopped the deportations in mid-November, perhaps now fearing, justifiably enough, that he would be held to account for them. In Budapest itself the remaining Jews were confined to ghetto quarters. By January 1945 there were 60,000 living in just 4,500 dwellings, sometimes fourteen to a room. Subject to repeated raids by Arrow Cross murder squads, the inhabitants were also soon starving, disease-ridden and suffering rapidly escalating death rates. A small group of inter-national diplomats in the Hungarian capital, among whom the Swedish representative Raoul Wallenberg was particularly prominent, made strenuous and partially successful attempts to protect the Jews, and succeeded in getting nearly 40,000 sets of exemption papers – many of them forged – recognized by the Arrow Cross.[22]

This was not quite the last major extermination of Jews in a European country. In August 1944 it became clear that the Slovakian military, led by the Defence Minister, were plotting to overthrow the puppet government that had run the country under German tutelage since 1939, and switch sides to the Allies. As a consequence, German troops occupied Slovakia on 29 August 1944. A full-scale uprising ensued. The nationalist and pro-Soviet insurgents could not co-ordinate their activities, however. The Western Allies thought it unnecessary to fly in support since the Red Army was already on the border. The Soviet forces failed to move quickly enough to come to the partisans' aid. By October 1944 the uprising had been brutally suppressed. Meanwhile the German occupiers had lost no time in ordering the resumption of the deportation of the country's remaining Jews, which the collaborationist regime there had brought to a halt in October 1942 after some 58,000 had been taken away to the extermination camps. The first trainloads left in September 1944 and continued until March 1945. By this time, almost 8,000 Slovakian Jews had been rounded up and deported to Auschwitz, more than 2,700 to Sachsenhausen and over 1,600 to Theresienstadt.[23] Not only Himmler's SS but also the German civilian and military authorities thus continued to pursue the Jews long after it had become clear to most of them that the war was lost. Revenge for the Jews' imagined role in the imminent defeat had become their prime motivation, and they pursued it to the bitter end.

II

A popular joke told in the summer of 1944 had a naive young man being shown a globe, on which, it was explained, the large green area was the Soviet Union, the huge red area the British Empire, the enormous mauve area the United States and the vast yellow area China. 'And that little blue spot?' he asks, pointing to the middle of Europe. 'That is Germany!' 'Oh! Does the Leader know how small it is?'[24] The rapid deterioration of the Reich's military situation in 1943–4 was obvious to everyone. As the self-proclaimed greatest military leader of all time, Hitler felt instinctively that Germany would still be winning if the generals had not been constantly undermining his strategy, disobeying his commands and deliberately retreating in the face of an enemy he alone knew how to defeat. Only a last effort, and everything would come right. He appointed Goebbels Reich Plenipotentiary for the Total War Effort on 18 July 1944, an initiative stemming from Goebbels himself, who was claiming his reward for his loyalty and presence of mind during the coup attempt. Goebbels's rival, Hermann Göring, felt himself outflanked, and sulked on his estate at Rominten for several weeks afterwards. In alliance now with Martin Bormann, Goebbels unleashed a flurry of measures, many of which were to be implemented not by the cumbersome bureaucracy of the state but by the Party Regional Leaders in the provinces. They concentrated in particular on trying to draft yet more men into the armed forces. This brought him up against Speer, who wanted more men for the arms industry. But Hitler overruled his former favourite. With the Leader's backing, Goebbels and Bormann summoned the Armaments Minister and told him bluntly that he was under their command. He was to make no further attempts to influence Hitler directly.[25]

Goebbels's renewed drive to 'total war' produced a series of labour-saving measures, as three-quarters of the staff of the Reich Culture Chamber were made redundant, and theatres, orchestras, newspapers, publishing houses and other institutions deemed inessential to the war effort were cut back or closed down. There was a fresh clampdown on consumer goods industries. Hitler himself vetoed Goebbels's suggestion to stop sending newspapers and magazines to soldiers at the front on the grounds that this would damage morale, but other cuts in the postal service went ahead, and redundancies in local government and administration brought further efficiency savings. The upper age-limit for women to be drafted into war industries was raised from forty-five to fifty-five, and some 400,000 women, most of them foreign, were moved out of domestic service into war-relevant areas of the economy. The attempt to merge the Prussian Ministry of Finance, over which the bomb plot conspirator Popitz had presided, into the Reich Finance Ministry proved too complex to resolve, but overall, the measures freed up more than 450,000 additional men for the war. With further men taken out of reserved occupations in war industries, all of this helped send a million more men to the front from the beginning of August to the end of December 1944. Yet over the same period, more than a million soldiers were killed, captured or wounded, and the area the Reich covered, and hence the number of people it could call upon, were shrinking fast. The Reich was running faster and faster to try to stay in the same place.[26]

By 20 November 1944 the Red Army had come within striking distance of Hitler's field headquarters at Rastenburg, and Hitler, yielding to the entreaties of Martin Bormann, left it for good, making his way back to the Reich Chancellery in Berlin. Yet the Red Army's advance now slowed down as it reached Germany itself, where the front narrowed between the Baltic and the Carpathians, and the German forces had interior communication lines. The Soviet forces were exhausted after their rapid advances, they had to regroup and reorganize themselves, and it took some time to solve the supply problems caused by the narrower gauge of the railway lines in the areas they were now entering, compared to the broad gauge used in the Soviet Union and the Balkans. The pause allowed Hitler to undertake one last attempt to reverse the situation in the west, where supply and manpower difficulties had also slowed down the Allied advance. By early December, the German armies had been forced back behind the fortifications of the West Wall. Hitler planned to break out with thirty freshly formed and equipped divisions, spear-headed by an armoured punch through the defences of the Americans, for whose fighting qualities he had nothing but contempt. This was to be a repeat in many ways of the campaign of 1940, dividing the enemy forces, pinning them against the sea and destroying them in a massive encirclement. The blow this would strike was intended to keep the Western Allies at bay while a new generation of 'wonder-weapons' was developed that would decisively turn the fortunes of war in Hitler's favour. If the offensive was really successful, indeed, and managed to capture Antwerp, Hitler and Jodl thought that it might even bring the Western Allies to the negotiating table. The generals and commanders to whom Jodl put the plans on 3 November 1944 dismissed it as wholly unrealistic. A rapid advance to the coast in 1940, against a confused and unprepared enemy, was one thing; under the conditions of December 1944, with a massively superior force ranged against them, and ham-pered by shortages of men, munitions and above all fuel, it was quite another. But Jodl told them there was no alternative. A mere tactical victory such as the recapture of Aachen would not suffice.[27]

On 11 December 1944, Hitler arrived at his new field headquarters near Bad Nauheim, close to the launch-point for the offensive. On 16 December 1944 the attack began. Aided both by surprise and by bad weather that prevented Allied planes from flying, 200,000 German troops and 600 tanks with 1,900 artillery pieces broke through the American lines, which were defended by 80,000 soldiers and 400 tanks, and pushed forwards 65 miles towards the river Meuse. But they soon began running out of petrol, and on Christmas Eve American armour fought them to a halt, supported by continual bombardment of the German lines by 5,000 Allied aircraft once the weather improved. Although the British, under the over-cautious Bernard Montgomery, failed to react quickly enough to cut off the German forces now occupy-ing a large salient that gave the encounter its name – the 'Battle of the Bulge' – the Americans under George Patton mounted a successful armoured counter-attack from the south. The German air force tried to neutralize Allied air supremacy by launching a series of raids with 800 fighters and bombers on Allied airfields on 1 January 1945, but this operation cost as many German planes as Allied ones – about 280 – and failed in its objective. A subsidiary German attack in Alsace also came to nothing. Frustrated by their failure to make the decisive breakthrough, the men of the SS First Panzer Division massacred a large number of American prisoners of war at Malmédy on 17 December 1944. This simply served to enrage the American forces now resuming their advance towards Germany. Altogether some 80,000 German and 70,000 American troops were killed, wounded or reported missing in the battle, and each side lost around 700 tanks and armoured vehicles. For the Germans, these losses were irreplaceable. The Americans made good their losses with ease from the vast quantities of men and equipment continually being transported across the Channel into the combat zone. Hitler's last major counter-attack had failed. On 3 January 1945 he recognized reality and withdrew his main forces from the battlefield to defensive positions further east.[28] Defeat now seemed inevitable. On 15 January 1945 Hitler boarded his special train and returned to Berlin.[29]

Increasingly, Hitler and the Nazi leadership turned their thoughts not to victory, but to revenge. In particular, Hitler hoped to develop the means to pay back the Allied bombing campaign in its own coin, and some more. Although he had from the very beginning of his career regarded terror as a key means of fighting his enemies, he had not initially regarded bombing raids on Rotterdam, London and other cities as what Allied propaganda referred to as 'terror raids'. Even the Blitz on London was aimed above all at the docks, while the notorious attack on Coventry was mounted because of the city's key function in armaments production. The purpose of such raids was to weaken the British war economy and bring Churchill to the negotiating table, not, as Hitler explicitly noted, to terrorize the civilian population. In April 1942, following the British raid on Lübeck, he had ordered the beginning of 'terror raids' on Britain. For many months, however, he lacked the means to undertake them to any effect. Meanwhile the rapidly intensifying Anglo-American raids on German towns and cities, during which – in 1943 – up to 70 per cent of high-explosive bombs and 90 per cent of incendiaries fell on residential areas – had created a widespread popular desire for retaliation, not in order to wreak revenge on the British but in order to force them to bring the destruction to a halt.

Propaganda Minister Goebbels was particularly exercised by the effects of the raids on popular morale. If Göring ('a disaster' in Goebbels's view) had failed to provide adequate protection against the raids, then something needed to be done to convince people that the regime had not failed altogether. Somewhat callously, Hitler initially took the view that the destruction offered the opportunity for urban improvement ('From the aesthetic viewpoint,' he opined, 'the towns do not present all that good a picture. Most industrial cities are badly laid out, fusty and abominably built. Here, the British air raids will give us space').[30] Nevertheless, he too became increasingly angered by the destruction, and declared that 'the British will stop only if their cities are destroyed ... Terror is broken by terror.'[31]

Characteristically, Goebbels favoured bombing the parts of British cities 'where the plutocrats live'.[32] To demand this degree of precision, however, was clearly unrealistic. Moreover, the German air force had no four-engined bombers, no high-altitude bombers, and no specialized night-bombers. Senior officers were delaying production of new models by demanding that they should be capable of dive-bombing enemy infantry and tanks. Göring declared in September 1942 that Germany's lack of long-distance bombers made him 'weep'.[33] Nevertheless, the air force scraped together some 440 bombers, mostly older models like the Ju88, for a raid on London on the night of 21–2 January 1944, derisively nicknamed the 'Baby Blitz' by the British. About 60 per cent of the 475 tons of bombs carried as payload were incendiaries: this was to be a retaliatory raid, causing maximum damage to the English capital city's housing stock. In the event, however, only 30 tons fell on the target, and indeed only half the bombs managed to hit the English mainland at all. Another raid a week later was no better. More than 100 planes suffered mechanical problems and had to turn back. Half the new Heinkel 177s were lost, four of them when their engines caught fire. The machine still had not been properly tried and tested. Hitler called it a 'crap machine ... probably the worst machine that was ever produced'.[34] Two dozen or so further raids followed on a variety of targets from Portsmouth to Torquay, each involving around 200 aircraft, until losses and mechanical failures reduced the numbers to little more than 100 towards the end of the campaign, in April and May 1944. The damage done was not very significant. Except in the successful raids on London on 18, 20 and 24 February and 21 March 1944, most bombs failed to reach their target, and the total tonnage dropped was tiny compared to what was hitting Germany. Long before the offensive came to an end in May 1944, it was clear that something new was required. A range of 'miracle' or 'wonder-weapons' was under development already. Hitler and Goebbels held out the promise that these would soon reverse the fortunes of war and snatch victory from the jaws of defeat.[35]

III

The first of these weapons to be deployed was a pilotless 'flying bomb'. It was named, with Hitler's immediate approval, the V-1 by Hans Schwarz van Berkl, a journalist on Goebbels's organ The Reich, on 17 June 1944. The name signified its function as a means of retaliation against the Allies, in revenge for the destruction of German towns and cities by Allied bombs, in a situation where raids by piloted bombers were clearly having no significant effect. The 'V' stood for Vergeltung, retribution, an appellation that already betrayed an unspoken assumption that their moral purpose was greater than their military effectiveness could ever be. The V-1 resulted from experimental projects developed in the mid-1930s, when the engineer Paul Schmidt had begun work on a pulsejet system that would operate through rapid intermittent explosions. To speed up progress, the Air Ministry had asked the Argus air-engine company to take the project over in 1939, and the pulsejet engine was tried out on a small fighter plane in 1941-2. However, its extreme noisiness and the vibrations it caused made it impossible to use in manned aircraft. The alternative was an 'aerial torpedo', or what would now be called a cruise missile, and in June 1942 the Air Ministry gave its formal approval to a full development programme to be carried out by the aircraft manufacturing firm of Fieseler. It took another two years to reach the production stage. On 13 June 1944, at Hitler's urgent command, the first ten V-1 flying bombs were catapulted from their coastal launch ramps towards London. Their fuel was calculated to run out over the British capital, when they would fall to the ground and explode. Londoners listened to the throbbing of the motors as the V-1s came over, waiting anxiously for them to cut out, then counting the seconds till the explosion. The psychological effect was considerable. Hitler ordered a massive boost in production late in June 1944. A total of 22,384 of the missiles were fired (1,600 from aircraft, the rest from launch ramps), but between a third and a half failed to reach their target. Some ran out of fuel too soon, while others were shot down by anti-aircraft fire or by fighter planes that could outfly the slow-moving missiles, whose speed of 375 mph they could easily better. Speer later thought that Hitler and his entourage, including himself, 'far overestimated its effects'. As the Allies overran the launch-sites, increasing numbers of V-1s were launched from Germany at Belgium, and particularly at Antwerp, which was hardly the purpose for which they had been designed. By September 1944 it was clear that the V-1 had failed to break British morale, and the programme was scaled back; the few that were launched at London from within Germany itself in 1945 had to carry much smaller warheads to enable them to cover the longer distance, and had little effect.[36]

The second and more technically sophisticated of the two 'V' weapons was a ballistic rocket developed by the army as a rival to the air force's V-1. Scientists had first begun working on liquid-fuel rockets at the end of the 1920s, in part inspired by a Fritz Lang film, *The Woman in the Moon*. A variety of groups, some backed by aircraft manufacturers like Hugo Junkers, experimented with various kinds of fuel, some of them dangerously volatile. By the late 1930s, a wealthy young aristocrat, Wernher von Braun, had emerged as the most important of the rocketry pioneers. Born in 1912, the young von Braun had grown up in a conservative, nationalist family; his father had lost his job as a civil servant as a result of supporting the Kapp putsch in 1920 and subsequently become a banker. In 1932 von Braun senior had become Minister of Agriculture in the reactionary government of Franz von Papen, but he had lost this job too when Hitler had come to power. The older von Braun's right-wing politics, however, provided his son with a set of attitudes that made it easy for him to enter the service of the Nazi government. After studying mechanical engineering at the Technical University of Berlin and completing a Ph.D. in applied physics, on liquid-fuel rocketry, Wernher von Braun got funding from the army and the air force, and set up a testing range at Peenemünde, a remote wilderness of beaches, marshes and dunes on the northern end of the island of Usedom, on the Baltic coast, where his grandfather had spent holidays many years before, hunting ducks. Joining the Nazi Party in 1937 and the SS three years later, von Braun possessed the credentials, connections, charm and charisma needed to persuade the military to increase the funds they devoted to this improbable project. The problems von Braun and his expanding team had to solve were formidable: the fuel had to be stable as well as powerful, the aerodynamics of the rockets had to be reliable, the guidance systems effective. Von Braun had to fight for allocations of key equipment like steel and indispensable components like gyroscopes, transmitters and turbopumps, and he had to acquire scientific experts and skilled workers against competition from areas of the war economy with a higher priority than the testing and development of experimental rockets.[37]

Crucially, however, von Braun managed to convince Albert Speer of the importance of the project. 'I liked mingling with this circle of non-political young scientists and inventors headed by Wernher von Braun – twenty-seven years old, purposeful, a man realistically at home in the future,' Speer later recalled.[38] Visiting Peenemünde shortly after his appointment as Armaments Minister, along with General Fromm, Field Marshal Milch and a representative of the navy, Speer watched the first firing of a remote-controlled rocket. 'With the roar of an unleashed giant,' he later recalled, 'the rocket rose slowly from its pad, seemed to stand upon its jet of flame for the fraction of a second, then vanished with a howl into the low clouds. Wernher von Braun was beaming.' Deeply impressed by this technical wizardry, Speer was being told by the technicians the 'incredible distances the projectile was covering, when, a minute and a half after the start, a rapidly swelling howl indicated that the rocket was falling in the immediate vicinity. We all froze where we stood. It struck the ground only a half a mile away.'[39] Not surprisingly, on hearing reports of the trial, Hitler was not convinced of the project's future. But his initial scepticism was overcome after Speer reported the first successful trial, on 14 October 1942, when one of the rockets travelled 120 miles and fell within two and a half miles of its target. Now it was Hitler's turn to be enthused. With a disregard for reality that was becoming obvious in other fields as well, he declared that 5,000 missiles had to be produced for launching against the British capital. A film presentation by von Braun convinced Hitler that the rocket would become 'the decisive weapon of the war'.[40]

With this backing, the rocket programme now prospered. Before long, however, it became necessary to shift production away from Peene-münde to somewhere more secure. Allied intelligence and reconnaissance flights had provided alarming information about this and other secret weapons sites, and a fleet of almost 600 bombers had been sent to the rocket development complex at Peenemünde to destroy it. The site survived the raid on 18 August 1943, but a good deal of damage had been caused none the less. Keen to extend his own power over the programme, Himmler persuaded Hitler that production should be relocated to an underground site well away from the destructive attention of Allied bombers. Himmler commissioned a senior SS officer, Hans Kammler, to set up this new manufacturing centre. Kammler had an engineering background and had played a significant role in the Air Ministry before moving across to help manage the building of the extermination camps at Auschwitz-Birkenau, Majdanek and Belzec. From early in 1942 he was in charge of the construction department of the SS Economy and Administration Head Office.[40] Speer thought he bore an uncanny resemblance to Reinhard Heydrich, 'blond, blue-eyed, long-headed, always neatly dressed, and well bred', but also 'a cold, ruthless schemer, a fanatic in the pursuit of a goal, and as carefully calculating as he was unscrupulous'. Yet, at first, Speer got on well with Kammler, describing him as 'in many ways my mirror image', a middle-class university graduate who 'had gone far and fast in fields for which he had not been trained', a man whose 'objective coolness' he found attractive.[41] After scouting various possibilities, Speer, Kammler and the rocket team settled on a complex of old gypsum mines near the town of Nordhausen in the Harz mountains in Thuringia. Kammler quickly began arranging the conversion of the mines into a new rocket production centre, known as the 'Central Works' (*Mittelwerk*) in a vague allusion to their geographical position, and organized the transfer of the salvageable equipment and papers from Peenemünde.[42]

To carry out the construction work, the SS established a sub-camp of Buchenwald, known as 'Work Camp Dora', at the site. By October 1943, 4,000 prisoners, most of them Russian, Polish and French, were at work in the mine, blasting, digging and mixing and pouring concrete; by the end of November 1943 their number had doubled. 'Pay no attention to the human cost,' declared Kammler. 'The work must go ahead, and in the shortest possible time.'[43] Rather than spend time and money on building barracks to house the prisoners outside the mines, as originally intended, Kammler had the SS wall off cross-tunnels 43 to 46 and got the prisoners to put together wooden bunk-beds, each of them four levels high. The damp atmosphere of the cold tunnels, where the temperature never rose above 15 degrees Celsius (59 degrees Fahrenheit), was made worse by constant dust from blasting work. There were no proper sanitary facilities, the water supplies were in no way sufficient, and the prisoners were unable to wash. Makeshift toilets consisted of large oil-drums sawn in half, with wooden boards placed over them. It was one of the SS guards' favourite jokes to approach the workers from behind as they sat on the boards and push them in. The prisoners, sleeping two or more to a bed, quickly became dirty, unkempt and lice-ridden.[44] One French prisoner described his arrival at the site on 14 October 1943:

The Kapos and SS drive us on at an infernal speed, shouting and raining blows down on us, threatening us with execution ... The noise bores into the brain and rends the nerves. The demented rhythm lasts for fifteen hours. Arriving at the dormitory ... we do not even try to reach the bunks. Drunk with exhaustion, we collapse onto the rocks, onto the ground. Behind, the Kapos press us on. Those behind trample over their comrades. Soon over a thousand despairing men, at the limit of their existence and racked with thirst, lie there hoping for sleep which never comes; for the shouts of the guards, the noise of the machines, the explosions and the ringing of the bell reach them even there.[45]

Prisoners were kept in the tunnels all the time, only seeing the light of day once a week, when they had to stand outside for hours on end during the weekly roll-call. Many had dysentery; those who were too weak to make their way to the parade-ground were beaten mercilessly by the SS, often until they were dead.[46]

At his subsequent trial in Nuremberg, Speer denied ever having visited a labour camp of any kind, and did not mention the Dora-Central Works complex.[47] In fact, however, as his Ministry's chronicle reveals, Speer visited the new V-2 production centre on 10 December 1943. He later professed himself appalled by the conditions under which the prisoners worked. According to his memoirs, he had immediately ordered the construction of proper accommodation for the prisoners, the improvement of sanitary facilities and the upgrading of their rations.[48] But his office chronicle made no mention of any protest; on the contrary, on 17 December 1943 Speer wrote to Kammler congratulating him on his success in setting up the new production centre in two months, an achievement 'that far exceeds anything ever done in Europe, and is unsurpassed even by American standards'.[49] It was not until 13 January 1944 that the Armaments Ministry's chief physician reported the terrible health situation at the camp, which led to a Ministry investigation. Deaths rose from eighteen in October 1943 to 172 in November 1943 and 670 in December 1943; within six months of the camp's opening, 2,882 prisoners had died. By March 1944 a crematorium had been installed to deal with the bodies. Only with the arrival of warmer weather and the completion of outside dormitories in May 1944 did the death rate begin to decline.[50] Eventually, 20,000 of the 60,000 men forced to work at the V-2 production plant and live in Dora or one of no fewer than thirty sub-camps dotted around the site died of disease, starvation and maltreatment.[51]

Meanwhile, no sooner had Speer fallen ill, on 18 January 1944, than Himmler moved in to try to take the enterprise over completely and turn it into yet another division of the burgeoning economic empire of the SS. Just over two months later, having failed to persuade Wernher von Braun to go along with his plans, Himmler had the rocketeer, his brother and two of his closest collaborators arrested on charges of belonging to a (completely fictional) left-wing resistance organization and trying to sabotage the rocket programme. Within a short time, however, Speer had pleaded with Hitler, during the Leader's visit to his sickbed, to order their release. Energetic pressure was also put on the Nazi Leader by Walter Dornberger, the army officer with overall responsibility for the V-2 programme. Himmler was obliged to order the rocketeers' release on the grounds of their scientific and technical indispensability, and his attempt to take the enterprise over came to nothing. Von Braun's arrest was to prove convenient when he came to defend his record during the Nazi years after the war by presenting himself as an unpolitical technical expert. His expertise was severely put to the test in the following months, as the rockets kept on blowing up during test flights and the first production models, rushed off the assembly-line at the Central Works, proved equally unsatisfactory. Not surprisingly, the poor physical condition, maltreatment and lack of expertise of the slave-workers led to workmanship of the poorest quality. Constant adjustments and refinements meant that no fewer than 65,000 changes were made to the blueprints by the end of the war. Even when conditions at Dora were improved by the provision of barracks and various amenities, the murderously brutal treatment of the prisoners by guards and overseers continued unabated, and there is no evidence that either Dornberger or von Braun, or for that matter Speer, ever did anything to try to improve the situation. Only in September 1944, when the teething troubles were finally solved, were the first rockets launched against London. Soon the factory was producing more than twenty a day, or up to 700 a month.[52]

By this time, the management of the production programme had been turned over from the army, which had lost enormously in power and influence after the July 1944 bomb plot, to a limited company set up by the rocketeers to try to forestall the growing influence of Kammler and the SS. Conditions at the Dora camp grew even worse with the arrival on 1 February 1945 of a new commandant, Richard Baer, who had previously served as the last commandant of Auschwitz, with orders to suppress the now-active resistance movement among the inmates. Baer had former German Communists bludgeoned to death and staged a number of mass executions, including one of 162 inmates in March 1945, which the other prisoners were forced to watch. Shortly afterwards the camp was evacuated. Only 600 workers, too sick to be moved, were left at Dora when Allied forces arrived, along with another 405 at a nearby sub-camp. The factory, together with the Peenemünde facility, had succeeded in constructing about 6,000 rockets by this time; the Central Works factory also made several thousand V-1 flying bombs. Altogether, 3,200 V-2 rockets had been successfully fired, most of them not at Britain but at targets in Belgium. There was no defence against them: they came down almost vertically at an unstoppable speed, something like 2,000 miles an hour. But they could not carry more than a small conventional payload of a ton of high explosive, and so were unable to cause significant destruction. The total number of people killed by the rocket was no more than 5,000. The V-2 was thus, as its historian Michael Neufeld has remarked, 'a unique weapon: more people died producing it than died from being hit by it'.[53]

IV

As early as the spring of 1942, as we have seen, General Fromm, who was to be arrested for his complicity in the bomb plot just over two years later, was already pessimistic about the outcome of the war. But

Fromm did not despair completely. He was convinced that the only thing that could win the war in the face of the massive arms programmes being implemented by Britain, America and the Soviet Union would be a super-bomb being developed by a group of physicists under the leadership of the leading theoretical physicists Otto Hahn and Werner Heisenberg. The attempt made by some extreme Nazi scientists in the 1930s to reject theoretical physics, and especially the theory of relativity, as 'Jewish' had been successfully rebuffed by the physics community at a dramatic confrontation in Munich on 15 November 1940.[54] Theory, it had resolved, was not Jewish but quintessentially German. A good deal of damage had been done in the meantime, however. The physicists pointed out that, while German scientists in 1927 had published forty-seven articles on nuclear physics, American and British scientists between them had managed only thirty-five. By 1939, however, the ratio had changed dramatically, and the Germans managed only 166 to the Anglo-Americans' 471. By this time, too, there were thirty particle accelerators in the USA against only one in Germany.[55] The potential military consequences were serious. As Hahn had discovered in 1938, if uranium was bombarded by neutrons, it released enough energy to set up a chain reaction with an almost incalculable destructive power. Yet Germany had clearly fallen behind in the race to turn this discovery to practical military use.[56]

Nevertheless, Heisenberg persisted in trying to develop a nuclear bomb. In doing so, however, he faced insurmountable problems. Although the Danish scientist Niels Bohr had worked out before the war that uranium-235 was the best material for this purpose, Heisenberg and Hahn never managed to calculate the quantity needed for a bomb, nor how to keep the fission process under control during production. They were right in thinking that 'heavy water' (an isotope of ordinary water) was needed for this latter purpose, and things looked set for success when the only factory in the world that could produce major quantities of it was captured in Norway in April 1940. But Allied intelligence realized its importance and effectively destroyed the factory in a series of raids by commandos and bomber planes in 1943. Even without this setback, Heisenberg's team failed to recognize the importance of graphite as well as heavy water in controlling nuclear fission. And even with a massive investment of money and resources it would take two, perhaps three years before an 'atomic bomb' could be ready.

Like the army generals, Speer knew that the Third Reich simply did not have the leisure to wait. The investment needed would simply divert much-needed resources from meeting the immediate needs of the war economy: aircraft, guns, tanks, ammunition, submarines, men and supplies that were required to inflict total defeat on the Red Army within the next few months, cut off the Atlantic supply-lines of the British, and get ready to meet the onslaught that was undoubtedly coming from the Americans. When lobbied by Heisenberg, Speer was impressed by the idea and gave it some financial resources. But these did not go nearly far enough. As early as the summer of 1942 the basic decision had been made only to allow development on a relatively small scale because Hitler and the leading German economic managers did not expect the war to last more than a few months more, so that the atom-bomb would have to wait until after it was over. The army, which in 1940 had taken over the main centre of research in this area, the Kaiser Wilhelm Institute for Physics, where Heisenberg was based, handed it back to the Reich Research Council, since it no longer seemed to be of direct military relevance.[57]

Had such a bomb existed, Speer thought later, Hitler would not have had any doubts or hesitations about using it. Watching a newsreel on the bombing of Warsaw in September 1939, ending with a montage showing a plane diving towards a map of the British Isles, which were then blown into the sky, Hitler had remarked to Speer: 'That is what will happen to them! That is how we will annihilate them!' Using funds provided by Speer, Heisenberg and his team built a cyclotron that succeeded in splitting an atomic nucleus by the summer of 1944. But there was not enough uranium available to go much further, and in view of the lack of any prospect of a bomb being completed in the near future, Speer ordered existing stocks of uranium and to be used for other purposes.[58] Moreover, in any case, the usual infighting within the regime militated against the concentration of effort needed. For there was another team besides Heisenberg's. It was led by the young physicist Manfred von Ardenne, backed, somewhat improbably, by Reich Postal Minister Wilhelm Ohnesorge. The latter's friend the court photographer Heinrich Hoffmann persuaded Hitler to take a personal interest in the research. Ardenne was assisted by Kurt Diebner, an army physicist, and a team of about 100 other researchers spread across seventeen different institutions. They made some progress in developing a tactical nuclear weapon of a different kind to Heisenberg's super-bomb, using enriched uranium. Later claims that Ardenne's team succeeded in carrying out test explosions on the Baltic island of Rügen in October 1944 and later in Thuringia on 3 and 12 March 1945 have met with a healthy dose of scepticism from historians, however. Here too, concentration camp prisoners were used in the construction process, and several hundred died while building the test site in March 1945. Whether or not Ardenne and Diebner were successful, it was all too late to make a difference. By this stage, the necessary supplies of uranium could not be obtained.[59] Hitler's backing was also no more than half-hearted, because he still believed at bottom that nuclear physics was a Jewish discipline, as did the Ministry of Education, which did nothing to support research in this area. In any case, even if the money, the men and the materials had been available, time was not. Germany lacked the resources that the United States devoted to the creation of the atomic bomb; and even there, it took until 1945 before the Manhattan Project, with its billions of dollars, huge numbers of scientists and limitless supply of materials, came up with a usable weapon.[60]

Potentially just as destructive were the nerve gases being developed by the I. G. Farben combine. In 1938 I. G. Farben scientists Schrader, Ambros, Rüdiger and Van der Linde had synthesized an extremely deadly organiphosphorus compound which they christened Sarin, after their surnames. As a director of I. G. Farben and head of the special committee in Speer's Ministry responsible for poison gas, Ambros was in a particularly strong position to develop such chemical agents, of which there was another one, called Tabun, ready to manufacture, and a third, called Soman, synthesized by scientists at the Kaiser Wilhelm Institute for Chemistry, led by Richard Kuhn, early in 1944. By 1942, factory production of Sarin and Tabun had begun at a site north of Breslau. 12,000 tonnes of Tabun had been produced by June 1944. These nerve agents were tested on animals, and it has been alleged that they were also tried out on concentration camp inmates, though there is no hard evidence for this. But there were serious problems to overcome before they could be deployed. During the development stage, the nerve gases, which were lethal if even a tiny amount came into contact with the skin, had caused convulsions or other injuries in over 300 workers (many of them forced labourers) and at least ten fatalities. The Nazi leader of the German Labour Front, Robert Ley, a chemist by training, was none the less enthusiastic about the new chemical weapons: Albert Speer later recalled him saying at this time, over the inevitable glasses of strong wine, stammering with excitement: 'You know we have this new poison gas – I've heard about it. The Leader must do it. He must use it. Now he has to do it! When else! This is the last moment. You too must make him realize that it's time.' Hitler did indeed consider using nerve gas against the Red Army. But Speer knew that the factories producing basic ingredients had been damaged so badly in Allied bombing raids that this idea could not be put into practice.[61]

In any case, there was no known effective protection against the gases. It was simply too dangerous to deploy them on the battlefield. Supposing the wind turned and blew them back on the German troops? Putting them into bombs or missiles was almost as dangerous. Mistakes always occurred, and nobody could be certain of the direction the gas cloud would take when a gas-bomb went off. Hitler's Plenipotentiary for Chemical Warfare, Karl Brandt (who was also his personal doctor), was convinced, like other scientists, that the Allies' superior resources must mean that they were more advanced in the development and production of nerve gases. If Germany started to use them, he reasoned, then Allied air supremacy would mean that there would be no defence if the Allies decided to retaliate. In the autumn of 1944, reflecting this thinking, gas-mask production in Germany was rapidly increased, and millions of masks were manufactured within the space of a few months. In fact, the Allies did not possess modern nerve gases, though they did have stocks of phosgene and mustard gas. They too were well equipped with gas masks, which had been distributed in their millions to the British population even before the war began. Whether such simple devices would have offered any protection against Sarin or Tabun, however, is extremely doubtful.[62]

Flying-bombs, rockets, atom-bombs and nerve gases were far from being the only technologically advanced devices under development in Germany during the war. As Speer remarked, by 1944 there was a whole variety of wonder-weapons in preparation:

We possessed a remote-controlled flying bomb, a rocket plane that was even faster than the jet plane, a rocket missile that homed on an enemy plane by tracking the heat rays from its motors, and a torpedo that reacted to sound and could thus pursue and hit a ship fleeing in a zigzag course. Development of a ground-to-air missile had been completed. The designer Lippisch had jet planes on the drawing board that were far in advance of anything so far known . . . We were literally suffering from an excess of projects in development. Had we concentrated on only a few types we would surely have completed some of them sooner.[63]

But none of these came to anything. The regime's inability to prioritize, based partly on in-fighting between different agencies, partly on a general overestimation of its ability to finance and construct such programmes, partly on a general underestimation of the time and resources needed to get from research and development to production, doomed them to failure. Instead of concentrating on the 'Waterfall' ground-to-air missile, for example, which in Speer's view would have played a vital role in reducing the impact of Anglo-American bombing raids, Hitler ordered a concentration of resources on the V-1 flying bomb and then the V-2 rocket. This left the missile programme to stagger on from one problem to another, denied the workforce and equipment that might have hastened its development to a point where it could actually have come into operation.[64] Speer and others were aware of the lack of co-ordination; some projects were being continued despite their obvious lack of practical military relevance. Yet the perpetual struggle for power within the regime meant that no one could do anything about it. The costs of these projects were enormous: there were more operational staff employed at the V-2 site in Peenemünde, for example, than there were on the Manhattan Project at Los Alamos. In the end, all these schemes imposed a huge financial burden on Germany without having any effect on the outcome of the war.[65]

It was a similar story with the jet-engined fighter, which might also have helped defend Germany's cities. The scientific and technological expertise was certainly available. By 1941 Ernst Heinkel had succeeded in developing and testing a jet engine, which was to be put into a revolutionary new fighter plane, the twin-engined Me262, giving it a speed of over 500 miles per hour. It first flew in July 1943. Speer was enthusiastic about the new aircraft, and blamed the subsequent failure to bring it into mass production on repeated interventions by Hitler, who first ordered a halt, then changed his mind but declared that it had to be a bomber instead of a fighter. Speer and many others, including the top commanders of the air force, tried to convince Hitler that the

Me262 would be able to inflict enormous damage on the British and American bombers now devastating Germany's towns and cities if it was developed and deployed as a fighter plane. But Hitler took this as criticism of his military and technical expertise and became so irritated with these repeated attempts to get him to change his mind that he banned all discussion of the Me262 from the autumn of 1944 onwards. In any case, Allied bombing was disrupting the plane's development and manufacturing sites well before this stage had been reached. Thus few were produced. Fuel supplies were being destroyed, the necessary supplies of metal alloys to construct the plane in large numbers were lacking, and the time and facilities for training pilots to fly the plane were absent. Most important of all, however, much more time was needed to test and refine the design until the inevitable teething troubles were dealt with and the plane could be flown safely and effectively. The Air Ministry committed itself whole-heartedly to developing the aircraft; Messerschmitt simply lacked the time and resources to bring the project to fruition.[66]

High hopes were entertained for a new generation of submarines, equipped with powerful batteries that would enable them to remain submerged for long periods so that they could not be detected by radar. The new craft were built for speed so that they could overtake convoys and sink them before the accompanying destroyers could steam into action. The first of the new U-boats was delivered in June 1944, and over 150 had been built by February 1945. But they had been rushed into production before being properly tried and tested, and many of them succumbed almost immediately to teething troubles. In any case, without aerial reconnaissance they would have found it difficult to locate their targets. A crash programme of construction of a long-range reconnaissance aircraft, the Ju290, had to be called off in the summer of 1944 after the damage inflicted by Allied air raids on production centres had made the futility of the project clear. Soon afterwards, the U-boat bases on the French coast fell into Allied hands. The new U-boats did not succeed in sinking a single ship, though the priority given to the construction programme, and the hopes held out for its success, convinced Hitler that the commander of the U-boat fleet, Admiral Dönitz, was one of the few remaining leaders in the armed forces who still possessed the will to victory that he demanded.[67]

Another wonder-weapon, dubbed the V-3, was intended purely as a measure of revenge against the British. An enormous gun with a barrel over 150 metres long, it was intended to shoot shells all the way from the Continent to the middle of London, boosting them with small explosions as they went up the barrel and so increasing their velocity. It was still under development when Allied bombs destroyed the firing site, and by the time the facilities had been repaired the war was irrevocably lost.[68] Yet another wonder-weapon, a four-stage rocket with powder instead of liquid fuel, was to lead eventually to the multi-stage, solid-fuel rockets of the postwar era, but the army never succeeded in producing more than two hundred, which were launched from the end of 1944 against Antwerp, but overshot the target. The only loss of life caused by this weapon was when a trial firing sent a rocket whizzing towards a nearby farm, killing several chickens and a dog and injuring two cows.[69] The list of wonder-weapons was seemingly endless. In early April 1945 Albert Speer encountered the Labour Front leader Robert Ley with Martin Bormann and others deep in discussion:

Ley came rushing towards me with the news: 'Death rays have been invented! A simple apparatus that we can produce in large quantities. I've studied the documentation; there's no doubt about it. This will be the decisive weapon!' With Bormann nodding confirmation, Ley went on, stuttering as always, to find fault with me. 'But of course your Ministry rejected the inventor. Fortunately for us, he wrote to me. But now you personally must get this project going. Immediately. At this moment there's nothing more important.'[70]

Speer's team soon found that the inventor was an eccentric amateur who was asking for equipment so out of date that it had not been manufactured for forty years.[71]

In the end, the main significance of the wonder-weapons was as a propaganda device that offered hope to those who still wanted Nazism to win. The German media carried lurid stories of the devastation caused by the V-1 and V-2, trying to satisfy people's demand for effective retaliatory action on the British that would bring the bombing raids to an end. Many of these were invented. In all, fewer than 6,000 V-1s fell on Britain and just over 1,000 V-2s. 31,600 houses were destroyed, mostly in London, and nearly 9,000 people were killed by the two weapons, with 24,000 being injured. This damage did not compare to the devastation inflicted by Allied bombing in Germany, and in no way met the demand for massive retaliation. People called the V-1 the

Volksverdummer Nr 1 (Stultifier of the People Number 1) or the *Versager Nr 1* (Failure Number 1). Goebbels's Propaganda Ministry was aware of this scepticism. So the co-ordinated media pumped out vague promises of new, as yet unspecified wonder-weapons of a far greater destructiveness. As early as 19 February 1943 Hitler was talking in public of 'hitherto unknown, unique weapons' that were on the way and would turn the tide of war.[72] Yet such promises soon lost any potency they might have had. Even in November the same year, a joke about them was doing the rounds. It revealed how well people knew that Germany's lack of resources was losing the war. '1950,' so went the imaginary report. 'Meeting in the Leader's headquarters about the date fixed for Vengeance. It is postponed once more because there is no agreement on whether the two airplanes should fly side-by-side or one in front of the other.'[73]

Towards the end of the war even the most optimistic and convinced followers of Nazism were beginning to have their doubts about the wonder-weapons. On 3 September 1944 Inge Molter wrote to her husband Alfred:

Fred, darling, we've got to keep going until the new weapons are ready, it can't be that the enemy will force us on to our knees before that happens. Darling, I simply can't believe that. Will it all have been in vain, will there be no more Germany? No, darling, I can't believe that. But unfortunately this view is very gradually trickling through into the shops and everywhere that one sees several people gathered together.[74]

On 12 November 1944 a concerned radio listener sent a letter to the head of the news service in the Propaganda Ministry, Hans Fritsche, asking: 'Why haven't at least some of the new weapons been put into action, when the enemy is standing so close before our borders to the west and the east?' He did not receive an answer.[75] By March 1945, Germany's situation, wrote the university student Lore Walb, was 'unspeakably bitter':

And in this situation the government is still talking of victory! In my innermost heart I too do not want to believe that our people are destined to downfall. But if you only think about them just a little, things look very black. You can't see any chink of light any more. The new weapons haven't turned up, and will most likely never turn up. I certainly believe that they were planned and that construction of them was begun, but at this point they won't succeed in getting them ready any more.[76]

'Until the last few days,' reported the Security Service of the SS at the end of March 1945, 'people retained a remnant of the belief in a miracle that has been so skilfully and purposefully nurtured by the propaganda about the new weapons.' But this small residue of hope had to be seen as a kind of psychological defence mechanism to cope with the despair that was now overwhelming the German people. The report concluded: 'Nobody believes that we can still escape a catastrophe with the methods and possibilities of waging war that have existed up to now. The last spark of hope remains rescue from outside, or a completely exceptional set of circumstances, or a secret weapon of enormous power. This hope too is being extinguished.'[77]

V

If new weapons could not rescue Germany, then perhaps new soldiers could. Already at the end of 1943 the call-up of increasingly older age-cohorts of men to the armed forces was prompting a variety of popular jokes. 'Vengeance will come,' so one went, 'when you see notices on the old people's homes: "Closed because of the call-up".'[78] On 26 September 1944, in a desperate attempt to deal with the shortage of military personnel, Hitler ordered the creation of the 'People's Storm' (*Volkssturm*), in which all men from the ages of sixteen to sixty were required to take up arms, and to undergo training for a final stand. They were to be organized by the Party, with the aim, Hitler said, of defending the German people against the attempt of its 'Jewish-international enemies' to annihilate them. All of them had to swear a personal oath of allegiance to Hitler, allegiance unto death. The official date for the launch of the People's Storm was chosen by Himmler as 18 October, the anniversary of the defeat of Napoleon's army in the 'Battle of the Nations' at Leipzig in 1813. This was to be a national uprising just like the one that – in popular legend – had ended French rule over Germany just over 130 years before. But the reality fell far short of the rhetoric. The men of the People's Storm were never going to be a very effective fighting force. They had no uniforms – there was no way of providing them by this stage – and had to come in their own clothes, bringing with them a rucksack, a blanket and cooking equipment. The arms and ammunition they needed were never fully forthcoming, and by the final stage of the war they were little more than a poor imitation of an army. Wandering out from his woodland hiding-place one day, the Social Democratic schoolboy Ullrich S. noted 400 men of the People's Storm come into the nearby village. 'Tired and exhausted, most of them were wearing uniforms borrowed from the air force, or plundered. A few only had their mufti. I only saw 5 soldiers in all who were bearing arms, the rest were not even carrying a bayonet.' With the characteristic disdain of the adolescent for the middle-aged, he added: 'Most of them were between 45 and 60 years of age. The whole crowd made a very pitiable impression on us. They almost looked like an old people's home on an outing.'[79] This view was widespread. 'Two men with shovels are walking across the graveyard,' went one popular joke of the day. 'An old man shouts after them: "So you want to dig out reinforcements for the People's Storm?"'[80] For the men of the People's Storm, however, enlistment was more than a joke. No fewer than 175,000 were eventually killed fighting against the professional armies of the Russians and the Western Allies.[81]

The draft for the People's Storm was deeply unpopular. People were well aware of its futility in military terms, and the sacrifices they were being asked to make were bitterly resented. In Stuttgart, the red posters put up around the city on 20 October 1944 advertising the creation of the People's Storm reminded citizens of the red placards used to announce executions. 'It's announcing an execution too,' people were reported saying, 'namely the execution of the German people.'[82] Recruitment was completely indiscriminate. The draft for the People's Storm thus caught many unsuspecting and reluctant men in its net. One of its victims was the theatre critic, writer and pseudo-aristocratic fantasist Friedrich Reck-Malleczewen. When the People's Storm was set up he was living peacefully on his little estate in the Bavarian hills with his second wife, Irmgard, whom he had married in March 1935, and their three daughters, born in 1939, 1941 and 1943. At this point, his own history of lies and deceptions came back to haunt him. Reck had boasted widely of having enjoyed a heroic military career during the First World War as a Prussian officer, so it was scarcely surprising that the leadership of the People's Storm in the nearby town of Seebruck asked him to enlist.

Reck, who had in fact never been on active service and never fired a shot at anybody in his life, ignored the request. Four days later, on 13 October 1944, he was arrested on the orders of the military recruitment office in Traunstein for undermining the German military effort and imprisoned for a week. The Gestapo now had their eye on Reck. They knew him apart from anything else as the author of books whose thrust was unmistakeably anti-Nazi, such as his study of the Anabaptists' reign of terror in sixteenth-century Münster (subtitled 'History of a Mass Delusion') and his account of Charlotte Corday's assassination of the French revolutionary Jean-Paul Marat, both published in 1937.

Unable to get at him on the basis of such subversive books because they had after all been published perfectly legitimately in Germany, with the approval of Goebbels's censorship apparatus, the Gestapo acted instead upon a denunciation passed to them by the director of the publishers Knorr and Hirth, in Munich, Alfred Salat, who had seen a letter sent to his colleague Fritz Hasinger by Reck on 10 July 1944 about his royalties. An aside in the letter that referred to the 'Mark of today' as being worth 'only half of what you get elsewhere for a more powerful coinage', coupled with general if rather vague complaints about the way publishers had treated their authors since 1933, was enough to have Reck arrested on 29 December 1944 on the charge of 'insulting the German currency' and 'statements denigrating the state'. When the jail where he was being held in Munich was destroyed by bombing, on 7–8 January 1945, Reck was transferred with the other prisoners to the concentration camp at Dachau, where the Gestapo ordered him to be kept for further interrogation. Conditions in the camp worsened rapidly in the last months of the war, and Reck soon fell ill. He was transferred to the block reserved for the sick, and, though he recovered sufficiently at one time to be released back into normal custody in the camp, he became sick again, and died at 8.30 a.m. on 16 February 1945. The death certificate gave the cause of death as enterocolitis, but a number of witnesses, including Reck's neighbour in the hospital block, the camp doctor who attended him in the final days and saw him die and the medical clerk in the camp, subsequently testified that he had died of typhus, a disease the presence of which in the camp officials even at this late stage were eager to deny.[83]

Not only older civilians like Reck, but also young boys and, increasingly, girls, were drafted in to man anti-aircraft guns and searchlights during bombing raids and take part in the war effort in other ways. Even Party officials were complaining in October 1944 of the 'recruitment of age-cohorts that are scarcely able to carry out any practical tasks', as adolescents from the Hitler Youth were called up for work on building defences 'on almost all borders of the Reich'.[84] On 17 March 1945, for example, all fourteen-to-sixteen-year-old pupils of the elite Napola secondary school at Oranienstein were enlisted to man the western defences. Five days later an SS instructor arrived to teach the other pupils how to use hand-held anti-tank guns.[85] Women too were drafted into the armed forces as auxiliaries and subjected to military discipline. One young East Prussian woman told how her unit of raw recruits had been together for three weeks, learning how to use a pistol, when enemy fighter-planes strafed their training camp. One girl who was on guard outside the camp ran for cover. For this she was condemned to death:

We were all forced to stand by the fence and watch our comrade being shot . . . A whole series of girls fainted. Then we were driven back to the camp . . . The impression that this execution had made on us was indescribable. All of us did nothing but stay in bed and cry for the whole day. None of us went to work. For this we were all locked into cells . . . We had to stay there for 4 days on nothing but bread and water. We were allowed to take a copy of *My Struggle* or the Bible with us, but I declined the offer.[86]

The futility of this final draft of young women into the armed forces was nowhere clearer than in the case of the twenty-three-year-old Rita H., a seamstress, whose duties consisted of little more than helping the evacuation of army administrative offices, including the burning of incriminating documents. As the women tried to light a fire in the pouring rain, 'the singed papers and files were lying around the whole area, for the wind was repeatedly rummaging through our little heaps of paper. It was strange,' she added, writing as a pious Catholic, 'and yet wonderful to stand there like that and in a way to experience the downfall of a Godless government.'[87]

'WE'LL TAKE A WORLD WITH US'

I

Hitler's last speech, broadcast on 30 January 1945, the twelfth anniversary of his appointment as Reich Chancellor, aroused more sympathy than enthusiasm among his listeners. He did not even bother to hold out the hope that the 'wonder-weapons' would turn the situation around. Instead, he railed as ever against the 'Jewish-international world conspiracy' that was hell-bent on the annihilation of Europe. Germans, he said, had to continue resisting until victory was achieved. There was to be no stab in the back as there had been in the First World War. Not even committed Nazis found the speech inspirational. As Melita Maschmann later wrote:

During the last months of the war I always had to fight back tears when I heard Hitler's voice on the radio or saw him on the newsreels. One's conscious mind might refuse to recognize the signs of an imminent collapse, which were becoming more and more obvious, but the immediate impressions one received through one's eyes and ears could not be falsified, and one's heart was gripped with fear at the appalling truth: the newsreels showed an ageing man, who walked with a stoop and glanced anxiously about him. His voice sounded shrill with despair. Was he, then, destined to fail? For us he embodied the unprecedented effort that had made the German nation take over the government of the continent. In looking at him one saw the sum total of all the countless sacrifices of lives, health and property which that effort had demanded. Had all this been in vain?[88]

Many of the most committed Nazis, or the most naive, continued to hope against hope that it had not. One fifteen-year-old girl, whose entire education had been aimed not least at building up an image of Hitler as a father-figure, could write in her diary after recording the latest military disasters: 'Our poor, poor Leader, he can't be sleeping at night any more, and yet he's had Germany's good in mind.'[89]

The tone of her remarks was far from exceptional in such circles. Now trained as an air force officer, Albert Molter joined in a party held to listen to Hitler's speech in his officers' mess. Patriotic songs were sung, and extracts from Hanns Johst's play *Schlageter* were performed.[90] Then the radio was switched on and everyone settled down to listen. 'As always,' Albert wrote to his wife Inge, 'it was wonderful to hear the Leader's voice. How heavy must be the burden he bears. Seen in this way it's almost mean to listen to the Leader's words in the hope that they will bring a decision. But actually a decision has been taken. No miracle will rescue us except that of German grit.'[91] In response, his wife compared the cause of National Socialism to that of Christianity, and Hitler's supposed sufferings to those of Jesus. Christ's life, she recalled, had ended in crucifixion. 'Fred, darling,' she asked her husband, 'are we to be asked for a similar sacrifice so that our idea can last for ever?'[92] Their identification with Hitler was complete. 'We must stand by Germany, by the Leader,' wrote Alfred to his wife on 9 March 1945, 'only in this way will we stand by ourselves.'[93] Shortly afterwards, his unit was sent to Berlin to fight alongside the infantry defending the German capital. Within a few weeks, the British had occupied Nienburg, where Inge was now living, and arrested her Nazi father. 'Our beloved, beautiful Germany,' she wrote in despair to her husband, 'all her sacrifices, all her heroism in vain.'[94] He never replied. By the time she wrote this letter, he had gone missing in action. His body was never found.[95]

While the most faithful of his followers wallowed in maudlin pity for his plight, Hitler's thoughts turned increasingly to suicide. Sheltering from an air raid in the bunker underneath the Reich Chancellery shortly after the German defeat in the Battle of the Bulge, Hitler briefly gave way to despair. The army had betrayed him, he said; the air force was a broken reed. 'I know the war is lost,' he told his adjutant, Nicolaus von Below, and he continued: 'Most of all, I'd like to put a bullet through my own head.' But if he was to perish, then Germany would perish too. 'We'll not capitulate. Never. We can go down. But we'll take a world with us.'[96] When it came to public propaganda, Hitler and Goebbels now focused increasingly on the threat of annihilation they saw coming from the east. Fear was to galvanize Germans into fighting on. On 21 January 1945, in an editorial for the *Reich*, Goebbels ranted despairingly against 'the world conspiracy of a parasitic race', the Jews, who had succeeded in mobilizing the entire world against National Socialism. Despite everything, he proclaimed defiantly, 'not Europe, but the Jews themselves will perish'.[97]

Despite such bluster, it was clear to most Germans that the war was now drawing to a rapid close as the Red Army, now regrouped and re-equipped after its rapid advances of the previous months, resumed the attack once more. After the loss of the Romanian oilfields, the German army desperately needed to cling on to its source of supplies in Hungary or there would be virtually no fuel left to power its remaining tanks, lorries, mobile artillery and transport vehicles. Hitler refused permission to the German forces in Budapest to withdraw, and the Hungarian capital was soon surrounded by Soviet forces. A major offensive aimed at breaking the encirclement failed in February 1945, with the loss of nearly 30,000 men killed or captured. An armoured thrust by the Sixth SS Panzer Army, taken out of the Battle of the Bulge, failed just as decisively, and by the end of March the Red Army had occupied almost the whole of Hungary. In the north, the German forces in Latvia held out, but they were completely isolated. The main Soviet attack came in the central sector, in mid-January, when armoured formations of the Red Army took advantage of the removal of key German units to the Hungarian campaign to pulverize the German front and crush the remaining German armour. By the end of January, the Red Army had occupied most of prewar Poland. Some pockets of resistance remained, notably the city of Breslau, which held out until May. But the Red Army now stood on the river Oder, at the gates of the German Reich. It had captured the major industrial area of Silesia and gained control over the oilfields of Hungary, and it was nearing Vienna. Its commanders paused to regroup and build up munitions and supplies for the final offensive.[98]

In the west, after the failure of the German counter-offensive in the Battle of the Bulge, 1.5 million Americans, more than 400,000 British and Canadians and 100,000 Free French troops assembled at the end of January for an attack on the Rhine. They took more than 50,000 prisoners as they advanced, driving the German forces across the river. On 7 March 1945, as American troops reached Remagen, they noticed German soldiers desperately trying to blow up the bridge across the river, the last one left standing. Rushing up reinforcements, they drove across and established a bridgehead the other side, allowing many troops across before the bridge finally collapsed. By the time the Rhine had been crossed, another 300,000 German troops had been captured and a further 60,000 killed or wounded. The Americans pushed on eastwards, towards Saxony, while Canadian forces advanced into Holland. British forces drove north-east towards Bremen and Hamburg, and yet more American divisions mounted a huge encirclement operation in the Ruhr, capturing more than 300,000 German prisoners. On 25 April 1945 American troops met their Red Army counterparts for a ceremonial handshake at the small town of Torgau on the river Mulde, a tributary of the Elbe. Others were heading south-east towards Munich, aiming to meet Allied forces advancing towards the Brenner Pass from northern Italy, where a final assault had begun on 9 April 1945. The Red Army had already entered Vienna on 3 April 1945, as American troops were pushing into Austria from the west. Amidst constant negotiation, the invading forces agreed a rough division of territory between themselves as the final reckoning approached. Despite some doubts on the British side, the German capital was left to the Red Army to take. Soviet forces now held complete command of the skies, and possessed overwhelming superiority in armour, artillery, ammunition and manpower on the ground. In fierce fighting in March and early April 1945, they destroyed almost all the remaining German armies, and the fortresses on which Hitler had set such hopes, in East Prussia and Pomerania, while Rokossovskii launched a massive assault into Mecklenburg in the north. By the middle of April 1945, two and a half million men were now poised for the final attack on Hitler's capital.

The German armed forces had little left to throw at the enemy. In March 1945, some 58,000 sixteen- and seventeen-year-olds were sent into the fray: their training was perfunctory, and however indoctrinated they might have been in the Nazi cause, they were no match for the tough veterans of the Red Army or the well-equipped battalions of the British and Americans and their allies.[99] German losses on the Eastern Front had risen from 812,000 in 1943 to 1,802,000 in 1944. By the end of the year, over three and a half million German troops had been killed or captured by the Red Army. Overall, more than 450,000 members of the German armed forces were killed in January 1945, 295,000 in February, 284,000 in March and 281,000 in April: indeed, over a third of all German troops killed during the war died in its last four and a half months. By the end of 1944 some 800,000 German troops were in the custody of the Western Allies, a figure that had climbed to over a million by April and four million by the time the war was over. 700,000 members of the German armed forces were in Soviet camps. By April 1945 there were 600,000 sick and wounded soldiers, airmen and sailors in hospital.[100] In the second half of 1944 alone, the air force lost more than 20,000 planes. The command of the skies passed to the Allied bombers, the Red Army and the invasion forces in the west.[101] Speer was redoubling his efforts to increase arms production, and in September 1944 almost 3,000 fighter planes were completed. But the more territory Germany lost, the faster the war economy shrank. In particular, the loss to the Red Army of major industrial areas in the east, notably Upper Silesia, deprived the Reich of key economic resources. It was no longer possible to recruit fresh forced labour from the occupied areas. Germany's sources of fuel in Romania and Hungary were gone. The attempt to provide a substitute by manufacturing synthetic fuel had proved futile. There was no longer any defence against the destruction now raining down continually on German cities from the air. The German armies were no longer disciplined, effective and motivated fighting forces but rapidly shrinking in number, demoralized and disorganized, little more than an armed rabble.[102]

II

Nazi propaganda now concentrated increasingly on instilling fear of the invader into the German people. Hitler's written message read out over the radio on 24 February 1945, the anniversary of the promulgation of the Nazi Party programme in 1920, warned that Germans would be shipped off to Siberia as slaves if the Red Army proved triumphant.[103] The next day, 25 February 1945, Goebbels warned, in an article in *The Reich*, that, if Germany surrendered, Stalin would immediately occupy south-eastern Europe, and 'an iron curtain would immediately fall on this huge territory, together with the vastness of the Soviet Union, and nations would be slaughtered behind it'.[104] Hitler's final appeal to the troops on the Eastern Front, issued to all ranks on 15 April 1945, used fear as its main weapon in calling for resistance to the last man: 'The deadly Jewish-Bolshevik enemy with his masses is beginning his final attack. He is attempting to destroy Germany and exterminate our people

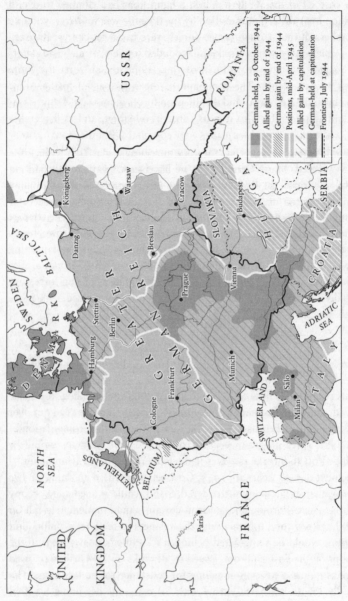

20. The End of the War

... The old men and children will be murdered, women and girls will be degraded as barracks whores. The remainder will march to Siberia.' But Germany would be spared this fate if they stood firm. 'The Bolshevik ... will bleed before the capital of the German Reich.'[105] Goebbels made a point of repeating these warnings in detail in these final weeks. He dragged up once more the allegation that the Allies intended to exterminate the German race. His warnings were echoed by Heinz Guderian, Chief of the Army General Staff, who declared that all the Red Army wanted to do in Germany was to rob, rape and kill.[106]

But such dire warnings had for some time been just as likely to backfire as to succeed. Many Germans, as we have seen, felt that they had no right to criticize the Red Army in view of the atrocities that Germany had committed itself. It was not just the Jews whose maltreatment aroused such feelings of guilt. A Party member in the Stuttgart area was reported to have asked rhetorically: 'Weren't our SS people frequently even more cruel towards Germans, their own fellow-citizens, than the Russians have been towards the East Prussians? We have shown the others how to deal with political enemies.'[107] Public exhortation to carry on fighting had equally little effect. On 24 February 1945 Bormann issued an appeal on the anniversary of the proclamation of the Nazi Party programme in 1920. Anyone who thought of retreat or surrender, he said, was a traitor to the nation. Self-sacrifice would be rewarded by victory. If only the German people's will stood firm, Germany would triumph.[108] Not long afterwards, in Berlin, three women were observed looking at a poster displayed in the shop window of the KdW department store, proclaiming: 'Berlin is working, fighting and standing.' A few more bombing raids like the previous day's, one was overheard saying, 'and the only thing standing will be ruins ... We didn't see much evidence of Berlin fighting last Sunday. The Americans dropped their bombs wherever they wanted. They flew all over the sky without any opposition, without any fighting.'[109] In the invaded areas, people began to seek a way of surrendering. Their attempts did not go down well with Nazi fanatics. 'In a session of the town council,' noted Lore Walb, who had gone back from Munich to her home town of Alzey in the Rhineland, 'Dr Sch. also pleaded for the surrender of the town, since further struggle is pointless, and in order to preserve everything that still remains. The District Leader [of the Nazi Party] was of course in favour of fighting to the finish.'[110] In one rural part of western Germany, soldiers who tried to set off explosive charges in front of the advancing Americans were attacked by local people with pitchforks.[111]

As propaganda failed, terror began to take its place. On 15 February 1945 Reich Justice Minister Otto-Georg Thierack ordered that anyone attempting to avoid his duty to fight on, thus jeopardizing Germany's determination to win, would be tried by a drumhead court-martial, consisting of a criminal court judge, a Nazi official and an officer of the armed forces, the Military SS or the police, and, if found guilty, executed on the spot.[112] As these makeshift courts swung into action, the more fanatical and energetic Nazi Party officials quickly dispensed with the rules. On 18 March 1945 Field Marshal Model ordered the military police to shoot any soldiers or civilians engaged in acts of sabotage. 'Where a white flag appears,' Himmler instructed his officers in the SS and police, 'all the male persons of the house concerned are to be shot. There must,' he added, 'be no hesitation in carrying out these measures.'[113] And in his last orders to the soldiers of the Eastern Front, in mid-April 1945, Hitler repeated that there was to be no retreat, no surrender: 'Anyone who gives you the order to retreat must be arrested immediately if you do not know exactly who he is, and if necessary is to be killed on the spot, quite irrespective of whatever rank he may carry.'[114] 'Strength Through Fear' became the slogan of the hour, replacing 'Strength Through Joy' – in German the initials, KdF, were the same.

Up to 10,000 people were summarily executed in this final phase of terror and repression.[115] They included a significant number of the 190,000 or so criminal offenders who now crowded Germany's state prisons and penitentiaries, many of them put there by political repression or the wartime crackdown on looting, theft and 'undermining morale'. As the Allied armies advanced, the prison authorities began to evacuate the jails. The governor of the women's penitentiary in Fordon, near Bromberg, took out the 565 inmates under guard on 21 January 1945, and marched them to another women's prison at Krone, 36 kilometres away. Only forty of them reached their destination. 'It was about minus 12 degrees,' reported the governor, 'and it was very icy. As a result, the prisoners as well as the warders were falling over all the time . . . During the march,' he continued, 'I observed numerous prisoners who were left behind, struggling to drag themselves forward. Many were sitting or lying by the side of the road, and nothing could induce them to get up again.'[116] When the Krone prisoners were evacuated in their turn, the same scenes repeated themselves. Coming across the column, an SS unit on the retreat gunned down one group of the prisoners, while other women prisoners were taken roughly out of the line by passing German soldiers and raped.[117]

All over Germany and the incorporated territories, state prisoners were forced to go on similar marches, some of them to concentration camps. Some, classified by penal officials as reformable, were released into a special formation of the Military SS. Thousands of the supposedly incorrigible, on the other hand, were simply taken out and shot. At Sonnenburg, a penitentiary located to the east of Berlin, the regional state prosecutor, Kurt-Walter Hanssen, a former personal assistant of Martin Bormann, had most of the prisoners murdered by a unit of SS and police officers brought in for the purpose on 30 January. The prisoners were made to kneel down in groups of ten, and were shot in the back of the neck; sick inmates were shot in their beds in the prison infirmary. More than 800 prisoners were killed in the space of a few hours, the majority of them foreign forced labourers who had been jailed for infringements of the harsh rules under which they had been obliged to live and work. The rest – a mere 150 – who had been classified as 'useful', were marched out in the direction of Berlin. For those left behind, conditions worsened dramatically with the arrival of evacuated prisoners from elsewhere; food supplies became even more scarce, disease was rife, and death rates rocketed. Reich Justice Minister Thierack personally ordered a large number of prison executions as late as April 1945. Army commanders who saw prison inmates as a military threat also ordered executions: Field Marshal Walter Model, surrounded by the Americans in the Ruhr area, ordered penitentiary inmates to be selected and executed if they were found to be 'dangerous': these included a number of German political prisoners as well as foreign workers. Altogether, 200 prisoners, including a number who were only on remand, were shot in this area over the following week.[118]

Model's murderous actions paralleled those of Hitler himself and reflected a similar mentality. The more desperate the military situation became, the more vital it seemed to such men to eliminate anyone who might threaten the regime from within. Obsessed to the end with the imaginary precedent of 1918, Hitler did not want another 'stab in the back'. 'I've ordered Himmler, in the event of there some day being reason to fear troubles back at home,' he had said some years earlier, on the night of 14–15 September 1941, 'to liquidate everything he finds in the concentration camps. Thus at a stroke the revolution would be deprived of its leaders.'[119] This included foreigners, such as the 141 French resistance workers who were shot in Natzweiler the day before the camp was evacuated in the face of the advancing Allied armies. Most of all, however, Hitler's murderous attention was turned towards his internal enemies.[120] The trials and executions of those involved in the bomb plot of 20 July 1944 continued almost to the end. On 4 April 1945 an evil chance led to the discovery of Admiral Canaris's personal diaries. Reading them in his Berlin bunker, Hitler convinced himself that Canaris and his fellow-conspirators had been working against him from the outset. All his remaining enemies had to be killed, he decided. He began by ordering the head of the SS Security Service, Ernst Kaltenbrunner, to do away with the surviving plotters. On 9 April 1945 Canaris, Oster, Bonhoeffer and two other political inmates of Flossenbürg concentration camp were stripped naked and hanged by crude ropes from wooden hooks in the courtyard. The bodies were immediately cremated. To Hitler's thirst for revenge was added Himmler's determination that prominent opponents of Nazism should not survive into the postwar era. As Gestapo chief Heinrich Müller told Helmuth von Moltke, 'We won't make the same mistake as in 1918. We won't leave out internal German enemies alive.'[121] On the same day as Canaris and the others were executed, as the Red Army was closing in on the concentration camp at Sachsenhausen, one of the inmates, Georg Elser, who had narrowly missed killing Hitler with a home-made time-bomb in November 1939, was moved out of his quarters in the camp to Dachau, where the commandant interviewed him briefly before having him taken out and shot in the back of the neck. Himmler had given orders for the execution, and instructed the camp authorities to attribute his death to a British air raid. A week later it was duly announced as such in the press.[122] A further series of murders took place between 20 and 24 April in Berlin, where the SS shot more of the people who had been involved in the bomb plot of July 1944.[123]

This was the kind of reckoning Hitler had carried out once before, when he had taken the opportunity of the purge of Ernst Röhm's storm-troopers at the end of June 1934 to settle old scores and eliminate possible members of an alternative government. But now it was being done on a much larger scale. Among the victims was the former Communist leader Ernst Thälmann. Incarcerated in a variety of prisons and camps since 1933, Thälmann had few illusions about his fate should the Red Army succeed in entering Germany. In August 1943 he was moved to the state prison at Bautzen, and a few months later his wife and daughter were arrested and taken to the Ravensbrück concentration camp. 'Thälmann,' Himmler jotted down in his notes for a meeting with Hitler on 14 August 1944, 'is to be executed.' Hitler signed the order, and three days later Thälmann was taken out of his cell and driven to the concentration camp at Buchenwald. Before he arrived, the prisoners, who included many former Communists, were locked into their barracks. One Polish inmate managed none the less to conceal himself near the entrance to the crematorium area, where the ovens were being stoked up in readiness for the disposal of Thälmann's corpse. He saw a large automobile arrive, and a broad-shouldered man get out, flanked by two Gestapo officers. The man was not wearing a hat, and the Pole noticed that he was bald. Prodded forward by the Gestapo, the man passed through the crematorium entrance, which was flanked by SS men. Immediately, three shots could be heard, then shortly afterwards, a fourth. The door was closed, then, twenty-five minutes later or so, they were reopened and the SS men came out. The Pole overheard their conversation. 'Do you know who that was?' one SS man asked his fellow officer. 'That was the Communist leader Thälmann,' came the answer. The official announcement of his death blamed it on a British air raid.[124]

A similar fate was clearly intended for a number of other prominent prisoners of the regime, including the ex-Chief of the Army General Staff General Franz Halder, the former Economics Minister Hjalmar Schacht, the sacked head of Army Procurement General Georg Thomas (all three arrested after the bomb plot), the last Austrian Chancellor Kurt Schuschnigg, the French politician and ex-Prime Minister Léon Blum, the Confessing Church leader Martin Niemöller, the former Hungarian Prime Minister Miklós Kalláy, the bomb plotter Fabian von Schlabrendorff, and the families of a number of his co-conspirators, including the Stauffenbergs, Goerdelers and von Hassells, along with a nephew of the Soviet Foreign Minister Molotov, assorted British agents, and army commanders from countries formerly allied to Germany. Some 160 people in all were gathered together in an SS convoy and taken to a mountainous area of the South Tyrol on 28 April 1945. Here, it had been decided, they were all to be shot and their bodies disposed of.

When a guard accidentally let slip their intended fate, one of the prisoners managed to contact the local German army commander, who sent a subordinate officer, Captain Wichard von Alvensleben, to investigate: gathering a posse of armed troops, the captain arrived at the scene, and before anything could happen, he used his aristocratic *hauteur* to browbeat the SS men into releasing their prisoners. They were all unharmed, but it had been a narrow escape.[125]

III

There were still some 700,000 prisoners in the concentration camps altogether at the beginning of 1945. As well as the main camps, there were at least 662 sub-camps dotted across the Reich and the incorporated territories at this time. By now, they held more prisoners in total than were housed in principal centres such as Auschwitz, Buchenwald, Sachsenhausen and Ravensbrück. As the Red Army advanced, Himmler ordered the camps in its path to be evacuated. Precisely when and how this was to be done was left largely to the commandants' own initiative. The largest of the camp complexes, at Auschwitz, held no fewer than 155,000 prisoners. Most of them were Poles and Russians. Roughly half of them were transported to camps further west. Huge quantities of material, equipment and personal effects went with the evacuees from Auschwitz. While the evacuation was in progress, work continued on new buildings, including a large set of additional facilities at Birkenau, dubbed 'Mexico' by the prisoners. Only in October 1944 was building work halted. The same month saw some 40,000 people perish in the existing gas chambers at Birkenau. In November, however, Himmler ordered all the gas chambers in every camp to be closed down and dismantled. At Auschwitz, the trenches used to incinerate corpses were levelled out, mass burial areas were filled up with earth and turfed over, the ovens and crematoria were dismantled, and the gas chambers destroyed or converted into air-raid bunkers.[126]

Now working for the concentration camp inspectorate, the former commandant of Auschwitz, Rudolf Höss, was sent by Oswald Pohl to the camp towards the end of 1944 'in the hope of reaching Auschwitz in time to make sure that the order for the destruction of everything important had been properly carried out', as he later recalled. Höss drove some distance across Silesia but was unable to reach the camp in the face of the relentless advance of the Red Army. 'On all the roads and tracks in Upper Silesia west of the Oder,' he reported, 'I now met columns of prisoners, struggling through the deep snow. They had no food. Most of the non-commissioned officers in charge of these stumbling columns of corpses had no idea where they were supposed to be going.' They requisitioned food from the villages through which they passed, but 'there was no question of spending the night in barns or schools, since these were all crammed with refugees'. Höss 'saw open coal trucks, loaded with frozen corpses, whole trainloads of prisoners who had been shunted on to open sidings and left there without food or shelter'. There were German refugees, too, in headlong flight from the advancing Russians, women 'pushing perambulators stacked high with their belongings'. The route taken by the 'miserable columns' of evacuated prisoners was easy to follow, he added, 'since every few hundred yards lay the bodies of prisoners who had collapsed or been shot'. Stopping his car by a dead body, he got out to investigate shots he heard near by 'and saw a soldier in the act of stopping his motor-cycle and shooting a prisoner leaning against a tree. I shouted at him, asking him what he thought he was doing, and what harm the prisoner had done him. He laughed impertinently in my face, and asked me what I proposed to do about it.' Höss's reaction to this challenge to his authority as a senior officer in the SS was unequivocal: 'I drew my pistol and shot him forthwith.'[127]

On 19 January 1945, despite Höss's failure to reach the camp, 58,000 prisoners began to make their way slowly out of Auschwitz westwards, most of them on foot, a few by train. SS guards shot stragglers and left their bodies by the roadside. As many as 15,000 of the prisoners died of starvation or cold or were killed by the SS. A few Poles defied the threats of the SS and gave some of them food or shelter; ethnic Germans stayed indoors. In the end, some 43,000 prisoners reached camps in the west. Only the very sick remained at Auschwitz, where the SS were desperately trying to blow up the remaining installations and burn incriminating documents before the Red Army arrived. The camp's building, administration and political department files were taken westwards; many ended up at Gross-Rosen. Medical equipment used in experimentation was dismantled or destroyed. In the chaos, the Special Detachment prisoners, key witnesses to mass murder, managed to melt into the crowds marching out of the camp and evade the SS, who had planned to kill them. The camp doctor Josef Mengele also absconded, taking his research notes and papers with him. On 20–21 January 1945, the SS guards abandoned the watchtowers, blew up the remains of the principal crematoria and set fire to the vast store of personal effects known to the inmates as 'Canada'. Executions continued right up to the last minute, until Crematorium V, where they took place, was blown up too, on 25–6 January 1945. The SS killed some 700 prisoners at the various camps and sub-camps belonging to the Auschwitz complex before they left, but they did not have the time to murder them all. On 27 January 1945 the Red Army marched in. 600 corpses were lying on the ground outside, but some 7,000 prisoners were still alive, many in a very weak condition. In the storerooms that had not been burned, the Russian soldiers painstakingly catalogued 837,000 women's coats and dresses, 44,000 pairs of shoes and 7.7 tons of human hair.[128]

Jewish prisoners were a particular target on the forced marches out of Auschwitz and other camps. When the prisoners employed on the manufacture of armoured personnel carriers at the Adler Works in Frankfurt were evacuated in March 1945 as the Americans approached the city, the SS pulled out the Jewish prisoners from the marching column and shot them; some of the victims were pointed out by their Polish fellow prisoners.[129] In East Prussia, some 5,000 mostly female Jewish prisoners were marched out of the various sub-camps belonging to Stutthof until they came to a halt at the fishing village of Palmnicken, where their way was blocked; the Regional Leader of East Prussia, together with the sub-camp commandants and local officers of the SS and the Todt Organization decided to kill them, and shot all apart from two or three hundred.[130] At a sub-camp of Flossenbürg, Helmbrechts, near the Franconian town of Hof, which housed mostly Polish and Russian women working in an arms factory, just over 1,100 prisoners were marched out in three groups on 13 April 1945, accompanied by forty-seven armed guards, male and female. Working their way towards no fixed destination, they had marched 195 miles by 3 May. Leaving the non-Jews behind after the first week, the guards proceeded southwards, beating and shooting the stragglers and the sick and depriving the prisoners of food and drink. More beatings were administered when local townspeople on occasion took pity on the prisoners and tried to throw them scraps of food. On 4 May, reaching the Czech border town of Prachtice, the column was attacked by an American plane, killing one of the guards; the remaining guards opened fire on the prisoners indiscriminately. Some of the survivors were marched up a nearby wooded hill and shot one by one as they collapsed with exhaustion. Before they fled, the guards set the others to walk into the town, where Czech townspeople gave them food and shelter. For many it was too late; twenty-six died before or shortly after the arrival of US troops, on 6 May 1945. Altogether at least 178 Jewish prisoners had perished on the march; a US army doctor later claimed that half the survivors were only saved by the prompt attentions of his medical team. Not for nothing were such aimless and murderous treks known by prisoners as 'death marches'. Many had no clear destination. Some of the marches, indeed, meandered across the country, even doubling back on themselves; a death march from Flossenbürg covered a good 250 miles, going north for a third of the way, then turning south, passing not far from the camp itself before continuing on to Regensburg.[131]

The evacuation of the concentration camp at Neuengamme, which housed, with its fifty-seven sub-camps, some 50,000 prisoners, was undertaken in co-operation with the Regional Leader of nearby Hamburg, Karl Kaufmann. Most of the sub-camp inmates were taken on murderous and exhausting 'death marches' to 'collection camps', including Bergen-Belsen, by mid-April. That still left 14,000 in the main camp. Kaufmann had already decided, after representations from business and military leaders, to surrender the city to the Allies. Kaufmann feared that if he had the prisoners released, they would descend upon the city in the search for food and shelter. By this time there were no other camps left on the German side of the front line to which they could be evacuated, so Kaufmann decided to put them on board ships. 4,000 Danish and Norwegian prisoners had already been taken to Sweden in March 1945 on the orders of Heinrich Himmler, with the agreement of Count Bernadotte, head of the Swedish Red Cross. Himmler hoped thereby to gain the confidence of the Swedish royal family, of which Bernadotte was a member, as intermediaries for the negotiations he felt (entirely without any justification) that he could carry out with the British. The remaining 10,000 prisoners from the main camp at Neuengamme were marched off to Lübeck between 21 and 26 April 1945 and put on to three ships Kaufmann had commandeered as 'floating concentration camps' – the freighters *Athens* and *Thielbeck*, and a luxury

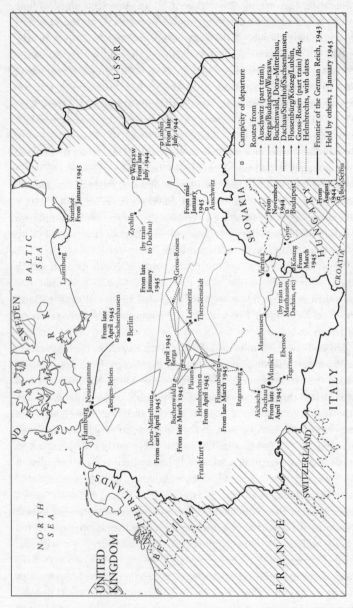

21. The Death Marches

liner, the *Cap Arcona*. No provision had been made for the prisoners, who were crammed into the holds, with no toilets and no water. Cauldrons of soup were lowered down when the SS opened the hatches, but there were no bowls or spoons, and much of the food spilled over on to the floor of the hold, mixing with the excrement now rapidly piling up. The SS took away the lifebelts to prevent escapes. Every day a launch brought out fresh water and returned to the shore with the corpses of prisoners who had died in the night. On 3 May 1945 British fighter-bombers spotted the ships, identified them as troop transports and attacked them with their rockets. The *Thielbeck* and *Cap Arcona* were badly hit. The *Thielbeck* sank, drowning all but fifty of the 2,800 prisoners on board. The *Cap Arcona* caught fire. Most of its lifeboats were destroyed in the inferno. As prisoners leaped into the icy waters of the Baltic, their clothes ablaze, a huge explosion ripped through the ship. It listed on to its port side and came to rest on the shallow bottom of the bay, half of the hull still above the water-line. 4,250 of the prisoners on board were drowned, burned to death, or shot by the bullets that filled the air as the planes exchanged fire with a group of U-boats in the nearby harbour. 350 prisoners were rescued after clinging to the hull for several hours. 400 of the 500 SS officers on board survived.[132]

Other evacuees from the camps were deliberately murdered en masse by the SS. A column of about a thousand prisoners evacuated from the Dora camp was penned into a barn at the town of Gardelegen for the night, and when the barn walls collapsed under the pressure of bodies, police and Hitler Youth poured petrol over the roof and burned those inside alive. Only a few were able to make their escape. The bodies were still burning when the Americans arrived the following day.[133] On some occasions, the local population in the areas through which the prisoners were marched joined in the killing. On 8 April 1945, for instance, when a column of prisoners scattered during a bombing raid on the north German town of Celle, ex-policemen and others, including some adolescents, helped hunt them down. Yet for all the particular sadism and violence directed by the SS against Jewish prisoners, the death marches were not, as has sometimes been claimed, simply the last chapter of the 'Final Solution'; many thousands of non-Jewish camp inmates, state prisoners, forced labourers and others had to endure them, and they can best be seen as the last act in the brutal and violent history of the

Third Reich's system of repression in general, rather than an exclusive exterminatory action directed against Jews.[134]

For those who survived to reach their destination, further horrors lay in store. The camps in the central area of the Reich became grossly overcrowded as a result of the arrival of the bedraggled columns of evacuees: the population of Buchenwald, for instance, went up from 37,000 in 1943 to 100,000 in January 1945. Under such conditions, death rates rose dramatically, and some 14,000 people died in the camp between January and April 1945, half of them Jews. At Mauthausen, the arrival of thousands of prisoners from sub-camps in the region led to a deterioration in conditions so drastic that 45,000 inmates died between October 1944 and May 1945. Conditions in the sub-camps that lasted to the end of the war were no better. Ohrdruf, a sub-camp of Buchenwald near Gotha, was the first to be discovered by the American army as it advanced through Thuringia. It had contained 10,000 prisoners engaged in excavating underground bunkers. The SS had marched out some of the inmates a few days before and shot many of them. The soldiers who discovered the camp on 5 April 1945 were so shocked by what they saw that their commander invited Generals Patton, Bradley and Eisenhower to visit it. 'More than 3,200 naked, emaciated bodies,' Bradley recalled later, 'had been flung into shallow graves. Lice crawled over the yellowed skin of their sharp, bony frames.' The generals came across a shed piled high with dead bodies. Bradley was so shaken that he was physically sick. Eisenhower reacted by ordering all his troops in the area to tour the camp. Similar scenes were repeated in many other places as the Americans advanced. Some of the former guards were still in the camp, disguised as prisoners; surviving inmates identified the former guards to the Allied troops, who sometimes shot the SS men in disgust; other guards had already been killed by angry prisoners wreaking their revenge.[135]

The terrible conditions prevailing in the camps in the final months of the war were most evident in the place that came to symbolize the inhumanity of the SS more than any other to the British, who liberated it at the end of the war: Belsen. The concentration camp at Bergen-Belsen had been converted from a prisoner-of-war camp early in 1943. Its special function was to serve as a place of temporary accommodation for a relatively small number of Jews from various European countries, and particularly from the Netherlands, whom Himmler and his allies in the Foreign Office thought might be used as bargaining chips or hostages in international negotiations. As the difficulty of carrying out exchanges of such prisoners became more apparent, the SS decided in March 1944 to use Bergen-Belsen as a 'convalescence camp', or, to put it more realistically, a dumping-ground, for sick and exhausted prisoners from other camps whose weakness made them incapable of work. Up to the end of 1944, some 4,000 such prisoners had been delivered to the camp, but since they were not provided with any adequate medical facilities, the death rate quickly rose to more than 50 per cent. In August 1944 the camp was further extended to include Jewish women, many of them from Auschwitz. By December 1944 there were more than 15,000 people in the camp, including 8,000 in the women's quarters. One of them was the young Dutch girl Anne Frank, who had been sent there at the end of October as an evacuee from Auschwitz; she died of typhus the following March. The commandant, Josef Kramer, appointed on 2 December 1944, was a long-time SS officer. He had previously served in Auschwitz-Birkenau, where he had recently overseen the murder of hundreds of thousands of Hungarian Jews in the gas chambers. A number of officials, including women guards, accompanied him. Kramer immediately removed the few privileges enjoyed by the 6,000 or so 'exchange Jews' who remained from the original camp contingent, and began a regime of rapidly increasing chaos and brutality.[136]

As Bergen-Belsen became the destination for prisoners evacuated from other camps in the face of the advancing Red Army, it became even more overcrowded. The number of inmates had increased to more than 44,000 by the middle of March 1945. Attempts to evacuate some of them to Theresienstadt ran into bomb attacks, and two trains were brought to a halt in open countryside on the way, when the guards absconded and Allied troops arrived to free the starving passengers, or those of them who were still alive. Meanwhile thousands more were still being delivered to Bergen-Belsen, including a large contingent from the Dora works, so that the total number of inmates reached 60,000 on 15 April 1945. Kramer had made no adequate or timely preparations for proper sanitary arrangements for them, so that these 60,000 had to make do with exactly the same number of washrooms, showers and toilets as had been provided a year earlier for a camp population of no more than 2,000. Soon excrement lay on the barrack floors up to a metre thick. Food supplies were completely inadequate; they ceased altogether as the war broke the last remaining communications. The water supply stopped when a bomb hit the pumping station, making the kitchens impossible to operate. Kramer did not bother to try to remedy the situation; yet after the British took over the camp on 15 April they were able to restore the water and food supplies and repair the cooking facilities within a few days. A doctor among the inmates later reported witnessing well over 200 cases of cannibalism among the prisoners. Kramer made things worse by constantly staging lengthy roll-calls in the open air, no matter how cold or wet the weather. Epidemics began to rage. Typhus killed thousands. But for the efforts of the doctors among the prisoners, the situation would have been even worse. Nevertheless, between the beginning of 1945 and the middle of April some 35,000 people died at Bergen-Belsen. The British, who took over the camp on 15 April 1945, were unable to rescue another 14,000, who were too weak, diseased or malnourished to recover.[137] Altogether, across Germany as a whole it has been estimated that between 200,000 and 350,000 concentration camp prisoners died on the 'death marches' and in the camps to which they were taken in these final months: up to half of the prisoners who were held in the camp system in January 1945, in other words, were dead four months later.[138]

IV

The final phases of the war saw some of the most devastating air raids of all. Bombing continued on an almost daily basis, sometimes with such intensity that firestorms were created similar to the one that had caused such destruction in Hamburg in the summer of 1943. In Magdeburg on 16 January 1945 a firestorm killed 4,000 people and totally flattened a third of the town; it was made worse by a raid by seventy-two Mosquitos the following night, dropping mines and explosives to disrupt the work of the fire brigades and clean-up squads. Increasingly, too, bombs with time-fuses were dropped, to make things even more dangerous. Small squadrons of fast, long-range Mosquito fighter-bombers flew at will over Germany's towns and cities, causing massive disruption by provoking repeated alarms and defensive mobilizations in the apprehension that a major raid was on the way. On 21 February 1945 more than 2,000 bombers attacked Nuremberg, flattening large areas of the city and cutting off water and electricity supplies. Two days later, on the night of 23–4 February 1945, 360 British bombers carried out the war's only raid on the south-west German town of Pforzheim, which they bombed so intensively over a period of 22 minutes that they created a firestorm that obliterated the city centre and killed up to 17,000 out of the town's 79,000 inhabitants. Berlin also saw its largest and most destructive raid of the war at this time. Over a thousand American bombers attacked the capital in broad daylight on 3 March 1945, pulverizing a large part of the city centre, rendering more than 100,000 people homeless, depriving the inhabitants of water and electricity, and killing nearly 3,000 people. At the request of the Soviet air force, more than 650 American bombers devastated the harbour of Swinemünde on 12 March, where many German refugees from the advancing Red Army had taken refuge. Some 5,000 people were killed, though popular legend soon had it that the death toll was many times higher. This was followed by an attack on Dortmund, like many of these other late raids aimed at destroying transport and communications hubs. On 16–17 March it was the turn of Würzburg, where 225 British bombers destroyed more than 80 per cent of the built-up area of the town and killed around 5,000 of its inhabitants. The last substantial British night-raid of the war was launched against Potsdam on 14–15 April 1945, killing at least 3,500.[139]

The most devastating air raid of the final phase of the war was carried out on Dresden. Up to this point, the baroque city on the Elbe had been spared the horrors of aerial bombardment. However, it was not just a cultural monument but also an important communications hub and a centre of the arms industry. The Soviet advance, now nearing the Elbe, was to be aided by Allied bombing raids intended to disrupt German road and rail communications in and around the city. And the German will to resist was to be further shattered. On 13 February 1945 two waves of British bombers attacked the city centre indiscriminately, un- opposed by flak batteries, which had been removed in order to man defences further east against the oncoming Red Army, or by German fighters, which remained grounded because they had no fuel. The weather was clear, and the pathfinder planes had an easy task. The British raids were followed by two daylight attacks by American bombers. The prolonged and concentrated succession of raids created a firestorm that destroyed the whole of the city centre and large parts of the suburbs. The city, wrote one inhabitant, 'was a single sea of flames as a result of the narrow streets and closely packed buildings. The night sky glowed blood-red.'[140] 35,000 people were killed.[141] Among the inhabitants of the city on those fatal days was Victor Klemperer. As one of the few remaining Jews in Germany, his life hitherto safeguarded by the loyalty of his non-Jewish wife, Eva, Klemperer had other things to worry about than the possibility of air raids. On the very morning of the first attack, an order arrived at the 'Jews' House', where he was being forced to live, announcing that the remaining Jews in Dresden were to be evacuated on the 16th. The order claimed that they would be required for labour duties, but since children were also named in the accompanying list, no one had any doubts as to what it really meant. Klemperer himself had to deliver copies of the circular to those affected. He himself was not on the list, but he had no illusions about the fact that he would be on the next one. Even in the final months of the war, the Nazis were grinding the machinery of extermination ever finer.[142]

That evening, while Klemperer was still contemplating his likely and imminent fate, the first wave of bombers flew over the city and began releasing their deadly cargo. At first, Klemperer hid in the cellar of the Jews' House. Then the house was hit by a bomb-blast. He went upstairs. The windows were blown in, and there was glass everywhere. 'Outside it was bright as day.' Strong winds were sweeping through the streets, caused by the immense firestorm in the city centre, and there were continual bomb-blasts. 'Then an explosion at the window close to me. Something hard and glowing hot struck the right side of my face. I put my hand up, it was covered in blood. I felt for my eye. It was still there.' In the confusion, Klemperer became separated from his wife. Taking her jewellery and his manuscripts in a rucksack, he scrambled out of the house, past the half-destroyed cellar and into a bomb crater and on to the street, joining a group of people who were making their way up through the public gardens to a terrace overlooking the city, where they thought it would be easier to breathe. The whole city was ablaze. 'Whenever the showers of sparks became too much for me on one side, I dodged to the other.' It began to rain. Klemperer wrapped himself in a blanket and watched towers and buildings in the city below glowing white and then collapsing in heaps of ashes. Walking to the edge of the terrace, he came by a lucky chance upon his wife. She was still alive. She had escaped death because someone had pulled her out of the Jews' House and taken her to a nearby cellar reserved for Aryans. Wanting to light a cigarette to relieve the stress, but lacking matches, she had seen that 'something was glowing on the ground, she wanted to use it – it was a burning corpse'.[143] Like many others, she had made her way out of the inferno to the park.

At this point, Klemperer's friend Eisenmann, another surviving Jew, came up to the couple, holding one of his children; the rest of his family had disappeared. Eisenmann dispensed some sound advice. 'I would have to remove my star,' Klemperer reported him as saying, 'just as he had already taken off his. Eva thereupon ripped the star from my coat with a pocket knife.' With this act, the Klemperers had effectively gone underground. In the chaos and destruction the Gestapo and other authorities would, for a time at least, have other things to do than to round up Dresden's remaining Jews, and all their lists had probably been destroyed anyway. Klemperer and his wife walked slowly along the river-bank:

Above us, building after building was a burnt-out ruin. Down here by the river, where many people were moving along or resting on the ground, masses of the empty, rectangular cases of the stick incendiary bombs stuck out of the churned-up earth. Fires were still burning in many of the buildings on the road above. At times, small and no more than a bundle of clothes, the dead were scattered across our path. The skull of one had been torn away, the top of the head was a dark red bowl. Once an arm lay there with a pale, quite fine hand, like a model made of wax such as one sees in barber's shop windows. Metal frames of destroyed vehicles, burnt-out sheds. Further from the centre some people had been able to save a few things, they pushed handcarts with bedding and the like or sat on boxes and bundles. Crowds streamed unceasingly between these islands, past the corpses and smashed vehicles, up and down the Elbe, a silent, agitated procession.[144]

Making their way through the still-burning city, they came to the Jews' House, to find it almost completely destroyed. Klemperer had his eye treated by an ambulance crew, then the couple reached a medical centre, where they were able to sleep and get a bite to eat, though not much more. Eventually they were all taken to an air base outside the city, where they received more food. Here Klemperer received further medical attention. He registered himself under his real name, but leaving out the tell-tale 'Israel' that he had been forced by law to carry since the beginning of 1939. Making their way out of Dresden to the north by train –

banned to Jews on pain of death – the Klemperers arrived at Piskowitz, where their former domestic servant Agnes lived; she assured them that she had not told anyone she had worked for a Jewish couple, and gave them shelter. Klemperer answered the inevitable question from the local mayor ('You are not of Jewish descent or of mixed race?') with a firm 'no'.[145] For them, as for a tiny number of other Jews, the chaos and destruction of the final months of the war offered a chance of survival. They took it gladly.

Only the most convinced Nazis saw the air raids as a spur to further defiance of the Allies. Shortly after the Allied bombing of Dresden, Luise Solmitz met an acquaintance who worked for the Propaganda Ministry:

When I said, 99 per cent of Hamburgers wanted these attacks to end, and what came afterwards would have to be borne, X shouted: 'But that's surely madness, that's the point of view of the stupid plebs! We have to stand before History with honour. You can't paint the consequences of a defeat in colours that are in any way adequate' . . . For him, Dresden is 'the biggest organized mass murder in history'.[146]

For the latter part of the war, she spent much of her time simply trying to keep her family alive. Although she was a non-smoker, she applied for a cigarette ration card because, as she noted, 'cigarettes are currency, hard currency'. Thus she was able to exchange them for food rations for her infant grandson. The gas connection to her home had been broken in the air raids at the end of July 1943 and not been restored until January 1944; but by early 1945 both gas and electricity supplies were in any case being regularly shut off for so-called 'gas-saving days' and 'current-saving days'. By this time, too, four-week ration cards were having to last for five weeks. At the end of 1944 official food rations began to be cut to levels which nobody could survive on. In the second week of January 1945 the monthly bread ration was cut from ten and a half kilos to 8,750 grams, and by mid-April it had fallen to 3,600 grams; the meat ration was reduced from 1,900 grams to 550 over the same period, the fat ration from 875 grams to 325.[147] The country's infrastructure was crumbling rapidly. 'I'm at the end of my strength, my will; completely exhausted and finished,' Luise Solmitz wrote despairingly on 9 April 1945.[148]

Under the impact of defeat and retreat, and worn out by the constant bombing raids on her home city of Hamburg, Luise Solmitz at last began to lose her faith in Hitler, though she was too cautious to say so too explicitly even in the privacy of her diary. Gathering together her thoughts about the Germans and their current situation on 8 September 1942, she had written:

For me, a great man is only one who knows how to moderate himself, because there is not just a present time in which revenge can be tasted, but also a future in which retribution will come. Bismarck could restrain himself, one of the few who resisted being swept away by the power of success, a man who opposed his own internal law to the kind of law of nature that carried the conqueror away. The inescapable fate of most conquerors is self-destruction.[149]

But it was not until her daughter Gisela left her newborn son Richard in her safekeeping that Luise Solmitz really turned against Hitler. It was bad enough to think that she and her husband Friedrich might die in the bombing, but the threat it posed to their baby grandchild, the innocent carrier of Germany's future, appalled her. By this time, she had only 'hate' and 'curses' for Hitler. 'I got into the habit of accompanying every bomb with a "Let Hitler die a miserable death" when we were amongst ourselves,' she wrote.[150] The family started to refer to the Nazis as 'Herr Jaspers', allowing them to discuss the decline and forthcoming end of the Nazi system without fear of being arrested if anyone overheard them. Every time Goebbels or another leading Nazi came on to the radio, they rushed across the room to switch it off.[151] The constant bombing was destroying what little was left of the popular belief in Hitler and support for the Nazi regime.

As the situation became more desperate, theft and illegal black-marketeering became the only ways to survive. Looting grew more widespread, above all from the summer of 1944 onwards. In Essen, for example, more than ninety grocery stores were looted in just two weeks in the autumn of 1944. People took advantage of the owners' absence during night-time air raids. Bomb damage provided them with further opportunities. Mostly they took small amounts of food and clothing. Police patrols were increased, and the Gestapo expanded its network of informers in the communities of foreign workers. In September 1944 Gestapo officers were authorized to carry out summary executions of looters, an order formalized by the Reich Security Head Office in early November 1944 initially only with regard to eastern workers, then to all. Local police and administrative authorities were thus, in effect, encouraged to take matters into their own hands. Members of the People's Storm were used to stand guard over bomb-damaged buildings, and to arrest and indeed to shoot eastern workers caught with loot from bomb-sites. In October 1944 one Gestapo officer in the west German town of Dalheim, not far from Cologne, coming across some eastern workers, all of them women, carrying what seemed to be looted goods, got his men to arrest seven of them; they confessed under interrogation and he had them all shot the following day. Sometimes local people would join in. Early in April 1945, for instance, a telephone operator on his way home from work in Oberhausen noticed four eastern workers coming out of a house the inhabitants of which had evidently taken refuge in an air-raid shelter; he gathered some other men, and arrested one of the workers, whom the men then started beating. The worker confessed to stealing some potatoes, and was taken to an office of the armed forces, where the telephone operator was given a gun. Taking his prisoner to a sports field, he was joined by a crowd, who also started beating the man with clubs and planks. The telephone operator then shot the man, but he did not die immediately; as he lay moaning on the ground the crowd gathered round and beat him to death.[152]

In such circumstances, it is not surprising that increasing numbers of foreign workers began to abscond or go underground. French workers given leave of absence to visit their families back home often simply failed to return – in the I. G. Farben factory in Ludwigshafen, for example, fully 68 per cent of the western European workers given leave to visit home in May and June 1943 never came back. To have banned home leave, however, would have caused widespread unrest among these workers, and punitive measures were not possible because they were from 'friendly' countries. Half or more of the workers who deserted their jobs were from the east, and these men and women were undoubtedly acting illegally. The chances of their actually making it back home were remote, but many of them managed to find work elsewhere, particularly if it was less demanding than the job they had left. Most tried their best to relocate to areas that were not threatened by bombing raids. The Gestapo tracked down and arrested a large number of them, organizing widespread manhunts and intensifying their checks on railway stations, bars and public places. By 1944 the number of escapes had increased to the staggering figure of half a million a year, at least according to Albert Speer, who insisted that, because of their importance to the war economy, the most that should be done to the absconding workers when they were arrested was to return them to their original place of work. Other foreign labourers increasingly signed themselves off sick, or simply worked more slowly. The police found the following chain-letter in the pocket of a French worker in May 1944: 'The Ten Commandments of a Perfect French Worker: 1. Walk slowly in the workshop. 2. Walk quickly after knocking off work. 3. Go to the toilet frequently. 4. Don't work too hard. 5. Annoy the foreman. 6. Court the beautiful girls. 7. Visit the doctor often. 8. Don't count on a vacation. 9. Cherish cleanliness. 10. Always have hope.'[153] Some workers deliberately sabotaged the weapons they were being forced to make. Others just produced shoddy work because they were tired and malnourished.

Resistance or refractoriness of this kind was almost always on an individual basis. In some places, Communist foreign labourers set up clandestine resistance movements, but these seldom did much more than organize escapes or identify and deal with informers. Far more common were gangs of escaped foreign workers hiding in bombed-out buildings and living off their wits, often together with young Germans. Their main source of support was usually the black market. With food in increasingly short supply, tobacco, as Luise Solmitz had noticed, became a kind of currency, to be exchanged when needed for bread or clothes. Western workers, especially the French, were better paid than their eastern counterparts, and often received food parcels from their relatives back home, so they were able to use this advantageous situation to build up a thriving clandestine market in the food so desperately needed by Soviet and Italian workers. Lacking purchasing power, Russian prisoners of war and civilian forced labourers began to make little toys and other knick-knacks from industrial waste and sell them on the streets or in the factories, though this was soon banned on the grounds that the materials they used were important for the war economy.[154] Large gangs began to emerge, building on their role in such often dangerous trades. By September 1944, encouraged by the approach of the Allied armies, these gangs were growing in number, especially in ruined west German towns like Cologne. They were often armed and were not afraid of shooting it out with the police. In Cologne, one gang of about thirty members, mainly eastern workers, was reported to be living off stolen and looted food, and when the Gestapo broke it up after a gunfight in

706 THE THIRD REICH AT WAR

which a police inspector was killed, the leading figure, Mishka Finn, found his way to another gang led by a former concentration camp inmate, a German. Most of the members were army deserters and escaped prisoners. This gang worked in turn with a more political group of younger working-class men known as the Edelweiss Pirates, who had been attacking members of the Hitler Youth and robbing grocery shops and other premises. When the group became more ambitious and started planning to blow up the Gestapo headquarters in the city, the police located and arrested its members. They hanged six of them, all eastern workers, in public, before a large crowd, on 25 October 1944, following this with the public execution of thirteen members of the German gang on 10 November 1944.[155]

However, this did not bring such activities in the city to an end; indeed, the head of the Cologne Gestapo was killed shortly afterwards in a shoot-out with yet another gang of eastern workers. One gang in Duisburg was a hundred strong and carried out break-ins on a more or less daily basis. The Gestapo responded to this mounting chaos with a policy of mass arrests and executions on an ever-larger scale. In Duisburg, twenty-four members of the eastern workers' gang were shot in February 1945, followed in March by sixty-seven more people, a number of them Germans suspected of sheltering members of the gang. In Essen the Gestapo chief, together with his superior officer from Düsseldorf, had thirty-five prisoners, mostly held on suspicion of looting or burglary, taken out of the police jail and shot. Thirty more eastern workers were executed on 20 March 1945 near Wuppertal, twenty-three in Bochum, and eleven in Gelsenkirchen. In Dortmund, the Gestapo shot some 240 men and women in March and April 1945, carrying on their killings right up to the moment when the Allied troops entered the city. Their victims were people imprisoned under suspicion of looting, theft, Communist resistance activities, espionage and a variety of other offences. Anger at Germany's impending defeat fuelled a spirit of vengeance, and a desire to restore a Nazi sense of order in a world rapidly descending into chaos, where people the Gestapo thought of as racially inferior were roaming almost unchecked through the major industrial cities of the German west. Gang activity in this region was driven more by a sense of survival than by any desire to offer overt resistance to the Nazi regime; but, as so often, the regime's response was political in its very essence, ideological to the last.[156]

V

According to the Soviet Union's own estimates, the Red Army's losses in the war totalled more than 11 million troops, over 100,000 aircraft, more than 300,000 artillery pieces, and nearly 100,000 tanks and self-propelled guns. Other authorities have put the losses of military personnel far higher, as high indeed as 26 million. Red Army troops were untrained, uneducated, often unprepared. The losses continued unabated right to the end of the war; indeed, more tanks were lost every day in the final battle for Berlin than had been lost even in the Battle of Kursk. Stalin sought victory at any price, and the price his men paid was astronomically high. Red Army officers and troops were told to obey orders without question and to avoid undertaking anything on their own initiative. Instead of mounting tactically sophisticated attacks, they often stormed the enemy lines in frontal assaults, incurring losses so heavy that it took time even with the vast resources at the Red Army's disposal to replace them. The result was that the war on the Eastern Front took far longer to win than it would have done with more intelligent and less profligate military leadership.[157] On top of this, however, the sufferings the troops had to endure and the enormous losses they suffered infused the Soviet soldiers' commitment to victory with a strong dose of bitterness and hatred for the enemy. This became apparent as soon as they reached the borders of Germany.

In July 1944 Soviet troops entered Majdanek, the first extermination camp to be discovered by any of the Allied armies. The barracks and yards were littered with corpses – Russians, Poles and many others, as well as Jews. Appalled reporters went round the gas chambers, which the Germans had not been able to dismantle in time. Thousands of Red Army soldiers were conducted round the camp at Majdanek to see for themselves. Pravda ('Truth'), the main Soviet daily newspaper, printed vivid reports, to add to the already well-known stories of the millions of Soviet prisoners of war deliberately starved and left to die by the Germans. As they made their way westwards into Germany, the Soviet forces discovered other killing centres, not only Auschwitz but smaller places like Klooga, near Tallinn, where photographers took pictures of the bodies of murdered Jews piled up with logs ready for a mass cremation that the Germans had not had time to begin. The deep impression made by such sights added fuel to the anger against the Germans built up over years of suffering at their hands. The memories of burned-out and looted cities like Kiev or Smolensk intensified as the troops entered a country whose standard of living seemed unimaginably high compared to their own. If Germany was so rich, then why had the Germans started the war? The contrast only seemed to deepen the Russian soldiers' fury. 'We will take revenge,' wrote one as he crossed into East Prussia in January 1945, 'revenge for all our sufferings . . . It's obvious from everything we see that Hitler robbed the whole of Europe to please his bloodstained Fritzes . . . Their shops are piled with goods from all the shops and factories of Europe.'[158] 'We hate Germany and the Germans deeply,' wrote another. 'You can often see civilians lying dead in the street . . . But the Germans deserve the atrocities that they unleashed. You only have to think about Majdanek.'[159] Political commissars, themselves the subject of a special murder order issued to the German forces in 1941, urged the troops on to take their revenge. 'The soldiers' rage in battle must be terrible,' went one widespread Soviet political slogan of the time. 'You said that we should do the same things in Germany as the Germans did to us,' wrote another soldier to his father. 'The court has begun already: they are going to remember this march by our army over German territory for a long, long time.'[160]

The Soviet military and civilian authorities ordered the occupied parts of Germany to be stripped bare. They carted off vast quantities of railway track, locomotives and wagons, weapons and ammunition, and much more besides, to replenish as far as they could the Soviet plant and equipment destroyed in the war. The Americans found that 80 per cent of Berlin's industrial machinery had been removed to the Soviet Union by the time they arrived in the city in 1945. Artworks were part of the officially sanctioned plunder too. In their hasty retreat, the Germans were forced to leave behind numerous collections, like others across Europe by this time placed for safe keeping in cellars, mines and other hiding places away from the heat of battle and the destructiveness of bombing raids. Special Soviet art recovery units roamed the countryside searching for these hoards, and those they succeeded in finding were carried off to a special repository in Moscow. In a deep quarry tunnel at the village of Groscotta near Dresden, they found numerous paintings stored by the Dresden museums, including Raphael's *Sistine Madonna* and Rembrandt's *Abduction of Ganymede*. The huge Pergamon Altar was dismantled and taken away. One and a half million cultural objects were eventually returned to East Germany, after 1949, but a good deal went astray. The mayor of Bremen, for example, had sent the city's art collection for safekeeping to a castle not far from Berlin, where Red Army troops found it. Arriving to inspect the collection, Viktor Baldin, a Russian architect enlisted in the Red Army, found the valuable works scattered around the area, and did his best to recover them, in one case trading a Russian soldier a pair of boots for an etching by Albrecht Dürer. While Baldin kept the hundreds of drawings he had found in safe keeping, seeking an opportunity to return his collection to Bremen, other items from the same collection began to turn up on the art market later on; one dealer gave a Berlin woman 150 marks and a pound of coffee in return for a Cranach as late as 1956. The Russians kept much of their 'trophy art' even after 1990, asking pointedly why they should return looted art to Germany when so many of their own cultural treasures had disappeared or been destroyed as a result of the actions of the invading German armies.[161]

Ordinary Red Army soldiers looted at will. The fierceness of the fighting in the final months of the war only added to the Soviet soldiers' fury. Perhaps, too, they were releasing the anger and frustration built up over many years of suffering, inflicted not only by Hitler but also by Stalin before him. Like the German soldiers entering Russia in 1941, they fought in close-knit groups united by a common ethos of masculine aggressiveness. The atrocities they committed were a symptom not of the breakdown of discipline and morale but of the group cohesion and collective mentality forged in the heat of battle. The Germans had plundered and destroyed, so why should they not do the same? Ordinary Soviet soldiers helped themselves to whatever they could find, irrespective of the military regulations. Food was the most important: soldiers plundered German military stores, broke into wine cellars and drank themselves into insensibility, and sent food parcels back to their families in enormous quantities. Officers took rare books, paintings, hunting rifles, typewriters, bicycles, bedding, clothes, shoes, musical instruments, and especially radios, a much-prized rarity back home. All of them stole wristwatches. At the railhead in Kursk, the monthly total of parcels arriving from soldiers in Germany jumped from 300 in January 1945 to 50,000 in April. By mid-May 1945, some 20,000 railway wagons of loot were waiting to be unloaded or sent on to their destinations. But there was violence and senseless destruction as well.[162] The Red Army soldiers torched houses, farms and even whole towns and villages; they shot civilians by the thousand, men, women and children. 'Happy is the heart,' wrote one soldier to his parents in February 1945, 'as you drive through a burning German town. We are taking revenge for everything, and our revenge is just. Fire for fire, blood for blood, death for death.'[163]

Driven by hatred, vengefulness and seemingly endless quantities of alcohol, the troops indulged in a systematic campaign of rape and sexual violence against German women. This had in the end very little to do with releasing months and years of sexual frustration and pent-up lust; other factors, notably hatred and aggression, were far more important. Most of the adult civilians the Red Army troops found in Germany were women: the men were dead, still fighting, or working in munitions factories. It was as women that the Germans became the object of the Soviet soldiers' wrath. Interviewed later on, German women typically recalled that, when they tried to protest, they were met not with counter-stories of German soldiers raping Russian women but with 'the image of a German soldier swinging a baby, torn from its mother's arms, against a wall – the mother screams, the baby's brains splatter against the wall, the soldier laughs.'[164] It had after all been the Germans who had invaded Russia, unprovoked, and caused an almost unimaginable degree of death, suffering and destruction. They would be given a lesson that would last a thousand years. As one Red Army soldier wrote: 'It's absolutely clear that if we don't really scare them now, there will be no way of avoiding another war in the future.'[165]

One young officer coming upon a unit that had overtaken a column of German refugees fleeing westward later recalled: 'Women, mothers and their children lie to the right and left along the route, and in front of each of them stands a raucous armada of men with their trousers down. The women who are bleeding or losing consciousness get shoved to one side, and our men shoot the ones who try to save their children.' A group of 'grinning' officers was standing near by, making sure 'that every soldier without exception would take part'.[166] Women and girls were subjected to serial rape wherever they were encountered. Rape was often accompanied by torture and mutilation and frequently ended in the victim being shot or bludgeoned to death. The raging violence was undiscriminating. Often, especially in Berlin, women were deliberately raped in the presence of their menfolk, to underline the humiliation.

The men were usually killed if they tried to intervene. In East Prussia, Pomerania and Silesia it is thought that around 1,400,000 women were raped, a good number of them several times. Gang-rapes were the norm rather than the exception. The two largest Berlin hospitals estimated that at least 100,000 women had been raped in the German capital. Many caught a sexually transmitted disease, and not a few fell pregnant; the vast majority of the latter obtained an abortion, or, if they did give birth, abandoned their baby in hospital. The sexual violence went on for many weeks, even after the war formally came to an end. German women learned to hide, especially after dark; or, if they were young, to take a Soviet soldier, preferably an officer, as a lover and protector. On 4 May 1945 an anonymous Berlin woman wrote in her diary: 'Slowly but surely we're starting to view all the raping with a sense of humour – gallows humour.'[167] She noted with a certain satisfaction that the Russian soldiers tended to prefer plump and well-fed women as their victims after the initial fury was over, and that these, unsurprisingly, were usually the wives of Nazi Party functionaries.[168]

Rightly afraid of what might happen to them when the Red Army arrived, millions of Germans fled before the advance of the Soviet troops. Pathetic columns like those of the women, children and old people who had taken to the roads of Europe from Belgium to Belarus in fear for their lives as the German armies marched into their countries in 1940 and 1941 could now be seen making their way back towards Germany in 1944 and 1945: only this time they consisted of Germans. The lucky ones carried their possessions on a car or a horse and cart, the less fortunate trudged along on foot. Many children froze to death on the journey. Some refugees still managed to find an undamaged railway line and a place on a train. Nazi officials in some towns piled people on to open goods wagons, shivering, and without food or drink. By the time one such trainload arrived in Schleswig-Holstein, it was reported, the refugees were 'in a dreadful state. They were riddled with lice and had many diseases such as scabies. After the long journey, there were many dead lying in the wagons.'[169] Towards the end of January 1945, up to 50,000 refugees were arriving in Berlin by rail every day. The Nazi authorities estimated in mid-February 1945 that more than 8 million people were fleeing westwards into the heart of the Reich. Along the Baltic coast, some half a million refugees were trapped in Danzig, and food parcels taken in by air or sea were frequently looted by starving

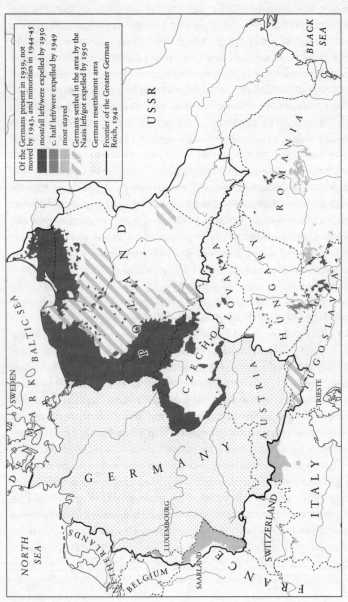

Of the Germans present in 1939, not moved by 1943, and minorities in 1944-45

▨ most/all left/were expelled by 1950

▨ c. half left/were expelled by 1949

▨ most stayed

Germans settled in the area by the Nazis left/got expelled by 1950

German resettlement area

— Frontier of the Greater German Reich, 1942

22. German Refugees and Expellees, 1944–50

German soldiers. Another 200,000 were bottled up by the fighting in the small port of Pillau. Local and regional officials began to organize their evacuation by sea. The 'Strength Through Joy' cruise liner *Wilhelm Gustloff* took some 6,600 from Gdynia on to the Baltic: a Soviet submarine came across it, fired three torpedoes and sank it with the loss of 5,300 lives. It was not the only refugee ship to be sunk in this way. Faced with bitter accusations of having committed a major atrocity, the Soviet navy claimed that the ship had been full of U-boat crewmen. It knew that Grand Admiral Dönitz had ordered that the evacuation of members of the armed forces had priority over that of civilians. In this case, however, it had made a terrible mistake. Nevertheless, the captain of the submarine that sank the ship was rewarded by being spared the prison sentence he faced because of the discovery of his long-term affair with a foreign woman; in 1990 he was posthumously awarded the title of Hero of the Soviet Union.[170]

Those Germans who remained in the occupied and conquered territories of the east faced a difficult future. During the war they had formed part of the often brutal and violent ruling ethnic elite. Now they were the vanquished. Over the following months, Czech, Polish and other re-established governments organized the forcible expulsion and expropriation of almost the entire ethnic German population of their states, driven out to join the millions who had already fled. Altogether perhaps 11 million German refugees and expellees arrived in the 'Old Reich' between 1944 and 1947. People fled in large numbers before the advancing Allied troops in the west as well. Back in her home town of Alzey in the Rhineland, Lore Walb saw people packing their bags as the Americans approached. 'The columns of cars have been going past our little house all evening in an unbroken procession,' she wrote on 26 March 1945. 'They were all coming from the Front and driving eastwards.' A quarter of the town's population, she reckoned, joined the columns of refugees.[171] Everywhere in Germany in the first months of 1945 people were on the move, living with the permanent threat of violence and death, waiting for the end with a mixture of fear and hope.

THE FINAL DEFEAT

I

In the mounting chaos and destruction of the last months of the war, Hitler's influence over the German masses finally disappeared. Even supporters of the regime, noted the SS Security Service on 28 March 1945, were criticizing him. Nobody believed his assurances of victory any longer.[172] 'Do you believe then,' some were reported as saying, 'that the German people has completely given up thinking? Do you think then that the German people can be kept going for much longer with empty phrases and promises?' In 1941 Hitler had announced that the last battle-ready Russian divisions had been destroyed. With the Russians now at the gates, 'who can take it badly when we don't believe the Leader's word any more?'[173] 'Doubts about our leadership,' the Security Service was forced to admit, 'are making no exception of the Leader's person.' When Hitler's proclamation of 24 February 1945 was read out over the radio, it did not make a favourable impression on listeners. 'The Leader is making another prophecy,' mocked a lower Nazi official in Lüneburg. 'It's the old record yet again,' said another.[174] Anger at the Nazi leadership had become general. People now feared the threat of the SS and of die-hard Nazi activists more than they feared defeat.[175] Among ordinary Germans, from whom his identity as a Jew was carefully kept hidden, Victor Klemperer now began to find spontaneous, mostly retrospective expressions of sympathy for the Jews, 'these poor people'.[176] Only a few still professed belief in Hitler, blaming others for Germany's defeat.[177] People began removing swastikas from buildings and destroying other Nazi insignia displayed in public places.[178]

There was increasing anger, too, at the Nazi leadership's failure to surrender when everything was so obviously lost. Those who remembered the First World War recalled that the military leaders of the day had thrown in the towel when they had realized that they were about to be defeated, thus saving many lives. 'What decent people Hindenburg and Ludendorff were by comparison,' one said. 'When they saw that the game was up, they brought it to an end and didn't let us go on being murdered, But *these people!* Just so they can rule for another couple of weeks . . .'[179] Millions were indeed dying in this final phase of the war. Lore Walb reflected bitterly on Hitler's 'really great guilt. Why,' she asked on 23 April 1945, 'doesn't he finally give up the fight – and why is he rushing us all into a civil war at the end as well?' She was deeply angered by what she called the 'unreason of the fanatics', amongst whom she now clearly numbered Hitler himself.[180] And indeed, far from deciding to bring the death and destruction to an end, Hitler was determined if anything to make it worse. Faced with an invasion of German territory by the autumn of 1944, and perhaps taking a leaf out of Stalin's book, he urged a policy of 'scorched earth', denying the enemy armies the ability to live off the land, just as the Russians had tried to do earlier in the war. The idea was completely unrealistic. Allied forces had ample supplies from their own bases. The only victims would have been German civilians. Government ministries agreed that the idea was impracticable, and Speer persuaded Hitler to disable industry in the battle zone by removing vital components rather than by blowing up factories or flooding mines. The armaments minister still thought that it would be possible to reoccupy the conquered territories in the near future and wanted essential production facilities to be ready for reuse. But after the Battle of the Bulge and the resumption of the Soviet advance at the beginning of 1945, Speer finally realized the inevitability of defeat. He decided that the German people would need as far as possible to inherit a functioning economy after the war was over, and he began, no doubt, to be concerned about his own reputation with the Allies. The main person now standing in the way of a managed surrender was Hitler himself. In mid-February 1945, according to his own later account, Speer conceived the idea of dropping poison gas down a ventilation shaft into Hitler's bunker beneath the Reich Chancellery. He managed to get the air filter system removed in response to Hitler's complaints that the air below ground was stuffy. But he was still casting around for a suitable chemical when Hitler, obsessed with security after the July bomb plot, recalled that poison gas was heavier than air, had a ten-foot chimney built over the air intake to the bunker and posted SS sentries all around the roof, which was now equipped with searchlights to identify anyone found lurking there at night. Speer quietly abandoned the project; whether it had ever existed outside his own fantasies remained unclear.[181]

On 18 March 1945 Speer sent Hitler a memorandum outlining plans for the preservation of Germany's economic infrastructure to allow reconstruction after the end of the war. Hitler told the military briefing that evening that there would be no point in taking such a course of action. The German nation had failed in the struggle for the survival of the fittest. The future belonged to the victors. Those Germans remaining after the struggle was over would be poor racial stock because the best had been killed. So it was not necessary to provide them with the basis for their future existence, on however primitive a level. Then he turned his anger on to Speer's memorandum. His response to it was to strip his Armaments Minister of most of his powers. On 19 March 1945 Hitler issued what quickly came to be known as his 'Nero order', after the Roman Emperor who had supposedly commanded the destruction of the city of Rome by fire. All military, transport, communication, industrial and supply installations and equipment within the Reich that might fall into the hands of the enemy were to be destroyed. 'It is an error,' Hitler said, 'to believe that after the recapture of lost areas it will be possible to use undamaged or only temporarily paralysed transport, communications, industrial and supply installations again for one's own purposes.' When the enemy was finally beaten back, he would 'leave only scorched earth behind him and . . . abandon all concern for the population'.[182] This was a fantasy on several different levels, of course. But it could cause immense suffering if implemented. Albert Speer determined to stop it. He toured the battle-fronts and arranged with sympathetic army commanders that Hitler's command to destroy everything should be ignored. Speer learned that the Regional Leaders were preparing to flood the coalmines, blow up the lift machinery and block the canals. Speer and his team quietly disposed of the explosives and other equipment that would be needed to carry out the plan, met with the Regional Leaders and went some way towards persuading them of its impracticality. He had already arranged with Heinrici, Model and Guderian to preserve the physical infrastructure of the invaded areas, east and west, as far as was possible under conditions of war.[183]

Back in Berlin, Hitler accused his Armaments Minister of trying to persuade the Regional Leaders to countermand his orders, and told him that he would only keep his job if he could convince himself that the war could still be won. Speer demurred. There was no doubt that the war was lost, he said. Hitler asked him again, in 'an almost pleading tone, and for a moment,' Speer later recalled, 'I thought that in his piteousness he was even more persuasive than in his masterful poses. Under other circumstances I would probably have weakened and given in. This time, what kept me from submitting to his spell was the thought of his destructive plans.'[184] Hitler gave him twenty-four hours to come up with an answer. Speer drafted a letter of refusal, but Hitler's secretaries informed him they had been forbidden to type it on the special large-character typewriter used for documents to be perused by the short-sighted Leader, so Hitler would not be able to read it. Speer gave in. Back in the Chancellery, he told Hitler: 'My Leader, I stand unreservedly behind you.' Hitler's eyes filled with tears of affection and relief. Speer had avoided dismissal. Indeed, he secured Hitler's authority to imple-ment the Nero order himself and regained most of his powers. On 30 March 1945, following this interview, Speer persuaded Hitler to issue a clarification of the Nero order, which laid down that the destruc-tion had to take place only in order to deny the enemy the use of industrial plant to bolster his own military strength. It was permissible to do this by crippling plant rather than destroying it. Speer continued to work against Party fanatics who wanted to destroy everything. In practice, too, by this stage both industrial firms and their workers had every incentive to protect their factories and mines from destruction, and many of them did so.[185] In any case, such arguments were becoming increasingly academic as the Allied troops advanced further into the heartland of Germany.

Hitler's mood of apocalyptic defeatism alternated during these final weeks with outward displays of defiant confidence in his ability to turn the situation round. He continued to hope for a split in the alliance between the Soviet Union and the Western powers. Some, like the Chief of the Army General Staff Heinz Guderian, advocated surrendering in the west and throwing all Germany's troops and resources into the defence of Berlin against the Red Army, in the hope that this would persuade Britain and America to join a new struggle against the Soviet domination of Central Europe. But Hitler would not hear of any kind of surrender, not even a partial one, and accused Guderian of committing high treason. For the moment he took no further action, but from late January 1945 onwards, his meetings with the Chief of the Army General Staff were held with Ernst Kaltenbrunner, head of the SS Security Service, a silently menacing witness, in attendance. Others too, however, thought of pursuing a similar line, including Ribbentrop and Göring. Yet they were unwilling to take any serious steps towards a negotiated peace in the west in the light of Hitler's intransigence. Hitler himself blamed Britain's persistence in opposing him on Churchill's love of conflict, but he also thought that it would be easier to make peace with Stalin, who would not have to contend with the kind of independent public opinion that hamstrung the Western leaders. At the same time, however, he did not think Stalin could be brought to the negotiating table unless the Red Army was so severely beaten before the gates of Berlin that he saw no alternative, so the end result was the same here too: Germany had no alternative but to fight on.[186]

Hitler had not survived the attempt to kill him on 20 July 1944 entirely unscathed. Although the blast temporarily cured his Parkinsonian tremor, most easily visible in the shaking of his left hand and lower arm, it was back by the middle of September 1944, and to it was added dizziness, an inability to stand for long periods, and a serious ear injury that took many weeks to overcome. On 23 September 1944 he had developed severe stomach cramps, and four days later symptoms of jaundice. He had become exhausted, developed a high temperature and taken to his bed. Only on 2 October 1944 had he begun to recover; by this time he had lost 16 pounds in weight. The doctor treating him for his ear problem had tried to blame his symptoms on the pills Morell was prescribing him, and he had won the support of Hitler's other attending physicians, including Karl Brandt, but Hitler's reaction had simply been to dismiss them all and reaffirm his faith in Morell's expertise. Indeed, the fact that Hitler had recovered while continuing to take the pills gave the lie to their assertion that Morell was trying to poison the Nazi Leader.[187] Nevertheless, in the last months of his life, according to Albert Speer, Hitler's health continued to deteriorate. By early 1945, Hitler was, he wrote,

shrivelling up like an old man. His limbs trembled; he walked stooped, with dragging footsteps. Even his voice became quavering and lost its old masterfulness. Its force had given way to a faltering, toneless manner of speaking. When he became excited, as he frequently did in a senile way, his voice would start breaking . . . His complexion was sallow, his face swollen; his uniform, which in the past he had kept scrupulously neat, was often neglected in this last period of life and stained by the food he had eaten with a shaking hand.[188]

Perhaps it was pity for him, Speer thought, that kept his entourage from raising any objections 'when, in the long since hopeless situation, he continued to commit non-existent divisions or to order units supplied by planes that could no longer fly for lack of fuel'.[189] They listened in silence when he told them that Stalin and the west would surely come to blows before they had won the war, or claimed that, in such a situation, the west would find it impossible to do without him. Speer himself was still happy enough to spend time with him poring over the plans they had drawn up for the rebuilding of Linz after the war. Yet Hitler's charisma was now ebbing away even amongst his immediate following. Speer noted later that where once everyone had stood when he entered a room, 'now conversations continued, people remained seated, servants took their orders from guests, associates who had drunk too much went to sleep in their chairs, and others talked loudly and uninhibitedly'.[190]

Hitler now spent increasing amounts of time in the bunker complex beneath the Reich Chancellery. Initially he still lunched in the undamaged part of the Chancellery, but his apartment had been destroyed along with much else in an air raid on 3 February 1945, and he worked and slept underground, coming up only to exercise his dog Blondi in the Chancellery garden, surrounded by heaps of rubble. He would rise at midday or shortly afterwards, shave and dress, then have lunch before conducting a conference on the military situation, attended not only by senior commanders but also by Himmler, Bormann, Kaltenbrunner and sometimes Ribbentrop. After dinner, at around eight, there would be another military briefing, after which he would retire to his study and hold forth in his accustomed manner to his entourage until he went to bed, often at five or six in the morning.[191] On 24 February 1945, on the anniversary of the promulgation of the Nazi Party programme in 1920, Hitler held a final meeting for the Nazi Party Regional Leaders in a still-standing hall in the Reich Chancellery. Arriving from all over Germany, the 'Old Fighters', many of whom had not seen him for some months, were shocked by the way he had aged. He shuffled rather than walked into the room, his eyes were bloodshot, his left hand and arm were visibly trembling, and he had to give up an attempt to raise a glass of water to his mouth to refresh himself. One participant noticed that he occasionally dribbled as he spoke. Attempting to rally them for one last effort, he promised yet again the arrival of wonder-weapons that would change the course of the war. They had to get the people of their districts to fight on until the new weapons were deployed, he said. Otherwise, if the German people were defeated, it would be clear that they did not deserve to win. The faith he expressed in the wonder-weapons was patently not sincere. But his belief in the Darwinian doom about to overtake the German people certainly was.[192]

II

By now, indeed, Hitler was looking mainly to what he imagined would be his place in history. Issuing a proclamation to the armed forces on 11 March 1945 ('Heroes' Memorial Day'), he announced that he had decided to provide the world with an example, going down, he implied, fighting, rather than surrendering cravenly as had been the case in 1918. Goebbels too decided that, if defeat was to come, then it would be a heroic defeat. He would devote his final weeks to creating inspiring images of Nazi self-sacrifice for future generations. Goebbels tried to persuade Hitler to broadcast to the nation again, but the Leader replied gloomily that he had nothing new to offer, and he was aware of reports from the Security Service of the SS that his proclamation of 24 February 1945 had not met with a positive reception. Goebbels was deeply frustrated. But Hitler knew that propaganda had finally failed in the face of the hard facts of invasion and defeat. At another level, as he moved increasingly depleted and in some cases non-existent armies around on his map in the bunker conference room, Hitler was now living a life almost entirely removed from reality. Such illusions were shared in full by Martin Bormann, who exercised his power over the Nazi Party by issuing a stream of directives, decrees and exhortations on a whole variety of issues. Goebbels complained that he was making a paper chancellery out of the Party Chancellery. The Regional Leaders, he thought, would not have the time to read the decrees, let alone the means to implement them. In government ministries, civil servants continued working despite their rapidly shrinking sphere of influence, like cartoon characters running off the edge of a cliff and keeping going despite the yawning abyss beneath.[193]

At the Berlin headquarters of the Hitler Youth at this time, wrote Melita Maschmann:

Every one of us worked with hectic energy. Countless projects were started up, knocked out by the effects of the war, abandoned, taken up again, cancelled, altered, rejected once again and so on. During the last months of this, the feeling crept over us that all this feverish activity on the part of the Reich Youth Leadership was hardly producing the slightest response in the country. Our office was like a termites' nest, gradually pervaded by a sense of the coming collapse without a single person daring to breathe a syllable about it . . . Our brains gave birth to plans and still more plans, lest we should have a moment to stop and think and then to have to recognize that all this bustle was already beginning to resemble the convulsions of a dance of death.[194]

In the last weeks of the war, she gave up anything more than the occasional appearance at the office, and busied herself with helping refugees fleeing from the Red Army. Coming across a group of injured anti-aircraft auxiliaries, all schoolboys, many weeping after a bomb had destroyed their emplacement and killed many of their comrades, she heard one say when asked if he was in pain: 'Yes, but it doesn't matter, Germany must triumph.'[195] 'From all those weeks which immediately preceded the collapse of Germany,' she recalled, 'I cannot remember a single conversation in which the probability of our defeat was mentioned.'[196] But she moved in circles of true Nazi believers, of course. And even here, the atmosphere began to take on the bizarre characteristics of the last days of a crumbling empire. While Berlin burned, Maschmann's boss, Reich Youth Leader Arthur Axmann, a man who boasted regularly of his working-class origins, held social evenings at the Youth Leadership's inn at Gatow, to the west of Berlin, where, according to the puritanical Maschmann, by her account a reluctant participant, 'the eating and drinking there was often sheer gluttony', and the party-goers included film starlets, 'charlatans and self-important egoists'.[197]

The death of US President Franklin D. Roosevelt on 12 April 1945 momentarily lifted the gloom in Hitler's Berlin bunker. For Hitler, waving a newspaper clipping at Speer, this was 'the miracle I always predicted. Who was right? The war isn't lost. Read it! Roosevelt is dead!'[198] Providence had come to his aid again. For a short while, fantastic schemes circulated round the corridors of the bunker. Speer would fly to meet Roosevelt's successor, Harry S. Truman, and peace would be signed. Hitler's study had a picture of Frederick the Great on the wall; the Prussian King had recovered during the Seven Years' War even after the Russians had occupied Berlin, and Hitler took inspiration from his example: indeed, Goebbels memorized the passage from Thomas Carlyle's biography of the King in which the author, addressing the monarch directly, reassured him that he would prevail in the end, then recited it to the Nazi Leader as an encouragement.[199] Hitler felt that the American President's death was just like this turning-point in the wars of Frederick the Great, when the Tsarina Elizabeth had died, and Russia suddenly abandoned the anti-Prussian coalition. Before long, however, as it became clear that Truman had no intention of reneging on the policies of his predecessor, the brief euphoria subsided.[200] On 20 April 1945 the Red Army opened the assault on Berlin. It was Hitler's fifty-sixth birthday.

In previous years the Leader's birthday had been the occasion for nationwide festivities. Remembering these amidst the ruins of Berlin was too painful, and Hitler banned the usual office celebrations, though his staff none the less lined up in the bunker to give him their congratulations. Hitler emerged into the open briefly to review a small detachment of Hitler Youth in the Chancellery garden, where they had gathered with representatives of the army and the SS. He congratulated the boys, none of them more than fourteen years old, on their bravery, patted one or two of them, and then vanished below again. It was his last public appearance, and the last time he was formally caught on camera. In the following days, most of the remaining senior figures in the regime left the centre of Berlin, driving out of the city through the smouldering rubble on the few roads still left open before the Russians closed the circle. Speer, Dönitz, Himmler, Kaltenbrunner, Ribbentrop, Rosenberg and a host of government ministers were among them. Hitler sent most of his personal staff away by plane to Berchtesgaden. Hermann Göring had already shipped much of his enormous art collection from his hunting lodge Carinhall, north of Berlin, to the south in a convoy of trucks, before saying his goodbyes to Hitler and departing for Bavaria himself. Only a few remained, notably Bormann, Hitler's long-term factotum Julius Schaub, and the top military men, including Keitel and Jodl. Hitler now gave way to hysteria. He threatened to have his doctor, Morell, shot for trying to drug him with morphine. On 22 April 1945 he ranted at the generals. Everyone had betrayed him, he shouted, even the SS. Breaking down in despair, he told them for the first time openly that he knew the war was lost. He would stay and shoot himself. All attempts to dissuade him failed. Eventually Goebbels, to whom he had ranted in similar vein over the telephone, arrived and calmed him down. They agreed that the Propaganda Minister, his wife and his six young children would come to stay in the bunker for the final days. Hitler's two remaining secretaries had also volunteered to stay. Meanwhile, Schaub burned Hitler's private documents and then left for Berchtesgaden to make sure the same was done there.[201]

Two days later Speer returned to speak with Hitler one last time. Speer's claim that he confessed his disobedience to Hitler in an outpouring of emotion was a later invention. The two men did not discuss their personal relationship at all, despite their years of friendship. Hitler simply asked him if he should give in to the entreaties of his entourage and leave Berlin for Berchtesgaden. Speer's reply confirmed Hitler's own intentions: he would stay on in the Reich capital, and kill himself to avoid being captured by the Russians. Eva Braun, his long-time companion, who had arrived in the bunker some weeks before, would die with him. Their bodies would be burned to avoid desecration. After an eight-hour stay, Speer flew out again, this time for good.[202] Shortly afterwards Hitler's resolve was strengthened when he learned of the fate that had overtaken Mussolini and his mistress Clara Petacci. The pair were picked up by partisans on 27 April 1945 in a column of cars, trucks and armoured vehicles full of German troops and Italian Fascists on its way to Italy's northern border, near Lake Como. An armed detachment led by the Communist partisan 'Colonel Valerio', who had spent five years in prison in the 1930s for anti-Fascist activities, put them up against a wall and shot them with a sub-machine gun in an act of 'Italian people's justice'. After executing fifteen more prisoners in the small town of Dongo, Valerio and his squad took all the bodies to Milan, where they dumped them on the Piazzale Loreto. A crowd gathered and desecrated the corpses in every possible way, spitting and urinating on them and shouting insults. Eventually Mussolini, Petacci and some of the others were hung upside-down from the gantry of a petrol station, where they were exposed to further insults.[203] If anything were needed to confirm Hitler's decision to kill himself, this was surely it.

Only now, at the very end, did Hitler's closest associates begin to desert him. Informed of Hitler's intentions by one of the generals present at the Leader's hysterical outburst on 22 April, Hermann Göring assumed that the 1941 decree naming him as head of state if Hitler was unable to carry out his duties would now come into force. He sent a telegram to the bunker announcing that he would take over if he heard nothing by 10 p.m. on 24 April. Persuaded by Göring's arch-enemy Bormann that this was an act of treason, Hitler sent a reply rescinding the 1941 decree and demanding the Reich Marshal resign all his offices for reasons of health. Göring did as he was told. Within a few hours he was under house arrest on the Obersalzberg. Himmler was next to defect. For several weeks, the head of the SS had been secretly negotiating with the Swedish Red Cross for the release of Scandinavian prisoners from the remaining concentration camps. On 23 April 1945, hearing of Hitler's decision to kill himself, he met his intermediary, Count Bernadotte. Himmler grandly declared that he was now effectively the leader of Germany, and drafted an instrument of surrender to be passed to the Western Allies. Once more, Hitler exploded when he learned of what he called 'the most shameful betrayal in human history'. He took out his fury on one of Himmler's subordinates who had the misfortune to be in the bunker at the time: Hermann Fegelein, a corrupt SS officer who had entered Hitler's entourage by marrying Eva Braun's sister. Earlier in the week, Fegelein had left the bunker without warning and disappeared. He had been discovered later, in his apartment, drunk, dressed in civilian clothes and in the company of a young woman who was not his wife. Around him were bags full of money, ready for his getaway. Fegelein was arrested and brought before Hitler, who threw furious accusations at him. He was working for Himmler, he had disappeared from the bunker to plot Hitler's arrest or assassination, he was a traitor. Hitler convened a drumhead court-martial which sentenced Fegelein to death. The guilty man was taken up to ground level and executed by firing-squad.[204]

All the while, Hitler was still convening his military conferences and directing the defence of Berlin. But the armies he was ordering to punch through the Soviet lines or break through the gathering encirclement from outside scarcely existed any more as coherent units. They numbered no more than a few score thousand, hardly enough to repel more than 2 million Soviet troops now pushing forward for the final assault. By 25 April 1945 the Soviet generals Zhukov and Konev had closed the ring around Berlin and begun advancing through the suburbs towards the city centre. As in Stalingrad, the war degenerated into bitter, unco-ordinated street fighting. General Gotthard Heinrici, whose reputation as a skilful commander of defensive operations had brought him command of the Army Group defending the capital, had maintained a semblance of order only by ignoring Hitler's injunctions to stand firm, but on 29 April he finally resigned his post, unable to cope any longer with the Leader's increasingly meaningless commands.[205] Heinrici's patriotic convictions, together with the habits of military discipline and the fear of what would happen if he surrendered to the Russians, were still shared by many German soldiers, who carried on fighting even when all was so obviously lost. The thousands of members of the People's Storm who were drafted in to defend the capital were not so determined; many of them deserted to go back to their families whenever the opportunity presented itself.[206]

By 29 April 1945 Soviet troops were entering the government quarter round the Potsdamer Platz at the heart of Berlin. The end was surely only hours away. Hitler made his last preparations. He summoned a city councillor, Walter Wagner, to the bunker. Now that there was no longer any need for concealment, he said, he would marry Eva Braun. As bombs and shells crashed down outside, Wagner performed the ceremony in front of Goebbels and Bormann as witnesses. A short champagne reception followed. At three in the morning, Hitler heard from Keitel that the last attempt at relieving Berlin from the outside had failed. As dawn broke, Soviet guns began bombarding the Reich Chancellery above. The military commanders told Hitler that it would all be over by the end of the day. After lunch, Hitler said farewell to his secretaries. All the remaining inhabitants of the bunker had been given prussic acid capsules, but Hitler did not entirely trust their effectiveness, although the previous day he had successfully had his dog Blondi put down with one. He retired to his study with Eva Braun at half-past three in the afternoon. Opening the door ten minutes or so later, Hitler's valet Heinz Linge, accompanied by Bormann, found Hitler's body on the sofa, blood oozing from a hole in his right temple, his pistol at his feet;

Eva Braun's body was next to his, giving off a strong smell of bitter almonds. She had taken poison. Following Hitler's prior instructions, his personal adjutant Otto Günsche, assisted by Linge and three SS men, took the bodies, wrapped in blankets, up into the Reich Chancellery garden, where, watched by Bormann, Goebbels and the two remaining senior military officers, Krebs and Burgdorf, they were doused in a large quantity of petrol and set alight. Observing the macabre scene from behind the partly opened bunker door, the funeral party raised their arms in a last 'Hail, Hitler!' and returned underground. Not long after six in the evening, Günsche sent two SS men to bury the charred remains. All that remained to identify them when Soviet investigators found them a few days later were dental bridges that the technician who had worked for Hitler's dentist since 1938 certified belonged to the former Nazi leader and his companion.[207]

Hitler left a brief private will, disposing of his personal possessions, and a much longer 'Political Testament', dictated to his secretary on 29 April 1945, in which he denied bringing about the war that had begun in 1939. It was remarkable for its scarcely veiled confession – or rather, boast – that he had had the Jews killed in revenge for the part he supposed they had played in starting the war. That war, he reaffirmed, 'was willed and incited exclusively by those international statesmen who either were of Jewish descent or worked for Jewish interests'. Recalling once more his prophecy of 30 January 1939, and thinking of the First World War and, perhaps, the Depression that had been so crucial in bringing him to power, he reminded his future readers that he had left nobody in any doubt

that the real people to blame for this murderous struggle would be: the Jews! I further left nobody in any doubt that this time not only would millions of . . . grown men suffer death and not only would hundreds of thousands of women and children be incinerated in the cities and bombed to death, but also that the real guilty parties would also have to expiate their guilt, even if by more humane means.

He ended by calling upon Germany and the Germans 'to observe the racial laws precisely and to resist pitilessly the world-poisoner of all peoples, international Jewry'.[208]

III

After the completion of Hitler's will, Goebbels had dictated a codicil of his own to the secretary. Weeping copiously, he said that for the first time he was going to disobey a direct order from his Leader. Hitler had told him to leave Berlin. But he was going to stay 'at the Leader's side to end a life which for me personally has no further value if it cannot be used in the service of the Leader and by his side'.[209] The day before, Magda Goebbels had written to her son by her first marriage, informing him that she was going to kill herself along with her husband and their children:

The world that will come after the Leader and National Socialism will not be worth living in, and therefore I have taken my children away. They are too dear to endure what is coming next, and a merciful God will understand my intentions in delivering them from it. We have now only one aim: loyalty unto death to the Leader. That we can end our lives with him is a mercy of fate that we never dared hope for.[210]

At twenty to nine in the evening of 30 April 1945, Helmut Kunz, an SS doctor, gave each of the six Goebbels children a morphine injection to put them to sleep, then Ludwig Stumpfegger, Hitler's physician in the last period of his life, put a phial of prussic acid into each child's mouth and crushed it, causing instant death. Goebbels and his wife climbed up the steps to the Reich Chancellery garden, and bit on their capsules. An SS man shot each body twice just to make sure they were dead. The bodies were then set alight, but there was very little petrol left over from the incineration of Hitler and Eva Braun's corpses, so the bodies of Joseph and Magda Goebbels were easily recognized by the Red Army troops when they came into the garden the following day.[211] The two remaining generals, Wilhelm Burgdorf and Hans Krebs (Hitler's last Chief of the Army General Staff) also killed themselves, along with the commander of Hitler's military escort, Franz Schädle. The rest of the bunker's inhabitants made their way into an underground railway tunnel in a desperate attempt to escape. Emerging into the open at the Friedrichstrasse station, they were confronted by a scene of unbelievable devastation, with shells falling everywhere, the buildings reduced to smoking rubble, and Soviet troops engaging small groups of German soldiers in the final assault. Amidst the noise and confusion, the secretaries and a few others somehow succeeded in evading capture and found their way to the west; others, including Günsche and Linge, were taken prisoner; many were killed by stray bullets or suspicious Soviet soldiers. Bormann and Stumpfegger managed to get as far as the Invalidenstrasse but found their way blocked by Red Army troops and took poison to avoid capture.[212]

The deaths in the bunker and the burned-out streets above were only the crest of a vast wave of suicides without precedent in modern history. Like Hitler, some senior Nazis killed themselves out of a warped sense of honour, fearing the indignity of being put on trial, the shame of being publicly condemned for their crimes, and the insults that would perhaps be done to their bodies. Hermann Göring was the most prominent among them. As American troops entered his Bavarian hideout near Berchtesgaden on 9 May 1945, he gave himself up voluntarily, evidently thinking he would be regarded as a significant figure from a defeated regime who would be used to negotiate terms of surrender. The American commander shook his hand and gave him a meal, after which reporters were allowed to quiz him on his role in the Third Reich and his views on what lay ahead ('I see a black future for Germany and the whole world'). A furious Eisenhower embargoed the reports and had Göring moved to prison, put on a diet, weaned off his drug dependency and subjected to gentle but persistent interrogation. Recovering much of his former energy, the ex-Reich Marshal charmed his interrogators and impressed his captors with the way he quickly came to dominate his fellow prisoners. Unrepentant and still proud of what he had done, he was condemned to death by hanging, and when his demand that he should be allowed to die an honourable soldier's death before a firing-squad was rejected, he obtained a poison capsule, probably through one of the guards, and killed himself on 15 October 1946.[213]

Almost a year before this, the former German Labour Front leader Robert Ley had hanged himself in the prison cell where he was awaiting trial. Ley's mental deterioration, caused by a combination of an air crash during the First World War and heavy drinking thereafter, accelerated under the conditions of confinement, and he occupied himself mainly by writing lengthy letters to his wife, Inge, who had herself committed suicide in 1942. He also wrote in the dead Inge's imaginary responses to his letters ('You have courageously portrayed the Leader as he really is: *The greatest German of all time*') and tried to communicate with the American automobile manufacturer Henry Ford, whom he regarded, not without some justification, as a fellow antisemite. On receiving his indictment for war crimes, Ley shouted: 'Stand us against the wall and shoot us! You are the victors!' He rejected the charges laid against him and killed himself, as he wrote in his suicide note, because he could not bear the shame of being treated as a criminal when he was none.[214] Heinrich Himmler also killed himself. Leaving Flensburg disguised with an eye-patch and a false passport, and accompanied by a few aides, including Otto Ohlendorf, Himmler had managed to cross the river Elbe before running into a British checkpoint, where he and his companions were arrested. On their arrival at an internment camp near Lüneburg, the commandant sent the others to their cells while detaining Himmler (a 'small, miserable-looking and shabbily dressed' man) for further questioning. Realizing the game was up, Himmler took off the eyepatch and put on a pair of spectacles instead. It was instantly obvious who he was, even before he whispered the name 'Heinrich Himmler'. He was searched, and a phial of poison was taken off him, but his interrogators were still not satisfied, and ordered a medical examination. When the doctor ordered Himmler to open his mouth, he noticed a small black object between the SS leader's teeth. As he took Himmler's head to turn it towards the light for a better look, Himmler snapped his teeth sharply together. There was a crunching sound, and he fell to the ground. He had bitten into a glass cyanide capsule and was dead within seconds. He was forty-four years old. Other leading SS officers followed his example, including Odilo Globocnik, who also took poison, Ernst Grawitz, the SS chief medical officer and enthusiastic experimenter on concentration camp inmates, who blew himself up together with his family by detonating two hand-grenades, and Friedrich Wilhelm Krüger, the SS and police chief who had made such trouble for Hans Frank in the Polish General Government.[215]

Hans Kammler, the senior SS officer who had been the key figure in the recruitment and exploitation of forced labour at the Dora-Central Works rocket factory, had acquired one last promotion from a grateful Hitler, who just before the end of the war had given him the entirely meaningless title 'Plenipotentiary of the Leader for Jet Aircraft'. After travelling across Germany trying to rally SS forces for a last stand, Kammler finally arrived in Prague, where he was shot by his adjutant, on his own command, at the very end of the war, desperate to avoid falling into the hands of Czech partisans.[216] Theodor Dannecker, the roving ambassasdor of death responsible for the deportation of many Jews to Auschwitz from different countries, fled to relatives in the north German town of Celle at the end of the war, but was arrested on a visit to his wife in Berlin on 9 December 1945, where he was denounced by her neighbours. The following day, he hanged himself in prison. On hearing of his death, his wife decided to kill herself along with their two young sons, but, as she was murdering the older boy, his cries awoke his younger brother, and she was unable to complete the killings. She was arrested and tried, but acquitted on grounds of diminished responsibility, and emigrated to Australia.[217] Another senior SS officer, Philipp Bouhler, head of Hitler's personal Chancellery and organizer of the 'euthanasia' murders of the mentally ill and handicapped, killed himself together with his wife on 19 May 1945.[218]

Reich Education Minister Bernhard Rust committed suicide on 8 May 1945, finally belying the reputation for indecision he had acquired during his years of office. Reich Justice Minister Otto-Georg Thierack was arrested by the British, and killed himself in an internment camp on 2 November 1946. The President of the Reich Supreme Court, Erwin Bumke, killed himself too, while the Reich Doctors' Leader Leonardo Conti, who was arrested and imprisoned prior to being tried in Nuremberg for his part in the murder of mental patients, hanged himself in his cell on 6 October 1945. Konrad Henlein, leader of the Sudeten German Nazis, killed himself after being captured by the Americans. Altogether, 8 out of 41 Regional Leaders, 7 out of 47 Higher SS and Police Leaders, 53 out of 554 army generals, 14 out of 98 air force generals and 11 out of 53 admirals killed themselves. Field Marshal Walter Model, Hitler's favourite military man, shot himself in a forest near Düsseldorf towards the end of April 1945 in order to avoid the shame of surrendering, in conformity with the injunction Hitler himself had issued to all German troops. Another general, Johannes Blaskowitz, who had been denied promotion after condemning German atrocities in Poland in 1939, was none the less arraigned for war crimes and eventually killed himself by jumping out of his cell window at Nuremberg on 5 February 1948. Regional Leader Jakob Sprenger of Hesse-Nassau committed suicide along with his wife as soon as he heard of Hitler's death.[219]

Many others contemplated suicide. Rudolf Höss, the former commandant of Auschwitz, considered death as an option in 1945. 'With the Leader gone, our world had gone. Was there any point in going on living?' Eventually, after much debate, Höss and his wife decided in the end to live on 'because of the children'. He later came to regret this decision. 'We were bound and fettered to that other world, and we should have disappeared with it.'[220]

His attitude was shared by many other Nazis, especially young people whose adult lives had been wholly bound up with the regime. Melita Maschmann

was firmly convinced that I would not outlive the 'Third Reich'. If it was condemned to go under, then so was I. The one thing would automatically follow the other without my having to do anything about it. I did not picture my death as a last sacrifice which I should have to make. Nor did I think of suicide. I was filled with a shadowy impression that 'my world' would be flung off its course, like a constellation in a cosmic catastrophe, and would drag me with it – like a tiny speck of dust – into outer darkness.[221]

She and her friends did not, she confessed, 'want anything to outlive the Third Reich'.[222] In the event, she too decided to live on and face the unknown terrors of a future without Nazism. Others were more determined. Interviewed by Gitta Sereny in 1991, Martin Bormann's son told how he had been driven to the Obersalzberg when his school, the Reich School of the Nazi Party at Feldafing, was closed on 23 April 1945, and was sitting with many of the staff from his father's office and the Berghof in a nearby inn on 1 May when the radio announced Hitler's death. Everyone was still and silent for a while, he remembered, 'but very soon afterwards, people started to go outside, first one – then there was a shot. Then another, and yet another. Not a word inside, no other sound except those shots from outside, but one felt that that was all there was, that all of us would have to die.' So the fifteen-year-old Bormann too went out, carrying his gun. 'My world was shattered; I couldn't see any future at all.' But in the back yard of the inn, 'where bodies were already lying all over the small garden', he saw another boy, aged eighteen, sitting on a log, and he 'told me to come and sit with him. The air smelled good, the birds sang, and we talked ourselves out of it.'[223]

Out of the many who contemplated killing themselves at this time, however, a good number did indeed take the fatal step. The wave of suicides went far beyond the ranks of committed Nazis. In a report on

popular behaviour and morale drawn up at the end of March 1945, the
Security Service of the SS recorded an atmosphere such as might be
found at the end of the world:

A large part of the people has become used to living only for the day. Any
kind of pleasures that present themselves are exploited. Even the most pointless
occasion is taken as an opportunity to drink down the last bottle, originally
reserved for the celebration of victory, the end of the blackout, the return of
husband and son. People are getting used to the idea of making an end to
themselves. Everywhere there is a great demand for poison, for a pistol, and for
other means of putting an end to life. Suicides out of genuine despair at the
catastrophe that is expected with certainty are on the agenda.[224]

Earlier the same month, the pastor at the Kaiser Wilhelm Memorial
Church in Berlin had felt it necessary to deliver a sermon against suicide.
But his words were not heeded. Official statistics recorded a jump from
238 suicides in the capital city in March 1945 to no fewer than 3,881
the following month, falling to 977 in May. Ordinary citizens were
disoriented, despairing, unable to see a future after the collapse of the
Third Reich. Suicide notes discovered by the police mentioned 'the
current situation', or 'fear of the Russian invasion', as a reason for
killing oneself, without going into further detail. As one said, 'life did
not have a point' any more after the end of the Third Reich. A number
of parents underlined their lack of a future perspective by killing their
children before they killed themselves.'[225]

Suicide rates rose almost everywhere, including in Catholic regions,
though here it is likely that they were affected by an influx of refugees
from Protestant areas, where the taboo on killing oneself was not so
strong. In Upper Bavaria, for example, there were 421 suicides in April
and May 1945, in comparison to only three to five in the same months
in previous years. But such increases were dwarfed by those recorded in
the areas invaded by the Red Army, including Berlin. In the city's district
of Friedrichshain, a grammar-school student reported that more than a
hundred people killed themselves the day the Russians arrived. 'A blessing that there is no gas,' she added, 'otherwise even more would have
taken their lives; perhaps we might also be dead.'[226] In the Pomeranian
village of Schivelbein, a Protestant clergyman reported that 'whole good,
churchgoing families took their lives, drowned themselves, hanged themselves, slit their wrists, or allowed themselves to be burned up along

with their homes' as soon as the Red Army arrived. Mass suicides were reported from other small Pomeranian towns – 500 in Schönlanke, for example, and 700 in Demmin, following the arrival of the Red Army. The burial register for the town of Teterow, where some 10,000 people lived in 1946, recorded 120 suicides in early May. Rapes by Russian soldiers were undoubtedly a major reason for this increase. In Teterow, shame and wounded masculinity after such incidents drove fathers of families to kill their wives and children, often with the woman's consent, before killing themselves. In the Sudetenland, it was reported that 'whole families would dress up in their Sunday finest, surrounded by flowers, crosses and family albums, and then kill themselves by hanging or poison'.[227]

Yet suicide was always a minority action. Many committed Nazis were thrown into confusion without succumbing to despair. Charlotte L., born in 1921 and employed doing welfare work in the Reich Labour Service, was a convinced Nazi who seems to have had no thought of killing herself. Political education had inspired a burning commitment in her. Writing in her diary on 5 February 1940, she had recorded the 'pleasure' with which she had taken a class on 'the consequences of Jewry'.[228] By 22 April 1945 the Americans had occupied her home town of Helmstedt, but Charlotte still refused to accept that the war was lost. 'I believe firmly in our Leader,' she wrote, '& that Germany has a future that we Germans deserve.' Her world collapsed when she heard that Hitler was dead. 'Our beloved Leader, who has done everything for us, for Germany.' She was disgusted at how many people were now changing their views. 'As wonderful as things were under the Leadership of Adolf Hitler,' she wrote on 3 June 1945, 'they can no longer be for a long time. The newspapers are telling lies and screwing up their propaganda beyond measure. Behind all this stands the Jew. Will the world ever realize that the Jew is the evil for us all?' she asked. Inge Molter, daughter of an active Nazi, also carried on hoping for victory until the very end. But gradually such people also began to achieve distance from the Nazi leadership. After her husband, the former stormtrooper Alfred, had gone missing during the final battle for Berlin, she obtained a job as a nurse in a hospital where a doctor told her at length of the atrocities the Nazis had committed. 'I often really don't know any more,' she wrote to her absent husband, in whose death she still refused to believe, 'how I regard all those things.

Sometimes I really have to think now that it wouldn't have been good if we had won the war.'[229]

IV

On 5 May 1945 the soldier and former stormtrooper Gerhard M. found time once more to write an entry in his diary. 'Our Leader Adolf Hitler,' he began, 'is no more.' But, he continued with evident puzzlement, 'This fact has not shattered us as one might have supposed.' With his comrades he had spent a little time reminiscing about the adventures of the previous twenty years. 'Then, however, everyday life carried on anyway, and we reconciled ourselves to it. Life goes on, even if the last Leader of the Great German Reich is no more.'[230] Similar reactions were reported by others. The German people had been officially told in a radio broadcast just before half-past ten at night on 1 May 1945 that Hitler had died heroically fighting to defend the capital of the Reich against the Bolshevik hordes. The truth would have undermined any further will to fight, and thereby destroyed any last remaining possibility of a negotiated settlement – a possibility that in fact only existed in the imagination of the new leaders of the Reich. Indeed, when the German commander in Berlin told his troops to lay down their arms, on 2 May 1945, he justified his order by telling them that Hitler had abandoned them by killing himself.[231] Many people refused to believe what seemed to them an unlikely story, and speculated that Hitler had taken poison. In any case, with his death, the last remaining reason for supporting Nazism had evaporated. There were no scenes of grief. No distraught citizens wept in public, as Russians were to do on the death of Stalin eight years later. The eighteen-year-old Erika S. went out on to the streets of Hamburg shortly after the announcement of Hitler's death to see how people were reacting. 'Strange,' she reported, 'nobody wept or even looked sad, although the beloved, honoured Leader, whom the total idiots regarded almost as a God, is no longer alive . . . Strange . . .' Only in school did she see a few girls weeping after the announcement in the morning assembly.[232]

Lore Walb, whose admiration of Hitler had been boundless five years before, now wrote, on 2 May 1945:

Hitler *fallen*, now he is at rest, it's surely the best thing for him. But ourselves? We're abandoned and delivered up to all and sundry and in our lifetime we can't rebuild any more what this war has destroyed. In the beginning the ideas Hitler wanted to realize were positive, and in domestic policy some good things happened. But he failed totally in foreign policy, and particularly as the supreme warlord. 'The path of an idea'. What a path! And the people must now pay for it ... What a bitter end ... Hitler is dead now. But we and those who are to come will carry throughout our lives the burden he laid on us.[233]

'That's now the end,' wrote a twenty-three-year-old office worker in Hamburg on 2 May 1945. 'Our Leader, who promised us so much, has achieved what nobody in power in Germany has so far achieved, he has left behind a Germany that is totally destroyed, he has taken away everyone's house and home, he has driven them from their homeland, he has caused millions to die, in short, he has achieved an appalling chaos.'[234]

After experiencing the bombing of her home town of Siegen and then hand-to-hand fighting between German and American troops as she cowered in a cellar, one fifteen-year-old girl who had believed in the promise that Germany would win at the last minute with new, secret weapons could see all was lost. 'I had to go into the dining room on my own, and there I threw myself on to the sofa and wept bitterly.' Everything had been destroyed. 'At first I didn't feel any resentment against the Leader ... but now, now I have fought through to the opinion that the Leader isn't worth feeling sorry for.' She felt betrayed by him, and by the other Nazi leaders, who were now committing suicide one after the other. Now indeed she could see the sense of the assassination attempt of 20 July 1944, which she had condemned so bitterly at the time. 'The men of 20th July had realized that the Leader's death was Germany's only salvation.'[235] In Hamburg on 30 April 1945, hearing of Hitler's death, which she believed to have been caused by his having poisoned himself, Luise Solmitz at last felt free to release the hatred that she had been building up for him over the previous months. He was, she wrote in her diary, 'the shabbiest failure in world history'. He was 'uncompromising, unbridled, irresponsible', qualities that had at first brought him success but then led to catastrophe. 'National Socialism,' she now thought, 'brought together all the crimes and depravities of all the centuries.' Twelve years previously she had thought very differently, but 'Hitler turned me from a meek and mild being into an opponent of war.' Goebbels was also dead: but 'no death can expunge such crimes'. As for Hitler: 'Now that we hopefully have his unimaginable crimes, lies, meannesses behind us, his botch-ups and his incompetence, his 5 years and 8 months of war, most Germans are saying: the best day of our life!' She noted: 'Hitler's promise: "Give me 10 years and you'll see what I've made out of Germany" has for months been his most often-quoted, out of bitterness.' On 5 May 1945 the Solmitzes burned their Nazi flag. But it was not just Nazism that was defeated. 'Never has a people supported such a bad cause with such enthusiasm,' she wrote on 8 May 1945, perhaps thinking of her own earlier attitudes, 'never so impelled itself to self-annihilation'. The Germans were 'lemmings' rushing to self-destruction. Not only the Nazis, but also the Germans, she concluded, had lost.[236]

Life went on not least because most people were far too busy trying to keep themselves alive amidst the ruins of the Reich to worry overmuch about Hitler's death, its meaning or its possible consequences. The arrangements Hitler made in his Political Testament for the continuation of government were an irrelevance in a situation where most of the Reich was now in the hands of the Allies. He rewarded Grand Admiral Karl Dönitz for his loyalty by making him Reich President, a post which Hitler had once said was so bound up with the memory of the previous incumbent, Paul von Hindenburg, that it should never be reinvented. Clearly, inconsistency was not going to get in the way of Hitler's own exclusive purchase on the title 'Leader'. Dönitz was also made head of the armed forces. Goebbels was named Reich Chancellor and Bormann Party Minister. Goebbels had managed finally to secure the dismissal of his hated and despised rival Joachim von Ribbentrop as Foreign Minister and his replacement by Arthur Seyss-Inquart, while Karl Hanke, a Regional Leader still resisting the Red Army in beleaguered Breslau, was named Himmler's successor as Reich Leader of the SS. The disloyal Speer was replaced as Armaments Minister by Karl-Otto Saur, and Goebbels's State Secretary Werner Naumann was promoted to the position of Propaganda Minister. A few existing ministers, like Backe, Funk, Schwerin von Krosigk and Thierack were allowed to continue in government. But by now they had virtually nothing left to govern. From his headquarters in Flensburg, near the Danish border in Schleswig-Holstein, Dönitz tried to buy time to allow the troops still fighting the

Red Army to withdraw to the west by agreeing to the surrender of the German forces in northern Italy, north-west Germany, Denmark and the Netherlands. The German armies in Austria and Bavaria capitulated as well, under orders from their commander, Albert Kesselring. Dönitz's tactic was partially successful, allowing over one and three-quarter million German troops to surrender to the Americans or the British instead of the Soviets, whose tally of prisoners amounted to less than a third of the total. But his bid to negotiate a separate general capitulation to the Western Allies met with a brusque rejection. Under threat of a continuation of bombing raids, Jodl agreed to a total and unconditional surrender, to be effective by the end of 8 May 1945, authorized reluctantly by Dönitz and signed in the early hours of 7 May 1945. The act was repeated with the full text drawn up earlier by all four Allies at Marshal Zhukov's headquarters outside Berlin two days later, backdated to the previous day. The war was over.[237]

AFTERMATH

I

For the vast majority of Germans, 8 May 1945 did not come as a
liberation, however much it might have appeared as such in retrospect.
Germany's defeat was unambiguous. People were struggling to adjust
their minds to the new situation, and to free themselves from the moral
and mental burden of Nazism. Many had already taken the first steps
along this road. The end of the war for the Germans was not a single
event but a process, affecting different people at different times, over a
period of months, as the Allied armies advanced slowly across the
Reich. Wherever and whenever they were overrun by the Allied armies,
however, the German people submitted meekly to their conquerors.
The partisan organization which Himmler and Bormann had hoped to
organize against the Allied occupation, in imitation of the Soviet partisans who had caused so much havoc in the German rear during the
previous years, was set up too late for any real momentum to develop.
Known as the 'Werewolf' movement, it tried to recruit fanatics of the
Hitler Youth generation for continuing resistance behind the lines. A
few units were formed, and on 25 March 1945 one of them managed
to assassinate Franz Oppenhoff, who had been installed as mayor
of Aachen by the invading Allies.[238] In the Bavarian mining town of
Penzberg, the workers deposed the Nazi mayor in order to open the way
for the advancing American troops to enter the area peacefully, but a
local army unit arrested them and executed them on the orders of the
Munich Regional Party Leader, and further executions took place when
a Werewolf unit arrived on the scene.[239] But such actions were isolated
and without wider-reaching consequences. For this, there were many
reasons.

To begin with, the Nazi Party, like the SS, the armed forces and virtually every other organization in the Third Reich, was in a state of complete disintegration and collapse. Large numbers of people who might in other circumstances have been able to provide leadership for a resistance movement were dead or captured. Communication was difficult if not impossible. The death of Hitler had in any case destroyed the factor that had cemented many people's loyalty to the Nazi cause. Many people had believed they were fighting for Hitler as much as for Germany; there seemed little reason to go on fighting now he was gone. More generally, Nazi dogma, repeated on innumerable occasions throughout the history of the Third Reich, proclaimed that 'might is right', that success carried its own justification with it. Germany's total defeat seemed therefore to confirm that the Allies after all had right on their side, a belief strengthened by the strong feelings of guilt for the extermination of the Jews that had begun to haunt the consciences of many Germans well before the end of the war. So complete was the defeat, so all-encompassing the devastation of Germany, that many patriots in any case blamed Hitler and the Nazis for it. Nobody could argue it away. Moreover, the Allied presence in Germany was pervasive, and the Allied occupying forces were very much alert to the threat of a partisan or resistance movement thanks to the propaganda pumped out by Goebbels's media urging young Germans to join it. On the other hand, the Allied forces, including even after the first few weeks the Russians and the French, proved less vengeful and more sympathetic than ordinary Germans had feared. Goebbels's prophecy that millions of Germans would be taken off to Siberia proved unfounded, even in the east. Resistance movements had indeed emerged to the German occupation of other European countries, but (with the exception of Yugoslavia) only after an initial period of two or three years when the vast majority of people were waiting to see which way the war would go, resigned to occupation at least for the time being. The same was the case in Germany. And finally, the Nazis had never won more than 37.4 per cent of the votes in a free national election. At times, notably following the victories of 1940, their popularity had been far greater. But popular opinion in Germany as elsewhere was commonly fickle and volatile, and by early 1945 support for the Nazis, as we have seen, had sunk to depths not plumbed since the middle of the 1920s.

Nevertheless, there were, of course, large numbers of committed Nazis

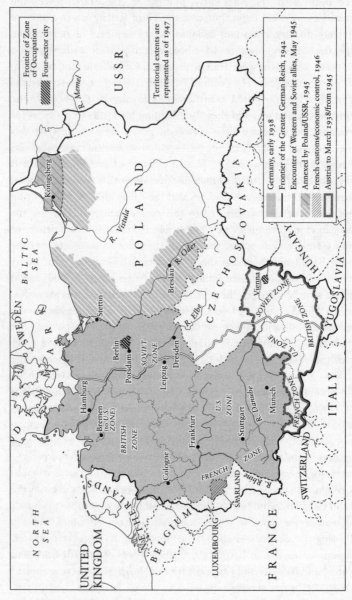

23. Post-War Arrangements in Central Europe

still at large in Germany at the end of the war despite all the suicides and deaths. To deal with them, and in particular to settle accounts with the remaining Nazi leaders, the Allies established an International Military Tribunal at Nuremberg. In a series of trials, beginning with the major war criminals (November 1945 to October 1946), Allied prosecutors presented a wealth of evidence of Nazi criminality, accusing Göring, Ribbentrop and others of waging an aggressive war of conquest, committing the mass murder of innocent civilians and carrying out a wide variety of atrocities and crimes against humanity and in violation of internationally agreed laws of war. The legitimacy of the proceedings was undermined to a degree by the participation of Soviet judges and by the Western Allies' carpet-bombing of German cities. It proved difficult to make some of the charges stick, notably the charge of conspiracy. Nevertheless, the Tribunal established a crucial precedent for the future. It was also widely publicized. The reporters present included William L. Shirer, who had left Germany in December 1940, possibly because he was told the Gestapo were compiling a dossier on his activities. Shirer subsequently used the documentary evidence compiled for the trial as an important source for his best-selling history of Nazi Germany, *The Rise and Fall of the Third Reich*, which he published in 1960 and which was still in print at the time of his death thirty-three years later. For the mass of ordinary Germans, however – some at least of whom had been made by Allied troops to help clear up the dead bodies of prisoners in concentration camps at the end of the war – the trials were further evidence, along with the bombing and the expulsions of ethnic Germans from Eastern Europe, that they were being singled out as victims in a war where justice was inevitably being meted out by the victors.[240]

The Nuremberg trial of the major war criminals resulted in a number of death sentences being handed out, one of them (Bormann) *in absentia*. Hans Frank (General Governor of Poland), Wilhelm Frick (Reich Interior Minister and Reich Protector of Bohemia and Moravia since 1943), Hermann Göring, General Alfred Jodl (head of operations at the Combined Armed Forces Supreme Command), Ernst Kaltenbrunner (head of the Security Service of the SS from 1943), Wilhelm Keitel (Jodl's superior), Joachim von Ribbentrop, Alfred Rosenberg, Fritz Sauckel, Arthur Seyss-Inquart and Julius Streicher were all sentenced to death; all were executed apart from Göring, who, as we have seen, committed suicide the night before he was due to be hanged. Rudolf Hess was sentenced to life imprisonment. He spent his last years as a solitary prisoner in Spandau jail and hanged himself in 1987 at the age of ninety-three, the last of the Nazi suicides. Hans Fritzsche, head of the news division in the Propaganda Ministry and a well-known radio commentator, was tried as a substitute for Goebbels, but it was clear that his crimes were in no way comparable to those of his boss, and he was acquitted. Hjalmar Schacht, the economics supremo in the 1930s, who had largely provided the funding for rearmament before the war, was also acquitted; he had after all retired some time before the war began. He wrote his memoirs and died in 1970 at the age of ninety-three. Walther Funk, his successor, received a life term but was released on health grounds in 1957, dying three years later. Karl Dönitz was sentenced to ten years' imprisonment, served his full term and died in 1980; his predecessor as head of the navy, Erich Raeder, was sentenced to life imprisonment but was released on health grounds in 1955, dying in 1960. Konstantin von Neurath received a fifteen-year sentence but was freed because of ill-health in 1954; he died two years later. His fellow aristocrat Franz von Papen, Hitler's Vice-Chancellor in 1933–4 and subsequently Ambassador to Austria and then Turkey, was acquitted, but rearrested and sentenced to eight years in prison for war crimes by a German court in 1947; he was released on appeal two years later and died in 1969. Baldur von Schirach, leader of the Hitler Youth and subsequently Regional Leader of Vienna, was sentenced to twenty years in jail; released on 1 October 1966, he died on 8 August 1974.[241]

Albert Speer was also sentenced to twenty years in jail at Nuremberg. He escaped a death sentence by presenting a subtle and sophisticated mixture of self-exculpation and self-blame. He had not known about Auschwitz, he said – a palpable untruth – but he should have done. Some thought his smooth, professional middle-class demeanour had won over the judges, and that he was as much to blame for the murderous exploitation of forced labour as was Fritz Sauckel, whose rough image earned him the noose instead. During his time at Spandau prison, Speer fought boredom and lassitude by measuring out during his daily constitutional an imaginary walk round the globe, and wrote a secret diary (on lavatory paper), as well as more than 25,000 letters, smuggled out by sympathetic visitors. He was released in 1966, and published a widely acclaimed set of memoirs. The book was remarkable for its frank appraisal of his relationship with Hitler, and for its shrewd judgements on the Nazi system of rule. But as time went on, it also became clear that the memoirs were less than honest. Speer embellished or edited many incidents, usually to his own credit, and concealed his knowledge of the extermination of the Jews. Towards the end of his life, in a remarkable series of interviews with the journalist Gitta Sereny, Speer was forced to retreat from the position he had adopted in his memoirs on many issues of detail, but, despite Sereny's claim to the contrary, he admitted no more to her about his knowledge of Auschwitz than he had to the court at Nuremberg. He died of a stroke during a visit to London in August 1981.[242]

There were other trials apart from those held at Nuremberg. Many of them were held in Poland, among them the trial of Rudolf Höss, former commandant of Auschwitz. At the end of the war, Höss went to the holiday island of Sylt, entering the Naval Intelligence School under a false identity. He managed to find work on a farm under an assumed name, but was finally tracked down and arrested on 11 March 1946. He had accidentally broken his little phial of poison two days before. He was harshly treated and complained of being beaten and he signed confessions that were not wholly accurate. The interrogators, he claimed, were all Jews. Höss did not abandon his Nazi convictions. Before the war, he thought, the concentration camps had been necessary and served a valuable purpose as re-education centres. But the extermination of the Jews had been 'fundamentally wrong' because it had not only drawn down on Germany 'the hatred of the entire world' but also 'in no way served the cause of antisemitism, but on the contrary brought the Jews far closer to their ultimate objective'.[243] Höss was brought to the Nuremberg War Crimes Tribunal on a number of occasions as a witness, most notably for the defence of Ernst Kaltenbrunner, but most of the time he was imprisoned in Cracow, where he wrote a lengthy autobiography, inaccurate in many details but unconsciously revealing the attitudes and beliefs that had made him the commandant of the largest murder factory in history. On 11 March 1947 Höss was brought into the dock in a trial attended by numerous foreign observers; he was found guilty of murder, sentenced to death and hanged in the main camp at Auschwitz, next to the SS camp administration building, on 16 April 1947.[244]

Later in the year, in November 1947, the Cracow Supreme Court tried forty SS officers and guards from the camp. Twenty-three were sentenced to death, including the camp leader, Hans Aumeier, and another former commandant, Arthur Liebehenschel. Others received prison sentences of varying length; one, the SS doctor Hans Münch, who had researched malnutrition among prisoners, was acquitted because of many testimonials on his behalf from former inmates. The engineer Kurt Prüfer, who had designed the gas chambers, was arrested in Erfurt in 1946 and sent to a Soviet labour camp, where he died in 1952. Ludwig Topf, co-owner of the firm Prüfer had worked for, Topf & Sons, committed suicide, but his brother, Ernst Wolfgang Topf, escaped unscathed and set up a new business in Wiesbaden making ovens for crematoria. Of the manufacturers of the poison gas Zyklon-B, two, the owner and chief executive of the Hamburg firm Tesch and Stabenow, were executed by a British military court, but others, including the general director of Degesch, Gerhard Peters, were acquitted.[245] Those executed after being tried for their crimes in various European countries included Friedrich Jeckeln, the SS commander who had been responsible for massacres of Jews in Riga and elsewhere; Otto Ohlendorf and Werner Naumann, who had led the murderous SS Task Forces in the east; the police chief Kurt Daluege; the SS commander who had destroyed the Warsaw ghetto uprising, Jürgen Stroop; the head of the concentration camp organization, Oswald Pohl; and the Nazi Party Regional Leaders Arthur Greiser and Albert Forster, who had ruled over the incorporated territories in Poland. Erich Koch, Regional Leader of East Prussia, was condemned to death by the Poles, but his sentence was commuted to life imprisonment on grounds of ill-health. Many others were condemned to lengthy terms of imprisonment.[246] The diarist Felix Landau, an Austrian SS man responsible for mass shootings as part of a Task Unit in occupied eastern Poland in 1941, and further murders carried out in his capacity as organizer of Jewish forced labour in the Lemberg district, was recognized in Linz by one of his former workers in 1946 and put in a prison camp by the Americans, but the following year he escaped. He lived as an interior decorator under a false name near Nördlingen until his arrest in 1959, followed by his trial and sentence to life imprisonment in 1962; he died in 1983.[247]

II

Apart from the trial of the 'major war criminals', twelve other trials at Nuremberg, involving 184 defendants, were held by the American occupying authorities to deal with a variety of lesser offenders. At the first of them, senior medical men were arraigned for carrying out cruel experiments on human beings without their consent, for killing the mentally ill and handicapped in the 'euthanasia' action, and other crimes. Among them were Viktor Brack and Karl Brandt: both were convinced they had done nothing wrong in ordering the killing of the handicapped; both were sentenced to death. In other trials, members of staff at the 'euthanasia' centres were tried for their crimes. Hermann Pfannmüller was sentenced to five years' imprisonment in 1951, and Friedrich Mennecke killed himself while under sentence of death.[248] The two medical scientists who had deliberately infected the Pontine marshes with malaria in 1943, causing in all probability 100,000 Italians to catch the disease and an unknown number to die of it, had mixed fortunes after the war. Ernst Rodenwaldt, denounced by his students for his Nazi affiliations, lost his chair, but he had the backing of a number of his colleagues, and was commissioned by the Allies to compile a report on hygiene in the Third Reich (from which he tactfully omitted his own special area of racial hygiene). He published an epidemiological atlas of the world and some works of medical history and issued a suitably discreet volume of memoirs. The Institute of War Medicine and Hygiene of the West German Army, located in Koblenz, was named after him in 1967.[249] Martini continued to publish as well, though he was not able to return to his post in Hamburg. In 1952 he published a fourth edition of his standard textbook on medical entomology. He died in 1960.[250]

Dr Josef Mengele, whose selections on the ramp at Auschwitz had sent so many to their deaths, left the camp before its dissolution, and worked briefly at Gross-Rosen, before joining an army unit headed by a former colleague. He was captured by the Americans but gave a false name and was released in July 1945, when he began working as a farmhand near Rosenheim in Bavaria. Fearing discovery, he obtained help from another former colleague to flee via Switzerland and northern Italy to Argentina, where he re-established himself, buying a half-share in a pharmaceutical company in 1955. In 1959 he moved to a German colony in Paraguay, but left for Brazil the following year. In the meantime he had divorced and remarried, both legal acts that drew attention for the first time to the fact that he was still alive. His flight and concealment owed a great deal to the help of clandestine networks of former Nazis. He continued to elude capture, and died in 1979 after suffering a heart attack while swimming. It was only in 1985 that his grave was located, and the body exhumed and identified from dental records.[251] By contrast, Mengele's mentor, Otmar von Verschuer, resumed his career after the war. He was elected President of the German Society for Anthropology in 1952 and two years later he became Dean of the Medical Faculty at Münster University, where he had been Professor of Genetics since 1951. In 1954 he published his book *Human Genetics*, which built on his *Hereditary Pathology*, published twenty years before. He eventually died in a car crash in 1969.[252]

Not only Josef Mengele but also Franz Stangl and Adolf Eichmann escaped to Latin America. Stangl was transferred to northern Italy when the death camp at Treblinka, where he had been commandant, was closed. His orders were to oversee the construction of defensive fortifications and the suppression of partisan movements. At the end of the war, he escaped to Austria but was arrested by American troops and interned. As war crimes investigations proceeded, his role in the euthanasia action was discovered, and the Americans appear to have discovered at some point that he had been commandant of a death camp. By this time, however, most Allied war crimes tribunals had ceased operation, and he was transferred to the Austrian authorities, who put him in an open prison in Linz. On 30 May 1948 he absconded and, using false identity papers he had acquired in jail, managed to cross the Alps into Italy, where he had made many useful contacts. Reaching Rome, he made contact at the Vatican with Bishop Alois Hudal, a priest and part of the circle of German and Austrian clerics with whom Pope Pius XII surrounded himself. Hudal was in charge of the German Catholic community in the Italian capital. An Austrian, he did a great deal to help his compatriot escape justice. He found him somewhere to stay, gave him money and kitted him out with a Red Cross passport before buying him a ticket for the sea passage to Syria. Stangl's family joined him there, and in 1951 they emigrated to Brazil. Many other former Nazis and SS men found the same route to safety. In Brazil, the Stangls, making no mention of Franz's past, found work and a social life in the expatriate

German community. The Stangls kept their name and made no attempt to hide, but, though Franz was on the official wanted list of the Austrian and German governments, he was only tracked down by the efforts of Simon Wiesenthal, who had established an information centre dedicated to locating and securing the arrest of former leading Nazis still at large. On 28 February 1967 Stangl was arrested by Brazilian police and deported to Germany, where he was tried for the 900,000 murders he had ordered at Treblinka. It was apparently only at this point that his wife, who travelled over from Brazil to attend the trial, learned of what he had really been doing in the camp. He was sentenced to life imprisonment on 22 December 1970 and died in prison on 28 June the following year.[253]

Towards the end of the war, Adolf Eichmann had formed a small partisan resistance movement in the Austrian Alps on the orders of Ernst Kaltenbrunner, with the assistance of Otto Skorzeny and the former Romanian Iron Guard leader Horia Sima. But Himmler soon put a stop to the enterprise, and Eichmann went underground, using forged identity papers. Fearing discovery, he too took advantage of the Vatican's policy of helping 'anti-Communist fighters' to escape to Latin America and arrived in Argentina, where the quasi-fascist dictatorship of Juan Peron provided a refuge for a variety of former Nazis and SS men. One of them was Otto Skorzeny, who had escaped from a prison camp in Germany in 1948 and lived in a variety of locations, including Spain and Ireland (he died in Germany in 1975). Eichmann's identity and location were discovered by the anti-Nazi state prosecutor in Hesse, Fritz Bauer, a Jewish German who had spent the war in exile in Sweden. At his prompting, the Israeli secret service kidnapped Eichmann in Buenos Aires in May 1960 and smuggled him to Jerusalem, where he stood trial for mass murder the following year amidst a blaze of publicity. He was sentenced to death and hanged at midnight on 31 May 1962.[254]

III

From the late 1940s to the late 1950s, the political climate of the Cold War militated against any major war crimes trials in West Germany. It was widely felt, both by the NATO Allies and by the West German government, that such trials would fuel East German charges that the country was rife with Nazi criminals, and perhaps also destabilize the Federal Republic's fledgling democracy by alienating large numbers of ex-Nazis who feared that they too might be brought before a court. By 1958, however, there were signs that the situation was beginning to change. The foundation of a Central Office of the Provincial Justice Administrations in Ludwigsburg laid the basis for the nationwide co-ordination of prosecutions. But it was the Eichmann trial that really put pressure on the West Germans to act. Once more, Fritz Bauer was the driving force behind the investigations. These culminated in the trial of a number of SS officers and guards in Frankfurt am Main in 1964. The last commandant of Auschwitz, Richard Baer, who was arrested in 1960 after having lived for many years as a forestry worker under a false name, was to have been a defendant, but he died before the trial began. In the dock were twenty-two men including block leaders, SS camp guards and others who were accused of specific acts of individual, physical violence against prisoners. More than 350 former inmates travelled to the court to give evidence. In August 1965, seventeen of the defendants were given mostly lengthy prison sentences. The trial proved a crucial turning-point in bringing the attention of the younger generation of West Germans to the crimes of the Third Reich; it was followed by four smaller trials in West Germany, in which more Auschwitz guards and block leaders were sentenced to imprisonment. The East Germans riposted with a trial of their own, arresting and executing the camp doctor Horst Fischer in 1966. He had been practising medicine openly in the communist state, under his own name, without hindrance, for more than twenty years before his arrest.[255]

The survival in positions of responsibility in postwar Germany of men like Fischer suggested strongly to many observers that the process of 'denazification' carried out by the Allies had been less than thorough. In the years immediately following the end of the war, millions of Germans were required to fill in and submit lengthy forms on their activities and beliefs under the Third Reich. They were then brought before tribunals, which heard evidence from interested parties and categorized the individual concerned as a Nazi, implicated in Nazism, a fellow traveller, or uninvolved. The process was vast in scope. More than 3,600,000 people in the western zones were affected, of whom 1,667 were classified as 'chief culprits', just over 23,000 as 'incriminated', and slightly more than 150,000 as 'less incriminated'. Thus under

5 per cent were judged to have been hard-core Nazis. 996,000 were categorized as merely nominal members of the Nazi Party (27 per cent), and 1,214,000 were exonerated (33 per cent). By the time the process was wound up, in 1948, 783,000 remained uncharged, 358,000 were amnestied, and 125,000 remained unclassified. In a similar process carried out in the Soviet Zone, more than 300,000 people were dismissed from their jobs, and 83,000 were banned from further employment altogether. Denazification could not, of course, ban all 6.5 million members of the Party from employment in positions of responsibility. The need for the expertise of judges, doctors, lawyers, scientists, engineers, bankers and many others was too great. Many of those who had condemned political offenders to death in the courts, taken part in 'euthanasia' killings in the hospitals, preached Nazi doctrines in the schools and universities, or participated in 'desk-top murders' in the civil service resumed their posts. The professions closed ranks and deflected criticism of their behaviour in the Third Reich, and a veil of silence descended over their complicity, not to be lifted until after the leading participants retired, towards the end of the century.[256]

The intrusiveness of the action alienated Germans, who wanted above all to forget, and popular approval of denazification as revealed in opinion polls fell from 57 per cent in March 1946 to 17 per cent in May 1949. The superficiality of the denazification process failed to change many of the Nazi views held by those it affected. And yet, overall, despite everything, the action was a success. The open expression of Nazi opinions became a taboo, and those who revealed them were generally forced to resign their posts. The internment, screening and trial before denazification tribunals of tens of thousands of hard-core Nazis opened the way for the re-emergence of anti-Nazis – Social Democrat, Catholic, liberal – and others who had taken no part in the regime, to occupy leading positions in politics, administration, culture and the media. Attempts to revive Nazism in the form of neo-Nazi political movements like the Socialist Reich Party or, later, the National Democratic Party never won more than marginal popular support; if they were too blatant, like the former, then they were legally suppressed. A postwar career like that of Werner Best, who survived more than one trial and condemnation to spend the rest of his long life – he died in 1989 – organizing help for former Nazis and campaigning for a general amnesty, was unusual. All the same, public opinion polls revealed that a majority continued well into the 1950s to regard Nazism as 'a good idea, badly carried out', and a worryingly large proportion of the population considered that Germany was better off without the Jews. It was not until the arrival of a new generation on the scene, symbolized by the year 1968, that a real confrontation with the past began. Nevertheless, the political culture of both East and West Germany was from the outset based on a vigorous repudiation of Nazi ideology and values, including the long tradition of German nationalism and militarism that had persuaded so many people to support it. The realities of the total defeat and, in the 1950s and 1960s, the prosperity generated by the 'economic miracle' persuaded the overwhelming majority of Germans to embrace the political culture of parliamentary democracy, European integration and international peace with growing enthusiasm and commitment.[257]

Few Germans found adjusting to this new world easy. Many still regretted the failure of the Third Reich. When Hitler's former military commanders came to write their memoirs, they took the opportunity to put forward the unrealistic but for many years widely accepted view that, if only Hitler had let them get on with the job, they could have won the war. The conduct of the German army on the Eastern Front went uncriticized in these works, and for decades, therefore, unquestioned. General Gotthard Heinrici was eventually captured on 28 May 1945 and did not get back to Germany until 1948. For the rest of his life he remained convinced that he had fought in a good cause – the German cause. He died peacefully on 13 December 1971.[258] Field Marshal Fedor von Bock was not so lucky. On 3 May 1945, in compulsory retirement since the summer of 1942, he was being driven with his wife, his step-daughter and a friend through the countryside towards Oldenburg, hoping to meet his friend Field Marshal Manstein to discuss the end of the war. The car was spotted by a British fighter plane, which swooped low over it and strafed it with bullets. The car burst into flames; Bock staggered out, the only survivor; he was picked up and taken to hospital, but died of his injuries the following day.[259] Among other senior military commanders, Walther von Brauchitsch died in a British prison in 1948, Gerd von Rundstedt was captured and interrogated by the British but never faced trial because of his heart condition, and died in 1953; Friedrich Paulus, who had surrendered at Stalingrad, lived in East Germany until his death in 1957, still outwardly committed to the Communist cause he had embraced in captivity; Erich von Manstein was sentenced to fifteen years' imprisonment by a British military court in 1949 for crimes against non-combatants, was released in 1953 and became a military adviser to the West German government, dying in 1973. Like the tank commander Heinz Guderian, who was briefly imprisoned after the war and died in 1954, Manstein was widely respected for his generalship; questions about his involvement in Nazism and its crimes went largely unanswered.

Lower down the military hierarchy, the diarist and letter-writer Wilm Hosenfeld was taken prisoner by a Red Army unit as he retreated from Warsaw on 17 January 1945 and put into a prison camp. His health deteriorated, and he suffered a stroke on 27 July 1947. By this time he was able to write letters to friends and family, and he desperately listed as many as he could remember of the Poles and Jews whom he had rescued, trying to get them to petition for his release. Some did. But it was to no avail. As a member of the German military administration during the Warsaw uprising of 1944, he was accused of war crimes, put on trial and sentenced to twenty-five years' imprisonment. On 13 August 1952 he suffered another stroke, this time fatal.[260] Many other German prisoners of war were kept in Soviet labour camps for a full decade after the war, until their final release in the mid-1950s. Civilian life proved difficult to adjust to for many of them. The soldier and long-time stormtrooper Gerhard M. found that the hardest thing to bear about the new political world he entered on 8 May 1945 was the fact that he was no longer able to wear a uniform. 'I have always liked wearing a uniform,' he confided to his diary, 'and indeed not just because of the many silver insignia . . . but mainly because of the forceful appearance of the breech-trousers and the better way the clothes fitted.'[261] He could not understand why he was not allowed to resume his prewar duties as a fireman. 'Yeah,' the new head of the fire service told him, 'you Nazis risked a very loud tone up to now, but now it's all over with that.' Gerhard M. found his dismissal incomprehensible. 'I absolutely couldn't pull myself together.' Bitterly he reflected on the war 'that our leaders, who had built Germany up in such exemplary fashion, unleashed a war of the strength of the world and thereby allowed the destruction of what not only they but also previous generations had created, merely because they wanted to go down in history as great military leaders'.[262] It took another nine years before he was able to resume his career in the fire service.[263]

Others found it equally difficult to come to terms with their new situation and achieve a self-critical distance to their Nazi past. As a former leading member of the League of German Girls, Melita Maschmann, afraid like many of Allied retribution, hid in Alpine valleys in Austria, using forged papers and living off bartered or stolen food, until mid-June 1945, when she was finally arrested and identified. Imprisonment finally brought home to her the fact that the Third Reich was over. The best thing about prison, she later recalled, was the enforced idleness, which gave her time to reflect and recuperate from the years of hard and unremitting effort she had put into the Nazi cause. The limited amount of 're-education' to which she was subjected was, she said, lamentable, and the re-educators were often less educated than middle-class women such as herself, who frequently bettered them in argument. She refused to believe the stories of the extermination camps and dismissed the photographs she was shown as fakes. When she listened to a radio relay of the closing speech of the head of the Hitler Youth, Baldur von Schirach, at the Nuremberg trial in 1946, she felt betrayed by his admission of guilt and put it down to the stress of imprisonment. She remained convinced, as she wrote in her notes at the time, 'that National Socialism as the idea of racial renewal, the Greater German Reich and a united Europe ... was one of the greatest political conceptions of modern times'. She thought it more honourable to undergo the process of denazification as a convinced Nazi than to be written off as a fellow traveller. And for some years afterwards, idealistic as ever, she devoted herself to helping former Nazis in distress, giving away much of her earnings in the process. It took a dozen years for her to achieve a degree of distance to the Nazi past, helped by religion, and in particular by her friendship with an Evangelical pastor. She enrolled as a university student and actively sought out the acquaintance of foreign students from other races. The final stage in her liberation from the ideology which had consumed her for much of her earlier life was her acceptance that the reports she began to read about the fate of individual Jews in Warsaw and the camps were true. Nazism, she concluded, had possessed the ability to attract many good, idealistic young people who were so carried away by their enthusiasm and dedication to the cause that they blinded themselves to what was really happening. She herself, however, remained susceptible to the appeal of ideologies, and later in her life became seriously interested in Indian spirituality.[264]

IV

German cultural life resumed relatively quickly after the war, encouraged by the Allies. But those who had been too closely involved in Nazi propaganda were unable to resume their careers. In the film world, Emil Jannings was forced to retire to his farm in Austria, dying in 1950; Leni Riefenstahl found it impossible to make films any more, and devoted her time to photography, celebrating the life of Nubian tribes and filming underwater life on coral reefs; she died in 2003, aged 101. Riefenstahl always claimed that she had been entirely unpolitical, but few who had seen *Triumph of the Will* were able to believe her. By contrast, Veit Harlan successfully defended his record in a denazification trial on the grounds that he was an artist, and the propaganda content of his films had been imposed on him by Goebbels. He made a few more films before he died in 1964.[265] Werner Egk, the leading modernist composer of the Third Reich, was able to resume his career, becoming a conservatory director and playing a central part in the reconstruction of musical life in West Germany; he died in 1983, laden with honours, a year after Carl Orff, whose postwar career was similarly successful. The former head of Goebbels's Chamber of Music, composer Richard Strauss, was perhaps too eminent to be disturbed by denazification proceedings; living quietly in Garmisch-Partenkirchen, he survived the war to produce a final sequence of limpid, Mozartian works that count among his best, from the *Metamorphoses* for string orchestra to the oboe concerto; he died in 1949 before he could hear the first performance of his final masterpiece, the *Four Last Songs*.[266]

The postwar career of the conductor Wilhelm Furtwängler was longer, but also more controversial. A denazification tribunal cleared him of all charges, and he continued to conduct and make recordings as a freelance up to his death in 1954, but the offer of an appointment as principal conductor of the Chicago Symphony Orchestra was rescinded in 1949 after protests by eminent Jewish musicians including Vladimir Horowitz and Artur Rubinstein. His fellow-conductor Bruno Walter, forced into exile under the Nazis because of his Jewish ancestry, told him forcefully that throughout the Nazi years

your art was used as a conspicuously effective means of propaganda for the Regime of the Devil, that you performed high service to this regime through your prominent image and great talent, that the presence and performance of an artist of your stature abetted every horrible crime against culture and morality, or at least, gave considerable support to them.[267]

Furtwängler claimed to have intervened on behalf of Jewish victims of the regime, as he had indeed done in a few individual cases early on in the Third Reich. But, Walter pointed out, he had never been in danger, and he had carried on his career as Germany's leading conductor throughout the whole period. 'In light of all that,' he concluded, 'of what significance is your assistance in the isolated cases of a few Jews?'[268]

Hitler's favourite sculptor, Arno Breker, was also brought before a denazification tribunal, but he could point in mitigation of his close association with Hitler to a number of instances in which he had helped people in distress, including a Jewish woman who modelled for Maillol, Dina Vierny. Breker had visited Heinrich Müller, head of the Gestapo, and secured her release from the French transit camp from which she was due to be deported to Auschwitz. He had also helped Picasso evade the attentions of the Gestapo in Paris. Breker's sculptures were popular not only with Hitler but also with Stalin, who offered him a commission in 1946 (Breker declined, saying: 'one dictatorship is sufficient for me'). All of this, bolstered by 160 affidavits testifying to the probity of his conduct during the Third Reich, succeeded in having him classified merely as a 'fellow traveller', with a fine of 100 Deutschmarks plus the costs of the trial (which he never paid). He subsequently rebuilt his career, partly with the help of architects from Speer's old office, and his admirers organized exhibitions of his work, but his campaign for rehabilitation did not succeed with the mainstream art world, which continued to regard him primarily as the state sculptor of the Third Reich all the way up to his death in 1991. A commentary in a leading conservative German newspaper on his ninetieth birthday the year before described him as 'the classic example of a seduced, deluded and also overbearing talent'.[269]

Of more immediate interest to the Allies after the war than artists and composers were the scientists and engineers who had worked so expertly, and to such little effect, on wonder-weapons like the V-1 and V-2. Special teams were put together by the Soviet and American authorities to locate and take key military technological equipment back home for further development. The inventors of the nerve gases Sarin and Tabun were arrested and interrogated; jet engines, advanced submarines, rocket planes and much more besides were dismantled and taken away for study. The Soviets removed several thousand scientists and engineers to work on updating their military technology and equipment, while the British and Americans turned their attention to the V-2 rocket team, Together with Wernher von Braun and some of his staff, they oversaw the launch of three V-2 missiles from the German North Sea coast in October 1945. 120 of the rocket programme staff, including von Braun, were taken off to a new base near El Paso, in Texas, to work on rocket development; they were not made available for the trial of those responsible for the crimes committed at Camp Dora. By 1950 the programme had been relocated to Huntsville, Alabama, where it became the leading missile development centre in the USA, eclipsing previous institutions like the Jet Propulsion Laboratory in Pasadena, California. Ten years later, building on the experience of the V-2, von Braun and the Huntsville team constructed the mighty Saturn rocket, which was used to launch men into space and within a decade to send them to the moon. Not only the Americans but also the Soviets, the British and the French used the expertise of members of the Peenemünde team wherever they could find them, in developing and building a new generation of intercontinental ballistic missiles, rendered infinitely more dangerous than their German predecessor by the invention of the atomic bomb.[270]

Other scientists, notably the pioneers of atom bomb research Otto Hahn and Werner Heisenberg, remained in Germany and resumed their careers. Hahn took over the directorship of the Kaiser Wilhelm Society in 1946, unsuccessfully opposing its renaming as the Max Planck Society at the behest of the British occupation authorities in the wake of the great scientist's death in 1947. What Hahn did succeed in doing, however, was to distance the Society successfully from its close involvement in Nazi research, a topic that remained undiscussed until almost the very end of the twentieth century. Hahn went to Stockholm to get his Nobel Prize for the discovery of nuclear fission, and died in Göttingen in 1968. Werner Heisenberg became director of the Max Planck Institute for Physics and rejoined the international scientific community, dying in 1971. His rivals, the champions of 'German Physics', did not prosper. Heisenberg had the pleasure of testifying against Johannes Stark at the latter's trial in 1947. Stark's sentence of four years' imprisonment was in the end not implemented, and he died, largely forgotten, in 1957. Ten years before, his mentor Philipp Lenard had died at the age of 85. Other, more minor figures in the German Physics movement were systematically shut out of academic life when it resumed again after the war.[271]

V

The ordinary, unassuming citizens whose voluminous and conscientiously kept diaries form such a vital record of everyday life under the Nazis suffered a variety of fates after the war. Dr Zygmunt Klukowski published a five-volume work on German war crimes and the underground resistance in the Zamość area. This led to his being called as a witness in one of the Nuremberg War Crimes Trials. Klukowski soon found himself living under another dictatorship, however, as the Soviet occupying power suppressed the Polish nationalist movement and installed a Communist regime in power. Klukowski now helped the Polish underground resistance to the Communists and kept a diary of the Communist terror, just as he had done of the Nazi. He was arrested by the Soviet political police twice, and, though he was not imprisoned, he was demoted from his long-held post of head of hospital to the status of a humble ward physician. In 1952 he was arrested again, while trying – unsuccessfully – to prevent his son Tadeusz from being executed for resistance activities, and spent four years in Wronki prison. In the thaw of 1956 he was pardoned and rehabilitated, and moved to Lublin, where he published his war diaries two years later. These made him famous: the book was quickly reprinted, and won a major literary prize, to go along with numerous other Polish national awards. By this time, however, Klukoswki was already suffering from cancer. He died on 23 November 1959, and was buried in Szczebrzeszyn, along with other soldiers of the Home Army: in 1986 the town erected a monument to him in the main square. His diaries reached a wider readership with their publication in English in 1993 on the initiative of his surviving son and grandson and remain the most vivid and detailed record we have of life in Poland under German occupation.[272]

Victor Klemperer and his wife Eva moved back into the house in the Dresden suburb of Dölzschen from which they had been evicted in 1939, and gradually put it back in order. At sixty-three, he had no intention of sinking into a quiet retirement. His ex-colleagues from the Technical

University at Dresden, who had avoided him during the Nazi period because he was Jewish, now spoke to him again as if nothing had happened in the intervening years. Former friends and neighbours, acquaintances and even complete strangers approached him for support in their claim that they were innocent of the Third Reich's crimes. Klemperer enjoyed his new-found status as one of the persecuted of the Third Reich. He was restored to his Professorship at the University, though he did not return to teach there, and then was appointed in rapid succession to more prestigious chairs at Greifswald, Halle and Berlin. He retrieved his manuscripts from his non-Jewish friend Annemarie Köhler, and published his study of Nazi language, *LTI*, which was immediately recognized as a classic. He resumed work on his study of eighteenth-century French literature, and this was published too. Dresden lay in the Soviet Zone of Occupation, and after some hesitation Klemperer joined the Communist Party, which he saw as the only convincing vehicle of retribution and reconstruction; for him, nothing else could give any assurance that the break with Nazism was complete. His membership opened up a wide range of cultural and educational work for him, and after the German Democratic Republic was founded in 1949 he became a deputy in the country's parliament, a position for which he was no more obliged to campaign or stand against an opponent than any other member was. The growing Stalinization of East Germany made him more sceptical; he ran into political criticism of his work, and he privately concluded that at bottom he was a liberal after all.[273]

In 1951 Klemperer's wife Eva, whose steadfast love had kept him alive during the Third Reich, died of a heart attack in her sleep shortly before her sixty-ninth birthday. 'I am quite alone,' he wrote in his diary, 'everything is valueless for me now.'[274] Initially, he took solace in work, but within a few months he began a relationship with the twenty-five-year-old Hadwig Kirchner, one of his students; despite feeling that he might be making a fool of himself, he fell in love, his sentiments were reciprocated, and the couple were married on 23 May 1952. He continued to teach French literature well into his seventies. In 1959 he fell seriously ill, and died on 11 February 1960 at the age of seventy-eight. There could be no question of publishing his voluminous diaries under the East German dictatorship, given their complete failure to follow the Communist Party line on either the Weimar Republic, the Third Reich or the postwar era; but after the fall of the Berlin Wall his widow made them available for publication, and they appeared in instalments through the 1990s, immediately establishing themselves as the most meticulous, vivid and honest account of the life of a Jew in Germany during the first six decades of the twentieth century.[275]

Luise Solmitz and her Jewish husband Friedrich also survived the war unscathed. They lived in quiet retirement in Hamburg. Luise continued to keep a daily record of her life, as she had done ever since 1905, filling one 700-page notebook with closely spaced lines of tiny, crabbed handwriting every year. In December 1953 she donated her diaries to the Hamburg State Archive as a historical record, but a year later, she found that she could not bear to be without them and retrieved them for her private use. She donated them again in 1967, but took them back home once more three months later, keeping them until her death in 1973 at the age of eighty-four. In the 1960s the Research Centre for the History of National Socialism in Hamburg secured her agreement to come in every day and dictate from the diaries for 1918–45 to a shorthand typist. As she went through them, she occasionally wondered at the views she had expressed in the early 1930s, views that had changed so radically by 1945. Coming across her description from January 1933 of Nazis singing about Jewish blood spurting from the knife, she added a comment: 'Who took that seriously then?'[276]

VI

Luise Solmitz's failure in the 1930s to recognize the violence that lay at the heart of Nazism was shared by many. As late as 1939 the great majority of Germans were hoping against hope that there would not be a general European war; and a large part of the euphoria that swept the country in the wake of the victory over France the following year expressed the relief that the traditional enemy had been defeated, and the humiliation of the 1919 Peace Settlement avenged, with what seemed to be a minimum of bloodshed. Yet Nazism was from the very beginning a creed based on violence and hatred, born of bitterness and despair. The depth and radicalism of the political, social and economic crises that assailed Germany under the Weimar Republic spawned a correspondingly deep and radical response. Germany's enemies within and without were to be utterly destroyed in order that Germany should rise again, this time to unprecedented heights of power and domination. Even the promises of economic reconstruction and social cohesion that won over so many Germans to the Nazi cause in the 1930s were subordinated in the end to the drive to war. In seeking to re-create the atmosphere of August 1914 – or what the Nazis imagined it to have been – internal conflict was to be banished and social and political divisions subsumed in the all-encompassing myth of the organic national and racial community of all Germans. The subversion that had supposedly led to the German army being stabbed in the back by Jewish revolutionaries feeding on domestic discontent in 1918 was to be prevented by ensuring that the Jews were removed from Germany by any means possible and that Germans themselves were well fed, racially pure and politically committed. These were aims that could only be achieved by the application of violence at its most ruthless and extreme.

The war that began in September 1939 unleashed it with a force that had so far only been apparent on specific occasions such as the maltreatment of the Jews of Vienna after the annexation of Austria in March 1938, or the nationwide pogrom of the 'Night of Broken Glass' the following November. The policies that unfolded in Poland in the opening months of the war set the tone for the Nazi occupation of other parts of Eastern Europe from the middle of 1941 onwards: expropriation, forcible deportation, imprisonment, mass shootings, murder on a hitherto unimaginable scale. These policies were applied to all the people who lived in the region apart from ethnic Germans, but they were applied with particular venom to the Jews, who were subjected to sadistic and systematic humiliation and torture, ghettoization and extermination by poison gas in facilities specially built for the purpose. Other groups, mainly though in many cases not exclusively German, were also killed in large numbers: the mentally ill and handicapped, Gypsies, homosexuals, Jehovah's Witnesses, 'asocials', petty criminals, the politically refractory and the socially marginal. Soviet prisoners of war were murdered in their millions, and people of many nationalities were taken forcibly to Germany and made to work and live under conditions that proved fatal for a large number of them. Some people who belonged to these other groups were, like many Jews, gassed to death; but only the Jews were singled out as the 'world enemy', a global threat to Germany's existence that had to be exterminated wherever it was found.

These policies were put into action to one degree or another by hundreds of thousands, even millions, of Germans, who were committed to the Nazi cause, or who – especially if they belonged to the younger generation – had been indoctrinated since 1933 with the belief that Slavs were subhuman, Jews were evil, Gypsies, criminals, the marginal and the deviant were at best a nuisance, at worst a threat. Nazism's encouragement of murderous violence, theft, looting and wanton destruction was not without its effect on the behaviour of German troops in Poland, the Soviet Union, Serbia and other parts of Europe. Only a very few, mostly impelled by a strong Christian conscience, raised their voices in criticism. Yet the majority of Germans felt uneasy at the mass murder of Jews and Slavs, and guilty that they were too afraid to do anything to stop it. In the case of the mentally ill and handicapped, who belonged in many cases to their own families and communities, they were upset enough to protest, at first indirectly and then, channelling their anger and despair through the Christian Churches, openly and to some effect.

In launching a war to be fought on a European scale with the goal of world domination as the long-term aim, Hitler and the Nazis were living out the fantasies that had impelled them into politics in the first place: fantasies of a great and resurgent Germany, expunging the stain of defeat in 1918 by establishing an imperial domination on a scale the world had never seen before. These fantasies were shared to a significant degree by key parts of the German Establishment, including the civil service, the professions and the top generals in the army. Despite their doubts, they all went along with it in the end. But Germany's economic resources were never adequate to turn these fantasies into reality, not even when the resources of a large part of the rest of Europe were added to them. No amount of 'mobilization for total war', no degree of economic rationalization, could alter this fundamental fact of life. Initially, the German armed forces managed to score a series of quick victories using tactics that defeated their enemies as much by surprise as by anything else. But they were unable to defeat Britain in 1940, and a stalemate ensued. This was the first major turning-point of the war.

The invasion of the Soviet Union the following year was in part an attempt to break this stalemate. But it was also the accelerated implementation of a desire long held by Hitler and the leading Nazis: the conquest of Eastern Europe, the acquisition of its notionally vast natural resources, and the racial subjugation and extermination of a large proportion of its inhabitants in order to make way for a new and permanent German hegemony. Operation Barbarossa inaugurated a war of attrition that the Third Reich could not win. The drive across North Africa to secure the prize of Middle Eastern oil could not succeed, for all Rommel's brilliance; the attempt to cut off the supplies sent to Britain and the Soviet Union in growing quantities from the United States failed because there were not enough U-boats to sustain it. A second turning-point in the war came at the end of 1941, when the German armies failed to take Moscow, and the United States brought their immense resources into the conflict on the Allied side. A third turning-point came a year later, in the catastrophic German defeat at Stalingrad.

Increasingly, the war came home to Germany, as Allied bombing fleets gained domination of the skies and brought devastation to Germany's cities. Until things began to go badly wrong in the war, the Nazis managed to pull the great mass of the German people along with them. German nationalism, belief in the greatness of Germany and resentment at the Peace Settlement of 1919 were present in every part of the population. They were behind the mass and undoubtedly genuine euphoria that greeted Germany's stunning military successes in 1939–40 and in a grimmer mood they sustained a large part of the German resistance to the Soviet invasion in 1944–5. Until the summer of 1944 cultural institutions and the mass media continued to offer a mixture of morale-boosting encouragement and soul-soothing escapism to the Germans at home, while food supplies and the basics of everyday life were sustained almost to the end. But the mass destruction of Germany's towns and cities that began in earnest in 1943 turned people against the Nazi regime even more than the realization after Stalingrad that the war was lost. The Nazi regime responded to disillusion at home and the decline of morale in the armed forces by intensifying the repression and terror that had always been a central part of its rule. The element of martyrdom and self-sacrifice in Nazi ideology was intensified too. Small numbers of Germans began to resist, but the only group capable of overthrowing Hitler, the military resistance, failed in the attempt in July 1944, inaugurating a further intensification of terror and destruction that ended in the downfall of the Third Reich just over nine months later.

The violence at the core of Nazism had in the end been turned back on Germany itself. As the German people – above all, German women – cleared away the last of the rubble, they began to experience something like a return to normality, reflected in the political and social atmosphere of the 1950s, with its emphasis on family values, material prosperity, social order, political stability and selective amnesia about the Nazi past. For many middle-aged and older Germans, there had been no real normality since before the First World War. Military conflict and material privation had been succeeded by revolution, hyperinflation, political violence, economic depression, dictatorship and war all over again. But the normality of the 1950s was also a new kind of normality. The Third Reich and the war it unleashed had changed many things. Nazism's promise of social equality was implemented, in ways it had not foreseen, during and after the war: the ferocious attack it launched on the German aristocracy after 20 July 1944, coupled with the break-up of the larger landed estates by the Allies after 1945 and the suppression of the Prussian military tradition at the same time, broke what remained of the social and political power of the titled nobility.

At the other end of the social scale, Nazism had destroyed the long-established traditions of the labour movement, already severely weakened by the Depression of 1929–33. Older workers quickly reorganized themselves into unions, reformed the Communist and Social Democratic Parties and launched a series of strikes in 1947 with the demand for the socialization of the means of production; but they had little support from the younger generations of workers, who had never belonged to a union or a left-wing party, and only wanted social peace and material prosperity. The strikes failed, the Communist Party in West Germany lost virtually all its support and was eventually banned, the Social Democrats abandoned their Marxist heritage in 1959, and the decline of heavy industry and the rise of a consumer society completed the process. In East Germany the flight of millions of professionals to the west and the egalitarian policies of the Communist regime created the same effect, albeit at a lower level of material prosperity. The old-style class-conflict that Nazism had put such store by overcoming had finally vanished. Germany had become a levelled-down, middle-class society, differing in its nature from east to west, but sharing a common transcendence of traditional class structures.

The power of nationalism had also been broken, so thoroughly that when elderly Germans came towards the end of the century to look back on the Third Reich and ask themselves why they had supported it, they could no longer remember that one of the main reasons had been because they had thought that it made Germany great again.[277] Germany, as the public celebrations accompanying its reunification in 1989–90 showed, may not have become a fully postnational society. The strong support of the vast majority of Germans for European integration may have been tempered by a continuing self-identification as Germans. But to be German in the second half of the twentieth century meant something very different from what it had meant in the first half: it meant, among other things, to be peace-loving, democratic, prosperous and stable, and it also meant having a critical attitude towards the German past, having a sense of responsibility for the death and destruction that Nazism caused, even feeling guilty about it.[278]

These matters continued to be widely debated, of course, and some at least also regarded the Germans themselves as victims of the Second World War. Yet in the early twenty-first century, Germany's capital city has a large public memorial to the Jewish victims of Nazism at its very centre, German concentration camps have become public museums to Nazi atrocities, and on the streets of a growing number of German towns and cities brass plates have been put on to the pavements outside houses and shops that belonged to Jews before 1933, with the names of their former owners inscribed on them. German historians have exposed the long-denied involvement of many sectors of the German population in the crimes of the Third Reich, from the officers and men of the army to the doctors and scientists who staffed Germany's hospitals and research institutes. Former slave labourers have launched successful actions to gain recognition and a small amount of compensation for their sufferings, and the businesses and companies that profited from the Nazi regime and its policies have opened their archives and admitted their complicity. Artworks and cultural objects expropriated from their Jewish owners under the Third Reich have been catalogued and galleries, museums and state authorities have opened the way for the restitution of those that have not yet been returned.

Not only historical knowledge about the Third Reich, but also public consciousness of what it did, has increased with distance in time from the Nazi regime; yet that regime has not lost any of its power to excite moral debate, rather, if anything, the reverse. Not long after the Second World War was over, the English historian Alan Bullock ended his great biography of Hitler by quoting the words inscribed on the tomb of the architect Sir Christopher Wren in the church he built in London, St Paul's Cathedral: *Si monumentum requiris, circumspice* – 'If you need a memorial, look around.'[279] In 1952, when Bullock published his book, the destruction wrought by the war was still to be seen in almost every part of Europe. More than half a century later, this is no longer the case. Bomb-sites have been cleared, battlefields levelled out, divisions healed, peace and prosperity restored to Europe. Most of those who lived through the Third Reich and fought in its wars are no longer with us. Within a few decades there will be no one left who remembers it at first hand. And yet its legacy is still alive in myriad ways. History does not repeat itself: there will be no Fourth Reich. Neo-Nazism still finds its supporters, but nowhere has it shown any signs of even coming close to achieving real political power. The legacy of the Third Reich is much wider. It extends far beyond Germany and Europe. The Third Reich raises in the most acute form the possibilities and consequences of the human hatred and destructiveness that exist, even if only in a small way, within all of us. It demonstrates with terrible clarity the ultimate potential consequences of racism, militarism and authoritarianism. It shows what can happen if some people are treated as less human than others. It poses in the most extreme possible form the moral dilemmas we all face at one time or another in our lives, of conformity or resistance, action or inaction in the particular situations with which we are confronted. That is why the Third Reich will not go away, but continues to command the attention of thinking people throughout the world long after it has passed into history.

Notes

Chapter 1. 'BEASTS IN HUMAN FORM'

1. Basic information from Paul Latawski, 'Polish Campaign', in Ian C. B. Dear (ed.), *The Oxford Companion to World War II* (Oxford, 2005 [1995]), 705–8; and Ian C. B. Dear, 'Animals', in ibid., 28–9; detailed account in Horst Rohde, 'Hitler's First Blitzkrieg and Its Consequences for North-eastern Europe', in Militärgeschichtliches Forschungsamt (ed.), *Germany and the Second World War* (10 vols., Oxford, 1990–; hereafter *GSWW*), II. 67–150 (table of German troop deployments at 92). For Hitler's orders, see Walther Hubatsch (ed.), *Hitlers Weisungen für die Kriegführung 1939–1945. Dokumente des Oberkommandos der Wehrmacht* (Frankfurt am Main, 1962), 17–19.

2. Latawski, 'Polish Campaign'; Rohde, 'Hitler's First Blitzkrieg', 101–18; brisk account in Gerhard L. Weinberg, *A World at Arms: A Global History of World War II* (Cambridge, 2005 [1994]), 48–64; also Józef Garlinski, *Poland in the Second World War* (London, 1985), 11–24; Wolfgang Jacobmeyer, 'Der Überfall auf Polen und der neue Charakter des Krieges', in Christoph Klessmann (ed.), *September 1939: Krieg, Besatzung, Widerstand in Polen: Acht Beiträge* (Göttingen, 1989), 16–37, at 19–20; for the alleged Polish cavalry charges, see Patrick Wright, *Tank: The Progress of a Monstrous War Machine* (London, 2000), 231–7.

3. William L. Shirer, *Berlin Diary* (London, 1970 [1941]), 167–8.

4. Contemporary details in Alcuin (pseud.), *I Saw Poland Suffer, by a Polish Doctor Who Held an Official Position in Warsaw under German Occupation* (London, 1941), 15; eyewitness reports in Dieter Bach and Wieslaw Lesiuk, *Ich sah in das Gesicht eines Menschen: Deutsch-polnische Begegnungen vor und nach 1945* (Wuppertal, 1995), 81–104.

5. Chaim A. Kaplan, *Scroll of Agony: The Warsaw Diary of Chaim A. Kaplan* (London, 1966), 20 (28 September 1939); the same scenes were also recorded by Adam Czerniakow, *The Warsaw Diary of Adam Czerniakow: Prelude to Doom* (New York, 1979 [1968]), 77 (28 September 1939).

6. Zygmunt Klukowski, *Diary from the Years of Occupation 1939–44* (Urbana, Ill., 1993 [1958]), vii–x, 16–17 (paragraphing dissolved).

7. Ibid., 17.

8. Ibid., 22.

9. Richard J. Evans, *The Third Reich in Power 1933–1939* (London, 2005), 689–95.

10. Rohde, 'Hitler's First Blitzkrieg', 118–26; Weinberg, *A World at Arms*, 60–63, details these border adjustments and the negotiations that preceded them.

11. Rohde, 'Hitler's First Blitzkrieg', 122–6; Garlinski, *Poland*, 25.

12. Ian Kershaw, *Hitler*, II: *1936–1945: Nemesis* (London, 2000), 235–9.

13. Shirer, *Berlin Diary*, 173.

14. Klaus Behnken (ed.), *Deutschland-Berichte der Sozialdemokratischen Partei Deutschlands (Sopade) 1934–1940* (7 vols., Frankfurt am Main, 1980), VI: *1939*, 980–82.

15. Heinz Boberach (ed.), *Meldungen aus dem Reich: Die geheimen Lageberichte des*

Sicherheitsdienstes der SS 1938–1945 (17 vols., Herrsching, 1984), II. 339 (Bericht zur innenpolitischen Lage (Nr. 2), 11 October 1939); Shirer, *Berlin Diary*, 182–4.

16. Martin Broszat, *Nationalsozialistische Polenpolitik* (Frankfurt am Main, 1965), 46–8.

17. Melita Maschmann, *Account Rendered: A Dossier on my Former Self* (London, 1964), 58–60.

18. Helmut Krausnick, *Hitlers Einsatzgruppen: Die Truppen des Weltanschauungskrieges 1938–1942* (Frankfurt am Main, 1985 [1981]), 267 n. 140; Broszat, *Nationalsozialistische Polenpolitik*, 51.

19. Kershaw, *Hitler*, II. 241–3; Wlodzimierz Jastrzebski, *Der Bromberger Blutsonntag: Legende und Wirklichkeit* (Poznań, 1990); Günter Schubert, *Das Unternehmen 'Bromberger Blutsonntag': Tod einer Legende* (Cologne, 1989). The official German Foreign Office publication of alleged Polish atrocities gave a total of 5,437 murders of Germans by Poles: Auswärtiges Amt (ed.), *Die polnischen Greueltaten an den Volksdeutschen in Polen* (Berlin, 1940), 5.

20. See the material compiled by two Polish war crimes prosecutors, Tadeusz Cyprian and Jerzy Sawicki, *Nazi Rule in Poland 1939–1945* (Warsaw, 1961), 11–70.

21. Evans, *The Third Reich in Power*, 614–15, 652–3, 678–88.

22. Günter Berndt and Reinhard Strecker (eds.), *Polen – ein Schauermärchen oder Gehirnwäsche für Generationen: Geschichtsschreibung und Schulbücher: Beiträge zum Polenbild der Deutschen* (Reinbek, 1971); Jacobmeyer, 'Der Überfall', 18. See also Antony Polonsky, 'The German Occupation of Poland during the First and Second World Wars', in Roy A. Prete and A. Hamish Ion (eds.), *Armies of Occupation* (Waterloo, Ontario, 1984), 97–142.

23. Broszat, *Nationalsozialistische Polenpolitik*, 9–13; Evans, *The Third Reich in Power*, 619, 689–92; Christoph Klessmann, *Die Selbstbehauptung einer Nation: Nationalsozialistische Kulturpolitik und polnische Widerstandsbewegung im Generalgouvernement 1939–1945* (Düsseldorf, 1971), 27–32.

24. Quoted in Jacobmeyer, 'Der Überfall', 16–17; see also Winfried Baumgart, 'Zur Ansprache Hitlers vor den Führern der Wehrmacht am 22. August 1939', *Vierteljahrshefte für Zeitgeschichte* (hereafter *VfZ*) 16 (1968), 120–49, and idem, and Hermann Boehm, 'Zur Ansprache Hitlers vor den Führern der Wehrmacht am 22. August 1939', *VfZ* 19 (1971), 294–304.

25. Elke Fröhlich (ed.), *Die Tagebücher von Joseph Goebbels* I: *Aufzeichnungen 1923–1941* (9 vols.); II: *Diktate 1941–1945* (15 vols.) (Munich, 1993–2000), I/VII. 147 (10 October 1939).

26. Hans-Günter Seraphim (ed.), *Das Politische Tagebuch Alfred Rosenbergs aus den Jahren 1934/35 und 1939/40* (Munich, 1964), 98–100; see more generally Tomasz Szarota, 'Poland and Poles in German Eyes during World War II', *Polish Western Affairs*, 19 (1978), 229–54, and Alexander B. Rossino, *Hitler Strikes Poland: Blitzkrieg, Ideology, and Atrocity* (Lawrence, Kans., 2003), 1–28.

27. Helmut Krausnick, 'Hitler und die Morde in Polen: Ein Beitrag zum Konflikt zwischen Heer und SS um die Verwaltung der besetzten Gebiete (Dokumentation)', *VfZ* 11 (1963), 196–209.

28. Broszat, *Nationalsozialistische Polenpolitik*, 13–37; for the administration of these areas, see ibid., 49–60; for the status of the General Government and the nature of its administration, ibid., 68–74; more detail in Czeslaw Madajczyk, *Die Okkupationspolitik Nazideutschlands in Polen 1939–1945* (Cologne, 1988 [1970]), 18–29, 30–44; for Frank, see Richard J. Evans, *The Coming of the Third Reich* (London, 2003), 179; Christoph Klessmann, 'Der Generalgouverneur Hans Frank', *VfZ* 19 (1971), 245–60; and Martyn Housden, *Hans Frank: Lebensraum and the Holocaust* (London, 2003), 1–76 (marred by gratuitous moralizing); for Forster, see Dieter Schenk, *Hitlers Mann in Danzig: Gauleiter Forster und die NS-Verbrechen in Danzig-Westpreussen* (Bonn, 2000). For a good recent account, see Mark Mazower, *Hitler's Empire: Nazi Rule in Occupied Europe* (London, 2008), 63–77.

29. Jan T. Gross, *Polish Society under German Occupation: The Generalgouvernement 1939–1944* (Princeton, N.J., 1979), 45–53; Frank relayed these views on 21 October 1939: see Werner Präg and Wolfgang Jacobmeyer (eds.), *Das Diensttagebuch des deutschen Generalgouverneurs in Polen 1939–1945* (Stuttgart, 1975), 52–3; see also the report in Franz Halder, *Kriegstagebuch* (ed. Hans-Adolf Jacobsen, 3 vols., Stuttgart, 1962–4), I. 107.

30. Christian Jansen and Arno Weckbecker, 'Eine Miliz im "Weltanschauungskrieg": Der "Volksdeutsche Selbstschutz" in Polen 1939/40', in Wolfgang Michalka (ed.), *Der Zweite Weltkrieg: Analysen – Grundzüge – Forschungsbilanz* (Munich, 1989), 482–500, at 490, cited in Kershaw, *Hitler*, II. 242–3.

31. Jansen and Weckbecker, 'Eine Miliz'; more detail in the same authors' *Der 'Volksdeutsche Selbstschutz' in Polen 1939/40* (Munich, 1992); Broszat, *Nationalsozialistische Polenpolitik*, 60–62; and Hans Umbreit, *Deutsche Militärverwaltungen 1938/39: Die militärische Besetzung der Tschechoslowakei und Polens* (Stuttgart, 1977), 176–8.

32. Michael Wildt, *Generation des Unbedingten: Das Führungskorps des Reichssicherheitshauptamtes* (Hamburg, 2002), 209–415; Saul Friedländer, *The Years of Extermination: The Third Reich and the Jews 1939–194* (New York, 2007), 679–81 n. 23.

33. Helmut Groscurth, *Tagebücher eines Abwehroffiziers 1938–1940* (ed. Helmut Krausnick and Harold C. Deutsch, Stuttgart, 1970), 201 (8 September 1939).

34. Kershaw, *Hitler*, II. 243; Groscurth, *Tagebücher*, 202 (9 September 1939).

35. Halder, *Kriegstagebuch*, I. 79 (19 September 1939), 81 (20 September 1939), 107 (18 October 1939); Rossino, *Hitler Strikes Poland*, 14–16; see also Heydrich's later reference to Hitler's order to exterminate the Polish intelligentsia in Krausnick, 'Hitler und die Morde in Polen'.

36. Broszat, *Nationalsozialistische Polenpolitik*, 221–2.

37. Krausnick, *Hitlers Einsatzgruppen*, 13–25; Wildt, *Generation des Unbedingten*, 420–28; Evans, *The Third Reich in Power*, 656–61, 678–9, 685 for Austria and Czechoslovakia.

38. Evans, *The Coming of the Third Reich*, 274; idem, *The Third Reich in Power*, 44, 52, 116; Rossino, *Hitler Strikes Poland*, 10–16.

39. Ibid., 29–57; see also Jens Banach, *Heydrichs Elite: Das Führerkorps der Sicherheitspolizei und des SD, 1936–1945* (Paderborn, 1998).

40. Rossino, *Hitler Strikes Poland*, 29–57; for von Woyrsch, see Evans, *The Third Reich in Power*, 36.

41. Quoted in Krausnick, *Hitlers Einsatzgruppen*, 29; also Kurt Pätzold (ed.), *Verfolgung, Vertreibung, Vernichtung: Dokumente des faschistischen Antisemitismus 1933 bis 1942* (Frankfurt am Main, 1984), 234.

42. Krausnick, *Hitlers Einsatzgruppen*, 31–4; Umbreit, *Deutsche Militärverwaltungen*, 162–73.

43. Krausnick, *Hitlers Einsatzgruppen*, 35–51; Rossino, *Hitler Strikes Poland*, 59–74; Jastrzebski, *Der Bromberger Blutsonntag*.

44. Klukowski, *Diary*, 68.

45. Ibid., 90–99 (21 June 1940).

46. Alcuin (pseud.), *I Saw Poland Suffer*, 73.

47. Broszat, *Nationalsozialistische Polenpolitik*, 44.

48. Jon Evans, *The Nazi New Order in Poland* (London, 1941), 51; the same incident also in Francis Aldor, *Germany's 'Death Space': The Polish Tragedy* (London, 1940), 187–92, based on accounts from Polish exiles in Paris.

49. Rossino, *Hitler Strikes Poland*, 87.

50. The obsession with *franc-tireurs* is a central theme in Jochen Böhler, *Auftakt zum Vernichtungskrieg: Die Wehrmacht in Polen 1939* (Frankfurt am Main, 2006), 54–168. For the terror more generally, see Madajczyk, *Die Okkupationspolitik*, 186–215.

51. Quoted in Krausnick, *Hitlers Einsatzgruppen*, 271 n. 177.

52. Keith Sword, 'Poland', in Dear (ed.), *The Oxford Companion to World War II*, 696; also Szymon Datner, 'Crimes Committed by the Wehrmacht during the September

Campaign and the Period of Military Government (1 Sept. 1939–25 Oct. 1939)', *Polish Western Affairs*, 3 (1962), 294–328; and Umbreit, *Deutsche Militärverwaltungen*, 197–9.

53. Karl Malthes, in *IR 309 marchiert an den Feind: Erlebnisberichte aus dem Polenfeldzuge 1939* (ed. Oberst Dr Hoffmann, Berlin, 1940), 158.

54. Heinrich Breloer (ed.), *Geheime Welten: Deutsche Tagebücher aus den Jahren 1939 bis 1947* (Cologne, 1999 [1984]), 27.

55. Ibid., 30.

56. Klukowski, *Diary*, 75, 77, 80–82; Evans, *The Nazi New Order*, 66–82; Broszat, *Nationalsozialistische Polenpolitik*, 102–10; Adam Tooze, *The Wages of Destruction: The Making and Breaking of the Nazi Economy* (London, 2006), 361–2.

57. Klukowski, *Diary*, 86–7 (19 May 1940); Wolfgang Jacobmeyer, *Heimat und Exil: Die Anfänge der polnischen Untergrundbewegung im Zweiten Weltkrieg (September 1939 bis Mitte 1941)* (Hamburg, 1973).

58. Housden, *Hans Frank*, 120–21; Gross, *Polish Society*, 87

59. Ulrich Herbert, *Hitler's Foreign Workers: Enforced Foreign Labor in Germany under the Third Reich* (Cambridge, 1997 [1985]), 79–94; Broszat, *Nationalsozialistische Polenpolitik*, 102–17; Gross, *Polish Society*, 78–81; Madajczyk, *Die Okkupationspolitik*, 216–32.

60. Klukowski, *Diary*, 31.

61. Böhler, *Auftakt*, 181–5.

62. Breloer (ed.), *Geheime Welten*, 27.

63. Housden, *Hans Frank*, 84–6; Madajczyk, *Die Okkupationspolitik*, 334–8.

64. Robert L. Koehl, *RKFDV: German Resettlement and Population Policy 1939–1945: A History of the Reich Commission for the Strengthening of Germandom* (Cambridge, Mass., 1957), 58; (Anon.), *The German New Order in Poland* (London, 1942), 262; Aldor, *Germany's 'Death Space'*, 147; Umbreit, *Deutsche Militärverwaltungen*, 222–72; Werner Röhr, 'Zur Wirtschaftspolitik der deutschen Okkupanten in Polen 1939–1945', in Dietrich Eichholtz (ed.), *Krieg und Wirtschaft: Studien zur deutschen Wirtschaftsgeschichte 1939–1945* (Berlin, 1999); Ryszard Kaczmarek, 'Die deutsche wirtschaftliche Penetration in Polen (Oberschlesien)', in Richard Overy *et al.* (eds.), *Die 'Neuordnung' Europas: NS-Wirtschaftspolitik in den besetzten Gebieten* (Berlin, 1997), 257–72.

65. Evans, *The Nazi New Order*, 83–96; Klukowski, *Diary*, 85; Alder, *Germany's 'Death Space'*, 147.

66. Martin Pöppel, *Heaven and Hell: The War Diary of a German Paratrooper* (Staplehurst, 1988), 21.

67. Alcuin (pseud.), *I Saw Poland Suffer*, 52–6.

68. Ibid., 69.

69. Ibid., 72–3; general survey in Madajczyk, *Die Okkupationspolitik*, 548–63. The question of whether German conduct towards the Poles can plausibly be called genocidal is dealt with sensibly in Gerhard Eitel, 'Genozid auch an Polen? Kein Thema für einen "Historikerstreit"', *Zeitgeschichte*, 18 (1990), 22–39.

70. Halder, *Kriegstagebuch*, I. 68 (10 September 1939).

71. Jansen and Weckbecker, *Der 'Volksdeutsche Selbstschutz'*, 175–80.

72. Quoted in Krausnick, *Hitlers Einsatzgruppen*, 63.

73. Ibid., 63–4.

74. Ibid., 55–6.

75. Ibid., 56–67; Rossino, *Hitler Strikes Poland*, 88–120, 174–85; Hans Meier-Welcker, *Aufzeichnungen eines Generalstabsoffiziers 1939–1942* (Freiburg im Breisgau, 1982), 39 (Cologne, 10 December 1939).

76. In Hans-Adolf Jacobsen (ed.), *Misstrauische Nachbarn: Deutsche Ostpolitik 1919/1970* (Düsseldorf, 1970), 137–41.

77. Ibid., 138.

78. Krausnick, *Hitlers Einsatzgruppen*, 78–88; Kershaw, *Hitler*, II. 247–8; Broszat, *Nationalsozialistische Polenpolitik*, 40–41.

79. For the collaboration of the army with the SS and ethnic German paramilitaries, see Böhler, *Auftakt*, 201–40.

80. Leon Poliakov and Josef Wulf (eds.), *Das Dritte Reich und seine Diener* (Frankfurt am Main, 1959), 385–6; Christopher Browning, *The Origins of the Final Solution: The Evolution of Nazi Jewish Policy, September 1939–March 1942* (Lincoln, Nebr., 2004), 16–24, 72–80.

81. Rossino, *Hitler Strikes Poland*, 174–85; Szymon Datner, *Crimes Committed by the Wehrmacht during the September Campaign and the Period of Military Government* (Posen, 1962); Janusz Gumkowski and Kazimierz Leszczynski, *Poland under Nazi Occupation* (Warsaw, 1961), 53–5.

82. Rossino, *Hitler Strikes Poland*, 263 n. 129; Böhler, *Auftakt*, 169–80. See also Mazower, *Hitler's Empire*, 78–96.

83. Koehl, *RKFDV*, 14–52; for Darré's schemes, see Evans, *The Third Reich in Power*, 421–5. These policies are placed in the context of postwar Polish policy by Michael G. Esch, 'Gesunde Verhältnisse': Die deutsche und polnische Bevölkerungspolitik in Ost-mitteleuropa 1939–1950* (Marburg, 1998); the fundamental work here remains Koehl, *RKFDV*, which first made clear the nature and dimensions of Nazi plans for the ethnic reordering of East-Central Europe. More recently, see Czeslaw Madajczyk *et al.* (eds.), *Vom Generalplan Ost zum Generalsiedlungsplan: Dokumente* (Munich, 1994); Götz Aly, 'Final Solution': Nazi Population Policy and the Murder of the European Jews* I (London, 1999 [1995]); and Isabel Heinemann, 'Rasse, Siedlung, deutsches Blut': Das Rasse- und Siedlungs-hauptamt der SS und die rassenpolitische Neuordnung Europas* (Göttingen, 2003).

84. Hitler speech in Max Domarus (ed.), *Hitler: Speeches and Proclamations 1932–1945: The Chronicle of a Dictatorship* (4 vols., London, 1990– [1962–63]), III: *The Years 1939 to 1940*, 1,836.

85. Koehl, *RKFDV*, 49–58, 247–9.

86. Ibid., 49–65; Broszat, *Nationalsozialistische Polenpolitik*, 62–5; Götz Aly and Susanne Heim, *Architects of Annihilation: Auschwitz and the Logic of Destruction* (Princeton, N.J., 2002), 73–114 (economically reductionist); see also Michael G. Esch, ' "Ohne Rücksicht auf historisch Gewordenes": Raumplanung und Raumordnung im besetzten Polen 1939–1944', in Götz Aly *et al.* (eds.), *Modelle für ein deutsches Europa: Ökonomie und Herrschaft im Grosswirtschaftsraum* (Berlin, 1992), 77–123; Philip T. Rutherford, *Prelude to the Final Solution: The Nazi Program for Deporting Ethnic Poles, 1939–1941* (Lawrence, Kans., 2007).

87. Broszat, *Nationalsozialistische Polenpolitik*, 43.

88. Klukowski, *Diary*, 60 (11 December 1939); Broszat, *Nationalsozialistische Polenpolitik*, 42–3.

89. Klukowski, *Diary*, 88; also 120–21 (14 October 1940).

90. Jacobmeyer, 'Der Überfall', 23–9; Klukowski, *Diary*, 104 (26 July 1940); Koehl, *RKFDV*, 126–60; overview and chronology in Aly, 'Final Solution', 14–52, and in Madajczyk, *Die Okkupationspolitik*, 233–58.

91. Wilm Hosenfeld, 'Ich versuche jeden zu retten': Das Leben eines deutschen Offiziers in Briefen und Tagebüchern* (ed. Thomas Vogel, Munich, 2004), 3, 302 (notes, 14 December 1939).

92. Ibid., 303 (note of 15 December 1939).

93. Koehl, *RKFDV*, 49–70; Broszat, *Nationalsozialistische Polenpolitik*, 118–37. For documentation of German racial policy, see Georg Hansen (ed.), *Schulpolitik als Volks-tumspolitik: Quellen zur Schulpolitik der Besatzer in Polen 1939–1945* (Münster, 1994), 23–80.

94. Wolfgang Michalka (ed.), *Das Dritte Reich* (2 vols., Munich, 1985), II: *Weltmacht-anspruch und nationaler Zusammenbruch 1939–1945*, 163–6.

95. Clarissa Henry and Marc Hillel, *Children of the SS* (London, 1976 [1975]), 182–90; Koehl, *RKFDV*, 143–5, 219–21; Cyprian and Sawicki, *Nazi Rule*, 83–91. For the 'Well of Life' scheme, see Evans, *The Third Reich in Power*, 521.

96. Koehl, *RKFDV*, 140–42.

97. Quoted in Broszat, *Nationalsozialistische Polenpolitik*, 129–30 (footnotes).

98. Klukowski, *Diary*, 240 (29 January 1943).

99. Präg and Jacobmeyer (eds.), *Das Diensttagebuch*, 53; see more generally Madajczyk, *Die Okkupationspolitik*, 42–146.

100. Koehl, *RKFDV*, 70–88, 125–40; Präg and Jacobmeyer (eds.), *Das Diensttagebuch*, 209–10, 251, 296–7, 303–4.

101. Broszat, *Nationalsozialistische Polenpolitik*, 137–57; (Anon.), *The German New Order*, 410–11; Aly and Heim, *Architects*, 130–59; Cyprian and Sawicki, *Nazi Rule*, 92–105; Boguslaw Drewniak, 'Die deutsche Verwaltung und die rechtliche Stellung der Polen in den besetzten polnischen Gebieten 1939–1945', *Deutsch-Polnisches Jahrbuch 1979–80*, 151–70.

102. Georg Hansen, ' "Damit wurde der Warthegau zum Exerzierplatz des praktischen Nationalsozialismus": Eine Fallstudie zur Politik der Einverleibung', in Klessmann (ed.), *September 1939*, 55-72; Klessmann, *Die Selbstbehauptung*, 19–26; Broszat, *Nationalsozialistische Polenpolitik*, 157–76; Georg Hansen, *Ethnische Schulpolitik im besetzten Polen: Der Mustergau Wartheland* (Münster, 1995). Documentation on language policy in Georg Hansen (ed.), *Schulpolitik*, 81–106. For Jäger, see Evans, *The Third Reich in Power*, 224. See also Präg and Jacobmeyer (eds.), *Das Diensttagebuch*, 314, for Frank's growing hostility to the Catholic Church in the General Government (19 December 1940).

103. Jochen August (ed.), *'Sonderaktion Krakau': Die Verhaftung der Krakauer Wissenschaftler am 6. November 1939* (Hamburg, 1997).

104. Klessmann, *Die Selbstbehauptung*, 54–61, 78–107; idem and Wazlaw Dlugoborski, 'Nationalsozialistische Bildungspolitik und polnische Hochschulen 1939–1945', *Geschichte und Gesellschaft*, 23 (1997), 535–59.

105. Präg and Jacobmeyer (eds.), *Das Diensttagebuch*, 53.

106. Hans-Christian Harten, *De-Kulturation und Germanisierung: Die nationalsozialistische Rassen- und Erziehungspolitik in Polen 1939–1945* (Frankfurt am Main, 1996), 170–87 (for cultural policy) and 188–264 (for education); Evans, *The Nazi New Order*, 113–37; Gross, *Polish Society*, 75–8.

107. Sword, 'Poland', 696–7; Gertrude M. Godden, *Murder of a Nation: German Destruction of Polish Culture* (London, 1943), 7–56.

108. Klukowski, *Diary*, 54, 72; see more generally Christoph Klessmann, 'Die kulturelle Selbstbehauptung der polnischen Nation', in idem (ed.), *September 1939*, 117–38; idem, *Die Selbstbehauptung*, 108–82; idem, 'Die Zerstörung des Schulwesens als Bestandteil deutscher Okkupationspolitik im Osten am Beispiel Polens', in Manfred Heinemann (ed.), *Erziehung und Schulung im Dritten Reich*, I: *Kindergarten, Schule, Jugend, Berufserziehung* (Stuttgart, 1980), 176–92; and the extensive documentation in Hansen (ed.), *Schulpolitik*, 107–411.

109. Klukowski, *Diary*, 146 (18 April 1941).

110. Ibid., 126 (25 November 1940); Madajczyk, *Die Okkupationspolitik*, 333–64. For the long-term effects, see Waclaw Dlugoborski, 'Die deutsche Besatzungspolitik und die Veränderungen der sozialen Struktur Polens 1939–1945', in idem (ed.), *Zweiter Weltkrieg und sozialer Wandel: Achsenmächte und besetzte Länder* (Göttingen, 1981), 303–63.

111. Koehl, *RKFDV*, 49, 76, 89–100, 254; Aly, *'Final Solution'*, 59–81.

112. Matthias Hamann, 'Erwünscht und unerwünscht: Die rassenpsychologische Selektion der Ausländer', in Götz Aly *et al.* (eds.), *Herrenmensch und Arbeitsvölker: Ausländische Arbeiter und Deutsche 1939–1945* (Berlin, 1986), 143–80; Koehl, *RKFDV*, 100–110.

113. Ibid., 209–37.

114. Ibid., 129, 160–61.

115. Klukowski, *Diary*, 253–4 (17 May 1943).

116. Ibid., 264–9 (2–11 July 1943), 274–5 (1 August 1943); wider context in Michael Hartenstein, *Neue Dorflandschaften: Nationalsozialistische Siedlungsplanung in den 'eingegliederten Ostgebieten': 1939 und 1944* (Berlin, 1998).

117. Aly and Heim, *Architects*, 275–9 (again overemphasizing economic motivations); Henry and Hillel, *Children*, 180–81; Housden, *Hans Frank*, 187–9, 203; Madajczyk, *Die Okkupationspolitik*, 422–30.

118. Klukowski, *Diary*, 271 (15 July 1943), 289 (28 November 1943).

119. Ibid., 277–8 (18–27 August 1943).

120. Götz Aly, 'The Posen Diaries of the Anatomist Hermann Voss', in Götz Aly *et al.*, *Cleansing the Fatherland: Nazi Medicine and Racial Hygiene* (Baltimore, Md., 1994), 99–155, at 127 (24 May 1941), 128 (2 June 1941), 130 (15 June 1941).

121. Jost Hermand, *Als Pimpf in Polen: Erweiterte Kinderlandverschickung 1940–1945* (Frankfurt am Main, 1993), 78–118.

122. Maschmann, *Account Rendered*, 110–19.

123. Ibid., 127–9.

124. Elizabeth Harvey, *Women and the Nazi East: Agents and Witnesses of Germanization* (London, 2003), esp. 78–118 (recruitment) and 119–90; more generally, for the varied attitudes of Germans towards the Poles, see Madajczyk, *Die Okkupationspolitik*, 166–85.

125. Alcuin (pseud.), *I Saw Poland Suffer*, 62–8.

126. Broszat, *Nationalsozialistische Polenpolitik*, 80–84; Joachim C. Fest, *The Face of the Third Reich* (London, 1979 [1963]), 322–31; Gross, *Polish Society*, 45–62, 145–59; Housden, *Hans Frank*, 154–76.

127. Quoted in Gross, *Polish Society*, 110; concern about the black market noted in Präg and Jacobmeyer (eds.), *Das Diensttagebuch*, 88 (16 January 1940).

128. Madajczyk, *Die Okkupationspolitik*, 596–602.

129. Klukowski, *Diary*, 70.

130. Ibid., 74.

131. Ibid., 119 (1 October 1940); see also Tomasz Szarota, *Warschau unter dem Hakenkreuz: Leben und Alltag im besetzten Warschau 1. 10. 1939 bis 31. 7. 1944* (Paderborn, 1985 [1973]), 80–81, 113–14.

132. Jacobmeyer, 'Der Überfall', 29–31.

133. Sword, 'Poland', 697; Czeslaw Luczak, 'Landwirtschaft und Ernährung in Polen während der deutschen Besatzungszeit 1939–1945', in Bernd Märtin and Alan S. Milward (eds.), *Agriculture and Food Supply in the Second World War* (Ostfildern, 1985), 117–27.

134. Natalija Decker, 'Die Auswirkungen der faschistischen Okkupation auf das Gesundheitswesen Polens und den Gesundheitszustand des polnischen Volkes', in Achim Thom and Genadij Caregorodcev (eds.), *Medizin unterm Hakenkreuz* (Berlin, 1989), 401–16; also Madajczyk, *Die Okkupationspolitik*, 261–307 for everyday life under the Germans.

135. Klukowski, *Diary*, 77 (19 February 1940), 105–6 (1 August 1940), 126 (23 November 1940), 132 (4 January 1941). For informers, see Wlodzimierz Borodziej, *Terror und Politik: Die deutsche Polizei und die polnische Widerstandsbewegung im Generalgouvernement 1939–1944* (Mainz, 1999), 136–61.

136. Klukowski, *Diary*, 85 (25 April 1940).

137. For comparisons, see Waclaw Dlugoborski, 'Deutsche und sowjetische Herrschaftssysteme in Ostmitteleuropa im Vergleich', in Gerhard Otto and Johannes Houwink ten Cate (eds.), *Das organisierte Chaos: 'Ämterdarwinismus' und 'Gesinnungsethik': Determinanten nationalsozialistischer Besatzungsherrschaft* (Berlin, 1999), 93–121; idem and Czeslaw Madajczyk, 'Ausbeutungssysteme in den besetzten Gebieten Polens und der UdSSR', in Friedrich Forstmeier and Hans-Erich Volkmann (eds.), *Kriegswirtschaft und Rüstung 1939–1945* (Düsseldorf, 1977), 375–416.

138. Janusz K. Zawodny, *Death in the Forest: The Story of the Katyn Forest Massacre* (London, 1971); Wladyslaw T. Bartoszewski, 'Foreword', in Salomon W. Slowes, *The Road to Katyn: A Soldier's Story* (Oxford, 1992), vii–xxxii; and, most recently, Gerd Kaiser, *Katyn: Das Staatsverbrechen – das Staatsgeheimnis* (Berlin, 2002), and Anna M. Cienciala *et al.*, *Katyn: A Crime without Punishment* (London, 2006).

139. Sword, 'Poland', 698–9; Garlinski, *Poland*, 32–7; Norman Davies, *God's Playground: A History of Poland* (2 vols., Oxford, 1981), II. 447–53; Jan T. Gross, *Revolution from Abroad: The Soviet Conquest of Poland's Western Ukraine and Western Belorussia* (Princeton, N.J., 1988), esp. 35–45 (intercommunal violence), 71–113 (plebiscites), 144–86 (prisons) and 187–224 (deportations).

140. Friedländer, *The Years of Extermination*, 43–8; see also more generally Norman Davies and Antony Polonsky (eds.), *Jews in Eastern Poland and the USSR, 1939–1946* (New York, 1991), and Jan T. Gross, 'A Tangled Web: Confronting Stereotypes Concerning Relations between Poles, Germans, Jews, and Communists', in István Déak *et al.* (eds.), *The Politics of Retribution in Europe: World War II and its Aftermath* (Princeton, N.J., 2000), 74–129, probably, however, underestimating Jewish collaboration with the Soviet administration (97–8): see the detailed investigation by Alexander B. Rossino, 'Polish "Neighbors" and German Invaders: Anti-Jewish Violence in the Bialystok District during the Opening Weeks of Operation Barbarossa', *Polin: Studies in Polish Jewry*, 16 (2003), 431–52; and Bogdan Musial, *'Konterrevolutionäre Elemente sind zu erschiessen': Die Brutalisierung des deutsch-sowjetischen Krieges im Sommer 1941* (Berlin, 2000), 57–73.

141. Mazower, *Hitler's Empire*, 96–101.

142. For Nazi antisemitism, see Evans, *The Coming of the Third Reich*, 172–4; idem, *The Third Reich in Power*, 536–610.

143. Wladyslaw Bartoszewski, 'Polen und Juden in der deutschen Besatzungszeit', in Klessmann (ed.), *September 1939*, 139–55, at 139–41; Evans, *The Third Reich in Power*, 605–7; Peter Longerich, *Politik der Vernichtung: Eine Gesamtdarstellung der national-sozialistischen Judenverfolgung* (Munich, 1998), 252; Friedländer, *The Years of Extermination*, 24–30.

144. Evans, *The Third Reich in Power*, 578–9; Sybil H. Milton, 'The Expulsion of Polish Jews from Germany, October 1938 to July 1939: A Documentation', *Leo Baeck Institute Yearbook*, 29 (1984), 169–74.

145. Longerich, *Politik*, 249–50; also Werner Röhr, 'Zum Zusammenhang von nazistischer Okkupationspolitik in Polen und dem Völkermord an den polnischen Juden', in idem *et al.* (eds.), *Faschismus und Rassismus: Kontroversen um Ideologie und Opfer* (Berlin, 1992), 300–316.

146. Rossino, *Hitler Strikes Poland*, 88–115; Halder, *Kriegstagebuch*, I. 67 (10 September 1939).

147. Walter Manoschek (ed.), *'Es gibt nur Eines für das Judentum: Vernichtung': Das Judenbild in deutschen Soldatenbriefen 1939–1941* (Hamburg, 1997 [1995]).

148. Quoted in Browning, *The Origins*, 114.

149. Otto Dietrich, *Auf den Strassen des Sieges Erlebnisse mit dem Führer in Polen: Ein Gemeinschaftsbuch* (Munich, 1939), quoted in Richard Breitman, *The Architect of Genocide: Himmler and the Final Solution* (London, 1991), 73.

150. Fröhlich (ed.), *Die Tagebücher*, I/VII. 177–9 (2 November 1939).

151. David Welch, *Propaganda and the German Cinema 1933–1945* (Oxford, 1983), 292–3.

152. Böhler, *Auftakt*, 197–200, for a brief general account; ibid., 188–97, for the antisemitic prejudices and actions of ordinary soldiers.

153. Kaplan, *Scroll*, 25 (4 October 1939), 28 (6 October 1939), 69 (16 December 1939); Umbreit, *Deutsche Militärverwaltungen*, 205–11; see the brief and somewhat inconclusive account of rapes in Böhler, *Auftakt*, 186–7, and the examples of the rape of Jewish women by German soldiers in ibid., 197–200.

154. Klukowski, *Diary*, 30, 45–8.

155. Ibid., 78; see also Gross, *Polish Society*, 92–109; further examples in Kaplan, *Scroll*, 30 (12 October 1939); for the Church, Dawid Sierakowiak, *The Diary of Dawid Sierako-wiak* (ed. Alan Adelson, London, 1996), 54; Anna Landau-Czajka, 'The Jewish Question in Poland: Views Expressed in the Catholic Press between the Two World Wars', *Polin: Studies in Polish Jewry*, 11 (1998), 263–78; Brian Porter, 'Making a Space for Antisemi-

tism: The Catholic Hierarchy and the Jews in the Early Twentieth Century', *Polin: Studies in Polish Jewry*, 16 (2003), 415–29; and Klukowski, *Diary*, 40.

156. Ibid., 45.

157. Ibid., 38–42.

158. Ibid., 52–3.

159. Ibid., 62–3.

160. Ibid., 83.

161. Präg and Jacobmeyer (eds.), *Diensttagebuch*, 176–7; Omer Bartov, *Hitler's Army: Soldiers, Nazis, and War in the Third Reich* (New York, 1991), 64; Alexander Rossino, 'Destructive Impulses: German Soldiers and the Conquest of Poland', *Holocaust and Genocide Studies*, 11 (1997), 351–65.

162. Gefr. H. K., 12 August 1940, quoted in Manoschek (ed.), *'Es gibt nur eines'*, 15.

163. O. Gefr. J. E., 30 December 1939, cited in ibid., 12.

164. Emanuel Ringelblum, *Notes from the Warsaw Ghetto: The Journal of Emanuel Ringelblum* (New York, 1958 [1952]), 24, 27, 34.

165. Ibid., 47, also 33, 254.

166. Ibid., 68.

167. Ibid., 79.

168. Ibid., 84.

169. Mark Spoerer, *Zwangsarbeit unter dem Hakenkreuz: Ausländische Zivilarbeiter, Kriegsgefangere und Häftlinge im Deutschen Reich und im besetzten Europa 1939–1945* (Stuttgart, 2001), 45; Böhler, *Auftakt*, 177–8; Shmuel Krakowski, 'The Fate of Polish Prisoners of War in the September 1939 Camps', *Yad Vashem Studies*, 12 (1977), 296–333.

170. Kaplan, *Scroll*, 29 (10 October 1939); further examples in Emanuel Ringelblum, *Polish-Jewish Relations during the Second World War* (Jerusalem, 1974), 23–57 (also with details of Polish participation).

171. Tatiana Berenstein *et al.* (eds.), *Faschismus – Getto – Massenmord: Dokumentation über Ausrottung und Widerstand der Juden in Polen während des Zweiten Weltkrieges* (Berlin, 1960), 219–21; Dieter Pohl, *Von der 'Judenpolitik' zum Judenmord: Der Distrikt Lublin des Generalgouvernements 1939–1944* (Frankfurt am Main, 1993), 22–5.

172. Sierakowiak, *The Diary*, 37 (10 September 1939), 38 (13 September 1939), 39 (15 September 1939), 40 (17 September 1939), 41 (19 September 1939), 52 (14 October 1939), 56 (27 October 1939), 63 (16 November 1939), 66 (30 November 1939), 69–70 (12 December 1939).

173. Ibid., 111 (9 September 1940).

174. See more generally Madajczyk, *Die Okkupationspolitik*, 258–60, for the deportation of Jews in the context of the German resettlement programme.

175. Longerich, *Politik*, 251–61; Hans Safrian, *Die Eichmann-Männer* (Vienna, 1993), 68–86; Christopher Browning, *The Path to Genocide: Essays on Launching the Final Solution* (Cambridge, 1992), 3–11; idem, *Nazi Policy, Jewish Workers, German Killers* (Cambridge, 2000), 1–15; idem, *The Origins*, 36–43; David Cesarani, *Eichmann: His Life and Crimes* (London, 2004), 78–81; Pohl, *Von der 'Judenpolitik'*, 15–21, 26–31, 47–55; Himmler's order for the deportation of all Jews from the incorporated territories reported on 31 October 1939 in Präg and Jacobmeyer (eds.), *Das Diensttagebuch*, 52; more details in Seev Goshen, 'Eichmann und die Nisko-Aktion im Oktober 1939: Eine Fallstudie zur NS-Judenpolitik in der letzten Etappe vor der "Endlösung" ', *VfZ* 29 (1981), 74–96, and idem, 'Nisko – Ein Ausnahmefall unter den Judenlagern der SS', *VfZ* 40 (1992), 95–106.

176. Safrian, *Die Eichmann-Männer*, 87–104.

177. Aly and Heim, *Architects*, 156–9; Longerich, *Politik*, 253–61.

178. Browning, *The Path to Genocide*, 28–30; idem, *The Origins*, 36–81, 89–110 (figures on 109); Longerich, *Politik*, 266–9.

179. Shirer, *Berlin Diary*, 197–8.

180. Evans, *The Third Reich in Power*, 660–61.

181. Gustavo Corni, *Hitler's Ghettos: Voices from a Beleaguered Society 1939–1944* (London, 2002), 22–4; Frank's concerns in Präg and Jacobmeyer (eds.), *Das Diensttagebuch*, 95, 146–7.

182. Sierakowiak, *The Diary*, 71 (15 December 1939).

183. Browning, *The Origins*, 111–18; also Berenstein *et al.* (eds.), *Faschismus*, 78–81, for the order of 10 December 1939; also Lucjan Dobroszycki (ed.), *The Chronicle of the Lodz Ghetto 1941–1944* (New Haven, Conn., 1984), especially the Introduction.

184. Friedländer, *The Years of Extermination*, 105–6.

185. Isaiah Trunk, *Judenrat: The Jewish Councils in Eastern Europe under Nazi Occupation* (New York, 1972), remains unsurpassed as the authoritative account of these institutions. For their inception, see ibid., 1–55. Famously, the political philosopher Hannah Arendt, in her brilliant, tough-minded book *Eichmann in Jerusalem* (New York, 1963), accused these bodies of complicity in the Third Reich's policy of mass murder. However, the room for manoeuvre open to them and to their members was minimal, as Friedländer, *The Years of Extermination*, xxiii–xxiv, points out; see also Aharon Weiss, 'Jewish Leadership in Occupied Poland: Postures and Attitudes', *Yad Vashem Studies*, 12 (1977), 335–65.

186. Browning, *The Origins*, 114–20; Corni, *Hitler's Ghettos*, 82–3; Aly and Heim, *Architects*, 186–214.

187. Corni, *Hitler's Ghettos*, 84–6; Isaiah Trunk, *Lodz Ghetto: A History* (Bloomington, Ind., 2006 [1962]), 32–103. For an eloquent defence of Rumkowski, see Gordon J. Horwitz, *Ghettostadt: Lodz and the Making of a Nazi City* (London, 2008), esp. 75–88 and 311–17.

188. Corni, *Hitler's Ghettos*, 24–31, 78–81; Präg and Jacobmeyer (eds.), *Das Diensttagebuch*, 91, 94.

189. Corni, *Hitler's Ghettos*, 27–9.

190. Friedländer, *The Years of Extermination*, 104–6.

191. Ringelblum, *Notes*, 86–7 (19 November 1940). Ringelblum was always careful to distinguish between regular soldiers, as here, SS men and Gestapo. See ibid., 114–15 for an example.

192. Berenstein *et al.* (eds.), *Faschismus*, 108–13; Browning, *The Origins*, 121–31.

193. Czerniakow, *The Warsaw Diary*, 237 (17 May 1941).

194. Nachman Blumenthal, 'A Martyr or Hero? Reflections on the Diary of Adam Czerniakow', *Yad Vashem Studies*, 7 (1968), 165–71; Joseph Kermish, 'Introduction', in Czerniakow, *The Warsaw Diary*, 1–24, at 19; Czerniakow, *The Warsaw Diary*, 295 (1 November 1941); Trunk, *Judenrat*; minutes of meeting of 6–7 June 1940 in Präg and Jacobmeyer (eds.), *Das Diensttagebuch*, 232, 239 (point 8).

195. Berenstein *et al.* (eds.), *Faschismus*, 138; Friedländer, *The Years of Extermination*, 105–7; Trunk, *Judenrat*, 165; see also Yisrael Gutman, *The Jews of Warsaw, 1939–1943: Ghetto, Underground, Revolt* (Bloomington, Ind., 1982).

196. Corni, *Hitler's Ghettos*, 204–7, 215.

197. Ringelblum, *Notes*, 241.

198. Ibid., 194, 181.

199. Berenstein *et al.* (eds.), *Faschismus*, 152–3.

200. Charles G. Roland, *Courage under Siege: Starvation, Disease, and Death in the Warsaw Ghetto* (New York, 1992), 39, 99–101, 154–65.

201. Klukowski, *Diary*, 168 (3 September 1941).

202. Ringelblum, *Notes*, 268.

203. Ibid., 224 (19 February 1941); Corni, *Hitler's Ghettos*, 119–56; Trunk, *Judenrat*, 96–9.

204. Ibid., passim, esp. 100–155; and especially Gunnar S. Paulsson, *Secret City: The Hidden Jews of Warsaw, 1940–1945* (London, 2003); and Yisrael Gutman and Shmuel Krakowski, *Unequal Victims: Poles and Jews during World War Two* (New York, 1986), 32–3.

205. Hosenfeld, 'Ich versuche', 534 (note of 27 September 1941).

206. Kaplan, Scroll, 221–2 (14 February 1941).

207. Szarota, Warschau, 46; Ringelblum, Notes, 181.

208. Maschmann, Account Rendered, 81–2.

209. Uff. H. Z., 30 June 1941, quoted in Manoschek (ed.), 'Es gibt nur Eines', 30.

210. Hosenfeld, 'Ich versuche', 452 (note of 3 March 1941).

211. Corni, Hitler's Ghettos, 139–56; Czerniakow, The Warsaw Diary, 363 (6 June 1942),
373 (2 July 1942); Ringelblum, Polish-Jewish Relations; Ringelblum, Notes.

212. Browning, The Origins, 175–8; see also Wolf Gruner, Die geschlossene Arbeitseinsatz
deutscher Juden: Zur Zwangsarbeit als Element der Verfolgung, 1938–1943 (Berlin,
1997); and Dieter Maier, Arbeitseinsatz und Deportation: Die Mitwirkung der Arbeitsverwaltung bei der nationalsozialistischen Judenverfolgung in den Jahren 1938–1945 (Berlin,
1994).

213. Friedländer, The Years of Extermination, 193–4; Hillel Levine, In Search of Sugihara:
The Elusive Japanese Diplomat Who Risked His Life to Rescue 10,000 Jews from the
Holocaust (New York, 1996).

214. Juliane Wetzel, 'Auswanderung aus Deutschland', in Wolfgang Benz (ed.), Die Juden in
Deutschland 1933–1945: Leben unter nationalsozialistischer Herrschaft (Munich, 1988),
413–98, esp. 472–98.

215. Volker Dahm, 'Kulturelles und geistiges Leben', in Benz (ed.), Die Juden, 75–267,
esp. 223–57 ('Kulturelles und geistiges Leben 1939–41').

216. Günter Plum, 'Deutsche Juden oder Juden in Deutschland?', in Benz (ed.), Die Juden,
35–74, esp. 71–2.

217. Browning, The Origins, 169–75; Eric A. Johnson, Nazi Terror: The Gestapo, Jews,
and Ordinary Germans (New York, 1999), 355–8, 382–95; 'racial defilement' cases in
Patricia Szobar, 'Telling Sexual Stories in the Nazi Courts of Law: Race Defilement in
Germany 1933–1945', Journal of the History of Sexuality, 11 (2002), 131–63. For
rationing, see Marion Kaplan, 'Jewish Daily Life in Wartime Germany', in David Bankier
(ed.), Probing the Depths of German Antisemitism: German Society and the Persecution
of the Jews, 1933–1941 (Jerusalem, 2000), 395–412, at 396–8.

218. Friedländer, The Years of Extermination, 93–4.

219. Ibid., 51–2.

220. Evans, The Third Reich in Power, 567–8, 601–2.

221. Victor Klemperer, I Shall Bear Witness: The Diaries of Victor Klemperer 1933–41
(London, 1998 [1995]), 114, 266–9, 279, 292–336, quotes at 324 (26 May 1940), 325
(26 May 1940), 336 (11 August 1940); idem, To the Bitter End: The Diaries of Victor
Klemperer 1942–45 (London, 1998 [1995]), 31 (24 March 1942).

222. Klemperer, I Shall Bear Witness, 337–99.

223. Evans, The Third Reich in Power, 524–7.

224. Michael Zimmermann, Rassenutopie und Genozid: Die nationalsozialistische 'Lösung
der Zigeunerfrage' (Hamburg, 1996), 193–9.

225. Browning, The Origins, 178–84; Henry Friedlander, The Origins of Nazi Genocide:
From Euthanasia to the Final Solution (Chapel Hill, N.C., 1995), 246–62; Sybil H. Milton,
' "Gypsies" as Social Outsiders in Nazi Germany', in Robert Gellately and Nathan Stolzfus
(eds.), Social Outsiders in Nazi Germany (Princeton, N.J., 2001), 212–32, esp. 223–5.

226. Guenter Lewy, The Nazi Persecution of the Gypsies (New York, 2000), 65–81;
Zimmermann, Rassenutopie, 167–84, 200–207.

227. Volker Riess, Die Anfänge der Vernichtung 'lebensunwerten Lebens' in den
Reichsgauen Danzig-Westpreussen und Wartheland 1939/40 (Frankfurt am Main, 1995),
21–24, 98.

228. Ibid., 355–8. For the gas wagons, see Matthias Beer, 'Die Entwicklung der Gaswagen
beim Mord an den Juden', VfZ 35 (1987), 403–17.

229. Klukowski, Diary, 76 (18 February 1940).

230. Longerich, Politik, 236–7; Ernst Klee (ed.), Dokumente zur 'Euthanasie' (Frankfurt am

Main, 1985), 70–81; Michael Burleigh, *Death and Deliverance: 'Euthanasia' in Germany, c.1900–1945* (Cambridge, 1994), 130–33.

231. Longerich, *Politik*, 234–5, 648 n. 36, arguing persuasively against the contention of Götz Aly that the killings stood in a causal connection with plans to resettle ethnic Germans in the area (Aly, *'Final Solution'*, 70–76; idem, 'Medicine against the Useless', in idem et al., *Cleansing the Fatherland: Nazi Medicine and Racial Hygiene* (Baltimore, Md., 1994), 22–98).

232. Riess, *Die Anfänge*, 359; also Ernst Klee, *'Euthanasie' im NS-Staat: Die 'Vernichtung lebensunwerten Lebens'* (Frankfurt am Main, 1985 [1983]), 95–8, 112–15; and Burleigh, *Death*, 130.

233. Quoted in Kurt Nowak, *'Euthanasie' und Sterilisierung im 'Dritten Reich' – Die Konfrontation der evangelischen und katholischen Kirche mit dem 'Gesetz zur Verhütung erbkranken Nachwuchses' und der 'Euthanasie'-Aktion* (Göttingen, 1984 [1977]), 63–4.

234. Evans, *The Coming of the Third Reich*, 35–8, 143–5, 377–8; idem, *The Third Reich in Power*, 506–15.

235. Hans-Walter Schmuhl, 'Die Patientenmorde', in Angelika Ebbinghaus and Klaus Dörner (eds.), *Vernichten und Heilen: Der Nürnberger Ärzteprozess und seine Folgen* (Berlin, 2001), 295–328, at 301; Klee (ed.), *Dokumente*, 35–64.

236. Quoted in Burleigh, *Death*, 97; Klee, *'Euthanasie'*, 76–7; Wagner quote in Eugen Kogon et al. (eds.), *Nationalsozialistische Massentötungen durch Giftgas: Eine Dokumentation* (Frankfurt am Main, 1983), 28–9; Hans-Walter Schmuhl, *Rassenhygiene, Nationalsozialismus, Euthanasie: Von der Verhütung zur Vernichtung 'lebensunwerten Lebens', 1890–1945* (Göttingen, 1987), 149–50, 178–81.

237. Riess, *Die Anfänge*, 281–90; Karl Heinz Roth and Götz Aly, 'Das "Gesetz über die Sterbehilfe bei unheilbar Kranken": Protokolle der Diskussion über die Legalisierung der nationalsozialistischen Anstaltsmorde in den Jahren 1938–1941', in Karl Heinz Roth (ed.), *Erfassung zur Vernichtung: Von der Sozialhygiene zum 'Gesetz über Sterbehilfe'* (Berlin, 1984), 101–79, at 104–11; Friedlander, *The Origins*, 39–44; Burleigh, *Death*, 93–100; Klee, *'Euthanasie'*, 77–81; Longerich, *Politik*, 234–5. The chronology of these events is reviewed exhaustively in Ulf Schmidt, 'Reassessing the Beginning of the "Euthanasia" Programme', *German History*, 17 (1999), 543–50, also effectively disposing of standard accounts of the name and case-history of the baby in Leipzig whose condition gave Hitler the pretext for launching the action. See also Ulf Schmidt, *Karl Brandt: The Nazi Doctor: Medicine and Power in the Third Reich* (London, 2007), 117–23 (for the case) and 123–46 (for the launching of the programme).

238. Roth and Aly, 'Das "Gesetz" ', 112–17; Burleigh, *Death*, 98–9; Friedlander, *The Origins*, 44–6.

239. Ibid., 67–8; Klee (ed.), *Dokumente*, 85–91; Christian Ganssmüller, *Die Erbgesundheitspolitik des Dritten Reiches: Planung, Durchführung und Durchsetzung* (Cologne, 1987), 158–70.

240. Klee, *'Euthanasie'*, 80–81.

241. Burleigh, *Death*, 99–101; Klee, *'Euthanasie'*, 82–95; Klee (ed.), *Dokumente*, 238–45, 295–307; Ganssmüller, *Die Erbgesundheitspolitik*, 150–55. For Binding and Hoche, see Evans, *The Coming of the Third Reich*, 145.

242. Götz Aly, 'Der Mord an behinderten Hamburger Kindern zwischen 1939 und 1945', in Angelika Ebbinghaus et al. (eds.), *Heilen und Vernichten im Mustergau Hamburg: Bevölkerungs- und Gesundheitspolitik im Dritten Reich* (Hamburg, 1984), 147–55; Burleigh, *Death*, 101–11; Schmuhl, 'Die Patientenmorde', 302; idem, *Rassenhygiene*, 182–9.

243. Quoted in Friedlander, *The Origins*, 50.

244. Aly, 'Der Mord', 151; Schmuhl, *Rassenhygiene*, 188–9.

245. Quoted in Aly, 'Der Mord', 148; see also Burleigh, *Death*, 100; Schmuhl, 'Die Patientenmorde', 305–6, and Gerhard Baader, 'Heilen und Vernichten: Die Mentalität der NS-Ärzte', in Ebbinghaus and Dörner (eds.), *Vernichten und Heilen*, 275–94.

246. Friedlander, *The Origins*, 68–9; Ganssmüller, *Die Erbgesundheitspolitik*, 155–7.

247. Good basic overview in Armin Trus, '... vom Leid erlösen': Zur Geschichte der nationalsozialistischen 'Euthanasie'-Verbrechen: Texte und Materialien für Unterricht und Studium (Frankfurt am Main, 1995), 91–7; more detail in Schmuhl, Rassenhygiene, 190–95.

248. Friedlander, The Origins, 65–6; Burleigh, Death, 113–14.

249. Friedlander, The Origins, 86–7; Schmuhl, Rassenhygiene, 195–7; Widmann quoted in Klee (ed.), Dokumente, 69.

250. Riess, Die Anfänge, 355–8.

251. Friedlander, The Origins, 86–94.

252. Ibid., 73–84; Klee, 'Euthanasie', 115–23; Klee (ed.), Dokumente, 92–104; Burleigh, Death, 128–9.

253. Schmuhl, Rassenhygiene, 202–3, 215–17.

254. Friedlander, The Origins, 83–5; Klee, 'Euthanasie', 174–90; Klee (ed.), Dokumente, 105–16, 184–90; Burleigh, Death, 135–46.

255. Quoted in Klee (ed.), Dokumente, 125 (box); see also, for the procedure, Friedlander, The Origins, 93–110.

256. Klee, 'Euthanasie', 149–52; Klee (ed.), Dokumente, 149–59; Burleigh, Death, 146–9; Schmuhl, Rassenhygiene, 203–8.

257. Friedlander, The Origins, 85.

258. Wirth quoted in Klee (ed.), Dokumente, 124–5; also more generally ibid., 119–42; Friedlander, The Origins, 102–6; and Burleigh, Death, 149–57.

259. Friedlander, The Origins, 109–10. See also Johannes Tuchel (ed.), 'Kein Recht auf Leben': Beiträge und Dokumente zur Entrechtung und Vernichtung 'lebensunwerten Lebens' im Nationalsozialismus (Berlin, 1984), and Roland Müller (ed.), Krankenmord im Nationalsozialismus: Grafeneck und die 'Euthanasie' in Südwestdeutschland (Stuttgart, 2001), a collection of conference papers.

260. Burleigh, Death, 169–73.

261. All quoted in Klee, 'Euthanasie', 310; see also Schmuhl, Rassenhygiene, 207–11.

262. Klee (ed.), Dokumente, 209; Friedlander, The Origins, 116–21; Lothar Gruchmann, 'Ein unbequemer Amtsrichter im Dritten Reich: Aus den Personalakten des Dr. Lothar Kreyssig', VfZ 32 (1984), 462–88.

263. Klee, 'Euthanasie', 255–8; see more generally Nowak, 'Euthanasie' und Sterilisierung.

264. Shirer, Berlin Diary, 398–401, 447–51.

265. Klee (ed.), Dokumente, 151–62 (reprinting the entire memorandum); Klee, 'Euthanasie', 285.

266. Quoted in Klee (ed.), Dokumente, 213–14.

267. Friedlander, The Origins, 113–14; Burleigh, Death, 166–9; Gansmüller, Die Erbgesundheitspolitik, 170–72; Schmuhl, Rassenhygiene, 312–46.

268. Ulrich von Hassell, The von Hassell Diaries: The Story of the Forces against Hitler inside Germany 1938–1944 (Boulder, Colo., 1994 [1946]), 150, 159, 165.

269. Klee (ed.), Dokumente, 143.

270. Klee, 'Euthanasie', 278–85; Burleigh, Death, 167–8.

271. Klee, 'Euthanasie', 234–53.

272. Beth A. Griech-Polelle, Bishop von Galen: German Catholicism and National Socialism (New Haven, Conn., 2002), 77; Evans, The Third Reich in Power, 515–16.

273. Ibid., 239.

274. Klee (ed.), Dokumente, 167–8, 193.

275. Ibid., 170–73; Griech-Polelle, Bishop von Galen, 76–7.

276. Klee (ed.), Dokumente, 182–4; Burleigh, Death, 174–6; Griech-Polelle, Bishop von Galen, 76–8 (but quoting Burleigh's words as though they were Faulhaber's).

277. Klee (ed.), Dokumente, 183.

278. Ibid., 184. The emphasis in these various documents on the illegitimacy of killing the innocent reflected the long-held support of the Catholic Church and its lay organizations for the death penalty: see Richard J. Evans, Rituals of Retribution: Capital Punishment in

Germany 1600–1987 (Oxford, 1996), 76–7, 332–3, 336–8, 432–3, 604–6, 654–5, 711–14, 797–9.

279. Klee (ed.), *Dokumente*, 193; overview in Schmuhl, *Rassenhygiene*, 346–54.

280. Klee (ed.), *Dokumente*, 178–86, 82–3.

281. Griech-Polelle, *Bishop von Galen*, 84–5, 186–96; Burleigh, *Death*, 176–8.

282. Trus, '. . . *vom Leid erlösen'*, 147–8.

283. Griech-Polelle, *Bishop von Galen*, 86; Klee, *'Euthanasie'*, 335–9.

284. Joachim Kuropka (ed.), *Meldungen aus Münster, 1924–1944: Geheime und vertrauliche Berichte von Polizei, Gestapo, NSDAP und ihren Gliederungen, staatlicher Verwaltung, Gerichtsbarkeit und Wehrmacht über die politische und gesellschaftliche Situation in Münster* (Münster, 1992).

285. Report in Boberach (ed.), *Meldungen*, IX. 3,175–8, also reprinted in Trus, '. . . *vom Leid erlösen'*, 138–41. See also Griech-Polelle, *Bishop von Galen*, 86–93; Burleigh, *Death*, 209–19; Karl Ludwig Rost, *Sterilisation und Euthanasie im Film des 'Dritten Reiches': Nationalsozialistische Propaganda in ihrer Beziehung zu rassenhygienischen Massnahmen des NS-Staates* (Berlin, 1984), 166–8; and Kurt Nowak, 'Widerstand, Zustimmung, Hinnahme: Das Verhalten der Bevölkerung zur "Euthanasie"', in Norbert Frei (ed.), *Medizin und Gesundheitspolitik in der NS-Zeit* (Munich, 1991), 235–51.

286. Lothar Gruchmann, 'Euthanasie und Justiz im Dritten Reich', *VfZ* 20 (1972), 235–79, at 278–9.

287. Ganssmüller, *Die Erbgesundheitspolitik*, 173; Gruchmann, 'Euthanasie', 277.

288. Burleigh, *Death*, 176–80, overstates the case against the Catholic Church; Friedlander, *The Origins*, 111–12, takes it more or less as read and credits public opinion rather than the Churches; Griech-Polelle, *Bishop von Galen*, 92–3, sums up the arguments judiciously, pointing out that Galen's sermons were expressing in religious terms what public opinion felt more generally.

289. Excellent analysis in Longerich, *Politik*, 241–2.

290. Thus the arguments in Omer Bartov, *The Eastern Front 1941–1945: German Troops and the Barbarization of Warfare* (London, 1985); and idem, *Hitler's Army*, dating these processes from the invasion of the Soviet Union onwards; see the critique in Rossino, *Hitler Strikes Poland*, 191, and the account of the many works that assume that the German war of racial extermination in the east only began in 1941 in Böhler, *Auftakt*, 9–16.

291. Tadeusz Piotrowski, *Poland's Holocaust: Ethnic Strife, Collaboration with Occupying Forces, and Genocide in the Second Republic, 1918–1947* (Jefferson, N.C., 1998); Böhler, *Auftakt*, 241–7.

292. Berndt and Strecker (eds.), *Polen*; Richard J. Evans (ed.), *Kneipengespräche im Kaiserreich: Die Stimmungsberichte der Hamburger Politischen Polizei 1892–1914* (Hamburg, 1989), 361–83.

293. Hosenfeld, *'Ich versuche'*, 292 (letter to son, 23 November 1939).

294. Johannes Hürter (ed.), *Ein deutscher General an der Ostfront: Die Briefe und Tagebücher des Gotthard Heinrici 1941/42* (Essen, 2001), 56 (letter to wife, 22 April 1941).

295. Ibid., 56 (letter to wife, 25 April 1941).

296. Ibid., 57 (letter to family, 30 April 1941).

297. Ibid.

298. Rossino, *Hitler Strikes Poland*, 121–43.

299. Evans, *The Coming of the Third Reich*, 61.

300. See Rossino, *Hitler Strikes Poland*, arguing against Jürgen Förster, 'Jewish Policies of the German Military, 1939–1942', in Asher Cohen *et al.* (eds.), *The Shoah and the War* (New York, 1992), 53–71, at 56, and Umbreit, *Deutsche Militärverwaltungen*, 137, 273.

Chapter 2. FORTUNES OF WAR

1. Roger Moorhouse, *Killing Hitler: The Third Reich and the Plots against the Führer* (London, 2006), 36–58, is the most recent account. See also Peter Hoffmann, *Hitler's Personal Security* (London, 1979), 105–11.

2. Moorhouse, *Killing Hitler*, 50–53; Heinz Höhne, *The Order of the Death's Head: The Story of Hitler's SS* (London, 1972 [1966]), 264–6.

3. Moorhouse, *Killing Hitler*, 43–50; Kershaw, *Hitler*, II. 271–5.

4. Boberach (ed.), *Meldungen*, III. 449: Bericht zur innenpolitischen Lage Nr. 15, 13 November 1939.

5. Shirer, *Berlin Diary*, 194–5 (9 November 1939).

6. Alan Bullock, *Hitler: A Study in Tyranny* (London, 1952), 522–3, claimed the Gestapo was responsible, as did Peter Padfield, *Himmler: Reichsführer-SS* (London, 1990), 283. See however Anton Hoch, 'Das Attentat auf Hitler im Münchener Bürgerbräukeller 1939', *VfZ* 17 (1969), 383–413, and especially Lothar Gruchmann (ed.), *Autobiographie eines Attentäters: Johann Georg Elser: Aussage zum Sprengstoffanschlag im Bürgerbräukeller, München, am 8. November 1939* (Stuttgart, 1970).

7. Moorhouse, *Killing Hitler*, 58.

8. Hans-Adolf Jacobsen (ed.), *Dokumente zur Vorgeschichte des Westfeldzuges 1939–1940* (Göttingen, 1956), 5–7. For the generals' previous caution, see Evans, *The Third Reich in Power*, 633, 642, 668–70.

9. International Military Tribunal, Nuremberg: ND 789-PS, 572–80: see Evans, *The Third Reich in Power*, 892.

10. Fedor von Bock, *Generalfeldmarschall Fedor von Bock: Zwischen Pflicht und Verweigerung: Das Kriegstagebuch* (ed. Klaus Gerbet, Munich, 1995), 78–9 (23 November 1939).

11. For the confrontation of 1938, see Evans, *The Third Reich in Power*, 668–71; for the arguments of 1939–40 and the revival of the plot, see Kershaw, *Hitler*, II. 262–71, and Johannes Hürter, *Hitlers Heerführer: Die deutschen Oberbefehlshaber im Krieg gegen die Sowjetunion 1941/42* (Munich, 2007), 163–71.

12. Tooze, *The Wages of Destruction*, 331–43. An exhaustive account of the airplane building programme is provided by Lutz Budrass, *Flugzeugindustrie und Luftrüstung in Deutschland* (Düsseldorf, 1998). The supply situation was a constant concern in Halder's diary during these months (Halder, *Kriegstagebuch*, I, *passim*).

13. Rolf-Dieter Müller, 'The Mobilization of the German Economy for Hitler's War Aims', *GSWW* V/I. 407–786, at 407–11; Tooze, *The Wages of Destruction*, 343–8.

14. Müller, 'The Mobilization', 453–85.

15. Evans, *The Third Reich in Power*, 364–5; for Todt see ibid., 322–5.

16. Weinberg, *A World at Arms*, 100–103; Catherine Merridale, *Ivan's War: The Red Army 1939–1945* (London, 2005), 67–70. For German policy, see Gerd R. Ueberschär, *Hitler und Finnland 1938–1941* (Wiesbaden, 1978).

17. Merridale, *Ivan's War*, 44–7, 57–60, 67–71.

18. Weinberg, *A World at Arms*, 105–7; John Erickson, *The Soviet High Command* (London, 1962), 541–52; Tomas Ries, *Cold Will: The Defence of Finland* (London, 1988); Geoffrey Roberts, *Stalin's Wars: From World War to Cold War, 1939–1953* (London, 2006), 46–55; Chris Bellamy, *Absolute War: Soviet Russia in the Second World War: A Modern History* (London, 2007), 69–98.

19. Thomas K. Derry, 'Norway', in Stuart J. Woolf (ed.), *European Fascism* (London, 1968), 217–30, at 217–24.

20. Derry, 'Norway', 224–6; Weinberg, *A World at Arms*, 114–15; Oddvar K. Hoidal, *Quisling: A Study in Treason* (Oslo, 1989); Carl-Axel Gemzell, *Raeder, Hitler und Skandinavien* (Lund, 1965). For Quisling's visit to Berlin in December 1939 and Raeder's key role in prewar planning, see Hans-Martin Ottmer, *'Weserübung': Der deutsche Angriff auf Dänemark und Norwegen im April 1940* (Munich, 1994), 24–6, 3–17.

21. Bernd Stegemann, 'Operation Weserübung', in *GSWW* II. 206–19, at 211–12; Ottmer, 'Weserübung', 67–79; Hubatsch (ed.), *Hitlers Weisungen*, 47–50.

22. Stegemann, 'Operation Weserübung', 207–11; Ottmer, 'Weserübung', 79–131.

23. Vidkun Quisling, *Quisling ruft Norwegen! Reden und Aufsätze* (Munich, 1942), 96–7, 102, 105, 137.

24. Stegemann, 'Operation Weserübung', 212–15.

25. Weinberg, *A World at Arms*, 119–21; Shirer, *Berlin Diary*, 254 (4 May 1940).

26. Meier-Welcker, *Aufzeichnungen*, 54 (21 March 1940).

27. Roy Jenkins, *Churchill* (London, 2001), 573–84.

28. Peter Clarke, *Hope and Glory: Britain 1900–1990* (London, 1996), 192–6.

29. Jacobsen (ed.), *Dokumente*, 64–5, 155–6; Hans-Adolf Jacobsen, *Fall Gelb: Der Kampf um den deutschen Operationsplan zur Westoffensive 1940* (Wiesbaden, 1957); Karl-Heinz Frieser, *Blitzkrieg-Legende: Der Westfeldzug 1940* (Munich, 1996 [1995]), 15–70 for the short-term, improvised nature of the plan, 71–116 for arguments about it within the military hierarchy.

30. Shirer, *Berlin Diary*, 275–6 (20 May 1940); Hans Umbreit, 'The Battle for Hegemony in Western Europe', in *GSWW* II. 227–326, at 270–80; Julian Jackson, *The Fall of France: The Nazi Invasion of 1940* (Oxford, 2003), 9–39; Ernest R. May, *Strange Victory: Hitler's Conquest of France* (New York, 2000).

31. Shirer, *Berlin Diary*, 276–9 (20 May 1940).

32. Weinberg, *A World at Arms*, 122–6.

33. Umbreit, 'The Battle', 37; Frieser, *Blitzkrieg-Legende*, 428.

34. Jackson, *The Fall of France*, 37–9; Frieser, *Blitzkrieg-Legende*, 135.

35. Bock, *Zwischen Pflicht und Verweigerung*, 101 (24 February 1940).

36. Jackson, *The Fall of France*, 42–7; Umbreit, 'The Battle', 278–304; vivid narrative in Tooze, *The Wages of Destruction*, 374–9; details of the amphetamine use in Werner Pieper (ed.), *Nazis on Speed: Drogen im 3. Reich* (Loherbach, 2002), 325–30; the best recent critical account in Frieser, *Blitzkrieg-Legende*, 173–361.

37. Jackson, *The Fall of France*, 9–12 (quote on 10).

38. Ibid., 58–62.

39. Ibid., 85–94, gives a judicious account of these much-contested events; see also Kershaw, *Hitler*, II. 295–6.

40. Bock, *Zwischen Pflicht und Verweigerung*, 135 (26 May 1940), 140 (30 May 1940); Hans-Adolf Jacobsen, *Dünkirchen: Ein Beitrag zur Geschichte des Westfeldzuges 1940* (Neckargemünd, 1958), 70–122, 203, and idem (ed.), *Dokumente zum Westfeldzug 1940* (Göttingen, 1960), 114–46, both pinning the responsibility on Rundstedt; Frieser, *Blitzkrieg-Legende*, 363–93, emphasizes Hitler's role.

41. Bock, *Zwischen Pflicht und Verweigerung*, 143 (2 June 1940).

42. Jackson, *The Fall of France*, 94–100.

43. Ibid., 101–6 (quote on 105).

44. Ibid., 107–73; Frieser, *Blitzkrieg-Legende*, 399–409; May, *Strange Victory*, 448–9, arguing for the buoyancy of French military morale in the early stages of the invasion.

45. Irène Némirovsky, *Suite Française* (London, 2007 [2004]), 50.

46. Ibid., 42.

47. Jackson, *The Fall of France*, 174–82; Hanna Diamond, *Fleeing Hitler: France 1940* (Oxford, 2007).

48. Meier-Welcker, *Aufzeichnungen*, 74 (12 June 1940).

49. Shirer, *Berlin Diary*, 328–32 (21 June, 1940).

50. Jackson, *The Fall of France*, 232; the best overall survey remains the same author's *France: The Dark Years 1940–1944* (Oxford, 2001).

51. Frieser, *Blitzkrieg-Legende*, 409–35.

52. Albert Speer, *Inside the Third Reich: Memoirs* (London, 1971 [1970]), 170–2 (also quoted in Lynn Nicholas, *The Rape of Europa: The Fate of Europe's Treasures in the Third Reich and the Second World War* (New York, 1994), 118).

53. Shirer, *Berlin Diary*, 260–63 (10–11 May 1940).

54. Lore Walb, *Ich, die Alte – ich, die Junge: Konfrontation mit meinen Tagebüchern 1933–1945* (Berlin, 1997), 179 (21 May 1940).

55. Boberach (ed.), *Meldungen*, IV. 1,163 (23 May 1940).

56. Ibid., 1,189 (30 May 1940), 1,261 (17 June 1940).

57. Ibid., 1,274–5 (20 June 1940).

58. Hosenfeld, *'Ich versuche'*, 294 (letter to his wife 25 November 1939).

59. Ibid., 356 (11 June 1940, letter to son).

60. Luise Solmitz, *Tagebuch* (Staatsarchiv der Freien- und Hansestadt Hamburg, 622–1, 11I511–13: Familie Solmitz; transcripts in Forschungsstelle für Zeitgeschichte, Hamburg), XI. 551, 560, 563, 565–6 (12 June 1940, 17 June 1940, 21 June 1940).

61. Gerhard L. Weinberg, 'Hitler and England, 1933–1945: Pretense and Reality', *German Studies Review*, 8 (1988), 299–309, argues that Hitler was never interested in a deal with Britain; see also Weinberg, *A World at Arms*, 89–95.

62. Frances Donaldson, *Edward VIII* (London, 1974), 191–206, 327–34, 358–77; Michael Bloch, *Operation Willi: The Plot to Kidnap the Duke of Windsor, July 1940* (London, 1984); Walter Schellenberg, *The Memoirs of Hitler's Spymaster* (London, 2006 [1956]).

63. Weinberg, *A World at Arms*, 118.

64. Charles S. Thomas, *The German Navy in the Nazi Era* (London, 1990), 191.

65. Shirer, *Berlin Diary*, 355, 358 (19–20 July 1940).

66. Walb, *Ich, die Alte*, 185 (17 June 1940).

67. Domarus (ed.), *Hitler*, III. 2,062 (19 July 1940), Kershaw, *Hitler*, II. 301–8. For the idea that a separate peace would have saved the British Empire, see John Charmley, *Churchill: The End of Glory: A Political Biography* (London, 1993), 422–32.

68. Karl Klee, *Das Unternehmen 'Seelöwe': Die geplante deutsche Landung in England 1940* (Göttingen, 1958); idem, *Dokumente zum Unternehmen 'Seelöwe': Die geplante deutsche Landung in England 1940* (Göttingen, 1959), both arguing that the problem was caused by lack of advance planning.

69. Walter Schellenberg, *Invasion 1940: The Nazi Invasion Plan for Britain* (London, 2000), esp. 1–114 ('Gestapo Handbook').

70. Richard J. Overy, *The Battle* (London, 2000), 60–63.

71. Ibid., esp. 161–2.

72. Ibid., 53–4, 80.

73. Tooze, *The Wages of Destruction*, 249–50, 400–401.

74. Shirer, *Berlin Diary*, 377 (17 August 1940).

75. Ulrich Steinhilfer and Peter Osborne, *Spitfire on My Tail: A View from the Other Side* (Bromley, 1989), 279 (19 August 1940).

76. Ibid., 289 (31 August). The original expression was *Horridoh!*

77. Domarus (ed.), *Hitler*, III. 2,086 (4 September 1940).

78. Ibid., 2,072 (1 August 1940, Directive no. 17); for the contrary view, see Kershaw, *Hitler*, II. 309; good discussion in Horst Boog, 'The Strategic Air War in Europe and Air Defence of the Reich', in *GSWW* VII. 9–458, at 357–67.

79. Overy, *The Battle*, 90–96; Klaus A. Maier, 'The Battle of Britain', in *GSWW* II. 374–407.

80. Overy, *The Battle*, 90–96; Alfred Price, *Blitz on Britain* (Shepperton, 1977); Tooze, *The Wages of Destruction*, 447–8.

81. Steinhilfer and Osborne, *Spitfire*, 295 (17 September 1940).

82. Ibid., 319 (letter to father, 19 October 1940).

83. Halder, *Kriegstagebuch*, II. 128 (7 October 1940).

84. Ibid., 99 (14 September 1940).

85. Walb, *Ich, die Alte*, 197 (10 September 1940).

86. F. Harry Hinsley, *British Intelligence in the Second World War* (5 vols., London, 1979–90), I. 316–18, 523–48.

87. Walb, *Ich, die Alte*, 200 (3 October 1940).

88. Meier-Welcker, *Aufzeichnungen*, 101 (31 December 1940).

89. Overy, *The Battle*, 97–135.

90. Quoted in Paul Preston, *Franco: A Biography* (London, 1993), 397–8.

91. Kershaw, *Hitler*, II. 329–30; Paul Preston, 'Franco and Hitler: The Myth of Hendaye 1940', *Contemporary European History*, 1 (1992), 1–16; idem, *Franco*, 399.

92. Richard Bosworth, *Mussolini's Italy: Life under the Dictatorship 1915–1945* (London, 2005), 415–20.

93. Denis Mack Smith, *Mussolini* (London, 1983 [1981]), 269–91; Umbreit, 'The Battle', 304–13.

94. Kershaw, *Hitler*, II. 331.

95. Detlef Vogel, 'German Intervention in the Balkans', in *GSWW* III. 451–55; Gerhard Schreiber, 'Germany, Italy and South-east Europe: From Political and Economic Hegemony to Military Aggression', ibid., 305–448 (statistics on 448); Smith, *Mussolini*, 298–302; Martin Clark, *Modern Italy 1871–1982* (Harlow, 1984), 285–8.

96. Dear (ed.), *The Oxford Companion to World War II*, 148–9; Smith, *Mussolini*, 308.

97. Clark, *Modern Italy*, 286.

98. Smith, *Mussolini*, 310–11; Dear (ed.), *The Oxford Companion to World War II*, 245–7.

99. Bernd Stegemann, 'The Italo-German Conduct of War in the Mediterranean and North Africa', in *GSWW* III. 643–754, at 673–80.

100. Halder, *Kriegstagebuch*, II. 377 (23 April 1941), III. 48 (6 July 1941).

101. Dear (ed.), *The Oxford Companion to World War II*, 748–9, 992–4; Weinberg, *A World at Arms*, 211–15, 222–5, 361–3; Stegemann, 'The Italo-German Conduct of War', 680–754; Reinhard Stumpf, 'The War in the Mediterranean Area 1942–1943: Operations in North Africa and the Central Mediterranean', in *GSWW* VI. 631–840, at 631–54 and 661–748.

102. Martin Gilbert, *The Holocaust: The Jewish Tragedy* (London, 1987 [1986]), 578; idem, *The Routledge Atlas of the Holocaust* (London, 2002 [1982]), Maps 59, 188; Robert Satloff, *Among the Righteous: Lost Stories from the Holocaust's Long Reach into Arab Lands* (New York, 2006).

103. Andreas Hillgruber (ed.), *Staatsmänner und Diplomaten bei Hitler: Vertrauliche Aufzeichnungen über Unterredungen mit Vertretern des Auslandes* (2 vols., Frankfurt am Main, 1967–70), I. 664–6.

104. Jeffrey Herf, *The Jewish Enemy: Nazi Propaganda during World War II and the Holocaust* (London, 2006), 76.

105. Tooze, *The Wages of Destruction*, 381–2.

106. Dear (ed.), *The Oxford Companion to World War II*, 744–5; Schreiber, 'Germany', 305–448, Weinberg, *A World at Arms*, 195–6; Jürgen Förster, 'Germany's Acquisition of Allies in South-east Europe', in *GSWW* IV. 386–428, at 386; Friedländer, *The Years of Extermination*, 166–9; Randolph L. Braham (ed.), *The Tragedy of Romanian Jewry* (New York, 1994); Mihail Sebastian, 'Voller Entsetzen, aber nicht verzweifelt': *Tagebücher 1935–44* (ed. Edward Kanterian, Berlin, 2005). For Romanian fascism and antisemitism, see Leon Volovici, *Nationalist Ideology and Antisemitism: The Case of Romanian Intellectuals in the 1930s* (Oxford, 1991) (esp. Stephen Fischer-Galati, 'The Legacy of Anti-Semitism', 1–28); Stanley G. Payne, *A History of Fascism 1914–45* (London, 1995), 134–8, 391–7; solid narrative of events in Keith Hitchins, *Rumania 1866–1947* (Oxford, 1994), 376–471 (esp. 451–71). By far the best account of Antonescu is now Dennis Deletant, *Hitler's Forgotten Ally: Ion Antonescu and His Regime, Romania 1940–44* (London, 2006): for a detailed narrative of the events recounted above, see ibid., 8–68. The slaughterhouse incident is recounted in Robert St John, *Foreign Correspondent* (London, 1960), 180.

107. Dear (ed.), *The Oxford Companion to World War II*, 1,011–2.

108. Kershaw, *Hitler*, II. 360–63; Vogel, 'German Intervention', 451–85.

109. Ibid., 497–526; Mark Mazower, *Inside Hitler's Greece: The Experience of Occupation 1941–44* (London, 1993), 1–8, 15–18; Peter Calvocoressi and Guy Wint, *Total War:*

Causes and Courses of the Second World War (Harmondsworth, 1974 [1972]), 154–60 (a little outdated, but still valuable); Weinberg, *A World at Arms*, 218–22.

110. Dear (ed.), *The Oxford Companion to World War II*, 213–15; Vogel, 'German Intervention', 527–55.

111. Dear (ed.), *The Oxford Companion to World War II*, 213–15.

112. Pöppel, *Heaven and Hell*, 67.

113. Quoted in Mazower, *Inside Hitler's Greece*, 23–4.

114. Ibid., 23–32; Rainer Eckert, *Vom 'Fall Marita' zur 'Wirtschaftlichen Sonderaktion': Die deutsche Besatzungspolitik in Griechenland vom 6. April 1941 bis zur Kriegswende im Februar/März 1943* (Frankfurt am Main, 1992), 85–142.

115. Mazower, *Inside Hitler's Greece*, 32–52.

116. Ibid., 85–96, 235–8; idem, *Salonica: City of Ghosts: Christians, Muslims and Jews 1430–1950* (London, 2004), 421–2.

117. Payne, *A History of Fascism*, 404–11; Ladislaus Hory and Martin Broszat, *Der kroatische Ustascha-Staat 1941–1945* (Stuttgart, 1965 [1964]), 13–38; Jozo Tomasevich, *War and Revolution in Yugoslavia, 1941–1945: Occupation and Collaboration* (Stanford, Calif., 2001), 47–174; Gert Fricke, *Kroatien 1941–1944: Der 'Unabhängige Staat' in der Sicht des Deutschen Bevollmächtigten Generals in Agram, Blaise v Hortenau* (Freiburg, 1972), 10, 25–67.

118. Hory and Broszat, *Der kroatische Ustascha-Staat*, 39–57.

119. Misha Glenny, *The Balkans 1804–1999: Nationalism, War and the Great Powers* (London, 1999), 498–502; Hory and Broszat, *Der kroatische Ustascha-Staat*, 75–106; Payne, *A History of Fascism*, 408–10; Friedländer, *The Years of Extermination*, 228–30; gruesome details and photographs in Edmond Paris, *Genocide in Satellite Croatia 1941–1945: A Record of Racial and Religious Persecution and Massacres* (Chicago, 1961), esp. 88–126 and 162–205.

120. Quoted in ibid., 109–10; see also ibid., 127–61 for the concentration camps.

121. Milan Ristović, 'Yugoslav Jews Fleeing the Holocaust, 1941–1945', in John K. Roth and Elisabeth Maxwell (eds.), *Remembering for the Future: The Holocaust in an Age of Genocide* (London, 3 vols., 2001), I. 512–26; Glenny, *The Balkans*, 300–302; Payne, *A History of Fascism*, 409–10; Hory and Broszat, *Der kroatische Ustascha-Staat*, 75–92; Tomasevich, *War and Revolution*, 380–415 for the Ustashe reign of terror, and 511–79 for the role of the Catholic Church. A careful analysis of numbers killed in the genocidal campaigns of the Ustashe can be found in Marko Hoare, *Genocide and Resistance in Hitler's Bosnia: The Partisans and the Chetniks, 1941–1943* (London, 2006), 19–28.

122. Evans, *The Coming of the Third Reich*, 316.

123. Kershaw, *Hitler*, II. 305.

124. Hitler, *Kriegstagebuch*, II. 214 (5 December 1940); Kershaw, *Hitler*, II. 307–8; Bernd Stegemann, 'Hitlers Kriegszeile im ersten Kriegsjahr 1939/40: Ein Beitrag zur Quellenkritik', *Militärgeschichtliche Mitteilungen*, 27 (1980), 93–105. For Stalinist antisemitism, see Herf, *The Jewish Enemy*, 93. For a detailed account of the decision to invade, see Jürgen Förster, 'Hitler's Decision in Favour of War against the Soviet Union', in *GSWW* IV. 13–51. For policy discussions and options in the summer of 1940, see Andreas Hillgruber, *Hitlers Strategie: Politik und Kriegführung 1940–41* (Frankfurt am Main, 1965), 144–277.

125. Roberts, *Stalin's Wars*, 30–46.

126. Tooze, *The Wages of Destruction*, 421–5.

127. Halder, *Kriegstagebuch*, II. 49 (31 July 1940).

128. Bock, *Zwischen Pflicht und Verweigerung*, 173 (1 February 1941); repeated on 14 June 1941 (ibid., 193).

129. Kershaw, *Hitler*, II. 331–7; Weinberg, *A World at Arms*, 198–205.

130. David M. Glantz, *Barbarossa: Hitler's Invasion of Russia 1941* (Stroud, 2001), 13–18.

131. Evan Mawdsley, *Thunder in the East: The Nazi–Soviet War 1941–1945* (London, 2005), 19–20; Tooze, *The Wages of Destruction*, 429–36.

132. Anthony F. Upton, *Finland 1939–40* (London, 1974); David Kirby, *Finland in the Twentieth Century* (London, 1979).

133. Förster, 'Germany's Acquisition', 398–408; see also Mark Axworthy *et al.*, *Third Axis, Fourth Ally: Romanian Armed Forces in the European War, 1941–1945* (London, 1995); and Hillgruber, *Hitler, König Carol und Marschall Antonescu*, 126–34; more generally, idem, *Hitlers Strategie*, 484–501.

134. Dear (ed.), *The Oxford Companion to World War II*, 431–3; Förster, 'Germany's Acquisition', 409–24.

135. Ibid., 421–8; Weinberg, *A World at Arms*, 274–8.

136. Quoted in Marshall Lee Miller, *Bulgaria during the Second World War* (Stanford, Calif., 1975), 1.

137. Hans-Jürgen Hoppe, *Bulgarien – Hitlers eigenwilliger Verbündeter* (Stuttgart, 1979); Miller, *Bulgaria*, 93–106; Richard Crampton, *Bulgaria* (Oxford, 2007), 248–65.

138. Quoted in Miller, *Bulgaria*, 76.

139. Klukowski, *Diary*, 158 (14 June 1941).

140. Tooze, *The Wages of Destruction*, 321; Heinrich Schwendemann, *Die wirtschaftliche Zusammenarbeit zwischen dem Deutschen Reich und der Sowjetunion von 1939 bis 1941: Alternative zu Hitlers Ostprogramm?* (Berlin, 1993), 373.

141. Weinberg, *A World at Arms*, 201–5; Roberts, *Stalin's Wars*, 61–70.

142. Quoted in Robert Service, *Stalin: A Biography* (London, 2004), 407.

143. Ibid., 406–9; Gabriel Gorodetsky, *Grand Delusion: Stalin and the German Invasion of Russia* (London, 1999); Roberts, *Stalin's Wars*, 70–81; Mawdsley, *Thunder in the East*, 32–41.

144. Glantz, *Barbarossa*, 28–32; for Soviet intelligence, see David M. Glantz, *Stumbling Colossus: The Red Army on the Eve of War* (Lawrence, Kans., 1998), 233–57.

145. Simon Sebag-Montefiore, *Stalin: The Court of the Red Tsar* (London, 2003), 317.

146. Kershaw, *Hitler*, II. 369–73, 378.

147. Quoted in Rainer F. Schmidt, 'Der Hess-Flug und das Kabinett Churchill: Hitlers Stellvertreten im Kalkül der britischen Kriegsdiplomatie Mai–Juni 1941', *VfZ* 42 (1994), 1–38, at 14–16.

148. Kershaw, *Hitler*, II. 369–81, effectively disposes of the numerous and often extremely bizarre conspiracy theories that were spun around Hess's flight at the time and later. Neither the claim that Hitler would have sanctioned, let alone ordered, such a hare-brained escapade, nor the idea that either Hess or Hitler was encouraged to mount such a mission by an influential 'peace party' in the British government and secret service – to take two of the less fanciful theories – has any basis in reality.

149. Gerhard Engel, *Heeresadjutant bei Hitler 1938–1943* (ed. Hildegard von Kotze, Stuttgart, 1974), 103–4.

150. Fröhlich (ed.), *Die Tagebücher*, I/IX. 309 (13 May 1941).

151. Quoted in Kershaw, *Hitler*, II. 939 n. 210.

152. Boberach (ed.), *Meldungen*, VII. 2,302 and 2,313 (15 and 19 May 1941).

153. Martin Broszat *et al.* (eds.), *Bayern in der NS-Zeit* (6 vols., Munich, 1977–83), I. 148 ('Aus Monatsbericht des Landrats, 31. 5. 1941').

154. Bock, *Zwischen Pflicht und Verweigerung*, 185 (10–12 May 1941).

155. Klemperer, *I Shall Bear Witness*, 368 (21 May 1941).

156. Walb, *Ich, die Alte*, 219 (15 May 1941).

157. Kershaw, *Hitler*, II. 166–7.

158. Quoted in Marie Vassiltchikov, *The Berlin Diaries of Marie 'Missie' Vassiltchikov 1940–1945* (London, 1987 [1985]), 51–2; Hassell, *The von Hassell Diaries*, 196, 204, and Gerhardt B. Thamm, *Boy Soldier: A German Teenager at the Nazi Twilight* (Jefferson, N.C., 2000), 34.

159. Hugh R. Trevor-Roper, 'The Mind of Adolf Hitler', in Adolf Hitler, *Hitler's Table Talk 1941–1944* (Oxford, 1988 [1953]), vii–xxxv, at xii–xiii.

160. Hitler, *Hitler's Table Talk*, 51 (10 October 1941).

161. Ibid., 38 (23 September 1941).

162. Ibid., 16 (27 July 1941).

163. Ibid., 24 (8/9 and 9/10 August 1941). For Hitler and Himmler's concept of the Ukraine as an imperial fiefdom, equivalent to British India, see Wendy Lower, *Nazi Empire-Building and the Holocaust in Ukraine* (Chapel Hill, N.C., 2005), 98–128.

164. Hitler, *Hitler's Table Talk*, 68–9 (17 October 1941).

165. Ibid., 61 (2 and 2/3 November 1941).

166. Ibid., 447 (27 April 1942).

167. Ibid., 578 (18 July 1942).

168. Ibid., 77 (17/18 October 1941).

169. Ibid., 69 (17 October 1941 and 22 July 1942).

170. Ibid., 62 (9 August 1942).

171. Longerich, *Politik*, 298; quote in Madajczyk, *Die Okkupationspolitik*, 92.

172. Alex J. Kay, 'Germany's Staatssekretäre, Mass Starvation and the Meeting of 2 May 1941', *Journal of Contemporary History*, 41 (2006), 685–700; Tooze, *The Wages of Destruction*, 475–80.

173. Madajczyk *et al.* (eds.), *Vom Generalplan Ost*; Mechthild Rössler and Sabine Schleier-macher, *Der 'Generalplan Ost': Hauptlinien der nationalsozialistischen Planungs- und Vernichtungspolitik* (Berlin, 1993); Thomas Podranski, *Deutsche Siedlungspolitik im Osten: Die verschiedenen Varianten des Generalplan Ost der SS* (Berlin, 2001).

174. Evans, *The Third Reich in Power*, 419–28.

175. Tooze, *The Wages of Destruction*, 463–76.

176. Hitler, *Hitler's Table Talk*, 8 (11/12 July 1941).

177. Ibid., 587 (22 July 1942).

178. Ibid., 624 (9 August 1942).

179. Halder, *Kriegstagebuch*, II. 317–20 (17 March 1941).

180. Ibid., 336–7 (30 March 1941).

181. Ibid.

182. Quoted in Longerich, *Politik*, 300–301; see also Hans-Adolf Jacobsen, 'The *Kommissarbefehl* and Mass Executions of Soviet Russian Prisoners of War', in Helmut Krausnick *et al.*, *Anatomy of the SS State* (London, 1968 [1965]), 505–35 (full translation of the order of 6 June on 532–4).

183. See also Jürgen Förster, 'Operation Barbarossa as a War of Conquest and Annihilation', in *GSWW* IV. 481–521.

184. Jacobsen, 'The *Kommissarbefehl*', 505–35, at 517; Kershaw, *Hitler*, II. 353–60; Bodo Scheurig, *Henning von Tresckow: Ein Preusse gegen Hitler* (Frankfurt am Main, 1987), 113–14; Christian Gerlach, 'Hitlergegner bei der Heeresgruppe Mitte und die "Verbrecher-ischen Befehle" ', in Gerd R. Ueberschär (ed.), *NS-Verbrechen und der militärische Wider-stand gegen Hitler* (Darmstadt, 2000), 62–76; Johannes Hürter, 'Auf dem Weg zur Militäropposition: Tresckow, Gersdorff, der Vernichtungskrieg und der Judenmord: Neue Dokumente über das Verhältnis der Heeresgruppe Mitte zur Einsatzgruppe B im Jahr 1941', *VfZ* 52 (2004), 527–62; Bock's views can be found in Bock, *Zwischen Pflicht und Verweigerung*, 190 (4 June 1941).

185. Quoted in Förster, 'Operation Barbarossa', 485.

186. Quoted in ibid., 514.

187. Quoted in ibid., 520.

188. Friedländer, *The Years of Extermination*, 210–11; see also Ortwin Buchbender, *Das tönende Erz: Deutsche Propaganda gegen die Rote Armee im Zweiten Weltkrieg* (Stuttgart, 1978), and for the senior commanders' attitude to the 'criminal orders', Hürter, *Hitlers Heerführer*, 247–65.

189. Longerich, *Politik*, 302–10, convincingly dealing with the specifics of the controversy between Christopher Browning, *Ordinary Men: Reserve Police Battalion 101 and the Final Solution in Poland* (London, 1998 [1992]), and Daniel Jonah Goldhagen, *Hitler's Willing Executioners: Ordinary Germans and the Holocaust* (London, 1996), though the

general issues raised by Goldhagen rightly continue to be debated. For the background, see Helmut Fangmann et al., 'Parteisoldaten': Die Hamburger Polizei im '3. Reich' (Hamburg, 1987); for indoctrination, see Jürgen Matthäus, 'Ausbildungsziel Judenmord? Zum Stellenwert der "weltanschaulichen Erziehung" von SS und Polizei im Rahmen der "Endlösung"', Zeitschrift für Geschichtswissenschaft, 47 (1999), 677–99; and idem et al. (eds.), Ausbildungsziel Judenmord? 'Weltanschauliche Erziehung' von SS, Polizei und Waffen-SS im Rahmen der 'Endlösung' (Frankfurt am Main, 2003).

190. Quoted in Longerich, Politik, 315.

191. Ibid., 310–20, provides a very careful consideration of the evidence, concluding that the postwar trial statements of defendants such as the Task Force leader Ohlendorf that a general command was given to kill all Jews indiscriminately lack credibility because of their exculpatory intent. After being condemned to death, indeed, Ohlendorf changed his story and said there had been no such command. See in particular Ralf Ogorreck, Die Einsatzgruppen und die 'Genesis der Endlösung' (Berlin, 1996). For the contrary view, see Breitman, The Architect of Genocide, 145–206. For Jews in the Soviet apparatus, see Friedländer, The Years of Extermination, 247–51; more detail in Mordechai Altschuler, Soviet Jewry on the Eve of the Holocaust: A Social and Demographic Profile (Jerusalem, 1998).

192. Glantz, Barbarossa, 35.

193. Brief summaries in Weinberg, A World at Arms, 264–6; Glantz, Barbarossa, 35; and Kershaw, Hitler, II. 393–9. John Erickson, Stalin's War with Germany, I: The Road to Stalingrad (London, 1975), remains the classic account, but has inevitably been overtaken by more recent research and particularly by Soviet documentation released since 1990. The same can be said of the even more detailed account in GSWW IV, in which the sections dealing with the Soviet Union are particularly outdated. The most recent narrative is Bellamy, Absolute War. See also the discussion of the senior generals' conduct of the campaign in Hürter, Hitlers Heerführer, 279–302.

194. Hürter (ed.), Ein deutscher General, 68 (letter to his wife, 11 July 1941).

195. Karl Reddemann (ed.), Zwischen Front und Heimat: Der Briefwechsel des münsterischen Ehepaares Agnes und Albert Neuhaus 1940–1944 (Münster, 1996), 223 (to Agnes Neuhaus, 25 June 1941).

196. Konrad Elmshäuser and Jan Lokers (eds.), 'Man muss hier nur hart sein': Kriegsbriefe und Bilder einer Familie (1934–1945) (Bremen, 1999), 92 (Kalendereintrag Hans-Albert Giese, 22 June 1941).

197. Hürter (ed.), Ein deutscher General, 63 (letter to family, 24 June 1941).

198. Quoted in Merridale, Ivan's War, 96–7 (also for the preceding details in this paragraph); Mawdsley, Thunder in the East, 59–69; Glantz, Barbarossa, 37–40. For the condition of the Red Army in 1941, see Glantz, Stumbling Colossus.

199. Merridale, Ivan's War, 86–7.

200. Ibid., 99.

201. Ibid., 99–100, 116, 122–3 (translation slightly amended).

202. Hürter, Hitlers Heerführer, 393–404.

203. Reddemann (ed.), Zwischen Front und Heimat, 225 (to Agnes Neuhaus, 27 June 1941).

204. Rudolf Stützel, Feldpost: Briefe und Aufzeichnungen eines 17jährigen 1940–1945 (Hamburg, 2005), 41; more generally Hannes Heer (ed.), 'Stets zu erschiessen sind Frauen, die in der Roten Armee dienen': Geständnisse deutscher Kriegsgefangener über ihren Einsatz an der Ostfront (Hamburg, 1995), 7, and Hürter, Hitlers Heerführer, 359–76.

205. Klukowski, Diary, 173 (4 October 1941).

206. Ibid., 173 (5 October 1941).

207. Merridale, Ivan's War, 123–5; Christian Streit, Keine Kameraden: Die Wehrmacht und die sowjetischen Kriegsgefangenen 1941–1945 (Stuttgart, 1978).

208. Quoted in ibid., 131; see also Hürter, Hitlers Heerführer, 377–93.

209. Hosenfeld, 'Ich versuche', 557 (letter to wife, 3 December 1941).

210. Streit, Keine Kameraden, 9.

211. Halder, *Kriegstagebuch*, III. 289 (14 November 1941); see more generally Vyacheslav M. Molotov *et al.*, *Soviet Government Statements on Nazi Atrocities* (London, 1945), 183–8.

212. Streit, *Keine Kameraden*, 201–88.

213. Andreas Hilger, *Deutsche Kriegsgefangene in der Sowjetunion, 1941–1956: Kriegs-gefangenenpolitik, Lageralltag und Erinnerung* (Essen, 2000), superseding earlier studies such as Kurt W. Böhme, *Die deutschen Kriegsgefangenen in sowjetischer Hand: Eine Bilanz* (Munich, 1966). For the statistics, see Hilger, *Deutsche Kriegsgefangene*, 137, 370, 389, 425; for political re-education, which was largely unsuccessful, 220–54.

214. Christian Streit, 'The Fate of the Soviet Prisoners of War', in Michael Berenbaum (ed.), *A Mosaic of Victims: Non-Jews Persecuted and Murdered by the Nazis* (London, 1990), 142–9; Alexander Dallin, *German Rule in Russia 1941–1945: A Study of Occupation Policies* (London, 1957), 409–27; Mawdsley, *Thunder in the East*, 102–5.

215. Bock, *Zwischen Pflicht und Verweigerung*, 298 (20 October 1941); see also ibid., 312–13 (9 November 1941), protesting that, 'According to military custom and law, the army is responsible for the life and safety of its prisoners of war, of whatever kind.'

216. Hürter, *Hitlers Heerführer*, 377–93.

217. Mawdsley, *Thunder in the East*, 102–5.

218. Service, *Stalin*, 410–24; Merridale, *Ivan's War*, 83; Sebag-Montefiore, *Stalin*, 330–33, also recording different versions of Stalin's statement by various memoirists, all equally vulgar; the version quoted here is attested by both Molotov and Chadaev. On Stalin's unpreparedness, see Roberts, *Stalin's Wars*, 61–70. Roberts's scepticism about Stalin's loss of nerve falls down on chronology by failing to realize that it came at the end of June, not immediately after the invasion (89–95).

219. Hoffmann, *Hitler's Personal Security*, 216–63; Kershaw, *Hitler*, II. 395–7; Fröhlich (ed.), *Die Tagebücher* II/I. 35 (9 July 1941).

220. Halder, *Kriegstagebuch*, III. 38 (3 July 1941).

221. Kershaw, *Hitler*, II. 405–7; Friedländer, *The Years of Extermination*, 199–200.

222. Quoted in Kershaw, *Hitler*, II. 405.

223. Ibid., 399 and 944 n. 40; Hitler, *Hitler's Table Talk*, 17 September 1941; Fröhlich (ed.), *Die Tagebücher* II/I. 29–39 (9 July 1941).

224. Walb, *Ich, die Alte*, 225 (30 June 1941).

225. Broszat *et al.* (eds.), *Bayern*, I. 149 ('Aus Monatsbericht der Gendarmerie-Station Heiligenstadt, 25. 6. 1941' and 'Aus Monatsbericht der Gendarmerie-Station Waischen-feld, 26. 6. 1941').

226. Solmitz, *Tagebücher*, 662 (23 June 1941).

227. Jochen Klepper, *Überwindung: Tagebücher und Aufzeichnungen aus dem Kriege* (Stutt-gart, 1958), 50 (22 June 1941).

228. Maschmann, *Account Rendered*, 91.

229. Broszat *et al.* (eds.), *Bayern*, I. 149–50 ('Aus Monatsbericht der Gendarmerie-Station Ebermannstadt, 27. 6. 1941').

230. Ibid., I. 152 ('Aus Monatsbericht des Gendarmerie-Kreisführers, 29. 8. 1941').

231. Merridale, *Ivan's War*, 84–7; Sebag-Montefiore, *Stalin*, 332–4.

232. Merridale, *Ivan's War*, 115–17.

233. Ibid., 114–16, also for the quotes; Roberts, *Stalin's Wars*, 95–103; Soviet reserves discussed in Glantz, *Barbarossa*, 15.

234. Bock, *Zwischen Pflicht und Verweigerung*, 210 (6 July 1941).

235. Halder, *Kriegstagebuch*, III. 53 (8 July 1941).

236. Rolf-Dieter Müller, 'The Failure of the Economic "Blitzkrieg Strategy" ', in *GSWW* IV. 1,081–8, esp. 1, 141–72; graphic details in Anatoly Kuznetsov, *Babi Yar: A Document in the Form of a Novel* (London, 1970 [1966]), 149–52.

237. Hürter (ed.), *Ein deutscher General*, 63 (diary, 23 June 1941).

238. Ibid., 64 (Heinrici to family, 4 July 1941).

239. Meier-Welcker, *Aufzeichnungen*, 124 (31 July 1941), 129 (24 August 1941).

240. Quoted in Theo J. Schulte, *The German Army and Nazi Policies in Occupied Russia* (Oxford, 1989), 109.

241. Birgit Beck, *Wehrmacht und sexuelle Gewalt: Sexualverbrechen vor deutschen Militär-gerichten 1939–1945* (Paderborn, 2004), 105–16 (for military brothels), 326–8 (for trials for rape).

242. Nicholas, *The Rape of Europa*, 185–201; also Molotov *et al.*, *Soviet Government Statements*, 198–209. For an analysis of mentions of theft and plunder in soldiers' letters, see also Martin Humburg (ed.), *Das Gesicht des Krieges: Feldpostbriefe von Wehr-machtssoldaten aus der Sowjetunion 1941–1944* (Opladen, 1998), 164–70. For treatment of civilians in general, see Hürter, *Hitlers Heerführer*, 465–508.

243. Elmshäuser and Lokers (eds.), *'Man muss hier nur hart sein'*, 93 (Hans-Albert Giese to Frieda Giese, 12 July 1941), and 102 (Hans-Albert Giese to Frieda Giese, 17 July 1941).

244. Hürter, *Hitlers Heerführer*, 442–9.

245. Ibid., 97 (23 October 1941).

246. Klaus Latzel, 'Tourismus und Gewalt Kriegswahrnehmungen in Feldpostbriefen', in Hannes Heer and Klaus Naumann (eds.), *Vernichtungskrieg: Verbrechen der Wehrmacht 1941–1944* (Hamburg, 1995), 449–51. See also Dieter Reifarth and Viktoria Schmidt-Linsenhoff, 'Die Kamera der Täter', in ibid., 475–503, and Bernd Hüppauf, 'Der entleerte Blick hinter der Kamera', in ibid., 504–50.

247. Alois Scheuer, *Briefe aus Russland: Feldpostbriefe des Gefreiten Alois Scheuer 1941–1942* (St Ingbert, 2000), 31 (15 August 1941).

248. Reddemann (ed.), *Zwischen Front und Heimat*, 286 (to Agnes, 16 August 1941).

249. Ibid., 431 (to Agnes, 28 February 1942).

250. Ibid., 500.

251. See Hitler's orders on the combating of partisans, in Hubatsch (ed.), *Hitlers Weisungen*, 201–9.

252. Hürter (ed.), *Ein deutscher General*, 62 (diary, 23 June 1941).

253. Ibid., 65 (letter to wife, 6 July 1941); more generally on the treatment of partisans, see idem, *Hitlers Heerführer*, 404–41.

254. Hürter (ed.), *Ein deutscher General*, 107 (7 November 1941).

255. Schulte, *The German Army*, 86–149.

256. Glantz, *Barbarossa*, 57–74.

257. Karel C. Berkhoff, *Harvest of Despair: Life and Death in Ukraine under Nazi Rule* (Cambridge, Mass., 2004), 15–17; Gross, *Revolution from Abroad*, 229.

258. Bock, *Zwischen Pflicht und Verweigerung*, 218–19 (15 July 1941), 229 (24 July 1941).

259. Horst Slesina, *Soldaten gegen Tod und Teufel: Unser Kampf in der Sowjetunion: Eine soldatische Deutung* (Düsseldorf, 1942), 164.

260. Scheuer, *Briefe aus Russland*, 30 (7 August 1941).

261. Hürter (ed.), *Ein deutscher General*, 69 (letter to wife, 20 July 1941). See also the vivid description of a Red Army counter-attack in Stützel, *Feldpost*, 54–6.

262. Rüdiger Overmans, *Deutsche militärische Verluste im Zweiten Weltkrieg* (Munich, 1999), 277–9; Hürter (ed.), *Ein deutscher General*, 177 n. 138.

263. Ibid., 70 (letter to wife, 22 July 1941).

264. Ibid., 72 (letter to wife, 3 August 1941), 76 (letter to wife, 23 August 1941).

265. Glantz, *Barbarossa*, 21–2, 75–84.

266. Halder, *Kriegstagebuch*, III. 117 (25 July 1941).

267. Ibid., III. 143 (2 August 1941).

268. Ibid., III. 170 (11 August 1941).

269. Ibid., III. 183 (17 August 1941) and 178 (15 August 1941).

270. Bock, *Zwischen Pflicht und Verweigerung*, 234 (29 July 1941), 236 (31 July 1941), 242 (7 August 1941).

271. Kleo Pleyer, *Volk im Feld* (Hamburg, 1943), 177.

272. Meier-Welcker, *Aufzeichnungen*, 168 (29 July 1942).

273. Glantz, *Barbarossa*, 21–2; Bock, *Zwischen Pflicht und Verweigerung*, 234–5.

274. Glantz, *Barbarossa*, 99–114 (quote on 114); Weinberg, *A World at Arms*, 268–78.

275. Bock, *Zwischen Pflicht und Verweigerung*, 255 (22 August 1941).

276. Ibid., 258 (25 August 1941).

277. Halder, *Kriegstagebuch*, III. 192 (22 August 1941).

278. Detailed account in Glantz, *Barbarossa*, 117–58; for Guderian's 'self-will', see Bock, *Zwischen Pflicht und Verweigerung*, 269–70 (5 September 1941).

279. Ibid., 277 (15 September 1941).

280. Fröhlich (ed.), *Die Tagebücher* II/I. 471–6 (23 September 1941).

281. Bock, *Zwischen Pflicht und Verweigerung*, 272 (7 September 1941); see also Hürter (ed.), *Ein deutscher General*, 85–91 (Heinrici was transferred from the Kiev front to Army Group Centre on 17 September 1941).

282. Kershaw, *Hitler*, II. 430–38; Glantz, *Barbarossa*, 84–96 (the Smolensk counter-offensive).

283. Humburg, *Das Gesicht*, 170–71; good critical discussion in Hürter, *Hitlers Heerführer*, 302–10; more generally, see Jehuda L. Wallach, *The Dogma of the Battle of Annihilation: The Theories of Clausewitz and Schieffen and their Impact on the German Conduct of Two World Wars* (Westport, Conn., 1980), 265–81.

284. Sebag-Montefiore, *Stalin*, 351–54.

285. Ibid.

286. Bock, *Zwischen Pflicht und Verweigerung*, 295 (15 October 1941), 297 (19 October 1941).

287. Meier-Welcker, *Aufzeichnungen*, 130–31 (1 September 1941), 136–8 (7 November 1941); also Bock, *Zwischen Pflicht und Verweigerung*, 307 (31 October 1941).

288. Hürter (ed.), *Ein deutscher General*, 94 (letter to wife 16 October 1941).

289. Sebag-Montefiore, *Stalin*, 356; Weinberg, *A World at Arms*, 278–82; Mawdsley, *Thunder in the East*, 195–217.

290. Bock, *Zwischen Pflicht und Verweigerung*, 301 (25 October 1941).

291. Ibid., 317 (14 November 1941).

292. Meier-Welcker, *Aufzeichnungen*, 156 (27 January 1942), 158 (3 March 1942).

293. Hürter (ed.), *Ein deutscher General*, 108 (report to family, 19 November 1941).

294. Christoph Rass, 'Das Sozialprofil von Kampfverbänden des deutschen Heeres 1939 bis 1945', in Militärgeschichtliches Forschungsant (ed.), *Das Deutsche Reich und der Zweite Weltkrieg* (hereafter *DRZW* (10 vols., Stuttgart/Munich, 1979–2008), IX/I (Munich, 2004), 641–741, at 700.

295. Hürter (ed.), *Ein deutscher General*, 116 (4 December 1941), 124 (11 December 1941).

296. Bock, *Zwischen Pflicht und Verweigerung*, 342 (7 December 1941).

297. Hürter, *Hitlers Heerführer*, 310–24.

298. Scheuer, *Briefe aus Russland*, 51 (letter to wife, 30 November 1941).

299. Ibid., 56 (letter to wife, 25 December 1941).

300. Kershaw, *Hitler*, II. 450–57.

301. Meier-Welcker, *Aufzeichnungen*, 145–6 (26 December 1941).

302. Ibid..

303. Hürter (ed.), *Ein deutscher General*, 131 (letter to wife 22 December 1941); for the frequency of themes such as bad weather, dirt, hunger and disease in soldiers' correspondence, see Humburg, *Das Gesicht*, 129–170.

304. Bock, *Zwischen Pflicht und Verweigerung*, 353–7 (16–22 December 1941); Hürter, *Hitlers Heerführer*, 310–28 (now superseding all previous accounts of the relations between Hitler and the senior generals in the crisis of December 1941 and January 1942).

305. Kershaw, *Hitler*, II. 451–5.

306. Reddemann (ed.), *Zwischen Front und Heimat*, 375 (to Agnes, 21 December 1941).

307. Hürter, *Hitlers Heerführer*, 325–6.

308. Weinberg, *A World at Arms*, argues repeatedly and convincingly, with many examples, that Hitler was always willing to entertain the idea of a tactical withdrawal. Once he

had taken a decision, however, he was temperamentally inclined to try to enforce it as undeviatingly and uncompromisingly as possible.

309. Hürter (ed.), *Ein deutscher General*, 135 (letter to wife, 24 December 1941).

310. Ibid., 138 (letter to wife 11 January 1942).

311. Halder, *Kriegstagebuch*, III. 373 (3 January 1942).

312. Hürter, *Hitlers Heerführer*, 341–2.

313. Ibid., 328–32.

314. Ibid., 332.

315. Ibid., 333–7.

316. Hürter (ed.), *Ein deutscher General*, 140–59 (21 January to 25 April 1942).

317. Brief narrative in Earl Ziemke, 'Moscow, Battle for', in Dear (ed.), *The Oxford Companion to World War II*, 593–5; more detail in Earl F. Ziemke, *Moscow to Stalingrad* (Washington, D.C., 1968).

318. Glantz, *Barbarossa*, 161–204; Overmans, *Deutsche militärische Verluste*, 239, 266.

319. Ibid., 238–9. The figures given in Glantz, *Barbarossa*, 161, at more than twice this number, seem exaggerated.

320. Weinberg, *A World at Arms*, 264.

Chapter 3. 'THE FINAL SOLUTION'

1. Ernst Klee *et al.* (eds.), *'Those Were the Days': The Holocaust as Seen by the Perpetrators and Bystanders* (London, 1991 [1988]), 28–33.

2. Ibid., 28–31.

3. Friedländer, *The Years of Extermination*, 207, and in more detail, Alfred Streim, 'Zur Eröffnung des allgemeinen Judenvernichtungsbefehls gegenüber den Einsatzgruppen', in Eberhard Jäckel und Jürgen Rohwer (eds.), *Der Mord an den Juden im Zweiten Weltkrieg: Entschlussbildung und Verwirklichung* (Stuttgart, 1985), 108–19 and Peter Klein (ed.), *Die Einsatzgruppen in der besetzten Sowjetunion 1941/42: Die Tätigkeits- und Lageberichte des Chefs des Sicherheitspolizei und des SD* (Berlin, 1997).

4. Quoted in Longerich, *Politik*, 324–5, 333–4; Klee *et al.* (eds.), *'Those Were the Days'*, 24–7.

5. Björn Felder, *Lettland im Zweiten Weltkrieg: Zwischen sowjetischen und deutschen Besatzern 1940–1946* (Paderborn, 2008).

6. Longerich, *Politik*, 325–6, 333–4.

7. Friedländer, *The Years of Extermination*, 219–25; Konrad Kwiet, 'Rehearsing for Murder: The Beginning of the Final Solution in Lithuania in June 1941', *Holocaust and Genocide Studies*, 12 (1998), 3–26; Jürgen Matthäus, 'Jenseits der Grenze: Die ersten Massenerschiessungen von Juden in Litauen (Juni–August 1941)', *Zeitschrift für Geschichtswissenschaft*, 44 (1996), 97–117; more generally Wolfgang Benz and Marion Neiss (eds.), *Judenmord in Litauen: Studien und Dokumente* (Berlin, 1999).

8. Reddemann (ed.), *Zwischen Front und Heimat*, 222 (to sister, 25 June 1941).

9. Quoted in Bernd Boll and Hans Safrian, 'Auf dem Weg nach Stalingrad: Die 6. Armee 1941/42', in Heer and Naumann (eds.), *Vernichtungskrieg*, 260–96, at 271; also quoted in full in Longerich, *Politik*, 324–5.

10. The diary of one Jew who escaped because his Christian neighbours assured the rampaging soldiers that there were no Jews in the house is reprinted in Aryeh Klonicki and Malwina Klonicki, *The Diary of Adam's Father: The Diary of Aryeh Klonicki (Klonymus) and His Wife Malvina* (Jerusalem, 1973).

11. Quoted in Longerich, *Politik*, 333, 352–7, 392; account of the movements and killing actions of Task Force A in ibid., 390–94, and Krausnick, *Hitlers Einsatzgruppen*, 151–6.

12. Browning, *The Origins*, 255–7.

13. Longerich, *Politik*, 334–7; the progress of Task Force B is documented in Krausnick, *Hitlers Einsatzgruppen*, 156–62.

14. Ben-Cion Pinchuk, *Shtetl Jews under Soviet Rule: Eastern Poland on the Eve of the Holocaust* (Oxford, 1990), 117–200.

15. Pleyer, *Volk im Feld*, 169, 184.

16. Longerich, *Politik*, 352–6.

17. Quoted in ibid., 358. See also Andrej Angrick and Dieter Pohl, *Einsatzgruppen C and D in the Invasion of the Soviet Union, 1941–1942* (London, 1999); Klein (ed.), *Die Einsatzgruppen*. English versions of the reports in Yitzhak Arad *et al.* (eds.), *The Einsatzgruppen Reports: Selections from the Dispatches of the Nazi Death Squads' Campaign against the Jews, July 1941–January 1943* (New York, 1989) (translations not always reliable); and Ogorreck, *Die Einsatzgruppen*.

18. For this event, see Evans, *The Third Reich in Power*, 621–3.

19. Longerich, *Politik*, 337–8.

20. Musial, '*Konterrevolutionäre Elemente*', 262–9.

21. Ibid., 200–248; see also Manoschek (ed.), '*Es gibt nur eines*', 31 (Gefr. F. B., 3 July 1941), and 51 (Lt. K., 13 February 1942).

22. Klee *et al.* (eds.), '*Those Were the Days*', 88–91.

23. Ibid., 91 (5 July 1941).

24. Ibid., 91 (5 July 1941); Musial, '*Konterrevolutionäre Elemente*', 175–99, also for the involvement of German soldiers in the pogroms and massacres in Lemberg and elsewhere, and for the events in Boryslaw; see also Manoschek (ed.), '*Es gibt nur eines*', 33 (letter of 6 July 1941).

25. Berkhoff, *Harvest of Despair*, 205–31; Longerich, *Politik*, 337–43.

26. Ibid., 343.

27. For Task Force C's movements, see Krausnick, *Hitlers Einsatzgruppen*, 162–9.

28. Klee *et al.* (eds.), '*Those Were the Days*', 96 (12 July 1941).

29. Ibid., 97 (12 July 1941).

30. Ibid., 101 (22 July 1941), 105 (2 August 1941); also in Longerich, *Politik*, 338–9.

31. Klee *et al.* (eds.), '*Those Were the Days*', 297–9; Friedlander, *The Years of Extermination*, 246–7.

32. Quoted in Latzel, 'Tourismus und Gewalt', 449–51. There is now a considerable literature on the value, or otherwise, of field-post letters as an historical source. See for example Humburg, *Das Gesicht*, 257–68.

33. Quoted in Hürter, *Hitlers Heerführer*, 443.

34. Hürter (ed.), *Ein deutscher General*, 67 (11 July 1941).

35. Longerich, *Politik*, 362.

36. Quoted in Kershaw, *Hitler*, II. 405; Browning, *The Origins*, 274, 310; Friedländer, *The Years of Extermination*, 200; Longerich, *Politik*, 362–6.

37. Fritz Baade *et al.* (eds.), '*Unsere Ehre heisst Treue': Kriegstagebuch des Kommandostabes Reichsführer-SS, Tätigkeitsberichte der 1. und 2. 33-Infanterie-Brigade, der 1. SS-Kav. Brigade und von Sonderkommandos der SS* (Vienna, 1965), 212.

38. Ibid., 96.

39. Ibid., 220 (Bericht 'Pripjet-Aktion').

40. Quoted in Klee *et al.* (eds.), '*Those Were the Days*', 66–7.

41. Ibid., 67; Berkhoff, *Harvest of Despair*, 65–9.

42. Peter Longerich, *Der ungeschriebene Befehl: Hitler und der Weg zur 'Endlösung'* (Munich, 2001), 106–7.

43. Klee *et al.* (eds.), '*Those Were the Days*', 75–86.

44. Brief account in Friedländer, *The Years of Extermination*, 282; more detail in Dieter Pohl, 'Hans Krüger and the Murder of the Jews in the Stanisławów Region (Galicia)', *Yad Vashem Studies*, 26 (1998), 257–64; idem, *Nationalsozialistische Judenverfolgung in Ostgalizien 1941–1944: Organisation und Durchführung eines staatlichen Massenverbrechens* (Munich, 1996) esp. 144–7; Thomas Sandkühler, '*Endlösung' in Galizien: Der Judenmord in Ostpolen und die Rettungsinitiativen von Berthold Beitz, 1941–1944* (Bonn, 1996) esp. 150; and Browning, *The Origins*, 348–50.

45. Bernd Boll, 'Zloczów, Juli 1941: Die Wehrmacht und der Beginn des Holocaust in Galizien', *Zeitschrift für Geschichtswissenschaft*, 50 (2002), 899–917.

46. Friedländer, *The Years of Extermination*, 215–19, documents in Klee *et al.* (eds.), '*Those Were the Days*', 137–54.

47. Quoted in ibid., 151; Groscurth, *Tagebücher*, 534–42.

48. Deletant, *Hitler's Forgotten Ally*, 127–30; more generally, Andrej Angrick, 'The Escalation of German–Rumanian Anti-Jewish Policy after the Attack on the Soviet Union', *Yad Vashem Studies*, 26 (1998), 203–38.

49. Deletant, *Hitler's Forgotten Ally*, 102–28 (quote at 116), convincingly countering the less hostile (though in many respects valuable) account by Larry Watts, *Romanian Cassandra: Ion Antonescu and the Struggle for Reform, 1916–1941* (Boulder, Colo., 1993).

50. Kurt Erichson (ed.), *Abschied ist immer: Briefe an den Bruder im Zweiten Weltkrieg* (Frankfurt am Main, 1994), 25 (letter to brother, 17 July 1941).

51. See Jean Ancel, *Transnistria* (3 vols., Bucharest, 1998).

52. Deletant, *Hitler's Forgotten Ally*, 197.

53. Ibid., 171–3, with accurate details and figures based on Romanian and German documents (other accounts seem to involve an element of double-counting); more generally, see Alexander Dallin, *Odessa, 1941–1944: A Case Study of Soviet Territory under Foreign Rule* (Iaşi, 1998 [1957]) esp. 74–5.

54. Deletant, *Hitler's Forgotten Ally*, 173–9.

55. Ibid., 179–87; Paul A. Shapiro, 'The Jews of Chisinau (Kishinev): Romanian Reoccupation, Ghettoization, Deportation', in Randolph L. Braham (ed.), *The Destruction of Romanian and Ukrainian Jews during the Antonescu Era* (New York, 1997), 135–94; Dennis Deletant, 'Ghetto Experience in Golta, Transnistria, 1942–1944', *Holocaust and Genocide Studies*, 18 (2004), 1–26; and Dalia Ofer, 'Life in the Ghettos of Transnistria', *Yad Vashem Studies*, 25 (1996), 229–74.

56. Jean Ancel, 'The Romanian Way of Solving the "Jewish Problem" in Bessarabia and Bukovina: June–July 1941', *Yad Vashem Studies*, 19 (1988), 187–232; idem, 'The "Christian" Regimes of Romania and the Jews, 1940–1942', *Holocaust and Genocide Studies*, 7 (1993), 14–29; Braham (ed.), *The Destruction of Romanian and Ukrainian Jews*; the fullest and most accurate account, convincingly stressing the racist character of these mass murders, is now in Deletant, *Hitler's Forgotten Ally*, 130–49 (quote on 141).

57. Friedländer, *The Years of Extermination*, 225, citing the International Commission on the Holocaust in Romania's *Final Report of the International Commission on the Holocaust in Romania, presented to Romanian President Ion Iliescu, 11 November 2004*; Deletant, *Hitler's Forgotten Ally*, 166–71.

58. Andrej Angrick, *Besatzungspolitik und Massenmord: Die Einsatzgruppe D in der südlichen Sowjetunion 1941–1943* (Hamburg, 2003), 174; Radu Ioanid, *The Holocaust in Romania: The Destruction of Jews and Gypsies under the Antonescu Regime, 1940–1944* (Chicago, 2000), 62–4.

59. Cited in Longerich, *Politik*, 388.

60. Ibid., 388–9; Breitman, *The Architect of Genocide*, 213–14.

61. For a detailed itinerary, see Krausnick, *Hitlers Einsatzgruppen*, 169–78; details in Longerich, *Politik*, 386–90; and Angrick, *Besatzungspolitik und Massenmord*.

62. Krausnick, *Hitlers Einsatzgruppen*, 118; Dear (ed.), *The Oxford Companion to World War II*, 1,011–16; Browning, *The Origins*, 334–5.

63. Walter Manoschek, 'Die Vernichtung der Juden in Serbien', in Ulrich Herbert (ed.), *Nationalsozialistische Vernichtungspolitik 1939–1945: Neue Forschungen und Kontroversen* (Frankfurt am Main, 1998), 209–34, at 209–12.

64. Quoted in Paul Hehn, *The German Struggle against Yugoslav Guerillas in World War II: German Counter-Insurgency in Yugoslavia 1941–1943* (New York, 1979), 28–9; Manoschek, 'Die Vernichtung', 214–15, 220.

65. Quoted in Ibid., 216–17.

66. Quoted in Manoschek (ed.), 'Es gibt nur eines', 39 (Lt. P. G., 29 July 1941).
67. Quoted in Manoschek, 'Die Vernichtung', 216.
68. Fröhlich (ed.), Die Tagebücher, II/I. 478 (24 September 1941).
69. Quoted in Browning, The Origins, 338.
70. Longerich, Politik, 458–9; quotation in Manoschek, 'Die Vernichtung', 222.
71. Quoted in ibid., 227; for the Gypsies, see ibid., 233, and especially Karola Fings et al.,
    '. . . einziges Land, in dem Judenfrage und Zigeunerfrage gelöst': Die Verfolgung der Roma
    im faschistisch besetzten Jugoslawien 1941–1945 (Cologne, n.d.).
72. Quoted in Glenny, The Balkans, 503.
73. Browning, The Origins, 341.
74. Quoted in Walter Manoschek, ' "Gehst mit Juden erschiessen?" Die Vernichtung der
    Juden in Serbien', in Heer and Naumann (eds.), Vernichtungskrieg, 39–56, at 46.
75. Walter Manoschek, 'Serbien ist judenfrei': Militärische Besatzungspolitik und Judenver-
    nichtung in Serbien 1941/42 (Munich, 1993), 155–8.
76. Manfred Messerschmidt, 'Partisanenkrieg auf dem Balkan, Ziele, Methoden, "Recht-
    fertigung" ', in Loukia Droulia and Hagen Fleischer (eds.), Von Lidice bis Kalavryta:
    Widerstand und Besatzungsterror: Studien zur Repressalienpraxis im Zweiten Weltkrieg
    (Berlin, 1999), 65–91; Walter Manoschek, 'Krajevo – Kragujevac – Kalavryta: Die Mas-
    saker der 717. Infanteriedivision bzw. 117. Jägerdivision am Balnak', in ibid., 93–104;
    idem, 'Partisanenkrieg und Genozid: Die Wehrmacht in Serbien 1941', in idem (ed.), Die
    Wehrmacht im Rassenkrieg: Der Vernichtungskrieg hinter der Front (Vienna, 1996),
    142–67.
77. Longerich, Politik, 405–10; Hannes Heer, 'Killing Fields: Die Wehrmacht und der
    Holocaust', in idem and Naumann (eds.), Vernichtungskrieg, 57–77.
78. Longerich, Politik, 418.
79. Browning, The Origins, 309–11.
80. Longerich, Der ungeschriebene Befehl, 107–11.
81. Werner Jochmann (ed.), Monologe im Führerhauptquartier 1941–44: Die Aufzeich-
    nungen Heinrich Heims (Hamburg, 1980), 106–8; see also Longerich, Der ungeschriebene
    Befehl, 114–15.
82. Browning, The Origins, 312; Longerich, Der ungeschriebene Befehl, 112.
83. Ibid., 112.
84. Weinberg, A World at Arms, 153–61; Saul Friedländer, Prelude to Downfall: Hitler
    and the United States, 1939–1941 (London, 1967); David Reynolds, From Munich to
    Pearl Harbor: Roosevelt's America and the Origins of the Second World War (Chicago,
    2001); idem, The Creation of the Anglo-American Alliance, 1937–1941: A Study in
    Competitive Co-operation (London, 1981).
85. Friedländer, The Years of Extermination, 201; Tooze, The Wages of Destruction, 406–7.
86. Weinberg, A World at Arms, 243–5.
87. Ibid., 245–63.
88. Domarus (ed.), Hitler, IV. 1,731. For details on the lack of Jewish influence on American
    policy at this time, see Herf, The Jewish Enemy, 79–82.
89. Ibid., 84–5.
90. Ibid., 98–104.
91. Fröhlich (ed.), Die Tagebücher, II/I. 32–5 (9 July 1941; the first dictated entry).
92. Herf, The Jewish Enemy, 105.
93. Ibid., 106–7, 281–3 (I have slightly adjusted Herf's figures since some of the headlines
    he cites do not mention Jews).
94. Ibid., 28–31.
95. A. N., 23 June 1941, quoted in Manoschek (ed.), 'Es gibt nur eines', 28.
96. Herf, The Jewish Enemy, 282.
97. Ibid., illustration, between 166 and 167.
98. Quoted in ibid., 113.
99. Friedländer, The Years of Extermination, 202–7; Wolfgang Benz, 'Judenvernichtung

aus Notwehr? Die Legenden um Theodore N. Kaufman', *VfZ* 29 (1981), 615–30; more generally, Philipp Gassert, *Amerika im Dritten Reich: Ideologie, Propaganda und Volksmeinung 1933–1941* (Stuttgart, 1997) esp. ch. 7, and Bianka Pietrow-Ennker, 'Die Sowjetunion in der Propaganda des Dritten Reiches: Das Beispiel der Wochenschau', *Militärgeschichtliche Mitteilungen*, 46 (1989), 79–120.

100. Cited in Herf, *The Jewish Enemy*, 108; for *The Reich*, see ibid., 20–21.

101. Longerich, *Politik*, 421–3 and 696 nn. 3, 5, 8; good discussion in Friedländer, *The Years of Extermination*, 78–9 n. 160.

102. Kershaw, *Hitler*, II. 410–12.

103. Fröhlich (ed.), *Die Tagebücher*, II/I. 269 (19 August 1941); see also Longerich, *Der ungeschriebene Befehl*, 113–14.

104. See in particular Gerhard Botz, *Wohnungspolitik und Judendeportation in Wien 1938 bis 1945: Zur Funktion des Antisemitismus als Ersatz nationalsozialistischer Sozialpolitik* (Vienna, 1975) 57–65.

105. Friedländer, *The Years of Extermination*, 238–9.

106. Longerich and Pohl, *Ermordung*, 157; see also idem, *Der ungeschriebene Befehl*, 114, and more generally, *Politik*, 421–34 (among other things, emphasizing the intensification of antisemitic propaganda at this time).

107. Longerich, *Der ungeschriebene Befehl*, 115. The argument of Friedländer, *The Years of Extermination*, 264, that Stalin would not have been impressed is beside the point; the point was to impress the German population at home.

108. Fröhlich (ed.), *Die Tagebücher*, II/I. 480–81 (24 September 1941); see also Longerich, *Der ungeschriebene Befehl*, 116–17.

109. Fröhlich (ed.), *Die Tagebücher*, II/I. 481 (24 September 1941).

110. Longerich, *Der ungeschriebene Befehl*, 115–17.

111. Klemperer, *I Shall Bear Witness*, 374–98 (23 June–1 July 1941).

112. Klemperer, *To the Bitter End*, 37 (12 April 1942).

113. Ibid., 33 (31 March 1942), 37 (18 April 1942), 41–2 (23 and 26 April 1942).

114. Ibid., 65 (6 June 1942).

115. Friedländer, *The Years of Extermination*, 228.

116. Klemperer, *I Shall Bear Witness*, 414–15 (18, 19 and 20 September 1941), also 424 (9 November 1941).

117. Ibid., 422 (31 October 1941).

118. Klemperer, *To the Bitter End*, 11 (6 February 1942).

119. Ibid., 62–3 (2 June 1942).

120. Friedländer, *The Years of Extermination*, 289.

121. Ibid., 368.

122. Klemperer, *To the Bitter End*, 50–53 (18–19 May 1942).

123. Longerich, *Politik*, 446–8.

124. Longerich, *Der ungeschriebene Befehl*, 121.

125. Friedländer, *The Years of Extermination*, 255–6.

126. Wolf Gruner, *Judenverfolgung in Berlin 1933–1945: Eine Chronologie der Behörden-massnahmen in der Reichshauptstadt* (Berlin, 1996), 84.

127. Friedländer, *The Years of Extermination*, 266–7, gives slightly varying figures; see also Longerich, *Der ungeschriebene Befehl*, 117–18. For the mechanics of deportation, and numerous stories of individual deportees, see the extraordinary study by Hans Georg Adler, *Der verwaltete Mensch: Studien zur Deportation der Juden aus Deutschland* (Tübingen, 1974).

128. Fröhlich (ed.), *Die Tagebücher*, II/II.340–41 (22 November 1941).

129. See Stadtarchiv München (ed.), '... *verzogen, unbekannt wohin': Die erste Deportation von Münchner Juden im November 1941* (Zurich, 2000); Dina Porat, 'The Legend of the Struggle of Jews from the Third Reich in the Ninth Fort Near Kovno, 1941–1942', *Tel Aviver Jahrbuch für deutsche Geschichte*, 20 (1991), 363–92.

130. Klemperer, *To the Bitter End*, 6 (1 January 1942).

131. Ibid., 13 (15 February 1942).
132. Ibid., 17 (21 February–6 March 1942).
133. Ibid., 25–7 (9–16 March 1942).
134. Ibid., 54–6 (23 May 1942).
135. Ibid., 81 (24 June 1942) (italics in original).
136. Ibid., 58 (27 May 1942).
137. Solmitz, *Tagebuch*, 652, 655, 679 (22 May 1941, 3 June 1941, 13 September 1941).
138. See the general discussion in Friedländer, *The Years of Extermination*, 263–7.
139. Quoted in Longerich, *Der ungeschriebene Befehl*, 119.
140. Quoted in ibid., 118.
141. Hillgruber (ed.), *Staatsmänner und Diplomaten*, I. 664.
142. Fröhlich (ed.), *Die Tagebücher* II/II. 222 (2 November 1941).
143. Avraham Tory, *Surviving the Holocaust: The Kovno Ghetto Diary* (Cambridge, 1990).
144. Ibid., 43–60; and Corni, *Hitler's Ghettos*, 35.
145. Ibid., 31–7.
146. Thus the persuasive argument of Pohl, *Von der 'Judenpolitik' zum Judenmord*, 179; for a survey of the endless debate over the exact dating of a supposed order, see Christopher R. Browning, 'The Decision-Making Process', in Dan Stone (ed.), *The Historiography of the Holocaust* (London, 2004), 173–96.
147. Quoted in Longerich, *Der ungeschriebene Befehl*, 23–4.
148. Christian Gerlach, *Kalkulierte Morde: Die deutsche Wirtschafts- und Vernichtungspolitik in Weissrussland 1941 bis 1944* (Hamburg, 1999), esp. 683–743, and 1,131–6; for the mentally ill and handicapped, see ibid., 1,067–74.
149. Herf, *The Jewish Enemy*, 124–7. The speech was subsequently published as a pamphlet, *The Iron Heart*.
150. Quoted in Longerich, *Der ungeschriebene Befehl*, 139; see also Jürgen Hagemann, *Die Presselenkung im Dritten Reich* (Bonn, 1970), 125, 146 n. 67.
151. Dieter Pohl, 'Schauplatz Ukraine: Der Massenmord an den Juden im Militärverwaltungsgebiet und im Reichskommissariat 1941–1945', in Norbert Frei *et al.* (eds.), *Ausbeutung, Vernichtung, Öffentlichkeit: Neue Studien zur nationalsozialistischen Lagerpolitik* (Munich, 2000), 135–73. See also Martin Dean, *Collaboration in the Holocaust: Crimes of the Local Police in Belorussia and the Ukraine, 1941–44* (New York, 2000); and Shmuel Spector, *The Holocaust of Volhynian Jews: 1941–1944* (Jerusalem, 1990).
152. Rudolf Höss, *Commandant of Auschwitz: The Autobiography of Rudolf Höss* (London, 1959 [1951]), 165.
153. Klee *et al.* (eds.), *'Those Were the Days'*, 68.
154. Longerich, *Der ungeschriebene Befehl*, 122–3.
155. Quoted in Klee *et al.* (eds.), *'Those Were the Days'*, 69.
156. Yitzhak Arad, *Belzec, Sobibor, Treblinka: The Operation Reinhard Death Camps* (Bloomington, Ind., 1999 [1987]), 10–11; Longerich, *Der ungeschriebene Befehl*, 123; idem, *Politik*, 441–2; further details in Beer, 'Die Entwicklung der Gaswagen'; killings of mental patients enumerated in Longerich, *Politik*, 403–4.
157. Peter Witte *et al.* (eds.), *Der Dienstkalender Heinrich Himmlers 1941/42* (Hamburg, 1999), 233–4 (13 October 1941 and note 35). Plans were also drawn up for the construction of killing centres in Riga and Mogilev, though they were never actually built.
158. Longerich, *Der ungeschriebene Befehl*, 122–3.
159. Friedländer, *The Years of Extermination*, 314–18; Grojanowski managed to escape, and told his story to Ringelblum in Warsaw, where he arrived in January 1942. See also Gilbert, *The Holocaust*, 502.
160. Longerich, *Der ungeschriebene Befehl*, 123; idem, *Politik*, 443.
161. Quoted in Klee *et al.* (eds.), *'Those Were the Days'*, 72–4.
162. Manoschek, 'Die Vernichtung', 228–34; also Menachem Schelach, 'Sajmiste – an Extermination Camp in Serbia', *Holocaust and Genocide Studies*, 2 (1987), 243–60; further details in Glenny, *The Balkans*, 504–6, and Browning, *The Origins*, 344–6, 421–3.

163. Mark Roseman, *The Wannsee Conference and the Final Solution: A Reconsideration* (New York, 2002), 81; Friedländer, *The Years of Extermination*, 728–31 n. 193.

164. Christian Gerlach, 'Die Wannsee-Konferenz, das Schicksal der deutschen Juden und Hitlers politische Grundsatzentscheidung, alle Juden Europas zu ermorden', *Werkstatt Geschichte*, 18 (1997), 7–44; Roseman, *The Wannsee Conference*, 86.

165. Ibid., 86.

166. Fröhlich (ed.), *Die Tagebücher*, II/II. 498–9 (13 December 1941); see also Longerich, *Der ungeschriebene Befehl*, 138.

167. Cited in ibid., 139.

168. Ibid., 140–42.

169. Präg and Jacobmeyer (eds.), *Das Diensttagebuch*, 457 (16 December 1941).

170. Ibid., 458.

171. Longerich, *Der ungeschriebene Befehl*, 133; idem, *Politik*, 461–5; Richard J. Evans, *Telling Lies About Hitler: The Holocaust, History and the David Irving Trial* (London, 2002), 84–8.

172. Longerich, *Der ungeschriebene Befehl*, 122–37.

173. Witte *et al.* (eds.), *Der Dienstkalender*, 294.

174. Cited in Longerich, *Der ungeschriebene Befehl*, 169–70.

175. Longerich, *Politik*, 447–8, stresses the existence by October 1941 of the *intention* but not a *plan* to exterminate the Jews of Europe; more generally, on the mass killings in the Wartheland and Lublin district see ibid., 450–58.

176. Roseman, *The Wannsee Conference*, 157–62, reprinting the original minutes of the meeting, usually known as 'The Wannsee Protocol'. Eberhard Jäckel, 'On the Purpose of the Wannsee Conference', in James S. Pacy and Alan P. Wertheimer (eds.), *Perspectives on the Holocaust: Essays in Honor of Raul Hilberg* (Boulder, Colo., 1995), 39–49, argues that the purpose of the meeting was to convince the participants that Hitler had personally commissioned Heydrich to carry out the genocide, a hypothesis for which there is no convincing evidence.

177. Roseman, *The Wannsee Conference*, 163–4.

178. Roseman, *The Wannsee Conference*, 165–72. For the details of the discussions and decisions on 'mixed-race' people, see Beate Meyer, *'Jüdische Mischlinge': Rassenpolitik und Verfolgungserfahrung 1933–1945* (Hamburg, 1999), 99–101; and Peter Longerich and Dieter Pohl (eds.), *Die Ermordung der europäischen Juden: Eine umfassende Dokumentation des Holocaust 1941–1945* (Munich, 1989), 167–9.

179. Tooze, *The Wages of Destruction*, 476.

180. Roseman, *The Wannsee Conference*, 136–40.

181. Longerich, *Politik*, 476–82; Tooze, *The Wages of Destruction*, 531–3.

182. Eichmann trial, 26 June 1961, 24 July 1961, quoted in Roseman, *The Wannsee Conference*, 144. For the view that the reference to road construction schemes was metaphorical, standing for slave labour of all kinds, see Friedländer, *The Years of Extermination*, 342.

183. Roseman, *The Wannsee Conference*, 136–40.

184. Ibid., 144–5, 148.

185. Ibid., 149–50.

186. Longerich, *Der ungeschriebene Befehl*, 143–8.

187. Domarus (ed.), *Hitler*, IV. 1,828–9 (30 January 1942).

188. Jochmann (ed.), *Adolf Hitler*, 227–9.

189. Longerich, *Der ungeschriebene Befehl*, 138–42.

190. Fröhlich (ed.), *Die Tagebücher*, II/III. 320–21 (15 February 1942).

191. Ibid. II/III. 561 (27 March 1942).

192. Ibid.

193. Domarus (ed.), *Hitler*, IV. 1,869.

194. Fröhlich (ed.), *Die Tagebücher*, II/IV. 184 (27 April 1942). For the so-called 'Schlegel-

berger Note', an undated memorandum reporting Hitler's repeated insistence to Lammers
that the Jewish problem would only be solved after the war, see Evans, *Telling Lies*,
89–94. If, as the document's place in the file suggests, the memorandum dated from the
spring of 1942, then it either referred to the specific problem of 'mixed-race' people and
'half-Jews' or it expressed Hitler's belief that the completion of the 'final solution' would
only occur after the end of the war, an event which at this time was still expected within
the year.

195. Quoted in Herf, *The Jewish Enemy*, 155.
196. Fröhlich (ed.), *Die Tagebücher*, II/IV. 350 (24 May 1942).
197. Ibid., 355.
198. Ibid., 406 (30 May 1942).
199. Roseman, *The Wannsee Conference*, 152–5.
200. Quoted in Berenstein *et al.* (eds.), *Faschismus*, 296; cf. also Evans, *Telling Lies*, 96.
201. Wolf Gruner, *Widerstand in der Rosenstrasse: Die Fabrik-Aktion und die Verfolgung der Mischehen 1943* (Frankfurt am Main, 2005); idem, 'Die Fabrik-Aktion und die Ereignisse in der Berliner Rosenstrasse: Fakten und Fiktionen um den 27. Februar 1943', *Jahrbuch für Antisemitismusforschung*, 11 (2002), 137–77. For the legend in its classical version, see Nathan Stoltzfus, *Resistance of the Heart: Intermarriage and the Rosenstrasse Protest in Nazi Germany* (New York, 1996), 209–58 (relying heavily on oral history interviews).
202. Jochen Klepper, *Unter dem Schatten deiner Flügel: Aus den Tagebüchern der Jahre 1932–1942* (Stuttgart, 1955), 798 (3 September 1939); idem, *Briefwechsel 1925–1942* (ed. Ernst G. Riemschneider, Stuttgart, 1973), 227–30 (exchange of letters with Frick).
203. Quoted in Klepper, *Unter dem Schatten*, 1,130 (8 December 1942).
204. Ibid., 1,130–31 (8 December 1942).
205. Ibid., 1,133 (10 December 1942).
206. Christian Goeschel, 'Suicide in Weimar and Nazi Germany' (Ph.D. dissertation, University of Cambridge, 2006), 135–59.
207. Longerich, *Der ungeschriebene Befehl*, 151–2.
208. Ibid., 149–6, 170–73. For a list of the deportations, see idem, *Politik*, 483–93.
209. Höhne, *The Order of the Death's Head*, 455–6; Detlev Brandes, *Die Tschechen unter deutschem Protektorat*, I: *Besatzungspolitik, Kollaboration und Widerstand im Protektorat Böhmen und Mähren bis Heydrichs Tod, 1939–1942* (Munich, 1969); Miroslav Kárny, '"Heydrichiaden": Widerstand und Terror im Protektorat Böhmen und Mähren', in Droulia and Fleischer (eds.), *Von Lidice bis Kalavryta*, 51–63.
210. Charles Whiting, *Heydrich: Henchman of Death* (London, 1999), 141–7.
211. Höhne, *The Order of the Death's Head*, 455–7; Kershaw, *Hitler*, II. 518–19; still useful for details: Charles Wighton, *Heydrich: Hitler's Most Evil Henchman* (London, 1962), 270–76; recent account using testimony of the surgeons in Mario R. Dederichs, *Heydrich: Das Gesicht des Bösen* (Munich, 2005), 185–212.
212. Cited in Günther Deschner, 'Reinhard Heydrich: Security Technocrat', in Ronald Smelser and Rainer Zitelmann (eds.), *The Nazi Elite* (London, 1993 [1989]), 85–97, at 87; idem, *Reinhard Heydrich – Statthalter der totalen Macht* (Munich, 1978).
213. Hitler, *Hitler's Table Talk*, 4 June 1942.
214. Höhne, *The Order of the Death's Head*, 149–50; Fest, *The Face of the Third Reich*, 152–70.
215. As reported later by his widow; see ibid., 161.
216. Felix Kersten, *The Kersten Memoirs 1940–1945* (London, 1956), 90–99.
217. Carl J. Burckhardt, *Meine Danziger Mission 1937–1939* (Munich, 1960), 55.
218. Ibid., 57.
219. Hitler, *Hitler's Table Talk*, 4 June 1942.
220. Ibid., 4 July 1942.
221. Jürgen Tampke, *Czech-German Relations and the Politics of Central Europe from*

Bohemia to the EU (London, 2003), 67–9; René Kupper, 'Karl Hermann Frank als Deutscher Staatsminister für Böhmen und Mähren', in Monika Glettler *et al.* (eds.), *Geteilt, Besetzt, Beherrscht: Die Tschechoslowakei 1938–1945: Reichsgau Sudetenland, Protektorat Böhmen und Mähren, Slowakei* (Essen, 2004), 31–52.

222. Tooze, *The Wages of Destruction*, 538–45. The importance of the food question was first highlighted in Christian Gerlach's *Krieg, Ernährung, Völkermord: Forschungen zur deutschen Vernichtungspolitik im Zweiten Weltkrieg* (Hamburg, 1998).

223. Berenstein *et al.* (eds.), *Faschismus*, 303.

224. Longerich, *Der ungeschriebene Befehl*, 168.

225. Domarus (ed.), *Hitler*, IV. 1,920 (30 September 1942); on this occasion Hitler used the word *Ausrottung* rather than the usual *Vernichtung*.

226. Cited in Friedländer, *The Years of Extermination*, 403.

227. Quoted in Herf, *The Jewish Enemy*, 169.

228. Domarus (ed.), *Hitler* IV. 1,937 (8 November 1942).

229. Helmut Heiber, *Goebbels-Reden* (2 vols., Düsseldorf, 1971–2). The version quoted in Jeremy Noakes (ed.), *Nazism 1919–1945*, IV: *The German Home Front in World War II: A Documentary Reader* (Exeter, 1998), 490–91, from the BBC radio monitoring service records shouts of 'Out with the Jews' from the audience after the last sentence.

230. Domarus (ed.), *Hitler*, IV. 1,991 (24 February 1943) and 2,001 (21 March 1943).

231. Frohlich (ed.), *Die Tagebücher* II/VIII. 287–90 (13 May 1943); see also Norman Cohn, *Warrant for Genocide: The Myth of the Jewish World-Conspiracy and the Protocols of the Elders of Zion* (London, 1967).

232. Quoted in Noakes (ed.), *Nazism*, IV. 497.

233. Herf, *The Jewish Enemy*, 281–7.

234. This is the thesis of Herf, ibid. See also ibid., 183–230, for a survey of antisemitic propaganda in 1943.

235. Quoted in Longerich, *Der ungeschriebene Befehl*, 181–2.

236. Arad, *Belzec*, 14–16.

237. Ibid., 16–22.

238. Gilbert, *The Holocaust*, 817; Arad, *Belzec*, 23–9, 68–74.

239. Klukowski, *Diary*, 191 (8 April 1942); the reference to electricity was clearly based on false information.

240. Ibid., 192 (12–13 April 1942).

241. Ibid., 195–6 (8 May 1942).

242. Ibid., 197 (9 May 1942).

243. Gitta Sereny, *Into that Darkness: An Examination of Conscience* (London, 1977 [1974]), 111–12.

244. Ibid., 21–55.

245. Arad, *Belzec*, 126–7.

246. Ibid., 30–37, 75–80.

247. Ibid., 30–36, 49–53, 75–80, 128–30, 171–3.

248. Michael MacQueen, 'The Conversion of Looted Jewish Assets to Run the German War Machine', *Holocaust and Genocide Studies*, 18 (2004), 27–45; Bertrand Perz and Thomas Sandkühler, 'Auschwitz und die "Aktion Reinhard" 1942–1945: Judenmord und Raubpraxis in neuer Sicht', *Zeitgeschichte*, 26 (2000), 283–316.

249. Friedländer, *The Years of Extermination*, 498–9.

250. Berenstein *et al.* (eds.), *Faschismus*, 412–21.

251. Arad, *Belzec*, 165–9, 171, 306–41, 373–5.

252. Ibid., 37–43.

253. Ibid., 81–94; Sereny, *Into that Darkness*, 200–207.

254. Ibid., 200–207, 358; Arad, *Belzec*, 89–99.

255. Ibid., 196–7.

256. Ibid., 101.

257. Ibid., 270–98; Sereny, *Into that Darkness*, 236–49.

258. Sereny, *Into that Darkness*, 248–9.
259. Arad, *Belzec*, 365–9.
260. Ibid., 170–78, 372–6; Sereny, *Into that Darkness*, 249–50.
261. Arad, *Belzec*, 379–80.
262. Peter Witte and Stephen Tyas, 'A New Document on the Deportation and Murder of Jews during "Einsatz Reinhard" 1942', *Holocaust and Genocide Studies*, 15 (2001), 468–86.
263. Gerald Fleming, *Hitler and the Final Solution* (Oxford, 1986 [1982]), 135–9. According to Eichmann during his later interrogation, the abridged report, when returned to his office, bore a note from Himmler: 'Leader has taken note, destroy, H.H.'.
264. Arad, *Belzec*, 379.
265. Sybille Steinbacher, *Auschwitz: A History* (London, 2005 [2004]), 5–27; Höss, *Commandant of Auschwitz*, 116–19; Nilli Keren, 'The Family Camp', in Yisrael Gutman and Michael Berenbaum (eds.), *Anatomy of the Auschwitz Death Camp* (Bloomington, Ind., 1994), 428–40. For a graphic memoir written by one of these prisoners, see Wieslaw Kielar, *Anus Mundi: Five Years in Auschwitz* (London, 1982 [1972]).
266. Höss, *Commandant of Auschwitz*, 231.
267. Ibid., 134–9; Steinbacher, *Auschwitz*, 89–91.
268. Tomasz Kranz, 'Das KL Lublin zwischen Planung und Realisierung', in Herbert *et al.* (eds.), *Die nationalsozialistischen Konzentrationslager*, I. 363–89.
269. Longerich, *Der ungeschriebene Befehl*, 124–5; Steinbacher, *Auschwitz*, 77.
270. Longerich, *Politik*, 444 (and 704 n. 114, for the disputed timing of these experiments).
271. Friedländer, *The Years of Extermination*, 236, 717 n. 147; Höss, *Commandant of Auschwitz*, 164.
272. Longerich, *Der ungeschriebene Befehl*, 124; Steinbacher, *Auschwitz*, 87–9.
273. Höss, *Commandant of Auschwitz*, 169.
274. Höss, *Commandant of Auschwitz*, 169.
275. Ibid., 166–7.
276. Longerich, *Der ungeschriebene Befehl*, 124–5; Jamie McCarthy *et al.*, 'The Ruins of the Gas Chambers: A Forensic Investigation of Crematoriums at Auschwitz I and Auschwitz-Birkenau', *Holocaust and Genocide Studies*, 18 (2004), 68–103. Michael Thad Allen, 'Not Just a "Dating Game": Origins of the Holocaust at Auschwitz in the Light of Witness Testimony', *German History*, 25 (2007), 162–91, argues persuasively that Crematorium II was designed from the start as a gas chamber in accordance with directives from Himmler in Berlin, criticizing arguments that the crematoria were only converted to gas chambers at a later date: see Robert Jan Van Pelt, 'A Site in Search of a Mission', in Gutman and Berenbaum (eds.), *Anatomy*, 93–156; and Sybille Steinbacher, *'Musterstadt' Auschwitz: Germanisierungspolitik und Judenmord in Ostoberschlesien* (Munich, 2000), 78.
277. Steinbacher, *Auschwitz*, 96–105.
278. Ibid., 119–21.
279. Ibid., 105–7; Höss, *Commandant of Auschwitz*, 211, 235.
280. Steinbacher, *Auschwitz*, 107.
281. Miroslav Kárny *et al.* (eds.), *Theresienstadt in der 'Endlösung der Judenfrage'* (Prague, 1992).
282. Steinbacher, *Auschwitz*, 108–9; Friedländer, *The Years of Extermination*, 354.
283. Ibid., 620; Steinbacher, *Auschwitz*, 108.
284. Ibid., 40–44; eadem, *'Musterstadt' Auschwitz*, 247.
285. Steinbacher, *Auschwitz*, 132–5.
286. Höss, *Commandant of Auschwitz*, 173.
287. Ibid., 172.
288. Ibid., 145.
289. Ibid., 172.
290. Ibid., 174.

291. Ibid., 175–6.

292. Czerniakow, *The Warsaw Diary*, 300 (19 November 1941), 341 (8–10 April 1942), 355 (18 May 1942), 366 (14 June 1942), 376–7 (8 July 1942).

293. Ibid., 384–5 (21–3 July 1942); Kermish, 'Introduction', in ibid., 23–4. Czerniakow's diary was preserved by unknown hands and came to light in 1959. There is an atmospheric account of the crucial meeting on 22 July 1942 in Marcel Reich-Ranicki, *The Author of Himself: The Life of Marcel Reich-Ranicki* (London, 2001 [1999]), 164–6. See also Wolfgang Scheffler, 'The Forgotten Part of the "Final Solution": The Liquidation of the Ghettos', *Simon Wiesenthal Centre Annual*, 2 (1985), 31–51.

294. Hosenfeld, *'Ich versuche'*, 628 (letter to wife, 23 July 1942). Hosenfeld's position in the military administration seems to have protected his letters from the attentions of the censor, though such an unqualified expression of criticism was still potentially very dangerous.

295. Ibid., 630 (diary, 25 July 1942).

296. Ibid., 642 (letter to son, 18 August 1942).

297. Klukowski, *Diary*, 208 (4 August 1942).

298. Kaplan, *Scroll*, Introduction and 271 (16 June 1942), 279–80 (25–6 June 1942); Gilbert, *The Holocaust*, 462; Corni, *Hitler's Ghettos*, 279. See also Jerzy Lewinski, 'The Death of Adam Czerniakow and Janusz Korcak's Last Journey', *Polin: Studies in Polish Jewry*, 7 (1992), 224–53.

299. Gutman, *The Jews of Warsaw*, 270–72.

300. Ringelblum, *Notes*, 310–11, also quoted in Corni, *Hitler's Ghettos*, 279.

301. Ibid., 293–315, 320–21; Hosenfeld, *'Ich versuche'*, 631 (diary, 25 July 1942).

302. Yisrael Gutman, *Resistance: The Warsaw Ghetto Uprising* (Boston, Mass., 1994); Shmuel Krakowski, *The War of the Doomed: Jewish Armed Resistance in Poland, 1942–1944* (New York, 1984); Reuben Ainsztein, *Revolte gegen die Vernichtung: Der Aufstand im Warschauer Ghetto* (Berlin, 1993).

303. Jürgen Stroop, *The Stroop Report: The Jewish Quarter of Warsaw Is No More!* (London, 1980 [1960]), 9.

304. Corni, *Hitler's Ghettos*, 315–21.

305. Hosenfeld, *'Ich versuche'*, 719 (diary, 16 June 1943).

306. Reich-Ranicki, *The Author of Himself*, 176–92.

307. Joseph Kermish, 'Introduction', in Ringelblum, *Polish-Jewish Relations*, vii–xxxi, at xxiii–xvi, and Ringelblum, *Notes*, ix–xxvii.

308. Weiss, 'Jewish Leadership'.

309. Friedländer, *The Years of Extermination*, 557.

310. Sierakowiak, *The Diary*, 77–90 (6 April–15 May 1941), 91–2 (16 May 1941), 133 (28 September 1941), 137–43 (4–23 October 1941).

311. Corni, *Hitler's Ghettos*, 280–81; Friedländer, *The Years of Extermination*, 314–15, 387–9; Avraham Barkai, 'Between East and West: Jews from Germany in the Lodz Ghetto', in Michael R. Marrus (ed.), *The Nazi Holocaust: Historical Articles on the Destruction of European Jews* (Westport, Conn., 1989), 378–439.

312. Dobroszycki (ed.), *The Chronicle of the Lodz Ghetto*, 163–5.

313. Sierakowiak, *The Diary*, 173 (25 May 1942), 238 (11 December 1942), 267–8 (14–15 April 1942); Corni, *Hitler's Ghettos*, 282–3.

314. Friedländer, *The Years of Extermination*, 531.

315. Ibid., 529–30; Alan Adelson and Robert Lapides (eds.), *Lódź Ghetto: Inside a Community under Siege* (New York, 1989), 328–31; Bernhard Chiari, *Alltag hinter der Front: Besatzung, Kollaboration und Widerstand in Weissrussland 1941–1944* (Düsseldorf, 1998).

316. Corni, *Hitler's Ghettos*, 309–10.

317. Yitzhak Arad, *Ghetto in Flames: The Struggle and Destruction of the Jews in Vilna in the Holocaust* (Jerusalem, 1980).

318. Philip Friedman, *Roads to Extinction: Essays on the Holocaust* (New York, 1980), 294–321.

319. Corni, *Hitler's Ghettos*, 283–4.

320. Antony Polonsky, 'Beyond Condemnation, Apologetics and Apologies: On the Complexity of Polish Behaviour Towards the Jews during the Second World War', in Roger Bullen, Hartmut Pogge Von Strandmann and Antony Polonsky (eds.), *Ideas into Politics: Aspects of European History 1880 to 1950* (London, 1984), 123–43, at 194.

321. Hosenfeld, '*Ich versuche*', 657–8 (diary, 1 September 1942).

322. Wolfram Wette, ' "Rassenfeind": Antisemitismus und Antislawismus in der Wehrmachtspropaganda', in Manoschek (ed.), *Die Wehrmacht im Rassenkrieg*, 55–73.

323. Manoschek, '*Es gibt nur eines*', 65 (Fw. E. E., 18 December 1942).

324. Ibid., 57 (Am. D. S., 17 May 1942).

325. Hans Safrian, 'Komplizen des Genozids: Zum Anteil der Heeresgruppe Süd an der Verfolgung und Ermordung der Juden in der Ukraine 1941', in Manoschek (ed.), *Die Wehrmacht im Rassenkrieg*, 90–115; Andrej Angrick, 'Zur Rolle der Militärverwaltung bei der Ermordung der sowjetischen Juden', in Babette Quinkert (ed.), '*Wir sind die Herren dieses Landes': Ursachen, Verlauf und Folgen des deutschen Überfalls auf die Sowjetunion* (Hamburg, 2002), 104–23.

326. Hürter, *Hitlers Heerführer*, 509–99, explores the mixture of utilitarian and ideological motives that led the senior army commanders on the Eastern Front to tolerate, encourage or lend logistical support to the mass murder of the Jewish population of the area.

327. Hosenfeld, '*Ich versuche*', 719 (diary, 16 June 1943).

Chapter 4. THE NEW ORDER

1. Richard Overy, 'Rationalization and the "Production Miracle" in Germany during the Second World War', in idem, *War and Economy in the Third Reich* (Oxford, 1994), 343–75 (quotes on 353–4).

2. Speer, *Inside the Third Reich*, 271–9; Tooze, *The Wages of Destruction*, 508–9.

3. Speer's account corrected in Gitta Sereny, *Albert Speer: His Battle with Truth* (London, 1995), 274–83; Max Müller, 'Der Tod des Reichsministers Dr Fritz Todt', *Geschichte in Wissenschaft und Unterricht* 18 (1967), 602–5; discussion in Kershaw, *Hitler*, II. 502–3.

4. Karl-Heinz Ludwig, *Technik und Ingenieure im Dritten Reich* (Düsseldorf, 1974), 403–72, and Müller, 'The Mobilization', 453–85.

5. Speer, *Inside the Third Reich*, 261–5, 275–7, 291; Sereny, *Albert Speer*, 291–2.

6. Müller, 'The Mobilization', 773–86.

7. Evans, *The Third Reich in Power*, 183–6; Alan S. Milward, *The German Economy at War* (London, 1985), 72–99.

8. See Evans, *The Third Reich in Power*, 183–6.

9. Speer, *Inside the Third Reich*, 262–3.

10. Quoted in Tooze, *The Wages of Destruction*, 506–7.

11. Halder, *Kriegstagebuch*, III. 309 (24 November 1941).

12. Budrass, *Flugzeugindustrie*, 724. A contributory factor may have been office intrigues against his position.

13. Tooze, *The Wages of Destruction*, 123–4, 508.

14. Ibid., 587–9; Overy, 'Rationalization', 356, 343–9.

15. Walter Naasner, *Neue Machtzentren in der deutschen Kriegswirtschaft 1942–1945* (Boppard, 1994), 471–2.

16. Speer, *Inside the Third Reich*, 280.

17. Ibid., 282–5.

18. Paul B. Jaskot, *The Architecture of Oppression: The SS, Forced Labor, and the Nazi Monumental Building Economy* (London, 2000), 80–113.

19. Speer, *Inside the Third Reich*, 287–300 (quote on 295–6); Milward, *The German Economy at War*, 54–71 (for Todt's achievements).

20. Overy, *War and Economy*, 356–70.

21. Tooze, *The Wages of Destruction*, 568–74.

22. Ibid., 578–84.

23. Overy, *War and Economy*, 356–67.

24. Weinberg, *A World at Arms*, 538.

25. Mark Harrison (ed.), *The Economics of World War II: Six Great Powers in International Comparison* (Cambridge, 1998), 26.

26. Edward R. Zilbert, *Albert Speer and the Nazi Ministry of Arms: Economic Institutions and Industrial Production in the German War Economy* (London, 1981), esp. 184–257; Budrass, *Flugzeugindustrie*, 738–9, 891.

27. Tooze, *The Wages of Destruction*, 587–9; Mark Harrison, *Accounting for War: Soviet Production, Employment and the Defence Burden, 1940–1945* (Cambridge, 1996); and John Barber and Mark Harrison, *The Soviet Home Front, 1941–1945: A Social and Economic History of the USSR in World War II* (London, 1991).

28. Tooze, *The Wages of Destruction*, 407; Müller, 'The Mobilization', 723; Boog, 'The Strategic Air War', 118.

29. Rolf-Dieter Müller, 'Albert Speer and Armaments Policy in Total War', *GSWW* V/II, 293–832, at 805.

30. Harrison (ed.), *The Economics of World War II*, 20–21.

31. Tooze, *The Wages of Destruction*, 383–5; Alan S. Milward, *The New Order and the French Economy* (Oxford, 1984), 81.

32. Many further examples in Götz Aly, *Hitler's Beneficiaries: Plunder, Racial War, and the Nazi Welfare State* (New York, 2007 [2005]); also Elmshäuser and Lokers (eds.), *'Man muss hier nur hart sein'*, 55, 62, 63, 68 etc.

33. Jeremy Noakes and Geoffrey Pridham (eds.), *Nazism 1919–1945*, III: *Foreign Policy, War and Racial Extermination: A Documentary Reader* (Exeter, 1988), 295; Alan S. Milward, *War, Economy and Society 1939–1945* (London, 1987 [1977]), 137.

34. Tooze, *The Wages of Destruction*, 386–8; Overy *et al.* (eds.), *Die 'Neuordnung' Europas*.

35. Milward, *War, Economy and Society*, 139–41.

36. Milward, *The New Order and the French Economy*, 111.

37. Harrison (ed.), *The Economics of World War II*, 22.

38. Milward, *War, Economy and Society*, 138–45.

39. Tooze, *The Wages of Destruction*, 389–91; Noakes and Pridham (eds.), *Nazism*, III. 297–8.

40. Harald Wixforth, *Die Expansion der Dresdner Bank in Europa* (Munich, 2006), 871–902.

41. Noakes and Pridham (eds.), *Nazism*, III. 274–80, at 280.

42. Alan Milward, *The Fascist Economy in Norway* (Oxford, 1972), 1, 3; idem, *War, Economy and Society*, 153–7; Ludolf Herbst, *Der totale Krieg und die Ordnung der Wirtschaft: Die Kriegswirtschaft im Spannungsfeld von Politik, Ideologie und Propaganda 1939–1945* (Stuttgart, 1982), 127–44.

43. Noakes and Pridham (eds.), *Nazism*, III. 283–4.

44. Ibid., 286.

45. Milward, *The New Order and the French Economy*, 23–8.

46. Tooze, *The Wages of Destruction*, 391–3.

47. Milward, *The New Order and the French Economy*, 147–80.

48. Noakes and Pridham (eds.), *Nazism*, III. 290.

49. Ibid., 292.

50. Ibid., 292.

51. Tooze, *The Wages of Destruction*, 409–10; Milward, *The New Order and the French Economy*, 293–4.

52. Tooze, *The Wages of Destruction*, 411–12.

53. Ibid., 418–19; Noakes and Pridham (eds.), *Nazism*, III. 298.

54. Tooze, *The Wages of Destruction*, 412–18.

55. Noakes and Pridham (eds.), *Nazism*, III. 304–9.

56. Franz Neumann, *Behemoth: The Structure and Practice of National Socialism 1933–1944* (New York, 1944 [1942]), 293.

57. Harold James, *The Deutsche Bank and the Nazi Economic War against the Jews: The Expropriation of Jewish-Owned Property* (Cambridge, 2001), 213–14.

58. Walter Naasner, *SS-Wirtschaft und SS-Verwaltung* (Düsseldorf, 1998), 164–7; Michael Thad Allen, *The Business of Genocide: The SS, Slave Labor, and the Concentration Camps* (Chapel Hill, N.C., 2002), 58–71, 107–12.

59. Naasner, *Neue Machtzentren*, 197–44; Georg Enno, *Die wirtschaftlichen Unternehmungen der SS* (Stuttgart, 1963), 70–71, 145.

60. Jan Erik Schulte, *Zwangsarbeit und Vernichtung: Das Wirtschaftsimperium der SS: Oswald Pohl und das SS-Wirtschafts-Verwaltungshauptamt 1933–1945* (Paderborn, 2001), 440–41.

61. Berenice A. Carroll, *Design for Total War: Arms and Economics in the Third Reich* (The Hague, 1968), 233.

62. Paul Erker, *Industrie-Eliten in der NS-Zeit: Anpassungsbereitschaft und Eigeninteresse von Unternehmen in der Rüstungs- und Kriegswirtschaft 1936–1945* (Passau, 1993), 73–5.

63. Johannes Bähr, *Die Dresdner Bank in der Wirtschaft des Dritten Reichs* (Munich, 2006), 477–570.

64. Peter Hayes, *From Cooperation to Complicity: Degussa in the Third Reich* (Cambridge, 2004), 190–91.

65. See Jonathan Steinberg, *The Deutsche Bank and its Gold Transactions during the Second World War* (Munich, 1999).

66. Erna Spiewack, television interview 1998, quoted in Hayes, *From Cooperation to Complicity*, 193.

67. Overy, 'Rationalization', 368.

68. Tooze, *The Wages of Destruction*, 567–9.

69. Peter W. Becker, 'Fritz Sauckel: Plenipotentiary for the Mobilisation of Labour', in Smelser and Zitelmann (eds.), *The Nazi Elite*, 194–201.

70. Ibid.; also Herbert, *Hitler's Foreign Workers*, 161–3; Edward L. Homze, *Foreign Labor in Nazi Germany* (Princeton, N.J., 1967), 111–53; Hans Pfahlmann, *Fremdarbeiter und Kriegsgefangene in der deutschen Kriegswirtschaft 1939–1945* (Darmstadt, 1968), 16–22.

71. See generally Ela Hornung et al., 'Zwangsarbeit in der Landwirtschaft', *DRZW* IX/II. 577–666.

72. Herbert, *Hitler's Foreign Workers*, 84–9; Christa Tholander, *Fremdarbeiter 1939 bis 1945: Ausländische Arbeitskräfte in der Zeppelin-Stadt Friedrichshafen* (Essen, 2001), 34–104.

73. Spoerer, *Zwangsarbeit*, 35–88, provides a detailed country-by-country account of recruitment; see also Pfahlmann, *Fremdarbeiter*, 82–103 and 176–92 for prisoners of war.

74. Herbert, *Hitler's Foreign Workers*, 95–111; see also the recent survey by Oliver Rathkolb, 'Zwangsarbeit in der Industrie', *DRZW* IX/II, 667–728.

75. Herbert, *Hitler's Foreign Workers*, 137–49.

76. Ibid., 157.

77. Ibid, 193–4; also Pfahlmann, *Fremdarbeiter*, 44–65.

78. Overmans, *Deutsche militärische Verluste*, 238–9.

79. Tooze, *The Wages of Destruction*, 513–14.

80. Herbert, *Hitler's Foreign Workers*, 273–8; Homze, *Foreign Labor*, 177–203; Richard Vinen, *The Unfree French: Life under the Occupation* (London, 2006), 183–214 (for prisoners of war), and 247–312 (for labour service); Pfahlmann, *Fremdarbeiter*, 31–44.

81. Quoted in Herbert, *Hitler's Foreign Workers*, 279.

82. Ibid., 278–82, 297–8.

83. Tooze, *The Wages of Destruction*, 519.

84. Bernard Bellon, *Mercedes in Peace and War: German Automobile Workers, 1903–1945* (New York, 1990), 250–51.

85. Quoted in Herbert, *Hitler's Foreign Workers*, 209–11; see also ibid., 211–17, and Bellon, *Mercedes*, 251; more generally, see Spoerer, *Zwangsarbeit*, 116–44; Pfahlmann, *Fremdarbeiter*, 193–217; Marcus Meyer, '... *uns 100 Zivilausländer umgehend zu beschaffen': Zwangsarbeit bei den Bremer Stadtwerken 1939–1945* (Bremen, 2002); Mark Spoerer, 'Die soziale Differenzierung der ausländischen Zivilarbeiter, Kriegsgefangenen und Häftlinge im Deutschen Reich', *DRZW IX/II*. 485–576, at 515–32.

86. Herbert, *Hitler's Foreign Workers*, 217–22; Andreas Heusler, *Ausländereinsatz: Zwangsarbeit für die Münchner Kriegswirtschaft 1939–1945* (Munich, 1996), 212–22; Spoerer, *Zwangsarbeit*, 199–200; Eginhard Scharf, '*Man machte mit uns, was man wollte': Ausländische Zwangsarbeiter in Ludwigshafen am Rhein 1939–1945* (Hamburg, 2004), 56–73; and Valentina Maria Stefanski, *Zwangsarbeit in Leverkusen: Polnische Jugendliche im I. G. Farbenwerk* (Osnabrück, 2000), 333–49; Katharina Hoffmann, *Zwangsarbeit und ihre gesellschaftliche Akzeptanz in Oldenburg 1939–1945* (Oldenburg, 2001), 96–161, 216–24; generally, Spoerer, 'Die soziale Differenzierung', 562–5.

87. Herbert, *Hitler's Foreign Workers*, 268–9; Spoerer, *Zwangsarbeit*, 200–205; Scharf, '*Man machte*', 237–42.

88. Behnken (ed.), *Deutschland-Berichte*, VII. 100–103 (February 1940).

89. Evans, *The Third Reich in Power*, 686–7.

90. Jill Stephenson, *Hitler's Home Front: Württemberg under the Nazis* (London, 2006), 281–5.

91. Herbert, *Hitler's Foreign Workers*, 116–36. Heusler, *Ausländereinsatz*, 387–417, gives a detailed account of social and sexual contacts with the German population in Munich. For the punishment of foreign labourers, see also Scharf, '*Man machte*', 246–50.

92. Herbert, *Hitler's Foreign Workers*, 69–94.

93. For Soviet prisoners of war in the Volkswagen factory, see Hans Mommsen and Manfred Grieger, *Das Volkswagenwerk und seine Arbeiter im Dritten Reich* (Düsseldorf, 1996), 544–65.

94. Quoted in Herbert, *Hitler's Foreign Workers*, 149.

95. Ibid., 149–67; Spoerer, *Zwangsarbeit*, 200–205.

96. Quoted in Herbert, *Hitler's Foreign Workers*, 171.

97. Tholander, *Fremdarbeiter*, 312–37, 365–9.

98. Herbert, *Hitler's Foreign Workers*, 176–80; Heusler, *Ausländereinsatz*, 172–222; Mommsen and Grieger, *Das Volkswagenwerk*, 566–98.

99. Quoted in Herbert, *Hitler's Foreign Workers*, 192.

100. Ibid., 182–92; Spoerer, *Zwangsarbeit*, 33, 90–115.

101. Solmitz, *Tagebuch* (7 March 1943).

102. Ibid., 840 (4 August 1943).

103. Rolf Keller, ' "Die kamen in Scharen hier an, die Gefangenen": Sowjetische Kriegsgefangene, Wehrmachtsoldaten und deutsche Bevölkerung in Norddeutschland 1941/42', in Detlef Garbe (ed.), *Rassismus in Deutschland* (Bremen, 1994), 35–53; Hoffmann, *Zwangsarbeit*, 315.

104. Solmitz, *Tagebuch*, 858 (2 September 1943) and 883 (29 December 1943, Nachtrag).

105. Richard J. Overy, 'Guns or Butter? Living Standards, Finance, and Labour in Germany, 1939–1942', in idem, *War and Economy in the Third Reich*, 259–314, at 303–4; Tilla Siegel, *Leistung und Lohn in der nationalsozialistischen 'Ordnung der Arbeit'* (Opladen, 1989), 161–73; and Leila J. Rupp, *Mobilizing Women for War: German and American Propaganda 1939–1945* (Princeton, N.J., 1978), 185–6.

106. Overy, 'Guns or Butter?', 307–11.

107. Matthew Stibbe, *Women in the Third Reich* (London, 2003), 91–6; Tim Mason, *Social Policy in the Third Reich: The Working Class and the 'National Community'* (Oxford, 1995), 19–40; Overy, 'Guns or Butter?', 309–10.

108. Quoted in Rupp, *Mobilizing Women*, 115.

109. Evans, *The Third Reich in Power*, 517–20.

110. Quoted in Rupp, *Mobilizing Women*, 122; for the above details, ibid., 115–16; also

Dörte Winkler, 'Frauenarbeit versus Frauenideologie: Probleme der weiblichen Erwerbs-tätigkeit in Deutschland, 1930–1945', *Archiv für Sozialgeschichte*, 17 (1977), 99–126, and the same author's *Frauenarbeit im 'Dritten Reich'* (Hamburg, 1977); also Annemarie Tröger, 'Die Frau im wesensgemässen Einsatz', in Frauengruppe Faschismusforschung (ed.), *Mutterkreuz und Arbeitsbuch: Zur Geschichte der Frauen in der Weimarer Republik und im Nationalsozialismus* (Frankfurt am Main, 1981), 246–72.

111. This is the overall argument of Rupp, *Mobilizing Women*.

112. Ibid., 185, and Winkler, 'Frauenarbeit', 126.

113. Stibbe, *Women*, 94–5.

114. Quoted in Herbert, *Hitler's Foreign Workers*, 189.

115. Ibid., 187–9.

116. Quoted in ibid., 307.

117. Stefanski, *Zwangsarbeit*, 339.

118. Ibid., 268–9; Stibbe, *Women*, 101–2; Klaus-Georg Siegfried, *Das Leben der Zwangs-arbeiter im Volkswagenwerk 1939–1945* (Frankfurt am Main, 1988), 235–55; Spoerer, *Zwangsarbeit*, 205–9.

119. Peter Hayes, *Industry and Ideology: IG Farben in the Nazi Era* (Cambridge, 1987), 349–56. For synthetic rubber, see Evans, *The Third Reich in Power*, 362–3, 375.

120. Hayes, *Industry and Ideology*, 358–67; Bernd C. Wagner, *IG-Auschwitz: Zwangsar-beit und Vernichtung von Häftlingen des Lagers Monowitz 1941–1945* (Munich, 2000), 37–90.

121. Martin Broszat, 'The Concentration Camps 1933–1945', in Helmut Krausnick *et al.*, *Anatomy of the SS State* (London, 1968), 460–71; figures amended in Nikolaus Wachs-mann, *Hitler's Prisons: Legal Terror in Nazi Germany* (London, 2004), 395; Hermann Kaienburg, 'KZ-Haft und Wirtschaftsinteresse: Das Wirtschaftsverwaltungshauptamt der SS als Leitungszentrale der Konzentrationslager und der SS-Wirtschaft', in idem (ed.), *Konzentrationslager und deutsche Wirtschaft 1939–1945* (Opladen, 1996), 29–60.

122. Quoted in Broszat, 'The Concentration Camps', 497.

123. Ibid., 498, and more generally, 473–98.

124. Ibid., 503–4; Jan Erik Schulte, 'Das SS-Wirtschafts-Verwaltungshauptamt und die Expansion des KZ-Systems', in Wolfgang Benz and Barbara Distel (eds.), *Der Ort des Terrors: Geschichte der nationalsozialistischen Konzentrationslager* (6 vols., Munich, 2005–7), I. 141–55; Hermann Kaienburg, 'Zwangsarbeit: KZ und Wirtschaft im Zweiten Weltkrieg', in ibid., 179–94.

125. 'Auschwitz', in ibid., V. 79–173.

126. Schulte, *Zwangsarbeit*, 441–5.

127. Jan Erik Schulte, 'Zwangsarbeit für die SS: Juden in der Ostindustrie GmbH', in Frei *et al.* (eds.), *Ausbeutung*, 43–74.

128. Manfred Grieger, 'Unternehmen und KZ-Arbeit: Das Beispiel der Volkswagenwerk GmbH', in Kaienburg (ed.), *Konzentrationslager*, 77–94; Mommsen and Grieger, *Das Volkswagenwerk*, 516–43, 566–98, 740–99; Christian Jansen and Arno Weckbecker, 'Zwangsarbeit für das Volkswagenwerk: Häftlingsalltag auf dem Laagberg bei Wolfsburg', in Frei *et al.* (eds.), *Ausbeutung*, 75–108.

129. Ludwig Eiber, 'Das KZ-Aussenlager Blohm und Voss im Hamburger Hafen', in Kaien-burg (ed.), *Konzentrationslager*, 227–38.

130. Neil Gregor, *Daimler-Benz in the Third Reich* (London, 1998), 194–6; Birgit Weitz, 'Der Einsatz von KZ-Häftlingen und jüdischen Zwangsarbeitern bei der Daimler-Benz AG (1941–1945): Ein Überblick', in Kaienburg (ed.), *Konzentrationslager*, 169–95, esp. 190. There are many local studies, including, for example, Annette Wienecke, '*Besondere Vorkommnisse nicht bekannt': Zwangsarbeit in unterirdischen Rüstungsbetrieben: Wie ein Heidedorf kriegswichtig wurde* (Bonn, 1996); and Wilhelm J. Waibel, *Schatten am Hohentwiel: Zwangsarbeiter und Kriegsgefangene in Singen* (Konstanz, 1997 [1995]), with interviews of former workers.

131. Broszat, 'The Concentration Camps', 501–2.

132. Quoted in ibid., 502.

133. Ibid., 497–9. See also Lutz Budrass and Manfred Grieger, 'Die Moral der Effizienz: Die Beschäftigung von KZ-Häftlingen am Beispiel des Volkswagenwerks und der Henschel Flugzeug-Werke', *Jahrbuch für Wirtschaftsgeschichte* (1993), 89–136.

134. Wagner, *IG-Auschwitz*, 204, 291; Rainer Fröbe, 'Der Arbeitseinsatz von KZ-Häftlingen und die Perspektive der Industrie, 1943–1945', in Ulrich Herbert (ed.), *Europa und der 'Reichseinsatz': Ausländische Zivilarbeiter, Kriegsgefangene und KZ-Häftlinge in Deutschland 1938–1945* (Essen, 1991), 351–83; Jaskot, *The Architecture of Oppression*, 37–8.

135. Spoerer, *Zwangsarbeit*, 183–90.

136. Tooze, *The Wages of Destruction*, 445–6; Hayes, *Industry and Ideology*, 361–5.

137. Hayes, *From Cooperation to Complicity*, 26–71; Heusler, *Ausländereinsatz*, 421; Spoerer, *Zwangsarbeit*, 186.

138. Ibid., 221–2.

139. A point first made by Carroll, *Design for Total War*, 245–7.

140. For an account of pre-Speer polycracy, see Müller, 'The Mobilization', 448–56, 630–38; also emphasized by Herbst, *Der totale Krieg*, 111–17; for continuing inter-institutional competition in the Speer era, see Carroll, *Design for Total War*, 245–7; for rivalry between Speer and the Reich Ministry of Economics, see Herbst, *Der totale Krieg*, 267–75.

141. Aly, *Hitler's Beneficiaries*, 75–179, 324–5; also Michael Wildt, 'Alys Volksstaat: Hybris und Simplizität einer Wissenschaft', *Sozial.Geschichte*, 20 (2005), 91–97, with further references. For a positive assessment of the contribution of foreign labour, see Pfahlmann, *Fremdarbeiter*, 226–35.

142. Harrison (ed.), *The Economics of World War II*, 10–11.

143. Naasner, *Neue Machtzentren*, 469–73. For the idea of 'crisis management' in wartime Germany, see Rolf-Dieter Müller, *Der Manager der Kriegswirtschaft: Hans Kehrl: Ein Unternehmer in der Politik des 'Dritten Reiches'* (Essen, 1999), esp. 101–3.

144. Speer, *Inside the Third Reich*, 446; for Sauckel in this period, see Homze, *Foreign Labor*, 233–9.

145. Milward, *The Fascist Economy in Norway*, 279.

146. Hans Umbreit, 'Auf dem Weg zur Kontinentalherrschaft', *DRZW* V/1. 3–345.

147. Ibid., 3–165 ('Stadien der territorialen "Neuordnung" in Europa' and 'Die vorgezogene "Neuordnung" '). For a good general account, see Mazower, *Hitler's Empire*.

148. For a detailed and sensitive study of the many different and often creative ways in which people in one area, the Loire Valley in France, coped with the German occupation, see Robert Gildea, *Marianne in Chains: In Search of the German Occupation 1940–1945* (London, 2002).

149. Quoted in Vinen, *The Unfree French*, 53.

150. The best recent account is Jackson, *France*; see also Vinen, *The Unfree French*; Ian Ousby, *Occupation: The Ordeal of France 1940–1944* (London, 1997); and the classic, pioneering study by Robert O. Paxton, *Vichy France: Old Guard and New Order, 1940–1944* (London, 1972).

151. Michael R. Marrus and Robert O. Paxton, *Vichy France and the Jews* (New York, 1981), 23–72; Paula Hyman, *From Dreyfus to Vichy: The Remaking of French Jewry, 1906–1939* (New York, 1979) and Pierre Birnbaum, *Anti-semitism in France: A Political History from Léon Blum to the Present* (Oxford, 1992 [1988]).

152. Marrus and Paxton, *Vichy France*, 177–314.

153. Friedländer, *The Years of Extermination*, 109–16; Longerich, *Politik*, 435. For the camps, see Regina M. Delacor, 'From Potential Friends to Potential Enemies: The Internment of "Hostile Foreigners" in France at the Beginning of the Second World War', *Journal of Contemporary History*, 35 (2000), 361–8; more generally, on the occupied zone, Philippe Burrin, *France under the Germans: Collaboration and Compromise* (New York, 1996).

154. David Carroll, *French Literary Fascism: Nationalism, Anti-Semitism, and the Ideology of Culture* (Princeton, N.J., 1995).

155. Anne Grynberg, *Les Camps de la honte: Les internes juifs des camps français, 1939–1944* (Paris, 1991); Marrus and Paxton, *Vichy France*, 121–76; Renée Poznanski, *Jews in France during World War II* (Hanover, 2001 [1994]), 42–55.

156. Friedländer, *The Years of Extermination*, 169–78.

157. Longerich, *Politik*, 435.

158. Ahrlich Meyer, *Täter im Verhör: Die Endlösung der Judenfrage in Frankreich 1940–1944* (Darmstadt, 2005), and Barbara Lambauer, 'Opportunistischer Antisemitismus: Der deutsche Botschafter Otto Abetz und die Judenverfolgung in Frankreich', *VfZ* 53 (2005), 241–73.

159. Friedländer, *The Years of Extermination*, 157–78; for Dannecker's background and deep-dyed antisemitism, see Claudia Steur, *Theodor Dannecker: Ein Funktionär der 'Endlösung'* (Essen, 1997), 14–91; for the race laws and their application in France, see Susan Zuccotti, *The Holocaust, the French, and the Jews* (New York, 1993), 51–64 (also 65–80 for the camps). More generally, see also the account in Jackson, *France*, 354–84.

160. Longerich, *Politik*, 434–40.

161. Gerald Schwab, *The Day the Holocaust Began: The Odyssey of Herschel Grynszpan* (New York, 1990).

162. Jacques Adler, *The Jews of Paris and the Final Solution: Communal Responses and Internal Conflicts, 1940–1944* (New York, 1987).

163. Marrus and Paxton, *Vichy France*, 281–340; see also Carmen Callil, *Bad Faith: A Forgotten History of Family and Fatherland* (London, 2007).

164. Friedländer, *The Years of Extermination*, 377.

165. Poznanski, *Jews in France*, 237–50.

166. Ibid., 303–55; Marrus and Paxton, *Vichy France*, 250–55; Zuccotti, *The Holocaust*, 103–17; Asher Cohen, *Persécutions et sauvetages: Juifs et Français sous l'Occupation et sous Vichy* (Paris, 1993), 269–7.

167. Richard I. Cohen, *The Burden of Conscience: French Jewish Leadership during the Holocaust* (Bloomington, Ind., 1987); Cohen, *Persécutions*, 125–90.

168. Michèle Cointet, *L'Église sous Vichy, 1940–1945: La répentance en question* (Paris, 1998).

169. Jackson, *France*, 221–4.

170. Witte *et al.* (eds.), *Der Dienstkalender*, 637.

171. Longerich, *Der ungeschriebene Befehl*, 178–9.

172. Cohen, *Persécutions*, 191–240, analyses changing public opinion in France; see also Jackson, *France*, 233–5.

173. Cohen, *Persécutions*, 496.

174. Jackson, *France*, 213–35, 389–426.

175. Martin Conway, *Collaboration in Belgium: Léon Degrelle and the Rexist Movement 1940–1944* (London, 1993), 22–7, 286–9.

176. Werner Warmbrunn, *The Dutch under German Occupation, 1940–1945* (London, 1963), 24–5, 32–4, 261–5; Gerhard Hirschfeld, *Nazi Rule and Dutch Collaboration: The Netherlands under German Occupation, 1940–1945* (Oxford, 1988 [1984]), 5–6. Konrad Kwiet, *Reichskommissariat Niederlande: Versuch und Scheitern nationalsozialistischer Neuordnung* (Stuttgart, 1968) argues that collaboration with the bourgeois establishment was less successful.

177. Bob Moore, *Victims and Survivors: The Nazi Persecution of the Jews in the Netherlands, 1940–1945* (London, 1997), 19–90.

178. Moore, *Victims and Survivors*, 146–89; Anne Frank, *The Diary of a Young Girl* (New York, 1995).

179. Moore, *Victims and Survivors*, 91–115, 195–206; Louis de Jong, 'The Netherlands and Auschwitz', *Yad Vashem Studies*, 7 (1968), 39–55; Gerhard Hirschfeld, 'Niederlande',

in Wolfgang Benz (ed.), *Dimension des Völkermords: Die Zahl der jüdischen Opfer des Nationalsozialismus* (Munich, 1991), 137–63.

180. Moore, *Victims and Survivors*, 102–4.

181. Ibid., 125–6.

182. Dan Michman (ed.), *Belgium and the Holocaust: Jews, Belgians, Germans* (Jerusalem, 1998).

183. Moore, *Victims and Survivors*, 2, 255; Maxime Steinberg, *La Persécution des Juifs en Belgique (1940–1945)* (Brussels, 2004), 77–108 (for economic measures) and 157–91 (for the role of the police).

184. William B. Cohen and Jörgen Svensson, 'Finland and the Holocaust', *Holocaust and Genocide Studies*, 9 (1995), 70–92; Longerich, *Politik*, 520.

185. Ibid., 531–2.

186. Paul A. Levine, *From Indifference to Activism: Swedish Diplomacy and the Holocaust, 1938–1944* (Uppsala, 1998); Friedländer, *The Years of Extermination*, 449, 454.

187. Jozef Lewandowski, 'Early Swedish Information about the Nazis' Mass Murder of the Jews', *Polin: Studies in Polish Jewry*, 13 (2000), 113–27; Steven Kublik, *The Stones Cry Out: Sweden's Response to the Persecution of the Jews, 1933–1945* (New York, 1988).

188. Ulrich Herbert, *Best: Biographische Studien über Radikalismus, Weltanschauung und Vernunft, 1903–1989* (Bonn, 1996), 323–41.

189. Longerich, *Politik*, 555–8; Herbert, *Best*, 360–73; Leni Yahil, *The Rescue of Danish Jewry: Test of a Democracy* (Philadelphia, Pa., 1969), 233–84; and Levine, *From Indifference to Activism*, 229–45. See also the controversy between Gunnar S. Paulsson, 'The Bridge over the Øresund: The Historiography on the Expulsion of the Jews from Nazi-occupied Denmark', in David Cesarani (ed.), *Holocaust: Critical Concepts in Historical Studies* (London, 2004), V. 99–127, and Hans Kirchhoff, 'Denmark: A Light in the Darkness of the Holocaust? A Reply to Gunnar S. Paulsson', ibid., 128–39.

190. Quoted in Longerich, *Politik*, 558.

191. Hassell, *The von Hassell Diaries*, 352.

192. Longerich, *Politik*, 558–60.

193. Mark Mazower, *Salonica: City of Ghosts: Christians, Muslims and Jews 1430–1950* (London, 2004), 421–42; Longerich, *Politik*, 526–7, 546–7, 561–2.

194. Götz Aly, 'Die Deportation der Juden von Rhodos nach Auschwitz', *Mittelweg*, 36 (2003), 79–88.

195. Deletant, *Hitler's Forgotten Ally*, 205–25.

196. Hillgruber (ed.), *Staatsmänner und Diplomaten*, II. 494; on Vatican intervention in Romania, see Theodore Lavi, 'The Vatican's Endeavors on Behalf of Romanian Jewry during the Second World War', *Yad Vashem Studies*, 5 (1963), 405–18.

197. Tzvetan Todorov, *The Fragility of Goodness: Why Bulgaria's Jews Survived the Holocaust* (London, 1999); more generally, Friedländer, *The Years of Extermination*, 452, 485 (quoting Ribbentrop); Deletant, *Hitler's Forgotten Ally*, 198–204; Crampton, *Bulgaria*, 264–6; Stephane Groueff, *Crown of Thorns: The Reign of King Boris III of Bulgaria, 1918–1943* (Lanham, Md., 1987), 316–31; and Frederick B. Chary, *The Bulgarian Jews and the Final Solution, 1940–1944* (Pittsburgh, Pa., 1972).

198. Hillgruber (ed.), *Staatsmänner und Diplomaten*, II. 256.

199. Longerich, *Politik*, 491–2, 563–5.

200. Livia Rothkirchen, 'The Situation of the Jews in Slovakia between 1939 and 1945', *Jahrbuch für Antisemitismusforschung*, 7 (1998), 46–70; Friedländer, *The Years of Extermination*, 372–4, 485–6 (quote at 373–4).

201. Ibid., 669; Rothkirchen, 'The Situation of the Jews'; John F. Morley, *Vatican Diplomacy and the Jews during the Holocaust, 1939–1945* (New York, 1980).

202. Marrus and Paxton, *Vichy France*, 215–80.

203. Ahlrich Meyer, *Die deutsche Besatzung in Frankreich 1940–1944: Widerstandbekämpfung und Judenverfolgung* (Darmstadt, 2000), 149–68.

204. Bob Moore 'Comparing Resistance and Resistance Movements', in idem (ed.), *Resistance in Western Europe* (Oxford, 2000), 249–62.
205. For Greece, see Mazower, *Inside Hitler's Greece*, esp. 265–354.
206. Klukowski, *Diary*, 197 (17 May 1942).
207. Ibid., 229–31 (7–14 December 1942).
208. Ibid., 235–7 (1–16 January 1943), 282 (29 September 1943), 286 (19 October 1943).
209. Ibid., 155–6 (12 June 1941), 159 (21 June 1941); Gross, *Polish Society*, 213–91.
210. Klukowski, *Diary*, 244–5 (22–5 February 1943).
211. Ibid., 299 (5 February 1944), 305 (2 March 1944).
212. Borodziej, *Terror und Politik*, 162–209.
213. Quoted in Hans Umbreit, 'Das unbewältigte Problem: Der Partisanenkrieg im Rücken der Ostfront', in Jürgen Förster (ed.), *Stalingrad: Ereignis: Wirkung und Symbol* (Munich, 1992), 130–49, at 142–3.
214. Peter Klein, 'Zwischen den Fronten: Die Zivilbevölkerung Weissrusslands und der Krieg der Wehrmacht gegen die Partisanen', in Quinkert (ed.), *'Wir sind die Herren dieses Landes'*, 82–103.
215. Friedländer, *The Years of Extermination*, 250.
216. Klukowski, *Diary*, 223–6 (4–20 November 1942).
217. Ibid., 227 (26 November 1942).
218. Dina Porat, 'The Vilna Proclamation of January 1, 1942, in Historical Perspective', *Yad Vashem Studies*, 25 (1996), 99–136.
219. Nechama Tec, *Ich wollte retten: Die unglaubliche Geschichte der Bielski-Partisanen 1942–1944* (Berlin, 2002).
220. Sven Erichson (ed.), *Abschied ist immer: Briefe an den Bruder im Zweiten Weltkrieg* (Frankfurt am Main, 1994), 78; more generally, Weinberg, *A World at Arms*, 408–17.
221. David M. Glantz and Jonathan M. House, *When Titans Clashed: How the Red Army Stopped Hitler* (Lawrence, Kans., 1995), 98–107.
222. Bock, *Zwischen Pflicht und Verweigerung*, 445 (15 June 1942).
223. Elmshäuser and Lokers (eds.), *'Man muss hier nur hart sein'*, 181 (letter to Frieda, 20 July 1942).
224. Weinberg, *A World at Arms*, 296–8, 412; Mawdsley, *Thunder in the East*, 118–48; Glantz and House, *When Titans Clashed*, 105–19; Bock, *Zwischen Pflicht und Verweigerung*, 470 (13–15 July 1942).
225. Kershaw, *Hitler*, II. 526–8.
226. Halder, *Kriegstagebuch*, III. 489 (23 July 1942).
227. Speer, *Inside the Third Reich*, 332.
228. Bellamy, *Absolute War*, 351–408; David Glantz, *The Siege of Leningrad 1941–1944: 900 Days of Terror* (London, 2004); Harrison E. Salisbury, *The 900 Days: The Siege of Leningrad* (London, 1969).
229. Quoted in Kershaw, *Hitler*, II. 531–2.
230. Meier-Welcker, *Aufzeichnungen*, 159 (9 April 1942).
231. Erichson, *Abschied*, 27 (letter to brother, 28 July 1942).
232. Ibid., 77 (letter of 18 August 1942).
233. Halder, *Kriegstagebuch*, III. 513 (30 August 1942).
234. Ibid., 517 (4 September 1942), 528 (24 September 1942).
235. Weinberg, *A World at Arms*, 408–17, 420–28; Kershaw, *Hitler*, II. 531–4; Bernd Wegner, 'Vom Lebensraum zum Todesraum: Deutschlands Kriegführung zwischen Moskau und Stalingrad', in Förster (ed.), *Stalingrad*, 17–38; Bernd Wegner, 'The War against the Soviet Union, 1942–1943', *GSWW* VI. 843–1,203, at 843–1,058.
236. Heinrich von Einsiedel, *The Shadow of Stalingrad: Being the Diary of a Temptation* (London, 1953), 7–8 (24 August 1942).
237. Ibid., 8–9.
238. Ibid.; Antony Beevor, *Stalingrad* (London, 1998), 92–5.
239. Ibid., 102–31.

240. Halder, *Kriegstagebuch*, III. 514 (31 August 1942).

241. Reddemann (ed.), *Zwischen Front und Heimat*, 631 (to Agnes, 3 October 1942).

242. Kershaw, *Hitler*, II. 536–8.

243. Beevor, *Stalingrad*, 127–33, 166–77.

244. Beevor, *Stalingrad*, 291–310.

245. Jens Ebert (ed.), *Feldpostbriefe aus Stalingrad: November 1942 bis Januar 1943* (Munich, 2006 [2000]). See also Katrin A. Kilian, 'Kriegsstimmungen: Emotionen einfacher Soldaten in Feldpostbriefen', *DRZW* IX/II. 251–88, for the decline in morale and hope for the end of the war, as expressed in soldiers' letters.

246. Beevor, *Stalingrad*, 189–235.

247. Ibid., 236–65; see also Mawdsley, *Thunder in the East*, 159–73, and Bellamy, *Absolute War*, 497–53.

248. Beevor, *Stalingrad*, 266–90.

249. Speer, *Inside the Third Reich*, 343.

250. Ebert (ed.), *Feldpostbriefe*, 81.

251. Beevor, *Stalingrad*, 333–6.

252. Ebert (ed.), *Feldpostbriefe*, 170.

253. Beevor, *Stalingrad*, 311–30.

254. Ebert (ed.), *Feldpostbriefe*, 216; more generally, ibid., 186–222.

255. Ibid., 163.

256. Ibid., 49.

257. Ibid., 27, 29; the caption to the illustration on 307, claiming the troops were not properly dressed for winter, is belied by the numerous mentions to the contrary in the letters (43, 159, 176, 205).

258. Ibid., 16, 38, 180, 236, 262.

259. Anatoly Golovchansky *et al.* (eds.), *'Ich will raus aus diesem Wahnsinn': Deutsche Briefe von der Ostfront 1941–1945* (Wuppertal, 1991), 164 (31 December 1942).

260. Groscurth, *Tagebücher*, 532.

261. Ebert (ed.), *Feldpostbriefe*, 242.

262. Golovchansky *et al.* (eds.), *'Ich will raus'*, 205 (10 January 1943).

263. Ibid., 202 (10 January 1943).

264. Ibid., 223 (15 January 1943).

265. Ebert (ed.), *Feldpostbriefe*, 304, 316; similarly on 270, 274, 281, 296, 305.

266. Rolf Dieter Müller, ' "Was wir an Hunger ausstehen müssen, könnt Ihr Euch gar nicht denken": Eine Armee verhungert', in Wolfram Wette and Gerd R. Ueberschär (eds.), *Stalingrad: Mythos und Wirklichkeit einer Schlacht* (Frankfurt am Main, 1992), 131–45; Beevor, *Stalingrad*, 335–8.

267. Ebert (ed.), *Feldpostbriefe*, 209; similarly on 124, 143, 161, 186.

268. Ibid., 306.

269. Ibid., 318, 322–4.

270. Boberach (ed.), *Meldungen*, XII. 4,698 (18 January 1943).

271. Beevor, *Stalingrad*, 352–73.

272. Quoted in Ebert (ed.), *Feldpostbriefe*, 341–2.

273. Quoted in ibid., 343.

274. Ibid., 342–4.

275. Beevor, *Stalingrad*, 374–431; Kershaw, *Hitler*, II. 543–57; Groscurth, *Tagebücher*, 95; for a detailed account, see Wegner, 'The War against the Soviet Union', *GSWW* VI. 1,058–72.

276. Karl-Heinz Frieser, *Krieg hinter Stacheldraht: Die deutschen Kriegsgefangenen in der Sowjetunion und das Nationalkomitee 'Freies Deutschland'* (Mainz, 1981), 55, 144–82, 188–9, 193–5; Kershaw, *Hitler*, II. 550–51.

277. Walb, *Ich, die Alte*, 260 (3 February 1943).

278. Wolfram Wette, 'Das Massensterben als "Heldenepos": Stalingrad in der NS-Propaganda', in Wette and Ueberschär (eds.), *Stalingrad*, 43–60; Heinz Boberach, 'Stim-

NOTES TO CHAPTER 4 811

mungsumschwung in der deutschen Bevölkerung', in ibid., 61–6; Bernhard R. Kroener, ' "Nun Volk, steh auf . . . !" Stalingrad und der "totale" Krieg 1942–1943', in Förster (ed.), *Stalingrad*, 151–70; Marlis Steinert, 'Stalingrad und die deutsche Gesellschaft', in ibid., 171–88.

279. Boberach (ed.), *Meldungen*, XII. 4,750–51 (4 February 1943) (italics in original).

280. Ibid.

281. Broszat *et al.* (eds.), *Bayern* I. 633 (Bericht der SD-Hauptaussenstelle Würzburg, 1 February 1943).

282. Ibid. (Bericht der SD-Aussenstelle Friedberg, 8 February 1943).

283. Ibid., 164–5 (Monatsbericht des Landrats, 2 February 1943).

284. Hassell, *The von Hassell Diaries*, 284.

285. Broszat *et al.* (eds.), *Bayern*, I. 633 (Bericht der SD-Hauptaussenstelle Würzburg, 1 February 1943).

286. Klemperer, *To the Bitter End*, 189–92 (5 and 14 February 1943).

287. Broszat *et al.* (eds.), *Bayern* I. 170 (Monatsbericht der Gendarmerie-Station Muggendorf, 19 March 1943).

288. Ibid., 170 (Monatsbericht der Gendarmerie-Station Waischenfeld, 19 March 1943).

289. Boberach (ed.), *Meldungen*, XIII. 5,146 (19 April 1943).

290. Cited in Noakes (ed.), *Nazism*, IV. 548.

291. Boberach (ed.), *Meldungen*, XIV. 5,445 (8 July 1943) (italics in original).

292. Ibid., 5,446 (italics in original); also Hassell, *The von Hassell Diaries*, 294 (March 1943).

293. Ibid., 5,447 (italics in original).

294. Willi A. Boelcke (ed.), *'Wollt Ihr den totalen Krieg?' Die geheimen Goebbels-Konferenzen 1939–1943* (Munich, 1969 [1967]), 414.

295. The version of the speech here, which differs from the published text, was monitored live by the BBC, and is reproduced from Noakes (ed.), *Nazism*, IV. 490–94. See also Iring Fetscher, *Joseph Goebbels im Berliner Sportpalast 1943: 'Wollt Ihr den totalen Krieg?'* (Hamburg, 1998) (speech reproduced in ibid., 63–98); and Günter Moltmann, 'Goebbels' Speech on Total War, February 18, 1943', in Hajo Holborn (ed.), *Republic to Reich: The Making of the Nazi Revolution: Ten Essays* (New York, 1973 [1972]), 298–342.

296. Boberach (ed.), *Meldungen*, XII. 4,833 (22 February 1943); Moltmann, 'Goebbels' Speech', 337 (for 'mass hypnosis').

297. Ibid., 309–16.

298. Kershaw, *Hitler*, II. 561–77.

299. Noakes (ed.), *Nazism*, IV. 238–40; Boberach (ed.), *Meldungen*, XIII. 5,136–40 (1 April 1943).

300. Boberach (ed.), *Meldungen*, XII. 4,826–30 (18 February 1943).

301. Tooze, *The Wages of Destruction*, 353–6.

302. Noakes (ed.), *Nazism*, IV. 510–18.

303. Ibid.

304. Overy, 'Guns or Butter?', 284–6; Josef Wulf, *Presse und Funk im Dritten Reich: Eine Dokumentation* (Gütersloh, 1964), 374.

305. Boberach (ed.), *Meldungen*, IX. 3,504–5 (23 March 1942).

306. Ibid.

307. Noakes (ed.), *Nazism*, IV. 521, 548.

308. Herbst, *Der totale Krieg*, 171–241.

309. Overy, 'Guns or Butter?', 259–64 (263 for the quote), criticizing Alan S. Milward, 'Hitlers Konzept des Blitzkrieges', in Andreas Hillgruber (ed.), *Probleme des Zweiten Weltkrieges* (Cologne, 1967), 19–40, and Burton H. Klein, *Germany's Economic Preparations for War* (Cambridge, Mass., 1959); see also Evans, *The Third Reich in Power*, 322–36, 349–50, 477–92.

310. Carroll, *Design for Total War*, 190.

311. Overy, 'Guns or Butter?', 264–71.

312. Ibid., 272; Tooze, *The Wages of Destruction*, 353–6; Aly, *Hitler's Beneficiaries*, 295–

300; Philipp Kratz, 'Sparen für das kleine Glück', in Götz Aly (ed.), *Volkes Stimme: Skepsis und Führervertrauen im Nationalsozialismus* (Frankfurt am Main, 2006), 59–79; Angelika Ebbinghaus, 'Fakten oder Fiktionen: Wie ist Götz Aly zu seinen weitreichenden Schluss-folgerungen gekommen?', *Sozial.Geschichte*, 20 (2005), 29–45, at 32; see also Christoph Buchheim, 'Die vielen Rechenfehler in der Abrechnung Götz Alys mit den Deutschen unter dem NS-Regime', *Sozial.Geschichte*, 20 (2005), 67–76.

313. Mathilde Wolff-Mönckeberg, *On the Other Side: To My Children from Germany 1940–1945* (London, 1982 [1979]), 96.

314. Boberach (ed.), *Meldungen*, XVI. 6,260–5 (quote on 6,262).

315. Overy, 'Guns or Butter?', 272–84.

316. Ibid., 285–91.

317. Hassell, *The von Hassell Diaries*, 173.

318. Pöppel, *Heaven and Hell*, 101.

319. Boberach (ed.), *Meldungen*, XII. 4,831 (22 February 1943) (italics in original).

320. Broszat *et al.* (eds.), *Bayern*, I. 169 (Landrat Ebermannstadt, Monatsbericht, 2 March 1943).

321. Ibid., 635 (Bericht der SD-Hauptaussenstelle Würzburg, 22 February 1943).

Chapter 5. 'THE BEGINNING OF THE END'

1. 'Aufsatz des Schülers Günter R. von der Dreikönigschule in Dresden, verfasst am 9. November 1934', No. 120, in Joachim S. Hohmann and Hermann Langer (eds.), *'Stolz, ein Deutscher zu sein...': Nationales Selbstverständnis in Schulaufsätzen 1914–1945* (Frankfurt am Main, 1995), 227–8.

2. Ralf Blank, 'Kriegsalltag und Luftkrieg an der "Heimatfront"', *DRZW* IX/I. 357–468, at 358 and 403–6.

3. Ursula Büttner, ' "Gomorrha" und die Folgen: Der Bombenkrieg', in Forschungsstelle für Zeitgeschichte in Hamburg (ed.), *Hamburg im 'Dritten Reich'* (Göttingen, 2005), 613–32, at 613–16; Horst Boog, 'The Anglo-American Strategic Air War over Europe and German Air Defence', in *GSWW* VI. 469–628, at 478–91.

4. Shirer, *Berlin Diary*, 441–2 (9 November 1940).

5. Boog, 'The Strategic Air War', 379–406.

6. Richard Overy, *Why the Allies Won* (London, 1995), 101–4 (also for the quotes); Boog, 'The Anglo-American Strategic Air War', 492–521.

7. Weinberg, *A World at Arms*, 572–7; Overy, *Why the Allies Won*, 104–12; Calvocoressi and Wint, *Total War*, 489–94; Jörg Friedrich, *Der Brand: Deutschland im Bombenkrieg 1940–1945* (Munich, 2002), 63–85. For a discussion of the doctrine of strategic bombing, its origins and evolution, see Boog, 'The Anglo-American Strategic Air War', 469–77.

8. Ibid., 565–6, 622–3.

9. Boog, 'The Strategic Air War', 367–8.

10. Boog, 'The Anglo-American Strategic Air War', 622–3.

11. Weinberg, *A World at Arms*, 577; Overy, *Why the Allies Won*, 109–10; Calvocoressi and Wint, *Total War*, 494; Friedrich, *Der Brand*, 86–7, 179–90; Boog, 'The Anglo-American Strategic Air War', 558–66. The Lancaster was still called the Manchester at this time.

12. Boberach (ed.), *Meldungen*, X. 3,597–9 (9 April 1942).

13. Solmitz, *Tagebuch*, 765 (8 September 1942).

14. Ibid., 733 (26 April 1942, 29 April 1942).

15. Overy, *Why the Allies Won*, 117–19; Weinberg, *A World at Arms*, 578–9; Calvocoressi and Wint, *Total War*, 494; Boog, 'The Anglo-American Strategic Air War', 566–621.

16. Quoted in Overy, *Why the Allies Won*, 117; Boog, 'The Strategic Air War', 9–15; and see also the classic official history by Charles Webster and Noble Frankland, *The Strategic Air Offensive against Germany 1939–1945* (4 vols., London, 1961), IV. 273–83.

17. Overy, *Why the Allies Won*, 114–22; Blank, 'Kriegsalltag', 366–8; Boog, 'The Strategic Air War', 22–9.

18. Fröhlich (ed.), *Die Tagebücher*, VII. 491 (7 March 1943).

19. Blank, 'Kriegsalltag', 369–70.

20. Tooze, *The Wages of Destruction*, 596–600.

21. Speer, *Inside the Third Reich*, 389–93, quoting his office journal.

22. Martin Middlebrook, *The Battle of Hamburg: Allied Bomber Forces against a German City in 1943* (London, 1980), 93–251; Boog, 'The Strategic Air War', 43–51.

23. Quoted in Middlebrook, *The Battle of Hamburg*, 264–5; ibid., 252–81, for details of the firestorm.

24. Ibid., 266–7.

25. Ibid., 282–327; Büttner, ' "Gomorrha" ', 616–18; Friedrich, *Der Brand*, 455; see also Christian Hanke *et al.*, *Hamburg im Bombenkrieg 1940–1945: Das Schicksal einer Stadt* (Hamburg, 2001); and Renate Hauschild-Thiessen (ed.), *Die Hamburger Katastrophe vom Sommer 1943 in Augenzeugenberichten* (Hamburg, 1991).

26. Wolff-Mönckeberg, *On the Other Side*, 79.

27. Ibid., 79; Büttner, ' "Gomorrha" ', 620–22.

28. Solmitz, *Tagebuch*, 840, 851 (4 August 1943, 19 August 1943).

29. Breloer (ed.), *Geheime Welten*, 41.

30. Ibid., 42.

31. Ibid., 43.

32. Solmitz, *Tagebuch*, 930 (21 June 1944), 943 (8 August 1944).

33. Ibid., 943 (8 August 1944).

34. Wolff-Mönckeberg, *On the Other Side*, 86.

35. Boberach (ed.), *Meldungen*, XV. 5,583 (9 August 1943) (italics in original).

36. Ibid., XV. 5.562, 5,575 (2 and 5 August 1943).

37. Joachim Szodrzynski, 'Die "Heimatfront" zwischen Stalingrad und Kriegsende', in Forschungsstelle für Zeitgeschichte in Hamburg (ed.), *Hamburg*, 633–86; for other localities, see for example Wilfried Beer, *Kriegsalltag an der Heimatfront: Alliierter Luftkrieg und deutsche Gegenmassnahmen zur Abwehr und Schadenbegrenzung, dargestellt für den Raum Münster* (Bremen, 1990); Gerd R. Ueberschär, *Freiburg im Luftkrieg 1939–1945* (Freiburg, 1990); Gerhard E. Sollbach (ed.), *Dortmund: Bombenkrieg und Nachkriegsalltag 1939–1945* (Hagen, 1996); Birgit Horn, *Die Nacht, als der Feuertod vom Himmel stürzte – Leipzig, 4. Dezember 1943* (Gudensberg-Gleichen, 2003).

38. Erichson, *Abschied*, 160–61 (letter to brother, 12 August 1943).

39. Boberach (ed.), *Meldungen*, XIV. 5,356 (17 June 1943).

40. Meike Wöhlert, *Der politische Witz in der NS-Zeit am Beispiel ausgesuchten SD-Berichte und Gestapo-Akten* (Frankfurt am Main, 1997), 50; Boberach (ed.), *Meldungen*, XIV. 5,619–20 (16 August 1943).

41. Boberach (ed.), *Meldungen*, XIV. 5,357.

42. Ibid.

43. Eva Gehrken, *Nationalsozialistische Erziehung in den Lagern der Erweiterten Kinderlandverschickung 1940 bis 1945* (Braunschweig, 1997), 16.

44. Gerhard Kock, 'Die Erweiterte Kinderlandverschickung und der Konflikt mit den Kirchen', in Martin Rüther (ed.), *'Zu Hause könnten sie es nicht schöner haben!': Kinderlandverschickung aus Köln und Umgebung 1941–1945* (Cologne, 2000), 209–42.

45. Gerhard Kock, 'Nur zum Schutz aufs Land gebracht? Die Kinderlandverschickung und ihre erziehungspolitischen Ziele', in ibid., 17–52; also Gehrken, *Nationalsozialistische Erziehung*, 16, 149, demonstrating that the camps were in fact a Party institution, contrary to the arguments of Gerhard Dabel (ed.), *KLV: Die erweiterte Kinder-Land-Verschickung* (Freiburg, 1981).

46. Katja Klee, ' "Nie wieder Aufnahme von Kindern" – Anspruch und Wirklichkeit der KLV in den Aufnahmegauen', in Rüther (ed.), *'Zu Hause'*, 161–94; Stephenson, *Hitler's Home Front*, 295–311.

47. Friedrich, *Der Brand*, 455–67; see also Olaf Gröhler, *Bombenkrieg gegen Deutschland* (Berlin, 1990).

48. Boberach (ed.), *Meldungen*, XV. 6,033.

49. Ibid., 6,025–8 (quote on 6,028).

50. Ibid., 6.029–30.

51. ibid., 6,030.

52. Ibid., 6,031.

53. Ibid., 6.032.

54. Fröhlich (ed.), *Die Tagebücher*, II/XIV. 409 (12 December 1944); ibid., 417–21, for the above; also Karl Christian Führer, 'Anspruch und Realität: Das Scheitern der national-sozialistischen Wohnungsbaupolitik 1933–1945', *VfZ* 45 (1997), 225–56.

55. Herwart Vorländer, *Die NSV: Darstellung und Dokumentation einer nationalsozialistischen Organisation* (Boppard, 1988), 127–75; also Armin Nolzen, ' "Sozialismus der Tat"? Die Nationalsozialistische Volkswohlfahrt (NSV) und der alliierte Luftkrieg gegen das deutsche Reich', in Dietmar Süss (ed.), *Deutschland im Luftkrieg: Geschichte und Erinnerung* (Munich, 2007), 57–70.

56. See generally Nicole Krämer, ' "Kämpfende Mütter" und "gefallene Heldinnen" – Frauen im Luftschutz', in Süss (ed.), *Deutschland im Luftkrieg*, 85–98.

57. Blank, 'Kriegsalltag', 391–4; Noakes (ed.), *Nazism*, IV. 562–5.

58. Blank, 'Kriegsalltag', 394–402, 421–5. A large complex of tunnels and rooms was also built into the mountainside at Hitler's Bavarian retreat on the Obersalzberg in the later stages of the war.

59. Hassell, *The von Hassell Diaries*, 157.

60. Blank, 'Kriegsalltag', 407–16; Fröhlich (ed.), *Die Tagebücher*, II/XI. 42 (3 January 1944).

61. Quoted in Blank, 'Kriegsalltag', 407–8.

62. Quoted in ibid., 410–11; see also Friedrich, *Der Brand*, 371–406.

63. Ibid., 406–34, and Bernhard Gotto, 'Kommunale Krisenbewältigung', in Süss (ed.), *Deutschland im Luftkrieg*, 41–56.

64. Quoted in Friedrich, *Der Brand*, 446.

65. Hans Wrobel (ed.), *Strafjustiz im totalen Krieg: Aus den Akten des Sondergerichts Bremen 1940 bis 1945* (Bremen, 1991), I. 168–71.

66. Ibid., 190–2.

67. Ralph Angermund, *Deutsche Richterschaft 1919–1945* (Frankfurt am Main, 1990), 209–15.

68. Speer, *Inside the Third Reich*, 396–8; Blank, 'Kriegsalltag', 372.

69. Speer, *Inside the Third Reich*, 395.

70. Blank, 'Kriegsalltag', 374–6.

71. Overy, *Why the Allies Won*, 120–22; Boog, 'The Strategic Air War', 54–76.

72. Overy, *Why the Allies Won*, 122–5; Boog, 'The Strategic Air War', 76–88, for a discussion of the crisis in the bombing campaign in 1943; ibid., 159–256 for the changing fortunes of German air defences.

73. Overy, *Why the Allies Won*, 125–3, 211.

74. Blank, 'Kriegsalltag', 459–60, briefly surveys the widely varying estimates.

75. Anthony C. Grayling, *Among the Dead Cities: Was the Allied Bombing of Civilians in WWII a Necessity or a Crime?* (London, 2006), effectively marshals the moral arguments against the bombing campaign. See also Lothar Kettenacker (ed.), *Ein Volk von Opfern? Die neue Debatte um den Bombenkrieg 1940–45* (Berlin, 2003).

76. Overy, *Why the Allies Won*, 128–33.

77. Pöppel, *Heaven and Hell*, 233.

78. Dietmar Süss, 'Nationalsozialistische Deutungen des Luftkrieges', in idem (ed.), *Deutschland im Luftkrieg*, 99–110.

79. Ibid., 379–80.

80. Ibid., 435–6.

81. Boberach (ed.), *Meldungen*, XV. 5,575 (5 August 1943); also XV. 5,885 (15 October 1943).

82. Blank, 'Kriegsalltag', 448–50. See also Friedrich, *Der Brand*, 481–90, and Barbara Grimm, 'Lynchmorde an alliierten Fliegern im Zweiten Weltkrieg', in Süss (ed.), *Deutschland im Luftkrieg*, 71–84.

83. Ibid., XVI, 6,302–3 (7 February 1944) (italics in original).

84. Dear (ed.), *The Oxford Companion to World War II*, 748–9, 992–4; Weinberg, *A World at Arms*, 211–15, 222–5, 361–3; Stumpf, 'The War in the Mediterranean Area', 631–840.

85. Kershaw, *Hitler*, II. 585.

86. Tooze, *The Wages of Destruction*, 401–2.

87. Basil H. Liddell Hart (ed.), *The Rommel Papers* (London, 1953), 507–24.

88. Walb, *Ich, die Alte*, 249, 253 (14 and 29 November 1942).

89. Crampton, *Bulgaria*, 374–81; Miller, *Bulgaria*, 135–48, carefully surveys the myriad theories about Boris's death and concludes that nobody had an obvious interest in bringing it about. Edward P. Thompson, *Beyond the Frontier: The Politics of a Failed Mission: Bulgaria 1944* (Woodbridge, 1997), recounts the death of the author's older brother Frank in the partisan war.

90. Denis Mack Smith, *Modern Italy: A Political History* (London, 1997 [1959]), 404–12; Kershaw, *Hitler*, II. 593.

91. Weinberg, *A World at Arms*, 593–6.

92. Smith, *Modern Italy*, 412–14; idem, *Mussolini* (London, 1987 [1981]), 341–6.

93. Christopher Duggan, *The Force of Destiny: A History of Italy since 1796* (London, 2007), 520–26; Boberach (ed.), *Meldungen*, XV. 5,755 (13 September 1943); Kershaw, *Hitler*, II. 593–8.

94. Boberach (ed.), *Meldungen*, XVI. 6,304 (7 February 1944) (italics in original).

95. Bosworth, *Mussolini's Italy*, 503–5; Herbert, *Hitler's Foreign Workers*, 282–7; Boberach (ed.), *Meldungen*, XIV. 5,724–5 (9 September 1943), and XV. 5,766 (13 September 1943) (italics in original).

96. Luigi Cajani, 'Die italienischen Militär-Internierten im nationalsozialistischen Deutschland', in Herbert (ed.), *Europa und der 'Reichseinsatz'*, 295–316, at 308; also Brunello Mantelli, 'Von der Wanderarbeit zur Deportation: Die italienischen Arbeiter in Deutschland 1938–1945', in ibid., 51–89; Ralf Lang, *Italienische 'Fremdarbeiter' im nationalsozialistischen Deutschland 1937–1945* (Frankfurt am Main, 1996), 83–110; Spoerer, *Zwangsarbeit*, 228.

97. Nicholas, *The Rape of Europa*, 229–72 (quote on 266–7).

98. Boberach (ed.), *Meldungen*, XIV. 5,540–41 (29 July 1943).

99. Smith, *Mussolini*, 348–67.

100. Ibid.; Boberach (ed.), *Meldungen*, XV. 5,755 (13 September 1943).

101. Friedländer, *The Years of Extermination*, 559–77; Longerich, *Politik*, 553–4, 560; Robert Katz, *The Battle for Rome: The Germans, the Allies, the Partisans, and the Pope, September 1943–June 1944* (New York, 2003), 61–85; idem, *Black Sabbath: A Journey through a Crime against Humanity* (London, 1969), 3–104.

102. See Evans, *Telling Lies*, 103–8; and Steur, *Theodor Dannecker*, 113–28.

103. Meir Michaelis, *Mussolini and the Jews: German–Italian Relations and the Jewish Question in Italy, 1922–1945* (Oxford, 1978); Susan Zuccotti, *The Italians and the Holocaust: Persecution, Rescue and Survival* (London, 1987); Katz, *Black Sabbath*, 105–292; Lilliana Picciotto Fargion, 'Italien', in Wolfgang Benz (ed.), *Dimension des Völkermords: Die Zahl der jüdischen Opfer des Nationalsozialismus* (Munich, 1991), 199–228; Jonathan Steinberg, *All or Nothing: The Axis and the Holocaust 1941–1943* (London, 1991); Susan Zuccotti, *Under His Very Windows: The Vatican and the Holocaust in Italy* (London, 2001).

104. Longerich, *Politik*, 561–2.

105. Ibid., 561.

106. Bosworth, *Mussolini's Italy*, 498–530 (statistics on 522).

107. Primo Levi, *If This Is a Man* (London, 1957 [1948]).

108. Frank Snowden, 'Latina Province 1944–1950', *Journal of Contemporary History*, 43/3 (2008), 509–26; Paul Weindling, *Epidemics and Genocide in Eastern Europe, 1890–1945* (Oxford, 2000), 2–3, 76–9, 376–8; Michael H. Kater, *Doctors under Hitler* (Chapel Hill, N.C., 1989).

109. Snowden, 'Latina Province'.

110. Weinberg, *A World at Arms*, 367–9

111. Ibid., 64–73; Tooze, *The Wages of Destruction*, 338–9, 397–9; Kershaw, *Hitler*, II. 585; detailed account in Werner Rahn, 'The War at Sea in the Atlantic and in the Arctic Ocean', *GSWW* VI. 301–468.

112. Klaus von Trotha, ' "Ran, Angreifen, Versenken!" Aus dem Tagebuch eines U-Boots Kapitäns', in Georg von Hase (ed.), *Die Kriegsmarine im Kampf um den Atlantik: Erlebnisberichte von Mitkämpfern* (Leipzig, 1942), 40–69.

113. Meier-Welcker, *Aufzeichnungen*, 98–103 (31 December 1940).

114. Michael Salewski, *Die deutsche Seekriegsleitung 1935–1945* (Frankfurt am Main, 1970), I. 175–207.

115. Weinberg, *A World at Arms*, 367–82.

116. Ibid., 235–7, 358, 382.

117. Ibid., 382–9.

118. Bernd Wegner, 'Von Stalingrad nach Kursk', in *DRZW* VII. 3–82, at 3–8.

119. Helmut Blume, *Zum Kaukasus 1941–1942: Aus Tagebuch und Briefen eines jungen Artilleristen* (Tübingen, 1993), 140 (letter to parents, 2 November 1942).

120. Ibid., 141 (letter to parents, 14 November 1942).

121. Wegner, 'The War against the Soviet Union', 1,022–59, 1,173–92.

122. Kershaw, *Hitler* II. 529–33; Wegner, 'The War against the Soviet Union'.

123. Reddemann (ed.), *Zwischen Front und Heimat*, 761 (to Agnes, 16 February 1943).

124. Ibid., Introduction. His widow never remarried.

125. Wegner, 'Von Stalingrad', 62.

126. Ibid., 63–9.

127. Ibid., 69–79; Karl-Heinz Frieser, 'Die Schlacht im Kursker Bogen', in *DRZW* VIII. 83–210, at 83–5.

128. Ibid., 83–102.

129. Quoted in ibid., 102; details in ibid., 102–3.

130. Ibid., 104–6.

131. Ibid., 106–12.

132. Ibid., 112–19.

133. Ibid., 119–39. Frieser's meticulous and radically revisionist account of Kursk supersedes all previous narratives of the battle.

134. Ibid., 140–72.

135. Ibid., 173–207.

136. Quoted in ibid., 200.

137. Ibid., 190–208 (quote on 208).

138. Karl-Heinz Frieser and Klaus Schönherr, 'Der Rückschlag des Pendels: Das Zurückweichen der Ostfront von Sommer 1943 bis Sommer 1944', in *DRZW* VIII. 277–490, at 277.

139. Karl-Heinz Frieser, 'Zusammenfassung', in *DRZW* VIII. 1,211–24.

140. Bernd Wegner, 'Die Aporie des Krieges', in *DRZW* VII. 211–76, at 256–69.

141. Ibid., 259–60.

142. Frieser and Schönherr, 'Der Rückschlag', 324–5.

143. Sven Oliver Müller, 'Nationalismus in der deutschen Kriegsgesellschaft 1939 bis 1945', in *DRZW* IX/II. 9–92, at 70–92.

144. Hürter (ed.), *Ein deutscher General*, 12–42.

145. Bock, *Zwischen Pflicht und Verweigerung*, Introduction, and 125–7.

146. Reinhard Stumpf, *Die Wehrmacht-Elite: Rang- und Herkunftsstruktur der deutschen Generale und Admirale 1933–1945* (Boppard, 1982), 298–302.

147. Quoted in Gerd R. Ueberschär and Winfried Vogel, *Dienen und Verdienen: Hitlers Geschenke an seine Eliten* (Frankfurt am Main, 2000 [1999]), 147–8; for the above details, see ibid., 146–82.

148. Rass, 'Das Sozialprofil', 712–18.

149. Ibid., 647.

150. Ibid., 651–7.

151. Ibid., 658–80.

152. Ibid., 682–3.

153. Ibid., 690.

154. Horst F. Richardson, *Sieg Heil! War Letters of Tank Gunner Karl Fuchs, 1937–1941* (Hamden, Conn., 1987), 124 (4 August 1941); more generally, Jürgen Förster, 'Geistige Kriegführung in Deutschland 1919 bis 1945', in *DRZW* IX/I. 469–640, esp. 469–559.

155. Ibid., 560–640.

156. Manoschek (ed.), *'Es gibt nur Eines'*, 52 (O'Gefr. A. G., 1 March 1942).

157. Ibid., 69 (Uffz. A. N., 29 May 1943).

158. Ibid., 74 (Uffz. O. D., 16 August 1944).

159. Hosenfeld, *'Ich versuche'*, 780–82 (diary, 28 December 1943).

160. Hürter (ed.), *Ein deutscher General*, 142.

161. Rass, 'Das Sozialprofil', 723–5, 733–5.

162. See the classic study of Edward A. Shils and Morris Janowitz, 'Cohesion and Disintegration in the *Wehrmacht* in World War II', *Public Opinion Quarterly*, 12 (1948), 280–315.

163. Thomas Kühne, 'Gruppenkohäsion und Kameradschaftsmythos in der Wehrmacht', in Rolf-Dieter Müller and Hans-Erich Volkmann (eds.), *Die Wehrmacht: Mythos und Realität* (Munich, 1999), 534–59; idem, 'Zwischen Männerbund und Volksgemeinschaft: Hitlers Soldaten und der Mythos der Kameradschaft', *Archiv für Sozialgeschichte*, 38 (1998), 165–89; more generally, idem, *Kameradschaft: Die Soldaten des nationalsozialistischen Krieges und das 20. Jahrhundert* (Göttingen, 2006).

164. Manfred Messerschmidt and Fritz Wüllner, *Die Wehrmachtjustiz im Dienste des Nationalsozialismus: Zerstörung einer Legende* (Baden-Baden, 1987), 50.

165. Ibid., 63–89.

166. Ibid., 69.

167. Ibid., 102.

168. Ibid., 102–3.

169. Ibid., 115; also 91, 132–68. Maria Fritsche, *Österreichische Deserteure und Selbstverstümmler in der Deutschen Wehrmacht* (Vienna, 2004).

170. Bernd Wegner, *Hitlers politische Soldaten: Die Waffen-SS 1933–1945: Studien zu Leitbild, Struktur und Funktion einer nationalsozialistischen Elite* (Paderborn, 1982), 210, 305, 316–17; Höhne, *The Order of the Death's Head*, 401–24.

171. Quoted in ibid., 425.

172. 'Die Rede Himmlers vor den Gauleitern am 3. August 1944', *VfZ* 1 (1953), 357–94.

173. Höhne, *The Order of the Death's Head*, 432–5.

174. Ibid., 435; Overmans, *Deutsche Militärische Verluste*, 257.

175. Quoted in Höhne, *The Order of the Death's Head*, 401–2.

176. Ibid., 436–7.

177. Ibid., 438–40.

178. Speer, *Inside the Third Reich*, 341.

179. Ibid., 409.

180. Boberach (ed.), *Meldungen*, XIII. 4,981–2 (22 March 1943); Kershaw, *Hitler*, II. 555–6.

181. Speer, *Inside the Third Reich*, 407–18.

182. Fritz Redlich, *Hitler: Diagnosis of a Destructive Prophet* (New York, 1998), 223–54.

183. Kershaw, *Hitler*, II. 564–6, 611–15.

184. Fröhlich (ed.), *Die Tagebücher* (25 July 1943).

185. Ludwig Metzger to Hans Fritsche, 12 September 1944, in Wulf, *Presse und Funk*, 359–60.

186. Speer, *Inside the Third Reich*, 271.

187. Kershaw, *Hitler*, II. 571–2.

188. Hassell, *The von Hassell Diaries*, 247

189. Fröhlich (ed.), *Die Tagebücher* II/VII, 447–51 (2 March 1943).

190. Noakes (ed.), *Nazism*, IV. 27–46; Dieter Rebentisch, *Führerstaat und Verwaltung im Zweiten Weltkrieg* (Stuttgart, 1989).

191. Kershaw, *Hitler*, II. 599.

192. Lammers to Bormann, 1 January 1945, quoted in Noakes (ed.), *Nazism*, IV. 35–7.

193. Ibid., 24–53.

194. Ibid., 54–91 (quotation on 90).

195. Ibid., 91–120.

196. Bärbel Wirrer (ed.), *Ich glaube an den Führer: Eine Dokumentation zur Mentalitätsgeschichte in nationalsozialistischen Deutschland 1942–1945* (Bielefeld, 2003), 243 (Inge to Alfred, 7 August 1944).

197. Quoted in Hans Engelhard (ed.), *Im Namen des deutschen Volkes: Justiz und Nationalsozialismus* (Cologne, 1989), 287.

198. Quoted in Lothar Gruchmann, *Justiz im Dritten Reich 1933–1940: Anpassung und Unterwerfung in der Ära Gürtner* (Munich, 1988), 921.

199. Wrobel (ed.), *Strafjustiz im totalen Krieg*, 46.

200. Ibid., 46–9; Engelhard (ed.), *Im Namen*, 149–50; Noakes (ed.), *Nazism*, IV. 121–35.

201. Evans, *Rituals*, 689–737.

202. Hitler, *Hitler's Table Talk*, 303 (8 February 1942).

203. Engelhard (ed.), *Im Namen*, 294.

204. Quoted in ibid., 293.

205. Evans, *Rituals*, 696–700; Martin Hirsch *et al.* (eds.), *Recht, Verwaltung und Justiz im Nationalsozialismus* (Cologne, 1984), 507–19; Engelhard (ed.), *Im Namen*, 267.

206. Hitler, *Hitler's Table Talk*, 637–45.

207. Hans Boberach (ed.), *Richterbriefe: Dokumente zur Beeinflussung der deutschen Rechtsprechung 1942–1944* (Boppard, 1975); Martin Broszat, 'Zur Perversion der Strafjustiz im Dritten Reich', *VfZ* 6 (1958), 390–443.

208. Boberach (ed.), *Richterbriefe*, 55–8.

209. Engelhard (ed.), *Im Namen*, 269; Patrick Wagner, 'Das Gesetz über die Behandlung Gemeinschaftsfremder: Die Kriminalpolizei und die "Vernichtung des Verbrechertums" ', in Götz Aly (ed.), *Feinderklärung und Prävention: Kriminalbiologie: Zigeunerforschung und Asozialenpolitik* (Berlin, 1988), 75–100.

210. For the willingness of the judiciary to go along with these measures, see Angermund, *Deutsche Richterschaft*.

211. Wachsmann, *Hitler's Prisons*, 284–306.

212. Ibid., 237–41.

213. Noakes (ed.), *Nazism*, IV. 135–6.

214. Wachsmann, *Hitler's Prisons*, 227–62, 392–7.

215. Quoted in Noakes (ed.), *Nazism*, IV. 168–9. More generally, see Georg Wagner-Kyora, ' "Menschenführung" in Rüstungsunternehmen der nationalsozialistischen Kriegswirtschaft', in *DRZW* IX/II. 383–476.

216. Höss, *Commandant of Auschwitz*, 90–91.

217. Karin Orth, 'Gab es eine Lagergesellschaft? "Kriminelle" und politische Häftlinge im Konzentrationslager', in Frei *et al.* (eds.), *Ausbeutung*, 109–33; Hermann Kaienburg, 'Deutsche politische Häftlinge im Konzentrationslager Neuengamme und ihre Stellung im Hauptlager', in Detlef Garbe (ed.), *Häftlinge in KZ Neuengamme: Verfolgungserfahrungen, Häftlingssolidarität und nationale Bindung* (Hamburg, 1999), 26–80; Lutz Niethammer (ed.), *Der 'gesäuberte' Antifaschismus: Die SED und die roten Kapos von Buchenwald* (Berlin, 1994); Benedikt Kautsky, *Teufel und Verdammte: Erfahrungen und*

Erkenntnisse aus sieben Jahren in deutschen Konzentrationslagern (Vienna, 1961), 159–63, quoted in Noakes (ed.), *Nazism*, IV. 162–4.

218. Ibid., 170–71; Wachsmann, *Hitler's Prisons*, 394–5; Garbe (ed.), *Häftlinge*, 203.

219. Kautsky, *Teufel*, quoted in Noakes (ed.), *Nazism*, IV. 167–8; see also Herbert Obenaus, 'Der Kampf um das tägliche Brot', in Ulrich Herbert *et al.* (eds.), *Die nationalsozialistischen Konzentrationslager: Entwicklung und Struktur* (2 vols., Göttingen, 1998), II. 841–73; and Florian Freund, 'Häftlingskategorien und Sterblichkeit in einem Aussenlager des KZ Mauthausen', in ibid., 874–86. See also the remarkable study by Stanislav Zamecnik, *Das war Dachau* (Frankfurt am Main, 2007 [2002]), esp. 226–322.

220. Quoted in Noakes and Pridham (eds.), *Nazism*, III. 618.

221. Steinbacher, *Auschwitz*, 59; Karin Orth, 'Die Kommandanten der nationalsozialistischen Konzentrationslager', in Herbert *et al.* (eds.), *Die nationalsozialistischen Konzentrationslager*, II. 755–86.

222. Burleigh, *Death*, 220; Schmuhl, *Rassenhygiene*, 217–19.

223. For Mennecke's letters and reports, see Peter Chroust (ed.), *Friedrich Mennecke: Innenansichten eines medizinischen Täters im Nationalsozialismus: Eine Edition seiner Briefe 1935–1947* (Hamburg, 1988); letter quoted in ibid., I. 242–4; see also Trus, '. . . vom Leid erlösen', 118–19.

224. Schmuhl, *Rassenhygiene*, 217–19; Burleigh, *Death*, 220–29.

225. Klee, '*Euthanasie*', 418.

226. Quoted in Gansmüller, *Die Erbgesundheitspolitik*, 174–5; see also Fridlof Kudlien, *Ärzte im Nationalsozialismus* (Cologne, 1985), 210.

227. Burleigh, *Death*, 239–45; Klee (ed.), *Dokumente*, 286–97; idem, '*Euthanasie*', 429–39.

228. Burleigh, *Death*, 238–48; Schmuhl, *Rassenhygiene*, 220–36.

229. Klee, '*Euthanasie*', 439–56.

230. Schmuhl, *Rassenhygiene*, 237–9; Burleigh, *Death*, 255–7.

231. Trus, '. . . vom Leid erlösen', 116, 129–30.

232. Burleigh, *Death*, 230–31.

233. Klee (ed.), *Dokumente*, 302–3; idem, '*Euthanasie*', 417–21.

234. Klee (ed.), *Dokumente*, 303.

235. Quoted in Schmuhl, *Rassenhygiene*, 346.

236. Klee, '*Euthanasie*', 421–5.

237. Gansmüller, *Die Erbgesundheitspolitik*, 175.

238. Klee (ed.), *Dokumente*, 300–301.

239. Ibid., 301–2.

240. Evans, *The Third Reich in Power*, 524–7.

241. Lewy, *The Nazi Persecution*, 65–106.

242. Ibid., 107–32 (quote on 130). The numbers killed in all these cases remains uncertain, and available estimates vary wildly.

243. Deletant, *Hitler's Forgotten Ally*, 187–96.

244. Lewy, *The Nazi Persecution*, 135.

245. Höss, *Commandant of Auschwitz*, 138–42.

246. Lewy, *The Nazi Persecution*, 167–228. See also Michael Zimmermann, 'Die nationalsozialistische Zigeunerverfolgung, das System der Konzentrationslager und das Zigeunerlager in Auschwitz-Birkenau', in Herbert *et al.* (eds.), *Die nationalsozialistischen Konzentrationslager*, II. 887–910.

247. Quoted in Noakes (ed.), *Nazism*, IV. 392.

248. Burkhard Jellonek, *Homosexuelle unter dem Hakenkreuz: Die Verfolgung Homosexueller im Dritten Reich* (Paderborn, 1990), 117.

249. Ibid., 257, 269–73, 282–7; Geoffrey Giles, 'The Denial of Homosexuality: Same-Sex Incidents in Himmler's SS and Police', in Dagmar Herzog (ed.), *Sexuality and German Fascism* (New York, 2005), 256–90, at 265–9.

250. Ibid., 269–90.

251. Jellonek, *Homosexuelle*, 329.

252. Geoffrey Giles, 'The Institutionalization of Homosexual Panic in the Third Reich', in Robert Gellately and Nathan Stoltzfus (eds.), *Social Outsiders in Nazi Germany* (Princeton, N.J., 2001), 233–55.

253. Noakes (ed.), *Nazism*, IV. 395.

254. Höss, *Commandant of Auschwitz*, 103–4.

255. Zamecnik, *Das war Dachau*, 230.

256. Till Bastian, *Homosexuelle im Dritten Reich: Geschichte einer Verfolgung* (Munich, 2000), 79–84.

257. See Evans, *The Third Reich in Power*, 529–35, also for the plight of homosexuals in Nazi Germany before 1939. For Jehovah's Witnesses, see ibid., 254–5.

258. Detlev J. K. Peukert, 'Arbeitslager und Jugend-KZ: Die Behandlung "Gemeinschaftsfremder" im Dritten Reich', in idem and Jürgen Reulecke (eds.), *Die Reihen fast geschlossen: Beiträge zur Geschichte des Alltags unterm Nationalsozialismus* (Wuppertal, 1981), 413–34, at 416.

259. Quoted in Norbert Frei, *Der Führerstaat: Nationalsozialistische Herrschaft 1933 bis 1945* (Munich, 1987), 202–8.

260. Peukert, 'Arbeitslager', 416.

Chapter 6. GERMAN MORALITIES

1. Quoted in Vandana Joshi, *Gender and Power in the Third Reich: Female Denouncers and the Gestapo, 1933–45* (London, 2003), 60.

2. Ibid., 59–61.

3. Rita Wolters, *Verrat für die Volksgemeinschaft: Denunziantinnen im Dritten Reich* (Pfaffenweiler, 1996), 59–61.

4. Joshi, *Gender*, 168–97.

5. Ibid., 152; more generally, see Birthe Kundrus, *Kriegerfrauen: Familienpolitik und Geschlechterverhältnisse im Ersten und Zweiten Weltkrieg* (Hamburg, 1995).

6. Noakes (ed.), *Nazism*, IV. 374.

7. Ibid.; see also Michelle Mouton, *From Nurturing the Nation to Purifying the Volk: Weimar and Nazi Family Policy, 1918–1945* (New York, 2007), 224–32.

8. Noakes (ed.), *Nazism*, IV. 368–9.

9. Ibid., 373.

10. Ibid., 375–84.

11. Dagmar Herzog, 'Hubris and Hypocrisy, Incitement and Disavowal: Sexuality and German Fascism', in eadem (ed.), *Sexuality and German Fascism*, 1–21, at 18–19.

12. Quoted in Stibbe, *Women*, 155.

13. Noakes, *Nazism*, IV. 385–90.

14. Boberach (ed.), *Meldungen*, XVI. 6,487 (italics in original); Mouton, *From Nurturing the Nation*, 186, 193–4.

15. Boberach (ed.), *Meldungen*, XVI. 6,487.

16. Ibid.; also Stibbe, *Women*, 159.

17. Wirrer (ed.), *Ich glaube an den Führer*, 324 (Inge to Fred, 17 April 1945).

18. Gerwin Udke (ed.), *'Schreib so oft Du kannst': Feldpostbriefe des Lehrers Gerhard Udke, 1940–1944* (Berlin, 2002), 73 (Gerhard to Dorothea Udke, 3 April 1942).

19. Benedikt Burkard and Friederike Valet (eds.), *'Abends wenn wir essen, fehlt uns immer einer': Kinder schreiben an die Väter, 1939–1945* (Heidelberg, 2000), 240 (1 November 1943).

20. John S. Conway, *The Nazi Persecution of the Churches 1933–1945* (London, 1968), 232–53; Evans, *The Third Reich in Power*, 220–60.

21. Ibid., 253, 220–60.

22. Hitler, *Hitler's Table Talk*, 555–6 (4 July 1942).

23. Ibid., 322 (20–21 February 1942).

24. Ibid., 323 (20–21 February 1942).

25. Ibid., 59 (14 October 1941).

26. Ibid., 51 (10 October 1941).

27. Ibid., 75–6 (19 October 1941).

28. Ibid., 145 (13 December 1941).

29. Ibid., 6–7 (11–12 July 1941).

30. Broszat et al. (eds.), Bayern, I. 423 (Aus Visitationsberichten Dekanat Hof (Ober-franken), 1941).

31. Conway, The Nazi Persecution, 259–60, 383–6.

32. Ian Kershaw, Popular Opinion and Political Dissent in the Third Reich: Bavaria 1933–1945 (Oxford, 1983), 331–40.

33. Broszat et al. (eds.), Bayern, I. 148 (Aus Monatsbericht des Landrats, 31 March 1941).

34. Kershaw, Popular Opinion, 331–57.

35. Broszat et al. (eds.), Bayern, I. 424 (Aus Visitationsberichten Dekanat Hof (Ober-franken), 1942).

36. Ibid.

37. Friedländer, The Years of Extermination, 302–3.

38. Griech-Polelle, Bishop von Galen, 195.

39. Friedländer, The Years of Extermination, 303.

40. Quoted in Michael Phayer, The Catholic Church and the Holocaust, 1930–1965 (Bloomington, Ind., 2000), 75.

41. Friedländer, The Years of Extermination, 559–74.

42. For this view, see John Cornwell, Hitler's Pope: The Secret History of Pius XII (London, 1999).

43. Zuccotti, Under His Very Windows; Robert S. Wistrich, 'The Vatican Documents and the Holocaust: A Personal Report', Polin: Studies in Polish Jewry, 15 (2002), 413–43.

44. Friedländer, The Years of Extermination, 56.

45. Ibid., 300.

46. Heinrich Hermelink (ed.), Kirche im Kampf: Dokumente des Widerstands und des Aufbaus in der evangelischen Kirche Deutschlands von 1933 bis 1945 (Tübingen, 1950), 654–8, 700–702; Theophil Wurm, Aus meinem Leben (Stuttgart, 1953), 88–177; he retired in 1949, aged eighty, and died in 1953.

47. Klemperer, To the Bitter End, 14 (15 February 1942).

48. Ibid., 5 (13 January 1942).

49. Ibid., 27 (16 March 1942).

50. Ibid., 148 (17 October 1942).

51. Ibid., 127 (29 August 1942).

52. Ibid., 361 (26 November 1944).

53. Otto Dov Kulka and Eberhard Jäckel (eds.), Die Juden in den Geheimen NS-Stimmungsberichten 1933–1945 (Düsseldorf, 2004), 489 (NSDAP Meinberg, March 1942).

54. Peter Longerich, 'Davon haben wir nichts gewusst!' Die Deutschen und die Juden-verfolgung 1933–1945 (Munich, 2006), 253–4.

55. Friedländer, The Years of Extermination, 294.

56. Klemperer, I Shall Bear Witness, 423 (1 November 1941).

57. Klemperer, To the Bitter End, 46 (8 May 1942), 50 (15 May 1942).

58. Friedländer, The Years of Extermination, 289.

59. Klemperer, To the Bitter End, 179 (8 January 1943).

60. Ibid., 282 (7 February 1944).

61. Ibid., 204 (16 April 1943).

62. Klemperer, I Shall Bear Witness, 404 (21 July 1941).

63. Friedländer, The Years of Extermination, 251–5; David Bankier, The Germans and the Final Solution: Public Opinion under Nazism (Oxford, 1992), 124–30. See also Frank

Bajohr and Dieter Pohl, *Der Holocaust als offenes Geheimnis: Die Deutschen, die NS-Führung und die Alliierten* (Munich, 2006); Ian Kershaw, *Hitler, the Germans and the Final Solution* (London, 2008); and Bernward Dörner, *Die Deutschen und der Holocaust: Was niemand wissen wollte, aber jeder wissen konnte* (Berlin, 2007).

64. Longerich, 'Davon', 175–81.

65. Kulka and Jäckel (eds.), *Die Juden*, 476–7 (SD-Aussenstelle Minden, 6 and 12 December 1941).

66. Ibid., 478 (SD Hauptaussenstelle Bielefeld, 16 December 1941).

67. Ibid., 503 (SD Aussenstelle Detmold, 31 July 1942), and 476–7 (SD Aussenstelle Minden, 6 December 1941).

68. Solmitz, *Tagebuch*, 691 (7 November 1941).

69. Ibid., 699 (5 December 1941).

70. Ibid., 747–9 (14 July 1942, 22 July 1942).

71. Ibid., 768–9, 776, 780, 782, 788, 796 (25 September 1942, 26 September 1942, 9 November 1942, 24 November 1942, 21 December 1942, 26 January 1943).

72. David M. Crowe, *Oskar Schindler: The Untold Account of His Life, Wartime Activities, and the True Story Behind The List* (Cambridge, Mass., 2004). The story was filmed by Steven Spielberg under the title *Schindler's List*.

73. Hosenfeld, 'Ich versuche', 710 (letter to wife, 31 March 1943), 739 (letter to wife, 29 July 1943).

74. Ibid., 108–11.

75. Wladyslaw Szpilman, *The Pianist: The Extraordinary True Story of One Man's Survival in Warsaw, 1939–1945* (London, 2002). The book became the basis for Roman Polanski's movie *The Pianist*.

76. Debórah Dwork and Robert Jan van Pelt, *Holocaust: A History* (London, 2002), 337–55.

77. Walter Laqueur, *The Terrible Secret: Suppression of the Truth about Hitler's 'Final Solution'* (London, 1980).

78. Saul Friedländer, *Kurt Gerstein oder die Zwiespältigkeit des Guten* (Gütersloh, 1968).

79. Friedländer, *The Years of Extermination*, 454–6.

80. David Engel, 'The Western Allies and the Holocaust: Jan Karski's Mission to the West, 1942–1944', *Holocaust and Genocide Studies*, 5 (1990), 363–446.

81. Bernard Wasserstein, *Britain and the Jews of Europe, 1939–1945* (London, 1979); excerpts in Herf, *The Jewish Enemy*, 174–5.

82. William D. Rubinstein, *The Myth of Rescue: Why the Democracies Could Not Have Saved More Jews from the Nazis* (London, 1997), puts the case, somewhat intemperately, against the claim that the Allies could have rescued the remaining Jews of Europe.

83. Longerich, 'Davon', 201–62, 325.

84. Boelcke (ed.), 'Wollt Ihr den totalen Krieg?', 410–11 (14–16 December 1942).

85. As argued in Goldhagen, *Hitler's Willing Executioners*.

86. Behnken (ed.), *Deutschland-Berichte*, VII. 157 (7 March 1940).

87. Kershaw, *Hitler, the Germans and the Final Solution*, 119–234.

88. Longerich, 'Davon', 290–91, 326–7.

89. Kulka and Jäckel (eds.), *Die Juden*, 525 (Parteikanzlei Munich, 12 June 1943).

90. Ibid., 527 (SD-Berichte zu Inlandsfragen, 8 July 1943); see also ibid., 531 (SD-Aussenstelle Schweinfurt, 6 September 1943).

91. Ibid., 528 (SD-Aussenstelle Würzburg, 3 August 1943).

92. Quoted in Noakes (ed.), *Nazism*, IV. 652.

93. Quoted in Wulf, *Presse und Funk*, 37 and 546.

94. David Welch, *The Third Reich: Politics and Propaganda* (London, 2002 [1993]), 159.

95. Fröhlich (ed.), *Die Tagebücher*, II/III. 377 (26 February 1942).

96. Evans, *The Third Reich in Power*, 207–18.

97. Birthe Kundrus, 'Totale Unterhaltung? Die kulturelle Kriegführung 1939 bis 1945 in Film, Rundfunk und Theater', in *DRZW* IX/I. 93–157; Peter Longerich, 'Nationalsozial-

istische Propaganda', in Karl Dietrich Bracher *et al.* (eds.), *Deutschland 1933–1945: Neue Studien zur nationalsozialistischen Herrschaft* (Düsseldorf, 1993), 291–314; Kaspar Maase, *Grenzenloses Vergnügen: Der Aufstieg der Massenkultur 1850–1970* (Frankfurt am Main, 1997), 206–34; David Welch, 'Nazi Propaganda and the *Volksgemeinschaft*: Constructing a People's Community', *Journal of Contemporary History*, 39 (2004), 213–38.

98. Reported in Jay W. Baird, *The Mythical World of Nazi War Propaganda, 1939–1945* (Minneapolis, Minn., 1974), 30.

99. Ibid.

100. Herf, *The Jewish Enemy*, 13, 22–6; Baird, *The Mythical World*, 28–31; Aristotle A. Kallis, *Nazi Propaganda and the Second World War* (London, 2005), 47–9, 59–62.

101. Ibid., 40–62.

102. Herf, *The Jewish Enemy*, 59–60.

103. Oron J. Hale, *The Captive Press in the Third Reich* (Princeton, N.J., 1964), 151, 234, 276–8, 287; William L. Combs, *The Voice of the SS: A History of the SS Journal 'Das Schwarze Korps'* (New York, 1986); Doris Kohlmann-Viand, *NS-Pressepolitik im Zweiten Weltkrieg* (Munich, 1991), 53–63; Richard Grunberger, *A Social History of the Third Reich* (London, 1974 [1971]), 504–5.

104. Shirer, *Berlin Diary*, 189–90.

105. Jan-Pieter Barbian, *Literaturpolitik im 'Dritten Reich': Institutionen, Kompetenzen, Betätigungsfelder* (Munich, 1995 [1993]), 238–44, 344–5, 373; Joseph Wulf, *Literatur und Dichtung im Dritten Reich: Eine Dokumentation* (Gütersloh, 1963), 222–3; Grunberger, *A Social History*, 453–6.

106. Ralf Schnell, *Literarische innere Emigration 1933–1945* (Stuttgart, 1976); Evans, *The Third Reich in Power*, 149–63.

107. Kundrus, 'Totale Unterhaltung?', 114–19.

108. Shelley Baranowski, *Strength Through Joy: Consumerism and Mass Tourism in the Third Reich* (Cambridge, 2004), 199–230; Kristin Semmens, *Seeing Hitler's Germany: Tourism in the Third Reich* (London, 2005), 154–86.

109. Boberach (ed.), *Meldungen*, IX. 3,371 (26 February 1942).

110. Telegram of 27 November 1939, quoted in Friederike Euler, 'Theater zwischen Anpassung und Widerstand: Die Münchner Kammerspiele im Dritten Reich', in Broszat *et al.*, (eds.), Bayern, II. 91–173, at 159.

111. Ibid., 160–72.

112. Kundrus, 'Totale Unterhaltung?', 119–21. See also Boguslaw Drewniak, *Das Theater im NS-Staat: Szenarium deutscher Zeitgeschichte 1933–1945* (Düsseldorf, 1983). For film and newsreel in the 1930s, see Evans, *The Third Reich in Power*, 125–33.

113. Wolf Donner, *Propaganda und Film im 'Dritten Reich'* (Berlin, 1993); Boguslaw Drewniak, *Der deutsche Film 1938–1945: Ein Gesamtüberblick* (Düsseldorf, 1987); Hilmar Hoffmann, *The Triumph of Propaganda: Film and National Socialism 1933–1945* (Oxford, 1996 [1988]); Eric Rentschler, *The Ministry of Illusion: Nazi Cinema and its Afterlife* (Cambridge, Mass., 1996); Harro Segeberg (ed.), *Mediale Mobilmachung*, I: *Das Dritte Reich und der Film* (Munich, 2004); Gerhard Stahr, *Volksgemeinschaft vor der Leinwand? Der nationalsozialistische Film und sein Publikum* (Berlin, 2001).

114. Kundrus, 'Totale Unterhaltung?', 101; Welch, *Propaganda and the German Cinema*, 217–18.

115. Kundrus, 'Totale Unterhaltung?', 105–7; however, see the more optimistic reports in Gerd Albrecht (ed.), *Film im Dritten Reich: Eine Dokumentation* (Karlsruhe, 1979), 225–32.

116. Welch, *Propaganda and the German Cinema*, 249.

117. Kundrus, 'Totale Unterhaltung?', 102–4; Welch, *Propaganda and the German Cinema*, 186–200; Kallis, *Nazi Propaganda*, 188–94.

118. Welch, *Propaganda and the German Cinema*, 238–80.

119. Boberach (ed.), *Meldungen*, VII. 2,293–5 (12 May 1941).

120. Welch, *Propaganda and the German Cinema*, 284–92.

121. Ibid., 292–301; Friedländer, *The Years of Extermination*, 19–24, 98–102, both excellent general introductory surveys. Public reactions are documented in Kulka and Jäckel (eds.), *Die Juden*, 434–40. For the reception, see David Culbert, 'The Impact of Anti-Semitic Film Propaganda on German Audiences: *Jew Süss* and *The Wandering Jew* (1940)', in Richard A. Etlin (ed.), *Art, Culture, and Media under the Third Reich* (Chicago, Ill., 2002), 139–57, at 139–47, and Karl-Heinz Reuband, ' "Jud Süss" und "Der ewige Jude" als Prototypen antisemitischer Filmpropaganda im Dritten Reich: Entstehungsbedingungen, Zuschauerstrukturen und Wirkungspotential', in Michel Andel *et al.* (eds.), *Propaganda, (Selbst-) Zensur, Sensation: Grenzen von Presse- und Wissenschaftsfreiheit in Deutschland und Tschechien seit 1871* (Essen, 2005), 89–148.

122. Shirer, *Berlin Diary*, 190. The movie he was referring to was *China Seas*, released in the USA in 1935, dubbed into German, as foreign-language films always were, and given a new title.

123. Mary-Elizabeth O'Brien, 'The Celluloid War: Packaging War for Sale in Nazi Home-Front Films', in Etlin (ed.), *Art*, 158–80.

124. Gerd Albrecht, *Nationalsozialistische Filmpolitik: Eine Soziologische Untersuchung über die Spielfilme des Dritten Reiches* (Stuttgart, 1969), 110.

125. Kundrus, 'Totale Unterhaltung?', 107; more generally, see Kallis, *Nazi Propaganda*, 194–217.

126. Boberach (ed.), *Meldungen*, XIII. 4,892 (4 March 1943); Welch, *Propaganda and the German Cinema*, 201–3, 222–4; Baird, *The Mythical World*, 217–27.

127. Welch, *Propaganda and the German Cinema*, 225–37; Kundrus, 'Totale Unterhaltung?', 107–8; Kallis, *Nazi Propaganda*, 153–84, for the general background; ibid., 198–202, for Kolberg; Fröhlich (ed.), *Die Tagebücher* II/XV, 542 (9 March 1945), for the Goebbels quote.

128. For radio in the 1930s, see Evans, *The Third Reich in Power*, 133–7.

129. Boberach (ed.), *Meldungen*, IX. 3,199 (22 January 1942); Uta C. Schmidt, 'Radioaneignung', in Inge Marssolek and Adelheid von Saldern (eds.), *Zuhören und Gehörtwerden* (2 vols., Tübingen, 1998), I: *Radio im Nationalsozialismus: Zwischen Lenkung und Ablenkung*, 243–360, at 351–3; Michael Kater, *Different Drummers: Jazz in the Culture of Nazi Germany* (New York, 1992), 111–25.

130. Wilhelm Schepping, 'Zeitgeschichte im Spiegel eines Liedes', in Günter Noll and Marianne Bröcker (eds.), *Musikalische Volkskunde aktuell* (Bonn, 1984), 435–64; Maase, *Grenzenloses Vergnügen*, 218–21.

131. Wulf, *Presse und Funk*, 358–61.

132. Boberach (ed.), *Meldungen*, IX. 3,166 (15 January 1942).

133. Johnson, *Nazi Terror*, 322–8.

134. Schmidt, 'Radioaneignung', 354 n. 435.

135. Evans, *Rituals*, 694–5.

136. Shirer, *Berlin Diary*, 206–7.

137. Horst J. P. Bergmeier and Rainer E. Lotz, *Hitler's Airwaves: The Inside Story of Nazi Radio Broadcasting and Propaganda Swing* (London, 1997), esp. 99–110, 136–77, 332–3.

138. Kater, *Different Drummers*, 102–10, 190–94; for jazz and the Swing Youth in the later 1930s, see Evans, *The Third Reich in Power*, 204–7.

139. For classical music in the 1930s, see ibid., 186–203.

140. Frederic Spotts, *Hitler and the Power of Aesthetics* (London, 2002), 232–3; Erik Levi, *Music in the Third Reich* (London, 1994), 209–12.

141. Hitler, *Hitler's Table Talk*, 242 (24–5 January 1942, also for general remarks by Hitler on his continuing love for Wagner's music).

142. Spotts, *Hitler*, 233–4, 259–63; Léhar, born in 1870, met Hitler in 1936; he died in 1948.

143. Levi, *Music in the Third Reich*, 195.

144. Ibid., 195–219.

145. Hitler, *Hitler's Table Talk*, 449 (30 April 1942).

146. Fröhlich (ed.), *Die Tagebücher*, II/XI. 82 (13 January 1944).

147. Richard J. Evans, *Rereading German History: From Unification to Reunification 1800–1996* (London, 1997), 187–93; Sam H. Shirakawa, *The Devil's Music Master: The Controversial Life and Career of Wilhelm Furtwängler* (New York, 1992), 290–93. The attempts of Shirakawa and Fred K. Prieberg, *Trial of Strength: Wilhelm Furtwängler and the Third Reich* (London, 1991 [1986]) to portray the conductor as a hero of the resistance to Hitler do not convince.

148. Quoted in Walter Klingler, *Nationalsozialistische Rundfunkpolitik 1942–1945: Organisation, Programm und die Hörer* (Mannheim, 1983), 137.

149. Boberach (ed.), *Meldungen*, XV. 5,808 (27 September 1943).

150. Ibid., 5,807.

151. Ibid.

152. Ibid.

153. Ibid., 5,809.

154. Michael H. Kater, *Composers of the Nazi Era: Eight Portraits* (New York, 2000), 248–59.

155. Quoted in Spotts, *Hitler*, 303. See also Evans, *The Third Reich in Power*, 187–90.

156. Fred K. Prieberg, *Musik im NS-Staat* (Frankfurt am Main, 1989 [1982]), 222–3.

157. Johann Peter Vogel, *Hans Pfitzner: Leben, Werke, Dokumente* (Berlin, 1999), 156–67, 182; Prieberg, *Musik*, 224–5.

158. Ibid., 318–24.

159. Ibid., 324–8.

160. Lyrics from the accompanying booklet to Anne Sofie von Otter *et al.*, *Terezín/Theresienstadt* (DGG, 2007). I am grateful to Chris Clark for the translation.

161. Ibid.

162. For the visual arts in the 1930s, see Evans, *The Third Reich in Power*, 164–80.

163. Peter Adam, *The Arts of the Third Reich* (London, 1992), 157.

164. Ibid., 158.

165. Ibid., 158–64; Gregory Maertz, *The Invisible Museum: The Secret Postwar History of Nazi Art* (New Haven, Conn., 2008).

166. Adam, *The Arts of the Third Reich*, 162, 169.

167. Ibid.

168. Evans, *The Third Reich in Power*, 167–8.

169. Adam, *The Arts of the Third Reich*, 202.

170. Ibid., 201.

171. Jonathan Petropoulos, *The Faustian Bargain: The Art World in Nazi Germany* (London, 2000), 218–38.

172. Evans, *The Third Reich in Power*, 400–409.

173. Nicholas, *The Rape of Europa*, 35–7, 44.

174. Ibid., 41–4; Petropoulos, *The Faustian Bargain*, 63–110.

175. See above, 375–82.

176. Nicholas, *The Rape of Europa*, 57–80; Housden, *Hans Frank*, 81–2.

177. Ibid., 84–6.

178. Nicholas, *The Rape of Europa*, 185–201.

179. Ibid., 83–114.

180. Ibid., 115–33. For the involvement of leading art dealers such as Karl Haberstock, see Petropoulos, *The Faustian Bargain*, 63–110.

181. Spotts, *Hitler*, 217–19.

182. Ibid., 219–20.

183. Quoted in Michael Grüttner, *Studenten im Dritten Reich* (Paderborn, 1995), 370.

184. Ibid., 371–3.

185. Ibid.; for education in the 1930s, see Evans, *The Third Reich in Power*, 261–90.

186. Reiner Lehberger, *Englischunterricht im Nationalsozialismus* (Tübingen, 1986), 196–208.

187. Bettina Goldberg, *Schulgeschichte als Gesellschaftsgeschichte: Die höheren Schulen im Berliner Vorort Hermsdorf (1893–1945)* (Berlin, 1994), 285–305; Willi Feiten, *Der nationalsozialistische Lehrerbund: Entwicklung und Organisation: Ein Beitrag zum Aufbau und zur Organisationsstruktur des nationalsozialistischen Herrschaftssystems* (Weinheim, 1981).

188. Hans-Dieter Arntz, *Ordensburg Vogelsang 1934–1945: Erziehung zur politischen Führung im Dritten Reich* (Euskirchen, 1986), 193–228.

189. Harald Schäfer, *Napola: Die letzten vier Jahre der Nationalpolitischen Erziehungs-anstalt Oranienstein bei Dietz an der Lahn 1941–1945: Eine Erlebnisdokumentation* (Frankfurt am Main, 1997), 94–5.

190. Grüttner, *Studenten*, 361–70, 487–8.

191. Ibid., 374–80.

192. Boberach (ed.), *Meldungen*, XI, 4,281 (5 October 1942). Italics in original.

193. Grüttner, *Studenten*, 383–5.

194. Ibid., 287–331, 387–414.

195. Ibid., 415–22; of the many studies of individual universities, most have relatively little to say about the war years; an exception is Mike Bruhn and Heike Böttner, *Die Jenaer Studenten unter nationalsozialistischer Herrschaft 1933–1945* (Erfurt, 2001), 85–166.

196. Grüttner, *Studenten*, 422–6, 457–71.

197. Christoph Cornelissen, *Gerhard Ritter: Geschichtswissenschaft und Politik im 20. Jahrhundert* (Düsseldorf, 2001), 292–369.

198. Michael Burleigh, *Germany Turns Eastward: A Study of Ostforschung in the Third Reich* (Cambridge, 1988), 155–249; Götz Aly, *Macht – Geist – Wahn: Kontinuitäten deutschen Denkens* (Berlin, 1997); Ingo Haar, *Historiker im Nationalsozialismus: Deutsche Geschichtswissenschaft und der 'Volkstumskampf' im Osten* (Göttingen, 2002); Winfried Schulze and Otto Oexle (eds.), *Deutsche Historiker im Nationalsozialismus* (Frankfurt am Main, 1999); more generally, Michael Fahlbusch, *Wissenschaft im Dienst nationalsozialistischer Politik? Die 'Volksdeutschen Forschungsgemeinschaften' von 1931–1945* (Baden-Baden, 1999); and Aly and Heim, *Architects*.

199. Quoted in Burleigh, *Germany*, 165.

200. Michael Grüttner, 'Wissenschaftspolitik im Nationalsozialismus', in Doris Kaufmann (ed.), *Geschichte der Kaiser-Wilhelm-Gesellschaft im Nationalsozialismus: Bestandsauf-nahme und Perspektiven der Forschung* (2 vols., Göttingen, 2000), II. 557–85.

201. Susanne Heim (ed.), *Autarkie und Ostexpansion: Pflanzenzucht und Agrarforschung im Nationalsozialismus* (Göttingen, 2002).

202. Susanne Heim, *Kalorien Kautschuk Karrieren: Pflanzenzüchtung und landwirtschaft-liche Forschung in Kaiser-Wilhelm-Instituten 1933–1945* (Göttingen, 2003), 249; Grüttner, 'Wissenschaftspolitik', 583.

203. Geoffrey Cocks, *Psychotherapy in the Third Reich: The Göring Institute* (New Bruns-wick, N.J., 1997 [1985]), 251–350.

204. Hans-Walter Schmuhl (ed.), *Rassenforschung an Kaiser-Wilhelm-Instituten vor und nach 1933* (Göttingen, 2003).

205. Heather Pringle, *The Master Plan: Himmler's Scholars and the Holocaust* (New York, 2006); Michael H. Kater, *Das Ahnenerbe der SS 1935–1945: Ein Beitrag zur Kulturpolitik des Dritten Reiches* (4th edn, Munich, 2006); Heinrich Harrer, *Seven Years in Tibet* (London, 1953). The book was later made into a Hollywood movie starring Brad Pitt. Harrer eventually died in 2006.

206. Robert N. Proctor, *Racial Hygiene: Medicine under the Nazis* (Cambridge, Mass., 1988), 217–22; Evans, *The Third Reich in Power*, 444–6.

207. Zamecnik, *Das war Dachau*, 262–75; Karl Heinz Roth, 'Tödliche Höhen: Die Unter-druckkammer-Experimente im Konzentrationslager Dachau und ihre Bedeutung für die

luftfahrtmedizinische Forschung des "Dritten Reichs" ', in Ebbinghaus and Dörner (eds.), *Vernichten und Heilen*, 110–51.

208. Karl Heinz Roth, 'Strukturen, Paradigmen und Mentalitäten in der luftfahrtmedizinischen Forschung des "Dritten Reichs": Der Weg ins Konzentrationslager Dachau', 1999. *Zeitschrift für Sozialgeschichte des 20. und 21. Jahrhunderts*, 15 (2000), 49–77.

209. Zamecnik, *Das war Dachau*, 275–84.

210. Ibid., 292–5.

211. Ibid., 285–92; Angelika Ebbinghaus and Karl Heinz Roth, 'Kriegswunden: Die kriegschirurgischen Experimente in den Konzentrationslagern und ihre Hintergründe', in Ebbinghaus and Dörner (eds.), *Vernichten und Heilen*, 177–218; Angelika Ebbinghaus, 'Zwei Welten: Die Opfer und die Täter der kriegschirurgischen Experimente', in ibid., 219–40; Loretta Walz, 'Gespräche mit Stanislawa Bafia, Wladyslawa Marczewska und Maria Plater über die medizinischen Versuche in Ravensbrück', in ibid., 241–72.

212. Schmidt, *Karl Brandt*, 263–4, also giving slightly differing numbers.

213. Thomas Werther, 'Menschenversuche in der Fleckfieberforschung', in Ebbinghaus and Dörner (eds.), *Vernichten und Heilen*, 152–73.

214. Schmidt, *Karl Brandt*, 257–62.

215. Ibid., 265–76.

216. Ibid., 276–9.

217. Ibid., 284–96.

218. Ernst Klee, *Auschwitz, die NS-Medizin und ihre Opfer* (Frankfurt am Main, 1997), 456–66; Robert Jay Lifton, *The Nazi Doctors: Medical Killing and the Psychology of Genocide* (London, 1986), 337–42.

219. Benoît Massin, 'Mengele, die Zwillingsforschung und die "Auschwitz-Dahlem Connection" ', in Carola Sachse (ed.), *Die Verbindung nach Auschwitz: Biowissenschaften und Menschenversuche an Kaiser-Wilhelm-Instituten: Dokumentation eines Symposiums* (Göttingen, 2003), 201–54.

220. Lifton, *The Nazi Doctors*, 347–60; Paul J. Weindling, *Health, Race and German Politics between National Unification and Nazism 1870–1945* (Cambridge, 1989), 55–63.

221. Lifton, *The Nazi Doctors*, 342–8.

222. Ibid., 360–83.

223. Klee, *Auschwitz*, 167–72, 436–45.

224. Jürgen Pfeiffer, 'Neuropathologische Forschung an "Euthanasie"-Opfern in zwei Kaiser-Wilhelm-Instituten', in Kaufmann (ed.), *Geschichte der Kaiser-Wilhelm-Gesellschaft*, I. 151–73.

225. Quoted in Evans, *Rituals*, 714–15.

226. Proctor, *Racial Hygiene*, 219–22; see also Rolf Winau, 'Medizinische Experimente in den Konzentrationslagern', in Benz and Distel (eds.), *Der Ort des Terrors*, I. 165–78.

227. Speer always denied in public that he had been present, but in a letter to Hélène Jeanty, the widow of a Belgian resistance leader, on 23 December 1971, he wrote: 'There is no doubt – I was present as Himmler announced on October 6 1943 that all Jews would be killed.' However, this too was a deception; Himmler did not say that they would be killed; he said they were being killed already, as Speer well knew (Kate Connolly, 'Letter proves Speer knew of Holocaust plan', *Guardian*, 13 March 2007).

228. Quoted in Longerich, *Der ungeschriebene Befehl*, 189.

229. Hans-Heinrich Wilhelm, 'Hitlers Ansprache vor Generalen und Offizieren am 26. Mai 1944', *Militärgeschichtliche Mitteilungen*, 20 (1976), 123–70 (quotation at 156).

230. Longerich, *Der ungeschriebene Befehl*, 188–91.

231. Quoted in Noakes and Pridham (eds.), *Nazism*, III. 617–18.

232. Randolph L. Braham, *The Politics of Genocide: The Holocaust in Hungary* (2 vols., New York, 1981), I. 391; Christian Gerlach and Götz Aly, *Das letzte Kapitel: Realpolitik, Ideologie und der Mord an den ungarischen Juden 1941/1945* (Munich, 2002).

233. Randolph L. Braham, 'The Role of the Jewish Council in Hungary: A Tentative Assessment', *Yad Vashem Studies*, 10 (1974), 69–109; Robert Rozett, 'Jewish and Hun-

garian Armed Resistance in Hungary', *Yad Vashem Studies*, 19 (1988), 269–88; Rudolf Vrba, 'Die missachtete Warnung: Betrachtungen über den Auschwitz-Bericht von 1944', *VfZ* 44 (1996), 1–24; and Yehuda Bauer, 'Anmerkungen zum "Auschwitz-Bericht" von Rudolf Vrba', *VfZ* 45 (1997), 297–307; Steur, *Theodor Dannecker*, 129–50.

234. Herf, *The Jewish Enemy*, 242.

235. Hillgruber (ed.), *Staatsmänner und Diplomaten*, II. 463–4.

236. Quoted in Phayer, *The Catholic Church*, 106.

237. Braham, *The Politics*, II. 607, 664–84, 762–74.

238. Weinberg, *A World at Arms*, 667–75; Frieser and Schönherr, 'Der Rückschlag', 447–50.

239. Weinberg, *A World at Arms*, 703–6; Karl-Heinz Frieser and Klaus Schönherr, 'Der Zusammenbruch im Osten: Die Rückzugskämpfe seit Sommer 1944', in *DRZW* VIII. 493–960.

240. Merridale, *Ivan's War*, 96; Weinberg, *A World at Arms*, 705–8.

241. Quoted in Norman Davies, *Rising '44: 'The Battle for Warsaw'* (London, 2003), 299–300.

242. Quoted in Kershaw, *Hitler*, II. 725.

243. Weinberg, *A World at Arms*, 709–12.

244. Hosenfeld, *'Ich versuche'*, 824 (letter to family, 8 August 1944).

245. Ibid., 856 (letter to family, 5 October 1944).

246. Ibid., 100–101, 834 (letter to family, 23 August 1944).

247. Weinberg, *A World at Arms*, 676–93, and Overy, *Why the Allies Won*, 134–79, for an overview; detailed account in Detlef Vogel, 'German and Allied Conduct of the War in the West', in *GSWW* VII. 459–702.

248. Kershaw, *Hitler*, II. 637–51.

249. Summary in Gerd R. Ueberschär, *Für ein anderes Deutschland: Der deutsche Widerstand gegen den NS-Staat 1933–1945* (Frankfurt am Main, 2006), 78–90, 116. Among many contributions, see Horst Duhnke, *Die KPD von 1933–1945* (Cologne, 1972); Detlev Peukert, *Die KPD im Widerstand: Verfolgung und Untergrundarbeit an Rhein und Ruhr 1933–1945* (Wuppertal, 1980); and idem, 'Der deutsche Arbeiterwiderstand 1933–1945', in Klaus-Jürgen Müller (ed.), *Der deutsche Widerstand 1933–1945* (Paderborn, 1986), 157–81.

250. Karin Hartewig, 'Wolf unter Wölfen? Die prekäre Macht der kommunistischen Kapos im Konzentrationslager Buchenwald', in Herbert *et al.* (eds.), *Die nationalsozialistischen Konzentrationslager*, II. 939–58; Niethammer (ed.), *Der 'gesäuberte' Antifaschismus*.

251. Ueberschär, *Für ein anderes Deutschland*, 133–40; Shareen Blair Brysac, *Resisting Hitler: Mildred Harnack and the Red Orchestra: The Life and Death of an American Woman in Nazi Germany* (New York, 2000); Almut Brunckhorst, *Die Berliner Widerstandsorganisation um Arvid Harnack und Harro Schluze-Boysen ('Rote Kapelle'): Kundschafter im Auftrag Moskaus oder integraler Bestandteil des deutschen Widerstandes gegen den Nationalsozialismus? Ein Testfall für die deutsche Historiographie* (Hamburg, 1998); Hans Coppi *et al.* (eds.), *Die Rote Kapelle im Widerstand gegen den Nationalsozialismus* (Berlin, 1994); Stefan Roloff, 'Die Entstehung der Roten Kapelle und die Verzerrung ihrer Geschichte im Kalten Krieg', in Karl Heinz Roth and Angelika Ebbinghaus (eds.), *Rote Kapellen – Kreisauer Kreise – Schwarze Kapellen: Neue Sichtweisen auf den Widerstand gegen die NS-Diktatur 1938–1945* (Hamburg, 2004), 186–205.

252. The League's story is told in the brilliant and moving book by Mark Roseman, *The Past in Hiding* (London, 2000).

253. Ueberschär, *Für ein anderes Deutschland*, 126–32; among a large literature, see especially Karl Heinz Jahnke, *Weisse Rose contra Hakenkreuz: Der Widerstand der Geschwister Scholl und ihrer Freunde* (Frankfurt am Main, 1969); idem, *Weisse Rose contra Hakenkreuz: Studenten im Widerstand 1942/43: Einblicke in viereinhalb Jahrzehnte Forschung* (Rostock, 2003); translated documents in Noakes (ed.), *Nazism*, IV. 457–9.

254. Breloer (ed.), *Geheime Welten*, 103.

255. Ibid., 113–15 (24 August and 10 September 1944).
256. Evans, *The Third Reich in Power*, 668–71.
257. Hassell, *The von Hassell Diaries*, 151–2.
258. Ueberschär, *Für ein anderes Deutschland*, 32–60, 66–77; Joachim C. Fest, *Plotting Hitler's Death: The German Resistance to Hitler 1933–1945* (London, 1996), provides a readable narrative of the evolution of the military-aristocratic conspiracy. Peter Hoffmann, *The History of the German Resistance 1933–1945* (Montreal, 1996 [1969]), is the most thorough and detailed account; Winfried Heinemann, 'Der militärische Widerstand und der Krieg', in *DRZW* IX/I. 743–892, is the most recent survey.
259. English version of extracts from the 9 August 1943 manifesto in Noakes (ed.), *Nazism*, IV. 614–16.
260. Hassell, *The von Hassell Diaries*, 283; Ueberschär, *Für ein anderes Deutschland*, 161–3.
261. Klemens von Klemperer, *German Resistance against Hitler: The Search for Allies Abroad 1938–1945* (Oxford, 1992); Hoffmann, *The History*, 205–50.
262. For the political aims and plans of the resisters, see Hoffmann, *The History*, 175–202. For documents of the resistance, see Hans-Adolf Jacobsen (ed.), *'Spiegelbild einer Verschwörung': Die Opposition gegen Hitler und der Staatsstreich vom 20. Juli 1940 in der SD-Berichterstattung: Geheime Dokumente aus dem ehemaligen Reichssicherheitshauptamt* (2 vols., Stuttgart, 1984).
263. Hans Mommsen, 'Social Views and Constitutional Plans of the Resistance', in Hermann Graml *et al.*, *The German Resistance to Hitler* (London, 1970 [1966]), 55–147.
264. Beate Ruhm von Oppen (ed.), *Helmuth James von Moltke: Letters to Freya, 1939–1945* (London, 1991); more generally, on the resisters' criticism of the conduct of the war in the east, see Heinemann, 'Der militärische Widerstand', 777–89.
265. Hassel, *The von Hassell Diaries*, 218.
266. Wolfgang Gerlach, *And the Witnesses Were Silent: The Confessing Church and the Persecution of the Jews* (Lincoln, Nebr., 2000 [1987]), 210–14; Hans Mommsen, 'Die Moralische Wiederherstellung der Nation: Der Widerstand gegen Hitler war von einer antisemitischen Grundhaltung getragen', *Süddeutsche Zeitung*, 21 July 1999, 15.
267. Ulrich Heinemann, ' "Kein Platz für Polen und Juden": Der Widerstandskämpfer Fritz-Dietlof Graf von der Schulenburg und die Politik der Verwaltung in Schlesien 1939/40', in Klessmann (ed.), *September 1939*, 38–54; Heinemann, 'Der militärische Widerstand', 751–76.
268. Evans, *The Third Reich in Power*, 576–7.
269. Quoted in Noakes (ed.), *Nazism*, IV. 633 (also for the views of Popitz and others).
270. Ueberschär, *Für ein anderes Deutschland*, 165–71; details of this and the other attempts on Hitler's life in Hoffmann, *The History*, 251–60.
271. Fest, *Plotting Hitler's Death*, 202–4, 212–15, 225–30.
272. Ibid., 202–26; Peter Hoffmann, *Claus Schenk Graf von Stauffenberg und seine Brüder* (Stuttgart, 1992), 15–268.
273. Fabian von Schlabrendorff, *Revolt against Hitler: The Personal Account of Fabian von Schlabrendorff* (London, 1948), 131.
274. Ueberschär, *Für ein anderes Deutschland*, 200–206; Fest, *Plotting Hitler's Death*, 237–60; Hoffmann, *The History*, 373–411; Heinemann, 'Der militärische Widerstand', 803–38.
275. Fest, *Plotting Hitler's Death*, 255–79; Hoffmann, *Claus Schenk*, 383–443.
276. Fest, *Plotting Hitler's Death*, 280–87; see also the gripping narrative in Kershaw, *Hitler*, II. 655–84.
277. Heinemann, 'Der militärische Widerstand', 838–40; Hoffmann, *The History*, 412–506.
278. Fest, *Plotting Hitler's Death*, 292–309; Kershaw, *Hitler*, II. 688–90; Speer, *Inside the Third Reich*, 511–28.
279. Quoted in Fest, *Plotting Hitler's Death*, 290.

280. Kershaw, *Hitler*, II. 691; Fest, *Plotting Hitler's Death*, 291–307.
281. Ibid., 297–317; Kershaw, *Hitler*, II. 692–3 (and 1,006 n. 43, discussing the evidence for and against Hitler having watched the film); Speer, *Inside the Third Reich*, 531.
282. Schlabrendorff, *Revolt*, 164.
283. Hürter (ed.), *Ein deutscher General*, 16, 48.
284. For an exhaustive account of the conspirators' foreign contacts, see Klemperer, *German Resistance against Hitler*.
285. Heinemann, 'Der militärische Widerstand', 840–43.
286. Quoted in Noakes (ed.), *Nazism*, IV. 634.

Chapter 7. DOWNFALL

1. Breloer (ed.), *Geheime Welten*, 76–8 (20–22 July 1944).
2. Ibid., 80 (10 August 1944).
3. Quoted in Manoschek (ed.), *'Es gibt nur eines'*, 73 (Uffz.E, 7 August 1944).
4. Wirrer (ed.), *Ich glaube an den Führer*, 235 (Alfred to Inge, 20 July 1944).
5. Ibid.
6. Pöppel, *Heaven and Hell*, 221, 237. See also the careful analysis of reactions in Ian Kershaw, *The 'Hitler Myth': Image and Reality in the Third Reich* (Oxford, 1989 [1987], 215–20.
7. Boberach (ed.), *Meldungen*, XVII. 6,684–6, and 6,700–701; Broszat *et al.* (eds.), *Bayern*, I. 185–6 (Ebermannstadt, 25 and 27 July 1944).
8. Herber (ed.), *Goebbels-Reden*, II. 394.
9. Ueberschär, *Für ein anderes Deutschland*, 224–8.
10. Broszat *et al.* (eds.), *Bayern*, I. 667.
11. Ibid., 664.
12. Ibid., 668.
13. Boberach (ed.), *Meldungen*, XVII. 6,651 (22 July 1944).
14. Ibid., XVII. 6,652.
15. Ibid., XVII. 6,693 (7 August 1944).
16. Ibid., XVII. 6,653
17. Ibid., XVII. 6,698.
18. Quoted in Kershaw, *The 'Hitler Myth'*, 220.
19. Quoted in ibid., 1,008–9 n. 91.
20. Weinberg, *A World at Arms*, 713–16; Kershaw, *Hitler*, II. 717–24.
21. Kershaw, *Hitler*, II. 734.
22. Tim Cole, *Holocaust City: The Making of a Jewish Ghetto* (London, 2003); Randolph L. Braham, *Eichmann and the Destruction of Hungarian Jewry* (New York, 1961); Kershaw, *Hitler*, II. 735–6; Longerich, *Politik*, 565–70.
23. Ibid., 563–4.
24. Hassell, *The von Hassell Diaries*, 351.
25. Speer, *Inside the Third Reich*, 532–4; Ralf Georg Reuth, *Goebbels: Eine Biographie* (Munich, 1995 [1990]), 561–6; Tooze, *The Wages of Destruction*, 637–8.
26. Kershaw, *Hitler*, II. 712–13.
27. Ibid., 731–42.
28. Ibid., 747, 757; Weinberg, *A World at Arms*, 757–71. For a detailed account of the land war in the west, see John Zimmermann, 'Die deutsche militärische Kriegsführung im Westen 1944/45', in *DRZW* X/I, 277–489. For the 'Battle of the Bulge', see Vogel, 'German and Allied Conduct of the War in the West', 863–97.
29. Kershaw, *Hitler*, II. 768–9.
30. Boog, 'The Strategic Air War', 369–73; Fröhlich (ed.), *Die Tagebücher*, II/VIII. 527–9 (25 June 1943).
31. Boog, 'The Strategic Air War', 375.
32. Fröhlich (ed.), *Die Tagebücher*, II/VII. 578 (18 March 1943).

33. Boog, 'The Strategic Air War', 381.

34. Ibid., 417.

35. Ibid., 406–20.

36. Speer, *Inside the Third Reich*, 481; Heinz Dieter Hölsken, *Die V-Waffen Entstehung – Propaganda – Kriegseinsatz* (Stuttgart, 1984), 178–202; Weinberg, *A World at Arms*, 561–2; Boog, 'The Strategic Air War', 413–15.

37. Michael J. Neufeld, *The Rocket and the Reich: Peenemünde and the Coming of the Ballistic Missile Era* (New York, 1995), 13, 22–3, 108–37; see also Rainer Eisfeld, *Mondsüchtig: Wernher von Braun und die Geburt der Raumfahrt aus dem Geist der Barbarei* (Hamburg, 2000).

38. Speer, *Inside the Third Reich*, 494.

39. Ibid., 495.

40. Ibid., 497.

41. Speer, *Inside the Third Reich*, 503–5; Neufeld, *The Rocket and the Reich*, 197–201.

42. Neufeld, *The Rocket and the Reich*, 197–238; Florian Freund, 'Die Entscheidung zum Einsatz von KZ-Häftlingen in der Raketenrüstung', in Kaienburg (ed.), *Konzentrationslager*, 61–74.

43. Quoted in Neufeld, *The Rocket and the Reich*, 209–10.

44. Ibid., 197–209; Sereny, *Albert Speer*, 402–5.

45. Neufeld, *The Rocket and the Reich*, 210.

46. Ibid.

47. Sereny, *Albert Speer*, 403. Sereny does not mention the letter to Kammler.

48. Speer, *Inside the Third Reich*, 500–501.

49. Quoted in Neufeld, *The Rocket and the Reich*, 211–12.

50. Ibid., 210–12.

51. Ibid., 264, 405; see also Jens Christian Wagner, 'Noch einmal: Arbeit und Vernichtung: Häftlingseinsatz im KL Mittelbau-Dora 1943–1945', in Frei *et al.* (eds.), *Ausbeutung*, 11–42.

52. Neufeld, *The Rocket and the Reich*, 226–30.

53. Ibid., 238–64 (quote on 264). Weinberg, *A World at Arms*, 562–3, gives a figure of 15,000 deaths; see also Allen, *The Business of Genocide*, 208–32.

54. Evans, *The Third Reich in Power*, 306–9; Alan D. Beyerchen, *Scientists under Hitler: Politics and the Physics Community in the Third Reich* (London, 1977), 168–98; Klaus Hentschel (ed.), *Physics and National Socialism: An Anthology of Primary Sources* (Basel, 1996), 281–4, 290–92.

55. Beyerchen, *Scientists*, 168–98.

56. Hentschel (ed.), *Physics*, lxvii.

57. Mark Walker, *German National Socialism and the Quest for Nuclear Power 1939–1949* (Cambridge, 1989); Speer, *Inside the Third Reich*, 315–17; Weinberg, *A World at Arms*, 568–71. Heisenberg's later claim that he deliberately slowed down progress on research so as to make sure that Hitler would not have an atom bomb before the war ended lacks all plausibility; even had he worked as fast as possible, it is still extremely unlikely that he would have put a working bomb together in time. See, among a voluminous literature, Thomas Powers, *Heisenberg's War: The Secret History of the German Bomb* (Boston, 1993); Jeremy Bernstein (ed.), *Hitler's Uranium Club: The Secret Recordings at Farm Hall* (New York, 2001), xxiv–xxv, xxvii–xxviii.

58. Speer, *Inside the Third Reich*, 317–18.

59. Rainer Karlsch, *Hitlers Bombe: Die geheime Geschichte der deutschen Kernwaffenversuche* (Stuttgart, 2005), 171–81, 215–19.

60. Speer, *Inside the Third Reich*, 316–20; for Lenard, see Evans, *The Third Reich in Power*, 306–9.

61. Speer, *Inside the Third Reich*, 553–4.

62. Schmidt, *Karl Brandt*, 284–96; also Florian Schmaltz, *Kampfstoff-Forschung im Nationalsozialismus: Zur Kooperation von Kaiser-Wilhelm-Instituten, Militär und*

Industrie (Göttingen, 2005), 143–77, 608–10; and idem, 'Neurosciences and Research on Chemical Weapons of Mass Destruction in Nazi Germany', *Journal of the History of the Neurosciences*, 15 (2006), 186–209; Weinberg, *A World at Arms*, 558–9.

63. Speer, *Inside the Third Reich*, 491.
64. Neufeld, *The Rocket and the Reich*, 233–8.
65. Ludwig, *Technik*, 451–63; Hentschel (ed.), *Physics*, 303, 327.
66. Speer, *Inside the Third Reich*, 488–91; Tooze, *The Wages of Destruction*, 620–21.
67. Weinberg, *A World at Arms*, 771–3.
68. Ibid., 537–8 (but a different, and evidently more accurate account, is given on page 563). See also Fritz Hahn, *Waffen und Geheimwaffen des deutschen Heeres, 1933–1945* (2 vols., Koblenz, 1986–7), I. 191–4.
69. Weinberg, *A World at Arms*, 563–4.
70. Speer, *Inside the Third Reich*, 620.
71. Ibid.
72. Quoted in Boog, 'The Strategic Air War', 413, 423, figures at 453–4.
73. Boberach (ed.), *Meldungen*, XV. 6,187 (27 December 1943).
74. Wirrer (ed.), *Ich glaube an den Führer*, 256 (Inge to Alfred, 3 September 1944).
75. Quoted in Wulf, *Presse und Funk*, 360.
76. Walb, *Ich, die Alte*, 301 (4 March 1945).
77. Boberach (ed.), *Meldungen*, XVII. 6,736 (28 March 1945). The printed text gives the words as 'einen ganz gewöhnlichen Umstand', a completely normal circumstance, but it only makes sense if one assumes this is a typing or printing error for 'einen ganz ungewöhnlichen Umstand', 'a completely unusual circumstance'.
78. Boberach (ed.), *Meldungen*, XV. 6,187 (27 December 1943).
79. Breloer (ed.), *Geheime Welten*, 87–8 (18 April 1945).
80. Hans-Jochen Gamm, *Der Flüsterwitz im Dritten Reich: Mündliche Dokumente zur Lage der Deutschen während des Nationalsozialismus* (Munich, 1990 [1963]), 180. The joke depends on an untranslatable pun – *ausheben* in German means both 'dig up' and 'recruit', depending on the context.
81. Klaus Mammach, *Der Volkssturm: Bestandteil des totalen Kriegseinsatzes der deutschen Bevölkerung 1944/45* (Berlin, 1981), 150; Franz Seidler, 'Deutscher Volkssturm': Der letzte Aufgebot 1944/45 (Munich, 1989), 374.
82. Roland Müller, *Stuttgart zur Zeit des Nationalsozialismus* (Stuttgart, 1988), 519.
83. Alphons Kappeler, *Ein Fall von 'Pseudologia phantastica' in der deutschen Literatur: Fritz Reck-Malleczewen: Mit Totalbibliographie* (Göppingen, 1975), 7–11. The widely repeated story that he was shot by the Gestapo has no basis in truth; for his earlier life, real and imagined, see Evans, *The Third Reich in Power*, 154–5, 251, 414–17, 419, 499, 587.
84. Boberach (ed.), *Meldungen*, XVII. 6,721 (28 October 1944).
85. Schäfer, *Napola*, 95–6.
86. Breloer (ed.), *Geheime Welten*, 226–7 (22 February 1945).
87. Ibid., 229.
88. Maschmann, *Account Rendered*, 176.
89. Breloer (ed.), *Geheime Welten*, 154 (27 January 1945).
90. For this play, see Evans, *The Coming of the Third Reich*, 417–18.
91. Wirrer (ed.), *Ich glaube an den Führer*, 293 (Albert to Inge, 30 January 1945).
92. Ibid., 295–6 (Inge to Alfred, 3–4 February 1945).
93. Ibid., 313 (Alfred to Inge, 9 March 1945).
94. Ibid., 321 (Inge to Alfred, 10 April 1945).
95. Ibid., 317.
96. Nicolaus von Below, *Als Hitlers Adjutant 1937–1945* (Frankfurt am Main, 1980), 398.
97. Quoted in Herf, *The Jewish Enemy*, 255–6.
98. Weinberg, *A World at Arms*, 798–802.

99. Jörg Echternkamp (ed.), *Kriegsschauplatz Deutschland 1945: Leben in Angst – Hoffnung auf Frieden: Feldpost aus der Heimat und von der Front* (Paderborn, 2006), 20–21.

100. Overmans, *Deutsche militärische Verluste*, 238–9.

101. For a detailed account, see Holst Boog, 'Die strategische Bomberoffensive der Alliierten gegen Deutschland und die Reichsluftverteidigung in der Schlussphase des Krieges', in *DRZW* X/I. 771–884.

102. Andreas Kunz, *Wehrmacht und Niederlage: Die bewaffnete Macht in der Endphase der nationalsozialistischen Herrschaft 1944 bis 1945* (Munich, 2005); 207–15; idem, 'Die Wehrmacht 1944/45: Eine Armee im Untergang', in *DRZW* X/II. 3–54.

103. Kershaw, *Hitler*, II. 781.

104. Quoted in Patrick Wright, *Iron Curtain: From Stage to Cold War* (London, 2007), 352. Churchill's first use of the term came shortly after this.

105. Hubatsch (ed.), *Hitlers Weisungen*, 310–11.

106. Baird, *The Mythical World*, 246–55.

107. Noakes (ed.), *Nazism*, IV. 652.

108. Ibid., 653.

109. Ibid., 651.

110. Walb, *Ich, die Alte*, 316 (26 March 1945).

111. Noakes (ed.), *Nazism*, IV. 654.

112. Ibid., 655–6.

113. Ibid., 658.

114. Hubatsch (ed.), *Hitlers Weisungen*, 311.

115. Gerhard Paul, ' "Diese Erschiessungen haben mich innerlich gar nicht mehr berührt": Die Kriegsendphasenverbrechen der Gestapo 1944/45', in idem and Klaus-Michael Mallmann (eds.), *Die Gestapo im Zweiten Weltkrieg: 'Heimatfront' und besetztes Europa* (Darmstadt, 2000), 543–68.

116. Wachsmann, *Hitler's Prisons*, 327.

117. Ibid.

118. Ibid., 334–7.

119. Hitler, *Hitler's Table Talk*, 29.

120. For Natzweiler, see Wolfgang Kirstin, *Das Konzentrationslager als Institution totalen Terrors: Das Beispiel des KL Natzweiler* (Pfaffenweiler, 1992), 13–16.

121. Quoted in Fest, *Plotting Hitler's Death*, 312.

122. Moorhouse, *Killing Hitler*, 58; Hoffmann, *The History*, 258.

123. Ueberschär, *Für ein anderes Deutschland*, 238–9.

124. Hannes Heer, *Ernst Thälmann in Selbstzeugnissen und Bilddokumenten* (Reinbek, 1975), 127–30.

125. Fest, *Plotting Hitler's Death*, 304; Ueberschär, *Für ein anderes Deutschland*, 238; Willi Dressen, 'Konzentrationslager als Tötungs- und Hinrichtungsstätten für Oppositionelle, Behinderte, Kriegsgefangene', in Benz and Distel (eds.), *Der Ort des Terrors*, I. 230–41.

126. Echternkamp (ed.), *Kriegsschauplatz*, 34–5.

127. Höss, *Commandant of Auschwitz*, 190–92.

128. Steinbacher, *Auschwitz*, 123–8.

129. Ernst Kaiser and Michael Knorn, '*Wir lebten und schliefen zwischen den Toten': Rüstungsproduktion, Zwangsarbeit und Vernichtung in den Frankfurter Adlerwerken* (Frankfurt am Main, 1994), 214–27.

130. Daniel Blatman, 'The Death Marches, January–May 1945: Who Was Responsible for What?', *Yad Vashem Studies*, 28 (2000), 155–201.

131. Goldhagen, *Hitler's Willing Executioners*, 327–71, provides a graphically detailed account, marred by anti-German rhetoric and the assumption that the marches only involved Jewish prisoners.

132. Wilhelm Lange, *Cap Arcona: Dokumentation* (Eutin, 1992); Detlef Garbe, 'Institutionen des Terrors und der Widerstand der Wenigen', in Forschungsstelle für Zeitgeschichte in Hamburg (ed.), *Hamburg*, 519–72, at 549–55; David Stafford, *Endgame 1945: Victory, Retribution, Liberation* (London, 2007), 291–306.

133. Neuman, *The Rocket and the Reich*, 264.

134. Daniel Blatman, 'Rückzug, Evakuierung und Todesmärsche 1944–1945', in Benz and Distel (eds.), *Der Ort des Terrors*, I. 296–312, at 306–8; for the death march in 1945 of Russian workers imprisoned by the Gestapo in Oldenburg, see Hoffmann, *Zwangsarbeit*, 288–92.

135. Harry Stein, 'Funktionswandel des Konzentrationslagers Buchenwald im Spiegel der Lagerstatistiken', in Herbert *et al.* (eds.), *Die Nationsozialistische Konzentrationslager*, I. 167–92; Michael Fabréguet, 'Entwicklung und Veränderung der Funktionen des Konzentrationslager Mauthausen 1938–1945', in ibid., 193–214; also Blatman, *Rückzug*; and Robert H. Abzug, *Inside the Vicious Heart: Americans and the Liberation of Nazi Concentration Camps* (New York, 1985), 21–30.

136. Eberhard Kolb, *Bergen-Belsen 1943–1945: Vom 'Aufenthaltslager' zum Konzentrationslager 1943–1945* (Göttingen, 2001), 21–4, 38–41.

137. Ibid., also Joanne Reilly, *Belsen: The Liberation of a Concentration Camp* (London, 1998), and Ben Shephard, *After Daybreak: The Liberation of Belsen, 1945* (London, 2005).

138. Daniel Blatman, 'Die Todesmärsche – Entscheidungsträger, Mörder und Opfer', in Herbert *et al.* (eds.), *Die nationalsozialistischen Konzentrationslager*, II. 1,063–92.

139. Blank, 'Kriegsalltag', 451–7; full details in Boog, 'Die Strategische Bomberoffensive'.

140. Quoted in Blank, 'Kriegsalltag', 455.

141. Evans, *Telling Lies*, 193–231; reliable accounts in Rudolf Förster, 'Dresden', in Marlene P. Hiller *et al.* (eds.), *Städte im 2. Weltkrieg: Ein internationaler Vergleich* (Essen, 1991), 299–315; Götz Bergander, *Dresden im Luftkrieg: Vorgeschichte, Zerstörung, Folgen* (Würzburg, 1998); and Frederick Taylor, *Dresden: Tuesday 13 February 1945* (London, 2004).

142. Klemperer, *To the Bitter End*, 387–9 (13 February 1945).

143. Ibid., 389–92 (22–4 February 1945).

144. Ibid., 393 (22–4 February 1945).

145. Ibid., 396–405 (15–27 February 1945).

146. Solmitz, *Tagebuch*, 998 (7 March 1945).

147. Noakes (ed.), *Nazism*, IV. 515.

148. Solmitz, *Tagebuch*, 983 (2 February 1945), 995 (27 February 1945), 1,010 (9 April 1945).

149. Solmitz, *Tagebuch*, 765 (8 September 1942).

150. Ibid., 888 (8 January 1944), 928 (10 June 1944), 943 (8 August 1944).

151. Ibid., 944 (3 September 1944), 958 (27 October 1944).

152. Herbert, *Hitler's Foreign Workers*, 359–64.

153. Ibid., 329 (quote) and 326–45.

154. Ibid., 326–8.

155. Ibid., 366–9; Fritz Theilen, *Edelweisspiraten* (Frankfurt am Main, 1984); Bernd-A. Rusinek, *Gesellschaft in der Katastrophe: Terror, Illegalität, Widerstand – Köln 1944/45* (Essen, 1989).

156. Herbert, *Hitler's Foreign Workers*, 369–71.

157. Frieser, 'Die Schlacht', 200–208.

158. Quoted in Merridale, *Ivan's War*, 260.

159. Ibid., 261.

160. Ibid., 261–2.

161. Nicholas, *The Rape of Europa*, 361–7.

162. Merridale, *Ivan's War*, 277–82.

163. Ibid., 267–9.

164. Atina Grossmann, 'A Question of Silence: The Rape of German Women by Occupation Soldiers', *October*, 72 (1995), 43–63, at 51.

165. Merridale, *Ivan's War*, 270.

166. Ibid., 267–8.

167. (Anon.), *A Woman in Berlin: Diary 20 April 1945 to 22 June 1945* (Oxford, 2006 [1955]), 173. The author was the journalist Masta Hillers (Grossmann, 'A Question of Silence', 54).

168. Ibid.

169. Quoted in Antony Beevor, *Berlin: The Downfall 1945* (London, 2002), 52.

170. Ibid., 46–55, 88; Heinrich Schwendemann, ' "Deutsche Menschen vor der Vernichtung durch den Bolschewismus zu retten": Das Programm der Regierung Dönitz und der Beginn einer Legendenbildung', in Bernd-A. Rusinek (ed.), *Kriegsende 1945: Verbrechen, Katastrophen, Befreiungen in nationaler und internationaler Perspektive* (Göttingen, 2004), 9–33.

171. Walb, *Ich, die Alte*, 313 (26 March 1945).

172. Kershaw, *The 'Hitler Myth'*, 200–225.

173. Boberach (ed.), *Meldungen*, XVII. 6,732–3.

174. Ibid., XVII. 6,733–4.

175. Klemperer, *To the Bitter End*, 443 (22 April 1945).

176. Ibid., 444 (22 April 1945).

177. Ibid., 453 (4 May 1945).

178. Ibid., 453 (5 May 1945).

179. Ibid., 419–27 (26 March–15 April 1945), quote on 419.

180. Walb, *Ich, die Alte*, 333 (23 April 1945).

181. Speer, *Inside the Third Reich*, 575–7.

182. Quoted in Noakes (ed.), *Nazism*, IV. 659–60; see also Kershaw, *Hitler*, II. 784–6.

183. Speer, *Inside the Third Reich*, 541–601; Kershaw, *Hitler*, II. 784.

184. Speer, *Inside the Third Reich*, 604.

185. Ibid., 610–18; Noakes (ed.), *Nazism*, IV. 659–61. For a critical discussion of Speer's actions in the final phase of the Third Reich, see Rolf-Dieter Müller, 'Der Zusammenbruch des Wirtschaftslebens und die Anfänge des Wiederaufbaus', in *DRZW* X/II, 55–378, at 74–106.

186. Kershaw, *Hitler*, II. 768–75, 782.

187. Redlich, *Hitler*, 207–9, 223–54.

188. Speer, *Inside the Third Reich*, 629.

189. Ibid.

190. Ibid., 631; Redlich, *Hitler*, 227.

191. Atmospheric account of Hitler's routine in Kershaw, *Hitler* II. 775–7.

192. Ibid., 780–81.

193. Ibid., 785–91.

194. Maschmann, *Account Rendered*, 146.

195. Ibid., 157.

196. Ibid., 163.

197. Ibid., 149.

198. Speer, *Inside the Third Reich*, 619.

199. Noakes (ed.), *Nazism*, IV. 666.

200. Ibid.

201. Kershaw, *Hitler*, II. 803–5.

202. Sereny, *Albert Speer*, 530–33; Speer, *Inside the Third Reich*, 635–47.

203. Duggan, *The Force of Destiny*, 529–32.

204. Kershaw, *Hitler*, II. 807–19.

205. Hürter (ed.), *Ein deutscher General*, 16.

206. Kershaw, *Hitler*, II. 802–19.

207. Ibid., 820–31, and 1,037–8 n. 156. See also the classic account by Hugh R. Trevor-

Roper, *The Last Days of Hitler* (London, 1962 [1947]), still well worth reading; detailed sifting of the evidence in Anton Joachimsthaler, *Hitlers End: Legenden und Dokumente* (Augsburg, 1999 [1994]).

208. Domarus (ed.), *Hitler*, IV. 2,236; Werner Maser (ed.), *Hitlers Briefe und Notizen: Sein Weltbild in handschriftlichen Dokumenten* (Düsseldorf, 1973), 326–66.

209. Kershaw, *Hitler*, 824.

210. Quoted in Christian Goeschel, 'Suicide at the End of the Third Reich', *Journal of Contemporary History*, 41 (2006), 153–73, at 167.

211. Reuth, *Goebbels*, 613–14; Trevor-Roper, *The Last Days*, 241–7.

212. Kershaw, *Hitler*, II. 831–3, 1,039 n. 15. The skeletons of both men were discovered during building work in 1972 and identified by their dental records.

213. Richard Overy, *Interrogations: The Nazi Elite in Allied Hands, 1945* (London, 2001), 145–6, 205.

214. Ibid., 165–8.

215. Höhne, *The Order of the Death's Head*, 534–6.

216. Neufeld, *The Rocket and the Reich*, 265.

217. Steur, *Theodor Dannecker*, 156–60, pointing out that she would hardly have done this had her husband not killed himself. Rumours that he survived were thus unfounded.

218. Burleigh, *Death*, 273, 351–84.

219. Goeschel, 'Suicide'; also idem, 'Suicide in Weimar and Nazi Germany', 196–200; Richard Bessel, *Nazism and War* (London, 2004), 154.

220. Höss, *Commandant of Auschwitz*, 193–4.

221. Maschmann, *Account Rendered*, 163.

222. Ibid., 164.

223. Sereny, *Albert Speer*, 543–4.

224. Boberach (ed.), *Meldungen*, XVII. 6,737.

225. Goeschel, 'Suicide in Weimar and Nazi Germany', 209–13.

226. Quoted in Bessel, *Nazism and War*, 155.

227. Damian van Melis, *Entnazifizierung in Mecklenburg-Vorpommern: Herrschaft und Verwaltung 1945–1948* (Munich, 1999), 23–4; Bessel, *Nazism and War*, 155; Naimark, *Fires of Hatred*, 117.

228. Breloer (ed.), *Geheime Welten*, 235.

229. Wirrer (ed.), *Ich glaube an den Führer*, 324 (Inge to Alfred, 4 August 1945). Breloer (ed.), *Geheime Welten*, 238 (22 April 1945) and 240 (3 June 1945).

230. Breloer (ed.), *Geheime Welten*, 44 (5 May 1945).

231. Kershaw, *Hitler*, II. 831–3.

232. Breloer (ed.), *Geheime Welten*, 123–4 (1 May 1945).

233. Walb, *Ich, die Alte*, 338, 344–5 (2 and 8 May 1945).

234. Breloer (ed.), *Geheime Welten*, 141.

235. Ibid., 163–5 (29 April 1945).

236. Solmitz, *Tagebuch*, 1,022 (30 April 1945), 1,031 (5 May 1945), 1,037 (8 May 1945).

237. Kershaw, *Hitler*, II. 822–3, 835–6; detailed account of the surrender of German forces in various parts of Europe in Klaus-Jürgen Müller and Gerd Ueberschär, *Kriegsende 1945: Die Zerstörung des deutschen Reiches* (Frankfurt am Main, 1994); see also Jörg Hillmann and John Zimmermann, *Kriegsende 1945 in Deutschland* (Munich, 2002) and Marlis Steinert, *Capitulation: A Story of the Dönitz Regime* (London, 1969).

238. Perry Biddiscombe, *Werwolf! The History of the National Socialist Guerilla Movement 1944–1946* (Cardiff, 1996), 38–9.

239. Klaus Tenfelde, 'Proletarische Provinz: Radikalisierung und Widerstand in Penzberg/ Oberbayern 1900 bis 1945', in Broszat *et al.* (eds.), *Bayern*, IV. 1–382.

240. Robert G. Moeller, *War Stories: The Search for a Usable Past in the Federal Republic of Germany* (Berkeley, Calif., 2001), 3, 6, 24, 43; Norbert Frei, *Adenauer's Germany and the Nazi Past: The Politics of Amnesty and Integration* (New York, 2002 [1997]), 303–12.

241. See Telford Taylor, *The Anatomy of the Nuremberg Trials* (London, 1993) and Overy, *Interrogations*.

242. Sereny, *Albert Speer*, 702–21; Matthias Schmidt, *Albert Speer: Das Ende eines Mythos: Speers wahre Rolle im Dritten Reich* (Bern, 1982); also Albert Speer, *Spandau: The Secret Diaries* (London, 1976 [1975]).

243. Höss, *Commandant of Auschwitz*, 195–201.

244. Steinbacher, *Auschwitz*, 137–9.

245. Ibid., 139–45.

246. Höhne, *The Order of the Death's Head*, 535–6.

247. Klee *et al.* (eds.), *'Those Were the Days'*, 297–9.

248. Burleigh, *Death*, 269–80; Schmidt, *Karl Brandt*, 351–84.

249. Kater, *Doctors under Hitler*, 2–3; Steven P. Remy, *The Heidelberg Myth: The Nazification and Denazification of a German University* (Cambridge, Mass., 2002), 198–203.

250. Horace W. Stunkard, 'Erich Martini (1880–1960)', *Journal of Parasitology*, 47 (1961), 909–10.

251. Lifton, *The Nazi Doctors*, 380–83.

252. Klee, *Auschwitz*, 488–91.

253. Sereny, *Into that Darkness*, 13, 16, 261–77, 301–7, 321–2, 339–66.

254. Cesarani, *Eichmann*, 200–323.

255. Steinbacher, *Auschwitz*, 145–52.

256. Konrad H. Jarausch, *After Hitler: Recivilizing Germans, 1945–1995* (New York, 2006), 54. The figure for the 'incriminated' does not include the British Zone. See also Clemens Vollnhals, *Entnazifizierung: Politische Säuberung und Rehabilitierung in den vier Besatzungszonen 1945–1949* (Munich, 1991); Lutz Niethammer, *Die Mitläuferfabrik: Die Entnazifizierung am Beispiel Bayerns* (Berlin, 1992).

257. Jarausch, *After Hitler*, 271–81. For Best, see Herbert, *Best*, 403–76, and more generally Norbert Frei (ed.), *Karrieren im Zwielicht: Hitlers Eliten nach 1945* (Frankfurt am Main, 2001). For problems of social adjustment immediately after the war, see Jörg Echternkamp, 'Im Schlagschatten des Krieges: Von den Folgen militärischer Herrschaft in der frühen Nachkriegszeit', in *DRZW* X/II. 657–97.

258. Hürter (ed.), *Ein deutscher General*, 16.

259. Bock, *Zwischen Pflicht und Verweigerung*, 11–25.

260. Hosenfeld, *'Ich versuche'*, 111–46.

261. Breloer (ed.), *Geheime Welten*, 44.

262. Ibid., 45.

263. Ibid., 273.

264. Maschmann, *Account Rendered*, 168–223 (quotation on page 190).

265. Steven Bach, *Leni – The Life and Work of Leni Riefenstahl* (New York, 2007), 252–92; Welch, *Propaganda and the German Cinema*, 125–34, 263, 307; Emil Jannings, *Theater, Film – Das Leben und Ich* (Munich, 1989 [1951]).

266. Kater, *Composers*, 3–30, 211–63.

267. Shirakawa, *The Devil's Music Master*, 364.

268. Ibid. More generally, see Toby Thacker, *Music after Hitler, 1945–1955* (London, 2007), 39–74.

269. Petropoulos, *The Faustian Bargain*, 239–53.

270. Neufeld, *The Rocket and the Reich*, 267–75.

271. Remy, *The Heidelberg Myth*, 54, 204–5.

272. Klukowski, *Diary*, x–xi, xv–xx.

273. Martin Chalmers, 'Introduction', in Victor Klemperer, *The Lesser Evil: The Diaries of Victor Klemperer 1945–59* (London, 2003 [1999]), vii–xvii.

274. Klemperer, *The Lesser Evil*, 359 (8 July 1951).

275. Ibid., 621–4.

276. Cited in Evans, *The Coming of the Third Reich*, 312–13; information from Staatsarchiv der Freien- und Hansestadt Hamburg.

277. Eric A. Johnson and Karl-Heinz Reuband, *What We Knew: Terror, Mass Murder, and Everyday Life in Nazi Germany: An Oral History* (New York, 2005), 337–44.

278. Bill Niven, *Facing the Nazi Past: United Germany and the Legacy of the Third Reich* (London, 2002), 233–41; Peter Reichel, *Politik mit der Erinnerung: Gedächtnisorte im Streit um die nationalsozialistische Vergangenheit* (Frankfurt am Main, 1999 [1995]).

279. Bullock, *Hitler*, 808.

Bibliography

Abzug, Robert H., *Inside the Vicious Heart: Americans and the Liberation of Nazi Concentration Camps* (New York, 1985).

Adam, Peter, *The Arts of the Third Reich* (London, 1992).

Adelson, Alan, and Lapides, Robert (eds.), *Lódź Ghetto: Inside a Community under Siege* (New York, 1989).

Adler, Hans Georg, *Der verwaltete Mensch: Studien zur Deportation der Juden aus Deutschland* (Tübingen, 1974).

Adler, Jacques, *The Jews of Paris and the Final Solution: Communal Responses and Internal Conflicts, 1940–1944* (New York, 1987).

Ainsztein, Reuben, *Revolte gegen die Vernichtung: Der Aufstand im Warschauer Ghetto* (Berlin, 1993).

Albrecht, Gerd (ed.), *Nationalsozialistische Filmpolitik: Ein Soziologische Untersuchung über die Spielfilme des dritten Reiches* (Stuttgart, 1969).

——, *Film im Dritten Reich: Eine Dokumentation* (Karlsruhe, 1979).

Alcuin (pseud.), *I Saw Poland Suffer, by a Polish Doctor Who Held an Official Position in Warsaw under German Occupation* (London, 1941).

Aldor, Francis, *Germany's 'Death Space': The Polish Tragedy* (London, 1940).

Allen, Michael Thad, *The Business of Genocide: The SS, Slave Labor, and the Concentration Camps* (Chapel Hill, N.C., 2002).

——, 'Not Just a "Dating Game": Origins of the Holocaust at Auschwitz in the Light of Witness Testimony', *German History*, 25 (2007), 162–91.

Altschuler, Mordechai, *Soviet Jewry on the Eve of the Holocaust: A Social and Demographic Profile* (Jerusalem, 1998).

Aly, Götz, 'Der Mord an behinderten Hamburger Kindern zwischen 1939 und 1945', in Angelika Ebbinghaus *et al.* (eds.), *Heilen und Vernichten im Mustergau Hamburg: Bevölkerungs- und Gesundheitspolitik im Dritten Reich* (Hamburg, 1984), 147–55.

——, 'Medicine against the Useless', in idem *et al.*, *Cleansing the Fatherland*, 22–98.

——, 'The Posen Diaries of the Anatomist Hermann Voss', in idem *et al.*, *Cleansing the Fatherland*.

——, *Macht – Geist – Wahn: Kontinuitäten deutschen Denkens* (Berlin, 1997).

——, *'Final Solution': Nazi Population Policy and the Murder of the European Jews* (London, 1999 [1995]).

——, 'Die Deportation der Juden von Rhodos nach Auschwitz', *Mittelweg*, 36 (2003), 79–88.

——, *Hitler's Beneficiaries: Plunder, Racial War, and the Nazi Welfare State* (New York, 2007 [2005]).

——, and Heim, Susanne, *Architects of Annihilation: Auschwitz and the Logic of Destruction* (Princeton, N.J., 2002).

——, *et al.*, *Cleansing the Fatherland: Nazi Medicine and Racial Hygiene* (Baltimore, Md., 1994).

Ancel, Jean, 'The Romanian Way of Solving the "Jewish Problem" in Bessarabia and Bukovina: June–July 1941', *Yad Vashem Studies*, 9 (1988), 187–232.

——, 'The "Christian" regimes of Romania and the Jews, 1940–1942', *Holocaust and Genocide Studies*, 7 (1993), 14–29.

——, *Transnistria* (3 vols., Bucharest, 1998).

Angermund, Ralph, *Deutsche Richterschaft 1919–1945* (Frankfurt am Main, 1990).

Angrick, Andrej, 'The Escalation of German-Rumanian Anti-Jewish Policy after the Attack on the Soviet Union', *Yad Vashem Studies*, 26 (1998), 203–38.

——, 'Zur Rolle der Militärverwaltung bei der Ermordung der sowjetischen Juden', in Quinkert (ed.), *'Wir sind die Herren dieses Landes'*, 104–23.

——, *Besatzungspolitik und Massenmord: Die Einsatzgruppe D in der südlichen Sowjetunion 1941–1943* (Hamburg, 2003).

——, and Pohl, Dieter, *Einsatzgruppen C and D in the Invasion of the Soviet Union, 1941–1942* (London, 1999).

(Anon.), *The German New Order in Poland* (London, 1942).

——, *A Woman in Berlin: Diary 20 April 1945 to 22 June 1945* (Oxford, 2006 [1955]).

Arad, Yitzhak, *Ghetto in Flames: The Struggle and Destruction of the Jews in Vilna in the Holocaust* (Jerusalem, 1980).

——, *Belzec, Sobibor, Treblinka: The Operation Reinhard Death Camps* (Bloomington, Ind., 1999 [1987]).

——, *et al.* (eds.), *The Einsatzgruppen Reports: Selections from the Dispatches of the Nazi Death Squads' Campaign against the Jews, July 1941–January 1943* (New York, 1989).

Arendt, Hannah, *Eichmann in Jerusalem* (New York, 1963).

Arntz, Hans-Dieter, *Ordensburg Vogelsang 1934–1945: Erziehung zur politischen Führung im Dritten Reich* (Eulskirchen, 1986).

August, Jochen (ed.), *'Sonderaktion Krakau' Die Verhaftung der Krakauer Wissenschaftler am 6. November 1939* (Hamburg, 1997).

Auswärtiges Amt (ed.), *Die polnischen Greueltaten an den Volksdeutschen in Polen* (Berlin, 1940).

Avni, Haim, *Spain, the Jews, and Franco* (Philadelphia, 1982).

Axworthy, Mark, *et al.*, *Third Axis, Fourth Ally: Romanian Armed Forces in the European War, 1941–1945* (London, 1995).

Baade, Fritz, *et al.* (eds.), *'Unsere Ehre heisst Treue': Kriegstagebuch des Kommandostabes Reichsführer-SS, Tätigkeitsberichte der 1. und 2. 33-Infanterie-Brigade, der 1. SS-Kav. Brigade und von Sonderkommandos der SS* (Vienna, 1965).

Baader, Gerhard, 'Heilen und Vernichten: Die Mentalität der NS-Ärzte', in Ebbinghaus and Dörner (eds.), *Vernichten und Heilen*, 275–94.

Bach, Dieter, and Lesiuk, Wieslaw, *Ich sah in das Gesicht eines Menschen: Deutsch-polnische Begegnungen vor und nach 1945* (Wuppertal, 1995).

Bach, Steven, *Leni – The Life and Work of Leni Riefenstahl* (New York, 2007).

Bähr, Johannes, *Die Dresdner Bank in der Wirtschaft des Dritten Reichs* (Munich, 2006).

Baird, Jay W., *The Mythical World of Nazi War Propaganda, 1939–1945* (Minneapolis, Minn., 1974).

Bajohr, Frank, and Pohl, Dieter, *Der Holocaust als offenes Geheinnis: Die Deutschen, die NS-Führung und die Alliierten* (Munich, 2006).

Banach, Jens, *Heydrichs Elite: Das Führerkorps der Sicherheitspolizei und des SD, 1936–1945* (Paderborn, 1998).

Bankier, David, *The Germans and the Final Solution: Public Opinion under Nazism* (Oxford, 1992).

Baranowski, Shelley, *Strength Through Joy: Consumerism and Mass Tourism in the Third Reich* (Cambridge, 2004).

Barber, John, and Harrison, Mark, *The Soviet Home Front, 1941–1945: A Social and Economic History of the USSR in World War II* (London, 1991).

Barbian, Jan-Pieter, *Literaturpolitik im 'Dritten Reich': Institutionen, Kompetenzen, Betätigungsfelder* (Munich, 1995 [1993]).

Barkai, Avraham, 'Between East and West: Jews from Germany in the Lodz Ghetto', in Marrus (ed.), *The Nazi Holocaust*, 378–439.

Bartoszewski, Wladyslaw T., 'Polen und Juden in der deutschen Besatzungszeit', in Klessmann (ed.), *September 1939*, 139–55.

——, 'Foreword', in Salomon W. Slowes, *The Road to Katyn: A Soldier's Story* (Oxford, 1992), vii–xxxii.

Bartov, Omer, *The Eastern Front 1941–1945: German Troops and the Barbarization of Warfare* (London, 1985).

——, *Hitler's Army: Soldiers, Nazis, and War in the Third Reich* (New York, 1991).

Bar-Zohar, Michael, *Beyond Hitler's Grasp: The Heroic Rescue of Bulgaria's Jews* (Holbrook, Mass., 1998).

Bastian, Till, *Homosexuelle im Dritten Reich: Geschichte einer Verfolgung* (Munich, 2000).

Bauer, Yehuda, 'Anmerkungen zum "Auschwitz-Bericht" von Rudolf Vrba', *VfZ* 45 (1997), 297–307.

Baumgart, Winfried, 'Zur Ansprache Hitlers vor den Führern der Wehrmacht am 22. August 1939', *VfZ* 16 (1968), 120–49.

——, and Boehm, Hermann, 'Zur Ansprache Hitlers vor den Führern der Wehrmacht am 22. August 1939', *VfZ* 19 (1971), 294–304.

Beck, Birgit, *Wehrmacht und sexuelle Gewalt: Sexualverbrechen vor deutschen Militärgerichten 1939–1945* (Paderborn, 2004).

Becker, Peter W., 'Fritz Sauckel: Plenipotentiary for the Mobilisation of Labour', in Smelser and Zitelman (eds.), *The Nazi Elite*, 194–201.

Beer, Matthias, 'Die Entwicklung der Gaswagen beim Mord an den Juden', *VfZ* 35 (1987), 403–17.

Beer, Wilfried, *Kriegsalltag an der Heimatfront: Alliierter Luftkrieg und deutsche Gegenmassnahmen zur Abwehr und Schadenbegrenzung, dargestellt für den Raum Münster* (Bremen, 1990).

Beevor, Antony, *Stalingrad* (London, 1998).

——, *Berlin: The Downfall 1945* (London, 2002).

Behnken, Klaus (ed.), *Deutschland-Berichte der Sozialdemokratischen Partei Deutschlands (Sopade) 1934–1940* (7 vols., Frankfurt am Main, 1980).

Bellamy, Chris, *Absolute War: Soviet Russia in the Second World War: A Modern History* (London, 2007).

Bellon, Bernard, *Mercedes in Peace and War: German Automobile Workers, 1903–1945* (New York, 1990).

Below, Nicolaus von, *Als Hitlers Adjutant 1937–1945* (Frankfurt am Main, 1980).

Benz, Wolfgang, 'Judenvernichtung aus Notwehr? Die Legenden um Theodore N. Kaufman', *VfZ* 29 (1981), 615–30.

—— (ed.), *Die Juden in Deutschland 1933–1945: Leben unter nationalsozialistischer Herrschaft* (Munich, 1988).

—— (ed.), *Dimension des Völkermords: Die Zahl der jüdischen Opfer des Nationalsozialismus* (Munich, 1991).

——, and Distel, Barbara (eds.), *Der Ort des Terrors: Geschichte der nationalsozialistischen Konzentrationslager* (6 vols., Munich, 2005–7).

——, and Neiss, Marion (eds.), *Judenmord in Litauen: Studien und Dokumente* (Berlin, 1999).

Berenstein, Tatiana, *et al.* (eds.), *Faschismus – Getto – Massenmord: Dokumentation über Ausrottung und Widerstand der Juden in Polen während des Zweiten Weltkrieges* (Berlin, 1960).

Bergander, Götz, *Dresden im Luftkrieg: Vorgeschichte, Zerstörung, Folgen* (Würzburg, 1998).

Bergmeier, Horst J. P., and Lotz, Rainer E., *Hitler's Airwaves: The Inside Story of Nazi Radio Broadcasting and Propaganda Swing* (London, 1997).

Berkhoff, Karel C., *Harvest of Despair: Life and Death in Ukraine under Nazi Rule* (Cambridge, Mass., 2004).

Berndt, Günter, and Strecker, Reinhard (eds.), *Polen – ein Schauermärchen oder Gehirnwäsche für Generationen: Geschichtsschreibung und Schulbücher: Beiträge zum Polenbild der Deutschen* (Reinbek, 1971).

Bernstein, Jeremy (ed.), *Hitler's Uranium Club: The Secret Recordings at Farm Hall* (New York, 2001).

Bessel, Richard, *Nazism and War* (London, 2004).

Beyerchen, Alan D., *Scientists under Hitler: Politics and the Physics Community in the Third Reich* (London, 1977).

Biddiscombe, Perry, *Werwolf! The History of the National Socialist Guerilla Movement 1944–1946* (Cardiff, 1996).

Birnbaum, Pierre, *Anti-semitism in France: A Political History from Léon Blum to the Present* (Oxford, 1992 [1988]).

Blank, Ralf, 'Kriegsalltag und Luftkrieg an der "Heimatfront"', *DRZW* IX/I. 357–468.

Blatman, Daniel, 'Die Todesmärsche – Entscheidungsträger, Mörder und Opfer', in Herbert *et al.* (eds.), *Die nationalsozialistischen Konzentrationslager*, II. 1,063–92.

——, 'The Death Marches, January–May 1945: Who Was Responsible for What?', *Yad Vashem Studies*, 28 (2000), 155–201.

——, 'Rückzug, Evakuierung und Todesmärsche 1944–1945', in Benz and Distel (eds.), *Der Ort des Terrors*, I. 296–312.

Bloch, Michael, *Operation Willi: The Plot to Kidnap the Duke of Windsor, July 1940* (London, 1984).

Blume, Helmut, *Zum Kaukasus 1941–1942: Aus Tagebuch und Briefen eines jungen Artilleristen* (Tübingen, 1993).

Blumenthal, Nachman, 'A Martyr or Hero? Reflections on the Diary of Adam Czerniakow', *Yad Vashem Studies*, 7 (1968), 165–71.

Boberach, Heinz (ed.), *Richterbriefe: Dokumente zur Beeinflussung der deutschen Rechtsprechung 1942–1944* (Boppard, 1975).

—— (ed.), *Meldungen aus dem Reich: Die geheimen Lageberichte des Sicherheitsdienstes der SS 1938–1945* (17 vols., Herrsching, 1984).

——, 'Stimmungsumschwung in der deutschen Bevölkerung', in Wette and Ueberschär (eds.), *Stalingrad*, 61–6.

Bock, Fedor von, *Generalfeldmarschall Fedor von Bock: Zwischen Pflicht und Verweigerung: Das Kriegstagebuch* (ed. Klaus Gerbet, Munich, 1995).

Boelcke, Willi A. (ed.), *'Wollt Ihr den totalen Krieg?' Die geheimen Goebbels-Konferenzen 1939–1943* (Munich, 1969 [1967]), 414.

Böhler, Jochen, *Auftakt zum Vernichtungskrieg: Die Wehrmacht in Polen 1939* (Frankfurt am Main, 2006).

Böhme, Kurt W., *Die deutschen Kriegsgefangenen in sowjetischer Hand: Eine Bilanz* (Munich, 1966).

Boll, Bernd, 'Zloczów, Juli 1941: Die Wehrmacht und der Beginn des Holocaust in Galizien', *Zeitschrift für Geschichtswissenschaft* 50 (2002), 899–917.

——, and Safrian, Hans, 'Auf dem Weg nach Stalingrad: Die 6. Armee 1941/42', in Heer and Naumann (eds.), *Vernichtungskrieg*, 260–96.

Boog, Horst, 'The Anglo-American Strategic Air War over Europe and German Air Defence', in *GSWW* VI. 469–628.

——, 'The Strategic Air War in Europe and Air Defence of the Reich', in *GSWW* VII. 9–458.

——, 'Die strategische Bomberoffensive der Alliierten gegen Deutschland und die Reichsluftverteidigung in der Schlussphase des Krieges', in *DRZW* X/I, 777–884.

Borodziej, Wlodzimierz, *Terror und Politik: Die deutsche Polizei und die polnische Widerstandsbewegung im Generalgouvernement 1939–1944* (Mainz, 1999).

Bosworth, Richard, *Mussolini's Italy: Life under the Dictatorship 1915–1945* (London, 2005).

Botz, Gerhard, *Wohnungspolitik und Judendeportation in Wien 1938 bis 1945: Zur Funktion des Antisemitismus als Ersatz nationalsozialistischer Sozialpolitik* (Vienna, 1975).

Braham, Randolph L., *Eichmann and the Destruction of Hungarian Jewry* (New York, 1961).

——, 'The Role of the Jewish Council in Hungary: A Tentative Assessment', *Yad Vashem Studies*, 10 (1974), 69–109.

——, *The Politics of Genocide: The Holocaust in Hungary* (2 vols., New York, 1981).

—— (ed.), *The Tragedy of Romanian Jewry* (New York, 1994).

—— (ed.), *The Destruction of Romanian and Ukrainian Jews during the Antonescu Era* (New York, 1997).

Brandes, Detlev, *Die Tschechen unter deutschem Protektorat*, I: *Besatzungspolitik, Kollaboration und Widerstand im Protektorat Böhmen und Mähren bis Heydrichs Tod, 1939–1942* (Munich, 1969).

Breitman, Richard, *The Architect of Genocide: Himmler and the Final Solution* (London, 1991).

Breloer, Heinrich (ed.), *Geheime Welten: Deutsche Tagebücher zus den Jahren 1939 bis 1947* (Cologne, 1999 [1984]).

Broszat, Martin, 'Zur Perversion der Strafjustiz im Dritten Reich', *VfZ* 6 (1958), 390–443.

——, *Nationalsozialistische Polenpolitik* (Frankfurt am Main, 1965).

——, 'The Concentration Camps 1933–1945', in Helmut Krausnick et al., *Anatomy of the SS State* (London, 1968), 397–504.

——, et al. (eds.), *Bayern in der NS-Zeit* (6 vols., Munich, 1977–83).

Browning, Christopher R., *The Path to Genocide: Essays on Launching the Final Solution* (Cambridge, 1992).

——, *Ordinary Men: Reserve Police Battalion 101 and the Final Solution in Poland* (London, 1998 [1992]).

——, *Nazi Policy, Jewish Workers, German Killers* (Cambridge, 2000).

——, 'The Decision-Making Process', in Dan Stone (ed.), *The Historiography of the Holocaust* (London, 2004), 173–96.

——, *The Origins of the Final Solution: The Evolution of Nazi Jewish Policy, September 1939–March 1942* (Lincoln, Nebr., 2004).

Bruhn, Mike, and Böttner, Heike, *Die Jenaer Studenten unter nationalsozialistischer Herrschaft 1933–1945* (Erfurt, 2001).

Brunckhorst, Almut, *Die Berliner Widerstandsorganisation um Arvid Harnack und Harro Schluze-Boysen ('Rote Kapelle'): Kundschafter im Auftrag Moskaus oder integraler Bestandteil des deutschen Widerstandes gegen den Nationalsozialismus? Ein Testfall für die deutsche Historiographie* (Hamburg, 1998).

Brysac, Shareen Blair, *Resisting Hitler: Mildred Harnack and the Red Orchestra: The Life and Death of an American Woman in Nazi Germany* (New York, 2000).

Buchbender, Ortwin, *Das tönende Erz: Deutsche Propaganda gegen die Rote Armee im Zweiten Weltkrieg* (Stuttgart, 1978).

Buchheim, Christoph, 'Die vielen Rechenfehler in der Abrechnung Götz Alys mit den Deutschen unter dem NS-Regime', *Sozial Geschichte*, 20 (2005), 67–76.

Budrass, Lutz, *Flugzeugindustrie und Luftrüstung in Deutschland* (Düsseldorf, 1998).

——, and Grieger, Manfred, 'Die Moral der Effizienz: Die Beschäftigung von KZ-Häftlingen am Beispiel des Volkswagenwerks und der Henschel Flugzeug-Werke', *Jahrbuch für Wirtschaftsgeschichte* (1993), 89–136.

Bullock, Alan, *Hitler: A Study in Tyranny* (London, 1952).

Burckhardt, Carl J., *Meine Danziger Mission 1937–1939* (Munich, 1960).

Burkhard, Benedikt, and Valet, Friederike (eds.), *'Abends wein wir essen, fehlt uns immer einer': Kinder schreiben and die Väter, 1939–1945* (Heidelberg, 2000).

Burleigh, Michael, *Germany Turns Eastwards: A Study of Ostforschung in the Third Reich* (Cambridge, 1988).

——, *Death and Deliverance: 'Euthanasia' in Germany, c.1900–1945* (Cambridge, 1994).

——, *Sacred Causes: Religion and Politics from the European Dictators to Al Qaeda* (London, 2006), 214–83.

Burrin, Philippe, *France under the Germans: Collaboration and Compromise* (New York, 1996).

Büttner, Ursula, ' "Gomorrha" und die Folgen: Der Bombenkrieg', in Forschungsstelle für Zeitgeschichte in Hamburg (ed.), *Hamburg*, 613–32.

Cajani, Luigi, 'Die italienischen Militär-Internierten im nationalsozialistischen Deutschland', in Herbert (ed.), *Europa und der 'Reichseinsatz'*, 295–316.

Callil, Carmen, *Bad Faith: A Forgotten History of Family and Fatherland* (London, 2007).

Calvocoressi, Peter, and Wint, Guy, *Total War: Causes and Courses of the Second World War* (Harmondsworth, 1974 [1972]).

Carroll, Berenice A., *Design for Total War: Arms and Economics in the Third Reich* (The Hague, 1968).

Carroll, David, *French Literary Fascism: Nationalism, Anti-Semitism, and the Ideology of Culture* (Princeton, N.J., 1995).

Cesarani, David, *Eichmann: His Life and Crimes* (London, 2004).

—— (ed.), *Holocaust: Critical Concepts in Historical Studies* (6 vols., London, 2004).

Chalmers, Martin, 'Introduction', in Klemperer, *The Lesser Evil*, vii–xvi.

Charmley, John, *Churchill: The End of Glory: A Political Biography* (London, 1993).

Chary, Frederick B., *The Bulgarian Jews and the Final Solution, 1940–1944* (Pittsburgh, Pa., 1972).

Chiari, Bernhard, *Alltag hinter der Front: Besatzung, Kollaboration und Widerstand in Weissrussland 1941–1944* (Düsseldorf, 1998).

Chroust, Peter (ed.), *Friedrich Mennecke: Innenansichten eines medizinischen Täters im Nationalsozialismus: Eine Edition seiner Briefe 1935–1947* (Hamburg, 1988).

Cienciala, Anna M., *et al.*, *Katyn: A Crime without Punishment* (London, 2006).

Clark, Martin, *Modern Italy 1871–1982* (Harlow, 1984).

Clarke, Peter, *Hope and Glory: Britain 1900–1990* (London, 1996).

Cocks, Geoffrey, *Psychotherapy in the Third Reich: The Göring Institute* (New Brunswick, N.J., 1997 [1985]).

Cohen, Asher, *Persécutions et sauvetages: Juifs et Français sous l'Occupation et sous Vichy* (Paris, 1993).

——, *et al.* (eds.), *The Shoah and the War* (New York, 1992).

Cohen, Richard I., *The Burden of Conscience: French Jewish Leadership during the Holocaust* (Bloomington, Ind., 1987).

Cohen, William B., and Svensson, Jörgen, 'Finland and the Holocaust', *Holocaust and Genocide Studies*, 9 (1995), 70–92.

Cohn, Norman, *Warrant for Genocide: The Myth of the Jewish World-Conspiracy and the Protocols of the Elders of Zion* (London, 1967).

Cointet, Michèle, *L'Église sous Vichy, 1940–1945: La répentance en question* (Paris, 1998).

Cole, Tim, *Holocaust City: The Making of a Jewish Ghetto* (London, 2003).

Combs, William L., *The Voice of the SS: A History of the SS Journal 'Das Schwarze Korps'* (New York, 1986).

Connolly, Kate, 'Letter Proves Speer Knew of Holocaust Plan', *Guardian*, 13 March 2007.

Conway, John S., *The Nazi Persecution of the Churches 1933–1945* (London, 1968).

Conway, Martin, *Collaboration in Belgium: Léon Degrelle and the Rexist Movement 1940–1944* (London, 1993).

Coppi, Hans, *et al.* (eds.), *Die Rote Kapelle im Widerstand gegen den Nationalsozialismus* (Berlin, 1994).

Cornelissen, Christoph, *Gerhard Ritter: Geschichtswissenschaft und Politik im 20. Jahrhundert* (Düsseldorf, 2001).

Corni, Gustavo, *Hitler's Ghettos: Voices from a Beleaguered Society 1939–1944* (London, 2002).

Cornwell, John, *Hitler's Pope: The Secret History of Pius XII* (London, 1999).

Crampton, Richard, *Bulgaria* (Oxford, 2007).

Crowe, David M., *Oskar Schindler: The Untold Account of His Life, Wartime Activities, and the True Story Behind The List* (Cambridge, Mass., 2004).

Culbert, David, 'The Impact of Anti-Semitic Film Propaganda on German Audiences: *Jew Süss* and *The Wandering Jew* (1940)', in Etlin (ed.), *Art*, 139–57.

Cyprian, Tadeusz, and Sawicki, Jerzy, *Nazi Rule in Poland 1939–1945* (Warsaw, 1961).

Czerniakow, Adam, *The Warsaw Diary of Adam Czerniakow: Prelude to Doom* (New York, 1979 [1968]).

Dabel, Gerhard (ed.), *KLV: Die erweiterte Kinder-Land-Verschickung* (Freiburg, 1981).

Dahm, Volker, 'Kulturelles und geistiges Leben', in Benz (ed.), *Die Juden*, 75–267.

Dallin, Alexander, *German Rule in Russia 1941–1945: A Study of Occupation Policies* (London, 1957).

——, *Odessa, 1941–1944: A Case Study of Soviet Territory under Foreign Rule* (Iaşi, 1998 [1957]).

Datner, Szymon, 'Crimes Committed by the Wehrmacht during the September Campaign and the Period of Military Government (1 Sept. 1939–25 Oct. 1939)', *Polish Western Affairs*, 3 (1962), 294–328.

——, *Crimes Committed by the Wehrmacht during the September Campaign and the Period of Military Government* (Posen, 1962).

Davies, Norman, *God's Playground: A History of Poland* (2 vols., Oxford, 1981).

——, *Rising '44: The Battle for Warsaw* (London, 2003).

——, and Polonsky, Antony (eds.), *Jews in Eastern Poland and the USSR, 1939–1946* (New York, 1991).

Dean, Martin, *Collaboration in the Holocaust: Crimes of the Local Police in Belorussia and the Ukraine, 1941–44* (New York, 2000).

Dear, Ian C. B. (ed.), *The Oxford Companion to World War II* (Oxford, 2005 [1995]).

——, 'Animals', in idem (ed.), *The Oxford Companion to World War II*, 28–9.

Decker, Natalija, 'Die Auswirkungen der faschistischen Okkupation auf das Gesundheitswesen Polens und den Gesundheitszustand des polnischen Volkes', in Thom and Caregorodcev (eds.), *Medizin unterm Hakenkreuz*, 401–16.

Dederichs, Mario R., *Heydrich: Das Gesicht des Bösen* (Munich, 2005).

Delacor, Regina M., 'From Potential Friends to Potential Enemies: The Internment of "Hostile Foreigners" in France at the Beginning of the Second World War', *Journal of Contemporary History*, 35 (2000), 361–8.

Deletant, Dennis, 'Ghetto Experience in Golta, Transnistria, 1942–1944', *Holocaust and Genocide Studies*, 18 (2004), 1–26.

——, *Hitler's Forgotten Ally: Ion Antonescu and His Regime, Romania 1940–44* (London, 2006).

Derry, Thomas K., 'Norway', in Stuart J. Woolf (ed.), *European Fascism* (London, 1968), 217–30.

Deschner, Günther, *Reinhard Heydrich – Statthalter der totalen Macht* (Munich, 1978).

——, 'Reinhard Heydrich: Security Technocrat', in Smelser and Zitelmann (eds.), *The Nazi Elite*, 85–97.

Diamond, Hanna, *Fleeing Hitler: France 1940* (Oxford, 2007).

Dietrich, Otto, *Auf den Strassen des Sieges: Erlebnisse mit dem Führer in Polen: Ein Gemeinschaftsbuch* (Munich, 1939).

Dlugoborski, Wlodimierz, 'Die deutsche Besatzungspolitik und die Veränderungen der sozialen Struktur Polens 1939–1945', in idem (ed.), *Zweiter Weltkrieg und sozialer Wandel: Achsenmächte und besetzte Länder* (Göttingen, 1981), 303–63.

——, 'Deutsche und sowjetische Herrschaftssysteme in Ostmitteleuropa im Vergleich', in Gerhard Otto and Johannes Houwink ten Cate (eds.), *Das organisierte Chaos: 'Ämterdarwinismus' und 'Gesinnungsethik': Determinanten nationalsozialistischer Besatzungsherrschaft* (Berlin, 1999), 93–121.

——, and Madajczyk, Czeslaw, 'Ausbeutungssysteme in den besetzten Gebieten Polens und der UdSSR', in Friedrich Forstmeier and Hans-Erich Volkmann (eds.), *Kriegswirtschaft und Rüstung 1939–1945* (Düsseldorf, 1977), 375–416.

Dobroszycki, Lucjan (ed.), *The Chronicle of the Lódź Ghetto 1941–1944* (New Haven, Conn., 1984).

Domarus, Max (ed.), *Hitler: Speeches and Proclamations 1932–1945: The Chronicle of a Dictatorship* (4 vols., London, 1990– [1962–63]).

Donaldson, Frances, *Edward VIII* (London, 1974).

Donner, Wolf, *Propaganda und Film im 'Dritten Reich'* (Berlin, 1995).

Dörner, Bernward, *Die Deutschen und der Holocaust: Was niemand wissen wollte, aber jeder wissen konnte* (Berlin, 2007).

Dressen, Willi, 'Konzentrationslager als Tötungs- und Hinrichtungsstätten für Oppositionelle, Behinderte, Kriegsgefangene', in Benz and Distel (eds.), *Der Ort des Terrors*, I. 230–41.

Drewniak, Boguslaw, 'Die deutsche Verwaltung und die rechtliche Stellung der Polen in den besetzten polnischen Gebieten 1939–1945', *Deutsch-Polnisches Jahrbuch* (1979–80), 151–70.

——, *Das Theater im NS-Staat: Szenarium deutscher Zeitgeschichte 1933–1945* (Düsseldorf, 1983).

——, *Der deutsche Film 1938–1945: Ein Gesamtüberblick* (Düsseldorf, 1987).

Droulia, Loukia, and Fleischer, Hagen (eds.), *Von Lidice bis Kalavryta: Widerstand und Besatzungsterror: Studien zur Repressalienpraxis im Zweiten Weltkrieg* (Berlin, 1999).

Duhnke, Horst, *Die KPD von 1933–1945* (Cologne, 1972).

Duggan, Christopher, *The Force of Destiny: A History of Italy since 1796* (London, 2007).

Dwork, Debórah, and van Pelt, Robert Jan, *Holocaust: A History* (London, 2002).

Ebbinghaus, Angelika, 'Zwei Welten: Die Opfer und die Täter der kriegschirurgischen Experimente', in Ebbinghaus and Dörner (eds.), *Vernichten und Heilen*, 219–40.

——, 'Fakten oder Fiktionen: Wie ist Götz Aly zu seinen weitreichenden Schlussfolgerungen gekommen?', *Sozial.Geschichte*, 20 (2005), 29–45.

——, and Dörner, Klaus (eds.), *Vernichten und Heilen: Der Nürnberger Ärzteprozess und seine Folgen* (Berlin, 2001).

——, and Roth, Karl Heinz, 'Kriegswunden: Die kriegschirurgischen Experimente in den Konzentrationslagern und ihre Hintergründe', in Ebbinghaus and Dörner (eds.), *Vernichten und Heilen*, 177–218.

Ebert, Jens (ed.), *Feldpostbriefe aus Stalingrad: November 1942 bis Januar 1943* (Munich, 2006 [2000]).

Echternkamp, Jörg (ed.), *Kriegsschauplatz Deutschland 1945: Leben in Angst – Hoffnung auf Frieden: Feldpost aus der Heimat und von der Front* (Paderborn, 2006).

Eckert, Rainer, *Vom 'Fall Marita' zur 'Wirtschaftlichen Sonderaktion': Die deutsche Besatzungspolitik in Griechenland vom 6. April 1941 bis zur Kriegswende im Februar/März 1943* (Frankfurt am Main, 1992).

Eiber, Ludwig, 'Das KZ-Aussenlager Blohm und Voss im Hamburger Hafen', in Kaienburg (ed.), *Konzentrationslager*, 227–38.

Einsiedel, Heinrich von, *The Shadow of Stalingrad: Being the Diary of a Temptation* (London, 1953).

Eisfeld, Rainer, *Mondsüchtig: Wernher von Braun und die Geburt der Raumfahrt aus den Geist der Barbarei* (Hamburg, 2000).

Eitel, Gerhard, 'Genozid auch an Polen? Kein Thema für einen "Historikerstreit"', *Zeitgeschichte*, 18 (1990), 22–39.

Elmshäuser, Konrad, and Lokers, Jan (eds.), *'Man muss hier nur hart sein': Kriegsbriefe und Bilder einer Familie (1934–1945)* (Bremen, 1999).

Engel, David, 'The Western Allies and the Holocaust: Jan Karski's Mission to the West, 1942–1944', *Holocaust and Genocide Studies*, 5 (1990), 363–446.

Engel, Gerhard, *Heeresadjutant bei Hitler 1938–1943* (ed. Hildegard von Kotze, Stuttgart, 1974).

Engelhard, Hans (ed.), *Im Namen des deutschen Volkes: Justiz und Nationalsozialismus* (Cologne, 1989).

Enno, Georg, *Die wirtschaftlichen Unternehmungen der SS* (Stuttgart, 1963).

Erichson, Kurt (ed.), *Abschied ist immer: Briefe an den Bruder im Zweiten Weltkrieg* (Frankfurt am Main, 1994).

Erickson, John, *The Soviet High Command* (London, 1962).

——, *Stalin's War with Germany*, I: *The Road to Stalingrad* (London, 1975).

Erker, Paul, *Industrie-Eliten in der NS-Zeit: Anpassungsbereitschaft und Eigeninteresse von Unternehmen in der Rüstungs- und Kriegswirtschaft 1936–1945* (Passau, 1993).

Esch, Michael G., ' "Ohne Rücksicht auf historisch Gewordenes": Raumplanung und Raumordnung im besetzten Polen 1939–1944', in Götz Aly *et al.* (eds.), *Modelle für ein deutsches Europa: Ökonomie und Herrschaft im Grosswirtschaftsraum* (Berlin, 1992).

——, *'Gesunde Verhältnisse': Die deutsche und polnische Bevölkerungspolitik in Ostmitteleuropa 1939–1950* (Marburg, 1998).

Etlin, Richard A. (ed.), *Art, Culture, and Media under the Third Reich* (Chicago, Ill., 2002).

Euler, Friederike, 'Theater zwischen Anpassung und Widerstand: Die Münchner Kammerspiele im Dritten Reich', in Broszat *et al.* (eds.), *Bayern*, II. 91–173.

Evans, Jon, *The Nazi New Order in Poland* (London, 1941).

Evans, Richard J. (ed.), *Kneipengespräche im Kaiserreich: Die Stimmungsberichte der Hamburger Politischen Polizei 1892–1914* (Hamburg, 1989).

——, *Rituals of Retribution: Capital Punishment in Germany 1600–1987* (Oxford, 1996).

——, *Rereading German History: From Unification to Reunification 1800–1996* (London, 1997).

——, *Telling Lies About Hitler: The Holocaust, History and the David Irving Trial* (London, 2002).

——, *The Coming of the Third Reich* (London, 2003).

——, *The Third Reich in Power 1933–1939* (London, 2005).

Fabruéget, Michel, 'Entwicklung und Veränderung der Funktionen des Konzentrationslager Mauthausen 1938–1945', in Herbert *et al.* (eds.), *Die nationalsozialistischen Konzentrationslager*, I. 193–214.

Fahlbusch, Michael, *Wissenschaft im Dienst nationalsozialistischer Politik? Die 'Volksdeutschen Forschungsgemeinschaften' von 1931–1945* (Wiesbaden, 1999).

Fangemann, Helmut, *et al.*, *'Parteisoldaten': Die Hamburger Polizei im '3. Reich'* (Baden-Baden, 1987).

Fargion, Lilliana Picciotto, 'Italien', in Benz (ed.), *Dimension des Völkermords*, 199–228.

Feiten, Willi, *Der nationalsozialistische Lehrerbund: Entwicklung und Organisation: Ein Beitrag zum Aufbau und zur Organisationsstruktur des nationalsozialistischen Herrschaftssystems* (Weinheim, 1981).

Felder, Björn, *Lettland im Zweiten Weltkrieg: Zwischen sowjetischen und deutschen Besatzern 1940–1946* (Paderborn, 2008).

Fest, Joachim C., *The Face of the Third Reich* (London, 1979 [1963]).

——, *Plotting Hitler's Death: The German Resistance to Hitler 1933–1945* (London, 1996).

Fetscher, Iring, *Joseph Goebbels im Berliner Sportpalast 1943: 'Wollt Ihr den totalen Krieg?'* (Hamburg, 1998).

Fings, Karola, *et al.*, *'. . . einziges Land, in dem Judenfrage und Zigeunerfrage gelöst': Die Verfolgung der Roma im faschistisch besetzten Jugoslawien 1941–1945* (Cologne, n.d.).

Fleming, Gerald, *Hitler and the Final Solution* (Oxford, 1986 [1982]).

Forschungsstelle für Zeitgeschichte in Hamburg (ed.), *Hamburg im 'Dritten Reich'* (Göttingen, 2005).

Förster, Jürgen, 'Hitlers Decision in Favour of War against the Soviet Union', in *GSWW* IV. 13–51.

——, 'Germany's Acquisition of Allies in South-east Europe', in *GSWW* IV. 386–428.

——, 'Operation Barbarossa as a War of Conquest and Annihilation', in *GSWW* IV. 481–521.

——, 'Jewish Policies of the German Military, 1939–1942', in Cohen *et al.* (eds.), *The Shoah and the War*, 53–71.

—— (ed.), *Stalingrad: Ereignis: Wirkung und Symbol* (Munich, 1992).

——, 'Geistige Kriegführung in Deutschland 1919 bis 1945', in *DRZW* IX/I. 469–640.

Förster, Rudolf, 'Dresden', in Marlene P. Hiller *et al.* (eds.), *Städte im 2. Weltkrieg: Ein internationaler Vergleich* (Essen, 1991), 299–315.

Frank, Anne, *The Diary of a Young Girl* (New York, 1995).

Frei, Norbert, *Der Führerstaat: Nationalsozialistische Herrschaft 1933 bis 1945* (Munich, 1987).

—— (ed.), *Karrieren im Zwielicht: Hitlers Eliten nach 1945* (Frankfurt am Main, 2001).

——, *Adenauer's Germany and the Nazi Past: The Politics of Amnesty and Integration* (New York, 2002 [1997]).

—— *et al.* (eds.), *Ausbeutung, Vernichtung, Öffentlichkeit: Neue Studien zur nationalsozialistischen Lagerpolitik* (Munich, 2000).

Freund, Florian, 'Die Entscheidung zum Einsatz von KZ-Häftlingen in der Raketenrüstung', in Kaienburg (ed.), *Konzentrationslager*, 61–76.

——, 'Häftlingskategorien und Sterblichkeit in einem Aussenlager des KZ Mauthausen', in Herbert *et al.* (eds.), *Die nationalsozialistischen Konzentrationslager*, II. 874–86.

Fricke, Gert, *Kroatien 1941–1944: Der 'Unabhängige Staat' in der Sicht des Deutschen Bevollmächtigten Generals in Agram, Blaise v Hortenau* (Freiburg, 1972).

Friedlander, Henry, *The Origins of Nazi Genocide: From Euthanasia to the Final Solution* (Chapel Hill, N.C., 1995).

Friedländer, Saul, *Prelude to Downfall: Hitler and the United States, 1939–1941* (London, 1967).

——, *Kurt Gerstein oder die Zwiespältigkeit des Guten* (Gütersloh, 1968).

——, *The Years of Extermination: The Third Reich and the Jews 1939–1945* (New York, 2007).

Friedman, Philip, *Roads to Extinction: Essays on the Holocaust* (New York, 1980).

Friedrich, Jörg, *Der Brand: Deutschland im Bombenkrieg 1940–1945* (Munich, 2002).

Frieser, Karl-Heinz, *Krieg hinter Stacheldraht: Die deutschen Kriegsgefangenen in der Sowjetunion und das Nationalkomitee 'Freies Deutschland'* (Mainz, 1981).

——, *Blitzkrieg-Legende: Der Westfeldzug 1940* (Munich, 1996 [1995]).

——, 'Die Schlacht im Kursker Bogen', in *DRZW* VIII. 83–210.

——, 'Der Zusammenbruch im Osten: Die Rückzugskämpfe seit Sommer 1944', in *DRZW* VIII. 493–960.

——, 'Zusammenfassung', in *DRZW* VIII. 1,211–24.

——, and Schönherr, Klaus, 'Der Rückschlag des Pendels: Das Zurückweichen der Ostfront von Sommer 1943 bis Sommer 1944', in *DRZW* VIII. 277–490.

Fritsche, Maria, *Österreichische Deserteure und Selbstverstümmler in der Deutschen Wehrmacht* (Vienna, 2004).

Fröbe, Rainer, 'Der Arbeitseinsatz von KZ-Häftlingen und die Perspektive der Industrie, 1943–1945', in Herbert (ed.), *Europa und der 'Reichseinsatz'*, 351–83.

Fröhlich, Elke (ed.), *Die Tagebücher von Joseph Goebbels*, I: *Aufzeichnungen 1923–1941* (9 vols.); II: *Diktate 1941–1945* (15 vols.) (Munich, 1993–2000).

Führer, Karl Christian, 'Anspruch und Realität: Das Scheitern der nationalsozialistischen Wohnungsbaupolitik 1933–1945', *VfZ* 45 (1997), 247–56.

Gamm, Hans-Jochen, *Der Flüsterwitz im Dritten Reich: Mündliche Dokumente zur Lage der Deutschen während des Nationalsozialismus* (Munich, 1990 [1963]).

Ganssmüller, Christian, *Die Erbgesundheitspolitik des Dritten Reiches: Planung, Durchführung und Durchsetzung* (Cologne, 1987).

Garbe, Detlef (ed.), *Häftlinge im KZ Neuengamme: Verfolgungserfahrungen, Häftlingssolidarität und nationale Bindung* (Hamburg, 1999).

——, 'Institutionen des Terrors und der Widerstand der Wenigen', in Forschungsstelle für Zeitgeschichte in Hamburg (ed.), *Hamburg*, 573–618.

Garlinski, Józef, *Poland in the Second World War* (London, 1985).

Gassert, Philipp, *Amerika im Dritten Reich: Ideologie, Propaganda und Volksmeinung 1933–1941* (Stuttgart, 1997).

Gehrken, Eva, *Nationalsozialistische Erziehung in den Lagern der Erweiterten Kinderlandverschickung 1940 bis 1945* (Braunschweig, 1997), 9, 16.

Gemzell, Carl-Axel, *Raeder, Hitler und Skandinavien* (Lund, 1965).

Gerlach, Christian, 'Die Wannsee-Konferenz, das Schicksal der deutschen Juden und Hitlers politische Grundsatzentscheidung, alle Juden Europas zu ermorden', *Werkstatt Geschichte*, 18 (1997), 7–44.

——, *Krieg, Ernährung, Völkermord: Forschungen zur deutschen Vernichtungspolitik im Zweiten Weltkrieg* (Hamburg, 1998).

——, *Kalkulierte Morde: Die deutsche Wirtschafts- und Vernichtungspolitik in Weissrussland 1941 bis 1944* (Hamburg, 1999).

——, 'Hitlergegner bei der Heeresgruppe Mitte und die "Verbrecherischen Befehle"', in Gerd R. Ueberschär (ed.), *NS-Verbrechen und der militärische Widerstand gegen Hitler* (Darmstadt, 2000), 62–76.

——, and Aly, Götz, *Das letzte Kapitel: Realpolitik, Ideologie und der Mord an den ungarischen Juden 1941/1945* (Munich, 2002).

Gerlach, Wolfgang, *And the Witnesses Were Silent: The Confessing Church and the Persecution of the Jews* (Lincoln, Nebr., 2000 [1987]).

Gilbert, Martin, *The Holocaust: The Jewish Tragedy* (London, 1987 [1986]).

——, *The Routledge Atlas of the Holocaust* (London, 2002 [1982]).

Gildea, Robert, *Marianne in Chains: In Search of the German Occupation 1940–1945* (London, 2002).

Giles, Geoffrey, 'The Institutionalization of Homosexual Panic in the Third Reich', in Robert Gellately and Nathan Stoltzfus (eds.), *Social Outsiders in Nazi Germany* (Princeton, N.J., 2001), 233–54.

——, 'The Denial of Homosexuality: Same-Sex Incidents in Himmler's SS and Police', in Herzog (ed.), *Sexuality and German Fascism*, 256–90.

Glantz, David M., *Stumbling Colossus: The Red Army on the Eve of World War* (Lawrence, Kans., 1998).

——, *Barbarossa: Hitler's Invasion of Russia 1941* (Stroud, 2001).

——, *The Siege of Leningrad 1941–1944: 900 Days of Terror* (London, 2004).

——, and House, Jonathan M., *When Titans Clashed: How the Red Army Stopped Hitler* (Lawrence, Kans., 1995).

Glenny, Misha, *The Balkans 1804–1999: Nationalism, War and the Great Powers* (London, 1999).

Godden, Gertrude M., *Murder of a Nation: German Destruction of Polish Culture* (London, 1943).

Goeschel, Christian, 'Suicide at the End of the Third Reich', *Journal of Contemporary History*, 41 (2006), 153–73.

——, 'Suicide in Weimar and Nazi Germany' (Ph.D. dissertation, University of Cambridge, 2006).

Goldberg, Bettina, *Schulgeschichte als Gesellschaftsgeschichte: Die höheren Schulen im Berliner Vorort Hermsdorf (1893–1945)* (Berlin, 1994).

Goldhagen, Daniel Jonah, *Hitler's Willing Executioners: Ordinary Germans and the Holocaust* (London, 1996).

Golovchansky, Anatoly *et al.* (eds.), *'Ich will raus aus diesem Wahnsinn': Deutsche Briefe von der Ostfront 1941–1945* (Wuppertal, 1991).

Gorodetsky, Gabriel, *Grand Delusion: Stalin and the German Invasion of Russia* (London, 1999).

Goshen, Seev, 'Eichmann und die Nisko-Aktion im Oktober 1939: Eine Fallstudie zur NS-Judenpolitik in der letzten Etappe vor der "Endlösung"', *VfZ* 29 (1981), 74–96.

——, 'Nisko – Ein Ausnahmefall unter den Judenlagern der SS', *VfZ* 40 (1992), 95–106.

Gotto, Bernhard, 'Kommunale Krisenbewältigung', in Süss (ed.), *Deutschland im Luftkrieg*, 41–56.

Grayling, Anthony C., *Among the Dead Cities: Was the Allied Bombing of Civilians in WWII a Necessity or a Crime?* (London, 2006).

Gregor, Neil, *Daimler-Benz in the Third Reich* (London, 1998).

Griech-Polelle, Beth A., *Bishop von Galen: German Catholicism and National Socialism* (New Haven, Conn., 2002).

Grieger, Manfred, 'Unternehmen und KZ-Arbeit: Das Beispiel der Volkswagenwerk GmbH', in Kaienburg (ed.), *Konzentrationslager*, 77–94.

Grimm, Barbara, 'Lynchmorde an alliierten Fliegern im Zweiten Weltkrieg', in Süss (ed.), *Deutschland im Luftkrieg*, 71–84.

Gröhler, Olaf, *Bombenkrieg gegen Deutschland* (Berlin, 1990).

Groscurth, Helmut, *Tagebücher eines Abwehroffiziers 1938–1940* (ed. Helmut Krausnick and Harold C. Deutsch, Stuttgart, 1970).

Gross, Jan T., *Polish Society under German Occupation: The Generalgouvernement 1939–1944* (Princeton, N.J., 1979).

——, *Revolution from Abroad: The Soviet Conquest of Poland's Western Ukraine and Western Belorussia* (Princeton, N.J., 1988).

——, 'A Tangled Web: Confronting Stereotypes Concerning Relations between Poles, Germans, Jews, and Communists', in István Déak *et al.* (eds.), *The Politics of Retribution in Europe: World War II and its Aftermath* (Princeton, N.J., 2000), 74–129.

Grossmann, Atina, 'A Question of Silence: The Rape of German Women by Occupation Soldiers', *October*, 72 (1995), 43–63.

Groueff, Stephane, *Crown of Thorns: The Reign of King Boris III of Bulgaria, 1918–1943* (Lanham, Md., 1987).

Gruchmann, Lothar (ed.), *Autobiographie eines Attentäters: Johann Georg Elser: Aussage zum Sprengstoffanschlag im Bürgerbräukeller, München, am 8. November 1939* (Stuttgart, 1970).

——, 'Euthanasie und Justiz im Dritten Reich', *VfZ* 20 (1972), 235–79.

——, 'Ein unbequemer Amtsrichter im Dritten Reich: Aus den Personalakten des Dr Lothar Kreyssig', *VfZ* 32 (1984), 463–88.

——, *Justiz im Dritten Reich 1933–1940: Anpassung und Unterwerfung in der Ära Gürtner* (Munich, 1988).

Grunberger, Richard, *A Social History of the Third Reich* (London, 1974 [1971]).

Gruner, Wolf, *Judenverfolgung in Berlin 1933–1945: Eine Chronologie der Behördenmassnahmen in der Reichshauptstadt* (Berlin, 1996).

——, *Die geschlossene Arbeitseinsatz deutscher Juden: Zur Zwangsarbeit als Element der Verfolgung, 1938–1943* (Berlin, 1997).

——, 'Die Fabrik-Aktion und die Ereignisse in der Berliner Rosenstrasse: Fakten und Fiktionen um den 27. Februar 1943', *Jahrbuch für Antisemitismusforschung*, 11 (2002), 137–77.

——, *Widerstand in der Rosenstrasse: Die Fabrik-Aktion und die Verfolgung der Mischehen 1943* (Frankfurt am Main, 2005).

Grüttner, Michael, *Studenten im Dritten Reich* (Paderborn, 1995).

——, 'Wissenschaftspolitik im Nationalsozialismus', in Kaufmann (ed.), *Geschichte der Kaiser-Wilhelm-Gesellschaft*, II. 557–85.

Grynberg, Anne, *Les Camps de la honte: Les internes juifs des camps français, 1939–1944* (Paris, 1991).

Gumkowski, Janusz, and Leszczynski, Kazimierz, *Poland under Nazi Occupation* (Warsaw, 1961).

Gutman, Yisrael, *The Jews of Warsaw, 1939–1945: Ghetto, Underground, Revolt* (Bloomington, Ind., 1982).

——, *Resistance: The Warsaw Ghetto Uprising* (Boston, Mass., 1994).

——, and Berenbaum, Michael (eds.), *Anatomy of the Auschwitz Death Camp* (Bloomington, Ind., 1994).

——, and Krakowski, Shmuel, *Unequal Victims: Poles and Jews during World War Two* (New York, 1986).

Haar, Ingo, *Historiker im Nationalsozialismus: Deutsche Geschichtswissenschaft und der 'Volkstumskampf' im Osten* (Göttingen, 2002).

Hagemann, Jürgen, *Die Presselenkung in Dritten Reich* (Bonn, 1970).

Hahn, Fritz, *Waffen und Geheimwaffen des deutschen Heeres, 1933–1945* (2 vols., Koblenz, 1986–7).

Halder, Franz, *Kriegstagebuch* (ed. Hans-Adolf Jacobsen, 3 vols., Stuttgart, 1962–4).

Hale, Oron J., *The Captive Press in the Third Reich* (Princeton, N.J., 1964).

Hamann, Matthias, 'Erwünscht und unerwünscht: Die rassenpsychologische Selektion der Ausländer', in Götz Aly *et al.* (eds.), *Herrenmensch und Arbeitsvölker: Ausländische Arbeiter und Deutsche 1939–1945* (Berlin, 1986), 143–80.

Hanke, Christian, *et al.*, *Hamburg im Bombenkrieg 1940–1945: Das Schicksal einer Stadt* (Hamburg, 2001).

Hansen, Georg, '"Damit wurde der Warthegau zum Exerzierplatz des praktischen Nationalsozialismus": Eine Fallstudie zur Politik der Einverleibung', in Klessmann (ed.), *September 1939*, 55–72.

—— (ed.), *Schulpolitik als Volkstumspolitik: Quellen zur Schulpolitik der Besatzer in Polen 1939–1945* (Münster, 1994).

——, *Ethnische Schulpolitik im besetzten Polen: Der Mustergau Wartheland* (Münster, 1995).

Harrer, Heinrich, *Seven Years in Tibet* (London, 1953).

Harrison, Mark, *Accounting for War: Soviet Production, Employment and the Defence Burden, 1940–1945* (Cambridge, 1996).

—— (ed.), *The Economics of World War II: Six Great Powers in International Comparison* (Cambridge, 1998).

Harten, Hans-Christian, *De-Kulturation und Germanisierung: Die nationalsozialistische Rassen- und Erziehungspolitik in Polen 1939–1945* (Frankfurt am Main, 1996).

Hartenstein, Michael, *Neue Dorflandschaften: Nationalsozialistische Siedlungsplanung in den 'eingegliederten Ostgebieten': 1939 und 1944* (Berlin, 1998).

Hartewig, Karin, 'Wolf unter Wölfen? Die prekäre Macht der kommunistischen Kapos im Konzentrationslager Buchenwald', in Herbert *et al.* (eds.), *Die nationalsozialistischen Konzentrationslager*, II. 939–58.

Harvey, Elizabeth, *Women and the Nazi East: Agents and Witnesses of Germanization* (London, 2003).

Hassell, Ulrich von, *The von Hassell Diaries: The Story of the Forces against Hitler inside Germany 1938–1944* (Boulder, Colo., 1994 [1946]).

Hauschild-Thiessen, Renate (ed.), *Die Hamburger Katastrophe vom Sommer 1943 in Augenzeugenberichten* (Hamburg, 1991).

Hayes, Peter, *Industry and Ideology: IG Farben in the Nazi Era* (Cambridge, 1987).

——, *From Cooperation to Complicity: Degussa in the Third Reich* (Cambridge, 2004).

Heer, Hannes, *Ernst Thälmann in Selbstzeugnissen und Bilddokumenten* (Reinbek, 1975).

——, 'Killing Fields: Die Wehrmacht und der Holocaust', in idem and Naumann (eds.), *Vernichtungskrieg*, 57–77.

—— (ed.), *'Stets zu erschiessen sind Frauen, die in der Roten Armee dienen': Geständnisse deutscher Kriegsgefangener über ihren Einsatz an der Ostfront* (Hamburg, 1995).

——, and Naumann, Klaus (eds.), *Vernichtungskrieg: Verbrechen der Wehrmacht 1941–1944* (Hamburg, 1995).

Hehn, Paul, *The German Struggle against Yugoslav Guerillas in World War II: German Counter-Insurgency in Yugoslavia 1941–1943* (New York, 1979).

Heiber, Helmut (ed.), *Goebbels-Reden* (2 vols., Düsseldorf, 1971–2).

Heim, Susanne (ed.), *Autarkie und Ostexpansion: Pflanzenzucht und Agrarforschung im Nationalsozialismus* (Göttingen, 2002).

——, *Kalorien, Kautschuk, Karrieren: Pflanzenzüchtung und landwirtschaftliche Forschung in Kaiser-Wilhelm-Instituten 1933–1945* (Göttingen, 2003).

Heinemann, Isabel, *'Rasse, Siedlung, deutsches Blut': Das Rasse- und Siedlungshauptamt der SS und die rassenpolitische Neuordnung Europas* (Göttingen, 2003).

Heinemann, Ulrich, '"Kein Platz für Polen und Juden": Der Widerstandskämpfer Fritz-Dietlof Graf von der Schulenburg und die Politik der Verwaltung in Schlesien 1939/40', in Klessmann (ed.), *September 1939*, 38–54.

Heinemann, Winfried, 'Der militärische Widerstand und der Krieg', in *DRZW* IX/I. 743–892.

Henry, Clarissa, and Hillel, Marc, *Children of the SS* (London, 1976 [1975]).

Hentschel, Klaus (ed.), *Physics and National Socialism: An Anthology of Primary Sources* (Basel, 1996).

Herbert, Ulrich (ed.), *Europa und der 'Reichseinsatz': Ausländische Zivilarbeiter, Kriegsgefangene und KZ-Häftlinge in Deutschland 1938–1945* (Essen, 1991).

——, *Best: Biographische Studien über Radikalismus, Weltanschauung und Vernunft, 1903–1989* (Bonn, 1996).

——, *Hitler's Foreign Workers: Enforced Foreign Labor in Germany under the Third Reich* (Cambridge, 1997 [1985]).

——, *et al.* (eds.), *Die nationalsozialistischen Konzentrationslager: Entwicklung und Struktur* (2 vols., Göttingen, 1998).

Herbst, Ludolf, *Der totale Krieg und die Ordnung der Wirtschaft: Die Kriegswirtschaft im Spannungsfeld von Politik, Ideologie und Propaganda 1939–1945* (Stuttgart, 1982).

Herf, Jeffrey, *The Jewish Enemy: Nazi Propaganda during World War II and the Holocaust* (London, 2006).

Hermand, Jost, *Als Pimpf in Polen: Erweiterte Kinderlandverschickung 1940–1945* (Frankfurt am Main, 1993).

Hermelink, Heinrich (ed.), *Kirche im Kampf: Dokumente des Widerstands und des Aufbaus in der evangelischen Kirche Deutschlands von 1933 bis 1945* (Tübingen, 1950).

Herzog, Dagmar, 'Hubris and Hypocrisy, Incitement and Disavowal: Sexuality and German Fascism', in eadem (ed.), *Sexuality and German Fascism*, 1–21.

—— (ed.), *Sexuality and German Fascism* (New York, 2005).

Heusler, Andreas, *Ausländereinsatz: Zwangsarbeit für die Münchner Kriegswirtschaft 1939–1945* (Munich, 1996).

Hilger, Andreas, *Deutsche Kriegsgefangene in der Sowjetunion, 1941–1956: Kriegsgefangenenpolitik, Lageralltag und Erinnerung* (Essen, 2000).

Hillgruber, Andreas, *Hitlers Strategie: Politik und Kriegführung 1940–41* (Frankfurt am Main, 1965).

—— (ed.), *Staatsmänner und Diplomaten bei Hitler: Vertrauliche Aufzeichnungen über Unterredungen mit Vertretern des Auslandes* (2 vols., Frankfurt am Main, 1967–70).

Hillmann, Jörg, and Zimmermann, John, *Kriegsende 1945 in Deutschland* (Munich, 2002).

Hinsley, F. Harry, *British Intelligence in the Second World War* (5 vols., London, 1979–90).

Hirsch, Martin, *et al.* (eds.), *Recht, Verwaltung und Justiz im Nationalsozialismus* (Cologne, 1984).

Hirschfeld, Gerhard, *Nazi Rule and Dutch Collaboration: The Netherlands under German Occupation, 1940–1945* (Oxford, 1988 [1984]).

——, 'Niederlande', in Benz (ed.), *Dimension des Völkermords*, 137–63.

Hitchins, Keith, *Rumania 1866–1947* (Oxford, 1994).

Hitler, Adolf, *Hitler's Table Talk 1941–1944* (Oxford, 1988 [1953]).

Hoare, Marko, *Genocide and Resistance in Hitler's Bosnia: The Partisans and the Chetniks, 1941–1943* (London, 2006).

Hoch, Anton, 'Das Attentat auf Hitler im Münchener Bürgerbräukeller 1939', *VfZ* 17 (1969), 383–413.

Hoffmann, Hilmar, *The Triumph of Propaganda: Film and National Socialism 1933–1945* (Oxford, 1996 [1988]).

Hoffmann, Katharina, *Zwangsarbeit und ihre gesellschaftliche Akzeptanz in Oldenburg 1939–1945* (Oldenburg, 2001).

Hoffmann, Peter, *Hitler's Personal Security* (London, 1979).

——, *Claus Schenk Graf von Stauffenberg und seine Brüder* (Stuttgart, 1992).

——, *The History of the German Resistance 1933–1945* (Montreal, 1996 [1969]).

Hohmann, Joachim S., and Langer, Hermann (eds.), 'Stolz, ein Deutscher zu sein...' *Nationales Selbstverständnis in Schulaufsätzen 1914–1945* (Frankfurt am Main, 1995), 227–8.

Höhne, Heinz, *The Order of the Death's Head: The Story of Hitler's SS* (London, 1972 [1966]).

Hoidal, Oddvar K., *Quisling: A Study in Treason* (Oslo, 1989).

Hölsken, Heinz Dieter, *Die V-Waffen: Entstehung – Propaganda – Kriegseinsatz* (Stuttgart, 1984).

Homze, Edward L., *Foreign Labor in Nazi Germany* (Princeton, N.J., 1967).

Hoppe, Hans-Jürgen, *Bulgarien – Hitlers eigenwilliger Verbündeter* (Stuttgart, 1979).

Horn, Birgit, *Die Nacht, als der Feuertod vom Himmel stürzte – Leipzig, 4. Dezember 1943* (Gudensberg-Gleichen, 2003).

Hornung, Ella, *et al.*, 'Zwangsarbeit in der Landwirtschaft', *DRZW* IX/II. 577–666.

Horwitz, Gordon J., *Ghettostadt: Lodz and the Making of a Nazi City* (London, 2008).

Hory, Ladislaus, and Broszat, Martin, *Der kroatische Ustascha-Staat 1941–1945* (Stuttgart, 1965 [1964]), 15–38.

Hosenfeld, Wilm, 'Ich versuche jeden zu retten': *Das Leben eines deutschen Offiziers in Briefen und Tagebüchern* (ed. Thomas Vogel, Munich, 2004).

Höss, Rudolf, *Commandant of Auschwitz: The Autobiography of Rudolf Höss* (London, 1959 [1951]).

Housden, Martyn, *Hans Frank: Lebensraum and the Holocaust* (London, 2003).

Hubatsch, Walther (ed.), *Hitlers Weisungen für die Kriegführung 1939–1945: Dokumente des Oberkommandos der Wehrmacht* (Frankfurt am Main, 1962).

Humburg, Martin (ed.), *Das Gesicht des Krieges: Feldpostbriefe von Wehrmachtssoldaten aus der Sowjetunion 1941–1944* (Opladen, 1998).

Hüppauf, Bernd, 'Der entleerte Blick hinter der Kamera', in Heer and Naumann (eds.), *Vernichtungskrieg*, 504–50.

Hürter, Johannes (ed.), *Ein deutscher General an der Ostfront: Die Briefe und Tagebücher des Gotthard Heinrici 1941/42* (Essen, 2001).

——, 'Auf dem Weg zur Militäropposition: Tresckow, Gersdorff, der Vernichtungskrieg und der Judenmord: Neue Dokumente über das Verhältnis der Heeresgruppe Mitte zur Einsatzgruppe B im Jahr 1941', *VfZ* 52 (2004), 527–62.

——, *Hitlers Heerführer: Die deutschen Oberbefehlshaber im Krieg gegen die Sowjetunion 1941/42* (Munich, 2007).

Hyman, Paula, *From Dreyfus to Vichy: The Remaking of French Jewry, 1906–1939* (New York, 1979).

Ioanid, Radu, *The Holocaust in Romania: The Destruction of Jews and Gypsies under the Antonescu Regime, 1940–1944* (Chicago, Ill., 2000).

IR 309 marchiert an den Feind: Erlebnisberichte aus dem Polenfeldzuge 1939 (ed. Oberst Dr Hoffmann, Berlin, 1940).

Jäckel, Eberhard, 'On the Purpose of the Wannsee Conference', in James S. Pacy and Alan P. Wertheimer (eds.), *Perspectives on the Holocaust: Essays in Honor of Raul Hilberg* (Boulder, Colo., 1995), 39–49.

Jackson, Julian, *France: The Dark Years 1940–1944* (Oxford, 2001).

——, *The Fall of France: The Nazi Invasion of 1940* (Oxford, 2003).

Jacobmeyer, Wolfgang, *Heimat und Exil: Die Anfänge der polnischen Untergrundbewegung im Zweiten Weltkrieg (September 1939 bis Mitte 1941)* (Hamburg, 1973).

——, 'Der Überfall auf Polen und der neue Charakter des Krieges', in Klessmann (ed.), *September 1939*, 16–37.

Jacobsen, Hans-Adolf (ed.), *Dokumente zur Vorgeschichte des Westfeldzuges 1939–1940* (Göttingen, 1956).

——, *Fall Gelb: Der Kampf um den deutschen Operationsplan zur Westoffensive 1940* (Wiesbaden, 1957).

——, *Dünkirchen: Ein Beitrag zur Geschichte des Westfeldzuges 1940* (Neckargemünd, 1958).

—— (ed.), *Dokumente zum Westfeldzug 1940* (Göttingen, 1960).

——, 'The *Kommissarbefehl* and Mass Executions of Soviet Russian Prisoners of War', in Helmut Krausnick *et al.*, *Anatomy of the SS State* (London, 1968 [1965]), 505–34.

—— (ed.), *Misstrauische Nachbarn: Deutsche Ostpolitik 1919/1970* (Düsseldorf, 1970).

—— (ed.), '*Spiegelbild einer Verschwörung': Die Opposition gegen Hitler und der Staatsstreich vom 20. Juli 1940 in der SD-Berichterstattung: Geheime Dokumente aus dem ehemaligen Reichssicherheitshauptamt* (2 vols., Stuttgart, 1984).

Jahnke, Karl Heinz, *Weisse Rose contra Hakenkreuz: Der Widerstand der Geschwister Scholl und ihre Freunde* (Frankfurt am Main, 1969).

——, *Weisse Rose contra Hakenkreuz: Studenten im Widerstand 1942/43: Einblicke in viereinhalb Jahrzehnte Forschung* (Rostock, 2003).

James, Harold, *The Deutsche Bank and the Nazi Economic War against the Jews: The Expropriation of Jewish-Owned Property* (Cambridge, 2001).

Jannings, Emil, *Theater, Film – Das Leben und ich* (Munich, 1989 [1951]).

Jansen, Christian, and Weckbecker, Arno, 'Eine Miliz im "Weltanschauungskrieg": Der "Volksdeutsche Selbstschutz in Polen 1939/40", in Wolfgang Michalka (ed.), *Der Zweite Weltkrieg: Analysen – Grundzüge – Forschungsbilanz* (Munich, 1989), 482–500.

——, *Der 'Volksdeutsche Selbstschutz' in Polen 1939/40* (Munich, 1992).

——, 'Zwangsarbeit für das Volkswagenwerk: Häftlingsalltag auf dem Laagberg bei Wolfsburg', in Frei *et al.* (eds.), *Ausbeutung*, 75–108.

Jarausch, Konrad H., *After Hitler: Recivilizing Germans, 1945–1995* (New York, 2006).

Jaskot, Paul B., *The Architecture of Oppression: The SS, Forced Labor, and the Nazi Monumental Building Economy* (London, 2000).

Jastrzebski, Wlodzimierz, *Der Bromberger Blutsonntag: Legende und Wirklichkeit* (Poznań, 1990).

Jellonek, Burkhard, *Homosexuelle unter dem Hakenkreuz: Die Verfolgung Homosexueller im Dritten Reich* (Paderborn, 1990).

Jenkins, Roy, *Churchill* (London, 2001).

Joachimsthaler, Anton, *Hitlers End: Legenden und Dokumente* (Augsburg, 1999 [1994]).

Jochmann, Werner (ed.), *Adolf Hitler: Monologe im Führerhauptquartier 1941–1944: Die Aufzeichnungen Heinrich Heims* (Hamburg, 1980).

Johnson, Eric A., *Nazi Terror: The Gestapo, Jews, and Ordinary Germans* (New York, 1999).

——, and Reuband, Karl-Heinz, *What We Knew: Terror, Mass Murder, and Everyday Life in Nazi Germany: An Oral History* (New York, 2005).

Jong, Louis de, 'The Netherlands and Auschwitz', *Yad Vashem Studies*, 7 (1968), 39–55.

Joshi, Vandana, *Gender and Power in the Third Reich: Female Denouncers and the Gestapo, 1933–45* (London, 2003).

Kaczmarek, Ryszard, 'Die deutsche wirtschaftliche Penetration in Polen (Oberschlesien)', in Overy *et al.* (eds.), *Die 'Neuordnung'*, 257–72.

Kaienburg, Hermann (ed.), *Konzentrationslager und deutsche Wirtschaft 1939–1945* (Opladen, 1996).

——, 'KZ-Haft und Wirtschaftsinteresse: Das Wirtschaftsverwaltungshauptamt der SS als Leitungszentrale der Konzentrationslager und der SS-Wirtschaft', in idem (ed.), *Konzentrationslager*, 29–60.

——, 'Deutsche politische Häftlinge im Konzentrationslager Neuengamme und ihre Stellung im Hauptlager', in Garbe (ed.), *Häftlinge*, 12–80.

——, 'Zwangsarbeit: KZ und Wirtschaft im Zweiten Weltkrieg', in Benz and Distel (eds.), *Der Ort des Terrors*, I. 179–94.

Kaiser, Ernst, and Knorn, Michael, '*Wir lebten und schliefen zwischen den Toten': Rüstungsproduktion, Zwangsarbeit und Vernichtung in den Frankfurter Adlerwerken* (Frankfurt am Main, 1994).

Kaiser, Gerd, *Katyn: Das Staatsverbrechen – das Staatsgeheimnis* (Berlin, 2002).

Kallis, Aristotle A., *Nazi Propaganda and the Second World War* (London, 2005).

Kaplan, Chaim A., *Scroll of Agony: The Warsaw Diary of Chaim A. Kaplan* (London, 1966).

Kaplan, Marion, 'Jewish Daily Life in Wartime Germany', in David Bankier (ed.), *Probing the Depths of German Antisemitism: German Society and the Persecution of the Jews, 1933–1941* (Jerusalem, 2000), 395–412.

Kappeler, Alphons, *Ein Fall von 'Pseudologia phantastica' in der deutschen Literatur: Fritz Reck-Malleczewen: Mit Totalbibliographie* (Göppingen, 1975).

Karlsch, Rainer, *Hitlers Bombe: Die geheime Geschichte der deutschen Kernwaffenversuche* (Stuttgart, 2005).

Kárny, Miroslav, ' "Heydrichiaden": Widerstand und Terror im Protektorat Böhmen und Mähren', in Droulia and Fleischer (eds.), *Von Lidice bis Kalavryta*, 51–63.

——, *et al.* (eds.), *Theresienstadt in der 'Endlösung der Judenfrage'* (Prague, 1992).

Kater, Michael H., *Doctors under Hitler* (Chapel Hill, N.C., 1989).

——, *Different Drummers: Jazz in the Culture of Nazi Germany* (New York, 1992).

——, *Composers of the Nazi Era: Eight Portraits* (New York, 2000).

——, *Das Ahnenerbe der SS 1935–1945: Ein Beitrag zur Kulturpolitik des Dritten Reiches* (Munich, 4th edn, 2006).

Katz, Robert, *Black Sabbath: A Journey through a Crime against Humanity* (London, 1969).

——, *The Battle for Rome: The Germans, the Allies, the Partisans, and the Pope, September 1943–June 1944* (New York, 2003).

Kaufmann, Doris (ed.), *Geschichte der Kaiser-Wilhelm-Gesellschaft im Nationalsozialismus: Bestandsaufnahme und Perspektiven der Forschung* (2 vols., Göttingen, 2000).

Kautsky, Benedikt, *Teufel und Verdammte: Erfahrungen und Erkenntnisse aus sieben Jahren in deutschen Konzentrationslagern* (Vienna, 1961).

Kay, Alex J., 'Germany's Staatssekretäre, Mass Starvation and the Meeting of 2 May 1941', *Journal of Contemporary History*, 41 (2006), 685–700.

Keller, Rolf, ' "Die kamen in Scharen hier an, die Gefangenen": Sowjetische Kriegsgefangene, Wehrmachtsoldaten und deutsche Bevölkerung in Norddeutschland 1941/42', in Detlef Garbe (ed.), *Rassismus in Deutschland* (Bremen, 1994), 35–53.

Keren, Nilli, 'The Family Camp', in Gutman and Berenbaum (eds.), *Anatomy*, 428–40.

Kermish, Joseph, 'Introduction', in Ringelblum, *Polish-Jewish Relations*, vii–xxxix.

——, 'Introduction', in Czerniakow, *The Warsaw Diary*, 1–24.

Kershaw, Ian, *Popular Opinion and Political Dissent in the Third Reich: Bavaria 1933–1945* (Oxford, 1983).

——, *The 'Hitler Myth': Image and Reality in the Third Reich* (Oxford, 1989 [1987]).

——, *Hitler*, II: *1936–1945: Nemesis* (London, 2000).

——, *Hitler, the Germans and the Final Solution* (London, 2008).

Kersten, Felix, *The Kersten Memoirs 1940–1945* (London, 1956).

Kettenacker, Lothar (ed.), *Ein Volk von Opfern? Die neue Debatte um den Bombenkrieg 1940–45* (Berlin, 2003).

Kielar, Wieslaw, *Anus Mundi: Five Years in Auschwitz* (London, 1982 [1972]).

Killian, Katrin A., 'Kriegsstimmungen: Emotionen einfacher Soldaten in Feldpostbriefen', in *DRZW* IX/II. 251–88.

Kirby, David, *Finland in the Twentieth Century* (London, 1979).

Kirchhoff, Hans, 'Denmark: A Light in the Darkness of the Holocaust? A Reply to Gunnar S. Paulsson', in Cesarani (ed.), *Holocaust*, V. 128–39.

Kirstin, Wolfgang, *Das Konzentrationslager als Institution totalen Terrors: Das Beispiel des KL Natzweiler* (Pfaffenweiler, 1992).

Klee, Ernst (ed.), *Dokumente zur 'Euthanasie'* (Frankfurt am Main, 1985).

——, *'Euthanasie' im NS-Staat: Die 'Vernichtung lebensunwerten Lebens'* (Frankfurt am Main, 1985 [1983]).

——, *Auschwitz, die NS-Medizin und ihre Opfer* (Frankfurt am Main, 1997).

——, *et al.* (eds.), *'Those Were the Days': The Holocaust as Seen by the Perpetrators and Bystanders* (London, 1991 [1988]).

Klee, Karl, *Das Unternehmen 'Seelöwe': Die geplante deutsche Landung in England 1940* (Göttingen, 1958).

——, *Dokumente zum Unternehmen 'Seelöwe': Die geplante deutsche Landung in England 1940* (Göttingen, 1959).

Klee, Katja, ' "Nie wieder Aufnahme von Kindern": Anspruch und Wirklichkeit der KLV in den Aufnahmegauen', in Rüther (ed.), *'Zu Hause'*, 161–94.

Klein, Burton H., *Germany's Economic Preparations for War* (Cambridge, Mass., 1959).

Klein, Peter (ed.), *Die Einsatzgruppen in der besetzten Sowjetunion 1941/42: Die Tätigkeits- und Lageberichte des Chefs der Sicherheitspolizei und des SD* (Berlin, 1997).

——, 'Zwischen den Fronten: Die Zivilbevölkerung Weissrusslands und der Krieg der Wehrmacht gegen die Partisanen', in Quinkert (ed.), *'Wir sind die Herren dieses Landes'*, 82–103.

Klemperer, Klemens von, *German Resistance against Hitler: The Search for Allies Abroad 1938–1945* (Oxford, 1992).

Klemperer, Victor, *I Shall Bear Witness: The Diaries of Victor Klemperer 1933–41* (London, 1998 [1995]).

——, *To the Bitter End: The Diaries of Victor Klemperer 1942–45* (London, 1998 [1995]).

——, *The Lesser Evil: The Diaries of Victor Klemperer 1945–59* (London, 2003 [1999]).

Klepper, Jochen, *Unter dem Schatten deiner Flügel: Aus den Tagebüchern der Jahre 1932–1942* (Stuttgart, 1955).

——, *Überwindung: Tagebücher und Aufzeichnungen aus dem Kriege* (Stuttgart, 1958).

——, *Briefwechsel 1925–1942* (ed. Ernst G. Riemschneider, Stuttgart, 1973).

Klessmann, Christoph, 'Der Generalgouverneur Hans Frank', *VfZ* 19 (1971), 245–66.

——, *Die Selbstbehauptung einer Nation: Nationalsozialistische Kulturpolitik und polnische Widerstandsbewegung im Generalgouvernement 1939–1945* (Düsseldorf, 1971).

——, 'Die Zerstörung des Schulwesens als Bestandteil deutscher Okkupationspolitik im Osten am Beispiel Polens', in Manfred Heinemann (ed.), *Erziehung und Schulung im Dritten Reich*, I: *Kindergarten, Schule, Jugend, Berufserziehung* (Stuttgart, 1980), 176–92.

——, 'Die kulturelle Selbstbehauptung der polnischen Nation', in idem (ed.), *September 1939*, 117–38.

—— (ed.), *September 1939: Krieg, Besatzung, Widerstand in Polen: Acht Beiträge* (Göttingen, 1989).

——, and Dlugoborski, Wazlaw, 'Nationalsozialistische Bildungspolitik und polnische Hochschulen 1939–1945', *Geschichte und Gesellschaft*, 23 (1997), 535–59.

Klingler, Walter, *Nationalsozialistische Rundfunkpolitik 1942–1945: Organisation, Programm und die Hörer* (Mannheim, 1983).

Klonicki, Aryeh and Malwina, *The Diary of Adam's Father: The Diary of Aryeh Klonicki (Klonymus) and His Wife Malwina* (Jerusalem, 1973).

Klukowski, Zygmunt, *Diary from the Years of Occupation 1939–44* (Urbana, Ill., 1993 [1958]).

Kock, Gerhard, 'Die Erweiterte Kinderlandverschickung und der Konflikt mit den Kirchen', in Rüther (ed.), *'Zu Hause'*, 209–42.

——, 'Nur zum Schutz aufs Land gebracht? Die Kinderlandverschickung und ihre erziehungspolitischen Ziele', in Rüther (ed.), *'Zu Hause'*, 17–52.

Koehl, Robert L., *RKFDV: German Resettlement and Population Policy 1939–1945: A*

History of the Reich Commission for the Strengthening of Germandom (Cambridge, Mass., 1957).

Kogon, Eugen, *et al.* (eds.), *Nationalsozialistische Massentötungen durch Giftgas: Eine Dokumentation* (Frankfurt am Main, 1983).

Kohlmann-Viand, Doris, *NS-Pressepolitik im Zweiten Weltkrieg* (Munich, 1991).

Kolb, Eberhard, *Bergen-Belsen 1943–1945: Vom 'Aufenthaltslager' zum Konzentrationslager 1943–1945* (Göttingen, 2001).

Krakowski, Shmuel, 'The Fate of Polish Prisoners of War in the September 1939 Camps', *Yad Vashem Studies* 12 (1977), 296–333.

——, *The War of the Doomed: Jewish Armed Resistance in Poland, 1942–1944* (New York, 1984).

Krämer, Nicole, ' "Kämpfende Mütter" und "gefallene Heldinnen": Frauen im Luftschutz', in Süss (ed.), *Deutschland im Luftkrieg*, 85–98.

Kranz, Tomasz, 'Das KL Lublin zwischen Planung und Realisierung', in Herbert *et al.* (eds.), *Die nationalsozialistischen Konzentrationslager*, I. 363–89.

Kratz, Philipp, 'Sparen für das kleine Glück', in Götz Aly (ed.), *Volkes Stimme: Skepsis und Führervertrauen im Nationalsozialismus* (Frankfurt am Main, 2006), 59–79.

Krausnick, Helmut, 'Hitler und die Morde in Polen: Ein Beitrag zum Konflikt zwischen Heer und SS um die Verwaltung der besetzten Gebiete (Dokumentation)', *VfZ* 11 (1963), 196–209.

——, *Hitlers Einsatzgruppen: Die Truppen des Weltanschauungskrieges 1938–1942* (Frankfurt am Main, 1985 [1981]).

Kroener, Bernhard R., 'The Manpower Resources of the Third Reich in the Area of Conflict between Wehrmacht, Bureaucracy and War Economy, 1939–1942', in *GSWW* V/I, 799–1,154.

——, ' "Nun Volk, steh auf . . . !" Stalingrad und der "totale" Krieg 1942–1943', in Förster (ed.), *Stalingrad*, 151–70.

Kublik, Steven, *The Stones Cry Out: Sweden's Response to the Persecution of the Jews, 1933–1945* (New York, 1988).

Kudlien, Fridlof, *Ärzte im Nationalsozialismus* (Cologne, 1985).

Kühne, Thomas, 'Zwischen Männerbund und Volksgemeinschaft: Hitlers Soldaten und der Mythos der Kameradschaft', *Archiv für Sozialgeschichte*, 38 (1998), 165–89.

——, 'Gruppenkohäsion und Kameradschaftsmythos in der Wehrmacht', in Rolf-Dieter Müller and Hans-Erich Volkmann (eds.), *Die Wehrmacht: Mythos und Realität* (Munich, 1999), 534–59.

——, *Kameradschaft: Die Soldaten des nationalsozialistischen Krieges und das 20. Jahrhundert* (Göttingen, 2006).

Kulka, Otto Dov, and Jäckel, Eberhard (eds.), *Die Juden in den Geheimen NS-Stimmungsberichten 1933–1945* (Düsseldorf, 2004).

Kundrus, Birthe, *Kriegerfrauen: Familienpolitik und Geschlechterverhältnisse im Ersten und Zweiten Weltkrieg* (Hamburg, 1995).

——, 'Totale Unterhaltung? Die kulturelle Kriegführung 1939 bis 1945 in Film, Rundfunk und Theater', in *DRZW* IX/I. 93–157.

Kunz, Andreas, *Wehrmacht und Niederlage: Die bewaffnete Macht in der Endphase der nationalsozialistischen Herrschaft 1944 bis 1945* (Munich, 2005).

——, 'Die Wehrmacht 1944/45: Eine Armee im Untergang', in *DRZW* X/II. 3–54.

Kupper, René, 'Karl Hermann Frank als Deutscher Staatsminister für Böhmen und Mähren', in Monika Glettler *et al.* (eds.), *Geteilt, Besetzt, Beherrscht: Die Tschechoslowakei 1938–1945: Reichsgau Sudetenland, Protektorat Böhmen und Mähren, Slowakei* (Essen, 2004), 31–52.

Kuropka, Joachim (ed.), *Meldungen aus Münster, 1924–1944: Geheime und vertrauliche Berichte von Polizei, Gestapo, NSDAP und ihren Gliederungen, staatlicher Verwaltung, Gerichtsbarkeit und Wehrmacht über die politische und gesellschaftliche Situation in Münster* (Münster, 1992).

Kuznetsov, Anatoly, *Babi Yar: A Document in the Form of a Novel* (London, 1970 [1966]).

Kwiet, Konrad, *Reichskommissariat Niederlande: Versuch und Scheitern nationalsozialistischer Neuordnung* (Stuttgart, 1968).

——, 'Rehearsing for Murder: The Beginning of the Final Solution in Lithuania in June 1941', *Holocaust and Genocide Studies*, 12 (1998), 3–26.

Lambauer, Barbara, 'Opportunistischer Antisemitismus: Der deutsche Botschafter Otto Abetz und die Judenverfolgung in Frankreich', *VfZ* 53 (2005), 241–73.

Landau-Czajka, Anna, 'The Jewish Question in Poland: Views Expressed in the Catholic Press between the Two World Wars', *Polin: Studies in Polish Jewry*, 11 (1998), 263–78.

Lang, Ralf, *Italienische 'Fremdarbeiter' im nationalsozialistischen Deutschland 1937–1945* (Frankfurt am Main, 1996).

Lange, Wilhelm, *Cap Arcona: Dokumentation* (Eutin, 1992).

Laqueur, Walter, *The Terrible Secret: Suppression of the Truth about Hitler's 'Final Solution'* (London, 1980).

Latawski, Paul, 'Polish Campaign', in Dear (ed.), *The Oxford Companion to World War II*, 705–8.

Latzel, Klaus, 'Tourismus und Gewalt: Kriegswahrnehmungen in Feldpostbriefen', in Heer and Naumann (eds.), *Vernichtungskrieg*, 447–59.

Lavi, Theodore, 'The Vatican's Endeavors on Behalf of Romanian Jewry during the Second World War', *Yad Vashem Studies*, 5 (1963), 405–18.

Lehberger, Reiner, *Englischunterricht im Nationalsozialismus* (Tübingen, 1986).

Levi, Erik, *Music in the Third Reich* (London, 1994).

Levi, Primo, *If This Is a Man* (London, 1957 [1948]).

Levine, Hillel, *In Search of Sugihara: The Elusive Japanese Diplomat Who Risked His Life to Rescue 10,000 Jews from the Holocaust* (New York, 1996).

Levine, Paul A., *From Indifference to Activism: Swedish Diplomacy and the Holocaust* (Uppsala, 1996).

Lewandowski, Jozef, 'Early Swedish Information about the Nazis' Mass Murder of the Jews', *Polin: Studies in Polish Jewry*, 13 (2000), 113–27.

Lewinski, Jerzy, 'The Death of Adam Czerniakow and Janusz Korcak's Last Journey', *Polin: Studies in Polish Jewry*, 7 (1992), 224–53.

Lewy, Guenter, *The Nazi Persecution of the Gypsies* (New York, 2000).

Liddell Hart, Basil H. (ed.), *The Rommel Papers* (London, 1953).

Lifton, Robert Jay, *The Nazi Doctors: Medical Killing and the Psychology of Genocide* (London, 1986).

Longerich, Peter, 'Nationalsozialistische Propaganda', in Karl Dietrich Bracher *et al.* (eds.), *Deutschland 1933–1945: Neue Studien zur nationalsozialistischen Herrschaft* (Düsseldorf, 1993), 291–314.

——, *Politik der Vernichtung: Eine Gesamtdarstellung der nationalsozialistischen Judenverfolgung* (Munich, 1998).

——, *Der ungeschriebene Befehl: Hitler und der Weg zur 'Endlösung'* (Munich, 2001).

——, *'Davon haben wir nichts gewusst!' Die Deutschen und die Judenverfolgung 1933–1945* (Munich, 2006).

——, and Pohl, Dieter (eds.), *Die Ermordung der europäischen Juden: Eine umfassende Dokumentation des Holocaust 1941–1945* (Munich, 1989), 167–9.

Lower, Wendy, *Nazi Empire-Building and the Holocaust in Ukraine* (Chapel Hill, N.C., 2005).

Luczak, Czeslaw, 'Landwirtschaft und Ernährung in Polen während der deutschen Besatzungszeit 1939–1945', in Bernd Martin and Alan S. Milward (eds.), *Agriculture and Food Supply in the Second World War* (Ostfildern, 1985), 117–27.

Ludwig, Karl-Heinz, *Technik und Ingenieure im Dritten Reich* (Düsseldorf, 1974).

Maase, Kaspar, *Grenzenloses Vergnügen: Der Aufstieg der Massenkultur 1850–1970* (Frankfurt am Main, 1997).

McCarthy, Jamie, *et al.*, 'The Ruins of the Gas Chambers: A Forensic Investigation of

Crematoriums at Auschwitz I and Auschwitz-Birkenau', *Holocaust and Genocide Studies*, 18 (2004), 68–103.

MacQueen, Michael, 'The Conversion of Looted Jewish Assets to Run the German War Machine', *Holocaust and Genocide Studies*, 18 (2004), 27–45.

Madajczyk, Czeslaw, *Die Okkupationspolitik Nazideutschlands in Polen 1939–1945* (Cologne, 1988 [1970]).

——, *et al.* (eds.), *Vom Generalplan Ost zum Generalsiedlungsplan: Dokumente* (Munich, 1994).

Maertz, Gregory, *The Invisible Museum: The Secret Postwar History of Nazi Art* (New Haven, Conn., 2008).

Maier, Dieter, *Arbeitseinsatz und Deportation: Die Mitwirkung der Arbeitsverwaltung bei der nationalsozialistischen Judenverfolgung in den Jahren 1938–1945* (Berlin, 1994).

Maier, Klaus A., 'The Battle of Britain', in *GSWW* II. 374–407.

Mammach, Klaus, *Der Volkssturm: Bestandteil des totalen Kriegseinsatzes der deutschen Bevölkerung 1944/45* (Berlin, 1981).

Manoschek, Walter, *'Serbien ist judenfrei': Militärische Besatzungspolitik und Judenvernichtung in Serbien 1941/42* (Munich, 1993).

——, ' "Gehst mit Juden erschiessen?" Die Vernichtung der Juden in Serbien', in Heer and Naumann (eds.), *Vernichtungskrieg*, 39–56.

—— (ed.), *Die Wehrmacht im Rassenkrieg: Der Vernichtungskrieg hinter der Front* (Vienna, 1996).

——, 'Partisanenkrieg und Genozid: Die Wehrmacht in Serbien 1941', in idem (ed.), *Die Wehrmacht im Rassenkrieg*, 142–67.

—— (ed.), *'Es gibt nur Eines für das Judentum: Vernichtung': Das Judenbild in deutschen Soldatenbriefen 1939–1941* (Hamburg, 1997 [1995]).

——, 'Die Vernichtung der Juden in Serbien', in Ulrich Herbert (ed.), *Nationalsozialistische Vernichtungspolitik 1939–1945: Neue Forschungen und Kontroversen* (Frankfurt am Main, 1998), 209–34.

——, 'Krajevo – Kragujevac – Kalavryta: Die Massaker der 717. Infanteriedivision bzw. 117. Jägerdivision am Balnak', in Droulia and Fleischer (eds.), *Von Lidice bis Kalavryta*, 93–104.

Mantelli, Brunello, 'Von der Wanderarbeit zur Deportation: Die italienischen Arbeiter in Deutschland 1938–1945', in Herbert (ed.), *Europa und der 'Reichseinsatz'*, 51–89.

Marrus, Michael R. (ed.), *The Nazi Holocaust: Historical Articles on the Destruction of European Jews* (5 vols., Westport, Conn., 1989).

——, and Paxton, Robert O., *Vichy France and the Jews* (New York, 1981).

Maschmann, Melita, *Account Rendered: A Dossier on my Former Self* (London, 1964).

Maser, Werner (ed.), *Hitlers Briefe und Notizen: Sein Weltbild in handschriftlichen Dokumenten* (Düsseldorf, 1973).

Mason, Tim, *Social Policy in the Third Reich: The Working Class and the 'National Community'* (Oxford, 1995).

Massin, Benoît, 'Mengele, die Zwillingsforschung und die "Auschwitz-Dahlem Connection" ', in Carola Sachse (ed.), *Die Verbindung nach Auschwitz: Biowissenschaften und Menschenversuche an Kaiser-Wilhelm-Instituten: Dokumentation eines Symposiums* (Göttingen, 2003), 201–54.

Matthäus, Jürgen, 'Jenseits der Grenze: Die ersten Massenerschiessungen von Juden in Litauen (Juni–August 1941)', *Zeitschrift für Geschichtswissenschaft*, 44 (1996), 97–117.

——, 'Ausbildungsziel Judenmord? Zum Stellenwert der "weltanschaulichen Erziehung" von SS und Polizei im Rahmen der "Endlösung" ', *Zeitschrift für Geschichtswissenschaft*, 47 (1999), 677–99.

——, *et al.* (eds.), *Ausbildungsziel Judenmord? 'Weltanschauliche Erziehung' von SS, Polizei und Waffen-SS im Rahmen der 'Endlösung'* (Frankfurt am Main, 2003).

Mawdsley, Evan, *Thunder in the East: The Nazi–Soviet War 1941–1945* (London, 2005).

May, Ernest R., *Strange Victory: Hitler's Conquest of France* (New York, 2000).

Mazower, Mark, *Inside Hitler's Greece: The Experience of Occupation 1941–44* (London, 1993).
——, *Salonica: City of Ghosts: Christians, Muslims and Jews 1430–1950* (London, 2004).
——, *Hitler's Empire: Nazi Rule in Occupied Europe* (London, 2008).
Meier-Welcker, Hans, *Aufzeichnungen eines Generalstabsoffiziers 1939–1942* (Freiburg im Breisgau, 1982).
Melis, Damian van, *Entnazifizierung in Mecklenburg-Vorpommern: Herrschaft und Verwaltung 1945–1948* (Munich, 1999).
Merridale, Catherine, *Ivan's War: The Red Army 1939–1945* (London, 2005).
Messerschmidt, Manfred, 'Partisanenkrieg auf dem Balkan, Ziele, Methoden, "Rechtfertigung" ', in Droulia and Fleischer (eds.), *Von Lidice bis Kalavryta*, 65–91.
——, and Wüllner, Fritz, *Die Wehrmachtjustiz im Dienste des Nationalsozialismus: Zerstörung einer Legende* (Baden-Baden, 1987).
Meyer, Ahlrich, *Die deutsche Besatzung in Frankreich 1940–1944: Widerstandbekämpfung und Judenverfolgung* (Darmstadt, 2000).
——, *Täter im Verhör: Die Endlösung der Judenfrage in Frankreich 1940–1944* (Darmstadt, 2005).
Meyer, Beate, *'Jüdische Mischlinge': Rassenpolitik und Verfolgungserfahrung 1933–1945* (Hamburg, 1999).
Meyer, Marcus, '... *uns 100 Zivilausländer umgehend zu beschaffen': Zwangsarbeit bei den Bremer Stadtwerken 1939–1945* (Bremen, 2002).
Michaelis, Meir, *Mussolini and the Jews: German–Italian Relations and the Jewish Question in Italy, 1922–1945* (Oxford, 1978).
Michalka, Wolfgang (ed.), *Das Dritte Reich* (2 vols., Munich, 1985).
Michman, Dan (ed.), *Belgium and the Holocaust: Jews, Belgians, Germans* (Jerusalem, 1998).
Middlebrook, Martin, *The Battle of Hamburg: Allied Bomber Forces against a German City in 1943* (London, 1980).
Militärgeschichtliches Forschungsamt (ed.), *Das Deutsche Reich und der Zweite Weltkrieg* (10 vols., Stuttgart/Munich, 1979–2008); English edn: *Germany and the Second World War* (10 vols., Oxford, 1990– [1979–]).
Miller, Marshall Lee, *Bulgaria during the Second World War* (Stanford, Calif., 1975).
Milton, Sybil H., 'The Expulsion of Polish Jews from Germany, October 1938 to July 1939: A Documentation', *Leo Baeck Institute Yearbook*, 29 (1984), 169–74.
——, ' "Gypsies" as Social Outsiders in Nazi Germany', in Robert Gellately and Nathan Stolzfus (eds.), *Social Outsiders in Nazi Germany* (Princeton, N.J., 2001).
Milward, Alan S., 'Hitlers Konzept des Blitzkrieges', in Andreas Hillgruber (ed.), *Probleme des Zweiten Weltkrieges* (Cologne, 1967), 19–40.
——, *The Fascist Economy in Norway* (Oxford, 1972).
——, *The New Order and the French Economy* (Oxford, 1984).
——, *The German Economy at War* (London, 1985).
——, *War, Economy and Society 1939–1945* (London, 1987 [1977]), 137.
Moeller, Robert G., *War Stories: The Search for a Usable Past in the Federal Republic of Germany* (Berkeley, Calif., 2001).
Molotov, Vyacheslav M. *et al.*, *Soviet Government Statements on Nazi Atrocities* (London, 1945).
Moltmann, Günter, 'Goebbels' Speech on Total War, February 18, 1943', in Hajo Holborn (ed.), *Republic to Reich: The Making of the Nazi Revolution: Ten Essays* (New York, 1973 [1972]), 298–342.
Mommsen, Hans, 'Social Views and Constitutional Plans of the Resistance', in Hermann Graml *et al.*, *The German Resistance to Hitler* (London, 1970 [1966]), 55–147.
——, 'Die moralische Wiederherstellung der Nation: Der Widerstand gegen Hitler war von einer antisemitischen Grundhaltung getragen', *Süddeutsche Zeitung*, 21 July 1999, 15.

——, and Manfred Grieger, *Das Volkswagenwerk und seine Arbeiter im Dritten Reich* (Düsseldorf, 1996), 544–65.

Moore, Bob (ed.), *Victims and Survivors: The Nazi Persecution of the Jews in the Netherlands, 1940–1945* (London, 1997).

——, *Resistance in Western Europe* (Oxford, 2000).

Moorhouse, Roger, *Killing Hitler: The Third Reich and the Plots against the Führer* (London, 2006).

Morley, John F., *Vatican Diplomacy and the Jews during the Holocaust, 1939–1945* (New York, 1980).

Mouton, Michelle, *From Nurturing the Nation to Purifying the Volk: Weimar and Nazi Family Policy, 1918–1945* (New York, 2007).

Müller, Klaus-Jürgen, and Ueberschär, Gerd, *Kriegsende 1945: Die Zerstörung des deutschen Reiches* (Frankfurt am Main, 1994).

Müller, Max, 'Der Tod des Reichsministers Dr Fritz Todt', *Geschichte in Wissenschaft und Unterricht* 18 (1967), 602–5.

Müller, Roland (ed.), *Stuttgart zur Zeit des Nationalsozialismus* (Stuttgart, 1988).

——, *Krankenmord im Nationalsozialismus: Grafeneck und die 'Euthanasie' in Südwestdeutschland* (Stuttgart, 2001).

Müller, Rolf-Dieter, 'The Failure of the Economic "Blitzkrieg Strategy" ', in *GSWW* IV. 1,061–8

——, 'The Mobilization of the German Economy for Hitler's War Aims', in *GSWW* V/I, 407–86.

——, ' "Was wir an Hunger ausstehen müssen, könnt Ihr Euch gar nicht denken": Eine Armee verhungert', in Wette and Ueberschär (eds.), *Stalingrad*, 131–45.

——, 'Albert Speer and Armaments Policy in Total War', in *GSWW* V/II, 293–832.

——, *Der Manager der Kriegswirtschaft: Hans Kehrl: Ein Unternehmer in der Politik des 'Dritten Reiches'* (Essen, 1999).

——, 'Der Zusammenbruch des Wirtschaftslebens und die Anfänge des Wiederaufbaus', in *DRZW* X/II, 55–378.

Müller, Sven Oliver, 'Nationalismus in der deutschen Kriegsgesellschaft 1939 bis 1945', in *DRZW* IX/II. 9–92.

Musial, Bogdan, *'Konterrevolutionäre Elemente sind zu erschiessen': Die Brutalisierung des deutsch-sowjetischen Krieges im Sommer 1941* (Berlin, 2000).

Naasner, Walter, *Neue Machtzentren in der deutschen Kriegswirtschaft 1942–1945* (Boppard, 1994).

——, *SS-Wirtschaft und SS-Verwaltung* (Düsseldorf, 1998).

Naimark, Norman M., *Fires of Hatred: Ethnic Cleansing in Twentieth-Century Europe* (London, 2001).

Némirovsky, Irène, *Suite Française* (London, 2007 [2004]).

Neufeld, Michael J., *The Rocket and the Reich: Peenemünde and the Coming of the Ballistic Missile Era* (New York, 1995).

Neumann, Franz, *Behemoth: The Structure and Practice of National Socialism 1933–1944* (New York, 1944 [1942]).

Nicholas, Lynn, *The Rape of Europa: The Fate of Europe's Treasures in the Third Reich and the Second World War* (New York, 1994).

Niethammer, Lutz (ed.), *Die Mitläuferfabrik: Die Entnazifizierung am Beispiel Bayerns* (Berlin, 1992).

——, *Der 'gesäuberte' Antifaschismus: Die SED und die rotten Kapos von Buchenwald* (Berlin, 1994).

Niven, Bill, *Facing the Nazi Past: United Germany and the Legacy of the Third Reich* (London, 2002).

Noakes, Jeremy (ed.), *Nazism 1919–1945*, IV: *The German Home Front in World War II: A Documentary Reader* (Exeter, 1998).

——, and Pridham, Geoffrey (eds.), *Nazism 1919–1945*, III: *Foreign Policy, War and Racial Extermination: A Documentary Reader* (Exeter, 1988).

Nolzen, Armin, ' "Sozialismus der Tat"? Die Nationalsozialistische Volkswohlfahrt (NSV) und der alliierte Luftkrieg gegen das deutsche Reich', in Süss (ed.), *Deutschland im Luftkrieg*, 57–70.

Nowak, Kurt, *'Euthanasie' und Sterilisierung im 'Dritten Reich' – Die Konfrontation der evangelischen und katholischen Kirche mit dem 'Gesetz zur Verhütung erbkranken Nachwuchses' und der 'Euthanasie'-Aktion* (Gottingen, 1984 [1977]).

——, 'Widerstand, Zustimmung, Hinnahme: Das Verhalten der Bevölkerung zur "Euthanasie" ', in Norbert Frei (ed.), *Medizin und Gesundheitspolitik in der NS-Zeit* (Munich, 1991), 235–51.

Obenaus, Herbert, 'Der Kampf um das tägliche Brot', in Herbert *et al.* (eds.), *Die nationalsozialistischen Konzentrationslager* II. 841–73.

O'Brien, Mary-Elizabeth, 'The Celluloid War: Packaging War for Sale in Nazi Home-Front Films', in Etlin (ed.), *Art*, 158–80.

Ofer, Dalia, 'Life in the Ghettos of Transnistria', *Yad Vashem Studies*, 25 (1996), 229–74.

Ogorreck, Ralf, *Die Einsatzgruppen und die 'Genesis der Endlösung'* (Berlin, 1996).

Orth, Karin, 'Die Kommandanten der nationalsozialistischen Konzentrationslager', in Herbert *et al.* (eds.), *Die nationalsozialistischen Konzentrationslager*, II. 755–86.

——, 'Gab es eine Lagergesellschaft? "Kriminelle" und politische Häftlinge im Konzentrationslager', in Frei *et al.* (eds.), *Ausbeutung*, 109–33.

Otter, Anne Sofie von, *et al.*, *Terezín/Theresienstadt* (Deutsche Grammophon Gesellschaft, 2007).

Ottmer, Hans-Martin, *'Weserübung': Der deutsche Angriff auf Dänemark und Norwegen im April 1940* (Munich, 1994).

Ousby, Ian, *Occupation: The Ordeal of France 1940–1944* (London, 1997).

Overmans, Rüdiger, *Deutsche militärische Verluste im Zweiten Weltkriege* (Munich, 1999).

Overy, Richard J., 'Guns or Butter? Living Standards, Finance, and Labour in Germany, 1939–1942', in idem, *War and Economy in the Third Reich*, 259–314.

——, 'Rationalization and the "Production Miracle" in Germany during the Second World War', in idem, *War and Economy in the Third Reich*, 343–56.

——, *War and Economy in the Third Reich* (Oxford, 1994).

——, *Why the Allies Won* (London, 1995).

——, *The Battle* (London, 2000).

——, *Interrogations: The Nazi Elite in Allied Hands, 1945* (London, 2001).

——, *et al.*, *Die 'Neuordnung' Europas: NS-Wirtschaftspolitik in den besetzten Gebieten* (Berlin, 1997).

Padfield, Peter, *Himmler: Reichsführer-SS* (London, 1990).

Paris, Edmond, *Genocide in Satellite Croatia 1941–1945: A Record of Racial and Religious Persecution and Massacres* (Chicago, Ill., 1961).

Pätzold, Kurt (ed.), *Verfolgung, Vertreibung, Vernichtung: Dokumente des faschistischen Antisemitismus 1933 bis 1942* (Frankfurt am Main, 1984).

Paul, Gerhard, ' "Diese Erschiessungen haben mich innerlich gar nicht mehr berührt": Die Kriegsendphasenverbrechen der Gestapo 1944/45', in idem and Klaus-Michael Mallmann (eds.), *Die Gestapo im Zweiten Weltkrieg: 'Heimatfront' und besetztes Europa* (Darmstadt, 2000), 543–68.

Paulsson, Gunnar S., *Secret City: The Hidden Jews of Warsaw, 1940–1945* (London, 2003).

——, 'The Bridge over the Øresund: The Historiography on the Expulsion of the Jews from Nazi-occupied Denmark', in Cesarani (ed.), *Holocaust*, V. 99–127.

Paxton, Robert O., *Vichy France: Old Guard and New Order, 1940–1944* (London, 1972).

Payne, Stanley G., *A History of Fascism 1914–45* (London, 2001 [1995]).

Pelt, Robert Jan Van, 'A Site in Search of a Mission', in Gutman and Berenbaum (eds.), *Anatomy*, 93–156.

Perz, Bertrand, and Sandkühler, Thomas, 'Auschwitz und die "Aktion Reinhard" 1942–1945: Judenmord und Raubpraxis in neuer Sicht', Zeitgeschichte, 26 (2000), 283–316.

Petropoulos, Jonathan, The Faustian Bargain: The Art World in Nazi Germany (London, 2000).

Peukert, Detlev J. K., Die KPD im Widerstand: Verfolgung und Untergrundarbeit an Rhein und Ruhr 1933–1945 (Wuppertal, 1980).

——, 'Arbeitslager und Jugend-KZ: Die Behandlung "Gemeinschaftsfremder" im Dritten Reich', in idem and Jürgen Reulecke (eds.), Die Reihen fast geschlossen: Beiträge zur Geschichte des Alltags unterm Nationalsozialismus (Wuppertal, 1981), 413–34.

——, 'Der deutsche Arbeiterwiderstand 1933–1945', in Klaus-Jürgen Müller (ed.), Der deutsche Widerstand 1933–1945 (Paderborn, 1986), 157–81.

Pfahlmann, Hans, Fremdarbeiter und Kriegsgefangene in der deutschen Kriegswirtschaft 1939–1945 (Darmstadt, 1968).

Pfeiffer, Jürgen, 'Neuropathologische Forschung an "Euthanasie"-Opfern in zwei Kaiser-Wilhelm-Instituten', in Kaufmann (ed.), Geschichte der Kaiser-Wilhelm-Gesellschaft, I. 151–73.

Phayer, Michael, The Catholic Church and the Holocaust, 1930–1965 (Bloomington, Ind., 2000).

Pieper, Werner (ed.), Nazis on Speed: Drogen im 3. Reich (Loherbach, 2002).

Pietrow-Ennker, Bianka, 'Die Sowjetunion in der Propaganda des Dritten Reiches: Das Beispiel der Wochenschau', Militärgeschichtliche Mitteilungen, 46 (1989), 79–120.

Pinchuk, Ben-Cion, Shtetl Jews under Soviet Rule: Eastern Poland on the Eve of the Holocaust (Oxford, 1990).

Piotrowski, Tadeusz, Poland's Holocaust: Ethnic Strife, Collaboration with Occupying Forces, and Genocide in the Second Republic, 1918–1947 (Jefferson, N.C., 1998).

Pleyer, Kleo, Volk im Feld (Hamburg, 1943).

Plum, Günter, 'Deutsche Juden oder Juden in Deutschland?', in Benz (ed.), Die Juden, 35–74.

Podranski, Thomas, Deutsche Siedlungspolitik im Osten: Die verschiedenen Varianten des Generalplan Ost der SS (Berlin, 2001).

Pohl, Dieter, Von der 'Judenpolitik' zum Judenmord: Der Distrikt Lublin des Generalgouvernements 1939–1944 (Frankfurt am Main, 1993).

——, Nationalsozialistische Judenverfolgung in Ostgalizien 1941–1944: Organisation und Durchführung eines staatlichen Massenverbrechens (Munich, 1996).

——, 'Hans Krüger and the Murder of the Jews in the Stanislawów Region (Galicia)', Yad Vashem Studies, 26 (1998), 259–64.

——, 'Schauplatz Ukraine: Der Massenmord an den Juden im Militärverwaltungsgebiet und im Reichskommissariat 1941–1945', in Frei et al. (eds.), Ausbeutung, 135–73.

Poliakov, Leon, and Wulf, Josef (eds.), Das Dritte Reich und seine Diener (Frankfurt am Main, 1959).

Polonsky, Antony, 'Beyond Condemnation, Apologetics and Apologies: On the Complexity of Polish Behaviour Towards the Jews during the Second World War', in David Cesarani (ed.), Holocaust: Critical Concepts in Historical Studies 5 vols., New York, (2004), II, 29–72.

——, 'The German Occupation of Poland during the First and Second World Wars', in Roy A. Prete and A. Hamish Ion (eds.), Armies of Occupation (Waterloo, Ontario, 1984), 97–142.

Pöppel, Martin, Heaven and Hell: The War Diary of a German Paratrooper (Staplehurst, 1988).

Porat, Dina, 'The Legend of the Struggle of Jews from the Third Reich in the Ninth Fort Near Kovno, 1941–1942', Tel Aviver Jahrbuch für deutsche Geschichte, 20 (1991), 363–92.

——, 'The Vilna Proclamation of January 1, 1942, in Historical Perspective', Yad Vashem Studies, 25 (1996), 99–136.

Porter, Brian, 'Making a Space for Antisemitism: The Catholic Hierarchy and the Jews in the Early Twentieth Century', Polin: Studies in Polish Jewry, 16 (2003), 415–29.

Powers, Thomas, *Heisenberg's War: The Secret History of the German Bomb* (Boston, 1993).

Poznanski, Renée, *Jews in France during World War II* (Hanover, 2001 [1994]).

Präg, Werner, and Jacobmeyer, Wolfgang (eds.), *Das Diensttagebuch des deutschen General-gouverneurs in Polen 1939–1945* (Stuttgart, 1975).

Preston, Paul, 'Franco and Hitler: The Myth of Hendaye 1940', *Contemporary European History*, 1 (1992), 1–16.

——, *Franco: A Biography* (London, 1993).

Price, Alfred, *Blitz on Britain* (Shepperton, 1977).

Prieberg, Fred K., *Musik im NS-Staat* (Frankfurt am Main, 1989 [1982]).

——, *Trial of Strength: Wilhelm Furtwängler and the Third Reich* (London, 1991 [1986]).

Pringle, Heather, *The Master Plan: Himmler's Scholars and the Holocaust* (New York, 2006).

Proctor, Robert N., *Racial Hygiene: Medicine under the Nazis* (Cambridge, Mass., 1988).

Quinkert, Babette (ed.), *'Wir sind die Herren dieses Landes': Ursachen, Verlauf und Folgen des deutschen Überfalls auf die Sowjetunion* (Hamburg, 2002).

Quisling, Vidkun, *Quisling ruft Norwegen! Reden und Aufsätze* (Munich, 1942).

Rahn, Werner, 'The War at Sea in the Atlantic and in the Arctic Ocean', in *GSWW* VI. 301–468.

Rass, Christoph, 'Das Sozialprofil von Kampfverbänden des deutschen Heeres 1939 bis 1945', in *DRZW* IX/I, 641–741.

Rathkolb, Oliver, 'Zwangsarbeit in der Industrie', in *DRZW* IX/II, 667–728.

Rebentisch, Dieter, *Führerstaat und Verwaltung im Zweiten Weltkrieg* (Stuttgart, 1989).

Reddemann, Karl (ed.), *Zwischen Front und Heimat: Der Briefwechsel des münsterischen Ehepaares Agnes und Albert Neuhaus 1940–1944* (Münster, 1996).

Redlich, Fritz, *Hitler: Diagnosis of a Destructive Prophet* (New York, 1998).

Reichel, Peter, *Politik mit der Erinnerung: Gedächtnisorte im Streit um die nationalsozial-istische Vergangenheit* (Frankfurt am Main, 1999 [1995]).

Reich-Ranicki, Marcel, *The Author of Himself: The Life of Marcel Reich-Ranicki* (London, 2001 [1999]).

Reifarth, Dieter, and Schmidt-Linsenhoff, Viktoria, 'Die Kamera der Täter', in Heer and Naumann (eds.), *Vernichtungskrieg*, 475–503.

Reilly, Joanne, *Belsen: The Liberation of a Concentration Camp* (London, 1998).

Remy, Steven P., *The Heidelberg Myth: The Nazification and Denazification of a German University* (Cambridge, Mass., 2002).

Rentschler, Eric, *The Ministry of Illusion: Nazi Cinema and its Afterlife* (Cambridge, Mass., 1996).

Reuband, Karl-Heinz, ' "Jud Süss" und "Der ewige Jude" als Prototypen antisemitischer Filmpropaganda im Dritten Reich: Entstehungsbedingungen, Zuschauerstrukturen und Wirkungspotential', in Michel Andel *et al.* (eds.), *Propaganda, (Selbst) Zensur, Sensation: Grenzen von Presse- und Wissenschaftsfreiheit in Deutschland und Tschechien seit 1871* (Essen, 2005), 89–148.

Reuth, Ralf Georg, *Goebbels: Eine Biographie* (Munich, 1995 [1990]).

Reynolds, David, *The Creation of the Anglo-American Alliance, 1937–1941: A Study in Competitive Co-operation* (London, 1981).

——, *From Munich to Pearl Harbor: Roosevelt's America and the Origins of the Second World War* (Chicago, 2001).

Richardson, Horst F., *Sieg Heil! War Letters of Tank Gunner Karl Fuchs, 1937–1941* (Hamden, Conn., 1987).

Ries, Tomas, *Cold Will: The Defence of Finland* (London, 1988).

Riess, Volker, *Die Anfänge der Vernichtung 'lebensunwerten Lebens' in den Reichsgauen Danzig-Westpreussen und Wartheland 1939/40* (Frankfurt am Main, 1995).

Ringelblum, Emanuel, *Notes from the Warsaw Ghetto: The Journal of Emanuel Ringelblum* (New York, 1958 [1952]).

——, *Polish-Jewish Relations during the Second World War* (Jerusalem, 1974), 23–57.

Ristović, Milan, 'Yugoslav Jews Fleeing the Holocaust, 1941–1945', in John K. Roth and Elisabeth Maxwell (eds.), *Remembering for the Future: The Holocaust in an Age of Genocide* (3 vols., London, 2001), I. 512–26.

Roberts, Geoffrey, *Stalin's Wars: From World War to Cold War, 1939–1953* (London, 2006).

Rohde, Horst, 'Hitler's First Blitzkrieg and Its Consequences for North-eastern Europe', in *GSWW* II. 67–150.

Röhm, Eberhard, and Thierfelder, Jörg, *Juden, Christen, Deutsche 1933–1945* (3 vols., Stuttgart, 1990–98).

Röhr, Werner, 'Zum Zusammenhang von nazistischer Okkupationspolitik in Polen und dem Völkermord an den polnischen Juden', in idem *et al.* (eds.), *Faschismus und Rassismus: Kontroversen um Ideologie und Opfer* (Berlin, 1992), 300–316.

——, 'Zur Wirtschaftspolitik der deutschen Okkupanten in Polen 1939–1945', in Dietrich Eichholtz (ed.), *Krieg und Wirtschaft: Studien zur deutschen Wirtschaftsgeschichte 1939–1945* (Berlin, 1999).

Roland, Charles G., *Courage under Siege: Starvation, Disease, and Death in the Warsaw Ghetto* (New York, 1992).

Roloff, Stefan, 'Die Entstehung der Roten Kapelle und die Verzerrung ihrer Geschichte im Kalten Krieg', in Karl Heinz Roth and Angelika Ebbinghaus (eds.), *Rote Kapellen – Kreisauer Kreise – Schwarze Kapellen: Neue Sichtweisen auf den Widerstand gegen die NS-Diktatur 1938–1945* (Hamburg, 2004), 186–205.

Roseman, Mark, *The Past in Hiding* (London, 2000).

——, *The Wannsee Conference and the Final Solution: A Reconsideration* (New York, 2002).

Rossino, Alexander B., 'Nisko – Ein Ausnahmefall unter den Judenlagern der SS', *VfZ* 40 (1992), 95–106.

——, 'Destructive Impulses: German Soldiers and the Conquest of Poland', *Holocaust and Genocide Studies*, 11 (1997), 351–65.

——, *Hitler Strikes Poland: Blitzkrieg, Ideology, and Atrocity* (Lawrence, Kans., 2003).

——, 'Polish "Neighbors" and German Invaders: Anti-Jewish Violence in the Bialystok District during the Opening Weeks of Operation Barbarossa', *Polin: Studies in Polish Jewry*, 16 (2003), 431–52.

Rössler, Mechthild, and Schleiermacher, Sabine, *Der 'Generalplan Ost': Hauptlinien der nationalsozialistischen Planungs- und Vernichtungspolitik* (Berlin, 1993).

Rost, Karl Ludwig, *Sterilisation und Euthanasie im Film des 'Dritten Reiches': Nationalsozialistische Propaganda in ihrer Beziehung zu rassenhygienischen Massnahmen des NS-Staates* (Berlin, 1984).

Roth, Karl Heinz, 'Strukturen, Paradigmen und Mentalitäten in der luftfahrtmedizinischen Forschung des "Dritten Reichs": Der Weg ins Konzentrationslager Dachau', *1999. Zeitschrift für Sozialgeschichte des 20. und 21. Jahrhunderts*, 15 (2000), 49–77.

——, 'Tödliche Höhen: Die Unterdruckkammer-Experimente im Konzentrationslager Dachau und ihre Bedeutung für die luftfahrtmedizinische Forschung des "Dritten Reichs" ', in Ebbinghaus and Dörner (eds.), *Vernichten und Heilen*, 110–51.

——, and Götz Aly, 'Das "Gesetz über die Sterbehilfe bei unheilbar Kranken": Protokolle der Diskussion über die Legalisierung der nationalsozialistischen Anstaltsmorde in den Jahren 1938–1941', in Karl Heinz Roth (ed.), *Erfassung zur Vernichtung: Von der Sozialhygiene zum 'Gesetz über Sterbehilfe'* (Berlin, 1984), 101–79.

Rothkirchen, Livia, 'The Situation of the Jews in Slovakia between 1939 and 1945', *Jahrbuch für Antisemitismusforschung*, 7 (1998), 46–70.

Rozett, Robert, 'Jewish and Hungarian Armed Resistance in Hungary', *Yad Vashem Studies*, 19 (1988), 269–88.

Rubinstein, William D., *The Myth of Rescue: Why the Democracies Could not Have Saved More Jews from the Nazis* (London, 1997).

Ruhm von Oppen, Beate (ed.), *Helmuth James von Moltke: Letters to Freya, 1939–1945* (London, 1991).

Rupp, Leila J., *Mobilizing Women for War: German and American Propaganda 1939–1945* (Princeton, N.J., 1978).

Rusinek, Bernd-A., *Gesellschaft in der Katastrophe: Terror, Illegalität, Widerstand – Köln 1944/45* (Essen, 1989).

Rüther, Martin (ed.), *'Zu Hause könnten sie es nicht schöner haben!' Kinderlandverschickung aus Köln und Umgebung 1941–1945* (Cologne, 2000).

Rutherford, Philip T., *Prelude to the Final Solution: The Nazi Program for Deporting Ethnic Poles, 1939–1941* (Lawrence, Kans., 2007).

Safrian, Hans, *Die Eichmann-Männer* (Vienna, 1993).

——, 'Komplizen des Genozids: Zum Anteil der Heeresgruppe Süd an der Verfolgung und Ermordung der Juden in der Ukraine 1941', in Manoschek (ed.), *Die Wehrmacht im Rassenkrieg*, 90–115.

Salewski, Michael, *Die deutsche Seekriegsleitung 1935–1945* (Frankfurt am Main, 1970).

Salisbury, Harrison E., *The 900 Days: The Siege of Leningrad* (London, 1969).

Sandkühler, Thomas, *'Endlösung' in Galizien: Der Judenmord in Ostpolen und die Rettungsinitiativen von Berthold Beitz, 1941–1944* (Bonn, 1996).

Satloff, Robert, *Among the Righteous: Lost Stories from the Holocaust's Long Reach into Arab Lands* (New York, 2006).

Schäfer, Harald, *Napola: Die letzten vier Jahre der Nationalpolitischen Erziehungsanstalt Oranienstein bei Dietz an der Lahn 1941–1945: Eine Erlebnis-Dokumentation* (Frankfurt am Main, 1997).

Scharf, Eginhard, *'Man machte mit uns, was man wollte': Ausländische Zwangsarbeiter in Ludwigshafen am Rhein 1939–1945* (Hamburg, 2004).

Scheffler, Wolfgang, 'The Forgotten Part of the "Final Solution": The Liquidation of the Ghettos', *Simon Wiesenthal Centre Annual*, 2 (1985), 31–51.

Schelach, Menachem, 'Sajmiste – An Extermination Camp in Serbia', *Holocaust and Genocide Studies*, 2 (1987), 243–60.

Schellenberg, Walter, *Invasion 1940: The Nazi Invasion Plan for Britain* (London, 2000).

——, *The Memoirs of Hitler's Spymaster* (London, 2006 [1956]).

Schenk, Dieter, *Hitlers Mann in Danzig: Gauleiter Forster und die NS-Verbrechen in Danzig-Westpreussen* (Bonn, 2000).

Schepping, Wilhelm, 'Zeitgeschichte im Spiegel eines Liedes', in Günter Noll and Marianne Bröcker (eds.), *Musikalische Volkskunde aktuell* (Bonn, 1984), 435–64.

Scheuer, Alois (ed.), *Briefe aus Russland: Feldpostbriefe des Gefreiten Alois Scheuer 1941–1942* (St Ingbert, 2000).

Scheurig, Bodo, *Henning von Tresckow: Ein Preusse gegen Hitler* (Frankfurt am Main, 1987).

Schlabrendorff, Fabian von, *Revolt against Hitler: The Personal Account of Fabian von Schlabrendorff* (London, 1948).

Schmaltz, Florian, *Kampfstoff-Forschung im Nationalsozialismus: Zur Kooperation von Kaiser-Wilhelm-Instituten, Militär und Industrie* (Göttingen, 2005).

——, 'Neurosciences and Research on Chemical Weapons of Mass Destruction in Nazi Germany', *Journal of the History of Neurosciences*, 15 (2006), 186–209.

Schmidt, Matthias, *Albert Speer: Das Ende eines Mythos: Speers wahre Rolle im Dritten Reich* (Bern, 1982).

Schmidt, Rainer F., 'Der Hess-Flug und das Kabinett Churchill', *VfZ* 42 (1994), 1–38.

Schmidt, Ulf, 'Reassessing the Beginning of the "Euthanasia" Programme', *German History*, 17 (1999), 543–50.

——, *Karl Brandt: The Nazi Doctor: Medicine and Power in the Third Reich* (London, 2007).

Schmidt, Uta C., 'Radioaneignung', in Inge Marssolek and Adelheid von Saldern (eds.), *Zuhören und Gehörtwerden* (2 vols., Tübingen, 1998), I: *Radio im Nationalsozialismus: Zwischen Lenkung und Ablenkung*, 243–360.

Schmuhl, Hans-Walter, *Rassenhygiene, Nationalsozialismus, Euthanasie: Von der Verhütung zur Vernichtung 'lebensunwerten Lebens', 1890–1945* (Göttingen, 1987).

——, 'Die Patientenmorde', in Ebbinghaus and Dörner (eds.), *Vernichten und Heilen*, 295–328.

—— (ed.), *Rassenforschung an Kaiser-Wilhelm-Instituten vor und nach 1933* (Göttingen, 2003).

Schnell, Ralf, *Literarische innere Emigration 1933–1945* (Stuttgart, 1976).

Schreiber, Gerhard, 'Germany, Italy, and South-east Europe: From Political and Economic Hegemony to Military Aggression', in *GSWW* III. 305–448.

Schubert, Günter, *Das Unternehmen 'Bromberger Blutsonntag': Tod einer Legende* (Cologne, 1989).

Schulte, Jan-Erik, 'Zwangsarbeit für die SS: Juden in der Ostindustrie GmbH', in Frei *et al.* (eds.), *Ausbeutung*, 43–74.

——, *Zwangsarbeit und Vernichtung: Das Wirtschaftsimperium der SS: Oswald Pohl und das SS-Wirtschafts-Verwaltungshauptamt 1933–1945* (Paderborn, 2001).

——, 'Das SS-Wirtschafts-Verwaltungshauptamt und die Expansion des KZ-Systems', in Benz and Distel (eds.), *Der Ort des Terrors*, I. 141–55.

Schulte, Theo J., *The German Army and Nazi Policies in Occupied Russia* (Oxford, 1989).

Schulze, Winfried, and Oexle, Otto (eds.), *Deutsche Historiker im Nationalsozialismus* (Frankfurt am Main, 1999).

Schwab, Gerald, *The Day the Holocaust Began: The Odyssey of Herschel Grynszpan* (New York, 1990).

Schwarz, Erika, *Tagesordnung: Judenmord: Die Wannsee-Konferenz am 20. Januar 1942* (Berlin, 1992).

Schwendemann, Heinrich, *Die wirtschaftliche Zusammenarbeit zwischen dem Deutschen Reich und der Sowjetunion von 1939 bis 1941: Alternative zu Hitlers Ostprogramm?* (Berlin, 1993).

——, ' "Deutsche Menschen vor der Vernichtung durch den Bolschewismus zu retten": Das Programm der Regierung Dönitz und der Beginn einer Legendenbildung', in Bernd-A. Rusinek (ed.), *Kriegsende 1945: Verbrechen, Katastrophen, Befreiungen in nationaler und internationaler Perspektive* (Göttingen, 2004), 9–33.

Sebag-Montefiori, Simon, *Stalin: The Court of the Red Tsar* (London, 2003).

Sebastian, Mihail, *'Voller Entsetzen, aber nicht verzweifelt': Tagebücher 1935–44* (ed. Edward Kanterian, Berlin, 2005).

Segeberg, Harro (ed.), *Mediale Mobilmachung*, I: *Das Dritte Reich und der Film* (Munich, 2004).

Seidler, Franz, *'Deutscher Volkssturm': Der letzte Aufgebot 1944/45* (Munich, 1989).

Semmens, Kristin, *Seeing Hitler's Germany: Tourism in the Third Reich* (London, 2005).

Seraphim, Hans-Günter (ed.), *Das Politische Tagebuch Alfred Rosenbergs aus den Jahren 1934/35 und 1939/40* (Munich, 1964).

Sereny, Gitta, *Into that Darkness: An Examination of Conscience* (London, 1977 [1974]).

——, *Albert Speer: His Battle with Truth* (London, 1995).

Service, Robert, *Stalin: A Biography* (London, 2004).

Shapiro, Paul A., 'The Jews of Chisinau (Kishinev): Romanian Reoccupation, Ghettoization, Deportation', in Braham (ed.), *The Destruction of Romanian and Ukrainian Jews*, 135–94.

Shephard, Ben, *After Daybreak: The Liberation of Belsen, 1945* (London, 2005).

Shils, Edward A., and Janowitz, Morris, 'Cohesion and Disintegration in the *Wehrmacht* in World War II', *Public Opinion Quarterly*, 12 (1948), 280–315.

Shirakawa, Sam H., *The Devil's Music Master: The Controversial Life and Career of Wilhelm Furtwängler* (New York, 1992).

Shirer, William L., *Berlin Diary* (London, 1970 [1941]).

Siegel, Tilla, *Leistung und Lohn in der nationalsozialistischen 'Ordnung der Arbeit'* (Opladen, 1989).

Siegfried, Klaus-Georg, *Das Leben der Zwangsarbeiter im Volkswagenwerk 1939–1945* (Frankfurt am Main, 1988).

Sierakowiak, Dawid, *The Diary of Dawid Sierakowiak* (ed. Alan Adelson, London, 1996).

Slesina, Horst, *Soldaten gegen Tod und Teufel: Unser Kampf in der Sowjetunion: Eine soldatische Deutung* (Düsseldorf, 1942).

Smelser, Ronald M., and Zitelmann, Rainer (eds.), *The Nazi Elite* (Basingstoke, 1993 [1989]).

Smith, Denis Mack, *Mussolini* (London, 1987 [1981]).

——, *Modern Italy: A Political History* (London, 1997 [1959]).

Snowden, Frank, 'Latina Province 1944–1950', *Journal of Contemporary History*, 43/3 (2008), 509–76.

Sollbach, Gerhard E. (ed.), *Dortmund: Bombenkrieg und Nachkriegsalltag 1939–1945* (Hagen, 1996).

Solmitz, Luise, *Tagebuch* (Staatsarchiv der Freien- und Hansestadt Hamburg, 622–1, 111511–13: Familie Solmitz; transcripts in Forschungsstelle für Zeitgeschichte, Hamburg).

Spector, Shmuel, *The Holocaust of Volhynian Jews: 1941–1944* (Jerusalem, 1990).

Speer, Albert, *Inside the Third Reich: Memoirs* (London, 1975 [1970]).

——, *Spandau: The Secret Diaries* (London, 1976 [1975]).

Spoerer, Mark, *Zwangsarbeit unter dem Hakenkreuz: Ausländische Zivilarbeiter, Kriegsgefangene und Häftlinge im Deutschen Reich und im besetzten Europa 1939–1945* (Stuttgart, 2001).

——, 'Die soziale Differenzierung der ausländischen Zivilarbeiter, Kriegsgefangenen und Häftlinge im Deutschen Reich', in *DRZW* IX/II. 485–576.

Spotts, Frederic, *Hitler and the Power of Aesthetics* (London, 2002).

Stadtarchiv München (ed.), '. . . verzogen, unbekannt wohin': Die erste Deportation von Münchner Juden im November 1941* (Zurich, 2000).

Stafford, David, *Endgame 1945: Victory, Retribution, Liberation* (London, 2007).

Stahr, Gerhard, *Volksgemeinschaft vor der Leinwand? Der nationalsozialistische Film und sein Publikum* (Berlin, 2001).

Stefanski, Valentina Maria, *Zwangsarbeit in Leverkusen: Polnische Jugendliche im I. G. Farbenwerk* (Osnabrück, 2000).

Stegemann, Bernd, 'Hitlers Kriegszeiele im ersten Kriegsjahr 1939/40: Ein Beitrag zur Quellenkritik', *Militärgeschichtliche Mitteilungen*, 27 (1980), 93–105.

——, 'The Italo-German Conduct of War in the Mediterranean and North Africa', in *GSWW* III. 643–754.

——, 'Operation Weserübung', in *GSWW* II. 206–19.

Stein, Henry, 'Funktionswandel des Konzentrationslagers Buchenwald im Spiegel der Lagerstatistiken', in Herbert *et al.* (eds.), *Die nationalsozialistischen Konzentrationslager*, I. 167–92.

Steinbacher, Sybille, *'Musterstadt' Auschwitz: Germanisierungspolitik und Judenmord in Ostoberschlesien* (Munich, 2000).

——, *Auschwitz: A History* (London, 2005 [2004]).

Steinberg, Jonathan, *All or Nothing: The Axis and the Holocaust 1941–1943* (London, 1991).

——, *The Deutsche Bank and Its Gold Transactions during the Second World War* (Munich, 1999).

Steinberg, Maxime, *La Persécution des Juifs en Belgique (1940–1945)* (Brussels, 2004).

Steinert, Marlis, *Capitulation 1945: A Story of the Dönitz Regime* (London, 1969).

——, 'Stalingrad und die deutsche Gesellschaft', in Förster (ed.), *Stalingrad*, 171–88.

Steinhilfer, Ulrich, and Osborne, Peter, *Spitfire on My Tail: A View from the Other Side* (Bromley, 1989).

Stephenson, Jill, *Hitler's Home Front: Württemberg under the Nazis* (London, 2006).

Steur, Claudia, *Theodor Dannecker: Ein Funktionär der 'Endlösung'* (Essen, 1997).

Stibbe, Matthew, *Women in the Third Reich* (London, 2003).

St John, Robert, *Foreign Correspondent* (London, 1960), 180.

Stoltzfus, Nathan, *Resistance of the Heart: Intermarriage and the Rosenstrasse Protest in Nazi Germany* (New York, 1996).

Streim, Alfred, 'Zur Eröffnung des allgemeinen Judenvernichtungsbefehls gegenüber den Einsatzgruppen', in Eberhard Jäckel and Jürgen Rohwer (eds.), *Der Mord an den Juden im Zweiten Weltkrieg: Entschlussbildung und Verwirklichung* (Stuttgart, 1985).

Streit, Christian, *Keine Kameraden: Die Wehrmacht und die sowjetischen Kriegsgefangenen 1941–1945* (Stuttgart, 1978).

——, 'The Fate of the Soviet Prisoners of War', in Michael Berenbaum (ed.), *A Mosaic of Victims: Non-Jews Persecuted and Murdered by the Nazis* (London, 1990), 142–9.

Stroop, Jürgen, *The Stroop Report: The Jewish Quarter of Warsaw Is No More!* (London, 1980 [1960]).

Stumpf, Reinhard, *Die Wehrmacht-Elite: Rang- und Herkunftsstruktur der deutschen Generale und Admirale 1933–1945* (Boppard, 1982).

——, 'The War in the Mediterranean Area 1942–1943: Operations in North Africa and the Central Mediterranean', in *GSWW* VI. 631–840.

Stunkard, Horace W., 'Erich Martini (1880–1960)', *Journal of Parasitology*, 147 (1961), 909–10.

Stützel, Rudolf, *Feldpost: Briefe und Aufzeichnungen eines 17jährigen 1940–1945* (Hamburg, 2005), 54–6.

Süss, Dietmar (ed.), *Deutschland im Luftkrieg: Geschichte und Erinnerung* (Munich, 2007).

——, 'Nationalsozialistische Deutungen des Luftkrieges', in idem (ed.), *Deutschland im Luftkrieg*, 99–110.

Sword, Keith, 'Poland', in Dear (ed.), *The Oxford Companion to World War II*, 695–705.

Szarota, Tomasz, 'Poland and Poles in German Eyes during World War II', *Polish Western Affairs*, 19 (1978), 229–54.

——, *Warschau unter dem Hakenkreuz: Leben und Alltag im besetzten Warschau 1. 10. 1939 bis 31. 7. 1944* (Paderborn, 1985 [1973]).

Szobar, Patricia, 'Telling Sexual Stories in the Nazi Courts of Law: Race Defilement in Germany 1933–1945', *Journal of the History of Sexuality*, 11 (2002), 131–63.

Szodrzynski, Joachim, 'Die "Heimatfront" zwischen Stalingrad und Kriegsende', in Forschungsstelle für Zeitgeschichte in Hamburg (ed.), *Hamburg*, 633–86.

Szpilman, Wladyslaw, *The Pianist: The Extraordinary True Story of One Man's Survival in Warsaw, 1939–1945* (London, 2002 [1999]).

Tampke, Jürgen, *Czech-German Relations and the Politics of Central Europe from Bohemia to the EU* (London, 2003).

Taylor, Frederick, *Dresden: Tuesday 13 February 1945* (London, 2004).

Taylor, Telford, *The Anatomy of the Nuremberg Trials* (London, 1993).

Tec, Nechama, *Ich wollte retten: Die unglaubliche Geschichte der Bielski-Partisanen 1942–1944* (Berlin, 2002).

Tenfelde, Klaus, 'Proletarische Provinz: Radikalisierung und Widerstand in Penzberg/Oberbayern 1900 bis 1945', in Broszat *et al.* (eds.), *Bayern*, IV. 1–382.

Thacker, Toby, *Music after Hitler, 1945–1955* (London, 2007).

Thamm, Gerhardt B., *Boy Soldier: A German Teenager at the Nazi Twilight* (Jefferson, N.C., 2000).

Theilen, Fritz, *Edelweisspiraten* (Frankfurt am Main, 1984).

Tholander, Christa, *Fremdarbeiter 1939 bis 1945: Ausländische Arbeitskräfte in der Zeppelin-Stadt Friedrichshafen* (Essen, 2001).

Thom, Achim, and Caregorodcev, Genadij (eds.), *Medizin unterm Hakenkreuz* (Berlin, 1989).

Thomas, Charles S., *The German Navy in the Nazi Era* (London, 1990).

Thompson, Edward P., *Beyond the Frontier: The Politics of a Failed Mission: Bulgaria 1944* (Woodbridge, 1997).

Todorov, Tzvetan, *The Fragility of Goodness: Why Bulgaria's Jews Survived the Holocaust* (London, 1999).

Tomasevich, Jozo, *War and Revolution in Yugoslavia, 1941–1945: Occupation and Collaboration* (Stanford, Calif., 2001).

Tooze, Adam, *The Wages of Destruction: The Making and Breaking of the Nazi Economy* (London, 2006).

Tory, Avraham, *Surviving the Holocaust: The Kovno Ghetto Diary* (Cambridge, 1990).

Trevor-Roper, Hugh R., *The Last Days of Hitler* (London, 1962 [1947]).

——, 'The Mind of Adolf Hitler', in Hitler, *Hitler's Table Talk* vii–xxxv.

Tröger, Annemarie, 'Die Frau im wesensgemässen Einsatz', in Frauengruppe Faschismusforschung (ed.), *Mutterkreuz und Arbeitsbuch: Zur Geschichte der Frauen in der Weimarer Republik und im Nationalsozialismus* (Frankfurt am Main, 1981), 246–72.

Trotha, Klaus von, ' "Ran, Angreifen, Versenken!" Aus dem Tagebuch eines U-Boots Kapitäns', in Georg von Hase (ed.), *Die Kriegsmarine im Kampf um den Atlantik: Erlebnisberichte von Mitkämpfern* (Leipzig, 1942), 40–69.

Trunk, Isaiah, *Judenrat: The Jewish Councils in Eastern Europe under Nazi Occupation* (New York, 1972).

——, *Lodz Ghetto: A History* (Bloomington, Ind., 2006 [1962]).

Trus, Armin, '. . . vom Leid erlösen': Zur Geschichte der nationalsozialistischen 'Euthanasie'-Verbrechen: Texte und Materialien für Unterricht und Studium* (Frankfurt am Main, 1995).

Tuchel, Johannes (ed.), *'Kein Recht auf Leben': Beiträge und Dokumente zur Entrechtung und Vernichtung 'lebensunwerten Lebens' im Nationalsozialismus* (Berlin, 1984).

Udke, Gerwin (ed.), *'Schreib so oft Du kannst': Feldpostbriefe des Lehrers Gerhard Udke, 1940–1944* (Berlin, 2002).

Ueberschär, Gerd R., *Hitler und Finnland 1938–1941* (Wiesbaden, 1978).

——, *Freiburg im Luftkrieg 1939–1945* (Freiburg, 1990).

——, *Für ein anderes Deutschland: Der deutsche Widerstand gegen den NS-Staat 1933–1945* (Frankfurt am Main, 2006).

——, and Vogel, Winfried, *Dienen und Verdienen: Hitlers Geschenke an seine Eliten* (Frankfurt am Main, 2000 [1999]).

Umbreit, Hans, *Deutsche Militärverwaltungen 1938/39: Die militärische Besetzung der Tschechoslowakei und Polens* (Stuttgart, 1977).

——, 'Auf dem Weg zur Kontinentalherrschaft', in *DRZW* V/I. 3–345.

——, 'The Battle for Hegemony in Western Europe', in *GSWW* II. 227–326.

——, 'Das unbewältigte Problem: Der Partisanenkrieg im Rücken der Ostfront', in Förster (ed.), *Stalingrad*, 130–49.

Upton, Anthony F., *Finland 1939–40* (London, 1974).

Vassiltchikov, Marie, *The Berlin Diaries 1940–1945 of Marie 'Missie' Vassiltchikov 1940–1945* (London, 1987 [1985]).

Vinen, Richard, *The Unfree French: Life under the Occupation* (London, 2006).

Vogel, Detlef, 'German Intervention in the Balkans', in *GSWW* III. 451–555.

——, 'German and Allied Conduct of the War in the West', in *GSWW* VII. 459–702.

Vogel, Johann Peter, *Hans Pfitzner: Leben, Werke, Dokumente* (Berlin, 1999).

Vollnhals, Clemens, *Entnazifizierung: Politische Säuberung und Rehabilitierung in den vier Besatzungszonen 1945–1949* (Munich, 1991).

Volovici, Leon, *Nationalist Ideology and Antisemitism: The Case of Romanian Intellectuals in the 1930s* (Oxford, 1991).

Vorländer, Herwart, *Die NSV: Darstellung und Dokumentation einer nationalsozialistischen Organisation* (Boppard, 1988).

Vrba, Rudolf, 'Die missachtete Warnung: Betrachtungen über den Auschwitz-Bericht von 1944', *VfZ* 44 (1996), 1–24.

Wachsmann, Nikolaus, *Hitler's Prisons: Legal Terror in Nazi Germany* (London, 2004).

Wagner, Bernd C., *IG-Auschwitz: Zwangsarbeit und Vernichtung von Häftlingen des Lagers Monowitz 1941–1945* (Munich, 2000).

Wagner, Jens Christian, 'Noch einmal: Arbeit und Vernichtung: Häftlingseinsatz im KL Mittelbau-Dora 1943–1945', in Frei *et al.* (eds.), *Ausbeutung*, 11–42.

Wagner, Patrick, 'Das Gesetz über die Behandluung Gemeinschaftsfremder: Die Kriminalpolizei und die "Vernichtung des Verbrechertums"', in Götz Aly (ed.), *Feinderklärung und Prävention: Kriminalbiologie: Zigeunerforschung und Asozialenpolitik* (Berlin, 1988), 75–100.

Wagner-Kyora, Georg, ' "Menschenführung" in Rüstungsunternehmen der nationalsozialistischen Kriegswirtschaft', in *DRZW* IX/II. 383–476.

Waibel, Wilhelm J., *Schatten am Hohentwiel: Zwangsarbeiter und Kriegsgefangene in Singen* (Konstanz, 1997 [1995]).

Walb, Lore, *Ich, die Alte – ich, die Junge: Konfrontation mit meinen Tagebüchern 1933–1945* (Berlin, 1997).

Walker, Mark, *German National Socialism and the Quest for Nuclear Power 1939–1949* (Cambridge, 1989).

Wallach, Jehuda L., *The Dogma of the Battle of Annihilation: The Theories of Clausewitz and Schlieffen and their Impact on the German Conduct of Two World Wars* (Westport, Conn., 1986).

Walz, Loretta, 'Gespräche mit Stanislawa Bafia, Wladyslawa Marczewska und Maria Plater über die medizinischen Versuche in Ravensbrück', in Ebbinghaus and Dörner (eds.), *Vernichten und Heilen*, 241–72.

Warmbrunn, Werner, *The Dutch under German Occupation, 1940–45* (London, 1963).

Wasserstein, Bernard, *Britain and the Jews of Europe, 1939–1945* (London, 1979).

Watts, Larry, *Romanian Cassandra: Ion Antonescu and the Struggle for Reform, 1916–1941* (Boulder, Colo., 1993).

Webster, Charles, and Frankland, Noble, *The Strategic Air Offensive against Germany 1939–1945* (4 vols., London, 1961).

Wegner, Bernd, *Hitlers politische Soldaten: Die Waffen-SS 1933–1945: Studien zu Leitbild, Struktur und Funktion einer nationalsozialistischen Elite* (Paderborn, 1982).

——, 'Vom Lebensraum zum Todesraum: Deutschlands Kriegführung zwischen Moskau und Stalingrad', in Förster (ed.), *Stalingrad*, 17–38.

——, 'Die Aporie des Krieges', in *DRZW* VII. 211–76.

——, 'Von Stalingrad nach Kursk', in *DRZW* VII. 3–82.

——, 'The War against the Soviet Union, 1942–1943', in *GSWW* VI. 843–1,230.

Weinberg, Gerhard L., 'Hitler and England, 1933–1945: Pretense and Reality', *German Studies Review*, 8 (1988), 299–309.

——, *A World at Arms: A Global History of World War II* (Cambridge, 2005 [1994]).

Weindling, Paul, *Health, Race and German Politics between National Unification and Nazism 1870–1945* (Cambridge, 1989).

——, *Epidemics and Genocide in Eastern Europe, 1890–1945* (Oxford, 2000).

Weiss, Aharon, 'Jewish Leadership in Occupied Poland: Postures and Attitudes', *Yad Vashem Studies*, 12 (1977), 335–65.

Weitz, Birgit, 'Der Einsatz von KZ-Häftlingen und jüdischen Zwangsarbeitern bei der Daimler-Benz AG (1941–1945): Ein Überblick', in Kaienburg (ed.), *Konzentrationslager*, 169–95.

Welch, David, *Propaganda and the German Cinema 1933–1945* (Oxford, 1983).

——, *The Third Reich: Politics and Propaganda* (London, 2002 [1993]).

——, 'Nazi Propaganda and the *Volksgemeinschaft*: Constructing a People's Community', *Journal of Contemporary History*, 39 (2004), 213–38.

Werther, Thomas, 'Menschenversuche in der Fleckfieberforschung', in Ebbinghaus and Dörner (eds.), *Vernichten und Heilen*, 152–73.

Wette, Wolfram, 'Das Massensterben als "Heldenepos": Stalingrad in der NS-Propaganda', in Wette and Ueberschär (eds.), *Stalingrad*, 43–60.

——, ' "Rassenfeind": Antisemitismus und Antislawismus in der Wehrmachtspropaganda', in Manoschek (ed.), *Die Wehrmacht im Rassenkrieg*, 55–73.

——, and Ueberschär, Gerd R. (eds.), *Stalingrad: Mythos und Wirklichkeit einer Schlacht* (Frankfurt am Main, 1992).

Wetzel, Juliane, 'Auswanderung aus Deutschland', in Benz (ed.), *Die Juden*, 413–98.

Whiting, Charles, *Heydrich: Henchman of Death* (London, 1999).

Wienecke, Annette, *'Besondere Vorkommnisse nicht bekannt': Zwangsarbeit in unterirdischen Rüstungsbetrieben: Wie ein Heidedorf kriegswichtig wurde* (Bonn, 1996).

Wighton, Charles, *Heydrich: Hitler's Most Evil Henchman* (London, 1962).

Wildt, Michael, *Generation des Unbedingten: Das Führungskorps des Reichssicherheitshauptamtes* (Hamburg, 2002).

——, 'Alys Volksstaat: Hybris und Simplizität einer Wissenschaft', *Sozial.Geschichte*, 20 (2005), 91–7.

Wilhelm, Hans-Heinrich, 'Hitlers Ansprache vor Generalen und Offizieren am 26. Mai 1944', *Militärgeschichtliche Mitteilungen*, 2 (1976), 123–70.

Winau, Rolf, 'Medizinische Experimente in den Konzentrationslagern', in Benz and Distel (eds.), *Der Ort des Terrors*, I. 165–78.

Winkler, Dörte, *Frauenarbeit im 'Dritten Reich'* (Hamburg, 1977).

——, 'Frauenarbeit versus Frauenideologie: Probleme der weiblichen Erwerbstätigkeit in Deutschland, 1930–1945', *Archiv für Sozialgeschichte*, 17 (1977), 99–126.

Wirrer, Bärbel (ed.), *Ich glaube an den Führer: Eine Dokumentation zur Mentalitätsgeschichte im nationalsozialistischen Deutschland 1942–1945* (Bielefeld, 2003).

Wistrich, Robert S., 'The Vatican Documents and the Holocaust: A Personal Report', *Polin: Studies in Polish Jewry*, 15 (2002), 413–43.

Witte, Peter, and Tyas, Stephen, 'A New Document on the Deportation and Murder of Jews during "Einsatz Reinhard" 1942', *Holocaust and Genocide Studies*, 15 (2001), 468–86.

Witte, Peter, *et al.* (eds.), *Der Dienstkalender Heinrich Himmlers 1941/42* (Hamburg, 1999).

Wixforth, Harald, *Die Expansion der Dresdner Bank in Europa* (Munich, 2006).

Wöhlert, Meike, *Der politische Witz in der NS-Zeit am Beispiel ausgesuchter SD-Berichte und Gestapo-Akten* (Frankfurt am Main, 1997).

Wolff-Mönckeberg, Mathilde, *On the Other Side: To My Children from Germany 1940–1945* (London, 1982 [1979]).

Wolters, Rita, *Verrat für die Volksgemeinschaft: Denunziantinnen im Dritten Reich* (Pfaffenweiler, 1996).

Wright, Patrick, *Tank: The Progress of a Monstrous War Machine* (London, 2000).

——, *Iron Curtain: From Stage to Cold War* (London, 2007).

Wrobel, Hans (ed.), *Strafjustiz im totalen Krieg: Aus den Akten des Sondergerichts Bremen 1940 bis 1945* (Bremen, 1991).

Wulf, Joseph, *Literatur und Dichtung im Dritten Reich: Eine Dokumentation* (Gütersloh, 1963).

——, *Presse und Funk im Dritten Reich: Eine Dokumentation* (Gütersloh, 1964).

Wurm, Theophil, *Aus meinem Leben* (Stuttgart, 1953).

Yahil, Leni, *The Rescue of Danish Jewry: Test of a Democracy* (Philadelphia, Pa., 1969).

Zamecnik, Stanislav, *Das war Dachau* (Frankfurt am Main, 2007 [2002]).

Zawodny, Janusz K., *Death in the Forest: The Story of the Katyn Forest Massacre* (London, 1971).

Ziemke, Earl F., *Moscow to Stalingrad* (Washington, D.C., 1968).

——, 'Moscow, Battle for', in Dear (ed.), *The Oxford Companion to World War II*, 593–5.

Zilbert, Edward R., *Albert Speer and the Nazi Ministry of Arms: Economic Institutions and Industrial Production in the German War Economy* (London, 1981).

Zimmermann, John, 'Die deutsche militärische Kriegsführung im Western 1944/45', in *DRZW* X/I. 277–489.

Zimmermann, Michael, *Rassenutopie und Genozid: Die nationalsozialistische 'Lösung der Zigeunerfrage'* (Hamburg, 1996).

——, 'Die nationalsozialistische Zigeunerverfolgung, das System der Konzentrationslager und das Zigeunerlager in Auschwitz-Birkenau', in Herbert *et al.* (eds.), *Die nationalsozialistischen Konzentrationslager*, II. 887–910.

Zuccotti, Susan, *The Italians and the Holocaust: Persecution, Rescue and Survival* (London, 1987).

——, *The Holocaust, the French, and the Jews* (New York, 1993).

——, *Under His Very Windows: The Vatican and the Holocaust in Italy* (New Haven, Conn., 2000).

Index

Numbers in **bold** indicate maps